Lecture Notes in Computer Science 1407

Edited by G. Goos, J. Hartmanis and J. van Leeuwen

T0189499

Springer

Berlin
Heidelberg
New York
Barcelona
Budapest
Hong Kong
London
Milan
Paris
Singapore
Tokyo

Hans Burkhardt   Bernd Neumann (Eds.)

Computer Vision – ECCV'98

5th European Conference on Computer Vision
Freiburg, Germany, June 2-6, 1998
Proceedings, Volume II

 Springer

Series Editors

Gerhard Goos, Karlsruhe University, Germany
Juris Hartmanis, Cornell University, NY, USA
Jan van Leeuwen, Utrecht University, The Netherlands

Volume Editors

Hans Burkhardt
Computer Science Department, University of Freiburg
Am Flughafen 17, D-79085 Freiburg, Germany
E-mail: burkhardt@informatik.uni-freiburg.de

Bernd Neumann
Computer Science Department, University of Hamburg
Vogt-Koelln-Str. 30, D-22527 Hamburg, Germany
E-mail: neumann@informatik.uni-hamburg.de

Cataloging-in-Publication data applied for

Die Deutsche Bibliothek - CIP-Einheitsaufnahme

Computer vision : proceedings / ECCV '98, 5th European Conference on Computer
Vision, Freiburg, Germany, June 2 - 6, 1998. Hans Burkhardt ; Bernd Neumann
(ed.). - Berlin ; Heidelberg ; New York ; Barcelona ; Budapest ; Hong Kong ;
London ; Milan ; Paris ; Santa Clara ; Singapore ; Tokyo : Springer.

Vol. 2. - (1998)
(Lecture notes in computer science ; Vol. 1407)
ISBN 3-540-64613-2

CR Subject Classification (1991): I.3.5, I.5, I.2.9-10, I.4

ISSN 0302-9743
ISBN 3-540-64613-2 Springer-Verlag Berlin Heidelberg New York

Typesetting: Camera-ready by author
SPIN 10637168   06/3142 – 5 4 3 2 1 0   Printed on acid-free paper

Preface

Following the highly successful conferences held in Antibes (ECCV '90), Santa Margherita Ligure (ECCV '92), Stockholm (ECCV '94), and Cambridge (ECCV '96), the Fifth European Conference on Computer Vision (ECCV '98) will take place from 2–6 June 1998 at the University of Freiburg, Germany. It is an honour for us to host this conference which has turned out to be one of the major events for the computer vision community. The conference will be held under the auspices of the European Vision Society (EVS) and the German Association for Pattern Recognition (DAGM).

ECCV is a single track conference consisting of highest quality, previously unpublished, contributed papers on new and original research on computer vision presented either orally or as posters. 223 manuscripts were reviewed double-blind each by three reviewers from the program committee. Forty-two papers were selected to be delivered orally and seventy to be presented at poster sessions.

Based on a generous donation from the OLYMPUS Europe Foundation "Science for Life" 10,000.- DM will be awarded for the best papers.

ECCV '98 is being held at the University of Freiburg, located in the lovely surroundings of the Black Forest. It is one of the oldest universities in Germany, founded in 1457, with an outstanding international reputation. This university with a long tradition has been recently enriched through the foundation of a new 15th Faculty for Applied Sciences consisting of two Institutes: the Institute of Computer Science which will host the ECCV '98 and the Institute of Microsystem Technology.

We wish to thank the members of the program committee and the conference board for their help in the reviewing process. It is their competence and hard work which provides the key for the continuing success of this conference series.

Our thanks are extended also to the University of Freiburg and its rector W. Jäger for hosting this conference; to Springer-Verlag in Heidelberg for their support of this conference through the proceedings; and to k&k for the local organization.

Finally we would like to express our appreciation to the members of our institutes and especially to Nikos Canterakis, to Christoph Schnörr, and to Helen Brodie for their never-ending patience and humour.

We wish all participants a successful and inspiring conference and a pleasant stay in Freiburg.

Freiburg, March 1998   Hans Burkhardt and Bernd Neumann

Conference Chairs

Hans Burkhardt	University of Freiburg
Bernd Neumann	University of Hamburg

Conference Board and Program Committee

N. Ayache	INRIA, Sophia Antipolis
R. Bajcsy	University of Pennsylvania
A. Blake	University of Oxford
P. Bouthemy	IRISA/INRIA, Rennes
M. Brady	University of Oxford
B. Buxton	University College London
H. Buxton	University of Sussex
S. Carlsson	KTH, Stockholm
H. Christensen	KTH, Stockholm
J. L. Crowley	INRIA, Rhône-Alpes
R. Cipolla	University of Cambridge
R. Deriche	INRIA, Sophia Antipolis
M. Dhome	Blaise Pascal University
J.-O. Eklundh	KTH, Stockholm
W. Enkelmann	IITB, Karlsruhe
O. Faugeras	INRIA, Sophia Antipolis
W. Förstner	University of Bonn
G. Granlund	Linköping University
B. M. ter Haar Romeny	University Hospital Utrecht
D. Hogg	Leeds University
R. Horaud	INPG, Grenoble
H. Knutsson	Linköping University
J. J. Koenderink	University of Utrecht
J. Malik	University of California at Berkeley
J. Mayhew	Sheffield University
R. Mohr	INPG, Grenoble
H.-H. Nagel	IITB, Karlsruhe
S. Peleg	The Hebrew University of Jerusalem
G. Sandini	University of Genova
W. von Seelen	Ruhr University at Bochum
F. Solina	Ljubljana University
G. Sparr	Lund University
M. Tistarelli	University of Genova
S. Tsuji	Wakayama University
L. Van Gool	Catholic University, Leuven
D. Vernon	Maynooth University, Ireland
A. Verri	University of Genova
J. J. Villanueva	Autonomous University of Barcelona
D. Weinshall	The Hebrew University of Jerusalem
A. Zisserman	University of Oxford
S. Zucker	Yale University

Contents of Volume II

Shading and Shape

Structure from Motion

Contents of Volume I

Stereo Vision and Calibration II

Colour and Indexing

Tracking, CONDENSATION

Matching and Registration

Matching Hierarchical Structures Using Association Graphs

Marcello Pelillo*, Kaleem Siddiqi, and Steven W. Zucker

Yale University
Center for Computational Vision & Control
{pelillo-marcello, siddiqi-kaleem, zucker-steven}@cs.yale.edu

Abstract. It is well known that the problem of matching two relational structures can be posed as an equivalent problem of finding a maximal clique in a (derived) "association graph." However, it is not clear how to apply this approach to computer vision problems where the graphs are hierarchically organized, i.e. are trees, since maximal cliques are not constrained to preserve the partial order. Here we provide a solution to the problem of matching two trees, by constructing the association graph using the graph-theoretic concept of connectivity. We prove that in the new formulation there is a one-to-one correspondence between maximal cliques and maximal subtree isomorphisms, and show how to solve the matching problem using simple "replicator" dynamical systems developed in theoretical biology. Such continuous solutions to discrete problems can motivate analog and biological implementations. We illustrate the power of the approach by matching articulated and deformed shapes described by shock trees.

1 Introduction

The matching of relational structures is a classic problem in computer vision and pattern recognition, instances of which arise in areas as diverse as object recognition, motion and stereo analysis. A well-known approach to solve this problem consists of transforming it into the equivalent problem of finding a maximum clique in an auxiliary graph structure, known as the *association graph* [2, 3]. The idea goes back to Ambler *et al.* [1], and has since been successfully employed in a variety of different problems, e.g., [5, 13, 21, 29, 28, 34, 36]. This framework is attractive because it casts relational structure matching as a pure graph-theoretic problem, for which a solid theory and powerful algorithms have been developed. Although the maximum clique problem is known to be NP-complete [10], powerful heuristics have been developed which efficiently find good approximate solutions [22].

In many computer vision problems, however, relational structures are organized in a hierarchical manner, i.e., are *trees* (see, for example, [17, 30, 32, 33,

---

* Permanent address: Dipartimento di Matematica Applicata e Informatica, Università "Ca' Foscari" di Venezia, Via Torino 155, 30173 Venezia Mestre, Italy, E-mail: pelillo@dsi.unive.it

37]). Since in the standard association graph formulation the solutions are not constrained to preserve the required partial order, it is not clear how to apply the framework in these cases. The extension of association graph techniques to tree matching problems is therefore of considerable interest. To illustrate the difficulties with the standard formulation, consider the problem of finding the largest subtree in the left tree of Figure 1 which is isomorphic to a subtree in the right tree. Up to permutations, the correct solution is clearly given by $3 \rightarrow$ a, $4 \rightarrow$ b, $5 \rightarrow$ c, $6 \rightarrow$ d, $7 \rightarrow$ f, and $8 \rightarrow$ g. In other words, the subtree rooted at node 3 is matched against that rooted at node a in the tree on the right. However, using the standard association graph formulation (*cfr.* [2, p. 366]), it is easily verified that the solutions induced by the maximum cliques correspond (up to permutations) to the following: $2 \rightarrow$ h, $3 \rightarrow$ a, $4 \rightarrow$ b, $5 \rightarrow$ c, $6 \rightarrow$ d, $7 \rightarrow$ f, and $8 \rightarrow$ g, which, while perfectly in accordance with the usual subgraph isomorphism constraints, *does* violate the requirement that the matched subgraphs be trees (note, in fact, that nodes 2 and h are isolated from the rest of the matched subtrees).

In this paper, we introduce a solution to this problem by providing a novel way of deriving an association graph from two (rooted) trees, based on the graph-theoretic notions of connectivity and the distance matrix. We prove that in the new formulation there is a one-to-one correspondence between maximal (maximum) cliques in the derived association graph and maximal (maximum) subtree isomorphisms. As an obvious corollary, the computational complexity of finding a maximum clique in such graphs is therefore the same as the subtree isomorphism problem, which is known to be polynomial in the number of nodes [10].

Following the development in [25], we use a recent generalization of the Motzkin-Straus theorem [20] to formulate the maximum clique problem as a quadratic programming problem. To (approximately) solve it we employ *replicator equations*, a class of simple continuous- and discrete-time dynamical systems developed and studied in various branches of biomathematics [12, 35]. We illustrate the power of the approach via several examples of matching articulated and deformed shapes described by *shock* trees [33].

2 Tree Isomorphism and Maximal Cliques

2.1 Notations and definitions

Before going into the details of the proposed framework, we need to introduce some graph-theoretical notations and definitions. More details can be found in standard textbooks of graph theory, such as [11]. Let $G = (V, E)$ be a graph, where V is the set of nodes and E is the set of (undirected) edges. The *order* of G is the number of nodes in V, while its *size* is the number of edges. Two nodes $u, v \in V$ are said to be *adjacent* (denoted $u \sim v$) if they are connected by an edge. A *path* is any sequence of distinct nodes $u_0 u_1 \ldots u_n$ such that for all $i = 1 \ldots n$, $u_{i-1} \sim u_i$; in this case, the length of the path is n. If $u_0 = u_n$ the path is called a *cycle*. A graph is said to be *connected* if any pair of nodes is

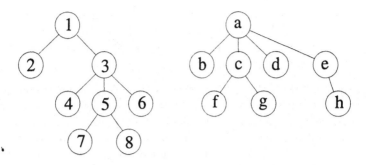

Fig. 1. An example of matching two trees. In the standard formulation of the association graph, the maximum cliques do not preserve the hierarchical structure of the two trees.

joined by a path. The *distance* between two nodes u and v, denoted by $d(u,v)$, is the length of the shortest path joining them (by convention $d(u,v) = \infty$, if there is no such path). Given a subset of nodes $C \subseteq V$, the *induced subgraph* $G[C]$ is the graph having C as its node set, and two nodes are adjacent in $G[C]$ if and only if they are adjacent in G.

A connected graph with no cycles is called a *tree*. A *rooted* tree is one which has a distinguished node, called the *root*. The *level* of a node u in a rooted tree, denoted by $\mathrm{lev}(u)$, is the length of the path connecting the root to u. Note that there is an obvious equivalence between rooted trees and directed trees, where the edges are assumed to be oriented. We shall therefore use the same terminology typically used for directed trees to define the relation between two adjacent nodes. In particular, if $u \sim v$ and $\mathrm{lev}(v) - \mathrm{lev}(u) = +1$, we say that u is the *parent* of v and, conversely, v is a *child* of u. Trees have a number of interesting properties. One which turns out to be very useful for our characterization is that in a tree any two nodes are connected by a *unique* path.

2.2 Deriving the association graph

Let $T_1 = (V_1, E_1)$ and $T_2 = (V_2, E_2)$ be two rooted trees. Any bijection $\phi : H_1 \rightarrow H_2$, with $H_1 \subseteq V_1$ and $H_2 \subseteq V_2$, is called a *subtree isomorphism* if it preserves the adjacency and hierarchical relations between the nodes and, in addition, the induced subgraphs $T_1[H_1]$ and $T_2[H_2]$ are trees. The former condition amounts to stating that, given $u, v \in H_1$, we have $u \sim v$ if and only if $\phi(u) \sim \phi(v)$, and u is the parent of v if and only if $\phi(u)$ is the parent of $\phi(v)$. A subtree isomorphism is *maximal* if there is no other subtree isomorphism $\phi' : H_1' \rightarrow H_2'$ with H_1 a strict subset of H_1', and *maximum* if H_1 has largest cardinality. The maximal (maximum) subtree isomorphism problem is to find a maximal (maximum) subtree isomorphism between two rooted trees.

We now introduce the notion of a *path-string*, which turns out to be of pivotal importance for our subsequent development.

Definition 1. *Let u and v be two distinct nodes of a rooted tree T, and let $u = x_0 x_1 \ldots x_n = v$ be the (unique) path joining them. The path-string of u and v, denoted by $\mathrm{str}(u,v)$, is the string $s_1 s_2 \ldots s_n$ on the alphabet $\{-1, +1\}$ where, for all $i = 1 \ldots n$, $s_i = \mathrm{lev}(x_i) - \mathrm{lev}(x_{i-1})$.*

The path-string concept has a very intuitive meaning. Suppose that you stand on a particular node in a rooted tree and want to move to another adjacent node. Because of the orientation induced by the root, only two types of moves can be done, i.e., going down to one of the children (if one exists) or going up to the parent (if you are not on the root). Let us assign to the first move the label $+1$, and to the second the label -1. Now, suppose that you want to move from node u to v, following the unique path joining them. Then, the path-string of u and v is simply the string of elementary moves you have to do in order to reach v, starting from u. It may be thought of as the degree of relationship between two relatives in a "family" tree.

The *association graph* of two rooted trees $T_1 = (V_1, E_1)$ and $T_2 = (V_2, E_2)$ is the graph $G = (V, E)$ where

$$V = V_1 \times V_2 \qquad (1)$$

and, for any two nodes (u, w) and (v, z) in V, we have

$$(u, w) \sim (v, z) \Leftrightarrow \mathrm{str}(u, v) = \mathrm{str}(w, z) \; . \qquad (2)$$

Intuitively, two nodes (u, w) and (v, z) are adjacent in G, if and only if the relationship between u and v in T_1 is the same as that between w and z in T_2. Note that this definition of association graph is stronger than the standard one used for matching arbitrary relational structures [2, 3]. A subset of vertices of G is said to be a *clique* if all its nodes are mutually adjacent. A *maximal* clique is one which is not contained in any larger clique, while a *maximum* clique is a clique having largest cardinality. The maximum clique problem is to find a maximum clique of G. The following result, which is the basis of the work reported here, establishes a one-to-one correspondence between the maximum subtree isomorphism problem and the maximum clique problem.

Theorem 1. *Any maximal (maximum) subtree isomorphism between two rooted trees induces a maximal (maximum) clique in the corresponding association graph, and vice versa.*

Proof (outline). Let $\phi : H_1 \to H_2$ be a maximal subtree isomorphism between rooted trees T_1 and T_2, and let $G = (V, E)$ denote the corresponding association graph, as defined above. The maximal clique induced by ϕ is simply the set of vertices $C_\phi \subseteq V$ defined as:

$$C_\phi = \{(u, \phi(u)) : u \in H_1\} \; .$$

Intuitively, the fact that C_ϕ is a clique follows from the observation that ϕ maps the path between any two nodes u and v onto the path joining $\phi(u)$ and $\phi(v)$. Trivially, C_ϕ is maximal because ϕ is, and this proves the first part of the theorem.

Suppose now that $C = \{(u_1, w_1), \cdots, (u_n, w_n)\}$ is a maximal clique of G, and define $H_1 = \{u_1, \cdots, u_n\} \subseteq V_1$ and $H_2 = \{w_1, \cdots, w_n\} \subseteq V_2$. Define $\phi : H_1 \to H_2$ as $\phi(u_i) = w_i$, for all $i = 1 \ldots n$. From the definition of the association graph and the hypothesis that C is a clique, it simple to see that ϕ is a one-to-one and onto correspondence between H_1 and H_2, which trivially preserves both the adjacency and the hierarchical relations between nodes. The fact that ϕ is maximal is a straightforward consequence of the maximality of C.

To conclude the proof we have to show that the induced subgraphs $T_1[H_1]$ and $T_2[H_2]$ are trees, and this is equivalent to showing that they are connected. Suppose by contradiction that this is not the case, and let $u_i, u_j \in H_1$ be two nodes which are not joined by a path in $T_1[H_1]$. Since both u_i and u_j are nodes of T_1, however, there must exist a path $u_i = x_0 x_1 \ldots x_m = u_j$ joining them in T_1. Let $x^* = x_k$, for some $k = 1 \ldots m$, be a node on this path which is not in H_1. Moreover, let $y^* = y_k$ be the k-th node on the path $w_i = y_0 y_1 \ldots y_m = w_j$ which joins w_i and w_j in T_2. It is easy to show that the set $\{(x^*, y^*)\} \cup C \subseteq V$ is a clique, and this contradicts the hypothesis that C is a maximal clique. This can be proved by exploiting the obvious fact that if x is a node on the path joining any two nodes u and v, then $\operatorname{str}(u, v)$ can be obtained by concatenating $\operatorname{str}(u, x)$ and $\operatorname{str}(x, v)$.

The "maximum" part of the statement is proved similarly. $\quad\square$

The next proposition provides us with a straightforward criterion to construct the association graph.

Proposition 1. *Let $T_1 = (V_1, E_1)$ and $T_2 = (V_2, E_2)$ be two rooted trees, $u, v \in V_1$, and $w, z \in V_2$. Then, $\operatorname{str}(u, v) = \operatorname{str}(w, z)$ if and only if the following two conditions hold:*

(a) $d(u,v) = d(w,z)$
(b) $\operatorname{lev}(u) - \operatorname{lev}(v) = \operatorname{lev}(w) - \operatorname{lev}(z)$

Proof. The proposition is a straightforward consequence of the following two observations. Let u and v be any two nodes in a tree, and let $\operatorname{str}(u, v) = s_1 s_2 \ldots s_n$ be the corresponding path-string. Then we have: (1) $\operatorname{lev}(u) - \operatorname{lev}(v) = \sum_i s_i$, and (2) $s_i = +1$ implies $s_j = +1$ for all $j \geq i$. $\quad\square$

This results allows us to efficiently derive the association graph by using a classical representation for graphs, i.e., the so-called *distance matrix* (see, e.g., [11]) which, for an arbitrary graph $G = (V, E)$ of order n, is the $n \times n$ matrix $D = (d_{ij})$ where $d_{ij} = d(u_i, u_j)$, the distance between nodes u_i and u_j.

3 Tree Matching Replicator Equations

Let $G = (V, E)$ be an arbitrary graph of order n, and let S_n denote the standard simplex of $\mathbb{R}^n$:

$$S_n = \{\, \mathbf{x} \in \mathbb{R}^n \;:\; \mathbf{e}'\mathbf{x} = 1 \text{ and } x_i \geq 0,\; i = 1 \ldots n \,\}$$

where $\mathbf{e}$ is the vector whose components equal 1, and a prime denotes transposition. Given a subset of vertices C of G, we will denote by $\mathbf{x}^c$ its *characteristic vector* which is the point in S_n defined as

$$x_i^c = \begin{cases} 1/|C|, & \text{if } i \in C \\ 0, & \text{otherwise} \end{cases}$$

where $|C|$ denotes the cardinality of C.

Now, consider the following quadratic function

$$f(\mathbf{x}) = \mathbf{x}'A\mathbf{x} + \frac{1}{2}\mathbf{x}'\mathbf{x} \tag{3}$$

where $A = (a_{ij})$ is the adjacency matrix of G, i.e., the $n \times n$ symmetric matrix defined as

$$a_{ij} = \begin{cases} 1, & \text{if } v_i \sim v_j \\ 0, & \text{otherwise} \end{cases}$$

A point $\mathbf{x}^* \in S_n$ is said to be a *global* maximizer of f in S_n if $f(\mathbf{x}^*) \geq f(\mathbf{x})$, for all $\mathbf{x} \in S_n$. It is said to be a *local* maximizer if there exists an $\varepsilon > 0$ such that $f(\mathbf{x}^*) \geq f(\mathbf{x})$ for all $\mathbf{x} \in S_n$ whose distance from $\mathbf{x}^*$ is less than ε, and if $f(\mathbf{x}^*) = f(\mathbf{x})$ implies $\mathbf{x}^* = \mathbf{x}$, then $\mathbf{x}^*$ is said to be a *strict* local maximizer.

The following theorem, recently proved by Bomze [6], expands on the Motzkin-Straus theorem [20], a remarkable result which establishes a connection between the maximum clique problem and certain standard quadratic programs. This has an intriguing computational significance in that it allows us to shift from the discrete to the continuous domain in an elegant manner.

Theorem 2. *Let C be a subset of vertices of a graph G, and let $\mathbf{x}^c$ be its characteristic vector. Then the following statements hold:*

(a) C is a maximum clique of G if and only if $\mathbf{x}^c$ is a global maximizer of the function f in S_n. In this case, $|C| = 1/2(1 - f(\mathbf{x}^c))$.

(b) C is a maximal clique of G if and only if $\mathbf{x}^c$ is a local maximizer of f in S_n.

(c) All local (and hence global) maximizers of f in S_n are strict.

Unlike the original Motzkin-Straus formulation, which is plagued by the presence of "spurious" solutions [26], the previous result guarantees us that *all* maximizers of f on S_n are strict, and are characteristic vectors of maximal/maximum cliques in the graph. In a formal sense, therefore, a one-to-one correspondence exists between maximal cliques and local maximizers of f in S_n on the one hand, and maximum cliques and global maximizers on the other hand.

We now turn our attention to a class of simple dynamical systems that we use for solving our quadratic optimization problem. Let W be a non-negative real-valued $n \times n$ matrix, and consider the following dynamical system:

$$\dot{x}_i(t) = x_i(t)\left[(W\mathbf{x}(t))_i - \mathbf{x}(t)'W\mathbf{x}(t)\right], \quad i = 1 \ldots n \tag{4}$$

where a dot signifies derivative w.r.t. time t, and its discrete-time counterpart

$$x_i(t+1) = x_i(t)\frac{(W\mathbf{x}(t))_i}{\mathbf{x}(t)'W\mathbf{x}(t)}, \quad i = 1 \ldots n . \tag{5}$$

It is readily seen that the simplex S_n is invariant under these dynamics, which means that every trajectory starting in S_n will remain in S_n for all future times. Moreover, it turns out that their *stationary points*, i.e. the points satisfying $\dot{x}_i(t) = 0$ for (4) or $x_i(t+1) = x_i(t)$ for (5), coincide and are the solutions of the equations

$$x_i[(W\mathbf{x})_i - \mathbf{x}'W\mathbf{x}] = 0, \quad i = 1 \ldots n . \tag{6}$$

A stationary point $\mathbf{x}$ is said to be *asymptotically stable* if every solution to (4) or (5) which starts close enough to $\mathbf{x}$, will converge to $\mathbf{x}$ as $t \to \infty$.

Both (4) and (5) are called *replicator equations* in theoretical biology, since they are used to model evolution over time of relative frequencies of interacting, self-replicating entities [12]. The discrete-time dynamical equations turn out to be a special case of a general class of dynamical systems introduced by Baum and Eagon [4] in the context of Markov chains theory. They also represent an instance of the original heuristic Rosenfeld-Hummel-Zucker relaxation labeling algorithm [31], whose dynamical properties have recently been clarified [24] (specifically, it corresponds to the 1-object, n-label case).

We are now interested in the dynamical properties of replicator dynamics; it is these properties that will allow us to solve our original tree matching problem.

Theorem 3. *If $W = W'$ then the function $\mathbf{x}(t)'W\mathbf{x}(t)$ is strictly increasing with increasing t along any non-stationary trajectory $\mathbf{x}(t)$ under both continuous-time (4) and discrete-time (5) replicator dynamics. Furthermore, any such trajectory converges to a stationary point. Finally, a vector $\mathbf{x} \in S_n$ is asymptotically stable under (4) and (5) if and only if $\mathbf{x}$ is a strict local maximizer of $\mathbf{x}'W\mathbf{x}$ on S_n.*

The previous result is known in mathematical biology as the Fundamental Theorem of Natural Selection [8, 12, 35] and, in its original form, traces back to Fisher [9]. As far as the discrete-time model is concerned, it can be regarded as a straightforward implication of the more general Baum-Eagon theorem [4]. The fact that all trajectories of the replicator dynamics converge to a stationary point has been proven more recently [15, 16].

In light of their dynamical properties, replicator equations naturally suggest themselves as a simple heuristic for solving the maximal subtree isomorphism problem. Let $T_1 = (V_1, E_1)$ and $T_2 = (V_2, E_2)$ be two rooted trees, and let A denote the N-node adjacency matrix of the corresponding association graph G, as defined in Section 2. By letting

$$W = A + \frac{1}{2}I_N$$

where I_N is the $N \times N$ identity matrix, we know that the replicator dynamical systems (4) and (5), starting from an arbitrary initial state, will iteratively maximize the function f defined in (3) over S_N and will eventually converge with probability 1 to a strict local maximizer which, by virtue of Theorem 2, will then correspond to the characteristic vector of a maximal clique in the association graph. As stated in Theorem 1, this will in turn induce a maximal subtree isomorphism between T_1 and T_2.

Clearly, in theory there is no guarantee that the converged solution will be a *global* maximizer of f, and therefore that it will induce a *maximum* isomorphism between the two original trees. Previous experimental work done on the maximum clique problem [7, 23], and also the results presented in the next section, however, suggest that the basins of attraction of optimal or near-optimal solutions are quite large, and very frequently the algorithm converges to one of them, despite its inherent inability to escape from local optima.

Since the process cannot leave the boundary of S_N, it is customary to start out the relaxation process from some interior point, a common choice being the barycenter of S_N, i.e., the vector $(\frac{1}{N}, \cdots, \frac{1}{N})'$. This prevents the search from being initially biased in favor of any particular solution.

4 An Example: Matching Shock Trees

We illustrate our framework with numerical examples of shape matching. We use a *shock graph* representation based on a coloring of the shocks (singularities) of a curve evolution process acting on simple closed curves in the plane [14]. Shocks are grouped into distinct types according to the local variation of the radius function along the medial axis. Intuitively, the radius function varies monotonically at a type 1, reaches a strict local minimum at a type 2, is constant at a type 3 and reaches a strict local maximum at a type 4. The shocks comprise vertices in the graph, and their formation times direct edges to form a basis for subgraph isomorphism; see [33] for details. An illustrative example appears in Figure 2. Each graph can be reduced to a unique rooted tree, providing the requisite hierarchical structure for our matching algorithm. The ability of shock trees to discriminate between classes of shapes, using *both* their topologies as well as metric/label information has been examined in [33]. Here we address the unlabeled version of the problem, and examine matching based on topology *alone*. We stress that our goal is to illustrate the power of the hierarchical structure matching algorithm.

We selected 22 silhouttes representing eight different object classes (Table 1, first column); the tools shapes were taken from the Rutgers Tools database. Each

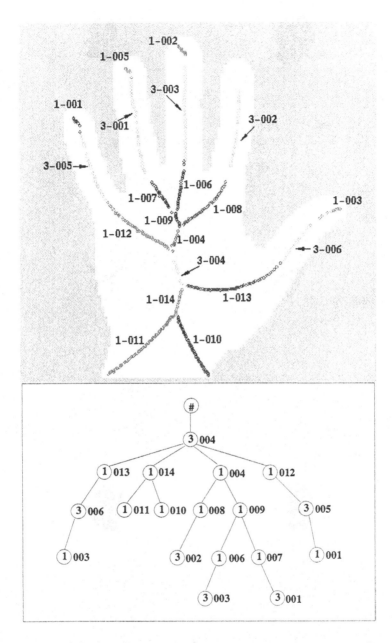

Fig. 2. An illustrative example of the shocks obtained from curve evolution (from [33]). TOP: The notation associated with the locus of shock points is of the form shock_type-identifier. BOTTOM: The tree has the shock_type on each node, and the identifier is adjacent. The last shock to form during the curve evolution process is the most "significant," and this appears under the root node labeled #.

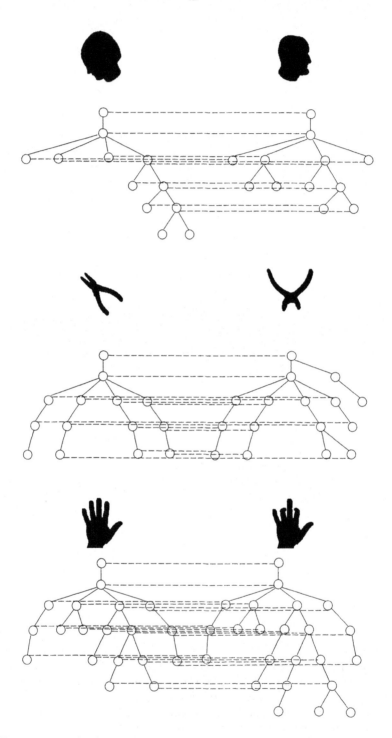

Fig. 3. Maximal subtree isomorphisms found for three illustrative examples.

entry was then matched against *all* entries in the database, and the size of the maximal clique found, normalized by the average number of nodes in the two trees, was recorded. Figure 3 shows the maximal subtree isomorphisms (each in one-to-one correspondence with a maximal clique) for three examples. The top 5 matches for each query shape, along with the associated scores, are shown in Table 1. The matching algorithm generally takes only two to three seconds to converge on a Sparc 10.

Note that despite the fact that metric/label information associated with nodes in the shock trees was discounted altogether, all exemplars in the same class as the query shape are within the top 5 matches, and typically in the top 3. It is evident that such a structural matching process for indexing into a database of shapes has great potential; with the addition of geometric information performance can only improve.

5 Conclusions

We have developed a formal approach for matching hierarchical structures by constructing an association graph whose maximal cliques are in one-to-one correspondence with maximal subtree isomorphisms. The framework is general and can be applied in a variety of computer vision domains: we have demonstrated its potential for shape matching. The solution is found by using a dynamical system, which makes it amenable to hardware implementation and offers the advantage of biological plausibility. In particular, the relaxation labeling equations are related to putative neuronal implementations [18, 19]. In [27] we extend the present framework to the problem of matching hierarchical structures with attributes. The attributes result in weights being placed on the nodes of the association graph, and a conversion of the maximum clique problem to a maximum weight clique problem.

Acknowledgements We thank Sven Dickinson for the use of shapes from the Rutgers Tools database. This work was supported by Consiglio Nazionale delle Ricerche (Italy), NSF and AFOSR.

References

1. A. P. Ambler, H. G. Barrow, C. M. Brown, R. M. Burstall, and R. J. Popplestone. A versatile computer-controlled assembly system. In *Proc. 3rd Int. J. Conf. Artif. Intell.*, pages 298–307, Stanford, CA, 1973.
2. D. H. Ballard and C. M. Brown. *Computer Vision.* Prentice-Hall, Englewood Cliffs, N.J, 1982.
3. H. G. Barrow and R. M. Burstall. Subgraph isomorphism, matching relational structures, and maximal cliques. *Inform. Process. Lett.*, 4(4):83–84, 1976.
4. L. E. Baum and J. A. Eagon. An inequality with applications to statistical estimation for probabilistic functions of markov processes and to a model for ecology. *Bull. Amer. Math. Soc.*, 73:360–363, 1967.

Query Shape	Top 5 Topological Matches				
	1	2	3	4	5
(hand)	1.00	.91	.81	.80	.79
(hand)	1.00	.81	.78	.72	.70
(hand)	1.00	.91	.78	.72	.70
(horse)	1.00	.70	.57	.57	.50
(horse)	1.00	.70	.69	.57	.50
(head)	1.00	1.00	.83	.80	.80
(head)	1.00	1.00	.83	.80	.80
(head)	1.00	.91	.86	.83	.83
(tool)	1.00	.96	.87	.83	.81
(tool)	1.00	.91	.87	.84	.82
(tool)	1.00	.96	.91	.87	.85
(tool)	1.00	.92	.87	.85	.81
(tool)	1.00	.92	.86	.82	.82
(wishbone)	1.00	.87	.86	.80	.79
(tool)	1.00	1.00	.80	.76	.75
(tool)	1.00	1.00	.80	.76	.75
(tool)	1.00	.80	.80	.80	.80
(tool)	1.00	.90	.87	.86	.86
(tool)	1.00	.95	.95	.90	.86
(tool)	1.00	.89	.89	.80	.80
(tool)	1.00	1.00	.95	.91	.89
(tool)	1.00	1.00	.95	.91	.89

Table 1. A tabulation of the top 5 matches for each query. The scores indicate the size of the maximal clique found, normalized by the average number of nodes in the two trees. Note that *only* the topology of the shock trees was used; the addition of geometric information permits finer comparisons [27].

5. R. C. Bolles and R. A. Cain. Recognizing and locating partially visible objects: The locus-feature-focus method. *Int. J. Robotics Res.*, 1(3):57–82, 1982.
6. I. M. Bomze. Evolution towards the maximum clique. *J. Global Optim.*, 10:143–164, 1997.
7. I. M. Bomze, M. Pelillo, and R. Giacomini. Evolutionary approach to the maximum clique problem: Empirical evidence on a larger scale. In I. M. Bomze, T. Csendes, R. Horst, and P. M. Pardalos, editors, *Developments in Global Optimization*, pages 95–108, Dordrecht, The Netherlands, 1997. Kluwer.
8. J. F. Crow and M. Kimura. *An Introduction to Population Genetics Theory*. Harper & Row, New York, 1970.
9. R. A. Fisher. *The Genetical Theory of Natural Selection*. Oxford University Press, London, UK, 1930.
10. M. Garey and D. Johnson. *Computer and Intractability: A Guide to the Theory of NP-Completeness*. Freeman, San Francisco, 1979.
11. F. Harary. *Graph Theory*. Addison-Wesley, Reading, MA, 1969.
12. J. Hofbauer and K. Sigmund. *The Theory of Evolution and Dynamical Systems*. Cambridge University Press, Cambridge, UK, 1988.
13. R. Horaud and T. Skordas. Stereo correspondence through feature grouping and maximal cliques. *IEEE Trans. Pattern Anal. Machine Intell.*, 11(11):1168–1180, 1989.
14. B. B. Kimia, A. Tannenbaum, and S. W. Zucker. Shape, shocks, and deformations I: The components of two-dimensional shape and the reaction-diffusion space. *Int. J. Comp. Vision*, 15:189–224, 1995.
15. V. Losert and E. Akin. Dynamics of games and genes: Discrete versus continuous time. *J. Math. Biol.*, 17:241–251, 1983.
16. Y. Lyubich, G. D. Maistrowskii, and Y. G. Ol'khovskii. Selection-induced convergence to equilibrium in a single-locus autosomal population. *Problems of Information Transmission*, 16:66–75, 1980.
17. D. Marr and K. H. Nishihara. Representation and recognition of the spatial organization of three-dimensional shapes. *Proc. R. Soc. Lond. B*, 200:269–294, 1978.
18. D. Miller and S. W. Zucker. Efficient simplex-like methods for equilibria of non-symmetric analog networks. *Neural Computation*, 4(2):167–190, 1992.
19. D. Miller and S. W. Zucker. Computing with self-excitatory cliques: A model and an application to hyperacuity-scale computation in visual cortex. *Neural Computation*, 1998. To be published.
20. T. S. Motzkin and E. G. Straus. Maxima for graphs and a new proof of a theorem of Turán. *Canad. J. Math.*, 17:533–540, 1965.
21. H. Ogawa. Labeled point pattern matching by delaunay triangulation and maximal cliques. *Pattern Recognition*, 19:35–40, 1986.
22. P. M. Pardalos and J. Xue. The maximum clique problem. *J. Global Optim.*, 4:301–328, 1994.
23. M. Pelillo. Relaxation labeling networks for the maximum clique problem. *J. Artif. Neural Networks*, 2:313–328, 1995.
24. M. Pelillo. The dynamics of nonlinear relaxation labeling processes. *J. Math. Imaging Vision*, 7:309–323, 1997.
25. M. Pelillo. A unifying framework for relational structure matching. Submitted, 1997.
26. M. Pelillo and A. Jagota. Feasible and infeasible maxima in a quadratic program for maximum clique. *J. Artif. Neural Networks*, 2:411–420, 1995.
27. M. Pelillo, K. Siddiqi, and S. W. Zucker. Attributed tree matching and maximum weight cliques. Submitted, 1997.

28. F. Pla and J. A. Marchant. Matching feature points in image sequences through a region-based method. *Comp. Vision Image Understanding*, 66:271–285, 1997.
29. B. Radig. Image sequence analysis using relational structures. *Pattern Recognition*, 17:161–167, 1984.
30. H. Rom and G. Medioni. Hierarchical decomposition and axial shape description. *IEEE Trans. Pattern Anal. Machine Intell.*, 15(10):973–981, 1993.
31. A. Rosenfeld, R. A. Hummel, and S. W. Zucker. Scene labeling by relaxation operations. *IEEE Trans. Syst. Man Cybern.*, 6:420–433, 1976.
32. H. Samet. *Design and Analysis of Spatial Data Structures*. Addison-Wesley, Reading, MA, 1990.
33. K. Siddiqi, A. Shokoufandeh, S. J. Dickinson, and S. W. Zucker. Shock graphs and shape matching. In *Proc. Int. Conf. Comp. Vision*, pages 222–229, Bombay, India, 1998.
34. V. Venkateswar and R. Chellappa. Hierarchical stereo and motion correspondence using feature groupings. *Int. J. Comp. Vision*, 15:245–269, 1995.
35. J. W. Weibull. *Evolutionary Game Theory*. MIT Press, Cambridge, MA, 1995.
36. B. Yang, W. E. Snyder, and G. L. Bilbro. Matching oversegmented 3D images using association graphs. *Image Vision Comput.*, 7:135–143, 1989.
37. S. Zhu and A. L. Yuille. FORMS: A flexible object recognition and modelling system. *Int. J. Comp. Vision*, 20(3):187–212, 1996.

Stereo Matching with Implicit Detection of Occlusions

Ralph Trapp[1], Siegbert Drüe, and Georg Hartmann

University of Paderborn, Department of Electrical Engineering,
Pohlweg 47-49, D-33098 Paderborn, Germany
{trapp, druee, hartmann}@get.uni-paderborn.de

Abstract. In this paper we introduce a new stereo matching algorithm, in which the matching of occluded areas is suppressed by a self-organizing process. In the first step the images are filtered by a set of oriented Gabor filters. A complex-valued correlation-based similarity measurement, which is applied to the responses of the Gabor filters, is used in the second step to initialize a self-organizing process. In this self-organizing network, which is described by coupled, non-linear evolution equations, the continuity and the uniqueness constraints are established. Occlusions are detected implicitly without a computationally intensive bidirectional matching strategy. Due to the special similarity measurement, dense disparity maps can be calculated with subpixel accuracy. Unlike phase-difference methods the disparity range is not limited to the modulation wavelength of the quadrature-filter. Therefore, there is no need for a hierachical coarse-to-fine control strategy in our approach.

1   Introduction

Stereo vision is a passive method used to recover the depth information of a scene, which is lost during the projection of a point in the 3D-scene onto the 2D image plane. In stereo vision, in which two or more views of a scene are used, the depth information can be reconstructed from the different positions in the images to which a physical point in the 3D-scene is projected. The displacement of the corresponding positions in the image planes is called disparity. The central problem in stereo vision, known as the correspondence problem, is to find corresponding points or features in the images. This task can be an ambiguous one due to several similar structures or periodic elements in the images. Furthermore, there may be occluded regions in the scene, which can be seen only by one camera. In these regions there is no solution for the correspondence problem. Interocular differences such as perspective distortions, differences in illumination and camera noise make it even more difficult to solve the correspondence problem. Due to these aspects, the correspondence problem is a ill-posed problem according to Hadamard [5, 25]. The strategies used in solving the correspondence

---

1 This work is supported by a grant from the DFG Graduate Center „Parallele Rechnernetzwerke in der Produktionstechnik", ME 872/4-1.

problem can be divided into three major categories: area-based, feature-based and phase-based techniques. The area-based strategies use the intensities of the images to match them locally at each pixel [23]. Stereo techniques, which match features derived from intensity images rather than image intensities themselves, are called "feature-based" [12, 18, 21, 22, 26]. Whereas area-based methods produce dense disparity maps, feature-based strategies are only able to calculate disparities at locations where features occur. Because of the ill-posed character of the correspondence problem both techniques often yield multiple candidates for the match of a feature or an image area. Thus additional mechanisms are required to choose the correct match from among all the candidates. For this purpose techniques such as relaxation labeling [4, 18, 21, 27], regularization theory [3, 10, 11, 19, 25, 29] and dynamic programming [2, 24] are used by many researchers to impose global consistency constraints. Techniques in which disparity is expressed in terms of phase differences in the output of local band-pass filters applied to the images are called "phase-based" methods [7, 8, 15, 28]. The main advantage of phase-based techniques is that disparity estimations are obtained with subpixel accuracy without a subpixel feature localization. In contrast to area-based or feature-based strategies, an additional mechanism for the purpose of disambiguation is not necessary because the disparity range is limited to the modulation wavelength of the filter. To treat stereo images with a large disparity range, hierachical, strategies with multiple resolutions are necessary to obtain correct measurements. In such strategies the coarse disparity measurements are used as an initialization of the next finer level. If no special mechanisms are provided, all techniques of the three categories tend to produce wrong disparity estimates in occluded areas.

Without the occurrence of occluded regions in the images, stereo matching is a one to one mapping of the two images. In general, however, there may be several objects in the scene with different distances in relation to the cameras which cause discontinuity in disparity and occlusions near intensity edges defining the boundaries of different object surfaces. Constraints such as uniqueness, smoothness or ordering of the disparity, which are utilized to simplify the matching process are invalid assumptions in occluded regions. If occlusions are not specially treated in the matching process, they may be incorrectly matched with regions in the other image. Although occlusions are one of the essential reasons for wrong matches in stereo analysis, there are only a few approaches which treat them explicitly. One way to avoid correspondence errors in occluded areas is a bidirectional or dual matching process [14, 16, 20, 31]. In this approach matching is carried out from the left to the right and from the right to the left image in two separate, but identical processes. Occluded areas, which are indicated by the mismatch between the two disparity maps, are marked in so called occlusion maps and they are excluded from further calculations. This technique is based on the assumption that the match with features or pixel intensities in occluded areas is not as good as the match with the correct regions in the matching process, which is carried out in the other direction. Due to interocular differences, this need not be generally true. Another disadvantage of these techniques is the high computational complexity of the bidirectional matching process.

In our approach we use a complex-valued similarity measurement applied to the output of oriented Gabor filters [9]. Similar to phase-based methods, this measurement is very robust with respect to interocular differences and provides dense data. Due to the correlation-based similarity measurement the disparity range is not limited, so coarse-to-fine control strategies are not required. We use the real part of this measurement to initialize a self-organizing process based on the pattern recognition equation introduced by Haken [13]. To each image point and to each possible disparity we assign a variable, which satisfies a non-linear evolution equation. The continuity constraint is established by a local cooperative coupling of the variables. All variables are involved in a competition so that after reaching the steady state of the dynamical process the variables with non-zero values represent the disparities at the image points. Contrary to the approach used by Reimann and Haken [27] the competition is arranged in a way that variables in occluded regions are prevented from winning the competition. Due to the special symmetry property of the similarity measurement no computationally intensive bidirectional match is required. After the correct disparities are determined by the self-organizing process, the imaginary part of the similarity measurement is used to improve the disparity estimation to subpixel accuracy.

2 Initial Processing

2.1 Gabor Filters

Since Sanger [28] proposed the use of the phase information in the output of local Gabor filters for binocular disparity measurements, many phase-based methods, which use quadrature-pairs of band-pass constant-phase filters, have been developed [7, 8, 15, 28]. The reason for the growing interest in these techniques are their numerous desirable properties. Disparity estimates are obtained with subpixel accuracy, dense disparity maps can be calculated, and no special treatment of the ambiguity of the correspondence problem is required. Furthermore, the measurements are robust with respect to smooth illumination differences between the two images because phase is amplitude invariant. In order to exploit some of these desirable properties, we decompose the images in the first step using a set of orientated Gabor filters.

Let $r(x)$ be the complex-valued result of the two-dimensional convolution of a Gabor filter $g(x)$ with an image $i(x)$ at the coordinate $x = [x_1, x_2]^T$.

$$r(x) = g(x) * i(x) \tag{1}$$

The Gabor filter $g(x)$ is tuned to an orientation ϕ and to a spatial frequency k_0.

$$g(x) = \frac{1}{2\pi ab} e^{-\frac{1}{2}x^T Ax} e^{jk_0^T x} \tag{2}$$

where $j^2 = -1$ and

$$A = RPR^T = \begin{bmatrix} \cos\phi & -\sin\phi \\ \sin\phi & \cos\phi \end{bmatrix} \begin{bmatrix} a^{-2} & 0 \\ 0 & b^{-2} \end{bmatrix} \begin{bmatrix} \cos\phi & \sin\phi \\ -\sin\phi & \cos\phi \end{bmatrix}. \tag{3}$$

The spatial support of the filter and the bandwidth respectively depend on the parameter matrix P.

2.2 Similarity Measurement

There are some reasons why we do not use the phase-difference of the Gabor filters directly for disparity estimation: The basis for phase-difference methods consists of the Fourier shift theorem. But because of the local spatial support of the filters used in practice, the Fourier shift theorem does not strictly apply. Furthermore, the limited disparity range requires some form of coarse-to-fine control strategy, in which an initial guess is provided from coarser levels to bring the images into the disparity range of the next finer level. This common strategy may fail if the coarsest channel yields a poor estimate. In this case the process may converge to an incorrect disparity. To prevent errors due to phase-instabilities, which may occur when the filter output passes through the origin in the complex plane and to avoid coarse-to-fine control strategies, we use a correlation-based approach, which preserves the desirable properties of phase-based techniques.

With the convolution of the product of the left filter response $r_l(x)$ and a spatial shifted complex conjugate version of the right filter response $r_r(x)$ with a small real valued window $w(x)$, we obtain a local, complex-valued measurement $\rho_{lr}(x, d)$ of the similarity between the filtered images. This measurement is normalized to the local energy of the filter responses:

$$\rho_{lr}(x, d) = \frac{w(x) * r_l(x) r_r^*(x + d)}{\sqrt{w(x) * |r_l(x)|^2} \sqrt{w(x) * |r_r(x + d)|^2}} \tag{4}$$

where the disparity $d = [d_1, d_2]^T$ acts as a two-dimensional spatial displacement of the right filter response. Due to the epipolar constraint, the vertical component of the disparity is zero if the conventional parallel axis stereo geometry is used. If a non-parallel axis stereo geometry is used, the images can be easily transformed into parallel axes images by rectification [1]. In this case the convolution in (4) can be reduced to a one-dimensional convolution. The window $w(x)$ is chosen to be a one-dimensional gaussian with a support equal to the horizontal support of the Gabor filter.

The real and the imaginary parts of (4) can be expressed in terms of magnitude $|r(x)|$ and phase $\varphi(x)$.

$$\text{Re}\{\rho_{lr}(x, d)\} = \frac{w(x) * |r_l(x)||r_r(x + d)| \cos(\varphi_l(x) - \varphi_r(x + d))}{\sqrt{w(x) * |r_l(x)|^2} \sqrt{w(x) * |r_r(x + d)|^2}}$$

$$\text{Im}\{\rho_{lr}(x, d)\} = \frac{w(x) * |r_l(x)||r_r(x + d)| \sin(\varphi_l(x) - \varphi_r(x + d))}{\sqrt{w(x) * |r_l(x)|^2} \sqrt{w(x) * |r_r(x + d)|^2}} \tag{5}$$

If the filter responses are locally similar, we expect a low phase difference. In this case there is a peak in the real part and we expect to find a zero-crossing in the imaginary part due to the approximately linear phase of the Gabor filter output. The peaks in the real part of the similarity measurement act as candidate disparities d between the two images with pixel accuracy. Unlike some other approaches, which use the superposition of similarity measurements applied to several filter channels tuned to different frequencies as a kind of voting strategy [7], we use the real part of the measurement to initialize a self-organizing process to disambiguate the disparities. The zero-crossings of the imaginary part in the proximity of correct disparities are used to obtain subpixel accurate disparity estimations, which is described in chapter 4.

A further important property of the similarity measurement, which is central to the detection of occlusions, is the following identity between the measurement, which is done from the right image to the left image and the measurement which is done in the opposite direction.

$$\rho_{lr}(x, d) = \rho_{rl}^*(x + d, -d) \qquad (6)$$

3 Correspondence by Self-organization

3.1 Related Work

One of the essential problems in stereo matching is that the correct correspondence may not be the one of the highest similarity. The reason for this is that the images may differ due to noise or distortions. Furthermore there may be points or areas in the image, which match equally well with several points or areas in the other images. These ambiguities, which are characteristic for ill-posed problems, can only be resolved by using natural constraints, which are general assumptions of the physical world. The most important constraints usually used in stereo vision are the uniqueness and the smoothness of the disparity map over the two-dimensional image plane first postulated by Marr and Poggio [21]. There are many approaches, which use these constraints to define energy functions, the global minimum of which is used to determine the correct correspondences. Strategies used to find the global minimum are, for instance, standard regularization theory [11, 25, 29] or stochastic relaxation [3, 10, 19]. To disambiguate the correspondence problem Reimann and Haken [27] use a kind of relaxation labeling algorithm. Similar to some other approaches of this category [4, 18] they assign a real-valued, time dependent variable $\xi(x, d, t)$ to each image coordinate x and to each possible disparity d. These variables, which are called binocular neurons, are involved in a dynamical process, which is described by coupled nonlinear evolution equations. The activity of these neurons is initialized by the output of an area-based matching technique. To satisfy the uniqueness constraint, the neurons are involved in a competition, which can be won only by one neuron at each image point. To get smooth disparity maps, each neuron is cooperatively connected to a small local area U representing the same disparity. The dynamics of the self-organizing process are described by the so-called coupled pattern recognition equations:

$$\dot{\xi}(x, d, t) = \left\{ \lambda(x, d) - (B + C) \sum_{d' \neq d} \xi^2(x, d', t) - C\xi^2(x, d, t) \right.$$

$$\left. + \sum_{x' \in U} D(x')\xi(x', d, t) \right\} \xi(x, d, t) \tag{7}$$

where the parameters B, C are positive constants. The first term $\lambda(x, d)$ represents an exponential growth of the amplitude $\xi(x, d, t)$ that depends on the area-based similarity between the images. The second term leads to a competition of all neurons at the same image point and the third term restricts the amplitude of $\xi(x, d, t)$. The fourth term represents the cooperative coupling, which is weighted by $D(x)$, of variables with the same disparity in a small local area in the image plane. It can be shown that only one of the variables at each image point reaches a non-zero stable fixed point and wins the competition in this way, while all of the other variables take the value zero. If we neglect the fourth term, we get the original pattern recognition equation introduced by Haken [13]. In this case the variable with the highest initial value always wins the competition. By adding the fourth term to the pattern recognition equation, variables, which have a strong cooperative area U, may win the competition even if they were initially smaller.

3.2 Initialization

In our approach, we use a modified version of the self-organizing process introduced by Reimann and Haken to disambiguate the disparity estimates resulting from the peaks in the real part of the similarity measurement defined in (4). For this purpose the variables of the dynamical process are initialized at the time $t = 0$ by a function f depending on the real part of the similarity measurement:

$$\xi(x, d, t = 0) = f\left(\sum_i c_i \mathrm{Re}\{\rho_{lr_i}(x, d)\} \right) \tag{8}$$

where the subscript i denotes the similarity measurements, which are applied to several filter channels. These channels are tuned to different orientations (e.g. $-30°, 0°, 30°$) but to the same spatial frequency k_0. The channels i can be weighted individually by the parameters c_i. The function f is used to map the values of the real part of the similarity measurement to a positive range by truncating the negative values. In the following sections the variables are involved in a special self-organizing process, in which natural constraints are exploited to solve the correspondence problem.

3.3 Treatment of Occluded Regions

Since there is no special treatment of occlusions in the approach of Reimann and Haken, an initialization of a variable in an occluded area with a non-zero value always results in a wrong disparity estimation, because there is no solution of the correspondence problem in this area. In order to prevent those correspondence errors, we define a new competition in a self-organizing process, which suppresses variables in occluded image regions.

Occlusions can be detected by a similarity measurement, which is carried out from left to right and vice versa. Figure 1 shows a random dot stereogram, in which a square area marked by the black frame is inserted in the images with a relative shift of ten pixels. The image point marked by the white point in the left image does not occur in the right image. The similarity measurement, which is carried out from left to right at this point shows a peak in the real part, which corresponds to the position marked by the black point in the right image. Due to its high similarity measurement this wrong disparity would probably win the competition. As a result of (6) the real part of the similarity measure carried out from right to left must show the same peak at the disparity with the opposite sign at the corresponding position in the right image. But in this measurement there is additionally a higher peak, which corresponds to the match with the correct image area in the left image marked by the black point. If the values of this measurement are also included in the competition, the disparity with the highest peak in this measurement is likely to win.

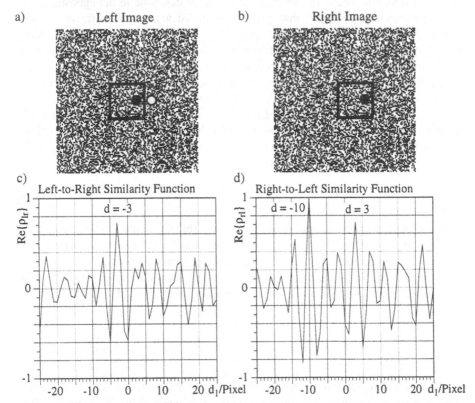

Fig. 1. a) and b) Random dot stereogram. c) Real part of the left-to-right similarity function of an occluded area marked by the white point in the left image. d) Real part of the right-to-left similarity function at the position marked by the black point in the right image, which corresponds to the maximum in c)

To prevent the match of occluded areas with other image points, we include both directions of the similarity measurement in the competition. By exploiting equation (6), which is also valid for the variables $\xi(x, d, t)$, the new competition term is given by:

$$\sum_{d' \neq d} \xi^2(x, d', t) + \xi^2(x + d - d', d', t) \tag{9}$$

Contrary to other bidirectional matching techniques [14, 16, 20, 31] the occlusion detection in our approach is done implicitly by a matching process, which is carried out in only one direction. Therefore, an explicit calculation of a computationally intensive bidirectional match is not necessary. Without loss of generality we refer in the following part only to the match, which is done from left to right.

3.4 Treatment of Matches between Occlusions

If a cooperative term as in (7) is used with a competitive term as shown in (9) a match of occluded image regions with areas seen from both views can be prevented even if the wrong match is locally higher than the correct match done in the opposite direction. Unfortunately, an object may produce occluded areas in both images, which occur on different sides of the object. So, if the established disparity range is large enough and a match between this occluded areas can be calculated, it is probable that a variable will win the competition, which represents a correspondence between the occluded areas. To treat this type of wrong correspondence, we consider a cyclopean camera, which was introduced by Julesz [16]. From the point of view of a cyclopean camera, the reconstructed 3D-coordinates of the correspondence between these occluded areas are found either in front of or behind the object that produces these occlusions. The cyclopean image coordinates x_c of a variable at the coordinates x in the left image and with disparity d are given by:

$$x_c = x + \frac{d}{2} \tag{10}$$

In this cyclopean image the variables representing the object and the correspondence between the occlusions have the same image coordinates. In order to suppress correspondences between occlusions, we extent the self-organizing process once again by involving all variables in the same competition, which show the same cyclopean image coordinates. This strategy can be implemented by using the following competition term:

$$\sum_{d' \neq d} \xi^2(x, d', t) + \xi^2(x + d - d', d', t) + \xi^2\left(x + \frac{d}{2} - \frac{d'}{2}, d', t\right) \tag{11}$$

Because occluded areas are unlikely to match better in large image areas than correct correspondences, matches between occlusions are suppressed by this technique. The dynamical behavior of the resulting self-organizing process is given by:

$$\dot{\xi}(x, d, t) = \left\{ A - C\xi^2(x, d, t) \right.$$

$$- \frac{B}{3N} \sum_{d' \neq d} \xi^2(x, d', t) + \xi^2(x + d - d', d', t) + \xi^2\left(x + \frac{d}{2} - \frac{d'}{2}, d', t\right) \quad (12)$$

$$\left. + \frac{D}{M} \sum_{x' \in U} \xi(x', d, t) \right\} \xi(x, d, t)$$

$$= F\{x, d, t\}$$

where the parameters A, B, C, D are positive constants. The terms that lead to the competition and to the cooperative coupling are normalized to the amount of involved variables N, M. For reasons of simplicity we choose the coupling constant D to be equal to all variables in the cooperative area U and the exponential growing term to be independent of the similarity measurement. In practice this self-organizing process can be easily implemented as an iterative algorithm if the differential equations are integrated numerically.

3.5   Properties of the Self-organizing Process

The parameters in equation (12) have to be chosen suitably in order to establish a competition and to insure the stability of the fixed points of the system. The fixed points $\xi_r(x, d)$ of (12) satisfy the condition $\dot{\xi}_r(x, d, t) = 0$. There are three possible solutions for the fixed points:

$$\xi_{r_1}(x, d) = 0$$

$$\xi_{r_{2/3}}(x, d) = \pm \sqrt{\frac{\Gamma(x, d)}{C}} \quad (13)$$

where $\Gamma(x, d)$ is given by:

$$\Gamma(x, d) = \left(A + \frac{D}{M} \sum_{x' \in U} \xi_r(x', d) \right.$$

$$\left. - \frac{B}{3N} \sum_{d' \neq d} \xi_r^2(x, d') + \xi_r^2(x + d - d', d') + \xi_r^2\left(x + \frac{d}{2} - \frac{d'}{2}, d'\right) \right) \quad (14)$$

By initializing the process with positive values, it can be shown (see appendix A) that the negative fixed points in (13) are never reached, thus we only consider the fixed points $\xi_{r_1}(x, d)$ and the positive fixed points $\xi_{r_2}(x, d)$.
Under certain conditions a competition can take place, in which variables with a strong cooperative support and a high initial value are likely to win (see appendix B). The winner of the competition is the variable that takes the stable fixed point solution $\xi_{r_2}(x, d)$. This fixed point should be reached only by one variable whereas all other variables, which are involved in the competition, should decrease to the fixed point solution $\xi_{r_1}(x, d)$. Furthermore, the parameters have to be chosen in a way that the sta-

bility of the fixed points is guaranteed under certain circumstances (see appendix A). The influence of the variables in the cooperative area on the self-organizing process is steered by the parameter D.

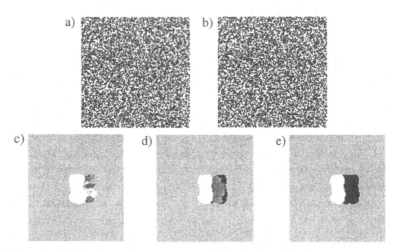

Fig. 2. a) and b) 50% Random dot stereogram. c) Disparity map without occlusion treatment. d) Disparity map generated by a self-organizing process with an extended competition defined by equation (9). e) Disparity map generated by using equation (12)

Figure 2 shows a random dot stereogram in which a rectangular area is inserted in the images with a relative displacement, which is equal to the width of the inserted rectangle. The results of the self-organizing process with different competition terms but equal parameters are shown by the disparity maps below the stereogram. The gray values in the disparity maps represent the disparities of the variables, which have reached the fixed point solution $\xi_{r_2}(x, d)$. If there is no variable at an image point that has reached the solution $\xi_{r_2}(x, d)$ the disparity remains undefined. These areas are marked black in the disparity maps. The disparity range was chosen to be twice as large as the width of the displaced rectangle. The left disparity map shown in figure 2c is calculated by a self-organizing process defined in (7). Because there is no special treatment of occlusions, the disparities on the right of the rectangle, represent false, accidental matches of the occluded area, because there are no correct correspondence partners in the right image.

The disparity map shown in figure 2d is generated by using an extended competition term defined in (9). In the occluded area only those variables have reached the fixed point $\xi_{r_2}(x, d)$, which represent matches with the occluded region in the right image. Because the disparities of these wrong matches are negative in this example, they are darker than the disparity of the rectangle. In the black areas none of the variables, which represent a match between the occluded areas in both images, have been initialized to a non-zero value by the function defined in (8). The disparity map in figure 2e is obtained by using the new self-organizing process introduced in (12). Due to the competition term defined in (11), all variables in the occluded area have been suppressed, and no disparity value has been calculated.

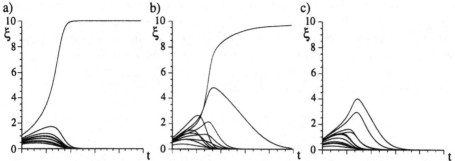

Fig. 3. Time dependent behavior of variable values at different image points. a) Image area without ambiguous matches. The variable with the highest initial value wins the competition. b) Image area with ambiguous matches. Due to the local cooperative coupling, a variable wins the competition, which was not the initially highest one. c) Competition in an occluded image area. No variable reaches the non-zero fixed point

The competition of variables lying at the same cyclopean image coordinates, which is established by (11), is related to the disparity gradient limit first proposed by Burt and Julesz [6]. In several approaches an approximation of the disparity gradient limit is used to disambiguate the correspondence problem (see for example [26]). Usually the disparity gradient is approximated by:

$$D_{pq} = \left| \frac{d_p - d_q}{x_p - x_q} \right| \tag{15}$$

where $x_{p/q}$ are the cyclopean image coordinates of the points p, q and $d_{p/q}$ the corresponding disparities. A match is only permitted if the disparity gradient is lower than a certain limit. For $D_{ij} < 2$ the disparity gradient limit is equal to the ordering constraint, which is often used in approaches using dynamic programming techniques (see for example [2]). In the steady state of our self-organizing process described in (12) there is at most one variable at the same cyclopean image point that reaches a non-zero fixed point. Therefore, matches are only prevented in our approach if their disparity gradient is infinity. This restriction of the disparity is much weaker than the ordering constraint or the disparity gradient limits used in practice.

4 Disparity Estimation with Subpixel Accuracy

As mentioned in chapter 2.2 the imaginary part of the similarity measurement introduced in (4) can be exploited to obtain a disparity estimation with subpixel accuracy. Due to the approximate linear phase of the Gabor filter, we expect to find a zero-crossing in the imaginary part of the similarity measurement close to a peak in the real part. After the self-organizing process has reached the steady state we interpolate the imaginary part at the position of variables with non-zero values, because they are likely to correspond to a peak in the real part of the similarity measurement. Then we use the position of the zero-crossings in the imaginary part as the new subpixel accurate disparity estimations. By using this technique we are able to obtain subpixel accurate disparity estimations without blurring of the discontinuities in the disparity map. The best results are obtained when the imaginary part of the similarity measurement is used, which gets its input from the filter orientation, in which the highest magnitude of the filter response occurs. Figure 4 shows a stereogram of white noise, in which one image is a copy of the other image, which is stretched horizontally by 10%.

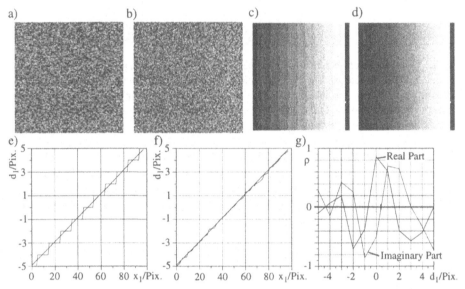

Fig. 4. a) + b) Stereogram generated with white noise. c) + e) Disparity map and disparity function with pixel accuracy. d) + f) Disparity map and disparity function with subpixel accuracy. g) Real and imaginary part of the similarity measurement

If the disparity is calculated by interpolating the zero-crossings in the imaginary part of the similarity measurement as shown in figure 4g, the root mean square of the quantization errors can be reduced in this example by 60%.

5 Experimental Results

The current algorithm has been tested on a number of real and artificial image pairs. In this section some of the results are presented. The parameters were chosen identically for all examples to $A = 0.4$, $B = 1.0$, $C = 0.01$, and $D = 0.61$. The cooperative area U was chosen to be a square area of 5x5 pixel. To reduce the computational expenditure, the horizontal disparity range was restricted to $|d_1| \leq 15$ pixel. The presented natural image pairs had been rectified, thus no vertical disparities had to be calculated. The Gabor filters were tuned to a modulation frequency of $k_0 = \pi/2$ and had a bandwidth of 0.6 octaves. The images were filtered by three channels tuned to the orientations $(-30°, 0°, 30°)$. The values of the superposed similarity measurements of the filter channels were truncated by their negative results and normalized to the number of channels by the function f to initialize the variables of the self-organizing process. Detected occlusions are marked black in the disparity maps. The disparity maps are registered in the right image coordinates.

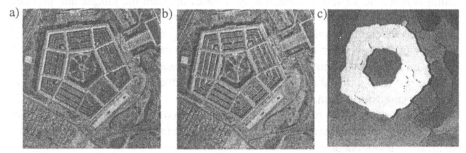

Fig. 5. a) Left and b) right image of the "Pentagon" stereo pair. c) Disparity map

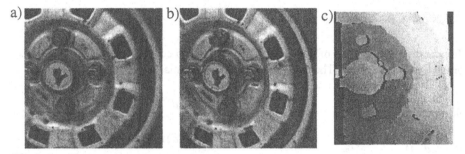

Fig. 6. Rectified a) left and b) right image of an old car tire. d) Disparity map

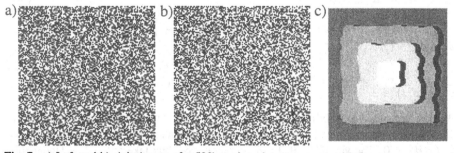

Fig. 7. a) Left and b) right image of a 50% random dot stereogram with four square areas of different disparity. c) Disparity map

6   Conclusion

In this paper we have outlined a new method for the estimation of disparities in stereo image pairs. In our approach we have combined some desirable properties of existing techniques such as the subpixel accuracy of phase-based techniques and the robustness and the high parallelization potential of cooperative approaches. Furthermore, we have implemented a new method of detecting occlusions in stereo images, which are one of the most important error sources in stereo matching. Due to a complex-valued, correlation-based technique, which is applied to the output of oriented Gabor filters, the algorithm is robust to smooth illumination differences between the images and provides dense, subpixel accurate disparity estimations. The continuity constraint and an extended version of the uniqueness constraint are applied in a self-organizing process. Because of this new technique occlusions are detected implicitly and no disparity estimates are calculated in this areas. As shown in some examples the algorithm produces reliable results in artificial and natural images, even if there are large occluded areas or disparity gradients in them.

Future work will include a fast, parallel implementation of this algorithm for the purpose of distance measurement and obstacle avoidance in order to navigate an autonomous robot manipulator.

Appendix A: Stability of the Fixed Points

To guarantee the stability of the fixed points, we have to consider the functional matrix of the linearized system. The non-zero elements of the matrix are:

$$\frac{\partial}{\partial \xi(x, d, t)} F(x, d, t)\big|_{\xi_r} = \Gamma(x, d) - 3C\xi_r^2(x, d)$$

$$\frac{\partial}{\partial \xi(x, d', t)} F(x, d, t)\big|_{\xi_r} = -2B\xi_r(x, d')\xi_r(x, d)/3N \quad \text{for } d' \neq d$$

$$\frac{\partial}{\partial \xi(x+d-d', d', t)} F(x, d, t)\big|_{\xi_r} = -2B\xi_r(x+d-d', d')\xi_r(x, d)/3N \quad \text{for } d' \neq d \quad (16)$$

$$\frac{\partial}{\partial \xi\left(x+\frac{d}{2}-\frac{d'}{2}, d', t\right)} F(x, d, t)\big|_{\xi_r} = -2B\xi_r\left(x+\frac{d}{2}-\frac{d'}{2}, d'\right)\xi_r(x, d)/3N \quad \text{for } d' \neq d$$

$$\frac{\partial}{\partial \xi(x', d, t)} F(x, d, t)\big|_{\xi_r} = \frac{D}{M}\xi_r(x, d) \quad \text{for } x' \in U$$

We now consider the stability of the fixed points under several different conditions. In the first case, we assume all variables of the competition to take the fixed point solution $\xi_{r_1}(x, d) = 0$. The variables of the cooperative area may take any value. Under this conditions the functional matrix has a diagonal sub-block of the form:

$$\frac{\partial}{\partial \xi(x, d, t)} F(x, d, t)\big|_{\xi_{r_1}} = A + \frac{D}{M}\sum_{x' \in U}\xi_r(x', d) \quad (17)$$

Due to the fact that A and D are positive constants and all variables are positive, this kind of fixed points is not stable, because the eigenvalues of this sub-block are positive. Thus not all of the variables, which are involved in the same competition process, can take the fixed point solution $\xi_{r_1}(x, d) = 0$ if they were initialized by a non-zero value.

If one of the variables takes the solution $\xi_{r_1}(x, d)$, whereas all other variables in the same competition process may take any non-negative value, the fundamental matrix has a diagonal sub-block, which is given by:

$$\frac{\partial}{\partial \xi(x, d, t)} F(x, d, t)\big|_{\xi_{r_1}} = \Gamma(x, d) \tag{18}$$

This fixed point is only stable if $\Gamma(x, d)$ is negative, otherwise it is unstable. Therefore, the variables are unable to take negative values if they are initialized by positive or zero values. Thus, the negative fixed point solution of (13) is never reached. We want to choose the parameters in a way that this kind of fixed points is stable if one variable in the competition process reaches the fixed point solution $\xi_{r_2}(x, d)$, which is given by (13). This leads to the inequality:

$$A - \frac{B}{3N} \xi_{r_2}^2(x, d) < 0 \tag{19}$$

The value of $\xi_{r_2}(x, d)$ can be approximated by the worst case, in which no variable in the cooperative area takes a non-zero value. The non-zero fixed point is then given by $\xi_{r_2}(x, d) = \sqrt{A/C}$. Under these conditions the parameters B, C, and N must fulfill the following inequality:

$$C < \frac{B}{3N} \tag{20}$$

The fixed point $\xi_{r_2}(x, d)$ should be stable if all other variables in the competition process have reached the fixed point solution $\xi_{r_1}(x, d)$. In this case the non-vanishing elements of this sub-block of the functional matrix are given by:

$$\frac{\partial}{\partial \xi(x, d, t)} F(x, d, t)\big|_{\xi_{r_2}} = -2\Gamma(x, d)$$

$$\frac{\partial}{\partial \xi(x', d, t)} F(x, d, t)\big|_{\xi_{r_2}} = \frac{D}{M} \xi_{r_2}(x, d) \quad \text{for } x' \in U \tag{21}$$

From the negative diagonal elements of this sub-block it follows using the theorem of Gerschgorin, that the eigenvalues of this sub-block are negative when the sum of the non-diagonal elements in each row is smaller than every diagonal element (see for example [30]). This is generally true if at least half of the variables in the cooperative area have reached also the fixed point solution $\xi_{r_2}(x, d)$.

Appendix B: Further Parameter Restrictions

To enable a competition, in which the variable with the greatest support of the cooperative area and with the highest value grows stronger than the other involved variables, the parameters need a further restriction.

Let $\xi(x_1, d_1, t)$ be the variable with the highest value in the competition and with the highest cooperative support $u(x_1, d_1, t) = \sum_{x' \in U_1} \xi(x', d_1, t)$,

$$\dot{\xi}(x_1, d_1, t) > \dot{\xi}(x, d, t) \quad \forall d \neq d_1 \text{ and } x \in \left\{ x_1, x_1 - d_1 - d, x_1 - \frac{d_1}{2} - \frac{d}{2} \right\}, \quad (22)$$

then follows from (12):

$$\xi(x_1, d_1, t) \left(A - \frac{B}{3N} s + \frac{B}{3N} \xi^2(x_1, d_1, t) - C\xi^2(x_1, d_1, t) + \frac{D}{M} u(x_1, d_1, t) \right) >$$

$$\xi(x, d, t) \left(A - \frac{B}{3N} s + \frac{B}{3N} \xi^2(x, d, t) - C\xi^2(x, y, t) + \frac{D}{M} u(x, d, t) \right) \qquad (23)$$

where s is the sum of the squares of all variable values involved in the competition.

$$s = \sum_{d'} \xi^2(x_1, d', t) + \xi^2(x_1 + d_1 - d', d', t) + \xi^2\left(x_1 + \frac{d_1}{2} - \frac{d'}{2}, d', t \right) \qquad (24)$$

Because the sum s is equal to all involved variables and the cooperative support of $\xi(x_1, d_1, t)$ is higher than the support of the other involved variables, the inequality (23) is fulfilled, if the following inequality is valid:

$$\left(\frac{B}{3N} - C \right) \xi^2(x_1, d_1, t) > \left(\frac{B}{3N} - C \right) \xi^2(x, d, t). \qquad (25)$$

Under the assumption made above this results in the parameter restriction:

$$\frac{B}{3N} > C. \qquad (26)$$

This inequality is always fulfilled if the stability of the fixed point $\xi_{r_1}(x, d)$ is guaranteed for the worst case discussed in appendix A (see equation (20)).

References

1. Ayache, N.; Hansen, C.: Rectification of Images for Binocular and Trinocular Stereovision. In Proc. of the 9th Intern. Conference on Pattern Recognition, pp. 11-16, Oktober 1988.
2. Baker, H. H.; Binford, T. O.: Depth from Edge and Intensity Based Stereo. In Proceedings of the 7th International Joint Conference on Artifical Intelligence, pp. 631-636, August 1981.
3. Barnard, S. T.: Stochastic stereo matching over scale. In International Journal of Computer Vision, vol. 2, pp. 17-32, 1989.
4. Barnard, S. T.; Thompson, W. B.: Disparity Analysis of Images. In Transactions on Pattern Analysis and Machine Intelligence, vol. PAMI-2, no. 4, pp. 333-340, July 1980.
5. Bertero, M.; Poggio, T. A.; Torre, V.: Ill-Posed Problems in Early Vision. In Proceedings of the IEEE, vol. 76, no. 8, pp. 869-889, August 1988.
6. Burt, P.; Julesz, B.: A Disparity Gradient Limit for Binocular Fusion. In Science, vol. 208, pp. 615-617, 1980.
7. Fleet, D. J.: Disparity from Local Weighted Phase-Correlation. In IEEE International Conference on Systems, Man and Cybernetics, pp. 48-56, San Antonio, October 1994.
8. Fleet, D. J.; Jepson, A. D.; Jenkin, M. R. M.: Phase-Based Disparity Measurement. In CVGIP: Image Understanding, vol. 53, no. 2, pp. 198-210, March 1991.

9. Gabor, D.: Theory of communication. In J. IEE, vol. 93, pp. 429-457, London, 1946.
10. Geman, S.; Geman, D.: Stochastic Relaxation, Gibbs Distributions, and the Bayesian Restoration of Images. In IEEE Transactions on Pattern Analysis and Machine Intelligence, vol. PAMI-6, no. 6, pp. 721-741, November 1984.
11. Gennert, M. A.: Brightness-based stereo matching. In International Conference on Computer Vision, pp. 139-143, 1988.
12. Grimson, W. E. L.: A computer implementation of a theory of human stereo vision. In Philosophical Transactions of the Royal Society of London, vol. B 292, pp. 217-253, 1981.
13. Haken, H.: Synergetic Computers and Cognition. Springer-Verlag, Berlin, 1991.
14. Hoff, W.; Ahuja, N.: Surfaces from Stereo: Integrating Feature Matching, Disparity Estimation, and Contour Detection. In IEEE Transactions on Pattern Analysis and Machine Intelligence, vol. 11, no. 2, February 1989.
15. Jenkin, M. R. M.; Jepson, A. D.: Recovering Local Surface Structure through Local Phase Difference Measurements. In Computer Vision, Graphics and Image Processing: Image Understanding, vol. 59, no. 1, pp. 72-93, January, 1994.
16. Jones, D. G.; Malik, J.: A computational framework for determining stereo correspondence from a set of linear spatial filters. In Proceedings of the 2nd European Conference on Computer Vision, Springer Verlag, Berlin, pp. 395-410, 1992
17. Julesz, B.: Foundations of cyclopean perception. University of Chicago Press, 1971.
18. Kim, Y. C.; Aggarwal, J. K.: Positioning Three-Dimensional Objects Using Stereo Images. In IEEE Journal of Robotics and Automation, vol. RA-3, no. 4, pp. 361-373, August 1987.
19. Konrad, J.; Dubois, E.: Multigrid Bayesian Estimation of Image Motion Fields Using Stochastic Relaxation. In Proceedings of the 2nd International Conference on Computer Vision, pp. 354-362, 1988.
20. Luo, A.; Burkhardt, H.: An Intensity-Based Cooperative Bidirectional Stereo Matching with Simultaneous Detektion of Discontinuities and Occlusions. In International Journal of Computer Vision, vol. 15, pp. 171-188, 1995.
21. Marr, D.; Poggio, T.: A computational theory of human stereo vision. In Proceedings of Royal Society of London, vol. B 204, pp. 301-328, 1979.
22. Medioni, G.; Nevatia, R.: Segment-Based Stereo Matching. In Computer Vision, Graphics, and Image Processing, vol. 31, pp. 2-18, 1985.
23. Moravec, H. P.: Towards automatic visual obstacle avoidance. In Proceedings of the 5th International Joint Conference on Artifical Intelligence, p. 584, 1977.
24. Otha, Y.; Kanade T.: Stereo by intra- and inter-scanline search. In IEEE Transactions on Pattern Analysis and Machine Intelligence, vol. PAMI-7, no. 2, pp. 139-154, March 1985.
25. Poggio, T. A.; Torre, V.; Koch, C.: Computational Vision and Regularization Theory. In Nature, vol. 317, pp. 314-319, 1985.
26. Pollard, S. B.; Mayhew, J. E. W.; Frisby, J. P.: PMF: A stereo correspondence algorithm using a disparity gradient constraint. In Perception, 14, pp. 449-470, 1985.
27. Reimann, D.; Haken, H.: Stereovision by Self-Organisation. In Biological Cybernetics, vol. 71, pp. 17-26, 1994.
28. Sanger, T. D.: Stereo Disparity Computation Using Gabor Filters. In Biological Cybernetics, vol. 59, pp. 405-418, 1988.
29. Terzopoulos, D.: Regularization of Inverse Visual Problems Involving Discontinuities. In IEEE Trans. Pattern Anal. and Machine Intel., vol. PAMI-8, no. 4, pp. 413-424, July 1986.
30. Varga, R. S.: Matrix Iterative Analyse. G. Forsythe (ed.), Prentice-Hall Series in Automatic Computation, New Jersey, 1962.
31. Weng, J.; Ahuja, N.; Huang, T. S.: Two-view matching. In Proceedings of the 2nd International Conference on Computer Vision, pp. 64-73, 1988.

A Solution for the Registration of Multiple 3D Point Sets Using Unit Quaternions

Raouf Benjemaa and Francis Schmitt

cole Nationale Suprieure des Tlcommunications
CNRS URA 820 - TSI dept
46 rue Barrault, F-75634 Paris Cedex 13, France
benjemaa@ima.enst.fr, schmitt@ima.enst.fr
WWW home page: http://www-ima.enst.fr/~benjemaa

Abstract. Registering 3D point sets is a common problem in computer vision. The case of two point sets has been analytically well solved by several authors. In this paper we present an analytic solution for solving the problem of a simultaneous registration of M point sets, $M > 2$, by rigid motions. The solution is based on the use of unit quaternions for the representation of the rotations.

We show that the rotation optimization can be decoupled from the translation one. The optimal translations are given by the resolution of a linear equation system which depends on the rotated centroid of the overlaps. The unit quaternions representing the best rotations are optimized by applying an iterative process on symmetric 4×4 matrices. The matrices correspond to the mutual overlaps between the point sets.

We have applied this method to the registration of several overlapping 3D surfaces sampled on an object. Our results on simulated and real data show that the algorithm works efficiently.

1 Introduction

Registering 3D point sets with 3D rigid motions is a common problem in computer vision and robotics. This problem typically occurs when 3D data are acquired from different viewpoints by stereo, range sensing, tactile sensing, *etc.*

We call **pairwise registration** the registration of two points sets. However, the case of a larger number of point sets overlapping each other occurs often. We can sequentially apply a pairwise registration by matching two by two the different sets. This widely used scheme doesn't take into account the whole correspondences between the data sets during a registration step. It remains essentially a local approach and it may cause error-distribution problems as pointed out in [10, 4, 15, 3]. For example the residual error of each individual pairwise registration can be low but unfortunately we have frequently observed a propagation and a cumulation of the registration errors.

Thus it appears to be much more efficient to register simultaneously the multiple point sets in order to keep the residual registration errors homogeneously distributed. We call **global registration** the simultaneous registration of multiple point sets which partially overlap each other and for which we know a correspondence between their points into each overlap.

In this paper we propose an analytic quaternion-based solution to solve the problem of the global registration of M point sets, with know correspondences, $M > 2$. The correspondence establishment depends on the type of data to be registered. To determine the correspondence between several point sets sampled on an object surface, the authors have proposed an efficient method based on a space partitioning with a multi-z-buffer technique [1,3]. By combining this fast correspondence establishment and the quaternion based global registration, the ICP (*Iterative Closest Point*) algorithm originally proposed by Besl and McKay [5] to register two point sets can be conveniently generalized to globally register multiple point sets.

The next section describes previous works on the registration of multiple data sets. We then recall some properties of the unit quaternions in section 3 and the classic quaternion-based solution for registering two point sets [7,8] in section 4 . In section 5 we state the problem of the global registration. The optimal solutions for the translations and then for the rotations are detailed in sections 6 and 7, respectively. Finally, experimental results on both synthetic and real data are shown in section 8.

2 Literature Review

Different analytic methods –singular value decomposition, polar decomposition and quaternion representation– have been proposed for registering two point sets with known correspondences. Each of them computes the rigid transformation, as a solution to a least squares formulation of the problem. For an overview and a discussion of these techniques see Kanatani [11] and references therein. Recently a comparative analysis of the various method was given in [12]. It was concluded that no one algorithm was found to be superior in all cases to the other ones.

Only few authors have investigated the registration of multiple point sets as a global problem. We may distinguish three different categories in the literature: **(a)** dynamic-system-based global registration, **(b)** iterative global registration, and **(c)** analytic global registration.

Kamgar-Parsi *et al.* [10] have developed a global registration method using a dynamic system for the 2D registration of multiple overlapping range images. The position of each range image is then optimized according to a 2D rigid transformation with three degrees of freedom (one for the rotation and two for the translation).

Recently Stoddart and Hilton [15] have also proposed a method in category (a) for the 3D global registration of multiple free-form surfaces. Their dynamic system is made of a set of springs of length null and whose extremities are connected between pairs of corresponding points on two overlapping surfaces. The registration is then obtained by solving the equation of the Lagrangian mechanic with an iterative Euler resolution.

In category (b), Bergevin *et al.* [4] have proposed an iterative algorithm based on a modified ICP algorithm to register multiple range images. At each iteration, each range image is successively matched with all the others, and its rigid transformation is estimated. The surfaces are simultaneously moved only at the end of the iteration, after the estimation of the complete set of rigid transformations.

Inspired by this work [4], the authors have developed an iterative method to simultaneously register multiple 3D unstructured data scattered on the surface of an object from different viewpoints [3]. This method is dramatically accelerated by using a multi-z-buffer space partitioning. Unlike Bergevin *et al.*'s method, each surface is immediately transformed when its rigid motion has been estimated. This way, the convergence is accelerated. In order to not favor any surface, its registration order is randomly chosen at each iteration.

The authors have recently proposed an analytic global registration solution based on a linearization of the rotations [2]. The optimal rigid transformation values are given by the simple resolution of two linear-equation systems. It is assumed that the rotation angles are small. Thus the method performs only when data sets are not too far from each others.

The global registration method presented in this paper belongs also to category (c) but the assumption of small rotation angles is not necessary. It is a generalization of the quaternion-based solution of the pairwise registration which has been independently proposed by Faugeras and Hebert [6, 7] and Horn [8].

3 Representing rotations by unit quaternions

The reader not familiar with quaternions can refer to [9, 14, 8, 13]. Quaternions will be denoted here by using symbols with dots above them.

A quaternion $\dot{q}$ can be seen as either a four-dimensional vector $(q_0, q_x, q_y, q_z)^t$, or a scalar q_0 and a tri-dimensional vector $(q_x, q_y, q_z)^t$, or a complex number with three different imaginary parts ($\dot{q} = q_0 + iq_x + jq_y + kq_z$).

The product on the left or on the right of a quaternion $\dot{q}$ by another quaternion $\dot{r} = (r_0, r_x, r_y, r_z)^t$, can conveniently be expressed in terms of the following products of the vector $\dot{q}$ by a 4×4 orthogonal matrix $\mathbb{R}$ or $\bar{\mathbb{R}}$ respectively:

$$\dot{r}\dot{q} = \begin{bmatrix} r_0 & -r_x & -r_y & -r_z \\ r_x & r_0 & -r_z & r_y \\ r_y & r_z & r_0 & -r_x \\ r_z & -r_y & r_x & r_0 \end{bmatrix} \dot{q} = \mathbb{R}\dot{q}, \tag{1}$$

or

$$\dot{q}\dot{r} = \begin{bmatrix} r_0 & -r_x & -r_y & -r_z \\ r_x & r_0 & r_z & -r_y \\ r_y & -r_z & r_0 & r_x \\ r_z & r_y & -r_x & r_0 \end{bmatrix} \dot{q} = \bar{\mathbb{R}}\dot{q}. \tag{2}$$

The unit quaternions are an elegant representation of rotation. Let recall some of their fundamental properties. A rotation R of angle θ around axe $\boldsymbol{u}$ can be represented by the unit quaternion $\dot{q} = (\cos\theta/2, \sin\theta/2\boldsymbol{u})$. This rotation applied to a vector $\boldsymbol{r}$ is then expressed as a multiplication of quaternions : $R(\boldsymbol{r}) = \dot{q}\dot{r}\dot{q}^*$, where $\dot{r}$ is a pure imaginary quaternion ($r_0 = 0$) and $\dot{q}^*$ denotes the conjugates of $\dot{q}$ ($\dot{q}^* = q_0 - iq_x - jq_y - kq_z$).

The scalar product h of two vectors $\boldsymbol{r}^i = (x^i, y^i, z^i)^t$ and $\boldsymbol{r}^j = (x^j, y^j, z^j)^t$ which are transformed by the rotations R^i and R^j respectively:

$$h = R^i(\boldsymbol{r}^i) \cdot R^j(\boldsymbol{r}^j),$$

can be written as:

$$h = (\dot{q}^i \dot{r}^i \dot{q}^{*i}) \cdot (\dot{q}^j \dot{r}^j \dot{q}^{*j}),$$

where $\dot{q}^i$ and $\dot{q}^j$ are the unit quaternions corresponding to R^i and R^j and $\dot{r}^i$ and $\dot{r}^j$ are the pure imaginary quaternions corresponding to $\boldsymbol{r}^i$ et $\boldsymbol{r}^j$, respectively.

Given that the dot product between two quaternions is preserved when multiplied by an unit quaternion, we can rewrite h in the following form

$$h = (\dot{q}^{*j} \dot{q}^i \dot{r}^i) \cdot (\dot{r}^j \dot{q}^{*j} \dot{q}^i).$$

Considering the matrix forms (1) and (2) of the quaternion product, it follows that

$$h = (\bar{\mathbb{R}}^i \dot{q}^{*j} \dot{q}^i) \cdot (\mathbb{R}^j \dot{q}^{*j} \dot{q}^i),$$

which also can be written in the form

$$h = (\dot{q}^{*j} \dot{q}^i)^t \mathbb{N}^{ij} (\dot{q}^{*j} \dot{q}^i), \tag{3}$$

where $\mathbb{N}^{ij} = \bar{\mathbb{R}}^{i^t} \mathbb{R}^j$ is a symmetric matrix having the form

$$\mathbb{N}^{ij} = \begin{bmatrix} a & e & f & g \\ e & b & h & k \\ f & h & c & l \\ g & k & l & d \end{bmatrix},$$

where

$$a = x^i x^j + y^i y^j + z^i z^j, \quad b = x^i x^j - y^i y^j - z^i z^j,$$
$$c = -x^i x^j + y^i y^j - z^i z^j, \; d = -x^i x^j - y^i y^j + z^i z^j,$$

and

$$e = y^i z^j - z^i y^j, \; f = z^i x^j - x^i z^j, \; g = x^i y^j - y^i x^j,$$
$$h = x^i y^j + y^i x^j, \; k = z^i x^j + x^i z^j, \; l = y^i z^j + z^i y^j.$$

By permuting the indexes i and j, the matrix $\mathbb{N}^{ji} = \bar{\mathbb{R}}^{j^t} \mathbb{R}^i$ can be written as follow:

$$\mathbb{N}^{ji} = \begin{bmatrix} a & -e & -f & -g \\ -e & b & h & k \\ -f & h & c & l \\ -g & k & l & d \end{bmatrix}.$$

This allows us to simply verify the useful following property:

$$\dot{q}^t \mathbb{N}^{ij} \dot{q} = \dot{q}^{*t} \mathbb{N}^{ji} \dot{q}^*, \quad \forall \dot{q}. \tag{4}$$

4 Pairwise registration using quaternions

Faugeras and Hebert [7], and Horn [8], have proposed a quaternion-based solution to register a set of n points $S^2 = \{P_i^2\}$ with a set of n points $S^1 = \{P_i^1\}$ where each point P_i^2 is in correspondence with the point P_i^1 with the same index. The rigid transformation T^2 to be applied to S^2, defined by the rotation R^2 and the translation t^2, is optimized by minimizing the following cost function:

$$E = \sum_{i=1}^{n} \| P_i^1 - R^2(P_i^2) - t^2 \|^2. \tag{5}$$

The optimal translation is given by the difference between the centroid of S^1 and the transformed centroid of S^2

$$t^2 = \bar{P}^1 - R^2(\bar{P}^2). \tag{6}$$

The unit quaternion representing the best rotation is the unit eigenvector corresponding to the maximum eigenvalue of the following 4×4 matrix:

$$\begin{bmatrix} S_{xx} + S_{yy} + S_{zz} & S_{yz} - S_{zy} & S_{zx} - S_{xz} & S_{xy} - S_{yx} \\ S_{yz} - S_{zy} & S_{xx} - S_{yy} - S_{zz} & S_{xy} + S_{yx} & S_{zx} + S_{xz} \\ S_{zx} - S_{xz} & S_{xy} + S_{yx} & -S_{xx} + S_{yy} - S_{zz} & S_{yz} + S_{zy} \\ S_{xy} - S_{yx} & S_{zx} + S_{xz} & S_{yz} + S_{zy} & -S_{xx} - S_{yy} + S_{zz} \end{bmatrix}$$

where $S_{xx} = \sum_{i=1}^{n} x'^2_i x'^1_i$, $S_{xy} = \sum_{i=1}^{n} x'^2_i y'^1_i$, ..., x'^j_i, y'^j_i and z'^j_i being the centered coordinates of the points P_i^j, $i = 1..n; j = 1..2$.

5 Specification of the global registration problem

We assume that there are M overlapping sets of points $S^1, S^2, ..., S^M$. The global registration process must find the best rigid transformations $T^1, T^2, ..., T^M$ to be applied to each point set.

We denote $O^{\alpha\beta} \subset S^\alpha$ the overlap of S^α with S^β, $\alpha, \beta \in [1..M]$. $O^{\alpha\beta}$ is composed of $N^{\alpha\beta}$ points $P_i^{\alpha\beta} \in S^\alpha$, $i = 1..N^{\alpha\beta}$. Each point $P_i^{\alpha\beta}$ is matched with a point $P_i^{\beta\alpha}$ belonging to $O^{\beta\alpha} \subset S^\beta$. Mutually, the point $P_i^{\beta\alpha}$ is matched with $P_i^{\alpha\beta}$. Then we have $N^{\alpha\beta} = N^{\beta\alpha}$.

The optimal rigid transformations are usually specified as the minimum of an objective function which can be chosen as the sum of the squared Euclidean distances between the matched points of all the overlaps:

$$E = \sum_{\alpha=1}^{M} \sum_{\beta=1}^{M} \sum_{i=1}^{N^{\alpha\beta}} \|T^{\alpha}(P_i^{\alpha\beta}) - T^{\beta}(P_i^{\beta\alpha})\|^2. \tag{7}$$

In order to simplify the notations, we introduce here $O^{\alpha\alpha}$ the overlap of the point set S^{α} with itself. Its contribution to error E having to remain always null, we just impose for each $\alpha \in [1..M]$:

$$N^{\alpha\alpha} = 0. \tag{8}$$

This cost function takes simultaneously into account the motions of the M surfaces. The residual errors will be homogeneously distributed in the whole mutual overlaps. One can notice that by taking $M = 2$ and by setting the transformation T^1 to the identity transformation, we retrieve equation (5).

6 Optimization of translations

We are looking for the translations which minimize the cost function (7). We show that this set of optimal translations is given by solving a linear equation system. We also show that the optimization of the rotations can be decoupled from the values of the translations.

6.1 Solution of optimal translations

Suppose that each rigid transformation T^{α} $(\alpha = 1, \ldots, M)$ is composed of the rotation R^{α} and the translation t^{α}, the cost function E, defined in equation (7) can be written:

$$E = \sum_{\alpha=1}^{M} \sum_{\beta=1}^{M} \sum_{i=1}^{N^{\alpha\beta}} \|R^{\alpha}(P_i^{\alpha\beta}) - R^{\beta}(P_i^{\beta\alpha}) + t^{\alpha} - t^{\beta}\|^2,$$

or,

$$E = \sum_{\alpha=1}^{M} \sum_{\beta=1}^{M} \left(\sum_{i=1}^{N^{\alpha\beta}} \|R^{\alpha}(P_i^{\alpha\beta}) - R^{\beta}(P_i^{\beta\alpha})\|^2 + 2[t^{\alpha} - t^{\beta}] \cdot \sum_{i=1}^{N^{\alpha\beta}} [R^{\alpha}(P_i^{\alpha\beta}) - R^{\beta}(P_i^{\beta\alpha})] \right.$$
$$\left. + N^{\alpha\beta}\|t^{\alpha} - t^{\beta}\|^2 \right).$$

However the right term of the scalar product can be expressed by $N^{\alpha\beta}[R^{\alpha}(\bar{P}^{\alpha\beta}) - R^{\beta}(\bar{P}^{\beta\alpha})]$ where $\bar{P}^{\alpha\beta}$ and $\bar{P}^{\beta\alpha}$ are the centroid of $O^{\alpha\beta}$ and $O^{\beta\alpha}$ respectively;

$$\bar{P}^{\alpha\beta} = \frac{1}{N^{\alpha\beta}} \sum_{i=1}^{N^{\alpha\beta}} P_i^{\alpha\beta}.$$

The cost function E can be written in the form:

$$E = E_R + E_{t,R},$$

where

$$E_R = \sum_{\alpha=1}^{M} \sum_{\beta=1}^{M} \sum_{i=1}^{N^{\alpha\beta}} \| R^\alpha(P_i^{\alpha\beta}) - R^\beta(P_i^{\beta\alpha}) \|^2,$$

and

$$E_{t,R} = \sum_{\alpha=1}^{M} \sum_{\beta=1}^{M} N^{\alpha\beta}(2[t^\alpha - t^\beta] \cdot [R^\alpha(\bar{P}^{\alpha\beta}) - R^\beta(\bar{P}^{\beta\alpha})] + \|t^\alpha - t^\beta\|^2),$$

We notice that E_R does not depend on translations. So the values of translations which minimize the cost function E will be given by the minimization of $E_{t,R}$. Let rewrite $E_{t,R}$ as follows:

$$E_{t,R} = C_1 + C_2,$$

where

$$C_1 = 2 \sum_{\alpha=1}^{M} \sum_{\beta=1}^{M} N^{\alpha\beta}[t^\alpha - t^\beta] \cdot [R^\alpha(\bar{P}^{\alpha\beta}) - R^\beta(\bar{P}^{\beta\alpha})],$$

$$= 4 \sum_{\alpha=1}^{M} [t^\alpha \cdot \sum_{\beta=1}^{M} N^{\alpha\beta}(R^\alpha(\bar{P}^{\alpha\beta}) - R^\beta(\bar{P}^{\beta\alpha}))],$$

and

$$C_2 = \sum_{\alpha=1}^{M} \sum_{\beta=1}^{M} N^{\alpha\beta}\|t^\alpha - t^\beta\|^2,$$

$$= 2 \sum_{\alpha=1}^{M} [t^{\alpha 2}(\sum_{\beta=1}^{M} N^{\alpha\beta})] - 2 \sum_{\alpha=1}^{M} \sum_{\beta=1}^{M} N^{\alpha\beta} t^\alpha \cdot t^\beta.$$

We have used here the data property $N^{\alpha\beta} = N^{\beta\alpha}$. $E_{t,R}$ can then be written in matrix form

$$E_{t,R} = 2(X^t \mathbf{A} X + 2X^t B), \qquad (9)$$

where, $X = (t^1, t^2, \ldots, t^M)^t$,

$$\mathbf{A} = \begin{bmatrix} N^1 & -N^{12} & \ldots & -N^{1M} \\ -N^{21} & N^2 & \ldots & -N^{2M} \\ \vdots & \vdots & \ddots & \vdots \\ -N^{M1} & -N^{M2} & \ldots & N^M \end{bmatrix},$$

(where $N^\alpha = \sum_{\beta=1}^{M} N^{\alpha\beta}$) and

$$
B = \begin{pmatrix}
\sum_{\beta=1}^{M} N^{1\beta}[R^1(\bar{P}^{1\beta}) - R^\beta(\bar{P}^{\beta 1})] \\
\sum_{\beta=1}^{M} N^{2\beta}[R^2(\bar{P}^{2\beta}) - R^\beta(\bar{P}^{\beta 2})] \\
\vdots \\
\sum_{\beta=1}^{M} N^{M\beta}[R^M(\bar{P}^{M\beta}) - R^\beta(\bar{P}^{\beta M})]
\end{pmatrix}.
$$

Minimizing $E_{t,R}$ is equivalent to the minimization of the function $Q(X)$:

$$
Q(X) = X^t \mathbf{A} X + 2X^t B. \tag{10}
$$

It should be noted that the matrix $\mathbf{A}$ is not invertible; its determinant is null, the sum of each line or each column being null. The cost function E is unchanged if the same rigid transformation is applied simultaneously to all M point sets. The reference frame of one point set should be chosen as an absolute one and only the $(M - 1)$ other sets should be moved. The choice of this set is arbitrary and does not affect the registration solution. Let fix the first set by setting $R^1 = I$ and $t^1 = 0$. Equation (10) becomes,

$$
Q(\bar{X}) = \bar{X}^t \bar{\mathbf{A}} \bar{X} + 2\bar{X}^t \bar{B}, \tag{11}
$$

where $\bar{X}$ and $\bar{B}$ are the vectors X and B deprived from their first element, and where

$$
\bar{\mathbf{A}} = \begin{bmatrix}
N^2 & \cdots & -N^{2M} \\
\vdots & \ddots & \vdots \\
-N^{M2} & \cdots & N^M
\end{bmatrix}.
$$

It may be of interest to note that despite the suppression of the first line and the first column of $\mathbf{A}$, the matrix $\bar{\mathbf{A}}$ still contains the terms $N^{\alpha 1}$ in the diagonal elements. Therefore the overlaps with the set S^1 are still considered.

$Q(\bar{X})$ is a quadratic form which is minimal when $\bar{\mathbf{A}}\bar{X} = -\bar{B}$. So, the value of the translations are simply obtained by the inversion of the matrix $\bar{\mathbf{A}}$:

$$
\bar{X}_{min} = -\bar{\mathbf{A}}^{-1}\bar{B}. \tag{12}
$$

The translations are given by a linear combination of the differences between the rotated centroids of the overlaps $O^{\alpha\beta}$ and $O^{\beta\alpha}$. Again if $M = 2$, we retrieve equation (6)) for a pairwise registration.

6.2 Decoupling between rotations and translations

Using the result of optimal translations, we show now that the optimization of the rotations can be decoupled from the translations.

For $\bar{X} = \bar{X}_{min}$, equation (11) becomes

$$
Q(\bar{X}_{min}) = -\bar{B}^t \bar{\mathbf{A}}^{-1} \bar{B}. \tag{13}
$$

We then obtain for the global cost function E: $E(\bar{X}_{min}) = E_R + E_{t,R} = E_R + 2Q(\bar{X}_{min})$; *i.e.* finally:

$$E(X_{min}) = \sum_{\alpha=1}^{M} \sum_{\beta=1}^{M} \sum_{i=1}^{N^{\alpha\beta}} \|R^{\alpha}(P_i^{\alpha\beta}) - R^{\beta}(P_i^{\beta\alpha})\|^2 - 2\bar{B}^t \bar{\mathbf{A}}^{-1} \bar{B}. \qquad (14)$$

The function E depends no more on translations as shown in equation (14). The rotations can then be optimized independently from translations .

7 Optimization of rotations using unit quaternions

In this section we solve the problem of the optimization of rotations by minimizing the cost function E defined in equation (14).

We start by rewriting expressing E as a function of quaternions in section 7.1. We show that minimizing E is equivalent to maximizing another cost function. Then a sequential algorithm is proposed in section 7.2 in order to maximize this new cost function. Finally, in section 7.3 we prove that this algorithm usually converges to a local minimum.

7.1 Rewriting expressing E with unit quaternions

Let $e_i^{\alpha\beta} = \|R^{\alpha}(P_i^{\alpha\beta}) - R^{\beta}(P_i^{\beta\alpha})\|^2$.

Using the preservation of norm by the rotations, we have:

$$e_i^{\alpha\beta} = \|P_i^{\alpha\beta}\|^2 + \|P_i^{\beta\alpha}\|^2 - 2R^{\alpha}(P_i^{\alpha\beta}) \cdot R^{\beta}(P_i^{\beta\alpha}).$$

The first term of E becomes,

$$\sum_{\alpha=1}^{M} \sum_{\beta=1}^{M} \sum_{i=1}^{N^{\alpha\beta}} e_i^{\alpha\beta} = -2 \sum_{\alpha=1}^{M} \sum_{\beta=1}^{M} \sum_{i=1}^{N^{\alpha\beta}} R^{\alpha}(P_i^{\alpha\beta}) \cdot R^{\beta}(P_i^{\beta\alpha}) + K \qquad (15)$$

where $K = 2\sum_{\alpha=1}^{M} \sum_{\beta=1}^{M} \sum_{i=1}^{N^{\alpha\beta}} \|P_i^{\alpha\beta}\|^2$ is a constant which does not depend on rotations. By combining equations (14) and (15) and by ignoring the constant term K, minimizing E is equivalent to maximizing

$$H = \sum_{\alpha=1}^{M} \sum_{\beta=1}^{M} \sum_{i=1}^{N^{\alpha\beta}} R^{\alpha}(P_i^{\alpha\beta}) \cdot R^{\beta}(P_i^{\beta\alpha}) + \bar{B}^t \bar{\mathbf{A}}^{-1} \bar{B}. \qquad (16)$$

Considering relation (3), the first term of H,

$$H_1 = \sum_{\alpha=1}^{M} \sum_{\beta=1}^{M} \sum_{i=1}^{N^{\alpha\beta}} R^{\alpha}(P_i^{\alpha\beta}) \cdot R^{\beta}(P_i^{\beta\alpha}),$$

can be written by using unit quaternions:

$$H_1 = \sum_{\alpha=1}^{M} \sum_{\beta=1}^{M} \sum_{i=1}^{N^{\alpha\beta}} (\dot{q}^{*\beta} \dot{q}^{\alpha})^{t} \mathbb{Q}_i^{\alpha\beta} (\dot{q}^{*\beta} \dot{q}^{\alpha}),$$

or also, by integrating the sum over i,

$$H_1 = \sum_{\alpha=1}^{M} \sum_{\beta=1}^{M} (\dot{q}^{*\beta} \dot{q}^{\alpha})^{t} \mathbb{Q}_R^{\alpha\beta} (\dot{q}^{*\beta} \dot{q}^{\alpha}), \qquad (17)$$

where $\mathbb{Q}_R^{\alpha\beta} = \sum_{i=1}^{N^{\alpha\beta}} \mathbb{Q}_i^{\alpha\beta} =$

$$\begin{bmatrix} S_{xx}^{\alpha\beta} + S_{yy}^{\alpha\beta} + S_{zz}^{\alpha\beta} & S_{yz}^{\alpha\beta} - S_{zy}^{\alpha\beta} & S_{zx}^{\alpha\beta} - S_{xz}^{\alpha\beta} & S_{xy}^{\alpha\beta} - S_{yx}^{\alpha\beta} \\ S_{yz}^{\alpha\beta} - S_{zy}^{\alpha\beta} & S_{xx}^{\alpha\beta} - S_{yy}^{\alpha\beta} - S_{zz}^{\alpha\beta} & S_{xy}^{\alpha\beta} + S_{yx}^{\alpha\beta} & S_{xy}^{\alpha\beta} + S_{yx}^{\alpha\beta} \\ S_{zx}^{\alpha\beta} - S_{xz}^{\alpha\beta} & S_{xy}^{\alpha\beta} + S_{yx}^{\alpha\beta} & -S_{xx}^{\alpha\beta} + S_{yy}^{\alpha\beta} - S_{zz}^{\alpha\beta} & S_{yz}^{\alpha\beta} + S_{zy}^{\alpha\beta} \\ S_{xy}^{\alpha\beta} - S_{yx}^{\alpha\beta} & S_{zx}^{\alpha\beta} + S_{xz}^{\alpha\beta} & S_{yz}^{\alpha\beta} + S_{zy}^{\alpha\beta} & -S_{xx}^{\alpha\beta} - S_{yy}^{\alpha\beta} + S_{zz}^{\alpha\beta} \end{bmatrix},$$

$$S_{xx}^{\alpha\beta} = \sum_{i=1}^{N^{\alpha\beta}} x_i^{\alpha\beta} x_i^{\beta\alpha}, \qquad S_{xy}^{\alpha\beta} = \sum_{i=1}^{N^{\alpha\beta}} x_i^{\alpha\beta} y_i^{\beta\alpha}, \qquad S_{xz}^{\alpha\beta} = \sum_{i=1}^{N^{\alpha\beta}} x_i^{\alpha\beta} z_i^{\beta\alpha}, ...,$$

with $(x_i^{\alpha\beta}, y_i^{\alpha\beta}, z_i^{\alpha\beta})^{t} = P_i^{\alpha\beta}$ and $(x_i^{\beta\alpha}, y_i^{\beta\alpha}, z_i^{\beta\alpha})^{t} = P_i^{\beta\alpha}$. In another side, as shown in appendix A, the quantity $\bar{B}^{t} \bar{A}^{-1} \bar{B}$ can be expressed in the form:

$$\bar{B}^{t} \bar{A}^{-1} \bar{B} = \sum_{\alpha=1}^{M} \sum_{\beta=1}^{M} (\dot{q}^{*\beta} \dot{q}^{\alpha})^{t} \mathbb{Q}_t^{\alpha\beta} (\dot{q}^{*\beta} \dot{q}^{\alpha}), \qquad (18)$$

(*cf.* appendix A for the expression of $\mathbb{Q}_t^{\alpha\beta}$). According to equations (17) and (18), equation (16) becomes :

$$\boxed{H = \sum_{\alpha=1}^{M} \sum_{\beta=1}^{M} (\dot{q}^{*\beta} \dot{q}^{\alpha})^{t} \mathbb{Q}^{\alpha\beta} (\dot{q}^{*\beta} \dot{q}^{\alpha})} \qquad (19)$$

where $\mathbb{Q}^{\alpha\beta} = \mathbb{Q}_R^{\alpha\beta} + \mathbb{Q}_t^{\alpha\beta}$.

$\mathbb{Q}_R^{\alpha\beta}$ and $\mathbb{Q}_t^{\alpha\beta}$ are 4×4 symmetrical matrices which have the same form than $\mathbb{N}^{ij}$ (*cf.* section 3). So $\mathbb{Q}^{\alpha\beta}$ verify the property (4).

7.2 Sequential algorithm

Let consider now the problem of maximizing the function H of equation (19) subject to the $4(M-1)$ vector $\mathbf{q} = (\dot{q}^{2}, \dot{q}^{3}, ..., \dot{q}^{M})^{t}$. The quaternion $\dot{q}^{1}$ is set to the identity quaternion, the reference frame of S_1 being chosen as the absolute one. We propose a sequential method to optimize the $(M-1)$ quaternions defined by the vector $\mathbf{q}$. The approach is the following one: at each iteration all the quaternions $\dot{q}^{j}$ are fixed excepted one of them. We determine this last one so that H is maximized. To be more precise, we start with an initial vector $\mathbf{q}_0$ which is arbitrarily defined or provided by a pre-computing step. We then construct a sequence of vectors $\mathbf{q}_m$, $m = 1, 2, \ldots$ where the transition from $\mathbf{q}_m$ to $\mathbf{q}_{m+1}$ is done in $(M - 1)$ steps: $\dot{q}_{m+1}^2$ is determined in the first step, then $\dot{q}_{m+1}^3, \ldots,$ and finally $\dot{q}_{m+1}^M$. The quaternion $\dot{q}_{m+1}^j$ is the unique solution of the following maximization problem: determine the quaternion $\dot{q}_{m+1}^j$ belonging to the unit quaternion set $\mathcal{Q}$ such as:

$$\begin{cases} H(\dot{q}_{m+1}^2, \ldots, \dot{q}_{m+1}^j, \dot{q}_m^{j+1}, \ldots, \dot{q}_m^M) \geq H(\dot{q}_{m+1}^2, \ldots, \dot{q}_{m+1}^{j-1}, \dot{q}^j, \dot{q}_m^{j+1}, \ldots, \dot{q}_m^M), \\ \forall \dot{q}^j \in \mathcal{Q} \end{cases}$$

(20)

When all the quaternions are fixed except $\dot{q}^j$, maximizing H (equation (19)) according to $\dot{q}^j$ becomes a simple problem. By ignoring the constant terms, this maximization is equivalent to the maximization of the following function $H(\dot{q}^j)$:

$$H(\dot{q}^j) = \sum_{\beta=1,\beta\neq j}^{M} (\dot{q}^{*\beta}\dot{q}^j)^t \mathbb{Q}^{j\beta} (\dot{q}^{*\beta}\dot{q}^j) + \sum_{\alpha=1,\alpha\neq j}^{M} (\dot{q}^{*j}\dot{q}^\alpha)^t \mathbb{Q}^{\alpha j} (\dot{q}^{*j}\dot{q}^\alpha),$$

$$= 2 \sum_{\beta=1,\beta\neq j}^{M} (\dot{q}^{*\beta}\dot{q}^j)^t \mathbb{Q}^{j\beta} (\dot{q}^{*\beta}\dot{q}^j) \qquad \text{(according property (4))}.$$

Then by using the matrix form of the quaternion product (1) :

$$H(\dot{q}^j) = 2 \sum_{\beta=1,\beta\neq j}^{M} (Q^{*\beta}\dot{q}^j)^t \mathbb{Q}^{j\beta} (Q^{*\beta}\dot{q}^j),$$

$$= 2 \sum_{\beta=1,\beta\neq j}^{M} \dot{q}^{j^t} (Q^{*\beta^t} \mathbb{Q}^{j\beta} Q^{*\beta}) \dot{q}^j,$$

which can be written into the form,

$$H(\dot{q}^j) = 2\dot{q}^{j^t} \mathbf{N}^j \dot{q}^j,$$

(21)

where $\mathbf{N}^j = \sum_{\beta=1,\beta\neq j}^{M} Q^{*\beta^t} \mathbb{Q}^{j\beta} Q^{*\beta}$.

$H(\dot{q}^j)$ is a quadratic form. The optimal unit quaternion which maximizes this function is then just the eigenvector corresponding to the highest eigenvalue of the matrix $\mathbf{N}^j$.

7.3 Algorithm convergence

We show that the sequential algorithm proposed in the previous section does always converge monotonically to a local maximum.

Let $\mathbf{q}_{m,j} = (\dot{q}_{m+1}^2, \ldots, \dot{q}_{m+1}^j, \dot{q}_m^{j+1}, \ldots, \dot{q}_m^M)$. We start to prove that the cost function H of equation (19) is upper bounded. Using the fact that the product of two unit quaternions is still a unit quaternion, we see that each quadratic term of the double sum of H is always smaller than the highest eigenvalue $\lambda_{max}^{\alpha\beta}$ of the 4×4 symmetric matrix $\mathbb{Q}^{\alpha\beta}$. By doing the summation over α and β we verify that for any set of quaternions $\dot{q}^1, \dot{q}^2, \cdots, \dot{q}^M$:

$$H(\dot{q}^1, \dot{q}^2, \cdots, \dot{q}^M) \leq \sum_{\alpha=1}^{M} \sum_{\beta=1}^{M} \lambda_{max}^{\alpha\beta}. \tag{22}$$

Thus the cost function H is upper bounded by the sum of the highest eigenvalue of the matrices $\mathbb{Q}^{\alpha\beta}$. Since, the series $H(\mathbf{q}_{m,j})$ is increasing by construction, this proves that our algorithm converges to a local maximum. If it converges to a global maximum is still an open question.

8 Experimental results

We have performed a global registration of M = 4 simulated sets containing each nine 3D points. Each set partially overlaps all the other ones. There are then $C_4^2 = 6$ different overlaps described by the subsets $O^{\alpha\beta}$. Each subset contains only 3 points in this simulation. The point coordinates vary between -100 and +100 units. The first point set is chosen as reference frame and is fixed. Each one of the three other sets is rotated by a random unit quaternion and translated by a random distance. In this example we do not add noise, thus the misregistration error value is expected to be very low.

We found that only 50 iterations were necessary to reduce the residual error from an initial value of 843 units to $0.2 \ 10^{-3}$ unit. The CPU time needed is very low, it is lower than one millisecond for each iteration on a Sun Sparc Station running at 300 MHz. It does not depend on the number of points taken into account in the overlaps, the matrices $\mathbb{Q}^{\alpha\beta}$ being precomputed.

In this problem ground truth is available and so we can compute the residual error of the obtained solution from the true values for the unit quaternions and the translations. The relative residual error for the angle of the quaternion is about 10^{-5} and the one for the translations is about 10^{-6}. These results show that the intrinsic precision of the algorithm is very high. Its accuracy allows its use for many registration applications in computer vision.

We have for example applied this quaternion-based global registration on 3D points sampled on surface of real objects with a laser range finder. The Greek bust shown in Figure 2 is a difficult object to scan due to the presence of deep concavities. In this example 12 different scans have been recorded by using translational motions with a step of 0.1 mm. They contain more than 2 million points. The resulting partially overlapping parts of the object are illustrated in Figure 1. A quick and rough interactive registration was first performed (Figure 2-left). Then all the scans were registered simultaneously (Figure 2-right) by using an

ICP approach. This global registration is an extension of the classical ICP algorithm proposed by Besl and McKay [5] to register two sets. Two steps are iterated until convergence. In the first step, a point-to-point correspondence is efficiently established between the mutual overlaps of the sampled surfaces by using the multi-z-buffer space partitioning described in [3]. In the second step, the quaternion-based registration proposed in this paper is applied to simultaneously optimize the rigid motions. Figure 3 shows the convergence of the ICP algorithm by displaying a curve of pseudo-time against RMS residual global error. The initial RMS error was 0.68 mm and after one iteration falls down to 0.19 mm. The RMS error for the 12 scans is 0.11 mm after 20 iterations. The CPU time required for each iteration of the global ICP registration is 15 seconds on a Sun Sparc Station running at 300 MHz .

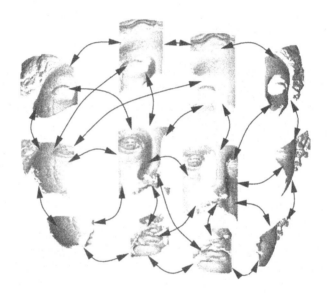

Fig. 1. Some pieces of a Greek bust mosaic (Hygia, Dion Museum, Greece).

A statuette was also digitized along 6 different views shown in Figure 4. Only four ICP iterations were needed to globally register these 6 views, the global RMS error decreasing from 0.61 mm to 0.21 mm. Figure 5 shows three renderings from different viewpoints of the registered data of the statuette.

9 Conclusion

We have proposed in this paper a complete solution to the problem of the global registration of multiple 3D point sets with known correspondences. It is based on the representation of the rotations by unit quaternions. Compared to our previous work based on a linearization of the rotations [2], this new approach

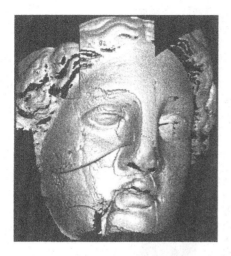

Fig. 2. The Greek bust after interactive (left) and global (right) registration of 12 scans.

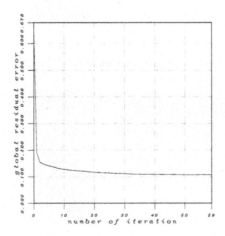

Fig. 3. ICP algorithm convergence of the 12 scans of the Greek bust.

does not require any assumption on the initial position of the point sets. It works well even when the data are initially faraway.

The experimental results have shown the excellent behaviour of the proposed algorithm to reach the optimum. With this solution the classic ICP algorithm which register only two point sets can be easily generalized into a **k-ICP** algorithm to register simultaneously k point sets ($k > 2$).

This method which has been successfully applied to the registration of several overlapping 3D sampled surfaces could be also very useful for other applications in computer vision.

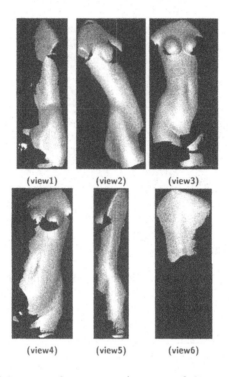

Fig. 4. Rendering of six views of a statuette (courtesy of the artist, Roland Coignard).

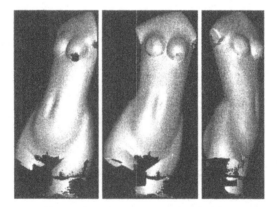

Fig. 5. Three different Renderings of the fusion of the six views of the statuette after their global registration.

Acknowledgment

This work was partly supported by the European ESPRIT project ARCHA-TOUR (EP III 9213).

Appendix A : development of $\bar{B}^t \bar{A}^{-1} \bar{B}$

We look here for the development of the form $\bar{B}^t \bar{A}^{-1} \bar{B}$ defined in section 6. Let denote $c^{\alpha\beta} = R^\alpha(N^{\alpha\beta}\bar{P}^{\alpha\beta})$ the transformed centroid of the overlap $O^{\alpha\beta}$ by the rotation R^α, multiplied by the number of points of $O^{\alpha\beta}$. We associate to each rotation R^α its unit quaternion $\dot{q}^\alpha$. Let denote a_{ij} the element (i,j) of the matrix $\bar{A}^{-1}$ where i and $j \in [2..M]$. In order to homogenize the indices of the sums, we introduce the following null terms with an index 1, $a_{1j} = a_{i1} = 0$. Then:

$$
\begin{aligned}
\bar{B}^t \bar{A}^{-1} \bar{B} &= \sum_{k=1}^{M}\sum_{l=1}^{M} a_{kl}[\sum_{\alpha=1}^{M}(c^{k\alpha} - c^{\alpha k}) \cdot \sum_{\beta=1}^{M}(c^{l\beta} - c^{\beta l})], \\
&= \sum_{k=1}^{M}\sum_{l=1}^{M} a_{kl} \sum_{\alpha=1}^{M}\sum_{\beta=1}^{M}(c^{\alpha k}\cdot c^{\beta l} - c^{\alpha k}\cdot c^{l\beta} - c^{k\alpha}\cdot c^{\beta l} + c^{k\alpha}\cdot c^{l\beta}), \\
&= \sum_{\alpha=1}^{M}\sum_{\beta=1}^{M}(\sum_{k=1}^{M}\sum_{l=1}^{M} a_{kl}c^{\alpha k}\cdot c^{\beta l}) - \sum_{\alpha=1}^{M}\sum_{l=1}^{M}(\sum_{k=1}^{M}\sum_{\beta=1}^{M} a_{kl}c^{\alpha k}\cdot c^{l\beta}) \\
&- \sum_{k=1}^{M}\sum_{\beta=1}^{M}(\sum_{\alpha=1}^{M}\sum_{l=1}^{M} a_{kl}c^{k\alpha}\cdot c^{\beta l}) + \sum_{k=1}^{M}\sum_{l=1}^{M}(\sum_{\alpha=1}^{M}\sum_{\beta=1}^{M} a_{kl}c^{k\alpha}\cdot c^{l\beta}).
\end{aligned}
$$

By appropriately changing some indices, this last quantity can be transformed into:

$$
\bar{B}^t \bar{A}^{-1} \bar{B} = \sum_{\alpha=1}^{M}\sum_{\beta=1}^{M}\sum_{k=1}^{M}\sum_{l=1}^{M} \mu_{kl}^{\alpha\beta} c^{\alpha k}\cdot c^{\beta l},
$$

where $\mu_{kl}^{\alpha\beta} = a_{kl} - a_{k\beta} - a_{\alpha l} + a_{\alpha\beta}$. Since $\bar{A}^{-1}$ is a symmetric matrix ($a_{ij} = a_{ji}$), we have $\mu_{kl}^{\alpha\beta} = \mu_{lk}^{\beta\alpha}$. Let use now equation (3) to develop $\bar{B}^t \bar{A}^{-1} \bar{B}$:

$$
\begin{aligned}
\bar{B}^t \bar{A}^{-1} \bar{B} &= \sum_{\alpha=1}^{M}\sum_{\beta=1}^{M}\sum_{k=1}^{M}\sum_{l=1}^{M} \mu_{kl}^{\alpha\beta} R^\alpha(N^{\alpha k}\bar{P}^{\alpha k}) \cdot R^\beta(N^{\beta l}\bar{P}^{\beta l}), \\
&= \sum_{\alpha=1}^{M}\sum_{\beta=1}^{M}\sum_{k=1}^{M}\sum_{l=1}^{M} \mu_{kl}^{\alpha\beta} (\dot{q}^{*\beta}\dot{q}^\alpha)^t \mathbb{N}_{kl}^{\alpha\beta}(N^{\alpha k}\bar{P}^{\alpha k}, N^{\beta l}\bar{P}^{\beta l})(\dot{q}^{*\beta}\dot{q}^\alpha) \\
&= \sum_{\alpha=1}^{M}\sum_{\beta=1}^{M} (\dot{q}^{*\beta}\dot{q}^\alpha)^t \mathbb{Q}_t^{\alpha\beta}(\dot{q}^{*\beta}\dot{q}^\alpha),
\end{aligned}
$$

where,

$$
\mathbb{Q}_t^{\alpha\beta} = \sum_{k=1}^{M}\sum_{l=1}^{M} \mu_{kl}^{\alpha\beta}\mathbb{N}_{kl}^{\alpha\beta}(N^{\alpha k}\bar{P}^{\alpha k}, N^{\beta l}\bar{P}^{\beta l}),
$$

$$
= \begin{bmatrix}
\bar{S}_{xx}^{\alpha\beta} + \bar{S}_{yy}^{\alpha\beta} + \bar{S}_{zz}^{\alpha\beta} & \bar{S}_{yz}^{\alpha\beta} - \bar{S}_{zy}^{\alpha\beta} & \bar{S}_{zx}^{\alpha\beta} - \bar{S}_{xz}^{\alpha\beta} & \bar{S}_{xy}^{\alpha\beta} - \bar{S}_{yx}^{\alpha\beta} \\
\bar{S}_{yz}^{\alpha\beta} - \bar{S}_{zy}^{\alpha\beta} & \bar{S}_{xx}^{\alpha\beta} - \bar{S}_{yy}^{\alpha\beta} - \bar{S}_{zz}^{\alpha\beta} & \bar{S}_{xy}^{\alpha\beta} + \bar{S}_{yx}^{\alpha\beta} & \bar{S}_{zx}^{\alpha\beta} + \bar{S}_{xz}^{\alpha\beta} \\
\bar{S}_{zx}^{\alpha\beta} - \bar{S}_{xz}^{\alpha\beta} & \bar{S}_{xy}^{\alpha\beta} + \bar{S}_{yx}^{\alpha\beta} & -\bar{S}_{xx}^{\alpha\beta} + \bar{S}_{yy}^{\alpha\beta} - \bar{S}_{zz}^{\alpha\beta} & \bar{S}_{yz}^{\alpha\beta} + \bar{S}_{zy}^{\alpha\beta} \\
\bar{S}_{xy}^{\alpha\beta} - \bar{S}_{yx}^{\alpha\beta} & \bar{S}_{zx}^{\alpha\beta} + \bar{S}_{xz}^{\alpha\beta} & \bar{S}_{yz}^{\alpha\beta} + \bar{S}_{zy}^{\alpha\beta} & -\bar{S}_{xx}^{\alpha\beta} - \bar{S}_{yy}^{\alpha\beta} + \bar{S}_{zz}^{\alpha\beta}
\end{bmatrix},
$$

50

where, $\bar{S}_{xx}^{\alpha\beta} = \sum_{k=1}^{M} \sum_{l=1}^{M} \mu_{kl}^{\alpha\beta} \bar{x}^{\alpha k} \bar{x}^{\beta l}$, $\qquad \bar{S}_{xy}^{\alpha\beta} = \sum_{k=1}^{M} \sum_{l=1}^{M} \mu_{kl}^{\alpha\beta} \bar{x}^{\alpha k} \bar{y}^{\beta l}, \ldots$
with $(\bar{x}^{\alpha k}, \bar{y}^{\alpha k}, \bar{z}^{\alpha k})^t = N^{\alpha k} \bar{P}^{\alpha k}$ and $(\bar{x}^{\beta l}, \bar{y}^{\beta l}, \bar{z}^{\beta l})^t = N^{\beta l} \bar{P}^{\beta l}$.

$\mathbb{Q}_t^{\alpha\beta}$ has the same form as $\mathbb{N}^{ij}$ (*cf.* section 3) so it verifies the property (4).

References

1. R. Benjemaa and F. Schmitt. Recalage rapide de surfaces 3D aprs projection dans des multi-zbuffers. *5th European Conferences on Rapid Prototyping - Paris, 11 pages*, October 1996.
2. R. Benjemaa and F. Schmitt. Recalage global de plusieurs surfaces par une approche algbrique (in frensh). *RFIA'98, 11me Congrs AFCET de Reconnaissance des Formes et Intelligence Artificielle, Clermont-Ferrand, France*, January 1997, "accepted".
3. R. Benjemaa and F. Schmitt. Fast global registration of 3D sampled surfaces using a multi-z-buffer technique. *Proceedings of the IEEE International Conference on Recent Advances in 3D Digital Imaging and Modeling, Ottawa-Canada*, pages 113–120, May 1997, Extended version to be published in the Journal Image and Vision Computing.
4. R. Bergevin, M. Soucy, H. Gagnon, and D. Laurendeau. Towards a general multi-view registration technique. *IEEE Trans. on PAMI*, 18(5):540–547, May 1996.
5. P. J. Besl and N. D. McKay. A method for registration of 3-D shapes. *IEEE Trans. on PAMI*, 14(2):239–256, February 1992.
6. O. D. Faugeras and M. Hebert. A 3D recognition and positioning algorithm using geometrical matching between primitive surfaces. *Int. Joint. Conf. Artificial Intelligence, Karlsruhe, Germany*, pages 996–1002, 1983.
7. O. D. Faugeras and M. Hebert. The representation and recognition and locating of 3-D objects. *Int. Jour. Robotic Research*, vol. 5(3):27–52, 1986.
8. B. K. P. Horn. Closed-form solution of absolute orientation using unit quaternions. *J. Opt. Soc. Am. A*, 4(4):629–642, April 1987.
9. T. D. Howell and J-C Lafon. The complexity of the quaternion product. Technical Report TR 75-245, Departement of Computer Science, Cornell University, Ithaca, N. Y., June 1975. ftp://ftp.netcom.com/pub/hb/hbaker/quaternion/cornellcstr75-245.ps.gz.
10. B. Kamgar-Parsi, J. L. Jones, and A. Rosenfeld. Registration of multiple overlapping range images: Scenes without distinctive features. *IEEE Trans. on PAMI*, 13(9):857–871, September 1991.
11. Kenichi Kanatani. Analysis of 3D rotation fitting. *IEEE Trans. on PAMI*, 16(5):543–549, May 1994.
12. A. Lorusso, D. W. Eggert, and R. B. Fisher. A comparison of four algorithms for estimating 3D rigid transformations. *British Machine Vision Conference, Birmingham, England*, pages 237–246, 1995.
13. L. Reyes-Avila. Quaternions : une reprsentation paramtrique systmatique des rotations finies. Technical Report 1303, INRIA-Rocquencourt, October 1990.
14. E. Salamin. Application of quaternions to computation with rotations. Technical report, Stanford AI Lab, 1979. ftp://ftp.netcom.com/pub/hb/hbaker/quaternion/stanfordaiwp79-salamin.ps.gz.
15. A. J. Stoddart and A. Hilton. Registration of multiple point sets. *ICPR'96, Vienna, Austria*, August 1996.

Robust Registration of Dissimilar Single and Multimodal Images

Christophoros Nikou[1,2], Fabrice Heitz[1], and Jean-Paul Armspach[2]

[1] LSIIT UPRES-A CNRS 7005, Université Strasbourg I
4 boulevard S. Brant, 67400 Illkirch, France
nikou@mondrian.u-strasbg.fr, Fabrice.Heitz@ensps.u-strasbg.fr
[2] Institut de Physique Biologique UPRES-A CNRS 7004
Faculté de Médecine, Université Strasbourg I
4, rue Kirschleger, 67085 Strasbourg, France
armspach@alsace.u-strasbg.fr

Abstract. In this paper, we develop data driven registration algorithms, relying on robust pixel similarity metrics, that enable an accurate (sub-pixel) rigid registration of dissimilar single and multimodal 2D/3D images. A "soft redescending" estimator is associated to a top down stochastic multigrid relaxation algorithm in order to obtain robust, data driven multimodal image registrations. With the stochastic multigrid strategy, the registration is not affected by local minima in the objective function and a manual initialization near the optimal solution is not necessary. The proposed robust similarity metrics are compared to the most popular standard similarity metrics, on synthetic as well as on real world image pairs showing gross dissimilarities. Two case-studies are considered: the registration of single and multimodal 3D medical images and the matching of multispectral remotely sensed images showing large overcast areas.

1 Introduction

Although a large variety of image registration methods have been proposed in the literature, only a few techniques have attempted to address the registration of images showing gross dissimilarities. If the case of single modal dissimilar images has been considered in [1], to our knowledge, no specific model has been proposed to handle *multimodal images* exhibiting large dissimilarities. The problem is indeed particularly difficult for multimodal images, showing both localized changes that have to be detected [2] and an "overall" difference (due to differences in the characteristics of the scene observed by multiple sensors). Medical imaging, with its wide variety of sensors (thermal, ultrasonic, X-Ray, MRI and nuclear) is probably one of the first application field, as are remote sensing, military imaging (visible, IR or radar) and multisensor computer vision.

In the present paper, we develop data driven registration methods, relying on pixel (or voxel) similarity metrics, that enable an accurate (subpixel) rigid registration of dissimilar single or multimodal 2D/3D images. Gross dissimilarities are handled by considering similarity measures related to robust M-estimators.

In particular, a novel pixel similarity metric is proposed for the multimodal case. This metric has shown very efficient for the registration of highly dissimilar images, on which conventional techniques fail. An example of such a multimodal image pair is given Fig. 5, showing two satellite images of France, taken at different optical wavelengths and at different dates. Gross dissimilarities, due to the presence of large overcast areas may be observed (Fig. 5(b)). Subpixel registrations have been obtained in this case (see Section 4).

The remainder of this paper is organized as following. Background and related approaches are presented in Section 2. In Section 3, we introduce two robust similarity metrics for the registration of single and multimodal images. The data-driven registration algorithm, based on these robust similarity measures, is described in the same section. In Section 4, the robust similarity metrics are compared to the most popular standard similarity metrics, on synthetic as well as on real world image pairs showing gross dissimilarities. The registration accuracy is evaluated for two case-studies: the registration of single modal (MRI/MRI) and multimodal (MRI/SPECT) 3D medical images and the matching of multi-spectral (visible/IR) satellite images showing large overcast areas. The proposed robust similarity measures compare favourably with all standard (non robust) techniques (including the quadratic similarity measure and the multimodality registration criterion devised by Woods *et al.* [3]). The multimodal robust similarity metrics shows also (excepted for one particular case) better performances than the recently proposed mutual information criterion [4,5], that has been recognized as the most efficient method in several recent studies.

2   Background and Standard Similarity Measures

A complete review of standard registration techniques may be found in [6], a classification in [7] and a comparison in [8]. Similarity measure-based approaches rely on the minimization of cost functions that express the pixel or voxel similarity of the images to be aligned. They have been proposed for both single and multimodal image registration [4,5,9–12]. Similarity metrics for the registration of 2D single modal images, that are to a certain extent robust to image changes have been described by Herbin *et al.* in [1]. Herbin *et al.* make use of deterministic and stochastic sign change criteria to obtain robust registrations of medical image sequences in critical situations corresponding for instance to lesion evolutions [1]. Contrary to the metrics described below, this method does not handle the case of multimodal images.

In this section we briefly present the most popular similarity metrics and describe their limitations. These similarity metrics will be compared, in Section 4, to the robust metrics we propose.

Pixel (or voxel) similarity metric-based registration consists in estimating the parameters Θ of the rigid transformation T_Θ minimizing a cost function $E\left(I_{ref}(.),\ I_{reg}(T_\Theta(.))\right)$, that expresses the similarity between the single or multimodal image pair:

$$\Theta^* = \arg\min_{\Theta}\left[E\left(I_{ref}(.),\ I_{reg}(T_\Theta(.))\right)\right], \qquad (1)$$

where $\Theta = (t_X, t_Y, t_Z, \hat{\theta}_X, \hat{\theta}_Y, \hat{\theta}_Z)^T$ is a vector containing the 3D translation parameters, (t_X, t_Y, t_Z) with respect to the X, Y and Z axis and the Euler rotation angles $(\hat{\theta}_X, \hat{\theta}_Y, \hat{\theta}_Z)$, $I_{ref}(.)$ represents the reference image and $I_{reg}(.)$ the image to be registered.

The classical quadratic similarity metric assumes that the two registered images differ only by an additive Gaussian noise [11], leading to the following *least squares cost function*:

$$E\left(I_{ref}(.), I_{reg}(T_\Theta(.))\right) = \sum_x [I_{ref}(x) - I_{reg}(T_\Theta(x))]^2 . \tag{2}$$

where x designates the pixel (or voxel) coordinates. Quadratic similarity metrics are related to gaussian sensor models [11], which do not take into account the interimage dissimilarities that may occur in real world applications.

A popular similarity measure for the registration of multimodal image pairs (widely used in medical imaging) is the multimodality similarity metric devised by Woods *et al.* [3]. The fundamental assumption related to Woods criterion is that a uniform region in the reference image corresponds, after registration, to a region that is also uniform in the second image (inter-image uniformity hypothesis).

The reference image is thus first partitioned into G grey level classes, where G denotes the number of grey levels of this image. The resulting spatial partition is projected on the image to be registered, yielding the same partition of this second image. The expected values μ_g, $g = 1, ..., G$ and the standard deviations σ_g, $g = 1, ..., G$ of each segmented region in the second image are then computed. If the two images are correctly registered, Woods assumes that the normalized variance $\frac{\sigma_g}{\mu_g}$ is minimum over the entire image [3]. The following *inter-image uniformity cost function* is thus defined:

$$E\left(I_{ref}(.), I_{reg}(T_\Theta(.))\right) = \sum_{g=1}^{G} \frac{N_g}{N} \frac{\sigma_g(T_\Theta(.))}{\mu_g(T_\Theta(.))} , \tag{3}$$

where:

$$\sigma_g(T_\Theta(.)) = \sqrt{\sum_{x|I_{ref}(x)=g} [I_{reg}(T_\Theta(x)) - \mu_g(T_\Theta(.))]^2} , \tag{4}$$

and:

$$\mu_g(T_\Theta(.)) = \frac{1}{N_g} \sum_{x|I_{ref}(x)=g} I_{reg}(T_\Theta(x)). \tag{5}$$

In (3), N represents the number of voxels in the images and N_g stands for the population of voxels having the value g in the reference image.

As pointed out by Woods [3], the inter-image uniformity hypothesis may only be a crude approximation when gross dissimilarities are present in the multimodal image pair. This is always the case when the multimodal pair is used for the complementary and non redundant information one image provides with respect to the other.

We finally consider the criterion based on the maximization of the mutual information proposed recently and independently in [4, 5]. This criterion is based on the same partitioning as in equation (3). The assumption is that the the mutual information is maximum when the two images are correctly registered, yielding the following *mutual information cost function* [4, 5]:

$$E\left(I_{ref}(.),\, I_{reg}(T_\Theta(.))\right) \;=\; -\sum_{g=1}^{G}\sum_{k=1}^{K} p(g,k)\log\frac{p(g,k)}{p(g)p(k)} \tag{6}$$

where G and K stand for the number of grey levels of I_{ref} and I_{reg}. The joint probabilities $p(g,k)$ are the elements of the cooccurrence matrix of $I_{ref}(.)$ and $I_{reg}(T_\Theta(.))$ and $p(g)$ and $p(k)$ are the marginal probabilities of $I_{ref}(.)$ and $I_{reg}(T_\Theta(.))$, both computed from the normalized histograms of the two images.

This criterion has been recognized, in several recent studies, as yielding the best results in multimodal medical image registration. It will be compared to our robust multimodal registration criterion in Section 4.

3 Robust Similarity Metrics-Based Registration

3.1 Robust similarity measures

Standard similarity-based approaches do not model the information differences between images in a single or multimodal pair and, as a consequence, are not robust with respect to them. To increase robustness, the cost function must thus be forgiving about outlying measurements.

Robust estimators have become popular in computer vision applications because they have proven effective in tolerating gross outliers in data [13, 14]. A review on robust estimators in computer vision may be found in [13]. A collection of non linear robust estimators, including least median of squares, least trimmed squares, M-estimators, Hough transforms, RANSAC and MINPRAN algorithms are presented in [15, 14]. The robustness of these estimators to situations in which mixture of data from multiple (coherent) structures plus gross outliers are to be handled is studied in depth in [14]. Stewart [14] shows that the estimated parameters may be heavily skewed in such situations.

In the following we consider the class of M-estimators [16] that has shown attractive properties (i.e., satisfactory breakdown points and moderate computational cost) in computer vision applications [15, 17]. This class of robust estimators reduces the optimization problem to a simple, low cost, weighted least squares problem, as explained in [15, 13]. A robust M-estimator of parameters Θ is obtained by introducing a robust error norm ("loss" function) ρ in the similarity metrics (2) and (3) [13].

For the single modality case, we consider the now standard *robust least squares cost function*:

$$E\left(I_{ref}(.),\, I_{reg}(T_\Theta(.))\right) \;=\; \sum_{x} \rho\left\{I_{ref}(x) - I_{reg}(T_\Theta(x)), C\right\}. \tag{7}$$

where C is a scale (noise) parameter and ρ is a non quadratic error norm (penalty function) associated with the M-estimator. Variants of this robust cost function have been used with success in image processing and computer vision problems such as surface reconstruction [15], image segmentation, computed imaging, optical flow measurement [18, 17], etc.

For multimodal images, we define a *robust inter-image uniformity cost function*:

$$E\left(I_{ref}(.), I_{reg}(T_\Theta(.))\right) = \sum_{g=1}^{G} \frac{N_g}{N} \widetilde{\sigma_g}(T_\Theta(.)) \tag{8}$$

where:

$$\widetilde{\sigma_g}(T_\Theta(.)) = \sqrt{\sum_{x|I_{ref}(x)=g} \rho\left\{I_{reg}(T_\Theta(x)) - \widetilde{\mu_g}(T_\Theta(.)), C\right\}}, \tag{9}$$

and

$$\widetilde{\mu_g}(T_\Theta(.)) = \arg\min_{\mu_g} \frac{1}{N_g} \sum_{x|I_{ref}(\bar{x})=g} \rho\left\{I_{reg}(T_\Theta(x)) - \mu_g, C\right\}, \tag{10}$$

Let us notice that the non robust cost functions (2) and (3) correspond to the special case $\rho(x, C) = x^2$ (for defining (8) we consider a non normalized version of (3), which has shown more efficient than the original Woods' criterion). In the single modal case (7), the cost function is simply defined as a robust error norm of the residual differences between the two registered images. In the multimodal case (8), a "robust variance" $\widetilde{\sigma_g}$ is computed for each region of the image to be registered, according to (9). This robust variance does take into account gross outliers in the registered image, thanks to the robust error norm ρ. A robust estimation of the expected value $\widetilde{\mu_g}$ (10) of the region is simultaneously computed by the same M-estimator.

For the experiments presented in this paper we have tested two "hard redescending" M-estimators [14] (namely the truncated quadratic ρ-function [15] and the Tukey "biweight" ρ-function), as well as a "soft redescending" estimator (the Geman-McClure ρ-function [15]). We privileged the Geman-McClure estimator because it required less calculations for almost the same accuracy as the Tukey "biweight" estimator. It showed less sensitive to initialization than the truncated quadratic. The Geman-McClure ρ-function [15] is defined by:

$$\rho(x, C) = \frac{x^2}{C^2 + x^2}.$$

As the magnitude of the residuals increases and grows beyond a point, its influence on the solution begins to decrease and the value of $\rho(x)$ approaches a constant. The scaling parameter C affects the point at which the influence of outliers begins to decrease.

The calculation of the registration parameters Θ involves the minimization of the non-linear cost functions (7) or (8) which depend on the scale parameter C. A good strategy [14] consists in starting the optimization procedure with a high value for C. The value of C decreases during the minimization process following the formula $C = \alpha.C$ with $0.8 < \alpha < 1$ until C reaches a predefined value. The effect of this procedure is that initially no data are rejected as outliers and a first, crude solution is obtained. During the following optimization steps the influence of the outliers is gradually reduced by decreasing C, leading to a reliable estimation of the rigid transformation parameters, which is robust to gross image differences. In other experiments we have also estimated C as the noise variance computed on homogeneous regions of the original images (other statistical methods for estimating C from the data may be found in [14]). These different strategies provided us with almost the same qualitative results.

3.2 The Multiresolution Stochastic Registration Algorithm

The robust estimators and the registration criteria considered previously are highly non linear, involving non convex cost functions having multiple local minima [19]. In most image registration methods based on the minimization of a cost function, deterministic optimization algorithms are applied. They are known to be very sensitive to local minima, unless they are initialized close to the optimal solution.

In order to increase robustness to local minima of the similarity function and to obtain data driven registrations, the parameter space has been discretized and a fast stochastic optimization algorithm has been applied. Stochastic optimization, based on random sampling, is far less sensitive to local minima, yielding better, often close to the optimal solutions [14]. The optimization technique used in our implementation is based on the Gibbs sampler [20]. A high value is adopted for the initial temperature in a simulated annealing procedure and a fast exponentially decreasing temperature schedule is considered instead of the optimal logarithmic descent [20]. The solution obtained after a given number of steps is further refined by a deterministic extension of the above algorithm, known as Iterated Conditional Modes (ICM). ICM is a deterministic Gauss-Seidel like algorithm, that only accepts configurations decreasing the cost function. It has fast convergence properties and local minima are not a problem, since the first stochastic optimization step provides a good initialization.

The optimization algorithm was applied on a sequence of multiresolution grids, using a standard top-down approach starting from the coarsest resolution level [17,21]. The solution obtained at a given resolution level is interpolated and forwarded to the next, finer resolution. The algorithm first carries out the calculations for every 81st (16th) voxel (pixel) in the 3D (2D) images. After the algorithm has converged, the resulting registration parameters represent the initial estimate for the next level, where every 27th (8th) voxel is processed, then every 9th (4th), every 3rd (2nd) and finally every voxel (pixel) in the image. The search space and the visited configurations were reduced while the resolution increases in order to gradually fine tune the solutions obtained on the coarser resolution levels. The first grids generally provided a good approximation of the final solution. Multigrid matching is usually motivated by the significant computational gain obtained in the registration. As noticed by several authors

[19], multigrid algorithms are also far less sensitive to local minima in the cost function than single resolution optimization schemes. It has indeed been conjectured that multigrid analysis may, to a certain extent, smooth the "landscape" of the objective function to minimize. This yields fast convergence towards good solutions [19].

4   Experimental Results

Registration experiments were performed with both 2D and 3D images. The following similarity measures have been implemented and compared:

- the standard least-squares (LS) similarity measure (Eq. 2) ;
- the inter-image uniformity (IU) criterion [3] (Eq. 3) ;
- the mutual information (MI) criterion [4, 5] (Eq. 6) ;
- the robust least-squares (RLS) similarity metrics (Eq. 7) ;
- the robust inter-image uniformity (RIU) criterion (Eq. 8).

LS and RLS may only be applied to single modal image registration, whereas the other methods (IU, RIU, MI) have been tested both in single and multimodal registration problems. Two representative case studies have been considered: the registration of single modal (MRI/MRI) and multimodal (MRI/SPECT) 3D medical images showing gross outliers or lesion evolution, and the matching of multispectral (visible/IR) remotely sensed images showing large overcast areas.

4.1   Single Modal Image Registration

Medical Images. A first class of experiments consisted in applying a known rigid transformation (3D translation and rotation) to a set of MRI volumes to create a second image set. 25% of the transformed images was then corrupted by salt and pepper noise, to simulate gross outliers (see Fig. 1(a-b)). For each method, the estimated registration parameters were compared to the true ones to determine the accuracy of the registration. Statistics on the registration errors were computed on a set of 20 different registrations problems, involving translation parameters between -20 and $+20$ voxels and rotations between -30 and $+30$ degrees. Let us notice that large rotations are generally difficult to handle with standard, deterministic approaches (in which initializations close to the desired solution are necessary). This is not the case of the stochastic sampling algorithm used here.

As we can see in Table 1, the robust algorithms achieved subvoxel registration errors while the non robust (LS and IU) techniques failed. The MI method, the "best" method referenced at the present time, also achieved subvoxel registration but its performances are slightly inferior to the results obtained by the RLS technique.

Figure 1(c) shows an example where the standard method (LS) failed to correctly register the MR slices shown in Figures 1(a) and 1(b), but where the RLS

58

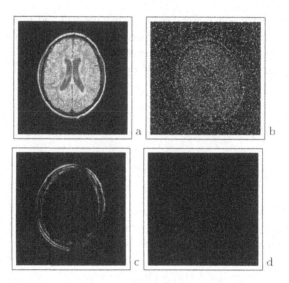

Fig. 1. Robust registration of MR images. **(a)** Reference image. **(b)** Image in (a) rotated by 20 deg, translated by 10 pixels along the x-axis, 10 pixels along the y-axis and corrupted at 25% with salt and pepper noise with large magnitude. **(c)** Difference between the (*noise free*) registered image and the image in (a) (*LS similarity metric*). **(d)** Difference between the (*noise free*) registered image and the image in (a) (*RLS similarity metric*)

achieved accurate matching by discarding outliers. The difference in accuracy is readily visible on the registration error shown in Figures 1(c) and 1(d).

We also show in Fig. 2 an example of the application of the RLS algorithm to the detection of changes in a set of MRI slices of a multiple sclerosis patient, acquired at different dates. Figure 2 illustrates a case on which small differences due to lesion evolution, which were not well distinguished previously due to misalignment by the standard LS similarity metric (Fig. 2(c)), are now clearly identified by simple image subtraction (Fig. 2(d)). This result has been validated by an expert physician from IPB.

Remotely Sensed Images. Two images of France, in the infra-red band of NOAA (Fig. 3(a-b), acquired at different dates and showing large overcast areas, were manually registered by an expert from LSIIT to establish ground truth. One of the images has been transformed using different 2D rotation and translation parameters and the registration algorithms were applied. This case, contrary to the example considered previously (Section 4.1), does not correspond to a corruption of the data by gross outliers, but to the presence of multiple coherent structures (i.e. ground and clouds) in the data. Mixture of data from multiple (coherent) structures introduces a significant bias in all robust estimators, as shown in a recent study by Stewart [14]. The performances of the robust methods are affected by this bias, as can be seen in Table 2 in which the different

Table 1. Single modal registration of $3D$ MRI images. An MR volume was artificially transformed using 20 different rigid transformations and the images were corrupted at 25% by salt and pepper noise. The average and the standard deviation of the registration errors computed from the 20 registrations are presented for the different approaches. Translation errors are given in voxels and rotation errors in degrees

Approach	Δt_x	Δt_y	Δt_z	$\Delta \hat{\theta}_x$	$\Delta \hat{\theta}_y$	$\Delta \hat{\theta}_z$
LS	2.30 ± 1.75	2.53 ± 1.56	2.77 ± 1.83	4.71 ± 2.89	5.33 ± 3.40	5.05 ± 3.51
IU	1.49 ± 1.40	1.56 ± 1.41	1.93 ± 1.63	3.75 ± 2.03	3.65 ± 2.54	2.99 ± 3.06
MI	0.05 ± 0.06	0.22 ± 0.15	0.09 ± 0.14	0.35 ± 0.35	0.27 ± 0.32	0.44 ± 0.69
RLS	0.04 ± 0.07	0.16 ± 0.11	0.06 ± 0.10	0.41 ± 0.21	0.16 ± 0.22	0.33 ± 0.24
RIU	0.09 ± 0.05	0.18 ± 0.14	0.10 ± 0.05	0.22 ± 0.34	0.24 ± 0.17	0.40 ± 0.59

approaches are compared. The registrations are not as accurate as in the previous case, although a subpixel accuracy is reached, and the difference between methods is less pronounced. The robust methods produce nevertheless the best results and compare favourably to the MI approach.

Figure 3 illustrates the contribution of the RLS metric with respect to a non robust LS metric, in the registration of the original infra-red image pair. The original images show a misregistration of about 3 pixels. Clouds in the second image lead the LS technique to a slight misalignment (Fig. 3(c)) while the RLS measure provides a more accurate registration (Fig. 3(d)). The difference is readily visible along the south-west coast of France. The registration errors presented in Figures 3(c-d) are obtained by subtraction of the registered image from the reference image in Figure 3(a), followed by contrast modifications for visualization purpose.

Table 2. Single modal registration of $2D$ remotely sensed infra-red images. Two images of the infra-red electromagnetic band of NOAA satellite acquired at different dates have been manually registered to create ground truth. One of the images has undergone 20 different rigid transformations using different translation and rotation values. The average and the standard deviation of the registration errors are presented for the different approaches. Translation errors are given in pixels and rotation errors in degrees

Approach	Δt_x	Δt_y	$\Delta \hat{\theta}$
LS	0.42 ± 0.18	0.31 ± 0.41	0.32 ± 0.18
IU	0.52 ± 0.21	0.77 ± 0.40	0.30 ± 0.25
MI	0.49 ± 0.54	0.63 ± 0.25	0.75 ± 0.89
RLS	0.36 ± 0.10	0.27 ± 0.37	0.30 ± 0.25
RIU	0.34 ± 0.17	0.70 ± 0.28	0.18 ± 0.13

4.2 Multimodal Registration

Medical Images. To evaluate the ability of the robust similarity metrics to handle multimodal image pairs, a 3D SPECT image volume has been manually

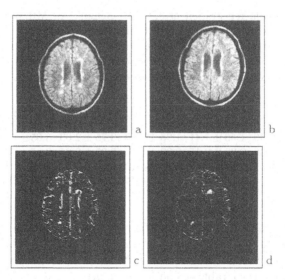

Fig. 2. Change detection in a MRI image sequence. **(a)** Multiple sclerosis patient MR image. **(b)** Image of the same patient acquired several months later. **(c)** Difference between the registered image and the image in (a) (*LS similarity metric*). **(d)** Difference between the registered image and the image in (a) (*robust RLS similarity metric*)

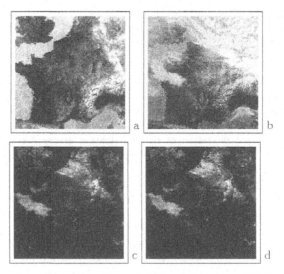

Fig. 3. Single modal registration of remotely-sensed images. **(a)** Image of France in the infra-red band of NOAA (*02/10/97*). **(b)** Image of France in the infra-red band of NOAA (*02/05/97*). **(c)** Registration error (*LS similarity metric*). **(d)** Registration error (*robust RLS similarity metric*)

registered to its corresponding MRI volume with the aid of an expert physician from IPB. The manually registered SPECT volume was then transformed using the same 3D translation and rotation parameters as in the previously described experiments (Section 4.1). To simulate outliers, 25% of the SPECT image was corrupted by salt and pepper noise. The robust inter-image uniformity technique RIU has been compared to the inter-image uniformity similarity function IU [3] and to the mutual information MI criterion [4, 5]. Table 3 shows the robustness of the different similarity measures to gross outliers. The error for the RIU method is about 1 voxel for the translation parameters and 1 degree for the Euler rotation angles. This is significantly more accurate than the IU approach. The proposed robust similarity metric also compares favourably to the MI criterion which yields registrations that are better than the IU criterion but are generally below RIU.

Table 3. Multimodal registration of 3D MRI/SPECT images. A 3D SPECT image volume manually pre-registered by an expert to its MRI counterpart was artificially transformed using 20 different translation and rotation parameters and corrupted at 25% by salt and pepper noise. The average and the standard deviation of the registration errors are presented for the different approaches. Translation errors are given in voxels and rotation errors in degrees

Approach	Δt_x	Δt_y	Δt_z	$\Delta\hat{\theta}_x$	$\Delta\hat{\theta}_y$	$\Delta\hat{\theta}_z$
IU	3.85 ± 5.59	3.02 ± 4.78	4.16 ± 4.38	8.33 ± 4.51	6.23 ± 3.52	6.80 ± 4.15
MI	1.41 ± 0.74	1.38 ± 1.23	2.06 ± 1.29	0.94 ± 1.58	1.04 ± 1.15	1.36 ± 0.77
RIU	0.82 ± 0.53	0.61 ± 0.50	0.83 ± 0.60	0.21 ± 0.48	1.14 ± 0.26	0.71 ± 0.94

Figure 4 shows a real example of a patient SPECT image volume registered with respect to its MRI counterpart by the robust algorithm. The accuracy of the registration has been evaluated by visual inspection and has been considered as satisfactory by an expert.

Remotely Sensed Images. We consider again the case of multispectral remotely sensed images, presenting coherent data corruption due to large overcast areas. Two images, one in the visible and one in the infrared band of NOAA, acquired at different dates (Fig. 5(a-b)) were manually registered to establish ground truth. One of the images has been transformed using different rotation and translation parameters and the multimodality registration algorithms were applied. The performances of the different methods are summarized in Table 4. As expected the robust RIU criterion provides registrations that are significantly more accurate than the non robust IU technique. The difference between the tested similarity metrics is however not as pronounced as for the medical images registration problem (in which gross outliers were considered). This may again be explained by the bias introduced by the mixture of data from multiple coherent structures on the robust estimation [14]. In this particular case, the mutual information MI criterion yields, in the average, the best results. Let us

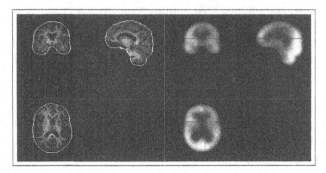

Fig. 4. Robust MRI/SPECT volume registration. The SPECT and MRI volumes with the SPECT contours superimposed on the MRI are shown (*multiplanar visualization*) after robust registration (*RIU similarity metric*)

however notice that the variance of the MI estimate is significantly higher than the variance of the robust RIU criterion (see Table 4), which tends to temper the conclusion in this case.

Table 4. Multimodal registration of $2D$ visible/infra-red images. Two images, one of the visible and one of the infra-red electromagnetic band of NOAA satellite acquired at different dates have been manually registered to create ground truth. One of the images has undergone 20 different rigid transformations using different translation and rotation values. The average and the standard deviation of the registration errors are presented for the different approaches. Translation error are given in pixels and rotation errors in degrees

Approach	Δt_x	Δt_y	$\Delta \hat{\theta}$
IU	1.34 ± 0.87	1.04 ± 0.34	0.34 ± 0.27
MI	0.40 ± 0.68	0.31 ± 0.74	0.24 ± 0.37
RIU	0.51 ± 0.34	0.76 ± 0.37	0.26 ± 0.20

Figure 5 presents the registration of the original multimodal pair. The images from the NOAA visible band (Fig. 5(a)) and from the NOAA infra-red band (Fig. 5(b)), acquired at different dates have been registered using the IU, RIU and MI approaches. In this particular case, the non robust IU metric and the MI criterion provided the same final registrations. As may be seen Fig. 5 (c), the IU metric, yields a misregistration, that is visible on the error image, along the south-west coast of France. This is not the case of the robust RIU similarity measure (Fig. 5 (d)) which provides an accurate registration of this dissimilar multimodal image pair. Let us notice that the multimodal registration error shown in Fig. 5 (c-d) is defined as the difference between the registered IR image and the IR image acquired at the same instant as the visible band reference image.

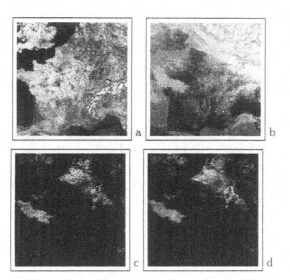

Fig. 5. Multimodal registration of visible/IR remotely-sensed images. (a) Image of France in the visible band of NOAA (*02/10/97*) (reference image). (b) Image of France in the infrared band of NOAA (*02/05/97*). (c) Registration error (*IU similarity metric*). (d) Registration error (*robust RIU similarity metric*). The registration error is defined as the difference between the registered IR image and the IR image acquired at the same instant as the visible band reference image (a)

The LS and RLS techniques require approximately the same average computation times: 20 mn cpu time for 3D $128 \times 128 \times 128$ images on a HP 715/80 workstation. For the same data size, the IU method takes 35 mn, the MI technique 40 mn and the RIU method needs 60 mn cpu time. In the case of 2D images (256×256), the RIU metric requires 4 mn cpu time while each of the other techniques takes approximately 1-2 minutes. As can be seen, the additional computational complexity introduced by the robust estimation is acceptable and these methods may thus be used with profit to improve the accuracy in many critical single or multimodal image registration problems.

5 Conclusion

The robust similarity metrics-based registration methods described in this paper were motivated by the lack, in existing approaches, of specific models for gross dissimilarities or outlying data that are often present in single and multimodal image pairs. The proposed stochastic multigrid registration algorithms have two major advantages over standard methods:

- No manual initialization near the optimal solution is required to obtain an accurate registration. Local minima, a major problem in standard image registration techniques, are avoided by the use of fast multigrid random sampling algorithms. This results in a fully data driven method that requires no human interaction.

– Gross image differences are taken into account efficiently by robust M-estimators. To our knowledge, the registration of *multimodal images* showing gross dissimilarities or mixture of data from multiple coherent structures has never been evoked until now.

As a conclusion, let us emphasize that the approach proposed in this paper is comprehensive and not limited to medical or remotely-sensed images. Other potential application fields [6] such as military imaging, multisensor robot vision or the multisource analysis of artistic patrimony [2] may benefit from the robustness of these methods.

Acknowledgments

This study has been supported by the Commission of the European Communities, DG XII, in the framework of the TMR program (Training and Mobility of Researchers), contract Nr ERBFMIBCT960701 and by the "Groupement d'Intérêt Scientifique" (CNRS, CEA, INRIA, MENESR) "Sciences de la Cognition".

The authors wish to thank Dr. Denis Bruckert (Groupement de Recherche en Télédétection et Radiométrie, LSIIT) for providing the NOAA images and Dr. Izzie-Jacques Namer (IPB) for providing and interpreting the MR and SPECT data.

References

1. M. Herbin, A. Venot, J. Y. Devaux, E. Walter, F. Lebruchec, L. Dubertet, and J. C. Roucayrol. Automated registration of dissimilar images: application to medical imagery. *Computer Vision, Graphics and Image Processing*, 47:77–88, 1989.

2. F. Heitz, H. Maître, and C. de Couessin. Event detection in multisource imaging: application to fine arts painting analysis. *IEEE Transactions on Acoustic, Speech and Signal Processing*, 38(4):695–704, 1990.

3. R. P. Woods, J. C. Mazziota, and S. R. Cherry. MRI-PET registration with automated algorithm. *Journal of Computer Assisted Tomography*, 17(4):536–546, 1993.

4. F. Maes, A. Collignon, D. Vandermeulen, G. Marchal, and P. Suetens. Multimodality image registration by maximization of mutual information. *IEEE Transactions on Medical Imaging*, 16(2):187–198, 1997.

5. W. Wells III, P. Viola, H. Atsumi, S. Nakajima, and R. Kikinis. Multimodal volume registration by maximization of mutual information. *Medical Image Analysis*, 1(1):33–51, 1996.

6. L. G. Brown. A survey of image registration techniques. *ACM Computing Surveys*, 24(4):325–376, 1992.

7. P. Van den Elsen, E. J. D. Paul, and M. A. Viergever. Medical image matching - a review with classification. *IEEE Engineering in Medicine and Biology*, 12(1):26–39, 1993.

8. J. West, M. Fitzpatrick, M. Wang, B. Dawan, C. Maurer, Jr. R. Maciunas, C. Barillot, D. Lemoine, A. Collignon, F. Maes, P. Suetens, D. Vandermeulen, P. Van den Elsen, S. Napel, T. Sumanaweera, B. Harkness, P. Hemler, D. Hill, D. Hawkes, C. Studholme, A. Mainz, M. Viergever, G. Malandain, X. Pennec, M. Noz, G. Maguire, Jr. M. Pollack, C. Pelizzari, R. Robb, D. Hanson, and R. Woods. Comparison and evaluation of retrospective intermodality brain image registration techniques. *Journal of Computer Assisted Tomography*, 21(4):554–566, 1997.

9. G. Malandain, S. Fernàndez-Vidal, and J. M. Rocchisani. Improving registration of 3D medical images using a mechanical-based method. *Lecture Notes in Computer Vision (ECCV'94)*, 801:131–136, 1994.

10. J. P. Thirion, A. Gourdon, O. Monga, A. Guéziec, and N. Ayache. Fully automatic registration of 3D CAT-scan images using crest lines. 14th *International Conference EMBS'92 (IEEE)*, pages 1888–1890, 1992.

11. G.E. Christensen, M.I. Miller, M.W. Vannier, and U. Grenander. Individualizing neuro-anatomical atlases using a massively parallel computer. *IEEE Computer*, pages 32–38, January 1996.

12. J. Sato and R. Cipolla. Image registration using multi-scale texture moments. *Image and Vision Computing*, 13(5):341–353, 1995.

13. P. Meer, D. Mintz, A. Rosenfeld, and D. Y. Kim. Robust regression methods for computer vision: a review. *International Journal of Computer Vision*, 6(1):59–70, 1990.

14. C. Stewart. Bias in robust estimation caused by discontinuities and multiple structures. *IEEE Transactions on Pattern Analysis and Machine Intelligence*, 19(8):818–833, 1997.

15. M. J. Black and A. Rangarajan. On the unification of line processes, outliers rejection and robust statistics in early vision. *International Journal of Computer Vision*, 19(1):57–91, 1996.

16. J. Huber. *Robust statistics*. John Wiley and sons, New York, 1981.

17. J. M. Odobez and P. Bouthemy. Robust multiresolution estimation of parametric motion models. *Journal of Visual Communication and Image Representation*, 6(4):348–365, 1995.

18. M. Black and P. Anandan. The robust estimation of multiple motions: parametric and piecewise-smooth flow fields. *Computer Vision and Image Understanding*, 63(1):75–104, 1996.

19. F. Heitz, P. Perez, and P. Bouthemy. Multiscale minimization of global energy functions in some visual recovery problems. *Computer Vision, Graphics and Image Processing : Image Understanding*, 59(1):125–134, 1994.

20. S. Geman and D. Geman. Stochastic relaxation, Gibbs distribution and the bayesian restoration of images. *IEEE Transactions on Pattern Analysis and Machine Intelligence*, 24(6):721–741, 1984.

21. D. Terzopoulos. Image analysis using multigrid relaxation methods. *IEEE Transactions on Pattern Analysis and Machine Intelligence*, 8(2):129–139, 1986.

Image Sequences and Video

Decoupling Fourier Components of Dynamic Image Sequences: A Theory of Signal Separation, Image Segmentation, and Optical Flow Estimation

David Vernon

Department of Computer Science
National University of Ireland, Maynooth
Ireland

Abstract. This paper presents a new Fourier-based approach to the separation or decoupling of m additive images from a time-sequence of the sum of these images where at least $m-1$ images are translating with distinct and unique velocity. A closed-form solution is presented for the case where $m = 2$. A generalization is then presented which extends the theory to embrace situations where the images are not additive but are, instead, formed by the superposition of an occluding object or objects on an occluded background. That is, the approach is generalized to effect a model-free segmentation of objects undergoing translatory fronto-parallel motion in dynamic image sequences. Object velocities of one pixel per frame are sufficient to guarantee segmentation.

We also show how the technique can be applied on a local basis to compute a dense instantaneous optical flow field for the image sequence, even in relatively featureless regions. The technique is evaluated using Otte's and Nagel's benchmark image sequence, for which ground-truth data is available, and results comparable with the ground-truth flow field are achieved. RMS errors of velocity magnitude and direction are computed and reported.

1 Introduction

Traditional approaches to segmentation typically exploit one of two broad approaches. These are (a) boundary detection, which depends on the detection of spatial intensity discontinuities (using first or second order gradient techniques) and their aggregation into contour-based object descriptions, and (b) region-growing, which depends on the identification of local regions that satisfy some regional similarity predicate (see [1] and [2] for an overview).

Equally, the measurement of object velocity in images normally exploits one of two primary techniques. The first involves the computation of the spatio-temporal gradient, differentiating the (filtered or unfiltered) image sequence with respect to time and subsequently computing the optical flow field (*e.g.* [3]). The second involves the segmentation of the object or feature in question using either region-based gradient (first or second order) filtering and analysis followed either by the computation of the optical flow field or by identification object correspondence, typically by matching contour or region primitives (*e.g.* [4]). A third, lesser-used, approach exploits the regularity in spatiotemporal-frequency representations of the image, such as the spatiotemporal Fourier Transform Domain, resulting from certain types of image motion, such as fronto-parallel translation [5–13]. Comparisons of the many variations of these approaches and the relationship between them can be found in [14–17].

In this paper, we develop the Fourier analysis of dynamic image sequences and we present a new approach (i) to the separation of additive signals (such as in the case of reflections superimposed on optical images), (ii) to the conventional segmentation of occluding and occluded objects, and (iii) to the estimation of instantaneous velocity (including estimation of optical flow). This is effected by processing the resultant Fourier phasors derived from the FFT of the composite image and by resolving each of them into the individual Fourier components corresponding to each object.

2 Theory

2.1 The Additive Model: Signal Separation

First, we show that it is possible to separate (or recover) m additive images, given only a time sequence of the sum of these images and given the assumption that at least $m - 1$ images are translating, each with a distinct and unique velocity. That is, given a composite image $\psi_{t_j}(x, y)$ at time t_j in a temporally-ordered image sequence:

$$\psi_{t_j}(x, y) = \sum_{i=1}^{m} \psi_{t_j}^i(x, y) \tag{1}$$

where $\psi_{t_j}^i(x, y)$ is the (unknown) i^{th} additive component image at time t_j, and assuming

$$\psi_{t_j}^i(x, y) = \psi_{t_0}^i(x - v_x^i j\delta t, y - v_y^i j\delta t) \tag{2}$$

where (v_x^i, v_y^i) is the spatial velocity of the ith component image and δt is the incremental time interval, it is possible to recover, or compute, each individual image $\psi_{t_0}^i(x, y), \forall i$.

This is accomplished by computing the Fourier transform $\mathsf{F}_{t_j}(k_x, k_y)$ of each image in the image sequence

$$\mathsf{F}_{t_j}(k_x, k_y) = \mathcal{F}\left(\psi_{t_j}(x, y)\right) \tag{3}$$

and then by decoupling the resultant (composite) Fourier component at each spatial frequency into the m individual Fourier components $\mathsf{F}_{t_0}^i(k_x, k_y)$ at time t_0. The required individual images are then computed using the inverse Fourier transform

$$\psi_{t_0}^i(x, y) = \mathcal{F}^{-1}\left(\mathsf{F}_{t_0}^i(k_x, k_y)\right) \tag{4}$$

In particular, the composite Fourier component at time t_j is a function of the m decoupled Fourier comonents $\mathsf{F}_{t_0}^i(k_x, k_y), 1 \le i \le m$ at time t_0 and of the incremental spatial frequency-dependent and velocity-dependent phase change $\Delta\Phi^i$ which results from the individual image translation where $\Delta\Phi^i$ is given by

$$\Delta\Phi^i = e^{-i(k_x v_x^i \delta t + k_y v_y^i \delta t)} \tag{5}$$

Specifically, we have

$$\mathsf{F}_{t_j}(k_x, k_y) = \sum_{i=1}^{m} \mathsf{F}_{t_0}^i(k_x, k_y)\left(\Delta\Phi^i\right)^j \tag{6}$$

If we have $i = m$ distinct individual images, equation 6 implies that we have $2m$ complex unknowns (*i.e.* $\mathsf{F}_{t_0}^i$ and $\Delta\Phi^{ij}$) and consequently we can solve for these $2m$ unknowns if we have $2m$ constraints. These constraints are derived from equation 6 by making $j = 2m$ observations for F_{t_j} (*i.e.* by using $j = 2m$ composite images in the temporal sequence). That is, for a given spatial frequency (k_x, k_y), we observe the Fourier transform F_{t_j} at time $t_0, t_1, \ldots, t_j, \ldots, t_{2m}$ and solve these $2m$ simultaneous equations of degree $2m - 1$ in complex unknowns $\mathsf{F}_{t_0}^i$ and $\Delta\Phi^i$.

In the simplest non-trivial case, $m = 2$, there are two distinct objects. In this case, and dropping the (k_x, k_y) for the sake of brevity while remembering that we are dealing with complex values defined on a 2-D domain, we have

$$\mathsf{F}_{t_0} = \mathsf{F}_{t_0}^1\left(\Delta\Phi^1\right)^0 + \mathsf{F}_{t_0}^2\left(\Delta\Phi^2\right)^0 \tag{7}$$

$$\mathsf{F}_{t_1} = \mathsf{F}_{t_0}^1\left(\Delta\Phi^1\right)^1 + \mathsf{F}_{t_0}^2\left(\Delta\Phi^2\right)^1 \tag{8}$$

$$\mathsf{F}_{t_2} = \mathsf{F}_{t_0}^1\left(\Delta\Phi^1\right)^2 + \mathsf{F}_{t_0}^2\left(\Delta\Phi^2\right)^2 \tag{9}$$

$$\mathsf{F}_{t_3} = \mathsf{F}_{t_0}^1\left(\Delta\Phi^1\right)^3 + \mathsf{F}_{t_0}^2\left(\Delta\Phi^2\right)^3 \tag{10}$$

This set of four simultaneous equations has a closed-form solution [18]:

$$\Delta\Phi^1 = \frac{-b + \sqrt{z}}{2a} \tag{11}$$

$$\Delta\Phi^2 = \frac{-b - \sqrt{z}}{2a} \tag{12}$$

$$\mathsf{F}_{t_0}^1 = \frac{\mathsf{F}_{t_0}\Delta\Phi^2 - \mathsf{F}_{t_1}}{\left(\Delta\Phi^2 - \Delta\Phi^1\right)} \tag{13}$$

$$\mathsf{F}_{t_0}^2 = \frac{\mathsf{F}_{t_0}\Delta\Phi^1 - \mathsf{F}_{t_1}}{\left(\Delta\Phi^1 - \Delta\Phi^2\right)} \tag{14}$$

where $a = \left(\mathsf{F}_{t_1}\right)^2 - \mathsf{F}_{t_0}\mathsf{F}_{t_2}$, $b = \mathsf{F}_{t_0}\mathsf{F}_{t_3} - \mathsf{F}_{t_1}\mathsf{F}_{t_2}$, $c = \left(\mathsf{F}_{t_2}\right)^2 - \mathsf{F}_{t_1}\mathsf{F}_{t_3}$, and $z = b^2 - 4ac = \alpha + i\beta$.

Note, however, that the assignment of $\Delta\Phi^1$ rather than $\Delta\Phi^2$ in equation 11 and *vice versa* in equation 12 (and, hence the assignment of $\mathsf{F}_{t_0}^1$ and $\mathsf{F}_{t_0}^2$

in equations 13 and 14) is arbitrary and the alternative assignment is equally valid. Consequently, once $F_{t_0}^1(k_x, k_y)$ and $F_{t_0}^2(k_x, k_y)$ have been solved for all spatial frequencies k_x, k_y, it is still necessary to sort these sets of $F_{t_0}^1(k_x, k_y)$ and $F_{t_0}^2(k_x, k_y)$. That is, we only have at this point two sets of phase changes $\{\Delta\Phi^A\}$ and $\{\Delta\Phi^B\}$ and two corresponding sets of Fourier components $\{F^A\}$ and $\{F^B\}$. These sets need to be sorted into two new sets $\{F^1\}$ and $\{F^2\}$ corresponding to the two individual component images. In [18], we presented a method of doing this based on the regularity of the incremental phase change $\Delta\Phi$ as a function of frequency (k_x, k_y). Specifically, we have:

$$\Delta\Phi(k_x, k_y) = e^{-i(v_x k_x \delta t + v_y k_y \delta t)}$$
$$= e^{i\delta\phi(k_x, k_y)} \tag{15}$$

For a given image i, (v_x^i, v_y^i) is constant. Thus a given image i will exhibit a phase change $\delta\phi(k_x, k_y)$:

$$\delta\phi(k_x, k_y) = -(v_x^i k_x \delta t + v_y^i k_y \delta t) \tag{16}$$

which will differ for each image i. Since we require $(v_x^i, v_y^i) \neq (v_x^j, v_y^j), i \neq j$, in order to sort the components of the two waves we simply need to identify the two velocities (v_x^1, v_y^1) and (v_x^2, v_y^2) which will, in turn, allow us to identify the corresponding expected phase change for images 1 and 2, respectively. Let these expected phase changes be denoted $\delta\phi_e^1(k_x, k_y)$ and $\delta\phi_e^2(k_x, k_y)$, respectively. Then we assign a component $F^A(k_x, k_y)$ to image 1, *i.e.* we include it in $\{F^1\}$, if $\left|\delta\phi_e^1 - \delta\phi^A\right| < \left|\delta\phi_e^2 - \delta\phi^A\right|$, otherwise we assign it to $\{F^2\}$; $F^B(k_x, k_y)$ is assigned to the other image.

It only remains, then, to identify the two velocities (v_x^1, v_y^1) and (v_x^2, v_y^2). We do this using a Hough transform. From equation 16 we have:

$$v_y = \frac{1}{k_y \delta t} \left(\delta\phi(k_x, k_y) - k_x v_x \delta t\right) \tag{17}$$

This equation represents a Hough transform in the two variables (v_x, v_y) which we solve for all $\delta\phi(k_x, k_y)$, k_x, k_y, and v_x. Note that

$$\delta\phi(k_x, k_y) = \arctan(\Im\Delta\Phi(k_x, k_y), \Re\Delta\Phi(k_x, k_y)) \tag{18}$$

Local maxima in this Hough transform space represent the velocities which are exhibited by the frequency components. In this case, there are two velocity maxima, one corresponding to image 1 and the other to image 2. The location of these maxima give us (v_x^1, v_y^1) and (v_x^2, v_y^2) and, thus, we can proceed to sort the components.

Note that the Hough transform equation 17 becomes degenerate if $k_y = 0$ in which case we use an alternative re-arrangement as follows:

$$v_x = \frac{1}{k_x \delta t} \left(\delta\phi(k_x, k_y)\right) \tag{19}$$

2.2   The Generalized Occlusion Model: Signal Segmentation

The foregoing theory assumes that the individual images combine additively to form the resultant image. Although there are many situations or applications where this assumption is valid, *e.g.* the superposition of reflections on an image acquired through a transparent medium, there are important situations where it is not. In particular, the common situation where a moving object occludes a (possibly moving) background violates the assumption. Although the foregoing approach does in fact produce a reasonable segmentation of the (occluding) forground objects from the (partially occluded) background, the results are inevitably imperfect. To deal with this, we next present a generalization of the foregoing theory to deal explicitly with the decoupling or segmentation of (non-additive) occluding objects undergoing translatory fronto-parallel motion in dynamic image sequences.

Recall equations 7 to 10. At time t_0, the situation where occlusion obtains is still accurately represented by equation 7, *i.e.* the composite image is the sum of the occluded object (or image) and the background object (or image), assuming the background occluded image signal has a zero value wherever the occluding image is non-zero, *i.e.* assuming that there is nothing behind the occluding object. Of course, this is not correct in most instances and there is a non-zero occluded signal. Whilst this does not invalidate equation 7, provided we allow the assumption, it does then cause a problem with equation 8 since, at time t_1, when the object and/or the background object has moved, there will be a change in the spectral content of the image due to the appearance of visual information in the background which was previously occluded at time t_0 and to the disappearance of visual information which is now occluded at time t_1 (remember that the velocities of the occluded and the occluding object are different). We will call this revealed/hidden signal the *occluded residue* or simply the *residue*. Consequently, to render equation 8 accurate again we must include a new term F^3 to represent the residue. Equation 8 now becomes

$$\mathsf{F}_{t_1} = \mathsf{F}_{t_0}^1 \left(\Delta \Phi^1 \right)^1 + \mathsf{F}_{t_0}^2 \left(\Delta \Phi^2 \right)^1 + \mathsf{F}^3 \tag{20}$$

Similarly, at time t_2, we must again add a new residue term F^4 and, in addition, we must alter the phase of the previous residue F^3 to reflect the translation of the background. Consequently, we must alter the phase either by $\Delta \Phi^1$ or by $\Delta \Phi^2$ depending on whether $\mathsf{F}_{t_0}^1$ or $\mathsf{F}_{t_0}^2$ is the background. Since we don't know which is the case at this point, we choose, arbitrarily, $\mathsf{F}_{t_0}^2$ as the background occluded image and $\mathsf{F}_{t_0}^1$ as the foreground occluding image. Later we will address the resolution of this arbitrary choice. Equation 9 then becomes:

$$\mathsf{F}_{t_2} = \mathsf{F}_{t_0}^1 \left(\Delta \Phi^1 \right)^2 + \mathsf{F}_{t_0}^2 \left(\Delta \Phi^2 \right)^2 + \mathsf{F}^3 \left(\Delta \Phi^2 \right)^1 + \mathsf{F}^4 \tag{21}$$

In the same way, equation 10 becomes:

$$\mathsf{F}_{t_3} = \mathsf{F}_{t_0}^1 \left(\Delta \Phi^1 \right)^3 + \mathsf{F}_{t_0}^2 \left(\Delta \Phi^2 \right)^3 + \mathsf{F}^3 \left(\Delta \Phi^2 \right)^2 + \mathsf{F}^4 \left(\Delta \Phi^2 \right)^1 + \mathsf{F}^5 \tag{22}$$

Now, instead of four complex unknowns as in the additive situation, we now have three additional unknowns, making a total of seven. Consequently, the system is underdetermined. Unfortunately, every time we add a new constraint, we also introduce an additional unknown representing a new residue. In order to make the problem tractable, we must adopt an alternative strategy.

There are three steps in this strategy. The first step involves a reduction in the number of unknowns, and the second and third steps concern the solution of these unknowns.

Approximation of the Residues If we assume that the occluding object velocity is small then it follows that the residues will be approximately the same and also that they will be small. Thus, we assume that $F^3(k_x, k_y) \approx F^4(k_x, k_y) \approx F^5(k_x, k_y)$. Adding a fifth constraint equation, we now have the following five simultaneous equations:

$$F_{t_0} = F_{t_0}^1 (\Delta\Phi^1)^0 + F_{t_0}^2 (\Delta\Phi^2)^0 \tag{23}$$

$$F_{t_1} = F_{t_0}^1 (\Delta\Phi^1)^1 + F_{t_0}^2 (\Delta\Phi^2)^1 + F^3 \tag{24}$$

$$F_{t_2} = F_{t_0}^1 (\Delta\Phi^1)^2 + F_{t_0}^2 (\Delta\Phi^2)^2 + F^3 (\Delta\Phi^2)^1 + F^3 \tag{25}$$

$$F_{t_3} = F_{t_0}^1 (\Delta\Phi^1)^3 + F_{t_0}^2 (\Delta\Phi^2)^3 + F^3 (\Delta\Phi^2)^2 + F^3 (\Delta\Phi^2)^1 + F^3 \tag{26}$$

$$F_{t_4} = F_{t_0}^1 (\Delta\Phi^1)^4 + F_{t_0}^2 (\Delta\Phi^2)^4 + F^3 (\Delta\Phi^2)^3 + F^3 (\Delta\Phi^2)^2 + \tag{27}$$
$$F^3 (\Delta\Phi^2)^1 + F^3$$

Recall that this system of equations assumes that $F_{t_0}^2$ corresponds to the occluded background image which is why we use the associated incremental phase change $\Delta\Phi^2$ in the residue terms. Note that if we let the residue equal zero then the equations are those of the purely additive case, *i.e.* equations 7 to 10, as one would expect.

Solution for the Incremental Phase Change We now have a system of five non-trivial simultaneous equations in five complex unknowns. Unfortunately, attempts at finding a well-posed closed-form analytical solution have been unsuccessful so far and an implementation of a gradient-descent numerical solution proved unreliable, principally because of the high-dimensionality of the solution space (it is a 10-D solution-space since there are five complex unknowns).

Instead, in order to solve these equations for $F_{t_0}^1$, $F_{t_0}^2$, $\Delta\Phi^1$, $\Delta\Phi^2$, and F^3, we exploit the velocity-dependent and frequency-dependent regularity of $\Delta\Phi^1$ and $\Delta\Phi^2$.

Recall from section 2.1 above that we used this relationship to sort the frequency components into the two distinct sets corresponding to each individual image in the case of additive images. In the occluded case which we are addressing in this paper, we solve for $\Delta\Phi^1$ and $\Delta\Phi^2$ as in the additive case using equations 11 and 12 above, *i.e.* by assuming the residue is zero. However, since the residue is not zero, the solution for each $\Delta\Phi^1$ and $\Delta\Phi^2$ will include an error $\delta_{\Delta\Phi^1}$ and $\delta_{\Delta\Phi^2}$. Since these errors are not systematic for all spatial frequencies (k_x, k_y), we can estimate the true value of $\Delta\Phi^1$ and $\Delta\Phi^2$ by fitting a plane to the erroneous values $\Delta\Phi^{1'} = \Delta\Phi^1 + \delta_{\Delta\Phi^1}$ and $\Delta\Phi^{2'} = \Delta\Phi^2 + \delta_{\Delta\Phi^2}$. Specifically, we use the values $\Delta\Phi^{1'}(k_x, k_y)$ and $\Delta\Phi^{2'}(k_x, k_y)$ for all spatial frequencies to identify the velocity (v_x^1, v_y^1) of the foreground occluding object and (v_x^2, v_y^2) of the background occluded image as described above. Having computed these velocities, we can then compute an estimate of the true incremental phase change $\Delta\Phi^1(k_x, k_y)$ and $\Delta\Phi^2(k_x, k_y)$ for each Fourier component, *i.e.* at each spatial frequency, from

$$\Delta\Phi^i = e^{-i(k_x v_x^i \delta t + k_y v_y^i \delta t)} \tag{28}$$

and, hence,

$$\Re(\Delta\Phi^i) = \cos(k_x v_x^i \delta t + k_y v_y^i \delta t) \tag{29}$$

$$\Im(\Delta\Phi^i) = \sin(k_x v_x^i \delta t + k_y v_y^i \delta t) \tag{30}$$

Solution for the Fourier Components At this point, we have 'solved' (or, rather, estimated) two of the unknowns $\Delta\Phi^1$ and $\Delta\Phi^2$, and it remains simply to solve for the remaining three $F_{t_0}^1$, $F_{t_0}^2$, and F^3. This can be accomplished in a straight-forward manner using equations 23, 24, and 25. These equations have the form

$$a + b - p = 0 \tag{31}$$

$$ad + be + c - q = 0 \tag{32}$$

$$ad^2 + be^2 + c(1 + e) - r = 0 \tag{33}$$

where a, b, and c are unknown. These three simultaneous equations yield the following solutions for a, b, and c:

$$c = \frac{p(de^2 - d^2 e) + q(d^2 - e^2) + r(e - d)}{(d^2 - e^2) + (1 + e)(e - d)} \tag{34}$$

$$b = \frac{q - pd - c}{e - d} \tag{35}$$

$$a = p - b \tag{36}$$

However, before we solve for $F_{t_0}^1$, $F_{t_0}^2$, and F^3 in this way, we must identify which is the occluding and which is the occluded component as we need to assign the appropriate known value of background phase change $\Delta\Phi^2$ to the term e in equations 34, 35, and 36.

We assume, arbitrarily, that the background velocity is smaller than that of the foreground occluding object. This provides the basis for deciding on which values of $F_{t_0}^1$, and $F_{t_0}^2$ are the occluding and occluded. Specifically,

$$d = \Delta \Phi^1 \atop e = \Delta \Phi^2 \Big\} \, |\Delta \Phi^1| > |\Delta \Phi^2|$$

and solve for $a = F_{t_0}^1$, $b = F_{t_0}^2$, and $c = F^3$. On the other hand

$$d = \Delta \Phi^2 \atop e = \Delta \Phi^1 \Big\} \, |\Delta \Phi^1| \leq |\Delta \Phi^2|$$

and solve for $a = F_{t_0}^2$, $b = F_{t_0}^2$, and $c = F^3$.

Note that equations 34 and 35 are degenerate if $d = e$, that is, if the incremental phase change of the occluded and occluding objects are equal: $\Delta \Phi^1(k_x, k_y) = \Delta \Phi^2(k_x, k_y)$. However, significant errors also arise as $d \to e$, i.e. as $\Delta \Phi^1 \to \Delta \Phi^2$, since the numerator in equations 34 and 35 involve estimates of d and e rather than exact values. Hence, the relative magnitude of the error inherent in this estimate grows exponentially as $(d - e) \to 0$; that is, as the denominator approaches zero. To eliminate the influence of these errors in the computation of the residue on the estimate of the occluded and occluding signal b and a, we simply set $c = (c' + \epsilon_c)$ equal to zero as $d \to e$. Specifically, we let $c = 0$ if

$$|e - d| \leq \tau v_{\max} \tag{37}$$

where τ is some specified toleralance and $v_{\max}$ is the magnitude of the maximum velocity exhibited by either the occluded or the occluding image.

However, we cannot effect the same strategy for b as $d \to e$ since this would be equivalent to the implementation of an ideal pulse-shaped band-stop filter. Instead, it is necessary to attenuate progressively the band-stop frequencies before computing the inverse FFT of the occluding and background images. The approach adopted in this paper is to attenuate frequencies satisfying equation 37 according to the function

$$G_{t_0}^{1,2}(k_x, k_y) = F_{t_0}^{1,2}(k_x, k_y) \left(\sin \left(\frac{e - d}{\tau} \times \frac{\pi}{2} \right) \right)^{2n}, \, |d - e| \leq \frac{\tau}{2} v_{\max}; \tag{38}$$

$$G_{t_0}^{1,2}(k_x, k_y) = F_{t_0}^{1,2}(k_x, k_y), \text{otherwise.} \tag{39}$$

The exponent $n \geq 1$ determines the slope of the filter cutoff. As $n \to \infty$, the filter approaches an ideal filter. In the following, we use values of $\tau = 0.2$ and $n = 1$ throughout.

2.3 Velocity Estimation: Computation of Instantaneous Optical Flow

We have seen above that the solution of the system of equations 7 – 10 (additive case) and equations 23 – 27 (generalized occluded case) yields not only the decoupled or segmented Fourier components but also the rate of change of phase and, hence, the velocity of the image translation. Consequently, we can exploit this approach to compute the local instantaneous velocity of a local region by treating it simply as a sub-image or image window. Unfortunately, the image data in such a region will exhibit a change due not only to the signal shift but also the translation of objects into the window and out of the the window. Consequently, there is a change in the spectral content of the window and not just a phase change as is assumed in the model. In order to reduce the impact of this 'edge effect', image data in a region is apodized or weighted as a function of its distance from the region centre. In this paper, a Gaussian weighting function is used and the Gaussian's standard deviation σ chosen such that the weighting at a some distance from the region centre is 50% of that at the region centre, where w is the length of the side of the 2-D region. Results are presented for Gaussian weighting functions of three standard deviations, each representing increased attenuation of image data toward the edge of the image (the three functions provide 50% weighting at $\frac{w}{8}$, $\frac{2w}{8}$, and $\frac{3w}{8}$ from the region centre). In the following, we will denote the three Gaussian functions as $\sigma_{\frac{w}{8}}$, $\sigma_{\frac{2w}{8}}$, and $\sigma_{\frac{3w}{8}}$.

3   Results and Evaluation

3.1   Image Separation and Segmentation

An image scenario which displays significant occlusion was used to test the approach. In each test, there are two objects, the foreground and the background, moving independently of one another with velocities (v_{x_1}, v_{y_1}) and (v_{x_2}, v_{y_2}), respectively. The technique was tested for velocities in the ranges: $(0,0) \leq (v_{x_1}, v_{y_1}) \leq (5,0)$ and $(0,0) \leq (v_{x_2}, v_{y_2}) \leq (5,5)$, in increments of one pixel. Due to lack of space, only quantitative results for $(v_{x_1}, v_{y_1}) = (0,0)$ are reported here although the images in figures 1 and 2 are derived from an image sequence where $(v_{x_1}, v_{y_1}) = (1,0)$. Nonetheless, the quantitative results for $(1,0) \leq (v_{x_1}, v_{y_1}) \leq (5,0)$ are comparable except where $(v_{x_1}, v_{y_1}) \rightarrow (v_{x_2}, v_{y_2})$ in which case the segmentation is unreliable and the RMS error is large.

The test scenario comprises two images, one of a child and the other of a sea-gull with a zero background. Figure 1 shows each individual image at time t_0 and the additive and occluding superposition of the seagull on the child background at time t_0. Figure 2 shows the result of computing (segmenting) the additively-generated composite images based on the sequence at time t_0, t_1, t_2, and t_3 using the original additive model. It also shows the result of segmenting the occlusion-based composite images using the generalized occlusion model.

Table 1 shows the RMS errors between the segmented occluding (foreground) image and the original occluding image for all combinations of image velocities (in the range specified above) for (i) the additive images segmented using the additive model, (ii) the occluded images using the additive model, and (iii) the occluded images using the occlusion model, respectively. Note that the values in this table are based on the RMS error computed using both the non-zero pixel values of foreground object and its surrounding zero pixel values (*i.e.* we take

Table 1. RMS error in reconstruction of gull foreground image computed for the complete image including its zero-valued backdrop; background image (child) velocity = (0, 0) pixels, foreground image (gull) velocity = (v_{x_2}, v_{y_2}) pixels.

RMS Error in Reconstruction of Foreground Image (i.e. Occluding Image including Zero Background)								
Type of Image Sequence	Decoupling Model	v_{x_2}	v_{y_2}					
			0	1	2	3	4	5
Additive	Additive	0	–	28.5	27.6	27.4	27.7	27.8
		1	18.5	13.4	12.0	14.0	14.1	14.6
		2	18.0	10.1	11.7	10.7	12.0	11.6
		3	18.2	11.3	10.6	12.0	11.1	12.0
		4	18.1	11.1	11.2	11.9	13.1	13.0
		5	18.2	11.5	12.0	11.9	12.4	14.0
Occlusion	Additive	0	–	50.2	46.9	47.8	49.3	49.9
		1	52.0	51.4	47.5	49.4	53.2	53.0
		2	49.4	48.2	46.4	49.0	51.5	52.0
		3	45.8	50.1	49.2	48.5	50.7	50.9
		4	46.4	48.2	49.1	50.5	51.1	52.1
		5	43.4	48.2	49.8	49.8	53.7	52.2
Occlusion	Occlusion	0	–	44.8	44.9	45.0	45.2	45.4
		1	44.2	46.1	46.2	46.1	46.0	46.2
		2	44.5	46.3	47.0	46.4	46.5	46.6
		3	44.6	45.8	46.6	47.2	47.3	46.9
		4	44.7	45.6	46.4	46.9	47.3	47.5
		5	44.9	45.8	46.7	46.9	47.7	48.0

into consideration the success of the technique in segmenting an occluding object and in reconstructing a zero-valued background).

3.2 Estimation of Optical Flow

Figure 3 demonstrates the results of applying the technique to four images in Otte's and Nagel's ground-truth test sequence [15]. Figure 3 (a) and (b) show images number 40 and 43 in the sequence whilst (c) shows the true optical flow field extracted directly from the Otte's and Nagel's ground-truth data (sampled every ten pixels). Figure 3 (d) shows the optical flow field computed using the technique described in this paper. All of the results shown in this paper were computed with a window size of 64 × 64 pixels. Flow vectors are plotted every ten pixels and their magnitude has been scaled by a factor of four.

Table 2 summarizes the mean magnitude and the mean direction of ground-truth data and the measured velocities; table 3 provides a summary of the RMS and mean errors of the measured velocities.

Note that all of the results presented in this paper are the unprocessed output of the algorithm (apart from interpolation); each velocity vector has been estimated independently and the vector field has not be subjected to median or mean filtering.

Table 2. Summary of mean and standard deviation of the magnitude and direction of the ground-truth data and the measured velocities.

Sequence	Gaussian Weighting	Magnitude		Direction	
		mean	standard deviation	mean	standard deviation
Image	Ground Truth	2.828	0.0	0.785	0.0
Translation	$\frac{3w}{8}$	2.428	0.126	0.786	0.054
Benchmark	$\frac{2w}{8}$	2.759	0.046	0.786	0.009
	$\frac{w}{8}$	2.748	0.063	0.784	0.063
Otte & Nagel	Ground Truth	1.573	0.641	0.306	0.202
Benchmark	$\frac{3w}{8}$	1.307	0.582	0.339	0.411
	$\frac{2w}{8}$	1.307	0.596	0.322	0.366
	$\frac{w}{8}$	1.311	0.616	0.312	0.337

Table 3. Summary of RMS and maximum errors in the measured velocities; errors are defined with respect to ground-truth data.

Sequence	Gaussian Weighting	RMS Error		Maximum Error	
		Magnitude (pixels)	Direction (radians)	Magnitude (pixels)	Direction (radians)
Image	$\frac{3w}{8}$	0.419	0.054	0.803	0.231
Translation	$\frac{2w}{8}$	0.083	0.009	0.211	0.049
Benchmark	$\frac{w}{8}$	0.102	0.049	1.028	0.814
Otte & Nagel	$\frac{3w}{8}$	0.479	0.154	5.369	2.494
Benchmark	$\frac{2w}{8}$	0.492	0.114	2.775	0.745
	$\frac{w}{8}$	0.529	0.124	5.625	1.601

4 Discussion

All of the images shown in figures 1 and 2 have a velocity of (1, 0) and (4, 0) pixels for each image, respectively. These velocities were chosen not because they provide the best results in each case but because they provide a reasonably typical example of a slowly translating background and a foreground translating in the same direction but with a larger velocity.

It is clear from figure 2 that the best segmentation is achieved for the additive case (using the additive model). This is to be expected since the problem is well-posed and exactly determined; any errors are due to the impossibility of solving for some spatial frequencies, specifically those for which the phase change is identical in foreground and background and those above a certain limiting range. The RMS errors in the cases of the occluded image sequence are inevitably larger since it is less well-posed and, as we have seen, requires an approximation in the solution. Finally, we note that the error in the computed velocity is consistently in the order of 0.1 to 0.2 pixels.

Concerning the computation of optical flow, we can see that, qualitatively, the approach described produces a dense and reasonably complete flow field (with the flow field associated with 'wider' weighting functions, *i.e.* the Gaussians with standard deviation $\sigma_{\frac{3w}{8}}$ and $\sigma_{\frac{2w}{8}}$ exhibiting somewhat poorer localization of the flow field). More importantly, however, is the accuracy of the technique. Otte and Nagel's [15] benchmark sequence was used to evaluate quantitatively the performance of the algorithm. This sequence has the major benefit that ground truth optical flow is available (*i.e.* the magnitude and direction of the optical flow of (almost) every point in the image). To compare the optical flow computed with the algorithm presented in this paper and ground-truth, the optical flow was estimated every ten pixels (for the three Gaussian weighting functions) and then a complete optical flow image was produced for both magnitude and direction by interpolating bi-linearly among these points. These were then compared to the ground-truth magnitude and direction images by estimating the RMS error (see table 3). Finally, the mean and standard deviation of the magnitude and direction of the ground-truth flow field and the three computed flow fields are given in table 2.

Referring to these images and tables, a number of points can be noted.

First, it is clear that the main errors occur at the occluding contours and, in particular, at the contour where the two objects are moving with significant velocities (as, for example, is the case with the white block and the large dark block in the foreground). Again, as expected, this error is greater for the wider weighting functions and, because the velocity estimate is based on a larger effective support, the error propagates into a bigger region around the occluding contour.

Second, the mean magnitudes and directions of the three computed flow fields are consistent and do not vary significantly (1.307, 1.307, and 1.311 pixels, and 0.339, 0.322, 0.312 radians, for mean magnitudes and directions, respectively). This compares with the ground-truth mean magnitude and direction values of 1.573 and 0.306, respectively. Clearly, there is a difference in the measured and ground-truth magnitude value. This apparent difference is evident in the vector-field (compare the field in 3 (c) and (d)) and shows up in the RMS error estimate. On average, the error in the estimate of the magnitude of the optical flow field is just over one quarter of a pixel and the error in direction is of the order of 0.02 radians radian or approximately one degree.

As the average magnitude error is significant, for comparison we also applied the technique to a trivial benchmark data set wherein an image is simply translated in the x and y direction by 2 pixels/frame. It should be emphasised that this test is intended to do no more than demonstrate the accuracy and the repeatability of the technique on real data with a known (and trivial) flow-field. Table 2 summarizes the mean magnitude and the mean direction of ground-truth data and the measured velocities; table 3 provides a summary of the RMS and maximum errors of the measured velocities. The chief point to note about these results is that, with the exception of the narrowest apodization window, the correct flow field is computed to within 0.1 pixels (magnitude) and 0.001 radians (direction). As it happens, the magnitude measurement accuracy is presently set at 0.1 pixels/frame as this is the sampling period of the (velocity) Hough transform space used in all of the work described in this paper. It remains to be seen whether or not this can be improved by increasing the decreasing the sampling period.

5 Conclusions

This paper presented and validated the theoretical basis for the use of Fourier techniques in separating additive images and in segmenting images which are formed by an occluding foreground and an occluded background. This theory facilitates the model-free segmentation of moving objects in dynamic image sequences in situations where the object velocity is constant and normal to the principal ray of the image sensor.

The significance of the approach and the main contribution of the work is that it allows model-free segmentation and, importantly, the visual complexity of the foreground and the background is irrelevant since the segmentation is effected independently for each individual spatial frequency in the Fourier domain.

The technique is also applied to the estimation of instantaneous optical flow by decoupling the Fourier transform of a local Gaussian-weighted window centred at every point at which the flow field is to be computed. The results compare very favourably with ground truth optical flow data for the benchmark image sequence used to test the approach. Problems remain at occluding contours because, so far, we have used the additive model for the optical flow estimation. However, since the generalized occlusion model computes the velocities of both objects in the local window around the occluding boundary, we expect to be able to improve this estimate even further in the future and to be able to compute the correct flow field on either side of the velocity discontinuity (*i.e.* the occluding boundary).

Acknowledgements

I would like to acknowledge the helpful comments of Dr. W. F. Lunnon, Department of Computer Science, National University of Ireland, Maynooth.

References

1. D. Vernon, *Machine Vision* Prentice-Hall International, London (1991).
2. D. Vernon and G. Sandini, *Parallel Computer Vision — The VIS a VIS System*, Ellis Horwood, London (1992).
3. J.H. Duncan and T.-C. Chou, "On the detection and the computation of optical flow", *IEEE Transactions on Pattern Analysis and Machine Intelligence*, **14(3)**, 346-352 (1992).
4. H. Shariat and K.E. Price, "Motion estimation with more than two frames", *IEEE Transactions on Pattern Analysis and Machine Intelligence*, **12(5)**, 417-434 (1990).
5. M.P. Cagigal, L. Vega, P. Prieto, "Object movement characterization from low-light-level images", *Optical Engineering*, **33(8)**, 2810-2812 (1994).
6. M.P. Cagigal, L. Vega, P. Prieto, "Movement characterization with the spatiotemporal Fourier transform of low-light-level images", *Applied Optics*, **34(11)**, 1769-1774 (1995).

7. S. A. Mahmoud, M.S. Afifi, and R. J. Green, "Recognition and velocity computation of large moving objects in images", *IEEE Transactions on Acoustics, Speech, and Signal Processing*, **36(11)**, 1790-1791 (1988).

8. S. A. Mahmoud, "A new technique for velocity estimation of large moving objects", *IEEE Transactions on Signal Processing*, **39(3)**, 741-743 (1991).

9. S.A. Rajala, A. N. Riddle, and W.E. Snyder, "Application of one-dimensional Fourier transform for tracking moving objects in noisy environments", *Computer Vision, Graphics, and Image Processing*, **21**, 280-293 (1983).

10. D. Vernon, "Phase-Based Measurement of Object Velocity in Image Sequences using the Hough Transform", *Optical Engineering* (1996).

11. D. J. Fleet and A.D. Jepson, "Hierarchical construction of orientation and velocity selective filters", *IEEE Transactions on Pattern Analysis and Machine Intelligence*, **11(3)**, 315-325 (1989).

12. D. J. Fleet and A.D. Jepson, "Computation of component image velocity from local phase information", *International Journal of Computer Vision*, **5**, 77-104 (1990).

13. D. J. Fleet and A.D. Jepson, "Stability in Phase Information", *IEEE Transactions on Pattern Analysis and Machine Intelligence*, **15(12)**, 1253-1268 (1993).

14. J.L. Barron, D.J. Fleet, and S. Beauchemin, "Performance of optical flow techniques", *Int. Journal of Computer Vision*, **12(1)**, 43-77 (1994).

15. M. Otte and H.-H. Nagel, "Optical flow estimation: advances and comparisons", *Lecture Notes in Computer Science*, J.O. Eklundh (Ed.), *Computer Vision – ECCV '94*, Springer-Verlag, Berlin, 51-60 (1994).

16. M. Tistarelli, "Multiple constraints for optical flow", *Lecture Notes in Computer Science*, J.O. Eklundh (Ed.), *Computer Vision – ECCV '94*, Springer-Verlag, Berlin, 61-70 (1994).

17. L. Jacobson and H. Wechsler, "Derivation of optical flow using a spatiotemporal-frequency approach", *Computer Vision, Graphics, and Image Processing*, **38**, 29-65 (1987).

18. D. Vernon, "Decoupling Fourier Components of Dynamic Image Sequences: Theory and Application to Segmentation and Estimation of Optical Flow", Technical Report, Department of Computer Science, National University of Ireland, Maynooth (1997).

19. D. Vernon, "Segmentation in Dynamic Image Sequences by Isolation of Coherent Wave Profiles", Proceedings of the 4th European Conference on Computer Vision, Springer-Verlag, 293-303 (1996).

20. P.V.C. Hough, 'Method and Means for Recognising Complex Patterns' U.S. Patent 3,069,654, (1962).

21. L. Hahn, *Complex Numbers and Geometry*, The Mathmatical Association of America, Washington, D.C. (1994).

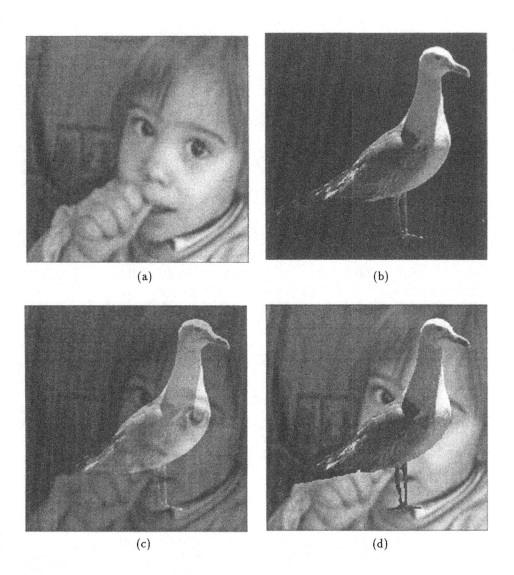

(a)   (b)

(c)   (d)

Fig. 1. Image separation and segmentation: (a) and (b) images 1 and 2 at time t_0 translating with velocities $(1, 0)$ and $(4, 0)$ pixels, respectively; (c) and (d) the additive and occluding superposition of the seagull on the child background at time t_0.

84

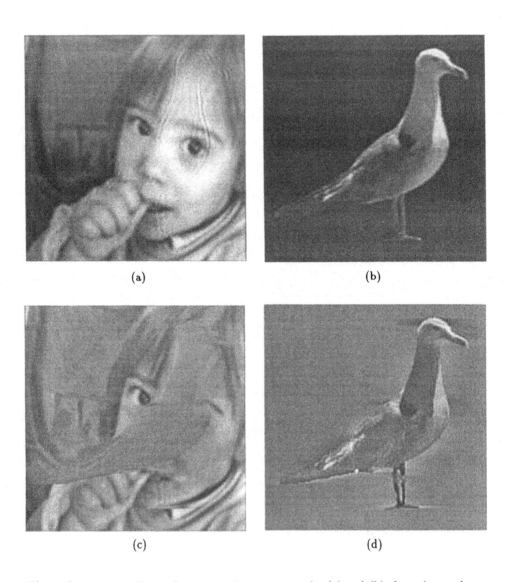

(a)

(b)

(c)

(d)

Fig. 2. Image separation and segmentation test scenario: (a) and (b) show the results of decoupling (segmenting) the additively-generated composite images based on the sequence at time t_0, t_1, t_2, and t_3 using the additive model; (e) and (f) show the results of segmenting the occlusion-based composite images using the generalized occlusion model.

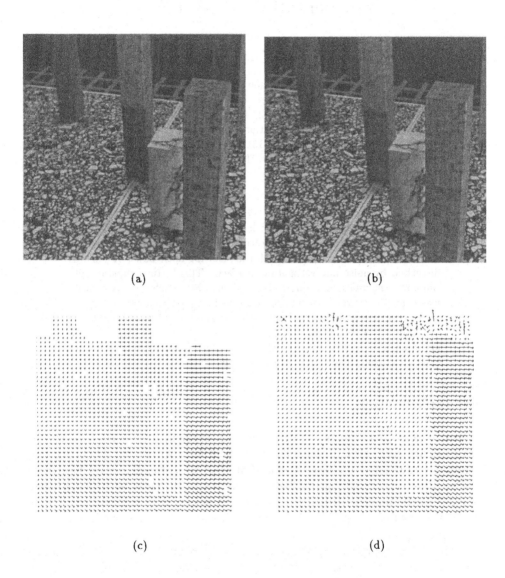

(a)   (b)

(c)   (d)

Fig. 3. (a) and (b) Images number 40 and 43 of Otte and Nagel's ground-truth motion sequence. (c) True optical flow field given by Otte and Nagel's ground-truth data (sampled every ten pixels) (d) Optical flow field computed using phase information: Gaussian weighting function with 50% weight at $\frac{w}{4}$ pixels from window centre (w, the window size, equals 64 pixels).

Spatiotemporally Adaptive Estimation and Segmentation of OF-fields

H.-H. Nagel[1,2] and A. Gehrke[1]

[1] Institut für Algorithmen und Kognitive Systeme
Fakultät für Informatik der Universität Karlsruhe (TH)
Postfach 6980, D-76128 Karlsruhe / Germany
[2] Fraunhofer-Institut für Informations- und Datenverarbeitung (IITB)
Fraunhoferstr. 1, D-76131 Karlsruhe / Germany
Tel. +49-721-6091-210; Fax +49-721-6091-413; email hhn@iitb.fhg.de

Abstract. A grayvalue *structure tensor* provides knowledge about a local grayvalue variation. This knowledge can be used to devise a *spatiotemporally adaptive* optic flow estimation process. Such an adaptive estimation lowers the level at which the resulting optic flow (OF) field is disturbed by noise and estimation artefacts. This in turn substantially simplifies the analysis of remaining – often subtle – effects which easily jeopardize a 'naive' segmentation approach. Appropriate treatment of such effects eventually results in a basically simple, but nevertheless surprisingly robust segmentation approach. Various stages of this approach are illustrated by examples for the extraction of moving vehicle images from a digitized road intersection video-sequence.

1 Introduction

In order to extract a weak, straight line edge segment from a noisy image, it is advantageous in general to employ a gradient filter with a suitably elongated support – see, e.g., [10]. The low-pass contribution to the derivative filter will then act *more along* the edge segment *than across* it. Evidently, such an approach implies a hen-and-egg dilemma: in order to extract the edge segment, one has to know its orientation, and in order to determine its orientation, one has to know the edge segment.

An analogous problem appears in the case where one has to *segment* an optic flow (OF) field to be estimated in the first place: segmentation of an OF-field requires the detection of discontinuities in an estimated vector field, i. e. it implies at first glance some kind of derivative operation, followed by a detection step which decides whether the local change appears significant enough to decide in favor of a discontinuity in the OF-field. Alternatively, one might consider region growing from some 'seed region'. For both alternatives, the hen-and-egg problem pops up in a different disguise: either location *and* structure of a segment boundary element or a seed region *together* with some appropriate stopping criterion for region growing have to be determined *simultaneously* in the OF vector field.

Optic flow – the apparent shift velocity of a grayvalue structure in the image plane – will be considered here as a threedimensional vector $\mathbf{u} = (u_1, u_2, 1)^T$ in an (x,y,t)-space formed by the image plane coordinates $\mathbf{x}' = (x, y)^T$ and time t. A location in this (x,y,t)-space will be given by the threedimensional vector $\mathbf{x} = (x, y, t)^T$. OF is usually *estimated* based on the postulate that the grayvalue $g(x, y, t)$ is locally stationary as a function of x, y, and t: $dg(x, y, t) = 0$. This results in the so-called 'Optic Flow Constraint Equation (OFCE)' [4]:

$$(g_x, g_y, g_t) \, \mathbf{u} = (\nabla g)^T \mathbf{u} = 0 \quad \text{with} \quad g_x = \frac{\partial g(x, y, t)}{\partial x}, \quad \text{etc.} \quad . \quad (1)$$

Due to space limitations, we refer to [1] for a general review of optic flow estimation. In the sequel, we first concentrate on our approach in order to provide a frame of reference for a discussion of related research in the concluding section.

2   The Grayvalue-Local-Structure-Tensor GLST

The gradient operator ∇ for the computation of $\nabla g(\mathbf{x})$ will be realized by a convolution of $g(\mathbf{x})$ with partial derivatives of a trivariate Gaussian $G(\mathbf{x})$ given by

$$G(\mathbf{x}) = \frac{1}{(2\pi)^{3/2}\sqrt{|\Sigma|}} \, e^{-\frac{1}{2}\mathbf{x}^T \Sigma^{-1} \mathbf{x}} \quad . \quad (2)$$

The covariance matrix Σ is initially set to

$$\Sigma_{\text{init}} = \begin{pmatrix} \sigma_x^2 & 0 & 0 \\ 0 & \sigma_y^2 & 0 \\ 0 & 0 & \sigma_t^2 \end{pmatrix} \quad (3)$$

with values for the standard deviations σ_x in the x-direction, σ_y in the y-direction, and σ_t in the t-direction chosen by the experimenter on the basis of a-priori knowledge.

Due to the fact that (1) is underdetermined at a single location $\mathbf{x}$, one modifies the estimation postulate into the requirement that the squared magnitude of the OFCE, averaged over some local environment, should be minimized by a suitable choice of $\mathbf{u}$:

$$\overline{|(\nabla g)^T \mathbf{u}|^2} = \overline{((\nabla g)^T \mathbf{u})^T ((\nabla g)^T \mathbf{u})} = \mathbf{u}^T \, \overline{\nabla g(\mathbf{x}) (\nabla g(\mathbf{x}))^T} \, \mathbf{u} \overset{!}{=} \min_{\mathbf{u}} \quad . \quad (4)$$

According to [7], let the spatiotemporal Gaussian introduced by (2) with covariance matrix 2Σ describe the local environment around a location $\mathbf{x}$. We then define the location-dependent 'Grayvalue-Local-Structure-Tensor (GLST)' as

$$GLST(\mathbf{x}) = \int\limits_{-\infty}^{+\infty} d\boldsymbol{\xi} \, \frac{\nabla g(\boldsymbol{\xi} - \mathbf{x}) (\nabla g(\boldsymbol{\xi} - \mathbf{x}))^T}{(2\pi)^{3/2}\sqrt{2|\Sigma|}} \, e^{-\frac{1}{4}(\boldsymbol{\xi} - \mathbf{x})^T \Sigma^{-1} (\boldsymbol{\xi} - \mathbf{x})} \quad . \quad (5)$$

By definition, the GLST is positive-semidefinite. $\text{GLST}_{\text{init}}$ denotes a Grayvalue-Local-Structure-Tensor computed by using Σ_{init} as given by (3).

Let $\mathbf{e}_{GLST_{\text{init}},i}$ denote the i-th eigenvector of $\text{GLST}_{\text{init}}$ and $\lambda_{\text{init},i}$ the corresponding eigenvalue, with $\lambda_{\text{init},1} \geq \lambda_{\text{init},2} \geq \lambda_{\text{init},3} \geq 0$. $\text{GLST}_{\text{init}}$ can then be written in the form

$$GLST_{\text{init}} =$$

$$(\mathbf{e}_{GLST_{\text{init}},1}, \mathbf{e}_{GLST_{\text{init}},2}, \mathbf{e}_{GLST_{\text{init}},3}) \begin{pmatrix} \lambda_{\text{init},1} & 0 & 0 \\ 0 & \lambda_{\text{init},2} & 0 \\ 0 & 0 & \lambda_{\text{init},3} \end{pmatrix} \begin{pmatrix} \mathbf{e}_{GLST_{\text{init}},1}^T \\ \mathbf{e}_{GLST_{\text{init}},2}^T \\ \mathbf{e}_{GLST_{\text{init}},3}^T \end{pmatrix} .$$

$$(6)$$

According to (4), optic flow is given as the projection of the GLST-eigenvector $\mathbf{e}_{GLST,3}(\mathbf{x}) = (e_{GLST,31}, e_{GLST,32}, e_{GLST,33})^T$, which corresponds to the smallest eigenvalue $\lambda_{GLST,3}(\mathbf{x})$ of $\text{GLST}(\mathbf{x})$, into the image plane. This is equivalent to the hypothesis that the eigenvector related to the smallest GLST-eigenvalue points into the direction of smallest *temporal* change, which in turn is ascribed to a grayvalue structure shifting smoothly in the (x, y, t)-space. The projection of this eigenvector into the image plane will be normalized to a unit value for the third (i. e. temporal) component in order to remain compatible with the definition given in Sect. 1:

$$\mathbf{u}(\mathbf{x}) = \left(\frac{e_{GLST,31}}{e_{GLST,33}} , \frac{e_{GLST,32}}{e_{GLST,33}} , \frac{e_{GLST,33}}{e_{GLST,33}} = 1 \right)^T . \tag{7}$$

3 An Adaptive Filter Based on the GLST

Let us substitute $\text{GLST}_{\text{init}}(\mathbf{x})$ for Σ^{-1} in (2) and recompute the gradient of $g(\mathbf{x})$. A large eigenvalue of $\text{GLST}_{\text{init}}(\mathbf{x})$ will severely restrict the extent over which grayvalues contribute to the partial derivative in the corresponding direction, whereas the low-pass action implied by the Gaussian will extend much more in the directions corresponding to $\mathbf{e}_{GLST_{\text{init}},2}$ and $\mathbf{e}_{GLST_{\text{init}},3}$. We thus obtain exactly the desired effect of *less* low-pass filtering in the direction of largest local grayvalue change than in the directions perpendicular to it. In general, the amount of low-pass filtering in the direction corresponding to an eigenvalue $\lambda_{\text{init},i}$ of $\text{GLST}_{\text{init}}(\mathbf{x})$ will be determined by the magnitude of this eigenvalue.

We may exploit this information in order to *improve the derivative operation*. Use of $\text{GLST}_{\text{init}}(\mathbf{x})$ instead of a constant Σ^{-1} during a *recomputation* of the gradient at each image location $\mathbf{x}$ automatically adapts the low-pass action of the Gaussian in the partial derivative operators to the local grayvalue structure.

3.1 Delimiting the Extent of an Adaptive Convolution Mask

There occur problems, however, unless we proceed with caution. In rather homogeneous image regions, the area of support can locally grow to a size where a standard implementation of a Finite Impulse Response (FIR) filter by a digital convolution operation may begin to fail. An uncontrolled adaptation can result, for example, in excessive mask sizes. On the other hand, it may well happen that an eigenvalue becomes very large in image areas with particularly strong gray-value transitions. As a consequence, the Gaussian in (2) will decrease so sharply that the sampling theorem may be violated upon conversion of the resulting filter to a digital version for a sampling grid given by the - already - digitized image sequence. We are thus forced to restrict the mask size to be used, without jeopardizing the desired adaptation effect whenever the eigenvalues of $\text{GLST}_{\text{init}}(\mathbf{x})$ remain compatible with the minimal and maximal mask size provided by the available implementation of a FIR digital convolution operation.

Let $\sigma^2_{\text{minsize}}$ be a parameter which forces a diagonal element in the covariance matrix for the Gaussian in (2) to remain compatible with the smallest admissible mask size. $\sigma^2_{\text{maxsize}}$ should be defined such that $\sigma^2_{\text{minsize}} + \sigma^2_{\text{maxsize}}$ determines the largest admissible mask size. Let

$$U = (\ \mathbf{e}_{GLST_{\text{init}},1}, \quad \mathbf{e}_{GLST_{\text{init}},2}, \quad \mathbf{e}_{GLST_{\text{init}},3}\ ) \tag{8}$$

denote the 3D rotation matrix in the (x, y, t)-space which aligns the coordinate axes with the eigenvector directions of $\text{GLST}_{\text{init}}(\mathbf{x})$. Denoting the 3x3 unit matrix by I and using $I = U(\mathbf{x})U^T(\mathbf{x})$, we introduce a *locally adapted* covariance matrix $\Sigma(\mathbf{x})$ as

$$\Sigma(\mathbf{x}) =$$

$$U(\mathbf{x}) \left(\sigma^2_{\text{minsize}} I + \begin{pmatrix} \dfrac{\sigma^2_{\text{maxsize}}}{1+\sigma^2_{\text{maxsize}}\lambda^w_1(\mathbf{x})} & 0 & 0 \\ 0 & \dfrac{\sigma^2_{\text{maxsize}}}{1+\sigma^2_{\text{maxsize}}\lambda^w_2(\mathbf{x})} & 0 \\ 0 & 0 & \dfrac{\sigma^2_{\text{maxsize}}}{1+\sigma^2_{\text{maxsize}}\lambda^w_3(\mathbf{x})} \end{pmatrix} \right) U^T(\mathbf{x})$$

$$\tag{9}$$

with $\lambda^w_i(\mathbf{x}) = \lambda_{\text{init},i}(\mathbf{x})$, $i \in \{1,2,3\}$. For experiments to be discussed shortly, we have chosen $\sigma^2_{\text{minsize}} = 0.5$ and $\sigma^2_{\text{maxsize}} = 4.0$. Let us assume for the moment that $\text{GLST}_{\text{init}}(\mathbf{x})$ has an eigenvalue $\lambda_{\text{init},3}$ close to zero due to lack of grayvalue variation in the corresponding direction. In the limit of zero for $\lambda_{\text{init},3}$, the third eigenvalue of $\Sigma(\mathbf{x})$ will become $\sigma^2_{\text{minsize}} + \sigma^2_{\text{maxsize}}$, thereby restricting a digitized version of the resulting Gaussian to the chosen maximal mask size. In case of a very *strong* straight line grayvalue transition front in the vicinity of image location $\mathbf{x}$, the first eigenvalue $\lambda_{\text{init},1}(\mathbf{x})$ of $\text{GLST}_{\text{init}}(\mathbf{x})$ will force the second contribution to the corresponding eigenvalue of $\Sigma(\mathbf{x})$ in (9) to be small, delimiting the sum of both terms from below by a suitably chosen $\sigma^2_{\text{minsize}}$.

Equation (9) will only yield acceptable results for the eigenvalues of $\Sigma(\mathbf{x})$, if the eigenvalues of $\text{GLST}_{\text{init}}$ range between $\sigma^2_{\text{minsize}}$ and $\sigma^2_{\text{maxsize}}$. If most of the initial eigenvalues, however, are far outside of this interval - by experience we have seen that most of the eigenvalues from $\text{GLST}_{\text{init}}$ range above 50 - the eigenvalues of $\Sigma(\mathbf{x})$ which are determined according to (9) are all close to $\sigma^2_{\text{minsize}}$

and therefore all are similar. Normalizing the eigenvalues by $\frac{1}{3}trace(GLST(\mathbf{x}))$ – i. e. setting $\lambda_i^w(\mathbf{x}) = \frac{\lambda_{\text{init},i}(\mathbf{x})}{\frac{1}{3}trace(GLST_{\text{init}}(\mathbf{x}))}$, $i \in \{1,2,3\}$ – forces the eigenvalues of $\Sigma(\mathbf{x})$ to vary between reasonable limits.

3.2 Estimation of an Improved GLST

The matrix $\Sigma(\mathbf{x})$ given by (9) describes the local grayvalue variation at location $\mathbf{x}$ in such a manner that the effects of noise on gradient computation will be reduced in comparison with that based on (3), since the low-pass filter action along the directions of smaller gray value variations will be increased. In addition, the influence of strong neighboring grayvalue structures is expected to be reduced due to a limitation of the filter extent in the direction of strong changes, which should lead to a less distorted gradient estimation at location $\mathbf{x}$. The choices for the parameters $\sigma_{\text{minsize}}^2$ and $\sigma_{\text{maxsize}}^2$ facilitate to incorporate a-priori knowledge about the spatiotemporal extent of semantically relevant grayvalue changes in an image sequence.

We may now exploit the knowledge about the local spatiotemporal grayvalue variation at image sequence location $\mathbf{x}$ in order to *recompute* the 'Grayvalue-Local-Structure-Tensor' as defined by (5), but this time using the spatiotemporally adaptive $\Sigma(\mathbf{x})$ given by (9) in the Gaussian of (2) instead of the constant Σ given by (3).

4 Adaptive Estimation of Optic Flow: Special Cases

Fig. 1. Image frame No. 424 from the image sequence 'dt_v'. The optical flow fields for the three selected windows will be illustrated subsequently in more detail.

In certain situations, a determination of the OF-vector according to (7) will not yield acceptable results. One condition occurs obviously at a location $\mathbf{x}$

where the local grayvalue is distributed so homogeneously that *all* eigenvalues of GLST practically vanish. This case can simply be detected by comparing trace(GLST(**x**)) – which represents the squared norm of the gradient averaged around **x** – against a minimal size threshold *min_norm_of_GLST*. We shall call pixel positions, where this threshold is *not* surpassed, as *neutral*. At such a location, it will not be possible to reliably detect any motion at all. A forteriori, it thus is not possible to decide at such a location whether the image of a scene surface element depicted at **x** moves relative to the recording camera against a non-contrasting background.

The convention which underlies (7) will lead to counter-intuitive results for a different situation, too. At a location **x** with a locally dominant *straight line* grayvalue transition front, all *spatial* gradients in the neighborhood around **x** point more or less into the same direction. Since $\Sigma(\mathbf{x})$ adapts to this local grayvalue structure, the GLST computed using $\Sigma(\mathbf{x})$ will have a very small component *perpendicular* to the prevailing *spatial* grayvalue gradient direction. It happens occasionally that this spatial variation is smaller than the temporal one, even if the local grayvalue structure shifts smoothly in the image plane with time. In such situations, one is confronted with the fact that the eigenvector corresponding to the smallest eigenvalue of GLST(**x**) *does not reflect the* apparent *shift* of a grayvalue structure *with time*.

We can detect this special condition by inspection of the third, i. e. temporal, component $e_{GLST,33}(\mathbf{x})$ of the eigenvector related to the smallest eigenvalue $\lambda_{GLST,3}(\mathbf{x})$ of GLST(**x**). If $e_{GLST,33}(\mathbf{x}) \leq e_{33_{\text{minflow}}}$, we consider the smallest eigenvalue to represent a *purely spatial* local grayvalue variation. We denote such a pixel as *spatially_tangent* since the eigenvector $\mathbf{e}_{GLST,3}(\mathbf{x})$ corresponding to the smallest eigenvalue is oriented in this case *within the image plane* to be tangential to an edge: it points into a direction with an essentially constant local grayvalue distribution. The characteristics of such a spatially_tangent location differ from those of a neutral one by exhibiting *at least one* eigenvalue significantly different from zero – see Fig. 2(c). Since the three eigenvectors of GLST(**x**) are mutually perpendicular to each other, any temporal variation at a ST-pixel must then be reflected by a vector in the normal plane to $\mathbf{e}_{GLST,3}(\mathbf{x})$. The direction of the smallest grayvalue variation with a temporal component will thus be given by the second eigenvector $\mathbf{e}_{GLST,2}(\mathbf{x})$ which corresponds to the middle eigenvalue.

5   Pixel Assignment to Categories

As a preparatory step for the segmentation of an OF-field, we first categorize each pixel by an hierarchical classification procedure according to its local spatiotemporal grayvalue structure. As will be seen, subtle characteristics of this spatiotemporal structure may substantially influence subsequent clustering, split, and merge steps.

The first test at a pixel location **x** determines if trace(GLST(**x**)) $\leq$ *min_norm_of_GLST* is true: such a pixel is assigned to the category *neutral* (*N*). In the case where trace(GLST(**x**)) $>$ *min_norm_of_GLST*, we can be sure that at

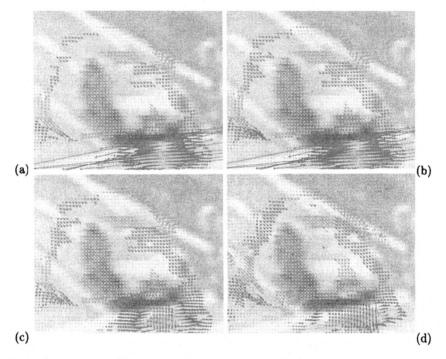

(a)   (b)

(c)   (d)

Fig. 2. Enlargement of window 2 in Figure 1. Overlaid are the OF-vectors wich are color-coded as follows: The yellow vectors show *regular_optical_flow (R_OF)*. The vectors at the *OF_discontinuity (OF_D)* locations are color-coded in red and at the *dominant_gradient_direction (DGD)* locations in turquoise. If a pixel could be assigned to the category *OF_discontinuity (OF_D)* and simultaneously complied with the criterion for the category *dominant_gradient_direction (DGD)*, it has nevertheless been assigned to the category *OF_discontinuity (OF_D)* and is, therefore, shown in red. The assignment of pixels to these categories is explained in Sect. 5. (a): The optic flow was estimated based on $GLST_{init}$. Note that the pixels, which have been assigned to the category *dominant_gradient_direction (DGD)*, are located at roadway markings with a homogeneous grayvalue structure in spatial direction. (b): Compared to panel (a), we have lowered the discontinuity_threshold. The number of locations assigned to category *OF_D* increases, thereby reducing the areas covered by accepted regular optic flow vectors. (c): Analogous to (b), but treating optical flow vectors at *spatially_tangent (S_T)* locations according to Sect. 4. The concerned pixels are mainly located at the roadway marking in front of the vehicle which exhibit a more or less homogenous grayvalue within the marking. At these locations, therefore, the OF-vector point along the direction of homogenous grayvalue, if we used the eigenvector corresponding to the smallest eigenvalue for the OF estimation – see panel (b). (d): Analogous to panel (c), but the overlaid estimated optical flow vectors are based on $GLST(x)$ as described in Sect. 3 rather than based on $GLST_{init}$. The number of pixels at the depicted vehicle image, which are *incorrectly* assigned to the category *OF_D*, is *smaller* than indicated in panel (c) although we use the same low discontinuity_threshold value as in panel (b) and (c). Simultaneously, the 'discontinuity wall' around the vehicle image in panel (d) contains less holes than the 'discontinuity wall' depicted in panel (c).

least one eigenvalue of GLST($\mathbf{x}$) differs significantly from zero. It thus is justified to speak about the *smallest* eigenvalue $\lambda_{GLST,3}(\mathbf{x})$ of GLST($\mathbf{x}$).

In case $e_{GLST,33}(\mathbf{x}) > e_{33_{minflow}}$ is true, the pixel at image location $\mathbf{x}$ is assigned to category *OF_discontinuity (OF_D)*, provided

$$\frac{\lambda_{GLST,3}(\mathbf{x})}{\frac{1}{3}trace\ (GLST(\mathbf{x}))} > discontinuity\_threshold \ . \tag{10}$$

Figure 2 shows the OF-vectors at these locations color-coded in red.

This test captures the observation that the temporal change – represented here by $\lambda_{GLST,3}(\mathbf{x})$ – is larger than deemed acceptable for a smooth shift of a grayvalue structure in the image plane. A large $\lambda_{GLST,3}(\mathbf{x})$ signifies that there is no direction with small grayvalue variation. According to (1) this means that there exist different OF-vectors in the local region considered. Please note that the left hand side of (10) varies by definition between 0 and 1 which allows to restrain the choice of a threshold to this range.

If, however, this location must be treated as *spatially_tangent (S_T)*, because $e_{GLST,33}(\mathbf{x}) \leq e_{33_{minflow}}$, the second eigenvalue $\lambda_{GLST,2}(\mathbf{x})$ indicates the smallest *temporal* change. Optic flow must then be defined as

$$\mathbf{u}(\mathbf{x}) = \left(\frac{e_{GLST,21}}{e_{GLST,23}} \ , \ \frac{e_{GLST,22}}{e_{GLST,23}} \ , \ \frac{e_{GLST,23}}{e_{GLST,23}} = 1 \right)^T \ , \tag{11}$$

see Fig. 2(c). In this case, the test for a discontinuity in the optic flow field must be applied to the second eigenvalue, i. e. location $\mathbf{x}$ is assigned to category *OF_D* if

$$\frac{\lambda_{GLST,2}(\mathbf{x})}{\frac{1}{3}trace\ (GLST(\mathbf{x}))} > discontinuity\_threshold \ . \tag{12}$$

Among the remaining image plane locations which are neither *neutral (N)* nor *OF_discontinuity (OF_D)*, we still have to detect any potential bias due to the aperture problem which occurs whereever the grayvalue structure is dominated by a straight line grayvalue transition front: the second eigenvalue differs from zero, but only by a small amount which may be insufficient to facilitate a reliable estimation of optic flow. We detect such situations, therefore, by the following test:

$$\frac{\lambda_{GLST,2}(\mathbf{x}) + \lambda_{GLST,3}(\mathbf{x})}{\frac{2}{3}trace\ (GLST(\mathbf{x}))} \leq threshold_{dominant\_gradient\_direction} \ , \tag{13}$$

Again, the left hand side of this equation varies by definition between 0 and 1.

All pixels not assigned in the course of this test sequence to one of the categories *neutral (N)*, *OF_discontinuity (OF_D)*, or *dominant_gradient_direction (DGD)*, will be treated as *regular_optical_flow (R_OF)* locations. These surviving locations are depicted in Fig. 2 through the yellow vectors.

6 Segmentation of Estimated Optic Flow Fields

The basic approach consists in identifying image locations where the temporal grayvalue change does not become small enough to justify a classification of the local spatiotemporal grayvalue variation as a smooth *temporal shift* of a characteristic *spatial* grayvalue structure. Ideally, such OF-discontinuity-locations should form a 'wall of discontinuities' around the image of an object moving relative to the camera with a velocity different from that of its environment. We proceed in four basic steps:

1. Each pixel is assigned – according to Sect. 5 – to one of the following categories:
   - neutral (N),
   - OF-discontinuity (OF_D),
   - dominant_gradient_direction (DGD),
   - regular_optical_flow (R_OF).
2. Pixels which have been assigned to the same category are clustered into 4-connected components, using a standard run-length algorithm as described, e. g., in [3].
3. If the variance of OF-vectors within a connected-component suggests two or more significant clusters, the originally obtained connected-component is split in order to increase the homogeneity of OF-vectors within a region.
4. Certain combinations of the connected components resulting from previous steps are merged in order to improve a mask covering the image of an object which potentially moves in the scene relative to the recording video camera.

6.1 'Discontinuity Walls'

The approach outlined above should result in clusters of R_OF-locations, surrounded by 'walls' of OF-discontinuity-(OF_D-)locations. In particular, a 'discontinuity wall' is expected around the image region corresponding to the image of an object moving in the scene relative to the camera.

As is shown in Fig. 2(a), a number of breaches can be detected in the 'discontinuity wall' around the depicted vehicle image. We may lower the discontinuity_threshold in order to detect more discontinuity locations in the hope to close many, if not all, of these breaches. As Figure 2(b) shows, a reduction of the discontinuity threshold from 0.03 to 0.023 does indeed close some holes, but only at the cost of many additional false alarms, i. e. a lot of spurious OF_D-locations are marked.

Figures 2(a) and (b) also illustrates that choosing the eigenvector associated with the smallest eigenvalue of the GLST may result in OF-vectors which are incompatible with intuition: as can be seen in Figs. 2(a) and (b), OF-vectors in the vicinity of strong, straight line grayvalue transition fronts tend to be oriented tangentially to these transition fronts – even in cases where a transition front (or a shadow cast in that image area) moves more or less in the gradient direction. Figure 2(c) demonstrates the improvement if we subject not the smallest, but the next larger eigenvalue to the discontinuity test in case of *(S_T)*-locations, using the same threshold as in Fig. 2(b).

So far, all depicted OF-vectors have been computed based on $GLST_{init}$. Figure 2(d) shows the result analogous to Fig. 2(c), but now computed on the basis of the locally adapted GLST(**x**) rather than on the basis of $GLST_{init}(\mathbf{x})$. It is seen that the 'discontinuity wall' contains less holes. Simultaneously, the number of spuriously detected discontinuities could be reduced, too.

6.2   Gaps at 'Dominant_Gradient_Direction'-Locations

The advantage of using this still very simple, but nevertheless more sensitive approach for the detection of discontinuities in the optic flow field consists not only in the fact that the number of 'breaches' in the 'discontinuity wall' is reduced. Even more important is the fact that a specific characteristic of the remaining gaps can be identified: the OF-vectors in gaps, which cause a connected-component determination to 'leak' into the background, do not differ significantly in magnitude and orientation from the acceptable ones covering the image of the moving object. One will notice, however, that the remaining weak points in the 'discontinuity wall' belong to the category *dominant_gradient_direction (DGD)* - see Fig. 2(d). This insight immediately suggests a remedy: in DGD-cases, it can not be decided reliably whether there is a discontinuity in an OF-field due to a straight line segment which delimits the object image in a direction parallel to the image motion, since the optic flow component in the direction of a strong gradient vanishes for locations which either belong to the image of the moving object or to the background occluded by it. The more or less homogeneous nature of the occluded background (or, analogously, of the occluding foreground) results in a dominant gradient direction due to the border between foreground and background. Since there is no motion perpendicular to this border, there is no way to check for a discontinuity of optic flow in this direction.

We thus decided to treat such DGD-situations as 'potential discontinuity' locations and to mark them separately. As a consequence, the connected-component subprocess will be prevented to extend across such a barrier and we obtain surprisingly clean masks covering the images of moving objects – *without* having to introduce any threshold on magnitude or orientation differences.

6.3   Splitting Connected-Components with a Significantly Inhomogeneous OF-Vector distribution

Optic flow in the background area differs significantly from flow vectors associated with a moving vehicle although we avoided so far to exploit a-priori knowledge about the fact that the camera remains stationary with respect to the background. We rather proceed on the *weaker* assumption that optic flow within the image area corresponding to a vehicle image differs significantly from that outside of this area.

The scatter plot in Fig. 4 shows the distribution of u_1 and u_2 components of optic flow within the right connected-component from Fig. 3(b). Two clusters

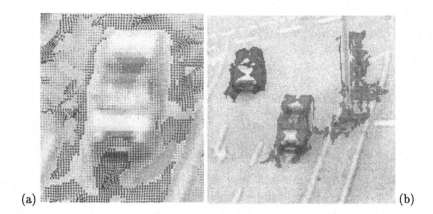

(a)   (b)

Fig. 3. (a): The same window as window no. 3 from Fig. 1, but recorded 80 msec later, has been enlarged and superimposed with OF-vectors estimated at the pixels which belong to the categories OF_D (dark vectors) and R_OF (bright vectors). One notices a gap at the right border of the depicted vehicle image in the 'discontinuity wall': white R_OF-vectors leak through the dark 'discontinuity wall' around the vehicle image into the background region. (b): A greater image region cropped around the area shown in panel (a). Superimposed are the masks for which all pixels at *regular_optical_flow (R_OF)* locations are connected, provided these locations are completely surrounded by pixels at *neutral (N)*, *OF_discontinuity (OF_D)*, or *dominant_gradient_direction (DGD)* locations. Due to the gap in the 'discontinuity wall', the right mask comprises a part of the background.

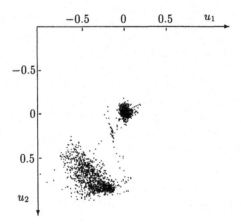

Fig. 4. The distribution of u_1 and u_2 components of the optical flow vectors within the larger connected-component (right hand side) from Fig. 3(b). One can clearly recognize an approximately circular cluster around $(u_1 = 0, u_2 = 0)$ corresponding to the stationary background, and another elliptical cluster centered around $(u_1 = -0.4, u_2 = 0.75)$ which corresponds to regular optic flow vectors associated with the moving vehicle.

pop out immediately which correspond to the two different segments of optic flow vectors contained in this connected-component. A standard clustering algorithm allows to detect and separate these two clusters automatically. It then is a straightforward procedure to separate the original connected-component into two segments, one corresponding to the image of the vehicle and the other corresponding to the background. Pixels, for which the estimated optic flow yields values in the uncertainty area between these two clusters, are simply suppressed: each pixel-cluster will only accept pixels with an OF-vector whose Mahalanobis distance from the nearest OF-cluster-center remains below a threshold.

6.4 Merging Certain Combinations of OF-Connected-Components

Although exclusion of DGD-locations helped to prevent 'leakage' of connected-components for vehicles into the background, it has the disadvantage to generate 'holes' within an object mask whenever the object image comprises marked straight line edge segments with substantial contrast. As can be seen in Fig. 5(b), such DGD-pixel locations can form connected-components of their own which are totally surrounded by R_OF locations. It should be noted that, in this case, the OF-vectors estimated for DGD-locations in the interior of the car image do not differ in an immediately noticeable manner from their surrounding R_OF-vectors.

We may now remove these 'Swiss-Cheese holes' by the simple requirement that a DGD-connected-component, which is completely surrounded by a R_OF-connected-component, can be merged into the surrounding component, provided the Mahalanobis distance between their mutual OF-vector distributions is compatible with the hypothesis that this distance vanishes. We thus first determine the cluster center coordinates $\mathbf{u}_{DGD}$ and $\mathbf{u}_{R\_OF}$, respectively, together with the corresponding covariance matrices Σ_{DGD} and Σ_{R_OF}. Subsequently, these two segments are merged, if

$$\left(\mathbf{u}_{DGD} - \mathbf{u}_{R\_OF}\right)^T \left(\Sigma_{DGD} + \Sigma_{R\_OF}\right)^{-1} \left(\mathbf{u}_{DGD} - \mathbf{u}_{R\_OF}\right)$$
$$\leq \quad threshold_{regionmerge-DGD-with-R\_OF} \quad . \quad (14)$$

As a result, we obtain a mask shown in Fig. 5(d).

Figure 6 presents an overlay of all 'object-image-masks' obtained in this manner for the entire frame. In order to simplify the visual detection of these masks by a viewer, we suppressed connected-components which either are smaller than 10 pixels or for which the average optic flow does not exceed a small threshold of 0.17 pixels per frame.

Since we sample video images of the depicted scene at a rate high compared to the temporal change related to scene motion, the apparent shift of object masks from frame to frame is small. The similarity of corresponding object masks from consecutive frames is further increased by the implied extended temporal averaging along the locally prevailing optic flow direction, an immediate consequence of the manner in which optic flow vectors are estimated in this approach.

Fig. 5. Enlargement of window No. 1 in Fig. 1. (a): Overlaid are the OF-vectors, which are estimated at pixel positions belonging to the category *regular_optical_flow (R_OF)* (colored with white) and *OF_discontinuity (OF_D)* (colored with black). (b): The OF-vectors colored black in this panel have been estimated at pixels which have been assigned to the category *dominant_gradient_direction (DGD)*. Note that most of these vectors are placed in the interior of the car image or around the high contrast road markings. The white OF-vectors have been estimated at pixels belonging to the category *neutral*. (c): Masks determined in analogy to those from Fig. 3. Due to pixels at DGD-locations, the depicted *regular_optical_flow (R_OF)*-mask exhibits a hole. (d): 'object-image-mask' resulting from the requirement to include DGD-segments, provided these are completely surrounded by R_OF-locations and the OF-vectors estimated at the DGD locations are similar (according to (14)) to the OF-vectors which are estimated at the *regular_optical_flow (R_OF)* -mask.

Fig. 6. Image frame as shown in Fig.1, with superimposed connected regions (indicated by their contour lines) determined according to the algorithm described in Sect. 6. The smaller masks in the top right quadrant as well as the one close to the top left corner correspond to moving people. Note the two masks around the top of a pole in the upper left quadrant: these two masks belong to a vehicle which is partially occluded by this pole.

7 Discussion of Related Research and Conclusion

[11] analysed potential error sources in the usual pseudo-inverse solution for differential OF-estimation and investigated a 'Total Least Squares' approach similar to the one underlying (4). These authors suggested the use of a filter set comprising various orientations, bandwidths, and resolutions. They had to devise means to combine results obtained by different filters – in contradistinction to our adaptive approach which obviates the need to recombine different filter results. [8], too, employ multiple filters based on Hermite polynomials and parameterize their OF-estimation approach directly by 3-D motion parameters. Their algorithm evaluates intermediate results in order to properly diagnose critical grayvalue configurations. These authors do not, however, determine an OF-field with the density and resolution required for the examples used above. No attempt has been made by these authors to actually segment the estimated OF-fields and to evaluate the segmentation results in order to facilitate an assessment of OF-estimation.

Xiong and Shafer [13, 14] investigated hypergeometric filters somewhat similar to Gabor filters (see, e. g., [13, Figure 5]) in order to estimate optic flow, too. Xiong and Shafer do not attempt to segment OF-fields estimated in this manner, nor do they apply their method to image sequences with discontinuities of the optical flow field comparable to those treated in this contribution. It thus remains open whether their approach could cope with such situations.

The idea of a 'structure tensor' had been investigated already way back by [6]. Subsequent generalizations of Knutsson's ideas to spatiotemporal grayvalue structures are discussed, e. g., by [12] who, however, only treated a few (fairly coarse) synthetic image examples. Knutsson also influenced the work of [5]. [2] recently extended the investigations of [5] and applied them to a few short image sequences. Neither [12] nor [5], however, exploited knowledge contained in the GLST about the local spatiotemporal grayvalue structure in order to devise a *matched derivative convolution filter*. These authors show several examples of estimated OF-fields although they do not explicitly generate masks covering images of moving objects. As far as can be inferred from their illustrations, the difficulties diagnosed and overcome by the algorithm described in the preceding sects. 4 through 6 had not yet even been recognized by these authors.

An adaptive spatiotemporal filter somewhat similar to the one described here has already been reported by [9] who assumed that relevant grayvalue structures could be modelled as spatiotemporal Gaussians. The authors exploited this assumption in an attempt to separate the covariance matrix defining a local grayvalue structure in an image sequence from the filter covariance matrix. Difficulties arose in areas where image noise becomes relevant or where the assumption about the underlying grayvalue structure begins to break down.

[7] used an adaptive filter in 2D which is constructed in a manner similar to the one described here. But no attemps have been made by [7] to apply the adaptive filter to the estimation and segmentation of optic flow fields.

Extended own investigations and a judicious combination of experiences reported in the literature suggested a renewed attempt to simultaneously estimate and segment an OF-field. We converted the knowledge provided by a GLST into a *spatiotemporally adaptive* OF-estimation approach. As can be seen from experimental evidence presented above, we thereby obtained a *much cleaner signal about what happens at a particular space-time location in an image sequence*. This improvement, in turn, greatly facilitated to identify *structural* criteria which distinguish various types of failures that may occur in estimation and segmentation steps.

This diagnostic capacity allowed us to design a fairly simple, but nevertheless robust segmentation algorithm for an OF-field which complies with our basic assumptions about motion and distances between objects in the scene relative to the recording video camera: objects, whose images have to be segmented from the background, move only a small distance – in comparison to their distance from the center of projection – during the time between consecutive video-frames, thus yielding essentially parallel and equal-magnitude OF-vectors. Obviously, our approach will have to be modified if the object motion is more complicated than a small translation, since only the latter results in a more or less homogeneous optic flow field.

Please note that we do not base our approach on an *explicit* a-priori characterization of similarity required between neighboring optic flow vectors: we just assume OF-vectors to be sufficiently similar due to the manner in which they have been estimated with a high overlap of their support areas. This 'inherited' similarity quickly breaks down, however, *near the boundary* of an image area corresponding to an object moving rigidly in the depicted scene.

The methodology underlying our approach exploits *entire image regions* with acceptably *homogeneous OF-vectors* as a *tool* for quickly identifying locations where the homogeneity assumption is violated: clustering pixel locations with equal characteristics into connected-components often *kind of magnifies* any estimation or segmentation *deficiency*. Such a deficiency is likely to result in counterintuive region boundaries which can be quickly identified and analysed. This 'methodological leverage' can only be applied, however, since the increased reliability of our *spatiotemporally adaptive OF-estimation* approach removes enough artefacts and noise effects that we obtain a chance to *structurally* analyse failures – as opposed to fiddling around endlessly with attempts to find 'the' optimal parameter combination.

As a result, we obtain 'moving object masks' whose derivation depends on intuitively accessible parameters – so far in an apparently uncritical manner. The resulting mask quality appears sufficient to initialize model-based tracking of vehicles. It may even facilitate a purely data-driven tracking approach in the picture domain. Further research into these directions has been started.

8 Acknowledgements

Partial support of these investigations by the Deutsche Forschungsgemeinschaft (DFG) is gratefully acknowledged.

References

1. J.L. Barron, D.J. Fleet, and S.S. Beauchemin: Performance of Optical Flow Techniques. International Journal of Computer Vision **12** (1994) 43-77
2. H. Haußecker and B. Jähne: A Tensor Approach for Precise Computation of Dense Displacement Vector Fields. E. Paulus and F.M. Wahl (Hrsg.), Mustererkennung 1997, 19. DAGM-Symposium, Braunschweig/Germany, 15.-17. September 1997; Informatik aktuell, Springer-Verlag Berlin Heidelberg 1997, pp. 199-208
3. R.M. Haralick and L.G. Shapiro: Computer and Robot Vision. Addison-Wesley Publishing Company, Reading / MA 1992 (Vol. I)
4. B.K.P. Horn: Robot Vision. The MIT Press, Cambridge/MA and London/UK 1986
5. B. Jähne: Spatio-Temporal Image Processing, Theory and Scientific Applications. Lecture Notes in Computer Science, Vol. 751, Springer-Verlag Berlin Heidelberg 1993.
6. H. Knutsson: Filtering and Reconstruction in Image Processing. Ph.D. Thesis, Department of Electrical Engineering; In: Linköping Studies in Science and Technology, Dissertations No. **88**, Linköping University, S-581 83, Linköping, Sweden, 1982.

7. T. Lindeberg, J. Gårding: Shape-Adapted Smoothing in Estimation of 3-D Depth Cues from Affine Distortions of Local 2-D Brightness Structure. Proc. 3rd European Conference on Computer Vision ECCV '94, 2–6 May 1994, Stockholm/S; J.-O. Eklundh (Ed.), Lecture Notes in Computer Science LNCS **800**, Springer-Verlag Berlin Heidelberg New York/NY 1994, pp. 389–400.

8. H. Liu, T.-H. Hong, M. Herman, and R. Chellappa: A General Motion Model and Spatio-Temporal Filters for Computing Optical Flow. International Journal of Computer Vision **22**:2 (1997) 141–172.

9. H.-H. Nagel, A. Gehrke, M. Haag, and M. Otte: Space- and Time-Variant Estimation Approaches and the Segmentation of the Resulting Optical Flow Field. Proc. Second Asian Conference on Computer Vision, 5-8 December 1995, Singapore, Vol. II, pp. 296–300.

10. V. S. Nalwa, T. O. Binford: On Detecting Edges. IEEE Transactions on Pattern Analysis and Machine Intelligence **PAMI-8** (1986) 699-714.

11. J. Weber and J. Malik: Robust Computation of Optical Flow in a Multi-Scale Differential Framework. Proc. Fourth International Conference on Computer Vision ICCV '93, 11-14 May 1993, Berlin/Germany, pp. 12-20; see, too, Int. Journal of Computer Vision **14**:1 (1995) 67–81.

12. C.-F. Westin: A Tensor Framework for Multidimensional Signal Processing. Ph.D. Thesis, Department of Electrical Engineering; In: *Linköping Studies in Science and Technology, Dissertations No.* **348**, (ISBN 91-7871-421-4) Linköping University, S-581 83, Linköping, Sweden, 1994.

13. Y. Xiong and S.A. Shafer: Moment and Hypergeometric Filters for High Precision Computation of Focus, Stereo and Optical Flow. International Journal of Computer Vision **22**:1 (1997) 25–59.

14. Y. Xiong and S.A. Shafer: Hypergeometric Filters for Optical Flow and Affine Matching. International Journal of Computer Vision **24**:2 (1997) 163–177.

Robust Video Mosaicing through Topology Inference and Local to Global Alignment

Harpreet S. Sawhney, Steve Hsu, and R. Kumar

Vision Technologies Laboratory
Sarnoff Corporation
CN5300, Princeton, NJ 08543, USA
{hsawhney,shsu,rkumar}@sarnoff.com

Abstract. The problem of piecing together individual frames in a video sequence to create seamless panoramas (*video mosaics*) has attracted increasing attention in recent times. One challenge in this domain has been to rapidly and *automatically* create high quality seamless mosaics using inexpensive cameras and relatively free hand motions.

In order to capture a wide angle scene using a video sequence of relatively narrow angle views, the scene needs to be scanned in a 2D pattern. This is like painting a canvas on a 2D manifold with the video frames using multiple connected 1D brush strokes. An important issue that needs to be addressed in this context is that of aligning frames that have been captured using a 2D scanning of the scene rather than a 1D scan as is commonly done in many existing mosaicing systems.

In this paper we present an end-to-end solution to the problem of video mosaicing when the transformations between frames may be modeled as parametric. We provide solutions to two key problems: (i) automatic inference of topology of the video frames on a 2D manifold, and (ii) globally consistent estimation of alignment parameters that map each frame to a consistent mosaic coordinate system. Our method iterates among automatic topology determination, local alignment, and globally consistent parameter estimation to produce a coherent mosaic from a video sequence, regardless of the camera's scan path over the scene. While this framework is developed independent of the specific alignment model, we illustrate the approach by constructing planar and spherical mosaics from real videos.

1   Motivation

Creation of panoramic images and mosaics from a video sequence or a collection of images has attracted tremendous attention from researchers and commercial practitioners alike. However, most previously developed systems for creating panoramas have either been limited by their use of special fixtures (e.g. tripods) for precisely controlled image capture [3] or have been restricted to a one-dimensional [1] scanning of a scene [8]. In this paper we present some key

---

[1] We use the term 1D scanning for an arrangement of frames in which each frame may overlap only with its two immediate temporal neighbors. In contrast 2D scanning of a scene allows frames to overlap even when they may not be temporal neighbors.

technical advances in automatically creating mosaics from video sequences that users create by smoothly moving a hand-held camera to cover the whole scene using multiple overlapping swaths (or 2D scanning). The overlap between consecutive swaths may be quite small relative to the width or height of individual images. Significant parts of this technology have been packaged into consumer level applications for various kinds of mosaicing scenarios under the commercial name of *VideoBrush^{TM}* [15].

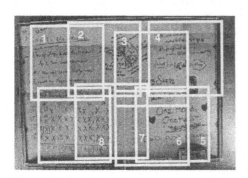

Fig. 1. An *S*-pattern for scanning a planar object.

Unlike the 1D case, in 2D scanning, there is a wrap-around and frames belonging to neighboring swaths must align with each other even though they are not temporally adjacent frames. Our framework is primarily motivated by the observation that although alignment of consecutive frames may be accurate, simply concatenating local alignment models leads to gross global misalignments. For example, in Fig. 1, if the capturing order of frames is $1 - 8$, and each frame is aligned with its predecessor, there is no guarantee that frames 1 and 8 will be aligned when warped to a global reference coordinate system.

There are two key problems in video mosaicing. First is to automatically infer the 2D neighborhood relations (topology) among frames. The input video sequence just provides a time ordered collection of frames that have captured overlapping parts of the scene. To create a mosaic, these frames need to be placed in their correct 2D topology. Second, the frames need to be stitched together so that the scene is represented as a single seamless whole even when the overlaps between frames may vary widely over the complete 2D scan. Previous work [4, 10, 13, 16] has addressed only a subset of the issues involved with alignment of frames but has not provided a comprehensive framework within which automatic inference of 2D topology is combined with local-to-global alignment for an end-to-end solution to the mosaicing problem.

The framework that we present has been applied to a number of different applications involving capture of a wide angle scene from multiple narrow angle views. In this work we will illustrate the framework through its applications to scanning planar objects with unrestricted camera motion, and creation of (hemi-)spherical mosaics by systematically scanning a scene from an approximately fixed position. Each of these applications highlights a different parameterization of the alignment model that is required for mosaicing. However, the framework within which the different parameterizations work is the same.

2 Issues and Related Work

For a video sequence of a planar scene, or of a 3D scene captured with approximately a fixed camera center, the process of creating a seamless mosaic of the scene involves the following major issues:

1. Determination of the 2D topology of the sequence of frames on a suitable 2D manifold.
2. Parameterization and estimation of the transformations that can be used to establish the geometric relationships between the various frames and a global mosaic reference frame.
3. Handling lens distortion.
4. Creation of a seamless mosaiced representation of the scene so that new views may be created.

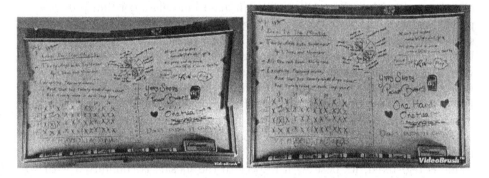

Fig. 2. Left: 75 frames captured using 3 successive horizontal swipes are poorly mosaiced using frame-to-frame plane projective parameters. **Right**: 75 frames captured using 3 successive horizontal swipes are successfully mosaiced using frame-to-mosaic plane projective parameters.

Previous approaches to the problem of video mosaicing have not addressed all these issues comprehensively or robustly. In particular, the important issue of automatic topology determination has been completely ignored. Early works on mosaics and image alignment like [4, 6, 9, 12, 14] essentially did 1D/2D mosaicing by solving for the alignment parameters of each frame individually. Each frame is registered to the previous frame in the sequence. The frame-to-frame registration parameters are concatenated to compute the global frame to mosaic alignment parameters. A mosaic is subsequently created by warping each frame to a reference coordinate system using the computed alignment parameters. The main problem with this approach is that the parameters obtained by the alignment of frames locally are not accurate enough to assemble a well aligned mosaic. Small errors in computing the frame-to-frame alignment parameters, or small deviations of the model from the true model, get compounded when they are concatenated to compute the global frame to mosaic alignment parameters.

An example of such a case is shown in Fig. 2 (left). A video sequence of 75 frames is captured of a planar white-board. Between each pair of consecutive frames, an 8-parameter projective transformation is solved for using a multi-resolution direct alignment technique [10, 12]. Finally, the center frame is chosen as the reference frame and each of the other frames is warped using the relevant concatenated pairwise parameters. It is to be emphasized that in spite of each of the pairwise frame alignments being almost perfect, the resulting mosaic suffers from gross misalignments. Therefore, one important issue to be addressed is how multiple frames can be constrained to create parameters that align all the frames accurately.

An improvement over frame to frame registration is to align each new frame to the mosaic as it is being built [10]. This provides a larger image context for aligning each new frame, and captures some constraints from spatially neighboring frames that are not temporally adjacent. Fig. 2 (right) shows the mosaic built using the frame-to-mosaic alignment algorithm. Unlike the frame-to-frame alignment algorithm (Fig. 2 (left)), the frame-to-mosaic algorithm produces a perfect mosaic. The frame-to-mosaic algorithm works well as long as there is sufficient overlap between frames in neighboring swaths, for instance in the top left-to-right and bottom right-to-left swaths in Fig. 1. However, when there is very little overlap, then the performance of the frame-to-mosaic algorithm is very similar to the frame-to-frame algorithm. Such an example can be seen in Fig. 3 (left). The frame-to-mosaic algorithm produces a poor alignment for one of frames in the bottom swath. This one poor alignment causes an overall error in the mosaic construction. The main problem with the frame-to-mosaic method is that computing the alignment is still a causal 1D processing chain. As each frame is registered, its pose with respect to the mosaic is committed with no possibility of improvement based on frames that are processed subsequently. If any link on this chain is bad, the overall mosaic construction is erroneous.

 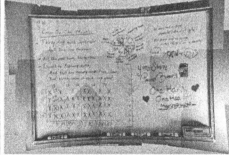

Fig. 3. Left:75 frames captured using 3 successive horizontal swipes are poorly mosaiced using frame-to-mosaic plane projective parameters.
Right:75 frames captured using 3 successive horizontal swipes are succesfully mosaiced using local-to-global plane projective parameters.

Some work in the area of image-based rendering has explicitly concentrated on creating closed mosaics on 1D manifolds for instance by projecting on cylindrical surfaces and then developing the surface [3, 7]. It has been explicitly assumed that the collection of images captures the complete 360° 1D manifold. This constraint has been enforced by using tripods and systematic angular steps between frames. In [5], for the 1D case, closure of the 1D mosaic is enforced by adjusting the focal length so that a complete 360° coverage is obtained. Therefore, in these works, it is assumed a priori that the collection of frames when mapped on a 1D manifold closes on itself.

Recently the problem of stitching together video frames on a 2D manifold has attracted attention. In a recent paper [13], Szeliski and Shum parameterize the 2D mosaicing problem using rotations and focal length of the camera that is moved around a fixed point. However, the various issues listed earlier have not been comprehensively addressed. The 2D topology was specified manually in their approach.

The determination of 2D topology or the relative placement of frames is critical in achieving simultaneous alignment of all the frames to create a seamless representation. In this paper, we combine automatic inference of 2D topology with a local to global alignment strategy. In our technique, each frame is able to constrain all other frames through constraints determined by the topology. For example, Fig. 3 (right) shows the perfect mosaic construction from the whiteboard video using the new algorithm, in contrast to the frame-to-mosaic alignment method (Fig. 3 (left)).

3 Our Approach

We provide a framework for the creation of mosaiced representations of a planar scene, or of a 3D scene from approximately a fixed viewpoint, by providing solutions to and integrating means for 2D topology determination, local alignment, and global consistency. Planar topology is adequate when the captured sequence can be represented as a whole on a planar surface. This is the case when the goal is to produce high resolution planar mosaics of paintings, white-boards and 3D scenes from relatively small total viewing angles. However, when the scene is captured through a sequence that closes on itself or covers the complete sphere or a significant part of a sphere around the fixed viewpoint, then the planar topology is not adequate for seamless representation of the scene since plane projective mappings will map points to infinity.

A 2D manifold, e.g. a plane or a sphere, may be explicitly used for representing planar images on the manifold. Alternatively, the specific transformations used to map points between frames can be implicitly used to represent the input frames on a manifold. In either case, 2D topology determination figures out which frames overlap and hence are neighbors on the appropriate manifold. The topology determination is an iterative process since it can be inferred only when frames are placed with respect to each other by solving for specific transformations. A hypothesis for a new neighborhood relationship is tested for reliability using a quality measure that is computed after coarse and fine alignment of the neighbors.

Local coarse registration estimates a low complexity (say, 2D translational only) mapping between neighbors. Fine local registration estimates a higher complexity mapping between neighbors or between a frame and the current estimate of the local mosaic. The step of globally consistent optimization infers all the reference-to-frame mappings by simultaneously optimizing them, such that they are maximally consistent with all the local registration information. Global consistency may be imposed by solving for purely parametric alignment models corresponding to the 2D manifold over which the mosaic is represented. This is similar to the bundle block adjustment used in photogrammetry [11]. In addition, misalignments due to departures from the global models are handled by quasi-parametric or piecewise parametric alignment between regions of overlap. However, in this paper we will not dwell on quasi-parametric alignment. For accurate alignment, we iterate between the coarse matching, topology determination and global consistency steps.

The complete process is depicted in Fig. 4.

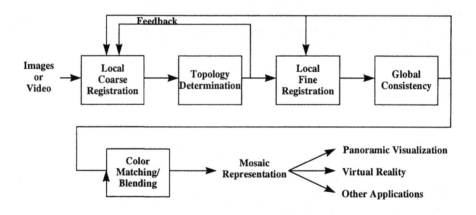

Fig. 4. Block diagram of the main steps.

While the previously described stages accomplish geometric alignment of the source images, color matching/blending adjusts for discrepancies in color and brightness between images. This is critical for avoiding seams in the mosaic. Another important real-world issue that needs to be taken care of especially for consumer cameras is that of handling lens distortion. We estimation lens distortion within the framework of multi-frame alignment in which we can solve for the alignment and lens distortion parameters without the need of a calibration object. The computed lens distortion parameter is applied as a correction to all the frames before mosaic creation. The reader is referred to [10] for details. We will not be dwelling on blending and lens distortion correction in this paper, but it is to be emphasized that in a real application, solutions to both are a must for creation of high quality mosaics on 2D manifolds.

4 Problem Formulation

The models that relate multiple frames when a camera is capturing a planar scene under arbitrary motion, or a 3D scene from a fixed viewpoint, can be parameterized as plane projective, or 3D rotations, or 3D rotations and translations with the 3D plane parameters. In order to create a seamless mosaic of a collection of frames, an optimal set of reference-to-image mappings need to be created: $\mathbf{u} = \mathbf{P_i}(\mathbf{x})$ of a parametric class, where $\mathbf{x}$ denotes a point on the reference surface and $\mathbf{u}$ is a point on the ith source image. In general, the shape of the reference surface and the source image surfaces can be any 2D manifold in 3D, such as planes and spheres.

Denote the mosaic image as $M(\mathbf{x})$, and the source images by $I_i(\mathbf{u})$. The $\mathbf{P_i}$'s need to be computed so that for each $\mathbf{x}$, the point $\mathbf{P_i}(\mathbf{x})$ in every image i corresponds to the same point in the physical scene. This condition assures that the mosaic image $M(\mathbf{x})$ constructed by combining pixels $\{I_i(\mathbf{P_i}(\mathbf{x})), \forall i\}$ will yield a spatially coherent mosaic, where each point $\mathbf{x}$ is in one-to-one correspondence with a point in the scene.

We formulate the problem of optimal mosaic creation as that of minimizing an objective function that measures the misalignment between frames as well as the redundancy in information. Formally, the following function is optimized:

$$\min_{\{\mathbf{P_i}\}} \sum_{\mathbf{x}} \mathrm{var}_i\{I_i(\mathbf{P_i}(\mathbf{x}))\} + \sigma^2(\text{Area of the mosaic}) \qquad (1)$$

where σ is a scale factor and $\mathrm{var}_i\{\cdot\}$ denotes the variance of the pixels from different frames that map to each $\mathbf{x}$. In words, the above Minimum Description Length cost function measures the compactness of representing a collection of frames in the form of a mosaic plus residuals of frames w.r.t. the mosaic. Note that the variances could be measured not just on the intensities directly, but alternatively on filtered representations of image intensities, or on the point locations $\mathbf{P_i}(\mathbf{x})$'s directly.

In order to optimize the error function of Equation (1), we need to maximize the overlap between warped frames in the mosaic coordinate system by finding the globally optimal alignment parameters. The optimization in general cannot be done in a closed-form. Therefore, we adopt an iterative technique. The technique is based on the observation that if the 2D topology of the input frames is known on an appropriate 2D manifold, and the local alignment parameters (or correspondences) are available between neighboring frames, then global bundle block adjustment can be used to solve for accurate $\mathbf{P_i}$'s. On the other hand if approximate knowledge of $\mathbf{P_i}$'s is available, then neighborhood relations can be inferred that can further establish new relationships between frames. Our approach switches between the two steps of topology determination and parameter estimation iteratively to reach a globally optimal solution. The topology determination step hypothesizes local neighborhood relations, and the global optimization step uses the local constraints to determine the parameters. In between these two steps, we need to establish correspondence relations between the neighboring frames and verify these with a quality measure. This is achieved using local coarse and fine alignment (see Fig. 4).

4.1 Topology Determination

The 2D topology refers to the set of pairs of input frames (i, j) whose local alignment information participates in globally consistent parameter estimation. Such pairs, henceforth called neighbors, are necessarily images with sufficient spatial overlap to make local estimation feasible.

At the start of the first iteration, there is typically no information on the $\mathbf{P_i}$'s whatsoever; hence, under the reasonable assumption that consecutive frames of a video sequence are overlapping, the initial topology defaults to a linear chain of temporal neighbors. Local alignment of such neighbors and global consistency—a trivial concatenation of motion models—yield the first estimate of $\mathbf{P_i}$.

In subsequent iterations, topology determination may become nontrivial and essential. Non-consecutive frames may be discovered to be neighbors, such as frames in adjacent swipes of an S pattern or pairs which close a loop or spiral scan. These patterns can be formed on any shape of reference surface if the direction of camera motion changes. In case of a closed shape like a sphere, moreover, loops can be formed even with constant camera motion, as typified by scanning a 360° panorama. Because topology is inferred from only approximate knowledge of $\mathbf{P_i}$ and because the choice of surface shape may be changed during the course of global consistency (e.g. from planar to spherical), it is possible that not all proper neighbors will be found during the second iteration; multiple iterations may be required to converge to agreement between topology and parameter estimation.

We update the topology at the start of each iteration by generating hypotheses for new neighbors, which get verified or refuted by local registration, and adding only verified neighbors as arcs in the neighbor relation graph, G. New candidates might be selected using various criteria, including influence on subsequent global estimation and proximity of the images.

1. The existing topology dictates where adding new arcs would have the most effect on the accuracy of the global parameter estimate. The first arc that closes a loop or ties together two swipes is significant, but not one which parallels many other nearby arcs. It is not essential to include every possible overlapping pair in the topology for accurate global alignment, nor is it computationally efficient. Therefore, it is desirable to limit the density of arcs within any local region.

2. The current topology and set of global parameter estimates $\mathbf{P_i}$ determine the relative spatial locations and uncertainty for any pair of frames under consideration. It is desirable to choose pairs which are most likely to overlap and to have least positional uncertainty so that local alignment need not search a large range.

The two desiderata are generally in direct conflict, since arcs of high payoff (influence) are very often image pairs with high risk (positional uncertainty). Our current experiments prioritize candidate arcs by greatest overlap rather than greatest influence, and additionally skip arcs too close to existing ones. It is expected that as iterations progress, global parameter estimates will increase in accuracy, drawing the high leverage pairs closer until they have reasonable overlap and uncertainty to get registered and added to G.

Specifically, candidates are added by considering their arc length d_{ij} in relation to path length D_{ij}. Arc length is defined by the distance between warped image centers $\mathbf{x_i}$, $\mathbf{x_j}$ on the mosaic surface, normalized by the warped frame "diameter" r_i, r_j:

$$d_{ij} = \frac{\max(0, |\mathbf{x_i} - \mathbf{x_j}| - |r_i - r_j|/2)}{\min(r_i, r_j)}$$

Path length D_{ij} is defined as the sum of arc lengths along the minimum sum path between nodes i, j in the existing graph. To add an arc, d_{ij} must not exceed a maximum limit and must be significantly shorter than D_{ij}, and the image reliability measure ρ_{ij} (see below) must be high. This heuristic tends to select arcs that both have good overlap and will add non-redundant constraints to the global bundle block adjustment.

4.2 Local Coarse and Fine Registration

Local alignment verifies the goodness of the neighborhood relationships suggested by topology determination by aligning images pairwise using parametric models. For each neighboring pair of images, the mapping $\mathbf{Q_{ij}}$ is estimated such that, for each point $\mathbf{u}$ in image i, the point $\mathbf{u'} = \mathbf{Q_{ij}}(\mathbf{u})$ in image j corresponds to the same point in the physical scene. Since the absolute pixel-to-scene calibration is typically not known in advance, this correspondence must be inferred by matching the appearance of $I_j(\mathbf{u'})$ and $I_i(\mathbf{u})$.

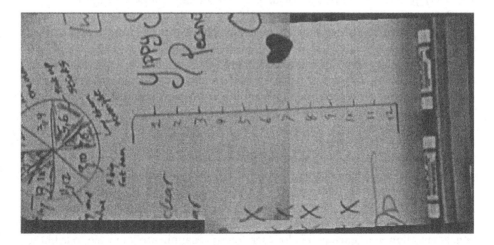

Fig. 5. Local plane projective registration between two neighboring frames of the *Whiteboard* video showing accurate automatic alignment even with small overlap. A mosaic of the two frames is shown. (The mosaic is rotated $90°$ to fit on the page.)

Often, $\mathbf{Q_{ij}}$ is restricted to a parametric family of mappings, such as projective mapping or pure translation. While a simple parametric model may only be an approximation of the true mapping, it is often faster and more reliable to estimate than a higher order model. Indeed, the kind of mapping does not even have to be the same as the mapping $\mathbf{P_j}$ to be estimated during global consistency.

In general, the magnitude of motion between temporally contiguous frames may be tens of pixels, and that between other neighbors may be as high as hundreds of pixels. We divide the local alignment problem into steps in which models of increasing complexity are estimated while establishing correspondence. Initially, a large range of 2D translations only is searched to establish robust rough correspondence. The image is divided into multiple blocks and each block establishes its correspondence through coarse-to-fine search with normalized correlation as a match measure. Majority consensus between the blocks is used to compute the 2D translation.

Once a reasonable guess of the translation is available, more accurate alignment is performed by fitting progressively complex models and minimizing the sum-of-squared-differences (SSD) error measure in a coarse-to-fine manner over a Laplacian pyramid [1]. At each level of the pyramid, the unknown parameters are solved for by:

$$\min_{\mathbf{Q_{ij}}} \sum_{\mathbf{u}} (I_j(\mathbf{Q_{ij}}(\mathbf{u})) - I_i(\mathbf{u}))^2 \qquad (2)$$

The initial 2D translation parameters at the coarsest level, and subsequently the refined parameters from each level are used to warp I_j and the next increment in the parameters is solved using a Levenberg-Marquardt iteration. Local alignment is done progressively using affine and then projective parameters to establish accurate correspondence between neighboring frames. In general, the progressive complexity technique provides good correspondences between frames even when the overlap may be as low as 10% as is shown in an example in Figure 5.

Before accepting the pair ij as neighbors, a reliability measure ρ_{ij} is computed. This measure is thresholded to discard poor estimates, and is also applied as a weight factor during global consistency. Using the computed $\mathbf{Q_{ij}}$, the resulting reference and warped images are compared by one of the following: (i) the mean (or median) absolute or squared pixel value error; (ii) normal flow magnitude; (iii) normalized correlation to compute ρ. We have found that normalized correlation gives the most reliable measure of alignment.

4.3 Global Consistency

The steps of topology determination and pairwise local alignment lead to local maximal overlaps between frames. If the local alignment parameters were globally consistent too then the cost function of Equation (1) would have been optimized. However, in general, the local alignment parameters provide good correspondences between neighboring frames but may still be far from providing consistent alignment parameters for each frame's mapping to a mosaic coordinate system. This was illustrated by the example in Figure 2. In order to optimize the error function of Equation (1), it is assumed that the topology determination and local alignment have achieved a local minimum of the second term, that is the area term. Now with the overlap between frames fixed, and based on the correspondences in the overlapping areas provided by local alignment, the first term is minimized with respect to the global alignment parameters.

The jointly optimum set of reference-to-image mappings $\mathbf{P_i}$ is computed by minimizing an alternative form for the first term of Equation (1) that measures point correspondence errors instead of image gray value errors.

$$\min_{\{\mathbf{P_i}\}} E = \sum_{ij \in G} E_{ij} + \sum_i E_i.$$

The term $E_{ij}(\mathbf{P_i}, \mathbf{P_j}; \mathbf{Q_{ij}})$ measures the alignment errors between points in neighboring images that, according to local alignment $\mathbf{Q_{ij}}$, are supposed to map to the same point in the mosaic coordinate system.

The regularization term $E_i(\mathbf{P_i})$ allows the inclusion of any kind of *a priori* desirable characteristic for the reference-to-image mappings. For example, for the case of projective mappings, E_i are designed to penalize the amount of distortion frames must undergo when warped to the mosaic. Another source of knowledge may be physical measurements of camera position and orientation. All such criteria can be expressed as functions of $\mathbf{P_i}$, constituting the error term E_i.

$\mathbf{P_i}$ is often restricted to a parameterized family of mappings, in which case the domain of this optimization problem is a finite-dimensional vector. Nevertheless, the global error criterion E is typically a complicated function of the unknown $\mathbf{P_i}$'s and only iterative solution is possible or practical. The optimization process is terminated either after a fixed number of iterations or when the error stops decreasing appreciably. In practice, typically five iterations of the global alignment have been found to be adequate.

The optimization should be initialized with some reasonable starting estimate of the $\mathbf{P_i}$'s. We choose a spanning tree T of the graph of neighbors G, and begin by optimizing $E = \sum_{ij \in T} E_{ij}$. Since there are no loops in subgraph T, it is possible to minimize this error by simply requiring $\mathbf{P_j}(\mathbf{x}) = \mathbf{Q_{ij}}(\mathbf{P_i}(\mathbf{x}))$ exactly for every pair of neighbors in T. As a special case, if T is all pairs of temporally adjacent frames, then this is nothing more than concatenating a linear chain of frame-to-frame mappings.

5 Examples

This section provides two example scenarios where different parameterizations are employed. Notation: for a 3D vector $\mathbf{X} = (X_1, X_2, X_3)$, define $\Pi(\mathbf{X}) = (X_1/X_3, X_2/X_3)$ and $\hat{v}(\mathbf{X}) = \mathbf{X}/|\mathbf{X}|$. For a 2D vector $\mathbf{u} = (u_1, u_2)$, define $\tilde{\mathbf{u}} = (u_1, u_2, 1)$. Also, a homography in $\mathcal{P}^2$ is written as $\mathbf{x} \approx \mathbf{A}\mathbf{X}$.

5.1 Planar Mosaic

In order to create a seamless mosaic of a planar surface from a video sequence acquired by a freely moving camera, the reference-to-image mappings as well as relative image-to-image mappings are well described by projective mappings.

Local coarse registration uses a pure translation mapping, for efficiency, while local fine registration uses projective mapping. Topology is recalculated once,

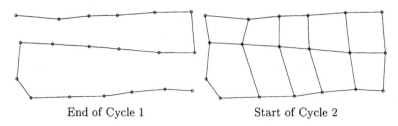

End of Cycle 1   Start of Cycle 2

Fig. 6. Topology refinement for an S pattern sequence: (1) Default topology of temporal neighbors only; (2) Topology of spatial neighbors. Topology converged after 2 cycles.

following the local coarse registration, whose translational shift estimates Q_{ij} are simply integrated to give preliminary estimates of P_i.

Global consistency endeavors to determine the jointly optimum reference-to-image mappings of the form $\tilde{\mathbf{u}} \approx A_i^{-1}\tilde{\mathbf{x}}$. The inverse mapping is then $\tilde{\mathbf{x}} \approx A_i\tilde{\mathbf{u}}$.

The complete E consists of two kinds of terms:

1. For each pair of neighboring images,

$$E_{ij} = \sum_{k=1}^{4} \left| \Pi(\mathbf{A_i}\tilde{\mathbf{u}_k}) - \Pi(\mathbf{A_j}\tilde{Q}_{ij}(\mathbf{u_k})) \right|^2$$

where the $\mathbf{u_k}$ are corners of the overlap between the images (typically four points). This term penalizes inconsistency between reference-to-image mappings and local registration.

2. For each image,

$$E_i = \sum_{k=1}^{2} \left| \Pi(\mathbf{A_i}\tilde{\alpha_k}) - \Pi(\mathbf{A_i}\tilde{\beta_k}) - (\alpha_k - \beta_k) \right|^2$$

where α_1, α_2, β_1, β_2 are the midpoints of the top, left, bottom, and right sides of the source image. This term penalizes scale, rotation, and distortion of the images when warped to the mosaic. Additionally, the term $|\Pi(\mathbf{A_1}(0,0,1))|^2$ is added to E_1 to fix the translation of one frame.

In the absence of these terms, the solution for $\{A_i\}$ is under-determined, since any projective transformation applied to the whole reference coordinate system would not affect E.

The global error is optimized as follows. First, the $\mathbf{A_i}$'s are initialized by concatenating the local registration projective mappings within a spanning tree. Second, the sum of E_i terms only is minimized with respect to the update $\mathbf{A_i} \leftarrow \mathbf{B_0}\mathbf{A_i}$ where $\mathbf{B_0}$ is a common projective mapping. Third, the complete E is minimized with respect to the update $\mathbf{A_i} \leftarrow \mathbf{B_i}\mathbf{A_i}$ where $\mathbf{B_i}$ is a per-image projective mapping. For the last two steps, optimization is done by Gauss-Newton method, which requires only first derivatives of the terms inside $|\cdot|^2$ with respect to the coefficients of $\mathbf{B}$; typically convergence is reached in 3–5 iterations for mosaics of dozens of frames.

The complete topology inference and local-to-global alignment framework for the example of Fig. 3 (right) is illustrated in Figure 6. The first cycle starts with the default topology of temporal neighbors only. The local estimator finds coarse translations Q_{ij}, and global estimation simply concatenates these translations into the reference-to-frame parameters P_i. The second cycle detects non-consecutive spatial neighbors, performs local estimation of projective models, then optimizes the global plane projective parameters. In this instance, topology converges in 2 cycles. The resulting mosaic was shown in Figure 3.

5.2 Spherical Mosaic

Fig. 7. 184 frames captured using 3 successive horizontal 360° swipes shown as over-lapping frames after the initial step of 2D translational alignment between consecutive frames. (The sequence has been broken into two parts for clarity.)

In order to illustrate that our framework for constructing a seamless mosaic representation is general, we now show the creation of seamless mosaics of any 3D scene from a video sequence acquired by a camera rotating about a fixed point. The camera parameters including lens distortion are unknown. In this situation the best shape for the reference surface is a sphere, which places no limitation on the angular extent of the mosaic representation. The image-to-image mappings are still well described by projective mappings, but the sphere-to-image mappings are not. The projective mappings are converted to 3D rotations and camera calibration parameters to infer the 2D topology on a sphere as well as to solve for globally consistent rotations and the calibration parameters.

Local coarse registration uses a 2D rotation/translation mapping, while local fine registration uses projective mapping. Topology is recalculated following the local coarse registration, whose translational shift estimates $\mathbf{Q}_{ij}$ are simply concatenated to give preliminary estimates of $\mathbf{P}_i$.

Global consistency endeavors to determine the jointly optimum reference-to-image mappings of the form $\mathbf{u} = \Pi(\mathbf{FR_i}^T\mathbf{X})$ where $\mathbf{F}$ is a upper triangular camera calibration matrix, $\mathbf{R_i}$ is an orthonormal rotation matrix, and $\mathbf{X}$ is a 3D point on the unit sphere reference surface. The method of [2] is used to estimate a common $\mathbf{F}$ from all the $\mathbf{Q}_{ij}$'s. Using this estimation the inverse mapping can be written as $\mathbf{X} = \mathbf{R_i}\hat{\mathbb{V}}(\mathbf{F}^{-1}\tilde{\mathbf{u}})$. It is assumed that the same $\mathbf{F}$ is valid for each frame.

The complete E consists solely of inconsistency terms for pairs of images

$$E_{ij} = \sum_{k=1}^{4} \left| \mathbf{R_i}\hat{\mathbb{V}}(\mathbf{F}^{-1}\tilde{\mathbf{u_k}}) - \mathbf{R_j}\hat{\mathbb{V}}(\mathbf{F}^{-1}\tilde{\mathbf{Q}}_{ij}(\mathbf{u_k})) \right|^2 .$$

For the central image in the mosaic, $\mathbf{R_{i_0}}$ is fixed as the identity.

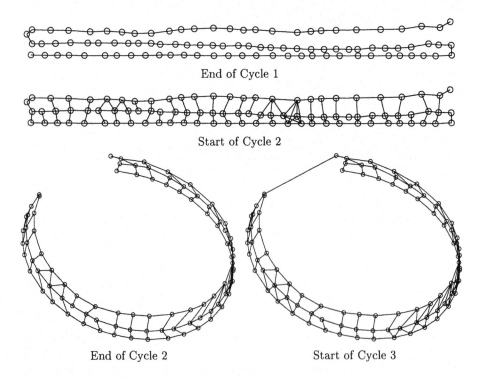

End of Cycle 1

Start of Cycle 2

End of Cycle 2   Start of Cycle 3

Fig. 8. Topology refinement for a 360° panoramic S pattern sequence: (1) Default topology of temporal neighbors only; (2,start) Planar toplogy of spatial neighbors; (2,end) Spherical topology due to global estimation; (3) Loop closure detected. Topology converged after 3 cycles.

The global error is optimized as follows. First, the $\mathbf{R_i}$'s are initialized by locally minimizing each E_{ij} in a spanning tree. Second, the complete E is minimized with respect to the update $\mathbf{R_i} \leftarrow \mathbf{B_i R_i}$ where $\mathbf{B_i}$ is a per-image rotation matrix, using a Gauss-Newton method. Note, an alternative strategy is to update both the common $\mathbf{F}$ matrix and the individual $\mathbf{R}$ matrices during each iteration of the non-linear optimization of function E.

The complete topology inference and local-to-global alignment framework for a spherical mosaic surface is illustrated in Figure 8 for a video sequence containing three successive horizontal 360° swipes. As a preprocessing step, lens distortion is estimated and compensated using the method of [10]. The first cycle is the same as the planar mosaic case, yielding P_i's which place the images on the reference surface as shown in Figure 7. The second cycle detects non-consecutive spatial neighbors, performs local estimation of projective models, estimates $\mathbf{F}$, then optimizes the global alignment using a spherical parameterization. The angular field of view of each frame implied by $\mathbf{F}$ is 37 × 29°. At the end of the second cycle, the 360° panorama does not quite close; however, the ends are near enough so that that during the third cycle the loop closure is hypothesized, verified, and incorporated into the globally consistent estimation. In this instance, topology converges in 3 cycles.

$\mathbf{F}$ estimation depends heavily on the non-affine parameters of the $\mathbf{Q_{ij}}$, which are in turn sensitive to alignment of the periphery of the field of view, namely the image area most affected by lens distortion. If lens distortion had not been compensated, the $\mathbf{F}$ estimated in this example would have implied a 29 × 23° field of view for each frame. This would have made the spherical topology at the end of the second cycle wrap only half-way around the circle, leaving the ends of the topology too distant for loop closure to be hypothesized.

The final seamless mosaic is shown in Figure 9. For hardcopy presentation, a Mercator projection readily portrays the full contents of the panoramic scene. For a compelling visual effect, however, it is preferable to view the spherical mosaic using a 3D graphics system, such as a VRML browser or stereo display.

6 Conclusions and Future Work

The new framework for robust image alignment and mosaic construction iterates among automatic topology determination, local alignment, and globally consistent parameter estimation to produce a coherent mosaic from a video sequence. The framework captures constraints missed by prior methods, namely constraints between non-consecutive but spatially neighboring frames, and non-causal constraints from frames appearing later in time. This approach allows any pattern of scanning of the scene.

We are extending the framework in several directions to improve its flexibility and efficiency. Quasi-parametric and explicit 3D recovery can be incorporated to handle scenes and scanning modes in which the parallax effects are significant. The local to global paradigm will be generalized to a hierarchy of local mosaics of clusters of frames. This multi-scale partitioning of the neighborhood constraints not only speeds up convergence of very large scale topologies but also allows relaxing the rigidity of parametric models.

References

[1] J. R. Bergen et al. Hierarchical model–based motion estimation. In *Proc. 2nd European Conference on Computer Vision*, pages 237–252, 1992.

[2] R. I. Hartley. Self-calibration from multiple views with a rotating camera. In *ECCV*, pages 471–478, 1994.

[3] Apple Computer Inc. An overview of apple's QuickTime VR technology, 1995. http://quicktime.apple.com/qtvr/qtvrtech5_25.html.

[4] M. Irani, P. Anandan, and S. Hsu. Mosaic based representations of video sequences and their applications. In *Proc. Intl. Conf. on Computer Vision*, pages 605–611, 1995.

[5] S. B. Kang and R. Weiss. Characterization of errors in compositing panoramic images. In *Proc. Computer Vision and Pattern Recognition Conference*, pages 103–109, 1997.

[6] S. Mann and R. W. Picard. Virtual bellows: Constructing high quality stills from video. In *ICIP*, 1994.

[7] L. McMillan and G. Bishop. Plenoptic modeling: An image-based rendering system. In *Proc. of SIGGRAPH*, pages 39–46, 1995.

[8] S. Peleg and J. Herman. Panoramic mosaics by manifold projection. In *CVPR*, pages 338–343, 1997.

[9] H. S. Sawhney, S. Ayer, and M. Gorkani. Model-based 2D&3D dominant motion estimation for mosaicing and video representation. In *Proc. Intl. Conf. on Computer Vision*, pages 583–590, 1995. ftp://eagle.almaden.ibm.com/pub/cs/reports/vision/dominant_motion.ps.Z.

[10] H. S. Sawhney and R. Kumar. True multi-image alignment and its application to mosaicing and lens distortion. In *CVPR*, pages 450–456, 1997.

[11] C. C. Slama. *Manual of Photogrammetry*. Amer. Soc. of Photogrammetry, Falls Church, VA, 1980.

[12] R. Szeliski. Image mosaicing for tele-reality applications. In *IEEE Wkshp. on Applications of Computer Vision*, pages 44–53, 1994.

[13] R. Szeliski and H. Shum. Creating full view panoramic image mosaics and environment maps. In *Proc. of SIGGRAPH*, pages 251–258, 1997.

[14] L. A. Teodosio and W. Bender. Salient video stills: Content and context preserved. In *ACM Intl. Conf. on Multimedia*, 1993.

[15] VideoBrush. http://www.videobrush.com.

[16] Y. Xiong and K. Turkowski. Creating image-based VR using a self-calibrating fisheye lens. In *Proc. Computer Vision and Pattern Recognition Conference*, pages 237–243, 1997.

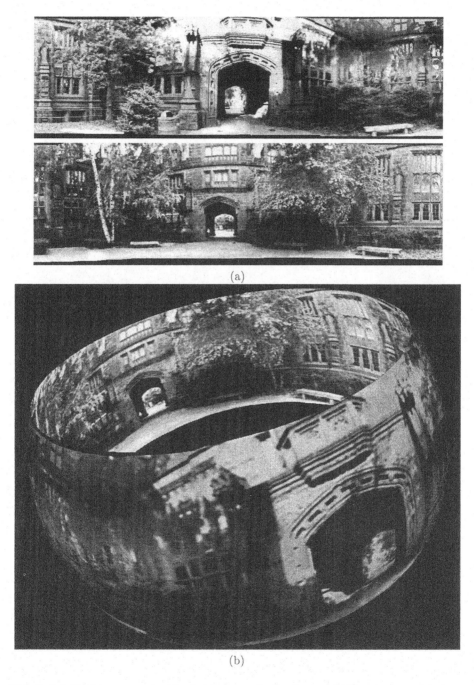

Fig. 9. (a) 184 frames captured using 3 successive horizontal 360° swipes are success-fully mosaiced using local-to-global spherical parameters. The Mercator projection of the mosaic is cut into two pieces for clarity. (b) Same mosaic rendered onto a spherical surface.

Matching and Registration
Shape and Shading
Motion and Flow
Medical IU and Rendering

Flexible Syntactic Matching of Curves

Yoram Gdalyahu and Daphna Weinshall

Institute of Computer Science, The Hebrew University,
91904 Jerusalem, Israel.
email:{yoram,daphna}@cs.huji.ac.il

Abstract. We present a flexible curve matching algorithm which performs qualitative matching between curves that are only weakly similar. While for model based recognition it is sufficient to determine if two curves are identical or not, for image database organization a continuous similarity measure, which indicates the amount of similarity between the curves, is needed. We demonstrate how flexible matching can serve to define a suitable measure. Extensive experiments are described, using real images of 3D objects. Occluding contours are matched under partial occlusion and change of viewpoint, and even when the two objects are different (such as the two side views of a horse and a cow). Using the resulting similarity measure between images, automatic hierarchical clustering of an image database is also shown, which faithfully capture the real structure in the data.

1 Introduction

Contour matching is an important problem in computer vision with a variety of applications, including model based recognition, depth from stereo and tracking. In these applications the two matched curves are usually very similar. For example, a typical application of curve matching to model based recognition would be to decide whether a model curve and an image curve are the same, up to an image transformation (e.g., translation, rotation and scale) and some permitted level of noise.

In this paper we are primarily interested in the case where the similarity between the two curves is weak. This is the situation, for example, when a recognition system is equipped with prototype shapes instead of specific exemplars. In this case the goal is to classify a given shape as belonging to a certain family, which is represented by the prototype. Another example (demonstrated in section 3) is the organization of an image database in a hierarchy of shape categories.

We use flexible curve matching to relate between feature points that are extracted on the boundaries of objects. We do not have a precise definition of what a reasonable matching between weakly similar curves is. As an illustrative example, consider two curves describing the shape of two different mammals: possibly we would like to see their limbs and head correspondingly matched. The matched pairs of points are then aligned using an optimal similarity transformation. From the residual distances between corresponding features we compute a robust dissimilarity measure between silhouettes.

To put our method in the context of existing curve matching methods, we first distinguish between dense matching and feature matching. Dense matching is usually formulated as a parameterization problem, with a cost function to be minimized. The cost might be defined as "elastic energy" needed to transform one curve to the other [4,7], but other alternatives also exist [2,10,9]. The main drawbacks of these methods are their high computational complexity (which is reduced significantly if only key points are matched), and the fact that none of them is invariant under both rotation and scaling. Computation of elastic energy (which is defined in terms of curvature) also requires an accurate evaluation of second order derivatives.

Feature matching methods may be divided into three groups: proximity matching, spread primitive matching, and syntactic matching. The idea behind proximity matching methods is to search for the best matching while permitting the rotation, translation and scaling (to be called alignment transformation) of each curve, such that the distances between matched key points are minimized [13,3,25]. The method is rather slow, and if scaling is permitted an erroneous shrinking of one feature set may result, followed by the matching of this set with a small number of features from the other set. One may avoid these problems by excluding many-to-one matches and by using the order of points, but then the method becomes syntactic (see below). As an alternative to the alignment transformation, features may be mapped to an intrinsic invariant coordinate frame [17,20,21]; the drawback of this approach is that it is global, the entire curve is needed to compute the mapping.

Features can be used to divide the curves into shape elements, or primitives. If a single curve is decomposed into shape primitives, it is reasonable to constrain the matching algorithm to preserve their order (see below). In the absence of any ordering information (like in stereo matching of many small fragments of curves), the matching algorithm may be called "spread primitive matching". In this category we find algorithms that seek isomorphism between attributed relational graphs [5,15,8], and algorithms that look for the largest set of mutually compatible matches. Here, compatibility means an agreement on the induced coordinate transformation, and a few techniques exist to find the largest set of mutually compatible matches (e.g., by constructing an association graph and searching for the maximal clique [14]).

For our purpose of matching complex outlines, it is advantageous to use the natural order of primitives and there is no need to solve the more general problem, which requires additional computational cost. Note that isomorphism of attributed relational graphs is found by different relaxation methods (sometimes called "relaxation labeling"), and they depend on successful choice of initial conditions. Scale and rotation invariance is achieved in these methods by using invariant relations, which suffer from the same drawbacks as invariant attributes (see below).

A syntactical representation of a curve is an *ordered* list of shape elements, having attributes like length, orientation, bending angle etc. Hence, many syntactical matching methods are inspired by efficient and well known string comparison algorithms, which use edit operations (substitution, deletion and insertion) to transform one string to the other [26, 18, 12]. The pattern recognition problem is different from the string matching problem in two major aspects, however: first, in pattern recognition invariance to certain geometrical transformations is desired; second, a resolution degradation (or smoothing) may create a completely different list of elements in the syntactical representation.

There are no syntactic algorithms available which satisfactorily solve both of these problems. If invariant attributes are used, the first problem is immediately addressed, but then the resolution problem either remains unsolved [1, 11, 16] or it is addressed by constructing for each curve a cascade of representations at different scales [24]. Moreover, invariant attributes are either non-local (e.g., length that is measured in units of the total curve length), or they are non-interruptible (see discussion in section 2.5). Using variant attributes is less efficient, but provides the possibility to define a merge operator which can handle noise [19, 22, 23], and might be useful (if correctly defined) in handling resolution change. However, the methods using variant attributes could not ensure rotation and scale invariance.

In this paper we present a local method which can cope both with occlusion and with image similarity transformations, and yet uses variant attributes that make it possible to cope with true scale (resolution) changes. The algorithm is presented in section 2. We are primarily concerned with the amount of flexibility that our method achieves, since we aim to apply it to weakly similar curves. Section 3 shows extensive experiments with real images, where excellent matching is obtained between weakly similar shapes. We demonstrate silhouette matching under partial occlusion, under substantial change of viewpoint, and even when the occluding contours describe different (but related) objects, like two different cars or mammals. Our method is efficient and fast, taking only a few seconds to match two curves.

2 The proposed method

The occluding contours of objects are extracted in a pre-processing stage. In the examples shown below, objects appear on a dark background, and segmentation is done using a standard clustering algorithm. The occluding contour is then approximated automatically by a polygon whose vertices are either points of extreme curvature, or points which are added to refine the approximation.

The polygon is our syntactic representation: the primitives are line segments, and the attributes are length and absolute orientation. The number of segments depends on the chosen scale and the shape of the contour, but typically is around 50. Coarser scale descriptions may be obtained using merge operators.

Our algorithm uses a variant of the edit algorithm, dynamic programming and heuristic search. We define a novel similarity measure between primitives, a novel merge operation, and introduce a penalty for interrupting a contour (in addition to the regular deletion/insertion penalty). The result is an algorithm that is robust, invariant under scaling and rigid transformations, suitable for partial matching, and fast.

2.1 Similarity between primitives

The similarity between two line segments is a function of their orientation and length attributes (θ, ℓ) and (θ', ℓ') respectively. Since global rotation and scale are arbitrary, the similarity between the segments cannot be determined independently, and at least one other pair of segments is needed for meaningful comparison. We pick two reference segments, (θ_0, ℓ_0) and (θ_0', ℓ_0'), which define the reference rotation $\theta_0 - \theta_0'$ and reference scale ℓ_0/ℓ_0'. The similarity between (θ, ℓ) and (θ', ℓ') is determined with respect to these reference segments.

Local and scale-invariant matching methods usually replace ℓ by the normalized length ℓ/ℓ_0, defining the scale similarity function as $S_\ell(\ell/\ell_0, \ell'/\ell_0')$. For example, the ratio between normalized lengths $\frac{\ell/\ell_0}{\ell'/\ell_0'}$ is used in [16, 15] (with global normalization the difference $|\ell/L - \ell'/L'|$ can be used [24, 22]). The ratio between normalized lengths may be viewed as the ratio between the relative scale $c = \ell/\ell'$ and the reference relative scale $c_0 = \ell_0/\ell_0'$.

We define a different measure of similarity between the two scales. Instead of dividing c by c_0, we map each scale factor to a direction in the (ℓ, ℓ')-plane, and we measure the angle between the two directions. The cosine of twice this angle is our measure of scale similarity (figure 1). This measure is numerically stable. It is not sensitive to small scale changes, nor does it diverge when c_0 is small. It is measured in intrinsic units between -1 and 1, in contrast with the scale ratio which is not bounded. The measure is symmetric, so that the labeling of the contours as "first" and "second" is arbitrary.

Let δ be the angle between the vectors $[\ell, \ell']$ and $[\ell_0, \ell_0']$. Our scale similarity measure can be expressed as:

$$S_\ell(\ell, \ell' | \ell_0, \ell_0') = \cos 2\delta = \frac{4cc_0 + (c^2 - 1)(c_0^2 - 1)}{(c^2 + 1)(c_0^2 + 1)} \tag{1}$$

The factor of 2 in the cosine argument simplifies the expression, lets it take values in the whole $[-1, 1]$ range (since $0 < \delta < \pi/2$), and reduces the sensitivity at the extreme cases (similar or unsimilar scales). S_ℓ thus depends explicitly on the scale values c and c_0 rather than on their ratio, hence it cannot be computed from the invariant attributes ℓ/ℓ_0 and ℓ'/ℓ_0'. The arbitrariness of labeling can be readily verified, since $S_\ell(c, c_0) = S_\ell(c^{-1}, c_0^{-1})$. Note that this property is not shared by the quantity $|c - c_0|$, which is not a good measure also because it depends explicitly on ℓ_0 and ℓ_0' rather than on their ratio.

We are familiar with only one other definition of a symmetric, bounded and scale invariant measure for segment length similarity [15]. The matching algorithm there is not syntactic and very different from ours. In addition, there is

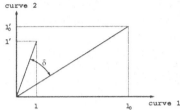

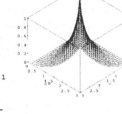 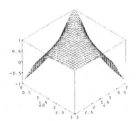

Fig. 1. Length similarity is measured by comparing the reference relative scale $c_0 = \ell_0/\ell_0'$ with the current relative scale $c = \ell/\ell'$. Each scale is mapped to a direction in the plane, and similarity is defined as $\cos(2\delta)$. This value is bounded by -1 and 1.

Fig. 2. Scale similarity: the scale $c = \ell/\ell'$ is compared with the reference scale $c_0 = \ell_0/\ell_0'$. Left: The binary relation used by Li [15] to measure scale similarity is $\exp(-|log(c/c0)|/\sigma)$ with $\sigma = 0.5$. Right: Our measure function (equation 1) is not sensitive to small scale changes, since it is flat near the line $c = c_0$.

an important qualitative difference between the two definitions (see figure 2), where our measure is more suitable for flexible matching.

We turn now to the orientation similarity S_θ between two line segments whose attributes are θ and θ' respectively. The relative orientation between them is measured in the trigonometric direction (denoted $\theta \rightarrow \theta'$) and compared with the reference rotation ($\theta_0 \rightarrow \theta_0'$):

$$S_\theta(\theta, \theta'|\theta_0, \theta_0') = \cos\left[(\theta \rightarrow \theta') - (\theta_0 \rightarrow \theta_0')\right]$$

As with the scale similarity measure, the use of the cosine introduces nonlinearity; we are not interested in fine similarity measurement when the two segments are close to being parallel or anti parallel. Our matching algorithm is designed to be flexible, in order to match curves that are only weakly similar; hence we want to encourage segment matching even if there is a small discrepancy between their orientations. Similarly, the degree of dissimilarity between two nearly opposite directions should not depend too much on the exact angle between them. On the other hand, the point of transition from acute to obtuse angle between the two orientations seems to have a significant effect on the degree of similarity, and therefore the derivative of S_θ is maximal when the line segments are perpendicular.

We note that a similar *linear* measure has been widely used by others [22, 23, 16, 8]. The non linear measure used by [15] differs from ours in exactly the same way as discussed above concerning length.

Finally, the combined similarity measure is defined as the weighted sum:

$$S = w_1 S_\ell + S_\theta$$

The weight w_1 (which equals 1 in all our experiments) controls the decoupling of scale and orientation similarity. In [19] a coupled measure is used: the segments are superimposed at one end, and their dissimilarity is proportional to the distance between their other ends. However, this measure is too complicated for our case, and it has the additional drawback that it is sensitive to the arbitrary reference scale and orientation (in the character recognition task of [19] it is assumed that characters are in the same scale and properly aligned).

2.2 Syntactic operations: gaps and merges

The goal of a classical string edit algorithm is to find a sequence of elementary edit operations, which transform one string into the other at a minimal cost. The elementary operations are substitution, deletion and insertion. Converting the algorithm to the domain of pattern recognition, substitution is interpreted as matching two shape primitives, and the symbol substitution cost is replaced by the dissimilarity between matched primitives. In our scheme we use a similarity function (instead of dissimilarity) and maximize the transformation gain (instead of minimizing cost). The similarity measure was discussed in the previous section. We now discuss the insertion/deletion gain, and the novel merge operation.

Gap opening: In string matching, the null string λ serves to define deletion and insertion operations, $a \rightarrow \lambda$ and $\lambda \rightarrow a$ respectively, where a is a string of length 1. In our case, a is a line segment and λ is interpreted as a "gap element". We define, customarily, the same gain for both operations, making the insertion of a into one sequence equivalent to the deletion of it from the other. This means that either the segment a is matched with some a' on the other curve, or the other curve is interrupted and a gap element λ is inserted into it, to be matched with a.

All the syntactical shape matching algorithms that we are familiar with make use of deletions and insertions as purely local operations, like in classical string matching. That is, the cost of inserting a sequence of gaps into a contour is equal to the cost of spreading the same number of gap elements in different places along the contour. We distinguish the two cases, since the first typically arises from occlusion or partial matching, while the second arises typically from curve dissimilarity. In order to make the distinction we adopt a technique frequently used in protein sequence comparison, namely, we assign a cost to the contour interruption itself, in addition to the deletion/insertion gain.

The gain from interrupting a contour and inserting ξ connected gap elements into it (that are matched with ξ consecutive segments on the other curve) is taken to be $w_2 \cdot \xi - w_3$. That is, a gain of w_2 for every individual match with a gap element, and a penalty of w_3 for the single interruption. This pre-defined quantity competes with continuous matching of the ξ segments (by substitutions), whose gain is lower only if the matching is poor. Note that $w_2 \cdot \xi - w_3$ is scale independent, since w_2 is a constant that does not depend on the length of the segment which is matched with the gap.

In all our experiments we used $w_2 = 0.8$ and $w_3 = 8.0$. (These values were determined in an ad-hoc fashion, and not by systematic optimization tuning, which is left for future research.) These numbers make it possible to match a gap with a long sequence of segments, as required when curves are partially occluded. On the other hand, isolated gaps are discouraged due to the high interruption cost. The parameters were so chosen because this mechanism is not intended to handle noise. Noise is better handled by the merging mechanism that we describe next.

Segment merging: One advantage of using variant attributes (length and absolute orientation) is that segment merging becomes possible. We use segment merging as the syntactic homologue of curve smoothing, accomplishing noise reduction by local resolution degradation. Segment merging, if defined correctly, should simplify a contour representation by changing its scale from fine to coarse.

A similar approach was taken in [24], but their use of invariant attributes made it impossible to realize the merge operator as an operation on attributes. Specifically, there is no analytical relation between the attributes being merged to the attributes of the equivalent primitive. Instead, a cascade of alternative representations is used, each one obtained by a different Gaussian smoothing of the two dimensional curve; a primitive sequence is replaced by its "ancestor" in the scale space description[1].

Merging was defined as an operation on attributes by [22], who also applied the technique to Chinese character recognition [23]. Their algorithm suffers from some drawbacks concerning invariance and locality[2]; below we concentrate on their merging mechanism, and compare it to our own.

Assume that the two line segments characterized by (ℓ_1, θ_1) and (ℓ_2, θ_2) are to be merged into one segment (ℓ, θ). In [22] $\ell = \ell_1 + \ell_2$, and θ is the weighted average between θ_1 and θ_2, with weights $\ell_1/(\ell_1+\ell_2)$ and $\ell_2/(\ell_1+\ell_2)$, and with the necessary cyclic corrections[3]. Usually, the polygonal shape that is obtained using this simple ad-hoc merging scheme *cannot* approximate the smoothed contour very well. Satisfactory noise reduction is achieved in one of the two extreme cases: either one segment is dominant (much longer than the other one). or the two segments have similar orientation. If two or more segments having large variance are merged, the resulting curve may not bear a direct relation to the shape of the original curve (figure 3). Hence, by performing segment merging on

---

[1] The primitive elements used in [24] are convex and concave fragments, which are bounded by inflection points. The attributes are the fragment length divided by total curve length (a non-local attribute), and the accumulated tangent angle along the fragment (a non-interruptible attribute). The algorithm cannot handle occlusions or partial distortions, and massive preprocessing is required to prepare the cascade of syntactical representations for each curve, with consistent fragment hierarchy.

[2] The primitives used by [22] are line segments, the attributes are relative length (with respect to the total length) and absolute orientation (with respect to the first segment). The relative length is, of course, a non-local attribute, and in addition the algorithm uses the total number of segments, meaning that the method cannot handle occlusions. The problem of attribute variance due to a possible rotation transformation remains in fact unsolved. The authors assume that the identity of the first segments is known. They comment that if this information is missing, one may try to hypothesize an initial match by labeling the segment that is near the most salient feature as segment number one.

[3] For example, an equal weight average between 0.9π and -0.9π is π and not zero.

130

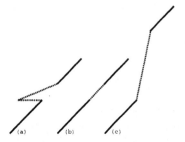

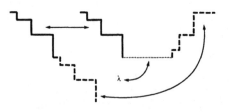

Fig. 3. Comparison between merging rules: (a) A polygonal approximation of a curve, with two dotted segments which are to be merged. (b) Merging result according to our scheme. A coarser approximation is obtained. (c) Merging according to Tsai and Yu [22]. The new polygon is not a good approximation.

Fig. 4. When the primitive attribute is measured relative to a preceding primitive, interrupting the sequence creates problems. Here, for example, the orientation information is lost when the dotted segment is matched with a gap element. As a result, the two contours may be matched almost perfectly to each other and considered as very similar.

a fine scale polygonal approximation, one typically does not obtain an acceptable coarse approximation of the shape.

We define a different merging rule: two adjacent line segments are replaced by the line connecting their two furthest endpoints. If the line segments are viewed as vectors oriented in the direction of propagation along the contour, then the merging operation of any number of segments is simply their vectorial sum.

Compare the polygonal approximation after merging with the polygon that would have been obtained if the curve was first smoothed and then approximated. The two polygons are not identical, since smoothing may cause displacement of features (vertices). However, a displaced vertex cannot be too far from a feature of the finest scale; the location error caused by "freezing" the feature points is clearly bounded by the length of the longest fragment in the initial (finest scale) representation.

To ensure good multi scaled feature matching our sub-optimal polygonal approximation is sufficient, and the expensive generation of the multi scale cascade is not necessary. Instead, the attributes of the coarse scale representation may be computed directly from the attributes of the finer scale.

2.3 The optimization algorithm

The optimization problem is constructed of two parts:

- finding the two reference segments $a_0 = (\ell_0, \theta_0)$ on contour A and $a'_0 = (\ell'_0, \theta'_0)$ on contour A'.
- finding the syntactic operations which maximize the matching gain.

The first part solves for the global alignment between the two curves, since matching the features a_0 and a'_0 uniquely determines the relative global rotation and scale of the curves. If A (A') is constructed of N (N') segments, then we assume that the optimal alignment transformation is approximated well by at least one of the $N \cdot N'$ possible selections of a_0 and a'_0.

We combine the alignment step and the matching step into one optimization problem. An optimal sequence of edit operations is found by standard dynamic programming, while at the same time a good reference pair is found by heuristic search.

Best syntactic operations: Let us assume for the moment that a reference pair of segments is given. Thus the optimal edit transformation between the sequence $\{a_0, a_1, \ldots, a_{N-1}\}$ and the sequence $\{a'_0, a'_1, \ldots, a'_{N'-1}\}$ can be found by dynamic programming. A virtual array $R_{N \times N'}$ is assigned (it is virtual since only a fraction of it really exists in memory), where the entry $R[i, j]$ holds the maximal gain that can be achieved when the first i elements of A are matched with the first j elements of A'. The updating scheme of R is "block completion", meaning that the upper left block of size $\mu \times \nu$ holds the evaluated elements, and in the next updating step the block is extended to size $(\mu + 1) \times \nu$ or to $\mu \times (\nu + 1)$. Every single entry is updated according to the following rule:

$$R[i, j] = \max\{r_1, r_2, r_3\} \tag{2}$$

where
$$r_1 = \max_{\alpha, \beta \in \Omega} \{R[\alpha, \beta] + S(\overline{\alpha i}, \overline{\beta j})\}$$

$$r_2 = \max_{0 < \alpha < i} \{R[\alpha, j] + w_2 \cdot (i - \alpha) - w_3\}$$

$$r_3 = \max_{0 < \beta < j} \{R[i, \beta] + w_2 \cdot (j - \beta) - w_3\}$$

$\overline{xy}$ denotes the vectorial sum of the segments $(x + 1), \ldots, y$.

Unlike in the "classical" editing algorithm, the term r_1 is computed over a domain Ω, generalizing the simple substitution operation to the substitution of merged segments. If $K - 1$ is the maximal number of segments that may be merged together, then

$$\Omega = \{\alpha, \beta \mid 0 < \alpha < i, \ 0 < \beta < j, \ (i - \alpha) + (j - \beta) \leq K\}$$

and the computation of r_1 involves $K(K - 1)/2$ evaluations of alternatives merges.

The single element deletion operation is generalized to the deletion of ξ consecutive elements, which is associated with an interruption penalty (w_3) and pre-insured gain ($w_2 \xi$). We keep one index (α_0) for each column j, such that $r_2 = R[\alpha_0, j] + w_2(i - \alpha_0) - w_3$. The initial value of α_0 is 1, and after entry $R[i, j]$ has been updated, the value of α_0 should be set to i if $R[i, j] - R[\alpha_0, j] \geq w_2(i - \alpha_0)$. A similar procedure applies to the computation of r_3. Hence both the computation of r_2 and r_3 have complexity $O(1)$.

Alignment of curves: The updating scheme of the virtual array $R_{N \times N'}$ is therefore completely defined, and only the last $\lfloor K/2 \rfloor$ rows and columns of R need to be stored in memory. We next show how to determine the pair of reference segments, a_0 and a'_0. A naive approach would be to try all the NN' possible selections of reference pairs (candidate alignments). One would then compute the matching gain for each candidate, and select the best result at the end. To avoid this massive computation we use two complementary strategies: heuristic search and statistical filtering.

The heuristic search is the familiar A^* algorithm, where the updating process of all the arrays R_l ($l \leq NN'$) becomes competitive. We define a potential function ("optimistic estimation") $f(R_l)$, which decreases monotonically during the update, and which gives an upper bound on R_l's score. The potential $f(R_l)$ is re-evaluated (decreased) after every block completion, which in turn is performed for the array with the largest potential. The process terminates when all the potentials are below the best score that has been already achieved, and an optimal solution is guaranteed, since $f(R_l)$ is based on optimistic estimation.

The potential $f(R)$ is defined as the maximum over entry potentials $f_{i,j}(R)$, where i (j) belongs to the last $\lfloor K/2 \rfloor$ rows (columns). The entry potential $f_{i,j}(R)$ is defined as[4]:

$$f_{i,j}(R) = R[i,j] + \epsilon(\eta - 1) + w_2(\zeta - \eta)$$
$$\eta = \min(N - i, N' - j)$$
$$\zeta = \max(N - i, N' - j)$$

and ϵ denotes the maximal segment similarity value ($\epsilon = 1 + w_1 = 2$ in our case).

While the heuristic search is only effective at the later stages, the complementary filtering strategy is effective at the initial stages. Assume that we try to match the first few (say, 10) segments in each array. Acquiring high score after an occasional (wrong) match of about 10 segments must be rare, and on the other hand the number of feasible starting points is of the order of $\min(N, N')$. Hence, the majority of the arrays which are associated with high potentials (after few updeting steps) will agree on the same global transformation (rotation and scale). As a result, we can rely on the high potential arrays for a reliable estimation of these global parameters.

Our statistical filtering strategy is therefore the following: we perform 10 updating steps for all the arrays, without evaluating their potentials. Then we look for central tendency among the rotations associated with the "best" arrays, and if such tendency is found - we eliminate all the arrays that are associated with a very different rotation angle.

2.4 Outliers removal

Since wrong matches are unavoidable, we use two different techniques for outliers detection. The first one is iterative elimination: in every iteration the matched

---

[4] Here we assume the worst case scenario, where $[i,j]$ is in a gap. Hence it is possible to increase the gain by extending the gap first, leaving space for a diagonal path of length $\eta - 1$ (the longest diagonal path from $[i,j]$ to the edge of R). We also assume that $w_3 > (w_2 - \epsilon/2)\min(N, N')$, otherwise the pre-insured gain is always higher than any other gain. In our case, since $\epsilon = 2$, this relation holds for $w_2 < 1$ and any value of N and N'.

pairs that are most distant are eliminated, and the rest are re-aligned. We chose to eliminate 10% of the pairs at every iteration. The motivation is the following: features are matched when the local pieces of curve around them have similar shape; if after alignment they are also proximal, meaning that they agree with the global alignment, then the match is likely to be correct.

Another pruning technique can be used when three related images are available (and not only two). Assume that a feature point p on contour 1 is matched with the point p' on contour 2, and p' is matched with p'' on contour 3. If the matching between 1 and 3 supports the mapping between p and p'', then the involved correspondences $(p - p', p' - p'', p - p'')$ are accepted. Note that the order of matching is arbitrary.

2.5 Discussion and comparison to other methods

Available syntactic matching methods usually achieve scale and rotation invariance (if at all) by using invariant attributes. The drawback is that invariant attributes cannot be smoothed by merging, and they are either non local or non interruptible. For example, in [16] the orientation of a line segment is measured with respect to its successor, hence the opening of a gap between segments introduces ambiguity into the representation (see figure 4). In [11] the attributes which describe curve fragments are Fourier coefficients, in [1] it is a measure called "sphericity". Both are invariant attributes, but non-interruptible[5].

Moreover, it seems to be impossible to find operators on invariant attributes that are equivalent to smoothing in real space. Instead, a cascade of different scale representations must be used [24], where few fragments may be replaced by a single one which is their "ancestor" in a scale space description. This requires massive preprocessing, building a cascade of syntactical representations for each curve with consistent fragment hierarchy.

The benefit of using invariant attributes is efficiency. Yet our algorithm is invariant with respect to scaling, rotation and translation without relying on invariant attributes, and is still efficient, capable of comparing complex real image curves in a few seconds. Furthermore, a novel merging operation was defined, which accomplished curve simplification and helped in noise reduction and resolution change.

---

[5] The Fourier coefficients are normalized individually, which means that if every fragment undergoes a different rigid or scaling transformation, the representation remains unchanged. The sphericity representation behaves in the same way. The relative size and orientation information is preserved as long as the sequence is not interrupted, since overlapping fragments are used. Note that in spite of this property the algorithms are applied to partial matching in the framework of model based recognition, since the solution that preserves the correct relative size and orientation information between primitives remains a valid solution, and the danger of finding an undesired solution (as is demonstrated in figure 4) is small.

Fig. 5. Qualitative matching between toy models of a horse and a wolf. Note the correct correspondence between the feet of the wolf to those of the horse, and the correspondence between the tails. The results are shown without outliers pruning. In this example, all the features to which no number is attached had been merged; e.g. the segment 9-10 on the horse outline was matched with 3 segments on the wolf outline.

3 Results

In Section 3.1 we present a few image pairs and triplets together with the matching results. This is a direct evaluation of the algorithm, using a highly subjective notion of success (as there is no "correct" way to match weakly similar curves). In Section 3.2 we present an indirect objective examination using the matching of a few thousands image pairs.

3.1 Subjective investigation

Figure 5 shows two images of different objects. There is geometrical similarity between the two silhouettes, which has nothing to do with the semantic similarity between them. The geometrical similarity includes five approximately vertical swellings or lumps (which describe the four legs and the tail). In other words, there are many places where the two contours may be considered locally similar. This local similarity is captured by our matching algorithm.

The two occluding contours of the two mammals and the feature points were automatically extracted in the pre-processing stage. Corresponding points are marked in figure 5 by the same numbers. Hence the tails and feet are nicely matched, although the two shapes are only weakly similar. The same matching result is obtained under arbitrarily large rotation and scaling of one image relative to the other.

Figure 6 demonstrates the local nature of our algorithm, namely, that partial matching can be found when objects are occluded. Since our method does not require global image normalization, the difference in length between the silhouette outlines does not impede the essentially perfect matching of the common parts. Moreover, the common parts are not identical (note the distance between the front legs and the number of ears) due to a small difference in viewpoint; this also does not impede the performance of our algorithm.

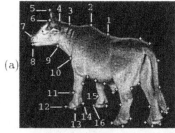

(a)

(b)

(c)

Fig. 6. Partial matching between three images. Points are mapped from (a) to (b) to (c) and back to (a). Only points which are mapped back to themselves are accepted (order is not important). The points on the tail in (a) are matched with the shadow (pointed by the arrow) in (b) , but matching (b) with (c) leaves the shadow unmatched. Hence the tail is not matched back to itself, and the correspondence with the shadow is rejected.

Figure 6 also demonstrates outliers pruning using three images. In image 6b there is a shadow between two of the leaves (pointed by the arrow), and as a result the outline penetrates inward. The feature points along the penetration are (mistakenly) matched with features along the tail in image 6a, since the two parts are locally very similar. However, we map the points of 6a to 6b, then to 6c and back to 6a. Only points which are mapped back to themselves are accepted as correct matches, which appear as common numbers in figure 6.

Figures 7 and 9 show the application of the algorithm to match images taken from very different points of view of different rigid objects. In figure 7 two different views of the same object are matched, and the method of iterative elimination of distances is demonstrated. Figure 9 shows matching between three different cars, subjected to both different orientations and to occlusion. Matching under a large viewpoint perturbation can be successful as long as the silhouettes remain similar enough. Note that preservation of shape under change of viewpoint is a quality that defines "canonical" or "stable" views. Stable images of 3D objects were proposed as the representative images in an appearance based approach to object representation [27].

The last example (figure 8) shows matching of human limbs at different body configurations.

We note again that all these examples were generated with the same values of parameters: $w_1 = 1$, $w_2 = 0.8$, $w_3 = 8.0$ and $K = 4$ (with the exception of figure 9, where $K = 5$). Each pairing assignment took only a few seconds (see next section).

3.2 Objective investigation

The test presented in this section is based on automatic matching of thousands of contours. The task was the partitioning of 90 images into hierarchical clus-

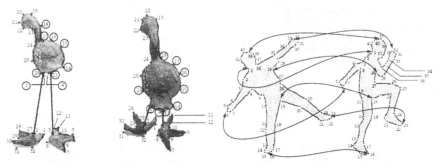

Fig. 7. Matching two views subjected to a large forthshortening effect. Rejected pairs (in circles) were detected in four iterations of eliminating the (10%) most distant pairs and re-aligning the others. 33 and 35 features were extracted on the two outlines; 32 pairs were initially matched, and 9 pairs were rejected (28%).

Fig. 8. Matching of human limbs at different body configurations. In this case the outlines were extracted with snakes rather than by gray level clustering (see acknowledgments). Original images are not shown.

ters. These were 90 images of 6 different objects (toy models of a cow, wolf, hippopotamus, two different cars, and a child). Each object contributed 15 images, taken from different points of view (in a sector range of 40° azimuth and 20° elevation).

The outlines were automatically extracted, and every two different contours were matched. The task involves matching 4005 image pairs, which took 6.5 hours on an INDY R4400 175Mhz workstation (5.8 seconds per match, on average).

Based on the matching results, a dissimilarity value was assigned to every pair of images, yielding a 90×90 dissimilarity matrix. It is beyond our scope here to describe in details how this value is defined. For our purpose it is sufficient to say that the dissimilarity value is computed from the residual distances between matched features. Hence, correct feature pairing is essential to achieve reliable dissimilarity estimation.

The dissimilarity matrix constituted the input to a newly developed clustering algorithm [6]. The algorithm has an additional scale parameter (called "temperature") which defines the level of specification. When this parameter is varied, the dendrogram shown in figure 10 is obtained. In the final level of classification (the lowest level in the hierarchy), the 90 images are grouped precisely according to their identity. Even the very similar car images are correctly separated at this level. More interesting is the hierarchical structure, which reflects our intuition regarding families of objects.

This kind of database structuring could not have emerged without the reliable estimation of the dissimilarities between weakly similar images. Hence the classification tree is an indirect and objective evidence to the quality of our matching method.

Fig. 9. Combination of various challenges: different models, different views and partial matching. The merging utility is used to overcome the different number of feature points around the wheels; the gap insertion utility is used to ignore the large irrelevant part.

4 Conclusions

This paper is concerned with a problem that is inherently ill posed, the matching of weakly similar curves. A simple heuristic was used, guided by the principle that matched features should lie on locally similar pieces of curve. Naturally, this principle cannot guarantee that results would agree with our own human intuition for "good" matching in specific examples, but our examples demonstrate that satisfactory and intuitive results are typically obtained. Note that "successful" matching depends on the application that the matching is used for. Our method is not suitable for recovering depth from stereo, but it is well suited for more qualitative tasks, such as the organization of image database, the selection of prototypical shapes, and image morphing for graphics or animation.

In order to achieve large flexibility we introduced a non linear measure of similarity between line segments, which was not sensitive to either very small or very large differences in their scale and orientation. Our specific choice of segment similarity, combined with a novel merging mechanism and an improved interruption operation, added up to a powerful and successful algorithm.

We demonstrated excellent results, matching similar curves under partial occlusion, matching similar curves where the curves depict the occluding contours of objects observed from different viewpoints, and matching different but related curves (like the silhouettes of different mammals or cars). Furthermore, we used the method to compare a range of curves, some of them very different, others rather similar. We then used the results to classify the data with an automatic hierarchical clustering algorithm, getting excellent results which faithfully captured the real structure in the data. This serves as indirect evidence to the quality of our matching algorithm.

138

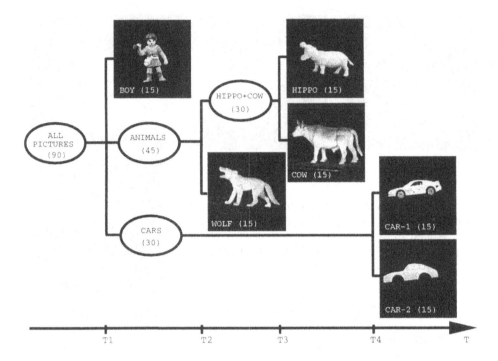

Fig. 10. The classification tree (dendrogram) obtained by hierarchical clustering algorithm, using the pairwise dissimilarity matrix of 90 images of 6 objects. The temperature axis (unscaled) determines the level of specification. At T1 three groups are identified, separating the pictures of the boy, animals and cars. At T2 and T3 the animal group is segmented into three sub groups, corresponding to the pictures of cow, wolf and hippo. Finally, at T4 the car group is segmented into two sub-groups, each containing images of a different car. The numerical values of the transitions are: T1=0.018, T2=0.029, T3=0.037 and T4=0.078. The final automatic classification is 100% correct, and the hierarchy reflects the true structure of the database.

Acknowledgments

We thank Marcello Blatt from the Weizmann institute for the clustering work, and Golan Yona from the Hebrew University for the discussions. Tyng-Luh Liu and Davi Geiger from New-York University are acknowledged for the data used to generate figure 8. This research is partialy founded by the Israeli ministry of science.

References

1. Ansari N., Delp E., "Partial shape recognition: a landmark based approach", PAMI 12, 470-489, 1990.
2. Arkin E., Paul Chew L., Huttenlocher D., Kedem K. and Mitchel J., "An efficiently computable metric for comparing polygonal shapes", PAMI 13, 209-216, 1991.

3. Ayach N. and Faugeras O., "HYPER: a new approach for the recognition and positioning of two dimensional objects", PAMI 8, 44-54, 1986.
4. Basri R., Costa L., Geiger D. and Jacobs D., "Determining the similarity of deformable shapes" *IEEE Workshop on Physics Based Modeling in Computer Vision*, 135-143, 1995.
5. Bhanu B. and Faugeras O., "Shape matching of two dimensional objects", PAMI 6, 137-155, 1984.
6. Blatt M., Wiseman S. and Domany E., "Data Clustering Using a Model Granular Magnet", Neural Computation 9, 1805-1842, 1997.
7. Brint A. and Brady M., "Stereo matching of curves", *Image and vision computing* 8, 50-56, 1990.
8. Christmas W., Kittler J. and Petrou M., "Structural matching in computer vision using probabilistic relaxation", PAMI 17, 749-764, 1995.
9. Del Bimbo A. and Pala P., "Visual image retrieval by elastic matching of user sketches", PAMI 19, 121-132, 1997.
10. Geiger D., Gupta A., Costa L. and Vlontzos J., "Dynamic programming for detecting, tracking and matching deformable contours", PAMI 17, 294-302, 1995.
11. Gorman J., Mitchell O. and Kuhl F., "Partial shape recognition using Dynamic programming", PAMI 10, 257-266, 1988.
12. Gregor J. and Thomason M., "Dynamic programming alignment of sequences representing cyclic patterns", PAMI 15, 129-135, 1993.
13. Huttenlocher D. and Ullman S., "Object recognition using alignment", Proc. ICCV (London), 102-111, 1987.
14. Koch M. and Kashyap R., "Using polygons to recognize and locate partially occluded objects", PAMI 9, 483-494, 1987.
15. Li S., "Matching: invariant to translations, rotations and scale changes", *Pattern Recognition* 25, 583-594, 1992.
16. Liu H. and Srinath M., "Partial shape classification using contour matching in distance transformation", PAMI 12, 1072-1079, 1990.
17. Lu C. and Dunham J., "Shape matching using polygon approximation and dynamic alignment", PRL 14, 945-949, 1993.
18. Marzal A. and Vidal E., "Computation of normalized edit distance and applications", PAMI 15, 926-932, 1993.
19. Rocha J. and Pavlidis T. "A shape analysis model with applications to a character recognition system", PAMI 16, 393-404, 1994.
20. Sclaroff S. and Pentland A., "Modal matching for correspondence and recognition", PAMI 17, 545-561, 1995.
21. Shapiro L. and Brady M., "Feature based correspondence: an eigenvector approach", *Image and vision computing* 10, 283-288, 1992.
22. Tsai W. and Yu S., "Attributed string matching with merging for shape recognition", PAMI 7, 453-462, 1985.
23. Tsay Y. and Tsai W., "Attributed string matching by split and merge for on-line chinese character recognition", PAMI 15, 180-185, 1993.
24. Ueda N. and Suzuki S., "Learning visual models from shape contours using multiscale covex/concave structure matching", PAMI 15, 337-352, 1993.
25. Umeyama S., "Parameterized point pattern matching and its application to recognition of object families", PAMI 15, 136-144, 1993.
26. Wang Y. and Pavlidis T., "Optimal correspondence of string subsequences", PAMI 12, 1080-1086, 1990.
27. Weinshall D. and Werman M., "On View Likelihood and Stability", PAMI 19, 97-108, 1997.

Holistic Matching

Andrew D. J. Cross and Edwin R. Hancock

Department of Computer Science
University of York
York, Y01 5DD, UK
email: erh,adjc@minster.york.ac.uk

Abstract. This paper describes a new approach to extracting affine structure from 2D point-sets. The novel feature is to unify the tasks of estimating transformation geometry and identifying point-correspondence matches. Unification is realised by constructing a mixture model over the bi-partite graph representing the correspondence match and by effecting optimisation using the EM algorithm. According to our EM framework the probabilities of structural correspondence gate contributions to the expected likelihood function used to estimate maximum likelihood affine parameters. This provides a means of rejecting structural outliers. We evaluate the technique on the matching of different affine views of 3.5in floppy discs. We provide a sensitivity study based on synthetic data.

1 Introduction

The estimation of transformational geometry is key to many problems of computer vision and robotics [11, 12]. Broadly speaking the aim is to recover a matrix representation of the transformation between image and world co-ordinate systems. In order to estimate the matrix requires a set of correspondence matches between features in the two co-ordinate systems [13]. Posed in this way there is a basic chicken-and-egg problem. Before good correspondences can be estimated, there need to be reasonable bounds on the transformational geometry. Yet this geometry is, after all, the ultimate goal of computation. This problem is usually overcome by invoking constraints to bootstrap the estimation of feasible correspondence matches [6, 9]. One of the most popular ideas is to use the epipolar constraint to prune the space of potential correspondences [6].

The aim in this paper is to develop a synergistic or holistic framework for matching. Specifically, we aim to facilitate feedback between the two problems of estimating transformational geometry and locating correspondence matches. We realise this goal using an architecture that is reminiscent of the hierarchical mixture of experts algorithm [7]. The key idea is to use a bi-partite graph to represent the current configuration of correspondence match. This graphical structure provides an architecture that can be used to gate contributions to the likelihood function for the geometric parameters using structural constraints. Correspondence matches and transformation parameters are estimated by applying the EM algorithm to the gated likelihood function. In this way we arrive at dual maximisation steps. Maximum likelihood parameters are found by minimising the structurally gated squared error residuals between features in the two images being matched. Correspondence matches are updated so as to maximise the *a posteriori* probability of the observed structural configuration on the bi-partite association graph.

It is important to stress that the idea of using a graphical model to provide structural constraints on parameter estimation is a task of generic importance. Although the EM algorithm has been used to extract affine and Euclidean parameters from point-sets [15, 5] or line-sets [10], there has been no attempt to impose structural constraints of the correspondence matches. Viewed from the perspective of graphical template matching [1, 8] our EM algorithm allows an explicit deformational model to be imposed on a set of feature points. Since the method delivers statistical estimates for both the transformation parameters and their associated covariance matrix it offers significant advantages in terms of its adaptive capabilities.

We provide a practical illustration for several matching tasks. These examples include the matching of images of floppy discs. Here we illustrate that the technique degrades gracefully even when there is severe perspective foreshortening. The second example focusses on aerial images where there is significant barrel distortion.

2 Affine Transformation of Point Sets

Our goal is to recover the parameters of a geometric transformation $\Phi^{(n)}$ that best maps a set of image feature points $\mathbf{w}$ onto their counterparts in a model $\mathbf{z}$. In order to do this, we represent each point in the image data set by an augmented position vector $\mathbf{w}_i = (x_i, y_i, 1)^T$ where i is the point index. This augmented vector represents the two-dimensional point position in a homogeneous coordinate system. We will assume that all these points lie on a single plane in the image. In the interests of brevity we will denote the entire set of image points by $\mathbf{w} = \{\mathbf{w}_i, \forall i \in \mathcal{D}\}$ where $\mathcal{D}$ is the point set. The corresponding fiducial points constituting the model are similarly represented by $\mathbf{z} = \{\mathbf{z}_j, \forall j \in \mathcal{M}\}$ where $\mathcal{M}$ denotes the index-set for the model feature-points $\mathbf{z}_j$.

In this paper we are interested in affine transformations. The affine transformation has six free parameters. These model the two components of translation of the origin on the image plane, the overall rotation of the co-ordinate system, the overall scale together with the two parameters of shear. These parameters can be combined succinctly into an augmented matrix that takes the form

$$\Phi^{(n)} = \begin{pmatrix} \phi_{1,1}^{(n)} & \phi_{1,2}^{(n)} & \phi_{1,3}^{(n)} \\ \phi_{2,1}^{(n)} & \phi_{2,2}^{(n)} & \phi_{2,3}^{(n)} \\ 0 & 0 & 1 \end{pmatrix} \tag{1}$$

With this representation, the affine tranformation of co-ordinates is computed using the following matrix multiplication

$$z_j^{(n)} = \Phi^{(n)} z_j \qquad (2)$$

Clearly, the result of this multiplication gives us a vector of the form $z_j^{(n)} = (x, y, 1)^T$. The superscript n indicates that the parameters are taken from the nth iteration of our algorithm. Our goal is to recover the elements $\phi_{i,j}^{(n)}$ of the parameter matrix $\Phi^{(n)}$, which describes a coordinate system transformation that will best bring the set image points $\mathbf{w}$ into registration with the model set $\mathbf{z}$.

Since the affine transformation can be represented in a linear fashion, the parameter recovery process is easily realised by matrix inversion. To be fully constrained, the recovery process requires three image points that are known to be in correspondence. There are several ways in which the correspondences may be established. One of the most popular is to use the epipolar constraint to search for candidate matches prior to parameter recovery. If more than three such points are available, then the parameter recovery process is over-constrained, and can be realised by least-squares fitting. If reliable correspondences are not available, then a robust fitting method must be employed. This involves removing rogue correspondences through outlier reject. A concrete example is furnished by the recent work of Torr [13].

In this paper we adopt a somewhat different approach to the affine recovery problem. We take the view that the available correspondences are at best uncertain and may contain a substantial proportion of errors. However, rather than rejecting those correspondences which give rise to a large affine registration error, we attempt to iteratively correct them. In a nutshell, our idea is to alternate between estimating affine parameters and refining correspondence matches. The framework for this study is furnished by a variant of the EM algorithm. Specifically, we use a gating process similar to that of Jordan and Jacob's [7] hierarchical mixture of experts architecture to control contributions to the log-likelihood function for the affine parameters.

The gating layer represents the state of correspondence match between the point-sets. Rather than using epipolar constraints to gauge consistency, we use constraints provided by the spatial proximity of the points. These constraints are elicited by separately triangulating the data and model points. The proximity constraints provided by the correspondences between two edges weight the contributions to the log-likelihood function. In the next Section we describe how the relational consistency of the correspondence match can be modelled in a probabilistic manner.

3 Relational Graph Matching

One of our goals in this paper is to exploit structural constraints to improve the recovery of transformation parameters from sets of feature points. We abstract the process as bi-partite graph matching. Because of its well documented robustness to noise and change of viewpoint, we adopt the Delaunay triangulation as our basic representation of image structure [14, 4]. We establish Delaunay triangulations on the data and the model, by seeding Voronoi tessellations from the feature-points.

The process of Delaunay triangulation generates relational graphs from the two sets of point-features. More formally, the point-sets are the nodes of a data graph $G_D = \{\mathcal{D}, E_D\}$ and a model graph $G_M = \{\mathcal{M}, E_M\}$. Here $E_D \subseteq \mathcal{D} \times \mathcal{D}$ and $E_M \subseteq \mathcal{M} \times \mathcal{M}$ are the edge-sets of the data and model graphs. Key to our matching process is the idea of using the edge-structure of Delaunay graphs to constrain the correspondence matches between the two point-sets. This correspondence matching is denoted by the function $f : \mathcal{M} \to \mathcal{D}$ from the nodes of the data-graph to those of the model graph. According to this notation the statement $f^{(n)}(i) = j$ indicates that there is a match between the node $i \in \mathcal{D}$ of the model-graph to the node $j \in \mathcal{M}$ of the data-graph at iteration n of the algorithm. We use the binary indicator

$$s_{i,j}^{(n)} = \begin{cases} 1 & \text{if } f^{(n)}(i) = j \\ 0 & \text{otherwise} \end{cases} \tag{3}$$

to represent the configuration of correspondence matches.

3.1 Relational Consistency

We exploit the structure of the Delaunay graphs to compute the consistency of match using the Bayesian framework for relational graph-matching recently reported by Wilson and Hancock [16]. Details are beyond the scope of this paper. Suffice to say that consistency of a configuration of matches residing on the neighbourhood $R_i = i \cup \{k \; ; \; (i,k) \in E_D\}$ of the node i in the data-graph and its counterpart $S_j = j \cup \{l \; ; \; (j,l) \in E_m\}$ for the node j in the model-graph is gauged by Hamming distance. The Hamming distance $H(i,j)$ counts the number of matches on the data-graph neighbourhood R_i that are inconsistently matched onto the model-graph neighbourhood S_j. According to Wilson and Hancock [16] the structural probability for the correspondence match $f(i) = j$ at iteration n of the algorithm is given by

$$\zeta_{i,j}^{(n)} = \frac{\exp\left[-\beta H(i,j)\right]}{\sum_{j \in \mathcal{M}} \exp\left[-\beta H(i,j)\right]} \tag{4}$$

In the above expression, the Hamming distance is given by

$$H(i,j) = \sum_{(k,l) \in R_i \bullet S_j} (1 - s_{k,l}^{(n)}) \tag{5}$$

where the symbol $\bullet$ denotes the composition of the data-graph relation R_i and the model-graph relation S_j. The exponential constant $\beta = \ln \frac{1-P_e}{P_e}$ is related to the uniform probability of structural matching errors P_e. This probability is set to reflect the overlap of the two point-sets. In the work reported here we set $P_e = \frac{2\|\mathcal{M}\| - |\mathcal{D}\|}{\|\mathcal{M}\| + |\mathcal{D}\|}$.

4 The Holistic Matching Algorithm

Our aim is to extract affine pose parameters and correspondences matches from the two point-sets using the EM algorithm. When couched probabilistically, the goal can be succinctly stated as that of jointly maximising the data-likelihood $p(\mathbf{w}|\mathbf{z}, f, \Phi)$ over the space of correspondence matches f and the matrix of affine parameters Φ. We realise this process using a dual-step or hierarchical version of the EM algorithm. According to the original work of Dempster *et al* [3] the expected likelihood function is computed by weighting the current log-probability density by the *a posteriori* measurement probabilities computed from the preceding maximum likelihood parameters. Here we wish to exploit Jordan and Jacobs [7] idea of augmenting the maximum likelihood process with a graphical model. From an architectural standpoint, the graphical model can be regarded as a supervisor network which effectively gates contributions to the expected log-likelihood function. The novelty of the work reported here is to develop a variant of this idea in which it is the bi-partite graph, i.e. f, which gates the likelihood function for the affine parameters Φ. This graph represent the current state of correspondence match between the two point-sets.

We extract both maximum likelihood perspective parameters and maximum *a posteriori* matching probabilities by applying coupled update operations to the gated likelihood function. In this way the consistency of the structural matching process can guide the pose recovery process. Likewise error probabilities derived from the position residuals are used to guide the correspondence matching process. When the joint likelihood function is maximised in this way, when the correspondence matches play the role of missing data.

In the spirit of Dempster, Laird and Rubin's EM algorithm [3], we aim to condition the updated parameter estimates (i.e. $\Phi^{(n+1)}$) on the most recently available correspondence matches (i.e. $f^{(n)}$). In other words, the maximum-likelihood parameters satisfy the following condition

$$\Phi^{(n+1)} = \arg\max_{\Phi} p(\Phi|\mathbf{w}, f^{(n)}) \qquad (6)$$

In a similar way, the *maximum a posteriori* matches are conditioned upon the most recently available parameter-estimates. The matching configuration therefore satisfies the following condition

$$f^{(n+1)} = \arg\max_{f} P(f|\mathbf{w}, \Phi^{(n)}) \qquad (7)$$

4.1 The gated likelihood function

We have recently shown how coupled updates of this form can be realised through the optimisation of single integrated expected likelihood function. Details of the formal development are outside the scope of this paper and can found in the recent account of Cross and Hancock [2]. Suffice to say that the parameters and the correspondence matches may be sought through joint optimisation of the quantity

$$Q(\Phi^{(n+1)}|\Phi^{(n)}) = \sum_{(i,j)\in f^{(n)}} P(z_j|w_i,\Phi^{(n)})\zeta_{i,j}^{(n)} \ln p(w_i|z_j,\Phi^{(n+1)}) \qquad (8)$$

The structure of this expected log-likelihood function requires further comment. The measurement densities $p(w_i|z_j,\Phi^{(n+1)})$ model the distribution of error-residuals between the observed model-point position w_i and the predicted position of the model point z_j under the current set of transformation parameter $\Phi^{(n+1)}$. The log-likelihood contributions at iteration $n+1$ are weighted by the *a posteriori* measurement probabilities $P(z_j|w_i,\Phi^{(n)})$ computed at the previous iteration n of the algorithm. Following Jordan and Jacobs [7] we gate the individual expected-likelihood contributions using the the structural matching probabilities $\zeta_{i,j}^{(n)}$. Finally, the summation extends over the set of correspondence matches $(i,j) \in f^{(n)}$ available at iteration n.

Using the Bayes rule, we can re-write the *a posteriori* measurement probabilities in terms of the of the conditional measurement densities

$$P(z_j|w_i,\Phi^{(n)}) = \frac{\alpha_j^{(n)} p(w_i|z_j,\Phi^{(n)})}{\sum_{j'\in\mathcal{M}} \alpha_{j'}^{(n)} p(w_i|z_{j'},\Phi^{(n)})} \qquad (9)$$

The mixing proportions $\alpha_j^{(n)}$ are computed by averaging the *a posteriori* probabilities over the set of data-points, i.e.

$$\alpha_j^{(n+1)} = \frac{1}{|\mathcal{D}|} \sum_{i\in\mathcal{D}} P(z_j|w_i,\Phi^{(n)}) \qquad (10)$$

In order to proceed with the development of a point registration process we require a model for the conditional measurement densities, i.e. $p(w_i|z_j,\Phi^{(n)})$. Here we assume that the required model can be specified in terms of a multivariate Gaussian distribution. The random variables appearing in these distributions are the error residuals for the position predictions of the jth model point delivered by the current estimated transformation parameters. Accordingly we write

$$p(w_i|z_j,\Phi^{(n)}) = \frac{1}{(2\pi)^{\frac{3}{2}}\sqrt{|\Sigma|}} \exp\left[-\frac{1}{2}\epsilon_{i,j}(\Phi^{(n)})^T \Sigma^{-1} \epsilon_{i,j}(\Phi^{(n)})\right] \qquad (11)$$

In the above expression Σ is the variance-covariance matrix for the vector of error-residuals $\epsilon_{i,j}(\Phi^{(n)}) = w_i - z_j^{(n)}$ between the components of the predicted measurement vectors $z_j^{(n)}$ and their counterparts in the data, i.e. w_i. Formally, the matrix is related to the expectation of the outer-product of the error-residuals i.e. $\Sigma = E[\epsilon_{i,j}(\Phi^{(n)})\epsilon_{i,j}(\Phi^{(n)})^T]$. With these ingredients, the expectation step of the EM algorithm simply reduces to computing the weighted squared error criterion

$$Q'(\Phi^{(n+1)}|\Phi^{(n)}) = \sum_{(i,j)\in f^{(n)}} P(z_j|w_i,\Phi^{(n)})\zeta_{i,j}^{(n)}\epsilon_{i,j}(\Phi^{(n+1)})^T \Sigma^{-1}\epsilon_{i,j}(\Phi^{(n+1)})$$

$$(12)$$

In other words, the *a posteriori* probabilities $P(z_j|w_i, \Phi^{(n)})$ and the structural matching probabilities $\zeta_{i,j}^{(n)}$ effectively regulate the contributions to the likelihood function. Matches for which there is little evidence contribute insignificantly, while those which are in good registration dominate.

4.2 Maximisation

As pointed out earlier, the maximisation step of our holistic matching algorithm is based on dual coupled update processes. The first of these aims to locate maximum *a posteriori* probability correspondence matches. The second update operation is concerned with locating maximum likelihood perspective parameters. We effect the coupling by allowing information flow between the two processes.

Maximum *a posteriori* probability matches: Point correspondences are sought so as to maximise the *a posteriori* probability of structural match. Individual point-correspondences should be updated in the following manner

$$f^{(n+1)}(i) = \arg\max_{j \in \mathcal{M}} P(z_j|w_i, \Phi^{(n)})\zeta_{i,j}^{(n)} \tag{13}$$

Once this update equation has been applied, the unmatched model-graph nodes are identified for removal from the triangulation. At this point the edited set of model feature-points is re-triangulated to correct potential structural errors. We provide more detials of this graph-editing process in Section 4.2.3. A full account of the method can be found in the recent paper of Wilson and Hancock [16]. The updated structural matching probabilities $\zeta_{i,j}^{(n+1)}$ are also updated using equations (4) and (5) as outlined in Section 3.

Maximum likelihood parameters: In the case of affine geometry, the transformation is linear in the parameters. This allows us to locate the maximum-likelihood parameters directly by solving the following system of saddle-point equations for the independent affine parameters $\phi_{k,l}^{(n+1)}$ running over the indices $k = 1, 2$ and $l = 1, 2, 3$

$$\frac{\partial Q'(\Phi^{(n+1)}|\Phi^{(n)})}{\partial \phi_{k,l}^{(n+1)}} = 0 \tag{14}$$

For the affine transformation the set of saddle-point equations is linear, and are hence easily solved by using matrix inversion. It is a straightforward to show that the updated matrix of affine parameters must satisfy the following implied system of linear equations

$$\sum_{(i,j) \in f^{(n)}} P(z_j|w_i, \Phi^{(n)})\zeta_{i,j}^{(n)} \left[(w_i - \Phi^{(n+1)} z_j)^T \Sigma^{-1} \right] z_j U = 0 \tag{15}$$

where the elements of the matrix U are the partial derivatives of the affine transformation matrix with respect to the individual parameters, i.e.

$$U = \begin{pmatrix} 1 & 1 & 1 \\ 1 & 1 & 1 \\ 0 & 0 & 0 \end{pmatrix} \tag{16}$$

As a result the updated solution matrix is given by

$$\Phi^{(n+1)} = \left[\sum_{(i,j) \in f^{(n)}} P(z_j | w_i, \Phi^{(n)}) \zeta_{i,j}^{(n)} z_j \ U^T \ z_j^T \ \Sigma^{-1} \right]^{-1}$$

$$\times \left[\sum_{(i,j) \in f^{(n)}} P(z_j | w_i, \Phi^{(n)}) \zeta_{i,j}^{(n)} w_i \ U^T \ z_j^T \ \Sigma^{-1} \right] \tag{17}$$

This allows us to recover a set of improved transformation parameters at iteration $n + 1$. Once these are computed, the *a posteriori* measurement probabilities may be updated by applying the Bayes formula to the measurement density function. The update procedure involves substituting the parameter matrix of equation (1) into the Gaussian density of equation (11) and applying the Bayes theorem.

Updating the triangulation: Once we have an estimate of the transformation parameters for iteration n, we can use these to project the model point set z onto the data point set w using the recovered transformational geometry as outlined in section 2. Our Delaunay graph structures are completely invariant to translations, uniform scalings and rotations. They are in addition robust to the effects of non-uniform scaling, shear and perspective foreshortening. However under severe deformations their structures do become perturbed. In order to overcome this source of potential structural corruption, at the end of each iteration we re-triangulate the graph in order to accurately reflect the structure of the points under the current estimate of the transformation parameters.

In addition to this structural modification, we can improve the robustness of parameter estimation by removing points in the model-set which have no correspondence in the data-set when computing the expected log-likelihood function in the expectation step of the EM algorithm. Once these points are removed we must once again re-triangulate the point set in order to reflect the change in structure. At each iteration of the maximisation stage, we also try re-introducing any deleted points back into the data set.

5   Results

In this section, we will provide experimental evaluation of our new coupled matching process. This investigation has two distinct directions. Firstly, we will experimentally compare our algorithm with some commonly used alternatives.

In particular we will compare our scheme with standard least squares parameter recovery. We will also make comparison with a purely structural correspondence matching scheme. This first pair of comparisons serve to demonstrate that the combined modeling of both point correspondences and transformation geometry yields significant advantages in terms of accuracy of convergence over their individual use. In other words, there are tangible advantages to our holistic approach. In the second part of the experimental investigation we will furnish examples showing the use of the holistic scheme on real world imagery. Here we will use two different data sets. The first of these involves perspective views of 3.5 inch floppy discs. The second example involves matching distorted aerial image data against a digital map.

5.1   Algorithm Comparison

The aim of this section is to demonstrate how the holistic matching algorithm performs in comparison with other, similar, schemes reported in the literature. The principal modes of comparison will be with

- **Standard Least Squares Fitting:** The aim of this investigation is to demonstrate that the structural component of the model can make a significant impact on the robust recovery of affine parameters. In this section we will demonstrate how, by making no other modifications to the standard expectation-maximisation scheme, other than weighting the contributions of the different feature-points according by their structural consistency, we can recover the parameters in a robust manner. This performance advantage persists right down to the limits imposed by the number of degrees of freedom of the projective transformation.
- **Standard Structural Matching:** In this set of experiments we aim to demonstrate how our EM methodology performs in comparison with standard structural matching [16]. Viewed from an alternative perspective, our EM approach can equivalently be seen as a natural way of weighting standard structural matching schemes using a model of the point set transformation. When viewed in this way, it is clearly important to investigate the role played by the explicit modeling of the transformational geometry.

The results of the comparative study have been obtained using random point sets. This allows us to compare algorithm sensitivity in a controlled manner under varying noise conditions. This experimental methodology also allows the results to be averaged over a large number of runs, and meaningful error bars to be derived from the whole population of trials. In each of the following experiments, 100 trials where made for each point on the graph. The reported error-bars are the standard errors over the set of trials.

Comparison With Least Squares Fitting Algorithms: Our aim in this experiment is to design a test that meaningfully demonstrates the overall effect of the structural component upon the recovery of affine projection parameters.

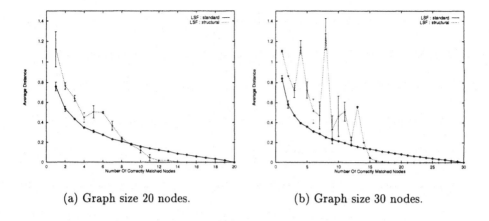

(a) Graph size 20 nodes.   (b) Graph size 30 nodes.

Fig. 1. Comparing the holistic matching scheme with a least squares approach.

With this aim in mind, we have taken random point sets and used these as the model graphs in our experiments. We generate data-graphs by deleting a controlled number of points and re-inserting random new ones into the original model graphs. The fraction of modified points is taken as a measure of structural corruption. As a measure of success we have used average, unweighted, distance between point correspondences. This figure of merit includes only points that have a direct correspondence match. In other words, we exclude nodes deleted from the graphs in the re-triangulation step.

Figure 1a shows a comparison of the holistic matching scheme and the standard, unweighted, least squares method of affine parameter estimation. Here we show the average registered point-distance as a function of the fraction of correct correspondence matches. It is clear from this plot that the structural component plays a significant role in reducing the effect of outliers on the converged image registration. Even when only 10 of the 20 nodes are correctly matched, then the structural approach successfully recovers solutions that have an average point error of less than 0.01 with an insignificant standard-error. Figure 1b repeats this experiment but for point sets with 30 nodes. Once again, we note that even when the fraction of outliers is as high as 50%, then our holistic scheme manages to recover solutions with a much smaller average residual point-distance.

Comparison With Standard Structural Matching: In order to demonstrate the relative stability of the holistic matching scheme we will compare it with a structural graph matching scheme. The algorithm used in this comparison is essentially the discrete relaxation process of Wilson and Hancock [16]. This structural matching technique results solely from the iteration of the MAP update process defined in equation (13), leaving the parameter estimates static. The aim of our study is to demonstrate the sensitivity of our method to isotropic

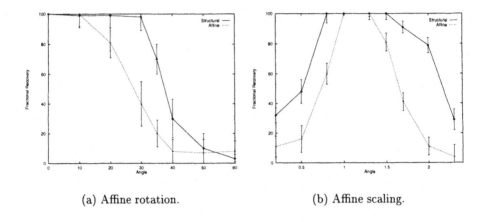

(a) Affine rotation. (b) Affine scaling.

Fig. 2. Sensitivity study.

image scale and rotation about the axis normal to the image plane. We will again base our study on large samples of random dot patterns.

The results of these sensitivity comparisons for rotation and scale are shown in Figure 2a and 2b respectively. In these figures, the x-axis shows the initial rotation (Figure 2a) or scale (Figure 2b) difference between the images being matched. The y axis, on the other hand, represents the fractional number of nodes correctly matched upon convergence. The dotted lines show the sensitivity of the standard structural matching scheme, while the solid lines are for the holistic matching method. It is clear that our holistic expectation-maximisation approach performs better than the standard relational matching scheme. In particular, the range of both rotation and scale over which the EM scheme successfully recovers meaningful results is significantly greater than that for the purely structural scheme. For instance, our method copes well with angle differences of up to 35 degrees, whereas the structural method must be initialised to within 10 degrees. In the case of the scale difference, the holistic method copes with differences in the range 0.7 to 1.6, whereas the the MAP scheme only functions effectively over the range 0.9 to 1.1. However, it must be stressed that the structural method can be rendered considerably more robust if affine invariant measures are used to compute the initial *a posteriori* matching probabilities.

5.2 Real World Imagery

In order to demonstrate the effectiveness of the new matching process on real world imagery we will consider the following two data-sets:

- **Disk Set:** This data set consists of a set of digital photographs of 3.5 inch floppy disks. This data-set was chosen since it allows for controlled shifts in viewpoint to be made. Both small viewpoint shifts that are nearly affine, and very large shifts where the controlled introduction of strong perspective foreshortening will be investigated. Experiments with this data are aimed at evaluating how our matching method degrades when the geometric transformation departs from the assumed affine model.

- **Road Network:** In this experiment we are concerned with the registration of aerial infra-red images against a digital map. The images were taken at night-time and the most prominent features are those that radiate absorbed heat. In the urban scenes under study these features are the tarmac roads. We therefore chose the road networks as the basis for our graph structures. The nodes in our graphs are junctions detected in the road network. It is important to note that these images are distorted due to the geometry of the line-scan process. The images are captured using horizontal line-scan as the aircraft moves in the vertical direction. The line-scan process is controlled by the rotation of a mirror. For this reason the images are subject to barrel distortion in the x-direction. In the y-direction there are also sampling irregularities due to the aircraft changing heading due to banking or turbulence.

We will first consider the task of recognising planer objects in different 3D poses, which is posed by the set of images of floppy disks. The object used in this study is placed on a desktop. The different object viewing angles are contrived so as to introduce increasing degrees of perspective foreshortening. The feature points used to triangulate the object are corners which are extracted by hand. Figure 3 shows a sequence of object-views with the triangulations of the hand segmented feature-points superimposed. The first oblique view in the sequence is taken as the object-model; the remaining object-poses are used to test the matching process.

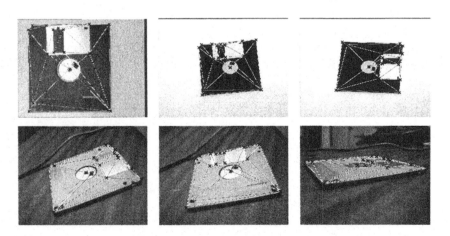

Fig. 3. The six views of used in the matching experiments.

Figure 4 shows the initial and final poses for the registration of the first and second images in the dataset. The fraction of correct initial correspondences

Fig. 4. a) An initial guess b) The final registration.

was found to be 50 percent. From the superimposed images it is clear that the recovered pose is accurate. Moreover, the ratio of the residual point registration error to the linear image dimension is 0.029.

Next, we provide an illustration of the iterative properies of our matching algorithm when one of the images under match exhibits a degree of perspective foreshortening. Clearly, in this case the affine transformation is no longer sufficient to represent the image deformation. Figure 5 shows the iterative registration for this experiment. The registration quickly converges upon a pose that is a good approximation to the full perspective transformation. In figure 6 we show the Delaunay triangulation iterating in synchronization with the image registration of figure 5. It is interesting to note the structure of the triangulation changing with iteration number. This clearly illustrates the effectivenness of the graph edit process in controlling the topology of the graph in the registration sequence.

Fig. 5. Iterative convergence using an affine transformation.

The final piece of experimentation involves the registration of a digital map against a set of aerial infra-red images. Figure 7 shows the map data together

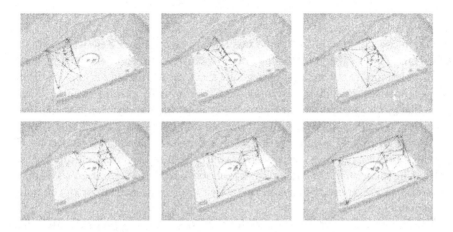

Fig. 6. The graphs iterating in synchronisation with the registration process.

Fig. 7. Aerial image registration: a) the digitial map; b) the registration with the high altitude image; c) the registration with the low altitude image.

with the raw images used in this example. The salient structure in this imagery is a road network. The feature points used in our matching experiments are junctions in the road network. These points are used to seed the Delaunay triangulation. There are three factors which complicate the matching process. Firstly, there are cartographic errors. As a result, there are features for which no correspondence exists even when the map is brought into exact registration with the images. Secondly, there is a significant amount of barrel distortion in these images. This process is not faithfully captured by our affine transformation model. Finally, the extracted Delaunay triangulations exhibit a significant degree of structural corruption. Figure 7 shows the final affine transformations of the map superimposed on the different aerial images. The matching process commences from a random initial estimate of the affine transformation matrix. It is clear that the recovered transformations are reasonably accurate given the poor geometric model.

6 Conclusions

Our main contribution in this paper has been to develop a new holistic matching algorithm. This two-step iterative process involves coupled operations to locate point-correspondences and estimate geometric transformation parameters. Point correspondences are located by maximum *a posteriori* graph-matching. Maximum likelihood parameters are recovered using the expectation-maximisation algorithm. These coupled iterative processes communicate by exchanging separate pieces of matching information. The point-correspondences passed by the matching process improve the robustness of maximum likelihood parameter estimation. In their turn, the maximum likelihood parameters are used to estimate *a posteriori* measurement probabilities which improve the accuracy of the point-correspondences.

We illustrate the effectiveness of the resulting matching process under affine geometry. This is a task of generic importance in computer vision with application in image mosaicking, pose recovery and camera calibration. Here the coupled matching process is shown to outperform structural matching. Moreover, the use of point-correspondences is shown to offer significant advantages in the control of added image noise.

In other words, we have presented a flexible matching method which unifies relational graph matching and pose-recovery. The framework is Bayesian and relies on some fairly non-restrictive assumptions concerning the Gaussian origin of measurement errors and observational independence. Our future plans revolve around the use of improved optimisation methods and more ambitious point-deformation models.

References

1. Y. Amit and A. Kong, "Graphical Templates for Model Registration", *IEEE PAMI*, **18**,, pp. 225–236, 1996.
2. A.D.J. Cross and E.R. Hancock, "Perspective Pose Recovery with a Dual Step EM Algorithm", *Advances in Neural Information Processing Systems*, **10**, Edited by M. Jordan, M. Kearns and S. Solla, MIT Press, 1998.
3. A.P. Dempster, Laird N.M. and Rubin D.B., "Maximum-likelihood from incomplete data via the EM algorithm", J. Royal Statistical Soc. Ser. B (methodological),**39**, pp 1-38, 1977.
4. O.D. Faugeras, E. Le Bras-Mehlman and J-D. Boissonnat, "Representing Stereo Data with the Delaunay Triangulation", *Artificial Intelligence*, **44**, pp. 41–87, 1990.
5. Gold S., Rangarajan A. and Mjolsness E., "Learning with pre-knowledge: Clustering with point and graph-matching distance measures", *Neural Computation*, **8**, pp. 787–804, 1996.
6. R.I. Hartley, "Projective Reconstruction and Invariants from Multiple Images", *IEEE PAMI*, **16**, pp. 1036—1041, 1994.
7. M.I. Jordan and R.A. Jacobs, "Hierarchical Mixtures of Experts and the EM Algorithm", *Neural Computation*, **6**, pp. 181-214, 1994.
8. M. Lades, J.C. Vorbruggen, J. Buhmann, J. Lange, C. von der Maalsburg, R.P. Wurtz and W.Konen, "Distortion-invariant object-recognition in a dynamic link architecture", *IEEE Transactions on Computers*, **42**, pp. 300–311, 1993

9. D.P. McReynolds and D.G. Lowe, "Rigidity Checking of 3D Point Correspondences under Perspective Projection", *IEEE PAMI*, **18** , pp. 1174–1185, 1996.
10. S. Moss and E.R. Hancock, "Registering Incomplete Radar Images with the EM Algorithm", *Image and Vision Computing*, **15**, 637–648, 1997.
11. D. Oberkampf, D.F. DeMenthon and L.S. Davis, "Iterative Pose Estimation using Coplanar Feature Points", *Computer Vision and Image Understanding*, **63**, pp. 495–511, 1996.
12. C. J. Poelman and T. Kanade, "A Para-perspective Factorization Method for Shape and Motion Recovery ", *IEEE PAMI*, **19**, 1997.
13. P. Torr, A. Zisserman and S.J. Maybank, "Robust Detection of Degenerate Configurations for the Fundamental Matrix", *Proceedings of the Fifth International Conference on Computer Vision*, pp. 1037–1042, 1995.
14. M. Tuceryan and T Chorzempa, "Relative Sensitivity of a Family of Closest Point Graphs in Computer Vision Applications", *Pattern Recognition*, **25**, pp. 361–373, 1991.
15. J. Utans, "Mixture Models and the EM Algorithms for Object Recognition within Compositional Hierarchies", *ICSI Berkeley Technical Report*, TR-93-004, 1993.
16. R.C. Wilson and E.R. Hancock, "Structural Matching by Discrete Relaxation", *IEEE PAMI*, **19**, pp. 634–648, 1997.

Creaseness from Level Set Extrinsic Curvature

Antonio M. López, Felipe Lumbreras, Joan Serrat

Computer Vision Center and Departament d'Informàtica, Campus UAB,
Edifici O, 08193–Bellaterra (Cerdanyola), Barcelona, Spain.
tel: +34 3 5812561, Fax: +34 3 5811670
antonio@cvc.uab.es

Abstract. Creases are a type of ridge/valley–like structures of a d dimensional image, characterized by local conditions. As creases tend to be at the center of anisotropic grey–level shapes, creaseness can be considered as a type of medialness. Among the several crease definitions, one of the most important is based on the extrema of the level set curvatures. In 2–d it is used the curvature of the level curves of the image landscape, however, the way it is usually computed produces a discontinuous creaseness measure. The same problem arises in 3–d with its straightforward extension and with other related creaseness measures. In this paper, we first present an alternative method of computing the level curve curvature that avoids the discontinuities. Next, we propose the Mean curvature of the level surfaces as creaseness measure of 3–d images, computed by the same method. Finally, we propose a natural extension of our first alternative method in order to enhance the creaseness measure.

Keywords: creaseness, level set curvatures, divergence, structure tensor.

1 Introduction

Ridge/valley–like structures (lines, surfaces, etc) of a d dimensional image, tend to be at the center of anisotropic grey–level objects. Therefore they are useful skeleton–like descriptors. As can be seen in [8] it is possible to characterize ridge/valley–like structures attending to the shape of the image landscape or to its hydrology, giving rise to different mathematical definitions. In the literature we can find a number of local characterizations [2]. We term here as *creases* the ridge/valley–like structures which are characterized locally. Creases have been proposed [5, 2] as a type of medial axis for grey–level objects as the skull in CT and MR images, vessels in arteriographies, roads in aerial photographs, fingerprints, etc.

One of the most useful definitions of creases, due to its invariance properties [2] and its relationship with the shape descriptor called Intensity Axis of Symmetry [5], is the one that is based on the level set curvatures. Given a function $L : \mathbf{R}^d \to \mathbf{R}$, a level set consists of the points $S_g = \{\mathbf{x}/L(\mathbf{x}) = g\}$. Different values of g give a sequence of sets S_g which are the level sets of L. For $d = 2$ the graph of L can be thought as a landscape. Then, the level sets are the level curves that appear in cartographic maps. In this case, creases are defined through the level curve curvature κ. Negative minima of κ along the level curve tangent direction $\mathbf{v}$, level by level, are valley–like curves and positive maxima are ridge–like curves. We refer here to this type of ridge–like and valley–like curves as *vertex curves*. They can be characterized by the local test

$$e = \nabla\kappa \cdot \mathbf{v} = 0 \qquad (1)$$

where $\nabla e \cdot \mathbf{v} < 0$ and $\kappa > 0$ means ridge–like and $\nabla e \cdot \mathbf{v} > 0$ and $\kappa < 0$ means valley–like (Fig. 1).

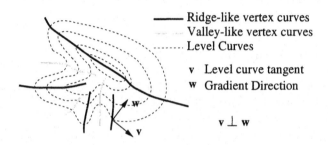

Ridge-like vertex curves
Valley-like vertex curves
Level Curves

$\mathbf{v}$ Level curve tangent
$\mathbf{w}$ Gradient Direction

$\mathbf{v} \perp \mathbf{w}$

Fig. 1. Vertex curves.

The extension of κ to 3–d is two times the Mean curvature κ_M of the level surfaces (see [13] p. 98 and [4] p. 337), which is an extrinsic differential geometric entity. Therefore, from now on we will refer to this extension for d dimensional images as the level set extrinsic curvature (LSEC) κ_d. In [2] we can find the generalization of Eq. (1) to extract r dimensional creases from d dimensional images, by the analysis of the principal curvatures of the level sets.

The computation of (1) or its generalization involves up to fourth order derivatives and the evaluation of complex expressions [5,2,10,14]. However, in many cases, as for elongated structures in 2–d and 3–d images, and plate–like structures in 3–d images, the extrema of curvature are so high that we can circumvent the problem by computing κ or κ_M as a creaseness measure and then applying a thresholding. In some applications the creaseness measure itself is sufficient (e.g. as feature for registration of CT/MR brain images [3]). The computation of these creaseness measures needs just up to second order derivatives and their equations are computationally much more cheaper than expressions derived from (1).

In this paper we propose the level curve curvature κ in 2–d, the Mean curvature of the level surfaces κ_M in 3–d and, in general, LSEC κ_d as creaseness measures. The level curve curvature has been already proposed as a creaseness measure. However, the traditional way of computing κ [3,9] gives raise to two problems. Firstly, it produces an extremely large dynamic range of values, but having only a few points with curvature at the upper and lower bounds, which we will call *outliers*. This makes creaseness to differ from medialness since these outliers are not 'more in the center' than other points with a high, but not outlier, creaseness value. Secondly it produces a discontinuous measure: gaps appear at places where we don't expect any reduction of creaseness for being at the center of some grey–level object.

In Sect. 2 we analyze the problems of computing LSEC by the traditional formula. In Sect. 3 we propose an alternative method to overcome them. In Sect. 4 we go a step further and propose a technique to enhance LSEC creaseness by incorporating the structure tensor analysis in the creaseness measure. As far as we know, it is the first time this technique is employed to compute a creaseness measure. In Sect. 5 we address the main computational aspects. In Sect. 6 we compare the output of our operators with existing creaseness measures. Finally, Sect. 7 summarizes the main conclusions.

2 LSEC Based on the Image Scalar Field

For $L : \mathbf{R}^d \to \mathbf{R}$ running on $\{x^1, ..., x^d\}$ coordinates, κ generalizes to κ_d according to tensorial calculus as (see [13] p. 98 and [4] p. 337):

$$\kappa_d = (L_\alpha L_\beta L_{\alpha\beta} - L_\alpha L_\alpha L_{\beta\beta})(L_\gamma L_\gamma)^{-\frac{3}{2}}, \quad \alpha, \beta, \gamma \in \{x^1, ..., x^d\} \tag{2}$$

where $L_\alpha = \partial L / \partial \alpha$, $L_{\alpha\beta} = \partial^2 L / \partial \alpha \partial \beta$ and the Einstein summation convention is used. Then, for $d = 2$ and using Cartesian coordinates we obtain the level curve curvature as:

$$\kappa = (2L_x L_y L_{xy} - L_y^2 L_{xx} - L_x^2 L_{yy})(L_x^2 + L_y^2)^{-\frac{3}{2}} \tag{3}$$

and for $d = 3$, two times the Mean curvature of the level surfaces:

$$2\kappa_{\mathrm{M}} = \Big(2(L_x L_y L_{xy} + L_x L_z L_{xz} + L_y L_z L_{yz}) - L_x^2(L_{yy} + L_{zz}) \\ -L_y^2(L_{xx} + L_{zz}) - L_z^2(L_{xx} + L_{yy}) \Big)(L_x^2 + L_y^2 + L_z^2)^{-\frac{3}{2}} \tag{4}$$

In 2—d, if we travel along the center of anisotropic structures we go up and down on the relief, passing through maxima, saddles and minima (e.g. Fig. 6(a)). We have found that computation of κ according to Eq. (3), produces gaps and outliers (Fig. 2) on the creaseness measure around this type of critical points (Fig. 3(c)), as well as on the center of elongated grey–level objects having a short dynamic range along it. We have checked [7] that this happens independently of the scheme of discretizing derivatives and even when the gradient magnitude $L_{\mathbf{w}} = (L_\gamma L_\gamma)^{1/2}$, for $\mathbf{w} = (L_{x^1}, ..., L_{x^d})^t$ being the gradient vector, is far away from the zero of the machine, this is, at pixels where Eq. (3) is well–defined. For example, in the case of ridge–like saddle points, as those in Fig. 6(a), κ not only goes down but also suffers from a 'change of sign barrier' on the path of the expected ridge–like curve (Fig. 6(c)). The reason is that the neighborhood of the saddle point is composed mainly of concave zones ($\kappa < 0$) but the sub–pixel ridge–like curve runs through convex zones ($\kappa > 0$) that discretization of Eq. (3) is not able to detect.

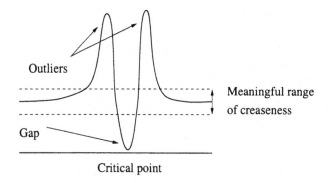

Fig. 2. Profile of κ along a crease which has a critical point on 'its way'.

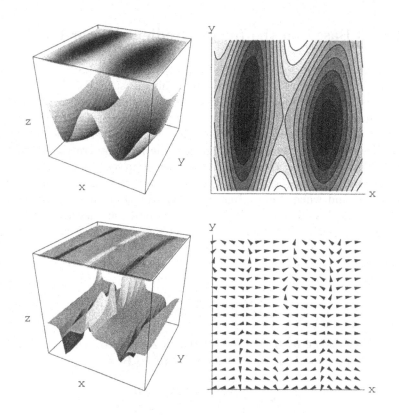

Fig. 3. From top to bottom and left to right: (a) Relief with two valley–like regions and a ridge–like one. (b) Relief's level curves. (c) κ. (d) Normalized gradient vector field.

Notice that gaps can not be distinguished locally from points that actually have low creaseness. This affects the use of the creaseness measure itself and the extraction of creases by thresholding the creaseness, since *crease finders* have to decide heuristically how to follow when they reach those discontinuities. To solve the problem of outliers we can use the cut–off transform

$$T(I(\mathbf{x}), g) = \begin{cases} g \text{ if } I(\mathbf{x}) > g \\ -g \text{ if } I(\mathbf{x}) < -g \\ I(\mathbf{x}) \quad \text{Otherwise} \end{cases} \tag{5}$$

for an experimentally given $g > 0$. If g is high we do not see clearly the creaseness measure, if g is low we get a thick response.

The 3-d operator κ_{M} computed according to Eq. (4) has analogous problems to κ in 2-d, as well as other more expensive 3-d creaseness measures as the ridgeness measure $L_{\mathbf{pp}}$ (second directional derivative of L along the direction $\mathbf{p}$ that minimizes the normal curvature of the level surfaces) or the valleyness measure $L_{\mathbf{qq}}$ (in this case $\mathbf{q}$ maximizes the normal curvature) [3,9].

3 LSEC Based on the Image Gradient Vector Field

To avoid the discretization problems of Eq. (2) when using LSEC as creaseness, we present an alternative way of computing this measure. For the sake of simplicity, consider the 2-d case. Equation (3) is the result of applying the implicit function theorem to a level curve defined as $L(\mathbf{x}) = g$, in order to define its local derivatives and then its curvature κ (see [13] p. 99). Another geometric relationship defines κ through the slopelines, this is, the lines integrating the gradient vector field $\mathbf{w}$, therefore, orthogonal to the level curves. Due to the orthogonality, when level curves are parallel straight lines, slopelines are also parallel and straight, and when the level curves bend, the slopelines diverge (Fig. 4). Therefore, it is clear that there is a connection between curvature of the level curves and the degree of parallelism of the slopelines. In vector calculus we have the divergence operator [12] which measures this degree of parallelism. The divergence of a d dimensional vector field $\mathbf{u} : \mathbf{R}^d \to \mathbf{R}^d, \mathbf{u}(\mathbf{x}) = (u^1(\mathbf{x}), ..., u^d(\mathbf{x}))^{\mathrm{t}}$ is defined as

$$\mathrm{div}(\mathbf{u}) = \sum_{i=1}^{d} \frac{\partial u^i}{\partial x^i} \ . \tag{6}$$

Now, if we denote by $\mathbf{0}_d$ the d dimensional zero vector, then we can define $\bar{\mathbf{w}}$, the normalized gradient vector field of $L : \mathbf{R}^d \to \mathbf{R}$, as

$$\bar{\mathbf{w}} = \begin{cases} \mathbf{w}/\|\mathbf{w}\| \text{ if } \|\mathbf{w}\| > 0 \\ \mathbf{0}_d \quad \text{ if } \|\mathbf{w}\| = 0 \end{cases} \tag{7}$$

and then it can be shown that

$$\kappa_d = -\mathrm{div}(\bar{\mathbf{w}}) \ . \tag{8}$$

Equations (2) and (8) are equivalent in the continuous. However, and this is one of the key points of this paper, the discretization of each equation gives different results, namely, Eq. (8) avoids the gaps and outliers that Eq. (2) produces on creases. Thus, from now on, for $d = 2$ we denote by κ and $\bar{\kappa}$ the discrete versions of LSEC according to Eqs. (2) and (8), respectively. Symbols $\kappa_M = \kappa_d/2$ and $\bar{\kappa}_M = \bar{\kappa}_d/2$ for $d = 3$ and κ_d and $\bar{\kappa}_d$ for $d > 3$ will be used analogously.

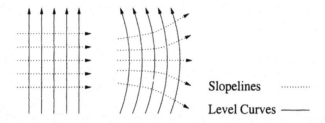

Slopelines ··········

Level Curves ———

Fig. 4. The divergence of the slopelines depends on the curvature of the level curves.

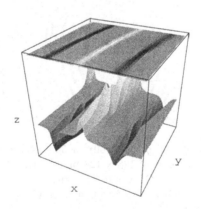

Fig. 5. $\bar{\kappa}$ computed from Fig. 3(d).

If we look at the gradient vector field $\bar{w}$ along a crease we appreciate as dominant the effect of attraction/repulsion of $\bar{w}$ even in the presence of critical points (Fig. 3(d)). This motivated us to compute[1] the level curve curvature from

---

[1] The definition of κ in terms of the divergence of $\bar{w}$ is used in other fields of computer vision as in non–linear scale–space. However this is done just to work with a compact notation, but κ is implemented by following Eq. (3) since it gives rise to a most straightforward discretization than using Eq. (8).

the normalized image gradient vector field instead of from the image scalar field L. In Fig. 5 we see the result of computing $\bar{\kappa}$. Notice how gaps are not present anymore, compared with Fig. 3(c). Furthermore, the dynamic range of $\bar{\kappa}_d$ is better than that of κ_d. Actually, it can be shown [7] that, for a d dimensional image, if we use centered finite differences to take derivatives, then the values of $\bar{\kappa}_d$ run on $[-d, d]$. The value is $-d$ at d dimensional minima and d at d dimensional maxima. The values of κ_d in the discrete case can also be bounded although having a much broader dynamic range that makes easier the existence of outliers. At Fig. 6 it is also analyzed the behavior of κ and $\bar{\kappa}$ around ridge–like saddle points in a synthetic image.

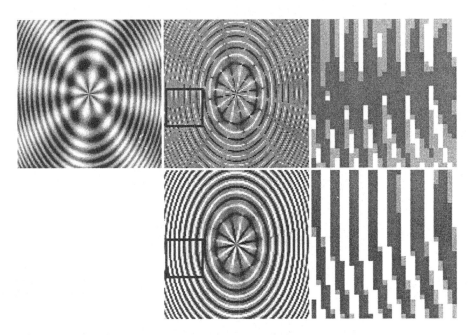

Fig. 6. From left to right: (a)$L(x, y) = \sin(60x^2 + 30y^2) + \sin(8 \arctan(y/x))$ sampled in $[-1, 1] \times [-1, 1]$ at a resolution of 128×128 pixels. **(b)** $T(\kappa, 1.0)$ with a region of interest (ROI). **(c)**. Zoom of the ROI. White lines: ridge–like creases after thresholding of κ, pixels where $\kappa > 0$ have been seted to lighter grey and $\kappa < 0$ to darker. **(d)** $\bar{\kappa}$. **(e)** Zoom of the previous ROI.

4 LSEC Based on the Image Structure Tensor Field

Once we have established $\bar{\kappa}_d$ as a good creaseness measure, we can go further and enhance it by modifying the gradient vector field of the image previously to apply the divergence operator. We want to filter the gradient vector field in such a way that the configurations of 7(a) approach those of Fig. 7(b) since

then attraction/repulsion and therefore creaseness, will be higher. At the same time, the qualitative behavior of the gradient vector field at regions where there is neither attraction nor repulsion, must remain unchanged. This filtering can be carried out in a natural way through the *structure tensor*, which is a well-known tool for analyzing oriented textures [1, 6, 11]. Moreover, without extra computational cost, we get a coarse measure of anisotropy that will allow us to attenuate the creaseness measure at zones in which we are not interested, like in flat regions.

Let's fix ideas in 2–d. To compute the dominant orientation, it is sufficient to analyze the behavior of the image gradient in a given neighborhood. We assume that, within a neighborhood of size σ_I centered at a given point $\mathbf{x}$, namely $\mathcal{N}(\mathbf{x}; \sigma_I)$, there is at most a single dominant orientation. Notice that the gradient of a function points towards the direction of maximum change, and the dominant orientation is perpendicular to this direction since anisotropy appears as similar grey values along one orientation and considerable fluctuations perpendicularly.

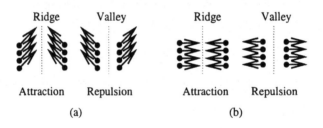

Fig. 7. Attraction and repulsion of vectors in (b) are higher than in (a).

The structure tensor is an operator represented by the following symmetric and semi-positive definite $d \times d$ matrix

$$\mathbf{M}(\mathbf{x}; \sigma_I) = \mathcal{N}(\mathbf{x}; \sigma_I) * (\mathbf{w}(\mathbf{x})^t \mathbf{w}(\mathbf{x})) \tag{9}$$

where the convolution '*' of the matrix $(\mathbf{w}(\mathbf{x})^t \mathbf{w}(\mathbf{x}))$ with the window $\mathcal{N}(\mathbf{x}; \sigma_I)$ is element–wise. A suitable choice for the window is a d dimensional Gaussian, i.e. $\mathcal{N}(\mathbf{x}; \sigma_I) = G(\mathbf{x}; \sigma_I)$. This choice implies that neighbors are weighted as a function of their distance.

The dominant gradient orientation is given by the eigenvector which corresponds to the highest eigenvalue of $\mathbf{M}$. However, we have assumed that every point has a preferred orientation. To verify this assumption we introduce a normalized confidence measure: to each orientation we associate a real value $\mathcal{C} \in [0, 1]$ which can be computed from the eigenvalues of the structure tensor. Similarity of the eigenvalues of the structure tensor implies isotropy and, as a result, $\mathcal{C}$ should be close to zero. Therefore, a logical choice consists of testing

whether the sum of quadratic differences in eigenvalues, namely

$$\lambda_\triangle(\mathbf{x};\sigma_\mathrm{I}) = \sum_{i=1}^{d} \sum_{j=i+1}^{d} (\lambda_i(\mathbf{x};\sigma_\mathrm{I}) - \lambda_j(\mathbf{x};\sigma_\mathrm{I}))^2, \tag{10}$$

exceeds a predefined threshold c characteristic for $\lambda_\triangle$ in the structure we want to enhance. A suitable function is

$$\mathcal{C}(\mathbf{x};\sigma_\mathrm{I}) = 1 - e^{-(\lambda_\triangle(\mathbf{x};\sigma_\mathrm{I}))^2/2c^2} \ . \tag{11}$$

Now we can obtain an enhanced creaseness measure by the following steps:

1. Compute the gradient vector field $\mathbf{w}$ and the tensor field $\mathbf{M}$.

2. Perform the eigenvalue analysis of $\mathbf{M}$. The normalized eigenvector $\mathbf{w}'$ corresponding to the highest eigenvalue gives the predominant gradient orientation. In the structure tensor analysis, opposite directions are equally treated. Thus, to recover the direction we put $\mathbf{w}'$ in the same quadrant in 2–d, or octant in 3–d, than $\mathbf{w}$. Then, we obtain the new vector field

$$\tilde{\mathbf{w}} = \mathrm{sign}(\mathbf{w}'^t\mathbf{w})\mathbf{w}' \tag{12}$$

where the function $\mathrm{sign}(x)$ returns $+1$ if $x > 0$, -1 if $x < 0$ and 0 if $x = 0$. In this way, attraction/repulsion of vectors is reinforced.

3. Compute the creaseness measure

$$\tilde{\kappa}_d = -\mathrm{div}(\tilde{\mathbf{w}}) \ . \tag{13}$$

4. Compute the confidence measure $\mathcal{C}$, tuning the constant c in Eq. (11) to reduce creaseness in the structures we are not interested, in order to take $\tilde{\kappa}_d\mathcal{C}$ as the final creaseness measure.

5 Computational Aspects

To obtain derivatives of a discrete image L in a well–posed manner [13, 4], we use the centered finite differences (CFDs) of a Gaussian smoothed version of the image:

$$L_\alpha(\mathbf{x};\sigma_\mathrm{D}) \approx \Delta_\alpha(L(\mathbf{x}) * G(\mathbf{x};\sigma_\mathrm{D})), \quad \alpha \in \{x^1, ..., x^d\} \tag{14}$$

where σ_D stands for the standard deviation of the Gaussian and Δ_α for the CFD along the α axis. Then, a method to calculate both κ and $\bar{\kappa}$ in 2–d, and κ_M and $\bar{\kappa}_\mathrm{M}$ in 3–d consists of computing the set of image derivatives and then applying the respective equations. In this case, $\bar{\kappa}$ and $\bar{\kappa}_\mathrm{M}$ require less memory and operations than κ and κ_M as can be seen in Table 1. However, in 3–d it is convenient to write an algorithm that scans the image voxel by voxel computing the respective expression. The reason is saving memory: by first computing all

Table 1. Number of operations at each pixel/voxel of a 2-d/3-d image. Addition and subtraction are assumed as equivalent, product and division too. The 1-d 1st order CFDs account as 1 addition plus a division and 2nd order CFDs as 3 additions and 1 division.

	κ	$\bar{\kappa}$	κ_M	$\bar{\kappa}_M$
Maximum number of images simultaneously in memory	6	5	9	7
Additions and subtractions	15	6	33	10
Products and divisions	8	4	13	6
Square roots	1	1	1	1
Divisions by a constant	5	4	9	6

the image derivatives involved in $\bar{\kappa}_M$ we need simultaneously 7 float 3-d images (see Table 1 and more details in [7]) which could mean a lot of memory. We have adopted the pixel/voxel scanning approach to minimize memory requirements and therefore disk throughput.

When running pixel/voxel by pixel/voxel computing $\bar{\kappa}$ or $\bar{\kappa}_M$ we have to buffer values to avoid the repetition of calculations [7]. In practice this makes $\bar{\kappa}$ and $\bar{\kappa}_M$ slightly more time consuming than κ and κ_M. Yet the difference is small as can be seen in Table 2. Computation of $\tilde{\kappa}_d$ consumes much more resources than κ_d and $\bar{\kappa}_d$ due to both the averaging of vectors and the eigensystem analysis.

Table 2. Time consuming in a 200 MHz Pentium Pro PC with 64MB of RAM memory under Linux OS. The swapping was needed only for the $250 \times 250 \times 180$ image. All the images are float since the operators are applied after a Gaussian smoothing, which was implemented by separable spatial convolutions but without exploiting Gaussian symmetry.

Image dimensions	Gaussian smoothing ($\sigma_D = 4.0$)	κ	$\bar{\kappa}$	$\tilde{\kappa}$ ($\sigma_I = 4.0$)
256×256	0.3 s	0.058 s	0.072 s	1.2 s
512×512	1.3 s	0.24 s	0.28 s	5.3 s
		κ_M	$\bar{\kappa}_M$	$\tilde{\kappa}_M$ ($\sigma_I = 4.0$)
$128 \times 128 \times 84$	50 s	1.8 s	2.1 s	50 s
$250 \times 250 \times 180$	360 s	23 s	23.3 s	720 s

6 Results

Results are presented within the framework that motivated our research in creaseness operators. It consists of the automatic registration of 3-d CT and MR brain volumes from the same patient as in [3]. This can be achieved by registering the surface that runs along the center of the skull from both images, which appears as a ridge–like structure in the CT image and a valley–like structure in the MR. The idea is to base the registration on a search through the space of the six 3–d rotation and translation parameters, using the correlation of the MR valleyness and the CT ridgeness to assess the goodness of each transform. Therefore we need continuous creaseness measures, with the creaseness in the skull bone enhanced.

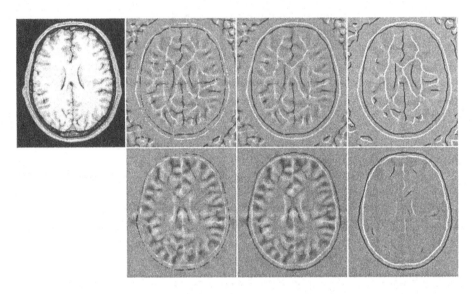

Fig. 8. From top to bottom and left to right: **(a)** 256×256 MR slice. The black fringe (valley–like structure) is the skull bone. In all cases we work with a Gaussian smoothed version of this image, for $\sigma_D = 4.0$ pixels. **(b)** $T(\kappa, 1.5)$ (see the cut-off transform T in Eq. (5)). **(c)** $\bar{\kappa}$. **(d)** $\tilde{\kappa}$ for $\sigma_I = 4.0$ pixels. **(e)** The well-known [3] operator $L_{vv} = -\kappa L_w$. **(f)** $-\bar{\kappa} L_w$. **(g)** $-\tilde{\kappa} \mathcal{C}$ for $c = 700$.

For 2–d data we obtain the results shown in Figs. 8 and 9. It is clearly distinguished that κ produces a number of gaps along the skull while $\bar{\kappa}$ and $\tilde{\kappa}$ give a continuous response. The $\tilde{\kappa}$ measure is more contrasted than $\bar{\kappa}$ and, when combined with the corresponding confidence measure $\mathcal{C}$, we can almost isolate creaseness on the skull (white response in Fig. 8(**g**) and black in 9(**g**)).

As the application is on 3–d data sets, the operators that we are actually using are $\bar{\kappa}_M$ and $\tilde{\kappa}_M$. Traditional operators such as L_{pp} and L_{qq} also have problems of continuity as can be seen in [3] at p. 386, where the authors used the same dataset. In Fig. 10 we can see the CT ridgeness and MR valleyness based on $\bar{\kappa}_M$. Notice how $\bar{\kappa}_M$ is quite continuous along the skull. However, response is also present within the brain. It is difficult to get rid of this response multiplying by the gradient magnitude L_w since we have then the same effect than in the 2–d case, this is, creaseness along the skull loss continuity as in Figs. 8(**f**) and

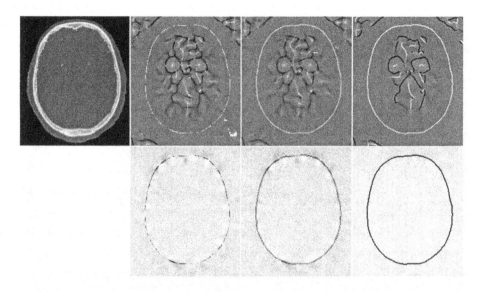

Fig. 9. From top to bottom and left to right: **(a)** 256 × 256 CT slice. The white fringe (ridge–like structure) is the skull bone. **(b)**–**(g)** have the same meaning and share the parameters of Fig. 8.

9(**f**) because along the center of the skull, the gradient magnitude is lower than in the skull boundary. In Fig. 11 we see the results based on the $\tilde{\kappa}_M$ operator multiplied by the confidence measure C. As in the 2–d case, the $\tilde{\kappa}_M$ operator itself gives a more contrasted creaseness measure as well as more homogeneous along the crease, and by its combination with C we get rid of the creaseness response in the background and within the brain.

7 Discussion

The level set extrinsic curvature (LSEC) is a creaseness measure that acts as a medialness measure for grey–level objects. In this paper, we first identified the problem of outliers and, mainly, gaps when computing this creaseness measure by classical schemes. Afterwards we have proposed an alternative method of computing LSEC that overcomes the mentioned problems. Moreover, the use of LSEC in 3–d ($\tilde{\kappa}_M$) as a creaseness measure is itself another key point of this paper since previous works went to 3–d on the basis of most computationally expensive principal curvature analysis of the level surfaces. Moreover, these measures suffer also from the problem of gaps while $\tilde{\kappa}_M$ does not. We have also proposed a new version of LSEC where the structure tensor analysis has been adapted from oriented texture analysis to enhance LSEC creaseness, which combined with the associated confidence measure gives a very clean creaseness measure along interesting objects. Results have been shown in the context of a real application,

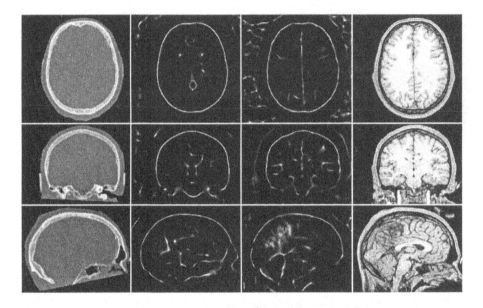

Fig. 10. Columns from left to right: **(a)** Transversal, coronal and sagital slices of a $250 \times 250 \times 180$ CT image with cubic voxels. **(b)** $\bar{\kappa}_M$ of the CT image after a Gaussian smoothing of $\sigma_D = 4.0$ voxels. **(c)** $\bar{\kappa}_M$ of the MR image at the same scale. **(d)** Same slices of a $250 \times 250 \times 180$ MR image with cubic voxels.

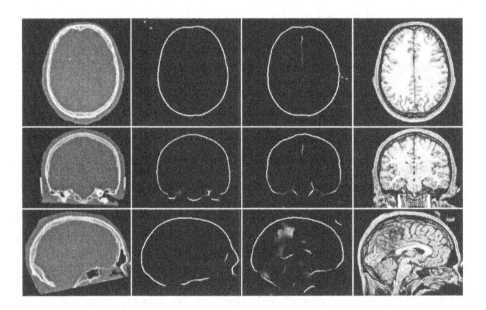

Fig. 11. All the columns have the same meaning than in Fig. 10 but showing the results of $\bar{\kappa}_M \mathcal{C}$ for $\sigma_D = \sigma_I = 4.0$ voxels and $c = 1000$.

namely, the registration of CT and MR brain volumes, where our operators have proved to give an excellent output.

Acknowledgments

This research has been partially funded by Spanish CICYT projects TIC97–1134–C02–02 and TAP96–0629–C04–03. The authors acknowledge also Dr. Petra van den Elsen from the 3D–CVG at the Utrecht University for providing us two 3-d CT and MR datasets.

References

1. J. Bigun, G. Granlund, and J. Wiklund. Multidimensional orientation estimation with applications to texture analysis and optical flow. *IEEE Trans. on Pattern Analysis and Machine Intelligence*, 13(8):775–790, 1991.
2. D. Eberly, R. Gardner, B. Morse, S. Pizer, and C. Scharlach. Ridges for image analysis. *Journal of Mathematical Imaging and Vision*, 4:353–373, 1994.
3. P. van den Elsen, J. Maintz, E-J. Pol, and M. Viergever. Automatic registration of CT and MR brain images using correlation of geometrical features. *IEEE Trans. on Medical Imaging*, 14:384–396, 1995.
4. L. Florack, B. ter Haar Romeny, J. Koenderink, and M. Viergever. Cartesian differential invariants in scale–space. *Journal of Mathematical Imaging and Vision*, 3:327–348, 1993.
5. J. Gauch and S. Pizer. Multiresolution analysis of ridges and valleys in grey–scale images. *IEEE Trans. on Pattern Analysis and Machine Intelligence*, 15:635–646, 1993.
6. B. Jahne. *Spatio–temporal image processing*, volume 751 of *Lecture Notes in Computer Science*, chapter 8, pages 143–152. Springer–Verlag, 1993.
7. A. López, F. Lumbreras, and J. Serrat. Efficient computing of local creaseness. Technical Report 15, Computer Vision Center, campus of the UAB. Spain., 1997.
8. A. López and J. Serrat. Ridge/valley–like structures: creases, separatrices and drainage patterns. Technical Report 21, Computer Vision Center, campus of the UAB. Spain., 1997.
9. J. Maintz, P. van den Elsen, and M. Viergever. Evaluation of ridge seeking operators for multimodality medical image matching. *IEEE Trans. on Pattern Analysis and Machine Intelligence*, 18:353–365, 1996.
10. O. Monga and S. Benayoun. Using partial derivatives of 3d images to extract typical surface features. *Computer Vision and Image Understanding*, 61:171–189, 1995.
11. W. Niessen, A. López, W. Van Enk, P. Van Roermund, B. ter Haar Romeny, and M. Viergever. In vivo analysis of trabecular bone architecture. In J. S. Duncan and G. Gindi, editors, *Information Processing and Medical Imaging*, volume 1230 of *Lecture Notes in Computer Science*, pages 435–440, 1997.
12. H. M. Schey. *DIV, GRAD, CURL and all that*. W. W. Norton & Company, 1973.
13. B. ter Haar Romeny and L. Florack. A multiscale geometric model of human vision. In W. Hendee and P. Well, editors, *The Perception of Visual Information*, pages 73–114. Springer–Verlag, 1993.
14. J. P. Thirion and A. Gourdon. Computing the differential characteristics of isointensity surfaces. *Computer Vision and Image Understanding*, 61:190–202, 1995.

Multichannel Shape from Shading Techniques for Moving Specular Surfaces

Günther Balschbach[1], Jochen Klinke[3], and Bernd Jähne[1,2,3]

[1] Institute for Environmental Physics, Heidelberg University
[2] Scripps Institution of Oceanography, La Jolla, CA, 92093-0230, USA
[3] Interdisciplinary Center for Scientific Computing, Heidelberg University

Abstract. This paper describes a shape from shading technique for the reconstruction of transparent moving specular surfaces such as the wind-driven wavy water surface. In contrast to classical shape from shading techniques that are based on reflection, the new technique is based on refraction. Specular surfaces require area-extended light sources in order to apply the shape from shading principle. With three or more properly arranged light sources, the surface gradient can be coded almost linearly in image irradiance ratios in order to achieve a maximum accuracy for the surface normals. This retrieval technique is also in first-order independent of the transmittance of the refracting surface. Two realizations of this system are discussed. The first system uses a color illumination scheme where the red, green, and blue channels of the light source radiance are changing linearly in different directions and a 3-CCD color camera. The second system uses a monochromatic light source with more than 16 000 LEDs and a four-way control electronic that generates four pulsed intensity wedges shortly after each other. Both systems have been used to retrieve the small-scale shape of wave-undulated water surfaces in wind/wave facilities and the ocean. This paper thus demonstrates a successful example how computer vision techniques have helped to solve a longstanding experimental problem in environmental sciences and now give an unprecedented insight into complex spatiotemporal phenomena.

1 Introduction

Shape form shading is one of the basic paradigms in computer vision for 3-D reconstruction [5]. This technique is based on the elementary interaction of surfaces with illumination. The object radiance that is perceived from an observer generally depends on the direction of the surface normal with respect to the incident rays from illumination sources and the ray reflected in the direction of the camera.

Unfortunately shape from shading techniques with a single illumination of the scene are nonlinear, ambiguous, and rather a qualitative than a quantitative technique for surface reconstruction. Deviations from the assumed bi-directional reflectance function cause significant systematic errors. Furthermore, standard shape from shading techniques cannot handle surfaces with specular reflectance.

a   b

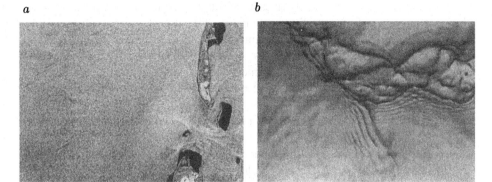

Fig. 1. a SAR image of the Dutch coast including the islands Fleeland and Terschelling taken with the SEASAT satellite. In the open ocean, ship tracks can be observed, while in the mud flats between the islands strong variations in the radar backscatter can be observed caused by strong tidal currents that are modulated by the varying water depth. Image courtesy of Dr. E. van Halsema, TNO, The Netherlands. **b** A microscale wave breaking event at 5 m/s wind speed as observed with the instrument shown in Fig. 11. The image sector is about $15 \times 20 \, \text{cm}^2$ (from [12]).

In environmental sciences, however, the surface of oceans, lakes, and rivers constitutes a surface with *purely specular* reflectance characteristics. Recently, the fine-scale structure of this surface in the millimeter to meter range undulated by wind- or flow-generated waves has received increasing interest for two reasons.

First, modern active remote sensing techniques based on microwaves (radar scatterometry) "see" these small structures [1, 17]. By various interactions between the small-scale features and larger-scale features the latter become visible in synthetic aperture radar (SAR) images [13]. As an example, Fig. 1a shows a SAR image of the Dutch coast in which ship tracks and tidal currents are visible. These processes at scales of a few meters become visible by their interaction with short wind waves with centimeter scales.

Second, short wind waves significantly influence the exchange processes between the atmosphere and the oceans. The regular wave motion may become unstable and break even on small scales without air entrainment and thus enhances the exchange, for instance, of climate relevant gases such as CO_2 significantly [15, 8]. Such an event, known as microscale wave breaking, is shown in Fig. 1b.

Thus there is a considerable interest to measure the small-scale shape of water surfaces. For almost a century, oceanographers tried to use optical techniques — mostly stereo photography — but without much success [9]. Thus this paper focuses on novel multichannel shape from shading techniques that is especially adapted to purely specular surfaces. Because of the dynamical nature of wind-driven, wavy water surfaces, techniques that retrieve the shape from a series of consecutive images are not suitable.

Multiple illuminations for surface reconstruction by shape from shading techniques (*photometric stereo*) were first considered by Woodham for industrial applications [20, 21]. Kozera [14] gives a thorough theoretical treatment of two-illumination shape from shading techniques. The use of colored illumination sources to obtain three illuminations simultaneously is discussed by [3, 22]. The extension of photmetric stereo to non-static scences is analyzed by [18]. The influence of specular reflections on photometric stereo was discussed among others by [16], but a discussion of photometric stereo techniques for *purely specular* surfaces is widely missing.

This paper first briefly reviews the principles for classical shape from shading technique based on reflectance for Lambertian surfaces in Sect. 2. Then it is discussed how multiple illuminations can be arranged to determine surface gradients in a simple way and independent of the surface reflectivity (Sect. 3). The principles worked out in these two sections are then applied to reflection-based and refraction-based techniques for purely specular surfaces in Sect. 4 and 5, respectively. Sect. 6 introduces multi-illumination setups for refraction-based techniques. The reconstruction of the height is discussed in Sect. 7 and some results are finally shown in Sect. 8.

2 Shape from Shading for Lambertian Surfaces

For the sake of simplicity, we assume that the surface is illuminated by parallel light. Then, the radiance of an Lambertian surface, L, is given by:

$$L = \frac{\rho(\lambda)}{\pi} E \cos \gamma, \tag{1}$$

where E is the irradiance and γ the angle between the surface normal and the light direction. The relation between the surface normal and the incident and exitant radiation can most easily be understood in the *gradient space*. This space is spanned by the gradient of the surface height $a(X, Y)$, s:

$$s = \nabla a = \left[\frac{\partial a}{\partial X}, \frac{\partial a}{\partial Y} \right]^T = [s_1, s_2]^T \tag{2}$$

which is related to the surface normal n by

$$n = \left[-\frac{\partial a}{\partial x}, -\frac{\partial a}{\partial Y}, 1 \right]^T = [-s_1, -s_2, 1]^T. \tag{3}$$

Without loss of generality, we set the direction of the light source as the x direction. Then, the light direction is given by the vector $l = (\tan \theta_i, 0, 1)^T$, and the radiance L of the surface can be expressed as

$$L = \frac{\rho(\lambda)}{\pi} E \frac{n^T l}{|n||l|} = \frac{\rho(\lambda)}{\pi} E \frac{-s_1 \tan \theta_i + 1}{\sqrt{1 + \tan^2 \theta_i} \sqrt{1 + s_1^2 + s_2^2}}. \tag{4}$$

The relation between the surface slope and measured radiance is nonlinear. This means that even if we take two different illuminations of the same surface, the surface slope may not be determined in a unique way.

3 Multi-Illumination Shape from Shading

As is was shown by several authors [21, 6, 11], the surface gradient and the surface reflectivity can be retrieved unambigiously when three or more images are taken from a scene with illumination from different directions. Here we will discuss the question as how to arrange the illuminiation directions in order to obtain an optimal retrieval of surface slope.

The three measured radiances L_i compose a vector $\boldsymbol{L} = [L_1, L_2, L_3]^T$. Using the unit vectors $\bar{\boldsymbol{n}} = \boldsymbol{n}/|\boldsymbol{n}|$ and $\bar{\boldsymbol{l}}_i = \boldsymbol{l}_i/|\boldsymbol{l}_i|$, the following linear equation system for the unit surface normal $\bar{\boldsymbol{n}}$ can be derived from (4):

$$\boldsymbol{L} = \rho(\lambda) E \begin{bmatrix} \bar{\boldsymbol{l}}_1^T \\ \bar{\boldsymbol{l}}_2^T \\ \bar{\boldsymbol{l}}_3^T \end{bmatrix} \bar{\boldsymbol{n}} \tag{5}$$

Generally, the solution of this equation can be given when the three illumination directions are not coplanar. We now search for special conditions to derive a simpler solution. We first observe that (4) gets a particular simple form for $l_1 = [0, 0, 1]^T$:

$$L_1 = \frac{\rho(\lambda)}{\pi} E \frac{1}{|\boldsymbol{n}|} \tag{6}$$

If we normalize the measured radiance for an arbitray illumination direction l_i by L_1 we obtain a much simpler equation

$$\frac{L_i}{L_1} = \frac{\boldsymbol{n}^T \boldsymbol{l}_i}{|\boldsymbol{l}_i|} == \boldsymbol{n}^T \bar{\boldsymbol{l}}_i. \tag{7}$$

In this equation the reflectivity of the surface is canceled out and the slope vector s is linearly related with the measured radiance. Only two equations of the type in (7) are required to determine the surface slope. The solution is particular simple if the illumination directions l_2 and l_3 are orthogonal to each other. Then we can write without loss of generality:

$$l_1 = [0, 0, 1]^T, l_2 = [\tan\theta_2, 0, 1]^T, l_3 = [0, \tan\theta_3, 1]^T. \tag{8}$$

and derive from (7)

$$s_{1,2} = \frac{L_{2,3}/L_1 \sqrt{1 + \tan^2\theta_{2,3}} - 1}{\tan\theta_{2,3}} \tag{9}$$

Now the equations are linear in s_1 and s_2 and — even better — they are decoupled: s_1 and s_2 depend only on L_2/L_1 and L_3/L_1, respectively. In conclusion we can summarize that an appropriate normalization together with orthogonal angles of azimuth for the illumination sources provides particular simple solutions for photometric stereo. We will use these principles in Sect. 6 for purely specular surfaces.

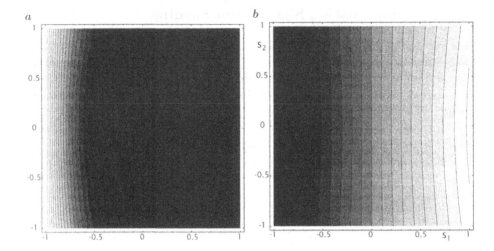

Fig. 2. Contour plots of the radiance maps for shape from ... technique with specular surfaces in gradient space: **a** Shape from reflection: camera with an incidence angle of 45° observing a scene illuminated by an infinitely extended isotropic light source. The distance between the contour lines is 0.05. **b** Shape from refraction with a telecentric illumination source whose radiance varies linearly in the x_1 direction. (From [7]).

4 Shape from Reflection for Specular Surfaces

For *specular* reflecting surfaces, point light sources or parallel illumination are not adequate for shape from shading techniques, since we would receive only individual specular reflexes. A well-known example is the *sun glitter* observed on a water surface as the direct reflection of sun light.

Thus, an area-extended diffuse light source is required. We discuss this approach under some simplified assumptions. Let us assume that we have an infinite light source with isotropic radiance. (A fully overcast sky is a good approximation to this ideal condition.) Then, the irradiance received from a specular surface depends only on the reflection coefficient ρ. The camera is inclined in order to obtain an irradiance that increases monotonically with one slope component. Then, the angle of incidence α is given as the angle between the direction of the reflected ray (towards the camera) $r = [\tan\theta_c, 0, 1]^T$ and the surface normal n (3) as

$$\alpha = \arccos(r, n) = \arccos\left(\frac{s_1 \tan\theta_c + 1}{\sqrt{1 + s_1^2 + s_2^2}\sqrt{1 + \tan^2\theta_c}}\right). \qquad (10)$$

The equation expresses the angle of incidence in terms of the camera inclination angle θ_c and the surface slope $s = [s_1, s_2]^T$. Since the radiance is assumed to be homogeneous and isotropic, the surface radiance is given by

$$L = \rho(\alpha)L_s, \tag{11}$$

where L_s and ρ are the radiance of the isotropic and homogeneous light source and the reflection coefficient as given by Fresnel's equations.

Results for unpolarized light with a camera inclination angle of $45°$ are shown in Fig. 2a and reveal the strong nonlinear relation between the surface slope and surface radiance, directly reflecting the dependence of the reflection coefficient on the inclination angle. These strong nonlinearities render this technique almost useless since only a narrow range of slopes can be measured with sufficient resolution. This technique, used for some time, is known as *Stilwell photography* in oceanography to measure the fine-scale shape of the ocean surface [19], but has had — not surprisingly — only limited success [9].

5 Shape from Refraction for Specular Surfaces

For transparent surfaces such as the water surface not only the reflection at the surface but also the *refraction* of light can be utilized for a shape from shading technique. Refraction has one significant advantage over reflection. While over a wide range of incidence angles only a small fraction of the incident light is reflected (at zero incidence only about 2 %), most light is transmitted through the water body. Thus much less intense light sources are required.

The base of the *shape from refraction* technique is a *telecentric illumination system* which converts a spatial radiance distribution into an angular radiance distribution (Fig. 3a). Then, all we have to do is to compute the relation between the surface slope and the angle of the refracted beam and to use a light source with an appropriate spatial radiance distribution.

Figure 3b illustrates the optical geometry for the simple case when the camera is placed far above and a light source below a transparent surface of a medium with a higher index of refraction. The relation between the surface slope s and the angle γ is given by [9] as

$$s = \tan\alpha = \frac{n\tan\gamma}{n - \sqrt{1 + \tan^2\gamma}} \approx 4\tan\gamma\left[1 + \frac{3}{2}\tan^2\gamma\right] \tag{12}$$

with $n = n_2/n_1$. The inverse relation is

$$\tan\gamma = s\frac{\sqrt{n^2 + (n^2 - 1)s^2} - 1}{\sqrt{n^2 + (n^2 - 1)s^2} + s^2} \approx \frac{1}{4}s\left(1 + \frac{3}{32}s^2\right). \tag{13}$$

In principle, the shape from refraction technique works for slopes up to infinity (vertical surfaces). In this limiting case, the ray to the camera grazes the surface (Fig. 3c) and

$$\tan\gamma = \sqrt{n^2 - 1}. \tag{14}$$

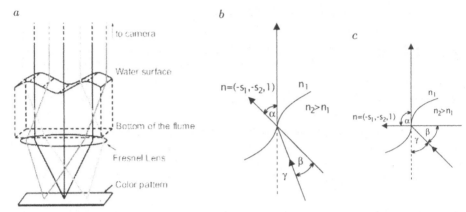

Fig. 3. a Telecentric illumination system for shape from refraction: an extended light source is located in the focal plane of a fresnel lens. **b** Rays emitted by the light source at an angle γ are refracted in the direction of the camera far above the water surface. **c** Even for a slope of infinity (vertical surface, $\alpha = 90°$), rays from the light source meet the camera.

The refraction law thus causes light rays to be inclined in a certain direction relative to the slope of the water surface. If we make the radiance of the light source dependent on the direction of the light beams, the water surface slope becomes visible. The details of the construction of such a system is described by [9]. Here we just assume that the radiance of the light rays is proportional to the $\tan \gamma$ in x_1 direction. Then we obtain the relation

$$L \propto s_1 \frac{\sqrt{n^2 + (n^2 - 1)s^2} - 1}{\sqrt{n^2 + (n^2 - 1)s^2} + s^2}. \tag{15}$$

Of course, we have again the problem that from a scalar quantity such as the radiance no vector component such as the slope can be inferred. The shape from refraction technique, however, comes very close to an ideal setup. If the radiance varies only linearly in the x_1 direction, as assumed, the radiance map in the gradient space is also almost linear (Fig. 2b). A slight influence of the cross slope (resulting from the nonlinear terms in (15) in s^2) becomes apparent only at quite high slopes.

6   Multi-Illumination Shape from Refraction

The shape form refraction technique described in the previous section with a single illumination source has been used extensively to compute wave number spectra from wave slope images [10] and is described in detail by [9]. New in this paper is the use of multiple illuminations simultaneously. Zhang and Cox [23] (see also [2]) were the first to describe a surface gradient instrument based on color imaging utilizing the HSI color space. Here we describe a simpler and

Fig. 4. Radiance of the extended light source for the shape from refraction instrument shown in Fig. 3: **a** green, **b** red, and **c** blue channel.

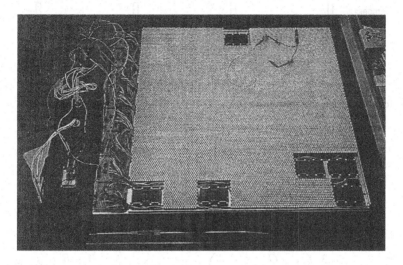

Fig. 5. Extended light source with LEDs. The diffuser screens and a few modules have been removed.

more accurate approach based on linear illumination gradients in the RGB color space based on the principles discussed in Sect. 3.

For color imaging a natural normalization is given by dividing the individual RGB image by the sum of all channels $R + G + B$. Then we are left with the hue and saturation of the color. In order to obtain a linear relation between the surface slope and the normalized colors, the RGB values must change linearly in different directions. Ideally, the luminance $R + G + B$ should not vary spatially and two wedges should be orthogonal to each other. These two conditions are met for instance with the following three color wedges (Fig. 4):

$$
\begin{aligned}
G &= (1/2 + cx_1)E_0(\boldsymbol{s}) \\
R &= [1/2 - c/2(x_1 + x_2)]E_0(\boldsymbol{s}) \\
B &= [1/2 - c/2(x_1 - x_2)]E_0(\boldsymbol{s}).
\end{aligned}
\tag{16}
$$

178

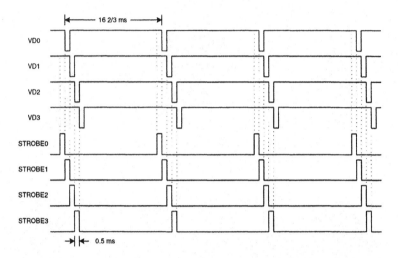

Fig. 6. Timing diagram of the vertical synchronization signals (VD) and the strobe signal for pulsed LED illumination with four shuttered CCD cameras.

The difference of the blue and red wedges yields a wedge orthogonal to the green wedge.

$$\frac{G}{R+G+B} = \frac{2}{3}\left(\frac{1}{2} + cx_1\right) \quad \text{and} \quad \frac{B-R}{R+G+B} = \frac{2}{3}cx_2. \tag{17}$$

Then the position on the wedge from which the light originates is given as

$$x_1 = \frac{3}{2c}\left(\frac{G}{G+R+B} - \frac{1}{3}\right) \quad \text{and} \quad x_2 = \frac{3}{2c}\frac{B-R}{G+R+B}. \tag{18}$$

From these position values, the x and y components of the slope can be computed using $\tan\gamma_{1,2} = x_{1,2}/f$ and (12).

An alternative to color imaging is a setup with multiple light sources of the same color. Figure 5 shows an array of more than 16 000 LEDs that can by set to four different states with different intensity patterns each. Separation between the different illuminations is then achieved by pulsing the light sources shortly after each other (timing diagram in Fig. 6). Shuttered cameras are synchronized in such a way that one camera sees only one light pulse. In this way, a quasi-simultaneous measurement with different illumination becomes possible. Such a system was used on a freely drifting buoy (Fig. 11) for ocean measurements to avoid errors caused by wavelength-dependent absorption and scattering in sea water.

7   Height Reconstruction

With the measured slope components s_x and s_y we have (at least a good approximation for) the surface gradient $s = (s_x, s_y) = \nabla h(x,y)$. We can now compute the original water height $h(x, y)$ using a simple Fourier transform technique except for an arbitrary offset [11]. The relation between height and gradient in object space and the corresponding relation in Fourier space is give by the following identities:

$$s_x(x, y) = \frac{\partial h(x, y)}{\partial x} \circ\!\!-\!\!\bullet \ \hat{s}_x(k_x, k_y) = ik_x\hat{h}(k_x, k_y) \tag{19}$$

$$\Rightarrow \ ik_x\hat{s}_x(k_x, k_y) = -k_x^2\hat{h}(k_x, k_y) \tag{20}$$

$$s_y(x, y) = \frac{\partial h(x, y)}{\partial y} \circ\!\!-\!\!\bullet \ \hat{s}_y(k_x, k_y) = ik_y\hat{h}(k_x, k_y) \tag{21}$$

$$\Rightarrow \ ik_y\hat{s}_y(k_x, k_y) = -k_y^2\hat{h}(k_x, k_y) \tag{22}$$

The two equations 20 and 22 are added and except for $k_x = k_y = 0$ divided by $-(k_x^2 + k_y^2) = -(\mid k \mid^2)$ to get

$$\hat{h}(k_x, k_y) = \frac{-i(k_x\hat{s}_x + k_y\hat{s}_y)}{\mid k \mid^2} \tag{23}$$

$$\Rightarrow h(x, y) = FT^{-1}\left(\frac{-i(k_x\hat{s}_x + k_y\hat{s}_y)}{\mid k \mid^2}\right) \tag{24}$$

Franklot [4] showed that $h(x, y)$ minimizes the error function

$$\sum_y \sum_x \left(\frac{\delta h(x, y)}{\delta x} - s_x(x, y)\right)^2 + \left(\frac{\delta h(x, y)}{\delta y} - s_y(x, y)\right)^2 \tag{25}$$

The algorithm is computed assuming a unique pixel distance in x and y direction. Therefore we first have to correct for the different spatial sampling of the image acquisition. The slope images are enlarged and mirrored in x and y direction to get periodic functions for s_x and s_y before computing the Fourier transform.

8 Results

One of the calibration techniques uses a spherical lens. Since this object shows a constant curvature, the slope components in x and y directions vary linearly in the corresponding directions. The original green, red, and blue images show considerable intensity decreases towards the edge of the calibration object (Fig. 7a–c). In the slope images, normalized using (18), this intensity drop is compensated (Fig. 7d, e).

The suppression of illumination inhomogeneities is nicely demonstrated in Fig. 8. This time, the color illumination source is directly observed through a flat water surface by removing the lens of the illumination system (Fig 3).

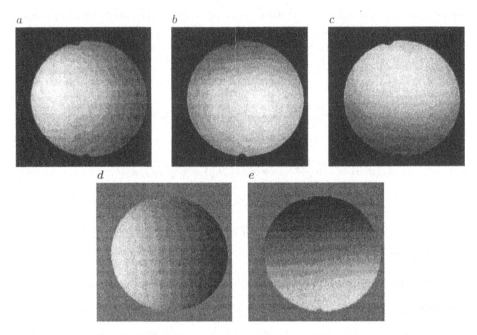

Fig. 7. Green (**a**), red **b**), and blue **c**) component of an RGB color image taken from a calibration target, a spherical lens. **d** , **e** Images showing the slope of a spherical lens in **a** x and **b** y direction retrieved from the images in Fig. 7a–c.

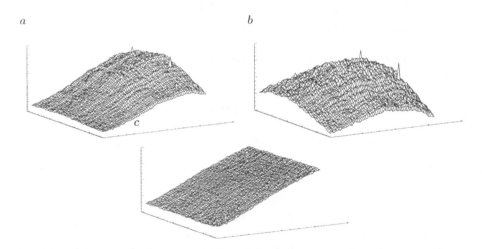

Fig. 8. Demonstration of the suppression of inhomogeneities in the luminance by the color shape from refraction technique. **a** original green component of the intensity wedge, **b** luminance of **a**, **c** normalized green component

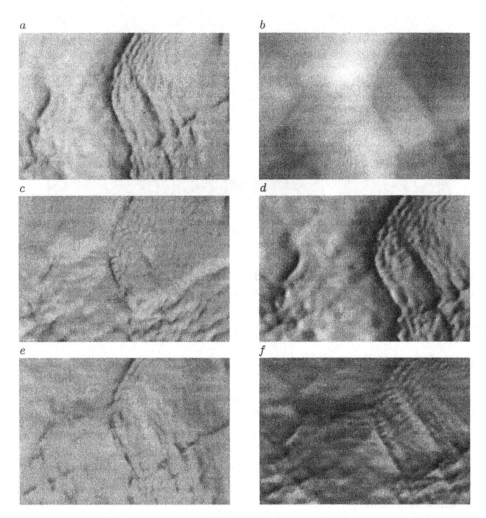

Fig. 9. **a**, **c**, and **e**, green, red, and blue component of the original color image, respectively. **b** Reconstructed height; **d** and **f** images of the slope in x and y direction, respectively.

Bubbles and dirt on the glass window at the bottom of the water channel lead to considerable small-scale spatial intensity fluctuations in the green channel (Fig. 8a). Furthermore, the intensity drop towards the edge of the illumination source makes the spatial intensity variation nonlinear and leads at the right edge even into an inversion of the direction of the spatial intensity gradient. The normalization technique according to (18) suppresses both errors and results in a linear intensity variation (Fig. 8c).

Figure 9 demonstrates the technique with real wave images taken in the circular wind/wave facility of Heidelberg University. The three components of

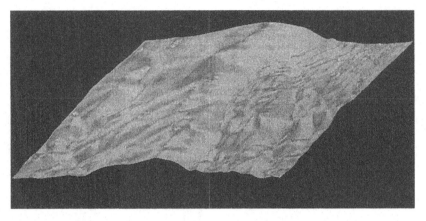

Fig. 10. Shaded plot of reconstructed water surface.

the original color image are shown in Fig. 9a, c, e. Figure 9b shows the height reconstruction using the images of the along-wind and cross-wind wave slope components (Fig. 9d, f). In Figure 10 a surface plot of the height function using a simple shading algorithm is shown.

9 Conclusions

The multiple-illumination shape from refraction techniques proved to be a useful technique to reconstruct the shape of dynamically changing, transparent and specular reflecting surfaces, such as water surfaces. Further work will concentrate on a careful error analysis, further improvement of the accuracy, measurements of very steep slopes, and field measurements with freely drifting buoys (Fig. 11).

Acknowledgments

Financial support for this research by the German Science Foundation (Deutsche Forschungsgemeinschaft, DFG) through the Forschergruppe "Bildfolgenanalyse zum Studium dynamischer Prozesse" (Jae 395/6-1) is gratefully acknowledged. Cooperation with Scripps Institution of Oceanography (SIO) and the field experiments were made possible by grants of the US National Science Foundation (Coastal Ocean Processes, CoOP) and the US Office of Naval Research (ONR) within the Marine Boundary Layer Accelerated Research Initiative (MBL/ARI).

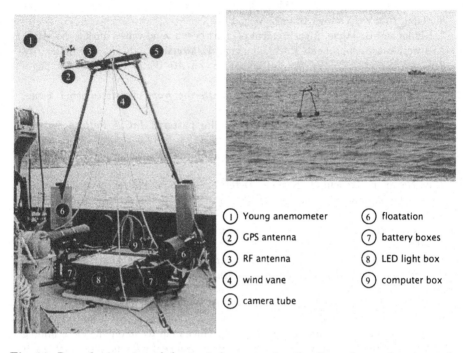

① Young anemometer   ⑥ floatation

② GPS antenna   ⑦ battery boxes

③ RF antenna   ⑧ LED light box

④ wind vane   ⑨ computer box

⑤ camera tube

Fig. 11. Buoy for imaging of short wind waves using the shape from refraction technique.

References

1. J. R. Apel. *Principles of Ocean Physics*, Academic Press, London, 1987.
2. D. Dabiri, X. Zhang, M. Gharib. Quantitative visualization of three-dimensional free surface slopes and elevations, *Altas of Visualization III*, Y. Nakayama, Y. Tanida (eds.) CRC Press, Boca Raton, 1997.
3. M. S. Drew. Robust specularity detection from a single multi-illuminant color image. *CVGIP: Image Understanding*, 59:320–327, 1994.
4. R. T. Frankot and R. Chellappa. A method for enforcing integrability in shape from shading algorithms, *IEEE Trans. on Patt. Anal. and Mach. Int. PAMI*, 10:439-451, 1988
5. B. K. P. Horn. Understanding image intensities, *Artificial Intelligence*, 8:201–231, 1977.
6. B. K. Horn. *Robot vision*. MIT Press, Cambridge, MA, 1986.
7. Jähne, B. *Practical Handbook on Digital Image Processing for Scientific Applications*. CRC-Press, Boca Raton, FL, USA, 1997.
8. B. Jähne and H. Haußecker. Air-Water Gas Exchange, *Annual Rev. Fluid Mech.*, 30:443–468.
9. B. Jähne, J. Klinke, and S. Waas. Imaging of short ocean wind waves: a critical theoretical review. *J. Optical Soc. Amer. A*, 11:2197–2209, 1994.
10. B. Jähne and K. Riemer. Two-dimensional wave number spectra of small-scale water surface waves, *J. Geophys. Res.*, 95:11,531–11,546, 1990.

11. R. Klette, A. Koschan, K. Schlüns. *Computer Vision, Räumliche Information aus digitalen Bildern.* Vieweg, Brauschweig, 1996.

12. J. Klinke and B. Jähne. Measurement of short ocean wind waves during the MBL-ARI west coast experiment. In B. Jähne and E. Monahan, editors, *Air-Water Gas Transfer, Selected Papers, 3rd Intern. Symp. on Air-Water Gas Transfer*, pages 165–173, Aeon, Hanau, 1995.

13. G. Komen and W. Oost, (eds.). *Radar scattering from modulated wind waves.* Reidel, Dordrecht, 1989.

14. R. Kozera. On shape recovery from two shading patterns. *Int. J. Pattern Recognition and Artificial Intelligence*, 6:673–698, 1993.

15. P. S. Liss and R. A. Duce (eds.). *The sea surface and global change*, Cambridge Univ. Press, Cambridge, UK, 1997.

16. S. K. Nayar, K. Ikeuchi, T. Kanade. Determining shape and reflectance of hybrid surfaces by photometric sampling. *IEEE Trans. Robotics & Automation*, 6:418–431, 1990.

17. R. H. Stewart. *Methods of Satellite Oceanography.* Univ. of California Press, Berkeley, 1985.

18. K. Schlüns. Eine Erweiterung des photometrischen Stereo zur Analyse nichtstatischer Szenen. *Proc. DAGM-Symposium Mustererkennung'92, Dresden*, Springer, Berlin, 405–410, 1992.

19. D. J. Stilwell. Directional energy spectra of the sea from photographs. *J. Geophys. Res.*, 74:1974–1986, 1969.

20. R. J. Woodham. Photometric stereo: a reflectance map technique for determining surface orientation from image intensity. *Proc. Image Understanding Systems & Industrial Applications*, SPIE Proc. Vol. 155, 136–143, 1978.

21. R. J. Woodham. Photometric method for determining surface orientation from multiple images. *Optical Eng.*, 19:139–144, 1980.

22. R. J. Woodham. Gradient and curvature from the photometric-stereo method, including local confidence estimation. *J. Optical Soc. America*, A11:3050–3068, 1994.

23. X. Zhang and C. S. Cox. Measuring the two dimensional structure of a wavy water surface optically: a surface gradient detector. *Exp. Fluids*, 17:225, 1994.

Modelling Objects Having Quadric Surfaces Incorporating Geometric Constraints

Naoufel Werghi, Robert Fisher, Craig Robertson, and Anthony Ashbrook

Department of Artificial Intelligence,
University of Edinburgh
5 Forrest Hill, EH1 2QL Edinburgh, UK
email:{naoufelw, rbf, craigr, anthonya }@dai.ed.ac.uk

Abstract. This paper deals with the constrained shape reconstruction of objects having quadric patches. The incorporation of geometric constraints in object reconstruction was used first by Porrill [10]. His approach combined the Kalman filter equations with linearized constraint equations. This technique was improved by De Geeter et al [5] to reduce the effects of linearization error. The nature and the specificity of this technique make it limited in scope and application.

In their approach for 3-D object pose estimation, Bolle et al [2] constrained some quadrics to have a certain shape (circular cylinder and sphere) by using a specific representation for these particular surfaces.

Our work uses a new approach to global shape improvement based on feature coincidence, position and shape constraints. The key idea is to incorporate user specific geometric constraints into the reconstruction process. The constraints are designed to fix some feature relationships (such as parallel surface separations, or cylindrical surface axis relationships) and then use least squares fitting to fix the remaining parameters. An optimization procedure is used to solve the reconstruction problem. In this paper, constraints for planar and general quadric surface classes are given. Results with quadric surfaces show much improvement in shape reconstruction for both constrained and unconstrained relationships. The proposed approach avoids the drawbacks of linearization and allows a larger category of geometric constraints. To our knowledge this work is the first to give such a large framework for the integration of geometric relationships in object modelling.

The technique is expected to have a great impact in reverse engineering applications and manufactured object modelling where the majority of parts are designed with intended feature relationships.

1 Introduction

There has been a recent flurry of effort on reconstructing 3D geometric models of objects from single [3, 6, 8] or multiple [2, 4, 12, 11, 13] range images, in part motivated by improved range sensors, and in part by demand for geometric models in the CAD and Virtual Reality (VR) application areas. However, an important aspect which has not been fully investigated is the exploitation of the geometric constraints defining the spatial or topological relationships between object features.

The work presented in this paper investigates reverse engineering, namely the combination of manufacturing knowledge of standard object shapes with the surface position information provided by range sensors.

The first motivation behind this work is that models needed by industry are generally designed with intended feature relationships so this aspect should be exploited rather than ignored. The consideration of these relationships is actually necessary because some attributes of the object would have no sense if the object modelling scheme did not take into account these constraints. For example, take the case when we want to estimate the distance between two parallel planes: if the plane fitting results gave two planes which are not parallel, then the distance measured between them would have no significance.

The second motivation is to see whether exploiting the available known relationships would be useful for reducing the effects of registration errors and mis-calibration. Thus improving the accuracy of estimated part features' parameters and consequently the quality of the modelling or the object localization.

In previous work [14] we have shown that this is quite possible for planar objects. A general incremental framework was presented whereby geometric relationships can be added and integrated in the model reconstruction process. The objects treated were polyhedral and the data was taken from single views only. An overview of the technique is given in Section 3.

In this paper we study the case of parts having quadric surfaces. Two types of quadric are treated here, cylinders and cones. Both single view data and registered multiple view data data have been used.

Section.2 discuss the related work and the originality of our contribution. In Section.3, we summarize the technique. More details can be found in [14]. Section.4 gives some mathematical preliminaries about quadrics in general and cylinders and cones in particular. Section.5 demonstrates the process on several test objects.

2 Related work

The main problem encountered in the incorporation of geometric relationships in object modelling is how to integrate these constraints in the shape fitting process. The problem is particularly crucial in the case of geometric constraints many of which are non-linear. In his pioneering work, Porrill [10] suggested a linearization of the nonlinear constraints and their combination with a Kalman filter applied to wire frame model construction. Porrill's method takes advantage of the recursive linear estimation of the KF, but it guarantees satisfaction of the constraints only to linearized first order. Additional iterations are needed at each step if more accuracy is required. This last condition has been taken into account in the work of De Geeter et al [5] by defining a "Smoothly Constrained Kalman Filter". The key idea of their approach is to replace a nonlinear constraint by a set of linear constraints applied iteratively and updated by new measurements in order to reduce the linearization error. However, the characteristics of Kalman filtering makes these methods essentially adapted for iteratively acquired data and many data samples. Moreover, there was no mechanism for determining how successfully the constraints have been satisfied. Besides, only lines and planes were considered in both of the above works.

The constraints considered by Bolle et al [2] in their approach to 3D object position covers only the shape of the surfaces. They chose a specific representation for the treated features: plane, cylinder and sphere.

Compared to Porrill's and De Geeter's work, our approach avoids the drawbacks of linearization, since the constraints are completely implemented. Besides our approach covers a larger category of feature shapes. Regarding the work of Bolles, the type of constraints which can be held by our approach go beyond the restricted set of surface shapes and cover also the geometric relationships between object features. To our knowledge the work appears the first to give such a large framework for the integration of geometric relationships in object modelling.

3 The optimization technique

Given sets of 3D measurement points representing surfaces belonging to a certain object, we want to estimate the different surfaces' parameters, taking into account the geometric constraints between these surfaces.

A state vector p is associated to the object, which includes the set of parameters related to the patches. The vector p has to best fit the data while satisfying the constraints. So, the problem that we are dealing with is a constrained optimization problem to which an optimal solution may be provided by minimizing the following function:

$$E(p) = F(p) + C(p) \tag{1}$$

where $F(p)$ is the objective function defining the relationship between the set of data and the parameters and $C(p)$ is the constraint function. $F(p)$ could be the likelihood of the range data given the parameters (with a negative sign since we want to minimize) or the least squares error function. The likelihood function has the advantage of considering the statistical aspect of the measurements. In a first step, we have chosen the least squares function as the integration of the data noise characteristics into the LS function can be done afterwards with no particular difficulty, leading to the same estimation of the likelihood function in the case of the Gaussian distribution.

Given M geometric constraints, the constraint function is represented by the following equation:

$$C(p) = \sum_{k=1}^{M} \lambda_k C_k(p) \tag{2}$$

where $C_k(p)$ is a vector function associated to constraint k. λ_k are weighting coefficients used to control the contribution of the constraints in the parameters' estimation. Each function is required to be convex since many robust techniques for minimizing convex functions are available in the literature. The objective function $F(p)$ is convex by definition, so therefore $E(p)$ is also convex.

Figure 1 shows the optimization algorithm that we have used, which has been simplified so that a single λ is associated to all the constraints. The algorithm starts with an initial parameter vector $p^{[0]}$ that satisfies the least squares function. Then we iteratively increase λ and solve for a new optimal parameter $p^{[n+1]}$ using the previous $p^{[n]}$. The new optimal vector is found by means of the standard Levenberg-Marquardt algorithm. The algorithm stops when the constraints are satisfied to the desired degree or when the parameter vector remains stable for a certain number of iterations. The initial value λ_0 has to be large enough to avoid the trivial null solution and to give the constraints a certain initial weight. A convenient value for the initial λ is : $\lambda_0 = F(p^{[0]})/C(p^{[0]})$

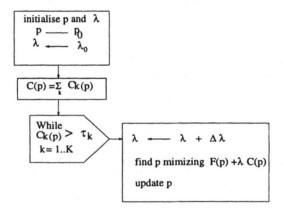

Fig. 1. The optimization algorithm *optim*

4 Preliminaries

This section give a brief overview about constraining quadrics and some particular shapes. A full treatment of these surfaces can be found in [1]. While the material contained here is largely elementary geometry, we present it in order to make clear how the set of constraints used for each surface type and relationship relate to the parameters of the generic quadric. The generic quadric form is used because it is easy to generate a least squares surface fit using the algebraic distance.

A general quadric surface is represented by the following quadratic equation:

$$f(x,y,z) = ax^2 + by^2 + cz^2 + 2hxy + 2gxz + 2fyz + 2ux + 2vy + 2wz + d = 0 \quad (3)$$

which can be written : $X^T A X + 2X^T B + C = 0$
where

$$A = \begin{bmatrix} a & h & g \\ h & b & f \\ g & f & c \end{bmatrix}, \quad B = [u, v, w]^T, \quad C = d; \quad X = [x, y, z]^T \qquad (4)$$

The type of the quadric depends on the discriminant of the quadric Δ and the cubic discriminant $\mathcal{D}$:

$$\Delta = \begin{vmatrix} a & h & g & u \\ h & b & f & v \\ g & f & c & w \\ u & v & w & d \end{vmatrix} \quad \mathcal{D} = \begin{vmatrix} a & h & g \\ h & b & f \\ g & f & c \end{vmatrix} \qquad (5)$$

and the cofactors of $\mathcal{D}$:

$$\mathcal{A} = bc - f^2 \qquad (6)$$
$$\mathcal{B} = ac - g^2$$
$$\mathcal{C} = ab - h^2$$
$$\mathcal{F} = gh - af$$
$$\mathcal{G} = hf - bg$$
$$\mathcal{H} = gf - ch$$

4.1 The cylinder

The quadric is a cylinder when $\Delta = \mathcal{D} = 0$, $u\mathcal{A} + v\mathcal{H} + w\mathcal{G} = 0$ and $\mathcal{A} + \mathcal{B} + \mathcal{C} > 0$. The equation of the cylinder axis is

$$\frac{x - \frac{u\mathcal{f}}{\mathcal{F}}}{1/\mathcal{F}} = \frac{y - \frac{v\mathcal{g}}{\mathcal{G}}}{1/\mathcal{G}} = \frac{z - \frac{w\mathcal{h}}{\mathcal{H}}}{1/\mathcal{H}} = 0 \qquad (7)$$

this means that the cylinder axis has as direction the vector $(1/\mathcal{F}, 1/\mathcal{G}, 1/\mathcal{H})$ and passes through the point $X_o(\frac{u\mathcal{f}}{\mathcal{F}}, \frac{v\mathcal{g}}{\mathcal{G}}, \frac{w\mathcal{h}}{\mathcal{H}})$. The axis orientation corresponds to the eigenvector of the matrix A related to the null eigenvalue. The two other eigenvalues are positive.

The circular cylinder For a circular cylinder, we can show that the parameters of the quadric should also satisfy the following conditions:

$$agh + f(g^2 + h^2) = 0 \qquad (8)$$
$$bhf + g(h^2 + f^2) = 0$$
$$cfg + h(f^2 + g^2) = 0$$
$$\frac{u}{f} + \frac{v}{g} + \frac{w}{h} = 0$$

A circular cylinder may be also represented by the canonical form:

$$(x - x_0)^2 + (y - y_0)^2 + (z - z_0)^2 - (n_x(x - x_0) + n_y(y - y_0) + n_z(z - z_0))^2 - r^2 = 0 \quad (9)$$

where $X_o = [x_0, y_0, z_0]^T$ is an arbitrary point on the axis, $n = [n_x, n_z, n_y]^T$ is a unit vector along the axis and r is the radius of the cylinder.

This form has the advantage of having a minimal number of parameters. However its implementation in the optimization algorithm may cause some complexity, indeed it is not possible with this form to get separate terms for the data and the parameters as in (3) (which allows the data terms to be computed off line). Consequently this may increase the computational cost dramatically.

The expansion of (9) and the identification with (3) yields

$$a = 1 - n_x^2 \tag{10}$$
$$b = 1 - n_y^2$$
$$c = 1 - n_z^2$$
$$h = -n_x n_y$$
$$g = -n_x n_z$$
$$f = -n_y n_z$$

These equations have the advantage of imposing implicitly the circularity constraints of the cylinder and avoid the problem when one of the parameters (f, g, h) vanishes. Besides, they make concrete the geometric relationships between the cylinder and other object features as we will see in Section 5.2.

4.2 The cone

A cone surface satisfies $\Delta \neq 0, \mathcal{D} = 0$. The summit of the cone is given by:

$$X_o = A^{-1} B \tag{11}$$

The axis of the cone corresponds to the eigenvector related to the negative eigenvalue of the matrix A. The two other eigenvalues are both positive.

Circular cone For a circular cone the parameters of the quadric equation have to satisfy the following conditions

$$\frac{af - gh}{f} = \frac{bg - hf}{g} = \frac{ch - fg}{h} \tag{12}$$

As for the cylinder case, a circular cone equation has a more compact form:

$$[(x-x_o)^2 + (y-y_o)^2 + (z-z_o)^2] \cos^2(\alpha) - [n_x(x-x_o) + n_y(y-y_o) + n_z(z-z_o)]^2 = 0 \tag{13}$$

where $[x_o, y_o, z_o]^T$ is the summit of the cone, $[n_x, n_y, n_z]^T$ is the unit vector defining the orientation of the cone axis and α is the semi-vertical angle. The quadric equation parameters can thus be expressed explicitly as a function of the above terms by :

$$a = n_x^2 - \cos^2\alpha \tag{14}$$

$$b = n_y^2 - \cos^2 \alpha$$
$$c = n_z^2 - \cos^2 \alpha$$
$$h = n_x n_y$$
$$g = n_x n_z$$
$$f = n_y n_z$$

For the same reasons mentioned in the cylinder case the compact form of the cone equation is not adequate for the optimization algorithm. Nevertheless it is useful to implicitly impose the conic constraints by means of equations (14) Instead of (12). Indeed in this form all the parameters (f, g, h) need to be different of zero.

4.3 Planes

A plane surface can be represented by this following equation:

$$n_x x + n_y y + n_z z + d = 0; \qquad (15)$$

where $n = [n_x, n_y, n_z]^T$ is unit normal vector ($\|n\| = 1$) to the plane and d is the distance to the origin.

5 Application on some test objects

The objects treated in this section are real parts. The data was acquired with a 3D triangulation range sensor. The range measurements were already segmented into groups associated with features by means of the *rangeseg* [7] program.

5.1 Notation

For the rest of the paper we need the following notations:
i_r is a vector which all the elements are null except the rth element which is equal to 1.
$j_{(r,s)}$ is a vector which all the elements are null except the rth and the sth elements which are equal to 1 and -1 respectively.
$M_{(r,s)}$ is a diagonal matrix which all the elements are null except the rth and the sth elements which are equal to 1 and -1 respectively.
$U_{(r,s)}$ is a diagonal matrix defined by

$$U_{(r,s)} = \begin{cases} U(i,i) = 1 & \text{if } r \leq i \leq s \\ U(i,i) = 0 & \text{otherwise} \end{cases}$$

$L_{(r,s,p)}$ a symmetric matrix defined by

$$L_{(r,s,p)} = \begin{cases} L(i,j) = L(j,i) = 1/2 & \text{if } i = r+t, \ j = s+t \ \ 0 \leq t \leq p \\ L(i,j) = L(j,i) = 0 & \text{otherwise} \end{cases}$$

5.2 The half cylinder

This object is composed of four surfaces. Three patches S_1, S_2 and S_3 have been extracted from two views represented in Figure 2(a,c). These surfaces correspond respectively to the base plane S_2, lateral plane S_1 and the cylindrical surface S_3 (Figure 2.b). The parameter vector is $p = [p_1{}^T, p_2{}^T, p_3{}^T]^T$, where $p_1 = [n_1{}^T, d_1]^T$, $p_2 = [n_2{}^T, d_2]^T$ and $p_3 = [a, b, c, h, g, f, u, v, w, d]^T$. The least squares error function is given by:

$$F(p) = p^T H p, \quad H = \begin{bmatrix} H_1 & O_{(4,4)} & O_{(4,10)} \\ O_{(4,4)} & H_2 & O_{(4,10)} \\ O_{(4,10)}^T & O_{(4,10)}^T & H_3 \end{bmatrix} \tag{16}$$

where H_1, H_2, H_3 are the data matrices related respectively to S_1, S_2, S_3:

$$H_i = \sum_j (X_j^i)(X_j^i)^T \text{ for } X_j^i \text{ belonging to surface } S_i$$

This object has the following constraints

1. S_1 and S_2 are perpendicular,
2. the cylinder axis is parallel to S_1's normal,
3. the cylinder axis lies on the surface S_2,
4. the cylinder is circular.

Constraint 1 is expressed by the following condition

$$C_{ang}(p) = (n_1{}^T n_2)^2 = (p^T L_{(1,5,2)} p)^2 = 0; \tag{17}$$

Constraint 2 is satisfied by equating the unit vector n in (9) to S_1's normal n_1. Constraint 3 is represented by two conditions: axis vector n is orthogonal to S_2's normal n_2, and one point of the axis satisfies S_2's equation. The first

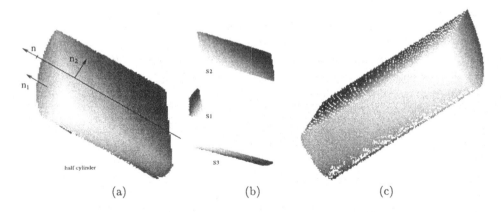

(a) (b) (c)

Fig. 2. Two views of the half cylinder and the extracted surfaces

condition is guaranteed by constraint 2 since n_2 is orthogonal to n_1. For the second condition the point X_o in Section 4.1 has to satisfy the equation:

$$C_{axe}(p) = (X_o^T n_2 + d_2)^2 = (-[u, v, w]^T n_2 + d_2)^2 = (i_8{}^T p - p^T L_{(5,15,2)}p)^2 = 0 \tag{18}$$

using equations (6) and (10).

The cylinder circularity constraint is implicitly defined by the equations (10). From these equations we extract the following constraints on the parameter vector p:

$$C_{circ_1}(p) = (i_9{}^T p + p^T U_{(1,1)}p - 1)^2 = 0 \tag{19}$$
$$C_{circ_2}(p) = (i_{10}{}^T p + p^T U_{(2,2)}p - 1)^2 = 0$$
$$C_{circ_3}(p) = (i_{11}{}^T p + p^T U_{(3,3)}p - 1)^2 = 0$$
$$C_{circ_4}(p) = (i_{12}{}^T p + p^T L_{(1,2,0)}p)^2 = 0$$
$$C_{circ_5}(p) = (i_{13}{}^T p + p^T L_{(1,3,0)}p)^2 = 0$$
$$C_{circ_6}(p) = (i_{14}{}^T p + p^T L_{(2,3,0)}p)^2 = 0$$

We group then all the above constraints in a single one

$$C_{circ}(p) = \sum_{k=1}^{6} C_{circ_k}(p) = 0 \tag{20}$$

Finally the normals n_1 and n_2 have to be unit. This is represented by:

$$C_{unit}(p) = (p^T U_{(1,3)}p - 1)^2 + (p^T U_{(5,7)}p - 1)^2 = 0 \tag{21}$$

The constraint function is then

$$C(p) = C_{unit}(p) + C_{ang}(p) + C_{axe}(p) + C_{circ}(p) \tag{22}$$

and optimisation function is

$$E(p) = p^T H p + \lambda(C_{unit}(p) + C_{ang}(p) + C_{axe}(p) + C_{circ}(p)) \tag{23}$$

Experiments In the first test, the algorithm *optim* has been applied to data extracted from a single view (Figure 2.c). The behaviour of the constraints (17),(18),(20) and (21) during the optimization have been mapped as a function of λ as well as the least squares residual (16) and the constraint function (22). The figures show a linear logarithmic decrease of the constraints with respect to λ. It is also noticed that at the end of the optimization all the constraints are highly satisfied. The least squares error converges to a stable value and the constraint function vanishes at the end of the optimization. The figures also show that it is possible to continue the optimization further until a higher tolerance is reached, however this is limited by the computing capacity of the machine. We have noticed that beyond a certain value of λ some numerical instabilities occurred.

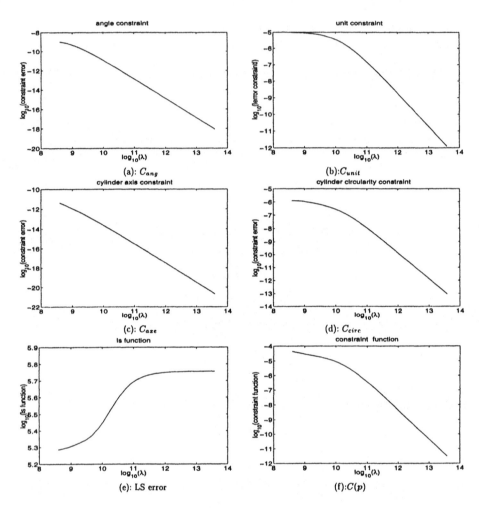

Fig. 3. (a),(b),(c),(d): decrease of the different constraints with respect to λ. (e),(f): variation of least squares function and the constraint function with respect to λ.

In the second test, registered data from view1 (Figure 2.a) and view2 (Figure 2.c) have been used. The registration was carried out by hand. Results similar to the first test have been obtained for the constraints.

Tables 1 and 2 represent the values of some object characteristics obtained from an estimation without considering the constraints and from the presented optimization algorithm. These are shown for the first and second test respectively.

The characteristics examined are the angle between plane S_1 and plane S_2, the distance between the cylinder axis's point X_o (see (4.1) and (9)) and the plane S_2 and the radius of the cylinder. The comparison of the tables' values for the two approaches show the clear improvement carried by the proposed technique. This is noticed in particular for the radius which the actual value is

$30mm$, although the extracted surface covers considerably less than a half of a cylinder. As we constrained the angle and distance relations, we expect these to be satisfied, as they are to almost an arbitrarily high tolerance, as seen in Fig.3. The radius was not constrained, but the other constraints on the cylinder have allowed the least squares fitting of the unconstrained parameters to achieve a much more accurate estimation of the cylinder radius in both cases.

view2	angle($S_1, S2$)(degree)	distance(X_o, S_2)(mm)	radius(mm)
without constraints	90.84	6.32	26.98
with constraints	90	0	29.68
actual values	90	0	30

Table 1. Improvement in shape and placement parameters with and without constraints from data from single view.

registered view1 and view2	angle($S_1, S2$)(degree)	distance(X_o, S_2)(mm)	radius(mm)
without constraints	89.28	2.23	30.81
with constraints	90	0	30.06
actual values	90	0	30

Table 2. Improvement in shape and placement parameters with and without constraints from data merged from two views.

5.3 The cone object

This object contain two surfaces: a plane (S_1) and a cone patch (S_2) (Figure4(c,d). Two views have been taken for this object (Figure4(a,b)

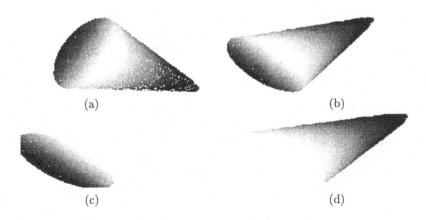

(a)

(b)

(c)

(d)

Fig. 4. (a,d): Two views of part , (c,d): extracted patches

The parameter vector is $p = [p_1{}^T, p_2{}^T]^T$, where $p_1 = [n_1{}^T, d_1]^T$ and $p_2 = [a, b, c, h, g, f, u, v, w, d]^T$. The least squares error function is given by:

$$F(p) = p^T H p, \quad H = \begin{bmatrix} H_1 & O_{(4,10)} \\ O_{(4,10)}^T & H_2 \end{bmatrix} \tag{24}$$

where H_1 and H_2 are the data matrices related to S_1 and S_2. This object involves the following constraints: 1) the cone axis is parallel to S_1, 2) the cone is circular Constraint 1 is imposed if S_1's normal is equated to the unit vector n of the cone axis. Eliminating $cos^2\alpha$ from the the cone circularity equations (14) and taking into consideration constraint 1, the circularity constraints are formulated as :

$$a - b = n_{1_x}^2 - n_{1_y}^2 \tag{25}$$
$$a - c = n_{1_x}^2 - n_{1_z}^2$$
$$b - c = n_{1_y}^2 - n_{1_z}^2$$
$$h = n_{1_x} n_{1_y}$$
$$g = n_{1_x} n_{1_z}$$
$$f = n_{1_y} n_{1_z}$$

A matrix formulation of these equations as a function of the parameter vector p is:

$$C_{circ_1}(p) = (j_{(5,6)}{}^T p - p^T M_{(1,2)} p)^2 = 0 \tag{26}$$
$$C_{circ_2}(p) = (j_{(5,7)}{}^T p - p^T M_{(1,3)} p)^2 = 0$$
$$C_{circ_3}(p) = (j_{(6,7)}{}^T p - p^T M_{(2,3)} p)^2 = 0$$
$$C_{circ_4}(p) = (i_8{}^T p - p^T L_{(1,2,0)} p)^2 = 0$$
$$C_{circ_5}(p) = (i_9{}^T p - p^T L_{(1,3,0)} p)^2 = 0$$
$$C_{circ_6}(p) = (i_{10}{}^T p - p^T L_{(2,3,0)} p)^2 = 0$$

which are grouped into a single constraint $C_{circ}(p) = \sum_{k=1}^{6} C_{circ_k}(p) = 0$. Considering as well the unit constraint related to the normal n_1 $C_{unit}(p) = (p^T U_{(1,3)} p - 1)^2 = 0$. The whole constraint function is : $C(p) = C_{unit}(p) + C_{circ}(p)$.

Experiments The optimization algorithm was applied to data from a single view and to registered data. The behaviour of the unit constraint, the circularity constraint, the least squares function and the constraint function during the optimization are qualitatively identical to that shown in Fig.3. As with the cylinder object, the constraints are satisfied up to a high tolerance.

For both the single view and the registered data, the angle between the cone axis and the plane normal, the distance from the cone summit to the plane and the semi vertical angle α have been computed. Table 3 and Table 4 show the estimated values.

We notice that the orthogonality of the plane and the cone axis is almost perfectly satisfied with the optimization. The actual values of the distance and the angle α are not known with high accuracy. Nevertheless the estimated values are within the errors' tolerances.

view1	angle(cone axis ,n_1)(degree)	distance(X_o, S_1)(mm)	α(degree)
without constraints	2.61	72.74	20.78
with constraints	0.00	72.55	19.68
True values	0	70	20

Table 3. Improvement in shape and placement parameters with and without constraints from data from a single view.

registered view1 and view2	angle(cone axis ,n_1)(degree)	distance(X_o, S_1)(mm)	α(degree)
without constraints	0.79	71.73	19.20
with constraints	0.00	70.09	19.59
True values	0	70	20

Table 4. Improvement in shape and placement parameters with and without constraints from data merged from two views.

5.4 The multi-quadric object

The third series of tests have been carried out on a more complicated object (Fig.5). It has two lateral planes S_1 and S_2, a back plane S_3, a bottom plane S_4, a cylindrical surface S_5 and a conic surface S_6. The cylindrical patch is less than

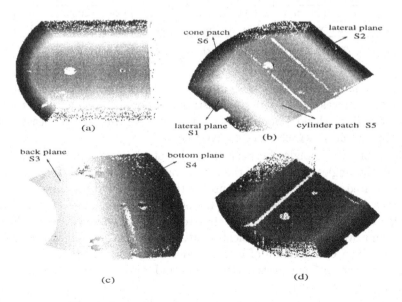

Fig. 5. four views of the multi-quadric object

a half cylinder (40% arc), the conic patch occupies a small area of the whole cone (less then 30%)

The vector parameter associated to this object is then $p^T = [p_1^T, p_2^T, p_3^T, p_4^T, p_5^T, p_6^T]$ where p_i is the parameter vector associated to the surface S_i.

The considered surfaces of the object have the following constraints

1. S_1 makes an angle of 120°[1] with S_2
2. S_1 and S_2 are perpendicular to S_3
3. S_1 and S_2 make an angle of 120° with S_4
4. S_3 is perpendicular to S_4
5. the axis of the cylindrical patch S_5 is parallel to S_3's normal
6. the axis of the cone patch S_6 is parallel to S_4's normal
7. the cylindrical patch is circular
8. the cone patch is circular

These constraints are then represented in the same manner as in Section 5.2 and Section 5.3.

Experiments Since the surfaces can not be recovered from a single view, four views (Fig.5) have been registered by hand. The results regarding the algorithm convergence are qualitatively identical to those shown in Fig.3. All the constraint functions vanish and are highly satisfied.

In order to check the robustness and the stability of the technique, we have carried out 100 optimizations, in each of them 50% of the surfaces' points are

angle	(S_1, S_2)	(S_1, S_3)	(S_1, S_4)	(S_2, S_3)	(S_2, S_4)	(S_3, S_4)
without constraints	119.76	92.08	121.01	87.45	119.20	90.39
with constraints	120.00	90.00	120.00	90.00	120.00	90.00
actual values	120	90	120	90	120	90

Table 5. Improvement of the surface's angle estimation.

selected randomly. The results shown below are the average of this tests. Our first intention was to compare the constrained approach with an object estimation method which does not consider constraints, in this case the least squares technique applied to each surface separately.

In Table 5 the angles between the different planes are mapped, we notice that all the angles converge to the actual values. Table 6 and Table 7 contain the estimated values of some attributes of the cylinder and the cone. The values show that each of the axis constraints are perfectly satisfied, the estimated radius and the cone half angle θ are quite close to the actual ones. We notice the good shape improvement of improvement, relative to the unconstrained least squares method, given by reduction of bias of about $12mm$ and 3° respectively in the radius and the half angle estimation. The standard deviation of the estimations have also been reduced.

---

[1] We consider the angle between normals.

The radius estimation is within the hoped tolerances, a systematic error of about $0.5mm$ is quite nice. However the cone half angle estimation seems to involve a larger systematic error (about $1.8°$). Two factors may contribute to this fact: 1) the registration error may be too large since it was made by hand and 2) the area of the cone patch covers less than 30 % of the whole cone. It is known that when a quadric patch does not contain enough information concerning the curvature, the estimation is very biased, even when robust techniques are applied, because it is not possible to predict the variation of the surface curvature.

cylinder parameters	angle(axis ,S_3's normal)	radius	standard deviation
without constraints	2.34	37.81	0.63
with constraints	0.00	59.65	0.08
actual values	0	60	0

Table 6. Improvement of the cylinder characteristic estimates.

cone parameters	angle(axis ,S_4's normal)	α	standard deviation
without constraints	6.0866	26.0108	0.3024
with constraints	0	31.8389	0.1337
actual values	0	30	0

Table 7. Improvement of the cone characteristic estimates.

angle	(S_1, S_2)	(S_1, S_3)	(S_1, S_4)	(S_2, S_3)	(S_2, S_4)	(S_3, S_4)
without constraints	119.76	92.08	121.48	87.45	119.20	90.39
with constraints	119.99	90.33	120.00	90.00	120.00	90.00
actual values	120	90	120	90	120	90

Table 8. Improvement of non-constrained angle estimates.

We have also investigated whether leaving some features unconstrained will affect the estimation since one can say that the satisfaction of the other constraints may push the unconstrained surfaces away from their actual positions. To test this, we have left the angles between the pair of planes (S_1, S_2) and (S_1, S_3) unconstrained. The results in Table 8 show that the estimated unconstrained angles are still close to the actual ones and the accuracy is improved compared to the non-constrained method. The computation time for this object in Matlab was $48s$ on a $200Mhz$ sun Ultrasparc workstation.

6   Conclusion

If we consider the objectives stated in the introduction which are : object shape reconstruction which satisfies the constraints and improves the estimation accuracy, we can say that these objectives have been reached. The experiments show that parameter optimization search does produce shape fitting that almost perfectly satisfied the constraints. The comparison of the results with the non-constrained fitting confirms that the proposed approach improves the quality of the fitting accuracy to a high degree. For the two objects having cylinder patches, the radius error is less then $0.5mm$. Results for the cone are reasonable but less satisfactory. This is mainly due to the relatively small area of the conic patch. Actually, we intentionally chose to work with small patches because it is the case when non-constrained fitting surface techniques fail to give reasonable estimation even with the robust algorithms. This is due to the "poorness" of the information embodied in the patch. However we intend to investigate a more robust form for the objective function which involves the data noise statistics.

Regarding the constraint representation, it is noticed that some constraints involve a large number of equations, in particular for the circularity constraint. One solution is to implicitly impose this constraints through the representation of the quadric equation ($(X - X_o)^T (I - nn^T)(X - X_o) - r^2 = 0$) for the cylinder and ($(X - X_o)^T (nn^T - cos^2(\alpha))(X - X_o) = 0$) for the cone. The main problem encountered with this representation is the complexity of the related objective function and the difficulty of separating the data terms from the parameter terms, but we are working on this issue. It will be also worthwhile to investigate some topological constraints between surfaces which have a common intersection. The adequate formulation of this type of constraints is the main problem to solve.

We are starting to investigate is how one might identify inter-surface relationships that can have a constraint applied. In manufacturing objects, simple angular and spatial relationships are given by design. It should be straightforward to define Mahalanobis distance tests for standard feature relationships, subject to the feature's statistical position distribution. With this analysis, a computer program could propose a variety of constraints that a human could either accept or reject, after which shape reconstruction could occur.

We have also investigated [14] an approach where constraints are incrementally added, for example by a human reverse engineer, but have found no essential difference in results. The batch satisfaction of all constraints as presented here takes very little computing time, so we no longer use the incremental algorithm.[2]

---

[2] Acknowledgements: the work presented in this paper was funded by UK EPSRC grant GR /L25110.

References

1. R.J.Bell *An elementary treatise on coordinate geometry.* McMillan and Co, London, 1910.
2. R.M.Bolle, D.B.Cooper *On Optimally Combining Pieces of Information, with Application to Estimating 3-D Complex-Object Position from Range Data.* IEEE Trans. PAMI, Vol.8, No.5, pp.619-638, September 1986.
3. K.L.Boyer, M.J.Mirza, G.Ganguly *The Robust Sequential Estimator.* IEEE Trans. PAMI, Vol.16, No.10, pp.987-1001 October 1994.
4. Y.Chen, G.Medioni *Object Modelling by Registration of Multiple Range Images.* Proc. IEEE Int. Conf. Robotics and Automation, Vol.2 pp.724-729, April, 1991.
5. J.De Geeter, H.V.Brussel, J.De Schutter, M. Decreton *A Smoothly Constrained Kalman Filter.* IEEE Trans. PAMI pp.1171-1177, No.10, Vol.19, October 1997.
6. P.J.Flynn, A.K.Jain *Surface Classification: Hypothesizing and Parameter Estimation.* Proc. IEEE Comp. Soc. CVPR, pp. 261-267. June 1988.
7. A. Hoover, G. Jean-Baptiste, X. Jiang, P. J. Flynn, H. Bunke, D. Goldof, K. Bowyer, D. Eggert, A. Fitzgibbon, R. Fisher *An Experimental Comparison of Range Segmentation Algorithms.* IEEE Trans. PAMI, Vol.18, No.7, pp.673-689, July 1996.
8. S.Kumar, S.Han, D.Goldgof, K.Boyer *On Recovering Hyperquadrics from Range data.* IEEE Trans. PAMI, Vol.17, No.11, pp.1079-1083, November 1995.
9. S.L.S. Jacoby, J.S Kowalik, J.T.Pizzo *Iterative Methods for Nonlinear Optimization Problems.* Prentice-Hall, Inc. Englewood Cliffs, New Jersey, 1972.
10. J.Porrill *Optimal Combination and Constraints for Geometrical Sensor Data.* International Journal of Robotics Research, Vol.7, No.6, pp.66-78, 1988.
11. M.Soucy, D.Laurendo *Surface Modelling from Dynamic Integration of Multiple Range Views.* Proc 11th Int. Conf. Pattern Recognition, pp.449-452, 1992.
12. H.Y.Shun, K.Ikeuchi, R.Reddy *Principal Component Analysis with Missing Data and its Application to Polyhedral Object Modelling.* IEEE Trans. PAMI, Vol.17, No.9, pp.855-867.
13. B.C.Vemuri, J.K Aggrawal *3D Model Construction from Multiple Views Using Range and Intensity Data.* Proc. CVPR, pp.435-437, 1986.
14. N.Werghi, R.B.Fisher, A.Ashbrook, C.Robertson *Improving Model Shape Acquisition by Incorporating Geometric Constraints.* Proc. BMVC, pp.530-539 Essex, September 1997.

Surface Reconstruction With Multiresolution Discontinuity Analysis

N.F. Law and R. Chung

Department of Mechanical and Automation Engineering,
The Chinese University of Hong Kong,
Shatin, N.T., Hong Kong.
email:{nflaw,rchung}@mae.cuhk.edu.hk

Abstract. The goal of surface reconstruction is to reconstruct a smooth surface while avoiding smoothing out discontinuities. In this paper, a new algorithm for surface reconstruction is proposed which can locate and identify discontinuities while reconstructing a smooth surface from a set of sparse and irregularly spaced depth measurements. This algorithm uses the wavelet transform technique to induce a multiresolution approach for recovering discontinuities. In particular, the wavelet modulus maxima representation is used which allows correlation between wavelet coefficients at different scales. These correlations can be used for feature correspondence across scales. By using this multiresolution information, the estimation of locations of discontinuities is refined. The performance of the algorithm is investigated and compared with a recently published bending moment-based algorithm. It can be seen that our approach can locate and preserve discontinuities while ensuring smoothness in most of the regions.

1 Introduction

Surface interpolation is a common problem encountered in computer vision, for instance in stereo imaging and visual motion analysis, when a dense depth map of the imaged scene is desirable. It refers to a process in which a piecewise smooth surface is reconstructed from a set of noisy measurements. As identifying and locating discontinuities such as edges and boundaries in the scene are important, we want not only to reconstruct the surface, but also to identify the location of discontinuous points in the reconstruction. This is the goal of the surface reconstruction problem.

As in the case of feature-based stereo imaging, the measurements are obtained through the feature correspondence between the left and right images. It thus gives an irregular sampling pattern and the sampling density could be very sparse. It may also happen that some parts in the image have no measurements as there may be no feature detectable in either the right or the left image. The reconstruction problem is therefore ill-posed in nature. Some additional constraints are needed in order to make the problem well-posed.

A popular approach to solve this ill-posed problem is by the regularization technique [1], [2]. It restricts the admissible solution to be a smooth function. The problem can be formulated as minimizing an error function defined as,

$$E = \sum_{k=1}^{K}(z_k - f(x_k, y_k))^2 + \lambda S(f) \tag{1}$$

where K is the total number of measurements available, the first term is the data constraint, i.e., the residual error in surface fitting to the measurements, the second term $S(f)$ is the smoothness requirement placed on f, and λ is a regularization constant which controls the tradeoff between the data constraint and the smoothness constraint. One popular choice for the functional $S(f)$ is the following quadratic form,

$$S(f) = \int \int [(D_x^2 f)^2 + 2(D_x D_y f)^2 + (D_y^2 f)^2] dx dy \tag{2}$$

where D_x and D_y are the differential operators with respect to x and y respectively.

As the smoothness constraint is applied globally to the entire scene, discontinuities present serious difficulties to the above formulation. Most often, discontinuities are blurred by minimizing E without a proper choice of λ. Different methods have been proposed to relax the global smoothness constraint in various ways so as to preserve visual discontinuities. The basic philosophy is to apply different degrees of smoothness to different parts of the image as in [2], [3], [4]. However, the discontinuities are analyzed using single resolution methods. As pointed out in [5], multiresolution analysis performs better than single resolution in discriminating between noise and desired features.

Another difficulty encountered in this minimization problem is the slow convergence rate. It becomes particularly serious when the size of the problem is large. A way to improve the convergence rate is to employ multigrid processing which basically uses the multiresolution concept in improving the convergence rate [2].

Wavelet transform provides a multiresolution picture of an object and thus enables multigrid processing. There are many different kinds of scheme for wavelet transform. One popular choice is the orthogonal wavelet transform as in [6]. An orthogonal wavelet is used as a preconditioning transform, i.e., the wavelet transform is applied to diagonalize the linear equation system. However, the discontinuities are found separately using the bending moment method rather than using the multiresolution property inherent to the wavelet transform [8]. In this paper, the scheme that we choose is the wavelet modulus maxima representation used by Mallat and Zhong [7]. This representation has a property that there exists strong correlation between the wavelet coefficients across scales. Noise would usually show up in the first few wavelet bands with its effect decreases drastically in the higher wavelet bands. In contrast strong edges will have their effects showing across all wavelet bands. Hence, by tracking the effects across wavelet bands, we can establish whether the response is due to noise or not, and how strong the edge is [8].

We propose to make use of this property to establish correlations between the wavelet coefficients across different scales. These correlations can then enhance the estimations of the wavelet coefficients at different scales and enable the discontinuities to be estimated robustly in a multiresolution manner. Experimental results show that our approach can locate and preserve discontinuities and reconstruct the surface with good quality even when the measurements are sparse.

In summary, our proposed algorithm allows surface reconstruction and discontinuities detection to be carried out simultaneously and under the same wavelet framework. Besides, the multiresolution approach inherent in the wavelet formulation allows a more robust performance in discontinuity detection.

2 Multiresolution Approach in the Wavelet Framework

Discretizing Eqns (1) and (2) gives the following expression for the surface reconstruction error,

$$E = \sum_{k=1}^{K}(z_k - f(m_k, n_k))^2 + \sum_{i,j} \lambda(i,j)A^2(i,j) \tag{3}$$

$$\sum_{i,j} \lambda(i,j)B^2(i,j) + 2\sum_{i,j} \lambda(i,j)C^2(i,j)$$

where

$$A(i,j) = f(i, j+1) - 2f(i,j) + f(i, j-1) \tag{4}$$
$$B(i,j) = f(i+1, j) - 2f(i,j) + f(i-1, j)$$
$$C(i,j) = f(i+1, j+1) - f(i+1, j)$$
$$- f(i, j+1) + f(i,j) \quad .$$

A, B and C are the discrete approximations to the differential operations D_x^2, D_y^2 and $D_x D_y$ respectively. The image up to a particular resolution can be represented using the quadratic spline wavelets as follows [5],

$$f_a(m,n) = \sum_i \sum_j h_a(m,i)s_a(i,j)h_a(n,j) \tag{5}$$

$$+ \sum_i \sum_j l_a(m,i)w^1{}_a(i,j)k_a(n,j)$$

$$+ \sum_i \sum_j k_a(m,i)w^2{}_a(i,j)l_a(n,j)$$

or in matrix-vector notation as,

$$\mathbf{f}_a = \mathbf{H}_a \mathbf{S}_a \mathbf{H}_a{}^T + \mathbf{L}_a \mathbf{W}^1{}_a \mathbf{K}_a{}^T + \mathbf{K}_a \mathbf{W}^2{}_a \mathbf{L}_a{}^T \tag{6}$$

where a is the resolution level, f_a is the image which consists of information only up to $(a-1)^{th}$ level, s_a is the lowpass version of f at level a, $w^1{}_a$ and $w^2{}_a$ are the wavelet coefficients at horizontal and vertical directions respectively, h_a, l_a and k_a are the reconstruction filters for s_a, $w^1{}_a$ and $w^2{}_a$ and are defined in [8].

Our approach is first to reconstruct an overly smooth solution and then refine the discontinuities iteratively in the overly smooth surface. In our formulation, the first smooth surface is the lowpass portion of the image at a particular resolution. The smooth surface estimation could be done by assuming $w^1{}_a$ and $w^2{}_a$ to be zero, and then choose the lowpass coefficient s_a so that the resultant f_a minimizes E. The minimization is done by the steepest descent search for simplicity. The gradient of E with respect to $s_a(m,n)$ is given by,

$$\frac{\partial E}{\partial s_a} = -2 \sum_{k=1}^{K} (z_k - f(m_k, n_k)) D(m_k, n_k, m, n) \qquad (7)$$

$$+ 2 \sum_{i,j} \lambda(i,j) A(i,j) A'(i,j)$$

$$+ 2 \sum_{i,j} \lambda(i,j) B(i,j) B'(i,j)$$

$$+ 4 \sum_{i,j} \lambda(i,j) C(i,j) C'(i,j)$$

where

$$A'(i,j) = D(i, j+1, m, n) - 2D(i, j, m, n) \qquad (8)$$
$$+ D(i, j-1, m, n)$$
$$B'(i,j) = D(i+1, j, m, n) - 2D(i, j, m, n)$$
$$+ D(i-1, j, m, n)$$
$$C'(i,j) = D(i+1, j+1, m, n) - D(i+1, j, m, n)$$
$$- D(i, j+1, m, n) + D(i, j, m, n)$$
$$D(i,j) = h_a(i,k) h_a(j,l) \qquad .$$

The derivative of E with respect to $w^1{}_a$ and $w^2{}_a$ can be obtained accordingly. The actual implementation is done in the Fourier domain for computational efficiency.

After having a set of coefficients for s_a, we then estimate the bandpass coefficients $w^1{}_a$ and $w^2{}_a$ so that the resultant surface with discontinuities minimizes E further. In this way, the bandpass information is progressively added into the reconstruction process. The derivative of E with respect to $w^1{}_a$ and $w^2{}_a$ can be obtained from Eq 4 in the same way as $\frac{\partial E}{\partial s_a}$ in Eq 7.

At the same time when the bandpass information is added to the reconstructed surface, we could track the wavelet modulus maxima positions across scales to find out whether the modulus maxima positions are due to noise (incorrect estimation) or due to discontinuities. Thus the estimations are improved by incorporating the multiresolution constraints inherent in our formulation. We could also impose the constraint that the modulus maxima cannot be created as one moves from fine to coarse scales. In this way, we could estimate where the discontinuities are robustly in the multiresolution framework.

The individual wavelet transform modulus maxima represent discontinuities. However, in two or higher dimensions, they are usually not independent features; they refer to points or extended boundaries and belong to certain lines or curves. Hence, we could link the individual wavelet modulus maxima to form contours and use these contours as primitives in feature correspondence across different scales.

In forming the wavelet modulus maxima contours, it is necessary to discard weak and short contours to facilitate the feature correspondence process. The boundaries of important coherent structures often generate long contour curves whereas contours resulting from noise are short. We thus remove any contour curve whose length is smaller than a given length threshold. Also, contour that has a low average amplitude corresponds to small variation in the image which is ignored. The length threshold and the amplitude threshold are set to be 30 % of their respective mean values of all contours in an image. We keep only those contours that satisfy both the length threshold and the amplitude threshold. Thus, the thresholds for both length and amplitude are set automatically for every test image.

The criteria used for features correspondence are position, sign and amplitude of the contours. The determining factor is the sign. If the sign between two modulus maxima contours at two scales are not the same, then they do not match with each other. If the sign is correct, check the position. The positional tolerance which is determined by the width of the wavelet reproducing kernels is used to decide whether the contours are close or not. If the contours are close together, check the amplitude to see if they are similar. It should be noted that the matching between the fine scale and the coarse scale can only be a many-to-one mapping, but not a one-to-many mapping. Since we match contours instead of individual pixels, we can either keep the contour if we find a match or remove the whole contour if no match is found.

If we consider the resolution level to be three, our algorithm can be summarized as follows,

1. Obtain a lowpass function s_3 by assuming no discontinuities;
2. Based on s_3, estimate w^1_3 and w^2_3 by using the gradient search to minimize the error defined in Eq 4. A rough estimate of the discontinuities points can be obtained based on f_3 and λ is updated accordingly.
3. Based on the above estimated f_3 (ie., w^1_3, w^2_3 and s_3 and hence s_2), estimate w^1_2 and w^2_2. Then extract the modulus maxima of both pairs w^1_2, w^1_3 and w^2_2, w^2_3 and apply the feature correspondence to shape w^1_2, w^1_3 and w^2_2, w^2_3. Through the above procedure, some unlikely or unmatched contours are clean up and smoothed out and we could estimate where the discontinuous points are and update λ accordingly.
4. Based on the above estimated f_2, estimate w^1_1 and w^2_1. Then apply feature correspondence to shape the wavelet coefficients at different scales and up-

date λ accordingly. Repeat this step until the estimated f does not change much.

A popular choice for $\lambda(i,j)$ is a binary set, ie., $\{0,1\}$. If a particular pixel (i,j) is known to be a discontinuous point, then the smoothness constraint is turned off by setting $\lambda(i,j)$ to zero, otherwise, the smoothness constraint is enforced by setting $\lambda(i,j)$ to one. We also adopt this approach except that $\lambda(i,j)$ in our case is determined by the wavelet maxima contours. At where the wavelet maxima contours are found, λ is set to zero and at where the wavelet maxima contours are not found, λ is set to one. In this way, we ensure that discontinuities are connected, they are not isolated features which could be due to noise or incorrect estimation.

3 Experimental Results

We provide some experimental results to illustrate the edge-detection and edge-preserving performance of our surface reconstruction algorithm. The proposed algorithm is applied to various data sets including both synthetic and real images. Its performance as a surface reconstruction algorithm was demonstrated on three images shown in Fig 1. For comparison purpose, a recently published bending moment-based algorithm [6] is also applied to the same images.

Fig 2 shows synthetic range measurements where zero-valued means no sample data and the intensity denotes the range. A sampling density of 10% of the range image is used. Fig 3 shows the discontinuities found and the reconstructed surface using our algorithm with three resolution levels and 50 iterations in each level. Fig 4 shows the discontinuities found and the reconstructed surface using the bending moment-based algorithm. A number of edge thresholds have been tried and the best discontinuity map is obtained by setting the threshold to be 150. It can be seen that the bending moment-based algorithm fails to reconstruct the three-level surface and the discontinuities detected are incorrect. Despite the sparse data available over a surface with a lot of discontinuities, our algorithm gives a good reconstruction.

In the bending moment-based algorithm, the discontinuities are detected using the bending moment method rather than using the multiresolution framework inherent to the wavelet transform. Moreover the off-diagonal terms of the preconditioned equation system are all approximated to be zero. The effect of this diagonalization depends on the regularization constant, the sampling density and the reconstruction level chosen. Thus, the diagonal assumption may not be valid at all times. In contrast, our algorithm uses the multiresolution information in constructing the discontinuity map which thus enhance the estimation of the wavelet coefficients and give a good solution.

In the second example, a checkerbox surface of size 128×128 is interpolated. The sampling density is also 10% and the sampled image is shown in Fig 5. Fig 6 shows the discontinuities found and the reconstructed surface using our algorithm with three resolution levels and 50 iterations in each level. Fig 7 shows

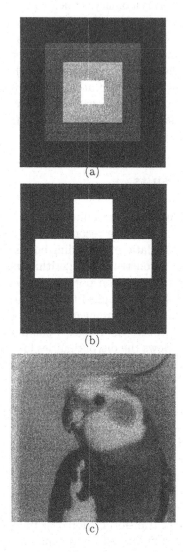

Fig. 1. The images used to test the surface reconstruction algorithm, (a) the wedding cake range image; (b) a checkerboard image; and (c) a bird image

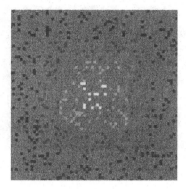

Fig. 2. 10 % sampling density of the wedding cake image. Dots indicate the sampled data, and the brightness on them indicate the depth. The brighter the point is, the closer to the viewer it is.

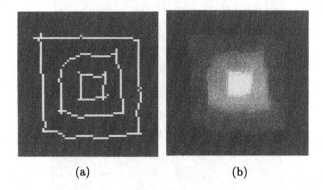

(a)   (b)

Fig. 3. The results obtained with the proposed algorithm for the 10 % wedding cake range data; (a) the discontinuities found and (b) the reconstructed surface.

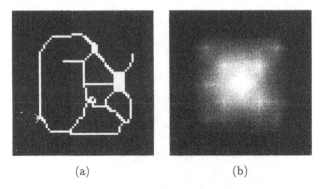

(a)   (b)

Fig. 4. The results obtained with the bending moment-based algorithm for the wedding cake range data; (a) the discontinuities found and (b) the reconstructed surface. The resolution level is set to be three and the edge threshold is 150.

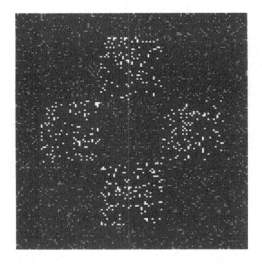

Fig. 5. A 10 % sampling density of the checkerboard image. Dots indicate the sampled data, and the brightness on them indicate the depth. The brighter the point is, the closer to the viewer it is.

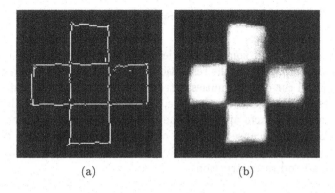

(a)   (b)

Fig. 6. The results obtained with the proposed algorithm for the 10 % checkerboard image; (a) the discontinuities found and (b) the reconstructed surface.

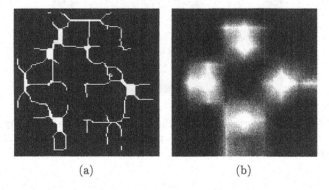

(a)   (b)

Fig. 7. The results obtained with the bending moment-based algorithm for the checkerboard image; (a) the discontinuities found and (b) the reconstructed surface. The resolution level is set to be four and the edge threshold is 150.

the edges found and the reconstructed surface using the bending moment-based algorithm.

We have experienced some difficulties in the bending moment-based algorithm in this example. When the resolution level is chosen to be four, the results are not good and the discontinuities detected using bending moment are messy. But if the resolution level is set to three, the reconstructed surface looks better except that some artifacts appear in the reconstructed surface as evidenced in Fig 8. This happens because the diagonalization assumption which depends on resolution level and the sampling density is not valid. However, our algorithm can still give a good reconstruction.

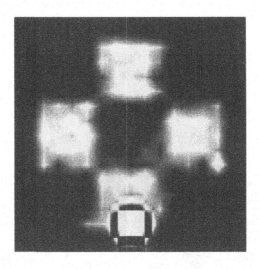

Fig. 8. The reconstructed surface using the bending moment-based approach. The resolution level is set to be three, and the number of iterations is two. Artifacts are obvious in the reconstructed surface.

In the above two examples, we can see that the bending moment-based algorithm do not give a good reconstruction when the sampling density is only 10 %. The discontinuity map which is obtained in a single resolution framework is also not as good as the multiresolution discontinuity detection. We have also tried on some higher sampling density case to see how the new algorithm compares with the bending moment-based algorithm. The results shown here are about the image of a bird. The sampling density is 30% in this example. Fig 9 shows the reconstructed surfaces using our algorithm and the bending moment-based algorithm. The reconstruction of the bending moment-based algorithm is improved. However, our algorithm again provides a better reconstruction.

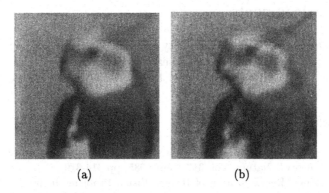

(a)   (b)

Fig. 9. The reconstructed surfaces obtained by (a) our proposed algorithm and (b) bending moment-based algorithm for a 30% sampling density of the bird image.

4   Conclusion

Global smoothness constraints intrinsic to standard regularization are inadequate near discontinuities. Since discontinuities play a vital role in inverse visual problems, some ways are needed to detect their locations so as to avoid smoothing over the discontinuous points. Typical ways to analyze discontinuities are, however, single resolution method in nature. We have presented in this paper a new surface reconstruction method which combines the multiresolution discontinuity tracking and the wavelet transform techniques to reconstruct from a sparse set of measurement a piecewise smooth surface that preserve discontinuities.

The new algorithm uses the wavelet modulus maxima representation [7]. Because of the multiresolution property of the representation and the existence of correlations between wavelet coefficients at different scales, feature correspondence across scales is possible. This improves the estimation of discontinuities and enhance the performance of the surface reconstruction algorithm.

The new algorithm starts with an overly smoothed surface. Discontinuities information which are characterized by the wavelet modulus maxima are added to the reconstructed surface progressively. Thus the discontinuity map undergoes refinement during surface reconstruction.

The new algorithm has been tested on a number of synthetic and real data sets. Simulation results show that the approach can preserve the discontinuities while ensuring smoothness in most regions. Comparison of the proposed algorithm with a recently published algorithm [6] has also been presented. From the experimental results, the performance of our algorithm has been shown to be superior in the surface reconstruction problem.

5 Acknowledgments

N.F. Law thanks the Chinese University of Hong Kong for the support under its Postdoctoral Fellowship on this research. The research was also partially supported by RGC of Hong Kong under the 1994-1995 Earmarked Grant.

References

1. Tomaso Poggio, Vincent Torre and Christof Koch, "Computational vision and regularization theory", Nature, Vol. 317, Sept 1985, pp 314-319.
2. D. Terzopoulos, "Regularization of Inverse Visual Problems Involving Discontinuities", IEEE Trans on Pattern Analysis and Machine Intelligence, Vol. 8, No. 4, July, 1986, pp 413 - 423.
3. D. Terzopoulos, "The Computation of Visible Surface Representations", IEEE Trans on Pattern Analysis and Machine Intelligence, Vol. 10, No. 4, July, 1988, pp 417-437.
4. M. Gokmen and C.C. Li, "Edge Detection and Surface Reconstruction Using Refined Regularization", IEEE Trans on Pattern Analysis and Machine Intelligence, Vol. 15, No. 5, May, 1993, pp 492-499.
5. A.W.C. Liew, "Multiscale Wavelet Analysis of Edges: Issues of Uniqueness and Reconstruction", PhD thesis, University of Tasmania, Australia, 1996.
6. Alex P Pentland, "Interpolation Using Wavelet Bases", IEEE Transactions on Pattern Analysis and Machine Intelligence, Vol. 16, No. 4, April, 1994, pp 410 - 414.
7. Stephane Mallat and Sifen Zhong, "Characterization of Signals from Multiscale Edges", IEEE Transactions on Pattern Analysis and Machine Intelligence, Vol. 14, No. 7, July 1992, pp 710 - 732.
8. N.F. Law and R. Chung, "Surface Reconstruction With Multiresolution Discontinuity Analysis", Technical Report, CUHK-MAE-98-04, The Chinese University of Hong Kong, 1998.

Shape from Chebyshev Nets

Jan Koenderink[1] and Andrea van Doorn[2]

[1] Helmholtz Instituut, Universiteit Utrecht, PO box 80000, 3508 TA Utrecht,
The Netherlands, j.j.koenderink@fys.ruu.nl
[2] Andrea J. van Doorn, Laboratory for Form Theory, Fac. of Industrial Design Eng.,
Technical University Delft, Jaffalaan 9, 2628 BX Delft, The Netherlands

Abstract. We consider a special type of wiremesh covering arbitrarily curved (but smooth) surfaces that conserves length in two distinct directions at every point of the surface. Such "Chebyshev nets" can be considered as deformations of planar Cartesian nets (chess boards) that conserve edge lengths but sacrifice orthogonality of the parameter curves. A unique Chebyshev net can be constructed when two intersecting parameter curves are arbitrarily specified at a point of the surface. Since any Chebyshev net can be applied to the plane, such nets induce mappings between any arbitrary pair of surfaces. Such mappings have many desirable properties (much freedom, yet conservation of length in two directions). Because Chebyshev nets conserve edge lengths they yield very strong constraints on the projection. As a result one may compute the shape of the surface from a single view if the assumption that one looks at the projection of a Chebyshev net holds true. The structure of the solution is a curious one and warrants attention. Human observers apparently are able to use such an inference witness the efficaciousness of fishnet stockings and body-suits in optically revealing the shape of the body. We argue that Chebyshev nets are useful in a variety of common tasks.

1 Introduction

The already well established field of photogrammetry has recently made remarkable progress[1993], largely because of innovative methods developed by the computer vision community. Modern methods make it viable to dispense largely with extensive camera (pre-)calibration and yet to obtain projective or affine solutions from two or more views. Such solutions can then be post-calibrated on the basis of known or assumed metric properties of the scene. Examples of such properties are parallelity, orthogonality and equipartition of length. The ideal scene would contain a Cartesian 3D-lattice. Of course, *if* such a fiducial structure were available one could actually dispense with the first step and unravel a single perspective view. In this paper we consider a generalization of this latter possibility: Shape from a single view on the basis of prior information concerning the metrical structure. We will focus on smooth, general *surfaces* on which a network of fiducial curves has been drawn.

Various authors have remarked upon the observation that the projection of such networks often allows the human observer to obtain a vivid 3D impression of the surface[1981, 1983, 1986]. However, this clearly need not hold for arbitrary networks: As a counterexample one could pick any network in the projection (e.g., a Cartesian grid) and use the inverse projection to put it on any surface. In such cases the impression is always that of a *flat*, frontoparallel object[1986], *even if the actual surface is highly curved*. One has speculated that such so called "shape from contour" is enabled by nets of principal curvature directions[1981]. For instance, Stevens, 1981 has: ... *to conclude anything about the sign of Gaussian curvature, the physical curves must be lines of curvature.* On the face of it this seems unlikely, and in this paper we consider more general possibilities.

2 Curvilinear "Cartesian grids"

Consider the problem of how to generalize the notion of "Cartesian grid" (chess board) on a general, curved surface. Clearly one has to do some concessions in order to be able to apply the net to the surface. Two obvious possibilities are, 1^{stly}, to keep all angles at $\pi/2$, or, 2^{ndly}, to preserve the equality of edge lengths. In the 1st case one obtains *conformal* nets. In general their edge lengths will vary from place to place. The nets of principal curvature directions are one possibility (since the principal directions are orthogonal), but infinitely many others exist. In the 2nd case one obtains the so called "Chebyshev nets". In that case the angles vary from place to place, *i.e.*, the mazes become parallelograms. In this paper we consider this 2nd possibility.

Chebyshev nets occur in real life (among more) as basket ball nets (part of a pseudosphere), nets used as hammocks, food containers, stretched over balloons, *etc.*, fishnet stockings and bodysuits. In figure 1 we show an example: A dancer's legs dressed in fishnet stockings. Notice the clarity with which the 3D shape is revealed, especially in the (complicated) knee region. Since the final category was presumably designed to bring out the body shape particularly clearly, one guesses that "shape from (Chebyshev) nets" will be possible. When we consider the edges of the net as freely rotatable about the vertices (the knots in a real wire net), such networks are evidently *deformable*. Indeed, the fishnet stockings probably started out as *planar* Cartesian nets (flat pieces of very tenuous cloth) which were then stretched over the body.

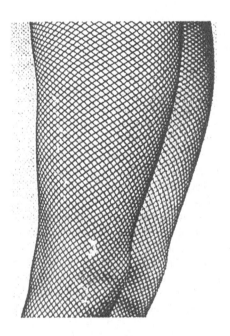

1. *Photograph of a dancer's legs clad with fishnet stockings. Notice how well the 3D shape is visually revealed from the projection. Notice especially the (geometrically) extremely complicated knee area.*

3 Chebyshev Nets

The main facts on Chebyshev nets are that 1^{stly}, they can be constructed with great freedom: One may specify two arbitrary (transversal) curves through any point of the surface and proceed to construct a unique Chebyshev net on them, maze by maze[1927]. Then, 2^{ndly}, each Chebyshev net can be applied to the plane (and hence to any other smooth surface). There are some limits to the validity of these statements though: They apply typically only to finite regions. Outside these regions the net "collapses" and needs to be "overstretched" which is forbidden by the constant edge length constraint[1882]. Indeed, the length of no diagonal can exceed double the edge length. In such cases one has to patch pieces together in other to "clothe" the surface. This introduces the notion of (tailor–like) "cutting and sewing". The classical reference is Chebyshev's lecture "On the cutting of our clothes". Chebyshev[1878] demonstrated how to construct a tight, sexy suit for the unit sphere from two pieces of "cloth". We illustrate how to cut the cloth for such a suit in figure 2. We are not aware of any such illustration in the literature, but presumably this mimics Chebyshev's solution for the problem. Two identical pieces of cloth should be cut—minding the weft and warp directions—and sewn together along corresponding points. The seam will run along the equator of the unit sphere (see figure 3). Of course the net will be in tension when applied over the sphere and a "crooked seam" will result in uneven tension. (Our example is exact, the edges being geodesic arcs of length 6°. Presumably Chebyshev used infinitesimal edge length; the difference should be slight though.) Notice that this method yields a nice (piecewise) "Cartesian" coordinate system for the unit sphere: This suggests another application for Chebyshev nets.

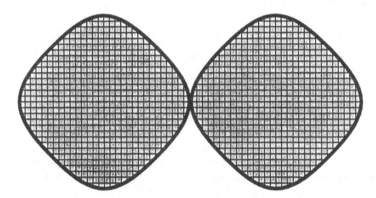

2. *How to cut the cloth in order to sew a tight suit for the unit sphere. The two identical pieces should be sewn together along corresponding points. In clothing the unit sphere the seam should run straight along the equator. The resulting fit should be perfect, though perhaps slightly uncomfortable since the cloth will be in tension.*

The 1st fundamental form (metric) for a Chebyshev net with parameters u, v (thus u =constant and v =constant are the "wires" of the net) is simply

$$ds^2 = du^2 + 2\cos\zeta\, du\, dv + dv^2,$$

where ζ denotes the angle between the wires (thus we obtain the Pythagorean theorem for $\zeta = \pi/2$). One easily shows that the Gaussian curvature is

$$K(u,v) = \frac{-1}{\sin\zeta}\frac{\partial^2\zeta}{\partial u\,\partial v}.$$

Notice that the diagonals of the mazes are orthogonal: If we use $\alpha = u+v$, $\beta = u-v$ as new parameters the metric becomes

$$ds^2 = \cos^2\frac{\zeta}{2}d\alpha^2 + \sin^2\frac{\zeta}{2}d\beta^2.$$

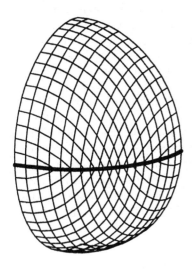

3. *A quadrant of the spherical suit. The "seam" is the equator of the sphere, the sides are the primeval weft and warp threads..*

In order to find examples of Chebyshev nets one may derive a system of 2nd order differential equations, essentially[1882]

$$\frac{\dfrac{\partial^2 x}{\partial u\partial v}}{\dfrac{\partial y}{\partial u}\dfrac{\partial z}{\partial v} - \dfrac{\partial z}{\partial u}\dfrac{\partial y}{\partial v}} = \frac{\dfrac{\partial^2 y}{\partial u\partial v}}{\dfrac{\partial z}{\partial u}\dfrac{\partial x}{\partial v} - \dfrac{\partial x}{\partial u}\dfrac{\partial z}{\partial v}} = \frac{\dfrac{\partial^2 z}{\partial u\partial v}}{\dfrac{\partial x}{\partial u}\dfrac{\partial y}{\partial v} - \dfrac{\partial y}{\partial u}\dfrac{\partial x}{\partial v}},$$

and solve for $(x(u,v), y(u,v), z(u,v))$. One easily checks that the class of surfaces of translation are a particular set of solutions. Solutions are only simple to obtain in special coordinate systems. For instance, for the unit sphere one finds[1882]

$$x(u,v) = \sin \operatorname{am}(u+v)\cos(u-v)k,$$
$$y(u,v) = \sin \operatorname{am}(u+v)\sin(u-v)k,$$
$$z(u,v) = \cos \operatorname{am}(u+v),$$

with am the Jacobi amplitude and k the modulus of the elliptic functions.

In figure 4 we illustrate a Chebyshev covering of the plane and in figures 5 and 6 of the sphere. Of course neither of these is unique. The planar case is an interesting one: In this case both the weft and warp families of threads are parallel curves. According to Stevens' speculations[1981] such families should be interpreted as (locally) *cylindrical.* Of course the "shape from Chebyshev net" solution will be planar.

Stevens would probably argue (our speculation) that the Chebyshev net assumption is not a natural one for human observers to make.

Evidently, it is a different problem to find Chebyshev nets on a *given* surface whereby two initial parameter curves can be specified freely. This leads to a 2nd order partial differential equation. We will not consider the problem here. The reader will find the necessary material in Bianchi[1927].

In practice one will often revert to finite methods because of several reasons. For instance, one might be interested in finite edge lengths to start with and consider the edges as rigid rods, freely rotatable about the vertices[1970]. (One may well speak of "finitesimal" nets, whereas the true Chebyshev nets are infinitesimal.) Or one might be interested in piecewise geodesic edges (a stretched wire *has* to be a geodesic). It turns out to be the case that (true) Chebyshev nets with geodesic wires are necessarily developable surfaces. In that case only one family (either the weft or the warp) can be geodesic[1882]. Since the developables form too restricted a class one has to consider

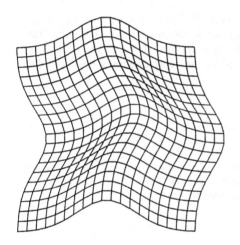

4. *A planar Chebyshev net. The weft and warp threads form parallel families.*

finitesimal nets with only piecewise geodesic wires (the edges). In such cases one most easily constructs the net maze by maze. In figure 5 we show a covering of the sphere obtained with such a piece–by–piece construction. Such purely geometric methods of course yield nets that will typically be mechanically unstable (statically that is). Examples are the planar nets of translation: Obviously only the subset of Cartesian nets is stable. One produces such stable nets by applying isotropic tension on the wires. In order to construct stable nets one has to consider the detailed static mechanical constraints. An example is the basket ball net: It assumes the form of a hyperbolically curved surface of revolution (constant Gaussian curvature), such that the wires are its asymptotic curves[1942].

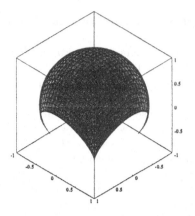

5. *A finitesimal spherical Chebyshev net. The edges are geodesic arcs of fixed length on the sphere. The net has been extended to its natural limits. This net was the basis for the computation of the cut needed to "dress" the sphere illustrated in figure 2.*

4   Shape from (Chebyshev) Nets

First consider an orthogonal projection of a finite Chebyshev net with straight edges on a plane. How does one compute the shape from the projection? One immediate observation is that the observed edge lengths λ_i (say) are related to the (unknown) true length Λ as $\lambda_i^2 + \Delta z^2 = \Lambda^2$, where Δz denotes the depth difference over the edge.

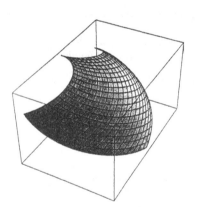

6. *A true (infinitesimal) spherical Chebyshev net: Of course only a few weft and warp threads at fine spacing could be drawn.*

Thus *if the true edge length were known* one could immediately regain the depth differences up to a sign. Since we don't assume the true edge length to be known this doesn't immediately apply. One has an additional constraint though: Surface consistency requires that the (algebraic) sum of the four depth differences over the edges of each maze vanishes. Thus we have (for any maze)

$$\sigma_1\sqrt{\Lambda^2 - \lambda_1^2} + \sigma_2\sqrt{\Lambda^2 - \lambda_2^2} + \sigma_3\sqrt{\Lambda^2 - \lambda_3^2} + \sigma_4\sqrt{\Lambda^2 - \lambda_4^2} = 0,$$

where $\sigma_j = \pm 1$. Clearly $\Lambda^2 \geq \max(\lambda_k)$. There is such an equation for each maze, the unknown Λ^2 being the same for all mazes. These equations generically determine Λ^2 and $\omega_i\{\sigma_1^i, \sigma_2^i, \sigma_3^i, \sigma_4^i\}$, with $\omega_i = \pm 1$, for all i (index i identifies the maze). In order to obtain the full solution we need to establish $\Omega\{\omega_1,\ldots,\omega_n\}$, where $\Omega = \pm 1$ and n denotes the number of mazes. Since Ω clearly represents an essential ambiguity (a "depth reversal") one may set one of the ω_i arbitrarily to ± 1.

In order to find the ω_i one compares adjoining mazes p and q (say): The depth interval over the common edge has to be the same for both mazes, this establishes $\omega_p\omega_q$. If one specifies $\omega_1 = 1$ (say), all the other ω_i generically follow from such a pairwise comparison. In case the data are essentially noise free and the case is generic such a scheme always lead to the solution. The pairwise comparison can for instance be implemented as a painting algorithm. One obtains the true edge length Λ and the true shape up to a depth displacement and a depth inversion. We have implemented the required synchronization of depth reversals for $2^N \times 2^N$ nets via the sequential synchronization of non–overlapping 2×2 subnets, each with elements of size $2^k \times 2^k$ ($k = 0,\ldots N - 1$). One easily handles even large nets this way.

With perfect data such reconstructions work very well and one obtains both the true edge length and the true shape (up to a global depth reversal of course) from any single view of the net, the solution is essentially exact and depends only on the number of digits carried in the calculations. (See figure 7.)

If the data are noisy it is the pairwise comparison that tends to break down first: At a certain noise level the distinction between a surface attitude and its depth reversal becomes insignificant. The synchronization of local depth reversals is then no longer feasible. (In order to obtain a robust solution one might attempt to find the set of ω_i's that globally minimizes the total failure at the common edges. Such a solution may be obtained via a simulated annealing procedure. However, the expected gain is perhaps not worth the effort.) When the noise level is just slightly bad, one expects failure due to synchronized depth reversal of larger areas. When the noise level is really bad one expects that the individual mazes will be depth reversed at random.

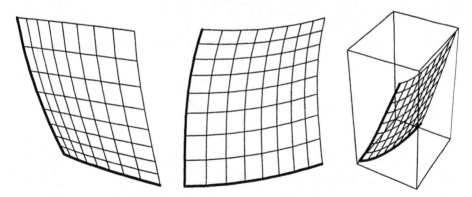

7. Typical example of "depth from nets": On the left two projections of the same net and on the right a reconstruction. With perfect data the reconstructions from one view are essentially exact. This net covers a paraboloid, the initial curves (drawn in bold line) are general curves, not geodesics.

In order to study the behavior of the solution in noisy conditions we considered a small (3x3 mazes) net. For such sizes one can still search for the global optimum of local depth reversals with an exhaustive search procedure. (Notice that the effort scales exponentially with the number of mazes.) We constructed a generic, finite

Chebyshev net (straight edges, vertices on the fiducial surface) on a paraboloid, using non–geodesic initial curves (or rather: edge progressions). The net was constructed exactly, maze by maze. We selected a projection in which the mazes had mutually quite different aspects. The projection was perturbed in the following manner: First we found the r.m.s. projected edge length. Next we added normally distributed random numbers to the Cartesian coordinates of the projected vertices, with zero mean and spread proportional to the r.m.s. projected edge length. The constant of proportionality will be referred to as the "noise level". This type of noise would be typical for data obtained by measurements of limited accuracy in the image (projection). We find the expected result, namely that:

— for low noise levels the reconstructions are essentially perfect. This regime extends to noise levels up to about 10^{-2};

— for high noise levels the synchronization of depth reversals breaks down completely. It is still possible to obtain reasonable estimates of the true edge length. This regime starts from noise levels roughly in the range 10^{-2}–10^{-1};

— in an intermediate region (here noise levels in a narrow range of about $3\,10^{-3}$ to $3\,10^{-2}$) one obtains mixed results. Sometimes the solution will be essentially good, merely somewhat deformed. Other times one witnesses depth reversal of local areas (larger than single mazes). In such cases a more intelligent algorithm (using prior information concerning smoothness for instance) might be expected to be able to "mend the damage". Sometimes one obtains really bad results, the depth reversals seem essentially random on the local (single maze) level.

Such behavior is indeed to be expected for a method that depends critically on the assessment of (often small) differences between Euclidean lengths (the true and the projected edge lengths). There is no way such a method could "deteriorate gracefully", rather, one is confronted with sudden breakdowns when critical noise levels are exceeded. Fortunately, the dangerous noise regime is pretty obvious from the image data themselves (histogram of projected edge lengths compared with tolerance).

We present an example in figures 8, 9 and 10. These illustrate three cases with noise level 1%. *Case A* illustrates an essentially correct reconstruction, the result is

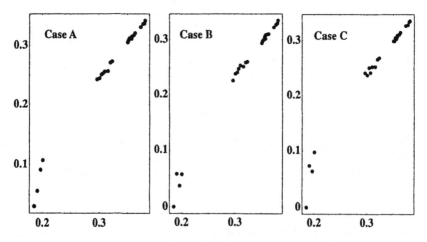

8. *Scatterplots of the recovered absolute differences over the (projected) edges against the veridical values. Notice that the results are quite acceptable in all three cases.*

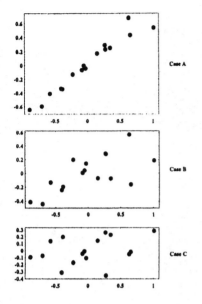

9. *Scatterplots of the recovered depths at the vertices (the average depth has arbitrarily set to zero) against the veridical values (average depths also set to zero). In case A the result is acceptable, in case B there is some correlation, but regional depth reversals make the result less than acceptable, though a smart algorithm might still be able to amend the problems. In case C we are left with a crumpled mess and the depths are essentially unrecoverable.*

merely somewhat distorted as compared with the fiducial shape. *Case B* illustrates the effect of local (but at a larger scale than the single mazes) depth reversals: The reconstruction is at least piece–wise correct. *Case C* illustrates a thoroughly crumpled reconstruction, this result is useless. In all three cases the (3D) edge length was estimated near to veridical (case A a deviation of 9.9%, case B a deviation of 11.5% and in case C a deviation of 11.0% from veridical). From figure 8 it is evident that the absolute depth differences over the edges are also well recovered in all cases (in case A we find a correlation of 99.2%, in case B of 99.1% and in case C of 98.7%). Because of the noise there are surface inconsistencies in all cases of the order of 10% of the true edge length (true edge length was 0.4 whereas the maximum surface consistency violation in case A was 0.029, in case B 0.056 and in case C 0.073). After the depth reversal synchronization procedure we were left with 1 sign violation (out of a total of 24) in case A and 9 sign violations in both cases B and C. Sometimes there were several solutions (with the same number of unresolved depth reversals), namely 2 in case A and a single solution in cases B and C. The unresolved depth reversals caused the major differences in the correlation of the recovered depths at the vertices with the veridical depths. These correlations were 97.5% in case A, 67.4% in case B and 31.1% in case C.

5 Conclusion

We have presented a method that lets us compute the shape of curved surfaces, covered with a wire mesh, from single views under the assumption that the net is the orthogonal, planar projection of a Chebyshev net. Such a reconstruction is robustly possible (given sufficiently precise data), explaining the informal but generally agreed upon fact that human observers can visually appraise the 3D shapes of such items

XY–plane YZ–plane ZX–plane

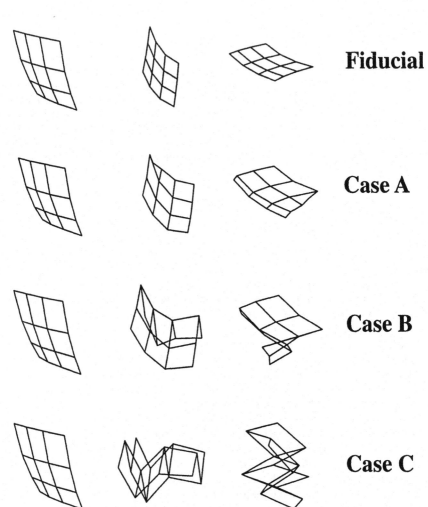

Fiducial

Case A

Case B

Case C

10. *Projections of the fiducial and the recovered nets on the coordinate planes. In this coordinate system the Z–axis is the depth dimension. Thus the projections on the XY–plane are very similar: Essentially the input image with 1% (projected) edgelength perturbations. Clearly case A represents an acceptable solution, case B nicely shows the result of regional depth reversals and case C is a crumpled mess due to essentially random local depth reversals.*

as basket ball nets, wire frames draped over balloons, used as packaging for foods, hammocks or fishnet stockings and bodysuits. The procedure radically differs from the established photogrammetic methods in that it is inherently Euclidean (it requires that the image plane carries a Euclidean metric). As such it is of interest as one extreme item in the toolbox of computer vision methods.

Although we have presented the case of orthogonal, planar projection, it is straightforward to generalize to the case of central projection provided the camera is fully calibrated. One simply changes to polar coordinates. Since the solution will be up to a scaling one may set the true edge length to unity and introduce the distance to the maze as the new unknown. Different from the present case this distance will vary from maze to maze, but the fact that Λ is the same for all mazes was not used in the solution anyway: Thus the solution essentially proceeds as described above and *conceptually* nothing new is gained, though such a solution may well prove to be of value in applications.

We envisage at least these three applications of Chebyshev nets in computer vision: 1^{stly}, they enlarge the set of fiducial objects on which one may draw to post–calibrate projective photogrammetic reconstructions, 2^{ndly}, the fact that "shape from (Chebyshev) nets" is viable and that humans seem able to perform this feat suggests their use in computer graphics. Renderings of Chebyshev nets may be used to provide the spectator with powerful depth cues. Finally, and 3^{rdly}, Chebyshev nets provide versatile parameterizations of surfaces for purposes of object representation. (For instance, we have presented a rather attractive parameterization of the hemisphere.) They are attractive because they are rather immediate generalizations of the planar Cartesian meshes (chess boards), yet they allow for much freedom, *e.g.*, can be naturally rotated about a point, deformed in various ways and applied to arbitrary other surfaces as—for instance—the plane. Thus any surface appears as a deformation of *e.g.* the plane such that lengths in two directions are conserved. This suggests many possible applications in CAD–CAM and object representation.

References

[1927] Bianchi, L.: Lezioni di geometria differenziale. 3rd ed., Vol. I, Part I, Nicola Zarichelli, Bologna (1927) 153–162

[1993] Faugeras, O.: Three–dimensional computer vision. The MIT Press, Cambridge, Mass. (1993)

[1986] Koenderink, J. J.: Optic Flow. Vision Research **26** (1986) 161–180

[1970] Sauer, R.: Differenzengeometrie. Springer, Berlin (1970)

[1981] Stevens, K. A.: The visual interpretation of surface contours. Artificial Intelligence **17** (1981) 47–73

[1983] Stevens, K. A.: The line of curvature constraint and the interpretation of 3–D shape from parallel surface contours. 8th Int.Joint Conf. on Artificial Intelligence (1983) 1057–1062

[1986] Stevens, K. A.: Inferring shape from contours across surfaces. In: From pixels to predicates. Ed. A. P. Pentland, Ablex Publ. Corp., Norwood, NJ. (1986)

[1942] Thomas, H.: Zur Frage des Gleichgewichts von Tschebyscheff–Netzen aus verknoteten und gespannten Fäden. Math.Z. **47** (1942) 66–77

[1878] Tschebyscheff, P. L.: Sur la coupe des vêtements. Association francaise pour l'avancement des sciences. Congrès de Paris (1878) 154

[1882] Voss, A.: Über ein neues Prinzip der Abbildung krummer Oberflächen. Math.Ann. **XIX** (1882) 1–25

Changes in Surface Convexity and Topology Caused by Distortions of Stereoscopic Visual Space

Gregory Baratoff[1] and Yiannis Aloimonos[2]

[1] Dept. of Neural Information Processing, University of Ulm,
89069 Ulm, GERMANY,
baratoff@neuro.informatik.uni-ulm.de,
[2] Center for Automation Research, University of Maryland,
College Park, MD 20742, USA,
yiannis@cfar.umd.edu

Abstract. We introduce the notion of a *distorted reconstruction* from two views, which need not satisfy the epipolar constraint. It can be computed from point correspondences and from a possibly inexact estimate of the stereo configuration. Thus, this scheme avoids the often costly and unstable minimization procedure for establishing the epipolar constraint, at the cost of introducing non-linear distortions. As a consequence, the convexity and topology of curves and surfaces can be changed.

The distorted reconstruction is related to the original scene structure by a quadratic Cremona transformation of space. By analyzing the distortion of curves and surfaces geometrically in terms of the singular elements of the associated Cremona transformation, we show that severe distortions are present particularly in the vicinity of the camera centers, thereby indicating that their consideration is of particularly high relevance for near regions of the stereo rig. Our main technical contribution is the derivation of the exact criteria governing changes in surface convexity and topology.

1 Introduction

One of the central tasks of a binocular (or stereoscopic) vision system is to reconstruct the scene from the projections of environmental structures onto the two views. The reconstruction computation is based on two pieces of information :

- a set of corresponding points (or lines) in the two views.
- the stereo configuration, i.e. the relative positions and orientations of the two cameras, and their internal parameters.

Corresponding points are usually obtained by a matching procedure based on purely visual attributes, whereas the stereo configuration can be obtained from either visual or by non-visual sources of information.

1.1 Reconstruction and the Epipolar Constraint

By whatever means it is obtained, the stereo configuration needs to be known exactly if the resulting reconstruction is to be veridical, i.e. if metric properties such as distances and angles are to be preserved. Unfortunately, obtaining the exact stereo configuration can be problematic. Estimates of the stereo configuration based on *non-visual* information are often not accurate enough. Furthermore, they are usually inconsistent with the epipolar constraint, which expresses the fact that corresponding rays issued by the two cameras should intersect in space. In order to exploit *visual* information, the cameras have to be calibrated individually, and their relative orientation has to be found, with both procedures in general requiring a non-linear minimization[16]. Especially in the presence of noise these computations are plagued by instabilities, and convergence can not in general be guaranteed.

Partial relief comes from recent advances in the field of computer vision showing that a projective reconstruction can still be obtained even if the internal parameters of both cameras are unknown[7]. A projective reconstruction is a projective transformation of the original scene structure, i.e. it is *linear* when expressed in terms of homogeneous coordinates. Furthermore, a projective reconstruction satisfies the epipolar constraint. A more practical reason for its attractiveness is the fact that a projective representation is adequate for a variety of tasks, such as recognition and navigation[5, 11].

But, just as is the case for the calibration of the stereo rig in the metric case, computing a projective reconstruction can be an unstable process[9]. In both cases the instability arises from the attempt to satisfy the epipolar constraint. The question we asked ourselves is whether this step could be avoided, and if so, what the nature of the resulting, necessarily *non-linear*, distortions would be.

1.2 Distorted Reconstruction

The reconstructed position of a point in space is usually defined as the intersection of the two corresponding rays. Therefore, the reconstruction is in general not even defined unless the epipolar constraint is satisfied. We remedy this by extending the definition of the reconstruction to point correspondences which are incompatible with the epipolar constraint. We call this new reconstruction a *distorted reconstruction*. There are many different ways of defining it, but we choose here a simple one that is at once geometrically intuitive and algebraically tractable : instead of the intersection of the two rays, the distorted reconstruction of a point is defined as the intersection of one of the rays and a plane containing the other ray.[1] This kind of distorted reconstruction can be termed a reconstruction with a *dominant camera*. The specific instance we will be using is shown in Figure 1, where the left camera is considered the dominant one, by virtue of providing the ray, whereas the right camera only provides a plane (the one defined by the x-coordinate).

---

[1] One alternative is the midpoint of the shortest segment connecting the two rays.

We do not claim originality for the *form* of the definition of the distorted reconstruction. Even in traditional approaches the reconstruction is sometimes computed in this manner, however only once an admissible stereo configuration has been found. Our approach represents, rather, a shift in emphasis : we consider the distorted reconstruction a *legitimate* reconstruction that is worthy of study. In going with this view, we take as the object of our analysis not the error in reconstruction, i.e. the difference between distorted and true structure, but the transformation relating the two. We call the transformation between the true and the distorted reconstruction of a scene the *shape distortion transformation*, or shape distortion for short. This also makes it more evident that we are considering the *systematic* relation between the two reconstructions arising from the use of an incorrect estimate of the stereo configuration, and not *random* errors due to image noise or matching errors. We have argued elsewhere[1] that both sources of error need to be considered, but in this article we concentrate on systematic errors.

The distorted reconstruction from image correspondences involves what we call the *apparent stereo configuration*, different from the *true stereo configuration* used in the projection of the scene onto the cameras. Furthermore, we refer to an *apparent space*, in which objects live that were reconstructed using the apparent configuration, and a *true space*, in which objects live that were reconstructed using the true configuration. In order to distinguish objects from the different spaces, we will always use primed symbols (e.g. $\mathbf{X}', \mathbf{m}'$) to refer to objects in the apparent space.

1.3 Related Work

The framework of distortions was introduced by [6] in the case of calibrated cameras, and under the assumption of infinitesimal motion. It was shown there that quadratic terms appeared in the reconstruction. Here, we show that the shape distortion transformation in the case of discrete displacements is a quadratic Cremona transformation for arbitrarily positioned and oriented, uncalibrated cameras. Thus, the framework applies to distortions of metric as well as projective reconstructions. Our application of global properties of Cremona transformations to qualitatively explain the shape distortion is novel; we first used it to study the distortions in the planar case [2, 3]. Quadratic distortions have been observed by photogrammetrists[13] in certain stereoscopes. In the Computer Vision literature, (plane) quadratic transformations have been used to describe the mapping between corresponding points in two image planes (e.g. [10]), but have not been applied in the analysis of transformations of reconstructed space.

2 The Shape Distortion

2.1 Double Algebra

In this and in the following sections we utilize the framework of Double Algebra[4] to derive and analyze the shape distortion. Double algebra was first used in Computer Vision by Svensson [15], and has gained interest in recent years. Specifically, we employ the double algebra of $\mathcal{R}^4$ to represent points, lines, and planes in projective space $\mathcal{P}^3$ by (linear) subspaces of $\mathcal{R}^4$ in terms of homogeneous vectors. Two homogeneous vectors $\mathbf{a}$ and $\mathbf{b}$ that are equal up to a non-zero scale factor k, i.e. $\mathbf{a} = k\mathbf{b}$ represent the same subspace, and we write $\mathbf{a} \cong \mathbf{b}$ when we do not wish to mention the scale factor.

Double Algebra provides the join and meet operators $\vee$ and $\wedge$ for combining subspaces in various ways. For example, one writes :

- $\mathbf{l} = \mathbf{A} \vee \mathbf{B}$ for the line $\mathbf{l}$ formed by joining the two points $\mathbf{A}$ and $\mathbf{B}$,
- $\mathbf{p} = \mathbf{l} \vee \mathbf{C}$ for the plane $\mathbf{p}$ formed by joining $\mathbf{l}$ to a third point $\mathbf{C}$,
- $\mathbf{D} = \mathbf{k} \wedge \mathbf{p}$ for the point $\mathbf{D}$ in which the line $\mathbf{k}$ meets the plane $\mathbf{p}$.

The meet and the join are both *anti-symmetric*, i.e. $\mathbf{A} \vee \mathbf{A} = 0$, expressing the fact that the join of a point with itself is undefined, and $\mathbf{p} \wedge \mathbf{p} = 0$, expressing the fact that the meet of a plane with itself is undefined. They are also *linear* in both arguments. Underlying the join and meet operators is the notion of a *bracket*, which is a coordinate-free abstraction of a determinant. In $\mathcal{P}^3$, the bracket is defined for any sequence of four points $\{\mathbf{X}_i\}_{i=1}^4$, and is written as $[\mathbf{X}_1\ \mathbf{X}_2\ \mathbf{X}_3\ \mathbf{X}_4]$. It vanishes when the four points are coplanar, which happens when the $\mathbf{X}_i$ are linearly dependent. We will also use the shortened form $[\mathbf{m}, \mathbf{X}_4]$ where $\mathbf{m} = \mathbf{X}_1 \vee \mathbf{X}_2 \vee \mathbf{X}_3$ is a plane.

2.2 Camera Geometry

We use the pinhole camera model, and use a representation of the camera in terms of its plane star [2].[2] Let $\mathbf{m}_1, \mathbf{m}_2, \mathbf{m}_3$ be the base planes of the camera.[3] From now on we use the terms plane star and camera interchangeably. The center of projection of a camera is given by $\mathbf{O}_M = \mathbf{m}_1 \wedge \mathbf{m}_2 \wedge \mathbf{m}_3$ as the point of intersection of the three base planes. We define the projection of a point $\mathbf{X}$ onto the camera M as $([\mathbf{m}_1, \mathbf{X}]\ [\mathbf{m}_2, \mathbf{X}]\ [\mathbf{m}_3, \mathbf{X}])^T$.

An alternative way to look at a camera is to interpret it as a line star, i.e. the collection of lines that pass through the camera center. Given a plane star M, we define the associated line star matrix $L_M = (\mathbf{x}_M\ \mathbf{y}_M\ \mathbf{z}_M)$, where $\mathbf{x}_M = \mathbf{m}_2 \wedge \mathbf{m}_3, \mathbf{y}_M = \mathbf{m}_3 \wedge \mathbf{m}_1, \mathbf{z}_M = \mathbf{m}_1 \wedge \mathbf{m}_2$ are the base lines.

Given a camera M, we define the x-plane $\mathbf{m}_x(\mathbf{X})$, the y-plane $\mathbf{m}_y(\mathbf{X})$, and the ray $\mathbf{l}_M(\mathbf{X})$ of M through a point $\mathbf{X}$ as follows :

$$\mathbf{m}_x(\mathbf{X}) \doteq -\mathbf{y}_M \vee \mathbf{X} = [\mathbf{m}_1, \mathbf{X}]\,\mathbf{m}_3 - [\mathbf{m}_3, \mathbf{X}]\,\mathbf{m}_1 \tag{1}$$

$$\mathbf{m}_y(\mathbf{X}) \doteq \mathbf{x}_M \vee \mathbf{X} = [\mathbf{m}_2, \mathbf{X}]\,\mathbf{m}_3 - [\mathbf{m}_3, \mathbf{X}]\,\mathbf{m}_2 \tag{2}$$

$$\mathbf{l}_M(\mathbf{X}) \doteq \mathbf{O}_M \vee \mathbf{X} = [\mathbf{m}_1, \mathbf{X}]\,\mathbf{x}_M + [\mathbf{m}_2, \mathbf{X}]\,\mathbf{y}_M + [\mathbf{m}_3, \mathbf{X}]\,\mathbf{z}_M \tag{3}$$

---

[2] A plane star is the 2-parameter family of planes through a common point. Any plane of the plane star can be generated as a linear combination of three base planes.

[3] The 3×4 matrix commonly used to represent a projective camera is given in terms of the plane star representation as $-M^T$, where $M = (\mathbf{m}_1\ \mathbf{m}_2\ \mathbf{m}_3)$. See [2].

Stereo Geometry Let C and D be two cameras. Then, a point $\mathbf{X}$ can be reconstructed by computing the meet of, say, the ray $\mathbf{l}_C(\mathbf{X})$ of C with the x-plane $\mathbf{d}_x(\mathbf{X})$ of D, i.e. $\mathbf{X} \cong \mathbf{l}_C(\mathbf{X}) \wedge \mathbf{d}_x(\mathbf{X})$. (See Fig. 1.) Note that there are other possible reconstructions (e.g. replace $\mathbf{d}_x(\mathbf{X})$ by $\mathbf{d}_y(\mathbf{X})$), but they are all equivalent if the apparent and true cameras are identical.

2.3   Distorted Reconstructions of Rays, Planes, and Points

In a distorted reconstruction we have an apparent stereo configuration, given by the pair of cameras C' and D', which are in general not identical with the true cameras C and D. We first define the distorted reconstructions of camera planes and rays (by modification of equations (1)–(3)) :

$$\mathbf{m}'_x(\mathbf{X}) = [\mathbf{m}_1, \mathbf{X}]\, \mathbf{m}'_3 - [\mathbf{m}_3, \mathbf{X}]\, \mathbf{m}'_1 \tag{4}$$

$$\mathbf{m}'_y(\mathbf{X}) = [\mathbf{m}_2, \mathbf{X}]\, \mathbf{m}'_3 - [\mathbf{m}_3, \mathbf{X}]\, \mathbf{m}'_2 \tag{5}$$

$$\mathbf{l}'_M(\mathbf{X}) = [\mathbf{m}_1, \mathbf{X}]\, \mathbf{x}'_M + [\mathbf{m}_2, \mathbf{X}]\, \mathbf{y}'_M + [\mathbf{m}_3, \mathbf{X}]\, \mathbf{z}'_M \tag{6}$$

These we call *direct* distorted planes and rays. They live in apparent space, whereas $\mathbf{X}$ lives in true space. Similarly, we also define the *reverse* distorted planes and rays for a point $\mathbf{X}'$ in the apparent space :

$$\mathbf{m}_x(\mathbf{X}') = [\mathbf{m}'_1, \mathbf{X}']\, \mathbf{m}_3 - [\mathbf{m}'_3, \mathbf{X}']\, \mathbf{m}'_1 \tag{7}$$

$$\mathbf{m}_y(\mathbf{X}') = [\mathbf{m}'_2, \mathbf{X}']\, \mathbf{m}_3 - [\mathbf{m}'_3, \mathbf{X}']\, \mathbf{m}_2 \tag{8}$$

$$\mathbf{l}_M(\mathbf{X}') = [\mathbf{m}'_1, \mathbf{X}']\, \mathbf{x}_M + [\mathbf{m}'_2, \mathbf{X}']\, \mathbf{y}_M + [\mathbf{m}'_3, \mathbf{X}']\, \mathbf{z}_M \tag{9}$$

These entities live in true space, whereas $\mathbf{X}'$ lives in apparent space. The direct distorted reconstruction of a point $\mathbf{X}$ is given by $\mathbf{l}'_C(\mathbf{X}) \wedge \mathbf{d}'_x(\mathbf{X})$. It is illustrated in Figure 1. We have the following result :

Theorem 1. *(Space Shape Distortion)*
Let (C, D) be the true stereo configuration, and (C', D') the apparent one. Then the shape distortion transformation $\mathbf{T}(\mathbf{X}) \doteq \mathbf{l}'_C(\mathbf{X}) \wedge \mathbf{d}'_x(\mathbf{X})$ is a quadratic space Cremona transformation. Its reverse is $\mathbf{T}'(\mathbf{X}') \doteq \mathbf{l}_C(\mathbf{X}') \wedge \mathbf{d}_x(\mathbf{X}')$.

Proof. That $\mathbf{T}$ is quadratic in $\mathbf{X}$ follows from the fact that both $\mathbf{l}'_C(\mathbf{X})$ and $\mathbf{d}'_x(\mathbf{X})$ are linear in $\mathbf{X}$, and from the linearity of the meet. The proof that $\mathbf{T}'$ is indeed the reverse transformation of $\mathbf{T}$ can be found in [2]. $\qquad\square$

3   Global Analysis of the Shape Distortion

In this section we review some established results on Cremona transformations [12], and then apply them to the shape distortion transformation.

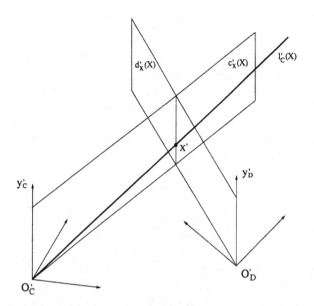

Fig. 1. Distorted reconstruction as the intersection of the distorted ray $l'_C(\mathbf{X}) = c'_x(\mathbf{X}) \wedge c'_y(\mathbf{X})$ of camera C with the distorted x-plane $d'_x(\mathbf{X})$ of camera D.

3.1 Cremona Transformations

A Cremona transformation is a *birational* transformation, i.e. a rational transformation whose inverse is also rational. This means that Cremona transformations are one-to-one mappings in general. A trivial example of a Cremona transformation is a collineation. It is one-to-one everywhere. However, for transformations of higher order there always exist exceptional points for which the transformation is not one-to-one.

A Cremona transformation $\mathbf{T}$ in $\mathcal{P}^3$ can be represented by a vector of 4 homogeneous polynomials $\mathcal{T}_i$:

$$\mathbf{T} : \mathbf{X} \mapsto \mathbf{X}' = (\mathcal{T}_1(\mathbf{X}) \; \mathcal{T}_2(\mathbf{X}) \; \mathcal{T}_3(\mathbf{X}) \; \mathcal{T}_4(\mathbf{X}))^T.$$

Cremona transformations have the property that the polynomials $\mathcal{T}_i$ all have the same degree; this is called the *order* of the transformation.

Since a Cremona transformation is a one-to-one mapping almost everywhere, its inverse $\mathbf{T}^{-1}$ is defined almost everywhere. One usually works instead with the *reverse* transformation $\mathbf{T}'$, which is equal to the inverse up to scale, i.e. $\mathbf{T}'(\mathbf{T}(\mathbf{X})) \cong \mathbf{T}^{-1}(\mathbf{T}(\mathbf{X})) = \mathbf{X}$. Since we are dealing with transformations between homogeneous coordinates, the scale does not affect the mapping of the non-homogeneous coordinates as long as it does not vanish. We write the reverse transformation as

$$\mathbf{T}' : \mathbf{X}' \mapsto \mathbf{X} = (\mathcal{T}'_1(\mathbf{X}') \; \mathcal{T}'_2(\mathbf{X}') \; \mathcal{T}'_3(\mathbf{X}') \; \mathcal{T}'_4(\mathbf{X}'))^T.$$

It has the same order as $\mathbf{T}$, since a Cremona transformation and its reverse always have the same order [12].

Singular Elements The exceptional elements at which $\mathbf{T}$ is not one-to-one are simply those at which $\mathbf{T}(\mathbf{X}) = \mathbf{0}$, i.e. where all polynomials $\mathcal{T}_i(\mathbf{X})$ vanish. The set of such points $\mathbf{X}$ forms the *base elements* of $\mathbf{T}$. For a *quadratic* space Cremona transformation, the base is made up of a base point $\mathbf{B}_1$, and a base conic $\mathbf{b}$. We will see that for our purposes the special case of a degenerate base conic $\mathbf{b}$ will be important; in this case $\mathbf{b}$ splits into two intersecting lines $\mathbf{b}_2$ and $\mathbf{b}_3$. Since $\mathbf{T}'$ is of the same order as $\mathbf{T}$, its base has exactly the same structure as that of $\mathbf{T}$. We denote its base elements by the corresponding primed quantities $\mathbf{B}_1'$ and $\mathbf{b}'$, respectively $\mathbf{b}_2', \mathbf{b}_3'$.

A further set of elements, which in a sense is dual to the base elements, is also relevant for the characterization of Cremona transformations. These are the *fundamental elements*. With a quadratic Cremona transformation is associated a fundamental plane $\mathbf{f}_1$, which is the plane containing the base conic $\mathbf{b}$, and a cone of fundamental lines, each generating line of which is formed by connecting the base point $\mathbf{B}_1$ to a point on the base conic $\mathbf{b}$. In the degenerate case of interest to us, $\mathbf{f}_1$ is spanned by $\mathbf{b}_2$ and $\mathbf{b}_3$, and the cone of fundamental lines splits into two planes $\mathbf{f}_2$ and $\mathbf{f}_3$ of fundamental lines. This configuration is illustrated in Figure 2. The fundamental elements of $\mathbf{T}'$ can be defined in an analogous way, and will be referred to by the corresponding primed quantities $\mathbf{f}_i'$.

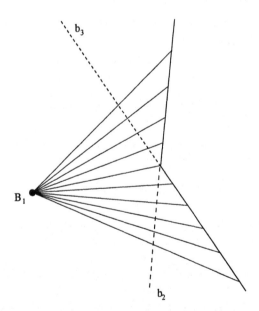

Fig. 2. Base elements of a quadratic space Cremona transformation with degenerate base conic.

The reason that we single out the fundamental elements is that $\mathbf{T}$ maps its fundamental elements onto the base elements of $\mathbf{T}'$, and vice versa. Specifically, $\mathbf{T}$ maps $\mathbf{f}_1$ onto $\mathbf{B}_1'$, and each fundamental line of $\mathbf{f}_2$ ($\mathbf{f}_3$) to a point of $\mathbf{b}_2$ ($\mathbf{b}_3$).

Similarly, $\mathbf{T}'$ maps $\mathbf{f}_1'$ onto $\mathbf{B}_1$, and each fundamental line of $\mathbf{f}_2'$ ($\mathbf{f}_3'$) to a point of $\mathbf{b}_2'$ ($\mathbf{b}_3'$).

Taken together, we call the base and the fundamental elements the *singular elements* of the Cremona transformation.

The Web of Quadrics A quadratic Cremona transformation maps a plane to a quadric surface. Thus, to the 3-parameter family of planes in true space there corresponds via $\mathbf{T}$ a 3-parameter family of quadrics in apparent space. Similarly, $\mathbf{T}'$ defines a 3-parameter family of quadrics in true space which are the images of planes in apparent space. Such a 3-parameter family is called a *web of quadrics*. An important property of the quadrics of a web is that each one of them contains the base elements of the associated quadratic Cremona transformation.

3.2 Properties of the Shape Distortion

In order to apply the global analysis to the shape distortion, the first step is to determine its singular elements. They are given in the following proposition :

Proposition 1. *(Singular Elements of the Space Shape Distortion)*
The singular elements of the space shape distortion $\mathbf{T}(\mathbf{X})$ *(from Thm. 1) are*

$$
\begin{aligned}
\mathbf{B}_1 &= \mathbf{O}_C & \mathbf{b}_2 &= \mathbf{y}_D & \mathbf{b}_3 &= \mathbf{f}_1 \wedge \mathbf{f}_2 \\
\mathbf{f}_1 &= \mathbf{d}_x(\mathbf{O}_C') & \mathbf{f}_2 &= \mathbf{c}(\mathbf{y}_D') & \mathbf{f}_3 &= \mathbf{B}_1 \vee \mathbf{b}_2,
\end{aligned}
\tag{10}
$$

and the singular elements of its reverse $\mathbf{T}'(\mathbf{X}')$ *are*

$$
\begin{aligned}
\mathbf{B}_1' &= \mathbf{O}_C' & \mathbf{b}_2' &= \mathbf{y}_D' & \mathbf{b}_3' &= \mathbf{f}_1' \wedge \mathbf{f}_2' \\
\mathbf{f}_1' &= \mathbf{d}_x'(\mathbf{O}_C) & \mathbf{f}_2' &= \mathbf{c}'(\mathbf{y}_D) & \mathbf{f}_3' &= \mathbf{B}_1' \vee \mathbf{b}_2'
\end{aligned}
\tag{11}
$$

The proof can be found in [2]. The proposition states several interesting facts :

- The dominant camera center $\mathbf{O}_C$ is the base point of the space shape distortion.
- The base conic splits into two base lines; one of them is $\mathbf{y}_D$, the y-axis of the non-dominant camera.
- The plane spanned by $\mathbf{O}_C$ and $\mathbf{y}_D$ is a plane of fundamental lines.

Since planes in general map onto quadrics passing through all three base elements, we can say that

Corollary 1. *The shape distortion is particularly severe in the vicinity of the dominant camera center and the Y-axis of the non-dominant camera.*

One can appreciate the severity of the distortion by imagining how the image of every plane must somehow converge to pass through the same base elements, for example the center of camera C. Thus, it is particularly important to take distortions into account in the near range of the stereo rig.

Our next result concerns changes in topology of a surface under the shape distortion :

Proposition 2. *(Topology Changes) The topology of a surface changes under the shape distortion iff the surface meets one of the following conditions :*

- *it intersects the fundamental plane f_1.*
- *it intersects one of the planes of fundamental lines f_2 and f_3 in such a way that it contains at least two distinct points of the same fundamental line.*

Proof. From section 3.1, we know that all points of a given fundamental element map to the same point. Thus, if a surface contains two distinct points belonging to the same fundamental element, the image of the surface will pass twice through the same point, thus creating a self-intersection, clearly a change of topology. A proper intersection with f_1 yields an entire curve, whereas an intersection with f_2 or f_3 does not necessarily intersect any of the fundamental lines within these planes twice. Thus, the additional requirement for f_2 and f_3. $\qquad\square$

3.3 Restriction to Preserved Planes

The space shape distortion is a complicated transformation. We could simplify the analysis if we considered the restriction of the space shape distortion to planes. However, we can not in general do this, since a plane maps into a (web) quadric, and not into a plane. A plane-to-plane mapping only exists if the web quadric is degenerate. Luckily, it turns out that there are enough of these degenerate quadrics for the purposes of our analysis. The next proposition tells us which ones they are :

Proposition 3. *Let $\mathbf{X}$ be a point which neither coincides nor is contained in any of the base elements of $\mathbf{T}$, and let $\mathbf{X'} = \mathbf{T}(\mathbf{X})$. Then,*

1. *the pencil of planes with axis $\mathbf{X} \vee \mathbf{B}_1$ maps to the pencil of planes with axis $\mathbf{X'} \vee \mathbf{B'_1}$.*
2. *the plane $\mathbf{X} \vee \mathbf{b}_i$ maps to the plane $\mathbf{X'} \vee \mathbf{b'_i}$, for $i = 2, 3$.*
3. *all other planes through $\mathbf{X}$ map to non-degenerate quadrics.*
4. *the line $\mathbf{X} \vee \mathbf{B}_1$ maps to the line $\mathbf{X'} \vee \mathbf{B'_1}$.*
5. *the pencil of lines with vertex $\mathbf{X}$ contained in the plane $\mathbf{X} \vee \mathbf{b}_i$ maps to the pencil of lines with vertex $\mathbf{X'}$ contained in the plane $\mathbf{X'} \vee \mathbf{b'_i}$.*
6. *all other lines through $\mathbf{X}$ map to non-degenerate conics.*

The proof can be found in [2], where it is also shown that the restriction of the space shape distortion to such preserved planes is a quadratic *plane* Cremona transformation. The structure of the planar transformation is similar to the space case, but its analysis is much simpler. Specifically, for a C-plane $\mathbf{p}$ (type 1 in Proposition 3), passing through $\mathbf{B}_1$, the base elements of the planar shape distortion are three base points : $\mathbf{B}_1$, plus the two points $\mathbf{p} \wedge \mathbf{b}_2$ and $\mathbf{p} \wedge \mathbf{b}_3$. A quadratic plane Cremona transformation in general maps a line to a conic. The set of images of lines form the *net of conics* associated with the transformation.

4 Distortion of Curvature

Our next task is to analyze the distortion of surface curvature. We first present results for the planar case, and then apply them to sections of surfaces by C-planes (type 1 in Proposition 3).

4.1 The Planar Case

A key result of the analysis of the planar shape distortion is the following :

Theorem 2. *Let C be a planar curve through the point $\mathbf{X}$, with its image C' under the planar shape distortion $\mathbf{T}$ passing through $\mathbf{X}' = \mathbf{T}(\mathbf{X})$. Let κ (κ') be the curvature of C (C') at $\mathbf{X}$ $(\mathbf{X}')$, and let κ_0 (κ_0') be the curvature of the net conic through $\mathbf{X}$ $(\mathbf{X}')$ with the same tangent there as C (C'). Then, the curvatures of C and C' are related as follows :*

$$\frac{\kappa'}{\kappa_0'} = 1 - \frac{\kappa}{\kappa_0} \tag{12}$$

A proof of this can be found in [2]. From the curvature formula (12) we obtain a simple rule for the sign of the curvature of the distorted curve :

$$\operatorname{sgn}(\kappa') = \begin{cases} \operatorname{sgn}(\kappa_0') & , \kappa < \kappa_0 \\ 0 & , \kappa = \kappa_0 \\ -\operatorname{sgn}(\kappa_0') & , \kappa > \kappa_0 \end{cases} \tag{13}$$

Thus, the curvature κ' changes sign when the curvature κ of the original curve crosses the threshold κ_0 set by the curvature of the net conic. The relationship between the two curvatures is illustrated in Figure 3. The four curves through

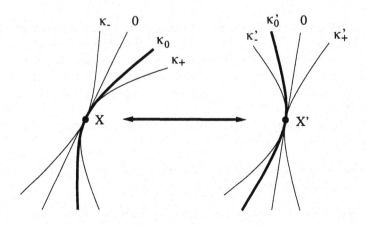

Fig. 3. Distortion of Curvature

$\mathbf{X}$ on the left map under $\mathbf{T}$ into four curves through $\mathbf{X}'$ on the right. The curves are labelled by their curvatures, and form the following pairs under $\mathbf{T}$: $\{(\kappa_-, \kappa'_-), (0, \kappa'_0), (\kappa_0, 0), (\kappa_+, \kappa'_+)\}$. The thick curves belong to the net of conics defined by the quadratic transformation. The existence of the middle intervals in Figure 3 is what distinguishes quadratic from projective (linear) transformations. It reflects the fact that a convex curve may transform into a curve with a concave segment, i.e. that changes of convexity can occur.

4.2 Distortion of Surface Curvature

The local surface curvature at a point $\mathbf{X}$ on a surface depends on the direction in the tangent plane in which it is measured. Euler's formula[8] gives the normal curvature as a function of angle α in the tangent plane as :

$$\kappa_n(\alpha) = \kappa_1 \cos^2(\alpha - \alpha_1) + \kappa_2 \sin^2(\alpha - \alpha_1) \tag{14}$$

where κ_1 and κ_2 are the principal curvatures, i.e. the maximal and minimal normal curvatures at $\mathbf{X}$, and α_1 is the angle corresponding to the direction associated with κ_1. The directions in which the principal curvatures occur are called principal directions. They are orthogonal. When κ_1 and κ_2 are of the same sign, the surface is locally elliptic, and when they are of opposite signs, the surface is hyperbolic. In the latter case there are locally two asymptotic directions in which the normal curvature vanishes. The asymptotic directions are bisectors of the principal directions.

If we take the section of a surface by a plane that is not normal to the surface, its curvature is given by Meusnier's Theorem[8] : $\kappa = \kappa_n / \cos\gamma$, where γ is the angle between the sectioning plane and the normal to the surface at $\mathbf{X}$. By combining this with (14), we can determine the curvature of an arbitrary section of a surface.

Curvature of a Web Quadric In the planar case discussed in section 4.1, the curvature of a curve was compared to the curvature of the net conic to determine whether the convexity of the curve changes. Here, we relate the curvature of a given surface to the curvature of the web quadric with the same tangent plane. We do this by considering their section by the pencil of preserved planes with axis $\mathbf{O}_C \vee \mathbf{X}$.

We now outline a way in which the curvature of a web-quadric can be determined. But first, we derive some useful properties :

Proposition 4. *The web quadrics associated with the space shape distortion and its reverse are hyperboloids of one sheet.*

Proof. In section 3.1 we saw that every web quadric contains all base elements. In particular, every web quadric of $\mathbf{T}$ contains the two (intersecting) base lines $\mathbf{b}_2$ and $\mathbf{b}_3$, and every web quadric of $\mathbf{T}'$ contains the two (intersecting) base line $\mathbf{b}'_2$ and $\mathbf{b}'_3$. The only non-degenerate quadrics that contain two intersecting lines are hyperboloids of one sheet [14]. $\qquad\square$

A hyperboloid has the property that at each of its points the surface is locally hyperbolic, i.e. its principal curvatures are of opposite sign. Additionally, for a hyperboloid of one sheet the two lines through $\mathbf{X}$ in the asymptotic directions are contained as a whole in the surface[14]. They are its generators. The next proposition shows that they belong to the family of preserved lines discussed in Section 3.3.

Proposition 5. *(Generators of Web Quadrics)*
Let $\mathcal{Q}$ be a web quadric of the space shape distortion $\mathbf{T}$ at a point $\mathbf{X}$, and let $\mathbf{m}$ be its tangent plane there. Then, the two generators of $\mathcal{Q}$ through $\mathbf{X}$ are the lines of intersection $\mathbf{l}_i$ of $\mathbf{m}$ with the planes $\mathbf{X} \vee \mathbf{b}_i$, $i = 2, 3$.

Proof. The web quadric $\mathcal{Q}$ is the image under $\mathbf{T}'$ of a plane $\mathbf{m}'$. Consider the pencil of lines in $\mathbf{m}'$ with vertex $\mathbf{X}'$. Of the lines of this pencil only two are preserved as lines under $\mathbf{T}'$, namely the lines $\mathbf{l}'_i = (\mathbf{X}' \vee \mathbf{b}'_i) \wedge \mathbf{m}'$ (type 5 in Proposition 3), which map to the lines $\mathbf{l}_i$, $i = 2, 3$. These two lines must therefore be the generators of $\mathcal{Q}$. $\square$

The construction of the generators described in the proposition is depicted in Figure 4. Since the directions in the tangent plane at $\mathbf{X}$ corresponding to

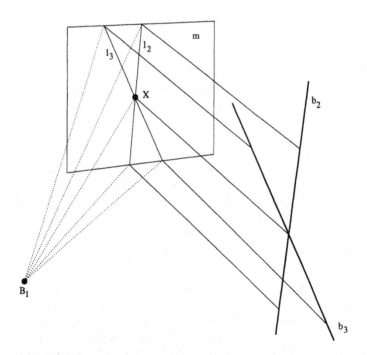

Fig. 4. The two generators $\mathbf{l}_2, \mathbf{l}_3$ through a point $\mathbf{X}$ of a web quadric with tangent plane $\mathbf{m}$ at $\mathbf{X}$ are the lines of intersection of $\mathbf{m}$ with the two planes $\mathbf{X} \vee \mathbf{b}_2$ and $\mathbf{X} \vee \mathbf{b}_3$.

the generators are asymptotic directions, we can find the principal directions

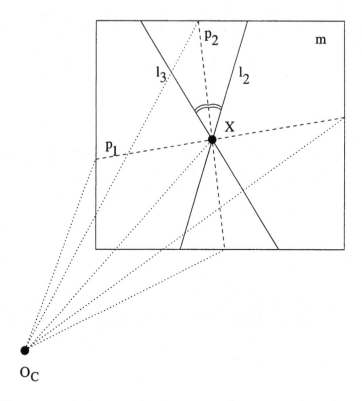

Fig. 5. The asymptotic directions in the tangent plane **m** are along the generators $l_i, i = 2, 3$, of the web quadric. The principal directions are bisectors of the asymptotic directions.

as their bisectors in **m**, as mentioned above. This is shown in Figure 5. The principal curvatures of the web quadric can thus be obtained as follows : one computes the curvatures $\tilde{\kappa}_1$ and $\tilde{\kappa}_2$ of the sections of the web quadric by the two C-planes through the principal directions (indicated in Figure 5 by the dotted lines). Additionally, one computes the angles γ_1 and γ_2 between these C-planes and the normal to **m**. Then, the principal curvatures of the web quadric are given by Meusnier's Theorem as $\kappa_i^0 = \tilde{\kappa}_i / \cos \gamma_i$.

Qualitative Description of Curvature Distortion Let κ_1 and κ_2 denote the principal curvatures at a point **X** of a surface with tangent plane **m** at **X**. Let α_1 denote the principal direction associated with κ_1. The normal curvature of the surface is given by (14). Let α_0 denote the principal direction associated with κ_1^0. The normal curvature of the web quadric is given by $\kappa_0(\alpha) = \kappa_1^0 \cos^2(\alpha - \alpha_0) + \kappa_2^0 \sin^2(\alpha - \alpha_0)$. The normal curvatures of the surface and of the web quadric are illustrated in Figure 6 (top figure). In each normal section, i.e. for each α, the interval in which $\kappa(\alpha)$ lies determines the interval in which the

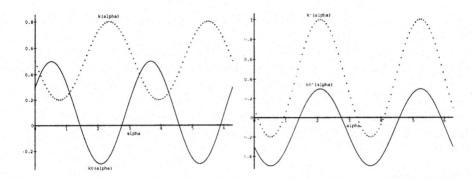

Fig. 6. Distortion of normal curvature in true space (left figure) and in apparent space (right figure). Solid curves represent the normal curvature of the web quadric as a function of direction. Dotted curves represent the normal curvature of the surface. See text for explanation.

distorted curvature $\kappa'(\alpha)$ lies. For example, if $\kappa(\alpha) > \kappa_0(\alpha)$, then $\kappa'(\alpha) > 0$. For certain values of α the graph of $\kappa(\alpha)$ intersects the graph of $\kappa_0(\alpha)$. These are the values of α at which the sign of the distorted curvature changes. It should be emphasized that this can happen independently of whether the true normal curvature function ever passes through zero. A situation where the surface in the true space is locally elliptic (all normal curvatures positive), but the distorted surface is locally hyperbolic, is shown in Figure 6. One sees there that the crossing of the graphs of $\kappa(\alpha)$ and $\kappa_0(\alpha)$ results in a zero-crossing of $\kappa'(\alpha)$. This is the criterion under which an elliptic patch of a surface can transform to a hyperbolic patch on the distorted surface, and vice-versa.

5 Conclusions

We derived the shape distortion transformation for the general case of uncalibrated, and arbitrarily positioned and oriented, cameras, and showed that the full range of distortions for a stereo rig, due to errors in intrinsic and extrinsic camera parameters, is exactly modelled by quadratic space Cremona transformations.

Our analysis of the shape distortion transformation in terms of global properties of quadratic Cremona transformations suggested that the distortions are particularly severe in the vicinity of the camera centers.

Global properties of quadratic Cremona transformations further show that the topology and convexity of curves and surfaces can change under the shape distortion. We showed how violations of topology are governed by the crossing of certain planes defined in terms of the stereo geometry. Regarding violations of convexity, we derived the criterion for the change of surface type from elliptic to hyperbolic.

In this work we have explored the geometrical structure of the shape distortion. Future work will proceed along two directions. Firstly, we intend to perform a quantitative evaluation of the magnitude of the distortion for commonly encountered stereo geometries. Secondly, we intend to examine which tasks could be performed based on a distorted reconstruction of a scene, similarly to what has successfully been done for affine and projective reconstructions [5,11].

References

1. G. Baratoff. Ordinal and metric structure of smooth surfaces from parallax. In *Proc. Int. Conf. on Pattern Recognition ICPR'96*, pages 275–279, 1996.
2. G. Baratoff. Distortion of stereoscopic visual space. Technical Report CAR-TR-861, PhD Thesis, Center for Automation Research, University of Maryland, College Park, USA, May 1997.
3. G. Baratoff. Distortions of stereoscopic visual space and quadratic cremona transformations. In *Proc. Computer Analysis of Images and Patterns CAIP'97*, pages 239–246, 1997.
4. M. Barnabei, A. Brini, and G. Rota. On the exterior calculus of invariant theory. *J. Algebra*, 96:120–160, 1985.
5. P. A. Beardsley, A. Zisserman, and D. W. Murray. Navigation using affine structure from motion. In *Proc. Europ. Conf. on Computer Vision ECCV'94*, pages 85–96, 1994.
6. L. Cheong and Y. Aloimonos. Iso-distortion contours and egomotion estimation. In *Proc. Int. Symp. on Computer Vision*, pages 55–60, 1995.
7. O. Faugeras. What can be seen in three dimensions with an uncalibrated stereo rig. In *Proc. Europ. Conf. on Computer Vision ECCV'92*, pages 563–578, 1992.
8. E. Kreyszig. *Differential Geometry*. Dover Publications, New York, 1991.
9. Q. T. Luong and O. Faugeras. The fundamental matrix : Theory, algorithms, and stability analysis. *Int. J. Computer Vision*, 17:43–75, 1996.
10. S. Maybank. *Theory of Reconstruction from Image Motion*. Springer-Verlag, Berlin, 1993.
11. L. Robert and O. D. Faugeras. Relative 3d positioning and 3d convex hull computation from a weakly calibrated stereo pair. In *Proc. Int. Conf. on Computer Vision ICCV'93*, pages 540–543, 1993.
12. J.G. Semple and L. Roth. *Introduction to Algebraic Geometry*. Oxford University Press, London, 1949.
13. C. C. Slama, C. Theurer, and S. W. Henriksen. *Manual of Photogrammetry*. American Society of Photogrammetry, 1980.
14. B. Spain. *Analytical Quadrics*. Pergamon Press, Oxford, UK, 1960.
15. L. Svensson. On the use of double algebra in computer vision. Technical Report TRITA-NA-P9310, Swedish Royal Institute of Technology, Stockholm, 1993.
16. J. Weng, N. Ahuja, and T.S. Huang. Optimal motion and structure estimation. *IEEE Trans. Pattern Analysis and Machine Intelligence*, 15:864–884, 1993.

Reconstruction of Smooth Surfaces with Arbitrary Topology Adaptive Splines

A. J. Stoddart and M. Baker

Centre for Vision, Speech and Signal Processing
University of Surrey, Guildford, Surrey GU2 5XH, UK,
a.stoddart@ee.surrey.ac.uk,
WWW: http://www.ee.surrey.ac.uk

Abstract. We present a novel method for fitting a smooth G^1 continuous spline to point sets. It is based on an iterative conjugate gradient optimisation scheme. Unlike traditional tensor product based splines we can fit arbitrary topology surfaces with locally adaptive meshing. For this reason we call the surface "slime".

Other attempts at this problem are based on tensor product splines and are therefore not locally adaptive.

1 Introduction

Range sensing is an area of computer vision that is being successfully applied to a variety of industrial problems. By combining several range images it is possible to build complete detailed surface models of real world objects for applications in VR, graphics and manufacturing [11,10,9].

Existing methods produce large datasets consisting of up to a million polygons. There is considerable interest in the use of more efficient representations such as spline surfaces [5,17,14]. Spline surfaces are much more efficient at representing smooth manufactured surfaces, e.g. car bodywork. For this reason splines are heavily used in CAD applications. Most of the spline surfaces commonly used in computer vision have severe limitations because they cannot have arbitrary topology and cannot be adaptively meshed.

In previous work [21] we presented a deformable surface that could have arbitrary topology, and we later went on to formulate a linear form that allowed fast computation [20]. In this paper we have developed a powerful scheme for surface reconstruction from point sets. The advances presented in this paper include

- A new method for constructing seed meshes.
- Techniques for locally adaptive spline surface representation. (Very few commonly used spline surfaces can be made locally adaptive.)
- Fast techniques for solving this optimisation problem based on an iterated conjugate gradient scheme.

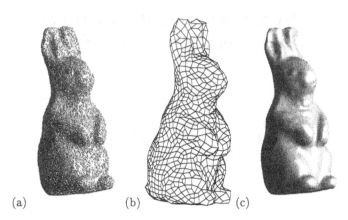

(a)   (b)   (c)

Fig. 1. Results from a surface fitted to a cloud of 15000 points (a) the point set (b) the control mesh (c) the fitted spline surface *flatshaded*

Our earlier work established a powerful representation. This work provides the tools necessary to use it in a variety of applications. Because of its special properties we have dubbed the surface 'slime'.

This work could be applied to a range of problems. We consider the following processing pipeline. Several range images are captured, registered and fused using a volumetric approach [11,10]. In this type of approach a volumetric field function is computed and the marching cubes algorithm can be used to obtain an isosurface. The result is a large piecewise flat mesh made up of triangular faces. Of course we may wish to reuse the original point measurements if accuracy has been lost by the volumetric representation. Volumetric approaches are limited by the processing considerations and memory usage rises rapidly as the voxel edge length is reduced below 1% of a side of the working volume.

This initial dense mesh and point set is taken as the starting point for our work. The aim of subsequent processing is to reduce the size of the representation, smooth the surface and increase the fidelity to the measured point set.

Accuracy is a key factor in commercial uptake of range sensing technology. A meaningful way of quoting accuracy independent of scale is to scale the working volume to lie inside a unit cube and express the rms error as a fraction of the cube size. The accuracy of commercially available range scanners varies between 1% and 0.01%. Mechanical Coordinate Measuring Machines (CMMs) can achieve 0.0001%. Any technique that proceeds via a discrete voxel approach has an error of the order of the voxel size. It is difficult to use small voxel sizes because routines for extracting an implicit surface (e.g. marching cubes) produce more than $O(10^5)$ triangles if the voxel size is reduced below 1%.

A sample set of results is now shown. In figure 1 we show a surface fitted to a cloud of 15000 points, the final spline control mesh (1459 patches) and a rendered view of the spline surface. *The rendered surface is rendered with flatshading, not a smoothed shading algorithm such as Gouraud shading as is common.*

2   Related work

Deformable curves and surfaces have been applied to many problems in computer vision. Medical imaging is an area where deformable surfaces are presently receiving much attention [18] due to the need for processing of volumetric data sets.

There has been much recent interest in shapes with non-trivial topology in computer vision in general and in deformable surfaces in particular. De Carlo and Metaxas have proposed an adaptive shape evolution scheme by blending together parts consisting of simple tensor product patches [5]. Another approach was presented by McInerney and Terzopoulos [17] who use a parallel 2D data structure to achieve a topologically adaptable snake. Related work includes that of Casselles *et al* [3] who proposed geodesic active contours based on a level set approach.

In the graphics community there is considerable interest in building models from range scanner data. Recent advances in fusion algorithms [11,10] allow the creation of detailed million polygon meshes and there is much interest in reducing the size of the representation by using higher order surfaces. Most recent work has concentrated on stitching together tensor product patches. [6,14].

3   The surface representation

The spline based surface that we use is a G^1 continuous arbitrary topology surface called a generalised biquadratic B-Spline (GBBS). It was first developed in the context of computer graphics by Loop and De Rose [15,16]. It is important to note that it is not possible to maintain C^1 continuity (first order parametric derivative) over an arbitrary topology surface. Instead the concept of G^1 continuity (first order geometric) is introduced. In effect it means that the tangent plane at a point on the surface varies continuously as the point moves on the surface.

We first presented an application of this surface to problems in computer vision in [21] and more recently [20] we succeeded in formulating a matrix form and a fast method of computation. The main weakness of the earlier work was the absence of algorithms for creating valid mesh topologies and adapting these topologies.

A full description of the GBBS would take up too much space so we present here only a brief summary of the salient points as they affect the algorithms. The reader is referred to the original papers for further details.

The GBBS is a powerful and elegant generalisation of the Biquadratic B-Spline. It automatically maintains G^1 continuity. The GBBS is defined by a set of M 3D control points $\mathbf{Q} = \{\mathbf{c}_m : \quad m = 1..M\}$ together with connectivity information K. The connectivity defines a mesh topology which is restricted to 4-sided faces, (see for example figure 2). Thus the surface is defined by $S = (\mathbf{Q}, K)$. The connectivity information can be summarised in a function $f(i, j, k, l)$ which is equal to 1 for each set of vertices i, j, k, l connected up to a face ordered

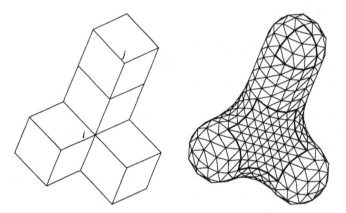

Fig. 2. A simple control mesh and the resulting spline surface (converted to triangles). Control point i generates the 6-sided patch and j generates the 3-sided patch.

anti-clockwise around an outward pointing normal. From this can be derived a function $e(i,j)$ equal 1 if i and j form an edge and 0 otherwise. It is also convenient to define $f(i,j)$ equal 1 if i and j are distinct but are part of the same face.

Each vertex gives rise to an n-sided surface patch where n is the number of 4-sided faces using that vertex. Patch m depends only on the $2n + 1$ element control vector $\mathbf{q}_m^\top = [c_m, c_k : f(m,k) = 1]$ consisting of c_m and the set of all vertices on adjacent faces, i.e. with k in the neighbourhood of m.

Previously we introduced a matrix-based scheme to compute the surface based on notation similar to that of [4]. The principal steps in computing the surface are as follows. The control vector $\mathbf{q}_m$ is converted to a vector of Bezier control points $\mathbf{r}_m$ by a matrix multiplication $\mathbf{r}_m = \mathbf{M}\mathbf{q}_m$ This is combined with a column vector containing all the Bezier polynomials $\mathbf{B}(p)$ to compute the point. Thus we obtain the surface patch S_m as a mapping from points $p = (u, v)$ contained in a regular n-gon domain D_n to a 3D surface

$$S_m = \{\mathbf{r}(p)|p \in D_n, \ \mathbf{r}(p) = \mathbf{B}^\top(p)\mathbf{M}\mathbf{q}_m\} \tag{1}$$

The whole surface S is the union of the patches S_m, $S = \bigcup_m S_m$. The control vector for patch m, $\mathbf{q}_m$ can be obtained from the vector of all control points $\mathbf{Q}^\top = [c_1..c_M]$ by a connectivity matrix $\mathbf{q}_m = G_m\mathbf{Q}$.

The simplest example of a Bezier polynomial is a Bezier curve [19,7]. When discussing Bezier curves it is useful to replace the usual single parameter u with two parameters $u_1(= u)$ and u_2 and a constraint that $u_1 + u_2 = 1$. A depth d Bezier curve $C = \{\mathbf{r}(u_1, u_2)| \ u_1 \epsilon[0,1], u_1 + u_2 = 1\}$ is defined in terms of $d + 1$ control points $\mathbf{r}_i$ and the Bernstein-Bezier polynomials $B_i^d(u_1, u_2)$ as follows

$$\mathbf{r}(u) = \mathbf{r}(u_1, u_2) = \sum_{i=0}^{d} \mathbf{r}_i B_i^d(u_1, u_2) = \sum_{i=0}^{d} \mathbf{r}_i \frac{d!}{i!(d-i)!} u_1^i u_2^{d-i} \tag{2}$$

The Bezier curve admits an elegant generalisation called a B-form that maps a $[(k+1)$-variate] k-dimensional parameter space onto any number of scalars. Firstly we must define multivariate Bernstein-Bezier polynomials. For these we will need a notation for multi-indices $\mathbf{i} = \{i_1, i_2, ...i_{k+1}\}$. The symbol $\hat{e}_j$ denotes a multi-index whose components are all zero except for the j component which is 1. It is useful to define a modulus of a multi-index as $|\mathbf{i}| = i_1 + i_2 + ... + i_{k+1}$. The k-variate depth d Bernstein-Bezier polynomials are a simple generalisation of equation (2).

$$B_\mathbf{i}^d(u_1, u_2, ...u_{k+1}) = \frac{d!}{i_1! i_2! ...i_{k+1}!} u_1^{i_1}, u_2^{i_2}, ...u_{k+1}^{i_{k+1}}, \qquad |\mathbf{i}| = d \qquad (3)$$

The Loop and De Rose scheme is based on S-patches, which are n-sided smooth patches which map a point $p = (u, v)$ inside n-sided domain polygon D to a 3D surface. Firstly we form n barycentric variables $l_i, i = 1..n$ defined as follows. Define the n vertices of the regular n-gon as p_i, $i = 1..n$. Define the fractional areas $\alpha_i(p)$ as the area of a triangle enclosed by points p, p_i, and p_{i+1} divided by the total area of D. Now form n new variables $\pi_i(p)$ by

$$\pi_i(p) = \alpha_1(p) \times ...\alpha_{i-2}(p)\alpha_{i+1}(p)...\alpha_n(p) \qquad (4)$$

Then form normalised variables $l_i(p)$

$$l_i(u, v) = l_i(p) = \frac{\pi_i(p)}{\pi_1(p) + ... + \pi_n(p)} \qquad (5)$$

The S-patch is now simply defined in terms of the variables $l_i(p)$ and the Bezier control points $\mathbf{r_i}$. It is a mapping $S = \{\mathbf{r}(u,v)|(u,v)\epsilon D_n\}$ where D_n is a n-sided domain polygon and

$$\mathbf{r}(u,v) = \sum_{|\mathbf{i}|=d} \mathbf{r_i}\, B_\mathbf{i}^d(l_1, l_2, ...l_n) \qquad (6)$$

Note that the n-sided patch uses a $k+1$ variate Bezier polynomial where $n = k+1$.

3.1 Computation

For details of computation of the matrix $\mathbf{M}$ the reader is referred to [20]. It contains constants so only needs to be computed once and stored. When repeated computation of a point p on a patch is required $\mathbf{B}^\top(p)\mathbf{M}$ may be pre-computed and stored. Then point evaluation consists of a weighted sum of the control points, and is very fast, $O(2n+1)$. This is typically what we use when rendering the surface. When an arbitrary point is required this can be slower for $n > 6$ because there are $\frac{(n+6)!}{6!(n+1)!}$ Bezier control points and in general we avoid patches with more than 6 sides.

4 Seeding

An important new result presented in this paper is a solution to the seeding problem. A valid slime surface must have a mesh of control points connected in a special way. The mesh must be made up of 4 sided faces and each non-boundary vertex must have 3 or more faces using it.

A precondition to adaptive meshing algorithms is a valid starting point. In our processing pipeline we indicated that our starting point is a triangular mesh. In our first paper [21] we suggested a method that would convert a triangular mesh to a mesh of four-sided faces. The idea was to subdivide each triangle into 3 four-sided faces. This was a valid solution, but not ideal, because it required the number of faces be increased by a factor of three.

A better option would be to group pairs of three-sided faces to form a four sided mesh with half the number of faces. This is a nontrivial problem because if even one triangle is unpaired the solution is of no use. It bears some superficial resemblance to the NP-hard problem of finding a Hamilton cycle on a graph.

The algorithm is now presented. It is based on region growing over the set of triangles t on the surface. Each triangle has edges e and the region boundary, denoted B is not allowed to self intersect. A pair of adjacent triangles is chosen as a seed and the seed boundary is passed to RegionGrow(B).

The region boundary is grown by adding a pair of adjacent triangles at a time. This operation can fail when the boundary self intersects and two non-connected regions each with an odd number of triangles are left outside the boundary. The algorithm backtracks from this point to the last boundary that contained no "elbows". By elbow we mean a part of the boundary where two adjacent boundary edges lie on the same triangle. The significance of this is that when a pair of triangles is grown there is no choice as to how the triangles are paired.

This is illustrated in figure 3 when the boundary encloses the shaded region and attempts to grow a pair of white triangles. If triangle 1 is added only triangle 2 can be paired with it. This is not the case for triangle 3 which can be paired with triangle 4 or 5.

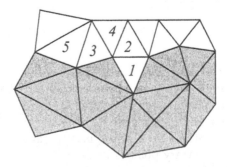

Fig. 3. The boundary contains an 'elbow' at triangle 1

The algorithm below is not guaranteed to succeed but has succeeded for all our data sets. A depth first recursive search is guaranteed to succeed but has worst case exponential complexity. The search presented here stores the last non-elbow boundary so it is a modification of a depth first search which only ever backtracks up one level. In practice, because there are many non-elbow boundaries, the algorithm is linear in the number of faces. Since the number of faces is potentially 10^6 this is welcome.

Pseudo code for the algorithm is presented below.

```
RegionGrow(B) {
    B' := B
    repeat {
        for each t₁ on B {
            for each t₂ adjacent t₁ outside B {
                B := B'
                ForcedGrow(B, t₁, t₂,pass)
                if (pass) exit loop over t₂ and t₁;
            }
        }
        if (not pass) report algorithm failed and exit.
        B' := B
    } until no more triangles to add.
}

ForcedGrow(B, t₁, t₂,pass) {
    Add t₁ and t₂ to B.
    If B self intersects set pass:=FALSE and return.
    If all triangles used up set pass:=TRUE and return.
    while (B contains elbow) {
        Add next two triangles to B at elbow.
        If B self intersects set pass:=FALSE and return.
        If all triangles used up set pass:=TRUE and return.
    }
    set pass:=TRUE and return.
}
```

Finally we show a sample output from the algorithm in figure 4. F 4(a) shows the input triangulated surface which is paired and the 4-sided mesh is shown in (b). This is a valid GBBS control mesh.

4.1 Limitations

The algorithm presented in this section has not been tested for open or closed surfaces with holes. This is because a region growing algorithm needs to have more that one boundary on such a surface. The algorithm will need to be extended for such surfaces.

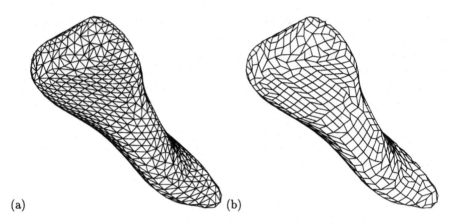

Fig. 4. Results from the seeding algorithm, (a) is the input mesh and (b) is a valid spline control mesh.

5 The energy function

Our approach to reconstructing the surface is similar to that of Hoppe [12]. Hoppe provided a comprehensive scheme that worked for piecewise flat surfaces. We have succeeded in generalising this approach to the case of GBBS surfaces.

The surface S is defined by a set of control points $\mathbf{Q}$ and a mesh topology K, i.e. $S = (K, \mathbf{Q})$. The goal of our spline optimisation is to find a surface which is a good fit to the point set $X = \{x_1..x_P\}$ with a small number of vertices. Thus we wish to minimise the energy function

$$E(K, \mathbf{Q}) = E_{dist}(K, \mathbf{Q}) + E_{rep}(K) + E_{spring}(K, \mathbf{Q}) \tag{7}$$

The first term depends on the quality of the fit to the point set. It is equal to the sum of the squared distances from the points $X = \{x_1..x_P\}$ to the surface.

$$E_{dist}(K, \mathbf{Q}) = \sum_{i=1}^{P} d^2(x_i, S(K, \mathbf{Q})) \tag{8}$$

The representation energy penalises meshes with many vertices. There are M vertices so

$$E_{rep}(K) = k_{rep}M \tag{9}$$

A regularisation term is needed during fitting (because the problem is under-constrained when no data points lie on a patch) and we use a simple spring-like term

$$E_{spring}(K, \mathbf{Q}) = k_{spring} \sum_{e(j,k)=1} |c_i - c_j|^2 \tag{10}$$

This term may be reduced to zero in the final stages of the optimisation, and so it need have no effect on the result. In particular it need not cause any smoothing of the surface.

6 Optimisation of the energy function

6.1 Fixed patch coordinates and fixed topology

We start by considering a simple case for optimisation. We consider only a single patch, S_m and those data points $\{x'_1 .. x'_R\}$ for which patch m is the closest patch. We assume that the closest point on patch m to point x'_i is $\mathbf{r}(p_i)$ with parametric coordinates p_i. Therefore we wish to optimise the energy function

$$E(\mathbf{q}) = \sum_{i=1}^{R} |x'_i - \mathbf{r}(p_i)|^2 + \sum_{e(i,j)=1} |c_i - c_j|^2 \tag{11}$$

with respect to the position of the patch control points $\mathbf{q}_m$. It is helpful to note that

$$\mathbf{r}(p_i) = \sum_{j:c_j \in \mathbf{q}_m} w_j(p_i)\mathbf{c}_j \tag{12}$$

where the weighting factors $w_j(p_i) = (\mathbf{B}^\top(p_i)\mathbf{M})_j$ are fixed numbers adding up to 1. This problem may be formulated as a matrix minimisation problem of the form $|Av - d|^2$ which can be solved rapidly. The column vector v is formed from the control points for the patch. The first R rows of the matrix A contain the weights $w_j(p_i)$ so that multiplication of row i with column vector v results in $\mathbf{r}(p_i)$. Correspondingly the first R rows in column vector d contain the data points x'_i.

The spring terms are attached along the edges of control mesh faces. For each edge there is another row of A and d. The row in d contains zero and the row of A contains a $\sqrt{k_{spring}}$ in column i and $-\sqrt{k_{spring}}$ in column j. It is easy to verify that $E(\mathbf{q})$ from equation (11)

$$E(\mathbf{q}) = |Av - d|^2 \tag{13}$$

It is worth noting that the above formulation is based on the column vectors v and d containing 3D vectors, but in fact it separates into 3 independent matrix equations to be solved for the x, y and z components. We have shown how the energy can be be reduced to a matrix equation for one patch, and the same procedure can easily be applied to generate a matrix equation for the whole mesh.

The matrix for the whole mesh is large but sparse. Such least square problems may be solved efficiently using the conjugate gradient method [8]. If we consider only one patch and fix all vertices except the central vertex then the problem reduces to 3 *quadratic* equations with straightforward analytic solutions.

6.2 Variable patch coordinates

The true cost in equation (11) depends on the distance to the closest point which varies as we vary the control points. We solve this iteratively by finding the closest point, then optimising over the control points and repeating the process until convergence. An attractive feature of the process is that the closest point step and the control point minimisation step both decrease the energy monotonically.

6.3 Variable mesh topology

Finally we wish to optimise the full energy function search over control point positions and mesh topologies. This is potentially a computationally expensive task especially if we aim to find a global optimum. However we can do a quite adequate job by local search techniques which can find a good local minimum.

Firstly we examine how mesh topology is allowed to change. The scheme used by Hoppe for triangles is reviewed in figure 5. It consists of 3 simple operations performed on edge $\{i, j\}$. It can be collapsed to a single vertex, split into two or swapped. It is worth noting that there are some conditions under which the

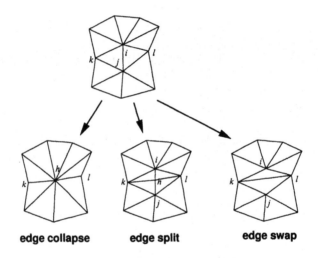

edge collapse   edge split   edge swap

Fig. 5. Topology editing operations for triangular meshes

edge collapse operation is not allowed and these are detailed in [12].

In the case of our mesh edge collapse is not an allowed operation since it can reduce 4-sided faces to 3-sided faces. Instead we use the operation of face collapse and its inverse face creation as shown in figure 6. We have not yet determined what conditions must be satisfied before face collapse is allowed, however we disallow face collapse when it results in a vertex used by 2 or fewer faces.

6.4 Closest Point Computation

The optimisation over control points is relatively quick, and the complexity of the computation is dominated by the nearest neighbour step. This is mirrored

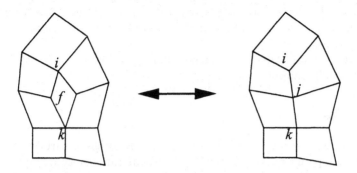

Fig. 6. Topology editing operations for 4-sided face meshes

in other problems such as surface registration by the iterated closest point algorithm [2] and also some formulations of the surface fusion problem.

The general closest point to point set problem can be solved in $O(N \log N)$ by use of appropriate spatial partitioning data structures. By encoding triangles into such a structure one can be guaranteed of finding all triangles within a threshold distance. Following this a routine for closest point to triangle is required, and it is worthwhile carefully optimising this routine.

Finding the closest point to a spline is slightly more computationally intensive. Each patch may be approximated to within a threshold by a piecewise planar triangular mesh according to a tessellation method of [13], see page 262. The nearest point to triangle routine may then be used. By decreasing the triangle size a very good approximation to the closest point may be found. In this way the closest point to spline can be found in less than 10 closest point to triangle operations.

In the first iteration the closest point search is performed over the entire mesh. Subsequent searches can be performed on a purely local basis, while the distance to the surface lies within a threshold.

6.5   Overall strategy

Our starting point is a detailed mesh and point set. A global search assigns each point to a triangle. Initially we proceed with a triangle optimisation scheme until the number of triangles has been reduced. This is mainly because the spline method is slower by about a factor of ten, so it saves time.

Then the seeding algorithm is applied to convert the triangular surface to a spline surface. Firstly all vertices are optimised followed by recomputing the closest point. These steps are iterated until convergence. Then local face collapse operations are performed. A face collapse is performed and the central vertex is optimised over position followed by a closest point computation for a few iterations. If the energy has been lowered the collapse is accepted, if not it is rejected.

The faces are sorted into ascending size and this forms a queue to be processed. Faces that fail to collapse are marked. When no faces can collapse the algorithm terminates.

We have not yet tested the face creation operation so we do not know if it can substantially improve the fit.

7 Results

We now present results for the foot dataset. The original surface is shown in figure 7 (a). A point set X is created by uniformly random sampling the original surface with 4000 points. We decimate to a triangular surface containing 118 faces. This is shown rendered in figure 7 (b) and also in figure 7 (d). The spline fit contains 59 faces (61 patches) and is shown rendered in 7 (c), the control mesh is shown in figure 7 (e). The rms distance from the point set may be computed.

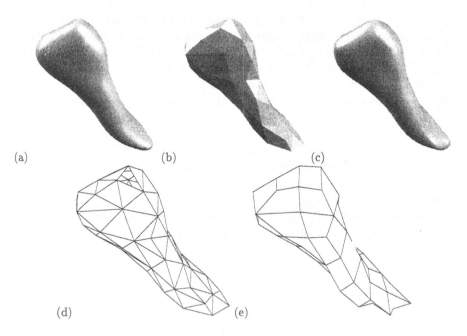

(a)　　　　　(b)　　　　　(c)

(d)　　　　　(e)

Fig. 7. Surface optimisation applied to the foot (a) original surface (b) best fit with 118 triangles - flat rendered (c) best fit with 59 spline patches - flat rendered (d) best fit with 118 triangles - line drawing (e) best fit with 59 spline patches - control mesh

The foot is firstly scaled to a unit cube. The triangular fit is 0.35% of the cube edge length and the spline fit is 0.18%. This is an improvement of a factor 2. A more dramatic improvement is to be expected in higher order derivatives such as the normal or curvature. This is apparent from the flat rendered versions in figure 7.

8 Conclusions

We have now provided a powerful new representation which can be used in a variety of applications in computer vision. We have previously developed a matrix formalism for easy algebraic manipulation in the same form as [4] and fast techniques for computing points on the spline. The matrices used for convenient computation of the GBBS surface have been made available on the Web [1].

In this paper we have developed a scheme for seeding the surface and adaptively remeshing the control points. An optimisation approach provides the framework for driving the adaptive meshing.

9 Future work

At present we can fit point sets of size 5000 in minutes on a workstation. We intend to optimise the code with the objective of dealing with point sets of size 500 000 in less than 30 minutes cpu time, followed by more detailed characterisation of the gains in accuracy over a number of data sets.

Extensions of the software are necessary to deal with open surfaces and internal crease edges.

10 Acknowledgements

This work was carried out as part of EPSRC Research Grants, GR/K04569 and GR/K91255. Both datasets were taken on a Cyberware scanner, the bunny is available on the Cyberware web site and the foot dataset was supplied by Tim McInerney.

References

1. A. J. Stoddart, Matrix data on the Web,
   http://www.ee.surrey.ac.uk/showstaff?A.Stoddart.
2. P. Besl and N. McKay. A method for registration of 3D shapes. *IEEE Trans. Pattern Analysis and Machine Intell.*, 14(2):239–256, 1992.
3. V. Casselles, R. Kimmel, and G. Sapiro. Geodesic active contours. In *5th Int. Conference on Computer Vision*, pages 694–699, Cambridge, Massachusetts, 1995.
4. R. Curwen and A. Blake. Dynamic contours: Real-time active contours. In *Active Vision*, pages 39–57, MIT Press, Cambridge, Mass, 1992.
5. D. DeCarlo and D. Metaxas. Adaptive shape evolution using blending. In *5th Int. Conference on Computer Vision*, pages 834–839, Cambridge, Massachusetts, 1995.
6. M. Eck and H. Hoppe. Automatic reconstruction of b-spline surfaces of arbitrary topological type. In *SIGGRAPH*, pages 325–334, New Orleans, 1996.
7. G. Farin. *Curves and Surfaces for Computer Aided Geometric Design*. Academic Press, Boston, 1990.
8. G. Golub and C. V. Loan. *Matrix Computations*. John Hopkins University Press, 1989.

9. A. Hilton, A. J. Stoddart, J. Illingworth, and T. Windeatt. Marching triangles: range image fusion for complex object modelling. In *1996 Int. Conference on Image Processing*, pages II381–384, Lausanne, Switzerland, 1996.

10. A. Hilton, A. J. Stoddart, J. Illingworth, and T. Windeatt. Reliable surface reconstruction from multiple range images. In *Fourth European Conference on Computer Vision*, pages 117–126, Cambridge, U.K., 1996.

11. H. Hoppe, T. DeRose, T. Duchamp, J. McDonald, and W. Stuetzle. Surface reconstruction from unorganized points. In *SIGGRAPH*, pages 71–78, 1992.

12. H. Hoppe, T. DeRose, T. Duchamp, J. McDonald, and W. Stuetzle. Mesh optimization. In *SIGGRAPH*, pages 19–25, 1993.

13. D. Kirk. *Graphics Gems*. Academic Press, London, U.K., 1992.

14. V. Krishnamurthy and M. Levoy. Fitting smooth surfaces to dense polygon meshes. In *SIGGRAPH*, pages 313–324, New Orleans, 1996.

15. C. T. Loop and T. D. DeRose. A multisided generalization of bezier surfaces. *ACM Trans. on Graphics*, 8(3):204–234, 1989.

16. C. T. Loop and T. D. DeRose. Generalized b-spline surfaces of arbitrary topology. *ACM Computer Graphics*, 24(4):347–356, 1990.

17. T. McInerney and D. Topologically adaptable snakes. In *5th Int. Conference on Computer Vision*, pages 840–845, Cambridge, Massachusetts, 1995.

18. T. McInerney and D. Terzopoulos. Deformable models in medical image analysis. *Medical Image Analysis*, 1(2):91–108, 1996.

19. M. E. Mortenson. *Geometric Modeling*. John Wiley and Sons, New York, 1985.

20. A. Saminathan, A. J. Stoddart, A. Hilton, and J. Illingworth. Progress in arbitrary topology deformable surfaces. In *British Machine Vision Conference*, pages 679–688, Colchester, England, 1997.

21. A. J. Stoddart, A. Hilton, and J. Illingworth. Slime: A new deformable surface. In *British Machine Vision Conference*, pages 285–294, York, England, 1994.

(Mis?)-Using DRT for Generation of Natural Language Text from Image Sequences

Ralf Gerber[1] and Hans–Hellmut Nagel[1,2]

[1] Institut für Algorithmen und Kognitive Systeme, Fakultät für Informatik der Universität Karlsruhe (TH), Postfach 6980, D–76128 Karlsruhe, Germany
[2] Fraunhofer–Institut für Informations– und Datenverarbeitung (IITB), Fraunhoferstr. 1, D–76131 Karlsruhe, Germany

Abstract. The abundance of geometric results from image sequence evaluation which is expected to shortly become available creates a new problem: how to present this material to a user without inundating him with unwanted details? A system design which attempts to cope not only with image sequence evaluation, but in addition with an increasing number of abstraction steps required for efficient presentation and inspection of results, appears to become necessary. The system-user interaction of a Computer Vision system should thus be designed as a natural language dialogue, assigned within the overall system at what we call the 'Natural Language Level'. Such a decision requires to construct a series of abstraction steps from geometric evaluation results to natural language text describing the contents of an image sequence. We suggest to use Discourse Representation Theory as developed by [14] in order to design the system-internal representation of knowledge and results at the Natural Language Level. A first implementation of this approach and results obtained applying it to image sequences recorded from real world traffic scenes are described.

1 Introduction

Creating a link between Computer Vision and Natural Language Processing becomes a research area of growing significance. This development – although unexpected at first sight – becomes more plausible once it is realized that methods for the automatic detection, initialisation, and tracking of moving objects in image sequences have matured significantly over the past years. As a consequence, results become available which are no longer restricted to tracking a single object through a short image sequence obtained from recording a controlled scene. It is now possible to evaluate extended image sequences recorded with a minimum of constraints from real world scenes, for example traffic scenes such as the one illustrated by Fig. 1. Results such as those illustrated by this figure will quickly exhaust the willingness and ability of researchers and users to scan through lists of data with scene coordinates of vehicles as a function of the frame number, i. e. of time. Even looking at the graphical representation of trajectories will soon loose its visual appeal which should not be underestimated

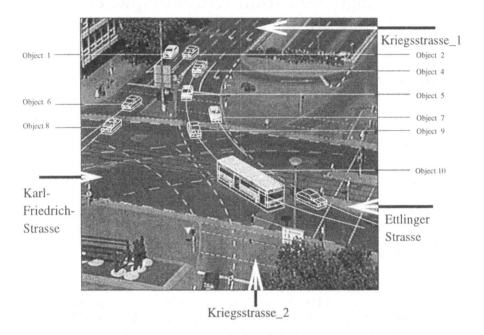

Fig. 1. Single frame of a real-world traffic scene recorded at an intersection. Vehicle trajectories obtained by automatic detection and model-based tracking are shown, together with the vehicle models used.

for a trained eye. Eventually, conceptual abstractions of relevant aspects covered by an image sequence will be desired, with the added complexity to facilitate specification of the desired aspect not at the time when the individual images of a sequence are processed, but at the time of inspection – possibly even depending on previous presentations of partial results from the same sequence.

We expect, therefore, that the geometric results from image sequence evaluation will be considered as a kind of data base which needs to be interrogated in the most flexible manner. Once one accepts such a scenario, it becomes obvious that the formulation of questions about a recorded scene in natural language terms and the expectation to obtain answers in the form of natural language text – at least as some kind of supplementary option – appear natural.

Our contribution should be understood as a step in this direction. We shall first outline our experimental approach in order to set the frame for a subsequent survey of the – not yet abundant – literature about links between computer vision and the generation of natural language text. Problems encountered in an attempt to generate natural language descriptions of different aspects captured about the temporal development within a scene by a video image sequence will then be presented in more detail.

A characteristic of our approach consists in that we do not develop ad-hoc solutions for the problems encountered, but rather investigate the possibility of adapting an established framework from computational linguistics. For this

(a)   (b)

Fig. 2. Frame #700 (a) and #1320 (b) of a gas station sequence, including the auto-matically derived trajectory for the moving vehicle 'object_2'.

purpose, *Discourse Representation Theory (DRT)*, see [14], is of particular inter-est to us since it discusses algorithms for the transformation of coherent natural language text into a computer-internal representation, based – to the extent pos-sible – on First Order Predicate Logic (FOPL). This formalism thus offers an immediate link to a representation which, on the one hand, incorporates logic for the manipulation of semantically relevant components of a description and, on the other hand, provides a framework which links logic-oriented representations to natural language text.

2 Outline of the System Structure of our Approach

Our image sequence *interpretation* process determines natural language descrip-tions of real-world vehicle traffic scenes. The structure of this interpretation process can be described as a Three-Layers-Architecture (see Fig. 3). The first layer comprises image evaluation steps like object detection and model-based vehicle tracking. Geometric results obtained in this *Signal Layer (SL)* comprise automatically generated trajectory data and the instantiation of various pieces of model knowledge underlying the model-based image evaluation steps. The first layer incorporates, too, the association of trajectory data with elementary motion verbs (see, e. g., [15]) and other conceptual primitives such as spatial or occlusion relations. These primitives provide the interface to the second layer, the so-called *Conceptual Layer (CL)*. The third layer, called *Natural Language Layer (NL)*, transforms results obtained in the CL into 'Discourse Representation Structures (DRS)' ([14]) which facilitate the derivation of natural language text.

In this contribution, we emphasize a discussion of the Natural Language Layer (NL). It will be shown that the generation of acceptable textual descrip-tions from a set of 'facts' obtained automatically by image sequence evaluation requires basic design decisions which justify to treat the NL as a separate compo-

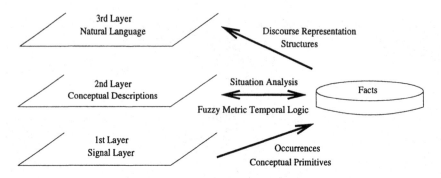

Fig. 3. The Three-Layers-Architecture of our Image Sequence Interpretation Process.

nent within an overall system concept. In doing so, we proceed on the assumption that sufficiently rich and reliable 'facts' about the temporal development within a traffic scene are provided by a robust SL, as described in [16] or [10]. The performance of the CL has been significantly improved in comparison with the state reported in [8, 9] by a transition from processing based on a procedural approach towards one based on 'Fuzzy Metric Temporal Logic' as described by [20].

This transition not only simplified a link to the logic-oriented representation of Discourse Representation Theory, but in addition facilitated to incorporate – in a most natural manner – a number of boundary conditions for natural language text generation from image sequence evaluation results. Initial results for such a logic-based intermediate conceptual representation have recently been published by [11].

3 Survey of Related Research

A comprehensive survey of advanced visual surveillance systems which interpret behavior of moving objects in image sequences can be found in [4]. In the sequel, we assume that the reader is familiar with the state described by [4], and concentrate mostly on more recent publications.

[18] suggested a 'Geometrical Scene Description (GSD)' as a suitable interface between the Computer Vision task and a conceptual representation level, discussed in the context of road traffic scenes. The natural language descriptions derived in NAOS ([18]) from a GSD, however, are based exclusively on synthetically generated trajectories in contradistinction to the work reported here.

As part of the project VITRA ([12]), the system SOCCER ([2]) and its subsystems derive natural language descriptions from soccer scenes. The authors use real-world image data as background, but have to interactively provide (synthetic) trajectories in order to study the performance of their approach. [4], too, are concerned with conceptual descriptions of traffic scenes, but do not derive natural language descriptions. These authors use Bayesian Belief Networks to perform the required inference steps for the extraction of a conceptual representation deemed suitable for the tasks envisaged by them.

[1] present a system which derives natural language descriptions of the location of renal stones found in radiographs. Since their system is based on the evaluation of single frames only, [1] do not take any kind of temporal relationships between the objects in the scene into account.

In contrast to the above–mentioned systems which derive conceptual descriptions from image sequences, the system PICTION ([22]) addresses the inverse problem of interpreting single images by exploiting accompanying linguistic information about the images, such as captions of newspaper photographs. In this case, the problem consists not in the generation of natural language descriptions, but in converting a conceptual description into an internal representation in order to use it for identifying objects in images.

In this context, two additional approaches should be mentioned which are concerned with an association between the output of some kind of image evaluation and the algorithmic generation of natural language text. [7] uses special so-called 'Lexical Conceptual Structures (LCS)' in order to represent the output expected from a computer vision system for language generation. His considerations, however, have not yet been applied to results obtained from real image data.

[3] describe a system for selecting excerpts from text documents treated as a digitized image. The goal consists in the extraction of summary sentences using algorithms based on the statistical characterization of word appearances in a document. Images are segmented to localize text regions, text lines, and words. Sentence and paragraph boundaries are identified. A set of word equivalence classes is computed. Word frequencies, word locations, and word image widths are used to rank equivalence classes as to their likelihood of being significant words. Subsequently, each sentence is scored based on the statistical appearance of significant words. The n best-scoring sentences are selected as an excerpt of the text. Although [3] generate natural language text based on image processing, these authors do not build up a system-internal representation for the *semantics* of the analysed text paragraphs. As a consequence, they are unable to generate independently formulated sentences.

A basically analogous task is pursued by [21] who developed an algorithm for *skimming* videos in order to automatically identify sections which comprise either 'important' audio or video information. Relative importance of each scene in the video is determined based on objects appearing in a segment, on associated words, and on the structure of the scene. Language analysis identifies 'important' audio regions by considering their frequency of occurrence. Words, for which the ratio of occurrence frequency divided by the corresponding frequency in a standard text exceeds a fixed threshold, are selected as keywords. A first level of analysis creates a reduced audio track, based on keywords. In order to increase comprehensibility of the audio track, 'keyphrases' are used which are obtained by starting with a keyword and extending segment boundaries to areas of silence or neighboring keywords. Although such a procedure provides a kind of 'semantic sieve', it does not allow to capture the semantics proper, for example to facilitate paraphrasing.

A similar problem has been taken up by [19] who developed 'Name–It', a system which associates faces and names in news videos. This system can either infer the name related to a given face, or it can locate faces in news videos based on a name obtained from caption text enclosed with the video image or from the related audio track. A natural language processing step utilizes a dictionary, a thesaurus, and a parser for lexical/grammatical analysis as well as knowledge about the structure of a typical news video. 'Name–It' calculates a normalized score for each word. A high score corresponds to a word which is assumed to correspond to a face. So, similar to [22], [19] address the inverse problem of interpreting image sequences by exploiting accompanying linguistic information.

Similar to [4], [13] use dynamic belief networks in order to reason about traffic events which have been recognized by tracking contours of vehicle images in highway traffic scenes. Associated with each moving object is a belief network which contains nodes corresponding to sensor values and nodes corresponding to descriptions derived from the sensor values. The knowledge about the domain of discourse is encoded in probabilities associated with each node. These probabilities can be learned provided enough examples are available. But in this case, the driving behaviour which has been modelled by these parameters is not represented in an explicitly intuitive way. The inspection of such probabilistic models is more difficult than in our hierarchical approach. Moreover, the underlying image data of [13] (highway scenes) does not contain as complex maneuvers as our image sequences. Though [13] operate in the image domain, they are able to treat certain occlusion relations by exploiting knowledge about the special camera pose.

[5, 6] describe their concurrent, hierarchical system SOO–PIN for high level interpretation of image sequences. These authors use a procedural programming language for geometric processing and an object–oriented logic programming language for symbolic reasoning. The domain of discourse is modelled by means of a network of concept–frames. Uncertainty is propagated using the Dempster–Shafer–Theory. While this system is well structured and the extracted high–level–descriptions are rich and facilitate consistency checks on a rather abstract level, the image processing level appears more brittle. Object recognition is performed by background subtraction and an object's speed is estimated by matching object candidates in only three consecutive frames. The resulting geometric data provides only a snapshot of the scene and, like [13], only refers to the *image domain*. In contradistinction, our system has been fed by automatically estimated trajectories of moving objects which have been tracked uninterruptedly over thousands of half frames in the *scene domain*. This enables us to precisely evaluate complex spatial relations, in particular occlusion relations. The large volume as well as the relatively high precision and reliability provided by this kind of image sequence evaluation stimulates extensive research into the use of abstract knowledge representation for the transformation of such data into natural language text.

The situation graph formalism for explicitly representing (traffic) situations is based on [17], which use conceptual graphs in order to represent state and action descriptions of situations. In this approach, the uncertainty of the input data was not exploited, and a procedural language was used for the implementation of the graph traversal algorithm. Now, we employ logic predicates for knowledge representation and an extended logic programming language developed by [20] in order to capture *fuzzy metric temporal predicates*. This facilitates the investigation of different graph traversal strategies by simply modifying some rules of the logic program.

4 Algorithmic Generation of Natural Language Text

The CL obtains descriptions regarding elementary facts derived by the Signal Layer in the form of *fuzzy metric temporal* predicates. Each such predicate comprises a relation identifier together with identifiers denoting the relation arguments, a degree_of_certainty in the form of a real number between 0.0 and 1.0, and a tuple consisting of the initial and final half-frame number defining the associated validity interval. Among the conceptual primitives, we distinguish motion-primitives, road-primitives, occlusion-primitives, and spatial relations. Motion-primitives characterize vehicle movements with respect to *mode* (such as forwards, stationary, backwards) and velocity (very slow, slow, normal, fast, very fast). The set of admissible movements comprises, too, the special 'movement' *to stand*.

Road-related primitives characterize details of the road model, in particular characteristics of lanes. The overall road model is structured hierarchically according to a type-hierarchy. Examples are *left_turning_lane(fobj_5)* which indicates that the object reference *fobj_5* refers to part of a left-turning lane. A predicate *kriegsstrasse(fobj_5)* indicates that *fobj_5* is part of a street named 'Kriegsstrasse'.

Occlusion primitives characterize in a deictic manner occlusion relations between road components, vehicles, and other objects.

4.1 Descriptions provided by the Conceptual Layer

The CL depends on what we call 'situation analysis' in order to construct abstractions from the facts provided by the SL. Trees of situation-graphs comprise the schematic knowledge about elementary 'occurrences' denoted by motion-primitives and their composition to more abstract concepts, for example characterizing sequences of vehicle manouvers, each of which is specified by a motion primitive. In this context, we speak about a *situation node* in a graph as comprising both a schematic *state description* of the agent within its current environment and an associated *action description* which specifies the action to be performed by an agent in the given state. The state description specifies all conditions which must be satisfied in order to enable the agent to perform the associated action.

```
GRAPH gr_get_petrol : get_petrol
{
    START SIT drive_to_pump
        : drive_to_pump(Lane),
          fill_in_petrol(Lane)
        {
            on(Agent, Lane);
            passing_lane(Lane);
            approaching(Agent);
        }
        { drive(Agent); }
    SIT fill_in_petrol
        : fill_in_petrol,
          leave_pump
        {
            on(Agent, filling_place: Fplace);
            velocity(Agent, zero);
        }
        { remain_standing(Agent); }
    FINAL SIT leave_pump
        : leave_pump(Lane)
        { on(Agent, Lane); passing_lane(Lane); }
        { leave(Agent); }
}
```

Fig. 4. Small part of a Situation-Graph in *SIT++*-notation. The subgraph *gr_get_petrol* includes situations which specialize the more common situation *get_petrol*. The defining part of a situation is introduced by the denotation 'SIT'. It is followed by the situation name and a list of possible successor situations sorted by decreasing priority. The first parenthesis includes the state scheme, the second parenthesis includes the action scheme associated with a situation.

The hierarchical arrangement of situation graphs enables the specification of subgraphs characterizing particular configurations of situations which occur sufficiently frequently to treat them as a conceptual unit. Several tree traversal strategies have been implemented for a traversal of this schematic knowledge base in the course of attempts to instantiate a particular sequence of situation nodes which is compatible with the stream of facts supplied by the SL. The instantiation process attempts to find at each half-frame time point the most specialized situation node which is compatible with the facts observed at that time point. Situation Trees are specified in a formal language illustrated in Fig. 4. Such specifications are translated automatically into metric temporal logic programs which can be evaluated by the metric temporal logic system *F-Limette* ([20]). F-Limette has generalized a tableau calculus by operations to treat metric temporal and fuzzy attributes.

Results at the level of situation analysis in our system are derived by the CL in the following manner. Traversal of the Situation Tree generates 'factual data' or 'facts' by instantiating situation descriptions which are compatible with geometric results provided by the SL. We distinguish between several types of facts. Those which characterize the *actual motion description* (i. e. corresponding to the current half-frame number) can be derived from the state-schema component of a situation-node schema. Facts which characterize *intentions* of an agent can be extracted from a-priori knowledge encoded in admissible paths through sequences of Situation-Graph nodes linked by edges of this graph: an intention is simply considered to be represented by a possible continuation of a partially instantiated path through the Situation-Graph. Facts related to actions terminating in some situation are characterized by the path through the Situation-Graph instantiated so far. All facts are considered to be true, i. e. we have not yet implemented the fuzzy logic equivalent of linguistic hedges.

In contradistinction to earlier, procedural approaches, the approach sketched here supports modelling several alternative 'views' on an image subsequence, for example differentiating with respect to the level of detail presented or by optional suppression of occlusion relations between selected objects in the scene.

4.2 Transformation of primitive descriptions into natural language text

[14] describe algorithms which transform a natural language English input text into a system-internal, logic-oriented representation called *Discourse Representation Structure (DRS)*. In analogy to the *Discourse Representation Theory (DRT)* of [14], we treat the stream of fuzzy metric temporal facts provided by the CL as a string of symbols, i. e. as a text, and convert it into DRSs. The grammar specifying the exchange of a symbol string between the CL and the NL is simpler than even the restricted English grammar used by [14]. The important point, however, consists in the conversion of symbol strings into a semantic representation which can be manipulated by standard logic operations. We thus had to devise conversion rules and an algorithm which evaluates these rules in order to convert the input stream of (abstracted) facts provided by the CL into suitable DRSs.

The syntax rules of the grammar specifying the 'language' used to communicate between the CL and the NL are used to first convert the stream of symbols into a syntax tree which is subsequently analysed according to rules corresponding to DRT-rules as described by [14]. The advantage of such a procedure consists in generating a system-internal representation which can – at least in principle – be manipulated by any program that is able to evaluate DRSs for the semantic content of a natural language text according to [14].

The DRS construction rules used in the current version of our system implementation differ somewhat from those described in [14]. Our language fragment differs from the fragment of the English language used by [14]. This pertains also to the syntax trees. In addition, [14] have designed their system to cope with texts generated outside their system, whereas the evaluation of 'text' transmitted within our system from the CL to the NL can exploit many presuppositions. The

$$\boxed{\begin{array}{c} x_1 \ y_1 \ t_1 \ e_1 \ \text{n} \ x_2 \ y_2 \ t_2 \ e_2 \\[4pt] \text{object\_2} \ (x_1) \\ \text{lower\_filling\_lane} \ (y_1) \\ e_1 = t_1 \\ t_1 < n \\[6pt] e_1: \boxed{x_1 \ \text{drive on} \ y_1} \\[6pt] x_2 = x_1 \\ \text{second\_filling\_place} \ (y_2) \\ e_2 = t_2 \\ t_2 < n \\ e_1 < e_2 \\[6pt] e_2: \boxed{x_2 \ \text{stop on} \ y_2} \end{array}}$$

Fig. 5. Simple Example of a DRS.

current version of our NL implementation thus does not have to cope with ambiguities. This implies, of course, that a particular semantics has to be encoded by the CL by selection of appropriate instances of facts.

Figure 5 illustrates a simple Discourse Representation Structure (DRS) which consists of the following two facts:

$$5 : 107 \ ! \ \text{drive\_on(object\_2, lower\_filling\_lane)}.$$
$$108 : 144 \ ! \ \text{stop\_on(object\_2, second\_filling\_place)}.$$

The first of these represents the statement valid between half-frame number 5 and 107, expressing that the object 'object_2' drives on the lower filling_lane. The second statement expresses the fact that this object stops during the half-frame interval 108 through 144 on the second filling_place. The first 'discourse referent (DR)' denotes the agent and is given by the first argument. The second argument denotes a reference object. Facts themselves are converted to event structures denoted by e_i which represent the duration of such an event. Since the second event of this example immediately succeeds the first one, we have that $e_1 < e_2$. Discourse referents t_i refer to temporal intervals comprising events. Since no such comprising intervals have been specified in our example, we have $e_i = t_i$. Since all facts are treated in retrospect, all intervalls in our example belong to the past, i. e. $t_i < n$ where n denotes the time at which the sentences are formulated, i. e. 'now'.

The transformation of DRS into natural language text does not belong to Computer Vision, but to Computational Linguistics. We nevertheless found it useful to implement a simple conversion from DRSs to natural language text in order to facilitate inspection of discourse representations created automatically by our system. This 'casual' implementation comprises a number of heuristics. It is our hope that the system approach will not be judged entirely on the

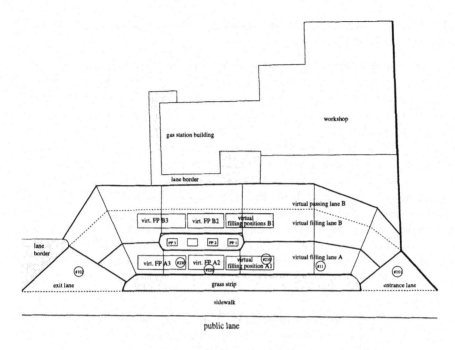

Fig. 6. Groundplane schematic map of the gas station.

insufficient quality of the natural language 'surface text'. We hope to eventually leave this transformation to professional linguists.

5 Experimental Results

The geometric evaluation process interpolates between fields of a digitized video sequence in order to obtain full-frame resolution with a sampling rate corresponding to a 20 msec interval between the resulting half-frames. The image sequence illustrated by Fig. 2 comprises about 8000 half-frames or almost three minutes of recording time. It thus becomes possible to test natural language text generation based on data sets which approach realistic proportions. This allows to compute several different natural language descriptions in order to study the formulation of texts which emphasize *different aspects* about the *same vehicle* as being relevant for the reader.

In order to simplify reference to details within images from this sequence, Fig. 6 shows a groundplane schematic map of the gas station in Fig. 2.

In the automatically generated texts of subsequent examples, the term *lower filling lane* refers to the 'virtual filling_lane A' from this map, whereas the term *upper filling lane* refers to 'virtual filling_lane B'. The term *filling_place* refers to a location which is situated on a filling lane, but next to a petrol pump (denoted as 'virtual filling_position' in Fig. 6). The text generation assumes that a vehicle obtains gas when it stops and remains standing for a while on a filling_place.

5.1 Stepwise introduction of knowledge about the relation between actions and locations

Our first example refers to 'object_2' which can be seen in the foreground of Fig. 2. The automatic generation of natural language text presented in Fig. 7 emphasizes actions of the agent (i. e. the vehicle 'object_2') as they can be observed for a particular time (i. e. half-frame number) interval. The verbphrase in a sentence thus exclusively comprises motion-verbs. The CL analyses *spatial relations* in this example *independently from actions* and, therefore, does not relate location and action with each other. In this case, action and location are only combined at the NL. It thus is difficult to extract statements about any *intention* of the agent from the information provided by the CL to the NL. This deficiency is compensated for by the fact that no a-priori knowledge about a particular scene is used. In this case, the system may generate reasonable statements about the vehicle even for situations where this agent does not behave according to some a-priori expectations, i. e. knowledge specific to a situation in this particular scene.

```
   5 :  119 ! drive_to(obj_2, dispensing_pump).
   5 : 1340 ! on(obj_2, lower_filling_lane).
   7 :  104 ! drive_slowly(obj_2).
 105 : 1164 ! remain_standing(obj_2).
 120 : 1222 ! take_in(obj_2, petrol).
1165 : 1366 ! drive_slowly(obj_2).
1223 : 1366 ! leave(obj_2, filling_station).
1341 : 1353 ! on(obj_2, upper_filling_lane).
```

Obj_2 slowly drove on the lower filling lane to the dispensing pump. Then it remained standing in order to take in petrol. After that, it slowly drove on the upper filling lane in order to leave the filling station.

Fig. 7. Natural language text automatically derived from facts generated by the 'Conceptual Layer (CL)'. The text refers to 'object_2', the vehicle shown in the foreground of Fig. 2. In this example, the 'Natural Language Layer (NL)' itself, i. e. without an explicit inference process by the CL, could relate an *action* ('remain standing') to an *intention* ('to take in petrol'), since this relation has been coded directly into the knowledge base of our system. This, in turn, is due to the fact that it has not yet been possible to automatically determine the activity 'to take in petrol' based on image sequence evaluation. This would require the analysis not only of moving *rigid*, but in addition of *nonrigid, jointed* bodies such as a human.

The last sentence refers to driving on the 'upper' filling lane since the *final* part of the vehicle trajectory overlapped also the 'virtual filling lane B' shown in Fig. 6.

In contradistinction to the example illustrated in Fig. 7, the text generation shown in the example of Fig. 8 exploits scene-specific knowledge provided by a situation-analysis based on a situation-graph. It thus becomes possible to identify 'intentions' of the agent and express this fact by introducing formulations like

```
     5 :   107 ! want_to_get_to(obj_2, free_dispensing_pump).
     5 :   107 ! drive_on(obj_2, lower filling lane).
   108 :   144 ! stop_on(obj_2, second filling place).
   145 : 1157 ! take_in(obj_2, petrol).
  1158 : 1164 ! start(obj_2).
  1158 : 1353 ! finish_getting(obj_2, gas).
  1158 : 1353 ! want_to_leave(obj_2, filling_station).
  1165 : 1353 ! drive_forward(obj_2).
  1354 : 1366 ! get(obj_2, petrol).
```

Obj_2 wanted to get to the free dispensing pump. So it drove on the lower filling lane. Later it stopped on the second filling place. Then it took in petrol. Then it started because it finished getting gas. Now it wanted to leave the filling station. It, therefore, drove forward.

Fig. 8. Second example of natural language text automatically derived from facts generated by the Conceptual Layer.

want to. Analogously, inferences about partial goals which have been reached by the agent will be formulated using the verb to *finish*.

In addition, the text generation attempts to take into consideration to which extent knowledge about the relation between the vehicle and stationary scene components influences the formulation of agent behavior, in particular regarding the actions performed as well as regarding potential intentions underlying these actions. These attempts result in the formulation of intermediate goals such as, for example, to reach a free filling_place.

5.2 Incorporation of quantified statements into the text

Other sequences are shorter – for example from the intersection scene illustrated by Fig. 1. They are used in order to demonstrate additional aspects of our approach. The third experiment documented in the following Fig. 9 demonstrates how statements about groups of vehicles are incorporated into the formulations. On the one hand, sentences refer to single vehicle behavior; on the other hand, the NL text generation uses quantorized statements, too. Such formulations are based on a situation analysis comprising *several* vehicles in order to associate their compound behavior with an appropriate natural language quantifier. The road names used in this text have been indicated in Fig. 1.

6 Discussion of Related Research and Conclusion

An increasing algorithmic ability to fast and reliably evaluate extended image sequences will result in voluminous sets of geometric data. A potential user is thus challenged to interactively interrogate this material according to a variety of aspects which in general can not be prespecified. As a consequence, the user is likely to formulate his question in natural language and will expect to obtain

> Obj_4 turned left on Kriegsstrasse into Ettlinger Strasse. It followed obj_5. It fell behind of obj_5 and obj_9.

> Most vehicles drove from Kriegsstrasse into Ettlinger Strasse. Some vehicles drove straight ahead on Kriegsstrasse. No vehicle turned right from Kriegsstrasse into Karl-Friedrich-Strasse. A few vehicles drove from Karl-Friedrich-Strasse into Ettlinger Strasse. No vehicle drove from Karl-Friedrich-Strasse into Kriegsstrasse. No vehicle turned left from Kriegsstrasse into Karl-Friedrich-Strasse. No vehicle drove from Ettlinger Strasse into Karl-Friedrich-Strasse. No vehicle drove from Ettlinger Strasse into Kriegsstrasse.

Fig. 9. Two examples of automatically generated natural language descriptions refering to the intersection sequence illustrated by Fig. 1.

either a natural language text answering his question or some segment of the video illustrating a possible system response. In order to analyse the desired question, the system will require the ability to analyse first the natural language question posed by the user. This analysis then provides the boundary condition for the extraction of facts from data obtained by image sequence evaluation and – equally important – for the manner in which this material will be presented to the user.

We thus expect that the abstraction process from digitized video to natural language text will be much more involved than a search for simple 'features' – either pictorial ones, acoustical ones in the accompanying audio track, or a combination of both. Only detailed knowledge about the scenes captured by the video and about the intentions of agents in the scene as well as about possible intentions of a user will enable a system to extract and present the desired information in a suitable manner.

A system living up to such a challenge will have to build a dynamic internal representation of both the discourse context of the user-system interaction and of the contents of video segments which have already been evaluated. In order to retain the flexibility expected, it appears best to convert both the natural language text analysis of the user-system interaction as well as the abstractions from the image sequence evaluation into a compatible structure which will facilitate a joint logic manipulation necessitated in the course of the interaction.

Our experience with the evaluation of extended real-world image sequences has shown that the gap between geometrical descriptions, which have been extracted by image evaluation steps, and appropriate natural language descriptions is too large in order to be bridged by a heuristically extended Geometric Scene Description (GSD). We, therefore, decided to use a much more formal approach in order to be able to *systematically study all intermediate steps*. It turned out to be advantageous to subdivide the abstraction process from geometric descriptions to a level expressible as natural language text into two additional layers: one is devoted to a logical manipulation of material (the CL), and the other to the selection of material to be presented to the user at a particular moment during an interaction. In addition, the latter step requires the ability to suitably *package* the selected material for presentation to the user. Selection and 'packaging' of evaluation results for the user at the appropriate level of abstraction is considered the task of the NL which is the topic of this contribution.

Although one might accuse us to 'misuse' Discourse Representation Theory (DRT) as developped by [14], DRT appears to us to offer an interesting framework for realizing a Natural Language Layer (NL). Looked at from this point of view, the NL as suggested in this contribution becomes a constituent part of an advanced Computer Vision System for the evaluation of image sequences. The examples given above illustrate that such an approach is at least feasible. All in all, data currently available to us comprise about fifty vehicles which have been detected and tracked automatically through subsequences extending sometimes through thousands of video frames. This allows to compute several different descriptions per vehicle in order to study the formulation of texts which emphasize *different aspects* about the *same vehicle* as being relevant for the reader.

Our initial attempts in the direction outlined in this contribution obviously still exhibit many limitations. We nevertheless consider the results obtained so far as encouraging future research.

Acknowledgement

We thank M. Haag for making image sequence evaluation data available for our experiments.

References

[1] A. Abella and J.R. Kender: *Description Generation of Abnormal Densities Found in Radiographs.* Proc. Workshop on Conceptual Descriptions from Images, Cambridge/UK, 19 April 1996, H. Buxton (Ed.), pp. 97-111.

[2] E. Andrè, G. Herzog, and T. Rist: *The System Soccer.* Proc. of the 8th European Conference on Artificial Intelligence, Munich/Germany, 1-5 August 1988, pp. 449-454.

[3] D.S. Bloomberg and F.R. Chen: *Document Image Summarization without OCR.* Proc. IEEE International Conference on Image Processing (ICIP '96), Lausanne/CH, 16-19 September 1996, Vol. II, pp. 229-232.

[4] H. Buxton and S. Gong: *Visual Surveillance in a Dynamic and Uncertain World.* Artificial Intelligence **78** (1995) 431-459.

[5] S. Dance, T. Caelli, and Z.-Q. Liu: *Picture Interpretation: A Symbolic Approach.* Series in Machine Perception and Artificial Intelligence Vol. **20**, World Scientific, Singapore a. o. 1995.

[6] S. Dance, T. Caelli, and Z.-Q. Liu: *A Concurrent, Hierarchical Approach to Symbolic Scene Interpretation.* Pattern Recognition **29**:11 (1996) 1891–1903.

[7] L. Friedman: *From Images to Language.* Proc. Workshop on Conceptual Descriptions from Images, Cambridge/UK, 19 April 1996, H. Buxton (Ed.), pp. 70-81.

[8] R. Gerber and H.-H. Nagel: *Berechnung natürlichsprachlicher Beschreibungen von Straßenverkehrsszenen aus Bildfolgen unter Verwendung von Geschehens- und Verdeckungsmodellierung.* In B. Jähne, P. Geißler, H. Haußecker und F. Hering

270

(Hrsg.), Mustererkennung 1996; 18. DAGM-Symposium, Heidelberg/Germany, 11.-13. September 1996, pp. 601-608 (in German).

[9] R. Gerber and H.-H. Nagel: *Knowledge Representation for the Generation of Quantified Natural Language Descriptions of Vehicle Traffic in Image Sequences.* Proc. IEEE International Conference on Image Processing (ICIP '96), Lausanne/CH, 16-19 September 1996, Vol. II, pp. 805-808.

[10] M. Haag, H.-H. Nagel: *Beginning a Transition from a Local to a More Global Point of View in Model–Based Vehicle Tracking.* H Burkhardt, B. Neumann (Eds.): Proc. European Conference on Computer Vision 1998 (ECCV '98), Freiburg/Germany, 2-6 June 1998.

[11] M. Haag, W. Theilmann, K.H. Schäfer, and H.-H. Nagel: *Integration of Image Sequence Evaluation and Fuzzy Metric Temporal Logic Programming.* KI-97: Advances in Artificial Intelligence, Proc. 21st Annual German Conference on Artificial Intelligence, Freiburg/Germany, 9-12 September 1997; G. Brewka, C. Habel, and B. Nebel (Eds.): Lecture Notes in Artificial Intelligence vol. **1303**, Springer-Verlag Berlin, Heidelberg, New York 1997, pp. 301-312.

[12] G. Herzog and P. Wazinski: *VIsual TRAnslator: Linking Perceptions and Natural Language Descriptions.* Artificial Intelligence Review Journal **8** (1994) 175-187.

[13] T. Huang, D. Koller, J. Malik, G. Ogasawara, B. Rao, S. Russell, and J. Weber: *Automatic Symbolic Traffic Scene Analysis Using Belief Networks.* Proc. 12th National Conference on Artificial Intelligence, Seattle/WA, 31 July – 4 August 1994, pp. 966-972.

[14] H. Kamp and U. Reyle: *From Discourse to Logic.* Kluwer Academic Publishers, Dordrecht/NL, Boston/MA, London/UK 1993.

[15] H. Kollnig und H.-H. Nagel: *Ermittlung von begrifflichen Beschreibungen von Geschehen in Straßenverkehrsszenen mit Hilfe unscharfer Mengen.* Informatik – Forschung und Entwicklung **8** (1993) 186-196 (in German).

[16] H. Kollnig and H.-H. Nagel: *3D Pose Estimation by Directly Matching Polyhedral Models to Gray Value Gradients.* International Journal of Computer Vision **23**:3 (1997) 283-302.

[17] H.-H. Nagel, H. Kollnig, M. Haag, and H. Damm: *The Association of Situation Graphs with Temporal Variations in Image Sequences.* Working Notes AAAI–95 Fall Symposium Series 'Computational Models for Integrating Language and Vision', R.K. Srihari (ed.), Cambridge/MA, 10–12 November 1995, pp. 1–8.

[18] B. Neumann und H.-J. Novak: *NAOS: Ein System zur natürlichsprachlichen Beschreibung zeitveränderlicher Szenen.* Informatik – Forschung Entwicklung **1** (1986) 83-92 (in German).

[19] S. Satoh, Y. Nakamura, and T. Kanade: *Name-It: Naming and Detecting Faces in Video by the Integration of Image and Natural Language Processing.* Proc. 15th International Joint Conference on Artificial Intelligence (IJCAI '97), 23-29 August 1997, Nagoya/Japan, Vol. II, pp. 1488-1493.

[20] K.H. Schäfer: *Unscharfe zeitlogische Modellierung von Situationen und Handlungen in Bildfolgenauswertung und Robotik.* Dissertation, Fakultät für Informatik der Universität Karlsruhe (TH), Juli 1996. Published in: Dissertationen zur Künstlichen Intelligenz (DISKI), Band **135**, infix–Verlag St. Augustin 1996 (in German).

[21] M.A. Smith and T. Kanade: *Video Skimming and Characterization through the Combination of Image and Language Understanding Techniques.* Proc. IEEE Conference on Computer Vision and Pattern Recognition (CVPR '97), 17-19 June 1997, San Juan, Puerto Rico, pp. 775-781.

[22] R.K. Srihari: *Linguistic Context in Vision.* Proc. IEEE Workshop on Context-Based Vision, Cambridge/MA, 19 June 1995, pp. 100–110.

The Structure of the Optic Flow Field

Mads Nielsen[1] and Ole Fogh Olsen[2]

[1] 3D-Lab, School of Dentistry,Nørre Alle 20, DK-2200 Copenhagen N, Denmark
[2] Department of Computer Science, University of Copenhagen, Universitetsparken 1, DK-2100, Copenhagen E, Denmark

Abstract. The optic flow field is defined as preserving the intensity along flow-lines. Due to singularities in the image at fixed time, poles are created in the optic flow field. In this paper we describe the generic types of flow singularities and their generic interaction over time. In a general analytic flow field, normally the topology is characterised by the points where the flow vanish again subdivided into repellers, attractors, whirls, and combinations hereof. We point out the resemblance, but also the important differences in the structure of a general analytic flow field, and the structure of the optic flow field expressed through its normal flow. Finally, we show examples of detection of these singularities and events detected from non-linear combinations of linear filter outputs.

Keywords: optic flow, scale-space, singularities, catastrophe theory, equivalence under deformation, transversality, flow structure, flow topology, turbulence, attention.

1 Introduction

Most work on optic flow has been devoted to its definition [7, 4] and to regularization schemes for its robust computation [7, 13, 2, 14, 17]. In this paper, we follow the Horn and Schunck definition of the optic flow field [7]. We do not regularize the solution, but only wish to classify it. The motivation is four fold: we seek a classification, in mathematical terms, of the flow field and its temporal changes. We want to emphasize that the events we describe or detect in images must be generic events. We will develop mechanisms for detecting these events, and finally we wish to indicate that this purely academical examination of the optic flow field may subserve the development of algorithms for many different visual task. In this paper we give simple examples using the flow structure for guiding an attention mechanism and for computing the degree of turbulence in a flow field. The inspiration is mainly from the analysis of autonomous dynamical systems [1] to which we will describe the analogy.

An object moving with respect to a camera induces a motion field on the image plane. This motion field is the projection of the motion of physical points fixed to the object, and will only under very restricted lightning and reflectance circumstances directly relate to the optic flow field [8]. We analyse the singularities of the data induced *optic flow field* while the singularities of the *motion field* have earlier been analysed for recovery of object motion parameters [10, 16]. Since we do not in this work relate the optic flow field to the motion field, we can not make similar observations.

The structure of a general analytic flow field is normally accessed through the singularities of the field, i.e. points where the flow vanishes[1]. The first order structure of the flow field round these points can classify the points as attractors, repellers, or whirls. The optic flow field is a special flow field since computed as a simple intensity preservation. Generically the optic flow field is not everywhere analytical. Furthermore, the tangential component of the flow is not determined by the constraint equation. These differences cause new flow structures to be created generically and ill-define the classical flow structures in an optic flow field. This paper analyses these differences, show examples, and applications.

A temporarily changing image may be obtained from imaging a dynamic scene. A physical conservation law then defines a spatial vector field temporarily connecting conserved properties. In computer vision the Horn and Schunck (HS) equation [7] expresses the preservation of intensity over time. The derived spatial vector field is the *optic flow field*. The HS equation only solves locally for one component of the vector field, giving rise to the so-called aperture problem. A unique representation of the optic flow field is given by the normal flow: the flow perpendicular to the local isophote.

The normal flow is well defined in all image points with non-vanishing spatial gradient, elsewhere the flow is undefined. However, in a neighbourhood round these singular points the flow field exhibits some typical behaviour. The flow magnitude typically increases towards infinity, the direction will be inwards, outwards, or combinations hereof. In Section 4 we analyse the flow around these singularities, categorise it, and see how these poles changes over time. The purpose of this exercise is to gain insight in the *structure of the optic flow field*.

In general analytic flow fields, vanishing flow points can describe the flow field structure. In optic flow fields only the normal flow is directly accessible and this will generically vanish at hyper-surfaces of codimension 1, i.e. at curves in 2D images. This means, that the standard classification of the flow field structure can not directly be applied to the normal flow fields. We can, however, define whirls in the normal flow field as second order temporal events and apply the detection of these to the quantization of turbulence.

A proper definition of structure change in the flow field needs a definition of *structure*. We do this through the mathematical concept of equivalence of flow fields under deformations. In Section 3 we review this method and its application to structural classification of analytical flow patterns. In Section 4 we define and derive the generic structure of the optic flow field.

Normally, the optic flow has been defined and computed directly based on pixel values, so as if they represent the true value of the intensity field. Recently [4] the optic flow definition and computation have been formulated in a scale-space framework taking the finite extent of pixels and filter-outputs into account. In Subsection 4.3 we comment on some aspects of the change of structure of the optic flow field when scale changes.

In Section 5 we describe how changes of flow field structure can be detected from outputs of linear filters. These events may be useful to detect violations of continuation models: structure emerging or disappearing, and thus guide an attention mechanism. We give examples of computations of the flow structure, and apply this to simple examples from computer vision and turbulent flow.

First, however, we look into the necessary notation and definitions.

2   Optic flow: notation and definitions

In this section we establish notations of what images, optic flow, normal flow, and the spatio-temporal iso-surface are. Furthermore we link the geometric properties of the spatio-temporal iso-surface to the flow and normal flow-field. We assume that I is sufficiently differentiable.

Definition 1 (Image sequence). *An image sequence* $I(x,t) : \mathbb{R}^D \times \mathbb{R} \mapsto \mathbb{R}$ *is a mapping from* D *spatial dimensions* $(x = (x_1, x_2, \ldots, x_D))$ *and a temporal dimension (t) into scalar values, normally denoted* intensities.

Definition 2 (Spatio-temporal optic flow field). *The spatio temporal optic flow field* $v : \mathbb{R}^{D+1} \mapsto \mathbb{R}^{D+1}$ *is any vector field preserving image sequence intensity along flow lines.*

The preservation of intensity along flow-lines of v is expressed through the full (or Lie) derivative along the flow:

$$\mathcal{L}_v I = v^{x_1} I_{x_1} + v^{x_2} I_{x_2} + \ldots + v^{x_D} I_{x_D} + v^t I_t = 0$$

where upper index denotes component of vector and lower index denotes partial differentiation. In the following we will often use notation from $2D$ (x,y) to simplify expressions: $\mathcal{L}_v I = v^x I_x + v^y I_y + v^t I_t = 0$.

2.1   Temporal gauge

The optic flow equation yields one equation in $D + 1$ unknowns. In general, the length of the vector is unimportant as only the actual connection of spatio-temporal points carries information. Often the length of the vectorfield is normalised to unit temporal component, i.e. $v^t = 1$. In this normalised flow field we denote the spatial components u. This reveals the well known Horn and Schunck equation

$$u^x I_x + u^y I_y + I_t = 0$$

We call (u^x, u^y) the spatial optic flow field or simply the optic flow field. This flow field answers the typical question asked by the computer vision programmer: in next frame of my image sequence, where did points move?

Definition 3 (Spatial optic flow field). *The spatial optic flow field* $u : \mathbb{R}^D \mapsto \mathbb{R}^D$ *is any vector field preserving image sequence intensity along flow lines of the spatio-temporal vector field* $v = \begin{bmatrix} u \\ 1 \end{bmatrix}$.

The normalisation of the temporal component is, however, only possible (finite) when $v^t \neq 0$. In cases where the temporal component vanishes, the above formulation yields singularities (poles) in the flow field. In Section 4, we analyse the flow field round these poles, show that they exists generically, and that they exhibit certain generic behaviours/interactions. In order to do this, even though the spatial flow field is our main concern, we must stay in the spatio-temporal formulation of the flow field. In this way, we can derive properties of the spatial flow field from simple geometric considerations.

2.2   Normal flow

The temporal gauge (or another normalisation) results in one equation in D unknowns. This shows the intrinsic degree of freedom in the flow, normally denoted the *aperture problem*. Using the temporal gauge, the spatial optic flow constraint equation reads $u\nabla I = -I_t$ where u is the spatial flow field and ∇ denotes the spatial gradient. The component of u along the spatial image gradient (the normal flow) is uniquely determined by the constraint equation, while any component in the iso-intensity tangent plane is unresolved. The normal flow will therefore often be considered the solution to the optic flow constraint equation, keeping in mind that any tangential component can be added.

2.3   Spatio-temporal iso-surfaces

When looking at the spatio-temporal flow at a given point in space-time (x_0, t_0) it is constrained to preserve intensity.

Definition 4 (Spatio-temporal iso-surface). *In every point (x_0, t_0) where $I_\alpha \neq 0$, $I(x,t) = I(x_0,t_0)$ defines the corresponding spatio-temporal iso-surface.*

Any flow line is though constrained to lie within the spatio-temporal surface. This surface is only defined for points where the spatio-temporal gradient I_α does not vanish. Whenever the image is continuous, the spatio-temporal surface is a closed surface differentiable to the same order as the image.

If $I_t(x_0,t_0) \neq 0$ then the spatio-temporal iso-surface can be locally parametrised by the spatial coordinates. In this situation, the intensity change in the time direction and the iso-surface will not locally be perpendicular to the spatial directions, i.e. the normal flow is not zero.

Definition 5 (Spatio-temporal iso-function). *The function $s(x) : \mathbb{R}^D \mapsto \mathbb{R}$ is defined in an open set round every point (x_0, t_0) where $I_t(x_0, t_0) \neq 0$ such that $I(x, s(x)) = I(x_0, t_0)$.*

The graph of the (spatio-temporal) iso-function is simply the iso-surface. The iso-function is linked to the local flow pattern through proposition 1:

Proposition 1 (iso-function normal flow). *The spatial normal flow through a point (x_0, t_0) is $u_n(x_0, t_0) = \|\nabla s\|^{-2} \nabla s$.*

Proof. The flow is determined by the equation $u\nabla I + I_t = 0$. By spatially differentiation of the definition of the iso-function $\partial_x I(x, s(x)) = 0$ we find $\nabla s = -\frac{\nabla I}{I_t}$ and thereby the optic flow equation reads $u(-I_t\nabla s) + I_t = 0$. This reduces to $u\nabla s = 1$ which is obviously fulfilled by $u = \frac{\nabla s}{\|\nabla s\|^2}$. Since ∇s is directed along the image gradient ∇I, this is the normal flow.

We are now capable of linking the geometric structure of the iso-function to the local normal flow. In the points where its tangent (hyper)plane coincide with the (hyper)plane spanned by the spatial dimensions, the normal flow is not defined, but in neighbouring points on the iso-surface, we can find the flow and categorize the undefined flow by its limiting structure.

In the following we will analyse the generic shape of the spatio-temporal iso-surfaces in terms of the spatio-temporal iso-function. Especially we will analyse the generic properties and the corresponding generic flow patterns.

3 Structure and genericity

We define, as in common catastrophe theory [6], structure as equivalence classes under deformations. That is, given a function $f(x, c) : \mathbb{R}^D \times \mathbb{R}^k \mapsto \mathbb{R}$, where x are the D spatial coordinates and c are the k control parameters of the function, define equivalence classes from a class of allowable deformations of x and c. In common catastrophe theory, we define $x' = \phi(x, c), c' = \psi(c)$, where ϕ and ψ are diffeomorphisms. Now the game is, given a function f, to choose ϕ, ψ such that $f(x', c')$ takes a special algebraic form. As an example, any point where the spatial gradient of f does not vanish, can by a correct choice of ϕ, ψ be put on the form $f(x', c') = x'_1$. We call this representation of f the normal form. Such an analysis of C^∞ functions leads to Thom's classification of catastrophes: regular points, critical points, folds, cusps, swallowtails, etc., each represented by a normal form.

An event is generic if one can not perturb it away with an infinitesimal perturbation. Mathematically that is, the event occurs in an open and dense set of all functions f. We expect to see only generic events in real image sequences, as all other events has measure zero in C^∞. Using the transversality theorem[6], one can argue on genericity simply by counting dimensions. In the product space of spatial coordinates and control parameters we expect an event to occur at a manifold of dimension $D + k$ minus the number of linear constraints on the functions jet to be satisfied for the event to take place.

In the case of flow fields, or dynamical systems, the class of diffeomorphisms is constrained since the flow field represents a connection of physical points. That is, the deformation of the coordinate system is not allowed to change the flow fields connection of physical points, only its coordinate representation. The result of this is that one cannot remove points of vanishing flow, and one cannot alter the eigenvalues of the matrix containing the spatial first order derivatives of the flow [1]. This leads to a very fine classification of flow fields since the eigenvalues index the equivalence class. Generically we find in a flow field at a given time instance points of vanishing flow (fixed points), and in 2D we categorize them according to their eigenvalues: two positive implies an unstable node (repeller), two negative a stable node (attractor or sink), two of opposite sign a bistable node (saddle node), and a pair of complex conjugate eigenvalues yields a spiralling flow called a focus and which may be stable or unstable according to the value of the real part of the eigenvalues.

When time varies the fixed points may interact changing the fixed point topology of the flow. Transitions which takes place generically when a single parameter (the time) is varied are called codimension 1 events. In case of the flow field, one generically meets three different events at codimension 1: scatter, saddle bifurcation, or Hopf bifurcation.

4 Structure of the optic flow field

In this section, we apply the general scheme outline above to the analysis of the structure of an optic flow field. An optic flow is defined through the conservation of image intensity along flow-lines. We define equivalence of the flow-field as identical up to a diffeomorphism of the image sequence:

Definition 6 (Image isophote equivalence). *Two images* $I(x,t) : \mathbb{R}^D \times \mathbb{R} \mapsto \mathbb{R}$ *and* $J(x,t) : \mathbb{R}^D \times \mathbb{R} \mapsto \mathbb{R}$ *are isophote equivalent or I-equivalent if* $I(x,t) = \tilde{J}(\tilde{x}, \tilde{t})$, *where*

$$\tilde{J}(x,t) = \eta(J(x,t)), \qquad \tilde{x} = \psi(x,t), \qquad \tilde{t} = \phi(t)$$

where $\eta_J > 0$ *and* $\phi_t > 0$ *since we want to distinguish also the direction of flow on flow-lines.*

Notice, that η is not a function of x or t. This is because the optic flow is dependent on the iso-intensity line (isophote) structure, and a varying diffeomorphism would change this structure. η can only change the intensity values, but not change the isophotes. Without further restrictions the classification of flow structure is rather crude, and we make the following smaller equivalence class, which leads to a finer classification.

Definition 7 (Image stationary equivalence). *Two images* $I(x,t) : \mathbb{R}^D \times \mathbb{R} \mapsto \mathbb{R}$ *and* $J(x,t) : \mathbb{R}^D \times \mathbb{R} \mapsto \mathbb{R}$ *are stationary equivalent or S-equivalent if they are I-equivalent with* $\psi(0,t) = 0$.

This more restrictive equivalence cannot change points of zero flow, unlike I-equivalence. None of them can remove critical points in the iso-functions. We introduce S-equivalence to make the analogy to nodes and foci of analytical flow fields. An even more restrictive equivalence class could be constructed, not allowing the spatial diffeomorphism to vary in time. This would be even more analogous to the classification of the analytical flows since the total first order flow structure would be invariant under the diffeomorphisms. This classification is, however, too fine in our taste and the S-equivalence suffices for our purposes, so we will not pursue this direction further in this paper.

We define local I-equivalence (local S-equivalence) in x_0, t_0 as being I-equivalent (S-equivalent) in an open set round x_0, t_0.

4.1 I-equivalent structure of the optic flow field

The normal flow is uniquely determined by the spatio-temporal iso-surface whenever the spatio-temporal image gradient does not vanish, and in positions where
its tangent plane is not parallel to the time axis, the flow is uniquely determined
by the spatio-temporal iso-function. Under I-equivalence the tangent plane of
the iso-surface can be tilted away from being parallel to the time axis, and we
need not treat this case separately. Hence we only analyse for general analytic
iso-functions and vanishing spatio-temporal gradient.

Proposition 2 (I-normal forms of 2D optic flow, codim 0). *At a fixed
time-slice $t = t_0$ the normal flow is generically in any point I-equivalent to one
of the following normal forms:*

$$n_0(x, y) = (1, 0)^T$$

$$n_2(x, y) = \frac{1}{x^2 + y^2} \begin{pmatrix} \pm x \\ \pm y \end{pmatrix}$$

where the sign combinations in n_2: $(+, -)$ and $(-, +)$ are equivalent.

*Proof. At a fixed time slice, the spatio-temporal gradient of the image will not
vanish generically (this happens at codimension 1), and thereby the iso-surface is
defined in every point. According to the arguments above we need only to analyse
analytic iso-functions. Any regular point on the iso-function are I-equivalent to
$s(x, y) = x$, and by using Prop. 1, we find n_0. The only generic critical points
are Morse critical points, which are I-equivalent to $s = \pm \frac{1}{2} x^2 \pm \frac{1}{2} y^2$. Again using
Prop. 1, we find n_2.*

The normal form n_2 has respectively identical spatial flow-lines to the stable
node $(-, -)$, the saddle $(-, +)$, and the unstable node $(+, +)$ of an analytical
flow field. However, the velocity increases towards plus/minus infinity when the
point approaches $(0, 0)$.

The classification of the flow follows directly from the classification of critical
points in analytical functions making the progress simple. The only twist is that
for codimension ≥ 1 there exists generically points where the iso-surface is not
defined.

Proposition 3 (I-normal forms of 2D optic flow, codim 1). *At a fixed
time-slice $t = t_0$ the normal flow is generically in any point I-equivalent with
codimension 1 to the normal forms of Prop. 2 or one of the following normal
forms:*

$$n_{2+1}(x, y) = \frac{1}{x^2 + y^2} \begin{pmatrix} xt \\ yt \end{pmatrix} \qquad n_3(x, y) = \frac{1}{(x^2 + t)^2 + y^2} \begin{pmatrix} x^2 + t \\ y \end{pmatrix}$$

where x, y, and t may independently change sign.

Proof. At codimension 0 we find the normal forms of Prop. 2. In codimension 1 we divide the analysis into two distinct case. Firstly we analyse the case where the spatio-temporal iso-surface is defined (the fold), secondly the case where it is not defined (the spatio-temporal critical point).

When the spatio-temporal surface is defined, we can using I-equivalence transform it into the normal form of general analytical functions. We use the theorem that iso-surfaces behave as generic functions [9], and find, at codimension 1, the only extra normal form compared to codimension 0 is the fold[6]: $s(x, y) = x^3 + tx + y^2$. By use of Prop. 1, we find n_3. Since I-equivalence only allows positive Jacobians in the diffeomorphisms, we must represent the signs of y and t explicitly.

When the spatio-temporal image gradient vanishes in (x_0, t_0), the iso-surface is not defined in this point. We can bring a spatio-temporal critical point on the following normal form by I-equivalence (up to signs of the individual terms): $I(x, y, t) = x^2 + y^2 + t^2$. We divide into two cases dependent on the sign of t, and find $s = \pm\sqrt{(I_0 - x^2 - y^2)}$, where I_0 is the intensity of the iso-surface. By Prop. 1 we find the normal flow:

$$n = \frac{\pm\sqrt{I_0 - x^2 - y^2}}{x^2 + y^2}\begin{pmatrix} x \\ y \end{pmatrix}$$

By substitution of the expression for $t = s(x, y)$ into this, the sign cancels out, and we find in both cases n_{2+1}.

Codimension one events take generically place in fixed time slices in a time sequence; The top of Figure 1 illustrates these events. A stable pole will always meet the saddle pole in its unstable direction while an unstable pole meets a saddle in its stable direction. This is illustrated in Figure 2.

Proposition 4 (I-normal forms of 2D optic flow, codim 2). *At a fixed time-slice $t = t_0$ the normal flow is generically in any point I-equivalent with codimension up to 2 to one of the normal forms in Prop. 2 or Prop. 3 or one of the following normal forms:*

$$n_{2+2}(x, y) = \frac{t_1^2 + t_2}{x^2 + y^2}\begin{pmatrix} x \\ y \end{pmatrix}$$

$$n_{3+1}(x, y) = \frac{t_1}{(x^2 + t_2)^2 + y^2}\begin{pmatrix} x^2 + t_2 \\ y \end{pmatrix}$$

$$n_4(x, y) = \frac{1}{(x^3 + t_2 x + t_1)^2 + y^2}\begin{pmatrix} x^3 + t_2 x + t_1 \\ y \end{pmatrix}$$

where x, y, and t_i may independently change sign. Any of the t_i may correspond to the physical time parameter.

Proof. The proof follows the lines of the proof in Prop. 3. First we divide into cases where the spatio-temporal iso-surface is defined or not. n_4 follows easily from a cusp in the iso-function: $s(x, y) = x^4 + t_2 x^2 + t_1 x + y^2$.

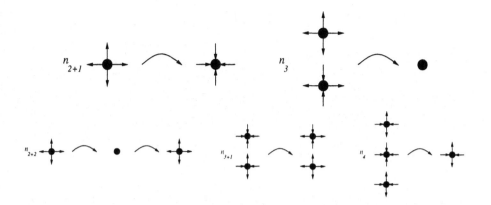

Fig. 1. Top, the generic events of codimension 1. n_{2+1} is a pole, where the directions of the flow are reversed. n_3 describes the interaction of two poles, where a saddle pole and a (un)stable pole interact and annihilate or are created. **Bottom**, the generic events of codimension 2. n_{2+2} is a pole that may change direction twice. n_{3+1} is an annihilation in t_2, but t_1 interchanges the stability of the poles. For instance, a stable pole and a saddle approach like at an annihilation, but they scatter and become a saddle and an unstable pole. n_4 is a pitchfork bifurcation. An example is a stable pole and two saddles approach, interact and become a single saddle.

In case of a vanishing spatio-temporal gradient, we subdivide into two cases dependent on whether I_{xx} or I_{tt} vanishes in the spatio-temporal critical point. In the first case we have a spatial fold as in n_3, but augmented by a vanishing temporal derivative, yielding n_{3+1}. In the latter case we have a spatially critical point in which a temporal fold happens, yielding n_{2+2}. The algebraic derivations are similar to the derivation of n_{2+1}.

In these normal forms we use two control parameters of which one is the time parameter and the other maybe most easily is visioned as a scale parameter even though these forms have not yet been proven to be the normal forms when the evolution along a control parameter is constrained as in the case of Gaussian scale space. Below we cite a theorem showing that even when the additional control parameter is a scale parameter, these normal forms are valid.

The codimension two events are illustrated schematically at the bottom of Figure 1. Assume t_1 is the time parameter, and t_2 is negative. Then when $t_1^2 > |t_2|$ n_{2+2} is an unstable pole, and when $t_1^2 < |t_2|$ it is a stable pole. If t_2 is positive, it is always unstable. Exactly when $t_2 = 0$, the pole disappears for $t_1 = 0$ but reappears with same orientation infinitesimally later.

4.2 S-equivalent structure of the optic flow field

The more restrictive S-equivalence cannot as I-equivalence remove vanishing flow. Hence, points with vanishing flow refines the classification. The intuitive

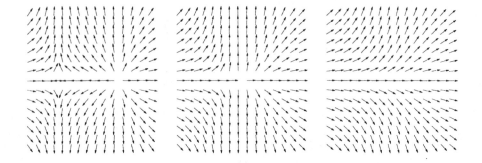

Fig. 2. The n_3 normal form for $t = -0.25, 0, 0.25$. A saddle and an unstable pole (left) meet (middle) and annihilate (right). Only the orientation of the flow is shown. The magnitude increases towards infinity near the poles.

key to the additional normal forms is the spatio-temporal surface of vanishing temporal derivative $T = \{x, y, t | I_t(x, y, t) = 0\}$. Since the image sequence is assumed to be differentiable, generically T will be a differentiable non self-intersecting surface.

Proposition 5 (S-normal forms of 2D optic flow, codim 0). *At a fixed time-slice $t = t_0$ the normal flow is generically in an open spatio-temporal neighbourhood round any point S-equivalent to one of the following normal forms:*

$$n_0(x, y) = (1, 0)^T$$
$$m_1(x, y) = (x - t, 0)^T$$
$$m_2(x, y) = (x - (y + 1)t, 0)^T$$
$$n_2(x, y) = \frac{1}{x^2 + y^2} \begin{pmatrix} \pm x \\ \pm y \end{pmatrix}$$

where the sign combinations in n_2: $(+, -)$ and $(-, +)$ are equivalent.

Proof. *The iso-surface is defined everywhere since at a fixed time the spatio-temporal image gradient is not generically zero. For non-vanishing temporal derivative we arrive at n_0 and n_2 for regular respectively critical spatial points. m_1 or m_2 occurs for $I_t = 0$. In a spatial coordinate system (v, w) where w is the image gradient direction, we find the parameters of the diffeomorphism such that the normal flow takes the form of m_1. This form of the diffeomorphism is only valid whenever $I_{tt} \neq 0$. For $I_{tt} = 0$ we find m_2. All these computations have been omitted in this paper due to the space limitations and their algebraic complexity.*

The number of linear constraining equations for a particular form determines the dimension of the set with points equivalent to the form. Hence, n_0, m_1 and n_2 points group in manifolds of dimension two, one and zero, respectively.

The normal form m_1 shows a line of zero normal flow, denoted a fixed line. Notice that S-equivalence do not distinguish attracting and repelling lines. m_2 counts for that the fixed line in a point does not move. The fixed line rotates locally round this point, and we denote this event a "whirl".

Proposition 6 (S-normal forms of 2D optic flow, codim 1). *At a fixed time-slice $t = t_0$ the normal flow is in a generic one-parameter family in an open spatio-temporal neighbourhood round any point S-equivalent to one of the normal forms of Prop. 5, Prop. 3, or the following:*

$$m_{1+2}(x,y) = (\pm y^2 \pm x^2 + t, 0)^T$$
$$m_{2+1}(x,y) = (x \pm (y^2 + 1)t, 0)^T$$
$$m_3(x,y) = (x - (y + 1)t^2, 0)^T$$

where the sign combinations in m_{1+2}: $(+,-)$ and $(-,+)$ are equivalent.

Proof. m_{1+2} follows from m_1 when also the spatial gradient of I_t vanishes. $m_{2+1}(x,y)$ follows from m_2 with the additional constraint that the spatio-temporal line of a whirl is locally orthogonal to the temporal dimension. m_3 follows from m_2 when $I_{ttt} = 0$. Again algebraic derivations have been omitted.

The event m_{1+2} is, for our purposes, the most important event arising from the S-equivalence next to m_1, if one is interested solely in the fixed lines. The latter describes that the normal flow vanishes at lines. m_{1+2} describes topology change of zero flow lines, denoted fixed lines. Depending on the signs, it is either a creation event $(-,-)$, an annihilation event $(+,+)$ or a fixed line saddle event $(+,-)$ or $(-,+)$. During an annihilation or creation event a circular zero flow line vanishes/appears. During the fixed line saddle event the connectivity of two zero flow lines changes. Four incoming lines meet in a cross exactly during the event. Before and after two different pairs of incoming lines are connected.

The event m_{2+1} describes the annihilation/creation of a pair of whirls. The two whirls will have opposite rotation directions. In a point they meet and annihilate. Even though m_2 does not distinguish the rotation direction, since two whirls of opposite rotation are S-equivalent, m_{2+1} constrains the whirls to having opposite rotation since the diffeomorphism can only change direction for both simultaneously. In Figure 3 top are m_{1+2} and m_{2+1} illustrated.

m_3 accounts for a locally stationary whirl. This point corresponds to a cusp in the function surface $I_t = 0$. Figure 3, bottom-left illustrates this. Going through the cusp, does not in codimension 1 change the rotation direction of the whirl. Whirls may change direction, but this event is not singled out since it is S-equivalent to the whirl itself. If one is interested in orientation of whirls another equivalence class must be constructed to subserve this analysis. However, what one can say directly is that in the real spatial plane, there will always be equally many left and right whirls. This holds for any subset of the plane where all fixed lines form closed curves, since a curve will after an infinitesimal perturbation cross the un-perturbed curve an even number of times, and these crossings will

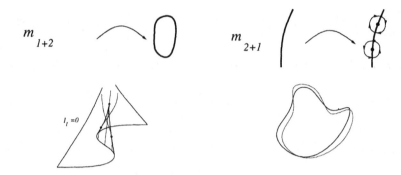

Fig. 3. Top, Two events of codimension 1: m_{1+2} and m_{2+1}. **Bottom,** left is the stationary fixed line whirl. Time is vertical. It corresponds to the cusp point of the surface of $I_t = 0$. The dashed lines are the fixed line at different time instances (horizontal planes cutting the surface). The dots are the corresponding whirls. They move on a parabola open in the direction towards the reader. Right is an illustration of the principle that a perturbed curve crosses the original curve an even number of times, and equally many times from inside as from outside.

be equally many outwards and inwards crossing. This is illustrated in Figure 3 (right).

The S-equivalence implies that on top of the poles, points of zero motion is the basis of the taxonomy of image sequence structure. The S-equivalence first picks up lines of zero flow, fixed lines. Then points where these lines do not move (whirls) and points where the fixed lines changes topology. It does not distinguish attracting and repelling lines.

4.3 A comment on the multi-scale optic flow structure

A scale space is constructed by convolving the image by Gaussians so that the scale-space fulfills the Heat equation $I_s = \triangle I$, where s is the scale parameter and $\triangle$ denotes the spatial, the temporal, or the spatio-temporal Laplacean dependent on which scale-space one constructs. The analysis of structure in scale-space can not be done by simply using transversality arguments and referring to Thom's classification. The proper analysis has been performed by Damon[3]. In conjunction with flow, however, we have proof, but leave it out here due to the space limitations, that under the heat equation, a spatio-temporal iso-surface is not constrained in its local deformation, only in its topology changes. The idea is that the second derivative across the surface, may make the surface evolve in any direction in its jet space. Similar has been proven by Kergosien and Thom [9] for iso-surfaces of general analytical functions. The importance of these two results are that we can argue of genericity simply by counting constraints on the iso-function: they translate to simple linear bands on the image jet. Thus in all the above normal forms, time may be exchanged with scale. The only limitation is that the time and the scale parameter may not coincide.

resolution. In general, intensities at larger scales will not be preserved since intensities will change weight under the Gaussian aperture functions due to the flow. This is treated in detail in [4]. The above normal forms are though still valid as they deal with the infinite resolution flow, but argued from a scale-space point of view, they can never be accessed.

5 Detection of structural changes

The change of topology in the poles or lines of zero normal flow is characterised by the corresponding normal forms. Thus, to detect change in the structure of the flow field we must detect when and where the normal forms apply. In table below we list the conditions for the events and name the events. In the table p denotes the direction in which the spatial second order image structure vanishes.

We compute derivatives of digital images as scale space derivatives. That is, we observe the image under a Gaussian aperture defining the spatial and temporal scale (inverse resolution). By differentiation of this spatio-temporal Gaussian prior to convolution, the computation of image derivatives is well-posed. The side effect is that it is not the image at grid resolution but at a lower resolution which is the object of analysis. We do not in this paper take into account the aspects due to the non-commutation of the Gaussian convolution and the deformation due to flow field. These effects have been analysed by Florack et al. [4].

n_0	Regular point	$\nabla I \neq 0$
n_2	Pole	$I_x = 0,\ I_y = 0$
n_{2+1}	Pole stability reversion	$I_x = 0,\ I_y = 0,\ I_t = 0$
n_3	Pole pair creation	$I_x = 0,\ I_y = 0,\ I_{xx}I_{yy} - I_{xy}^2 = 0$
n_{2+2}	Pole stability fold	$I_x = 0,\ I_y = 0,\ I_t = 0,\ I_{tt} = 0$
n_{3+1}	Pole scatter	$I_x = 0,\ I_y = 0,\ I_t = 0,\ I_{xx}I_{yy} - I_{xy}^2 = 0$
n_4	Pole pitchfork bifurcation	$I_x = 0,\ I_y = 0,\ I_{xx}I_{yy} - I_{xy}^2 = 0,\ I_{ppp} = 0$
m_1	Fixed line	$I_t = 0$
m_2	Fixed line whirl	$I_t = 0,\ I_{tt} = 0$
m_{1+2}	Fixed line creation	$I_t = 0,\ I_{xt} = 0,\ I_{yt} = 0$
m_{2+1}	Fixed line whirl creation	$I_t = 0,\ I_{tt} = 0,\ I_{ty}I_{ttx} - I_{tx}I_{tty} = 0$
m_3	Stationary fixed line whirl	$I_t = 0,\ I_{tt} = 0,\ I_{ttt} = 0$

The zero locus of pre-computed differential expression is computed using an algorithm similar to the Marching Cubes algorithm [12]. For each differential expression, the zero locus is computed, and the intersection of loci is computed using an algorithm assembling the Marching Lines algorithm [15]. In this way the normal flow events are detected and their spatio-temporal position simultaneously computed.

In the following we detect some of these in two different image sequences. First, we detect the poles and their temporal interaction in a sequence of a person walking in a hall way. Secondly, we detect the lines of fixed flow and their interaction in a sequence of turbulent flow, and use the scale interaction for quantifying the amount of turbulence in the sequence.

5.1 Temporal pole evolution

Figure 4 illustrates the detection of flow poles and their temporal interaction in a sequence of a person appearing in a hall way. We see poles due to critical image points at the scale at hand. These are distributed all over the image, and most have close to constant positions. However, in the center region, where the person appears in the hall way we see poles created and annihilated. These points corresponds to points where the topology of the flow pattern changes. That is, these creation/annihilation points are invariant to any additional flow added to the normal flow. In this way they are not influenced by quantitative aspects such as speed, orientation etc. We suggest that they may be used for guiding an attention mechanism.

5.2 Fixed line scale-evolution

In turbulent flow, the degree of turbulence can be accessed through the scaling properties of the "eddies". Kolmogorov introduced the cascade models of turbulent flow, looking at the energy transport from large scale eddies to small scale eddies [11]. Frisch introduced a variant of these called the β-model [5] where the variable of interest is the scaling properties of the space filling of eddies. The so-called structure function characterising the flow is defined in terms of the scaling exponent of the space filling of the eddies. In the following, we sketch how this can be accessed through the multi-scale optic flow structure.

At every scale a number of whirls is present. As an approximation we assume that a whirl corresponds to an eddy and that its space filling corresponds to its area, that is its spatial scale squared. The scaling exponent of the energy as a function of scale may then be estimated from counting whirls at a number of different scales.

In Figure 5, smoke induced into a ventilated pigsty is shown. The smoke is illuminated by a laser scanning through a plane such that the smoke in a vertical 2D plane in the 3D pigsty is imaged. In Figure 5 bottom-right the scale evolution of whirls in the Pigsty sequence is shown including annihilation (and the few creation) events. As indicated above the scaling properties of the whirls may be used for accessing the degree of turbulence in the flow. From the number of detected whirls as a function of scale we find approximately that $V \propto s^{0.5}$. That is, only 70 percent of the energy is transported to whirls at the half length scale[1]. This computation is, though, based only on approximately 100 whirls and a scaling interval of a single decade. This is clearly insufficient to state that we have proven self similarity or precisely computed the degree of turbulence. We have merely indicated a direction in which the structure of the optic flow field as suggested in this paper can be used for more practical exercises.

---

[1] Dimensional analysis indicates a scaling of S^0, so this is not a trivial result

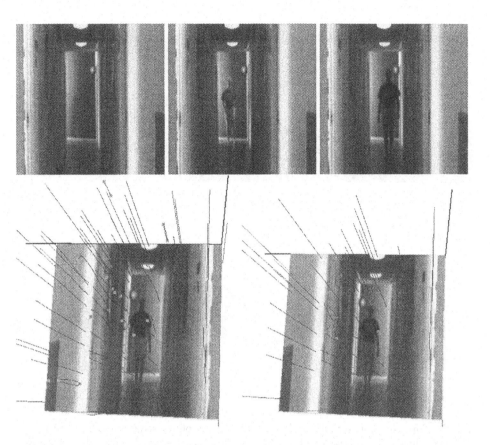

Fig. 4. Top, the first, middle, and last frame of the hall way sequence. **Bottom**,The spatio-temporal curves of the poles and their creation points for spatial scale $s = 5$ (left) and $s = 8$ (right). Temporal scale is 2. Sequence is $256 \times 256 \times 32$ pixels cubed

6 Summary

We have introduced two equivalence classes of optic flow and derived normal forms of codimension 0, 1, and 2 (the latter only in case of I-equivalence). I-equivalence leads to a definition of structure as the poles in the flow field whereas the S-equivalence leads also to fixed points.

The major differences to normal analytical flow fields as in autonomous dynamical systems, is the presence of poles and that the tangential component of the optic flow field is undefined. The poles can only be avoided by a regularization of the flow field as is normally done in computer vision algorithms [7]. An arbitrary "gauge condition" could be imposed to fix the tangential component and in this way fixed points as in dynamical systems can be introduced. Restricting the equivalence class of flows could make the analogy to dynamical systems even larger.

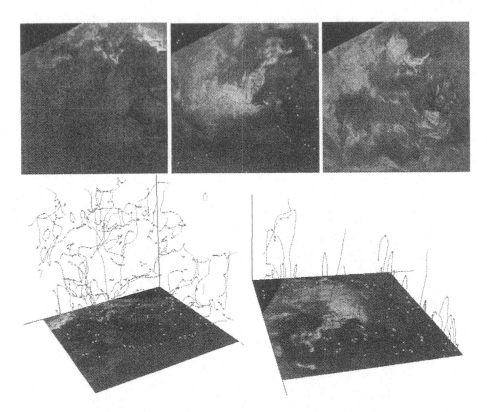

Fig. 5. Top, the first, middle, and last frame of the pigsty sequence. The fixed lines and the whirls are superimposed on the middle frame. **Bottom**, left is the temporal evolution of whirls and their creation/annihilation points. Right are the whirls in the middle frame as a function of scale. Points mark annihilations or creations.

We have introduced a concept of whirls. These however have a very different nature than the nodes in dynamical systems since the whirl include second order temporal structure, and the analogy to nodes is not clear.

The natural continuation of the research presented in this paper is to look at a gauge fixed tangential flow, and to introduce temporarily constant diffeomorphisms for definition of the equivalence of flow. In this way the only difference to dynamical systems may be the poles.

The theoretical results in this paper has been applied to two simple examples: computation of spatio-temporal points in which the topology of the flow field changes, as a mechanism for guiding attention, and computation of the scaling properties of whirls as to characterize turbulent flow.

References

1. Vladimir I. Arnol'd. *Ordinary Differential Equations*. Springer Verlag, 3 edition, 1992.
2. J. Arnspang. Notes on local determination of smooth optic flow and the translational property of first order optic flow. Technical Report 88-1, Institute of Datalogy, University of Copenhagen, Denmark, 1988.
3. J. Damon. Local Morse theory for solutions to the heat equation and Gaussian blurring. *Journal of Differential Equations*, 1993.
4. Luc Florack, Wiro Niessen, and Mads Nielsen. The intrinsic structure of optic flow incorporating measurement duality. *International Journal on Computer Vision*, 1997. (In Press).
5. U. Frisch, P. Sulem, and M. Nelkin. A simple model of intermittent fully developed turbulence. *Journal of Fluid Mechanics*, 87(4):719–736, 1987.
6. Robert Gilmore. *Catastrophe Theory for Scientist and Engineers*. Dover, 1981.
7. B. Horn and B. Schunck. Determining optical flow. *Artificial Intelligence*, 23:185–203, 1981.
8. B. Jähne. *Spatio-Temporal Image Processing-Theory and Scientific Applications*. Lecture Notes in Computer Science, VOLUME = 751, PUBLISHER =.
9. Y. L. Kergosien and R. Thom. Sur les points parabolique des surfaces. Technical Report 290:705–710, C.R. Acad. Sci. Paris t., 1980.
10. J. J. Koenderink and A. J. van Doorn. Second order optic flow. *Journal of the Optical Society of America*, 8(2):530–538, 1992.
11. A. N. Kolmogorov. The local structure of turbulence in incressible viscious fluids for very large reynolds numbers. Technical report, C R Acad. Sci. USSR 30, 301, 1941.
12. William E. Lorenson and Harvey E. Cline. Marching cubes: A high resolution 3d surface reconstruction algorithm. *Computer Graphics*, 21(4), 1987.
13. H. H. Nagel. Displacement vectors derived from second-order intensity variations in image sequences. *Comp. Graph. and Image Proc.*, 21:85–117, 1983.
14. M. Otte and H. H. Nagel. Optical flow estimation: Advances and comparisons. In J.-O. Eklundh, editor, *Proc. Europ. Conf. on Computer Vision*, pages 51–60, Stockholm, Sweden, 1994.
15. Jean Philip Thirion and Alexis Gourdon. The marching lins algorithm: new results and proofs. Technical Report 1881, INRIA, 1993.
16. A. Verri, F. Girosi, and V. Torre. Mathematical properties of the two-dimensional motion field: from singular points to motion parameters. *Journal of the Optical Society of America-A*, 6(5):698–712, 1989.
17. P. Werkhoven. *Visual Perception of Successive Order*. PhD thesis, Utrecht University, University of Utrecht, Dept. of Physics of Man, Princetonplein 5, 3508 TA Utrecht, the Netherlands, May 1990.

Optical Flow Using Overlapped Basis Functions for Solving Global Motion Problems

Sridhar Srinivasan and Rama Chellappa *

Department of Electrical Engineering and Center for Automation Research
University of Maryland, College Park, MD 20742, U.S.A.
{shridhar,rama}@cfar.umd.edu

Abstract. Motion problems in which the scene motion largely conforms to a low order global motion model are called global motion problems, examples of which are stabilization, mosaicking and motion super-resolution. In this paper, we propose a two-step solution for robustly estimating the global motion parameters that characterize global motion problems. Our primary contribution is an improved estimation algorithm for modeling the optical flow field of a sequence using overlapped basis functions. Moreover, we show that the parametrized flow estimates can be consolidated through an iterative process that estimates global deformation while ensuring robustness to systematic errors such as those caused by moving foreground objects or occlusion. We demonstrate the validity of our model and accuracy of the algorithm on synthetic and real data. Our technique is computationally efficient, and is ideally suited for the application areas discussed here, *viz.* stabilization, mosaicking and super-resolution.

1 Introduction

Motion problems in which the scene motion largely conforms to a global motion model are termed global motion problems. Electronic stabilization of video, creating mosaics from image sequences and performing motion super-resolution are examples of global motion problems. These are often encountered in surveillance, navigation (tele-operation), automatic target recognition (ATR) and forensic science. Reliable motion estimation is critical to these tasks, which is particularly challenging when the sequences display random as well as highly structured systematic errors. The former is usually a result of sensor noise, atmospheric turbulence, etc. while the latter is caused by occlusion, shadows and independently moving foreground objects. The goal in global motion problems is to maintain the integrity of the solution in the presence of both types of errors.

Prior work on global motion problems can be classified into *flow based, direct* and *feature based* approaches. A low-order model is fit to the dense flow

* The support of this research by the Defense Advanced Research Projects Agency (DARPA Order No. C635) and the Office of Naval Research under Contract N00014-95-1-0521 is gratefully acknowledged. We also thank the anonymous reviewers for their valuable comments and criticism.

field estimated from the sequence in the flow based approach [1], [4], [11]. Direct methods estimate the motion parameters from the original sequence in one step [2], [13], [18], while feature based methods match sparse feature sets extracted from each image for registering successive images [16], [25]. The shortcoming of flow based methods is that estimating a dense flow field is both ill-conditioned and an overkill for the global motion problem, besides complicating the process of consolidating the flow field into global motion parameters. On the other hand, estimating the motion parameters directly from the luminance data saves computations at the cost of failure in the presence of structured errors. Finally, feature based methods suffer due to their excessive dependence on reliable feature extraction and correspondence.

In this paper, we propose a two step algorithm for solving the global motion problem. The first and critical step of the algorithm is based on a new optical flow estimator which models the flow field as a linear combination of an overlapped set of basis functions. Consolidation of the flow field into global motion parameters, which is the second step, is performed in the parameter (feature) space, like in the feature based methods. While the flow field model is similar to spline based motion computation [23], the estimation process is very different. Indeed, we show that our estimate of the flow field parameters is relatively unaffected by errors in the estimates of spatial gradients. Moreover, we develop a computationally efficient strategy for single-scale motion estimation. Since the consolidation process operates on the model weights which are far fewer in number than the image size, the dimensionality of the problem is small. This permits robust and efficient computation of the global motion parameters. In practice, we have achieved rates of over 5 frame/s on a sequential workstation for image stabilization.

This paper is organized as follows: section 2 introduces the optical flow model, an estimation methodology together with a mathematical justification for its robustness and an efficient algorithm for its solution. Consolidation of the flow model is covered in section 3. Section 4 describes our experiments and tabulates the results obtained by our algorithm.

2   Optical Flow Modeling and Estimation

When the projected time-varying image field of a scene is given by $\psi = \psi(x, y, t)$, preservation of luminance patterns implies the *gradient constraint equation*

$$\frac{\partial \psi}{\partial t} + u\frac{\partial \psi}{\partial x} + v\frac{\partial \psi}{\partial y} = 0 \qquad \forall\, x, y, t \,. \tag{1}$$

u and v in (1) denote the horizontal and vertical velocities, as functions of space and time, respectively. Together, they constitute the optical flow field of the sequence. For every triplet (x, y, t) in (1), there are two unknowns, making the problem of computing the optical flow ill-conditioned.

The problem of estimating a pixelwise flow field has been approached by regularization of the optical flow constraint [3], [6], [8]-[10], [14], [15], [17]. In these methods, the process of estimating optical flow is converted to a non-linear optimization problem, although (1) is linear in the velocity field (u, v). Results obtained by these techniques are often significantly off the mark, highly sensitive to numerical precision, determined only at a sparse set of points with reasonable confidence and carry with them the pitfalls associated with nonlinear optimization [6].

Our proposed technique models the optical flow field as a linear combination of an overlapped set of basis functions that is solved by a linear system of equations. This system is sparse and its solution involves a sparse matrix inversion. A numerically stable solution is obtained by using the method of conjugate gradients, giving a dense and reliable flow field even when the matrix is ill conditioned.

An alternative to computing the optical flow on a pixelwise basis is to model the motion fields u and v in terms of a weighted sum of basis functions and to estimate the weights which constitute the flow model parameters [20], [22], [23]. In this approach, the motion field is force-fitted to the model and derives the smoothness properties from the model basis functions. Let $\{\phi = \phi(x, y, t)\}$ be a family of basis functions, and let the flow field be modeled as

$$u = \sum_{k=0}^{K} u_k \phi_k \text{ and } v = \sum_{k=0}^{K} v_k \phi_k . \tag{2}$$

The patchwise constant, affine or polynomial model is a special case of (2), for instance setting ϕ_k to a rectangular window function is equivalent to the constant-in-a-patch model. Likewise, choosing a wavelet basis for $\{\phi_k\}$ is tantamount to performing a multiresolution optical flow computation. Since the optical flow field of a sequence is largely smooth, it seems reasonable to model the field using (2) and an appropriate basis $\{\phi_k\}$.

Substituting (2) into (1), we get

$$\frac{\partial \psi}{\partial t} + \sum_k u_k \phi_k \frac{\partial \psi}{\partial x} + \sum_k v_k \phi_k \frac{\partial \psi}{\partial y} = 0 \quad \forall x, y, t . \tag{3}$$

This continuum of equations in 3-space (3) can be reduced to a scalar equation for each instant of time by integrating with a multiplicative kernel $\theta = \theta(x, y)$,

$$\int \frac{\partial \psi}{\partial t} \theta dx dy + \sum_k u_k \int \phi_k \frac{\partial \psi}{\partial x} \theta dx dy + \sum_k v_k \int \phi_k \frac{\partial \psi}{\partial y} \theta dx dy = 0 . \tag{4}$$

Equation (4) exists for every square integrable kernel θ, and every instant of time. In order to solve for $\{u_k, v_k\}$, it is necessary to choose appropriate kernels in (4).

2.1 Solutions

System (3) is linear in the unknowns $\{u_k, v_k\}$ and is analogous to the matrix-vector system

$$Ax \rightarrow b \quad A \in \mathbb{R}^{M \times N}, M > N , \tag{5}$$

where x corresponds to the vector $(u_0, v_0, \ldots)'$. The analogy implies the applicability of solutions and results of (5) to (3). In the discrete domain, the analogy is obvious since an equation of the type (3) exists for each pixel in the current frame, corresponding to one row of the composite matrix $[A|b]$. The least squares (LS) solution of (5) is given by $A'Ax = A'b$. Likewise, choosing θ from the family $\{\phi_k \frac{\partial \psi}{\partial x}, \phi_k \frac{\partial \psi}{\partial y}\}$ gives the LS solution of (3). In practice, only discretized data is available for the image luminance field ψ. The LS solution assumes knowledge of the spatial derivatives of ψ, which may not be known reliably. Any minor and random non-compliance of (1) is accounted by the observation error in b. A robust approach must try to minimize sensitive dependence of the solution on the spatial as well as temporal derivatives. In other words, in the analogue (5), the solution must be accurate and robust to errors in A as well as in b, which can be stated as:

Assume x_0 is the exact solution for the overconstrained linear system $Ax \to b$. Let Δ and δ be zero mean, independent additive observation noise in A and b respectively, i.e. the quantities $\hat{A} = A + \Delta$ and $\hat{b} = b + \delta$ are observed. Find an 'optimal' estimate x of x_0 given $\hat{A}$ and $\hat{b}$.

In the remainder of this section, we analyze three solutions *viz.* the LS, total least squares (TLS) and our proposed method we refer to as the extended least squares (ELS), in terms of their optimality quantified by the bias and variance of estimates. We assume Δ and δ to be uncorrelated with A and b, and the matrix $A'A$ to be invertible. In addition, we assume the availability of the observation $\hat{A}'A$ for the ELS estimate, the existence of which we prove later. The symbol $\approx$ denotes a first order approximation. R_Δ denotes the covariance matrix of rows of Δ and r_δ is the variance of δ_i, assuming that the rows are *iid*.

LS solution. The LS solution of (5) is $x_{LS} = (\hat{A}\hat{A}')^{-1}\hat{A}'b$. The error associated with this solution can be shown to be

$$e_{LS} \approx (A'A)^{-1}A'(\delta - \Delta x_0) - \underbrace{(A'A)^{-1}A'R_\Delta x_{LS}}_{\text{bias}} . \tag{6}$$

x_{LS} is the minimizer of $\|Ax - b\|_2$ when the observation error is present only in $\hat{b}$. Bias sets in when $\hat{A} \neq A$. The two random components of e_{LS} are independent by the assumption of independence of Δ and δ. A modification of LS, the corrected least squares (CLS) method removes bias while preserving the error covariance. However, this assumes knowledge of the covariance matrix R_Δ.

TLS solution. The TLS principle has emerged as an alternative to LS since it is capable of handling errors in potentially all observations in a linear system, not merely on the 'right hand side' [12]. The TLS solution is obtained by minimally perturbing the composite observation matrix $[\hat{A}|\hat{b}]$ to reduce its rank to N. x_{TLS}, the TLS estimate, is given by $x_{TLS} = -v_{n+1}^{(n)}/v_{n+1,n+1}^{(n)}$, where $v_{n+1}^{(n)}$ is the vector formed by the first n components of v_{n+1}, which is the eigenvector of $[\hat{A}|\hat{b}]'[\hat{A}|\hat{b}]$

corresponding to its smallest eigenvalue μ. $v_{n+1,n+1}$ is the $n+1$th component of v_{n+1}.

e_{TLS} is not easy to determine for the TLS case, even when the observation errors are small. Setting $E[e_{\text{TLS}}] = 0$ gives a necessary condition for a zero bias estimate

$$(r_\delta I - R_\Delta) x_0 \to 0 \ . \tag{7}$$

Thus, the TLS estimate is unbiased *only if* the error in estimating the temporal gradient is equal in variance to the error in estimating the (windowed) spatial gradient. However, in typical image sequence problems, the temporal gradient is calculated over a smaller number of frames than the spread of the spatial gradient operator. In order to satisfy (7), it becomes necessary to discard useful information by narrowing down the support of the spatial gradient operator, which is not desirable. In addition, it has been argued in [12] that the covariance of an unbiased TLS estimate is larger than that of the LS estimate, in the first order approximation as well as in simulations. There is, therefore, no fundamental gain in choosing the TLS over the LS solution.

ELS solution. Neither the LS nor the TLS solutions of (5) are unbiased in the general case, and the CLS solution shows sensitive dependence on the errors in $\hat{A}$ as well as in $\hat{b}$. Interestingly, if an additional observation, *viz.* $\hat{G} = \hat{A}'A$ is available, the ELS solution proposed here shows no dependence on the error Δ in the observation of A. Moreover, the observation corresponding to $\hat{G}$ is available for (3). The ELS solution of (5) is the solution of $\hat{G}x = \hat{A}'\hat{b}$,

$$x_{\text{ELS}} = \hat{G}^{-1} \hat{A}' \hat{b} \ . \tag{8}$$

A linearized analysis shows the corresponding estimation error to be

$$e_{\text{ELS}} = \underbrace{\hat{G}^{-1}}_{\approx (A'A)^{-1}} [\Delta' \underbrace{(Ax_0 - b)}_{=0} + \underbrace{\Delta'\delta + A'\delta}_{O(2)}] \approx (A'A)^{-1} A'\delta \ , \tag{9}$$

proving the claim. The subtle difference between x_{LS} and x_{ELS} leads to the replacement of the error term $-(A'A)^{-1} A'\Delta x_0$ in (6) by $\hat{G}^{-1}\Delta'\delta$ in (9). Assuming small observation errors, the latter is insignificant. Therefore, x_{ELS} is unbiased, and has a smaller covariance than x_{LS} or x_{CLS}. In the original problem (3), the ELS solution is obtained when θ in (4) is chosen from the family $\{\phi_k \frac{\partial\hat{\psi}}{\partial x}, \phi_k \frac{\partial\hat{\psi}}{\partial y}\}$ where the quantity $\frac{\partial\hat{\psi}}{\partial\{x,y\}}$ is an *estimate* of the derivative, giving

$$\int \frac{\partial\hat{\psi}}{\partial t}\phi_l \frac{\partial\hat{\psi}}{\partial x} + \sum_k u_k \int \phi_k \frac{\partial\psi}{\partial x}\phi_l \frac{\partial\hat{\psi}}{\partial x} + \sum_k v_k \int \phi_k \frac{\partial\psi}{\partial y}\phi_l \frac{\partial\hat{\psi}}{\partial x} = 0$$

$$\int \frac{\partial\hat{\psi}}{\partial t}\phi_l \frac{\partial\hat{\psi}}{\partial y} + \sum_k u_k \int \phi_k \frac{\partial\psi}{\partial x}\phi_l \frac{\partial\hat{\psi}}{\partial y} + \sum_k v_k \int \phi_k \frac{\partial\psi}{\partial y}\phi_l \frac{\partial\hat{\psi}}{\partial y} = 0 \tag{10}$$

where the integrals are over XY and the estimated temporal derivative is $\frac{\partial\hat{\psi}}{\partial t}$. We now prove the availability of the observations $\hat{G} = \hat{A}'A$ and $\hat{A}'\hat{b}$, which is equivalent to proving the computability of the integrals in (10), under certain weak assumptions on the functional form of ϕ_k and the estimate $\frac{\partial\hat{\psi}}{\partial\{x,y\}}$.

2.2 Eliminating Derivatives

Consider the integral $I(y) = \int \phi_k \frac{\partial\psi}{\partial x} \phi_l \frac{\partial\hat{\psi}}{\partial x} dx$. Assume that the estimate $\frac{\partial\hat{\psi}}{\partial\{x,y\}}$ has a differentiable functional form, $i.e.$ the derivative $\frac{\partial}{\partial\{x,y\}} \frac{\partial\hat{\psi}}{\partial\{x,y\}}$ is known exactly. This holds for even the simplest of discrete gradient masks like $(-1,1)$ since the masks assume a smooth underlying functional form. Also, assume that $\{\phi_k\}$ are differentiable and that $\phi_k(x,y) \to 0$ as $x \to \pm\infty$ or $y \to \pm\infty$. Integrating $I(y)$ by parts over $(-\infty,\infty)$, we get

$$I(y) = \underbrace{\left[\phi_k\phi_l\frac{\partial\hat{\psi}}{\partial x}\psi\right]_{-\infty}^{\infty}}_{=0} - \int_{-\infty}^{\infty} \psi\frac{\partial\phi_k\phi_l\frac{\partial\hat{\psi}}{\partial x}}{\partial x}dx \tag{11}$$

which is computable reliably without knowing the exact derivatives $\frac{\partial\psi}{\partial\{x,y\}}$. Applying this reasoning to (10) gives

$$\sum_k u_k \int \frac{\partial\phi_k\phi_l\frac{\partial\hat{\psi}}{\partial x}}{\partial x}\psi + \sum_k v_k \int \frac{\partial\phi_k\phi_l\frac{\partial\hat{\psi}}{\partial x}}{\partial y}\psi = \int \frac{\partial\hat{\psi}}{\partial t}\phi_l\frac{\partial\hat{\psi}}{\partial x}$$

$$\sum_k u_k \int \frac{\partial\phi_k\phi_l\frac{\partial\hat{\psi}}{\partial y}}{\partial x}\psi + \sum_k v_k \int \frac{\partial\phi_k\phi_l\frac{\partial\hat{\psi}}{\partial y}}{\partial y}\psi = \int \frac{\partial\hat{\psi}}{\partial t}\phi_l\frac{\partial\hat{\psi}}{\partial y} \tag{12}$$

with the following desirable properties:

- The accuracy of spatio-temporal image derivatives is not critical to the accuracy of computation.
- The computed image flow is force-fitted on a model. The only conditions on the model are that it be space-limited and differentiable.
- With finite extent basis functions ϕ_k, the system of equations gives a sparse, banded matrix structure.

It is only by eliminating derivatives that the ELS method is achievable. In practice, the gains of using ELS are eroded because of the following reasons. We have implicitly assumed that noise is introduced only on differentiation while in reality even the image data ψ is noisy. Also, the integrals in (12) are evaluated from discretely sampled data and are not true integrals. Although the difference between $\hat{G}$ and $\hat{A}'\hat{A}$ is small, it is sufficient to prove the empirical superiority of the ELS.

2.3 Choice of Basis Functions

As in all estimation problems, there is an inevitable tradeoff between sensitivity and selectivity, or equivalently, between accuracy and localization. The specific basis function family $\{\phi_k\}$ determines the shape of the ROC curve, and its density (defined as the number of basis functions per unit area) fixes the operating point on the curve. Not all differentiable, compactly supported curves are meaningful to the problem at hand. Since the variations in optical flow are typically high-frequency and localized or low-frequency and global, periodic bases do not offer any advantage. Orthogonal bases do not lead to a simpler solution than non-orthogonal bases because there are no integrals of the form $\int \phi_k \phi_l$. However, for every non-overlapping pair $\{\phi_i, \phi_j\}$, the corresponding entries in the observation matrix $\hat{G}$, $\hat{G}_{ij}$ and $\hat{G}_{ji}$, are zero. Thus, from the computational aspect, it is desirable to minimize the number of overlapping pairs. Besides, since systematic errors show spatial concentration, a locally supported basis function set ensures that the damage caused by a systematic error is limited to one or a few model weights determining the flow field.

The reasoning thus far, including the final linear system (12), holds for any choice of basis functions which are differentiable and which decay to zero. In the remainder of this section, we place certain additional restrictions on the choice of $\{\phi_k\}$ that ensure computational ease and have intuitive appeal for modeling a motion field. We construct $\{\phi_k\}$ from translations of a prototype function ϕ_0 along a uniformly spaced square grid of spacing w, with the following additional requirements:

- *Separability:* $\phi_0(x, y) = \phi_0(x)\phi_0(y)$
- *Symmetry about the origin:* $\phi_0(x) = \phi_0(-x)$
- *Peak at the origin:* $|\phi_0(x)| \leq \phi_0(0) = 1$
- *Compact support:* $\phi_0(x) = 0 \quad \forall |x| > w$
- *Constancy:* $\phi_0(x) + \phi_0(x - w) \simeq 1, \forall x \in [0, w]$
- *Linearity:* $\phi_0(x) + \lambda\phi_0(x - w) \simeq 1 + (\lambda - 1)\frac{x}{w} \; \forall x \in [0, w]$

Compact support ensures that each basis function overlaps with exactly nine of its neighbors, in the cardinal and diagonal directions. *Constancy* is essential for modeling the simple case of uniform translation, and *linearity* is necessary for exactly modeling an affine flow field. *Constancy* is implied by *linearity*.

The spacing w of the grid at which the basis functions are centered determines the density of the basis functions, thereby determining the position of the algorithm on the ROC curve. A larger spacing implies a larger support for ϕ_k which reduces error in estimates of the integrals in (12). However, increasing w means that the parameter space spans fewer dimensions, giving fewer degrees of freedom for modeling the flow field. Trying to fit a stiff model leads to non-compliance at motion discontinuities. Therefore, w determines the tradeoff between robustness and accuracy of the algorithm.

2.4 Sparse Matrix Inversion

In our experiments, we used the cosine window

$$\phi_0(x) = \frac{1}{2}\left[1 + \cos(\frac{\pi x}{w})\right] \quad x \in [-w, w] \tag{13}$$

as the prototype basis function. The entire bases is generated from shifts of the prototype along a rectangular grid with spacing w. The *linearity* property is only approximately satisfied for this choice. The observation matrix $\hat{G}$ is block tridiagonal, given by

$$\hat{G} = \begin{bmatrix} D_1 & U_1 & 0 & 0 \\ L_2 & D_2 & U_2 & 0 \\ 0 & L_3 & D_3 & U_3 \\ & & & \ddots \end{bmatrix} \cdots , \quad D_i, U_i, L_i \sim \begin{bmatrix} \times & \times & 0 & 0 \\ \times & \times & \times & 0 \\ 0 & \times & \times & \times \\ & & & \ddots \end{bmatrix} \cdots \tag{14}$$

where each of the submatrices D_i, U_i and L_i are in turn block tridiagonal, and $\times$ denotes a 2 by 2 submatrix with data dependent coefficients. In addition, $\hat{G}$ is block diagonal dominant, *almost* symmetric and *almost* positive semidefinite[1]. In order to solve (12), we employ the method of *Preconditioned Biconjugate Gradients (PBCG)* [5], [19]. The structure of $\hat{G}$ allows for a good choice of useful preconditioners, one of which is the matrix $\tilde{G}$ formed by the symmetric component of the diagonal 2 x 2 submatrices of $\hat{G}$. In effect, $\tilde{G}$ is the component of $\hat{G}$ comprised purely of within-grid interactions.

3 Consolidation

With a good choice of local basis functions, the proposed flow algorithm yields model parameters $\{u_k, v_k\}$ that largely conform to the global motion model. Parameters corresponding to areas showing systematic errors like moving foreground regions show large deviations from the global model. In order to compute the global motion model parameters, it is necessary to simultaneously segment out the "good" parameters. This is achieved by consolidation.

Since there may exist foreground areas moving quite differently from the background, the distribution of flow velocities, even when estimated without error, may be multimodal. Model parameter estimation involves locating the fundamental mode and its membership - a robust estimation problem with no mathematically concise solution. Also, although the optical flow is computed over the whole image, its reliability is local gradient dependent. Areas which have large gradients are typically, though not always, associated with more reliable flow estimates. In the first pass, grids showing significant gradient content are picked out as "reliable" and the flow estimates at these grid points are combined in a least squares framework to give a set of model parameters. These parameters are recomputed after rejecting a fraction of the data points with the worst fit.

---

[1] Since $\hat{G} = \hat{A}'A \approx A'A$.

This step is repeated a few times giving the final global motion model parameters. The above process is known as iterative weighted least squares.

While pruning the flow field model coefficients used for computing the global motion parameters, the angular error measure employed in [6] is used. Assume that the true and computed flows at a point (x, y) in a particular frame are $(u_0, v_0)'$ and $(u, v)'$ respectively. Define vectors $\mathbf{v_0} = (u_0, v_0, 1)'$ and $\mathbf{v} = (u, v, 1)'$. The error angle ϵ at (x, y) is given by $\epsilon = \arccos\left(\frac{\mathbf{v_0} \cdot \mathbf{v}}{\|\mathbf{v_0}\| \|\mathbf{v}\|}\right)$. ϵ is insensitive to the magnitude of the motion vector and offers a normalized measure against which a range of velocities can be compared meaningfully.

4 Results

In this paper, we claim that the proposed technique is well suited to the class of global motion problems. The first step in proving our claim is to demonstrate that the optical flow algorithm proposed here does indeed model and estimate optical flow accurately. This is covered in the next section, followed by experimental results on the global motion problems of stabilization, mosaicking and super-resolution in the following sections.

4.1 Performance of Optical Flow Algorithm

For demonstrating the quantitative performance of the proposed optical flow method, we perform a series of experiments on synthetic data along the lines of [6]. Exact flows are known for this data, which consists of the *sinusoid, square, translating tree, diverging tree* and *Yosemite* sequences. *Sinusoid* is a uniformly translating modulated 2D pattern with a wavelength of 6 pixels. *Square* is the simple case of a white square moving against a dark background. The *tree* sequences are synthesized from realistic data simulating camera translation with respect to the 2D scene. *Yosemite* is a 2D rendering of a 3D model, with motion discontinuities introduced along the edges of the mountains. Moreover, the clouds in this sequence translate uniformly across the image while undergoing a steady luminance change. In addition, there is significant aliasing near the lower portions of the image making this sequence particularly challenging.

First, we verify the validity of the optical flow field model by fitting the known correct flows of the sequences to the model using a least squares estimator. Computed model parameters are used to generate flow fields and the mean error metric $\bar{\epsilon}$ is calculated between the original flow field and its model. This is indicated in Tables 1 and 2 as the *Perfect Model Estimate*.

Computed flows for *sinusoid* and *square* sequences, suitably downsampled and rescaled, are shown in Fig. 1. The error metric ϵ for these scenes is tabulated, together with the standard deviation $\bar{\sigma}_\epsilon$, which indicates the spread of errors over the image frame, in Tables 1 and 2. For a comparison, the error values of the conventional optical flow techniques obtained from [6] are shown in the tables as well. Since the subspace flow method gives a dense flow estimate, the comparison with alternative optical flow techniques is limited to those yielding a dense flow

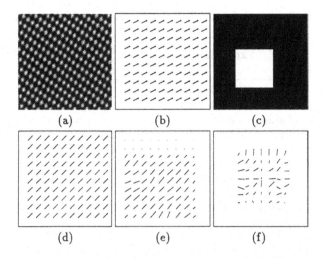

Fig. 1. *Sinusoid* sequence: (a) center frame, (b) computed flow (visually identical to true flow). *Square* sequence: (c) center frame (d) true flow, computed flow using (e) proposed algorithm and (f) Anandan's algorithm.

field. Even among these, many algorithms estimate optical flow only within an inscribed region whose margin width is determined by the spread of the gradient operator, while the proposed technique gives a corner to corner flow estimate.

For the *Sinusoid* data set (Fig. 1 (a)-(b), Table 1), the proposed technique ranks after Fleet and Jepson's. The latter benefits greatly from the sharp frequency spectrum of the input sinusoid, while Singh's method which is comparable in accuracy to ours. The proposed technique is the best for *Square* (Fig. 1 (c)-(f), table 1) by a wide margin. For this sequence, Fleet and Jepson's algorithm is unable to produce a 100% dense flow field, and $\bar{\epsilon}$ of Singh's algorithm is greater than twice $\bar{\epsilon}$ of the proposed. Interestingly, while the "true" flow field of *Square* has been deemed to be a uniform translation across the image (Fig. 1 (d)), it is a moot point whether the background is indeed moving along with the white square. The output of our algorithm (Fig. 1 (e)) shows mainly the square in motion, which is an interpretation as credible as the "true" flow. On the other hand, Anandan's algorithm which ranks second in Table 1, computes flow only for approximately half the image area due to border effects, and the computed flow pattern is visually meaningless (Fig. 1 (f)). Our algorithm performs very well for the synthetic data sets *diverging tree*, *translating tree* and *Yosemite* (Table 2). It ranks at the top for *translating tree* and *Yosemite* and in the second place for *diverging tree*. For the latter sequence, the flow can be made more accurate by changing w. Indeed, $\bar{\epsilon} \approx 2.1$ when w is decreased from 32 to 16 for this case, making the proposed algorithm the best in the list. However, we have chosen to compare the performance of our algorithm with no hand-adjustment of parameters whatsoever. Note that the error standard deviation $\bar{\sigma}$ is significantly

Table 1. Performance of optical flow algorithm on *sinusoid* and *square* data

Experiment	Sinusoid		Square	
	$\bar{\epsilon}$	$\bar{\sigma}$	$\bar{\epsilon}$	$\bar{\sigma}$
Horn & Schunck (original)	4.19	0.50	47.21	14.60
Horn & Schunck (mod.)	2.55	0.59	32.81	13.67
Lucas & Kanade	2.47	0.16	×	×
Uras *et. al.*	2.59	0.71	×	×
Nagel	2.55	0.93	34.57	14.38
Anandan	30.80	5.45	31.46	18.31
Singh ($n = w = 2, N = 2$)	2.24	0.02	49.03	21.38
Singh ($n = w = 2, N = 4$)	91.71	0.04	45.16	21.10
Fleet & Jepson ($\tau = 1.25$)	0.03	0.01	×	×
Perfect Model Estimate	0.10	0.08	0.12	0.09
Proposed	2.46	0.03	20.71	22.11

smaller than $\bar{\sigma}$ of the other techniques. The results indicate that the proposed technique is consistently accurate over the range of synthetic imagery.

The difference between using the ELS and LS solutions is less dramatic, although the ELS consistently shows a smaller $\bar{\epsilon}$. The difference is largest for *square* whose ELS and LS estimate errors are 20.714 and 20.765 respectively. For the other sequences, the differences are in the third decimal place.

Table 2. Performance of proposed algorithm on *translating tree, diverging tree* and *Yosemite* sequences

Experiment	Trans. Tree		Diverg. Tree		Yosemite	
	$\bar{\epsilon}$	$\bar{\sigma}$	$\bar{\epsilon}$	$\bar{\sigma}$	$\bar{\epsilon}$	$\bar{\sigma}$
Horn and Schunck (original)	38.72	27.67	12.02	11.72	31.69	31.18
Horn and Schunck (modified)	2.02	2.27	2.55	3.67	9.78	16.19
Uras *et. al.* (unthresholded)	0.62	0.52	4.64	3.48	8.94	15.61
Nagel	2.44	3.06	2.94	3.23	10.22	16.51
Anandan	4.54	3.10	7.64	4.96	13.36	15.64
Singh (step 1, $n = 2, w = 2$)	1.64	2.44	17.66	14.25	15.28	19.61
Singh (step 2, $n = 2, w = 2$)	1.25	3.29	8.60	5.60	10.44	13.94
Perfect Model Estimate	0.09	0.09	1.40	1.04	3.03	6.48
Proposed	0.61	0.26	2.94	1.64	8.94	10.63

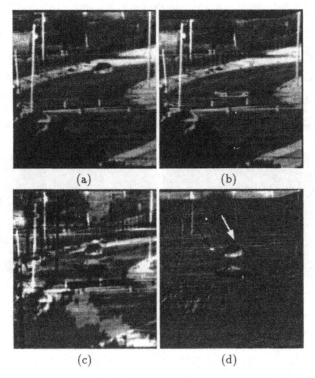

(a)   (b)

(c)   (d)

Fig. 2. *TI car* sequence: (a) frame 1, (b) stabilized frame 42, (c) difference between unstabilized frames, and (d) difference between stabilized frames

4.2 Stabilization

We present two sequences, reflecting disparate operating conditions, for demonstrating the performance of the stabilization algorithm. The first sequence is a dynamic scene comprising a car, a cyclist, two pedestrians and ruffling foliage. This scene, shown in Fig. 2, is imaged by an infra-red camera fixated on the cyclist. It is impossible to locate the cyclist without stabilizing for camera motion. The camera undergoes panning with no rotation about the optical axis, and no translation. The first and forty-second frames are shown in Figs. 2 (a) and (b), and the difference between these frames without and with stabilization is shown in Figs. 2 (c) and (d) respectively. The effect of stabilization in locating moving objects, especially the cyclist and pedestrians is obvious in the figure. Notice that the cyclist shows up in the stabilized frame difference as a dark and a bright spot near the car (corresponding to his/her position in the first and last frames respectively), indicated by arrows.

The second image sequence reflects a navigation scenario where a forward looking camera is mounted on a moving platform. The platform motion involves translation and rotation about all three axes. The camera has a wide field of

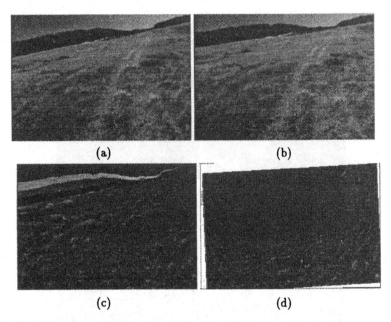

Fig. 3. *Radius* sequence: (a) frame 3, (b) frame 20, (c) unstabilized difference, and (d) stabilized difference between frame 20 and frame 3

view, and this implies a large coverage of the foreground as well. The third and twentieth frames are shown in Figs. 3 (a) and (b). Unstabilized and stabilized frame differences shown in Figs. 3 (c) and (d) demonstrate the ability of the algorithm to compensate for unwanted motion. The six parameter affine motion model is used for both these examples.

4.3 Mosaicking

We consider two cases of generating a wide angle view by forming a mosaic from (i) a panning camera and (ii) a camera translating along the optical axis. While the former leads to a topologically correct reconstruction, the latter can be, at best, a qualitative approximation of a true wide angle view.

The first case, presented in Fig. 4, is an interesting application of mosaicking. The input sequence is a zoomed and panned shot of a moving bus which nearly fills a third to a half of the image area. While constructing the mosaic, only newly appearing areas are included, and the center one-third band is ignored in the consolidation process. The clearance between the front of the bus and the left boundary of the image is sufficient to ensure that data is available to reconstruct the background despite severe occlusion by the moving bus. Although apriori knowledge is incorporated by deleting the central horizontal band, portions of the moving bus often spill out into the "useful" area. Fig. 4 (d) shows the reconstructed mosaic from the first 128 frames, registered to the coordinate

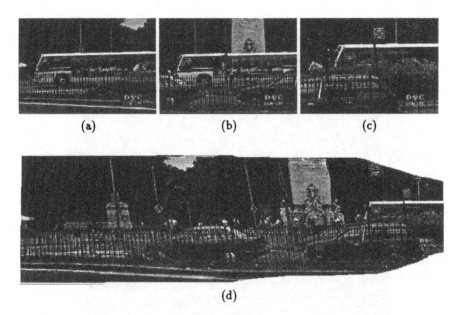

Fig. 4. *Bus* sequence: (a) frame 125, (b) frame 63, (c) frame 0, (d) mosaic using 120 frames

system of the first frame. Zooming is evident from the shape of the envelope of the mosaic. Since our method is based on frame-to-frame registration, errors tend to propogate. This can be seen from the slight slant in the central portion of the mosaic. It must be borne in mind that since the slant is built up over around 60 frames, the per-frame erroneous warping is miniscule, and mosaicking is accurate.

The second example shown in Fig. 5 is a scene richly structured in 3D. The dominant motion of the camera is translation along the optical axis. It is impossible to reconstruct the true wide angle view since there exist regions in the scene that would be imaged by wide angled optics but do not appear in the sequence. Nevertheless, this situation arises commonly in teleoperation of robotic vehicles. It is desirable to present contextual information to the teleoperator in the form of snippets from previous scenes that are not visible in the current scene. This effect can be realized by building a mosaic using a low degree of freedom global motion model on the image sequence. In our experiment, we used 36 frames of a sequence whose first and last frames are shown in Fig. 5 (a) and (b) respectively. Since the current frame is used as the reference, the mosaic construction proceeds in the opposite sense to the previous example, with the latest view overwriting the previous views. The qualitative mosaic reconstructed by our algorithm is presented in Fig. 5 (c). We have used the six parameter affine model for the two examples of mosaicking.

302

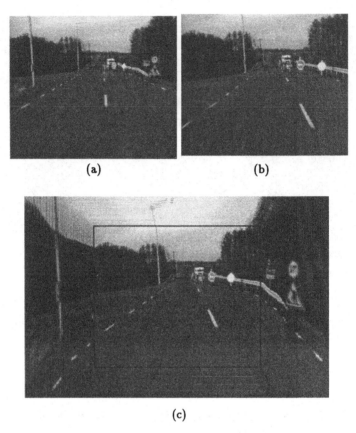

(a)   (b)

(c)

Fig. 5. *Saab* sequence: (a) frame 1, (b) frame 36, (c) qualitative mosaic using 36 frames

4.4   Motion Super-resolution

The last experiment we present here demonstrates the ability of our algorithm
to perform super-resolution. An image sequence gathered by an aerial platform
was regenerated from an MPEG compressed bitstream. The first frame is shown
in Fig. 6 (a). Vehicles on the highway at the bottom of the image are at most
few pixels in size and move with velocities < 1 pixel/frame. In order to identify
these moving vehicles, we build a 2× super-resolved mosaic of 20 frames (shown
in Fig. 6 (c)). Temporal filtering eliminates the foreground objects, which are in
turn recovered by deleting the computed background from the images. Fig. 6 (b)
shows the moving vehicles as dark spots. Without the ability to resolve at the
sub-pixel level, the targets are liable to be lost in the quantization noise of
lossy MPEG encoding. The algorithm is resistant to compression artifacts while
producing accurate results.

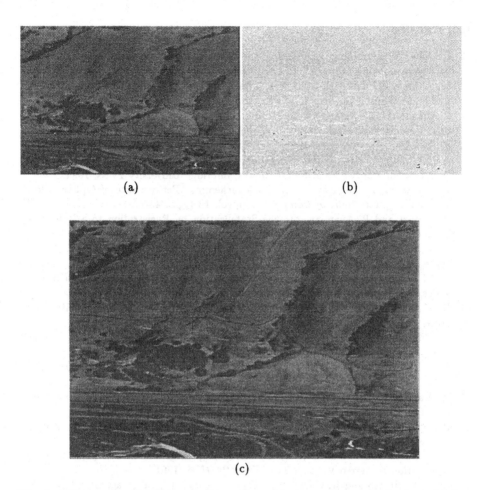

(a)   (b)

(c)

Fig. 6. *S69* sequence: (a) frame 1, (b) moving objects marked as dark spots, (c) 2× super-resolved image

4.5 Concluding Remarks

In this paper, we have proposed an alternative approach for solving global motion problems. We claim that the proposed method is superior in its robustness to random and systematic errors in the image sequence. We have shown the theoretical performance of the subspace optical flow technique and demonstrated, through numerous experiments, the ability of the algorithm to perform accurate optical flow estimation, stabilization, mosaicking and motion super-resolution, in support of our claim.

References

1. G. Adiv, "Determining 3-D Motion and Structure from Optical Flow Generated by Several Moving Objects", *IEEE PAMI*, vol. 7, no. 4, 1985.
2. M. S. Alam *et. al.*, "High-resolution Infrared Image Reconstruction using Multiple Randomly Shifted Low-resolution Aliased Frames", *Proc. SPIE 3063*, 1997.
3. P Anandan, "Measuring Visual Motion from Image Sequences", Ph. D. dissertation, University of Massachusetts, Amherst, 1987.
4. P. Anandan *et. al.*, "Real-time Scene Stabilization and Mosaic Construction", *ARPA Image Understanding Workshop*, 1994.
5. O. Axelsson, *Iterated Solution Methods*, Cambridge University Press, 1994.
6. J. L. Barron, D. J. Fleet and S. S. Beauchemin, "Performance of Optical Flow Techniques", *Int. Jour. of Comp. Vision*, vol. 12:1, pp. 43-77.
7. P. J. Burt and P. Anandan, "Image Stabilization by Registration to a Reference Mosaic", *ARPA Image Understanding Workshop*, 1994.
8. D. J. Heeger, "Model for the Extraction of Image Flow", *Jour. Opt. Soc. Amer.*, vol. 4, pp. 1455-1471.
9. B. K. P. Horn and B. G. Schunck, "Determining Optical Flow", *Artificial Intelligence*, vol. 17, pp. 185-204, 1981.
10. D. J. Fleet and A. D. Jepson, "Computation of Component Image Velocity from Local Phase Information", *Int. Jour. Comp. Vision*, vol. 5, pp. 77-104.
11. N. Gupta and L. Kanal, "Recovering 3-D motion from a Motion Field", *Special Issue on Computer Vision*, 1995.
12. S. V. Huffel and J. Vandewalle, *The Total Least Squares Problem - Computational Aspects and Analysis*, SIAM, 1991.
13. M. Irani and S. Peleg, "Improving Resolution by Image Registration", *Comp. Vision Graphics Image Proc.*, vol. 53, pp. 231-239.
14. H. Liu, "A General Motion Model and Spatio-Temporal Filters for 3-D Motion Interpretations", Ph. D. dissertation, Univ. of Maryland, 1995.
15. B. D. Lucas and T. Kanade, "An Iterative Image Registration Technique with an Application to Stereo Vision", *Proc. DARPA IUW*, 1991.
16. C. H. Morimoto and R. Chellappa, "Fast Electronic Digital Image Stabilization", *Proc. of IEEE ICPR*, 1996.
17. H. H. Nagel, "On the Estimation of Optical Flow", *Artificial Intelligence*, vol. 33, pp. 299-324, 1987.
18. S. Negahdaripour and B. K. P. Horn, "Direct Passive Navigation", *IEEE PAMI*, vol. 9, no. 1, pp. 168-176, 1987.
19. W. H. Press *et. al.*, *Numerical Recipes in C (2 ed.)*, Cambridge University Press, 1992.
20. S. Rakshit and C. H. Anderson, "Computation of Optical Flow Using Basis Functions", *IEEE IP*, vol. 6, no. 9, pp. 1246-1254, 1997.
21. A. Singh, "An Estimation-Theoretic Framework for Image-Flow Computation", *Proc. IEEE ICCV*, 1990.
22. S. Srinivasan and R. Chellappa, "Robust Modeling and Estimation of Optical Flow with Overlapped Basis Functions", CAR-TR-845, Univ. of Maryland, 1996.
23. R. Szeliski and J. Coughlan, "Spline-Based Image Registration", DEC-TR-CRL-94/1, Cambridge Research Laboratory, 1994.
24. S. Uras *et. al.*, "A Computational Approach to Motion Perception", *Biological Cybernetics*, vol. 60, pp. 79-97, 1988.
25. Y. S. Yao, "Electronic Stabilization and Feature Tracking in Long Image Sequences", Ph. D. dissertation CAR-TR-790, Univ. of Maryland, 1996.

The Role of Total Least Squares in Motion Analysis

Matthias Mühlich and Rudolf Mester

Inst. f. Applied Physics, J. W. Goethe-Universität Frankfurt/Main, Germany
(muehlich|mester)@iap.uni-frankfurt.de

Abstract. The main goal of this paper is to put well-established techniques for two-view motion analysis in the context of the theory of Total Least Squares and to make clear that robust and reliable motion analysis algorithms cannot be designed without a thorough statistical consideration of the consequences of errors in the input data.
We focus on the non-iterative 8+n-point algorithm for estimating the fundamental matrix and present a comprehensive statistical derivation of the compelling necessity for one of the normalization transforms proposed by Hartley [1, 2]. It turns out that without these transformations the results of the well-known non-iterative methods for two-view motion analysis are biased and inconsistent. With some further improvements proposed in this paper, the quality of the algorithm can even be enhanced beyond what has been reported in the literature before.

1 Introduction

The computation of relative orientation is one of the key points in two-view motion analysis. The early investigations of Longuet-Higgins [3] and Tsai & Huang [4] have led to a family of non-iterative[1] algorithms that have attracted considerable attention due to their moderate computational effort. Unfortunately, the quality of the results that are obtained from these algorithms decreases dramatically as soon as measurement errors enter the input data, and even the usage of far more data than is minimally required – the approved recipe: 'redundancy combats noise' – does not significantly defuse this situation.

We will consider in the following the non-iterative algorithm for the determination of the fundamental matrix as it is rather compactly described in [2], and which goes back to [4] (although the early papers are dealing with the case of calibrated cameras and employ the *essential matrix* which is a special case of the fundamental matrix).

---

[1] These algorithms are non-iterative except for the solution of eigensystem equations or the determination of the singular value decomposition which play a key role in these procedures. Sometimes these algorithms are called linear, but this is rather misleading since the computation of the eigensystem and the SVD is definitely nonlinear.

2 The ideal case: no measurement error in the input data

Let us first briefly review the 8+n-point algorithm. Let $u = (u_1, u_2, 1)^T$ and $v = (v_1, v_2, 1)^T$ be the homogeneous coordinates of the projection of the same rigid object point in two images B_u and B_v. If the vectors u and v are error–free, it is well known that they are related to each other by the equation

$$v^T \cdot \mathbf{F} \cdot u = 0 \tag{1}$$

with a 3×3-matrix $\mathbf{F}$, the *fundamental matrix*, which is identical for all pairs of corresponding vectors u_i, v_i. The matrix $\mathbf{F} = (f_{ij})$ is the entity we are interested in, since it encapsulates all the information on motion or relative orientation that can be extracted from the given image pair. The matrix $\mathbf{F}$ is necessarily rank-deficient, i.e. rank $(\mathbf{F}) = 2$ [4,5]. By 'vectorizing' the matrix $\mathbf{F}$, i. e. stacking the matrix elements f_{ij} to form a vector f which is (dropping double indices)

$$\mathbf{F} \rightarrow f = (f_{11}, f_{12}, f_{13}, f_{21}, f_{22}, f_{23}, f_{31}, f_{32}, f_{33})^T = (f_1, \dots, f_9)^T \,,$$

equation (1) can be expressed as

$$a^T \cdot f = 0 \ \text{ with } \ a^T = (v_1 u_1, \ v_1 u_2, \ v_1, \ v_2 u_1, \ v_2 u_2, \ v_2, \ u_1, \ u_2, \ 1) \,. \tag{2}$$

Each point correspondence $(u_i \leftrightarrow v_i)$ can be expressed in the form of equation (2) and from N correspondences we obtain a linear equation system

$$\mathbf{A}_0 \cdot f = 0 \tag{3}$$

where the coefficient vectors a_i^T $(i = 1, \dots, N)$ are row vectors of a $N \times 9$-matrix $\mathbf{A}_0$ (subscript 0 denoting the unperturbed matrix).

If the correspondences between each pair u_i, v_i were perfect, matrix $\mathbf{A}_0$ would have rank 8 for $N \geq 8$ except for degenerate configurations[2] of the object points in the 3D-space [6], so 8 point correspondences would be sufficient for determining vector f and thus the fundamental matrix $\mathbf{F}$ as well. In this error-free case, equation (3) can be solved exactly, and the solution vector (or vectors, as in the case of degenerate configurations) correspond to the basis vector(s) of the nullspace of matrix $\mathbf{A}_0$.

3 The realistic case: input data with measurement errors

In the presence of errors, the matrix will not be of rank 8, i.e. there is no non-trivial solution to eqn.(2). Traditionally, the approach taken in this situation is as follows:

---

[2] It is not true that in the case of degenerate configurations no solution can be extracted at all; instead, we obtain a linear manifold of solution vectors, which could possibly be valuable information as well.

Step 1: initial estimate of F. Since it follows from rank $(\mathbf{A}) = 9$ that there is no $\boldsymbol{f} \neq 0$ that solves eqn.(3) exactly, we try to find a unit vector $\boldsymbol{f}$ for which the right hand side is at least close to $\mathbf{0}$. This means that we minimize $|\mathbf{A}\boldsymbol{f}|^2$ subject to the constraint $|\boldsymbol{f}|^2 = \boldsymbol{f}^T\boldsymbol{f} = 1$. The solution to this constrained minimization problem obtained by means of Lagrangian multipliers is given by the eigenvector of $\mathbf{A}^T\mathbf{A}$ corresponding to the smallest eigenvalue of $\mathbf{A}^T\mathbf{A}$. In other words (see [7]), $\boldsymbol{f}$ is the right hand singular vector corresponding to the smallest singular value of matrix $\mathbf{A}$.

Step 2: enforcement of rank $(\mathbf{F}) = 2$. Since the true fundamental matrix $\mathbf{F}$ must have rank 2, the vector $\boldsymbol{f}$ obtained so far is rearranged to matrix form and the resulting matrix is enforced to have rank 2 by expanding the current estimate of $\mathbf{F}$ in a sum of rank 1 matrices and suppressing the matrix with the lowest Frobenius norm. Practically, this is done by means of the *singular value decomposition* (SVD).

This procedure is correct under certain conditions that we will discuss later. However, it blocks the view onto a much more general framework which allows a consideration of the detailed statistical structure of the disturbances.

3.1 Error models and metrics for optimum estimation

Let us look a bit closer onto equation (3). It necessarily holds for error free data, i. e. for vector pairs $(\boldsymbol{u}_i \leftrightarrow \boldsymbol{v}_i)$ containing no measurement errors and, consequently, for row vectors $\boldsymbol{a}_i^T$ being numerically correct. However, in practice there *are* errors in our input data and we have the following situation: $\mathbf{A}\boldsymbol{f} \neq 0$ due to the fact that the matrix $\mathbf{A}$ we actually have is related to the true, but unknown matrix $\mathbf{A}_0$ by $\mathbf{A} = \mathbf{A}_0 + \mathbf{D}$, introducing the error matrix $\mathbf{D} \neq 0$.

$$(\mathbf{A}_0 + \mathbf{D})\boldsymbol{f} = \mathbf{A}_0\boldsymbol{f} + \mathbf{D}\boldsymbol{f} = \mathbf{D}\boldsymbol{f} \neq 0$$

In this situation the search for the solution vector $\boldsymbol{f}$ boils down to *estimate* the true matrix $\mathbf{A}_0$, and given its corrupted version $\mathbf{A}$ this is equivalent to estimate the error matrix $\mathbf{D}$. In other words, given a rank 9 matrix $\mathbf{A}$ we have to find a plausible (whatever that may denote) estimate of a matrix $\mathbf{D}$ that lowers the rank of $\mathbf{A} - \mathbf{D} = \hat{\mathbf{A}}_0$ to 8, since for $N \times 9$-matrices $\hat{\mathbf{A}}_0$ of rank ≤ 8 the equation $\hat{\mathbf{A}}_0\boldsymbol{f} = 0, \boldsymbol{f} \neq 0$ has one (or several) solution(s). The credibility of the estimate $\mathbf{D}$ is inevitably related to a consideration of the structure of the stochastic process that generates the error matrix $\mathbf{D}$.

Let us assume for the moment (until we still look a bit closer) that the error matrix $\mathbf{D}$ is a realization of a random matrix process with the following characteristics:

Model 1 (Zero-mean i.i.d. error matrix D)

$$\mathsf{E}\,[\mathbf{D}] = 0 \quad \Leftrightarrow \quad \mathsf{E}\,[d_{ij}] = 0 \quad \text{for all } i, j$$

$$\mathsf{Var}\,[d_{ij}] = \mathsf{E}\,\left[(d_{ij} - \mathsf{E}\,[d_{ij}])^2\right] = \mathsf{E}\,[d_{ij}^2] = \sigma^2 \quad \text{for all } i, j$$

$$\mathsf{Cov}\,[d_{ij}, d_{km}] = \mathsf{E}\,[(d_{ij} - \mathsf{E}\,[d_{ij}])(d_{km} - \mathsf{E}\,[d_{km}])] = \begin{cases} \sigma^2 & : \quad i, j = k, m \\ 0 & : \quad else \end{cases}$$

Here E [·] denotes expectation, and Var [·] and Cov [·] are the variances and covariances of their arguments. The matrix elements complying to these conditions are called *independent identically distributed* (i.i.d.) and zero mean, and the matrix itself is called a zero mean i.i.d. random matrix.

Under these conditions, a *least squares estimate*[3] of matrix $\mathbf{A}_0$ is performed by determining the error matrix $\mathbf{D}$ that is lowest in Frobenius norm $\|\mathbf{D}\|_F = \left(\sum_{ij} d_{ij}^2\right)^{1/2} \to$ min and lowers the rank of matrix $\mathbf{A}$ such that rank $(\mathbf{A} - \mathbf{D}) = 8$ holds, i.e. the Frobenius norm serves as a metric.

If additionally the random matrix process $\{\mathbf{D}\}$ is Gaussian (and this is *not* required for the least squares process to be reasonable!), this very solution is also the *maximum likelihood* (ML) estimate of $\mathbf{A}_0$ and consequently of f as well, with all the advantageous characteristics of ML estimation applying.

The answer to the question how this least squares estimate of $\mathbf{A}_0$ is obtained is provided by the *Eckart-Young-Mirsky theorem (Eckart & Young 1936, Mirsky 1960):*

Theorem 1. *Let $\mathbf{A}$ be a $N \times M$ matrix of* rank $(\mathbf{A}) = r$ *and let $\mathbf{A} = \mathbf{USV}^T = \sum_{i=1}^r s_i \mathbf{u}_i \mathbf{v}_i^T$ with singular values $s_1 \geq s_2 \geq \ldots \geq s_{r-1} > s_r > 0$ be the singular value decomposition of $\mathbf{A}$.*

If $k < r$ then $\mathbf{A}_k = \sum_{i=1}^k s_i \mathbf{u}_i \mathbf{v}_i^T$ is the solution to the minimization problem

$$\|\mathbf{A} - \hat{\mathbf{A}}_0\|_F \longrightarrow \textit{min} \quad \textit{subject to} \quad \text{rank}\left(\hat{\mathbf{A}}_0\right) \overset{!}{=} k$$

In our case, the actual rank of $\mathbf{A}$ is 9 and the desired rank is 8, so we have

$$\hat{\mathbf{A}} = \sum_{i=1}^8 s_i \mathbf{u}_i \mathbf{v}_i^T \qquad \text{and} \qquad \hat{\mathbf{D}} = s_9 \mathbf{u}_9 \mathbf{v}_9^T \tag{4}$$

Since we are ultimately looking for the vector f that solves $\hat{\mathbf{A}} f = 0$, we see from equation (4) that $\mathbf{v}_9$ (the right singular vector corresponding to the smallest singular value s_9) is the solution to our problem, since it is the only vector that is orthogonal to all of the vectors $\mathbf{v}_i, i = 1, \ldots, 8$. This vector is, as it is known from the theory of singular value decomposition [7], identical to the eigenvector of $\mathbf{A}^T \mathbf{A}$ corresponding to the smallest eigenvalue. Here, it becomes obvious that the solution of step 1 and step 2 both reduce to the rank reduction of a given matrix, controlled by a given (or tacitly assumed) error metric. Note that this proceeding, stacking two approximation problems on top of each other does not necessarily provide a rank 2 matrix that is optimum with respect to the metric defined in step 1.

Thus, we have apparently derived the very same result as it is known for a long time by making a considerable detour. However, we will show in the following that this detour is really worthwhile, since it opens the door to a very valuable theory, from which we can use methods and tools for adjusting our solution to

---

[3] Note that this is not a *linear* least squares problem.

the precise requirements given by the algebraic and statistical structure of the problem at hand. This framework is the theory of *total least squares estimation,* also known as *errors-in-variables-modeling* (EIV) or *orthogonal regression.*

4 Total Least Squares

What we have done so far is in fact to use the basic procedure of Total Least Squares estimation. [8–11]:

Definition 1 (Total Least Squares problem). *We are given an overdetermined set of N equations $a^T x = b$ in M unknowns x, compiled to a matrix equation $\mathbf{A}x = b$. Both the vector b as well as the matrix $\mathbf{A}$ are subject to errors. The total least squares problem consists in finding an $N \times M$ matrix $\hat{\mathbf{A}}$ and an M-vector $\hat{b}$ for which the equation*

$$\hat{\mathbf{A}}x = \hat{b} \tag{5}$$

has an exact solution, (i.e. $\hat{b}$ is in the column space of $\hat{\mathbf{A}}$) under the condition that the deviation between $(\mathbf{A}|b)$ and $(\hat{\mathbf{A}}|\hat{b})$ is minimal in terms of the Frobenius norm:

$$\|(\mathbf{A}|b) - (\hat{\mathbf{A}}|\hat{b})\|_F \longrightarrow min \tag{6}$$

Once a minimizing approximation $(\hat{\mathbf{A}}|\hat{b})$ has been found, any vector x satisfying eqn.(5) is called a TLS solution.

In the last decade, this basic TLS problem has been extended to a considerable number of generalizations and specializations, such as *Generalized Total Least Squares (GTLS), Structured Total Least Squares (STLS)* and many more, cf. [8–10, 12, 13]. One of the most important motivations for the development of these specialized versions of TLS is the need for a metric that differs from the Frobenius norm, either due to a prescribed structure of the true matrix $\mathbf{A}_0$ (e.g. Toeplitz) or due to disturbances in $\mathbf{A}$ that do not have the simple statistical structure given by a zero-mean i.i.d. matrix $\mathbf{D}$.

Van Huffel [10] gives a comprehensive overview on the statistical properties of TLS solutions, including conditions for consistency of the estimate, i.e. the requirement that the estimate converges towards the true parameter vector as the number of measurements is increased.

If the errors in $\mathbf{A}$ and b are uncorrelated with zero mean and equal variance, then under mild conditions the TLS solution $\hat{x}$ is a strongly consistent estimate of the solution of the unperturbed equation $\mathbf{A}_0 x = b_0$.

If, however, this is *not* the case, for instance if the errors are correlated and of unequal size, or if some columns of $\mathbf{A}$ are error-free, an adequate estimate can be obtained by use of the Generalized Total Least Squares technique [10] which essentially consists in replacing the metric given in eqn.(6) by

$$\left\| \mathbf{W}_1 \cdot \Big((\mathbf{A} \mid b) - (\tilde{\mathbf{A}} \mid \tilde{b}) \Big) \cdot \mathbf{W}_2 \right\|_F \longrightarrow min. \tag{7}$$

with suitably chosen weight matrices $\mathbf{W}_1$ and $\mathbf{W}_2$ which perform a so-called *equilibration*. The case of matrices $\mathbf{A}$ known to contain *exact*, i.e. error-free columns is handled by Demmel [14].

We are now equipped with a sufficient repertoire of techniques to handle non-standard problems of type TLS; but let us first have a look on the subject of data normalization before we investigate the statistical structure of the specific problem we are dealing with.

5 Input data normalization

5.1 Normalized eight-point algorithm

The 'classic' 8+n-point algorithm is known to be very susceptible to noise. In 1995 Hartley pointed out that a considerable improvement in performance could be achieved by a normalization of the input data (point correspondences) and it was demonstrated by examples that the quality of the results of the normalized 8+n-point algorithm is significantly better than the standard procedure, and comparable to the best iterative algorithms [1]. A second paper [2] exposed the principle in more detail, describing several variants of data normalization. However, an analysis of the statistical input-output relation, referring to the central entities of any estimation procedure, namely bias, variance and consistence, is missing in both of these papers.

Hartley's proposal is centred in the observation that a valid solution for the initially given problem $\mathbf{A}f = 0$ (which is, as we know, a TLS problem) can be obtained as well, if the initially given correspondence data which may be specified in arbitrary coordinate frames are linearly transformed to a canonical coordinate frame which is derived from the distribution of the data. Let $\mathbf{R}$ and $\mathbf{S}$ be two non-singular 3×3 matrices which are used to obtain the transformed correspondence data $v_i' = \mathbf{S}v_i$ and $u_i' = \mathbf{R}u_i$ from the initially given data u_i and v_i. Instead of looking for a solution to $v_{i0}^T \mathbf{F} u_{i0} = 0$, a solution for

$$\underbrace{v_i^T \mathbf{S}^T}_{v_i'} \underbrace{(\mathbf{S}^T)^{-1} \mathbf{F} \mathbf{R}^{-1}}_{\mathbf{F}'} \underbrace{\mathbf{R} u_i}_{u_i'} = 0 . \tag{8}$$

is sought. In the new coordinate frame, matrix $\mathbf{F}'$ is determined the same way as before: Find a TLS solution, rearrange it in matrix form and enforce the rank 2 constraint using the Eckart-Young-Mirsky-theorem. The inverse transformation $\mathbf{F} = \mathbf{S}^T \mathbf{F}' \mathbf{R}$ will yield the desired matrix $\mathbf{F}$. Hartley points out that the TLS solution of eqn.(1) is not identical to the TLS solution of eqn.(8), and this is really what is intended: By selection of proper matrices $\mathbf{R}$ and $\mathbf{S}$ the initial TLS can be solved under a problem-adapted metric.[4]

---

[4] Unfortunately, the coordinate transform can help only in step 1 of the estimation process, but not in step 2 (reduction to rank 2).

5.2 Choice of the transformation matrices

Hartley proposes to apply the transformations both to vectors $\{u_i\}$ and vectors $\{v_i\}$. We will now describe the transformation $v_i' = \mathbf{S}v_i$. Since the third component of the homogeneous vector should not be changed, possible transformations will consist of a translation, a rotation and a scaling in the first two components.

$$\mathbf{S} = \text{diag}\,\{\alpha_1, \alpha_2, 1\} \cdot \begin{pmatrix} \cos\phi & \sin\phi & 0 \\ -\sin\phi & \cos\phi & 0 \\ 0 & 0 & 1 \end{pmatrix} \cdot \begin{pmatrix} 1 & 0 & -\frac{1}{N}\sum_{i=1}^{N} v_{i1} \\ 0 & 1 & -\frac{1}{N}\sum_{i=1}^{N} v_{i2} \\ 0 & 0 & 1 \end{pmatrix} \qquad (9)$$

The righthand matrix translates the new coordinate frame into the center of gravity of the point set. The middle matrix may rotate the coordinate frame and the lefthand matrix is a scaling matrix.

Hartley proposes two different normalizing schemes. Whereas the translation and the rotation into the principal axes frames are identical in his papers, the scaling is not. In [1] the scaling is designed with the aim to make the mean *absolute value* of the new coordinates equal to 1, whereas in [2] the points are normalized with the aim to make the mean *square* of the coordinates equal to 1. In our experiments we have found only very small differences between the results obtained with these two normalization schemes[5], which we will denote by `Hartley1` and `Hartley2`.

6 Perturbation of the TLS solution

As the determination of the SVD, which is the central operation in our algorithm, involves the solution of an eigensystem problem, we will now consider the influence of an error matrix on the eigenvectors of the unperturbed matrix.

6.1 Perturbation of the eigenvectors

Golub & van Loan [9, chapter 7.2.4] give a linear approximation of the perturbation in eigenvectors. But whereas they regard arbitrary $N \times N$-matrices with complex elements we are only interested in symmetric matrices with real elements. Therefore their equations simplify considerably.

Theorem 2. *Let* $\mathbf{B} \in \mathbb{R}^{n \times n}$ *be a symmetric matrix with distinct eigenvalues* $\lambda_1, \lambda_2, \ldots, \lambda_n$ *and eigenvectors* x_k. *Assume* $\mathbf{C} \in \mathbb{R}^{n \times n}$ *satisfies* $\|\mathbf{C}\|_2 = 1$. *We are looking for the eigenvectors of* $\mathbf{B} + \varepsilon\mathbf{C}$.

A Taylor expansion of $x_k(\varepsilon)$ *has the following form:*

$$x_k(\varepsilon) = x_k + \delta_{x_k} + O(\varepsilon^2) \qquad (10)$$

---

[5] Hartley also proposes an algorithm with isotropic scaling and no rotation at all in his second paper, which has not been considered here.

with

$$\delta_{x_k} = \sum_{\substack{i=1 \\ i \neq k}}^{n} \frac{x_i^T C x_k}{(\lambda_k - \lambda_i)} x_i = \left(\sum_{\substack{i=1 \\ i \neq k}}^{n} \frac{x_i x_i^T}{(\lambda_k - \lambda_i)} \right) C x_k \qquad (11)$$

Thus, we have made a very important observation: If $E[C] = 0$ holds, it follows that $E[\delta_{x_k}] = 0$:

$$E[\delta_{x_k}] = E\left[\left(\sum_{\substack{i=1 \\ i \neq k}}^{n} \frac{x_i x_i^T}{(\lambda_k - \lambda_i)} \right) C x_k \right] = \left(\sum_{\substack{i=1 \\ i \neq k}}^{n} \frac{x_i x_i^T}{(\lambda_k - \lambda_i)} \right) E[C] x_k = 0 . \qquad (12)$$

Now we have shown that

$$E[\text{EigVec}(B + \varepsilon C)] = \text{EigVec}(B) \quad \text{if} \quad E[C] = 0 , \qquad (13)$$

where $\text{EigVec}(\cdot)$ denotes the set of eigenvectors of a given matrix.

6.2 Perturbation of the singular vectors

We assume that the vectors u_i in the first image are error-free whereas the corresponding point coordinates v_i in the second image are corrupted by zero-mean measurement errors, i.e. $u_i = u_{i0}$ and $v_i = v_{i0} + b_i$ with $E[b_i] = 0$. Since b_i is zero-mean, we have $\text{Cov}[b_i] = C_{b_i} = E[b_i b_i^T]$, and in the absence of further information we may assume $C_{b_i} = \text{diag}\{\sigma_b^2, \sigma_b^2, 0\}$. The row vectors of A (called a_i^T) are corrupted with an error d_i^T ($a_i = a_{i0} + d_i$) and for d_i we get:

$$d_i^T = (b_{i1} u_{i01}, \ b_{i1} u_{i02}, \ b_{i1}, \ b_{i2} u_{i01}, \ b_{i2} u_{i02}, \ b_{i2}, \ 0, \ 0, \ 0) . \qquad (14)$$

We see that the last three elements are error-free. It is seen easily that $E[d_i] = 0$ for all i holds as well.

We are looking for the eigenvectors[6] of $A_0^T A_0$ which we denote as x_{i0} (actually we are only interested in the eigenvector x_{90} corresponding to the smallest eigenvalue).

$$A^T A = A_0^T A_0 + \underbrace{A_0^T D + D^T A_0}_{\Delta_1} + \underbrace{D^T D}_{\Delta_2} = A_0^T A_0 + \Delta \qquad (15)$$

$A_0^T A_0$ is perturbed with two different error matrices; a term Δ_1 which is linear in D (with $E[\Delta_1] = 0$) and a quadratic term Δ_2 (with $E[\Delta_2] \neq 0$). Since $A_0^T A_0$ is symmetric, we can apply eqn.(11) to δ_{x_9} and get (for small D) an expression for the error in x_9

$$\delta_{x_9} = \left(\sum_{i=1}^{8} \frac{x_{i0} x_{i0}^T}{(\lambda_{90} - \lambda_{i0})} \right) \Delta \cdot x_{90} \qquad (16)$$

In order to obtain an unbiased estimator we have to ensure that $E[\delta_{x_9}] \stackrel{!}{=} 0$ holds. In general this will *not* be true due to $E[\Delta] \neq 0$.

---

[6] The subscript 0 denotes the *true* eigenvalues and eigenvectors of $A_0^T A_0$.

6.3 Requirements for the statistical structure of matrix A

We can formulate the last requirement in another way as well: we would like to achieve that the expected eigenvectors (at least the ninth) of the perturbed matrix do not differ from the eigenvectors of the unperturbed matrix. Thus the stochastic process that generates the perturbation matrices $\mathbf{\Delta}$ should be such that

$$\mathsf{E}\left[\mathsf{EigVec}\left(\mathbf{A}_0^T\mathbf{A}_0 + \mathbf{\Delta}\right)\right] \stackrel{!}{=} \mathsf{EigVec}\left(\mathbf{A}_0^T\mathbf{A}_0\right) \tag{17}$$

holds. In section 6 we have already derived with eqn. (13) that eqn. (17) would hold in linear approximation if $\mathsf{E}\left[\mathbf{\Delta}\right] = \mathbf{0}$, which is not the case. However, we will see that even a weaker requirement is sufficient in order to make eqn. (17) hold.

Proposition: If $\mathsf{E}\left[\mathbf{\Delta}\right] = c\mathbf{I}$ holds, the requirement (17) assuring unbiasedness holds as well.

In order to prove this proposition, we first note that $\mathsf{EigVec}\left(\mathbf{A} + c\mathbf{I}\right) = \mathsf{EigVec}\left(\mathbf{A}\right)$ for any matrix $\mathbf{A}$ ([15]). Now we define $\mathbf{\Delta}' = \mathbf{\Delta} - c\mathbf{I}$. Obviously $\mathsf{E}\left[\mathbf{\Delta}'\right] = \mathbf{0}$ holds, thus eqn.(13) can be applied and we obtain:

$$\mathsf{E}\left[\mathsf{EigVec}\left(\mathbf{A}_0^T\mathbf{A}_0 + \mathbf{\Delta}\right)\right] = \mathsf{E}\left[\mathsf{EigVec}\left((\mathbf{A}_0^T\mathbf{A}_0 + c\mathbf{I}) + \mathbf{\Delta}'\right)\right]$$
$$= \mathsf{EigVec}\left(\mathbf{A}_0^T\mathbf{A}_0 + c\mathbf{I}\right) = \mathsf{EigVec}\left(\mathbf{A}_0^T\mathbf{A}_0\right) .$$

Therefore, we have to ensure that

$$\mathsf{E}\left[\mathbf{\Delta}\right] = \mathsf{E}\left[\mathbf{\Delta}_1\right] + \mathsf{E}\left[\mathbf{\Delta}_2\right] = \mathsf{E}\left[\mathbf{A}_0^T\mathbf{D} + \mathbf{D}^T\mathbf{A}_0\right] + \mathsf{E}\left[\mathbf{D}^T\mathbf{D}\right] \stackrel{!}{=} c\mathbf{I} \tag{18}$$

holds. From $\mathsf{E}\left[\mathbf{D}\right] = \mathbf{0}$ follows $\mathsf{E}\left[\mathbf{\Delta}_1\right] = \mathbf{0}$, and therefore our requirement can be transformed into the simple form

$$\mathsf{E}\left[\mathbf{D}^T\mathbf{D}\right] \stackrel{!}{=} c\mathbf{I} \tag{19}$$

We see that, for small errors, it does not depend on the *linear* perturbation terms whether the estimator is unbiased but solely on the *quadratic* term $\mathbf{D}^T\mathbf{D}$.

Let us now regard the matrix $\mathbf{D}^T\mathbf{D}$. Its element (j, k) is obtained from the scalar product of the j-th and the k-th column of $\mathbf{D}$: $(\mathbf{D}^T\mathbf{D})_{jk} = \sum_{i=1}^{N} d_{ij}d_{ik}$. Therefore our requirement is $\sum_{i=1}^{N} \mathsf{E}\left[d_{ij}d_{ik}\right] \stackrel{!}{=} \delta_{jk}c$. In matrix form we can express eqn. (19) as follows:

$$\sum_{i=1}^{N} \mathsf{Cov}\left[\mathbf{a}_i\right] = \sum_{i=1}^{N} \mathsf{E}\left[\mathbf{d}_i\mathbf{d}_i^T\right] = \sum_{i=1}^{N} \mathbf{C}_{d_i} \stackrel{!}{=} c\mathbf{I} . \tag{20}$$

If we look at $\mathbf{d}_i$ (eqn.(14)) we realize that the last three columns of $\mathbf{A}$ are error-free and therefore in $\mathbf{C}_{d_i} = \mathsf{Cov}\left[\mathbf{a}_i\right]$ the last three columns and rows will be 0.

However, this is no serious problem. On the contrary, we can turn it into an advantage since we have *more* information about the possible error structure in matrix $\mathbf{A}$. We can replace the normal TLS estimation procedure with the already mentioned special form of TLS that minimizes the error matrix norm subject to the constraint that a certain number of columns (here: three) are free of errors. Two different but equivalent TLS-FC (Total Least Squares - Fixed Columns) algorithms are described by Golub, Hoffman & Steward [16] and Demmel [14]. We use the second algorithm which is based on the SVD of the matrix $\mathbf{A}$.

Our modified requirement is:

$$\sum_{i=1}^{N} \mathbf{C}_{d_i} \stackrel{!}{=} c\tilde{\mathbf{I}} \quad \text{with } \tilde{\mathbf{I}} = \text{diag}\{1,1,1,1,1,1,0,0,0\} \tag{21}$$

7 Derivation of optimum normalization transforms

Now we recall Hartley's idea and perform a transformation of the input data $\boldsymbol{u}_i$ and $\boldsymbol{v}_i$.

$$\boldsymbol{u}_i' = \mathbf{R}\boldsymbol{u}_i = \mathbf{R}\boldsymbol{u}_{i0} = \boldsymbol{u}_{i0}' \quad \text{and} \quad \boldsymbol{v}_i' = \mathbf{S}\boldsymbol{v}_i = \mathbf{S}\boldsymbol{v}_{i0} + \mathbf{S}\boldsymbol{b}_i = \boldsymbol{v}_{i0}' + \boldsymbol{b}_i'$$

In contrast to Hartley we will now deduce the matrices $\mathbf{R}$ and $\mathbf{S}$ from the requirement we set up in the last section. The matrices $\mathbf{R}$ and $\mathbf{S}$ must be non-singular (otherwise eqn.(8) could not hold) and have the following structure

$$\mathbf{R} = \begin{pmatrix} r_{11} & r_{12} & r_{13} \\ r_{21} & r_{22} & r_{23} \\ 0 & 0 & 1 \end{pmatrix} \quad \text{and} \quad \mathbf{S} = \begin{pmatrix} s_{11} & s_{12} & s_{13} \\ s_{21} & s_{22} & s_{23} \\ 0 & 0 & 1 \end{pmatrix} \tag{22}$$

The third rows are $(0,0,1)$ because the third component of the homogenous vectors $\boldsymbol{u}_i$ and $\boldsymbol{v}_i$ shall remain 1. Now we look at the expectation and the covariance matrix of $\boldsymbol{b}_i'$:

$$\mathsf{E}\left[\boldsymbol{b}_i'\right] = \mathsf{E}\left[\mathbf{S}\boldsymbol{b}_i\right] = \mathbf{S}\mathsf{E}\left[\boldsymbol{b}_i\right] = \mathbf{S}0 = \mathbf{0} \tag{23}$$

$$\mathbf{C}_{b'} = \text{Cov}\left[\boldsymbol{b}_i'\right] = \mathsf{E}\left[\boldsymbol{b}_i' \boldsymbol{b}_i'^T\right] = \mathsf{E}\left[\mathbf{S}\boldsymbol{b}_i \boldsymbol{b}_i^T \mathbf{S}^T\right] = \mathbf{S}\mathsf{E}\left[\boldsymbol{b}_i \boldsymbol{b}_i^T\right] \mathbf{S}^T$$

$$= \mathbf{S}\begin{pmatrix} \sigma_b^2 & 0 & 0 \\ 0 & \sigma_b^2 & 0 \\ 0 & 0 & 0 \end{pmatrix} \mathbf{S}^T = \begin{pmatrix} c_{11} & c_{12} & 0 \\ c_{21} & c_{22} & 0 \\ 0 & 0 & 0 \end{pmatrix} \tag{24}$$

After considering the statistical properties of the transformed input data we can now use this knowledge. In the new coordinate frame we have

$$\boldsymbol{d}_i'^T = (b_{i1}' u_{i1}', \ b_{i1}' u_{i2}', \ b_{i1}', \ b_{i2}' u_{i1}', \ b_{i2}' u_{i2}', \ b_{i2}', \ 0, \ 0, \ 0) \ . \tag{25}$$

The vector $\boldsymbol{d}_i'$ is zero-mean because $\boldsymbol{b}_i'$ is zero-mean (see eqn.(23)). We obtain:

$$\text{Cov}\left[\boldsymbol{d}_i'\right] = \mathbf{C}_{d_i'} = \begin{pmatrix} c_{11}\mathbf{X}_i & c_{12}\mathbf{X}_i & 0 \\ c_{21}\mathbf{X}_i & c_{22}\mathbf{X}_i & 0 \\ 0 & 0 & 0 \end{pmatrix} \quad \text{with } \mathbf{X}_i \stackrel{def}{=} \begin{pmatrix} u_{i1}'^2 & u_{i1}' u_{i2}' & u_{i1}' \\ u_{i1}' u_{i2}' & u_{i2}'^2 & u_{i2}' \\ u_{i1}' & u_{i2}' & 1 \end{pmatrix}$$

$$\tag{26}$$

Using the Kronecker matrix product $\otimes$ this can be written as:

$$\mathbf{C}_{d'_i} = \mathbf{C}_{b'} \otimes \mathbf{X}_i \tag{27}$$

With the requirement expressed by eqn.(21) we obtain:

$$\sum_{i=1}^{N} \mathbf{C}_{d'_i} = \sum_{i=1}^{N} \mathbf{C}_{b'} \otimes \mathbf{X}_i = \mathbf{C}_{b'} \otimes \left(\sum_{i=1}^{N} \mathbf{X}_i \right) \overset{!}{=} c\tilde{\mathbf{I}} \tag{28}$$

This means that the following two equations must hold simultaneously:

$$\mathbf{C}_{b'} = \mathbf{S} \cdot \mathbf{C}_d \cdot \mathbf{S}^T \overset{!}{=} \begin{pmatrix} k_1 & 0 & 0 \\ 0 & k_1 & 0 \\ 0 & 0 & 0 \end{pmatrix} \tag{29}$$

$$\sum_i \mathbf{X}_i = \begin{pmatrix} \sum_i u'_{i1}u'_{i1} & \sum_i u'_{i1}u'_{i2} & \sum_i u'_{i1} \\ \sum_i u'_{i2}u'_{i1} & \sum_i u'_{i2}u'_{i2} & \sum_i u'_{i2} \\ \sum_i u'_{i1} & \sum_i u'_{i2} & \sum_i 1 \end{pmatrix} = \sum_i \mathbf{R} u_i u_i^T \mathbf{R}^T \overset{!}{=} \begin{pmatrix} k_2 & 0 & 0 \\ 0 & k_2 & 0 \\ 0 & 0 & k_2 \end{pmatrix} \tag{30}$$

This can also be seen from eqn.(26). Since $\mathbf{C}_b$ is already assumed to be diag $\{\sigma_b^2, \sigma_b^2, 0\}$, $\mathbf{S}$ may be an arbitrary matrix of the following structure:

$$\mathbf{S} = \alpha \cdot \begin{pmatrix} \cos\phi & \sin\phi & 0 \\ -\sin\phi & \cos\phi & 0 \\ 0 & 0 & 1 \end{pmatrix} \cdot \begin{pmatrix} 1 & 0 & t_1 \\ 0 & 1 & t_2 \\ 0 & 0 & 1 \end{pmatrix}$$

with arbitrary values for the parameters α, ϕ, t_1, t_2 except $\alpha \neq 0$. This looks very similar to the transformation given by eqn.(9) except for the fact that α is no diagonal matrix, i.e. only *isotropic* scaling is allowed for the vectors v_i. In contrast to this requirement Hartley is performing an *anisotropic* scaling of the 'second' vector v_i as well. However, this will cause problems only if two principal moments of the vectors v_i are notably different.

We continue regarding eqn.(30). If we require that the third component of vector u'_i remains to be 1, this fixes the otherwise arbitrary constant k_2 to be N. Solutions for $\mathbf{R}$ can be found by considering that from eqn.(30) and the requirement that $\mathbf{R}$ be nonsingular we obtain

$$\sum_i u'_i u'_i{}^T = N \cdot \mathbf{R}^{-1} \left(\mathbf{R}^T \right)^{-1} \tag{31}$$

This fixes the 3×3-matrix $\mathbf{R}$ except for a premultiplication by an arbitrary orthonormal 3×3 matrix. In any case, from eqn.(30) we clearly see that the matrix $\mathbf{R}$ must inevitably yield

$$\sum_i u'_{i1} = \sum_i u'_{i2} = 0 \tag{32}$$

$$\sum_i (u'_{i1})^2 = \sum_i (u'_{i2})^2 = N \tag{33}$$

$$\sum_i u'_{i1} u'_{i2} = 0 \tag{34}$$

These are exactly the non-isotropic scaling prescriptions proposed by Hartley [2] as one of several options. Our derivation has shown that this scaling process is absolutely necessary *for the vectors* u_i. Finally, the difference between the method derived in our paper and Hartley's method is that firstly the transformation S is isotropic, and secondly that we use the TLS-FC algorithm instead of plain TLS.

8 Experimental results

The different approaches discussed so far have been implemented in *Mathematica*, using synthetic data with an exactly known setup and exactly controllable measurement errors. We would like to stress the point that these experimental results are reported here in order to illustrate several effects that have been observed in a very large set of experiments. Due to the huge number of parameters, the derivation of generally valid conclusions is only possible on the basis of theoretical considerations, and experiments are to be understood as attempts to check whether the theory can be in accordance with reality.

We considered the case of the essential matrix (known camera parameters, enabling us to analyze the algorithms' performance in a Euclidean space) and performed a large number of simulations for different settings of the true motion (by now: pure translation in varying directions) and using 'objects' determined by a set of N random points inside of a cube given by world coordinates $x, y, z \in [-1, 1]$. These points have been projected onto the image plane yielding a set of N vector pairs u, v. Examples of such point sets visualized as displacement vector fields are shown in fig. 1 and fig. 8.

Errors in the point correspondences have been introduced by adding noise vectors (d_1, d_2) drawn from a uniform distribution $d_1, d_2 \in [-\epsilon/2, \epsilon/2]$ to the v_i vectors (u_i remaining undisturbed) with ϵ varying in the range between 0 and 30 units. Thus the variance of the error components d_i is $\epsilon^2/12$. The focal length was 256 units. The virtual image area had a width and height of 400 units.

For a fixed motion situation and a fixed 'object', 500 experiments have been performed for each of 10 different values of ϵ, respectively. What we were most interested in was the difference between the true motion vector direction and the estimates of this entity as produced by the four different algorithm variations which have been under investigation. As the translation direction can only be computed up to a scale factor, we used the angular difference between the two unit vectors (true and estimated direction) as a measurement of quality.

We did not only compute the mean angular error (MAE) between the estimated and the true direction of translation (each simulation yields one angular error, MAE = mean of all these errors), but also the angular error between the true translation direction and the mean estimated translation direction (compute mean estimated direction *first* and *then* the angular error of this quantity; AEM = angular error of mean direction). Whereas the MAE reflects the overall dispersion of the estimation result, the AEM measure will flag situations where the expectation of the estimated direction is not in coincidence with the true direction of translation. Thereby a more differentiated analysis of the algorithms' output is possible and cases where the considered algorithm is biased can be detected. The four algorithm variants considered here are

- standard algorithm: no normalization; application of plain TLS for first estimation step and subsequent rank reduction.
- "Hartley1": anisotropic scaling of both u and v; application of plain TLS for first estimation step and subsequent rank reduction.
- "Hartley2": anisotropic normalization of both u and v; application of plain TLS for first estimation step and subsequent rank reduction.
- new algorithm: anisotropic normalization of u, shift to the center of mass and isotropic scaling for v; application of TLS with fixed columns according to [14].

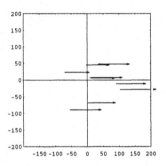

Fig. 1. Example of a displacement vector field used in our experiments; motion parallel to image plane (x direction), N=9

In our experiments, the theoretically predicted problems with the standard algorithm and the two variants proposed by Hartley did in fact occur. We list the different observations:

- The standard algorithm (solid line in all figures) is extremely susceptible to noise in the input data. Even for a rather moderate amount of error in the correspondences, the mean angular error increases very rapidly and settles in the area of about 60 degrees. It can be shown rather easily that the mean angular error to be expected when the direction of translation is *guessed* (i. e. uniform distribution on the unit sphere), is about 57 degrees. So we can only join the choir of authors stating that the plain 8+n-points algorithm is virtually useless due to its lack of stability.
- The standard algorithm is strongly biased towards the viewing direction. This is a known – but not widely known – fact (cf. [17] and the related case discussed in [18]). This bias gets visible from a comparison of figures 2, 4,

318

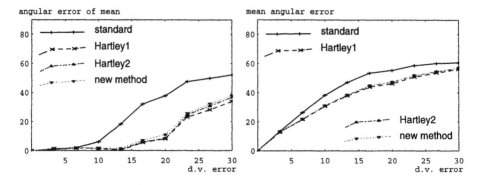

Fig. 2. Angular difference of mean direction estimate to true direction (AEM); here: motion in *x* direction, N=9

Fig. 3. Mean angular difference between estimated and true motion direction (MAE); motion type = *x* direction, N=9

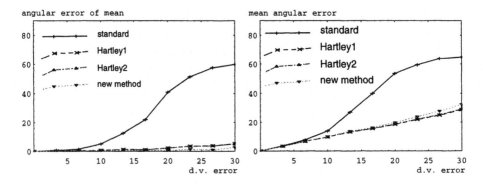

Fig. 4. AEM; here: motion in *x* direction, N=18

Fig. 5. MAE; motion type = *x* direction, N=18

and 6 (translation parallel to image plane; 9, 18 and 36 correspondences) versus figure 9 (translation in viewing direction, 9 correspondences) which is representative for the behaviour of 18, 36 and 60 correspondences as well. The apparently excellent behaviour of the standard algorithm with respect to the AEM measure in fig. 9 is caused by the fact that the true motion direction is in exact coincidence with the bias of the estimator.

- The performance of Hartley's variants with respect to the AEM criterion does not provide any clue for a bias (cf. figs. 2, 4, 6, and 9), and neither does our new algorithm, which is almost indistinguishable from the latter two with respect to the AEM criterion. Thus the results of the experiments are compatible with our claim that the normalization procedure eliminates the bias, as indented.
- When we performed the first experiments, we were rather astonished to stumble upon the strange behaviour of the 'Hartley-normalized' algorithms with respect to the mean angular error (MAE) for the case that the direction of translation is identical to the viewing direction (translation in

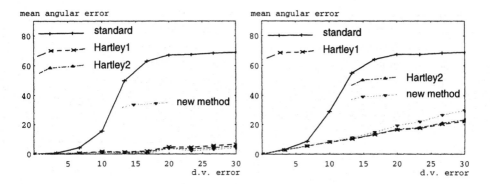

Fig. 6. AEM; here: motion in x direction, N=36

Fig. 7. MAE; motion type = x direction, N=36

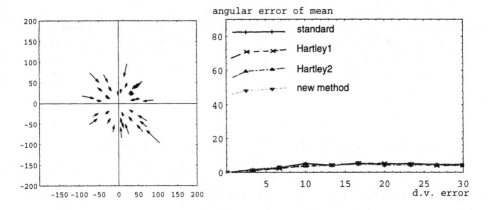

Fig. 8. Displacement vector field for motion in z direction (in viewing direction), N=36

Fig. 9. AEM; here: motion in z direction, N=9

z-direction): Comparing figs.10, 11, 12, and 13 one finds that the MAE, and therefore the uncertainty of the estimation result, *increases* if more data (point correspondences) are added. Obviously, the regarded estimator is not consistent.

- For the method proposed in this paper, the MAE remains moderate for all situations investigated here, and – more important – it does not increase with increasing number of point correspondences as can be seen in figures 10 – 13.

9 Conclusions

We have shown that a proper analysis of the statistical structure of errors in the input data of a motion estimation algorithm can provide valuable information about the sensitive parts of a given procedure. Moreover, this type of error

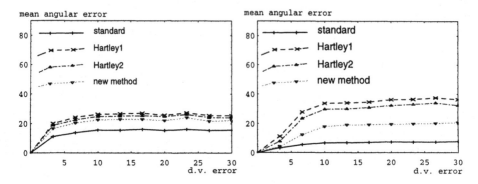

Fig. 10. MAE; motion type $= z$ direction, N=9

Fig. 11. MAE; motion type $= z$ direction, N=18

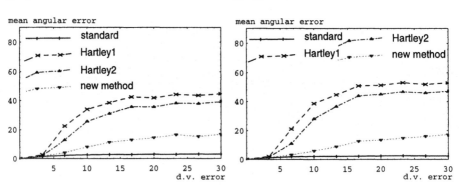

Fig. 12. MAE; motion type $= z$ direction, N=36

Fig. 13. MAE; motion type $= z$ direction, N=60

analysis can be the starting point for modifications that provide the algorithm with extensions that significantly improve its overall performance in terms of precision, stability and reliability.

We are convinced that the concept of Total Least Squares estimation will become established in the field of motion analysis, since many estimation tasks currently under investigation in various research groups do precisely belong to the class of problems the TLS method is aiming at.

It shall not be held back that even in the context of the specific problem discussed in this paper there are still several open questions, for instance the optimum estimation of a rank 2 fundamental matrix. For the moment being, we must confine ourselves to the remark that the Frobenius norm is certainly *not* the correct metric for performing the constraint enforcement step; instead, the correct metric is implicitly given by the covariance structure of the F-matrix estimate obtained in the first step. Here, further investigations are required and we hope to be able to present results before long.

Finally, we would like to express our confidence in that non-iterative algorithms for the two-view motion analysis problem will eventually perform at least as well as the best iterative procedures as soon as a comprehensive exploitation of the statistical input-output relation has been performed. As it has been pointed out in Hartley's 1997 paper, the gap to be bridged is not very large.

References

1. Hartley, R.I.: In defence of the 8-point-algorithm. In: Proc. Fifth International Conference on Computer Vision, IEEE Computer Society Press, S.1064-1070, June 1995.
2. Hartley, R.I.: In defence of the 8-point-algorithm. IEEE Trans. on Pattern Analysis and Machine Intelligence, Vol. 19, no.6, June 1997.
3. Longuet-Higgins, H.C.: A computer algorithm for reconstructing a scene from two projections. *Nature*, vol. 293, September 1981, S.433-435
4. Tsai, R.Y.; Huang, T.S.: Uniqueness and estimation of three-dimensional motion parameters of rigid objects with curved surfaces. IEEE Trans. Pattern Analysis and Machine intelligence, vol.6, pp.13-27, 1984
5. Weng, J.; Huang, T.S.; Ahuja, N.: Motion and structure from image sequences. Springer Verlag, Series in Information Science, vol. 29, 1993.
6. Maybank, S.J.: The projective geometry of ambiguous surfaces. Phil. Trans. R.Soc.Lond., vol.A332, pp.1-47, 1990
7. Strang, G.: Linear algebra and its applications. 3rd edition, Harcourt Brace Jovanovich, Inc., 1988.
8. Golub, G.H.; van Loan, C.F.: An analysis of the total least squares problem, SIAM J. Matrix Anal. Appl., Vol. 17, No. 6, pp 883-893, 1980.
9. Golub, G.H.; van Loan, C.F.: Matrix computations. John Hopkins University Press 2nd ed., 1989.
10. van Huffel, S., Vandewalle, J.: The total least squares problem: Computational aspects and analysis. SIAM (Society for Industrial and Applied Mathematics), Philadelphia, 1991
11. Therrien, C.W.: Discrete random signals and statistical signal processing. Prentice Hall, 1992.
12. van Huffel, S.; Vandewalle, J.: Analysis and properties of the generalized total least squares problem $AX \approx B$, when some or all columns are subject to error. SIAM J. Matrix Anal. Appl., Vol. 10, no. 3, pp 294-315, 1989.
13. Mendel, J.: Lessons in estimation theory for signal processing, communications, and control. Prentice Hall, Englewood Cliffs, 1995
14. Demmel, J.W.: The smallest perturbation of a submatrix which lowers the rank and constrained total least squares problems. SIAM J. Numer. Anal. 24, pp. 199-206.
15. Rao, C.R.; Toutenburg, H.: Linear models: least squares and alternatives. Springer Series in Statistics, 1995.
16. Golub, G.H.; Hoffman, A.; Stewart, G.W.: A generalization of the Eckart-Young-Mirsky Matrix Approximation Theorem, Linear Algebra and its Applications, 88/89: 317-327, 1987
17. Kanatani, K.; Geometric computation for machine vision: a geometric viewpoint. Oxford University Press, U.K., 1993.
18. Earnshaw, A.M.; Blostein, S.D.: The performance of camera translation direction estimators from optical flow: analysis, comparison, and theoretical limits. IEEE Trans. Patt. Anal. and Machine Intell., vol.18, No. 9, 1996, pp.927-932

Study of Dynamical Processes with Tensor-Based Spatiotemporal Image Processing Techniques

B. Jähne[1,2,4], H. Haußecker[1], H. Scharr[1], H. Spies[1], D. Schmundt[1,3], and U. Schurr[3]

[1] Research Group Image Processing, Interdisciplinary Center for Scientific Computing, Heidelberg University, Im Neuenheimer Feld 368, 69120 Heidelberg
[2] Institute for Environmental Physics, Heidelberg University
Im Neuenheimer Feld 366, 69120 Heidelberg
[3] Institute of Botany, Heidelberg University
Im Neuenheimer Feld 360, 69120 Heidelberg,
[4] Scripps Institution of Oceanography, University of California, San Diego
La Jolla, CA, 92093-0230, USA,

Abstract. Image sequence processing techniques are used to study exchange, growth, and transport processes and to tackle key questions in environmental physics and biology. These applications require high accuracy for the estimation of the motion field since the most interesting parameters of the dynamical processes studied are contained in first-order derivatives of the motion field or in dynamical changes of the moving objects. Therefore the performance and optimization of low-level motion estimators is discussed. A tensor method tuned with carefully optimized derivative filters yields reliable and dense displacement vector fields (DVF) with an accuracy of up to a few hundredth pixels/frame for real-world images. The accuracy of the tensor method is verified with computer-generated sequences and a calibrated image sequence. With the improvements in accuracy the motion estimation is now rather limited by imperfections in the CCD sensors, especially the spatial nonuniformity in the responsivity. With a simple two-point calibration, these effects can efficiently be suppressed. The application of the techniques to the analysis of plant growth, to ocean surface microturbulence in IR image sequences, and to sediment transport is demonstrated.

1 Introduction

Since December 1995, the Interdisciplinary Center for Scientific Computing, the Institute for Environmental Physics, and the Institute for Botany cooperate in a DFG-funded interdisciplinary research unit ("Forschergruppe") to study transport, exchange, and growth processes. The oceanographic applications are investigated in close cooperation with the Scripps Institution of Oceanography, University of California, San Diego. The combination of novel visualization techniques and image sequence processing techniques gives an unprecedented insight into complex dynamic processes. This approach allows studying key scientific questions for which previously no adequate experimental techniques were available. A close and interdisciplinary cooperation between applications and fundamental research in image analysis is the most distinct feature of the research unit. The application areas currently include

- small-scale air sea interaction processes, especially air-water gas transfer and wind-generated waves [14,11],

- plant leaf growth processes including the measurement of the physiological relevant parameters, and

- analysis of the pollution plumes (especially NO_x) from biomass burning and industrial areas using multispectral image sequences of the GOME instrument on the ERS2 satellite.

The "objects" encountered in the research unit differ from those normally studied in computer vision and thus pose new challenges for image sequence processing and analysis:

Accuracy. The displacements between consecutive frames must be determined with a relative accuracy much better than 1 %. This requirement results in an error for the interframe displacement of no larger than a few hundredth pixels.

Derivatives of motion field. For plant growth studies and the analysis of turbulent flows the optical flow is not of primary interest but spatial derivatives of the motion field such as divergence and vorticity.

Estimate of dynamical changes. The objects are non-rigid undergoing dynamical changes. New parts may gradually appear when studying the growth of plant leaves or roots or when new waves are generated by the wind at the ocean surface.

Multichannel motion estimation. An adequate study of dynamic processes often requires the simultaneous acquisition of image sequences of many parameters. Therefore the image sequence processing techniques must be set up in a way that they can also be used with multichannel images. This means more than just using multiple channels to determine a *single* velocity. Often the different channels show slightly *different* velocities, which are significant to characterize the underlying dynamical process. In the plumes from biomass burning, for example, different tracers have different life times. Or, if multiple tracers are used to study the transfer processes across the ocean surface, different diffusivities lead to different concentration patterns from which important clues about the underlying mechanisms can be drawn.

Speed of processing. Systematic studies of the dynamical processes investigated require processing of huge amounts of image sequences. Thus the algorithms used must also be fast.

The requirements summarized above caused us to revisit the basic approaches to image sequence processing. While there is a wealth of different concepts to compute optical flow (for a recent review see, e. g., [1]), much less work has been devoted to analyze the performance of optical flow algorithms with real-world image sequences and to optimize their implementation for accuracy and speed.

In this paper we report significant improvements in the accuracy of a tensor-based technique analyzing motion as orientation in spatiotemporal images. After briefly reviewing the tensor technique in Sect. 2, the focus in this paper is on an accurate and fast implementation in Sect. 3. One key point is a new nonlinear filter optimization technique minimizing the error in the direction of gradient operators (Sect. 3.2). In Sect. 4 the accuracy of the new approach is first verified with computer generated and calibrated real-world image sequences. Then it is shown that a careful radiometric calibration of the camera is required to avoid systematic errors in the motion field due to the photoresponse nonuniformity (PRNU) of the imaging sensor. Finally, various applications of the research unit are shown and discussed in Sect. 5.

2 Theory of the Structure Tensor

2.1 Motion as Orientation in Spatiotemporal Images

The displacement of gray value structures in spatiotemporal images yields inclined image structures with respect to the temporal axis. The relation between the orientation angle and the optical flow is given by

$$u = - [\tan \varphi_1, \tan \varphi_2]^T , \tag{1}$$

where $u = [u_x, u_y]^T$ denotes the optical flow on the image plane and the angles φ_1 and φ_2 define the angles between the plane normal to the lines of constant gray value and the x and y axes, respectively [7]. This basic property of spatiotemporal images allows to estimate the optical flow from a 3-D orientation analysis, searching for the orientation of constant gray value in xt-space. Orientation is different from direction. While the direction (e. g., of a gradient vector) is defined for the full angular range of 360°, the orientation is invariant under a rotation of 180° and thus has only a definition range of 180°.

In order to determine local orientation locally, Bigün and Granlund [2] proposed a tensor representation of the local grey value distribution. Using directional derivatives, Kass and Witkin [12] came to a solution that turned out to be equivalent to the tensor method. Searching for a general description of local orientation Knutsson [13] concluded that local structure in an n-dimensional space can be represented by a symmetric $n \times n$ tensor. Rao [19] used a similar tensor representation for 2D texture analysis.

2.2 Total Least Squares Optimization

The orientation of gray-value structures can mathematically be formulated as a total least squares optimization problem [3]. The scalar product between a vector r, representing the orientation for constant gray values in the image sequence, and the spatiotemporal gradient $\nabla_{xt} g(x, t)$ is a semi-positive definite bilinear form that expresses the local deviation of the spatiotemporal gray value structure from an ideally oriented structure. If the gradient is perpendicular to

r, the product is zero. It reaches a maximum when the gradient is either parallel or antiparallel to r. Thus the expression

$$\int\limits_{-\infty}^{\infty} h(x - x', t - t') \left(r^T(x,t) \nabla_{xt} g(x',t')\right)^2 \, d^2 x' dt', \qquad (2)$$

has to be minimized in a local neighborhood. The size of the local neighborhood around the central point (x,t) is given by the shape of the window-function $h(x - x', t - t')$. Equation (2) can be rewritten as a matrix equation

$$r^T \left[h * \left(\nabla_{xt} g \, \nabla_{xt} g^T\right)\right] r = r^T J r \to \min, \qquad (3)$$

with the 3D *structure tensor*

$$J(x) = \int\limits_{-\infty}^{\infty} h(x - x', t - t') \nabla_{xt} g(x',t') \nabla_{xt} g^T(x',t') \, d^2 x' dt'. \qquad (4)$$

The components of this tensors are abbreviated by

$$G_{pq} = h * \left(\frac{\partial g}{\partial p} \frac{\partial g}{\partial q}\right) \quad \text{with} \quad p, q \in \{x, y, t\} \qquad (5)$$

Equation (3) reaches a minimum if the vector r is given by the *eigenvector* of the tensor J to the *minimum eigenvalue* [2,18]. The estimation of local orientation therefore reduces to an *eigenvalue analysis* of the tensor J.

The eigenvalues $\lambda_1 \geq \lambda_2 \geq \lambda_3$ of the tensor can be used to characterize the spatiotemporal gray value structure [6], where the smallest eigenvalue λ_3 reflects the noise level in the image sequence. If it is significantly higher than expected from the noise level, the neighborhood shows no constant motion. If the smallest eigenvalue is consistent with the noise level and the two others are significantly larger than the noise level, both components of the optical flow can be estimated and are given by the eigenvector e_s to the smallest eigenvalue:

$$u = \left(\frac{e_{s,x}}{e_{s,t}}, \frac{e_{s,y}}{e_{s,t}}\right). \qquad (6)$$

If two eigenvalues are in the order of the noise level, an image structure with linear symmetry (spatial local orientation) moves with a constant velocity. This is the well known *aperture problem* in optical flow computation. The eigenvector to the largest eigenvalue, e_l, points normal to the plane of constant gray values in the spatiotemporal domain and can be used to compute the normal optical flow $u_\perp$:

$$u_\perp = -\frac{e_{l,t}}{\sqrt{e_{l,x}^2 + e_{l,y}^2}}. \qquad (7)$$

The tensor approach accounts for errors in *all* components of the spatiotemporal gradient. In contrast, the classical differential approach [15]

$$\begin{bmatrix} G_{xx} & G_{xy} \\ G_{xy} & G_{yy} \end{bmatrix} \begin{bmatrix} u_1 \\ u_2 \end{bmatrix} = - \begin{bmatrix} G_{xt} \\ G_{yt} \end{bmatrix} \tag{8}$$

which is a solution of the least-squares minimization problem

$$h * \left(\boldsymbol{u} \boldsymbol{\nabla} g + \frac{\partial g}{\partial t} \right)^2 \rightarrow \min, \tag{9}$$

accounts only for errors in the temporal derivate $\partial g / \partial t$.

2.3 Analytical Performance Analysis

It was shown analytically by [7,9] that the tensor method — as well as other approaches — yield *exact* estimates of the optical flow under the ideal condition of a spatial pattern moving with a constant velocity. The different techniques, however, distinguish themselves in the way they respond to deviations and distortions from the ideal case. The tensor method shows — in contrast to the standard least squares differential approach — no bias of the estimate in images with isotropic normal distributed noise. Inhomogeneous and accelerated motion also causes a surprisingly low bias in the motion estimate [9].

The analysis summarized here refers to continuous spatiotemporal images. It thus does not include errors caused by the discretization. In Sect. 3.2 we will discuss that the largest error in the motion estimate is due to an inadequate discretization of the spatial and temporal derivates.

3 Accurate and Fast Implementation

3.1 Computing the Structure Tensor by Spatiotemporal Filtering

The implementation of the tensor components can be carried out very efficiently by simple spatiotemporal filter operators. Identifying the convolution in (4) with a 3D spatiotemporal smoothing of the product of partial derivatives with the window function $h(\boldsymbol{x}, t)$, each component of the structure tensor can be computed as

$$J_{pq} = \mathcal{B} \left(\mathcal{D}_p \cdot \mathcal{D}_q \right), \tag{10}$$

with the 3D spatiotemporal smoothing operator $\mathcal{B}$ and the differential operators $\mathcal{D}_p$ in the direction of the coordinate x_p.

Using a binomial operator the smoothing can be performed very efficiently on a multigrid data structure [5,8]. With this approach, the displacement vector field is stored on the next coarser level of a pyramid. Thus the number of computations for any subsequent processing — especially the eigenvalue analysis (Sect. 3.3) — is also reduced by a factor of four.

The smoothing and derivative filters can be computed very efficiently in integer arithmetic using modern multimedia instruction sets such as Intel's MMX or Sun's VIS [10].

3.2 Optimal Derivative Filters

The most critical point is the choice of an appropriate differential operator. A difference operator is only an approximation of a derivative operator. For an accurate computation of the structure tensor only deviations in the direction of the gradient are of importance as can be seen directly from (2). This means that for an optimal difference filter, it is not required to approximate the ideal transfer function of the derivative filter, ik_q. It suffices to approximate a more general transfer function

$$\hat{D}_q(\boldsymbol{k}) = \hat{f}(|\boldsymbol{k}|)k_q, \tag{11}$$

where $\hat{f}(|\boldsymbol{k}|)$ is an arbitrary isotropic function and k_q is the component of the wave number in the direction q (for the time axis this is the circular frequency ω). The transfer function (11) includes the classes of all regularized derivative filters that smooth the images before the discrete differences are computed.

The standard symmetric difference filter is a bad choice to compute the structure tensor. This filter has the transfer function

$$\hat{D}_q = i\sin(\pi \tilde{k}_q), \tag{12}$$

where $\tilde{k}$ is the wave number normalized to the Nyquist wave number. Consequently the direction of the 2-D spatial gradient is given by

$$\phi = \arctan \frac{\sin(\pi \tilde{k} \sin \phi)}{\sin(\pi \tilde{k} \cos \phi)}. \tag{13}$$

A Taylor expansion of this expression in $\tilde{k}$ gives the angle error, $\Delta\phi$, in the approximation of small $\tilde{k}$ as

$$\Delta\phi = \frac{(\pi \tilde{k})^2}{24} \sin 4\phi + O(\tilde{k}^4). \tag{14}$$

The error is substantial, it is more than $5°$ at $\tilde{k} = 0.5$. The error of other standard derivative filters is not much lower. The error for the Sobel filter, for example, is only two times lower in the approximation for small wave numbers [8].

The general form of the transfer function in (11) suggests that an ansatz of a derivative filter with cross-smoothing in all directions except the direction in which the derivation is applied seems to be a good choice. (The symmetric difference filter contains already a certain degree of smoothing.) For the sake of an efficient computation, separable filters of the form:

$$\boldsymbol{D}_{x,\text{opt}} = \boldsymbol{D}_x * \boldsymbol{B}_y * \boldsymbol{B}_t, \quad \boldsymbol{D}_x = \frac{1}{2}[1,0,-1], \quad \boldsymbol{B}_{y,t} = [p/2, 1-p, p/2]^T \tag{15}$$

are used with the transfer function

$$\hat{D}_{x,\text{opt}}(p) = i\sin(\pi \tilde{k}_x)((1-p) + p\cos(\pi \tilde{k}_y))\,((1-p) + p\cos(\pi \tilde{\omega})) \tag{16}$$

The equations above show the separable filter for derivation in x direction. The derivative filters in the other direction just show permuted indices for the directions.

The ansatz in (15) and (16) has one degree of freedom. It is optimized with a nonlinear functional that describes the deviation of the direction of the gradient built with the filters and contains an arbitrary wave number dependent weighting function so that the filters can be optimized for selected wave number ranges. Further details of the optimization technique and its generalization to larger filter kernels can be found in [20]. With rational filter coefficients, a value of $p = 6/16$ turned out to be an optimal choice. For wave numbers $\tilde{k}$ up to 0.5, the error in the direction of the gradient is well below $0.4°$. The maximum error is thus more than ten times lower than for the Sobel filter. The nonlinear optimization procedure used here also produces significantly better filters than a similar approach by Farid and Simoncelli [4] based on a linear optimization technique.

3.3 Fast Eigenvalue Analysis

The *Jacobi transformation* [17] proved to be an efficient and robust algorithm to determine the eigenvalues and eigenvectors of the structure tensor. In all cases no more than 8 elementary Jacobi rotations were required. Interestingly, the Jacobi algorithm required a maximum of only three iterations with a spatially oriented gray value structure (aperture problem, rank one structure tensor). Since edges are generally more common than corners, the Jacobi algorithm is thus very efficient in the mean.

Preselecting interesting image regions could further speed up the eigenvalue analysis. If the *trace* of the structure tensor (sum of the eigenvalues) is below a certain noise dependent threshold, it indicates a homogeneous region in which the computation of the eigenvalues and eigenvectors is not required since no significant motion estimate can be retrieved then.

4 Results

4.1 Computer Generated Image Sequences

First computer generated sequences were used to test the ultimate accuracy of the implementation of the tensor method. In order to get realistic spatial structures, we used frame 13 (Fig. 2a) of the calibrated sequence taken by the IITB in Karlsruhe [16]. From this image a sequence was produced using optimized interpolation filters [8]. The result for a motion in x direction with 0.456 pixels/frame of a sequence to which zero mean normal distributed noise with a standard deviation of 2.0 bits was added is shown in Fig. 1. For the optimized filter and the Sobel filter, the standard deviation of the error in the velocity estimate is well below 0.01 pixels/frame. In contrast the simple symmetric filter shows both a systematic offset of almost 0.1 pixels/frame and a significant wider distribution in x direction. This test clearly shows that highly accurate motion estimation is possible under ideal condition with a constant motion field.

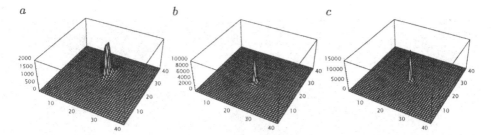

Fig. 1. 2-D histogram of the error in the motion estimation for a constant shift of 0.456 pixels/frame of one image of the IITB sequence. In addition, a zero-mean normal distributed noise with a standard deviation of 2.0 was added to each image of the computer generated sequence. One unit in the diagram corresponds to 0.01 pixels/frame, zero error is in the center at [20, 20]. Results with the tensor technique using **a** a symmetric derivative filter $1/2[1\ 0\ -1]$, **b** a 3-D Sobel filter, and **c** the optimized $3 \times 3 \times 3$ filter described in Sect. 3.2.

4.2 Calibrated Real-world Sequence

The IITB image sequence [16] is one of the few calibrated image sequences available. It has also been used to test the error in the motion estimation with real image sequences. Fig. 2 shows the results. At the highly textured floor, a dense velocity field could be computed, while it is rather sparse at the marble columns (Fig. 2c). The smallest eigenvalue of the structure tensor shows the deviation from an ideally spatiotemporal structure with constant motion. Therefore parts of the edges of the columns appear bright in Fig. 2d. The error maps for the velocity estimates are shown in Fig. 2e and f, respectively. It is not surprising that the errors are high at motion discontinuities, because the structure tensor averages over a local spatiotemporal neighborhood defined by the size of the smoothing mask in (10). Again the much better performance of the optimized filter can be observed. The simple symmetric difference filter (Fig. 2e) shows a considerable systematic error that grows with increasing shifts in x direction (see Fig. 2b).

A 2-D histogram of the error maps for the velocity estimate is shown for three different derivative filters in Fig. 3. The optimized filter results in a standard deviation less than 0.03 pixels/frame. This is about a two times lower standard deviation than the best results in Table 1 from Otte and Nagel [16]. Their results are based on averaging over a $5 \times 5 \times 5$ neighborhood, while the smoothing used with the multigrid binomial filters in the tensor method effectively averages only over a sphere with a radius of 1.73 pixels or a volume of 22 pixels and thus preserves a higher spatial resolution. The non-optimized filters show significantly broadened distributions with standard deviations comparable to those found by Otte and Nagel [16] (Fig. 3a, b).

Fig. 2. Motion analysis using the calibrated sequence from the IITB, Karlsruhe [16]. **a** Frame 13 of the sequence. **b** x component of the true motion field. **c** Motion field determined with the tensor technique. Areas where no 2-D velocity could be determined are masked out. **d** Smallest eigenvalue of the structure tensor. **e** Error map (range [-0.2, 0.2] pixels/frame) for the $1/2$ [1 0 -1] filter. **f** same as **e** for the optimized $3 \times 3 \times 3$ derivative filter (Sect. 3.2).

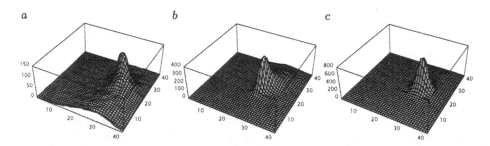

Fig. 3. 2-D histogram of the error in the motion estimation for the calibrated IITB sequence. Results with the tensor technique using **a** a symmetric derivative filter $1/2[1\ 0\ -1]$,. **b** a 3-D Sobel filter, and **c** the optimized $3 \times 3 \times 3$ filter.

a   b

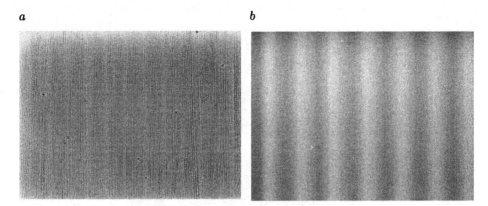

Fig. 4. Radiometric calibration of a standard CCD camera (Jai CV-M10): **a** Image of the relative responsivity in a range of ±3%. **b** Fixed pattern noise (without any illumination) in a range of ±0.5.

4.3 Influence of Sensor Imperfections

One may wonder why the standard deviations with real sensor data are significantly higher than those obtained with computer generated sequences (compare Fig. 1 und 3). The higher errors are related to imperfections of the CCD sensor/camera system.

A radiometric calibration study showed that standard CCD cameras show significant large-scale and small-scale spatial variations in the order of about 1%, which cannot be neglected (Fig. 4a). The fixed pattern noise without illumination is less serious. In the example shown in Fig. 4b the amplitude of the patterns is well below one. Since these patterns are static, they are superimposed to the real motion in the sequence. In parts of the sequence where the local contrast is low, the static patterns dominate the structure and thus a lower or even zero velocity is measured.

The influence of static patterns can nicely be demonstrated if objects with low contrast are moving such as the slightly textured elephant in Fig. 5. On the glass window of the CCD sensor, dirt causes spatial variations in the responsivity of the sensor (Fig. 5a, d). At the edges of the speckles, the smallest eigenvalue of the structure tensor shows high values indicating motion discontinuities (Fig. 5b). The motion field indeed shows drops at the positions of the speckles (Fig. 5c). If a simple two-point calibration is performed using the measured responsivity and an image with a dark pattern, the influence of the speckles is no longer visible both in the smallest eigenvalue and the motion field (Fig. 5e, f)

5   Application Examples

The structure tensor technique was applied to a variety of application examples from oceanography (IR ocean surface images), botany (growth processes), and

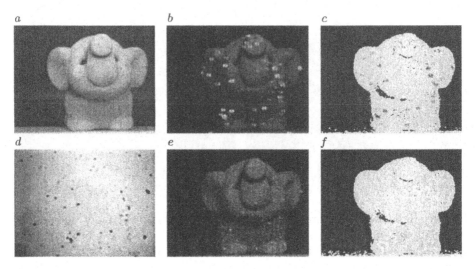

Fig. 5. Demonstration of the influence of spatial sensitivity variations of the CCD sensor on motion estimation: **a** One image of the elephant sequence. **b** Lowest eigenvalue of the structure tensor. **c** Velocity component in x direction. **d** Contrast enhanced relative responsivity. **e** Lowest eigenvalue of the structure tensor for a sequence corrected for the spatial responsivity changes. **f** Velocity component in x direction for the corrected sequence.

to traffic scenes. It proved to work well without any adaptation to the image content. Fig. 6 shows example motion fields of such sequences. The application to the IR sequences (Fig. 6a) demonstrates that the tensor technique is also suitable for noisy imagery.

The accuracy of the estimated velocity can also be demonstrated by computing first-order derivatives of the velocities. These are the most interesting quantities for the study of the dynamical processes we are investigating. The divergence of the motion field, for instance, directly gives the area-resolved growth rate (relative increase in area, see Fig. 7a). For the study of the microscale turbulence at the ocean surface, the divergence of the motion field is related to divergence and convergence zones at the interface (Fig. 7a).

Another interesting example is the study of sediment transport in the beds of rivers. Figure 8 shows the evaluation of a sequence where a strong flow in the river induced the transport of sand particles in the sediment. Despite the bad quality of the sequence taken by an endoscope put into the sand, reliable motion fields could be computed. The nature of these processes becomes evident in the images showing the divergence and rotation of the flow.

a

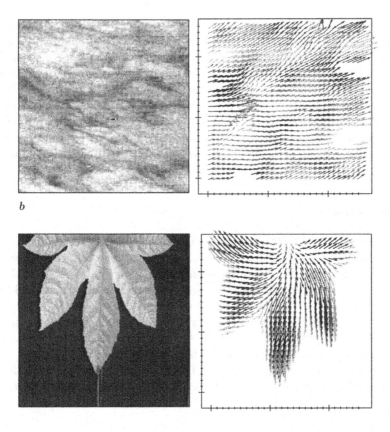

b

Fig. 6. Displacement vector fields computed with the tensor method. **a** IR images of the ocean surface for heat transfer studies, **b** growing leaf of a castor-oil plant. The arrows visualize the computed displacement field. Black arrows mean high certainty, lighter arrows lower certainty.

Fig. 7. Divergence of the motion field of a growing leaf of a castor-oil plant. The scale for the divergence ranges from -2.0 to 6.0 permille/min.

6 Conclusions

In this paper some recent research results of an interdisciplinary research unit were discussed. It is shown that the accuracy of motion estimation can significantly be improved over previous approaches by using a tensor method with carefully optimized derivative filters. The tensor approach also gives direct measures for the quality of the estimated motion. Some of the next steps of our research will include the extension to model-based motion estimation, multichannel image sequence processing, and the direct modeling of parameters of the dynamical processes. It is the long-term goal of our research to merge image sequence processing, 3-D image processing, and spectroscopic imaging into 5-D imaging as a powerful tool to study complex scientific problems.

Acknowledgments

Financial support for this research by the German Science Foundation (Deutsche Forschungsgemeinschaft, DFG, Jae 395/6-1) through the research unit (Forschergruppe) "Bildfolgenanalyse zum Studium dynamischer Prozesse", the US National Science Foundation (Coastal Ocean Processes, CoOP) and the US Office of Naval Research (ONR) through the Marine Boundary Layer Accelerated Research Initiative (MBL/ARI) is gratefully acknowledged. Sediment transport is being studied in a project funded by the German Federal Waterways Engineering and Research Institute (BAW), Karlsruhe (Dipl.-Ing. H.-J. Köhler). H. S. is supported by a scholarship within the DFG-Graduiertenkolleg "Modellierung und Wissenschaftliches Rechnen in Mathematik und Naturwissenschaften".

References

1. S. S. Beauchemin and J. L. Barron, 1997. The computation of optical flow, *ACM Computing Surveys, 27(3)*, pp. 433–467.
2. J. Bigün and G. Granlund, 1987. Optimal orientation detection of linear symmetry. Proc. *First Intern. Conf. on Comp. Vision, ICCV'87*, London, June 8-11, 1987, pp. 433–438.
3. C. H. Chu and E. J. Delp, 1989. Estimating displacement vectors from an image sequence, *J. Opt. Soc. Am. A6(6)*, pp. 871–878.
4. H. Farid and E.P. Simoncelli, 1997. Optimally rotation-equivariant directional derivative kernels. *7th Int. Conf. Computer Analysis of Images and Patterns*, Kiel, pp. 207–214.
5. H. Haußecker, 1995. Mehrgitter-Bewegungssegmentierung in Bildfolgen mit Anwendung zur Detektion von Sedimentverlagerungen, Diploma thesis, Univ. Heidelberg.
6. H. Haußecker and B. Jähne, 1997. A tensor approach for precise computation of dense displacement vector fields, Proc. *Mustererkennung 1997*, Braunschweig, 15–17. September 1997, E. Paulus und F. M. Wahl (Hrsg.), Informatik Aktuell, Springer, Berlin, pp. 199–208.
7. B. Jähne, 1993. *Spatio-Temporal Image Processing, Theory and Scientific Applications*, Lecture Notes in Computer Science, Vol. 751, Springer, Berlin, 1993.

8. B. Jähne, 1997. *Practical Handbook on Digital Image Processing for Scientific Applications*, CRC-Press, Boca Raton, FL, USA.

9. B. Jähne, 1997. Performance characteristics of low-level motion estimators in spatiotemporal images, Proc. *DAGM-Workshop Performance Characteristics and Quality of Computer Vision Algorithms*, Braunschweig, September 18, 1997, W. Foerstner (ed.), Institute of Photogrammetry, Univ. Bonn.

10. B. Jähne, 1997. SIMD-Bildverarbeitungsalgorithmen mit dem Multimedia Extension-Instruktionssatz (MMX) von Intel, *Automatisierungstechnik AT, 10*, pp. 453–460.

11. B. Jähne and H. Haußecker, 1998. Air-Water Gas Exchange, *Annual Rev. Fluid Mech., 30*, pp. 443–468.

12. M. Kass, and A. Witkin, 1987. Analyzing Oriented Patterns, *Comp. Vision Graphics Image Proc., 37*, pp. 362–385.

13. H. Knutsson, 1989. Representing local structure using tensors, *6th Scandinavian Conf. Image Analysis*, Oulu, Finland, pp. 244–251.

14. P. S. Liss and R. A. Duce (eds.). *The Sea Surface and Global Change*, Cambridge Univ. Press, Cambridge, UK, 1997.

15. B. D. Lucas, and T. Kanade. An iterative image-registration technique with an application to stereo vision, Proc. *DARPA Image Understanding Workshop*, pp. 121–130.

16. M. Otte, and H.-H. Nagel, 1994. Optical flow estimation: advances and comparisons, Proc. *ECCV'94, Vol. II*, J. O. Eklundh (ed.), Springer, Berlin, pp. 51–60.

17. W. H. Press, S. A. Teukolsky, W. T. Vetterling, B. P.:Flannery, 1992. *Numerical recipes in C: The Art of Scientific Computing*, Cambridge Univ. Press

18. A. R. Rao and B. G. Schunck, 1989. Computing oriented texture fields, *Proceedings CVPR'89*, San Diego, CA, pp. 61–68, IEEE Computer Society Press, Los Alamitos.

19. A. R. Rao, 1990. *A Taxonomy for Texture Description and Identification*, Springer, New York

20. H. Scharr, S. Körkel, and B. Jähne, 1997. Numerische Isotropieoptimierung von FIR-Filtern mittels Querglättung, Proc. *Mustererkennung 1997*, Braunschweig, 15–17. September 1997, E. Paulus und F. M. Wahl (Hrsg.), Informatik Aktuell, Springer, Berlin, pp. 367–374.

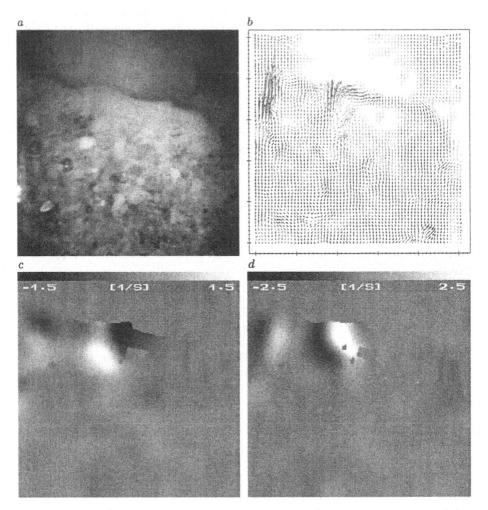

Fig. 8. Example for the study of flow in sediments. **a** One of the images of the flow of sand particles in the sediment observed with an embedded endoscope. **b** Displacement vector field computed with the tensor method. **c** Divergence and **d** rotation of the vector field as a color overlay on the original image; a color scale is included at the top of each image.

Motion Recovery from Image Sequences: Discrete Viewpoint vs. Differential Viewpoint[*]

Yi Ma, Jana Košecká, and Shankar Sastry

Electronics Research Laborotory
University of California at Berkeley,
Berkeley CA 94720-1774, USA,
{mayi,janka,sastry}@robotics.eecs.berkeley.edu

Abstract. The aim of this paper is to explore intrinsic geometric methods of recovering the three dimensional motion of a moving camera from a sequence of images. Generic similarities between the discrete approach and the differential approach are revealed through a parallel development of their analogous motion estimation theories.

We begin with a brief review of the (discrete) essential matrix approach, showing how to recover the 3D displacement from image correspondences. The space of normalized essential matrices is characterized geometrically: the unit tangent bundle of the rotation group is a double covering of the space of normalized essential matrices. This characterization naturally explains the geometry of the possible number of 3D displacements which can be obtained from the essential matrix.

Second, a differential version of the essential matrix constraint previously explored by [19, 20] is presented. We then present the precise characterization of the space of differential essential matrices, which gives rise to a novel eigenvector-decomposition-based 3D velocity estimation algorithm from the optical flow measurements. This algorithm gives a unique solution to the motion estimation problem and serves as a differential counterpart of the SVD-based 3D displacement estimation algorithm from the discrete case.

Finally, simulation results are presented evaluating the performance of our algorithm in terms of bias and sensitivity of the estimates with respect to the noise in optical flow measurements.

Keywords: optical flow, epipolar constraint, motion estimation.

---

[*] Research is supported by ARO under the MURI grant DAAH04-96-1-0341, "An Integrated Approach to Intelligent Systems".

1 Introduction

The problem of estimating structure and motion from image sequences has been studied extensively by the computer vision community in the past decade. Various approaches differ in the types of assumptions they make about the projection model, the model of the environment, or the type of algorithms they use for estimating the motion and/or structure. Most of the techniques try to decouple the two problems by estimating the motion first, followed by the structure estimation. In spite of the fact that the robustness of existing motion estimation algorithms has been studied quite extensively, it has been suggested that the fact that the structure and motion estimation are decoupled typically hinders their performance [12]. Some algorithms address the problem of motion and structure (shape) recovery simultaneously either in batch [16] or recursive fashion [12].

The approaches to the motion estimation only, can be partitioned into the discrete and differential methods depending on whether they use as an input set of point correspondences or image velocities. Among the efforts to solve this problem, one of the more appealing approaches is the *essential matrix approach*, proposed by Longuet-Higgins, Huang and Faugeras *et al* in 1980s [7]. It shows that the relative 3D displacement of a camera can be recovered from an *intrinsic* geometric constraint between two images of the same scene, the so-called *Longuet-Higgins constraint* (also called the *epipolar or essential constraint*). Estimating 3D motion can therefore be decoupled from estimation of the structure of the 3D scene. This endows the resulting motion estimation algorithms with some advantageous features: they do not need to assume any *a priori* knowledge of the scene; and are computationally simpler (comparing to most non-intrinsic motion estimation algorithms), using mostly linear algebraic techniques. Tsai and Huang [18] then proved that, given an essential matrix associated with the Longuet-Higgins constraint, there are only two possible 3D displacements. The study of the essential matrix then led to a three-step SVD-based algorithm for recovering the 3D displacement from noisy image correspondences, proposed in 1986 by Toscani and Faugeras [17] and later summarized in Maybank [11].

Being motivated by recent interests in dynamical motion estimation schemes (Soatto, Frezza and Perona [14]) which usually require smoothness and regularity of the parameter space, the geometric property of the essential matrix space is further explored: the unit tangent bundle of the rotation group, *i.e.* $T_1(SO(3))$, is a double covering of the space of normalized essential matrices (full proofs are given in [9]).

However, the essential matrix approach based on the Longuet-Higgins constraint only recovers *discrete* 3D displacement. The velocity information can only be approximately obtained from the inverse of the exponential map, as Soatto *et al* did in [14]. In principle, the displacement estimation algorithms obtained by using epipolar constraints work well when the displacement (especially the translation) between the two images is relatively large. However, in real-time applications, even if the velocity of the moving camera is not small, the relative displacement between two consecutive images might become small due to a high sampling rate. In turn, the algorithms become singular due to the small translation and the estimation results become less reliable.

A differential (or continuous) version of the 3D motion estimation problem is to recover the 3D velocity of the camera from optical flow. This problem has also been explored by many researchers: an algorithm was proposed in 1984 by Zhuang *et al* [20] with a simplified version given in 1986 [21]; and a first order algorithm was given by Waxman *et al* [8] in 1987. Most of the algorithms start from the basic bilinear constraint relating optical flow to the linear and angular velocities and solve for rotation and translation separately using either numerical optimization techniques (Bruss and Horn [2]) or linear subspace methods (Heeger and Jepson [3,4]). Kanatani [5] proposed a linear algorithm reformulating Zhuang's approach in terms of essential parameters and twisted flow. However, in these algorithms, the similarities between the discrete case and the differential case are not fully revealed and exploited.

In this paper, we develop in parallel to the discrete essential matrix approach developed in the literature, as a review see Ma *et al* [9] or Maybank [11], a *differential essential matrix approach* for recovering 3D velocity from optical flow. Based on the differential version of the Longuet-Higgins constraint, so called *differential essential matrices* are defined. We then give a complete characterization of the space of these matrices and prove that there exists exactly one 3D velocity corresponding to a given differential essential matrix. As a differential counterpart of the three-step SVD-based 3D displacement estimation algorithm, a four-step eigenvector-decomposition-based 3D velocity estimation algorithm is proposed.

2 Discrete Essential Matrix Approach Review

We first introduce some notation which will be frequently used in this paper. Given a vector $p = (p_1, p_2, p_3)^T \in \mathbb{R}^3$, we define $\hat{p} \in so(3)$ (the space of skew symmetric matrices in $\mathbb{R}^{3 \times 3}$) by:

$$\hat{p} = \begin{pmatrix} 0 & -p_3 & p_2 \\ p_3 & 0 & -p_1 \\ -p_2 & p_1 & 0 \end{pmatrix}. \tag{1}$$

It then follows from the definition of cross product of vectors that, for any two vectors $p, q \in \mathbb{R}^3$: $p \times q = \hat{p}q$. The matrices of rotation by θ radians about y-axis and z-axis are respectively denoted by:

$$R_Y(\theta) = \begin{pmatrix} \cos(\theta) & 0 & \sin(\theta) \\ 0 & 1 & 0 \\ -\sin(\theta) & 0 & \cos(\theta) \end{pmatrix}, \quad R_Z(\theta) = \begin{pmatrix} \cos(\theta) & -\sin(\theta) & 0 \\ \sin(\theta) & \cos(\theta) & 0 \\ 0 & 0 & 1 \end{pmatrix}. \tag{2}$$

The camera motion can be modeled as a rigid body motion in $\mathbb{R}^3$. The displacement of the camera belongs to the special Euclidean group $SE(3)$:

$$SE(3) = \{(p, R) : p \in \mathbb{R}^3, R \in SO(3)\} \tag{3}$$

where $SO(3)$ is the space of 3×3 rotation matrices (unitary matrices with determinant $+1$) on $\mathbb{R}$. An element $g = (p, R)$ in this group is used to represent the 3D translation and orientation (the displacement) of a coordinate frame F_c attached to the camera relative to an inertial frame which is chosen here as the initial position of the camera frame F_o. By an abuse of notation, the element $g = (p, R)$ serves both as a specification of the configuration of the camera and as a transformation taking the coordinates of a point from F_c to F_o. More precisely, let $q_o, q_c \in \mathbb{R}^3$ be the coordinates of a point q relative to frames F_o and F_c, respectively. Then the coordinate transformation between q_o and q_c is given by:

$$q_o = Rq_c + p. \tag{4}$$

In this paper, we use bold letters to denote quantities associated with the image. The image of a point $q \in \mathbb{R}^3$ in the scene is then denoted by $\mathbf{q} \in \mathbb{R}^3$. As the model of image formation, we consider both *spherical projection* and *perspective projection*. For the spherical projection, we simply choose the imaging surface to be the unit sphere: $S^2 = \{q \in \mathbb{R}^3 : \|q\| = 1\}$, where the norm $\| \cdot \|$ always means 2-norm unless otherwise stated. Then the spherical projection is defined by the map π_s from $\mathbb{R}^3$ to S^2:

$$\pi_s : q \mapsto \mathbf{q} = \frac{q}{\|q\|}.$$

For the perspective projection, the imaging surface is chosen to be the plane of unit distance away from the optical center. The perspective projection onto this plane is then defined by the map π_p from $\mathbb{R}^3$ to the projective plane $\mathbb{RP}^2 \subset \mathbb{R}^3$:

$$\pi_p : q = (q_1, q_2, q_3)^T \mapsto \mathbf{q} = (\frac{q_1}{q_3}, \frac{q_2}{q_3}, 1)^T.$$

The approach taken in this paper only exploits the intrinsic geometric relations which are preserved by both projection models. Thus, theorems and algorithms to be developed are true for both cases. We simply denote both π_s and π_p by the same letter π. The image of the point q taken by the camera at the initial position then is $\mathbf{q}_o = \pi(q_o)$, and the image of the same point taken at the current position is $\mathbf{q}_c = \pi(q_c)$. The two corresponding image points $\mathbf{q}_o$ and $\mathbf{q}_c$ have to satisfy an intrinsic geometric constraint, the so-called *Longuet-Higgins* or *epipolar constraint* [7]:

$$\mathbf{q}_c^T R^T \hat{p} \mathbf{q}_o \equiv 0. \tag{5}$$

The matrices which have the form $E = R^T \hat{p}$ with $R \in SO(3)$ and $\hat{p} \in so(3)$ play an important role in recovering the displacement (p, R). Such matrices are called *essential matrices*; and the set of all essential matrices is called the *essential space*, defined to be

$$\mathcal{E} = \{RS \mid R \in SO(3), S \in so(3)\}. \tag{6}$$

The following theorem is a stronger version of Huang and Faugeras' theorem and gives a characterization of the essential space:

Theorem 1. (Characterization of the Essential Matrix)
A non-zero matrix E is an essential matrix if and only if the singular value decomposition (SVD) of E: $E = U\Sigma V^T$ satisfies: $\Sigma = diag\{\lambda, \lambda, 0\}$ for some $\lambda > 0$ and $U, V \in SO(3)$.

The condition $U, V \in SO(3)$ was not in the original theorem given by Huang or Faugeras, but it is convenient for the following theorem which shows how to explicitly recover the displacement from an essential matrix. One may refer to the full paper [9] for the proof of this extra condition.

Theorem 2. (Uniqueness of the Displacement Recovery from the Essential Matrix)
There exist exactly two 3D displacements $g = (p, R) \in SE(3)$ corresponding to a non-zero essential matrix $E \in \mathcal{E}$. Further, given the SVD of the matrix $E = U\Sigma V^T$, the two displacements (p, R) that solve $E = R^T\hat{p}$ are given by:

$$(R_1^T, \hat{p}_1) = (UR_z^T(+\frac{\pi}{2})V^T, VR_z(+\frac{\pi}{2})\Sigma V^T)$$
$$(R_2^T, \hat{p}_2) = (UR_z^T(-\frac{\pi}{2})V^T, VR_z(-\frac{\pi}{2})\Sigma V^T). \tag{7}$$

This theorem is a summary of results presented in [18, 14]. A rigorous proof of this theorem is given in [9]. A natural consequence of Theorem 1 and 2 is the three-step SVD-based displacement estimation algorithm proposed by Toscani and Faugeras [17], which is summarized in [11] or [9].

Motivated by recent interests in dynamic (or recursive) motion estimation schemes [14], differential geometric properties of the essential space $\mathcal{E}$ have been explored. Since the Longuet-Higgins condition is an homogeneous constraint, the essential matrix E can only be recovered up to a scale factor. It is then customary to set the norm of the translation vector p to be 1. Thus the normalized essential space, defined to be

$$\mathcal{E}_1 = \{RS \mid R \in SO(3), S = \hat{p}, \|p\| = 1\}, \tag{8}$$

is of particular interest in motion estimation algorithms.

Theorem 3. (Characterization of the Normalized Essential Space)
The unit tangent bundle of the rotation group $SO(3)$, i.e. $T_1(SO(3))$, is a double covering of the normalized essential space $\mathcal{E}_1$, or equivalently speaking, $\mathcal{E}_1 = T_1(SO(3))/\mathbb{Z}_2$.

The proof of this theorem, as well as a more detailed differential geometric characterization of the normalized essential space is given in [9]. As a consequence of this theorem, the normalized essential space $\mathcal{E}_1$ is a 5-dimensional connected compact manifold embedded in $\mathbb{R}^{3\times3}$. This property validates estimation algorithms which require certain smoothness and regularity on the parameter space, as dynamic algorithms usually do.

3 Differential Essential Matrix Approach

The differential case is the infinitesimal version of the discrete case. To reveal the similarities between these two cases, we now develop the *differential essential matrix approach* for estimating 3D velocity from optical flow in a parallel way as developed in the literature for the discrete essential matrix approach for estimating 3D displacement from image correspondences [9, 11]. After deriving a differential version of the Longuet-Higgins constraint, the concept of differential essential matrix is defined; we then give a thorough characterization for such matrices and show that there exists exactly one 3D velocity corresponding to a non-zero differential essential matrix; as a differential version of the three-step SVD-based 3D displacement estimation algorithm [11], a four-step eigenvector-decomposition-based 3D velocity estimation algorithm is proposed.

3.1 Differential Longuet-Higgins Constraint

Suppose the motion of the camera is described by a smooth curve $g(t) = (p(t), R(t)) \in SE(3)$. According to (4), for a point q attached to the inertial frame F_o, its coordinates in the inertial frame and the moving camera frame satisfy: $q_o = R(t)q_c(t) + p(t)$. Differentiating this equation yields: $\dot{q}_c = -R^T \dot{R} q_c - R^T \dot{p}$.

Since $-R^T \dot{R} \in so(3)$ and $-R^T \dot{p} \in \mathbb{R}^3$ (see Murray, Li and Sastry [13]), we may define $\omega = (\omega_1, \omega_2, \omega_3)^T \in \mathbb{R}^3$ and $v = (v_1, v_2, v_3)^T \in \mathbb{R}^3$ to be:

$$\hat{\omega} = -R^T \dot{R}, \quad v = -R^T \dot{p}. \tag{9}$$

The interpretation of these velocities is: $-\omega$ is the angular velocity of the camera frame F_c relative to the inertial frame F_i and $-v$ is the velocity of the origin of the camera frame F_c relative to the inertial frame F_i. Using the new notation, we get:

$$\dot{q}_c = \hat{\omega} q_c + v. \tag{10}$$

From now on, for convenience we will drop the subscript c from q_c. The notation q then serves both as a point fixed in the spatial frame and its coordinates with respect to the current camera frame F_c. The image of the point q taken by the camera is given by projection: $\mathbf{q} = \pi(q)$, and it's optical flow $\mathbf{u}$, $\mathbf{u} = \dot{\mathbf{q}} \in \mathbb{R}^3$. The following is the differential version of the Longuet-Higgins constraint, which has been independently referenced and used by many people in computer vision.

Theorem 4. (Differential Longuet-Higgins Constraint)
Consider a camera moving with linear velocity v and angular velocity ω with respect to the inertial frame. Then the optical flow $\mathbf{u}$ at an image point $\mathbf{q}$ satisfies:

$$(\mathbf{u}^T, \mathbf{q}^T) \begin{pmatrix} \hat{v} \\ s \end{pmatrix} \mathbf{q} = 0 \tag{11}$$

where s is a symmetric matrix defined by $s := \frac{1}{2}(\hat{\omega}\hat{v} + \hat{v}\hat{\omega}) \in \mathbb{R}^{3 \times 3}$.

Proof. From the definition of the map π's, there exists a real scalar function $\lambda(t)$ ($\|q(t)\|$ or $q_3(t)$, depending on whether the projection is spherical or perspective) such that: $q = \lambda \mathbf{q}$. Take the inner product of the vectors in (10) with $(v \times \mathbf{q})$:

$$\dot{q}^T (v \times \mathbf{q}) = (\hat{\omega} q + v)^T (v \times \mathbf{q}) = q^T \hat{\omega}^T \hat{v} \mathbf{q}. \tag{12}$$

Since $\dot{q} = \dot{\lambda} \mathbf{q} + \lambda \dot{\mathbf{q}}$ and $\mathbf{q}^T (v \times \mathbf{q}) = 0$, from (12) we then have: $\lambda \dot{\mathbf{q}}^T \hat{v} \mathbf{q} - \lambda \mathbf{q}^T \hat{\omega}^T \hat{v} \mathbf{q} = 0$. When $\lambda \neq 0$, we have: $\mathbf{u}^T \hat{v} \mathbf{q} + \mathbf{q}^T \hat{\omega} \hat{v} \mathbf{q} \equiv 0$. For any skew symmetric matrix $A \in \mathbb{R}^{3 \times 3}$, $\mathbf{q}^T A \mathbf{q} = 0$. Since $\frac{1}{2}(\hat{\omega} \hat{v} - \hat{v} \hat{\omega})$ is a skew symmetric matrix, $\mathbf{q}^T \frac{1}{2}(\hat{\omega} \hat{v} - \hat{v} \hat{\omega}) \mathbf{q} = \mathbf{q}^T s \mathbf{q} - \mathbf{q}^T \hat{\omega} \hat{v} \mathbf{q} = 0$. Thus, $\mathbf{q}^T s \mathbf{q} = \mathbf{q}^T \hat{\omega} \hat{v} \mathbf{q}$. We then have: $\mathbf{u}^T \hat{v} \mathbf{q} + \mathbf{q}^T s \mathbf{q} \equiv 0$.

3.2 Characterization of the Differential Essential Matrix

We define the space of 6×3 matrices given by:

$$\mathcal{E}' = \left\{ \begin{pmatrix} \hat{v} \\ \frac{1}{2}(\hat{\omega} \hat{v} + \hat{v} \hat{\omega}) \end{pmatrix} \middle| \omega, v \in \mathbb{R}^3 \right\} \subset \mathbb{R}^{6 \times 3}. \tag{13}$$

to be the *differential essential space*. A matrix in this space is called a *differential essential matrix*. Note that the differential Longuet-Higgins constraint (11) is homogeneous in the linear velocity v. Thus v may be recovered only up to a constant scale. Consequently, in motion recovery, we will concern ourselves with matrices belonging to *normalized differential essential space*:

$$\mathcal{E}'_1 = \left\{ \begin{pmatrix} \hat{v} \\ \frac{1}{2}(\hat{\omega} \hat{v} + \hat{v} \hat{\omega}) \end{pmatrix} \middle| \omega \in \mathbb{R}^3, v \in S^2 \right\} \subset \mathbb{R}^{6 \times 3}. \tag{14}$$

The skew-symmetric part $\hat{v}$ of a differential essential matrix simply corresponds to the velocity v. The characterization of the (normalized) essential matrix only focuses on the characterization of the symmetric part of the matrix: $s = \frac{1}{2}(\hat{\omega} \hat{v} + \hat{v} \hat{\omega})$. We call the space of all the matrices of such form the *special symmetric space*:

$$\mathcal{S} = \left\{ \frac{1}{2}(\hat{\omega} \hat{v} + \hat{v} \hat{\omega}) \middle| \omega \in \mathbb{R}^3, v \in S^2 \right\} \subset \mathbb{R}^{3 \times 3}. \tag{15}$$

A matrix in this space is called a *special symmetric matrix*. The motion estimation problem is now reduced to the one of *recovering the velocity* (ω, v) *with* $\omega \in \mathbb{R}^3$ *and* $v \in S^2$ *from a given special symmetric matrix* s.

The characterization of special symmetric matrices depends on a characterization of matrices in the form: $\hat{\omega} \hat{v} \in \mathbb{R}^{3 \times 3}$, which is given in the following lemma. This lemma will also be used in the next section to prove the uniqueness of the velocity recovery from special symmetric matrices. Like the (discrete) essential matrices, matrices with the form $\hat{\omega} \hat{v}$ are characterized by their singular value decomposition (SVD): $\hat{\omega} \hat{v} = U \Sigma V^T$, and moreover, the unitary matrices U and V are related.

Lemma 1. *A matrix $Q \in \mathbb{R}^{3 \times 3}$ has the form $Q = \hat{\omega}\hat{v}$ with $\omega \in \mathbb{R}^3$, $v \in S^2$ if and only if the SVD of Q has the form:*

$$Q = -V R_Y(\theta) diag\{\lambda, \lambda \cos(\theta), 0\} V^T \tag{16}$$

for some rotation matrix $V \in SO(3)$. Further, $\lambda = \|\omega\|$ and $\cos(\theta) = \omega^T v / \lambda$.

Proof. We first prove the necessity. The proof follows from the geometric meaning of $\hat{\omega}\hat{v}$: for any vector $q \in \mathbb{R}^3$, $\hat{\omega}\hat{v}q = \omega \times (v \times q)$. Let $b \in S^2$ be the unit vector perpendicular to both ω and v: $b = \frac{v \times \omega}{\|v \times \omega\|}$ (if $v \times \omega = 0$, b is not uniquely defined. In this case, pick any b orthogonal to v and ω, then the rest of the proof still holds). Then $\omega = \lambda e^{\hat{b}\theta} v$ for some $\lambda \in \mathbb{R}_+$ and $\theta \in \mathbb{R}$ (according this definition, λ is the length of ω; θ is the angle between ω and v, and $0 \le \theta \le \pi$). It is direct to check that if the matrix V is defined to be: $V = (e^{\hat{b}\frac{\pi}{2}}v, b, v)$. Q has the form given by (16).

We now prove the sufficiency. Given a matrix Q which can be decomposed in the form (16), define the unitary matrix $U = -V R_Y(\theta) \in O(3)$. For matrix $\Sigma_\sigma = diag\{\sigma, \sigma, 0\}$ with $\sigma \in \mathbb{R}$, it is direct to check that matrices $R_Z(+\frac{\pi}{2})\Sigma_\sigma$ and $R_Z(-\frac{\pi}{2})\Sigma_\sigma$ are skew matrices. So $W R_Z(\pm\frac{\pi}{2})\Sigma_\sigma W^T$ are also skew for any $W \in O(3)$. Let $\hat{\omega}$ and $\hat{v}$ given by the formulae:

$$\hat{\omega} = U R_Z(\pm\frac{\pi}{2})\Sigma_\lambda U^T, \quad \hat{v} = V R_Z(\pm\frac{\pi}{2})\Sigma_1 V^T \tag{17}$$

where $\Sigma_\lambda = diag\{\lambda, \lambda, 0\}$ and $\Sigma_1 = diag\{1, 1, 0\}$. Then:

$$\hat{\omega}\hat{v} = U R_Z(\pm\frac{\pi}{2})\Sigma_\lambda U^T V R_Z(\pm\frac{\pi}{2})\Sigma_1 V^T = U R_Z(\pm\frac{\pi}{2})\Sigma_\lambda(-R_Y^T(\theta)) R_Z(\pm\frac{\pi}{2})\Sigma_1 V^T$$

$$= U diag\{\lambda, \lambda \cos(\theta), 0\} V^T = Q. \tag{18}$$

Since ω and v have to be, respectively, the left and the right zero eigenvectors of Q, the reconstruction given in (17) is unique.

The following theorem gives a characterization of the special symmetric matrix.

Theorem 5. (Characterization of the Special Symmetric Matrix)
A matrix $s \in \mathbb{R}^{3 \times 3}$ is a special symmetric matrix if and only if s can be diagonalized as $s = V \Sigma V^T$ with $V \in SO(3)$ and: $\Sigma = diag\{\sigma_1, \sigma_2, \sigma_3\}$, with $\sigma_1 \ge 0, \sigma_3 \le 0$ and $\sigma_2 = \sigma_1 + \sigma_3$.

Proof. We first prove the necessity. Suppose s is a special symmetric matrix, there exist $\omega \in \mathbb{R}^3$, $v \in S^2$ such that $s = \frac{1}{2}(\hat{\omega}\hat{v} + \hat{v}\hat{\omega})$. Since s is a symmetric matrix, it is diagonalizable, all its eigenvalues are real and all the eigenvectors are orthogonal to each other. It then suffices to check its eigenvalues satisfy the given conditions.

Let the unit vector b and the rotation matrix V be the same as in the proof of Lemma 1, so are θ and γ. Then according to Lemma 1:

$$\hat{\omega}\hat{v} = -V R_Y(\theta) diag\{\lambda, \lambda \cos(\theta), 0\} V^T.$$

Since $(\hat{\omega}\hat{v})^T = \hat{v}\hat{\omega}$, it yields

$$s = \frac{1}{2}V\left(-R_Y(\theta)diag\{\lambda, \lambda\cos(\theta), 0\} - diag\{\lambda, \lambda\cos(\theta), 0\}R_Y^T(\theta)\right)V^T.$$

Define the matrix $D(\lambda, \theta) \in \mathbb{R}^{3\times3}$ to be

$$D(\lambda, \theta) = -R_Y(\theta)diag\{\lambda, \lambda\cos(\theta), 0\} - diag\{\lambda, \lambda\cos(\theta), 0\}R_Y^T(\theta)$$
$$= \lambda\begin{pmatrix} -2\cos(\theta) & 0 & \sin(\theta) \\ 0 & -2\cos(\theta) & 0 \\ \sin(\theta) & 0 & 0 \end{pmatrix}. \tag{19}$$

Directly calculating its eigenvalues and eigenvectors, we obtain that

$$D(\lambda, \theta) = R_Y\left(\frac{\theta}{2} - \frac{\pi}{2}\right)$$
$$\times diag\{\lambda(1 - \cos(\theta)), -2\lambda\cos(\theta), \lambda(-1 - \cos(\theta))\}R_Y^T\left(\frac{\theta}{2} - \frac{\pi}{2}\right) \tag{20}$$

Thus $s = \frac{1}{2}VD(\lambda, \theta)V^T$ has eigenvalues:

$$\left\{\frac{1}{2}\lambda(1 - \cos(\theta)), \quad -\lambda\cos(\theta), \quad \frac{1}{2}\lambda(-1 - \cos(\theta))\right\}, \tag{21}$$

which satisfy the given conditions.

We now prove the sufficiency. Given $s = V_1 diag\{\sigma_1, \sigma_2, \sigma_3\}V_1^T$ with $\sigma_1 \geq 0, \sigma_3 \leq 0$ and $\sigma_2 = \sigma_1 + \sigma_3$ and $V_1^T \in SO(3)$, these three eigenvalues uniquely determine $\lambda, \theta \in \mathbb{R}$ such that the σ_i's have the form given in (21):

$$\begin{cases} \lambda = \sigma_1 - \sigma_3, & \lambda \geq 0 \\ \theta = \arccos(-\sigma_2/\lambda), & \theta \in [0, \pi] \end{cases}$$

Define a matrix $V \in SO(3)$ to be $V = V_1 R_Y^T\left(\frac{\theta}{2} - \frac{\pi}{2}\right)$. Then $s = \frac{1}{2}VD(\lambda, \theta)V^T$. According to Lemma 1, there exist vectors $v \in S^2$ and $\omega \in \mathbb{R}^3$ such that $\hat{\omega}\hat{v} = -VR_Y(\theta)diag\{\lambda, \lambda\cos(\theta), 0\}V^T$. Therefore, $\frac{1}{2}(\hat{\omega}\hat{v} + \hat{v}\hat{\omega}) = \frac{1}{2}VD(\lambda, \theta)V^T = s$.

3.3 Uniqueness of 3D Velocity Recovery from the Special Symmetric Matrix

Theorem 5 is given in Kanatani [6] as exercise 7.12. However, we are going to use this property and its constructive proof to propose a new motion recovery algorithm. This algorithm is based upon the following theorem whose proof explicitly gives all the possible ω's and v's which can be recovered from a special symmetric matrix.

Theorem 6. (Uniqueness of the Velocity Recovery from the Special Symmetric Matrix)
There exist exactly four 3D velocities (ω, v) with $\omega \in \mathbb{R}^3$ and $v \in S^2$ corresponding to a non-zero special symmetric matrix $s \in \mathcal{S}$.

Proof. Suppose (ω_1, v_1) and (ω_2, v_2) are both solutions for $s = \frac{1}{2}(\hat{\omega}\hat{v} + \hat{v}\hat{\omega})$, we have: $\hat{v}_1\hat{\omega}_1 + \hat{\omega}_1\hat{v}_1 = \hat{v}_2\hat{\omega}_2 + \hat{\omega}_2\hat{v}_2$. From Lemma 1, we may write:

$$\hat{\omega}_1\hat{v}_1 = -V_1 R_Y(\theta_1)diag\{\lambda_1, \lambda_1\cos(\theta_1), 0\}V_1^T$$
$$\hat{\omega}_2\hat{v}_2 = -V_2 R_Y(\theta_2)diag\{\lambda_2, \lambda_2\cos(\theta_2), 0\}V_2^T. \tag{22}$$

Let $W = V_1^T V_2 \in SO(3)$, then: $D(\lambda_1, \theta_1) = W D(\lambda_2, \theta_2)W^T$. Since both sides have the same eigenvalues, according to (20), we have: $\lambda_1 = \lambda_2, \theta_2 = \theta_1$. We then can denote both θ_1 and θ_2 by θ. It is direct to check that the only possible rotation matrix W which satisfies the preceding equation is given by $I_{3\times3}$ or:

$$\begin{pmatrix} -\cos(\theta) & 0 & \sin(\theta) \\ 0 & -1 & 0 \\ \sin(\theta) & 0 & \cos(\theta) \end{pmatrix} \quad or \quad \begin{pmatrix} \cos(\theta) & 0 & -\sin(\theta) \\ 0 & -1 & 0 \\ -\sin(\theta) & 0 & -\cos(\theta) \end{pmatrix}. \tag{23}$$

From the geometric meaning of V_1 and V_2, all the cases give either $\hat{\omega}_1\hat{v}_1 = \hat{\omega}_2\hat{v}_2$ or $\hat{\omega}_1\hat{v}_1 = \hat{v}_2\hat{\omega}_2$. Thus, according to the proof of Lemma 1, if (ω, v) is one solution and $\hat{\omega}\hat{v} = U diag\{\lambda, \lambda\cos(\theta), 0\}V^T$, then all the solutions are given by:

$$\hat{\omega} = UR_Z(\pm\frac{\pi}{2})\Sigma_\lambda U^T, \quad \hat{v} = VR_Z(\pm\frac{\pi}{2})\Sigma_1 V^T;$$
$$\hat{\omega} = VR_Z(\pm\frac{\pi}{2})\Sigma_\lambda V^T, \quad \hat{v} = UR_Z(\pm\frac{\pi}{2})\Sigma_1 U^T \tag{24}$$

where $\Sigma_\lambda = diag\{\lambda, \lambda, 0\}$ and $\Sigma_1 = diag\{1, 1, 0\}$.

Given a non-zero differential essential matrix $E \in \mathcal{E}'$, its special symmetric part gives four possible solutions for the 3D velocity (ω, v). However, only one of them has the same linear velocity v as the skew-symmetric part of E does. We thus have:

Theorem 7. (Uniqueness of Velocity Recovery from the Differential Essential Matrix)
There exists only one 3D velocity (ω, v) with $\omega \in \mathbb{R}^3$ and $v \in \mathbb{R}^3$ corresponding to a non-zero differential essential matrix $E \in \mathcal{E}'$.

In the discrete case, there are two 3D displacements corresponding to an essential matrix. However, the velocity corresponding to a differential essential matrix is unique. This is because, in the differential case, the twist-pair ambiguity (see Maybank [11]), which is caused by a 180° rotation of the camera around the translation direction, is avoided.

It is clear that the normalized differential essential space $\mathcal{E}'_1$ is a 5-dimensional differentiable submanifold embedded in $\mathbb{R}^{6\times3}$. Further considering the symmetric and anti-symmetric structures in the differential essential matrix, the embedding space can be naturally reduced from $\mathbb{R}^{6\times3}$ to $\mathbb{R}^9$. This property is useful when using estimation schemes which require some regularity on the parameter space, for example, the dynamic estimation scheme proposed by Soatto *et al* [14].

3.4 Algorithm

Based on the previous study of the differential essential matrix, in this section, we propose an algorithm which recovers the 3D velocity of the camera from a set of (possibly noisy) optical flow vectors.

Let $E = \begin{pmatrix} \hat{v} \\ s \end{pmatrix} \in \mathcal{E}_1'$ with $s = \frac{1}{2}(\hat{\omega}\hat{v} + \hat{v}\hat{\omega})$ be the essential matrix associated with the differential Longuet-Higgins constraint (11). Since the submatrix $\hat{v}$ is skew symmetric and s is symmetric, they have the following forms:

$$v = \begin{pmatrix} 0 & -v_3 & v_2 \\ v_3 & 0 & -v_1 \\ -v_2 & v_1 & 0 \end{pmatrix}, \quad s = \begin{pmatrix} s_1 & s_2 & s_3 \\ s_2 & s_4 & s_5 \\ s_3 & s_5 & s_6 \end{pmatrix}. \tag{25}$$

Define the (differential) *essential vector* $\mathbf{e} \in \mathbb{R}^9$ to be:

$$\mathbf{e} = (v_1, v_2, v_3, s_1, s_2, s_3, s_4, s_5, s_6)^T. \tag{26}$$

Define a vector $\mathbf{a} \in \mathbb{R}^9$ associated to optical flow $(\mathbf{q}, \mathbf{u})$ with $\mathbf{q} = (x, y, z)^T \in \mathbb{R}^3$, $\mathbf{u} = (u_1, u_2, u_3)^T \in \mathbb{R}^3$ to be[1]:

$$\mathbf{a} = (u_3 y - u_2 z, u_1 z - u_3 x, u_2 x - u_1 y, x^2, 2xy, 2xz, y^2, 2yz, z^2)^T. \tag{27}$$

The differential Longuet-Higgins constraint (11) can be then rewritten as: $\mathbf{a}^T \mathbf{e} = 0$. Given a set of (possibly noisy) optical flow vectors: $(\mathbf{q}^i, \mathbf{u}^i)$, $i = 1, \ldots, m$ generated by the same motion, define a matrix $A \in \mathbb{R}^{m \times 9}$ associated with these measurements to be: $A = (\mathbf{a}^1, \mathbf{a}^2, \ldots, \mathbf{a}^m)^T$, where $\mathbf{a}^i$ are defined for each pair $(\mathbf{q}^i, \mathbf{u}^i)$ using (27). In the absence of noise, the essential vector $\mathbf{e}$ has to satisfy: $A\mathbf{e} = 0$. In order for this equation to have a unique solution for $\mathbf{e}$, the rank of the matrix A has to be eight. Thus, *for this algorithm, in general, the optical flow vectors of at least eight points are needed to recover the 3D velocity, i.e. $m \geq 8$*, although the minimum number of optical flows needed is 5 (see Maybank [11]).

When the measurements are noisy, there might be no solution of $\mathbf{e}$ for $A\mathbf{e} = 0$. As in the discrete case, we choose the solution which minimizes the error function $\|A\mathbf{e}\|^2$. This can be mechanized using the following lemma. It is straight forward to see that (Theorem 6.1 of Maybank [11]):

Lemma 2. *If a matrix $A \in \mathbb{R}^{n \times n}$ has the singular value decomposition $A = U\Sigma V^T$ and $c_n(V)$ is the nth column vector of V (the singular vector associated to the smallest singular value σ_n), then $\mathbf{e} = c_n(V)$ minimizes $\|A\mathbf{e}\|^2$ subject to the condition $\|\mathbf{e}\| = 1$.*

Since the differential essential vector $\mathbf{e}$ is recovered from noisy measurements, the symmetric part s of E directly recovered from $\mathbf{e}$ is not necessarily a special symmetric matrix. Thus one can not directly use the previously derived results for special symmetric matrices to recover the 3D velocity. In the algorithms

---

[1] For perspective projection, $z = 1$ and $u_3 = 0$ thus the expression for $\mathbf{a}$ can be simplified.

proposed in Zhuang [20, 21], such s, with the linear velocity v obtained from the skew-symmetric part, is directly used to calculate the angular velocity ω. This is a over-determined problem since three variables are to be determined from six independent equations; on the other hand, erroneous v introduces further error in the estimation of the angular velocity ω.

We thus propose a different approach: first extract the special symmetric component from the first-hand symmetric matrix s; then recover the four possible solutions for the 3D velocity using the results obtained in Theorem 6; finally choose the one which has the closest linear velocity to the one given by the skew-symmetric part of E. In order to extract the special symmetric component out of a symmetric matrix, we need a projection from the space of all symmetric matrices to the special symmetric space $\mathcal{S}$.

Theorem 8. (Projection to the Special Symmetric Space)
If a symmetric matrix $F \in \mathbb{R}^{3 \times 3}$ is diagonalized as $F = V diag\{\lambda_1, \lambda_2, \lambda_3\}V^T$ with $V \in SO(3)$, $\lambda_1 \geq 0, \lambda_3 \leq 0$ and $\lambda_1 \geq \lambda_2 \geq \lambda_3$, then the special symmetric matrix $E \in \mathcal{S}$ which minimizes the error $\|E - F\|_f^2$ is given by $E = V diag\{\sigma_1, \sigma_2, \sigma_2\}V^T$ with:

$$\sigma_1 = \frac{2\lambda_1 + \lambda_2 - \lambda_3}{3}, \quad \sigma_2 = \frac{\lambda_1 + 2\lambda_2 + \lambda_3}{3}, \quad \sigma_3 = \frac{2\lambda_3 + \lambda_2 - \lambda_1}{3}. \quad (28)$$

Proof. Define $\mathcal{S}_\Sigma$ to be the subspace of $\mathcal{S}$ whose elements have the same eigenvalues: $\Sigma = diag\{\sigma_1, \sigma_2, \sigma_3\}$ with $\sigma_1 \geq \sigma_2 \geq \sigma_3$. Thus every matrix $E \in \mathcal{S}_\Sigma$ has the form $E = V_1 \Sigma V_1^T$ for some $V_1 \in SO(3)$. To simplify the notation, define $\Sigma_\lambda = diag\{\lambda_1, \lambda_2, \lambda_3\}$. We now prove this theorem by two steps.

Step One: We prove that the special symmetric matrix $E \in \mathcal{S}_\Sigma$ which minimizes the error $\|E - F\|_f^2$ is given by $E = V\Sigma V^T$. Since $E \in \mathcal{S}_\Sigma$ has the form $E = V_1 \Sigma V_1^T$, we get:

$$\|E - F\|_f^2 = \|V_1 \Sigma V_1^T - V\Sigma_\lambda V^T\|_f^2 = \|\Sigma_\lambda - V^T V_1 \Sigma V_1^T V\|_f^2. \quad (29)$$

Define $W = V^T V_1 \in SO(3)$. Then:

$$\|E - F\|_f^2 = \|\Sigma_\lambda - W\Sigma W^T\|_f^2 = tr(\Sigma_\lambda^2) - 2tr(W\Sigma W^T \Sigma_\lambda) + tr(\Sigma^2). \quad (30)$$

Using the fact that $\sigma_2 = \sigma_1 + \sigma_3$ and W is a rotation matrix, we get:

$$tr(W\Sigma W^T \Sigma_\lambda) = \sigma_1(\lambda_1(1 - w_{13}^2) + \lambda_2(1 - w_{23}^2) + \lambda_3(1 - w_{33}^2))$$
$$+ \sigma_3(\lambda_1(1 - w_{11}^2) + \lambda_2(1 - w_{21}^2) + \lambda_3(1 - w_{31}^2)). \quad (31)$$

Minimizing $\|E - F\|_f^2$ is equivalent to maximizing $tr(W\Sigma W^T \Sigma_\lambda)$. From (31), $tr(W\Sigma W^T \Sigma_\lambda)$ is maximized if and only if $w_{13} = w_{23} = 0$, $w_{33}^2 = 1$, $w_{21} = w_{31} = 0$ and $w_{11}^2 = 1$. Since W is a rotation matrix, we also have $w_{12} = w_{32} = 0$ and $w_{22}^2 = 1$. All possible W give a unique matrix in $\mathcal{S}_\Sigma$ which minimizes $\|E - F\|_f^2$: $E = V\Sigma V^T$.

Step Two: From step one, we only need to minimize the error function over the matrices which have the form $V \Sigma V^T \in \mathcal{S}$. The optimization problem is then converted to one of minimizing the error function:

$$\|E - F\|_f^2 = (\lambda_1 - \sigma_1)^2 + (\lambda_2 - \sigma_2)^2 + (\lambda_3 - \sigma_3)^2 \tag{32}$$

subject to the constraint: $\sigma_2 = \sigma_1 + \sigma_3$. The formula (28) for $\sigma_1, \sigma_2, \sigma_3$ are directly obtained from solving this minimization problem.

An important property of this projection is that it is statistically unbiased [9]. That is, if components of the essential vector e are corrupted by identically independent (symmetric) zero-mean noise, this projection gives an unbiased estimate of the true special symmetric matrix.

Remark 1. For symmetric matrices which do not satisfy conditions $\lambda_1 \geq 0$ or $\lambda_3 \leq 0$, one may simply choose $\lambda_1' = max(\lambda_1, 0)$ or $\lambda_3' = min(\lambda_3, 0)$.

We then have an eigenvector-decomposition based algorithm for estimating 3D velocity from optical flow:

Four-Step 3D Velocity Estimation Algorithm:

1. **Estimate Essential Vector:** For a given set of optical flows: $(\mathbf{q}^i, \mathbf{u}^i)$, $i = 1, \ldots, m$, find the vector e which minimizes the error function $V(\mathbf{e}) = \|A\mathbf{e}\|^2$ subject to the condition $\|\mathbf{e}\| = 1$;
2. **Recover the Special Symmetric Matrix:** Recover the vector $v_0 \in S^2$ from the first three entries of e and the symmetric matrix $s \in \mathbb{R}^{3 \times 3}$ from the remaining six entries.[2] Find the eigenvalue decomposition of the symmetric matrix $s = V_1 diag\{\lambda_1, \lambda_2, \lambda_3\} V_1^T$ with $\lambda_1 \geq \lambda_2 \geq \lambda_3$. Project the symmetric matrix s onto the special symmetric space $\mathcal{S}$. We then have the new $s = V_1 diag\{\sigma_1, \sigma_2, \sigma_3\} V_1^T$ with: $\sigma_1 = (2\lambda_1 + \lambda_2 - \lambda_3)/3$, $\sigma_2 = (\lambda_1 + 2\lambda_2 + \lambda_3)/3$, and $\sigma_3 = (2\lambda_3 + \lambda_2 - \lambda_1)/3$.
3. **Recover Velocity from the Special Symmetric Matrix:** Define $\lambda = \sigma_1 - \sigma_3 \geq 0$ and $\theta = \arccos(-\sigma_2/\lambda) \in [0, \pi]$. Let $V = V_1 R_Y^T \left(\frac{\theta}{2} - \frac{\pi}{2}\right) \in SO(3)$ and $U = -V R_Y(\theta) \in O(3)$. Then the four possible 3D velocities corresponding to the special symmetric matrix s are given by:

$$\hat{\omega} = U R_Z(\pm\frac{\pi}{2})\Sigma_\lambda U^T, \quad \hat{v} = V R_Z(\pm\frac{\pi}{2})\Sigma_1 V^T$$

$$\hat{\omega} = V R_Z(\pm\frac{\pi}{2})\Sigma_\lambda V^T, \quad \hat{v} = U R_Z(\pm\frac{\pi}{2})\Sigma_1 U^T \tag{33}$$

where $\Sigma_\lambda = diag\{\lambda, \lambda, 0\}$ and $\Sigma_1 = diag\{1, 1, 0\}$;
4. **Recover Velocity from the Differential Essential Matrix:** From the four velocities recovered from the special symmetric matrix s in step 3, choose the pair (ω^*, v^*) which satisfies: $v^{*T} v_0 = max_i\, v_i^T v_0$. Then the estimated 3D velocity (ω, v) with $\omega \in \mathbb{R}^3$ and $v \in S^2$ is given by: $\omega = \omega^*, v = v_0$.

---

[2] In order to guarantee v_0 to be of unit length, one needs to "re-normalize" e, *i.e.* multiply e by a scalar such that the vector determined by the first three entries is of unit length.

Both v_0 and v^* contain recovered information about the linear velocity. However, experimental results show that, statistically, within the tested noise levels (next section), v_0 always yields a better estimate than v^*. We thus simply choose v_0 as the estimate. Nonetheless, one can find statistical correlations between v_0 and v^* (experimentally or analytically) and obtain better estimate, using both v_0 and v^*. Another potential way to improve this algorithm is to study the systematic bias introduced by the least square method in step 1. A similar problem has been studied by Kanatani [5] and an algorithm was proposed to remove such bias from Zhuang's algorithm [20].

Remark 2. Since both $E, -E \in \mathcal{E}_1'$ satisfy the same set of differential Longuet-Higgins constraints, both $(\omega, \pm v)$ are possible solutions for the given set of optical flows. However, one can discard the ambiguous solution by adding the "positive depth constraint".

Remark 3. By the way of comparison to the Heeger and Jepson's algorithm [3], note that the equation $Ae = 0$ may be rewritten to highlight the dependence on optical flow as: $[A_1(\mathbf{u}) \mid A_2]e = 0$, where $A_1(\mathbf{u}) \in \mathbb{R}^{m \times 3}$ is a linear function of the measured optical flow and $A_2 \in \mathbb{R}^{m \times 6}$ is a function of the image points alone. Heeger and Jepson compute a left null space to the matrix A_2 ($C \in \mathbb{R}^{(m-6) \times m}$) and solve the equation: $CA_1(\mathbf{u})v = 0$ for v alone. Then they use v to obtain ω. Our method simultaneously estimates $v \in \mathbb{R}^3, s \in \mathbb{R}^6$. We make a simulation comparison of these two algorithms in section 4.

Note this algorithm is not optimal in the sense that the recovered velocity does not necessarily minimize the originally picked error function $\|Ae(\omega, v)\|^2$ on $\mathcal{E}_1'$ (same for the three-step SVD based algorithm in the discrete case [9]). However, this algorithm only uses linear algebra techniques and is thus simpler and does not try to optimize on the submanifold $\mathcal{E}_1'$.

4 Experimental Results

We carried out initial simulations in order to study the performance of our algorithm. We chose to evaluate it in terms of bias and sensitivity of the estimate with respect to the noise in the optical flow measurements. Preliminary simulations were carried out with perfect data which was corrupted by zero-mean Gaussian noise where the standard deviation was specified in terms of pixel size and was independent of velocity. The image size was considered to be 512x512 pixels.

Our algorithm has been implemented in Matlab and the simulations have been performed using example sets proposed by [15] in their paper on comparison of the egomotion estimation from optical flow[3]. The motion estimation was performed by observing the motion of a random cloud of points placed in front

---

[3] We would like to thank the authors in [15] for making the code for simulations of various algorithms and evaluation of their results available on the web.

of the camera. Depth range of the points varied from 2 to 8 units of the focal length, which was considered to be unity. The results presented below are for fixed field of view (FOV) of 60 degrees. Each simulation consisted of 500 trials with a fixed noise level, FOV and ratio between the image velocity due to translation and rotation for the point in the middle of the random cloud. Figures 1 and 2 compare our algorithm with Heeger and Jepson's linear subspace algorithm. The presented results demonstrate the performance of the algorithm while translating along X-axis and rotating around Z-axis with rate of $23°$ per frame. The analysis of the obtained results of the motion estimation algorithm was performed using benchmarks proposed by [15]. The bias is expressed as an angle between the average estimate out of all trails (for a given setting of parameters) and the true direction of translation and/or rotation. The sensitivity was computed as a standard deviation of the distribution of angles between each estimated vector and the average vector in case of translation and as a standard deviation of angular differences in case of rotation. We further evaluated the

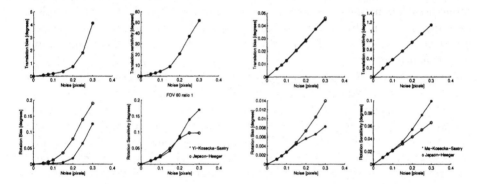

Fig. 1. The ratio between the magnitude of linear and angular velocity is 1.

Fig. 2. The ratio between the magnitude of linear and angular velocity is 10.

algorithm by varying the direction of translation and rotation and their relative speed. The choice of the rotation axis did not influence the translation estimates. In the case of the rotation estimate our algorithm is slightly better compared to Heeger and Jepson's algorithm. This is due to the fact that in our case the rotation is estimated simultaneously with the translation so its bias is only due to the bias of the initially estimated differential essential matrix obtained by linear least squares techniques. This is in contrary to the rotation estimate used by Jepson and Heeger's algorithm which uses another least-squares estimation by substituting already biased translational estimate to compute the rotation. The translational estimates are essentially the same since the translation was estimated out from v_0, skew symmetric part of the differential essential matrix. Increasing the ratio between magnitudes of translational and angular velocities improves the bias and sensitivity of both algorithms.

The evaluation of the results and more extensive simulations are currently underway. We believe that through thorough understanding of the source of translational bias we can obtain even better performance by utilizing additional information about linear velocity, which is embedded in the symmetric part of the differential essential matrix. In the current simulations translation was estimated only from v_0 skew symmetric part of **e**.

5 Conclusions and Future Work

This paper presents a unified view of the problem of egomotion estimation using discrete and differential Longuet-Higgins constraint. In both (discrete and differential) settings, the geometric characterization of the space of (differential) essential matrices gives a natural geometric interpretation for the number of possible solutions to the motion estimation problem. In addition, in the differential case, understanding of the space of differential essential matrices leads to a new egomotion estimation algorithm, which is a natural counterpart of the three-step SVD based algorithm developed for the discrete case by [17].

In order to exploit temporal coherence of motion and improve algorithm's robustness, a dynamic (recursive) motion estimation scheme, which uses implicit extended Kalman filter for estimating the essential parameters, has been proposed by Soatto *et al* [14] for the discrete case. The same ideas certainly apply to our algorithm.

In applications to robotics, a big advantage of the differential approach over the discrete one is that it can make use of nonholonomic constraints (*i.e.* constraints that confine the infinitesimal motion of the mobile base but not the global motion) and simplify the motion estimation algorithms [9]. An example study of vision guided nonholonomic system can be found in [10]. In this paper, we have assumed that the camera is ideal. This approach can be extended to uncalibrated camera case, where the motion estimation and camera self-calibration problem can be solved simultaneously, using the differential essential constraint [19,1]. In this case, the essential matrix is replaced by the fundamental matrix which captures both motion information and camera intrinsic parameters. It is shown in [1], that the space of such fundamental matrices is a 7-dimensional algebraic variety in $\mathbb{R}^{3\times3}$. Thus, besides five motion parameters, only two extra intrinsic parameters can be recovered.

References

1. Michael J. Brooks, Wojciech Chojnacki, and Luis Baumela. Determining the egomotion of an uncalibrated camera from instantaneous optical flow. *in press*, 1997.
2. A. R. Bruss and B. K. Horn. Passive navigation. *Computer Graphics and Image Processing*, 21:3–20, 1983.
3. D. J. Heeger and A. D. Jepson. Subspace methods for recovering rigid motion I: Algorithm and implementation. *International Journal of Computer Vision*, 7(2):95–117, 1992.
4. A. D. Jepson and D. J. Heeger. Linear subspace methods for recovering translation direction. *Spatial Vision in Humans and Robots, Cambridge Univ. Press*, pages 39–62, 1993.

5. K. Kanatani. 3D interpretation of optical flow by renormalization. *International Journal of Computer Vision*, 11(3):267–282, 1993.
6. Kenichi Kanatani. *Geometric Computation for Machine Vision*. Oxford Science Publications, 1993.
7. H. C. Longuet-Higgins. A computer algorithm for reconstructing a scene from two projections. *Nature*, 293:133–135, 1981.
8. Waxman A. M., Kamgar-Parsi B., and Subbarao M. Closed form solutions to image flow equations for 3d structure and motion. *International Journal of Computer Vision 1*, pages 239–258, 1987.
9. Yi Ma, Jana Košecká, and Shankar Sastry. Motion recovery from image sequences: Discrete viewpoint vs. differential viewpoint. *Electronic Research Laboratory Memorandum, UC Berkeley*, UCB/ERL, June 1997.
10. Yi Ma, Jana Košecká, and Shankar Sastry. Vision guided navigation for a nonholonomic mobile robot. *Electronic Research Laboratory Memorandum, UC Berkeley*, UCB/ERL(M97/42), June 1997.
11. Stephen Maybank. *Theory of Reconstruction from Image Motion*. Springer Series in Information Sciences. Springer-Verlag, 1993.
12. Philip F. McLauchlan and David W. Murray. A unifying framework for structure and motion recovery from image sequences. In *Proceeding of Fifth International Conference on Computer Vision*, pages 314–320, Cambridge, MA, USA, 1995. IEEE Comput. Soc. Press.
13. Richard M. Murray, Zexiang Li, and Shankar S. Sastry. *A Mathematical Introduction to Robotic Manipulation*. CRC press Inc., 1994.
14. S. Soatto, R. Frezza, and P. Perona. Motion estimation via dynamic vision. *IEEE Transactions on Automatic Control*, 41(3):393–413, March 1996.
15. T. Y. Tian, C. Tomasi, and D. J. Heeger. Comparison of approaches to egomotion computation. In *Proceedings of 1996 IEEE Computer Society Conference on Computer Vision and Pattern Recognition*, pages 315–20, Los Alamitos, CA, USA, 1996. IEEE Comput. Soc. Press.
16. Carlo Tomasi and Takeo Kanade. Shape and motion from image streams under orthography. *Intl. Journal of Computer Vision*, 9(2):137–154, 1992.
17. G. Toscani and O. D. Faugeras. Structure and motion from two noisy perspective images. *Proceedings of IEEE Conference on Robotics and Automation*, pages 221–227, 1986.
18. Roger Y. Tsai and Thomas S. Huang. Uniqueness and estimation of three-dimensional motion parameters of rigid objects with curved surfaces. *IEEE Transactions on Pattern Analysis and Machine Intelligence*, PAMI-6(1):13–27, January 1984.
19. T. Vieville and O. D. Faugeras. Motion analysis with a camera with unknown, and possibly varying intrinsic parameters. *Proceedings of Fifth International Conference on Computer Vision*, pages 750–756, June 1995.
20. Xinhua Zhuang and R. M. Haralick. Rigid body motion and optical flow image. *Proceedings of the First International Conference on Artificial Intelligence Applications*, pages 366–375, 1984.
21. Xinhua Zhuang, Thomas S. Huang, and Narendra Ahuja. A simplified linear optic flow-motion algorithm. *Computer Vision, Graphics and Image Processing*, 42:334–344, 1988.

Discrete Wavelet Analysis: A New Framework for Fast Optic Flow Computation

Christophe P. Bernard

Centre de Mathématiques Appliquées
École Polytechnique
91128 Palaiseau cedex, France
bernard@cmapx.polytechnique.fr

Abstract. This paper describes a new way to compute the optical flow based on a discrete wavelet basis analysis. This approach has thus a low complexity ($O(N)$ if one image of the sequence has N pixels) and opens the way to efficient and unexpensive optical flow computation. Features of this algorithm include multiscale treatment of time aliasing and estimation of illumination changes.

Keywords Analytic wavelets, Image compression, Optic flow, Illumination, Discrete wavelets.

1 Introduction

Optic flow detection consists in computing the motion field $\mathbf{v} = (v_1, v_2)$ of the features of an image sequence in the image plane. Applications range from moving image compression to real scene analysis and robotics.

Given an image sequence $I_t(x_1, x_2)$ we want to measure the optical flow $\mathbf{v} = (v_1, v_2)$ that matches the well known *optical flow equation*

$$I_{t+\delta t}(x_1 + v_1\delta t, x_2 + v_2\delta t) = I_t(x_1, x_2) \ , \tag{1}$$

or its differential counterpart

$$\frac{\partial I_t}{\partial x_1}v_1 + \frac{\partial I_t}{\partial x_2}v_2 + \frac{\partial I_t}{\partial t} = 0 \ . \tag{2}$$

No point-wise resolution of (2) is possible, since on each location and each time, this would consist in solving a single scalar equation for two scalar unknowns. This is the *aperture problem*.

1.1 Previous Work

Horn & Schunck [13] [14] wrote a pioneering paper on the subject in 1980. Then, several methods where proposed: region matching methods [2], differential methods [16] and spatiotemporal filtering methods [1] [6] [9] [11] [12], on which Barron & al. made an extensive review [3]. Later, Burns & al. developed a discrete wavelet spatiotemporal filtering technique [4], and Weber & Malik designed a filtered differential method [21].

In this profusion of methods, two points always arise:

Additional assumption The only way to get rid of aperture is to do an additional assumption on the optic flow, expressed or implied. Horn & Schunck minimize a smoothness functional; region based matching methods, and filtering based methods [2] [1] [6] [9] [11] [12] [4] [21] rely explicitly on the assumption that the optic flow is constant over quadrangular domains.

Multiscale approach Because of *time aliasing*, the optic flow measurement must be performed on a multi-scale basis. Coarse scales for detection of large displacements and finer scales for smaller displacements.

1.2 Motivation

This work was motivated by the belief that wavelet bases, as described by Ingrid Daubechies [7] Stéphane Mallat [17] are a very well designed tool for our purpose for several reasons:

- Wavelet bases have a natural multiscale structure;
- As a local frequency analysis tool, wavelet analysis compares favorably to filtering (as used in [1] [6] [9] [11] [12] [21]) because it is far less computation intensive, and still provides a complete information on this signal;
- With the additional assumption that the optic flow is locally constant, they provide an easy way to solve the aperture problem.

1.3 Road Map

In Sect. 2, we show how we solve the aperture problem. Section 3 is devoted to numerical experimentation. Time aliasing problems are addressed in Sect. 4, and Sect. 5–6 respectively focus on stability enhancement with analytic wavelets, and to the design of dyadic filter bank wavelets that are specific to the optic flow measurement, and are a key point in achieving these measurements in a short time.

2 Suggested Solution

2.1 Wavelet Notations

We start from a set of mother wavelets $(\psi^s)_{s=1...S}$ in $L_2(\mathbb{R}^2)$. We then define a discrete wavelet family $(\psi_{j\mathbf{k}}^s)_{s=1...S, j \in \mathbb{Z}, \mathbf{k} \in \mathbb{Z}^2}$ by

$$\psi_{j\mathbf{k}}^s(\mathbf{x}) = 2^j \psi^s(2^j \mathbf{x} - \mathbf{k})$$

where j is a resolution index and $\mathbf{k} = (k_1, k_2)$ a 2-dimensional translation index, and $\mathbf{x}$ a 2-dimensional variable $\mathbf{x} = (x_1, x_2)$.

EXAMPLE —In image processing, a set of three mother wavelets is commonly used. These wavelets are built as tensor products of a scaling function $\phi \in L_2(\mathbb{R})$ and a wavelet $\psi \in L_2(\mathbb{R})$:

$$\psi^1(\mathbf{x}) = \psi(x_1)\phi(x_2) \tag{3}$$
$$\psi^2(\mathbf{x}) = \phi(x_1)\psi(x_2) \tag{4}$$
$$\psi^3(\mathbf{x}) = \psi(x_1)\psi(x_2) \tag{5}$$

Note that a wavelet $\psi_{j\mathbf{k}}^s$ is located around $(2^{-j}k_1, 2^{-j}k_2)$, and spreads over domain of size proportional to 2^{-j}.

2.2 Local Systems

Given such a basis, we do an inner product of (2) with all the S different wavelets that we have at scale j and location $\mathbf{k}$, getting thus S different equations.

$$\iint \left(\frac{\partial I_t}{\partial x_1} v_1(\mathbf{x}) + \frac{\partial I_t}{\partial x_2} v_2(\mathbf{x}) + \frac{\partial I_t}{\partial t} \right) \psi_{j\mathbf{k}}^s(\mathbf{x}) dx_1 dx_2 = 0 \quad \forall s = 1\ldots S \tag{6}$$

Using the notation $< f, g >= \iint f(\mathbf{x})g(\mathbf{x})dx_1 dx_2$, this can also be written as

$$\left\langle \frac{\partial I_t}{\partial x_1} v_1, \psi_{j\mathbf{k}}^s \right\rangle + \left\langle \frac{\partial I_t}{\partial x_2} v_2, \psi_{j\mathbf{k}}^s \right\rangle + \left\langle \frac{\partial I_t}{\partial t}, \psi_{j\mathbf{k}}^s \right\rangle = 0 \quad \forall s = 1\ldots S \tag{7}$$

For a given resolution j and translation index $\mathbf{k}$, we do the following assumption:

$(A_{j\mathbf{k}})$: $v_1(\mathbf{x})$ and $v_2(\mathbf{x})$ are constant over support[1] $(\psi_{j\mathbf{k}}^s)$ for all $s = 1..S$

Equation (7) then becomes

$$\left\langle \frac{\partial I_t}{\partial x_1}, \psi_{j\mathbf{k}}^s \right\rangle v_1 + \left\langle \frac{\partial I_t}{\partial x_2}, \psi_{j\mathbf{k}}^s \right\rangle v_2 + \frac{\partial}{\partial t} \left\langle I_t, \psi_{j\mathbf{k}}^s \right\rangle = 0 \quad \forall s = 1\ldots S$$

and after an integration by parts

$$\boxed{\left\langle I_t, \frac{\partial \psi_{j\mathbf{k}}^s}{\partial x_1} \right\rangle v_1 + \left\langle I_t, \frac{\partial \psi_{j\mathbf{k}}^s}{\partial x_2} \right\rangle v_2 = \frac{\partial}{\partial t} \left\langle I_t, \psi_{j\mathbf{k}}^s \right\rangle} \quad \forall s = 1\ldots S \ . \tag{8}$$

For j and $\mathbf{k}$ fixed, we have a *local system* of 3 equations with 2 unknowns v_1 and v_2, that has to be compared to the single equation (2): now we have found a way around aperture.

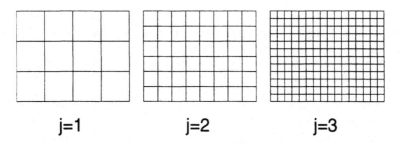

Fig. 1. Measure grids at several scales

2.3 Solving the Local Systems

For some scale indexes $j = 1, 2, 3$, the corresponding discrete grids $\{2^{-j}(k_1, k_2)\}$ are displayed in Fig. 1. At each node of each of these, we have a local system (8).

A question arises: what grid should we choose for our optic flow measurement? The answer depends on several factors.
— Arguments towards finer scale grids are (1) that we get a finer knowledge of the space dependence of the optic flow and (2) that the needed assumptions on the optic flow $\mathcal{A}_{j\mathbf{k}}$ are looser when the scale is finer.
— However, there is a strong argument against going towards finer scales: time aliasing (see Sect. 4). Time aliasing limits reliable estimation of the flow at a given scale j to flows that are smaller than $\alpha 2^{-j}$, where α is some constant of $[0, 1/2)$.

2.4 Adaptive Choice of the Measure Scale

The time aliasing limitation making fine scale measurements unreliable, we will start with coarse scale measures and then refine our measure. The behavior of a local system at a given scale j and location $2^{-j}(k_1, k_2)$ hints us whether at a given location, we stick at the current scale, or we use finer scale estimation.

1. If the system has a unique solution (v_1, v_2), we get a straightforward estimation of the optic flow at $2^{-j}\mathbf{k}$. Thus the measure scale j is suitable.
2. If the system has no solution, it means that our assumption $\mathcal{A}_{j\mathbf{k}}$ is incorrect. In such a case, we try to do finer scale measurements, since they rely on looser assumptions $\mathcal{A}_{j+1,\mathbf{k}'}$.

   If for example our measure region overlaps two regions where the flow is different, we have to split our measure region in subregions, to perform again this measure on each of these subregions, where hopefully the optic flow is locally constant.

---

[1] For the simplicity of our statement, we will consider the interval where most of the $L_2(\mathbb{R})$–energy of the wavelets is concentrated, and suppose that this support is $2^{-j}\mathbf{k} + [-2^{-j-1}; 2^{-j-1}]^2$.

3. If on the contrary, the system has infinitely many solutions, this means that the pattern at the location we are looking at is too poor to tell us how it is moving. The aperture problem remains.

   A typical case is a locally translation invariant pattern, because then it is impossible to measure its translation along his translation invariance axis.

As a safeguard against errors induced by time aliasing, we add two tests. The first is done in case 1, where we reject measures (v_1, v_2) that are above the time aliasing threshold (ie $|(v_1, v_2)| > \alpha \times 2^{-j}$). The second is done in case 2, where we make a least-squares estimate of $\mathbf{v}$. If $|\mathbf{v}| > \alpha \times 2^{-j-1}$, we give up any estimation at that location, since even finer scale estimations are false because of aliasing.

3 Numerical Experimentation

The algorithm was implemented with a dedicated set of *analytic* mother wavelets. The motivation of their use as well as their construction are described in Sect. 5.

3.1 True Sequences

Image sequences were downloaded from Barron & al.'s FTP site at *csd.uwo.ca*. The algorithm was tested on the rubik sequence (a rubik's cube on a rotating plate), the taxi sequence (where three vehicles are moving respectively towards East, West and Northwest) and the NASA sequence, which a is zoom on a Coke can.

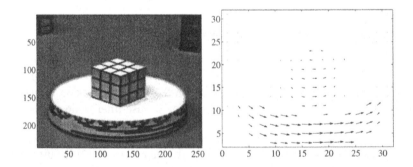

Fig. 2. Rubik sequence and flow

3.2 Synthetic Sequences

The described algorithm was also run on classical synthetic sequences (including Yosemite), and the result was compared to classical methods (Heeger, Fleet &

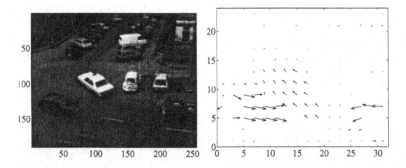

Fig. 3. Taxi sequence

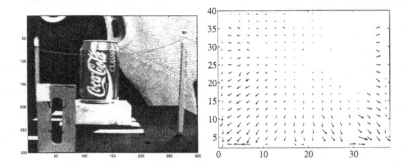

Fig. 4. NASA sequence

Jepson, Weber & Malik). The estimations errors are about 1.2 times higher, and are thus a little weaker. Reasons for this are that

- the suggested method is a two-frame method, while others rely on a number of frames ranging from 10 to 64;
- there no is coarse scale oversampling, and no coarse scale error averaging. The small loss of accuracy induced by this is counterbalanced by a much lower computational cost.

3.3 Illumination Changes

We use a new optic flow equation

$$\frac{\partial I_t}{\partial x}v_x + \frac{\partial I_t}{\partial y}v_y + \frac{\partial I_t}{\partial t} = \lambda I_t$$

instead of (2) where $\lambda = \frac{\partial}{\partial t}\log L$ is the logarithmic derivative of the illumination factor L. We use an additional wavelet shape $\psi^0(x,y) = \phi(x)\phi(y)$ of nonzero integral, and perform illumination change measurements, that is, estimate the new unknown parameter λ.

A synthetic sequence (moving white noise, with increasing illumination of Gaussian shape) was created. Three pictures of the sequence (Fig. 5) and the corresponding measured flow and illumination map (Fig. 6) are displayed. The real optic flow is of $(1.2, 0.8)$ pixels per frame, and the average error in degrees as measured by Barron & al. is less than 1.

Fig. 5. Moving random pattern with varying illumination

4 Time Aliasing

Since our picture sequence is time sampled, the computation of the right–hand side coefficient in (8)

$$\frac{\partial}{\partial t}\left\langle I_t, \psi^s_{j\mathbf{k}}\right\rangle$$

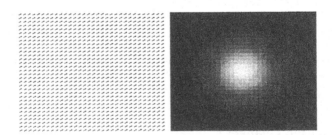

Fig. 6. Measured flow and illumination maps

relies on a finite difference approximation of the picture time derivative $\frac{\partial}{\partial t}I_t$ in time, like $\frac{\partial}{\partial t}I_t \simeq I_{t+1} - I_t$. We will see that the error of such estimations is high if the displacement (v_1, v_2) between two pictures I_t and I_{t+1} is large with regard to the wavelet scale 2^{-j}.

Note that this phenomenon always arises in some form in optic flow computation and has been pointed out by many authors [15]. Also note that this very problem motivates a multiscale approach to optic flow computation [2] [4] [18] [21].

Let us suppose that for a given j and $\mathbf{k}$, the picture is translating uniformly over the support of our wavelets $\psi_{j\mathbf{k}}^s$ for all s, ie

$$I_t(\mathbf{x}) = I(\mathbf{x} - t\mathbf{v})$$

4.1 Error Bound

The simplest time derivative approximation is a two step finite difference

$$\frac{\partial I_t}{\partial t} \simeq I_{t+1} - I_t$$

In this paper however, we will use higher order estimate, and measure the optic at each $t + 1/2$, between two successive pictures, based on the following approximation:

$$\frac{\partial I_{t+1/2}}{\partial t} \simeq I_{t+1} - I_t$$

Now we also need to compute coefficients of the left hand side of (8) at $t + 1/2$: $< \frac{\partial}{\partial x_i} \psi_{j\mathbf{k}}^s, I_{t+1/2} >$, because we only know them at integer times. This is done with the following estimation:

$$\frac{\partial}{\partial t} I_{t+1/2} \simeq \frac{I_t + I_{t+1}}{2}$$

At a given resolution j, these approximations lead respectively to the following coefficient approximations:

$$< \frac{\partial I_{t+1/2}}{\partial t}, \psi_{j\mathbf{k}} > \simeq \langle I_{t+1} - I_t, \psi_{j\mathbf{k}} \rangle \qquad (9)$$

$$< I_{t+1/2}, \psi_{j\mathbf{k}} > \simeq \left\langle \frac{I_{t+1} + I_t}{2}, \psi_j \mathbf{k} \right\rangle \qquad (10)$$

which can be rewritten after variable changes and integrations by parts

$$< I_{t+1/2}, \mathbf{v}.\nabla\psi_{j\mathbf{k}} > \simeq \langle I_{t+1/2}, \psi_{j\mathbf{k}}(\mathbf{x} + \mathbf{v}/2) - \psi_{j\mathbf{k}}(\mathbf{x} - \mathbf{v}/2) \rangle \qquad (11)$$

$$< I_{t+1/2}, \psi_{j\mathbf{k}} > \simeq \left\langle I_{t+1/2}, \frac{\psi_{j\mathbf{k}}(\mathbf{x} + \mathbf{v}/2) + \psi_{j\mathbf{k}}(\mathbf{x} - \mathbf{v}/2))}{2} \right\rangle \qquad (12)$$

4.2 Design Rule

Each approximation (11) and (12) is the approximation of a linear functional of $L_2(\mathbb{R})$ with another one. We take as a design rule that the following approximations be true:

$$\mathbf{v}.\nabla\psi_{jk} \simeq \psi_{jk}(\mathbf{x}+\mathbf{v}/2) - \psi_{jk}(\mathbf{x}-\mathbf{v}/2) \tag{13}$$

$$\psi_{jk} \simeq \frac{\psi_{jk}(\mathbf{x}+\mathbf{v}/2) + \psi_{jk}(\mathbf{x}-\mathbf{v}/2))}{2} \tag{14}$$

With a Taylor expansion of ψ, we can prove that there exists some constant M such that the sum of the relative errors of (13) and (14) is less than $M \times (|\mathbf{v}|2^j)$. This sum has been numerically estimated for the wavelets we use later in this algorithm, and lead to the constraint

$$\boxed{|\mathbf{v}| \le 0.42 \times 2^{-j}}$$

5 Analytic Wavelets

Standard real valued wavelets are displayed in Fig. (7–a-d). If we use wavelets ψ^1, ψ^2 and ψ^3 to compute the optic flow, the determinants of the system of equations (8) will be real valued and highly oscillating in space.

For these two reasons, they will vanish very often and make the flow estimation poor and unstable.

5.1 A Problem: Extinction

Going back to the one–dimensional case, we can write the velocity estimation as

$$v(k/2^j) \simeq \frac{\frac{\partial}{\partial t}\int I_t(x)\psi_{jk}(x)dx}{\int I_t(x)\psi'_{jk}(x)dx} \tag{15}$$

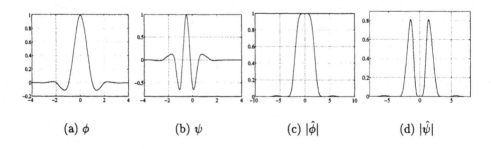

(a) ϕ (b) ψ (c) $|\hat{\phi}|$ (d) $|\hat{\psi}|$

Fig. 7. ϕ, ψ and their Fourier transforms

If ψ is a classical real-valued wavelet, as displayed in Fig. (7–a,c), its time and frequency behavior can be described with a local cosine model:

$$\psi(x) \simeq g(x)\cos(x) = \mathrm{Re}(g(x)e^{ix}) \tag{16}$$

where $g(x)$ is an even function with a frequency content significantly narrower that 2π. As a consequence, we can make the following approximation:

$$\psi'(x) = \mathrm{Re}(ig(x)e^{ix})$$

In this case, the denumerator of (15) is equal to

$$D(k/2^j) = \mathrm{Re}\left(i2^j \int I_t(x)g(2^jx - k)e^{i(2^jx-k)}dx\right)$$

$$= \mathrm{Re}\left(i2^je^{-ik} \int I_t(x)e^{i2^jx}g(2^jx - k)dx\right)$$

$$= \mathrm{Re}\left(ie^{-ik} \int I_t(2^{-j}y)e^{iy}g(y - k)dy\right) \quad \text{by setting } y = 2^jx$$

where the integral is a convolution C of two functions

$$y \mapsto I_t(y2^{-j})e^{iy}$$
$$\text{and } y \mapsto g(-y) = g(y)$$

Because g has a narrow spectrum, so has C, and thus our denumerator is

$$D(k/2^j) = \mathrm{Re}(ie^{-ik}C(k))$$

where C is slowly varying. Therefore,

$$D(k/2^j) = \cos(k - \mathrm{Arg}\,C(k) + \pi/2) \times |C(k)| \tag{17}$$

where $\mathrm{Arg}(C(k))$ and $|C(k)|$ are slowly varying. The denumerator thus roughly behaves like a cosinus function. It is thus very likely to vanish or to be close to 0 for some k.

5.2 A Solution: Analytic Wavelets

If instead of this real valued wavelet ψ, we use its positive frequency analytic part ψ^+ defined as

$$\hat{\psi}^+(\xi) = 2 \times 1_{(\xi \geq 0)} \times \hat{\psi}(\xi)$$

equation (16) becomes

$$\psi(x) \simeq g(x)e^{ix}$$

that is the same formula now without the "real–part" operator. As a result, the cosine function is replaced by a complex exponential in (17) that becomes

$$D(k/2^j) = e^{i(k - \text{Arg } C(k) + \pi/2)} \times |C(k)|$$

The modulus of $D(k/2^j)$ is now $|C(k)|$ instead of $|\cos((k - \text{Arg } C(k) + \pi/2) \times |C(k)|$ and is less often close to zero.

Two–dimension analytic wavelets This suggests us to replace our three real wavelets ψ^1, ψ^2 and ψ^3 as defined in equations (3–5), with the four following wavelets

$$\Psi^1(\mathbf{x}) = \psi^+(x_1)\phi(x_2) \tag{18}$$

$$\Psi^2(\mathbf{x}) = \phi(x_1)\psi^+(x_2) \tag{19}$$

$$\Psi^3(\mathbf{x}) = \psi^+(x_1)\psi^+(x_2) \tag{20}$$

$$\Psi^4(\mathbf{x}) = \psi^+(x_1)\psi^-(x_2) \tag{21}$$

where $\psi^-(t) = \overline{\psi^+(t)}$. It is easy to prove that if $(\psi^s_{jk})_{s=1..3, j \in \mathbb{Z}, k \in \mathbb{Z}^2}$ is a basis of $L_2(\mathbb{R})$, then $(\Psi^s_{jk})_{s=1..4, j \in \mathbb{Z}, k \in \mathbb{Z}^2}$ is a frame.

Analytic measure functions are also used in spatiotemporal filtering techniques, where velocity tuned filters are analytic [9]. Note, however, that the Hilbert transform is also used to make filters direction selective and not analytic [4] [20].

Psychophysical evidence also supports the use of analytic wavelets. Daugman [8] identified a pair of (real valued) Gabor filters with a $\pi/2$ phase shift between them

$$f_1 = e^{-(\mathbf{X} - \mathbf{X}_0)^2/2\sigma} \cos \mathbf{k}.\mathbf{X}$$

$$f_2 = e^{-(\mathbf{X} - \mathbf{X}_0)^2/2\sigma} \sin \mathbf{k}.\mathbf{X}$$

Such a pair can equivalently be seen as a single complex filter

$$f = e^{-(\mathbf{X} - \mathbf{X}_0)^2/2\sigma} e^{i\mathbf{k}.\mathbf{X}} \tag{22}$$

that now has a non-symmetric spectrum, and is thus an approximation of an analytic transform of f_1.

6   Dyadic Filter Bank Wavelets

For computational efficiency, we need wavelets implementable with dyadic filter banks, so that the computation of the system coefficients in (8) can be done with a fast wavelet transform. We will use separable wavelets $\psi(x_1, x_2) = f(x_1)g(x_2)$, and can therefore limit ourselves to the one-dimensional case.

Wavelet coefficients in the one–dimensional case can be computed with a dyadic pyramid filtering and subsampling scheme when the wavelet is an infinite convolution of discrete FIR[2] filters, which can be written in Fourier domain as

---

[2] finite impulse response

$$\hat{\psi}(\xi) = \prod_{j=1}^{+\infty} m_j \left(\frac{\xi}{2^j} \right) \tag{23}$$

where the m_j's are trigonometric polynomials. For computational efficiency purposes, the functions m_j should be all the same, up to the very first ones.

There exist plenty of dyadic filter bank wavelets. More difficult points are the computation of wavelet derivative coefficients also with dyadic filter banks, as well as the design of *analytic* dyadic filter bank wavelets.

6.1 Dyadic Filter Bank Wavelet Derivatives

If a function ψ is an infinite convolution of discrete filters

$$\hat{\psi}(\xi) = \prod_{j=1}^{+\infty} m_j \left(\frac{\xi}{2^j} \right)$$

then

$$\widehat{\psi'}(\xi) = \prod_{j=1}^{+\infty} m'_j \left(\frac{\xi}{2^j} \right)$$

where

$$m'_j(\xi) = \begin{cases} \frac{2m_j(\xi)}{e^{i\xi}+1} & \text{if } j \geq 2 \\ 2(e^{i\xi}-1)m_1(\xi) & \text{if } j = 1 \end{cases}$$

Proof. Thanks to the following identity

$$\prod_{j=1}^{+\infty} \frac{e^{i\xi/2^j}+1}{2} = \frac{e^{i\xi}-1}{i\xi}$$

we get,

$$\prod_{j=1}^{+\infty} m'_j \left(\frac{\xi}{2^j} \right) = i\xi \prod_{j=1}^{+\infty} m_j \left(\frac{\xi}{2^j} \right) = \widehat{\psi'}(\xi)$$

This shows that the derivative a dyadic filter bank wavelet is also implementable with a filter bank and gives us the rule to find the corresponding coefficients. The extension to partial derivatives of two–dimensional wavelets is straightforward.

6.2 Analytic Dyadic Filter Bank Wavelets

Using a true Hilbert transform to compute analytic wavelet coefficients is not possible in practice because of its computational cost. The purpose of this section is thus to approximate the Hilbert transform ψ^+ of a real wavelet ψ with an almost analytic wavelet $\psi^\#$ that can still be implemented with a FIR^2 filter bank.

We want our wavelet $\psi^{\#}$ to have most of its energy on the positive frequency peak, and we want to keep the relationship $\psi = 2\,\mathrm{Re}(\psi^{\#})$, the same way as for the true Hilbert transform, $\psi = 2\,\mathrm{Re}(\psi^{+})$.

Starting from any FIR filter pair m_0 and m_1 defining a wavelet as

$$\hat{\psi}(\xi) = m_1\left(\frac{\xi}{2}\right)\prod_{j=2}^{+\infty} m_0\left(\frac{\xi}{2^j}\right) \tag{24}$$

ψ and its Fourier transform are displayed in (7-a,b).

If m_2 is a Deslauriers-Dubuc interpolation filter, then $\hat{\psi}^{\#}(\xi) = \hat{\psi}(\xi)m_2(\xi/2 - \pi/4)$ is a good approximation of $\hat{\psi}^{+}(\xi)$, since most of the negative frequency peak of ψ is canceled by a vanishing $m_2(\xi)$. $\hat{\psi}$ (solid) and $m_2(\xi - \pi/4)$ (dashed) are displayed together in 8-a, and the resulting $\widehat{\psi^{\#}}$ in 8-b. The remaining negative frequency content of $\psi^{\#}$ is not 0, but is less than 2% of $\psi^{\#}$'s total L_2 norm. Also we have the relationship $\psi = 2\,\mathrm{Re}(\psi^{\#})$, because

$$m_2(\xi) + m_2(\xi + \pi) = 1 \quad \text{and} \quad m_2(\xi) = m_2(-\xi) \quad \forall \xi$$

Thanks to the way $\psi^{\#}$ is defined, inner products $\int I(x)\psi^{\#}(x)dx$ are computed the same way as $\int I(x)\psi(x)dx$ up to a single additional discrete filtering step.

Conclusion

The method presented in this paper is an improvement of the existing ones in terms of reduced computational complexity. This reduction is gained because

- the optic flow is computed with only two frames.
- the pyramid filtering and subsampling scheme structure allows to measure displacements at several scales without massive convolutions. As a consequence, optic flow of a standard sequence can be computed on a single processor computer in few seconds.

Acknowledgments

The author would like to express his gratefulness to Stéphane Mallat for very helpful comments and discussions and Jean-Jacques Slotine for stimulating discussions on possible applications in robotics.

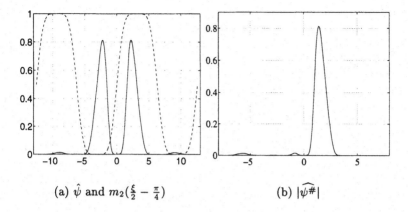

(a) $\hat{\psi}$ and $m_2(\frac{\xi}{2} - \frac{\pi}{4})$ (b) $|\widehat{\psi^{\#}}|$

Fig. 8. Approximation $\psi^{\#}$ of ψ^{+} and its Fourier transform

References

1. E. H. Adelson and J. R. Bergen, "Spatiotemporal Energy Models for the Perception of Vision," *J. Opt. Soc. Amer.*, Vol A2, pp. 284-299, 1985.
2. P. Anandan, "A Computational Framework and an Algorithm for the Measurement of Visual Motion," *International Journal of Computer Vision*, Vol. 2, pp. 283-310, 1989.
3. J.L. Barron, D.J. Fleet and S.S. Beauchemin, "Performance of Optical Flow Techniques," *International Journal of Computer Vision*, Vol. 12:1, pp. 43-77, 1994.
4. T.J. Burns, S.K. Rogers, D.W. Ruck and M.E. Oxley, "Discrete, Spatiotemporal, Wavelet Multiresolution Analysis Method for Computing Optical Flow," *Optical Engineering*, Vol. 33:7, pp. 2236-2247, 1994.
5. P.J. Burt and E.H. Adelson, "The Laplacian Pyramid as a Compact Image Code," *IEEE. Trans. Communications*, Vol. 31, pp. 532-540, 1983.
6. C.W.G. Clifford, K. Langley and D.J. Fleet, "Centre-Frequency Adaptive IIR Temporal Filters for Phase-Based Image Velocity Estimation," *Image Processing and its Applications*, Vol. 4-6, pp. 173-177, 1995.
7. I. Daubechies, *Ten Lectures on Wavelets*, Society for Industrial and Applied Mathematics, Philadelphia, 1992.
8. J. G. Daugman, "Complete Discrete 2-D Gabor Transforms by Neural Networks for Image Analysis and Compression," *IEEE Trans. Acoust., Speech, Signal Processing*, Vol. 36:7, pp. 1169-1179, 1988.
9. D.J. Fleet and A.D. Jepson, "Computation of Component Image Velocity from Local Phase Information," *International Journal of Computer Vision*, Vol. 5, pp. 77-104, 1990.
10. W.T. Freeman and E.H. Adelson, "The Design and Use of Steerable Filters," *IEEE Trans. on Pattern Analysis and Machine Intelligence*, Vol. 13:9, pp. 891-906, 1991.
11. M. Gökstorp and P-E. Danielsson, "Velocity Tuned Generalized Sobel Operators for Multiresolution Computation of Optical Flow," *IEEE*, pp. 765-769, 1994.
12. D.J. Heeger, "Optical Flow Using Spatiotemporal Filters," *International Journal for Computer Vision*, Vol. 1, pp. 279-302, 1988.

13. B.K.P Horn and B.G. Schunck, "Determining Optical Flow," *A.I. Memo No. 572, Massachusetts Institute of Technology*, 1980.
14. B.K.P Horn and B.G. Schunck, "Determining Optical Flow," *Artificial Intelligence*, Vol. 17, pp. 185-204, 1981.
15. B. Jähne, "Spatio-Temporal Image Processing," *Lecture Notes in Computer Science* vol. 751, Springer Verlag, 1993.
16. B. D. Lucas and T. Kanade, "An Iterative Image Registration Technique with an Application to Stereo Vision," *Proc. DARPA Image Understanding Workshop*, pp. 121-130, 1981.
17. S.G. Mallat, "A Theory for Multiresolution Signal Decomposition," *IEEE Trans. on Pattern Analysis and Machine Intelligence*, Vol. 11:7, pp. 674-693, 1989.
18. E.P. Simoncelli, W.T. Freeman, "The Steerable Pyramid: a Flexible Architecture for Multi-Scale Derivative Computation," *2nd Annual IEEE International Conference on Image Processing, Washington DC*, 1995.
19. A.B. Watson, "The Cortex Transform: Rapid Computation of Simulated Neural Images," *Computer Vision, Graphics, and Image Processing*, Vol. 39:3, pp. 311-327, 1987.
20. A.B. Watson and A.J. Ahumada, Jr, "Model of Human Visual-Motion Sensing," *Journal of Optical Society of America*, Vol. A:2-2, pp. 322-342, 1985.
21. J. Weber and J. Malik, "Robust Computation of Optical Flow in a Multi-Scale Differential Framework," *International Journal of Computer Vision, Vol. 14:1, pp. 5-19, 1995*

Automatic Detection and Labelling of the Human Cortical Folds in Magnetic Resonance Data Sets

Gabriele Lohmann, D. Yves von Cramon

Max-Planck-Institute of Cognitive Neuroscience
Inselstr. 22 - 26, 04103 Leipzig, Germany
Ph: ++49-341-9940 217, Fax: ++49-341-9940 221
email: lohmann,cramon@cns.mpg.de

Abstract. The folding of the cortical surface of the human brain varies dramatically from person to person. However, the folding pattern is not arbitrary. The cortical folds (also called "sulci") often serve as landmarks for referencing brain locations, and the most pronounced sulci have names that are well established in the neuroanatomical literature.

In this paper, we will present a method that both automatically detects and attributes neuroanatomical names to these folds using image analysis methods applied to magnetic resonance data of human brains. More precisely, we subdivide each fold into a number of substructures which we call *sulcal basins*, and attach labels to these basins. These sulcal basins form a complete parcellation of the cortical surface.

The algorithm reported here is important in the context of human brain mapping. Human brain mapping aims at establishing correspondences between brain function and brain anatomy. One of the most intriguing problems in this field is the high inter-personal variability of human neuroanatomy which makes studies across many subjects very difficult. Most previous attempts at solving this problem are based on various methods of image registration where MR data sets of different subjects are warped until they overlap. We believe that in the process of warping too much of the individual anatomy is destroyed so that relevant information is lost. The approach presented in this paper allows inter-personal comparisons without having to resort to image warping. Our concept of sulcal basins allows to establish a complete parcellation of the cortical surface into separate regions. These regions are neuroanatomically meaningful and can be identified from MR data sets across many subjects. At the same time, the parcellation is detailed enough to be useful for brain mapping purposes.

1 Introduction

The folding of the cortical surface of the human brain varies dramatically from person to person. However, the folding pattern is not arbitrary. In fact, the cortical folds (also called "sulci") often serve as landmarks for referencing brain locations, and the more pronounced sulci have names that are well established in the neuroanatomical literature [1].

In this paper, we will present a method that both automatically detects and attributes neuroanatomical names to these folds. More precisely, we subdivide each fold into a number of substructures which we call *sulcal basins*, and attach labels to these substructures. The reason why we introduce the concept of a sulcal basin is that we believe that sulcal basins have a lower degree of interpersonal variability than entire sulci.

Our method is important in the context of human brain mapping. Human brain mapping aims at establishing correspondences between brain function and brain anatomy. One of the most intriguing problems in this field is the high inter-personal variability of human neuroanatomy which makes studies across many subjects very difficult.

Most previous attempts at solving this problem are based on various methods of image registration where MR data sets are registered and warped onto a brain atlas [2],[3],[4],[5],[6]. A related approach is that by Gueziec et al. [7] and also Declerck et al. [8] who presented methods for extracting and matching lines in multiple MR data sets. However, in the process of warping much of the individual anatomy is destroyed by geometric distortions so that relevant information is lost. In particular, size and shape information is destroyed.

The approach presented in this paper allows inter-personal comparisons without having to resort to image warping. Our concept of sulcal basins allows to establish a complete parcellation of the cortical surface into separate regions. These regions are neuroanatomically meaningful and can be identified from MR data sets across many subjects. At the same time, the parcellation is detailed enough to be useful for brain mapping purposes.

The work closest in spirit to ours is that by Mangin et al. [9],[10],[11] who also seek to obtain a structural description of the cortical topography. It differs from ours in that they do not use use the concept of a sulcal basin which is fundamental to our approach. Instead, they use an approach based on structural decompositions of sulcal skeletons.

The paper is organized as follows. We begin by defining the concept of a sulcal basin and present an algorithm for extracting sulcal basins from MR images of the human brain. We then introduce a brain model consisting of sulcal basins and their spatial relationships. Finally, we present a graph matching approach that performs an automatic labelling of the sulcal basins.

2   Sulcal basins

2.1   The concept of a sulcal basin

The notion of a sulcal basin has not been used in the literature before. Let us therefore begin by defining this concept. Figure 1a shows a volume rendering of a MR data set depicting a top right view of a healthy subject's brain. The sulci are clearly visible as dark valleys. Figure 1b shows the top part of the same brain. This time however, we removed the grey matter so that the white matter surface becomes visible and the sulci become more pronounced. Corresponding locations in both images are indicated by labels.

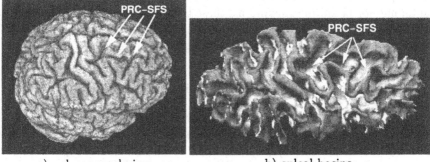

a) volume rendering   b) sulcal basins

Figure 1: Sulcal basins

Note that the fold labelled "prc-sfs (precentral/superior frontal sulcus)" which appears to consist of one large part in the volume rendering decomposes into three separate concave basins in the figure 1b. In fact, all sulci decompose into several such substructures, which we call "sulcal basins".

More precisely, sulcal basins are defined to be concavities in the white matter surface which are bounded by convex ridges that separate one basin from the next so that adjacent sulcal basins meet at the top of the ridge. Figure 2 illustrates this definition. The entire white matter surface is covered by such concavities so that a decomposition into sulcal basins yields a complete parcellation of the surface.

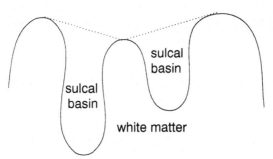

Figure 2: Sulcal basins

There are two principal advantages in introducing the concept of a sulcal basin. Firstly, in subdividing sulci into atomic parts we obtain a spatially more precise definition of brain loci. As we are ultimately interested in inter-subject comparisons, this is an important consideration.

Secondly, the high interpersonal variability in sulcal patterns can at least be partly attributed to different forms of groupings of sulcal basins. The two sets of sulcal basins below for instance can be easily matched, even though the two groups formed in each set cannot be matched:

The post-central sulcus for instance usually consists of two basins, a superior and an inferior basin. In some brains, these two basins are connected to form a coherent sulcus. In others, there are completely disconnected. Thus, sulcal basins are much more useful as entities for matching than entire sulci.

2.2 Automatic detection of sulcal basins from magnetic resonance data sets

Several approaches to automatic sulcus detection from MR images have been reported in the literature [12], [13], [14] which either seek surface representations of the cortical folds or are based on skeletonization methods.

The concept of sulcal basins is new, and consequently no methods for extracting them from MR images have existed so far. In the following, we will describe our approach.

Sulcal basins are concave indentations in the white matter surface, so that in principle it would be possible to detect sulcal basins by simply computing curvature properties of the white matter surface. Parts of the surface which belong to a sulcal basin are concave so that both the mean curvature and the Gaussian curvature are positive. Boundaries between basins are either saddles or ridges and have negative or zero curvature values.

However, the white matter surface is highly convoluted and the MR data sets have a limited spatial resolution, so that the computation of second order differentials becomes quite inaccurate. As a consequence, we found that curvature computations are not feasible for our purpose. In addition, there are also some parts of a sulcal basin wall which are convex and yet they do not constitute a boundary between basins as illustrated below:

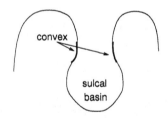

Therefore, we use a different approach which is not based on curvature properties. The method consists of a sequence of image analysis steps of which the first four are illustrated in figure 3.

The input data set (fig 3a) is first subjected to a white matter segmentation which separates white matter from other tissue classes (fig. 3b). This step helps to make the sulcal indentations more pronounced and thus more easily identifiable.

A large number of segmentation algorithms are known from the literature. Any suitable segmentation procedure can be used here. A general segmentation algorithm that produces satisfactory results for all types of input data does not exist at this point, so that the choice of a suitable algorithm and its parameters still very much depends on the type of data at hand. In our experiments, we used both simple thresholding techniques, as well as a new algorithm based on region growing [15].

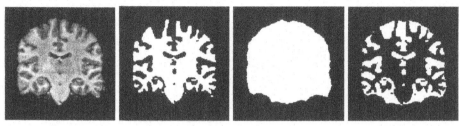

a) MR image   b) white matter   c) closing   d) sulcal interiors

Figure 3: The first four steps of the algorithm

We then close the sulci using a 3D morphological closing filter [16] to obtain an idealized smoothed surface (fig. 3c). We use a structuring element of spherical shape with a very large diameter. The exact size of the diameter is not critical as long as it is large enough. We subtract the white matter from the morphologically closed image so that only the sulcal interiors remain (fig. 3d).

At this point in the procedure, the processed image contains the union of all sulcal basins. We now need to separate the individual basins by trying to find the ridges between them. The main idea is based on the observation that each sulcal basin has a locally deepest point (or a small set of locally deepest points) which may be used to guide the search.

The sulcal depth is computed with respect to the smoothed surface (fig. 3c) using a 3D distance transform [17]. The distance transform attaches a value to each white voxel which encodes its distance towards the nearest black voxel so that each sulcal interior point of figure 3d receives a depth label. In essence, we first try to detect small "islands" of locally deepest points assuming that each such island represents one sulcal basin.

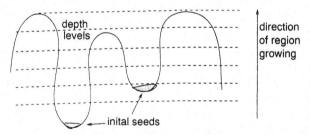

Figure 4: Region growing

We search for locally deepest points by moving a search window of size $n \times n \times n$ across the image where typically $n = 7$. Adjoining deepest points that are of almost equal depth and are close are merged into one larger patch so that perturbations due to noise are eliminated.

Finally, we let each initial island grow in a manner similar to region growing until a separating ridge is encountered. During region growing, successively higher levels are processed so that at each stage in the procedure only voxels of a given depth are added to a sulcal basin. Figure 4 illustrates this process, and figure 5 shows a data flow diagram of the entire procedure.

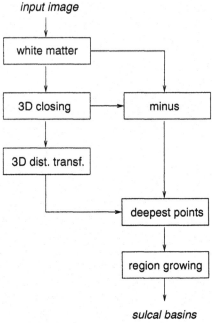

Figure 5: Flow diagram

3 Knowledge representation

In the following, we will describe a method of automatically attaching neuroanatomical labels to the sulcal basins that have been identified using the procedures described in the previous sections. We will begin by describing our knowledge representation scheme.

The neuroanatomical knowledge we use for describing sulcal basins consists of two parts: firstly, we use a *unary model* that describes unary predicates of a sulcal basin such as location, depth or size. Secondly, we use a *relational model* that describes spatial relationships between basins.

The unary model was obtained as follows. We first rotate all data sets into a standard coordinate system where the origin is taken to be half-way between CA (commissura anterior) and CP (commissura posterior) making our coordinate system analogous to the one proposed in [18].

We then performed a hand labelling of four data sets of which the sulcal basins had been extracted beforehand. We identified a set of 29 neuroanatomical labels which are listed in table I.

These labels were chosen because they represent all primary and secondary sulci, covering the most part of the lateral brain surface. The structures that are not represented here are the medial sulci which reside along the inter-hemispheric cleft, the basal sulci which are located along the bottom of the brain, the Sylvian fissure, and some tertiary sulci which have a high degree of interpersonal variability so that no well established neuroanatomical names exist for them.

Each sulcal basin of the above list is represented by its centroid, which is computed from the four hand-labelled data sets. Figure 6 shows these centroids against the sulcal pattern of one of these four data sets (the sulcal lines shown here for better orientation were extracted using the algorithm described in [19]).

id	neuroanatomical name	abbreviation
1	superior central sulcus	cs sup
2	central sulcus broca's knee	cs broca
3	inferior central sulcus	cs inf
4	superior precentral sulcus	prc sup (fef)
5	medial precentral sulcus	prc med
6	inferior precentral sulcus	prc inf
7	superior frontal sulcus 1 (posterior part)	sfs 1
8	superior frontal sulcus 2	sfs 2
9	superior frontal sulcus 3	sfs 3
10	superior frontal sulcus 4 (anterior part)	sfs 4
11	intermediate frontal sulcus (posterior part)	imfs 1
12	intermediate frontal sulcus (anterior part)	imfs 2
13	inferior frontal sulcus (posterior part)	ifs 1 (post)
14	inferior frontal sulcus (anterior part)	ifs 2 (ant)
15	superior post-central sulcus	poc sup
16	inferior post-central sulcus	poc inf
17	intraparietal sulcus (anterior)	ips asc
18	intraparietal sulcus (medial)	ips hor
19	intraparietal sulcus (descending)	ips desc
20	superior temporal sulcus 1 (posterior part)	sts 1 (post)
21	superior temporal sulcus 2	sts 2
22	superior temporal sulcus 3	sts 3
23	superior temporal sulcus 4 (anterior part)	sts 4
24	medial temporal sulcus	mts
25	inferior temporal sulcus 1 (posterior part)	its 1 (post)
26	inferior temporal sulcus 2	its 2
27	inferior temporal sulcus 3	its 3
28	inferior temporal sulcus 4 (anterior part)	its 4
29	occipital sulcus	occ

Table I: list of neuroanatomical labels

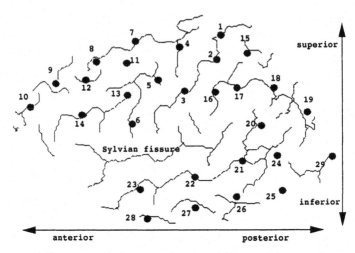

Figure 6: The left hemisphere model

Spatial relations between sulcal basins are defined with respect to the standard coordinate system to which all data sets have been aligned by the preprocessing routine. The relational model describes spatial relationships of three different kinds.

The first type of relation is the "anterior-posterior" relation which describes a basin's position with respect to the coordinate axis along the front/back direction as indicated in figure 6. For instance, basin 4 is anterior with respect to basin 2, but posterior to basin 7. This relation can be easily computed from the basin centroid's address as it is directly related to one of the three coordinate axes of the standard coordinate system.

Likewise, we define a relation called "superior/inferior" (top/bottom) which is determined by a direction orthogonal to the first. The third direction aligned along the third principal axis of the coordinate system is less interesting as the brain extends mostly along the first two axes so that it has less discriminative power.

Instead, we use another relation called "sulcal connectedness" which describes whether the ridge that separates two adjacent basins is "strong" or not. More precisely, two basins are said to be "connected" if the ridge between them is lower than a given threshold. Note that the height of the separating ridge can be easily determined from the distance transform. However, we use this particular relation quite cautiously, as the sulcal connectedness is quite variable from person to person. Only very few sulcal connections can be definitely established. For instance, the basins belonging to the central sulcus must always be connected.

The three relations defined above are represented by three adjacency matrices where each entry in a matrix describes the degree to which the relation between any two basins holds. At present, we distinguish between three degrees: "0" (the relation does not hold), "1" (unknown) and "2" (the relation holds). For instance, basin 5 is always superior to basin 6. However, it is unknown whether it is superior or inferior to basin 3, because in some brains it is superior to basin 3 whereas in others it is inferior. The adjacency matrix representing the connectedness relation contains mostly "unknowns". However, it is useful in establishing the central sulcus.

4 Graph matching

Sulcal basins of some data set can now be labelled by matching them against the model described in the previous section. The technique we use for this purpose is an adaptation of the widely used association graph matching [20, pp.365 ff] which will be explained in the following.

The sulcal basin model described in the previous section yields a graph

$$G_1 \; = \; (V_1, R)$$

where V_1 denotes the set of 29 nodes which represent the centroids of the model basins. Each node $v \in V_1$ has a both a neuroanatomical label and a set of descriptors which include its 3D coordinate in the standard coordinate system and its average size or depth. The relational model R is represented by the list of adjacency matrices as defined above.

Likewise, each new data set is represented by a graph

$$G_2 \; = \; (V_2, R)$$

where V_2 is a list of nodes which represent the centroids of the sulcal basins which have been extracted from the data set using the algorithm described in section 2. The spatial relationships between these basins are documented in the list of adjacency matrices contained in R.

The association graph

$$A \; = \; (U, S)$$

contains possible associations between the two graphs G_1 and G_2 such that the neuroanatomical labellings of G_1 are inherited by G_2 while the constraints imposed by the adjacency matrices are preserved. Nodes in the association graph represent possible matches. More precisely, a node u of the association graph is a pair $u = (v_1, v_2) \in U$ where $v_1 \in V_1$ and $v_2 \in V_2$ such that the distance

$$d \; = \; ||v_1 \; - \; v_2||$$

does not exceed a given threshold. In our experiments, we used a threshold value of 15 mm. As a further restriction, we only allowed three possible matches for each model node so that in cases where more than three nodes of G_2 were within a 15 mm radius of a model node we only admitted the three closest nodes. Such restrictions help to reduce the complexity.

Two nodes in the association graph are linked by an edge if they exhibit compatible spatial relationships. More precisely, two nodes $a = (v_1, v_2)$ and $b = (u_1, u_2)$ are connected if either

$$R(v_1, u_1) \; = \; R(v_2, u_2) \neq 1, \; \text{ or } R(v_1, u_1) \; = \; 1.$$

Thus, links in the association graph enforce spatial constraints as imposed by the adjacency matrices. If the spatial relationship between any two basins is known (i.e. $R(v_1, u_1) \neq 1$), then compatibility only holds iff the spatial relationship is the same in both the model graph and the data graph. If the spatial relationship is not known (i.e. $R(v_1, u_1) = 1$) then the link is established anyhow so as not to impose unnecessary constraints.

The process of finding matches between the model graph and the data graph consists in finding maximal cliques in the association graph. A clique is defined as a subset C of nodes such that any two nodes of C are linked by an edge. A maximal clique is a clique which cannot be extended without destroying its clique property.

In the context of graph matching, a clique in the association graph represents a set of matches between model and data graph such every pair of nodes obeys the spatial constraints. If such a clique is maximal, it contains the largest possible number of matches.

Note that there may be more than one maximal clique in the association graph, so that we need to define a criterion that selects a "best" maximal clique. In our experiments, we used the following function to evaluate the quality of a clique:

$$ f(M) = \sum_{(u,v) \in M} \sum_{(u',v') \in M} \| (\|u - u'\| - \|v - v'\|) \| $$

where $M \subset U$ denotes a clique in the association graph, and u, u', v, v' denote spatial addresses of nodes in the graphs G_1 and G_2, respectively. The function $f(M)$ measures how well distances between any two nodes in the model graph agree with distances in the data graph. It attains a low value if distances are well preserved, and a high value otherwise.

A large number of algorithms for finding maximal cliques are known from the literature [21]. In our experiments, we used the algorithm described in [20, p. 367]. Regardless of which particular algorithm we use, the problem of finding maximal cliques in a graph is in principal of exponential complexity. Therefore, it is not feasible to seek cliques in an association graph using all 29 basin labels at the same time. We circumvent this problem by following an incremental approach. We begin by first identifying the most prominent and least variable sulci which are the central, precentral, lower postcentral and the anterior intraparietal sulci. We then proceed by identifying the remaining sulci belonging to the frontal lobe, the parietal lobe and finally the temporal lobe, so that the entire identification process is split into four stages. At each stage, approximately eight basin labels are processed.

In spite of the fact that we do not process all labels at the same time, we can still enforce the entire set of constraints across all labels so that the resulting clique obeys all constraints. This is possible as the clique finding method we use supports incremental updates.

5 Experiments

Our input data consisted of T1-weighted magnetic resonance images (MRI) of healthy volunteers. The spatial resolution between planes was approx. $1.5mm$ and the within-plane resolution was set to approx. $0.95mm \times 0.95mm$. The images were subsequently resampled to obtain isotropic voxels of size $1mm \times 1mm \times 1mm$ so that each data set contained 160 slices with 200×160 pixels in each slice. As noted before, all data sets were rotated into a standard coordinate system. In addition, we applied an automatic procedure to extract brain from non-brain material. For a more detailed description of our preprocessing procedure see [22].

Our sulcus detection method was initially applied to four MR data sets so that the unary model could be generated. This model was then used to label sulcal basins which had been extracted from 17 other data sets. None of these 17 data sets had been used for the unary model. So far, we have only processed left hemispheres.

The graph matching algorithm produced maximal cliques which on the average contained 25.4 out of 29 possible matches. In two cases, only 21 and 22 matches were found, in all other cases at least 25 matches were found. An average of 1.1 of the matches found were false. Figure 7 shows a few results.

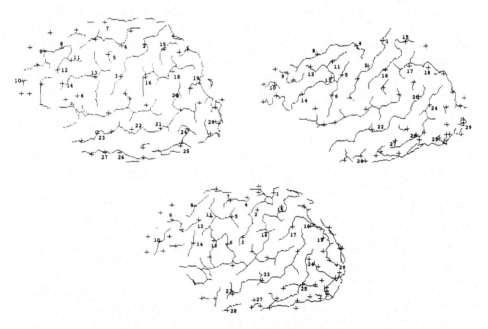

Figure 7: Results of the automatic labelling process

The computation time for the basin identification procedure was approximately 100 seconds. The automatic labelling procedure took approximately 37 seconds.

6 Discussion

We have presented a method that automatically detects and attributes neuroanatomical names to substructures of the cortical folds which we call sulcal basins using magnetic resonance data of healthy human brains. We believe that our method is relevant in the context of human brain mapping because it helps to identify brain loci in a way that is anatomically meaningful and easily reproducible across many subjects so that inter-personal comparisons become possible.

Future work will focus on the following aspects. Firstly, we intend to extend the list of anatomical labels so that brain loci which are not modelled at present (the Sylvian fissures, the medial and basal sulci and some tertiary sulci) can be identified as well. The aim will be to obtain a complete parcellation of the human cortex. At present, the method covers most of the lateral brain surface.

The number of basins varies somewhat between subjects. Therefore, there is some ambiguity in the identification process. For instance, the superior frontal sulcus (basins 7,8,9,10) sometimes contains one basin more or less than our model. In future work, we intend to modify our method so that deviations from the standard model can be dealt with. However, in our experiments so far we found that deviations from the standard model are surprisingly small.

Another aspect of our future work will of course be to improve the accuracy and reliability of the method. At present, the method identifies roughly 85 percent of the sulcal basins with one or two erroneous matches. Improvements can be achieved in several ways. Firstly, the unary model which contains average voxel addresses of the model basins should be incrementally updated as new data sets are processed so that the model begins to "learn". Secondly, other types of spatial relationships between basins will be added. And thirdly, the graph matching procedure will be extended to include probabilistic reasoning.

References

1. M. Ono, S. Kubik, C.D. Abernathy. *Atlas of the cerebral sulci.* Georg Thieme Verlag, Stuttgart, New York, 1990.
2. J.C. Maziotta, A.W. Toga, A. Evans, P. Fox, J. Lancaster. A probabilistic atlas of the human brain: theory and rationale for its development. *Neuroimage*, 2:89–101, 1995.
3. P. Thompson, A.W. Toga. A surface-based technique for warping three-dimensional images of the brain. *IEEE Transactions on Medical Imaging*, 15(4):402–417, 1996.
4. P.M. Thompson, D. MacDonald, M.S. Mega, C.J. Holmes, A.C. Evans, A.W. Toga. Detection and mapping of abnormal brain structure with a probabilistic atlas of cortical surfaces. *Journal of Computer Assisted Tomography*, 21(4):567–581, 1997.
5. G. Rizzo, P. Scifo, M.C. Gilardi, V. Bettinardi, F. Grassi, S. Cerutti, F. Fazio. Matching a computerized brain atlas to multimodal medical images. *NeuroImage*, 6(1):59–69, 1997.
6. S. Sandor, R. Leahy. Surface-based labeling of cortical anatomy using a deformable atlas. *IEEE Transactions on Medical Imaging*, 16(1):41–54, Feb. 1997.

7. A. Guéziec, N. Ayache. Smoothing and matching of 3-d space curves. *International Journal of Computer Vision*, 12(1):79–104, 1994.
8. J. Declerck, G. Subsol, J.-P. Thirion, N. Ayache. Automatic retrieval of anatomical structures in 3D medical images. In N. Ayache, editor, *Computer Vision, Virtual Reality and Robotics in Medicine*, pages 153–162, Nice, France, April 1995. Springer Lecture Notes, 905.
9. J.-F. Mangin, V. Frouin, I. Bloch, J. Régis, and J. López-Krahe. From 3-D magnetic resonance images to structured representations of the cortex topography using topology preserving deformations. *Journal of Mathematical Imaging and Vision*, 5(4):297–318, 1995.
10. J.F. Mangin, V. Frouin, J. Regis, I. Bloch, P. Belin, Y. Samson. Towards better management of cortical anatomy in multi-modal multi-individual brain studies. *Physica medica*, XII(Supplement 1):103–107, June 1996.
11. A. Manceaux-Demiau, J.F. Mangin, J. Regis, Olivier Pizzato, V. Frouin. Differential features of cortical folds. In *CVRMed*, Grenoble, France, 1997.
12. M. Valliant, C. Davatzikos, R.N. Bryan. Finding 3D parametric representations of the deep cortical folds. In *Proc. Mathematical Methods in biomedical image analysis (MMBIA 96)*, pages 151–157, San Francisco, CA, June 1996. IEEE Computer Society.
13. M. Valliant, C. Davatzikos. Mapping the cerebral sulci: application to morphological analysis of the cortex and to non-rigid registration. In *Int. Conf. on Information Processing in Medical Imaging (IPMI 97)*, pages 141–154, Poultney, Vermont, USA, June 9–13 1997.
14. M. Näf, O. Kübler, R. Kikinis, M.E. Shenton, G. Szekely. Characterization and recognition of 3D organ shape in medical image analysis using skeletonization. In *Proc. Mathematical Methods in biomedical image analysis (MMBIA 96)*, pages 139–150, San Francisco, CA, June 1996. IEEE Computer Society.
15. G. Lohmann. A new approach to white matter segmentation in MR images. Technical report, Max-Planck-Institute of Cognitive Neuroscience, Leipzig, Germany, 1997.
16. P. Maragos, R.W. Schafer. Morphological systems for multidimensional signal processing. *Proc. of the IEEE*, 78(4):690–709, 1990.
17. G. Borgefors. Distance transforms in arbitrary dimensions. *Computer Vision, Graphics, and Image Processing*, 27:321–345, 1984.
18. P.T. Fox, J.S. Perlmutter, M.E. Raichle. A stereotactic method of anatomical localization for positron emission tomography. *Journal of Computer Assisted Tomography*, 9(1):141–153, Jan./Feb. 1985.
19. G.Lohmann. Extracting line representations of sulcal and gyral patterns in MR images of the human brain. Technical report, Max-Planck-Institute of Cognitive Neuroscience, Leipzig, Germany, July 1997.
20. D. Ballard, C.M. Brown. *Computer Vision*. Prentice Hall, Englewood Cliffs, NJ, 1982.
21. E.A. Akkoyunlu. The enumeration of maximal cliques of large graphs. *SIAM J. Comput.*, 2(1), March 1973.
22. F. Kruggel, G.Lohmann. Automatic adaptation of the stereotactical coordinate system in brain MRI data sets. In J. Duncan, editor, *Int. Conf. on Information Processing in Medical Imaging (IPMI 97)*, Poultney, Vermont, USA, June 9–13 1997.

Efficient 3-D Scene Visualization by Image Extrapolation*

Tomáš Werner, Tomáš Pajdla, Václav Hlaváč

Center for Machine Perception
Faculty of Electrical Engineering, Czech Technical University
121 35 Prague 2, Karlovo náměstí 13, Czech Republic
http://cmp.felk.cvut.cz

Abstract. Image-based scene representation is believed to be an alternative to the 3-D model reconstruction and rendering. In attempt to compare generality of image-based and model-based approaches we argue that it is plausible to distinguish three approaches to 3-D scene visualization: image interpolation, image extrapolation, and 3-D model reconstruction and rendering. We advocate that image extrapolation is a useful trade-off between simple but limited interpolation and general but difficult 3-D model reconstruction and rendering. Image extrapolation is able to visualize correctly the part of a 3-D scene that is visible from two reference images. In fact, it is equivalent to reconstructing a projective 3-D model from two reference images and rendering it. In the second part of the work, we present an algorithm for rendering a projective model. Our approach is more efficient than the ray-tracing-like algorithm by Laveau and Faugeras [6]. We show that visibility can be solved by z-buffering, and that virtual images can be synthesized by transferring triangles from a reference image via a homography or an affinity. Such algorithms are often supported by hardware on graphics work stations, which makes a step towards the real-time synthesis. The results are presented for real scenes.

1 Introduction

This work considers visualization of a real 3-D scene described by a set of intensity *reference images* taken from different viewpoints. The novel images of the scene, not captured by any real camera, are called *virtual images*. Traditional scene visualization proceeds in two steps: (i) reconstruction of a 3-D model, (ii) rendering of the model.

Image-based scene representation is believed to be an alternative. It proposes to display a real 3-D scene from any viewpoint without using its 3-D model. The scene is represented only by a collection of 2-D reference images. A virtual image is then constructed directly from the reference images using correspondences

---
* This research was supported by the Grant Agency of the Czech Republic, grants 102/97/0480 and 102/97/0855, by European Union, grant Copernicus CP941068, and by the Czech Ministry of Education, grant VS96049.

among them. The aim of such a procedure is to avoid the difficult reconstruction of a consistent 3-D model.

It was thought [1, 6, 8, 10, 15, 5] that displaying a 3-D scene from 2-D reference images is quite a different process from rendering a 3-D model. The difference seemed to follow from the observation of Ullman [14] who has proposed that the objects could be recognized just on the basis of linear combination of corresponding points in their orthographic images. It was in deep contrast to recognition based on verification of a 3-D model projected to the image.

Ullman's approach has attracted new attention since Shashua showed that a trilinear function replaces the linear one [11] for a perspective camera, and since Laveau and Faugeras [6] and Hartley [4] made clear that any projective reconstruction of the scene suffices for the visualization itself. Tedious calibration of the camera has been thus avoided in the case of visualization.

Seitz and Dyer [10] have stressed that visualizing an object by interpolating close views is a well-posed process and therefore a perfect correspondence algorithm and removal of hidden surfaces are not ultimately needed for certain limited tasks. Other works have demonstrated that even quite complicated scenes can be visualized by interpolating between the reference views [8, 15].

The above results make an impression that virtual images of a general scene can be constructed by an image-based approach. However, knowledge about geometry of isolated points is not sufficient for constructing virtual images because *occlusion* must be also considered.

To display the scene by a camera revolving around it in a circle, quite many reference images were needed in [15] to make visual effect realistic enough. This is caused by the principal deficiency of image interpolation, namely by its *inability to show a general object from an arbitrary view point using the images and the correspondences obtained from a sparse set of viewpoints*. This deficiency is caused by occlusion. Surprisingly, no object, not even a convex polyhedron, can be completely visualized by mere interpolating between finite number of reference images.

Consider the situation illustrated in Fig. 1 when the reference views $C_1, \ldots, C_6$ are located around a simple convex polyhedron. The images taken by the virtual camera C, lying in the segment $C_2 C_3$, cannot be constructed by interpolating between reference views C_2 and C_3 since the camera C_2 does not see both sides of the polyhedron which are seen by the camera C. It will not help to move one of the reference cameras, e.g. C_3, closer to B_1 in hope to avoid the malfunction of the view synthesis. By moving C_3 to B_1, the same problem appears on the segment $C_3 C_4$. The only solution would be to increase the density of views near B_1 to infinity. Indeed, the algorithm for automatic finding the optimal sparse set of reference views [16] has tended to select many reference images near places like B_1.

In the light of this observation, we believe that the following questions must be clarified: How general are image-based approaches? Can an arbitrary virtual image of an arbitrary scene be constructed by an approach avoiding 3-D model reconstruction?

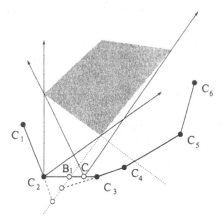
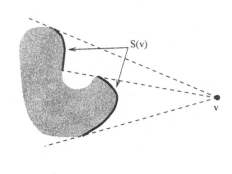

Fig. 1. Virtual view C cannot be constructed by interpolation from the views C_2 and C_3 but can be extrapolated from C_3 and C_4.

Fig. 2. The set $S(v)$ of scene points visible from the viewpoint v.

In the first part of the work, Section 2, we attempt to compare generality of image-based and model-based approaches. We show that it is plausible to distinguish three qualitatively different approaches to constructing virtual images. The simplest one, *image interpolation*, is similar to Seitz's and Dyer's approach [10]. In *image extrapolation*, visibility must be solved explicitly. *3-D Model reconstruction and rendering* is the most general approach, the only one which can be used if both the scene and the position of virtual camera are general. It requires fusing parts of the virtual image transferred from different sets of reference images.

Since the applicability of image interpolation is limited and 3-D model reconstruction is difficult, we advocate *image extrapolation* as a trade-off useful in practice. The application can be, e.g., observing a scene described by a pair of uncalibrated photographs. In Section 3 we present an efficient algorithm for synthesizing virtual images by image extrapolation. The algorithm is similar to rendering a Euclidean 3-D model, however, no Euclidean reconstruction is needed and visibility can be solved in image planes. In contrary to Laveau and Faugeras [6], the rendering algorithm allows using hardware-supported graphics functions available on some work stations. Therefore, the synthesis of virtual images can be faster.

2 Analysis of Approaches to 3-D Scene Visualization

In this section the following questions are addressed: *Can an image-based approach be used to construct an arbitrary virtual image of an arbitrary 3-D scene? If not, for which configurations of the scene and virtual and reference viewpoints can it be used?*

2.1 Used Concepts

A *scene* is one or more rigid opaque bodies in a fixed relative position. *Scene points* are the points on the surface of the scene. *Viewpoints* are points that are not inside the scene nor on its surface. We will denote the *set of scene points visible from the viewpoint v* by $\mathcal{S}(v)$. The set $\mathcal{S}(v)$ for an example configuration is shown in[1] Fig. 2. Each viewpoint is a possible center of a camera. If it is a real camera, the viewpoint is called the *reference* viewpoint. If it is a center of a non-existing camera for which a novel view of the scene is to be created, it is called the *virtual* viewpoint.

We assume that an algorithm able to find corresponding pairs of pixels in two reference images is available. We further assume that there exists an algorithm that allows to compute the position of an image point in the virtual image from the positions of corresponding image points in some subset of reference images (this subset usually contains only two images). This algorithm is often called *transfer*. Approaches to transfer can be found in [12, 4, 2, 13].

2.2 Three Approaches to Constructing Virtual Images

The considered task is to construct virtual images of a scene from a captured set of reference images. The virtual viewpoint will be denoted by v and two reference viewpoints by v', v''.

If the scene were a cloud of isolated points we could construct an arbitrary virtual image by transferring all corresponding points from a pair of arbitrary reference images to the virtual image (in fact, this is image interpolation described below). Since scene surfaces occlude each other this simple approach cannot be used in some situations.

Possible configurations of the scene, the reference viewpoints and the virtual viewpoint can be divided into three qualitatively different classes. A different approach to constructing virtual images is suitable for each class so that:

- The virtual image is *complete*, that is, no part of the scene is missing in it.
- Possible *hidden surfaces are correctly removed* in the virtual image.
- The approach is as *simple and efficient* as possible.

The three classes of approaches are summarized in Table 1 and described in the following three sections. For each class, necessary and sufficient condition for configuration of the scene and the viewpoints is formulated in terms of $\mathcal{S}(v), \mathcal{S}(v'), \mathcal{S}(v'')$.

Image Interpolation. Image interpolation allows synthesizing the virtual image from two reference images of the scene by transferring points in an arbitrary order from the reference images to the virtual one.

Once we find the correspondence, the synthesis of the virtual image is simple and fast. The following algorithm can perform image interpolation:

---

[1] In this figure, as well as in other figures in the paper, the scene is shown as two-dimensional for simplicity.

Table 1. Three approaches to constructing virtual images.

Approach	Condition	Solving visibility necessary?	Fusion necessary?
image interpolation	$\mathcal{S}(v) = \mathcal{S}(v') \cap \mathcal{S}(v'')$	no	no
image extrapolation	$\mathcal{S}(v) \subset \mathcal{S}(v') \cap \mathcal{S}(v'')$	yes	no
model reconstruction and rendering	$\mathcal{S}(v) \not\subset \mathcal{S}(v') \cap \mathcal{S}(v'')$	yes	yes

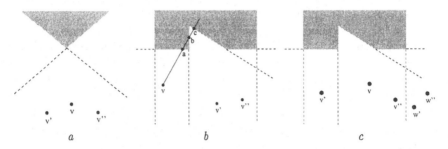

Fig. 3. Configurations of the scene and the virtual and reference images corresponding to image interpolation (a), image extrapolation (b), and model reconstruction and rendering (c).

1. Find the correspondences in the two reference images by a stereo algorithm. Sparse correspondences of salient features are sufficient.
2. For each pair of corresponding points in the reference images, compute the position of the corresponding point in the virtual image by a transfer.
3. Construct a triangulation on the set of transferred points in the virtual image. Warp the interiors of the triangles from one reference image to the virtual image. This is similar to morphing, well-known in computer graphics.

Let v be the virtual viewpoint and v', v'' the reference viewpoints. The necessary and sufficient condition for image interpolation to yield a correct and complete virtual image is:

$$S(v) = S(v') \cap S(v'') . \tag{1}$$

It means that exactly the part of the scene visible from both v' and v'' has to be visible from v. Figure 3a shows an example configuration when the virtual image that can be correctly constructed by image interpolation. Viewpoints v, v', v'' must not leave the domain bounded by dashed lines.

This method is similar to "image interpolation" by Seitz and Dyer [10].

Image Extrapolation. The example in Fig. 3b shows scene points a, b, c transferred to the same image point in the virtual image. One has to decide which of them is visible. If visibility is not explicitly solved (like in image interpolation), an incorrect virtual image can obtained.

An algorithm for image extrapolation is image interpolation augmented with an explicit removal of hidden surfaces. The removal can be done in a way similar to ray tracing [6] or, more efficiently, by z-buffering distances from the epipole, described in Section 3.3. In contrary to image interpolation, sparse correspondences of salient features need not be sufficient. The reason is that a part of the scene can be occluded by a surface with no salient features.

The necessary and sufficient condition for image extrapolation to yield a complete virtual image is the following:

$$S(v) \subset S(v') \cap S(v'') , \qquad (2)$$

i.e. the part of the scene visible from the viewpoint v has to be a *subset* of the parts visible from both v' and v''.

3-D Model Reconstruction and Rendering. Sometimes, two reference images do not allow to construct a complete virtual image because some parts of the scene visible from the virtual viewpoint are not visible from both reference viewpoints. In this case, we have to use other pairs of reference images and *fuse* multiply reconstructed image parts. The fusion makes this approach practically equal to the reconstruction and rendering of a consistent (projective) 3-D model[2].

Images taken from reference viewpoints v' and v'' do not suffice to construct the complete virtual image from the viewpoint v if

$$S(v) \not\subset S(v') \cap S(v'') , \qquad (3)$$

that means, a part of the scene visible from v is invisible from either v' or v''. An example configuration is in Fig. 3c.

Since two reference images are not enough, it is necessary to use another pair of reference viewpoints, e.g. w' and w'' in Fig. 3c. If

$$S(v) \subset [S(v') \cap S(v'')] \cup [S(w') \cap S(w'')] \qquad (4)$$

the transfer from v' and v'' to v combined with the transfer from w' and w'' to v yields the complete virtual image (otherwise, other pairs of reference images have to be added). A difficulty occurs if

$$[S(v') \cap S(v'')] \cap [S(w') \cap S(w'')] \neq \emptyset \qquad (5)$$

because some parts of the scene will be constructed *twice* in the virtual image. Since these two parts will not be exactly the same due to noise, they have to be fused. Thus we have to cope with fusion of multiply reconstructed scene parts, which is one of the most difficult issues in 3-D model reconstruction.

---

[2] This approach seems to work with a view-centered representation whereas a model-based approach works with an object-centered representation. But this is not significant because (i) there is no qualitative difference between transfer and projective reconstruction–reprojection, and (ii) it is convenient to express reconstructions from different subsets of reference images in a common projective coordinate system in order to construct a single virtual image v, which is in fact an object-centered representation.

2.3 Comparison of the Three Approaches

Which approach should be used for a given application? In order to visualize a general scene from a general viewpoint, we showed that only 3-D model reconstruction/rendering yields correct and complete virtual images.

Image interpolation is on the opposite end of the spectrum. It has nice properties in its well-posedness [10], relative insensitivity to errors in correspondence, and no care about possible hidden surfaces. However, the domain of its validity is limited and it is difficult to find this domain automatically for a general scene.

Image extrapolation is a trade-off between the two limit approaches. For a general scene and general viewpoints, it does not ensure completeness (i.e., some part of the scene can be missing in the virtual image) yet it guarantees reconstructed parts to be visualized with correctly solved visibility. Obviously, image extrapolation is the most general method for visualizing a scene described by two reference images only.

While it is reasonable to call image interpolation an image-based approach, and 3-D model reconstruction/rendering a model-based one, we could hesitate about image extrapolation. This may indicate that using the concepts "image-based" and "model-based" can sometimes cause misunderstanding.

3 Image Extrapolation from Uncalibrated Images

Three issues are involved in image extrapolation:

1. Reconstruction of a partial 3-D model from several (often only two) reference images. The model is partial because only scene parts that are visible from all these reference images *at the same time* are reconstructed. This is important, as it distinguishes image extrapolation from the reconstruction of a complete consistent 3-D model from a large number of reference images.
2. Virtual camera positioning.
3. Rendering the partial 3-D model.

This section presents an efficient algorithm for the issue 3. However, we will also briefly introduce issues 1 and 2 to have a necessary background.

We will consider only uncalibrated reference images. In that case, at most *projective* 3-D model can be reconstructed [9]. This situation is important especially when the reference images cannot be calibrated, e.g., if we want to visualize scene parts visible in a set of photographs taken by an unknown cameras.

We will denote camera centers by C, image planes by π, image points by $\mathbf{u}_i = [u_i \; v_i \; w_i]^\top$, scene points by $\mathbf{X}_i = [X_i \; Y_i \; Z_i \; W_i]^\top$, and 3×4 camera projection matrices by $\mathbf{M}$. The points are elements of a projective space and represented by homogeneous coordinates. Entities related to the virtual camera and the reference cameras will be distinguished by primes. Thus, C is a center of the virtual camera and C', C'' are centers of the first and second reference camera; π, π' and π'' are respectively the virtual image plane, the first reference and the second reference image plane; etc.

3.1 Reconstructing a Projective Model

We assume that a reconstructed projective model is available and that it is represented by the following data:

- The *set of corresponding pairs [image point, scene point]*, $\{[\mathbf{u}_i', \mathbf{X}_i], \; i = 1, \ldots, N\}$. This is the result of a projective reconstruction (e.g., [9]) from the set of corresponding image points $\{[\mathbf{u}_i' \; \mathbf{u}_i''], \; i = 1, \ldots, N\}$. It is

$$\rho_i' \mathbf{u}_i' = \mathbf{M}' \mathbf{X}_i \, , \quad \rho_i'' \mathbf{u}_i'' = \mathbf{M}'' \mathbf{X}_i \, , \tag{6}$$

  where $\mathbf{M}', \mathbf{M}''$ are camera matrices of the reference cameras, $\{\mathbf{X}_i, \; i = 1, \ldots, N\}$ is the set of reconstructed scene points, and $\rho_i' \neq 0$, $\rho_i'' \neq 0$. Points $\mathbf{X}_i$ differ from an underlying Euclidean structure by an unknown projective transformation.
- The *triangulation* on the set $\{\mathbf{X}_i, \; i = 1, \ldots, N\}$. The triangulation approximates the underlying scene surface. Since only the surface that is visible from both reference cameras can be reconstructed, there is a one-to-one mapping between this surface and the reference image plane π'. Therefore the triangulation can conveniently be done in π' rather than in the projective space of the scene.
- The *reference image* captured from the viewpoint C'. It is used to store *texture* which will be warped to the the virtual image during the rendering process. (The texture from the other reference images is currently not used.)

3.2 Virtual Camera Positioning

The reconstructed points $\mathbf{X}_i$ are projected to the virtual image as

$$\rho_i \mathbf{u}_i = \mathbf{M} \mathbf{X}_i \, , \tag{7}$$

where $\rho \neq 0$. The camera matrix $\mathbf{M}$ specifies the virtual view, in other words, it *positions the virtual camera*. If Euclidean reconstruction were available, $\mathbf{M}$ could be easily computed from extrinsic and intrinsic camera parameters. Virtual camera positioning in projective space is a difficult task, which has not yet drawn too much attention, however. It has a connection to the theory of self-calibration and Kruppa equations [3]. We will assume that a matrix $\mathbf{M}$ specifying the required virtual image is available.

3.3 Rendering a Projective Model

The rendering of the projective model involves two problems to be solved: (i) explicit removal of invisible parts of the scene, (ii) correct and efficient filling pixels in the virtual image plane. Let us discuss them in more detail.

A part of the scene visible in reference images (and therefore reconstructed) can be invisible in the virtual image for the following reasons:

- *This part is behind the virtual camera.* If the projection to the virtual image plane π is done exactly according to (7), the virtual camera cannot distinguish between scene points in front of it and behind it, both can be projected into an image point in π. To model a real situation correctly, the scene points behind π must be explicitly distinguished from the scene points in front of π, and their rendering must be suppressed. The solution has been suggested using oriented projective geometry [7].
- *This part is occluded by another scene part.* Scene points X_1, X_2 projected in two image points u'_1, u'_2 distinct in π' can be projected in a common point $u_1 = u_2$ in π. This means that either X_1 occludes X_2 or *vice versa* if the scene is observed from C. The decision which of these two cases occurs can be done according to the distance of points u'_1, u'_2 from the epipole e' in π' [6,7]. Equation (10) below gives the exact formulation. We will use this distance to remove occluded surfaces by z-buffering.

Let us focus on how to fill pixels in the virtual image plane π. A naive way is to transfer pixels in a random order from π' to π. The drawback is that some pixels in π remain unfilled because of different sampling frequencies in π and π'.

Ray tracing remedies this drawback. It allows warping texture and solving visibility correctly. It is interesting that the rays can be traced directly in image planes [6]. Ray tracing is time-consuming since an intersection of the scene and rays going through all pixels in π must be found.

A more efficient approach is *transfer by triangles*. First, the vertices of each triangle are transferred from π' to π. Second, the interior of each triangle is transferred by an appropriate transformation. Visibility can be solved by z-buffering. We will show that this approach can result in a very efficient implementation.

Transferring Triangles via Homography. Let us consider two corresponding triangles T and T'. The triangle T lies in the virtual image plane π and has the vertices u_1, u_2, u_3. The triangle T' lies in the reference image plane π' and has the vertices u'_1, u'_2, u'_3. We know u_1, u_2, u_3 from (7) and u'_1, u'_2, u'_3 from (6). T is rendered by transferring the interior points from T' to T. The interiors of T and T' are related via a homography:

$$u \simeq Hu' \tag{8}$$

where u lies inside T and u' lies inside T'.

We need four corresponding point pairs to determine H. We show that we can use the pairs $[u_1, u'_1], [u_2, u'_2], [u_3, u'_3]$, and $[e, e']$. The first three pairs can be used obviously as they are vertices of T and T'. Figure 4 illustrates why $[e, e']$ can be used as the fourth pair. The triangle $X_1 X_2 X_3$ corresponds[3] to T in π and also to T' in π'. The plane $X_1 X_2 X_3$ and the line CC' intersect in the point X_4. The epipoles e and e' are the corresponding images of X_4 and therefore the fourth corresponding pair. In projective space, X_4 exists even if the plane $X_1 X_2 X_3$ and the line CC' are parallel.

---

[3] The situation is simplified by one dimension in Fig. 4, therefore X_3 is not shown.

H is used for computing intensities of pixels inside T in the virtual image (i.e., transferring texture from T' to T) and removing hidden pixels by z-buffering.

Transferring texture. The intensity function[4] in the image point $\mathbf{u}'$ in the reference image is denoted by $I'(\mathbf{u}')$ and in the corresponding image point $\mathbf{u}$ in the virtual image by $I(\mathbf{u})$. Currently, we assume that $I(\mathbf{u}) = I'(\mathbf{u}')$ for each pair $[\mathbf{u}', \mathbf{u}]$ (that is, we neglect changes due to photommetry). Synthesis of the virtual image means computing an intensity in each its pixel $\mathbf{u}$. This intensity $I(\mathbf{u})$ is obtained as

$$I(\mathbf{u}) = I'(\mathbf{u}') = I'(\mathbf{H}^{-1}\mathbf{u}) \,. \tag{9}$$

Transferring depth. The visibility in the virtual view can be solved by z-buffering in π. Let us assign values of the following function $d'(\mathbf{u}')$ to points in π':

$$d'(\mathbf{u}') = o(\mathbf{e}') \; \sigma\left(\left\|\left[\frac{u'}{w'} \; \frac{v'}{w'}\right] - \left[\frac{e'}{g'} \; \frac{f'}{g'}\right]\right\|^2\right) \tag{10}$$

where $\mathbf{u}' = [u' \; v' \; w']^\top$, $\mathbf{e}' = [e' \; f' \; g']^\top$, $\|[\frac{u'}{w'} \; \frac{v'}{w'}] - [\frac{e'}{g'} \; \frac{f'}{g'}]\|$ is the distance of the point $\mathbf{u}'$ from the epipole $\mathbf{e}'$, and σ is an arbitrary monotonic function. The function $o(\mathbf{e}')$ equals 1 resp. -1 if C lies in front resp. from behind of π' (see [7] for explanation). The values of $z(\mathbf{u})$ in the z-buffer[5] for each pixel $\mathbf{u}$ in π are obtained in terms of $d'(\mathbf{u}')$:

$$z(\mathbf{u}) = d'(\mathbf{u}') = d'(\mathbf{H}^{-1}\mathbf{u}) \,. \tag{11}$$

Approximating the Homography by Affinity. Equations (9) and (11) allow to synthesize virtual images in a similar manner as a Euclidean 3-D model is rendered in computer graphics. This rendering can be very fast especially on work stations with hardware-supported texture warping and z-buffering (e.g. Silicon Graphics). We want to enable utilizing these hardware-supported functions.

Sometimes only warping via an affine transformation is supported, rather than via a homography as in (9) and (11). If T is small compared to the whole image and the maximum difference in depth of the interior points of T is also small, **H** can be approximated by an affinity. Since an affine transformation leaves length ratios unchanged, the relation $\mathbf{u}' = \mathbf{H}^{-1}(\mathbf{u})$ can be conveniently approximated using barycentric coordinates, $\mathbf{u}' = \alpha_1\mathbf{u}'_1 + \alpha_2\mathbf{u}'_2 + \alpha_3\mathbf{u}'_3$, where α_i are determined by $\mathbf{u} = \alpha_1\mathbf{u}_1 + \alpha_2\mathbf{u}_2 + \alpha_3\mathbf{u}_3$, $\alpha_1 + \alpha_2 + \alpha_3 = 1$. Then (9) changes to

$$I(\mathbf{u}) = I'(\mathbf{u}') = I'(\alpha_1\mathbf{u}'_1 + \alpha_2\mathbf{u}'_2 + \alpha_3\mathbf{u}'_3) \,. \tag{12}$$

---

[4] For simplicity, the notation $I(\mathbf{u})$ is used for intensity in an image point even if $\mathbf{u} = [u \; v \; w]^\top$ is in projective coordinates and the function I usually takes points in Cartesian coordinates. $I(\mathbf{u})$ can be considered as an abbreviation for $I([\frac{u}{w} \; \frac{v}{w}]^\top)$.

[5] Unlike in rendering a Euclidean model for which z-buffer is usually used, $z(\mathbf{u})$ does not mean the Euclidean depth in $\mathbf{u}$ here but rather an increasing function of it.

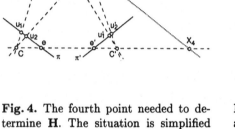

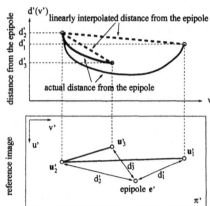

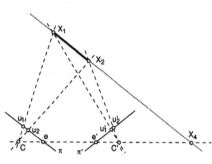

Fig. 4. The fourth point needed to determine **H**. The situation is simplified by one dimension, therefore $\mathbf{X}_3$ is not shown.

Fig. 5. The error in visibility due to the approximation of (11) by (14). The segment $\mathbf{u}_2'\mathbf{u}_3'$ is incorrectly determined as visible.

Similarly, we can approximate (11):

$$z(\mathbf{u}) = d'(\mathbf{u}') = d'(\alpha_1\mathbf{u}_1' + \alpha_2\mathbf{u}_2' + \alpha_3\mathbf{u}_3') \ . \tag{13}$$

However, this requires evaluating (10) for each pixel in π. A more efficient way is to further approximate (13) in a way similar to Goraud shading well-known from computer graphics:

$$z(\mathbf{u}) = \alpha_1 d'(\mathbf{u}_1') + \alpha_2 d'(\mathbf{u}_2') + \alpha_3 d'(\mathbf{u}_3') \ . \tag{14}$$

Note that (14) becomes identical to the exact relation (13) if $d'(\mathbf{u}')$ is *linear* in coordinates of $\mathbf{u}'$.

Thus, (12) and (14) are approximations of the exact relations (9) and (11) and allow using hardware-supported warping via an affine transformation.

Artifacts Due to the Approximations. The approximation of (9) by (12) causes the texture inside T to be distorted. This distortion becomes more significant near the middle of T and increases with the size of T and with the maximal depth difference of its points. It will vanish for orthographic cameras.

We will show that the approximation of (11) by (14) can cause determining the visibility of T incorrectly on some conditions. In Fig. 5, there are two triangles, $\mathbf{u}_1'\mathbf{u}_2'$ and $\mathbf{u}_2'\mathbf{u}_3'$. Since the situation is simplified by one dimension, these triangles are illustrated as line segments. The correct decision whether the segment $\mathbf{u}_2'\mathbf{u}_3'$ occludes $\mathbf{u}_1'\mathbf{u}_2'$ or *vice versa* should be done according to the actual distance of the segments' interior points from the epipole $\mathbf{e}'$. When this actual distance ($d'(\mathbf{u}')$ in (11), solid-line plots in Fig. 5) is approximated by a linear interpolation from end points ($d'(\mathbf{u}')$ in (14), dashed-line plots), the segment $\mathbf{u}_2'\mathbf{u}_3'$ is incorrectly determined as visible.

This error can be avoided by an appropriate choice of the function σ in (10) so that $d'(\mathbf{u}')$ is *linear* in coordinates of $\mathbf{u}'$ because then (13) and (14) will be equal. It is not obvious, however, if expressing $d'(\mathbf{u}')$ as a linear function in $\mathbf{u}'$ is possible and when. We will show that it is possible if $\mathbf{e}'$ lies outside the convex hull of all image points $\mathbf{u}'$. Then we can replace (10) with

$$d'(\mathbf{u}') = \mathbf{n}'^{\top} \mathbf{u}' \qquad (15)$$

where $\mathbf{n}'$ is a vector such that $\mathbf{n}'^{\top}(\mathbf{u}'_i - \mathbf{e}')$ has the same sign for all image points $\mathbf{u}'_i$. Such a vector exists only if $\mathbf{e}'$ lies outside the image. This sign has to be positive, resp. negative if $\mathbf{C}$ lies in front of π' resp. behind π'. In fact, (15) describes a projection of the ray $\mathbf{e}'\mathbf{u}'$ to a vector that is "parallel enough" to the image of the optical axis of the reference camera. This projection can be written as $d'(\mathbf{u}') = \mathbf{n}'^{\top}(\mathbf{u}' - \mathbf{e}')$, hence (15) after omitting the constant $-\mathbf{n}'^{\top}\mathbf{e}'$.

4 Experimental Results

We will describe experiments with image extrapolation on two real scenes. The first scene (Teeth) was a plaster cast of human teeth arch, its dimensions were approx. $8 \times 8 \times 8$ cm. The second scene (Doll) was a small ceramic statue of about the same dimensions.

Figure 6 shows the reference images. Figs. 6a, c show images in π', b, d show images in π''. Image sizes are 250×160 pixels for the Teeth scene and 384×278 pixels for the Doll scene.

Reconstruction of the partial projective model. We found sparse correspondences of the two reference images by tracking edges in a dense image sequence between the reference images [17]. The edges were obtained in rows using Deriche edge detector with subpixel precision. Any standard feature-based stereo algorithm would also suffice. The matched edges for the first scene are shown in Fig. 6e, f.

Projective reconstruction was done, using the corresponding edge points.

Next, triangulation of the projective model was constructed by using Delaunay triangulation on the set of the matched points in π'. There were 4183 triangles for the Teeth scene (Fig. 6g) and 12408 triangles for the Doll scene.

Virtual camera positioning. We set the elements of the virtual camera matrix $\mathbf{M}$ (see (7)) experimentally so that it yielded an acceptable virtual image. Resolving the front-behind ambiguity, i.e. marking a single image point in π as well as the epipole $\mathbf{e}'$ in π' as projected from front or from behind, was specified by the user.

Rendering the projective model. Equation (12) was used to warp texture from π' (i.e., Fig. 6a or c) to π. Removing hidden pixels by z-buffering was done according to (14). We used for computing $d'(\mathbf{u}')$ (15) if $\mathbf{e}'$ was outside the convex hull of $\mathbf{u}'_i$ and (10) otherwise. The function σ was linear.

We used hardware-supported z-buffering on a Silicon Graphics Indigo 2 work station. About 4 grey-scale images for the Teeth scene and 2 color images for the

Doll scene were synthesized per second, image sizes being about 500×500 pixels. We hope that if also texture warping were supported by hardware (as is the case for some other workstations) real-time synthesis could have been achieved.

The resulting virtual images are shown in Fig. $6h-l$. Incorrectly reconstructed triangles due to errors in the correspondence can be noticed in $6b, c$. The cusp on the doll's nose in $6l$ is caused by the existence of only one salient feature (edge) on the tip of the nose. Figure $6m$ shows a virtual image with the following error in visibility: C was incorrectly marked in (10) as lying behind π' instead of in front of π'.

5 Conclusion

This paper presented two main results. First, image-based visualization was shown to be closely related to model-based one, because a consistent 3-D model must be used for a perfect visualization of a general scene from a general viewpoint. Fusion and visibility must be explicitly solved like in 3-D model reconstruction/rendering. We distinguished three approaches to visualization: (i) image interpolation (simplest, correct only for a special configuration of a scene and viewpoints), (ii) image extrapolation (correctly removing hidden surfaces but some parts of the scene can be missing), and (iii) 3-D model reconstruction/rendering (difficult, correct in a general situation).

Second, image extrapolation was introduced and advocated as a useful tradeoff between simplicity and generality. It was shown to be equivalent to the reconstruction and rendering of a partial projective model. An efficient algorithm for rendering a projective model was presented. It includes transfer from the reference images to the virtual one by triangles via a homography and solving visibility by z-buffering. The derived relations were approximated so that the resulting algorithm could use warping via affine transformation. We showed that qualitative errors in visibility can be caused by these approximation and when they can be avoided.

Examples of virtual images of two real scenes were presented. The synthesis was close to real time when using triangle warping supported by hardware on a Silicon Graphics Indigo workstation.

References

1. Shenchang Eric Chen and Lance Williams. View interpolation for image synthesis. In James T. Kajiya, editor, *Computer Graphics (SIGGRAPH '93 Proceedings)*, volume 27, pages 279–288, August 1993.
2. O. Faugeras and B. Mourrain. On the geometry and algebra of the point and line correspondences between N images. In *Proceedings of the 5th International Conference on Computer Vision*, pages 951–956, Boston, USA, June 1995. IEEE.
3. Olivier D. Faugeras, Q. T. Luong, and S. J. Maybank. Camera self-calibration: Theory and experiments. In *European Conference on Computer Vision*, pages 321–333, 1992.

4. R. I. Hartley. A linear method for reconstruction from lines and points. In *Proceedings of the 5th International Conference on Computer Vision*, pages 882–887, Boston USA, June 1995. IEEE Computer Society Press.

5. R. Kumar, P. Anadan, M. Irani, J. Bergen, and K. Hanna. Representation of scenes from collection of images. In *Proceedings of the Visual Scene Representation Workshop, Boston, MA., USA, June 24*, pages 10–17. IEEE Computer Society Press, 1995.

6. S. Laveau and O. Faugeras. 3-D scene representation as a collection of images. In *Proc. of 12th International Conf. on Pattern Recognition, Jerusalem, Israel*, pages 689–691, October 9–13 1994.

7. S. Laveau and O. Faugeras. Oriented projective geometry for computer vision. In *Proceedings of the 4th European Conference on Computer Vision'96*, volume I, pages 147–156. Springer-Verlag, April 1996.

8. Leonard McMillan and Gary Bishop. Plenoptic modeling: An image-based rendering system. In Robert Cook, editor, *SIGGRAPH'95 Conference Proceedings*, pages 39–46. Addison Wesley, August 1995.

9. Charlie Rothwell, Gabriela Csurka, and Olivier Faugeras. A comparison of projective reconstruction methods for pairs of views. Technical Report 2538, INRIA, Sophia-Antipolis, France, April 1995.

10. S. M. Seitz and C. R. Dyer. Physically-valid view synthesis by image interpolation. In *Proceedings of the Visual Scene Representation Workshop, Boston, MA., USA, June 24*, pages 18–27. IEEE Computer Society Press, 1995.

11. A. Shashua. On geometric and algebraic aspects of 3D affine and projective structures from perspective 2D views. Technical Report AI Memo No. 1405, Massachusetts Institute of Technology, Artifical Intelligence Laboratory, July 1993.

12. A. Shashua and M. Werman. Trilinearity of three perspective views and its associated tensor. In *Proceedings of the 5th International Conference on Computer Vision*, pages 920–925. IEEE Computer Society Press, May 1995.

13. M. Spetsakis and J. Alomoinos. A unified theory of structure from motion. In *Proceedigs ARPA Image Understanding Workshop*, pages 271–283, Pittsburg, PA, USA, 1990.

14. S. Ullman and R. Basri. Recognition by linear combination of models. *IEEE Transactions of Pattern Analysis and Machine Intelligence*, 13(10):992–1005, October 1991.

15. T. Werner, R.D. Hersch, and V. Hlaváč. Rendering real-world objects using view interpolation. In *Proceedings of the 5th International Conference on Computer Vision*, pages 957–962, Boston, USA, June 1995. IEEE Computer Society Press.

16. T. Werner, V. Hlaváč, A. Leonardis, and T. Pajdla. Selection of reference views for image-based representation. In *Proceedings of the 13th International Conference on Pattern Recognition*, volume I – Track A: Computer Vision, pages 73–77, Vienna, Austria, August 1996. IEEE Computer Society Press, Los Alamitos, CA., USA.

17. Tomáš Werner, Tomáš Pajdla, and Václav Hlaváč. Correspondence by tracking edges in a dense sequence for image-based scene representation. In *Proceedings of the Czech Pattern Recognition Workshop '97*, pages 64–68, Milovy, Czech Republic, Feb 1997. Czech Pattern Recognition Society. Available from http://cmp.felk.cvut.cz.

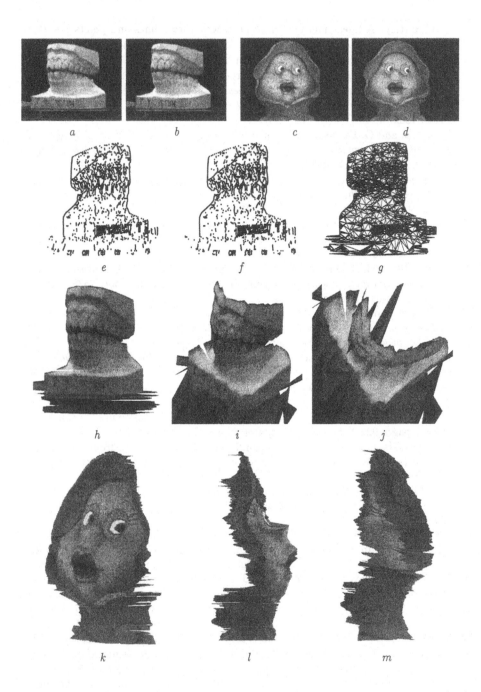

Fig. 6. The reference images for the Teeth scene (a,b) and for the Doll scene (c,d). Matched edge elements in the reference images of the first scene are in e,f. Subfigure g shows the triangulation on the set of edgels in e. The synthesized virtual images of the Teeth scene (h,i,j) and of the Doll scene k,l. Subfigure m shows the result if visibility is solved incorrectly.

Shading and Shape

What Shadows Reveal About Object Structure

David J. Kriegman and Peter N. Belhumeur

Center for Computional Vision and Control, Yale University, New Haven CT 06520
david.kriegman@yale.edu and belhumeur@yale.edu
http://cvc.yale.edu

Abstract. *In a scene observed from a fixed viewpoint, the set of shadow curves in an image changes as a point light source (nearby or at infinity) assumes different locations. We show that for any finite set of point light sources illuminating an object viewed under either orthographic or perspective projection, there is an equivalence class of object shapes having the same set of shadows. Members of this equivalence class differ by a four parameter family of projective transformations, and the shadows of a transformed object are identical when the same transformation is applied to the light source locations. Under orthographic projection, this family is the generalized bas-relief (GBR) transformation, and we show that the GBR transformation is the only family of transformations of an object's shape for which the complete set of imaged shadows is identical. Finally, we show that given multiple images under differing and unknown light source directions, it is possible to reconstruct an object up to these transformations from the shadows alone.*

1 Introduction

In his fifteenth century *Treatise on Painting* [15], Leonardo da Vinci errs in analysis of shadows while comparing painting and relief sculpture:

> As far as light and shade are concerned low relief fails both as sculpture and as painting, because the shadows correspond to the low nature of the relief, as for example in the shadows of foreshortened objects, which will not exhibit the depth of those in painting or in sculpture in the round.

It is true that – when illuminated by the same light source – a relief surface and a surface "in the round" will cast different shadows. However, Leonardo's statement appears to overlook the fact that for any flattening of the surface relief, there is a corresponding change in the light source direction such that the shadows appear the same. This is not restricted to classical reliefs but, as we will later show, applies equally to a greater set of projective transformations.

Original   Transformed   Original (2)   Transformed (2)

Fig. 1. An illustration of the effect of applying a generalized perspective bas-relief (GPBR) transformation to a scene composed of a teapot resting on a supporting plane. The first image shows the original teapot. The second image shows the teapot after having undergone a GPBR transformation $(a_1, a_2, a_3, a_4) = (.05, .05, .05, 1)$ with respect to the viewpoint used to generate the first image. Note that the attached and cast shadows as well as the occluding contour are identical in first two images. The third image shows the original teapot from a second viewpoint. The fourth image reveals the nature of the GPBR transformation, showing the transformed teapot from the same viewpoint as used for the third image.

More specifically, when an object is viewed from a fixed viewpoint, there is a four parameter family of projective transformations of the object's structure and the light source locations such that the images of the shadows remain the same. It follows then, that when light source positions are unknown one cannot determine the Euclidean structure of an object from its shadows alone. Yet in all past work on reconstruction from shadows, it is explicitly assumed that the direction or location of the light source *is known*. An implication of these results is that two objects differing by these transformations cannot be recognized solely from their shadow lines.

In early work, Waltz considered labelings of shadow edges in line drawing interpretation [27]. Subsequently, Shafer showed how geometric constraints on surface orientation could be obtained from labeled line drawings using shadow and surface outlines under orthographic projection [23]. The Entry-Exit method was developed to segment and label shadow curves using information about the projection onto the image plane of the light source direction [11]. Kender and his colleagues have undertaken a series of studies pertaining to metric reconstruction of surfaces from the shadows in multiple images of an object in fixed pose when the light source direction is known [12, 17, 29]. Shadows have also been used in the interpretation of aerial images, particularly to locate and reconstruct buildings when the sun direction is known [6, 13, 14, 20].

Here we consider shadows on unknown objects produced by light sources whose directions are also unknown. In the next section we show that seen from a fixed viewpoint under perspective projection, two surfaces produce the same shadows if they differ by a particular projective transformation – which we call the Generalized Perspective Bas-Relief (GPBR) transformation. See Figure 1 for an example of this transformation. This result holds for any number of proximal or distant point light sources. Furthermore, under conditions where perspective can be approximated by orthographic projection, this transformation is the Generalized Bas-Relief (GBR) transformation [3]. As will be shown in Section 3, the GBR transformation is unique in that any two smooth surfaces which produce the same shadows must differ by a GBR.

In Section 4, we propose an algorithm for reconstructing, from the attached shadow boundaries, the structure of an object up to a GBR transformation. The algorithm assumes that the object is viewed orthographically and that it is illuminated by a set of point light sources at infinity. We do not propose this algorithm with the belief that its present form has great applicability, but rather we give it to demonstrate that under ideal conditions information from shadows alone is enough to determine the structure of the object up to a GBR transformation.

2 Shadowing Ambiguity

Let us define two objects as being *shadow equivalent* if there exists two sets of point light sources S and S' such that for every light source in S illuminating one object, there exists a light source in S' illuminating the second object, such that the shadowing in both images is identical. Let us further define two objects as being *strongly shadow equivalent* if for *any* light source illuminating one object, there exists a source illuminating the second object such that shadowing is identical – i.e., S is the set of all point light sources. In this section we will show that two objects are shadow equivalent if they differ by a particular set of projective transformations.

Consider a camera-centered coordinate system whose origin is at the focal point, whose x and y axes span the image plane, and whose z-axis points in the direction of the optical axis. Let a smooth surface f be defined with respect to this coordinate system and lie in the halfspace $z > 0$. Since the surface is smooth, the surface normal $\mathbf{n}(\mathbf{p})$ is defined at all points $\mathbf{p} \in f$.

We model illumination as a collection of point light sources, located nearby or at infinity. Note that this is a restriction of the lighting model presented by Langer and Zucker [19] which permits anisotropic light sources whose intensity is a function of direction. In this paper, we will represent surfaces, light sources, and the camera center as lying in either a two or three dimensional real projective space ($\mathbb{RP}^2$ or $\mathbb{RP}^3$). (For a concise treatment of real projective spaces, see [21].) This allows a unified treatment of both point light sources that are nearby (proximal) or distant (at infinity) and camera models that use perspective or orthographic projection.

When a point light source is proximal, its coordinates can be expressed as $\mathbf{s} = (s_x, s_y, s_z)$. In projective (homogeneous) coordinates, the light source $\mathbf{s} \in \mathbb{RP}^3$ can be written as $\mathbf{s} = (s_x, s_y, s_z, 1)$. (Note that different fonts are used to distinguish between Euclidean and projective coordinates.) When a point light source is at infinity, all light rays are parallel, and so one is concerned with the direction of the light source. The direction can be represented as a unit vector in $\mathbb{R}^3$ or as point on an illumination sphere $\mathbf{s} \in S^2$. In projective coordinates, the fourth homogeneous coordinate of a point at infinity is zero, and so the light source can be expressed as $\mathbf{s} = (s_x, s_y, s_z, 0)$. (Note that when the light source at infinity is represented in projective coordinates, the antipodal points from S^2 must be equated.)

For a single point source $\mathbf{s} \in \mathbb{RP}^3$, let us define the set of *light rays* as the lines in $\mathbb{RP}^3$ passing through $\mathbf{s}$. For any $\mathbf{p} \in \mathbb{RP}^3$ with $\mathbf{p} \neq \mathbf{s}$, there is a single light ray passing through $\mathbf{p}$. Naturally it is the intersection of the light rays with the surface f which determine the shadows. We differentiate between two types of shadows: *attached shadows* and *cast shadows* [2, 25]. See Figures 2 and 3. A surface point $\mathbf{p}$ lies on the border of an *attached shadow* for light source $\mathbf{s}$ if and only if it satisfies both a local and global condition:

Local Attached Shadow Condition: The light ray through $\mathbf{p}$ lies in the tangent plane to the surface at $\mathbf{p}$. Algebraically, this condition can be expressed as $\mathbf{n}(\mathbf{p}) \cdot (\mathbf{p} - \mathbf{s}) = 0$ for a nearby light source and as $\mathbf{n}(\mathbf{p}) \cdot \mathbf{s} = 0$ for a distant light source. A point $\mathbf{p}$ which satisfies at least the local condition is called a *local attached shadow boundary point*.

Global Attached Shadow Condition: The light ray does not intersect the surface between $\mathbf{p}$ and $\mathbf{s}$, i.e., the light source is not occluded at $\mathbf{p}$.

Now consider applying an arbitrary projective transformation $a : \mathbb{RP}^3 \to \mathbb{RP}^3$ to both the surface and the light source. Under this transformation, let $\mathbf{p}' = a(\mathbf{p})$ and $\mathbf{s}' = a(\mathbf{s})$.

Lemma 1. *A point $\mathbf{p}$ on a smooth surface is a local attached shadow boundary point for point light source $\mathbf{s}$ iff $\mathbf{p}'$ on a transformed surface is a local attached shadow boundary point for point light source $\mathbf{s}'$.*

Proof. At a local attached shadow boundary point $\mathbf{p}$, the line defined by $\mathbf{p} \in \mathbb{RP}^3$ and light source $\mathbf{s} \in \mathbb{RP}^3$ lies in the tangent plane at $\mathbf{p}$. Since the order of contact (e.g., tangency) of a curve and surface is preserved under projective transformations, the line defined by $\mathbf{p}'$ and $\mathbf{s}'$ lies in the tangent plane at $\mathbf{p}'$.

Cast shadows occur at points on the surface that face the light source, but where some other portion of the surface lies between the shadowed points and the light source. A point $\mathbf{p}$ lies on the boundary of a cast shadow for light source

s if and only if it similarly satisfies both a local and global condition:

> **Local Cast Shadow Condition:** The light ray through **p** grazes the surface at some other point **q** (i.e., **q** lies on an attached shadow). A point **p** which satisfies at least the local condition is called a *local cast shadow boundary point.*

> **Global Attached Shadow Condition:** The only intersection of the surface and the light ray between **p** and **s** is at **q**.

Lemma 2. *A point* **p** *on a smooth surface is a local cast shadow boundary point for point light source* **s** *iff* **p′** *on a transformed surface is a local cast shadow boundary point for point light source* **s′**.

Proof. For a local cast shadow boundary point $\mathbf{p} \in \mathbb{RP}^3$ and light source $\mathbf{s} \in \mathbb{RP}^3$, there exists another point $\mathbf{q} \in \mathbb{RP}^3$ on the line defined by **p** and **s** such that **q** lies on an attached shadow. Since collinearity is preserved under projective transformations, **p′**, **q′** and **s′** are collinear. From Lemma 1, **q′** is also an attached shadow point.

Taken together, Lemmas 1 and 2 indicate that under a projective transformation of a surface and light source, the set of local shadow curves is a projective transformation of the local shadow curves of the original surface and light source. However, these two lemmas do not imply that the two surfaces are shadow equivalent since the transformed points may project to different image points, or the global conditions may not hold.

2.1 Perspective Projection: GPBR

We will further restrict the set of projective transformations. Modeling the camera as a function $\pi : \mathbb{RP}^3 \to \mathbb{RP}^2$, we require that for any point **p** on the surface $\pi(\mathbf{p}) = \pi(a(\mathbf{p}))$ where a is a projective transformation – that is **p** and $a(\mathbf{p})$ must project to the same image point. We will consider two specific camera models in turn: perspective projection π_p and orthographic projection π_o.

Without loss of generality, consider a pinhole perspective camera with unit focal length located at the origin of the coordinate system and with the optical axis pointed in the direction of the z-axis. Letting the homogeneous coordinates of an image point be given by $\mathbf{u} \in \mathbb{RP}^2$, then pinhole perspective projection of $\mathbf{p} \in \mathbb{RP}^3$ is given by $\mathbf{u} = \Pi_p \mathbf{p}$ where

$$\Pi_p = \begin{bmatrix} 1 & 0 & 0 & 0 \\ 0 & 1 & 0 & 0 \\ 0 & 0 & 1 & 0 \end{bmatrix}. \tag{1}$$

For $\pi_p(\mathbf{p}) = \pi_p(a(\mathbf{p}))$ to be true for any point **p**, the transformation must move **p** along the optical ray between the camera center and **p**. This can be accomplished by the projective transformation $a : \mathbf{p} \mapsto A\mathbf{p}$ where

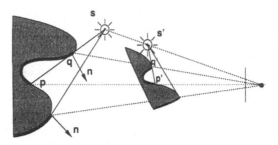

Fig. 2. In this 2-d illustration of the generalized perspective bas-relief transformation (GPBR), the lower shadow is an attached shadow while the upper one is composed of both attached and cast components. A GPBR transformation has been applied to the left surface, yielding the right one. Note that under GPBR, all surface points and the light source are transformed along the optical rays through the center of projection. By transforming the light source from **s** to **s'**, the shadows are preserved.

$$A = \begin{bmatrix} 1 & 0 & 0 & 0 \\ 0 & 1 & 0 & 0 \\ 0 & 0 & 1 & 0 \\ a_1 & a_2 & a_3 & a_4 \end{bmatrix}. \tag{2}$$

We call this transformation the Generalized Perspective Bas-Relief (GPBR) transformation. In Euclidean coordinates, the transformed surface and light source are given by

$$\mathbf{p'} = \frac{1}{\mathbf{a} \cdot \mathbf{p} + a_4}\mathbf{p} \qquad \mathbf{s'} = \frac{1}{\mathbf{a} \cdot \mathbf{s} + a_4}\mathbf{s} \tag{3}$$

where $\mathbf{a} = (a_1, a_2, a_3)^T$. Figure 2 shows a 2-d example of GPBR being applied to a planar curve and a single light source. The effect is to move points on the surface and the light sources along lines through the camera center in a manner that preserves shadows. The sign of $\mathbf{a} \cdot \mathbf{p} + a_4$ plays a critical role: if it is positive, all points on f move inward or outward from the camera center, remaining in the halfspace $z > 0$. On the other hand, if the sign is negative for some points on f, these points will move through the camera center to points with $z < 0$, i.e., they will not be visible to the camera. The equation $\mathbf{a} \cdot \mathbf{p} + a_4 = 0$ defines a plane which divides $\mathbb{R}^3$ into these two cases; all points on this plane map to the plane at infinity. A similar effect on the transformed light source location is determined by the sign of $\mathbf{a} \cdot \mathbf{s} + a_4$.

Proposition 1. *The image of the shadow curves for a surface f and light source $\mathbf{s}$ is identical to the image of the shadow curves for a surface f' and light source $\mathbf{s'}$ transformed by a GPBR if $\mathbf{a} \cdot \mathbf{s} + a_4 > 0$ and $\mathbf{a} \cdot \mathbf{p} + a_4 > 0$ for all $\mathbf{p} \in f$.*

Proof. Since GPBR is a projective transformation, Lemmas 1 and 2 show that the local attached and cast shadow curves on the transformed surface f' from light source $\mathbf{s}'$ are a GPBR of the local shadow curves on f from light source $\mathbf{s}$. For any point $\mathbf{p}$ on the surface and any GPBR transformation A, we have $\Pi_p \mathbf{p} = \Pi_p A \mathbf{p}$, and so the images of the local shadow curves are identical

To show that the global condition for an attached shadow is also satisfied, we note that projective transformations preserve collinearity; therefore, the only intersections of the line defined by $\mathbf{s}'$ and $\mathbf{p}'$ with f' are transformations of the intersections of the line defined by $\mathbf{s}$ and $\mathbf{p}$ with f. Within each light ray (a projective line), the points are subjected to a projective transformation; in general, the order of the transformed intersection points on the line may be a combination of a cyclic permutation and a reversal of the order of the original points. However, the restriction that $\mathbf{a} \cdot \mathbf{p} + a_4 > 0$ for all $\mathbf{p} \in f$ and that $\mathbf{a} \cdot \mathbf{s} + a_4 > 0$ has the effect of preserving the order of points between $\mathbf{p}$ and $\mathbf{s}$ on the original line and between $\mathbf{p}'$ and $\mathbf{s}'$ on the transformed line.

It should be noted for that for any $\mathbf{a}$ and a_4, there exists a light source $\mathbf{s}$ such that $\mathbf{a} \cdot \mathbf{s} + a_4 < 0$. When f is illuminated by such a source, the transformed source passes through the camera center, and the global shadowing conditions may not be satisfied. Hence two objects differing by GPBR are not strongly shadow equivalent. On the other hand, for any bounded set of light sources and bounded object f, there exists a set of $a_1, \ldots, a_4$ such that $\mathbf{a} \cdot \mathbf{s} + a_4 > 0$ and $\mathbf{a} \cdot \mathbf{p} + a_4 > 0$. Hence, there exist a set of objects which are *shadow equivalent*.

Since the shadow curves of multiple light sources are the union of the shadow curves from the individual light sources, this also holds for multiple light sources. It should also be noted that the occluding contour (silhouette) of f and f' are identical, since the camera center is a fixed point under GPBR and the occluding contour is the same as the attached shadow curve produced by a light source located at the camera center.

Figure 1 shows an example of the GPBR transformation being applied to a scene containing a teapot resting on a support plane. The images were generated using the VORT ray tracing package – the scene contained a single proximal point light source, the surfaces were modeled as Lambertian, and a perspective camera model was used. When the light source is transformed with the surface, the shadows are the same for both the original and transformed scenes. Even the shading is similar in both images, so much so that it is nearly impossible to distinguish the two surfaces. However, from another viewpoint, the effect of the GPBR on the object's shape is apparent.

This result compliments past work on structure from motion in which the aim of structure recovery is a weaker non-Euclidean representation, such as affine [18, 22, 24, 26], projective [9], or ordinal [10].

2.2 Orthographic Projection: GBR

When a camera is distant and can be modeled as orthographic projection, the visual rays are all parallel to the direction of the optical axis. In $\mathbb{RP}^3$, these rays intersect at the camera center which is a point at infinity. Without loss of generality consider the viewing direction to be in the direction of the z-axis

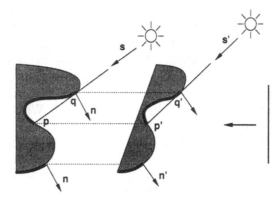

Fig. 3. The image points that lie in shadow for a surface under light source **s** are identical to those in shadow for a transformed surface under light source **s'**. In this 2-d illustration, the lower shadow is an attached shadow while the upper one is composed of both attached and cast components. A generalized bas-relief transformation with both flattening and an additive plane has been applied to the left surface, yielding the right one.

and the x and y axes to span the image plane. Again, letting the homogeneous coordinates of an image point be given by $\mathbf{u} \in \mathbb{RP}^2$, orthographic projection of $\mathbf{p} \in \mathbb{RP}^3$ can be expressed as $\mathbf{u} = \Pi_o \mathbf{p}$ where

$$\Pi_o = \begin{bmatrix} 1 & 0 & 0 & 0 \\ 0 & 1 & 0 & 0 \\ 0 & 0 & 0 & 1 \end{bmatrix}. \tag{4}$$

Now, let us consider another set of projective transformations $g : \mathbb{RP}^3 \to \mathbb{RP}^3$. For $\pi_o(\mathbf{p}) = \pi_o(g(\mathbf{p}))$ to be true for any point $\mathbf{p}$, the transformation g must move $\mathbf{p}$ along the viewing direction. This can be accomplished by the projective transformation $g : \mathbf{p} \mapsto G\mathbf{p}$ where

$$G = \begin{bmatrix} 1 & 0 & 0 & 0 \\ 0 & 1 & 0 & 0 \\ g_1 & g_2 & g_3 & g_4 \\ 0 & 0 & 0 & 1 \end{bmatrix} \tag{5}$$

with $g_3 > 0$. The mapping g is an affine transformation which was introduced in [3] and was called the generalized bas-relief (GBR) transformation. Consider the effect of applying GBR to a surface parameterized as the graph of a depth function, $(x, y, f(x, y))$. This yields a transformed surface

$$\begin{bmatrix} x' \\ y' \\ z' \end{bmatrix} = \begin{bmatrix} x \\ y \\ g_1 x + g_2 y + g_3 f(x, y) + g_4 \end{bmatrix}.$$

See Figure 3 for an example. The parameter g_3 has the effect of scaling the relief of the surface, g_1 and g_2 characterize an additive plane, and g_4 provides a depth offset. As described in [3], when $g_1 = g_2 = 0$ and $0 < g_3 < 1$, the resulting transformation is simply a compression of the surface's relief, as in relief sculpture.

Proposition 2. *The image of the shadow curves for a surface f and light source s are identical to the image of the shadow curves for a surface f' and light source s' transformed by any GBR.*

Proof. The proof follows that of Proposition 1.

It should be noted that Proposition 2 applies to both nearby light sources and those at infinity. However, in contrast to the GPBR transformation, nearby light source do not move to infinity nor do light sources at infinity become nearby light sources since GBR is an affine transformation which fixes the plane at infinity. Since Proposition 2 holds for *any* light source, all objects differing by a GBR transformation are *strongly shadow equivalent*.

An implication of Propositions 1 and 2 is that when an object is observed from a fixed viewpoint (whether perspective or orthographic projection), one can at best reconstruct its surface up to a four parameter family of transformations (GPBR or GBR) from shadow or occluding contour information, irrespective of the number of images and number of light sources. Under the same conditions, it is impossible to distinguish (recognize) two objects that differ by these transformations from shadows or silhouettes.

3 Uniqueness of the Generalized Bas-Relief Transformation

Here we prove that under orthographic projection the generalized bas-relief (GBR) transformation is unique in that there is no other transformation of an object's surface which preserves the set of shadows produced by illuminating the object with all possible point sources at infinity. We consider only the simplest case – an object with convex shape casting no shadows on its own surface – and show that the set of attached shadow boundaries are preserved *only* under a GBR transformation of the object's surface.

Recall that an attached shadow boundary is defined as the contour of points $(x, y, f(x, y))$ satisfying $\mathbf{n} \cdot \mathbf{s} = 0$, for some $\mathbf{s}$. For a convex object, the global attached shadow condition holds everywhere. Here the magnitude and the sign of the light source are unimportant as neither effects the location of the attached shadow boundary. Thus, let the vector $\mathbf{s} = (s_x, s_y, s_z)^T$ denote in homogeneous coordinates a point light source at infinity, where all light sources producing the same attached shadow boundary are equated, i.e., $(s_x, s_y, s_z)^T \equiv (ks_x, ks_y, ks_z)^T \ \forall k \in \mathbb{R}, k \neq 0$. With this, the space of light source directions S is equivalent to the real projective plane ($\mathbb{RP}^2$), with the line at infinity given by coordinates of the form $(s_x, s_y, 0)$. Note that in the previous section, we represented light sources as points in $\mathbb{RP}^3$; here, we restrict our selves only to distant light sources lying on the plane at infinity of $\mathbb{RP}^3$, (a real projective plane).

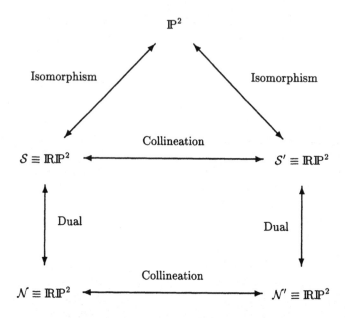

Fig. 4. The relation of different spaces in proof of Proposition 3.

Let $\mathbf{n} = (n_x, n_y, n_z)^T$ denote the direction of a surface normal. Again, the magnitude and sign are unimportant, so we have $(n_x, n_y, n_z)^T \equiv (kn_x, kn_y, kn_z)^T$ $\forall k \in \mathbb{R}, k \neq 0$. Thus, the space of surface normals $\mathcal{N}$ is, likewise, equivalent to $\mathbb{R}\mathbb{P}^2$. Note that under the equation $\mathbf{n} \cdot \mathbf{s} = 0$, the surface normals are the dual of the light sources. Each point in the $\mathbb{R}\mathbb{P}^2$ of light sources has a corresponding line in the $\mathbb{R}\mathbb{P}^2$ of surface normals, and vice versa.

Let us now consider the image contours defined by the points (x, y) satisfying $\mathbf{n} \cdot \mathbf{s} = 0$, for some $\mathbf{s}$. These image contours are the attached shadow boundaries orthographically projected onto the image plane. For lack of a better name, we will refer to them as the imaged attached shadow boundaries.

The set of imaged attached shadow boundaries for a convex object forms an abstract projective plane $\mathbb{P}^2$, where a "point" in the abstract projective plane is a single attached shadow boundary, and a "line" in the abstract projective plane is the collection of imaged attached shadow boundaries passing through a common point in the image plane. To see this, note the obvious projective isomorphism between the real projective plane of light source directions S and the abstract projective plane of imaged attached shadow boundaries $\mathbb{P}^2$. Under this is isomorphism, we have bijections mapping points to points and lines to lines.

Now let us say that we are given two objects whose visible surfaces are described by respective functions $f(x, y)$ and $f'(x, y)$. If the objects have the same set of imaged attached shadow boundaries as seen in the image plane (i.e., if the objects are strongly shadow equivalent), then the question arises: How are the two surfaces $f(x, y)$ and $f'(x, y)$ related?

Proposition 3. *If the visible surfaces of two convex objects f and f' are strongly shadow equivalent, then the surfaces are related by a generalized bas-relief transformation.*

Proof. As illustrated in Figure 4, we can construct a projective isomorphism between the set of imaged attached shadow boundaries $\mathbb{P}^2$ and the real projective plane of light source directions S illuminating surface $f(x, y)$. The isomorphism is chosen to map the collection of imaged attached shadow boundaries passing through a common point (x, y) in the image plane (i.e., a line in $\mathbb{P}^2$) to the surface normal $\mathbf{n}(x, y)$. In the same manner, we can construct a projective isomorphism between $\mathbb{P}^2$ and the real projective plane of light source directions S' illuminating the surface $f'(x, y)$. The isomorphism is, likewise, chosen to map the same collection of imaged attached shadow boundaries passing through (x, y) in the image plane to the surface normal $\mathbf{n}'(x, y)$. Under these two mappings, we have a projective isomorphism between S and S' which in turn is a projective transformation (collineation) [1]. Because $\mathcal{N}$ and $\mathcal{N}'$ are the duals of S and S' respectively, the surface normals of $f(x, y)$ are also related to the surface normals of $f'(x, y)$ by a projective transformation, i.e., $\mathbf{n}'(x, y) = P\mathbf{n}(x, y)$ where P is a 3×3 invertible matrix.

The transformation P is further restricted in that the surface normals along the occluding contour of f and f' are equivalent, i.e., the transformation P pointwise fixes the line at infinity of surface normals. Thus, P must be of the form

$$P = \begin{bmatrix} 1 & 0 & p_1 \\ 0 & 1 & p_2 \\ 0 & 0 & p_3 \end{bmatrix}$$

where $p_3 \neq 0$. The effect of applying P to the surface normals is the same as applying G in Eq. 5 to the surface if $p_1 = -g_1/g_3$, $p_2 = -g_2/g_3$ and $p_3 = 1/g_3$. That is, P has the form of the generalized bas-relief transformation. Note that the shadows are independent of the translation g_4 along the line of sight under orthographic projection.

4 Reconstruction from Attached Shadows

In the previous section, we showed that under orthographic projection with distant light sources, the only transformation of a surface which preserves the set of imaged shadow contours is the generalized bas-relief transformation. However, Proposition 3 does not provide a prescription for actually reconstructing a surface up to GBR. In this section, we consider the problem of reconstruction from the attached shadow boundaries measured in n images of a surface, each illuminated by a single distant light source. We will show that it is possible to estimate the n light source directions and the surface normals at a finite number of points, all up to GBR. In general, we expect to reconstruct the surface normals at $O(n^2)$ points. From the reconstructed normals, an approximation to the underlying surface can be computed for a fixed GBR. Alternatively, existing shape-from-shadow methods can be used to reconstruct the surface from the estimated light

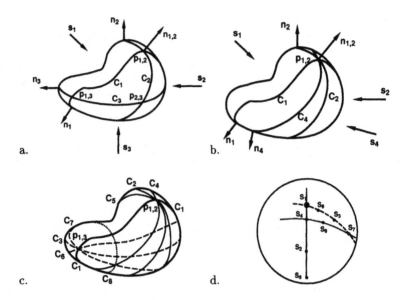

Fig. 5. Reconstruction up to GBR from attached shadows: For a single object in fixed pose, these figures show superimposed attached shadow contours C_i for light source direction s_i. The surface normal where C_i intersects the occluding contour is denoted by n_i. The normal at the intersection of C_i and C_j is denoted by $n_{i,j}$. a) The three contours intersect at three points in the image. b) The three contours meet at a common point implying that s_1, s_2 and s_3 lie on a great circle of the illumination sphere. c) Eight attached shadow boundaries of which four intersect at $p_{1,2}$ and four intersect at $p_{1,3}$; the direction of the light sources $s_1 \ldots s_8$ and the surface normals at the intersection points can be determined up to GBR. d) The structure of the illumination sphere S^2 for the light source directions generating the attached shadow boundaries in Fig. 5.c.

source directions (for a fixed GBR) and from the measured attached and cast shadow curves [12, 17, 29].

First, consider the occluding contour (silhouette) of a surface which will be denoted C_0. This contour is equivalent to the attached shadow produced by a light source whose direction is the viewing direction. Define a coordinate system with $\hat{x}$ and $\hat{y}$ spanning the image plane, and with $\hat{z}$ pointing in the viewing direction. For all points p on the occluding contour, the viewing direction lies in the tangent plane (i.e., $n(p) \cdot \hat{z} = 0$), and the surface normal $n(p)$ is parallel to the image normal. Hence if the normal to the image contour is (n_x, n_y), the surface normal is $n = (n_x, n_y, 0)^T$. In $\mathbb{RP}^2$, the surface normals to all points on the occluding contour correspond to the line at infinity.

Now consider the attached shadow boundary C_1 produced by a light source whose direction is s_1. See Figure 5.a. For all points $p \in C_1$, s_1 lies in the tangent plane, i.e., $s_1 \cdot n(p) = 0$. Where C_1 intersects the occluding contour, the normal n_1 can be directly determined from the measured contour as described above. It should be noted that while C_1 and the occluding contour intersect transversally on the surface, their images generically share a common tangent and form the crescent moon image singularity [8]. Note that by measuring $\mathbf{n}_1$ along the occluding contour, we obtain a constraint on the light source direction, $\mathbf{s}_1 \cdot \mathbf{n}_1 = 0$. This restricts the light source to a line in $\mathbb{RP}^2$ or to a great circle on the illumination sphere S^2. The source $\mathbf{s}_1$ can be expressed parametrically in the camera coordinate system as

$$\mathbf{s}_1(\theta_1) = \cos\theta_1 \mathbf{n}_1 + \sin\theta_1 \hat{\mathbf{z}}.$$

From the shadows in a single image, it is not possible to further constrain $\mathbf{s}_1$ nor does it seem possible to obtain any further information about points on C_1.

Now, consider a second attached shadow boundary C_2 formed by a second light source direction $\mathbf{s}_2$. Again, the measurement of $\mathbf{n}_2$ (where C_2 intersects C_0) determines a projective line in $\mathbb{RP}^2$ (or a great circle on S^2) that the light source $\mathbf{s}_2$ must lie on. In general, C_1 and C_2 will intersect at one or more visible surface points. If the object is convex and the Gauss map is bijective, then they only intersect at one point $\mathbf{p}_{1,2}$. For a nonconvex surface, C_1 and C_2 may intersect more than once. However in all cases, the direction of the surface normal $\mathbf{n}_{1,2}$ at the intersections is

$$\mathbf{n}_{1,2} = \mathbf{s}_1(\theta_1) \times \mathbf{s}_2(\theta_2). \tag{6}$$

Thus from the attached shadows in two images, we directly measure $\mathbf{n}_1$ and $\mathbf{n}_2$ and obtain estimates for $\mathbf{n}_{1,2}$, $\mathbf{s}_1$, and $\mathbf{s}_2$ as functions of θ_1 and θ_2.

Consider a third image illuminated by $\mathbf{s}_3$, in which the attached shadow boundary C_3 *does not* pass through $\mathbf{p}_{1,2}$ (Fig. 5.a). Again, we can estimate a projective line (great circle on S^2) containing $\mathbf{s}_3$. We also obtain the surface normal at two additional points, the intersections of C_3 with C_1 and C_2. From the attached shadow boundaries for a convex surface measured in n images – if no three contours intersect at a common point – the surface normal can be determined at $n(n-1)$ points as a function of n unknowns $\theta_i, i = 1 \ldots n$.

However, the number of unknowns can be reduced when three contours intersect at a common point. Consider Fig. 5.b where contour C_4 intersects C_1 and C_2 at $\mathbf{p}_{1,2}$. In this case, we can infer from the images that $\mathbf{s}_1, \mathbf{s}_2$ and $\mathbf{s}_4$ all lie in the tangent plane to $\mathbf{p}_{1,2}$. In $\mathbb{RP}^2$, this means that $\mathbf{s}_1, \mathbf{s}_2, \mathbf{s}_4$ all lie on the same projective line. Since $\mathbf{n}_4$ can be measured, $\mathbf{s}_4$ can be expressed as a function of θ_1 and θ_2, i.e.,

$$\mathbf{s}_4(\theta_1, \theta_2) = \mathbf{n}_4 \times (\mathbf{s}_1(\theta_1) \times \mathbf{s}_2(\theta_2)).$$

Thus, a set of attached shadow curves (C_1, C_2, C_4 in Fig. 5.b) passing through a common point ($\mathbf{p}_{1,2}$) is generated by light sources ($\mathbf{s}_1, \mathbf{s}_2, \mathbf{s}_4$ in Fig. 5.d) located on a great circle of S^2. The light source directions can be determined up to two degrees of freedom θ_1 and θ_2. Now, if in addition a second set of light sources lies along another projective line (the great circle in Fig 5.d containing $\mathbf{s}_1, \mathbf{s}_3, \mathbf{s}_6, \mathbf{s}_7$), the corresponding shadow contours (C_1, C_3, C_6, C_7 in Fig 5.c) intersect at another point on the surface ($\mathbf{p}_{1,3}$). Again, we can express the location of light sources (s_6, s_7) on this great circle as functions of the locations of two other sources (s_1 and s_3):

$$s_i(\theta_1, \theta_3) = n_i \times (s_1(\theta_1) \times s_3(\theta_3)).$$

Since s_1 lies at the intersection of both projective lines, we can estimate the direction of any light source located on either line up to just three degrees of freedom θ_1, θ_2, and θ_3. Furthermore, the direction of any other light source (s_8 on Fig. 5.d) can be determined if it lies on a projective line defined by two light sources whose directions are known up to θ_1, θ_2 and θ_3. From the estimated light source directions, the surface normal can be determined using Eq. 6 at all points where the shadow curves intersect. As mentioned earlier, there are $O(n^2)$ such points – observe the number of intersections in Fig. 5.c. It is easy to verify algebraically that the three degrees of freedom θ_1, θ_2 and θ_3 correspond to the degrees of freedom in GBR g_1, g_2 and g_3. The translation g_4 of the surface along the line sight cannot be determined under orthographic projection.

5 Discussion

We have defined notions of shadow equivalence for object, showing that two objects differing by a four parameter family of projective transformations (GPBR) are shadow equivalent under perspective projection. Furthermore, under orthographic projection, two objects differing by a generalized bas-relief (GBR) transformation are strongly shadow equivalent – i.e., for any light source illuminating an object, there exits a light source illuminating a transformed object such that the shadows are identical. We have proven that GBR is the only transformation having this property. While we have shown that the occluding contour is also preserved under GPBR and GBR, it should be noted that image intensity discontinuities (step edges) arising from surface normal discontinuities or albedo discontinuities are also preserved under these transformations since these points move along the line of sight and are viewpoint and (generically) illumination independent. Consequently, edge-based recognition algorithms should not be able to distinguish objects differing by these transformations, nor should edge-based reconstruction algorithms be able to perform Euclidean reconstruction without additional information.

In earlier work where we concentrated on light sources at infinity [4, 3], we showed that for any set of point light sources, the shading as well as the shadowing on an object with Lambertian reflectance are identical to the shading and shadowing on any generalized bas-relief transformation of the object, i.e., the illumination cones are identical. This is consistent with the effectiveness of well-crafted relief sculptures in conveying a greater sense of the depth than is present. It is clear that shading is not preserved for GPBR or for GBR when the light sources are proximal; the image intensity falls off by the reciprocal of the squared distance between the surface and light source, and distance is not preserved under these transformations. Nonetheless, for a range of transformations and for some sets of light sources, it is expected that the intensity may only vary slightly.

Furthermore, we have shown that it is possible to reconstruct a surface up to GBR from the shadow boundaries in a set of images. To implement a reconstruction algorithm based on the ideas in Section 4 requires detection of cast and attached shadow boundaries. While detection methods have been presented [5, 28], it is unclear how effective these techniques would be in practice. In particular, attached shadows are particularly difficult to detect and localize since for a Lambertian surface with constant albedo, there is a discontinuity in the intensity gradient or shading flow field, but not in the intensity itself. On the other hand, there is a step edge at a cast shadow boundary, and so extensions of the method described in Section 4 which use information about cast shadows to constrain the light source direction may lead to practical implementations.

Leonardo da Vinci's statement that shadows of relief sculpture are "foreshortened" is, strictly speaking, incorrect. However, reliefs are often constructed in a manner such that the cast shadows will differ from those produced by sculpture in the round. Reliefs have been used to depict narratives involving numerous figures located at different depths within the scene. Since the sculpting medium is usually not thick enough for the artist to sculpt the figures to the proper relative depths, sculptors like Donatello and Ghiberti employed rules of perspective to determine the size and location of figures, sculpting each figure to the proper relief [16]. While the shadowing for each figure is self consistent, the shadows cast from one figure onto another are incorrect. Furthermore, the shadows cast onto the background, whose orientation usually does not correspond to that of a wall or floor in the scene, are also inconsistent. Note however, that ancient Greek sculpture was often painted; by painting the background of the Parthenon Frieze a dark blue [7], cast shadows would be less visible and the distortions less apparent. Thus, Leonardo's statement is an accurate characterization of complex reliefs such as Ghiberti's East Doors on the Baptistery in Florence, but does not apply to figures sculpted singly.

Acknowledgments

Many thanks to David Mumford for leading us to the proof of Proposition 3, and to Alan Yuille for many discussions about the GBR.

References

1. E. Artin. *Geometric Algebra*. Interscience Publishers, Inc., New York, 1957.
2. M. Baxandall. *Shadows and Enlightenment*. Yale University Press, New Haven, 1995.
3. P. Belhumeur, D. Kriegman, and A. Yuille. The bas-relief ambiguity. In *Proc. IEEE Conf. on Comp. Vision and Patt. Recog.*, pages 1040–1046, 1997.
4. P. N. Belhumeur and D. J. Kriegman. What is the set of images of an object under all possible lighting conditions. In *Proc. IEEE Conf. on Comp. Vision and Patt. Recog.*, pages 270–277, 1996.

5. P. Breton and S. Zucker. Shadows and shading flow fields. In *CVPR96*, pages 782–789, 1996.
6. F. Cheng and K. Thiel. Delimiting the building heights in a city from the shadow in a panchromatic spot-image. 1 test of 42 buildings. *JRS*, 16(3):409–415, Feb. 1995.
7. B. F. Cook. *The Elgin Marbles*. Harvard University Press, Cambridge, 1984.
8. L. Donati and N. Stolfi. Singularities of illuminated surfaces. *Int. J. Computer Vision*, 23(3):207–216, 1997.
9. O. Faugeras. Stratification of 3-D vision: Projective, affine, and metric representations. *J. Opt. Soc. Am. A*, 12(7):465–484, 1995.
10. C. Fermuller and Y. Aloimonos. Ordinal representations of visual space. In *Proc. Image Understanding Workshop*, pages 897–904, 1996.
11. L. Hambrick, M. Loew, and R. Carroll, Jr. The entry-exit method of shadow boundary segmentation. *PAMI*, 9(5):597–607, September 1987.
12. M. Hatzitheodorou. The derivation of 3-d surface shape from shadows. In *Proc. Image Understanding Workshop*, pages 1012–1020, 1989.
13. A. Huertas and R. Nevatia. Detection of buildings in aerial images using shape and shadows. In *Proc. Int. Joint Conf. on Art. Intell.*, pages 1099–1103, 1983.
14. R. Irvin and D. McKeown. Methods for exploiting the relationship between buildings and their shadows in aerial imagery. *IEEE Systems, Man, and Cybernetics*, 19(6):1564–1575, 1989.
15. M. Kemp, editor. *Leonardo On Painting*. Yale University Press, New Haven, 1989.
16. M. Kemp. *The Science of Art: Optical Themes in Western Art from Brunelleschi to Seurat*. Yale University Press, New Haven, 1990.
17. J. Kender and E. Smith. Shape from darkness. In *Int. Conf. on Computer Vision*, pages 539–546, 1987.
18. J. Koenderink and A. Van Doorn. Affine structure from motion. *JOSA-A*, 8(2):377–385, 1991.
19. M. Langer and S. Zucker. What is a light source? In *Proc. IEEE Conf. on Comp. Vision and Patt. Recog.*, pages 172–178, 1997.
20. G. Medioni. Obtaining 3-d from shadows in aerial images. In *CVPR83*, pages 73–76, 1983.
21. J. Mundy and A. Zisserman. *Geometric invariance in computer vision*. MIT Press, 1992.
22. R. Rosenholtz and J. Koenderink. Affine structure and photometry. In *Proc. IEEE Conf. on Comp. Vision and Patt. Recog.*, pages 790–795, 1996.
23. S. Shafer and T. Kanade. Using shadows in finding surface orientation. *Comp. Vision, Graphics, and Image Proces.*, 22(1):145–176, 1983.
24. L. Shapiro, A. Zisserman, and M. Brady. 3D motion recovery via affine epipolar geometry. *Int. J. Computer Vision*, 16(2):147–182, October 1995.
25. A. Shashua. *Geometry and Photometry in 3D Visual Recognition*. PhD thesis, MIT, 1992.
26. S. Ullman and R. Basri. Recognition by a linear combination of models. *IEEE Trans. Pattern Anal. Mach. Intelligence*, 13:992–1006, 1991.
27. D. L. Waltz. Understanding line drawings of scenes with shadows. In P. Winston, editor, *The Psychology of Computer Vision*, pages 19–91. McGraw-Hill, New York, 1975.
28. A. Witkin. Intensity-based edge classification. In *Proc. Am. Assoc. Art. Intell.*, pages 36–41, 1982.
29. D. Yang and J. Kender. Shape from shadows under error. In *Proc. Image Understanding Workshop*, pages 1083–1090, 1993.

Shape Representations from Shading Primitives

John Haddon and David Forsyth

Computer Science Division
University of California, Berkeley CA 94720
Phone: +1-510-643-6763, +1-510-642-9582
Fax: +1-510-643-1534
haddon@eecs.berkeley.edu, daf@cs.berkeley.edu

Abstract

Diffuse interreflections mean that surface shading and shape are related in ways that are difficult to untangle; in particular, distant and invisible surfaces may affect the shading field that one sees. The effects of distant surfaces are confined to relatively low spatial frequencies in the shading field, meaning that we can expect signatures, called shading primitives, corresponding to shape properties. We demonstrate how these primitives can be used to support the construction of useful shape representations. Approaches to this include testing hypotheses of geometric primitives for consistency with the shading field, and looking for shading events that are distinctive of some shape event. We show that these approaches can be composed, leading to an attractive process of representation that is intrinsically bottom up. This representation can be extracted from images of real scenes, and that the representation is diagnostic.

1 Background

Changes in surface brightness are a powerful cue to the shape of a surface; the study of extracting shape information from image shading starts with [12] and is comprehensively summed up in Brooks' book [13]. The approach views shading as a local effect; surface brightness is modelled as a product of a visibility term and a non-negative function of the Gauss map, leading to a partial differential equation—the *image irradiance equation*—which expresses the relationship between surface geometry and image brightness. Shape from shading theories that view shading as a local effect are now widely agreed to be unsatisfactory, for three reasons: the local shading model omits the effects of diffuse interreflections, a source of substantial effects in the brightness of surfaces; the underlying shape representation, a dense depth map, contains excess detail for most recognition applications; and the necessary assumptions are unrealistically restrictive. New models of shape from shading can be obtained by changing either the type of shape representation sought in the shading field [9], or the model of shading [18, 19, 16].

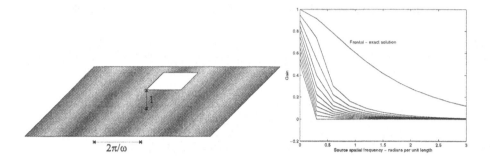

Fig. 1. *A patch with a frontal view of an infinite plane which is a unit distance away and carries a radiosity* $\sin \omega x$ *is shown on the left; this patch is small enough that its contribution to the plane's radiosity can be ignored. If the patch is slanted by* σ *with respect to the plane, it carries radiosity that is nearly periodic, with spatial frequency* $\omega \cos \sigma$. *We refer to the amplitude of the component at this frequency as the gain of the patch. The graph shows numerical estimates of the gain for patches at ten equal steps in slant angle, from 0 to* $\pi/2$, *as a function of spatial frequency on the plane. The gain falls extremely fast, meaning that large terms at high spatial frequencies must be regional effects, rather than the result of distant radiators. This is why it is hard to determine the pattern in a stained glass window by looking at the floor at foot of the window.*

1.1 Distant surfaces and their effects

Very few techniques for extracting shape information from shading fields are robust to the effects of diffuse interreflections—some approaches appear in [28, 21, 27, 29]. A problem arises outside controlled environments, however, because there may be surfaces that are not visible, but radiate to the objects in view (so called "distant surfaces"). Mutual illumination has a characteristic smoothing effect; as figure 1 shows, shading effects that have a high spatial frequency and a high amplitude generally cannot come from distant surfaces.

The extremely fast fall-off in amplitude with spatial frequency of terms due to distant surfaces (shown in figure 1) means that, if one observes a high amplitude term at a high spatial frequency, *it is very unlikely to have resulted from the effects of distant, passive radiators* (because these effects die away quickly). This effect suggests that the widely established convention (e.g. [3, 14, 17]) of classifying effects in shading as due to reflectance if the spatial frequency is high ("edges") and the dynamic range is relatively low, and due to illumination otherwise, can be expanded. There is a mid range of spatial frequencies that are largely unaffected by mutual illumination from distant surfaces, because the gain is small. Spatial frequencies in this range cannot be "transmitted" by distant passive radiators unless these radiators have improbably high radiosity. As a result, spatial frequencies in this range can be thought of as *regional properties*, which can result only from interreflection effects within a region.

2 Primitives

Object representation is a fundamental problem in recognition tasks. In particular, one would like to have some ability to abstract objects—recognise them at a level above that of specific instances. The classical approach to alleviating difficulties with abstraction is to view recognition in terms of assemblies of stylised primitives. In this view, which has been espoused in a variety of forms [1, 2, 20, 22], objects are represented as assemblies of shapes taken from a collection of parametric families with "good" properties. A classical difficulty with this view of representation is that it is hard to know what the primitives should be.

One important feature of geometric primitives is that their **appearance is stereotyped**. In particular, the most useful form of primitive is one where it is possible to test an assembly of image features and say whether it is likely to have come from a primitive or not. A second feature of a useful primitive is that it is **significant**. For example, a cylinder is a significant property, because many objects are made of crude cylinders. A third useful property is **robustness**; cylindrical primitives are quite easy to find even in the presence of some deformations.

In the work described in [8], it was shown that viewing objects as assemblies of primitives can be used successfully, if crudely, to find images containing horses. The program first finds the primitives—in this case, cylindrical body segments, which appear in an image as regions that are hide-like in colour and texture and have nearly parallel and nearly straight sides—and then tries to form assemblies of the primitives that are consistent with the animal's joint kinematics. Our horse finder has low recall—about 15%—but marks only 0.65% of pictures without horses, and has been extensively tested on a large set of images [7].

The weakness in this program lies in the fact that there are so many sets of nearly-parallel, nearly-straight edges (potentially body segments) that, if the number is not reduced, the kinematic tests become overwhelmed. For the horse finder, this problem can be alleviated by requiring that only segments that have hide-like pixels in the interior could be body segments. This approach can be made more general, by considering the fact that shading across a cylinder-like surface is quite constrained.

2.1 Shading primitives

Traditional shape from shading requires an impractical local shading model to produce a dense depth map. For our purposes a dense depth map is heavily redundant—instead, we will concentrate on finding stylised events in the shading field that are strongly coupled to shape, which we call *shading primitives*. In [16], Koenderink observed that deep holes and grooves in surfaces have characteristic shading properties—they are usually dark, because it is "hard" to get light into them. This is clearly an important component of the appearance of surfaces. For example, the lines on human foreheads—geometrically so trivial that they tend not to appear in depth maps—are easily visible and used by humans for communication *because they almost always have a small attached shadow, which gives them high contrast.* These shadows are largely independent of the details of the local shape of the surface—a deep groove will be dark, and the shape of the bottom of the groove is irrelevant. The appearance of grooves is stereotyped—grooves almost always appear in images as narrow, dark bars— and so they are easily found. This combination of significance, robustness, and stereotypical appearance is precisely what is required from a primitive.

There are two forms of test in which a shading primitive might appear. In the first case, one uses shading to test an hypothesis about shape; the test must be constructed to be robust to light reflected from distant surfaces, and to yield useful results. As we show, tests meeting these requirements can be built, *because one knows what kind of shape is expected.* In the second case, the shading is the primary object that establishes the hypothesis; for example, grooves have a characteristic appearance that can be found using a template matching like approach. Typically, complex objects will require multiple tests, and we show in section 4 that one can build composite representations using shading primitives.

3 Shading on a primitive

Cylinders are natural primitives for programs that attempt to find people or animals, like the horse-finding program above. The geometric approach to finding image regions that could represent cylinders involves finding boundaries, constructing local symmetries between boundary points (as in [4, 13]) and then constructing collections of symmetries that have the same length and whose centers lie roughly on a straight line to which they are roughly perpendicular.

In this case, exploiting shading is easy because there is already an hypothesis as to the underlying geometry (as in [10]). In particular, we can test the shading along a symmetry to see whether it is consistent with the shading across a limb.

3.1 Method

Testing whether the shading across a symmetry represents the shading across a limb cross-section requires a classifier of some form. To determine this classifier, we developed a simple geometric model of a limb cross-section, and then applied a simple shading model to the limb model to generate typical shading cross-sections. We then used these analytically determined shading cross-sections to train a classifier. Passing the segment under test to the classifier tells us whether the shading is consistent with that on a limb.

The geometrical model of a limb is approximately cylindrical, with a few variations. The cross-section of the limb is taken to be elliptical, with a randomly chosen aspect ratio, and the major axis at any angle to the observer. Since limbs are certainly not perfectly elliptical in cross-section, we add a couple of bumps or grooves to the surface. Using our shading model, we calculate the shading distribution on this shape as in figure 2. It is these theoretical predictions of shading, rather than experimental data, which are used to train the classifier. However, the theoretical model does have some parameters, such as the range of aspect ratios, and number and size of bumps, which were tuned to give a reasonable match to the experimental data.

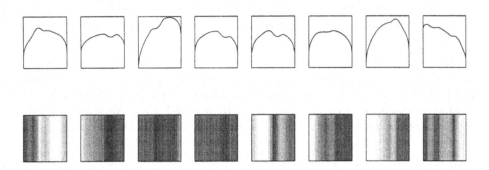

Fig. 2. *Typical limbs from our model. In each case, the plot shows the upper cross-section of the limb, while the image below it shows the shading that will be result on a limb of that shape. The bumps on the surface are intended to capture muscle definition.*

To predict the shading on our geometrical limb model, we use the same shading model as in [11]. The radiosity at any point on the limb is modelled as the sum of two components: the first due to distant radiators, which is uniform (because any spatial frequency high enough to be non-uniform over the support of the cylinder was suppressed by the low gain at high spatial frequencies); and the second due to a single point source, modeled as a source at infinity. This is a version of a model suggested by Koenderink [15] and also used by Langer *et al.*[18].

Because the limb has translational symmetry, we can model the "sky" (distant radiators) as an infinitely long half cylinder above the limb with its axis collinear with that of the limb. We can then write the brightness at a point **u** on the limb as:

$$B(\mathbf{u}) = \frac{E_a}{2}[\sin(\theta_1 - \theta_u) - \sin(\theta_0 - \theta_u)] + E_p\cos(\theta_p - \theta_u)$$

where θ_1 and θ_0 are the polar angles of the edges of the unobscured sky (measured from the zenith), θ_u is the polar angle of the the normal at **u**, θ_p is the polar angle of the point light source, and E_a and E_p are the brightnesses of the ambient and point light sources. This simple model allows us to predict the radiosity given a particular limb shape.

In images, limbs appear in a variety of sizes. In order to compare limbs of different sizes, we linearly interpolate between the samples we have to create a cross section of a given width. We then project this cross section onto the most significant principal components of the positive training data, in order to generate a data point in a lower-dimensional feature space. In addition to the principal components, we also consider the residual, a measure of the amount of variation in the signal which is not captured by the principal components. Signals similar to those yielding the principal components will be described fairly completely by the projection onto those principal components. However, signals unlike the positive data will not be described very well by the projection onto the principal components, and the difference between the original signal and its projection onto the space of principal components will be quite large. It is the energy of this difference which we call the residual.

For our classifier, we trained a support vector machine [5] using the projection onto principal components and the residual. In contrast to the use of SVMs in [24] and [23], we culled our positive training data from the results of our theoretical shading model applied to the geometrical limb model. Negative training data consisted of randomly oriented lines selected from randomly chosen images.

3.2 Results

In order to validate our geometric limb model, we compared the principal components of the images from the model, images of real limbs, and real images of things that aren't limbs. The principal components were ordered from most significant to least significant, and we then determined the matrix which transforms one set of principal components into another. The first n rows and columns of this matrix give the best map from the first n principal components in the first set to the first n principal components in the second set. The nth leading principal minor (the determinant of this $n \times n$ matrix) indicates the reduction in volume of a polytope in the first subspace when projected onto the second subspace. If the two subspaces are similar (so the $n \times n$ matrix is nearly a rotation) there will be very little reduction in volume, and the determinant will be close to one. If the subspaces are orthogonal, the polytope will collapse, and the determinant will be close to zero. Figure 3(a) shows the first thirty leading principal minors for the mappings between the three data sets. While the negatives and positives cease to describe the same subspace after only a few principal components, the theoretical and real positive data have a very strong correlation through fifteen principal components. This is a strong indication that our theoretical model is capturing the essential characteristics of shading on real limbs, because the principal components span the same space.

Since we are using this classifier as a tool to discard cross-sections which are apparently not from a limb, we require the false negative rate to be low—while it is always possible to discard a section at a higher level, once discarded at a low level, it will be very difficult to retrieve. Thus, we choose a 5% false negative rate on real cross-sections, which allows the classifier to reject 57% of negatives. While this is certainly not perfect, this does represent a significant reduction in the number of segments to be passed on for further analysis.

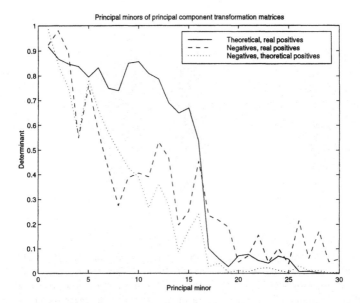

Fig. 3. *The first thirty leading principal minors of the mappings between negative, real positive and theoretical positive data. The determinant is a measure of the similarity between the subspaces described by the first n principal components in each set. The positives are very similar through the first fifteen components, while the negatives differ significantly from both positive sets after only eight components.*

3.3 Shading tests as a system component

The contribution of any visual cue should be evaluated in the context of a larger task. We have proposed to use shading cues to evaluate the hypothesis that a cylindrical primitive is present in a recognition system to find people or animals. It is natural to ask whether this improves the overall recognition process. It is difficult to give a precise answer to this question, because the learned predicates that determine whether an assembly of segments represents a person or animal are currently extremely crude. This means that we have no measure of performance that can be reliably assigned to any particular cause.

However, it is possible to estimate the extent of the contribution that testing shading makes. The standard problem with assembling symmetries is that the process produces vast numbers of symmetries, which overwhelm later grouping stages. One measure of success for measurements of shading is that they reduce this number of symmetries, without removing assemblies that could represent limbs. Since we see a shading test as more likely to be helpful in understanding large image segments (obtained using, for example, Shi's [25] normalized cut method), rather than in segmentation itself, we can apply this test on images of isolated human figures. For each of 20 images showing human figures in quite complex poses, taken from [26], we measured the rate at which the shading test rejected *symmetries* without losing body *segments*. To determine whether

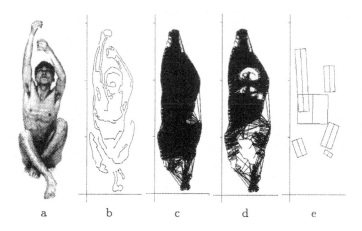

a   b   c   d   e

Fig. 4. *Over a test set of 20 images, symmetries are accepted by the shading test at a median rate of 61%. (a) A typical image from our test set. Notice that there is muscle definition, hair and light shadowing on the body segments, and that segments shadow other segments. The other figures on the bottom illustrate our process. Edges are shown in figure (b); figure (c) shows all symmetries found. Notice the large number of symmetries, and the spurious symmetries linking the legs. Figure (d) shows the symmetries that pass the shading test. Notice that the number of symmetries has gone down substantially, and that body segments are all represented. Figure (e) shows the segments manually determined to correspond to body segments; we have accepted that the arms, being straight, correspond to single long segments, and that one thigh is not visible as a segment, so we regard this output as containing all body segments.*

the test rejects important symmetries, we identified by hand the human body segments (upper arm/leg, lower arm/leg and torso) which did not have corresponding image segments and were visible with clear boundaries in the image. The requirement for clear boundaries ensures that errors in edge detection are not ascribed to the shading test. While this test is notably subjective, it allows some assessment of the performance of the shading cue, which is generally good—in the presence of shadows, muscle definition and the like, about half (median rejection rate is 39%) of the set of *symmetries* in a given image is rejected. The median rate at which *segments* are missed in an image is about one per two images; 10 of the images have no segments absent, five have one segment absent, and five have two absent. There appears to be some correlation with pose, which probably has to do with reduced contrast for body segments occluding other segments.

These shading tests are currently being used in a program that seeks to extract a human figure from an image. The shading test eliminates a large number of segments which are clearly not human limbs, without rejected significant numbers of actual limb segments.

4   Composite shading primitives

In [11], we developed a technique for finding grooves and folds. We applied our shading model to a geometrical model of the shape, and used these theoretical predictions to train a support vector machine to recognize grooves or folds. In that work, we were merely concerned with finding isolated shading primitives. However, difficult recognition tasks require rich representations (or, equivalently, multiple cues with multiple tests). It is therefore natural to compose tests for shading primitives. In this section, we demonstrate building a representation for a back as a near elliptical cylinder with a groove in it, by composing the tests for grooves and for limbs.

4.1   Local Properties

After finding the groove and localising it, we determine its width. Once we know how much of the figure has been affected by the presence of the groove, we can discount that part of the cross-section (which we do by "filling in" the groove) and can then determine whether the rest of the cross-section is consistent with the shading on a "limb".

The centre of the groove is easily found by non-maximum suppression. Currently, we only find the widths of vertical grooves, but it is easy to perform this search at arbitrary orientations, since the groove finder works at all orientations.

We search for grooves from finest to coarsest scale, linking response from scale to scale. Because the intensity pattern associated with a groove decays fairly smoothly at its boundaries, the response to a groove is essentially constant as the scale of the matching process increases, until the scale exceeds that of the groove, when the response decays slowly (see figure 5(b)). As a result, by matching from finest to coarsest scale we can reject noise responses (which do not have corresponding matches at coarser scales) and estimate the width of the groove. We fit the groove response data with two linear segments: the first, horizontal; and the second, the true line of best fit to the last values. The intersection between these lines gives us an estimate of the width of the groove.

This procedure actually improves our groove detection ability. While the groove finder does respond to the edge of a figure, it responds equally well at all scales—since there *is* no groove, it never sees the edge of the groove (see figure 5(c)). This means that, unlike real grooves, there will be no knee in the curve, allowing us to reject boundary points.

Once we have found a groove and determined its width, we can discount its effect on the shading of the back. For simplicity, we set the intensity values within the groove by linearly interpolating betwen the intensity values on either side of the groove, which gives an effect rather like filling in the groove (figure 6). While there are probably better ways of interpolating over the groove—one might use the expectation maximisation [6] algorithm to fill in this "missing" data—our approach gives perfectly acceptable results. In fact, in our current implementation, we have not actually found it necessary to discount the effect of the grooves.

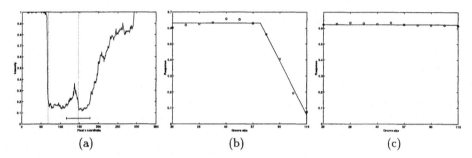

Fig. 5. *The process of finding the width of a groove. (a) The intensity values perpendicular to the line of the groove. (b) The response of the groove detector at different scales to the groove at $x = 147$ in (a). The response is constant for small groove sizes, and then starts to drop when the size of the detector matches the size of the groove. We fit two line segments to the data, and their intersection gives the size of the groove. The calculated extent of the groove is shown by the bar in (a). (c) The response of the groove detector to the putative groove at $x = 68$ in (a). In fact, this is simply the edge of the figure, and not a groove. Thus, the groove detector has an almost constant response over all widths. Any putative groove with this signature is rejected.*

However, we expect that as our tests become more accurate, it will be necessary to account for the presence of the groove in the shading pattern across the back.

Results Figure 7 shows three typical images in the left column. In the middle column, the grey sections indicate cross-sections with limb-like shading. The top image, of a back, gives a positive response for most of the length of the back. The segments containing hair are not considered to be limb-like. The middle image is of a very flat back, with almost uniform shading, which therefore does not match the model of shading on a cylinder. It may be possible to extend our model to capture this behaviour as well. The bottom image is a fishing lure, which has many sections with limb-like shading, since its shape is roughly cylindrical, with a groove-like reflectance pattern in the centre.

4.2 Global properties

As we have seen, the shading field along a single cross-section can give us some indication as to whether the cross-section comes from a back. However, it is a much more powerful test to look at the global structure, and compare the spatial relationship of grooves and limb symmetries.

Method Because the groove detector is sensitive to orientation, we run the groove detector over the image at different orientations. Currently, we are doing this at only one scale. We find the centres of the groove by finding a high response, and stepping along the groove in the direction corresponding to the

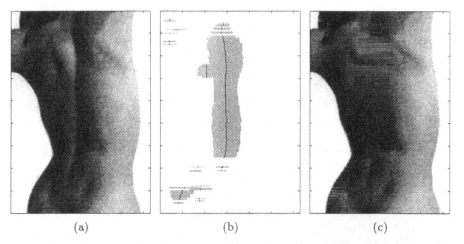

Fig. 6. *The process of groove detection and interpolation. (a) The original image. (b) Grooves in the image. The centres of the grooves are marked in black, and the widths are marked in grey. Currently, we do not follow the groove down the back while searching for widths, but it is expected that this process will allow the groove detector to jump the gaps. (c) The image with grooves filled in. The intensities at either side of the groove are interpolated linearly across the width of the groove.*

orientation with the highest response. Repeating this process until the response drops below a threshold allows us to trace out potential grooves. This process yields many potential grooves, only some of which correspond to the spine. To remove spurious grooves, we trained a support vector machine on two images, where grooves corresponding to the spine are marked as positives, and all others are marked as negatives. The features we used in the classifier were the number of points in the groove, the ratio of the number of points to the distance between the endpoints, average deviation from a straight line, and average difference between the orientation at a given point and the tangent to the groove.[1]

Using the symmetry finder discussed in subsection 3.3, we now determine which pairs of possible spine grooves and symmetry axes are consistent. The spine should be approximately parallel to the sides of the back, close to the symmetry axis, and have a region of support overlapping with the region of symmetry.

Results The spine groove classifier is effective at extracting grooves which may correspond to the spine. Out of ten images, it fails to find the spine in three cases, because the groove making up the spine is incorrectly connected to other grooves (see figure 9(a)). However, a better groove following procedure—one that tries to

---

[1] The orientation is determined by the maximum response at a given point, while the flow of the groove is determined by the maximum response at surrounding points.

426

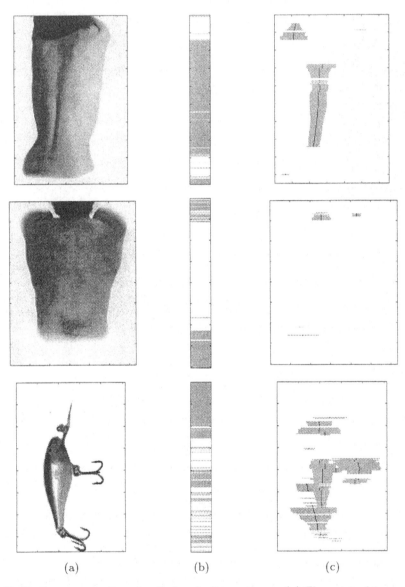

(a)   (b)   (c)

Fig. 7. *Testing cross-sections locally for shading patterns. (a) The original image. (b) Horizontal cross-sections of (a) with limb-like shading patterns are marked in grey. The breaks in the responses could be corrected by using some sort of hysteresis in the matching process. (c) Grooves in the image. The centre of each groove is marked in black, and the groove extent is marked in grey. The top row shows a back with a shading pattern consistent with the model. The middle row shows a shading pattern inconsistent with the model—the back is very flat, which creates very little variation in the intensity across the image. The bottom row shows a fishing lure, which has a shading pattern somewhat similar to many backs.*

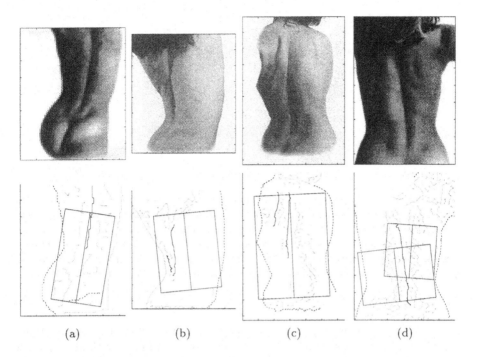

(a) (b) (c) (d)

Fig. 8. *By using spatial reasoning, we can find which grooves are consistent with the groove due to the spine down the middle of the back. Top row: The original image. Bottom row: All grooves are marked with a dotted line. Grooves which could be spine grooves are marked with dashed lines. Spine grooves consistent with the axis of symmetry are solid lines. The axis of symmetry, with its length and width, are described by the rectangle.*

find straight grooves—should allow us to find the spine in these cases. In many cases, the classifier picks up the sides of the figure, since these are reasonably straight, and, out of context, are similar to spine grooves. However, these are rejected using spatial reasoning.

Overall, the conjunction of the groove primitive and the limb primitive works well. Out of seven test images in which we can find the spine, we end up with a single consistent axis of symmetry in four cases (figure 8), and two possible axes of symmetry in two more cases. In the last case, a single spurious horizontal groove allows four symmetry axes to pass the consistency tests, in addition to the two symmetry axes consistent with the actual spine groove (figure 9(d)). These horizontal symmetries, however, may be considered an artefact of the airbrushing of the image.

Out of four control images, two have one possible spine groove, which is not consistent with any axis of symmetry. In the dice example (figure 10), the edge of one die is marked as a possible groove, and is consistent with the symmetry formed by two parallel edges. However, a test that compares the orientations

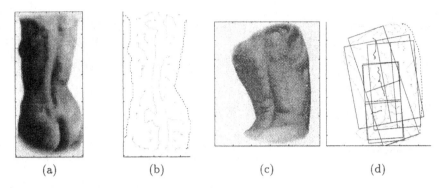

$$(a) \qquad (b) \qquad (c) \qquad (d)$$

Fig. 9. *Examples of problems with the symmetry groove reasoning. Image (a) has too many other grooves, making it too difficult to find the spine groove. Image (c) has many spurious symmetries (probably due to airbrushing) and one spurious horizontal groove, causing several spurious symmetry-groove pairs. This could be rejected by examining how the shading pattern changes as one moves up and down the groove. Note that the spine grooves are marked, with the symmetry axis that would be consistent with that.*

of the grooves as compared to the orientation of the symmetry cross-sections should reject such axis-groove pairs—a true groove will have dark and light on *opposite* sides from the dark and light sides from the overall shading pattern. In this case, they are on the same side, so we should be able to reject the image.

5 Conclusions and future work

In this paper, we have demonstrated a practical use for a recognition technique based on shape from shading. Using a geometrical model of a limb, and a simple shading model, we are able to reject a large number of possible limb segments suggested by a symmetry finder. As a part of a program which finds geometric primitives and pieces them together to construct a body, this performs the valuable task of reducing the number of image segments which need to be considered as part of the kinematic chain.

Secondly, we suggested that it is possible to compose different shading primitives in order to create a more powerful decision mechanism. We showed the feasibility of composing the groove primitive with the limb primitive to get a clear description of a back.

The shading model does not take into account the effects of shadows cast by other objects. In general, it is exceedingly difficult to account for such shadows, since the object casting the shadow will not always be visible. However, the model is robust to the effects of some shadows. In figure 4, the shading test does accept even limb segments which are partially in shadow from other limb segments.

In its present form, our shading model assumes that the reflectance of the surface is approximately constant. However, the essential characteristics of shad-

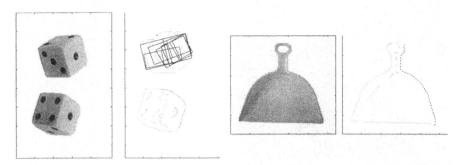

Fig. 10. *Control images. The edge of the die is marked as a possible groove, and is consistent with the symmetries found from the other edges of the die. By testing the orientations of the groove and symmetry axis, such false positives should be rejected. While the dustpan has a single groove which might be a spine, it is not in the correct position with respect to other edges in the images, and is therefore inconsistent with an image of a back.*

ing will remain across reflectance boundaries, so, in principle, there is no reason why we could not find, for example, a lycra-clad arm (since lycra is tight, the shape of the arm wearing lycra will be the same as the naked arm). Because changes in reflectance tend to be high-frequency changes, we can isolate these changes and concentrate on the mid-frequency shading effects as cues to surface shape.

Up to this point, we have demonstrated three shading primitives: folds, grooves, and limbs. We would like to extend the "shading dictionary" to include many more primitives which may be combined together to create useful, abstract representations of shape to aid in object recognition. Many shading primitives likely have very significant spatial relationships, which we would like to exploit. For example, it is relatively rare to see a single fold in clothing worn by people—typically there are several folds. (See figure 11.) Furthermore, these folds do not come in arbitrary orientations; instead, they tend to be approximately parallel. Because these spatial relationships between primitives exist, we envision a robust description of objects in terms of these groups of primitives.

The suggestion of extending the shading dictionary to include more primitives raises the question about what kinds of things are useful primitives. A useful primitive has a distinctive shading pattern which results from some class of geometric shapes. Furthermore, once one has selected a primitive, how can one best model it? The geometric models for folds, grooves and limbs all had several parameters which were tuned to give better performance. It is unclear how to tune the parameters for a given model to improve the performance.

As in all classification problems, the problem of feature selection is a difficult one. It is not clear that we have chosen the best features in this work, and the question remains as to how to select features that will best describe a given shading primitive. With the set of features we are currently using, when

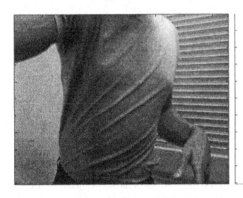

Fig. 11. *Folds in clothing have a very characteristic structure, which can be predicted from theories of buckling of shells. By grouping sets of folds with common directions, we can obtain some clue as to whether a clothed person may be found in an image. The figure on the right shows one of about twenty groups of parallel folds that are automatically extracted from the image. Note that the extent of the folds roughly corresponds to the region occupied by the torso in the image.*

the classifier gives unexpected results on given data, it can be very difficult to understand this misclassification.

References

1. I. Biederman. Recognition-by-components: A theory of human image understanding. *Psych. Review*, 94(2):115–147, 1987.
2. T. Binford. Visual perception by computer. In *Proc. IEEE Conference on Systems and Control*, 1971.
3. A. Blake. Boundary conditions for lightness computation in mondrian world. *Computer Vision, Graphics and Image Processing*, 32:314–327, 1985.
4. J. Brady and H. Asada. Smoothed local symmetries and their implementation. *International Journal of Robotics Research*, 3(3), 1984.
5. C. Cortes and V. Vapnik. Support-vector networks. *Machine Learning*, 20(3):273–97, 1995.
6. A. Dempster, N. Laird, and D. Rubin. Maximum likelihood from incomplete data via the EM algorithm. *Journal of the Royal Statistical Society B*, 39, 1977.
7. D. Forsyth and M. Fleck. Body plans. In *IEEE Conf. on Computer Vision and Pattern Recognition*, 1997.
8. D. Forsyth, J. Malik, M. Fleck, and J. Ponce. Primitives, perceptual organisation and object recognition. in review.
9. D. Forsyth and A. Zisserman. Reflections on shading. *IEEE T. Pattern Analysis and Machine Intelligence*, 13(7):671–679, 1991.
10. A. D. Gross and T. E. Boult. Recovery of shgcs from a single intensity view. *IEEE T. Pattern Analysis and Machine Intelligence*, 18(2):161–180, 1996.
11. J. Haddon and D. Forsyth. Shading primitives: Finding folds and shallow grooves. In *Int. Conf. on Computer Vision*, 1998.
12. B. Horn. Shape from shading : a method for obtaining the shape of a smooth opaque object from one view. Ai tr-232, MIT, 1970.
13. B. Horn and M. Brooks. *Shape from shading*. MIT Press, 1989.
14. B. K. P. Horn. Determining lightness from an image. *Computer Vision, Graphics and Image Processing*, 3:277–299, 1974.

15. J. Koenderink. Vignetting and reflexes. Shading Course Notes.
16. J. Koenderink and A. V. Doorn. Geometrical modes as a method to treat diffuse interreflections in radiometry. *J. Opt. Soc. Am.*, 73(6):843–850, 1983.
17. E. Land and J. McCann. Lightness and retinex theory. *J. Opt. Soc. Am.*, 61(1):1–11, 1971.
18. M. Langer and S. Zucker. Shape-from-shading on a cloudy day. *Journal of the Optical Society of America A*, 11(2):467–78.
19. M. Langer and S. Zucker. Diffuse shading, visibility fields, and the geometry of ambient light. In *IEEE Conf. on Computer Vision and Pattern Recognition*, pages 138–47, 1993.
20. D. Marr and K. Nishihara. Representation and recognition of the spatial organization of three-dimensional shapes. *Proc. Royal Society, London*, B-200:269–294, 1978.
21. S. Nayar, K. Ikeuchi, and T. Kanade. Shape from interreflections. *IJCV*, 6(3):173–195, August 1991.
22. R. Nevatia and T. Binford. Description and recognition of complex curved objects. *Artificial Intelligence*, 8:77–98, 1977.
23. M. Oren, C. Papageorgiou, P. Sinha, and E. Osuna. Pedestrian detection using wavelet templates. In *IEEE Conf. on Computer Vision and Pattern Recognition*, pages 193–9, 1997.
24. E. Osuna, R. Freund, and F. Girosi. Training support vector machines: an application to face detection. In *IEEE Conf. on Computer Vision and Pattern Recognition*, pages 130–6, 1997.
25. J. Shi and J. Malik. Normalized cuts and image segmentation. In *IEEE Conf. on Computer Vision and Pattern Recognition*, 1997.
26. unknown. *Pose file 6.* unknown, unknown. A collection of photographs of human models, annotated in Japanese.
27. T. Wada, H. Ukida, and T. Matsuyama. Shape from shading with interreflections under proximal light source-3d shape reconstruction of unfolded book surface from a scanner image. In *Int. Conf. on Computer Vision*, pages 66–71, 1995.
28. R. Woodham. Photometric method for determining surface orientation from multiple images. *Optical Engineering*, 19(1):139–44, 1980.
29. J. Yang, N. Ohnishi, D. Zhang, and N. Sugie. Determining a polyhedral shape using interreflections. In *IEEE Conf. on Computer Vision and Pattern Recognition*, pages 110–115, 1997.

A Comparison of Measures for Detecting Natural Shapes in Cluttered Backgrounds

Lance R. Williams   Karvel K. Thornber

Dept. of Computer Science   NEC Research Institute
University of New Mexico   4 Independence Way
Albuquerque, NM 87131   Princeton, NJ 08540

Abstract. We propose a new measure of perceptual saliency and quantitatively compare its ability to detect natural shapes in cluttered backgrounds to five previously proposed measures. As defined in the new measure, the saliency of an edge is the fraction of closed random walks which contain that edge. The transition probability matrix defining the random walk between edges is based on a distribution of natural shapes modeled by a stochastic motion. Each of the saliency measures in our comparison is a function of a set of affinity values assigned to pairs of edges. Although the authors of each measure define the affinity between a pair of edges somewhat differently, all incorporate the Gestalt principles of good-continuation and proximity in some form. In order to make the comparison meaningful, we use a single definition of affinity and focus instead on the performance of the different functions for combining affinity values. The primary performance criterion is accuracy. We compute false-positive rates in classifying edges as signal or noise for a large set of test figures. In almost every case, the new measure significantly outperforms previous measures.

1 Introduction

The goal of segmentation is to partition a set of image measurements (e.g., edges) into equivalence classes corresponding to distinct objects. In this paper, we consider a somewhat simpler grouping problem which (following [11]) we call the *saliency problem.* The goal of the saliency problem is to assign a value to each edge which is correlated with whether that edge belongs to a shape or is background noise (see Figure 1). Given the distribution of saliency values, it is then often possible to choose a threshold which will segment the edges into shape and noise classes.

Each of the saliency measures proposed in the literature is a function of a set of affinity values assigned to pairs of edges. Although the authors of each measure define the affinity between a pair of edges somewhat differently, all incorporate the Gestalt principles of good-continuation and proximity in some form. A *saliency function* maps the set of affinities between all pairs of oriented or directed edges (i.e., the *affinity matrix*) to a *saliency vector.* In this paper, we have chosen to compare the definitions of saliency—not affinity. The differences in the authors' definitions of affinity prevents a direct comparison since

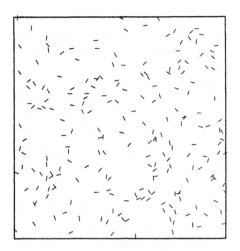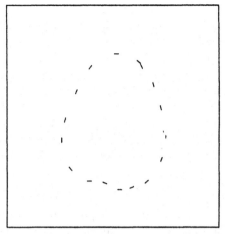

Fig. 1. Left: Seventeen edges from the boundary of a pear in a background of two-hundred edges of random position and orientation. Right: The most salient edges (where saliency is defined as the fraction of closed random walks which contain that edge.)

each requires its own set of parameters. The choice was either to 1) optimize the performance of each measure over its required parameters and compare the different measures with each using its optimal parameter setting; or 2) replace the individual affinity functions with a single function and compare performance using a single parameter setting. Apart from requiring an impractical amount of work, the first approach has the disadvantage of confounding the definitions of affinity and saliency so that the relative merits of each are difficult to disentangle. The shortcoming of the second approach (which is the one we adopted) is that while providing the best comparison of the saliency functions, it says nothing about the relative merits of the affinity functions. Although unlikely, it also ignores possible dependencies between the specific affinity and saliency functions used in a given measure.

The affinity functions can be divided into three classes. Functions in the first class are based on co-circularity[3, 5, 14]. The disadvantage of these functions is that they are non-generic—a circle does not have sufficient degrees of freedom to smoothly join two arbitrary positions and orientations in the plane. They are also difficult to motivate using arguments based on the statistics of natural shapes. Functions in the second class are based on curves of least energy[4, 11]. The affinity between two directed edges is inversely related to the energy, $\int_\Gamma ds\,(\alpha\,\kappa^2(s) + \beta)$, in the curve of least energy joining the two edges. Functions in the third class are based on an explicit prior probability distribution of natural shapes modeled by a stochastic motion[7, 13, 16]. A particle travels with constant speed in the direction $\theta(t)$. Change in direction is a normally distributed random variable with zero mean. Consequently, $\theta(t)$ is a Brownian motion. The variance of the random variable reflects the prior expectation of smoothness. In addition, a constant fraction of particles decay per unit time. The half-life reflects the prior expectation of shortness. The affinity between two edges, i and j, is defined as the sum of the probabilities over all paths joining the two edges, i.e., $P'(j\,|\,i)$. Curves of least energy and stochastic motions are closely related. In fact, it is possible to show that the energy of the curve of least energy is a linear function of the log-likelihood of the maximum likelihood stochastic motion[7, 16]. It follows that the function $P'(j\,|\,i)$ behaves very similiarly to $\exp[-\int_\Gamma dt\,(\alpha\kappa^2(t) + \beta)]$ when Γ is a curve of least energy. This is because the probability associated with Γ (and curves of similiar shape) dominates the probabilities summed over all paths.

To facilitate the exposition, we will introduce a single nomenclature for describing all of the saliency measures. One of the major differences between the measures is whether they are formulated using orientations or directions. By direction we mean an angular quantity with a unique value over its 2π range. By orientation we mean an angular quantity where a direction, e.g., θ, and its opposite direction, e.g., $\theta + \pi$ are identified with each other. Orientations assume values in the range zero to π. We will use $\mathbf{x}$ to represent a vector of values associated with edge directions and $\mathbf{y}$ to represent a vector of values associated with edge orientations. If a stimulus contains n edge segments then the saliency vector, $\mathbf{x}$, has $2n$ components while the saliency vector, $\mathbf{y}$, has n components. The saliency vectors $\mathbf{x}$ and $\bar{\mathbf{x}}$ are identical except for a permutation which exchanges opposite directions. For example, if x_i represents the saliency associated with some edge with direction, θ, then $\bar{x}_i$ represents the saliency of the same edge, but in the opposite direction, $\theta + \pi$.

All of the saliency measures in our comparison associate an affinity value with a pair of oriented or directed edges. We will use the $n \times n$ matrix A to represent the affinity values between all pairs of oriented edges and the $2n \times 2n$ matrix P to represent the affinity values between all pairs of directed edges. An important distinction between saliency measures based on orientation and those based on direction involves the symmetry (or non-symmetry) of the affinity matrices. While the affinity oriented edge i has for j equals the affinity that oriented edge j has for i, this does not (generally) hold for directed edges. Basically, $A_{ij} = A_{ji}$ (i.e., $A = A^T$) but in general, $P_{ij} \neq P_{ji}$. For reasons we will describe later (see Figure 4), this difference is critical in understanding the relative performance of the various measures.

Although not symmetric, P exhibits another kind of symmetry. If we use the subscript $\bar{i}$ to denote the opposite direction to i then $P_{ij} = P_{\bar{j}\,\bar{i}}$. This is termed *time-reversal* symmetry. For the purposes of our comparison, we will define A_{ij} to be $\max(P_{i\,j}, P_{\bar{i}\,j}, P_{i\,\bar{j}}, P_{\bar{i}\,\bar{j}})$, that is, the affinity between two orientations is defined to be the maximum of the affinities among all combinations of directions.

2 Saliency Measures

In the following section, we provide short synopses of the saliency measures used in the comparison.

2.1 Shashua and Ullman (SU)

Shashua and Ullman[11] were the first to use the term saliency in the sense that it is being used in this paper. Building on earlier work by Montanari[6], they described a saliency measure which could be computed by a local parallel network.[1] Using our nomenclature, the saliency of a network element (one for each position and direction) at time $t+1$ is related to the saliencies of neighboring elements at time t by the following update equation:

$$x_i^{(t+1)} = 1 + \max_j P_{ij}\, x_j^{(t)}$$

Recently, Alter and Basri[1] have done an extensive analysis of Shashua and Ullman's method and give expressions for the saliency measure for the case of continuous curves. The saliency of a directed edge i equals the maximum of the saliencies of all continuous curves, Γ, which begin at that edge:

$$\Phi(i) = \max_{\Gamma \in C(i)} \Phi(\Gamma)$$

The saliency of a continuous curve, Γ, is given by the following expression:

$$\Phi(\Gamma) = \int_{s_1}^{s_n} ds\ \sigma(s) \cdot \rho^{\int_{s_1}^{s} dt\,(1-\sigma(t))} \cdot e^{-\int_{s_1}^{s} dt\,\kappa^2(t)}$$

where $\sigma(.)$ is an indicator function which equals one where the curve lies on an edge element (and equals zero elsewhere), ρ is a parameter in the interval $[0,1)$ which controls the rate of convergence, and $\kappa^2(.)$ is the square of the curvature. The overall effect is that the Shashua-Ullman measure favors long smooth curves containing only a few short gaps. For the special case of a curve threading a sequence of n edges of negligible length, we have the following simplification:

$$\Phi(\Gamma) = \sum_{i=1}^{n} e^{-\int_{s_1}^{s_i} dt\,(\kappa^2(t) - \ln \rho)}$$

We observe that the first two terms of this series will dominate all subsequent terms unless the radius of curvature is large and the curve is densely sampled. Consequently, for visual patterns consisting of a sparsely sampled curve in a background of noise, the Shashua and Ullman measure becomes local and greedy. We will see that this seriously limits its performance on such patterns in the presence of correlated noise.

---

[1] In our nomenclature, Montanari's update equation is $x_i^{(t+1)} = \min(-\ln P_{ij} + x_j^{(t)})$. After t time-steps, $x_i^{(t)}$ equals the energy of the minimum energy curve of length t beginning at edge i. In general, this quantity will not converge to a finite value as t goes to infinity.

2.2 Hérault and Horaud (HH)

Hérault and Horaud[5] cast the problem of segmenting a set of oriented edges into figure and ground as a quadratic programming problem which is solved by simulated annealing. The objective function consists of two terms, $-E_{saliency}-E_{constraint}$:

$$\min -\frac{1}{2}\mathbf{y}^T H \mathbf{y} - b^T \mathbf{y} \text{ for } \mathbf{y} \in \{-1, +1\}^n$$

where $H_{ij} = A_{ij} - \alpha$ and $b_i = \sum_j (A_{ij} - \alpha)$. The affinity function used by Hérault and Horaud is based on co-circularity, smoothness and proximity. Hérault and Horaud say only that α is a parameter related to the signal-to-noise ratio but do not say how it is chosen or provide the value they used in their experiments. Experimentally, we have found that their method is very sensitive to the choice of this parameter. If α is too large, the solution consists of all -1's (i.e., all ground) while if it is too small it consists of all $+1$'s (i.e., all figure). Determining the proper value of α makes the job of fairly comparing Hérault-Horaud with measures lacking a comparable parameter difficult. Therefore (for the comparison) we decided to maximize $E_{saliency}$ over 0-1 solution vectors with exactly m components equal to 1:

$$\max \mathbf{y}^T A \mathbf{y} \text{ for } \mathbf{y} \in \{0, 1\}^n \text{ and } \mathbf{y}^T \mathbf{y} = m$$

where m is the number of figure edges and n is the total number of edges. Although in a real application, we would generally not know the value of m, we do know this value for all of our test patterns. For this reason, the modified problem should provide a lower bound on the false-positive rate for the Hérault-Horaud measure.

2.3 Sarkar and Boyer (SB)

Sarkar and Boyer[10] describe a saliency measure and apply it to the problem of distinguishing developed and undeveloped land in aerial images. Although this is a somewhat different application than the one considered in this paper, the similarity between Sarkar and Boyer's computation and our own makes a comparison worthwhile. In addition to good-continuation and proximity, Sarkar and Boyer's affinity function incorporates pairwise measures useful for detecting clusters of buildings such as parallelism, perpendicularity and closure.[2] The affinity function we used in the comparison is the same one we used with the other methods (i.e., only a subset of the relations proposed by Sarkar and Boyer). Given an affinity matrix, A, Sarkar and Boyer propose that the saliency vector, $\mathbf{y}$, maximizes the Raleigh Quotient:

$$\frac{\mathbf{y}^T A \mathbf{y}}{\mathbf{y}^T \mathbf{y}}$$

---

[2] The closure between a pair of edges equals the closure of the group of edges containing that pair. Closed groups must be identified in advance.

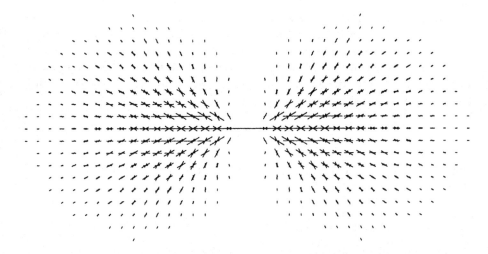

Fig. 2. In the Yen and Finkel[17] saliency computation, the support for oriented edge i due to all other oriented edges j is given by the linear relaxation labeling step, $y_i^{(t+1)} = \sum_j A_{ji} y_j^{(t)} / \sum_j \sum_k A_{jk} y_k^{(t)}$. Because Yen and Finkel's intention was to model the visual cortex, the linear relaxation step is implemented as repeated convolution with a large kernel filter followed by normalization. The symmetry of the A matrix manifests itself in the plane as mirror image symmetry in the kernel. In general, this iteration will converge to the eigenvector associated with the largest positive real eigenvalue of A, i.e., it computes the same measure as Sarkar and Boyer[10].

When A is symmetric, the Raleigh Quotient is maximized by the eigenvector, **y**, associated with the largest positive real eigenvalue of A:

$$\lambda \mathbf{y} = \mathbf{A}\mathbf{y}$$

This measure can also be optimized using the following recurrence equation (which has been independently proposed as a saliency computation by Yen and Finkel[17]):

$$y_i^{(t+1)} = \sum_j A_{ij} y_j^{(t)} / \sum_j \sum_k A_{jk} y_k^{(t)}$$

From linear algebra, we know that the vector **y** will converge to the eigenvector associated with the largest positive real eigenvalue of A. Viewed this way, we see that A is being used as a linear relaxation labeling operator and that Sarkar and Boyer are solving a linear relaxation labeling problem as defined by Rosenfeld, Hummel and Zucker[9] (see Figure 2).

2.4 Guy and Medioni (GM)

Guy and Medioni[3] describe a saliency computation which involves the summation of vector voting patterns based on co-circularity and proximity. The distribution of votes which accumulate at a point in the plane is represented by its 2×2 covariance matrix. The predominant orientation at a point is determined by the eigenvector of the covariance matrix with largest eigenvalue. Neglecting the clever device of representing the vote distributions by their covariance matrices, it is possible to interpret Guy and Medioni's voting patterns as representing the correlation between orientations at different locations in the image plane. In our nomenclature, the saliency at an edge would be the sum of the voting patterns due to all other edges:

$$y_i = \sum_j A_{ij}$$

which is essentially one iteration of linear relaxation labeling using the operator A and a constant input vector.

2.5 Williams and Jacobs (WJ)

Williams and Jacobs[16] describe a method for computing a representation of illusory contours and occluded surface boundaries which they call a *stochastic completion field*. The magnitude of the stochastic completion field at (u, v, ϕ) is the probability that a particle following a stochastic motion (representing the prior distribution of boundary completion shapes) will pass through (u, v, ϕ) on a path joining two boundary fragments. Although not portrayed as a saliency measure, it is easy and natural to use this method to compute saliency. The saliency of an edge is defined to be the probability that a particle following a stochastic motion will pass through that edge on a path joining two others. The saliency vector is given by $\mathbf{x}\,\bar{\mathbf{x}}$ where each component of $\mathbf{x}$ is:

$$x_i = \sum_j P_{ij}$$

The value of x_i is the probability that a particle will reach directed edge i from some other edge j. The saliency of i is just x_i multiplied by $\bar{x}_i$ (i.e., the probability that a particle will reach the same edge but with opposite direction). From time-reversal symmetry, we see that this equals the probability that a particle starting at any edge will pass through edge i and eventually reach another edge.[3]

3 A New Measure (WT)

We define the salience of an edge to be the fraction of closed random walks which contain that edge. It is important to distinguish between *random walks* and *stochastic motions*. By random walk, we mean a sequence of edges visited by a particle subject to the random process with transition probability matrix, P. By stochastic motion, we mean the path in the plane followed by a particle when $\theta(t)$ is a Brownian motion. These two concepts are necessarily related, since the probability that a particle located at edge i at time-step t will be at edge j at

---

[3] It is also worth noting that the WJ measure can be computed very efficiently using a multi-resolution method. See [15].

time-step $t + 1$ is defined to be the sum over the probabilities of all stochastic motions between i and j, i.e., $P_{ji} \equiv P'(j \mid i)$. It follows that the distribution of random walks of length $t + 1$ is related to the distribution of random walks of length t through multiplication by the matrix, P. If $x_i^{(t)}$ represents the fraction of random walks of length t which end at directed edge i, then $x_i^{(t+1)}$ (i.e., the fraction of length $t + 1$ random walks), is given by the following recurrence equation (see Figure 3):

$$x_i^{(t+1)} = \sum_j P_{ij} x_j^{(t)} / \sum_j \sum_k P_{jk} x_k^{(t)}$$

The $\sum_j \sum_k P_{jk} x_k^{(t)}$ term in the denominator is a normalization factor. Without the normalization after each step, the vector $\mathbf{x}$ would quickly approach zero, because random walks of increasing length have decreasing probability. In the steady-state, this normalization factor equals λ:

$$\lambda \mathbf{x} = \mathbf{P} \mathbf{x}$$

where the eigenvector, $\mathbf{x}$, represents the fraction of random walks located at any given edge and the eigenvalue, λ, represents the ratio of the number of random walks which reach one more edge to the number which drift off or die in every step of the random process.[4] In the steady-state, the variation of the eigenvalue equals zero (i.e., $\delta\lambda/\delta\mathbf{x} = 0$) and the eigenvalue itself is given by the following equation:

$$\lambda = \frac{\bar{\mathbf{x}}^{\mathbf{T}} \mathbf{P} \mathbf{x}}{\bar{\mathbf{x}}^{\mathbf{T}} \mathbf{x}}$$

While λ can be set equal to other expressions, the significance of the above form is that it makes explicit the relationship between error in $\mathbf{x}$ and error in λ. Specifically, it shows that if $\mathbf{x}$ were in error by $\delta\mathbf{x}$, the calculated λ would be in error by only $(\delta\mathbf{x})^2$. Note that while this is a variational-principle for the eigenvalue, unlike the Raleigh Quotient, it is not a maximum-principle.[5]

It is possible to view the eigenvector, $\mathbf{x}$, as the distribution of random walks which survived in all past-times and (from time-reversability) to view $\bar{\mathbf{x}}$ as the distribution of random walks which will survive in all future-times. By taking the product, $\mathbf{x}\bar{\mathbf{x}}$, we are constructing the distribution of random walks which survive in all past *and* future times. It follows that $\mathbf{x}\bar{\mathbf{x}}$ represents the distribution of closed random walks through the edges.

The use of directions (as opposed to orientations) is essential—even for non-directional stimuli.[6] Using only orientations, it is impossible to enforce tangent

---

[4] Unlike a Markov process, λ is usually very small—the great majority of particles never reach another edge. In a Markov process, the probabilities in every column of the transition matrix must sum to one. Consequently, the largest eigenvalue also equals one.

[5] In particular, there is no guarantee that a process which starts at a random vector and repeatedly applies the recurrence equation will converge to an eigenvector.

[6] The explicit representation of two directions is the motivation behind the design of the bipole cell in the boundary contour system of Grossberg and Mingolla[2]. It is also a feature of Ullman's model of illusory contour shape[14].

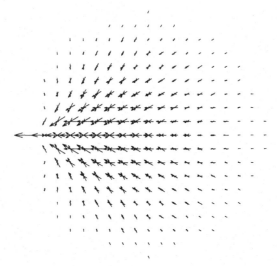

Fig. 3. In the saliency computation proposed in this paper, the support for directed edge i due to all other directed edges j is given by the linear relaxation labeling step, $x_i^{(t+1)} = \sum_j P_{j\,i}\, x_j^{(t)} / \sum_j \sum_k P_{j\,k}\, x_k^{(t)}$. Because P is not symmetric, this iteration is not guaranteed to converge. The salience of edge i is given by the product of x_i and $\bar{x}_i$ where x is the eigenvector associated with the largest positive real eigenvalue of P. This quantity represents the relative number of closed random walks through edge i.

continuity at i. The consequence of not representing both directions is the presence of cusps (sudden reversals of direction) in the particle's paths (see Figure 4).

To develop some intuition for the meaning of the eigenvalue, it will be useful to consider an idealized situation. We know from linear algebra that the eigenvalues of P are solutions to the equation $\det(P - \lambda I) = 0$. Now, consider a closed path, Γ, threading m directed edges. The probability that a particle following this path will reach directed edge, $\Gamma_{i \bmod m+1}$, given that it is located at directed edge, Γ_i, equals $P'(\Gamma_{i \bmod m+1} | \Gamma_i)$. Assuming that the probability of a particle traveling from directed edge Γ_i to Γ_j when Γ_j does not immediately follow Γ_i on the closed path is negligible (i.e., $P_{j\,i} = P'(\Gamma_j | \Gamma_i)$ when $j = i \bmod m + 1$ and $P_{j\,i} = 0$ otherwise) then:

$$\lambda(\Gamma) = \left(\prod_{i=1}^{m} P'(\Gamma_{i \bmod m+1} | \Gamma_i) \right)^{\frac{1}{m}}$$

satisfies $\det(P - \lambda I) = 0$. This is the *geometric mean* of the transition probabilities in the closed path.[7] Normally long contours have very low probability: $\prod_{i=1}^{m} P'(\Gamma_{i \bmod m+1} | \Gamma_i)$. However, the properties of the geometric mean are such that smoothness and closure are favored and long contours suffer no penalty. It

---

[7] Equivalently, minus one times the logarithm of the eigenvalue equals the *average transition energy*: $-\ln \lambda(\Gamma) = -\sum_{i=1}^{m} \ln P'(\Gamma_{i \bmod m+1} | \Gamma_i)/m$.

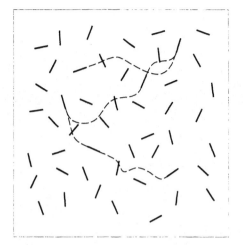
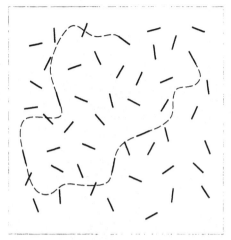

Fig. 4. The explicit representation of two directions (i.e., **x** and **x̄**) and the use of a *non-symmetric* linear relaxation labeling operator (i.e., P) is essential if the intermediate states of the relaxation labeling process (i.e., $x_i^{(t)}$, $x_i^{(t+1)}$, etc.) are to be interpreted as distributions of random walks which are continuous in tangent. Repeated application of a *symmetric* linear relaxation labeling operator (i.e., A) to a vector of saliencies associated with orientations (i.e., **y**) yields distributions of random walks which can reverse direction at edge locations (left). After the initial iteration, this process tends to increase the salience of the noise edges as much as the signal edges. This explains why the performance of Guy and Medioni's saliency computation (essentially one iteration of linear relaxation labeling using the operator A and a constant input vector) is superior to that of Sarkar and Boyer[10]. It also explains why direction-based measures (e.g., WJ and WT) outperform both.

is useful to compare this to the saliency which Shashua and Ullman assigns to a curve, which is given by the following geometric series:

$$\Phi(\Gamma) = \sum_{j=1}^{\infty} \prod_{i=1}^{j} P'(\Gamma_{i+1} | \Gamma_i)$$

Shashua and Ullman desired a saliency measure which favored long, smooth contours yet converged to a finite value for contours of infinite length (i.e., for closed contours). Unfortunately, the rate at which this series converges depends critically on the values of the $P'(\Gamma_{i+1} | \Gamma_i)$. If the transition probabilities are too small, the series will converge too rapidly (and the measure becomes local and greedy). Conversely, if they are too large, the series will converge too slowly. In summary, we see that the geometric mean has the properties Shashua and Ullman wanted but lacks other undesirable properties.

4 Results

The first comparison used test patterns which consisted of short oriented edges spaced uniformly around the perimeter of a circle in a background of edges

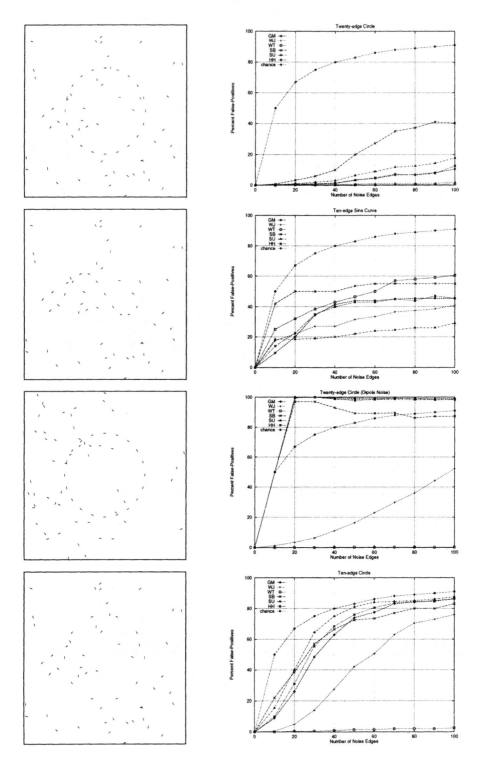

Fig. 5. (a) twenty-edge circle. (b) ten-edge sine curve. (c) twenty-edge circle (dipole noise) (d) ten-edge circle. All patterns are shown at a noise-level of fifty.

with random positions and orientations (see Figure 5 (a)).[8] We computed the saliency of both shape and noise edges using each of the six measures: SU, HH, SB, GM, WJ, and WT. The edges were then sorted in ascending order based on their saliencies. The salience of the most salient edge is ϕ_1 and the salience of the least salient edge is ϕ_n. Given m shape edges, we define a false-positive as a noise edge which is assigned a salience larger than ϕ_{m+1}. The false-positive rate for each measure was computed for patterns consisting of different numbers of shape and noise edges. The false-positive rate for each combination (e.g., 20 shape edges and 70 noise edges) was estimated by averaging the false-positive rate for ten trials using different noise patterns.[9] The right half of Figure 5(a) is a plot of the percentage false-positives versus the number of noise edges for the twenty-edge circle.

All of the measures perform reasonably well (less than 10% false-positive rate) at the low noise-levels (40 noise edges or less). At higher noise-levels, the performance of the measures begins to diverge. It is interesting that GM significantly outperforms SB, since GM is essentially one iteration of SB. We speculate that the false-positive rate is increased by additional relaxation-labeling steps using the non-directional operator. We also observe that GM performs comparably to HH—even though the HH measure is significantly more expensive to compute. Finally, at the lower signal-to-noise ratios, WJ and WT have significantly lower false-positive rates.

The second comparison was identical to the first except that the shape edges formed an open-ended sine curve (see Figure 5 (b)). The right half of Figure 5 (b) is a plot of the percentage false-positives versus the number of noise edges for the ten-edge sine curve. The relatively poor performance of the WT measure compared to the other measures can be attributed to its explicit reliance on closure. Nevertheless, it still outperforms the SB measure for higher signal-to-noise ratios and has an error rate comparable to that of SB (i.e., within 5%) at lower signal-to-noise ratios. As in the previous comparison, the performance of GM and HH are nearly identical. The false-positive rates of these measures is somewhat larger than that of the WJ measure. The SU measure had the best performance.

In the third comparison, we used a background consisting of correlated (i.e., dipole) noise (see Figure 5(c)). A dipole consists of two collinear edges separated by a gap of size equal to the distance between successive edges of the circle. Because the two edges forming a dipole are collinear, the affinity between the edges forming a dipole is greater than between adjacent circle edges. Consequently, it is impossible to distinguish noise edges from shape edges using purely

---

[8] The radius of the circle equals 32 and the noise edges are uniformly distributed within a square of size 64.

[9] We wanted to ensure that HH was not unfairly penalized because of the inherent difficulty of solving the combinatorial optimization problem. We therefore computed the value of $\mathbf{y}^T \mathbf{A} \mathbf{y}$ for the perfect segmentation and accepted a trial only when the simulated annealing procedure returned a greater or equal value. After ten failed attempts, we restarted that trial with a new noise-pattern.

local measures. Indeed, all of the measures but WJ and WT have nearly a 100% false-positive rate. In the case of the SU measure, this is because (for gaps of this size) the geometric series is dominated by the first two terms.[10]

In the fourth comparison (see Figure 5(d)), we used a ten-edge circle. This is a challenging pattern because the sampling rate is so low—only one edge per 36 degrees of circumference. Most of the measures perform poorly, even at relatively high signal-to-noise ratios. For a noise-level of 80, the GM, SU and HH measures are performing almost at chance, or 90% false-positive rate. The SB and WJ measures perform slightly better, with false-positive rates of 80% and 70%, respectively. In contrast, the false-positive rate for WT is under 5%.

Our intention in the last comparison was to test the saliency measures on a collection of "real images" but to do so in a way which would allow meaningful error rates to be estimated. In the past, when new grouping methods have been proposed, their performance has not been systematically compared to others from the literature. Although the proposed methods are typically demonstrated on two or three "real images," because the computational goal is often not well defined, performance is impossible to gauge. Consequently, it is unclear whether or not the methods represent genuine improvements in the state of the art.

We decided to construct test patterns from pairs of real images in such a way that performance on the saliency problem could be objectively measured. Nine different fruits and vegetables were placed in front of a uniformly colored background (three of these are shown in Figure 6(a-c)). This allowed their silhouettes to be extracted using straightforward methods. The orientation at points uniformly spaced along the silhouette was then estimated using a robust line fitting technique (see Figure 6(d-f)).

Next, we selected nine images of natural texture from the MIT Media Lab texture database (these of these are shown in Figure 6(g-i)). The Canny edge detector was applied to a 64×64 block from each texture and the resulting edges were filtered on contrast to create a set of nine masking patterns consisting of approximately 800 edges each (see Figure 6(j-l)).

Edges from the nine fruit and vegetable silhouettes (signal) and nine natural texture masking patterns (noise) were then combined to construct a set of 405 test patterns. These patterns represent all 81 silhouette and texture combinations at five different signal-to-noise ratios (see Figure 6(m-o)).[11] Each of the six saliency measures was run on all of the test patterns and false-positive rates were computed as before. The results are plotted in Figure 7. For a signal-to-noise ratio of 0.2, the false-positive rate for the SB measure is 72% (i.e., 8% better than chance performance). The false-positive rates for SU, GM, HH and WJ are all approximately 50%. In contrast, the false-positive rate for the WT measure is 20% (i.e., 60% better than chance performance). Furthermore, after the signal-to-noise ratio is reduced by a factor of two, the false-positive rate for the WT measure remains under 50%.

---

[10] For the thirty-edge circle, the geometric series converges more slowly. Presumably, SU would continue to improve (relative to the other measures) as the size of the gaps decreases.

[11] The texture edges are undersampled to achieve a given signal-to-noise ratio.

5 Conclusion

In this paper, we introduced a new measure of perceptual saliency and quantitatively compared its ability to detect natural shapes in cluttered backgrounds to five previously proposed measures. The saliency measure is based on the distribution of closed random walks through the edges. We computed false-positive rates in classifying edges as signal or noise for a large set of test figures. In almost every case, the new measure significantly outperforms previous measures.

6 Appendix

In this Appendix, we give the analytic expression for the affinity function used in the comparisons (see [13] for its derivation).[12] We define the affinity, P_{ji}, between two directed edges, i and j, to be:

$$P_{ji} \equiv P'(j \mid i) = \int_0^\infty dt\, P(j \mid i; t) \approx F\, P(j \mid i; t_{opt})$$

where $P(j \mid i; t)$ is the probability that a particle which begins its stochastic motion at (x_i, y_i, θ_i) at time 0 will be at (x_j, y_j, θ_j) at time t. The affinity between two edges is the value of this expression integrated over stochastic motions of all durations, $P'(j \mid i)$. This integral is approximated analytically using the method of steepest descent. The approximation is the product of P evaluated at the time at which the integral is maximized (i.e., t_{opt}), and an extra factor, F. The expression for P at time t is:

$$P(j \mid i; t) = \frac{3\exp[-\frac{6}{Tt^3}(a\,t^2 - b\,t + c)] \cdot \exp(\frac{-t}{\tau})}{\sqrt{\pi^3 T^3\ t^7/2}}$$

where

$$a=[2 + \cos(\theta_j - \theta_i)]\,/\,3$$
$$b=[x_{ji}(\cos\theta_j + \cos\theta_i) + y_{ji}(\sin\theta_j + \sin\theta_i)]/v$$
$$c=(x_{ji}^2 + y_{ji}^2)/v^2$$

for $x_{ji} = x_j - x_i$ and $y_{ji} = y_j - y_i$. The parameters T, τ and v determine the distribution of shapes (where T is the diffusion coefficient, τ is particle half-life and v is speed). In all of our experiments, $T = 0.002$, $\tau = 5.0$ and $v = 1$. The expression for P should be evaluated at $t = t_{opt}$, where t_{opt} is real, positive, and satisfies the following cubic equation:

$$-7t^3/4 + 3(a\,t^2 - 2\,b\,t + 3\,c)/T = 0$$

---

[12] For a derivation of a related affinity function, see the recent paper of Sharon, Brandt and Basri[12].

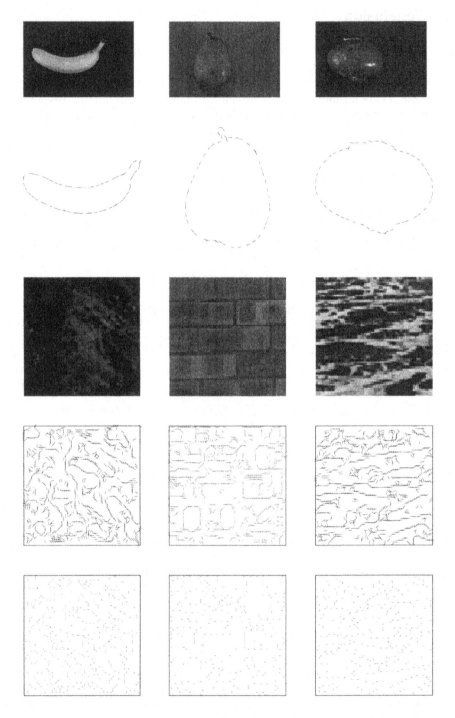

Fig. 6. (a-c) Banana, pear, red onion (d-f) Banana edges, pear edges, red onion edges (g-i) Terrain, brick, water (j-l) Terrain edges, brick edges, water edges (m-o) Banana with terrain mask, pear with brick mask, red onion with water mask.

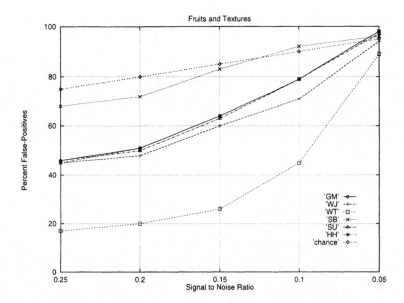

Fig. 7. False-positive rate for fruit and vegetable silhouettes with natural texture backgrounds.

If more than one real, positive root exists, then the root maximizing $P(j \mid i; t)$ is chosen.[13] Finally, the extra factor F is:

$$F = \sqrt{2\pi t_{opt}^5 / [12(3\,c - 2\,b\,t_{opt})/T + 7\,t_{opt}^3/2]}$$

For our purposes here, we ignore the $\exp(-t/\tau)$ factor in the steepest descent approximation for t_{opt}. We note that by increasing v, the distribution of contours can be uniformly scaled.

Acknowledgments The authors wish to thank Hong Pan for providing the silhouettes of fruits and vegetables. Thanks also to Shyjan Mohamud and Majd Sakr for their assistance in running experiments and plotting results. Finally, we are grateful to David Jacobs and Michael Langer for many helpful discussions.

References

1. Alter, T. and R. Basri, Extracting Salient Contours from Images: An Analysis of the Saliency Network, *Proc. IEEE Conf. on Comp. Vision and Pattern Recognition (CVPR '96)*, pp. 13-20, San Francisco, CA, 1996.

---

[13] For a discussion on solving cubic equations, see [8].

2. Grossberg, S., and E. Mingolla, Neural Dynamics of Form Perception: Boundary Completion, Illusory Figures, and Neon Color Spreading, *Psychological Review* **92**, pp. 173-211, 1985.

3. Guy, G. and G. Medioni, Inferring Global Perceptual Contours from Local Features, *Intl. Journal of Computer Vision* **20**, pp. 113-133, 1996.

4. Horn, B.K.P., The Curve of Least Energy, MIT AI Lab Memo No. 612, MIT, Cambridge, Mass.,1981.

5. Hérault, L. and R. Horaud, Figure-Ground Discrimination: A Combinatorial Optimization Approach, *IEEE Trans. on Pattern Analysis and Machine Intelligence* **15**, pp. 899-914, 1993.

6. Montanari, U., On the Optimal Detection of Curves in Noisy Pictures, *Comm. of the Assoc. for Computing Machinery* **14**, pp. 335-345, 1971.

7. Mumford, D., Elastica and Computer Vision, *Algebraic Geometry and Its Applications*, Chandrajit Bajaj (ed.), Springer-Verlag, New York, 1994.

8. Press, W.H., Flannery, B.P., Teukolsky, S.A., and W.T. Vetterling, *Numerical Recipes in C*, Cambridge University Press, 1988.

9. Rosenfeld, A., Hummel R., and S. Zucker, Scene Labeling by Relaxation Operations, *IEEE Trans. on Systems Man and Cybernetics* **6**, pp. 420-433, 1976.

10. Sarkar, S. and K. Boyer, Quantitative Measures of Change based on Feature Organization: Eigenvalues and Eigenvectors, *Proc. IEEE Conf. Computer Vision and Pattern Recognition (CVPR '96)*, pp. 478-483, San Francisco, CA, 1996.

11. Shashua, A. and S. Ullman, Structural Saliency: The Detection of Globally Salient Structures Using a Locally Connected Network, *2nd Intl. Conf. on Computer Vision*, Clearwater, FL, 1988.

12. Sharon, E., Brandt, A., and R. Basri, Completion Energies and Scale, *Proc IEEE Conf. Computer Vision and Pattern Recognition (CVPR '97)*, pp. 884-890, San Juan, Puerto Rico, 1997.

13. Thornber, K.K. and L.R. Williams, Analytic Solution of Stochastic Completion Fields, *Biological Cybernetics* **75**, pp. 141-151, 1996.

14. Ullman, S., Filling-in the Gaps: The Shape of Subjective Contours and a Model for Their Generation, *Biological Cybernetics* **21**, pp. 1-6, 1976.

15. Williams, L.R., Wang, T. and K.K. Thornber, Computing Stochastic Completion Fields in Linear-Time Using a Resolution Pyramid, *Proc. of 7th Intl. Conf. on Computer Analysis of Images and Patterns (CAIP '97)*, Kiel, Germany, 1997.

16. Williams, L.R. and D.W. Jacobs, Stochastic Completion Fields: A Neural Model of Illusory Contour Shape and Salience, *Neural Computation* **9**, pp. 849-870, 1997.

17. Yen, S. and L. Finkel, "Pop-Out" of Salient Contours in a Network Based on Striate Cortical Connectivity, *Investigative Opthalmology and Visual Science (ARVO)*, Vol. **37**, No. 3, 1996.

Bias-Variance Tradeoff for Adaptive Surface Meshes

Richard C. Wilson and Edwin R. Hancock

Department of Computer Science
University of York
York, Y01 5DD, UK
email: wilson,erh@minster.york.ac.uk

Abstract. This paper presents a novel statistical methodology for exerting control over adaptive surface meshes. The work builds on a recently reported adaptive mesh which uses split and merge operations to control the distribution of planar or quadric surface patches. Hitherto, we have used the target variance of the patch fit residuals as a control criterion. The novelty of the work reported in this paper is to focus on the variance-bias tradeoff that exists between the size of the fitted patches and their associated parameter variances. In particular, we provide an analysis which shows that there is an optimal patch area which minimises the variance in the fitted patch parameters. This area offers the best compromise between the noise-variance, which decreases with increasing area, and the model-bias, which increases in a polynomial manner with area. The computed optimal areas of the local surface patches are used to exert control over the facets of the adaptive mesh. We use a series of split and merge operations to distribute the faces of the mesh so that each resembles as closely as possible its optimal area. In this way the mesh automatically selects its own model-order by adjusting the number of control-points or nodes. We provide experiments on both real and synthetic data. This experimentation demonstrates that our mesh is capable of efficiently representing high curvature surface detail.

1 Introduction

Adaptive meshes [3, 18, 19] have proved popular in both the segmentation [25, 12, 4, 13, 16, 8] and efficient representation [6] of volumetric surface data . The literature is rich with examples. For instance De Floriani et al [6, 7] have developed a multi-scale mesh which has been exploited not only for surface representation, but also for stereoscopic reconstruction. Several authors have reported variable topology meshes. Bulpitt and Efford [1] have a mesh that adapts itself so as to minimise curvature and goodness of fit criteria. The "slime" surface of Stoddart et al [20] uses region merge operations of refine a B-spline mesh surface.

These surfaces are effectively driven by geometric criteria [18, 19]. In a recent series of papers we have developed a surface mesh which is statistically motivated [27, 26]. Each node in our mesh represents a local quadric patch that is fitted to a support neighbourhood on the surface. Specifically, we have shown how a series of node split and merge operations can be used to both refine and decimate the mesh so as to deliver a surface of predefined target variance. These operations not only control the surface topology, they also iteratively modify the support neighbourhoods for the quadric patch representation. Analysis of the mesh reveals that the equilibrium distribution of mesh nodes is such that the density is proportional to the underlying curvature of the surface. The surface has been demonstrated to produce useful segmentations that can be used for subsequent differential analysis [26].

The aim in this paper is to focus more closely on the statistical criterion that underpins the control of the mesh split and merge operations. In particular we consider the variance-bias tradeoff [10] which underpins the choice of the support neighbourhood for the estimation of surface parameters. Simple split-and-merge operations based on a target 'goodness of fit' can result in biased or noisy patch estimates. This has undesirable effects on the recovered differential structure of the surface [17, 22, 23]. It is for this reason that we present a detailed analysis of parameter variance. The main conclusion of this analysis is that the variance has a two-component structure. The first component results from the effects of noise and decreases with increasing area of estimation. The second term results from the model-bias and increases with the area of estimation. As a result of the interplay between these two terms, there is an optimal choice of the area of estimation that results in a joint minimisation of both the noise variance of the estimated parameters and the model bias.

The optimal local area of estimation is used to exert control over the split [19] and merge [18] operations that underpin our adaptive mesh. By driving the adaptation of the mesh from the optimal local patch area we provide a natural means of controlling the model-order for our surface representation. Using these split and merge operations, a mesh is generated which has faces of area equal to the optimal area of estimation. If surface patches are placed at each of these faces, the subsequent piecewise representation is optimal in the sense that the error to the underlying surface parameters is minimal. The parameters of the patch are sufficient to represent the surface to within the accuracy limits imposed by the noise.

2 Approximating the surface from noisy data-points

Following Besl and Jain [2] our aim is to fit increasingly complex variable order surface models to potentially noisy data-points. Viewed from the perspective of local surface geometry this can be viewed as sequentially estimating derivatives of increasing order through the fitting of an appropriate surface patch. When couched in this intrinsically hierarchical way, each derivative relies on the estimation of the preceding and lower order derivatives. As a concrete example, in order to estimate curvature through a second-order quadric patch, we must first fit zero and first order models to determine the surface height and surface normal direction. Subject to the limitations imposed by the level of image noise, this process can obviously be extended to any model-order to estimate the desired derivative.

In practice however, there is a problem of variance-bias tradeoff that hinders the parameter estimation process. By increasing the size of the sample or surface area used to estimate the model parameters, the effects of noise variance may be minimised. In other words, the temptation is to increase the size of the local surface patches so as to increase the accuracy of the estimated derivatives. Unfortunately, as the surface facet is increased in area problems of model bias emerge. In a nutshell, the problem is that the model order is insufficient to represent genuine structure in the data. The basic issue addressed in this paper is how to resolve this dilemma for the important and generic problem of adaptive mesh control. It must be stressed that variance-bias issues are ones of pivotal philosophical and practical importance in data fitting [10].

We commence our discussion with a set of 3-dimensional data-points $P = \{\mathbf{p}_i | \forall i\}$ derived from range data. In realistic tasks, these points are invariable uncertain in the sense that they deviate from the true surface due to some noise process. In the following, we denote the function of the underlying surface as $f(x,y)$ and the equation of points on this underlying surface is therefore $z = f(x,y)$. The data-point $\mathbf{p}_i = (x_i, y_i, z_i)$ is related to the true surface by $z_i = f(x_i, y_i) + n_i$, where n_i is the additive noise process. Now consider the Taylor expansion of the true surface function.

$$f(x_i, y_i) = f(x_o, y_o) + \left\{ \frac{\partial f}{\partial x} \right\}_o (x_i - x_o) + \left\{ \frac{\partial f}{\partial y} \right\}_o (y_i - y_o)$$
$$+ \left\{ \frac{\partial^2 f}{\partial x^2} \right\}_o (x_i - x_o)^2 + \left\{ \frac{\partial^2 f}{\partial x \partial y} \right\}_o (x_i - x_o)(y_i - y_o) + \left\{ \frac{\partial^2 f}{\partial y^2} \right\}_o (y_i - y_o)^2$$

$$(1)$$

If we wish to estimate, for example, first order derivatives (corresponding to the surface normal), we must first estimate the height $z_o = f(x_o, y_o)$ and remove it's contribution to the Taylor expansion by moving the origin of the coordinate system to $(x_o, y_o, f[x_o, y_o])$. The derivatives $\frac{\partial f}{\partial x}$ and $\frac{\partial f}{\partial x}$ can the be estimated by fitting the tangent plane $z = ax + by$. Similarly, the surface curvature can be determined by transforming co-ordinates to remove zero and first order contributions. The necessary second-order derivatives are estimated by fitting the quadric patch $f(x,y) = \alpha x^2 + \beta xy + \gamma y^2$ to the transformed height data.

In the remainder of this section, we provide an analysis of the errors in the fitted local surface models for each derivative in turn, commencing with the estimation of surface location. In each case we provide an analysis of variance for the fitted surface parameters. This commences from the known variances of the surface fit-residuals. These residuals are propagated through into the estimation of surface parameter variances. This analysis reveals the area dependence of the parameter variances. It is this analysis which allows us to estimate the optimal patch-area which results in the best variance-bias tradeoff.

2.1 Estimating the average surface height

We first consider the estimation of the height of the local origin of co-ordinates on the surface. We denote this point by the vector of co-ordinates $o = (x_o, y_o, z_o)^T$. This location of the origin can be estimated by the mean height of the data-points. If S denotes the index-set of the sample of available points and n_i represents the additive noise present in the height measurement z_i, then

$$o = \frac{1}{|S|} \sum_{i \in S} \begin{pmatrix} x_i \\ y_i \\ z_i \end{pmatrix} = \frac{1}{|S|} \sum_{i \in S} \begin{pmatrix} x_i \\ y_i \\ f(x_i, y_i) + n_i \end{pmatrix} \tag{2}$$

If the sampled points are uniformly distributed over $x - y$ footprint of the surface patch, then the x and y co-ordinates of the origin are located at the centre-of-mass of the support neighbourhood. The height distribution, on the other hand, is governed both by the sampling noise and the bias introduced by the underlying surface shape in the sampling window. The two processes have very different origins. The noise process is stochastic and requires an explicit statistical model. The bias is a measure of the inappropriateness of the surface shape model adopted in the local sampling window.

The contributions from the various sources can be evaluated by again using the Taylor expansion. Our estimate of the local location of the surface is given by the average height of the sample data-points thus;

$$z_{est} = \frac{1}{|S|} \sum_{i \in S} [n_i + z_o + \Delta x_i \frac{\partial f}{\partial x} + \Delta y_i \frac{\partial f}{\partial y} + \Delta x_i^2 \frac{\partial^2 f}{\partial x^2} + \Delta x_i \Delta y_i \frac{\partial^2 f}{\partial x \partial y} + \Delta y_i^2 \frac{\partial^2 f}{\partial y^2} \tag{3}$$

where $\Delta x_i = x_i - x_o$ and $\Delta y_i = y_i - y_o$. Because we have chosen a symmetrical sampling window, the odd spatial moments $\sum_{i \in S} \Delta x_i$, $\sum_{i \in S} \Delta y_i$ and $\sum_{i \in S} \Delta x_i \Delta y_i$ are zero. As a result, the estimated height-intercept is given by

$$z_{est} = z_o + \frac{1}{|S|} \sum_{i \in S} n_i + \frac{1}{|S|} \frac{\partial^2 f}{\partial x^2} \sum_{i \in S} \Delta x_i^2 + \frac{1}{|S|} \frac{\partial^2 f}{\partial y^2} \sum_{i \in S} \Delta y_i^2 + \dots \tag{4}$$

In other words, the estimated height-intercept is deviates from the average z-value by an amount that is determined by the second-order derivatives of the surface. The variance of the fit-residuals, i.e. $\sigma_{est}^2 = \frac{1}{|S|} \sum_{i \in S} (z_i - z_o)^2$ therefore has a two-component structure. The first of these results from averaging the raw image noise over the $|S|$ samples in the local surface patch. When the noise n_i is assumed to follow a Gaussian distribution with variance σ^2 and zero mean, then the average noise variance is equal to $\frac{1}{|S|} \sigma^2$. The second contribution to the variance of the fitted height originates from the derivative bias terms, of which the most significant terms are the second order derivatives of the surface. As a result, the total variance is given by

$$\sigma_{est}^2 = \frac{\sigma^2}{|S|} + \left\{ \frac{\partial^2 f}{\partial x^2} \right\}_o^2 \left(\sum_{i \in S} \Delta x_i^2 \right)^2 + \left\{ \frac{\partial^2 f}{\partial y^2} \right\}_o^2 \left(\sum_{i \in S} \Delta y_i^2 \right)^2$$

$$+ \left\{ \frac{\partial^2 f}{\partial x^2} \right\}_o \left\{ \frac{\partial^2 f}{\partial y^2} \right\}_o \sum_{i \in S} \Delta x_i^2 \sum_{i \in S} \Delta y_i^2 \tag{5}$$

If the data-points are uniformly distributed over the x-y footprint of the surface patch, then the expectation values of the second-order moments $\sum_{i \in S} \Delta x_i^2$ and $\sum_{i \in S} \Delta y_i^2$ can be calculated from the geometric moments of the support neighbourhood. Of course, the exact values of these moments depend on both the size and shape of the support neighbourhood. For simplicity, we will evaluate the moments for a circular region around the origin. In order to make the role of the area A of the support neighbourhood explicit, we replace the number of points in the sample-set by the expression $|S| = \rho A$ where ρ is the surface-density of data-points. As a result, the expectation value for $\sum_{i \in S} \Delta x_i^2$ is given, in the circular case, by

$$E(\sum_{i \in S} \Delta x_i^2) = \rho \int_A x^2 dA = \frac{\rho A^2}{8\pi} \tag{6}$$

Substituting for the expectation values of the second-order surface-moments, the final expression for the total variance is given by

$$\sigma(A)_{est}^2 = \frac{\sigma^2}{\rho A} + \frac{A^2}{64\pi^2} \left[\left\{ \frac{\partial^2 f}{\partial x^2} \right\}_o^2 + \left\{ \frac{\partial^2 f}{\partial x^2} \right\}_o \left\{ \frac{\partial^2 f}{\partial y^2} \right\}_o + \left\{ \frac{\partial^2 f}{\partial y^2} \right\}_o^2 \right]$$
$$= \frac{\sigma^2}{\rho A} + k_0 A^2$$

The two component area dependence of the total variance is now made explicit. The first term represents the propagation of raw noise variance. As the area of the support neighbourhood used in the estimation of the origin increases, then so the effect of noise-variance on the fitted parameters decreases. The second term, on the other hand, represents the model bias in the extracted parameters. In the case of estimating the origin, the bias depends on the second derivatives, or curvature, of the local surface. The bias term increases with increasing surface area. It is clear that there is critical value of the area which results in minimum total variance. We locate the minimum area by fitting an empirical model to the measured height variance observed for various support neighbourhood areas. This fitting process returns estimates of the two model parameters σ^2 and k_0. When these have been extracted from the the variance-area data, the optimal area is given by

$$A_{min} = \left(\frac{\sigma^2}{2\rho k_0} \right)^{\frac{1}{3}} \tag{7}$$

In the Sections 2.2 and 2.3, we extend our analysis to the estimation of local surface orientation and curvature. In both cases, there is a similar variance-bias structure to the total variance.

2.2 Estimation of the surface normal

By translating to the local system of co-ordinates centred on the origin o, we we can again perform the Taylor expansion for the local surface patch. In the translated co-ordinate system,

$$z' = \left\{\frac{\partial f}{\partial x}\right\}_o x' + \left\{\frac{\partial f}{\partial y}\right\}_o y' + \left\{\frac{\partial^2 f}{\partial x^2}\right\}_o x'^2 + \left\{\frac{\partial^2 f}{\partial x \partial y}\right\}_o x'y' + \left\{\frac{\partial^2 f}{\partial y^2}\right\}_o y'^2 \quad (8)$$

where $x' = x - x_o$ and $y' = y - y_o$ are the translated co-ordinates. In the transformed co-ordinate system the height intercept of the local surface patch is zero. Hence, the tangent-plane may be estimated directly from the data-points in this new coordinate system.

Both the parameter estimation process and the propagation of variance is more complicated than in the case of the origin. Parameter estimation is realised by the least-squares fit of a tangent plane through the origin $z' = ax' + by'$. Again we choose a set of sample data-points S. We denote the parameters of the tangent plane by $\mathbf{P} = (a, b)^T$. The positions of the sample points are represented by the design matrix

$$\mathbf{X}_p = \begin{pmatrix} x'_1 & y'_1 \\ x'_2 & y'_2 \\ \vdots & \vdots \end{pmatrix}$$

while the corresponding height data is represented by the column-vector $\mathbf{Z}_p = (z'_1, z'_2, ...)^T$. The least-squares fit for the parameters is given by $\hat{\mathbf{P}} = \mathbf{L}_p \mathbf{Z}_p$ where $\mathbf{L}_p = (\mathbf{X}_p^T \mathbf{X}_p)^{-1} \mathbf{X}_p^T$ is the pseudo-inverse of the design matrix.

When the parameter-vector $\mathbf{P}$ is estimated in this way, then its covariance structure can be found by propagating the variance in the transformed height data $\mathbf{Z}_p$. If Σ_{Z_p} is the covariance matrix for the transformed height data, then the the covariance matrix for the plane parameters, i.e. $E[(\mathbf{P} - \hat{\mathbf{P}})(\mathbf{P} - \hat{\mathbf{P}})^T]$, is given by

$$\Sigma_p = \mathbf{L}_p \Sigma_{Z_p} \mathbf{L}_p^T \quad (9)$$

As in the case of the origin, the total covariance matrix has a two-component structure which reflects the two sources of error in the estimation of the surface normals. The first component is due to the propagation of noise in the surface-data-point positions, while the second component is a bias term that results from the higher order terms in the Taylor expansion. We make this two-component structure more explicit by writing

$$\Sigma_p = \mathbf{L}_p \Sigma_N \mathbf{L}_p^T + \mathbf{L}_p \Sigma_B \mathbf{L}_p^T \quad (10)$$

The noise component of the parameter covariance matrix is modelled under the assumption that transformed height data is subject to independent identically distributed Gaussian noise of zero mean and variance σ^2. Under this assumption the noise variance of the least-squares parameter estimates is given by

$$\mathbf{L}_p \Sigma_N \mathbf{L}_p^T = \sigma^2 \begin{pmatrix} \sum_{i \in S} x_i'^2 & \sum_{i \in S} x_i' y_i' \\ \sum_{i \in S} x_i' y_i' & \sum_{i \in S} y_i'^2 \end{pmatrix}^{-1} \quad (11)$$

In other words, the noise-component to the total covariance matrix depends on the second-order moments of the points in the surface patch. As before we assume a circular support neighbourhood. In this case, the expectation values of the odd co-ordinate moments are zero. The expectation values of the even moments can be computed along the same lines as outlined in the previous subsection. As a result the noise contribution has a diagonal covariance matrix Specifically,

$$L_p \Sigma_N L_p^T = \frac{12\sigma^2}{\rho A} I \tag{12}$$

where I is the 2x2 identity matrix.

The bias contribution is more complex and depends, as before, on the second-order, and higher, derivatives of the local surface. We model the bias term to second-order by computing the covariance matrix for the local deviations from the planar approximation. Accordingly, we write bias-component of the covariance matrix as

$$\Sigma_\mathbf{B} = \begin{pmatrix} \epsilon_1 \epsilon_1 & \epsilon_1 \epsilon_2 & \dots & \epsilon_1 \epsilon_n \\ \epsilon_2 \epsilon_1 & \ddots & & \\ \vdots & & & \end{pmatrix} \tag{13}$$

where $\epsilon_i = \frac{\partial^2 f}{\partial x^2}(x_i - x_o)^2 + \frac{\partial f}{\partial x}\frac{\partial f}{\partial y}(x_i - x_o)(y_i - y_o) + \frac{\partial^2 f}{\partial y^2}(y_i - y_o)^2 + \dots$ is the non-planar deviation of the point indexed i.

Details of the bias model are outside the scope of this paper. Suffice to say that, we can compute the expectation values for the elements of the non-planar bias covariance matrix in much the same way as for the case of estimating the patch height, neglecting higher order terms of the expansion. Under this condition, the bias can be represented as a second-order polynomial in the patch area A. If $\mathbf{K_0}$, $\mathbf{K_1}$ and $\mathbf{K_2}$ represent co-efficient matrices whose elements depend on the second order and higher derivatives of the surface function, then

$$L_p \Sigma_B L_p^T = \mathbf{K_0} + \mathbf{K_1} A + \mathbf{K_2} A^2 + \dots \tag{14}$$

Collecting together terms, we find that the total parameter covariance matrix can be expressed as

$$\Sigma_p(A) = \frac{12\sigma^2}{\rho A} \mathbf{I} + \mathbf{K_0} + \mathbf{K_1} A + \mathbf{K_2} A^2 + \dots \tag{15}$$

Again, the noise propagation term is inversely proportional to the area of the estimating patch. The bias terms, on the other hand, are polynomial in area. As a result the parameter covariance matrix can be minimised with respect to the patch area.

The problem of determining the optimal area of estimation for surface normals is more complicated than in the case of the average height. The main difficulty stems from the fact that we are dealing with a covariance matrix rather than a single scalar quantity. However, since the noise component of Σ_p is diagonal, we confine our attention to minimising the trace of the covariance matrix.

To first order in area, the trace is given by

$$Tr[\Sigma_{\mathbf{p}}] = \sigma_a^2 + \sigma_b^2 = 2\left[(\frac{12\sigma^2}{\rho A} + k_0 + k_1 A)\right] \tag{16}$$

where σ_a^2 and σ_b^2 are the measured variances for the plane parameters a and b. Again, we can fit the predicted area dependance to the observed sum of variances $\sigma_a^2 + \sigma_b^2$ to estimate the semi-empirical parameters σ, k_0 and k_1. The minimum error surface patch area is given by

$$A_{min} = \left[\frac{\rho k_1}{12\sigma^2}\right]^{\frac{1}{2}} \tag{17}$$

2.3 Estimation of the surface curvature

The estimation of surface curvature proceeds in much the same way as for the surface normals. We begin by transforming the coordinate system in such a way as to remove both zero order and first order terms of the Taylor expansion. From a geometric perspective this is equivalent to translating the origin and rotating into the local tangent plane. If the local co-ordinate system is located at the point $\boldsymbol{o}$, then the z-axis of co-ordinates is directed along the surface normal. The x and y axes are orthogonal to one-another and are oriented arbitrarily in the local tangent plane of the surface. In the local coordinate system, the Taylor expansion is now given by

$$f(x'', y'') = \left\{\frac{\partial^2 f}{\partial x''^2}\right\}_o x''^2 + \left\{\frac{\partial^2 f}{\partial x'' \partial y''}\right\}_o x'' y'' + \left\{\frac{\partial^2 f}{\partial y''^2}\right\}_o y''^2 + O(x''^3) \tag{18}$$

It is now clear that the natural approximate representation of this surface in the local coordinate system is a quadric patch

$$f(x'', y'') = \alpha x''^2 + \beta x'' y'' + \gamma y''^2 \tag{19}$$

In other words, the vector of parameters $\mathbf{Q} = (\alpha, \beta, \gamma)^T$ represents the estimate of the second order derivatives of the surface around the origin $\boldsymbol{o}$ of the local coordinate system. We obtain estimates of the parameters $\hat{\mathbf{Q}} = (\hat{\alpha}, \hat{\beta}, \hat{\gamma})^T$ using least-squares fitting over the raw data-points that associate with a support neighbourhood of area A on the surface. The solution vector is given by $\hat{\mathbf{Q}} = \mathbf{L}_q \mathbf{Z}_q$ where the design matrix of transformed sample-points is given by

$$\mathbf{X}_q = \begin{pmatrix} x''^2_1 & x''_1 y''_1 & y''^2_1 \\ x''^2_2 & x''_2 y''_2 & y''^2_2 \\ & \vdots & \end{pmatrix}$$

and the transformed height data is now represented by the column-vector $\mathbf{Z}_q = (z''_1, z''_2, ...)^T$. Again the pseudo-inverse of the design matrix $\mathbf{L}_q$ is given by $\mathbf{L}_q = (\mathbf{X}_q^T \mathbf{X}_q)^{-1} \mathbf{X}_q^T$.

The parameter covariance matrix again has a variance-bias structure. We make this explicit by writing

$$\Sigma_Q = L_q \Sigma_N L_q^T + L_q \Sigma_B L_q^T \tag{20}$$

The covariance component originating from additive noise is related to the fourth-order moments of the x and y co-ordinates in the support neighbourhood. Specifically, we find

$$L_q \Sigma_N L_q^T = \sigma^2 \begin{pmatrix} \sum_{i \in S} x_i''^4 & \sum_{i \in S} x_i''^3 y_i'' & \sum_{i \in S} x_i''^2 y_i''^2 \\ \sum_{i \in S} x_i''^3 y_i'' & \sum_{i \in S} x_i''^2 y_i''^2 & \sum_{i \in S} x_i'' y_i''^3 \\ \sum_{i \in S} x_i''^2 y_i''^2 & \sum_{i \in S} x_i'' y_i''^3 & \sum_{i \in S} y_i''^4 \end{pmatrix}^{-1} \tag{21}$$

The expectation values of the matrix elements can be estimated as before, and are given by

$$< \sum_{i \in S} x_i''^4 > = \rho \int_A x''^4 dA = \frac{\rho A^3}{8\pi^2} \tag{22}$$

and

$$< \sum_{i \in S} x_i''^2 y_i''^2 > = \rho \int_A x''^2 y''^2 dA = \frac{\rho A^3}{24\pi^2} \tag{23}$$

The expectation-values for the remaining fourth-order moments which involve odd-powers of x or y are zero. Hence we may write the noise component of the covariance matrix explicitly in terms of the area of the support neighbourhood in the following manner

$$L_q \Sigma_N L_q^T = \frac{3\pi^2 \sigma^2}{\rho A^3} \begin{pmatrix} 3 & 0 & -1 \\ 0 & 8 & 0 \\ -1 & 0 & 3 \end{pmatrix} = \frac{3\pi^2 \sigma^2}{\rho A^3} K_N \tag{24}$$

Details of the analysis of the bias in the deviations from the local quadratic is more complicated and beyond the scope of this paper. Suffice to say that the bias component can be expanded in terms of a polynomial in A in the following manner

$$L_q \Sigma_B L_q^T = K_0 + A K_1 + A^2 K_2 + \ldots \tag{25}$$

where K_0 and K_1 are matrices whose elements depend on the third order derivatives of the surface.

We can now write the covariance matrix of the quadric patch parameters in terms of the area of estimation (to first order terms) thus:

$$\Sigma_Q = \frac{3\pi^2 \sigma^2}{\rho A^3} K_N + K_0 + A K_1 \tag{26}$$

Since the noise covariance matrix, i.e. $L_q \Sigma_N L_q^T$ is no longer diagonal, we can no-longer strictly recover the optimal patch area by minimising the trace of Σ_Q. However, from equation (24) it is clear that the off-diagonal elements are insignificant compared to the trace. Therefore, in the case of the quadric patch parameters we approximate the optimal surface area by fitting a semi-empirical model to the measured trace of the quadric patch covariance matrix Σ_Q.

$$Tr[\Sigma_Q] = \sigma_\alpha^2 + \sigma_\beta^2 + \sigma_\gamma^2 = \left[\frac{42\pi^2\sigma^2}{\rho A^3} + k_0 + Ak_1 \right] \tag{27}$$

where σ_α^2, σ_β^2 and σ_γ^2 are the measured variances for each of the quadric patch parameters in turn. As before, we calculate the values of the semi-empirical parameters σ^2, k_0 and k_1 by fitting the predicted area dependance to the measured variances. In this case the optimal surface area which minimises $Tr[\Sigma_q]$ is given by

$$A_{min} = \left[\frac{\rho k_1}{14\pi^2\sigma^2} \right]^{\frac{1}{4}} \tag{28}$$

3 Controlling the Mesh

In the previous section, we provided an analysis of variance for the sequential extraction of a local surface origin, the local tangent plane, and, finally, the local patch curvature parameters. In each case we demonstrated that the fit covariance parameters could be minimised with respect to the area of the sample neighbourhood. In other words, there is an optimal choice of estimation area. This area can be viewed as providing the best tradeoff between model bias and underlying data variance. Our overall aim in this paper is to exploit this property to control the area of surface patches in an adaptive surface mesh. Since the area of the patches determines the number of nodes needed to represent the surface, the use of the optimal local patch area effectively corresponds to controlling the model-order of the surface representation. The interpretation of the mesh depends on the quantity which is being estimated over the surface. For example, in the case of surface normals, the centre of each face represents a point at which the surface normal is sampled. The surface is represented by the piecewise combination of the tangent planes associated with these sample normals. The mesh adapts itself to the data using a series of split and merge operations which are aimed at delivering a mesh which optimally represents the surface.

3.1 Optimal area estimation

Here we aim to use the minimum parameter-covariance area to control the split and merge operations. We directly estimate the optimal local patch-size and adjust the mesh topology accordingly. In an ideal world, the optimal area could be determined by varying the area of estimation and noting the value that minimises the parameter covariances. However there is an obstacle to the direct implementation of this process. In practice, the random nature of the noise component of the data-points results in multiple local minima.

The bias-variance relationships developed in the previous section allow us to overcome this difficulty. In particular, they suggest the overall model-dependance between the variance in model parameters and the area of estimation. By fitting this semi-empirical model to the computed parameter variances we can smoothly estimate the position of the global minimum corresponding to the optimal area. The strategy that we adopt in determining the optimal local patch area is as follows. For each point on the surface we gradually increase the local patch area and compute the associated parameter variances. This gives a set of data points to which we can fit an appropriate empirical form of the bias-variance curve. The fitted parameters can be used to extract the value of the minimum local patch-area in a stable manner.

3.2 Mesh Adaptation

The optimal areas of estimation vary over the surface, and suggest that the level of representation, i.e. the model-order, required by the surface should also vary in line with the variance-bias criteria outlined in Section 2. To achieve this goal, we will adopt an adaptive mesh representation of the surface. In this representation, nodes of the mesh represent salient points on the surface; the distance between these points is such that there is the best trade-off between noise and bias in the positions of the points. The mesh points then represent the minimal accurate representation of the surface.

Our mesh is based on the Delaunay triangulation of a set of control points or nodes [24, 18, 19, 8, 9, 6]. In contrast to the bulk of the work reported in the literature which focus on the optimal positioning of the nodes [8, 24], in this paper it is the triangular faces of the mesh to which we turn our attention. The basic update process underpinning our surface involves adjusting the mesh-topology by splitting and merging surface-triangles. This process is realised by either inserting or deleting nodes from the mesh. The net effect of the two operations is to modify the node, edge and face sets of the mesh. The node insertion and deletion operations take place with the objective of delivering a set of faces whose areas are consistent with the optimal values dictated by the bias-variance criteria outlined in section 2. In this way the density of nodes is such as to strike a compromise between over-fitting the data and over-smoothing genuine surface detail. In other words, we seek the minimum model-order (i.e. the total number of nodes) such that each of the triangular faces is as close as possible to its optimal area.

Triangle merging is realised by deleting a node from the mesh as illustrated in the left-hand panel of Figure 1. The basic aim is to merge triangles if the aggregate area is more consistent with the optimal area than the original area. Suppose that the set of triangles M_j is to be merged to form a new triangle with area A_j. The average area of the configuration of triangles is

$$A_j^{merge} = \frac{1}{|M_j|} \sum_{i \in M_j} A_i \qquad (29)$$

The triangles are merged if the fractional difference between the average area and the optimal area is greater than 10%. In other words, we instantiate the merge if

$$\frac{A_j^{optimal} - A_j^{merge}}{A_j^{optimal}} > 0.1 \tag{30}$$

This tolerancing can be viewed as providing the adaptation of the mesh with a degree of hysteresis.

The geometry of the split operation is illustrated in the right-hand panel Figure 1. A new node is introduced at the centroid of the original triangle. The new node-set is re-triangulated to update the edge and face sets of the triangulation. The condition for initiating a split operation is that the current fractional difference between the triangle area and it optimal value is greater than 10%. The split condition can therefore be stated as

$$\frac{A_j - A_j^{optimal}}{A_j^{optimal}} > 0.1 \tag{31}$$

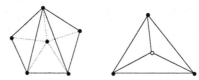

Fig. 1. Merging and splitting triangles

4 Experiments

In this Section we provide some experimental evaluation of our new bias-variance controlled surface. There are several aspects to this study. We commence by considering synthetic data. The aim here is to illustrate that the two-component variance model described in Section 3 does provide a good description for the distribution of the parameter variances as a function of patch-area. The second aspect of our experimentation focuses on real world data-sets. Here we consider range-data from the Michigan State University data-base.

4.1 Synthetic Data

The main aim under this heading is to illustrate that the variance-bias description presented in Section 3 provides an accurate model of the distribution of the fitted parameter variances under controlled conditions. Moreover, we also aim to show that the simple parametric models developed in Section 4.1 are capable of fitting the observed distribution of variance as a function of the area used in the estimation process.

Figure 2a shows a series of plots of the parameter variance as a function of the area of estimation. Here we investigate the effect of quadric patch fitting on two different synthetic surfaces. The points marked with a cross show the computed variances when the surface is itself quadric. Here the parameter variances follow a distribution which monotonically decays with area. In other words, because the model is well matched to the data, the bias component of the parameter variance is zero and there is no local minimum area. The diamonds, on the other hand, show the variance for a surface of the form $f(z) = \cos(x)\cos(y)$. This surface is not well matched to the quadric patch approximation, and we may anticipate the model-bias term to emerge. This is evident from the fact that the variance shows a local minimum when the estimating area is approximately 500 points. In order to investigate the effectiveness of our analysis of variance in describing the observed distribution, the boxes show the result of plotting the prediction of the model outlined in Section 2.3. Although the agreement between the two curves is by no means perfect, the main features are captured by the model. Most importantly for the successful implementation of our adaptive mesh, there is good agreement in the location of the minimum variance area.

To illustrate the behavior of the parameter variance on realistic data, Figure 2b shows an example distribution for a range-image. Here there is genuine data-point noise and there is considerably more structure than in the case of the synthetic surface. However, the distribution maintains the same gross structure. There is a clear decaying component due to the surface noise together with an increasing component due to the bias term. The interplay between these two components results in a well defined global minimum. In other words, fitting an appropriately parameterised distribution should meet with success when attempting to estimate the minimum variance area.

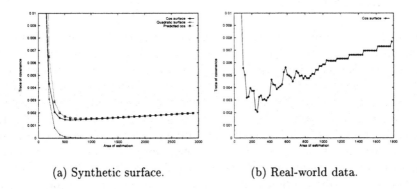

(a) Synthetic surface.　　　　　(b) Real-world data.

Fig. 2. Trace of the curvature covariance matrix for simulated surface.

4.2 Real World Data

In this Section we provide experiments on real world data-sets from the Michigan State University range-image archive. We commence by showing a sequence of results for a range image of a Renault part. Figure 3a shows the surface normals estimated using the local fitting process outlined in Section 3.1. The associated patches are shown in Figure 3b. In Figure 3c we shown the rendered surface patches. The main points to note from this sequence of images are as follows. Firstly, the extracted surface normals provide a faithful representation of the high curvature surfaces details. This is particularly evident around the sharp machined edges of the part. The second point to note is the distribution of surface triangles. In the flat portions of the image these are sparse. By contrast, in the highly curved regions of the surface, the density increases to account for the local curvature of the surface.

Figures 4a-4c show an analogous sequence of images for a range-image of a bust of the composer Mozart. This range-image contains considerably more fine detail than the Renault-part. The main point to note is the effectiveness of the mesh at representing areas of different curvature with mesh points of varying density.

The planar patch information is refined in Figure 4d where we show the mean curvature extracted from the subsequent quadric patch fit. The mean curvature is given $K = \alpha + \gamma$ where α and γ are the coefficients of the quadric patch as defined in equation 19. The estimated curvatures are signed. The maximum negative and positive values appear as extreme light and dark regions in the figure. The important feature to note from the figure is the fine detail in both the cravat and collar of the bust. There is also well defined detail around the concave features of the face (i.e. the eye sockets, the lips and the ridge of the nose).

5 Conclusions

The main contribution in this paper have been twofold. In the first instance, we have provided an analysis of variance for the various stages in establishing the derivatives of surface fits to range data. This analysis reveals that there is a two component structure to the variance of the fitted parameters. The first component of results from the propagation of noise variance and decreases with the increasing area of the patch. The second variance contribution originates from the model bias. This term is polynomial in the patch area. The main conclusion is that there is a local patch area which offers optimal tradeoff between noise-variance propagation and model bias in the minimisation of the fit residuals.

Our second contribution is to exploit this property to control the area of the facets of a triangulated surface mesh. By locally varying the patch area we minimise the parameter variance. This minimisation is realised by splitting and merging the triangular faces of the mesh until they each have a near optimal area.

463

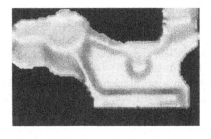

(a) Surface normals.

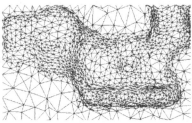

(b) Adaptive mesh.

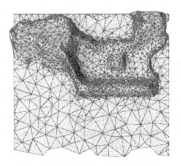

(c) Rendering

Fig. 3. Analysis of the Renault part.

References

1. A.J. Bulpitt and N.D. Efford, "An efficient 3d deformable model with a self-optimising mesh", *Image and Vision Computing*, **14**, pp. 573–580, 1996.
2. P. J. Besl and R. C. Jain, "Segmentation through variable order surface fitting", *IEEE Transactions on Pattern Analysis and Machine Intelligence*, **10**:2 pp167-192 1988
3. X. Chen and F. Schmill. Surface modeling of range data by constrained triangulation", *Computer-Aided Design*, **26**, pp. 632—645 1994.
4. I. Cohen, L.D. Cohen and N. Ayache, "Using deformable surfaces to segment 3D images and infer differential structure", *CVGIP*, **56**, pp. 243–263, 1993.
5. I. Cohen and L.D. Cohen, "A hybrid hyper-quadric model for 2-d and 3-d data fitting", *Computer Vision and Image Understanding*, **63**, pp. 527–541, 1996.
6. L. De Floriani, " A pyramidal data structure for triangle-based surface description", *IEEE Computer Graphics and Applications*, **9**, pp. 67–78, 1987.
7. L. De Floriani, P. Marzano and E. Puppo, " Multiresolution models for topographic surface description.", *Visual Computer*, **12**:7, pp. 317–345, 1996.
8. H. Delingette, "Adaptive and deformable models based on simplex meshes", *IEEE Computer Society Workshop on Motion of Non-rigid and Articulated Objects*, pp. 152–157, 1994.

9. H. Delingette, M. Hebert and K. Ikeuchi, "Shape representation and image segmentation using deformable surfaces", *IEEE Computer Society Conference on Computer Vision and Pattern Recognition*, pp. 467–472, 1991.

10. D. Geman, E. Bienenstock and R. Doursat, "Neural networks and the bias variance dilemma", *Neural Computation,*, **4**, pp.1-58, 1992.

11. J. O. Lachaud and A. Montanvert, "Volumic segmentation using hierarchical representation and triangulates surface", *Computer Vision, ECCV'96, Edited by B. Buxton and R. Cipolla, Lecture Notes in Computer Science, Volume 1064*, pp. 137–146, 1996.

12. R. Lengagne, P. Fua and O. Monga, "Using crest-lines to guide surface reconstruction from stereo", *Proceedings of th 13th International Conference on Pattern Recognition*, Volume A, pp. 9–13, 1996.

13. D. McInerney and D. Terzopoulos, "A finite element model for 3D shape reconstruction and non-rigid motion tracking", *Fourth International Conference on Computer Vision*, pp. 518–532, 1993.

14. D. McInerney and D. Terzopoulos, "A dynamic finite-element surface model for segmentation and tracking in multidimensional medical images with application to cardiac 4D image-analysis", *Computerised Medical Imaging and Graphics*, **19**, pp. 69–83, 1995.

15. M. Moshfeghi, S. Ranganath and K. Nawyn, "Three dimensional elastic matching of volumes", *IEEE Transactions on Image Processing*, **3**, pp. 128–138,

16. W. Neuenschwander, P. Fua, G. Szekely and O. Kubler, "Deformable Velcro Surfaces", *Fifth International Conference on Computer Vision*, pp. 828–833, 1995.

17. P.T. Sander and S.W. Zucker, "Inferring surface structure and differential structure from 3D images", IEEE PAMI, **12**, pp 833-854, 1990.

18. F. J. M. Schmitt, B. A. Barsky and Wen-Hui Du, "An adaptive subdivision method for surface fitting from sampled data", *SIGGRAPH '86*, **20**, pp. 176–188, 1986

19. W.J.Schroeder, J.A. Zarge and W.E. Lorenson, "Decimation of triangle meshes", *Computer Graphics*, **26** pp. 163–169, 1992.

20. A.J. Stoddart, A. Hilton and J. Illingworth, "SLIME: A new deformable surface", *Proceedings British Machine Vision Conference*, pp. 285–294, 1994.

21. A. J. Stoddart, J. Illingworth and T. Windeatt, "Optimal Parameter Selection for Derivative Estimation from Range Images" *Image and Vision Computing*, **13**, pp629–635, 1995..

22. M. Turner and E.R. Hancock, "Bayesian extraction of differential surface structure", *in Computer Analysis of Images and Patterns, Lecture Notes in Computer Science, Volume 970, Edited by V. Havlac and R. Sara*, pp. 784–789, 1995.

23. M. Turner and E.R. Hancock, "A Bayesian approach to 3D surface fitting and refinement", *Proceedings of the British Machine Vision Conference*, pp. 67–76, 1995.

24. G. Turk, "Re-tiling polygonal surfaces", *Computer Graphics*, **26**, pp. 55–64, 1992.

25. M. Vasilescu and D. Terzopoulos, "Adaptive meshes and shells", *IEEE Computer Society Conference on Computer Vision and Pattern Recognition* , pp. 829–832, 1992.

26. R. C. Wilson and E. R. Hancock, "Refining Surface Curvature with Relaxation Labeling", *Proceedings of ICIAP97*, Ed, A. Del Bimbo, Lecture Notes in Computer Science 1310, Springer pp. 150-157 1997.

27. R. C. Wilson and E. R. Hancock, "A Minimum-Variance Adaptive Surface Mesh", *CVPR'97*, pp. 634-639 1997.

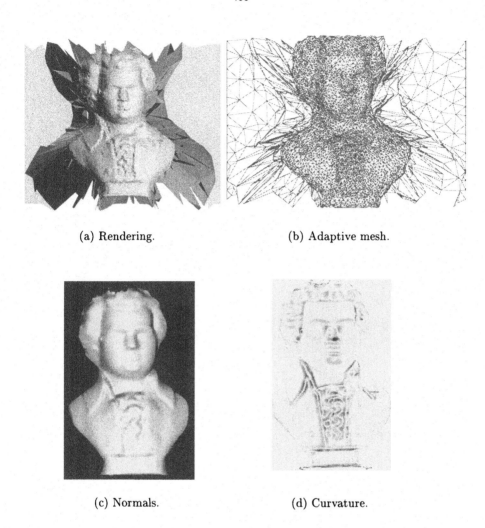

(a) Rendering.

(b) Adaptive mesh.

(c) Normals.

(d) Curvature.

Fig. 4. Analysis of the range-data for the Mozart bust.

Appearance and Recognition

Recognizing 3-D Objects with Linear Support Vector Machines

Massimiliano Pontil[1], Stefano Rogai[2], and Alessandro Verri[3]

[1] Center for Biological and Computational Learning, MIT, Cambridge MA (USA)
[2] INFM - DISI, Università di Genova, Genova (I)

Abstract. In this paper we propose a method for 3-D object recognition based on linear Support Vector Machines (SVMs). Intuitively, given a set of points which belong to either of two classes, a linear SVM finds the hyperplane leaving the largest possible fraction of points of the same class on the same side, while maximizing the distance of either class from the hyperplane. The hyperplane is determined by a subset of the points of the two classes, named *support vectors*, and has a number of interesting theoretical properties. The proposed method does not require feature extraction and performs recognition on images regarded as points of a space of high dimension. We illustrate the potential of the recognition system on a database of 7200 images of 100 different objects. The remarkable recognition rates achieved in all the performed experiments indicate that SVMs are well-suited for aspect-based recognition, even in the presence of small amount of occlusions.

1 Introduction

Support Vector Machines (SVMs) have recently been proposed as a very effective method for general purpose pattern recognition [12, 3]. Intuitively, given a set of points which belong to either of two classes, a SVM finds the hyperplane leaving the largest possible fraction of points of the same class on the same side, while maximizing the distance of either class from the hyperplane. According to [12], given fixed but unknown probability distributions, this hyperplane – called the Optimal Separating Hyperplane (OSH) – minimizes the risk of misclassifying the *yet-to-be-seen* examples of the test set.

In this paper an aspect-based method for the recognition of 3–D objects which makes use of SVMs is described. In the last few years, aspect-based recognition strategies have received increasing attention from both the psychophysical [10, 4] and computer vision [7, 2, 5] communities. Although not naturally tolerant to occlusions, aspect-based recognition strategies appear to be well-suited for the solution of recognition problems in which geometric models of the viewed objects can be difficult, if not impossible, to obtain. Unlike other aspect-based methods, recognition with SVMs (*a*) does not require feature extraction or data reduction, and (*b*) can be performed directly on images regarded as points of an N-dimensional object space, *without* estimating pose. The high dimensionality of the object space makes OSHs very effective decision surfaces, while the recognition stage is reduced to deciding on which side of an OSH lies a given point in object space.

The proposed method has been tested on the COIL database[3] consisting of 7200 images of 100 objects. Half of the images were used as training examples, the remaining half as test images. We discarded color information and tested the method on the remaining images corrupted by synthetically generated noise, bias, and small amount of occlusions. The remarkable recognition rates achieved in all the performed experiments indicate that SVMs are well-suited for aspect-based recognition. Comparisons with other pattern recognition methods, like perceptrons, show that the proposed method is far more robust in the presence of noise.

The paper is organized as follows. In Section 2 we review the basic facts of the theory of SVMs. Section 3 discusses the implementation of SVMs adopted throughout this paper and describes the main features of the proposed recognition system. The obtained experimental results are illustrated in Section 4. Finally, Section 5 summarizes the conclusions that can be drawn from the presented research.

2 Theoretical overview

We recall here the basic notions of the theory of SVMs [12, 3]. We start with the simple case of linearly separable sets. Then we define the concept of support vectors and deal with the more general nonseparable case. Finally, we list the main properties of SVMs. Since we have only used linear SVMs we do not cover the generalization of the theory to the case of nonlinear separating surfaces.

2.1 Optimal separating hyperplane

In what follows we assume we are given a set S of points $\mathbf{x}_i \in \mathbb{R}^n$ with $i = 1, 2, \ldots, N$. Each point $\mathbf{x}_i$ belongs to either of two classes and thus is given a label $y_i \in \{-1, 1\}$. The goal is to establish the equation of a hyperplane that divides S leaving all the points of the same class on the same side while maximizing the distance between the two classes and the hyperplane. To this purpose we need some preliminary definitions.

Definition 1. The set S is *linearly separable* if there exist $\mathbf{w} \in \mathbb{R}^n$ and $b \in \mathbb{R}$ such that

$$y_i(\mathbf{w} \cdot \mathbf{x}_i + b) \geq 1, \tag{1}$$

for $i = 1, 2, \ldots, N$.

The pair $(\mathbf{w}, b)$ defines a hyperplane of equation $\mathbf{w} \cdot \mathbf{x} + b = 0$ named the *separating hyperplane* (see Figure 1(a)). If we denote by w the norm of $\mathbf{w}$, the

---

[3] The images of the COIL database (Columbia Object Image Library) can be downloaded through anonymous ftp from www.cs.columbia.edu.

signed distance d_i of a point $\mathbf{x}_i$ from the separating hyperplane $(\mathbf{w}, b)$ is given by

$$d_i = \frac{\mathbf{w} \cdot \mathbf{x}_i + b}{w}, \tag{2}$$

with w the norm of $\mathbf{w}$. Combining inequality (1) and equation (2), for all $x_i \in S$ we have

$$y_i d_i \geq \frac{1}{w}. \tag{3}$$

Therefore, $1/w$ is the lower bound on the distance between the points $\mathbf{x}_i$ and the separating hyperplane $(\mathbf{w}, b)$.

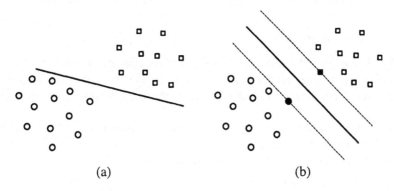

Fig. 1. Separating hyperplane (a) and OSH (b). The dashed lines in (b) identify the margin.

We now need to establish a one-to-one correspondence between separating hyperplanes and their parametric representation.

Definition 2. Given a separating hyperplane $(\mathbf{w}, b)$ for the linearly separable set S, the *canonical representation* of the separating hyperplane is obtained by rescaling the pair $(\mathbf{w}, b)$ into the pair $(\mathbf{w}', b')$ in such a way that the distance of the closest point, say $\mathbf{x}_j$, equals $1/w'$.

Through this definition we have

$$\min_{\mathbf{x}_i \in S} \{y_i (\mathbf{w}' \cdot \mathbf{x}_i + b')\} = 1.$$

Consequently, for a separating hyperplane in the canonical representation, the bound in inequality (3) is tight. In what follows we will assume that a separating hyperplane is always given in the canonical representation and thus write $(\mathbf{w}, b)$ instead of $(\mathbf{w}', b')$. We are now in a position to define the notion of OSH.

Definition 3. Given a linearly separable set S, the *optimal separating hyperplane* is the separating hyperplane for which the distance of the closest point of S is maximum.

Since the distance of the closest point equals $1/w$, the OSH can be regarded as the solution of the problem of minimizing $1/w$ subject to the constraint (1), or

Problem **P1**
Minimize $\frac{1}{2}\mathbf{w} \cdot \mathbf{w}$
subject to $y_i(\mathbf{w} \cdot \mathbf{x}_i + b) \geq 1,\, i = 1, 2, \ldots, N$

Note that the parameter b enters in the constraints but not in the function to be minimized. The quantity $2/w$, the lower bound of the minimum distance between points of different classes, is named the *margin*. Hence, the OSH can also be seen as the separating hyperplane which maximizes the margin (see Figure $1(b)$). We now study the properties of the solution of Problem **P1**.

2.2   Support vectors

Problem **P1** is usually solved by means of the classical method of Lagrange multipliers. In order to understand the concept of SVs it is necessary to go briefly through this method. For more details and a thorough review of the method see [1].

If we denote with $\boldsymbol{\alpha} = (\alpha_1, \alpha_2, \ldots, \alpha_N)$ the N nonnegative Lagrange multipliers associated with the constraints (1), the solution to Problem **P1** is equivalent to determining the *saddle point* of the function

$$L = \frac{1}{2}\mathbf{w} \cdot \mathbf{w} - \sum_{i=1}^{N} \alpha_i \left\{ y_i(\mathbf{w} \cdot \mathbf{x}_i + b) - 1 \right\}. \tag{4}$$

with $L = L(\mathbf{w},\, b,\, \boldsymbol{\alpha})$. At the saddle point, L has a minimum for $\mathbf{w} = \bar{\mathbf{w}}$ and $b = \bar{b}$ and a maximum for $\boldsymbol{\alpha} = \bar{\boldsymbol{\alpha}}$, and thus we can write

$$\frac{\partial L}{\partial b} = \sum_{i=1}^{N} y_i \alpha_i = 0, \tag{5}$$

$$\frac{\partial L}{\partial \mathbf{w}} = \mathbf{w} - \sum_{i=1}^{N} \alpha_i y_i \mathbf{x}_i = 0 \tag{6}$$

with

$$\frac{\partial L}{\partial \mathbf{w}} = (\frac{\partial L}{\partial w_1}, \frac{\partial L}{\partial w_2}, \ldots, \frac{\partial L}{\partial w_N}).$$

Substituting equations (5) and (6) into the right hand side of (4), we see that Problem **P1** reduces to the maximization of the function

$$\mathcal{L}(\boldsymbol{\alpha}) = \sum_{i=1}^{N} \alpha_i - \frac{1}{2} \sum_{i,j=1}^{N} \alpha_i \alpha_j y_i y_j \mathbf{x}_i \cdot \mathbf{x}_j, \tag{7}$$

subject to the constraint (5) with $\boldsymbol{\alpha} \geq 0$[4]. This new problem is called the *dual problem* and can be formulated as

---

[4] In what follows $\boldsymbol{\alpha} \geq 0$ means $\alpha_i \geq 0$ for every component α_i of any vector $\boldsymbol{\alpha}$.

Problem **P2**

Maximize $\quad -\frac{1}{2}\alpha^\mathsf{T} D\alpha + \sum \alpha_i$

subject to $\quad \sum y_i \alpha_i = 0$

$\qquad\qquad \alpha \geq 0,$

where both sums are for $i = 1, 2, \ldots, N$, and D is an $N \times N$ matrix such that

$$D_{ij} = y_i y_j \mathbf{x}_i \cdot \mathbf{x}_j. \tag{8}$$

As for the pair $(\bar{\mathbf{w}}, \bar{b})$, from equation (6) it follows that

$$\bar{\mathbf{w}} = \sum_{i=1}^{N} \bar{\alpha}_i y_i \mathbf{x}_i, \tag{9}$$

while $\bar{b}$ can be determined from $\bar{\alpha}$, solution of the dual problem, and from the Kühn-Tucker conditions

$$\bar{\alpha}_i \left(y_i (\bar{\mathbf{w}} \cdot \mathbf{x}_i + \bar{b}) - 1 \right) = 0, \quad i = 1, 2, \ldots, N. \tag{10}$$

Note that the only $\bar{\alpha}_i$ that can be nonzero in equation (10) are those for which the constraints (1) are satisfied with the equality sign. This has an important consequence. Since most of the $\bar{\alpha}_i$ are usually null, the vector $\bar{\mathbf{w}}$ is a linear combination of a relatively small percentage of the points $\mathbf{x}_i$. These points are termed *support vectors* (SVs) because they are the closest points from the OSH and the only points of S needed to determine the OSH (see Figure 1(b)). Given a support vector $\mathbf{x}_j$, the parameter $\bar{b}$ can be obtained from the corresponding Kühn-Tucker condition as $\bar{b} = y_j - \bar{\mathbf{w}} \cdot \mathbf{x}_j$.

2.3 Linearly nonseparable case

If the set S is not linearly separable or one simply ignores whether or not the set S is linearly separable, the problem of searching for an OSH is meaningless (there may be no separating hyperplane to start with). Fortunately, the previous analysis can be generalized by introducing N nonnegative variables $\boldsymbol{\xi} = (\xi_1, \xi_2, \ldots, \xi_N)$ such that

$$y_i (\mathbf{w} \cdot \mathbf{x}_i + b) \geq 1 - \xi_i, \quad i = 1, 2, \ldots, N. \tag{11}$$

The purpose of the variables ξ_i is to allow for a small number of misclassified points. If the point $\mathbf{x}_i$ satisfies inequality (1), then ξ_i is null and (11) reduces to (1). Instead, if the point $\mathbf{x}_i$ does not satisfy inequality (1), the extraterm $-\xi_i$ is added to the right hand side of (1) to obtain inequality (11). The generalized OSH is then regarded as the solution to

Problem **P3**

Minimize $\quad \frac{1}{2}\mathbf{w} \cdot \mathbf{w} + C\sum \xi_i$

subject to $\quad y_i (\mathbf{w} \cdot \mathbf{x}_i + b) \geq 1 - \xi_i \; i = 1, 2, \ldots, N$

$\qquad\qquad \boldsymbol{\xi} \geq 0.$

The purpose of the extraterm $C \sum \xi_i$, where the sum is for $i = 1, 2, \ldots, N$, is to keep under control the number of misclassified points. The parameter C can be regarded as a regularization parameter. The OSH tends to maximize the minimum distance $1/w$ for small C, and minimize the number of misclassified points for large C. For intermediate values of C the solution of problem **P3** trades errors for a larger margin. The behavior of the OSH as a function of C is studied in detail in [8].

In analogy with what was done for the separable case, Problem **P3** can be transformed into the *dual*

Problem **P4**
Maximize $\quad -\frac{1}{2}\alpha^T D\alpha + \sum \alpha_i$
subject to $\quad \sum y_i \alpha_i = 0$
$\qquad\qquad 0 \leq \alpha_i \leq C, \qquad i = 1, 2, \ldots, N$

Note that the dimension of **P4** is given by the size of the training set, while the dimension of the input space gives the rank of D. From the constraints of Problem **P4** it follows that if C is sufficiently large and the set S linearly separable, Problem **P4** reduces to **P2**. The vector $\mathbf{w}$ is still given by equation 9, while $\bar{b}$ can again be determined from $\bar{\alpha}$, solution of the dual problem **P4**, and from the new Kuhn-Tucker conditions

$$\bar{\alpha}_i \left(y_i(\bar{\mathbf{w}} \cdot \mathbf{x}_i + \bar{b}) - 1 + \bar{\xi}_i \right) = 0 \tag{12}$$

$$(C - \bar{\alpha}_i)\bar{\xi}_i = 0 \tag{13}$$

where the $\bar{\xi}_i$ are the values of the ξ_i at the saddle point. Similarly to the separable case, the SVs are the points $\mathbf{x}_i$ for which $\bar{\alpha}_i > 0$. The main difference is that here we have to distinguish between the SVs for which $\bar{\alpha}_i < C$ and those for which $\bar{\alpha}_i = C$. In the first case, from condition (13) it follows that $\bar{\xi}_i = 0$, and hence, from condition (12), that the SVs lie at a distance $1/\bar{w}$ from the OSH. These SVs are termed *margin vectors*. The SVs for which $\bar{\alpha}_i = C$, are instead: misclassified points if $\xi_i > 1$, points correctly classified but closer than $1/\bar{w}$ from the OSH if $0 < \xi \leq 1$, or margin vectors if $\xi_i = 0$. Neglecting this last rare (and degenerate) occurrence, we refer to all the SVs for which $\alpha_i = C$ as *errors*. All the points that are not SVs are correctly classified and lie outside the margin strip.

We conclude this section by listing the main properties of SVMs.

2.4 Mathematical properties

The first property distinguishes SVMs from previous nonparametric techniques, like nearest-neighbors or neural networks. Typical pattern recognition methods are based on the minimization of the *empirical risk*, that is on the attempt to minimize the misclassification errors on the training set. Instead, SVMs minimize the *structural risk*, that is the probability of misclassifying a previously unseen data point drawn randomly from a fixed but unknown probability distribution. In particular, it follows that, if the VC-dimension [11] of the family of decision surfaces is known, then the theory of SVMs provides an upper bound for the probability of misclassification of the test set for any possible probability distributions of the data points [12].

Secondly, SVMs condense all the information contained in the training set relevant to classification in the support vectors. This (a) reduces the size of the training set identifying the most important points, and (b) makes it possible to perform classification efficiently.

Thirdly, SVMs can be used to perform classification in high dimensional spaces, even in the presence of a relatively small number of data points. This is because, unlike other techniques, SVMs look for the optimal separating hyperplane. From the quantitative viewpoint, the margin can be used as a measure of the difficulty of the problem (the larger the margin the lower the probability of misclassifying a yet-to-be-seen point).

3 The recognition system

We now describe the recognition system we devised to assess the potential of the theory. We first review the implementation developed for determining the SVs and the associated OSH.

3.1 Implementation

In Section 2 we have seen that the problem of determining the OSH reduces to Problem **P4**, a typical problem of quadratic programming. The vast literature of nonlinear programming covers a multitude of problems of quadratic programming and provides a plethora of methods for their solution. Our implementation makes use of the equivalence between quadratic programming problems and *Linear Complementary* Problems (LCPs) and is based on the *Complementary Pivoting Algorithm* (CPA), a classical algorithm able to solve LCPs [1].

Since CPA spatial complexity goes with the square of the number of examples, the algorithm cannot deal efficiently with much more than a few hundreds of examples. This has not been a fundamental issue for the research described in this paper, but for problems of larger size one definitely has to resort to more sophisticated techniques [6].

3.2 Recognition stages

We have developed a recognition system based on three stages:

1. Preprocessing
2. Training set formation
3. System testing

We now describe these three stages in some detail.

Preprocessing The COIL database consists of 72 images of 100 objects (for a total of 7200 images), objects positioned in the center of a turntable and observed from a fixed viewpoint. For each object, the turntable is rotated by 5° per image. Figures 2 shows a selection of the objects in the database. Figures 3 shows one every three views of one particular object. As explained in detail by Murase and Nayar[5], the object region is re-sampled so that the larger of the two dimensions fits the image size. Consequently, the apparent size of an object may change considerably from image to image, especially for the objects which are not symmetric with respect to the turntable axis.

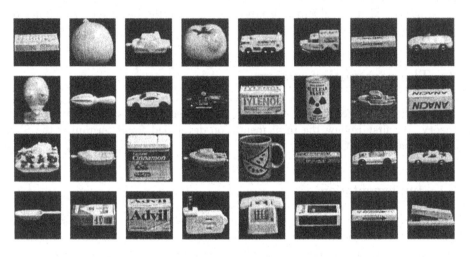

Fig. 2. Images of 32 objects of the COIL database.

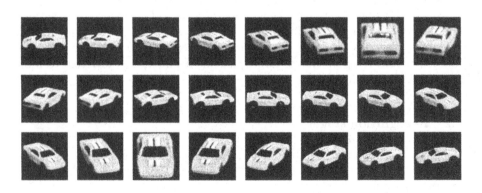

Fig. 3. Twentyfour of the 72 images of a COIL object.

The original images were color images (24 bits for each of the RGB channels) of 128 × 128 pixels. In the preprocessing stage each image was transformed into an 8-bit grey-level image rescaling the obtained range between 0 and 255. Finally, the image spatial resolution was reduced to 32 × 32 by averaging the grey values over 4 × 4 pixel patches. The aim of these transformations was to reduce the dimensionality of the representation given the relatively small number of images available. The effectiveness of this considerable data reduction is explained elsewhere [9].

Forming the training set The training set consists of 36 images (one every 10°) for each object. After the preprocessing stage, each image can be regarded as a vector $\mathbf{x}$ of $32 \times 32 = 1024$ components.

Depending on the classification task, a certain subset of the 100 objects (from 2 to 32) has been considered. Then, the OSHs associated to each pair of objects i and j in the subset were computed, the SVs identified, and the obtained parameters, $\mathbf{w}(i,j)$ and $b(i,j)$, stored in a file. We have never come across errors in the classification of the training sets. The reason is essentially given by the high dimensionality of the object space compared to the small number of examples. The images corresponding to some of the SVs for a specific pair of objects are shown in Figure 4.

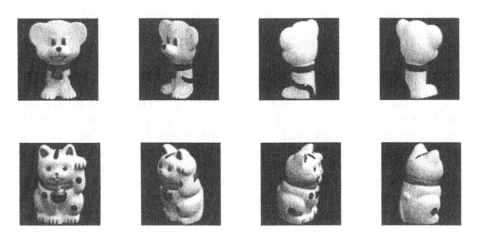

Fig. 4. Eight of the SVs for a specific object pair.

Typically, we have found a number of SVs ranging from 1/3 to 2/3 of the 72 training images for each object pair. This large fraction of SVs can be explained by the high dimensionality of the object space combined with the small number of examples.

System testing Given a certain subset σ of the 100 objects and the associated training set of 36 images for each object in σ, the test set consists of the remaining

36 images per object in σ. Recognition was performed following the rules of a tennis tournament. Each object is regarded as a *player*, and in each *match* the system temporarily classifies an image of the test set according to the OSH relative to the pair of players involved in the match. If in a certain match the players are objects i and j, the system classifies the viewed object of image **x** as object i or j depending on the sign of

$$\mathbf{w}(i,j) \cdot \mathbf{x} + b(i,j).$$

If, for simplicity, we assume there are 2^K players, the first round 2^{K-1} matches are played and the 2^{K-1} losing players are out. The 2^{K-1} match winners advance to the second round. The $(K-1)$-th round is the final between the only 2 players that won all the previous matches. This procedure requires $2^K - 1$ classifications. Note that the system recognizes object identity without estimating pose.

We are now ready to present the experimental results.

4 Experimental results

We describe here the experimental results of the recognition system on the COIL database. We first considered the images exactly as downloaded from the Net and afterwords verified what amount of noise the system can tolerate.

4.1 COIL images

We tested the proposed recognition system on sets of 32 of the 100 COIL objects. The training sets consisted of 36 images for each of 32 objects and the test sets the remaining 36 images for each object. For all 10 random choices of 32 of the 100 objects we tried, the system reached perfect score. Therefore, we decided to select by hand the 32 objects *most difficult* to recognize (*i.e.* the set of objects separated by the smallest margins). By doing so the system finally mistook a packet of chewing gum for another very similar packet of chewing gum in one case (see Figure 5).

(a)   (b)

Fig. 5. The only misclassified image (*a*) and corresponding erroneously recognized object (*b*).

To gain a better understanding of how an SVM perform recognition, it may be useful to look at the relative weights of the components of the vector **w**. A grey valued encoded representation of the absolute value of the components of the vector **w** relative to the OSH of the two objects of Figure 4 is displayed in Figure 6(a) (the darker a point, the higher the corresponding **w** component). Note that the background is essentially irrelevant, while the larger components (in absolute value) can be found in the central portion of the *image*. Interestingly, the image of Figure 6(a) resembles the visual appearance of both the "dog" and "cat" of Figure 4. The graph of Figure 6(b) shows the convergence of $\sum w_i x_i$ to the dot product $\mathbf{w} \cdot \mathbf{x}$ for one of the "cat" image, with the components w_i sorted in decreasing order. From the graph it clearly follows that less than half of the 1024 components are all that is needed to reach almost perfect convergence, while a reasonably good approximation is already obtained using only the largest 100 components. The graph of Figure 6(b) is typical with a few exceptions corresponding to very similar object pairs.

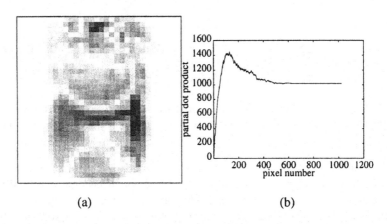

(a)   (b)

Fig. 6. Relative weights of the components of the normal vector **w**. See text for details.

In conclusion the proposed method performs recognition with excellent percentages of success even in the presence of very similar objects. It is worthwhile noticing that while the recognition time is practically negligible (requiring the evaluation of 31 dot products), the training stage (in which all the $32 \times 31/2 = 496$ OSHs must be determined) takes about 15 minutes on a SPARC10 workstation.

4.2 Robustness

In order to verify the effectiveness and robustness of the proposed recognition system, we performed experiments under increasingly difficult conditions: pixelwise random noise, bias in the registration, and small amounts of occlusion.

Noise corrupted images We added zero mean random noise to the grey value of each pixel and rescaled the obtained grey levels between 0 and 255. Restricting the analysis to the 32 objects most difficult to recognize, the system performed equally well for maximum noise up to ±100 grey levels and degrades gracefully for higher percentages of noise (see Table 1). Some of the noise corrupted images from which the system was able to identify the viewed object are displayed in Figure 7.

Table 1. Average overall error rates for noise corrupted images. The noise is in grey levels.

Noise	±25	±50	±75	±100	±150	±200	±250
32 Objects	0.3%	0.8%	1.1%	1.6%	2.7%	6.2%	11.0%
30 Objects	0.0%	0.1%	0.2%	0.2%	0.7%	1.8%	5.8%

Fig. 7. Eight images synthetically corrupted by white noise, spatially misregistrated and their combination. All these images were correctly classified by the system.

By inspection of the obtained results, we noted that most of the errors were due the three chewing gum packets of Figure 2 which become practically indistinguishable as the noise increases. The same experiments leaving out two of the three packets produced much better performances (see rightmost column of Table 1). It must be said that the very good statistics of Table 1 are partly due to the "filtering effects" of the reduction of the image size from 128×128 to 32×32 pixels obtained by spatial averaging.

From the obtained experimental results, it can be easily inferred that the method achieves very good recognition rates even in the presence of large amount of noise.

Shifted images We checked the dependence of the system on the precision with which the available images are spatially registered. We thus shifted each image of the test set by n pixels in the horizontal direction and repeated the same recognition experiments of this section on the set of the 32 most difficult objects. As can be appreciated from Table 2, the system performs equally well for small shifts ($n = 3, 5$) and degrades slowly for larger displacements ($n = 7, 10$).

We have obtained very similar results (reported in [9]) when combining noise and shifts. It is concluded that the spatial registration of images is important but

Table 2. Average overall error rates for shifted images (the shifts are in pixel units).

Shift	3	5	7	10
32 Objects	0.6%	2.0%	6.7%	18.6%
30 Objects	0.1%	0.8%	4.8%	12.5%

that spatial redundancy makes it possible to achieve very good performances even in the presence of a combination of additive noise and shift. Here again it must be noted that the quality of the results is partly due to the "filtering effects" of the preprocessing step.

Occlusions In order to verify the robustness of the system against occlusions we performed two more series of experiments. In the first series we randomly selected a subwindow in the rescaled test images (32×32) and assigned a random value between 0 and 255 to the pixels inside the subwindow. The obtained error rates are summarized in Table 3. In the second experiment we randomly selected n columns and m rows in the rescaled images and assigned a random value to the corresponding pixels. The obtained error rates are summarized in Table 4. Some of the images from which the system was able to identify partially occluded objects are displayed in Figure 8. Comparing the results in Tables 3 and 4 it is evident that the occlusion concentrated in a subwindow of the image poses more problems. In both cases, however, we conclude that the system tolerates small amounts of occlusion.

Fig. 8. Eight images with small occlusions correctly classified by the system.

Table 3. Average overall error rates for images occluded by squared window of k pixel per edge.

k	4	6	8	10
32 Objects	0.7%	2.0%	5.7%	12.7%
30 Objects	0.4%	1.2%	4.3%	10.8%

Table 4. Average overall error rates for images occluded by n columns and m rows.

n	m	32 objects	30 objects
1	1	2.1%	1.3%
1	2	3.2%	1.9%
2	1	4.5%	2.8%
2	2	6.1%	3.2%

4.3 Comparison with perceptrons

In order to gain a better understanding of the relevance of the obtained results we run a few experiments using perceptrons instead of SVMs. We considered two objects (the first two toy cars in Figure 2) and run the same experiments described in this section. The results are summarized in table 5. The perceptron column gives the average of the results obtained with ten different perceptrons (corresponding to 10 different random choices of the initial weights). The poor performance of perceptrons can be easily explained in terms of the margin associated with the separating hyperplane of each perceptron as opposed to the SVM margin. In this example, the perceptron margin is between 2 and 10 times smaller than the SVM margin. This means that both SVMs and perceptrons separate exactly the training set, but that the perceptron margin makes it difficult to classify correctly novel images in the presence of noise. Intuitively, this fact can be explained by thinking of noise perturbation as a motion in object space: if the margin is too small, even a slight perturbation can bring a point across the separating hyperplane (see Figure 1).

Table 5. Comparison between SVMs and perceptrons in the presence of noise.

Noise	±50	±100	±150	±200	±250	±300
SVM	0.0%	0.0%	0.0%	0.0%	0.1%	4.1%
Mean Perc.	2.6%	7.1%	15.5%	23.5%	30.2%	34.7%

5 Discussion

In this final section we compare our results with the work of [5] and summarize the obtained results.

The images of the COIL database were originally used by Murase and Nayar as a benchmark for testing their appearance-based recognition system. Our results seem to compare favorably with respect to the results reported in [5] especially in terms of computational cost. This is not surprising because thanks to the design of SVMs, we make use of all the available information with no need of data reduction. Note that SVMs allow for the construction of training sets of much smaller size than the training sets of [5]. Unlike Murase and Nayar's method, however, our method does not identify object's pose.

It would be interesting to compare our method with the classification strategy suggested in [5] on the same data points. After the construction of parametric eigenspaces, Murase and Nayar classify an object by computing the minimum of the distance between the point representative of the object and the manifold of each object in the database. A possibility could be the use of SVMs for this last stage.

In conclusion, in this paper we have assessed the potential of linear SVMs in the problem of recognizing 3-D objects from a single view. As shown by the comparison with other techniques, it appears that SVMs can be effectively *trained* even if the number of examples is much lower than the dimensionality of the object space. This agrees with the theoretical expectation that can be derived by means of VC-dimension considerations [12]. The remarkably good results which we have reported indicate that SVMs are likely to be very useful for direct 3-D object recognition, even in the presence of small amounts of occlusion.

References

1. Bazaraa, M., Shetty, C.M.: Nonlinear programming. (John Wiley, New York, 1979).
2. Brunelli, R., Poggio, T.: Face Recognition: Features versus Templates. IEEE Trans. on PAMI, **15** (1993) 1042-1052
3. Cortes C., Vapnik, V.N.: Support Vector Network. Machine learning **20** (1995) 1-25
4. Edelman, S., Bulthoff, H., Weinshall, D.: Stimulus Familiarity Determines Recognition Strategy for Novel 3-D Objects. AI Memo No. 1138, MIT, Cambridge (1989)
5. Murase, N., Nayar, S.K.: Visual Learning and Recognition of 3-D Object from Appearance. Int. J. Comput. Vision **14** (1995) 5-24
6. Osuna, E., Freund, R., Girosi, F.: Training Support Vector Machines: an Applications to Face Detection. Proc. Int. Conf. Computer Vision and Pattern Recognition, Puerto Rico, (1997)
7. Poggio, T., Edelman, S.: A Network that Learns to Recognize Three-Dimensional Objects. Nature **343** (1990) 263-266
8. Pontil, M., Verri, A.: Properties of Support Vector Machines. Neural Computation **10** (1998) 977-966
9. Pontil, M., Verri, A.: Support Vector Machines for 3-D Objects Recognition. IEEE Trans. on PAMI (to appear)
10. Tarr, M., Pinker, S.: Mental Rotation and Orientation-Dependence in Shape Recognition. Cognitive Psychology **21** (1989) 233-282
11. Vapnik, V.N., Chervonenkis, A.J.: On the uniform convergence of relative frequencies of events to their probabilities. Theory Probab Appl. **16** (1971) 264-280
12. Vapnik, V.N.: The Nature of Statistical Learning Theory. (Springer-Verlag, New York, 1995).

Active Appearance Models

T.F. Cootes, G.J. Edwards, and C.J. Taylor

Wolfson Image Analysis Unit,
Department of Medical Biophysics,
University of Manchester,
Manchester M13 9PT, U.K.
tcootes@server1.smb.man.ac.uk
http://www.wiau.man.ac.uk

Abstract. We demonstrate a novel method of interpreting images using an Active Appearance Model (AAM). An AAM contains a statistical model of the shape and grey-level appearance of the object of interest which can generalise to almost any valid example. During a training phase we learn the relationship between model parameter displacements and the residual errors induced between a training image and a synthesised model example. To match to an image we measure the current residuals and use the model to predict changes to the current parameters, leading to a better fit. A good overall match is obtained in a few iterations, even from poor starting estimates. We describe the technique in detail and give results of quantitative performance tests. We anticipate that the AAM algorithm will be an important method for locating deformable objects in many applications.

1 Introduction

Model-based approaches to the interpretation of images of variable objects are now attracting considerable interest [6][8][10] [11][14] [16][19][20]. They can achieve robust results by constraining solutions to be valid instances of a model. In addition the ability to 'explain' an image in terms of a set of model parameters provides a natural basis for scene interpretation. In order to realise these benefits, the model of object appearance should be as complete as possible - able to synthesise a very close approximation to any image of the target object.

Although model-based methods have proved successful, few of the existing methods use full, photo-realistic models which are matched directly by minimising the difference between the image under interpretation and one synthesised by the model. Although suitable photo-realistic models exist, (e.g. Edwards *et al* [8] for faces), they typically involve a large number of parameters (50-100) in order to deal with variability in the target objects. Direct optimisation using standard methods over such a high dimensional space is possible but slow [12].

In this paper, we show a direct optimisation approach which leads to an algorithm which is rapid, accurate, and robust. In our proposed method, we do not attempt to solve a general optimisation each time we wish to fit the model to a new image. Instead, we exploit the fact the optimisation problem is similar each time - we can learn these similarities off-line. This allows us to find directions of rapid convergence even though the search space has very high dimensionality. This approach is similar to that of Sclaroff and Isidoro [18], but uses a statistical rather than 'physical' model.

In this paper we discuss the idea of image interpretation by synthesis and describe previous related work. In section 2 we explain how we build compact models of object appearance which are capable of generating synthetic examples similar to those in a training set. The method can be used in a wide variety of applications, but as an example we will concentrate on interpreting face images. In section 3 we describe the Active Appearance Model algorithm in detail and in 4 demonstrate its performance.

1.1 Interpretation by Synthesis

In recent years many model-based approaches to the interpretation of images of deformable objects have been described. One motivation is to achieve robust performance by using the model to constrain solutions to be valid examples of the object modelled. A model also provides the basis for a broad range of applications by 'explaining' the appearance of a given image in terms of a compact set of model parameters. These parameters are useful for higher level interpretation of the scene. For instance, when analysing face images they may be used to characterise the identity, pose or expression of a face. In order to interpret a new image, an efficient method of finding the best match between image and model is required.

Various approaches to modelling variability have been described. The most common general approach is to allow a prototype to vary according to some physical model. Bajcsy and Kovacic [1] describe a volume model (of the brain) that also deforms elastically to generate new examples. Christensen *et al* [3] describe a viscous flow model of deformation which they also apply to the brain, but is very computationally expensive. Turk and Pentland [20] use principal component analysis to describe face images in terms of a set of basis functions, or 'eigenfaces'. Though valid modes of variation are learnt from a training set, and are more likely to be more appropriate than a 'physical' model, the eigenface is not robust to shape changes, and does not deal well with variability in pose and expression. However, the model can be matched to an image easily using correlation based methods.

Poggio and co-workers [10] [12] synthesise new views of an object from a set of example views. They fit the model to an unseen view by a stochastic optimisation procedure. This is slow, but can be robust because of the quality of the synthesised images. Cootes *et al* [5] describe a 3D model of the grey-level surface, allowing full synthesis of shape and appearance. However, they do not suggest a plausible search algorithm to match the model to a new image. Nastar *at al* [16] describe a related model of the 3D grey-level surface, combining physical and statistical modes of variation. Though they describe a search algorithm, it requires a very good initialisation. Lades *at al* [13] model shape and some grey level information using Gabor jets. However, they do not impose strong shape constraints and cannot easily synthesise a new instance.

Cootes *et al* [6] model shape and local grey-level appearance, using Active Shape Models (ASMs) to locate flexible objects in new images. Lanitis *at al* [14] use this approach to interpret face images. Having found the shape using an ASM, the face is warped into a normalised frame, in which a model of the intensities of the shape-free face is used to interpret the image. Edwards *at al* [8] extend this work to produce a combined model of shape and grey-level appearance, but again rely on the ASM to locate faces in new images. Our new approach can be seen as a further extension of this idea, using all the information in the combined appearance model to fit to the image.

In developing our new approach we have benefited from insights provided by two earlier papers. Covell [7] demonstrated that the parameters of an eigen-feature model can be used to drive shape model points to the correct place. The AAM described here is an extension of this idea. Black and Yacoob [2] use local, hand crafted models of image flow to track facial features, but do not attempt to model the whole face. The AAM can be thought of as a generalisation of this, in which the image difference patterns corresponding to changes in each model parameter are learnt and used to modify a model estimate.

In a parallel development Sclaroff and Isidoro have demonstrated 'Active Blobs' for tracking [18]. The approach is broadly similar in that they use image differences to drive tracking, learning the relationship between image error and parameter offset in an off-line processing stage. The main difference is that Active Blobs are derived from a single example, whereas Active Appearance Models use a training set of examples. The former use a single example as the original model template, allowing deformations consistent with low energy mesh deformations (derived using a Finite Element method). A simply polynomial model is used to allow changes in intensity across the object. AAMs learn what are valid shape and intensity variations from their training set.

Sclaroff and Isidoro suggest applying a robust kernel to the image differences, an idea we will use in later work. Also, since annotating the training set is the most time consuming part of building an AAM, the Active Blob approach may be useful for 'bootstrapping' from the first example.

2 Modelling Appearance

In this section we outline how our appearance models were generated. The approach follows that described in Edwards *et al* [8] but includes extra normalisation and weighting steps. Some familiarity with the basic approach is required to understand the new Active Appearance Model algorithm.

The models were generated by combining a model of shape variation with a model of the appearance variations in a shape-normalised frame. We require a training set of labelled images, where key landmark points are marked on each example object. For instance, to build a face model we require face images marked with points at key positions to outline the main features (Figure 1).

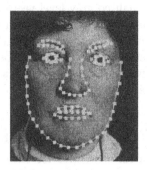

Fig. 1. Example of face image labelled with 122 landmark points

Given such a set we can generate a statistical model of shape variation (see [6] for details). The labelled points on a single object describe the shape of that object. We align all the sets into a common co-ordinate frame and represent each by a vector, $\mathbf{x}$. We then apply a principal component analysis (PCA) to the data. Any example can then be approximated using:

$$\mathbf{x} = \bar{\mathbf{x}} + \mathbf{P}_s \mathbf{b}_s \qquad (1)$$

where $\bar{\mathbf{x}}$ is the mean shape, $\mathbf{P}_s$ is a set of orthogonal *modes of variation* and $\mathbf{b}_s$ is a set of shape parameters.

To build a statistical model of the grey-level appearance we warp each example image so that its control points match the mean shape (using a triangulation algorithm). We then sample the grey level information $\mathbf{g}_{im}$ from the *shape-normalised* image over the region covered by the mean shape. To minimise the effect of global lighting variation, we normalise the example samples by applying a scaling, α, and offset, β,

$$\mathbf{g} = (\mathbf{g}_{im} - \beta \mathbf{1})/\alpha \qquad (2)$$

The values of α and β are chosen to best match the vector to the normalised mean. Let $\bar{\mathbf{g}}$ be the mean of the normalised data, scaled and offset so that the sum of elements is zero and the variance of elements is unity. The values of α and β required to normalise $\mathbf{g}_{im}$ are then given by

$$\alpha = \mathbf{g}_{im} \cdot \bar{\mathbf{g}} \ , \ \ \beta = (\mathbf{g}_{im} \cdot \mathbf{1})/n \qquad (3)$$

where n is the number of elements in the vectors.

Of course, obtaining the mean of the normalised data is then a recursive process, as the normalisation is defined in terms of the mean. A stable solution can be found by using one of the examples as the first estimate of the mean, aligning the others to it (using 2 and 3), re-estimating the mean and iterating.

By applying PCA to the normalised data we obtain a linear model:

$$\mathbf{g} = \bar{\mathbf{g}} + \mathbf{P}_g \mathbf{b}_g \qquad (4)$$

where $\bar{\mathbf{g}}$ is the mean normalised grey-level vector, $\mathbf{P}_g$ is a set of orthogonal *modes of variation* and $\mathbf{b}_g$ is a set of grey-level parameters.

The shape and appearance of any example can thus be summarised by the vectors $\mathbf{b}_s$ and $\mathbf{b}_g$. Since there may be correlations between the shape and grey-level variations, we apply a further PCA to the data as follows. For each example we generate the concatenated vector

$$\mathbf{b} = \begin{pmatrix} \mathbf{W}_s\mathbf{b}_s \\ \mathbf{b}_g \end{pmatrix} = \begin{pmatrix} \mathbf{W}_s\mathbf{P}_s^T(\mathbf{x} - \bar{\mathbf{x}}) \\ \mathbf{P}_g^T(\mathbf{g} - \bar{\mathbf{g}}) \end{pmatrix} \tag{5}$$

where $\mathbf{W}_s$ is a diagonal matrix of weights for each shape parameter, allowing for the difference in units between the shape and grey models (see below). We apply a PCA on these vectors, giving a further model

$$\mathbf{b} = \mathbf{Q}\mathbf{c} \tag{6}$$

where $\mathbf{Q}$ are the eigenvectors and $\mathbf{c}$ is a vector of *appearance* parameters controlling both the shape and grey-levels of the model. Since the shape and grey-model parameters have zero mean, $\mathbf{c}$ does too.

Note that the linear nature of the model allows us to express the shape and grey-levels directly as functions of $\mathbf{c}$

$$\mathbf{x} = \bar{\mathbf{x}} + \mathbf{P}_s\mathbf{W}_s\mathbf{Q}_s\mathbf{c} \;,\; \mathbf{g} = \bar{\mathbf{g}} + \mathbf{P}_g\mathbf{Q}_g\mathbf{c} \tag{7}$$

where

$$\mathbf{Q} = \begin{pmatrix} \mathbf{Q}_s \\ \mathbf{Q}_g \end{pmatrix} \tag{8}$$

An example image can be synthesised for a given $\mathbf{c}$ by generating the shape-free grey-level image from the vector $\mathbf{g}$ and warping it using the control points described by $\mathbf{x}$.

2.1 Choice of Shape Parameter Weights

The elements of $\mathbf{b}_s$ have units of distance, those of $\mathbf{b}_g$ have units of intensity, so they cannot be compared directly. Because $\mathbf{P}_g$ has orthogonal columns, varying $\mathbf{b}_g$ by one unit moves $\mathbf{g}$ by one unit. To make $\mathbf{b}_s$ and $\mathbf{b}_g$ commensurate, we must estimate the effect of varying $\mathbf{b}_s$ on the sample $\mathbf{g}$. To do this we systematically displace each element of $\mathbf{b}_s$ from its optimum value on each training example, and sample the image given the displaced shape. The RMS change in $\mathbf{g}$ per unit change in shape parameter b_s gives the weight w_s to be applied to that parameter in equation (5).

2.2 Example: Facial Appearance Model

We used the method described above to build a model of facial appearance. We used a training set of 400 images of faces, each labelled with 122 points around the main features (Figure 1). From this we generated a shape model with 23 parameters, a shape-free grey model with 114 parameters and a combined appearance model with only 80 parameters required to explain 98% of the observed variation. The model uses about 10,000 pixel values to make up the face patch.

Figures 2 and 3 show the effects of varying the first two shape and grey-level model parameters through ±3 standard deviations, as determined from the training set. The first parameter corresponds to the largest eigenvalue of the covariance matrix, which gives its variance across the training set. Figure 4 shows the effect of varying the first four appearance model parameters, showing changes in identity, pose and expression.

Fig. 2. First two modes of shape variation (±3 sd) **Fig. 3.** First two modes of grey-level variation (±3 sd)

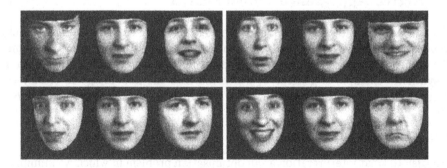

Fig. 4. First four modes of appearance variation (±3 sd)

2.3 Approximating a New Example

Given a new image, labelled with a set of landmarks, we can generate an approximation with the model. We follow the steps in the previous section to obtain **b**, combining the shape and grey-level parameters which match the example. Since **Q** is orthogonal, the combined appearance model parameters, **c** are given by

$$\mathbf{c} = \mathbf{Q}^T\mathbf{b} \tag{9}$$

The full reconstruction is then given by applying equations (7), inverting the grey-level normalisation, applying the appropriate pose to the points and projecting the grey-level vector into the image.

For example, Figure 5 shows a previously unseen image alongside the model reconstruction of the face patch (overlaid on the original image).

Fig. 5. Example of combined model representation (right) of a previously unseen face image (left)

3 Active Appearance Model Search

We now address the central problem: We have an image to be interpreted, a full appearance model as described above and a reasonable starting approximation. We propose a scheme for adjusting the model parameters efficiently, so that a synthetic example is generated, which matches the new image as closely as possible. We first outline the basic idea, before giving details of the algorithm.

3.1 Overview of AAM Search

We wish to treat interpretation as an optimisation problem in which we minimise the difference between a new image and one synthesised by the appearance model. A difference vector $\delta\mathbf{I}$ can be defined:

$$\delta\mathbf{I} = \mathbf{I_i} - \mathbf{I_m} \tag{10}$$

where $\mathbf{I_i}$ is the vector of grey-level values in the image, and $\mathbf{I_m}$, is the vector of grey-level values for the current model parameters.

To locate the best match between model and image, we wish to minimise the magnitude of the difference vector, $\Delta = |\delta\mathbf{I}|^2$, by varying the model parameters,

c. Since the appearance models can have many parameters, this appears at first to be a difficult high-dimensional optimisation problem. We note, however, that each attempt to match the model to a new image is actually a similar optimisation problem. We propose to learn something about how to solve this class of problems in advance. By providing a-priori knowledge of how to adjust the model parameters during during image search, we arrive at an efficient runtime algorithm. In particular, the spatial pattern in δI, encodes information about how the model parameters should be changed in order to achieve a better fit. In adopting this approach there are two parts to the problem: learning the relationship between δI and the error in the model parameters, δc and using this knowledge in an iterative algorithm for minimising Δ.

3.2 Learning to Correct Model Parameters

The simplest model we could choose for the relationship between δI and the error in the model parameters (and thus the correction which needs to be made) is linear:

$$\delta c = A \delta I \qquad (11)$$

This turns out to be a good enough approximation to achieve acceptable results. To find A, we perform multiple multivariate linear regression on a sample of known model displacements, δc, and the corresponding difference images, δI. We can generate these sets of random displacements by perturbing the 'true' model parameters for the images in which they are known. These can either be the original training images or synthetic images generated with the appearance model. In the latter case we know the parameters exactly, and the images are not corrupted by noise.

As well as perturbations in the model parameters, we also model small displacements in 2D position, scale, and orientation. These four extra parameters are included in the regression; for simplicity of notation, they can be regarded simply as extra elements of the vector δc. To retain linearity we represent the pose using (s_x, s_y, t_x, t_y) where $s_x = s \cos(\theta)$, $s_y = s \sin(\theta)$. In order to obtain a well-behaved relationship it is important to choose carefully the frame of reference in which the image difference is calculated. The most suitable frame of reference is the shape-normalised patch described in section 2.

We calculate a difference thus: Let c_0 be the known appearance model parameters for the current image. We displace the parameters by a known amount, δc, to obtain new parameters $c = \delta c + c_0$. For these parameters we generate the shape, x, and normalised grey-levels, g_m, using (7). We sample from the image, warped using the points, x, to obtain a normalised sample g_s. The sample error is then $\delta g = g_s - g_m$.

The training algorithm is then simply to randomly displace the model parameter in each training image, recording δc and δg. We then perform multi-variate regression to obtain the relationship

$$\delta c = A \delta g \qquad (12)$$

The best range of values of $\delta\mathbf{c}$ to use during training is determined experimentally. Ideally we seek to model a relationship that holds over as large a range errors, $\delta\mathbf{g}$, as possible. However, the real relationship is found to be linear only over a limited range of values. Our experiments on the face model suggest that the optimum perturbation was around 0.5 standard deviations (over the training set) for each model parameter, about 10% in scale and 2 pixels translation.

Results For The Face Model We applied the above algorithm to the face model described in section 2.2. After performing linear regression, we can calculate an R^2 statistic for each parameter perturbation, δc_i to measure how well the displacement is 'predicted' by the error vector $\delta\mathbf{g}$. The average R^2 value for the 80 parameters was 0.82, with a maximum of 0.98 (the 1st parameter) and a minimum of 0.48.

We can visualise the effects of the perturbation as follows. If $\mathbf{a}_i$ is the ith row of the regression matrix $\mathbf{A}$, the predicted change in the ith parameter, δc_i is given by

$$\delta c_i = \mathbf{a}_i.\delta\mathbf{g} \tag{13}$$

and $\mathbf{a}_i$ gives the weight attached to different areas of the sampled patch when estimating the displacement. Figure 6 shows the weights corresponding to changes in the pose parameters, (s_x, s_y, t_x, t_y). Bright areas are positive weights, dark areas negative. As one would expect, the x and y displacement weights are similar to x and y derivative images. Similar results are obtained for weights corresponding to the appearance model parameters

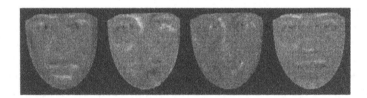

Fig. 6. Weights corresponding to changes in the pose parameters, (s_x, s_y, t_x, t_y)

Perturbing The Face Model To examine the performance of the prediction, we systematically displaced the face model from the true position on a set of 10 test images, and used the model to predict the displacement given the sampled error vector. Figures 7 and 8 show the predicted translations against the actual translations. There is a good linear relationship within about 4 pixels of zero. Although this breaks down with larger displacements, as long as the prediction has the same sign as the actual error, and does not over-predict too far, an iterative updating scheme should converge. In this case up to 20 pixel displacements in x and about 10 in y should be correctable.

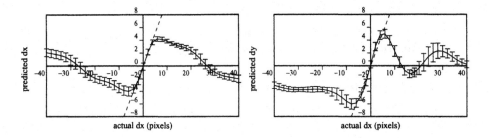

Fig. 7. Predicted *dx* vs actual *dx*. Error-bars are 1 standard error

Fig. 8. Predicted *dy* vs actual *dy*. Error-bars are 1 standard error

We can, however, extend this range by building a multi-resolution model of object appearance. We generate Gaussian pyramids for each of our training images, and generate an appearance model for each level of the pyramid. Figure 9 shows the predictions of models displaced in *x* at three resolutions. L0 is the base model, with about 10,000 pixels. L1 has about 2,500 pixels and L2 about 600 pixels.

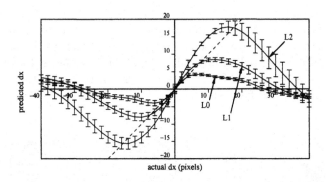

Fig. 9. Predicted *dx* vs actual *dx* for 3 levels of a Multi-Resolution model. L0: 10000 pixels, L1: 2500 pixels, L2: 600 pixels. Errorbars are 1 standard error

The linear region of the curve extends over a larger range at the coarser resolutions, but is less accurate than at the finest resolution. Similar results are obtained for variations in other pose parameters and the model parameters.

3.3 Iterative Model Refinement

Given a method for predicting the correction which needs to made in the model parameters we can construct an iterative method for solving our optimisation problem.

Given the current estimate of model parameters, c_0, and the normalised image sample at the current estimate, g_s, one step of the iterative procedure is as follows:

- Evaluate the error vector $\delta\mathbf{g}_0 = \mathbf{g}_s - \mathbf{g}_m$
- Evaluate the current error $E_0 = |\delta\mathbf{g}_0|^2$
- Compute the predicted displacement, $\delta\mathbf{c} = \mathbf{A}\delta\mathbf{g}_0$
- Set $k = 1$
- Let $\mathbf{c}_1 = \mathbf{c}_0 - k\delta\mathbf{c}$
- Sample the image at this new prediction, and calculate a new error vector, $\delta\mathbf{g}_1$
- If $|\delta\mathbf{g}_1|^2 < E_0$ then accept the new estimate, $\mathbf{c}_1$,
- Otherwise try at $k = 1.5$, $k = 0.5$, $k = 0.25$ etc.

This procedure is repeated until no improvement is made to the error, $|\delta\mathbf{g}|^2$, and convergence is declared.

We use a multi-resolution implementation, in which we iterate to convergence at each level before projecting the current solution to the next level of the model. This is more efficient and can converge to the correct solution from further away than search at a single resolution.

Examples of Active Appearance Model Search We used the face AAM to search for faces in previously unseen images. Figure 10 shows the best fit of the model given the image points marked by hand for three faces. Figure 11 shows frames from a AAM search for each face, each starting with the mean model displaced from the true face centre.

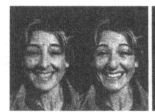

Fig. 10. Reconstruction (left) and original (right) given original landmark points

As an example of applying the method to medical images, we built an Appearance Model of part of the knee as seen in a slice through an MR image. The model was trained on 30 examples, each labelled with 42 landmark points. Figure 12 shows the effect of varying the first two appearance model parameters. Figure 13 shows the best fit of the model to a new image, given hand marked landmark points. Figure 14 shows frames from an AAM search from a displaced position.

495

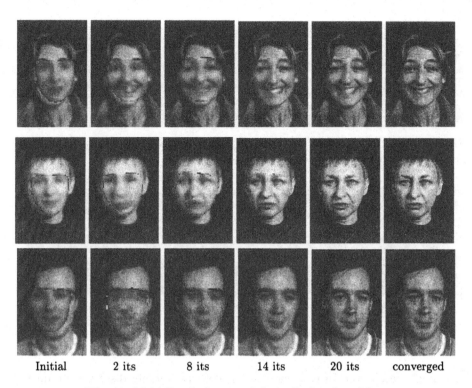

| Initial | 2 its | 8 its | 14 its | 20 its | converged |

Fig. 11. Multi-Resolution search from displaced position

4 Experimental Results

To obtain a quantitative evaluation of the performance of the algorithm we trained a model on 88 hand labelled face images, and tested it on a different set of 100 labelled images. Each face was about 200 pixels wide.

On each test image we systematically displaced the model from the true position by ±15 pixels in x and y, and changed its scale by ±10%. We then ran the multi-resolution search, starting with the mean appearance model. 2700 searches were run in total, each taking an average of 4.1 seconds on a Sun Ultra. Of those 2700, 519 (19%) failed to converge to a satisfactory result (the mean point position error was greater than 7.5 pixels per point). Of those that did converge, the RMS error between the model centre and the target centre was (0.8, 1.8) pixels. The s.d. of the model scale error was 6%. The mean magnitude of the final image error vector in the normalised frame relative to that of the best model fit given the marked points, was 0.88 (sd: 0.1), suggesting that the algorithm is locating a better result than that provided by the marked points. Because it is explicitly minimising the error vector, it will compromise the shape if that leads to an overall improvement of the grey-level fit.

Figure 15 shows the mean intensity error per pixel (for an image using 256 grey-levels) against the number of iterations, averaged over a set of searches

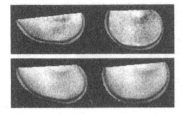

Fig. 12. First two modes of appearance variation of knee model

Fig. 13. Best fit of knee model to new image given landmarks

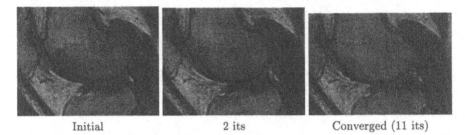

Initial   2 its   Converged (11 its)

Fig. 14. Multi-Resolution search for knee

at a single resolution. In each case the model was initially displaced by up to 15 pixels. The dotted line gives the mean reconstruction error using the hand marked landmark points, suggesting a good result is obtained by the search.

Figure 16 shows the proportion of 100 multi-resolution searches which converged correctly given starting positions displaced from the true position by up to 50 pixels in x and y. The model displays good results with up to 20 pixels (10% of the face width) displacement.

5   Discussion and Conclusions

We have demonstrated an iterative scheme for fitting an Active Appearance Model to new images. The method makes use of learned correlation between model-displacement and the resulting difference image. Given a reasonable initial starting position, the search converges quickly. Although it is slower than an Active Shape Model [6], since all the image evidence is used, the procedure should be more robust than ASM search alone. We are currently investigating further efficiency improvements, for example, sub-sampling both model and image.

The algorithm can be thought of as a differential optic flow method, in which we learn the patterns of changes associated with varying each parameter. Like differential optic flow, it can only cope with relatively small changes (though the training phase makes it more robust). To deal with larger displacements we are exploring techniques akin to correlation -based optic flow, in which sub-regions of the model are systematically displaced to find the best local correction.

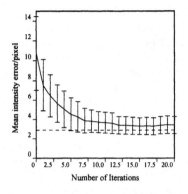

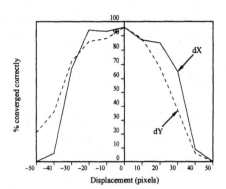

Fig. 15. Mean intensity error as search progresses. Dotted line is the mean error of the best fit to the landmarks.

Fig. 16. Proportion of searches which converged from different initial displacements

We are attempting to find the parameters $\mathbf{c}$ of some vector valued model $\mathbf{v}(\mathbf{c})$ which minimises $\Delta = |\mathbf{v}_{im} - \mathbf{v}(\mathbf{c})|^2$, where $\mathbf{v}_{im}$ may vary as $\mathbf{c}$ varies. With no other information, this would be difficult, but could be tackled with general purpose algorithms such as Powells, Simplex, Simulated Annealing or Genetic Algorithms [17]. However, by obtaining an estimate of the derivative, $\frac{\partial \mathbf{x}}{\partial \mathbf{c}}$ we can direct the search more effectively. The algorithm described above is related to steepest gradient descent, in which we use our derivative estimate, combined with the current error vector, to determine the next direction to search. It may be possible to modify the algorithm to be more like a conjugate gradient descent method, or to use second order information to use the Levenberg-Marquardt algorithm [17], which could lead to faster convergence.

The nature of the search algorithm makes it suitable for tracking objects in image sequences, where it can be shown to give robust results [9]. In the experiments above we have examined search from relatively large displacements. In practise, a good initial starting point can be found by a variety of methods. We could use an ASM, which by searching along profiles can converge from large displacements. Alternatively we could train a rigid eigen-feature type model [15] [4] which can be used to locate the object using correlation. A few iterations of the AAM would then refine this initial estimate.

We anticipate that the AAM algorithm will be an important method of locating deformable objects in many applications.

References

1. Bajcsy and A. Kovacic. Multiresolution elastic matching. *Computer Graphics and Image Processing*, 46:1–21, 1989.
2. M. J. Black and Y. Yacoob. Recognizing facial expressions under rigid and non-rigid facial motions. In 1st *International Workshop on Automatic Face and Gesture Recognition 1995*, pages 12–17, Zurich, 1995.

3. G. E. Christensen, R. D. Rabbitt, M. I. Miller, S. C. Joshi, U. Grenander, T. A. Coogan, and D. C. V. Essen. *Topological Properties of Smooth Anatomic Maps*, pages 101–112. Kluwer Academic Publishers, 1995.

4. T. Cootes, G. Page, C. Jackson, and C. Taylor. Statistical grey-level models for object location and identification. *Image and Vision Computing*, 14(8):533–540, 1996.

5. T. Cootes and C. Taylor. Modelling object appearance using the grey-level surface. In E. Hancock, editor, 5th *British Machine Vison Conference*, pages 479–488, York, England, September 1994. BMVA Press.

6. T. F. Cootes, C. J. Taylor, D. H. Cooper, and J. Graham. Active shape models - their training and application. *Computer Vision and Image Understanding*, 61(1):38–59, January 1995.

7. M. Covell. Eigen-points: Control-point location using principal component analysis. In 2nd *International Conference on Automatic Face and Gesture Recognition 1997*, pages 122–127, Killington, USA, 1996.

8. G. J. Edwards, C. J. Taylor, and T. Cootes. Learning to identify and track faces in image sequences. In 8th *British Machine Vison Conference*, Colchester, UK, 1997.

9. G. J. Edwards, C. J. Taylor, and T. Cootes. Face recognition using the active appearance model. In 5th *European Conference on Computer Vision*, 1998.

10. T. Ezzat and T. Poggio. Facial analysis and synthesis using image-based models. In 2nd *International Conference on Automatic Face and Gesture Recognition 1997*, pages 116–121, Killington, Vermont, 1996.

11. U. Grenander and M. Miller. Representations of knowledge in complex systems. *Journal of the Royal Statistical Society B*, 56:249–603, 1993.

12. M. J. Jones and T. Poggio. Multidimensional morphable models. In 6th *International Conference on Computer Vision*, pages 683–688, 1998.

13. M. Lades, J. Vorbruggen, J. Buhmann, J. Lange, C. von der Malsburt, R. Wurtz, and W. Konen. Distortion invariant object recognition in the dynamic link architecture. *IEEE Transactions on Computers*, 42:300–311, 1993.

14. A. Lanitis, C. Taylor, and T. Cootes. Automatic interpretation and coding of face images using flexible models. *IEEE Transactions on Pattern Analysis and Machine Intelligence*, 19(7):743–756, 1997.

15. B. Moghaddam and A. Pentland. Probabilistic visual learning for object recognition. In 5th *International Conference on Computer Vision*, pages 786–793, Cambridge, USA, 1995.

16. C. Nastar, B. Moghaddam, and A. Pentland. Generalized image matching: Statistical learning of physically-based deformations. In 4th *European Conference on Computer Vision*, volume 1, pages 589–598, Cambridge, UK, 1996.

17. W. Press, S. Teukolsky, W. Vetterling, and B. Flannery. *Numerical Recipes in C (2nd Edition)*. Cambridge University Press, 1992.

18. S. Sclaroff and J. Isidoro. Active blobs. In 6th *International Conference on Computer Vision*, pages 1146–53, 1998.

19. L. H. Staib and J. S. Duncan. Boundary finding with parametrically deformable models. *IEEE Transactions on Pattern Analysis and Machine Intelligence*, 14(11):1061–1075, 1992.

20. M. Turk and A. Pentland. Eigenfaces for recognition. *Journal of Cognitive Neuroscience*, 3(1):71–86, 1991.

Estimating Coloured 3D Face Models from Single Images: An Example Based Approach

Thomas Vetter and Volker Blanz

Max-Planck-Institut für biologische Kybernetik
Spemannstr. 38   72076 Tübingen – Germany
Email: [thomas.vetter/volker.blanz]@tuebingen.mpg.de

Abstract. In this paper we present a method to derive 3D shape and surface texture of a human face from a single image. The method draws on a general flexible 3D face model which is "learned" from examples of individual 3D-face data (Cyberware-scans). In an analysis-by-synthesis loop, the flexible model is matched to the novel face image.
From the coloured 3D model obtained by this procedure, we can generate new images of the face across changes in viewpoint and illumination. Moreover, nonrigid transformations which are represented within the flexible model can be applied, for example changes in facial expression.
The key problem for generating a flexible face model is the computation of dense correspondence between all given 3D example faces. A new correspondence algorithm is described which is a generalization of common algorithms for optic flow computation to 3D-face data.

1 Introduction

Almost an infinite number of different images can be generated from the human face. Any system that tries to analyse images of faces is confronted with the problem of separating different sources of image variation. For example, in order to identify a face of a person, the system must be able to ignore changes in illumination, orientation and facial expression, but it must be highly sensitive to attributes that are characteristic of identity. One approach to solving this problem is to transform the input image to a feature vector which is then compared to stored representations. In these 'bottom-up' strategies, the crucial problem is to choose appropriate features and criteria for comparison. An alternative approach is to build an explicit model of the variations of images. An image analysis is performed by matching an image model to a novel image, thereby coding the novel image in terms of a known model.

This paper focuses on the analysis and synthesis of images of a specific object class – that is on images of human faces. A model of an entire object class, such as faces or cars, with all objects sharing a common similarity, can be learned from a set of prototypical examples. Developed for the analysis and synthesis of images of a specific class of objects, it must solve two problems simultaneously:

- The model must be able to synthesize images that cover the whole range of possible images of the class.

– Matching the model to a novel image must be possible, avoiding local minima.

Recently, two-dimensional image-based face models have been constructed and applied for the synthesis of rigid and nonrigid face transformations [1, 2, 3]. These models exploit prior knowledge from example images of prototypical faces and work by building flexible image-based representations (*active shape models*) of known objects by a linear combination of labeled examples. These representations are used for image search and recognition or synthesis [3]. The underlying coding of an image of a new object or face is based on linear combinations of prototypical images in terms of both two-dimensional shape (warping fields), and color values at corresponding locations (texture).

For the problem of synthesizing novel views to a single example image of a face, we have developed over the last years the concept of *linear object classes* [4]. This image-based method allows us to compute novel views of a face from a single image. On the one hand, the method draws on a general flexible image model which can be learned automatically from examples images, and on the other hand, on an algorithm that allows this flexible model to be matched to a novel face image. The novel image can now be described or coded by means of the internal model parameters which are necessary to reconstruct the image. The design of the model also allows new views of the face to be synthesized.

In this paper we replace the two-dimensional image model by a three-dimensional flexible face model. A flexible three-dimensional face model will lead on the one hand to a more efficient data representation, and on the other hand to a better generalization to new illumination conditions.

In all these techniques, it is crucial to establish the correspondence between each example face and a single reference face, either by matching image points in the two-dimensional approach, or surface points in the three-dimensional case. Correspondence is a key step posing a difficult problem. However, for images of objects which share many common features, such as faces all seen from a single specific viewpoint, automated techniques seem feasible. Techniques applied in the past can be separated in two groups, one which establishes the correspondence for a small number of feature points only, and techniques computing the correspondence for every pixel in an image. For the first approach models of particular features such as the eye corners or the whole chin line are developed off line and then matched to a new image [3]. The second technique computes the correspondence for each pixel in an image by comparing this image to a reference image using methods derived from optical flow computation[2, 5].

In this paper, the method of dense correspondence, which we have already applied successfully to face images [4], will be extended to the three-dimensional face data. Firstly, we describe the flexible three-dimensional face model and compare it to the two-dimensional image models we used earlier. Secondly we describe an algorithm to compute dense correspondence between individual 3D models of human faces. Thirdly we describe an algorithm that allows us to match the flexible face model to a novel image. Finally we show examples for synthesizing new images from a single image of a face and describe future improvements.

2 Flexible 3D face models

In this section we will give a formulation of a flexible three-dimensional face model which captures prior knowledge about faces exploiting the general similarity among faces. The model is a straightforward extension of the linear object class approach as described earlier[4]. Exploiting the general similarity among faces, prototypical examples are linked to a general class model that captures regularities specific for this object class.

Three-dimensional models
In computer graphics, at present the most realistic three-dimensional face representations consist of a 3D mesh describing the geometry, and a texture map capturing the color data of a face. These representations of individual faces are obtained either by three-dimensional scanning devices or by means of photogrammetric techniques from several two-dimensional images of a specific face [6, 7]. Synthesis of new faces by interpolation between such face representation was already demonstrated in the pioneering work of Parke (1974). Recently the idea of forming linear combinations of faces has been used and extended to a general three-dimensional flexible face model for the analysis and synthesis of two-dimensional facial images [1, 4].

Shape model: The three-dimensional geometry of a face is represented by a shape-vector $\mathbf{S} = (X_1, Y_1, Z_1, X_2, ..., Y_n, Z_n)^T \in \Re^{3n}$, that contains the X, Y, Z-coordinates of its n vertices. The central assumption for the formation of a flexible face model is that a set of M example faces $\mathbf{S}_i$ is available. Additionally, it is assumed that all these example faces $\mathbf{S}_i$ consist of the same number of n consistently labeled vertices, in other words all example faces are in full correspondence (see next section on correspondence). Usually this labeling is defined on an average face shape, which is obtained iteratively, and which is often denoted as reference face $\mathbf{S}_{ref}$. Additionally, all faces are assumed to be aligned in an optimal way by rotating and translating them in three-dimensional space. Under this assumptions a new face geometry $\mathbf{S}_{model}$ can be generated as a linear combination of M example shape-vectors $\mathbf{S}_i$ each weighted by c_i

$$\mathbf{S}_{model} = \sum_{i=1}^{M} c_i \, \mathbf{S}_i \, . \tag{1}$$

The linear shape model allows for approximating any given shape $\mathbf{S}$ as a linear combination with coefficients that are computed by projecting $\mathbf{S}$ onto the example shapes $\mathbf{S}_i$. The coefficients c_i of the projection then define a coding of the original shape vector in this vector space which is spanned by all examples.

Texture model: The second component of a flexible three-dimensional face or head model is texture information, which is usually stored in a *texture map*. A texture map is simply a two-dimensional color pattern storing the brightness or color values (ideally only the *albedo* of the surface). This pattern can be recorded in a scanning process or generated synthetically.

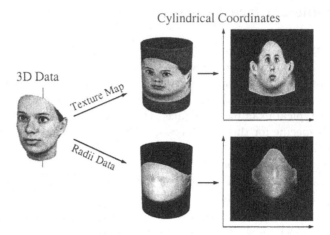

Fig. 1. *Three-dimensional head data represented in cylindrical coordinates result in a data format which consists of two 2D-images. One image is the texture map (top right), and in the other image the geometry is coded (bottom right).*

A u, v coordinate system associates the texture map with the modeled surface. The texture map is defined in the two-dimensional u, v coordinate system. For polygonal surfaces as defined by a shape vector $\mathbf{S}$, each vertex has an assigned u, v texture coordinate. Between vertices, u, v coordinates are interpolated.

The linear texture model, described in [1] starts from a set of M example face textures $\mathbf{T}_i$. Equivalent to the shape model described earlier, it is assumed that all M textures $\mathbf{T}_i$ consist of the same number of n consistently labeled texture values, that is all textures are in full correspondence. For texture synthesis linear models are used again. A new texture $\mathbf{T}_{model}$ is generated as the weighted sum of M given example textures $\mathbf{T}_i$ as follows

$$\mathbf{T}_{model} = \sum_{i=1}^{M} b_i \mathbf{T}_i, \tag{2}$$

Equivalent to the linear expansion of shape vectors (equation 1), the linear expansion of textures can be understood and used as an efficient coding schema for textures. A new texture can be coded by its M projection coefficients b_i in the 'texture vector space" spanned by M basis textures.

3 3D Correspondence with Optical Flow

In order to construct a flexible 3D face model, it is crucial to establish correspondence between a reference face and each individual face example. For all vertices of the reference face, we have to find the corresponding vertex location on each face in the dataset. If, for example, vertex j in the reference face is located on the tip of the nose, with a 3D position described by the vector components X_j, Y_j, Z_j in $\mathbf{S}_{ref}$, then we have to store the position of the tip of the nose of face i in the vector components X_j, Y_j, Z_j of $\mathbf{S}_i$. In general, this is a difficult problem, and it is difficult to formally specify what correct correspondence is supposed to be. However, assuming that there are no categorical differences such as some having a beard and others not, an automatic method is feasible for computing the correspondence.

The key idea of the work described in this paragraph is to modify an existing optical flow algorithm to match points on the surfaces of three-dimensional objects instead of points on 2D images.

Optical Flow Algorithm

In video sequences, in order to estimate the velocities of scene elements with respect to the camera, it is necessary to compute the vector field of optical flow, which defines the displacements $(\delta x, \delta y) = (x_2 - x_1, y_2 - y_1)$ between points $p_1 = (x_1, y_1)$ in the first image and corresponding points $p_2 = (x_2, y_2)$ in the following image.

A variety of different optical flow algorithms have been designed to solve this problem (for a review see [8]). Unlike temporal sequences taken from one scene, a comparison of images of completely different scenes or faces may violate a number of important assumptions made in optical flow estimation. However, some optical flow algorithms can still cope with this more difficult matching problem.

In previous studies [4], we built flexible image models of faces based on correspondence between images, using a coarse-to-fine gradient-based method [9] and following an implementation described in [10]:

For every point x, y in an image $I(x, y)$, the algorithm attempts to minimize the error term $E(x, y) = \sum_{R(x,y)} (I_x \delta x + I_y \delta y - \delta I)^2$ for $\delta x, \delta y$, with I_x, I_y being the spatial image derivatives and δI the difference of grey-levels of the two compared images. The region R is a 5x5 pixel neighbourhood of (x, y). Solving this optimization problem is achieved in a single iteration.

Since this is only a crude approximation to the overall matching problem, an iterative coarse-to-fine strategy is required. The algorithm starts with an estimation of correspondence on low-resolution versions of the two input images. The resulting flow field is used as an initial value to the computation on the next higher level of resolution. Iteratively, the algorithm proceeds to full resolution.

In our applications, results were dramatically improved if images on each level of resolution were computed not only by downsampling the original (Gaussian Pyramid), but also by band-pass filtering (Laplacian Pyramid). The Laplacian Pyramid was computed from the Gaussian pyramid adopting the algorithm proposed by [11].

Three-dimensional face representations.

The adaptation and extension of this optical flow algorithm to face surfaces in 3D is straightforward due to the fact that these two-dimensional manifolds can be parameterized in terms of two variables: In a cylindrical representation (see figure 1), faces are described by radius and color values at each angle ϕ and height h. Images, on the other hand, consist of grey-level values in image coordinates x,y. Thus, in both cases correspondence can be expressed by a mapping C : $\Re^2 \rightarrow \Re^2$ in parameter space.

In order to compute correspondence between different heads, both texture and geometry were considered simultaneously. The optical flow algorithm described above had to be modified in the following way. Instead of comparing scalar grey-level functions $I(x,y)$, our modification of the algorithm attempts to find the best fit for the vector function

$$\mathbf{F}(h, \phi) = \begin{pmatrix} radius(h, \phi) \\ red(h, \phi) \\ green(h, \phi) \\ blue(h, \phi) \end{pmatrix}$$

in a norm

$$\|(radius, red, green, blue)^T\|^2 = w_1 \cdot radius^2 + w_2 \cdot red^2 + w_3 \cdot green^2 + w_4 \cdot blue^2.$$

The coefficients $w_1 ... w_4$ correct for the different contrasts in range and color values, assigning approximately the same weights to variations in radius as to variations in all color channels taken together.

Radius values can be replaced by other surface properties such as Gaussian curvature or surface normals in order to represent the shapes of faces more appropriately.

The displacement between corresponding surface points is expressed by a correspondence function

$$C(h, \phi) = (\delta h(h, \phi), \delta \phi(h, \phi)). \tag{3}$$

Interpolation in low-contrast areas.
It is well known that in areas with no contrast or with strongly oriented intensity gradients, the problem of optical flow computation cannot be uniquely solved based on local image properties only (aperture problem). In our extension of the algorithm to surfaces of human faces, there is no structure to define correct correspondence on the cheeks, along the eyebrows and in many other areas, and indeed the method described so far yields spurious results here. While these problems might remain undetected in a simple morph between two faces, they still have significant impact on the quality of the flexible face model.

The ambiguities of correspondence caused by the aperture problem can be resolved if the flow field is required to be smooth. In a number of optical flow algorithms, smoothness constraints have been implemented as a part of an iterative optimization of correspondence [12, 13, 14].

In our algorithm, smoothing is performed as a separate process after the estimation of flow on each level of resolution. For the smoothed flow field $(\delta h'(h, \phi), \delta \phi'(h, \phi))$, an energy function is minimized using conjugate gradient descent such that on the one hand, flow vectors are kept as close to constant as possible over the whole domain, and on the other hand as close as possible to the flow field $(\delta h(h, \phi), \delta\phi(h, \phi))$ obtained in the computation described above. The first condition is enforced by quadratic potentials that increase with the square distances between each individual flow vector and its four neighbours. These interconnections have equal strength over the whole domain. The second condition is enforced by quadratic potentials that depend on the square distance between $(\delta h'(h, \phi), \delta\phi'(h, \phi))$ and $(\delta h(h, \phi), \delta\phi(h, \phi))$ in every position (h, ϕ). These potentials vary over the (h, ϕ) domain: If the gradient of colour and radius values, weighted in the way described above, is above a given threshold, the coupling factor is set to a fixed, high value in the direction along the gradient, and zero in the orthogonal direction. This allows the flow vector to move along an edge during the relaxation process. In areas with gradients below threshold, the potential is vanishing, so the flow vector depends on its neighbours only. With our choice of the threshold, only 5% of all flow-vectors were set free in the low-resolution step, but 85% in the final full-resolution computation.

4   Matching the flexible 3D model to a 2D image

Based on an example set of faces which are already in correspondence, new 3D shape vectors S^{model} and texture maps T^{model} can be generated by varying the coefficients c_i and b_i in equations (1) and (2). Combining model shape and model texture results in a complete 3D face representation which can now be rendered to a new model image I^{model}. This model image is not fully specified by the model parameters c_i and b_i, but it also depends on some projection parameters p_j and on the parameters r_j of surface reflectance properties and illumination used for rendering. For the general problem of matching the model to a novel image I^{novel} we define the following error function

$$E(\mathbf{c}, \mathbf{b}, \mathbf{p}, \mathbf{r}) = \frac{1}{2} \sum_{x,y} \left[I^{novel}(x,y) - I^{model}(x,y) \right]^2 \tag{4}$$

where the sum is over all pixels (x, y) in the images, I^{novel} is the novel image being matched and I^{model} is the current guess for the model image for a specific parameter setting $(\mathbf{c}, \mathbf{b}, \mathbf{p}, \mathbf{r})$. Minimizing the error yields the model image which best fits the novel image with respect to the L_2 norm.

However, the optimization of the error function in equation (4) is extremely difficult for several reasons. First, the function is not linear in most of the parameters, second, the number of parameters is large (> 100) and additionally, the whole computation is extremely expensive since it requires the rendering of the three-dimensional face model to an image for each evaluation of the error function.

In this paper we will simplify the problem by assuming the illumination parameters $\mathbf{r}$ and also the projection parameters $\mathbf{p}$, such as viewpoint, are known. This assumption allows us to reduce the amount of rendering and also to use image modeling techniques developed earlier [15, 16]. By rendering images from all example faces under fixed illumination and projection parameters, the flexible

3D model is transformed into a flexible 2D face model. This allows us to generate new model images depicting faces in the requested spatial orientation and under the known illumination. After matching this flexible 2D model to the novel image (see below), the optimal model parameters are used within the flexible 3D model to generate a three-dimensional face representation which best matches the novel target image.

4.1 Linear image model

To build the flexible 2D model, first we render all 3D example faces under the given projection and illumination parameters to images $I_0, I_1, \ldots, I_M$. Let I_0 be the reference image, and let positions within I_0 be parameterized by (u, v). Pixelwise correspondences between I_0 and each example image are mappings $\mathbf{s}_j : \mathcal{R}^2 \to \mathcal{R}^2$ which map the points of I_0 onto I_j, i.e. $\mathbf{s}_j(u, v) = (x, y)$, where (x, y) is the point in I_j which corresponds to (u, v) in I_0. We refer to $\mathbf{s}_j$ as a *correspondence field* and interchangeably as *2D shape vector* for the vectorized I_j.

The 2D correspondence s_j between each pixel in the rendered reference image I_0 and its corresponding location in each rendered example image I_i, can be directly computed from the projection P of the differences of 3D shapes between all 3D faces and the reference face, $PS_j - PS_0$.

Warping image I_j onto the reference image I_0, we obtain $\mathbf{t}_j$ as:

$$\mathbf{t}_j(u, v) = I_j \circ \mathbf{s}_j(u, v) \Leftrightarrow I_j(x, y) = \mathbf{t}_j \circ \mathbf{s}_j^{-1}(x, y).$$

So, $\{\mathbf{t}_j\}$ is the set of shape-normalized prototype images, referred to as *texture vectors*. They are normalized in the sense that their shape is the same as the shape of the chosen reference image.

The flexible image model is the set of images I^{model}, parameterized by $\mathbf{c} = [c_0, c_1, \ldots, c_M], \mathbf{b} = [b_0, b_1, \ldots, b_M]$ such that

$$I^{model} \circ \left(\sum_{i=0}^{M} c_i s_i \right) = \sum_{j=0}^{M} b_j t_j. \tag{5}$$

The summation $\sum_{i=0}^{M} c_i s_i$ constrains the 2D shape of every model image to be a linear combination of the example 2D shapes. Similarly, the summation $\sum_{j=0}^{M} b_j t_j$ constrains the texture of every model image to be a linear combination of the example textures.

For any values for c_i and b_i, a model image can be rendered by computing $(x, y) = \sum_{i=0}^{M} c_i s_i(u, v)$ and $g = \sum_{j=0}^{M} b_j t_j(u, v)$ for each (u, v) in the reference image. Then the (x, y) pixel is rendered by assigning $I^{model}(x, y) = g$, that is by warping the texture into the model shape.

4.2 Matching a 2D face model to an image

For matching the flexible image model to a novel image we used the method described in [15, 16]. In 2D, the error function as defined in equation (4) is reduced to a function of the model parameters **c** and **b**.

$$E(\mathbf{c}, \mathbf{b}) = \frac{1}{2} \sum_{x,y} \left[I^{novel}(x, y) - I^{model}(x, y) \right]^2$$

In order to compute I^{model} (see equation (5)) the shape transformation ($\sum c_i s_i$) has to be inverted or one has to work in the coordinate system (u, v) of the reference image, which is computationally more efficient. Therefore, the shape transformation (given some estimated values for **c** and **b**) is applied to both I^{novel} and I^{model}. From equation (5) we obtain

$$E = \frac{1}{2} \sum_{u,v} [I^{novel} \circ (\sum_{i=0}^{M} c_i s_i(u, v)) - \sum_{j=0}^{M} b_j t_j(u, v)]^2.$$

Minimizing the error yields the model image which best fits the novel image with respect to the L_2 norm. The optimal model parameters **c** and **b** are found by a stochastic gradient descent algorithm [17], a method that is fast and has a low tendency to be caught in local minima.

The robustness of the algorithm is further improved using a coarse-to-fine approach [11]. In addition to the textural pyramids, separate resolution pyramids are computed for displacement fields s in x and y.

Separate matching of facial subregions.

In the framework described above, the flexible face model has M degrees of freedom for texture and M for shape, if M is the number of example faces. The number of degrees of freedom can be increased by dividing faces into independent subregions which are optimized independently [18], for example into eyes, nose, mouth and a surrounding region. Once correspondence is established, it is sufficient to define these regions on the reference face. In the linear object class, this segmentation is equivalent to splitting down the vector space of faces into independent subspaces. The process of fitting the flexible face model to given images is modified in the following ways: First, model parameters **c** and **b** are estimated as described above, based on the whole image. Starting from these initial values, each segment is then optimized independently, with its own parameters **c** and **b**. The final 3D model is generated by computing linear combinations for each segment separately and blending them at the borders according to an algorithm proposed for images by [11, 19] .

5 Novel view synthesis

After matching the 2D image model to the novel image, the 2D model parameters **c** and **b** can be used in the three-dimensional flexible face model as defined in equations (1) and (2). The justification of this parameter transfer is discussed

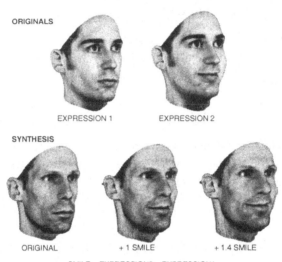

ORIGINALS

EXPRESSION 1   EXPRESSION 2

SYNTHESIS

ORIGINAL   + 1 SMILE   + 1.4 SMILE

SMILE = EXPRESSION2 – EXPRESSION1

Fig. 2. *Correspondence between faces allows us to map expression changes from one face to the other. The difference between the two expressions in the top row is mapped on the left face in the lower row multiplied by a factor of 1 (center) or by 1.4 (lower right)*

in detail under the aspect of *linear object classes* in [4]. The output of the 3D flexible face model is an estimate of the three-dimensional shape from the two-dimensional image. Since this result is a complete 3D face model, new images can be rendered from any viewpoint or under any illumination condition.

The correspondence between all faces within this flexible model allows for mapping non-rigid face transitions 'learned' from one face onto all other faces in the model. In figure 2, the transformation for a smile is extracted from one person and then mapped onto the face of another person. Computing the correspondence between two examples of one person's face, one example showing the face smiling and the other showing the face in a neutral expression, results in a correspondence field or deformation field which captures the spatial displacement for each vertex in the model according to the smile. This expression specific correspondence field is formally identical to the correspondence fields between different persons described earlier. Such a 'smile-vector' can now be added or subtracted from each face which is in correspondence to one of the originals, making a neutral looking face more smily or giving a smiling face a more emotionless expression.

6 Data set

We used a 3D data set obtained from 200 laser scanned ($Cyberware^{TM}$) heads of young adults (100 male and 100 female).

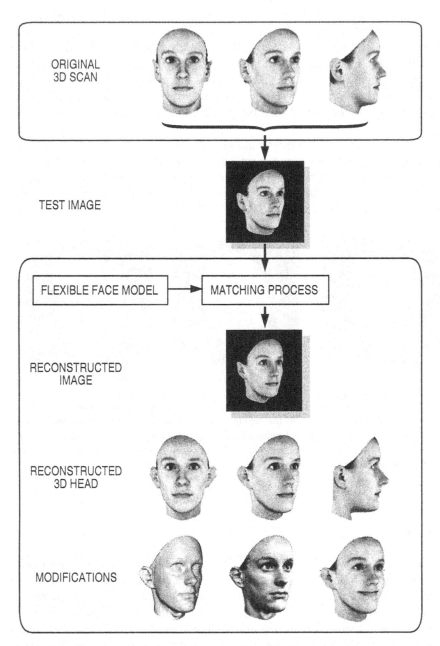

Fig. 3. *Three-dimensional reconstruction of a face from a single two-dimensional image of known orientation and illumination. The test image is generated from an original 3D scan (top) which is not part of the training set of 100 faces. Using the flexible face model derived from the training set, the test image can be reconstructed by optimizing parameters in a 2D matching process. These model parameters also describe the estimated 3D structure of the reconstructed head. The bottom row illustrates manipulations of surface properties, illumination and facial expression (left to right).*

The laser scans provide head structure data in a cylindrical representation, with radii of surface points sampled at 512 equally-spaced angles, and at 512 equally spaced vertical distances. Additionally, the RGB-color values were recorded in the same spatial resolution and were stored in a texture map with 8 bit per channel. All faces were without makeup, accessories, and facial hair. After the head hair was removed digitally (but with manual editing), individual heads were represented by approximately 70000 vertices and the same number of color values.

We split our data set of 200 faces randomly into a training and a test set, each consisting of 100 faces. The training set was used to 'learn' a flexible model. From the test set, images were rendered showing the faces 30° from frontal, and using mainly ambient light. The image size used in the experiments was 256-by-256 pixel and 8 bit per color channel.

ORIGINAL   NO SEGMENTATION   SEGMENTATION

Fig. 4. *In order to recover more of the characteristics of a test image (left), after optimizing model parameters for the whole face (center), separate sets of parameters are optimized for different facial subregions independently (right). As subregions, we used eyes, nose, mouth and the surrounding area. Improvements can be seen in the reconstructed shape of lips and eyes.*

7 Results

Correspondence between all 3D example face models and a reference face model was computed automatically. The results were correct (visual inspection) for almost all 200 faces, in only 7 cases obvious correspondence errors occurred.

Figure 3 shows an example of a three-dimensional face reconstruction from a single image of known orientation and illumination. After matching the model to the test image, the model parameters were used to generate a complete three-dimensional face reconstruction. Figure 3 illustrates the range of images that can be obtained when a full 3D head is reconstructed, including both manipulations of viewpoint, surface material or illumination, and changes of internal properties such as facial expression.

At present, evaluation of the three-dimensional face reconstructions from single images is only based on visual inspection. Out of 100 reconstructions, 72 faces were highly similar and often hard to distinguish from the original in a 30° view. In 27 cases, persons were still easy to identify, but images displayed some differences, for example in the shape of cheeks or jaw. Only one reconstruction showed a face clearly unlike the original, yet a face that could very well exist.

We rated the example shown in figure 3 as highly similar, but within this category it is average. While the reconstructed head appears very similar to the original image in a 30° view, it is not surprising to notice that front and profile views reveal a number of differences.

Since texture vectors in the flexible 2D face model only code points that are part of the face, no particular background colour is specified. Performance should be roughly the same for any background that produces clear contours, and indeed results are almost identical for test images with black and light brown backgrounds.

The flexible model approach can also be applied to faces that are partially occluded, for example wearing sunglasses, or for persons with unusual features such as beards or moles. In each iteration of the matching process, contributions are ignored for those pixels which have the largest disagreement in color values with respect to the original image [15]. Along with a relatively stable reconstruction of all visible areas, the system yields an estimate of the appearance of occluded areas, based on the information available in the image and the internal structure of the face model (figure 5). Moreover, the approach allows detection of conspicious image areas. Conspiciousness of an individual pixel can be measured in different ways, for example by plain disagreement of reconstructed colour values with the original image, by the required change in model parameters to fit the original (used in figure 5), or by the loss in overall matching quality for fitting this specific pixel within the flexible face model. The second and third measures take into account that in some regions small changes of the model parameters lead to considerable changes in color value, while other regions show only small variations.

ORIGINAL   RECONSTRUCTION   CONSPICIOUS PIXELS

Fig. 5. *Reconstruction of a partly occluded face. In the matching process, pixels with large disagreement in colour values were ignored. No segmentation was applied. The approach allows detection of conspicious image areas (right, see text).*

8 Conclusions

We presented a method for approximating the three-dimensional shape of a face from just a single image. In an analysis-by-synthesis loop, a flexible 3D-face model is matched to a novel image. The novel image can now be described or coded by means of the model parameters reconstructing the image. Prior knowledge of the three-dimensional appearance of faces, derived from an example set of faces, allows new images of a face to be predicted. The results presented in this paper are preliminary. We plan to apply a more sophisticated evaluation of reconstruction quality based on ratings by naive human subjects and automated similarity measures.

Clearly, the present implementation with its intermediate step of generating a complete 2D face model can not be the final solution. Next, we plan for each iteration step to form linear combinations in our 3D-representation, render an image from this model and then perform a comparison with the target image. This requires several changes in our matching procedure to keep the computational costs tolerable.

Conditions in our current matching experiments were simplified in two ways. Firstly, all images were rendered from our test set of 3D-face scans. Secondly, projection parameters and illumination conditions were known. The extension of the method to face images taken under arbitrary conditions, in particular to any photograph, will require several improvements. Along with a larger number of free parameters in the matching procedure, model representations need to be more sophisticated, especially in terms of the statistical dependence of the parameters. Reliable results on a wider variety of faces, such as different age groups or races, can only be obtained with an extended data set.

While the construction of 3D-models from a single image is very difficult and often an ill-posed problem in a bottom-up approach, our example-based technique allows us to obtain satisfying results by means of a maximum likelihood estimate. The ambiguity of the problem is reduced when several images of an object are available, a fact that is exploited in stereo or motion-based techniques. In our framework, we can make use of this additional information by simultaneously optimizing the model parameters c and b for all images, while the camera and lighting parameters p and r are adjusted for each image separately.

The method presented in this paper appears to be complementary to non model-based techniques such as stereo. While our approach is limited to results within a fixed model space, these techniques are often not reliable in areas with little structure. For the future, we plan to combine the benefits of both techniques.

References

1. C. Choi, T. Okazaki, H. Harashima, and T. Takebe, "A system of analyzing and synthesizing facial images," in *Proc. IEEE Int. Symposium of Circuit and Syatems (ISCAS91)*, pp. 2665–2668, 1991.

2. D. Beymer, A. Shashua, and T. Poggio, "Example-based image analysis and synthesis," A.I. Memo No. 1431, Artificial Intelligence Laboratory, Massachusetts Institute of Technology, 1993.
3. A. Lanitis, C. Taylor, T. Cootes, and T. Ahmad, "Automatic interpretation of human faces and hand gestures using flexible models," in *Proc. International Workshop on Face and Gesture Recognition* (M.Bichsel, ed.), (Zürich, Switzerland), pp. 98–103, 1995.
4. T. Vetter and T. Poggio, "Linear objectclasses and image synthesis from a single example image," *IEEE Transactions on Pattern Analysis and Machine Intelligence*, vol. 19, no. 7, pp. 733–742, 1997.
5. D. Beymer and T. Poggio, "Image representation for visual learning," *Science*, vol. 272, pp. 1905–1909, 1996.
6. F. Parke, "A parametric model of human faces," doctoral thesis, University of Utah, Salt Lake City, 1974.
7. T. Akimoto, Y. Suenaga, and R. Wallace, "Automatic creation of 3D facial models," *IEEE Computer Graphics and Applications*, vol. 13, no. 3, pp. 16–22, 1993.
8. J. Barron, D. Fleet, and S. Beauchemin, "Performance of optical flow techniques," *Int. Journal of Computer Vision*, pp. 43–77, 1994.
9. J. Bergen, P. Anandan, K. Hanna, and R. Hingorani, "Hierarchical model-based motion estimation," in *Proceedings of the European Conference on Computer Vision*, (Santa Margherita Ligure, Italy), pp. 237–252, 1992.
10. J. Bergen and R. Hingorani, "Hierarchical motion-based frame rate conversion," technical report, David Sarnoff Research Center Princeton NJ 08540, 1990.
11. P. Burt and E. Adelson, "The Laplacian pyramide as a compact image code," *IEEE Transactions on Communications*, no. 31, pp. 532–540, 1983.
12. B. K. P. Horn and B. G. Schunck, "Determining optical flow," *Artificial Intelligence*, vol. 17, pp. 185–203, 1981.
13. E. Hildreth, *The Measurement of Visual Motion*. Cambridge: MIT Press, 1983.
14. H. H. Nagel, "Displacement vectors derived from second order intensity variations in image sequences.," *Computer Vision, Graphics and Image Processing*, vol. 21, pp. 85–117, 1983.
15. M. Jones and T. Poggio, "Model-based matching by linear combination of prototypes," a.i. memo no., Artificial Intelligence Laboratory, Massachusetts Institute of Technology, 1996.
16. T. Vetter, M. J. Jones, and T. Poggio, "A bootstrapping algorithm for learning linear models of object classes," in *IEEE Conference on Computer Vision and Pattern Recognition – CVPR'97*, (Puerto Rico, USA), IEEE Computer Society Press, 1997.
17. P. Viola, "Alignment by maximization of mutual information," A.I. Memo No. 1548, Artificial Intelligence Laboratory, Massachusetts Institute of Technology, 1995.
18. T. Vetter, "Synthestis of novel views from a single face image," *International Journal of Computer Vision*, no. in press.
19. P. Burt and E. Adelson, "Merging images through pattern decomposition," in *Applications of Digital Image Processing VIII*, no. 575, pp. 173–181, SPIE The International Society for Optical Engeneering, 1985.

A Comparison of Active Shape Model and Scale Decomposition Based Features for Visual Speech Recognition

Iain Matthews, J. Andrew Bangham, Richard Harvey, and Stephen Cox

School of Information Systems, University of East Anglia, Norwich, NR4 7TJ, UK
Email: {iam,ab,rwh,sjc}@sys.uea.ac.uk

Abstract. Two quite different strategies for characterising mouth shapes for visual speech recognition (lipreading) are compared. The first strategy extracts the parameters required to fit an active shape model (ASM) to the outline of the lips. The second uses a feature derived from a one-dimensional multiscale spatial analysis (MSA) of the mouth region using a new processor derived from mathematical morphology and median filtering. With multispeaker trials, using image data only, the accuracy is 45% using MSA and 19% using ASM on a letters database. A digits database is simpler with accuracies of 77% and 77% respectively. These scores are significant since separate work has demonstrated that even quite low recognition accuracies in the vision channel can be combined with the audio system to give improved composite performance [16].

1 Introduction

The emerging field known as speechreading is of importance both as a tough problem on which to test generic vision algorithms and also as a problem of considerable value in its own right. It is known that speech recognition systems fail in those poor signal-to-noise conditions that humans manage successful discourse. Furthermore, it is known that a speech reading system with even quite poor performance can provide useful improvements in recognition accuracy under noisy conditions [16].

There is useful information conveyed about speech in the facial movements of a speaker. Hearing-impaired listeners can learn to use lipreading techniques very successfully and are capable of understanding fluently spoken speech. Even for untrained human listeners, being able to see the face of a speaker is known to significantly improve intelligibility particularly under noisy conditions [17, 39]. Likewise the pose of the head affects intelligibility [33]. There is evidence that visual information is used to compensate for those elements the audio signal that are vulnerable in acoustic noise, for example the cues for place of articulation are usually found above 1kHz, and these are easily lost in noise [40]. In practice, some signals which are easily confused in the audio domain (e.g. 'b' and 'e', 'm' and 'n', etc.) are distinct in the visual domain. The intimate relation between the audio and visual sensory domains in human recognition can be seen with audio-visual illusions [30] where the perceiver "hears" something other than what was said acoustically. These effects have even been observed in infants [24].

Early evidence that vision can help speech recognition by computer was presented by Petajan [35]. Using a single talker and custom hardware to quantify mouth opening together with linear and dynamic time warping, he showed that an audio-visual system was better than either alone. Others mapped power spectra from the images [42], or used optic flow [28] and achieved similar results. At around that time a major improvement in audio speech recognition systems emerged with the development of hidden Markov models (HMM's) [25]. HMM's were first applied to visual speech recognition by Goldschen using an extension of Petajan's mouth blob extraction hardware [18]. HMM's were also used for audio-visual recognition with a vector quantised codebook of images and were shown to enhance accuracy in the presence of audio noise [37].

A number of recognition systems which demonstrate improved audio-visual speech recognition compared to audio alone have been reported. As with all recognition systems, the key lies in a good choice of feature space in which to operate. A major problem in generating visual speech features, common to most pattern recognition problems, is that of too much information. Each frame contains thousands of pixels from which a feature vector of between, perhaps, 10 to 100 elements must be extracted. One may categorise ways of reducing the image data to the feature vector ranging from: what might be called a "low level" approach, where features are obtained by direct analysis of the image, for example simple blob analysis, grey scale statistics, etc. and a "high level" approach, where features are obtained by using prior information, such as a model. In practice there is a continuum [21] between these two extremes, but the distinction helps us to show how our approach fits into that framework. Provided the correct model is used then a high level model based system might be expected to be the more robust.

Current high level models either explicitly or implicitly define shape. They take the form of dynamic contours [10, 23] deformable templates [13, 21] and active shape models [27]. Although there has been considerable success attaching shape models to images of some objects, e.g. [14] and the process looks most attractive, it is not easy to fit them to lips under varying lighting conditions and in real-time. Using blue lipstick chroma-key extraction [1] or small stick-on reflectors [15] makes the process easier but such techniques are useful for research purposes only. As the model tracks the mouth so the parameters required to maintain tracking are used to form the visual feature vector. A particular problem of shape models lies in what exactly to include in the model. There is evidence, for example, that using both the inner and outer lip contours is more effective than just the outer edge [27], but what else should one include? The high level model used in this paper is our implementation of active shape models [14].

Examples of the low level approach include the blob extraction of [35] and the 'eigenlips' approaches of [9, 11] in which the greyscale image is subsampled and the principal components accounting for the variance during articulation form the features. A variant we have tried that is designed to reduce the impact of changing lighting conditions is robust blob extraction via an area sieve [4, 8]. A sieve, Sect. 3.2, is used to extract the dark blob representing the mouth aperture using a method analogous to a band-pass filter [19]. The disadvantage is that blob area measurements take little account of shape.

A measure of shape may be obtained by applying a one-dimensional sieve along each of the vertical lines of the mouth image [19]. The effect is to measure the vertical lengths and positions of all the image features, such as the opening between the lips, lip width, etc. at all positions across the mouth. This represents a coding of the mouth shape, teeth, tongue, etc. In other words it is a mapping of the original image [3, 4] with no information reduction. However, in this new domain it turns out that even an unsophisticated data reduction method, such as finding the distribution of these lengths still preserves useful information. This can readily be seen in real-time by watching the histogram change as the shape of the mouth is changed (the algorithm has been implemented at 30 frames per second on a Silicon Graphics O2 workstation).

The high and low level approaches are fundamentally different. The shape models are attractive because they instantiate a model that corresponds closely to our understanding of what we think might be important in lipreading. However, there can be significant problems fitting the models to moving lips under varying lighting conditions and there is an open question on exactly what the shape model should include. On the other hand the low level approach generates a simpler length histogram that is very fast to compute and for which there is evidence that it can robustly reject noise [8]. However, it is hard to see how to introduce prior information into the low level model. One might expect a combination of both methods to be the best solution [9]. In this paper we try to get some intuition into how the high and low level methods compare.

2 Databases

In the audio-visual speech community there remains the need for a large standard database on which to build statistically sound models and form comparative results. This is being addressed by, for example, BT Labs [12] and AT&T [36].

In the absence of a standard database each research group has collected their own, invariably small, database. Two easily obtained are the *Tulips* database of isolated digits recorded by Javier Movellan at UCSC [32] and our own *AVletters* database of isolated letters [16, 19, 29]. Here we compare both of these.

The AVletters database consists of three repetitions by each of ten talkers, five male (two with moustaches) and five female (none with moustaches), of the letters A–Z, a total of 780 utterances. Recording took place in the campus TV studio under normal studio ceiling lighting conditions. All recording was of the full face and stored on SVHS quality videotape. The output of a studio quality tie-clip microphone was adjusted for each talker through a mixing desk and fed to the video recorder. Talkers were prompted using an autocue that presented each of three repetitions of the alphabet in a non-sequential, non-repeating order. Each talker returns their mouth to the neutral position. No restraint was used but the talkers do not move out of a close-up frame of their mouth.

Each utterance was digitised at quarter frame PAL resolution (376 × 288 at 25fps) using a Macintosh Quadra 600AV in ITU-R BT.601 8-bit headroom greyscale. Audio was simultaneously recorded at 22.05kHz, 16-bit resolution. This database is available on CDROM by contacting the authors. The mouth images were further cropped to 80 × 60 pixels after locating the centre of the mouth in the middle frame of each utterance. Each utterance was hand segmented using the visual data such that each utterance began and ended with the talkers mouth in the neutral position.

The Tulips database contains two repetitions of the digits 1–4 by each of 12 talkers, 9 male and 3 female, a total of 96 utterances. This was recorded using office ceiling lights with an additional incandescent lamp at the side to simulate office working conditions. Talkers were not restrained but could view their mouths and asked not to move out of shot.

The database was digitised at 100 × 75 resolution at 30fps using a Macintosh Quadra 840AV in ITU-R BT.601 8-bit headroom greyscale. Audio was simultaneously recorded at 11kHz, 8-bit resolution. This database is available from http://cogsci.ucsd.edu/~movellan/. Each utterance was hand segmented so that the video and audio channels extended to one frame either side of an interval containing the significant audio energy. If the lips were clearly moving before or after this time up to an additional three extra frames were included.

Table 1 shows the comparison between both databases.

Table 1. Comparison of databases

Database	Task	Talkers	Reps.	Utts.	Frames	Image size	Lighting
AVletters	'A'–'Z'	10	3	780	18,562	80 × 60	ceiling
Tulips	'1'–'4'	12	2	96	934	100 × 75	ceiling & side

3 Methods

3.1 Active Shape Models

Active shape models are the application of point distribution models (PDM's) [14] to locate image objects. A point distribution model is defined from the statistics of a set of labelled points located in a set of training images. Examples of the positions of the points used for the AVletters database and the Tulips database are shown as crosses in Fig. 2. Notice that the AVletters database includes two talkers with moustaches and has less direct lighting so does not emphasise the lip contour as much as the Tulips database. Active shape models have been successfully used in visual speech recognition by [26,27]. The implementation described here follows that of [27].

To form the PDM a mean shape, $\bar{\mathbf{x}}$, is calculated from points hand located in 469 images (AVletters) or 223 images (Tulips) and principal component analysis (PCA) applied to identify the directions of the variations about this shape. It is imperative that points are labelled consistently throughout the training set otherwise modes are formed that represent labelling errors. To minimise our labelling error we spline smooth secondary points to be equidistant between a few reliably locatable primary points. Any valid shape, $\mathbf{x}$, in the sense of the training data, can then be approximated by adding the weighted sum of a reduced subset, t, of these modes to the mean shape,

$$\mathbf{x} = \bar{\mathbf{x}} + \mathbf{Pb} \tag{1}$$

where $\mathbf{P}$ is a matrix containing the first t eigenvectors and $\mathbf{b}$ is a vector of t weights.

The order of the point distribution model is chosen such that 95% of the variance of the models is represented in the first t modes of variation. The first six modes (out of seven) for each of the databases are shown in Fig. 1. The first two modes from AVletters represent the degree of vertical and horizontal mouth opening. These modes are interchanged for the Tulips database. The third mode in both cases alters the 'smile' and the remaining modes account for pose variation and lip shape assymetry. It is gratifying to find the six modes are similar when training independently on two databases.

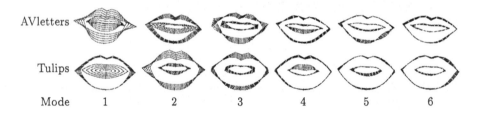

Fig. 1. First six modes of variation at ± 2 standard deviations about the mean for both AVletters and Tulips databases. Note, modes 3–6 are the same for both databases and modes 1 and 2 are interchanged.

To actively fit a PDM to any image we require a cost function that can be evaluated in terms of the model weight parameters $\mathbf{b}$ and a rotation, translation and scaling of resulting points. The standard method for ASM's [14] is to build statistical models of the grey levels along the normal of each model point, Fig. 2. In common with [27] we concatenate all the model normals into a single vector and, in analogy to building a PDM, perform PCA to find the mean $\bar{\mathbf{x}}_g$ and t modes of variation of the this concatenated grey level profile vector. This is a grey-level profile distribution model (GLDM).

$$\mathbf{x}_g = \bar{\mathbf{x}}_g + \mathbf{P}_g \mathbf{b}_g \tag{2}$$

519

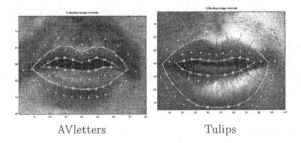

AVletters   Tulips

Fig. 2. Example point models from AVletters and Tulips with grey level profile normals. The speaker in the AVletters example has a moustache and the lighting does not emphasise the lips.

The sum of squares error between the concatenated grey level normals vector and the t modes of the GLDM is,

$$R_g^2 = (x_g - \overline{x}_g)^T (x_g - \overline{x}_g) - b_g^T b_g \qquad (3)$$

To locate modelled features the model is placed at an initial location on an image and 3 is iteratively minimised using the simplex algorithm [34] for translation, rotation, scale and model parameters until convergence. During minimisation shape and grey level profile model parameters are constrained to lie within $\pm 3\sigma$ of the mean. In the majority of utterances the converged models fitted well, in a few cases they fitted poorly and in far fewer the fit was bad. Fig. 3 shows some examples.

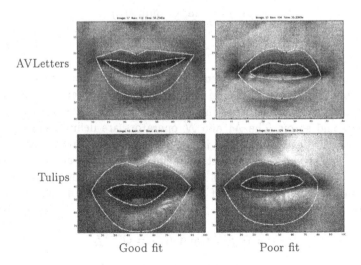

Good fit   Poor fit

Fig. 3. Examples of good and poor ASM fits for AVletters and Tulips.

Observation vectors are formed using the shape model weight parameters b obtained after the ASM has converged for each frame. To speed up the fitting process the model is initialised at its previous position for the next frame. Running on an SGI O2 workstation each simplex iteration takes approximately 0.5ms. This can accurately track video at 15 frames per second or faster given lower termination tolerances.

3.2 Multiscale Spatial Analysis

The low level method we use has its theoretical roots in mathematical morphology and is similar to granulometry. The system used here is related to alternating sequential filters (formed from openings and closings) and multiscale recursive median filters known as *sieves*. Sieves preserve scale-space causality [4–6] and, like certain wavelets, they can transform the signal to another domain, called granularity, and such a transformation is invertible [3]. The granularity domain can be useful for pattern recognition [2]. Another feature of sieves that is important for lip-reading, lies in the observation that sieves preserve edges well by robustly rejecting random and clutter noise [8].

The sieve may be defined in any number of dimensions by defining the image as a set of connected pixels with their connectivity represented as a graph [20], $G = (V, E)$ where the set of vertices, V, are pixel labels and E, the set of edges, represent the adjacencies. Defining $C_r(G)$ as the set of connected subsets of G with r elements allows the definition of $C_r(G, x)$ as those elements of $C_r(G)$ that contain x.

$$C_r(G, x) = \{\xi \in C_r(G) | x \in \xi\} \tag{4}$$

Morphological openings and closings, over a graph, may be defined as

$$\psi_r f(x) = \max_{\xi \in C_r(G,x)} \min_{u \in \xi} f(u) \tag{5}$$

$$\gamma_r f(x) = \min_{\xi \in C_r(G,x)} \max_{u \in \xi} f(u) \tag{6}$$

The effect of an opening of size one, ψ_2, is to remove all *maxima* of area one when working in 2D. In 1D it would remove all maxima of length one. γ_2 would remove *minima* of scale one. Applying ψ_3 to $\psi_2 f(x)$ will now remove all maxima of scale two and so on. The $\mathcal{M}$ and $\mathcal{N}$ operators are defined as $\mathcal{M}^r = \gamma_r \psi_r$ and $\mathcal{N}^r = \psi_r \gamma_r$. Sieves, and filters in their class such as alternating sequential filters with flat structuring elements, depend on repeated application of such operators at increasing scale. This cascade structure is key, since each stage removes maxima and/or minima of a particular scale. The output at scale r is denoted by $f_r(x)$ with

$$f_1 = \mathcal{Q}^1 f = f \text{ and } f_{r+1} = \mathcal{Q}^{r+1} f_r \tag{7}$$

where $\mathcal{Q}$ is one of the γ, ψ, $\mathcal{M}$ or $\mathcal{N}$ operators. Illustrations of sieves and formal proofs of their properties appear elsewhere [4]. The differences between successive stages of a sieve, called *granule functions*, $d_r = f_r - f_{r+1}$, contain non-zero regions, called *granules*, of only that scale.

In one-dimension the graph, (4), becomes an interval

$$C_r(x) = \{[x, x + r - 1] \,|\, x \in \mathbf{Z}\} \qquad (8)$$

where $\mathbf{Z}$ is the set of integers and C_r is the set of intervals in $\mathbf{Z}$ with r elements and the sieves so formed give decompositions by length. It is this that is of importance to lip-reading. The 1D sieve is used to measure the lengths of features seen vertically down the face in the mouth region and these vary as the mouth opens and shuts.

The sieves used in this paper differ in the order in which they process extrema. In 1D the effect of applying an opening of size one, ψ_2, is to remove all maxima of length one, an *o*-sieve. Likewise a γ_2 would remove minima of length one, a *c*-sieve. A 1D alternating sequential filter would remove either maxima and then minima at each, increasing scale, an *N*-sieve, or remove minima and then maxima at each scale an *M*-sieve.

For this lip-reading work, we use a novel variant in which the maxima and minima are removed in a single pass. This is equivalent to applying a recursive median filter at each scale [6]. The sieve so formed is called an *m*-sieve. It inherits the ability to robustly reject noise in the manner of medians and furthermore is much quicker to compute than conventional scale-space preserving schemes.

A granularity is obtained for each image of an utterance, in turn, by applying a one-dimensional sieve along each vertical line in the region of the mouth. A large number granules are obtained and the problem is how to reduce the number of values to manageable proportions. Here, we take the simple step of creating a histogram of granule scales. This is a rough measure of the shape of the mouth. It provides a simple method of substantially reducing the dimensionality from that of the raw image data to the maximum scale used in the sieve. In these examples between 60 and 100 scales are used. The observation vector for the HMM classification is formed by further processing each "scale-histogram".

The simplest form of scale-histogram is obtained by counting the number of granules found at each scale, from 1 to maximum scale and plotting this as a histogram, *sh*. An alternative is to calculate "granule energy" by summing the squared amplitudes, a^2. Other alternatives include summing the raw amplitudes, a and the absolute amplitudes, $|a|$, noting that granules can have negative amplitude. Examples of these are shown in Fig. 4. The number of granules of around scale 8 is associated with the mouth being open.

The changes in scale-histogram can be followed over time in Fig. 5 where the $|a|$ histogram is plotted over time. The scale-histogram is plotted as intensity, white represents a large number of granules. The top row is the smallest scale and the bottom the largest. There is a clear association between each word and the pattern formed by the scale-histogram over time. There is a strong analogy between these patterns and spectrograms formed from an audio signal.

Figure 6 shows another example scale-histogram as it evolves over time. The top panel shows four frames from the image sequence of the utterance "D-G-M", the first is a neutral mouth position and the others taken from the centre of

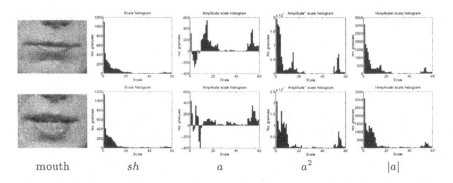

mouth	*sh*	*a*	a^2	$|a|$

Fig. 4. Comparison of scale-histograms for closed, top panel and open, bottom panel, mouths. Abscissa runs from scale 0 to scale 60 and the ordinate shows a function of the number of granules.

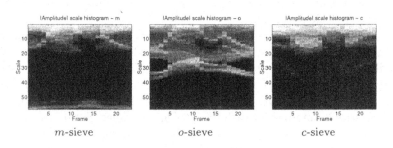

m-sieve	*o*-sieve	*c*-sieve

Fig. 5. The changes in three different $|a|$ histograms over time observed for the utterance *M*. Intensity is a function of absolute amplitude, the abscissa is time and the ordinate scale with small scale granules shown at the top. Left panel, *m*-sieve, middle panel *o*- and right panel *c*-sieve.

each of the utterances. The scale-histogram clearly changes during articulation and remains stationary between utterances. As expected, motion is present just before and after the acoustic utterance which confirms that visual features can be used to provide audio cues. The dimensionality of the scale-histograms is further reduced to 5, 10, 15 or 20 features by principal component analysis.

4   Results

For the AVletters database recognition experiments were performed using the first two utterances from each of the ten talkers as a training set (20 training examples per utterance) and the third utterance from each talker as a test set (10 test examples per utterance). For the Tulips database recognition was performed using the first utterance from each of the twelve talkers as a training set (12 examples per utterance) and the second utterance from each talker as a test set (12 examples per utterance).

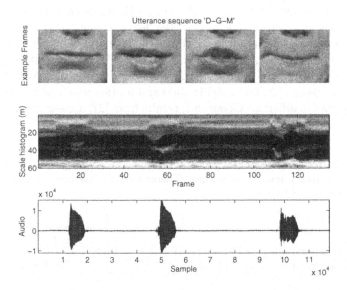

Fig. 6. Showing the temporal relationship between the visual information in a scale-histogram (middle panel) and the audio signal (bottom panel). The utterances were *D-G-M*.

Classification was done using left to right HMM's, each state associated with a one or more Gaussian densities with a diagonal covariance matrix. All HMM's were implemented using the HMM Toolkit HTK V2.1 [41].

4.1 Active Shape Models

Building the PDM is laborious since the model needs to be trained by hand placing example points on images until the PDM has converged. In both ASM cases (Tulips and AVletters) the PDM's have converged, adding new data does not significantly alter any of the modes. In both cases two complete utterances from each talker were used (for Tulips it was '1' and '3', 223 images (9812 points) and for AVletters it was 'A' and 'O', 469 images (20636 points) which represents a significant amount of manual input). The grey level distribution models always have a great many modes; for example, about 15 account for 95% of the variance for an individual and 48 modes for a whole-database model on AVletters. This suggests that whole database GLDM's are too general for accurate tracking. In our recognition system, separate GLDM's are used for each speaker to improve the chances of tracking reliably (not practical in a real situation). Equivalent data for the Tulips database is 12 modes for a greyscale model of a single person and 44 modes for all speakers.

Having fitted ASM's to all images we use the shape model weight vector as the observation vector for a HMM. Table 2 shows the recognition accuracy obtained using various HMM model parameters. The best recognition on the Tulips database was obtained using a 9 state HMM with a single Gaussian mode.

This result differs slightly from that shown in [27]. However, here we have used multi-talker training and testing and not the 'leave-one-out' or jacknife method. It should be emphasised that although the methods are the same we have used an our own MATLAB implementation of ASM's and we have reduced the grey level profile lengths to 10 points in order to decrease convergence time. Also, although the number of points in the model is comparable, the actual positions defined during training are different. Given this, results from [27] appear consistent with those shown here.

Table 2. ASM recognition accuracies, %, for Tulips and AVletters with variations in the HMM parameters: no. states and no. Gaussian modes per state. Dashes indicate that models could not be trained

States	3			5			7			9		
Modes	1	3	5	1	3	5	1	3	5	1	3	5
AVletters	10.8	15.0	13.5	15.8	17.7	14.2	17.3	**18.8**	17.3	17.7	-	-
Tulips	56.2	56.2	47.9	58.3	56.2	-	75.0	-	-	**76.7**	-	-

4.2 Multiscale Spatial Analysis

There is little collective experience of how one might use either granulometry or granularity to characterise a gesture sequence such as the mouth movements during speaking, nor is there any readily accessible analysis to steer by. We therefore find some ground rules by exploring *all* combinations of the following variables:

1. Figure 5 shows that the type of MSA could affect the result. Test: m-sieve, o-sieve, c-sieve;
2. It is observed that the DC (baseline) component of the raw image affects the result obtained using MSA. Test: preserve DC, ignore DC;
3. In acoustic speech recognition features are typically evaluated faster than video frame rate. Others have found that using temporally interpolated visual features can improve performance. Test: interpolated, non-interpolated;
4. Test: the number of principal components;
5. PCA can be calculated in a square or non-square pattern space. Test: using covariance and correlation matrices;
6. Test: the number of states in the HMM;
7. Test: the number of Gaussian modes per state.

We form features using principle component analysis (PCA) so all that needs to be determined are the eigenvectors of the covariance or correlation matrix. Exploring all the above variables was a lengthy computational task, however, the results show several trends that allow us to dispense with a number of the options and present the interesting results. For example the experiments show that it is generally better to ignore the DC component when using MSA and to use the covariance matrix when calculating the PCA.

It would be expected that most of the information would be associated with the boundary of the dark interior of the mouth. This is most effectively distinguished by a closing granulometry, and very badly characterised by an opening granulometry. We therefore concentrate on results from the c and m-sieve, which is bipolar and more robust [8].

The remaining results are summarised in Fig. 7. Using nine states and three Gaussian modes per state are preferred. There also seems to be a slight advantage in using interpolated data. The best results are obtained using the $|a|$ histograms from a c-sieve, followed closely by the m-sieve. The best results, 44.6% and 40.8%, are obtained with interpolated $|a|$ histograms for c and m-sieves respectively.

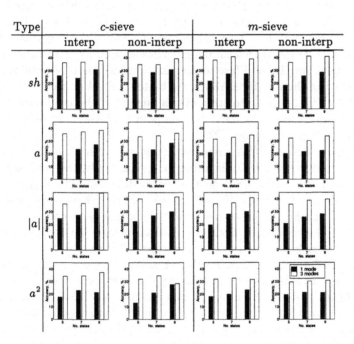

Fig. 7. Left c-sieve. Right m-sieve. Shows how varying the HMM parameters: number of states (abscissa) and Gaussian modes (white columns, 3, black, 1) effects recognition accuracy (ordinate) for interpolated and non-interpolated AVletters data.

The trends in the results shown for the AVletters database are reflected in the results obtained with the Tulips database. Table 3 shows a direct comparison of results obtained using the best MSA options ($|a|$ histogram using a c-sieve, ignoring DC, PCA with covariance matrix).

The MSA Tulips result, 77% correct is identical to that obtained using ASM's. However, for the larger and more complex AVletters database the MSA result, 45%, is much higher than the ASM result, 19%.

Table 3. MSA recognition accuracies, %, for Tulips and AVletters with variations in the HMM parameters: no. states and no. Gaussian modes per state. Top panel shows results for 10 PCA coefficients, bottom panel for 20 PCA coefficients.

States	5		7		9	
Modes	1	3	1	3	1	3
AVletters 10	16.5	30.8	25.4	37.7	30.0	37.3
AVletters 20	24.6	36.1	27.3	36.5	32.7	**44.6**
Tulips 10	66.7	54.2	**77.1**	58.3	75.0	72.9
Tulips 20	62.5	52.1	66.7	58.3	64.6	68.7

5 Conclusion

The results presented here compare two different methods for visual speech recognition. The results suggest that multiscale spatial analysis (MSA) scales better to a larger task than active shape models (ASM's). This might be due to the ASM incorporating inaccurate prejudice as well as good priors or that the lip contour is simply to diffuse to accurately track. Another problem is that as a proportion of the database ASM's are better trained on the smaller Tulips database. It is impracticable to train over a quarter of the (still unrealistically small) AVletters database by hand placing points. Methods to help automate this process are being developed [22].

Results show that the MSA based method is more robust, quicker and more accurate. With multispeaker trials, using image data only, the accuracy is 45% using MSA and 19% using ASM on the letters database. The digits database is simpler with accuracies of 77% and 77% respectively. This is the first time a mathematical morphology based low level method has been compared directly with a high level model based method for the same task. The results show that a low level approach can be very effective, especially when scaling to the more complex letters database. It also has the advantage that it can run in real-time using existing hardware, without consuming all system resources.

A significant omission from the MSA system is a method for normalising the scale. This might be solved when an automatic head tracker is included in the system, such an approach has been implemented elsewhere [9,31]. This suggests significant improvement might be obtained by combining the two methods presented here.

References

1. A. Adjoudani and C. Benoît. *On the Integration of Auditory and Visual Parameters in an HMM-based ASR*, pages 461–471. In Stork and Hennecke [38], 1996.
2. J. A. Bangham, T. G. Campbell, and R. V. Aldridge. Multiscale median and morphological filters used for 2d pattern recognition. *Signal Processing*, 38:387–415, 1994.
3. J. A. Bangham, P. Chardaire, C. J. Pye, and P. Ling. Mulitscale nonlinear decomposition: The sieve decomposition theorem. *IEEE Trans. Pattern Analysis and Machine Intelligence*, 18(5):529–539, 1996.

4. J. A. Bangham, R. Harvey, P. Ling, and R. V. Aldridge. Morphological scale-space preserving transforms in many dimensions. *Journal of Electronic Imaging*, 5(3):283–299, July 1996.

5. J. A. Bangham, R. Harvey, P. Ling, and R. V. Aldridge. Nonlinear scale-space from n-dimensional sieves. *Proc. European Conference on Computer Vision*, 1:189–198, 1996.

6. J. A. Bangham, P. Ling, and R. Young. Mulitscale recursive medians, scale-space and transforms with applications to image processing. *IEEE Trans. Image Processing*, 5(6):1043–1048, 1996.

7. C. Benoît and R. Campbell, editors. *Proceedings of the ESCA Workshop on Audio-Visual Speech Processing*, Rhodes, Sept. 1997.

8. A. Bosson, R. Harvey, and J. A. Bangham. Robustness of scale space filters. In *BMVC*, volume 1, pages 11–21, 1997.

9. C. Bregler and S. M. Omohundro. Learning visual models for lipreading. In M. Shah and R. Jain, editors, *Motion-Based Recognition*, volume 9 of *Computational Imaging and Vision*, chapter 13, pages 301–320. Kluwer Academic, 1997.

10. C. Bregler, S. M. Omohundro, and J. Shi. *Towards a Robust Speechreading Dialog System*, pages 409–423. In Stork and Hennecke [38], 1996.

11. N. M. Brooke, M. J. Tomlinson, and R. K. Moore. Automatic speech recognition that includes visual speech cues. *Proc. Institute of Acoustics*, 16(5):15–22, 1994.

12. C. C. Chibelushi, S. Gandon, J. S. D. Mason, F. Deravi, and R. D. Johnston. Desing issues for a digital audio-visual integrated database. In *IEE Colloquium on Integrated Audio-Visual Processing*, number 1996/213, pages 7/1–7/7, Savoy Place, London, Nov. 1996.

13. T. Coianiz, L. Torresani, and B. Caprile. *2D Deformable Models for Visual Speech Analysis*, pages 391–398. In Stork and Hennecke [38], 1996.

14. T. F. Cootes, A. Hill, C. J. Taylor, and J. Haslam. The use of active shape models for locating structures in medical images. *Image and Vision Computing*, 12(6):355–366, 1994.

15. P. Cosi and E. M. Caldognetto. *Lips and Jaw Movements for Vowels and Consonants: Spatio-Temporal Characteristics and Bimodal Recognition Applications*, pages 291–313. In Stork and Hennecke [38], 1996.

16. S. Cox, I. Matthews, and A. Bangham. Combining noise compensation with visual information in speech recognition. In Benoît and Campbell [7], pages 53–56.

17. N. P. Erber. Interaction of audition and vision in the recognition of oral speech stimuli. *Journal of Speech and Hearing Research*, 12:423–425, 1969.

18. A. J. Goldschen. *Continuous Automatic Speech Recognition by Lipreading*. PhD thesis, George Washington University, 1993.

19. R. Harvey, I. Matthews, J. A. Bangham, and S. Cox. Lip reading from scale-space measurements. In *Proc. Computer Vision and Pattern Recognition*, pages 582–587, Puerto Rico, June 1997. IEEE.

20. H. J. A. M. Heijmans, P. Nacken, A. Toet, and L. Vincent. Graph morphology. *Journal of Visual Computing and Image Representation*, 3(1):24–38, March 1992.

21. M. E. Hennecke, D. G. Stork, and K. V. Prasad. *Visionary Speech: Looking Ahead to Practical Speechreading Systems*, pages 331–349. In Stork and Hennecke [38], 1996.

22. A. Hill and C. J. Taylor. Automatic landmark generation for point distribution models. In *Proc. British Machine Vision Conference*, 1994.

23. R. Kaucic, B. Dalton, and A. Blake. Real-time lip tracking for audio-visual speech recognition applications. In *Proc. European Conference on Computer Vision*, volume II, pages 376–387, 1996.

24. P. K. Kuhl and A. N. Meltzoff. The bimodal perception of speech in infancy. *Science*, 218:1138–1141, Dec. 1982.

25. S. E. Levinson, L. R. Rabiner, and M. M. Sondhi. An introduction to the application of the theory of probabilistic functions of a markov process to automatic speech recognition. *The Bell System Technical Journal*, 62(4):1035–1074, Apr. 1983.

26. J. Luettin. Towards speaker independent continuous speechreading. In *Proc. of the European Conference on Speech Communication and Technology*, 1997.

27. J. Luettin. *Visual Speech and Speaker Recognition*. PhD thesis, University of Sheffield, May 1997.

28. K. Mase and A. Pentland. Automatic lipreading by optical-flow analysis. *Systems and Computers in Japan*, 22(6):67–75, 1991.

29. I. Matthews, J. A. Bangham, and S. Cox. Scale based features for audiovisual speech recognition. In *IEE Colloquium on Integrated Audio-Visual Processing*, number 1996/213, pages 8/1–8/7, Savoy Place, London, Nov. 1996.

30. H. McGurk and J. McDonald. Hearing lips and seeing voices. *Nature*, 264:746–748, Dec. 1976.

31. U. Meier, R. Stiefelhagen, and J. Yang. Preprocessing of visual speech under real world conditions. In Benoît and Campbell [7], pages 113–116.

32. J. R. Movellan. Visual speech recognition with stochastic networks. In G. Tesauro, D. Touretzky, and T. Leen, editors, *Advances in Neural Information Processing Systems*, volume 7, 1995.

33. K. K. Neely. Effect of visual factors on the intelligibility of speech. *Journal of the Acoustical Society of America*, 28(6):1275–1277, Nov. 1956.

34. J. A. Nelder and R. Mead. A simplex method for function minimisation. *Computing Journal*, 7(4):308–313, 1965.

35. E. D. Petajan. *Automatic Lipreading to Enhance Speech Recognition*. PhD thesis, University of Illinois, Urbana-Champaign, 1984.

36. G. Potamianos, Cosatto, H. P. Graf, and D. B. Roe. Speaker independent audiovisual database for bimodal ASR. In Benoît and Campbell [7], pages 65–68.

37. P. L. Silsbee. *Computer Lipreading for Improved Accuracy in Automatic Speech Recognition*. PhD thesis, The University of Texas, Austin, Dec. 1993.

38. D. G. Stork and M. E. Hennecke, editors. *Speechreading by Humans and Machines: Models, Systems and Applications*. NATO ASI Series F: Computer and Systems Sciences. Springer-Verlag, Berlin, 1996.

39. W. H. Sumby and I. Pollack. Visual contribution to speech intelligibility in noise. *Journal of the Acoustical Society of America*, 26(2):212–215, Mar. 1954.

40. Q. Summerfield. Some preliminaries to a comprehensive account of audio-visual speech perception. In B. Dodd and R. Campbell, editors, *Hearing by Eye: The Psychology of Lip-reading*, pages 3–51. Lawrence Erlbaum Associates, London, 1987.

41. S. Young, J. Jansen, J. Odell, D. Ollason, and P. Woodland. *The HTK Book*. Cambridge University, 1996.

42. B. P. Yuhas, M. H. Goldstein, Jr., and T. J. Sejnowski. Integration of acoustic and visual speech signals using neural networks. *IEEE Communications Magazine*, 27:65–71, 1989.

Motion Segmentation

Motion Segmentation and Depth Ordering Based on Morphological Segmentation

Lothar Bergen and Fernand Meyer

bergen@cmm.ensmp.fr, meyer@cmm.ensmp.fr,
Centre de Morphologie Mathématique, Ecole des Mines de Paris,
35, rue Saint-Honoré, 77305 Fontainebleau Cedex, France

Abstract. In this paper the motion segmentation and depth ordering problem for monocular image sequences with and without camera motion is addressed. We show how a new multiscale morphological segmentation technique, based on the watershed, can produce a superset of the motion boundaries. Regions with similar motion then have to be merged. The difficulties of motion estimation at object boundaries with occlusion are analyzed and a solution combining segmentation and robust estimation is presented. Region merging is then performed using the obtained motion parameters. We then present a new technique for the depth ordering of the resulting image partition. We show how the modelling error on either side of the motion boundary can be used to indicate the occlusion relationship of the objects. The algorithm is then applied to several synthetic and natural image sequences. The results demonstrate that the technique is robust and that the depth ordering requires only minimal motion to perform correctly. This is due to the fact that, unlike existing techniques for depth ordering, the motion between two frames only has to be analyzed. We then point out possible improvements and indicate how temporal integration of the information can further increase stability.

1 Introduction

The increasing availability of audiovisual material in digital form creates a demand for new functionalities like interactivity, integration of objects of different nature, etc.. The new standard MPEG-4 meets these demands by allowing a scene to be represented as a composition of objects rather than just pixels. It does not specify, however, how the decomposition of a scene into objects is performed.

A first step in the semantic analysis of a scene is the segmentation into objects with coherent motion. A second step then consists in establishing the depth ordering of the resulting image partition: to establish which object moves in front of which.

For the motion segmentation two possible starting points exist.

We can start with a motion field we want to segment: in this case, the field needs to be dense and accurate. Motion estimation unfortunately produces poor results precisely at motion boundaries.

The use of grey level segmentation is the alternative starting point. The hypothesis underlying this approach is that such a segmentation produces a superset of the motion boundaries: the motion boundaries are contained in the segmentation. The problem then consists in merging regions with similar motion, which also proves challenging at object boundaries with occlusion.

The techniques that perform motion segmentation and depth ordering found in literature rely exclusively on motion information: some approaches try to detect motion boundaries directly in sparse motion fields calculated through token matching [6, 7]. A more recent technique is based on a decomposition of the scene into layers with coherent motion. The evolution of these layers in time is then used to extract information concerning depth ordering [2].

In this paper, we address the motion segmentation and depth ordering problem for monocular image sequences with and without camera motion. We use a morphological grey level segmentation as our starting point. We then show how robust parameter estimation techniques improve motion estimation at motion boundaries and how this permits regions with similar motion to be merged. A new technique for the depth ordering of the resulting image partition is then presented.

Figure 1 shows a schematic overview of our algorithm which also corresponds to the structure of this article.

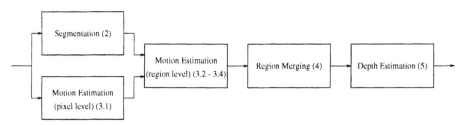

Fig. 1. The steps of the motion segmentation and depth ordering

2 Segmentation

Segmentation generally produces a superset of the motion boundaries: the motion boundaries are included in the grey level segmentation. This is due to the fact that the surface properties or the illumination of the objects in the scene often differ.

Figure 2 shows, as an example, image no. 50 from the "Foreman" sequence in QCIF format. Next to the original we see the morphological gradient, the difference between the dilated and eroded image, which indicates discontinuities in the luminance (shown with $\gamma = 5$ for better visualization).

We can confirm that the motion boundary (the contour of the upper body) corresponds to areas with high gradient almost everywhere.

The segmentation we have used for this work is a multiscale morphological segmentation technique, based on volumic closings of the gradient image and the watershed transform [1]. The result is a series of mosaic images with increasing

 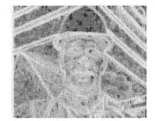

Original   Morphological Gradient ($\gamma = 5$)

Fig. 2. "Foreman"

resolution verifying the following property: each contour present in a given mosaic is also present in all finer mosaics. Figure 3 shows such a series of mosaics for the above example.

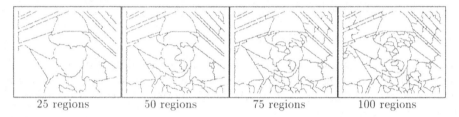

25 regions   50 regions   75 regions   100 regions

Fig. 3. Hierarchy of segmentations

This segmentation is extremely fast, since all resolution levels are constructed simultaneously in the same run. Hence, it is easy to choose the best starting point for studying the motion.

Two basic strategies are possible: we can choose a segmentation with a resolution high enough to obtain a superset of the motion boundaries, in which case regions have to be successively merge based on their motion.

Another strategy, which will not be presented in this article, consists in choosing a segmentation with an intermediate resolution and to split regions if the robust motion estimation indicates that it contains more than a single type of motion. The segmentation also allows for this kind of strategy: the resolution can simply be increased within the region concerned. This allows a closed loop between segmentation and motion estimation to be established.

3 Motion Estimation

The motion information available for an individual pixel is incomplete due to the aperture problem: only the motion component normal to iso-brightness contours can be measured. Therefore, the measurements of several pixels have to be combined to obtain a complete motion vector. The regions of our segmentation provide us with an ideal support for this combination because they generally correspond to a single object in the scene.

We will first present the technique used to measure the normal motion of each pixel and then introduce the model that is used to integrate the partial motion information inside each region.

3.1 Pixel Level

We use a differential technique (without regularization) to estimate the normal motion at pixel level [4]. This yields higher precision for fine motion than standard correlation techniques and is computationally very simple.

Two images have to be prefiltered to prepare for differentiation and to increase the signal-to-noise ratio. We use a cube shaped spatio-temporal gaussian filter with a side length of 7 pixels / frames (i.e. the filtered value is calculated from the values of its neighbours in a cube, which extends 3 frames in time and 3 pixels in x and y to either side).

If we now assume that the intensity is conserved, $dI(x, t)/dt = 0$, the gradient constraint equation can be derived:

$$(\nabla I(x,t))^T v + I_t(x,t) = 0 \ , \tag{1}$$

where $\nabla I(x, t)$ is the gradient and I_t the partial temporal derivative of the intensity. This equation gives us the motion component normal to spatial contours with constant intensity: $v_n = v_n n$, where the normal velocity and the normal direction are given by:

$$v_n(x,t) = \frac{-I_t(x,t)}{\|\nabla I(x,t)\|} \quad \text{and} \quad n(x,t) = \frac{\nabla I(x,t)}{\|\nabla I(x,t)\|} \ . \tag{2}$$

3.2 Region Level

In order to integrate the partial motion information of the individual pixels at region level we use a parametric model. We have decided to employ a nodal representation. A fixed number of nodes $\{x_i\}$ is chosen depending on the motion type and complexity.

The modelling then consists in computing a "model velocity" $\phi(x_i)$ at each node x_i, such that the interpolated velocity field based on the nodal velocities is as close as possible to the observed velocity field within the region [3].

Being velocities, the parameters of the model have a small range of variation, of the same magnitude as the motion in the sequence, which contributes to the robustness of the computations.

The interpolation technique we use is a linear technique called kriging. The velocity of each point of the region is then a linear function of the velocities at the fixed nodes:

$$v(x, \{\phi(x_i)\}) = \sum_i \lambda_i(x)\phi(x_i) \ . \tag{3}$$

In this equation the $\phi(x_i)$ represent the node velocities that have to be determined, the $\lambda_i(x)$ are the corresponding weights for the interpolation given by kriging.

Using kriging as interpolation method has two important advantages. On the one hand, it is very flexible: it is possible to model the structure of the motion field by choosing an appropriate covariance model. In our case, we have chosen a covariance model yielding a spline interpolation. On the other hand, the weights only depend on the geometry, i.e. the position of the pixel and the position of the nodes to be interpolated. This allows the interpolation weights $\lambda_i(x)$ to be tabulated once and for all.

The number and the placement of the nodes determines the motion complexity that can be represented: a single node corresponds to a simple translation, three nodes with a non collinear placement yield an affine model, more than three nodes produce models with increasing complexity.

The number of motion measurements, which depends on the region's size, limits the number of model parameters that can be estimated reliably. For the integration of the motion information in each region we use models with up to four nodes (which corresponds to a maximum of eight parameters to be estimated). Figure 4 shows the chosen node placements for 3 and 4 node models.

Fig. 4. Node placement

To estimate the motion parameters of a region R we replace v in the gradient constraint (1) with our model $v(x, \{\phi(x_i)\})$ so that the measurement in each point of R yields a constraint on the motion parameters $\phi(x_i)$:

$$(\nabla I(x,t))^T v(x, \{\phi(x_i)\}) + I_t(x,t) = 0 \ . \tag{4}$$

The over-determined set of linear equations now has to be solved. The standard least-square approach consists in minimizing the following sum:

$$\sum_R ((\nabla I(x,t))^T v(x, \{\phi(x_i)\}) + I_t(x,t))^2 \ , \tag{5}$$

which with (2) can also be written:

$$\sum_R \|\nabla I(x,t)\|^2 (nv(x, \{\phi(x_i)\}) - v_n)^2 \ , \tag{6}$$

where v_n is the normal velocity and n the normal direction.

The second expression can be interpreted as a weighted over-determined set of equations. In each point of the region the equation

$$nv(x, \{\phi(x_i)\}) - v_n = 0 \tag{7}$$

gives the normal velocity $v_n = v_n n$. Each of these equations is weighted with $\|\nabla I(x, t)\|^2$. The weight controls the influence of each measurement in the parameter estimation.

In general it makes sense to give higher weight to measurements from areas with high gradient: noise is less likely to corrupt those measurements (i.e. they have a higher signal-to-noise ratio).

This, however, does not hold true at motion boundaries, as will be shown in the following section.

3.3 Motion Estimation at Object Boundaries with Occlusion

We have seen that the aperture problem restricts local motion measurement to only the normal component. But even to estimate this normal component, estimation techniques have to take into account a small neighbourhood. Correlation techniques, for example, require a minimum window size, differential techniques combine information through prefiltering.

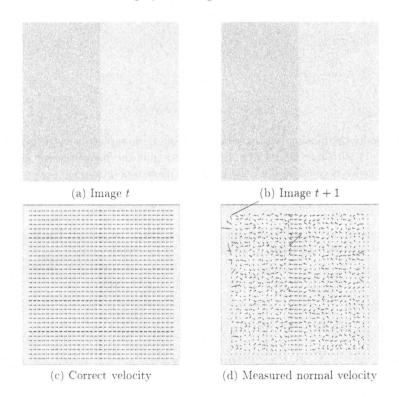

(a) Image t (b) Image $t + 1$

(c) Correct velocity   (d) Measured normal velocity

Fig. 5. Occlusion

The effect that this has on motion estimation around object boundaries will be shown in an example. Figure 5 shows a synthetic sequence (size: 100 × 100) with occlusion: two surfaces move towards each other with the surface on the right occluding the surface on the left. The two surfaces have random texture with grey values drawn uniformly from the intervals $[200, 210]$ and $[220, 230]$. Their velocities are $(1, 0)$ and $(-1, 0)$ as shown in Fig. 5(c) (the velocity field is subsampled by a factor 3 and scaled by a factor 2). In order to compare the measured normal velocity with the known correct velocity, we evaluate the following error:

$$\text{error} = |nv_c - v_n| , \tag{8}$$

where v_c represents the known correct velocity. This is simply the difference between the measured normal velocity v_n and the projection of the correct velocity v_c onto the normal direction.

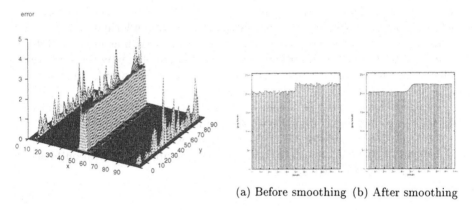

(a) Before smoothing (b) After smoothing

Fig. 6. Error at occlusion   **Fig. 7.** Image profile at $y = 50$

Figure 6 shows the situation around the motion boundary at $x = 50$: the error is negligible on the side of the occluding region but significant on the side of the occluded region. The error on the side of the occluded object is about 2 in a narrow band next to the contour: this indicates that the motion measured corresponds to the occluding object. This error is due to the small neighbourhood that contributes to the motion information in each pixel. Figure 7 shows how filtering affects the motion measurement: the discontinuity is smoothed and spread into the occluded region. The motion measured in this area therefore corresponds to the occluding object.

The width of the area with erroneous measurements depends on the size of the neighbourhood that contributes to the motion measurement and the relative motion of the two regions. We can observe this kind of error even if the grey level difference between the regions is very small as long as the relative motion of the regions has a non-zero component in the direction normal to the motion boundary.

The motion parameters for a simple translation estimated through minimizing (6) are $\{(-0.942, 0.004), (-0.994, 0.003)\}$. As expected, the parameters calculated for the occluded region do not reflect the correct motion (for this example they are even almost identical with the occluding region). The main reason for the bad performance is that a certain number of measurements contributing to the motion estimation are erroneous. The problem is then aggravated by the weighting with the square gradient: the erroneous measurements receive higher weight since they come from an area with high gradient. The parameters we obtain without the weighting are $\{(0.413, 0.012), (-1.002, 0.002)\}$.

In the next section we show how robust estimation techniques can help to overcome this problem.

3.4 Robust Regression

In the previous section we saw that the parameter estimation has to be able to cope with erroneous motion measurements in order to perform correctly at motion boundaries. Those motion boundaries are not the only source for erroneous measurements, all kinds of noise can corrupt the motion information.

In statistics all these erroneous measurements are known as *outliers*. Robust estimation techniques allow outliers to be detected and eliminate (or limit) their influence on the estimation: they yield the parameters that best fit the majority of the measurements [5, 8].

We have concentrated on a class of techniques called *M-estimators* that can be easily implemented as iterative reweighted least-square estimation.

First we simplify our notation. Then we show why the least-square approach we used above lacks in robustness and how M-estimators cope with outliers.

In the following we will refer to

$$|\boldsymbol{nv}(\boldsymbol{x}, \{\phi(\boldsymbol{x}_i)\}) - v_{\mathrm{n}}| \tag{9}$$

as the absolute residuals which will be noted as $r(\boldsymbol{x})$ or simply as r.

Instead of noting the motion parameters as vectors (the node velocities $\phi(\boldsymbol{x}_i)$) we replace them by a set of scalar parameters p_j with $j = 1, \ldots, m$, where m is twice the node number.

If we now abandon the gradient weighting, for the reasons shown above, (6) can now be written as

$$\min \sum_R r^2(\boldsymbol{x}) \ . \tag{10}$$

We see that each residual contributes with its square to the sum we have to minimize. This explains why even a single erroneous measurement with a large error can wreak havoc on the estimation: due to the squaring of the residuals the influence on the sum is so big that the parameters get pulled away from the correct solution during minimization.

M-estimator minimize the following sum:

$$\min \sum_R \rho(r/\hat{\sigma}) \ . \tag{11}$$

In this equation ρ is the function that replaces the square and $\hat{\sigma}$ is a robust estimate for the standard deviation of the residuals which serves as a scale parameter. The robust estimate $\hat{\sigma}$ is given by

$$\hat{\sigma} = 1.4826[1 + 5/(n - m)] \text{ median}(r) , \qquad (12)$$

where m is the number of parameters to be estimated and n the number of measurements in the region.

In order to be able to cope with outliers, the function ρ has to be less increasing than square. The literature proposes a multitude of functions from which we have retained the functions *Fair* and *Geman-McClure* whose formulas are given in Table 1 and which are depicted in Fig. 8.

type	$\rho(x)$	$\psi(x)$	$w(x)$
L_2	$\frac{x^2}{2}$	x	1
Fair	$c^2\left[\frac{|x|}{c} - \log(1 + \frac{|x|}{c})\right]$	$\frac{x}{1+|x|/c}$	$\frac{1}{1+|x|/c}$
Geman-McClure	$\frac{x^2/2}{1+x^2}$	$\frac{x}{(1+x^2)^2}$	$\frac{1}{(1+x^2)^2}$

Table 1. Least-square and used M-Estimators

FAIR

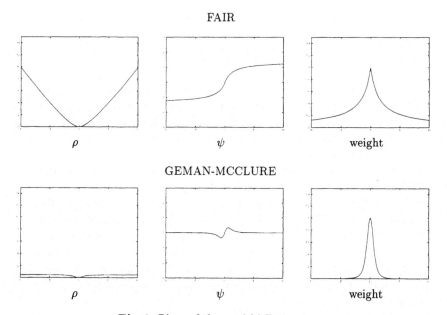

GEMAN-MCCLURE

Fig. 8. Plots of the used M-Estimators

We will now show how the minimization of (11) can be solved as an iterated reweighted least-square problem.

The minimization of (11) is equivalent to the solution of the following linear system:

$$\sum_R \psi(r/\hat{\sigma})\frac{\partial r}{\partial p_j} = 0, \; j = 1,\dots,m \; , \tag{13}$$

where $\psi = d\rho(x)/dx$ is called the *influence function*. If we then define a *weight function*

$$\omega(x) = \frac{\psi(x)}{x} \; , \tag{14}$$

(13) can be written as

$$\sum_R \omega(r/\hat{\sigma})r\frac{\partial r}{\partial p_j} = 0, \; j = 1,\dots,m \; . \tag{15}$$

The previous equation is now equivalent to the following weighted least-square problem

$$\min \sum_R \omega(r/\hat{\sigma})r^2 \; , \tag{16}$$

where $\omega(r/\hat{\sigma})$ represents the weight for each of the residuals.

Figure 9 illustrates the iterative nature of the solution.

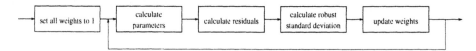

Fig. 9. Robust regression scheme

Without any prior knowledge about the reliability of the individual measurements or the model parameters, we start by setting all the weights to 1. We then calculate the parameters p_j and the corresponding residuals. The robust estimate for the standard deviation is evaluated and serves to scale the residuals for the weight computation.

In Fig. 8 we can see that large residuals are assigned low weights for the next iteration and therefore their influence is reduced.

The main difference between the two functions ρ we use is that the Geman-McClure function can completely exclude residuals from the modelling by assigning zero weights, whereas the Fair function always yields non-zero weights. The Geman-McClure function is more severe but does not always guarantee good convergence: we therefore use the Fair function at the beginning of the iteration.

The iteration stops when $\hat{\sigma}$ no longer decreases or when a fixed number of iteration is reached.

If we apply the robust approach to our occlusion problem we, in fact, obtain the correct motion parameters $\{(1,0),(-1,0)\}$.

Let us now look at a more challenging problem with multiple occlusions and added random noise.

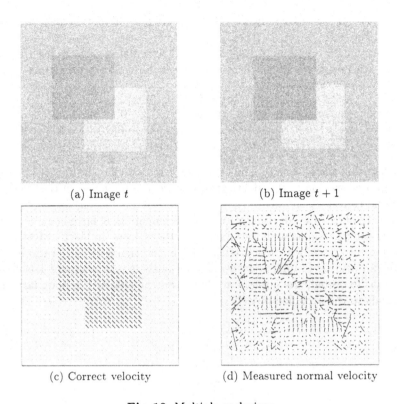

(a) Image t (b) Image $t + 1$

(c) Correct velocity (d) Measured normal velocity

Fig. 10. Multiple occlusions

Figure 10 (a) and (b) show two diagonally translating squares in front of a stationary background. Their velocities are $(1, -1)$ for square 1 (top left) and $(-1, 1)$ square 2 (bottom right) as shown in (c). As for the previous synthetic example, the different textures are obtained by drawing grey values uniformly from the intervals $[180, 190]$, $[200, 210]$ and $[220, 230]$. To all the pixels of the resulting sequence Gaussian noise with $\sigma = 5$ is added independently (Fig. 11 shows the histogram before and after the addition of the noise).

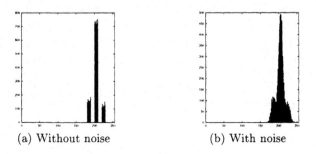

(a) Without noise (b) With noise

Fig. 11. Histograms

This noise introduces significant error into the normal motion measurements (c.f. Fig. 10 (d)).

The following table compares the translation calculated with the least-square (with and without gradient weighting) and the robust parameter estimation:

	Background	Square 1	Square 2
Least-square (weighted)	$(0.032, -0.062)$	$(0.273, -0.266)$	$(-0.037, 0.035)$
Least-square	$(-0.016, -0.071)$	$(0.548, -0.670)$	$(-0.369, 0.296)$
Robust	$(0.032, -0.070)$	$(0.993, -0.999)$	$(-0.940, 0.960)$

The fact that the background motion is well estimated in all three cases is due to the opposed motion of the identical squares whose influence on the occluded background cancels itself out.

Figure 12 shows the location of the measurements that have been classified as outliers (in grey) along with the contours of the objects (in black). Most of the outliers fall into areas with low gradient where the signal-to-noise ratio is very low. We can also see a high concentration of outliers where square 1 occludes square 2: as expected, the outliers are found on the side of the boundary that corresponds to the occluded object.

Fig. 12. Outliers

4   Region Merging

Now that we are able to calculate the correct motion parameters for the regions of the segmentation, we can group the regions that have similar motion. This will be done as an iterative region merging: at each iteration, all pairs of adjacent regions are candidates for merging. Instead of trying to compare the motion in the parameter space, we calculate a new set of motion parameters for each of the region pairs and evaluate the resulting modelling quality. Quality measures based on the motion compensated images (i.e. PSNR) have been tested but have proven inconsistent and time consuming. We use the mean modelling error of the motion instead:

$$\text{error}(R, \boldsymbol{p}) = \frac{1}{\text{size}(R)} \sum_{R} \omega(\boldsymbol{x})(\boldsymbol{n}\boldsymbol{v}(\boldsymbol{p}) - v_n)^2 \ , \tag{17}$$

where $\omega(\boldsymbol{x})$ are the weights we have calculated through robust regression and $\boldsymbol{p}$ our m motion parameters.

The merging criterion can then be based on the individual errors before the merging $\{\text{error}(R_1, \boldsymbol{p}_1), \text{error}(R_2, \boldsymbol{p}_2)\}$ and the modelling errors when the joint model parameters have been used $\{\text{error}(R_1, \boldsymbol{p}_{12}), \text{error}(R_2, \boldsymbol{p}_{12})\}$.

If two regions have similar motion, the jointly calculated motion parameters yield small errors $\{\text{error}(R_1, \boldsymbol{p}_{12}), \text{error}(R_2, \boldsymbol{p}_{12})\}$ when applied to the individual regions: we therefore consider the motion of two regions as similar if the following criterion

$$C = \max\{\text{error}(R_1, \boldsymbol{p}_{12}), \text{error}(R_2, \boldsymbol{p}_{12})\} \tag{18}$$

is small.

The different steps of the merging procedure with an exhaustive evaluation of the similarity criterion C for all region couples are the following:

1. Evaluation of the similarity criterion C for all couples of adjacent regions,
2. merging of the couple with the most similar motion (smallest C),
3. updating of the criteria for all the region pairs involved in the merging (i.e. all the region couples that contained one of the two merged regions),
4. iteration from point 2.

This exhaustive approach at first seems very costly. However this is not the case: the joint modelling of two regions requires only the solution of one over-determined linear system in the least-square sense (since we keep the weights already established through robust estimation) for which efficient numerical tools exist. In particular, we may reuse parts of the calculus for the individual motion parameters to calculate the joint parameters.

The merging will be stopped when a predefined error threshold is exceeded or when the criterion rises abruptly. The functioning of the merging will be shown along with the results of the depth ordering we shall introduce in the next section.

5 Depth Ordering

As seen in Sect. 3.3, occlusion causes significant error on the side of the occluded object. This error makes it possible to deduce the depth ordering of the involved objects.

As mentioned before, measurements at locations with high gradient are less sensitive to noise and thus yield more reliable values. We therefore have to distinguish two main classes of outliers: regions with low gradient which are likely to be corrupted by noise and regions with high gradient which generally correspond to occluded objects (or if the segmentation is not fine enough they might also indicate multiple types of motion in a region).

Figure 12, which we have already seen, shows both types: spread unevenly across the image we find outliers that correspond to the first class; at the motion boundary between the two squares the outliers are due to occlusion.

A simple and elegant way to separate the two types of outliers is to make use of the gradient information: we weight the absolute residuals $r(\boldsymbol{x})$ obtained through robust estimation with the modulus of the gradient

$$r_{\text{weighted}}(\boldsymbol{x}) = |\nabla I(\boldsymbol{x},t)| r(\boldsymbol{x}) \ , \tag{19}$$

and reestimate $\hat{\sigma}$. We then recalculate the weights $\omega(r/\hat{\sigma})$ with the chosen weight function. The measurements which are now classified as outliers (i.e. have zero weight) correspond to true modelling errors: the occluded regions.

The location of the measurements that are classified as outliers in this way are shown in Fig. 13.

In order to quantify this information we compute the spatial outlier density in a narrow band on either side of the motion frontier. The width of the band depends linearly on the relative motion of the two regions normal to the contour and on the size of the prefilter used. For our test we have used a width of three pixels.

Figure 14(a) shows these bands for the occluding square example.

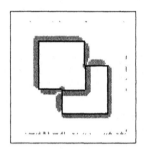
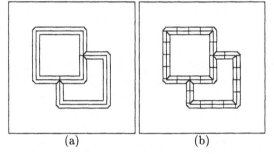

(a)   (b)

Fig. 13. Outliers (weighted)   **Fig. 14.** Bands used in the depth evaluation

We now have to establish an ordering based on these two densities. If we define two thresholds t_{low} and t_{high} we can distinguish between situations with and without a clear depth ordering. A clear ordering exists when one density is below t_{low} and the other above t_{high}. In all other cases, we cannot make any statement about the ordering. The low threshold allows for a certain number of false outliers and the high threshold indicates the minimum number of outliers for a region to be considered occluded.

In this initial form, the approach only works for simple cases. Let us consider the situation where a narrow rectangle translates in the direction of its longer sides in front of a stationary background. Error due to occlusion can only be observed at the short sides: the outlier density in the background therefore will be very small and normally does not exceed t_{high}. This is why we partition the bands into short strips (c.f. Fig. 14(b)) and use a kind of "voting" mechanism: only the pairs of strips with a clear ordering contribute to the depth detection. With this approach, a correct depth ordering becomes possible for the previous example and for most natural scenes.

In our examples, we have used a length of 20 pixels for the partitioning of the bands and we set the threshold to $t_{\text{low}} = 0.2$ and $t_{\text{high}} = 0.8$.

This relative ordering is represented in the form of a directed graph: nodes correspond to the regions and the edges indicate relative depth. We can now perform (if there are no cycles) a topological sort on the graph: as a result, we obtain an image in which low grey values correspond to objects close to the observer and high grey values to more distant ones.

Figure 15 shows the different depths for the translating square sequence (with white indicating the most distant object).

Fig. 15. Depth

Let us now see how the algorithm performs on natural scenes. The results for the image sequences "Foreman" and "Claire" are show in Fig. 16 and 17 (the velocity fields are subsampled by a factor 5 and scaled by a factor 4). The image size, the number of the frame treated in the sequence and the number of regions used in the segmentation are given in the following table:

name	size	frame no.	region no.
"Foreman"	QCIF (176 × 144)	50	75
"Claire"	QCIF (176 × 144)	15	20

For these examples a model with three nodes which is capable of representing affine motion has been used.

The normal velocity for "Foreman" in Fig. 16(b) shows two different types of motion: the upper body moves to the left and the background moves up to the right (due to the camera motion down to the left). As we have already seen, the segmentation with 75 regions contains the major motion boundaries. We can also see that the region merging is then correctly performed. Note however that there is a small region on the right that has merged with the person's shoulder although it belongs to the background. This is due the fact that the region is relatively narrow: the majority of its motion measurements yield the motion of the occluding object, in which case the robust estimation produces the foreground motion. This problem can easily be resolved by imposing a minimum region size or a morphological constraint on the segmentation's regions. The depth ordering then yields the correct depths: the person shown in grey is situated in front of the background in white.

The motion in the sequence "Claire" (Fig. 17(b)) is quite small. We can see that the head moves downwards and that the upper body and the background are practically still. Also note that some of the motion measurements in the background (mostly at the top and on the right), due to some form of interference, indicate large motion. Due to the relative simplicity of the grey-level image, a region number of 20 is sufficient for the segmentation. The correct result of the merging shows that the robust technique has coped well with the

546

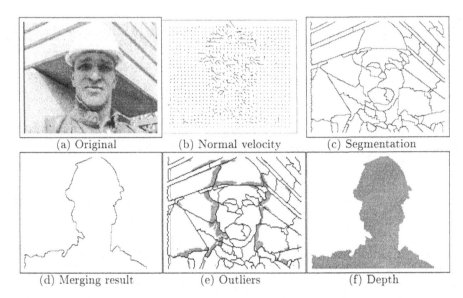

(a) Original   (b) Normal velocity   (c) Segmentation

(d) Merging result   (e) Outliers   (f) Depth

Fig. 16. "Foreman"

erroneous measurements in the background. The calculated depth correctly reflects the structure of the scene, which demonstrates that the depth ordering also performs well for small motion.

6 Conclusion

We have shown how morphological segmentation, combined with robust parameter estimation techniques, can be used to segment the motion of a scene with multiple occluding objects. We have then presented a new technique that performs depth ordering of the resulting image partition: the modelling error at the motion boundaries is used to indicate the occlusion relationship.

The main advantage of this approach lies in the fact that the motion has to be analyzed between only two frames to perform the depth ordering, unlike existing techniques [2, 6, 7] which require three frames.

This becomes possible through the combination of the morphological segmentation, which provides precise contour placement, and the robust estimation, which indicates modelling errors due to occlusion.

The effect that this has on performance is twofold. It allows to deduce depth ordering even if the motion is very small and it provides high robustness.

The use of a closed loop containing segmentation and motion estimation, as mentioned above, is a step towards more flexibility. A step towards more stability then consists of the integration of motion and depth information across several image frames. The information at time t can be used to initialize segmentation, robust motion estimation and depth ordering at time $t + 1$. All this information can then be accumulated over multiple frames which will allow a scene to be segmented correctly into objects even if, temporarily, no motion is present.

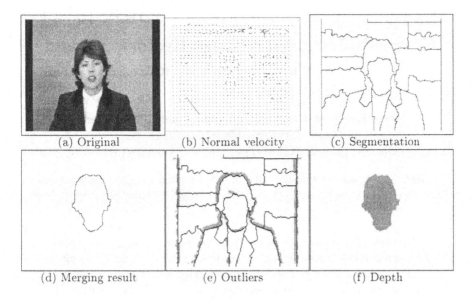

| (a) Original | (b) Normal velocity | (c) Segmentation |
| (d) Merging result | (e) Outliers | (f) Depth |

Fig. 17. "Claire"

Acknowledgments

This work has been financed by CNET France Telecom.

References

1. J. Cichosz and F. Meyer. Morphological multiscale image segmentation. In *Workshop on Image Analysis for Multimedia Interactive Services (WIAMIS'97)*, pages 161–166, Louvain-la-Neuve (Belgium), June 1997.
2. Trevor Darrell and David Fleet. Second-order method for occlusion relationships in motion layers. Technical Report 314, MIT Media Lab Vismod, 1995.
3. E. Decencière Ferrandière, C. de Fouquet, and F. Meyer. Applications of kriging to image sequence coding. *Accepted for publication in Signal Processing: Image Communication*, 1997.
4. B. K. P Horn and B. G. Schunck. Determining optical flow. *Artificial Intelligence*, 17:185–203, 1981.
5. Peter Meer, Doron Mintz, Dong Yoon Kim, and Azriel Rosenfeld. Robust regression methods for computer vision: A review. *International Journal of Computer Vision*, 6(1):59–70, April 1991.
6. K. M. Mutch and W. B. Thompson. Analysis of accretion and deletion at boundaries in dynamic scenes. *IEEE Transactions on Pattern Analysis and Machine Intelligence*, 7:133–138, 1985.
7. W. B. Thompson, K. M. Mutch, and V. A. Berzins. Dynamic occlusion analysis in optical flow fields. *IEEE Transactions on Pattern Analysis and Machine Intelligence*, 7:374–383, 1985.
8. Zhengyou Zhang. Parameter estimation techniques: A tutorial with application to conic fitting. Technical Report 2676, Institut National de Recherche en Informatique et en Automatique, Sophia-Antipolis Cedex, France, October 1995.

Image Sequence Restoration : A PDE Based Coupled Method for Image Restoration and Motion Segmentation

Pierre Kornprobst[1,2], Rachid Deriche[1], and Gilles Aubert[2]

Pierre.Kornprobst@sophia.inria.fr

http://www.inria.fr/robotvis/personnel/pkornp/pkornp-eng.html

[1] INRIA, 2004 route des Lucioles, BP 93, 06902 Sophia-Antipolis Cedex, France
[2] Laboratoire J.A Dieudonné, UMR n° 6621 du CNRS, 06108 Nice-Cedex 2, France

Abstract. This article deals with the problem of restoring and segmenting noisy image sequences with a static background. Usually, motion segmentation and image restoration are tackled separately in image sequence restoration. Moreover, segmentation is often noise sensitive. In this article, the motion segmentation and the image restoration parts are performed in a coupled way, allowing the motion segmentation part to positively influence the restoration part and vice-versa. This is the key of our approach that allows to deal simultaneously with the problem of restoration and motion segmentation. To this end, we propose a theoretically justified optimization problem that permits to take into account both requirements. A suitable numerical scheme based on half quadratic minimization is then proposed and its stability demonstrated. Experimental results obtained on noisy synthetic data and real images will illustrate the capabilities of this original and promising approach.

1 Introduction

Automatic image sequence restoration is clearly a very important problem. Applications areas include image surveillance, forensic image processing, image compression, digital video broadcasting, digital film restoration, medical image processing, remote sensing ... See, for example, the recent work done within the European projects, fully or in part, involved with this important problem : *AURORA, NOBLESSE, LIMELIGHT, IMPROOFS,*... Image sequence restoration is tightly coupled to motion segmentation. It requires to extract moving objects in order to separately restore the background and each moving region along its particular motion trajectory. Most of the work done to date mainly involves motion compensated temporal filtering techniques with appropriate 2D or 3D Wiener filter for noise suppression, 2D/3D median filtering or more appropriate morphological operators for removing impulsive noise [5, 16, 17, 14, 11, 24, 7, 6]. However, and due to the fact that image sequence restoration is an emerging domain compared to 2D image restoration, the literature is not so abundant than the one related to the problem of restoring just a single image. For example, numerous PDE based algorithms have been recently proposed to tackle the problems of noise removal, 2D image enhancement and 2D image restoration in real images with a particular emphasis on preserving the grey level discontinuities during the enhancement/restoration process. These methods, which have been proved to be very efficient, are based on evolving nonlinear partial differential equations (PDE's) (See the work of Perona & Malik [27], Nordström,Shah, Osher & Rudin [29], Proesman et al. [28], Cottet and Germain, Alvarez et al [2], Cohen [8], Weickert [34], Malladi & Sethian [23], Aubert et al. [3], You et al. [36], Sapiro et al. [30], Kornprobst & Deriche [21, 19], ...).

It is the aim of this article to tackle the important problem of image sequence restoration by applying this PDE based methodology, which has been proved to be very successful in anisotropically restoring images. Therefore, considering the case of an image sequence with some moving objects, we have to consider both motion segmentation and image restoration problems. Usually, these two problems are tackled separately in image sequence restoration. However, it is clear that these two problems must be tackled simultaneously in order to achieve better results. In this article, the motion segmentation and the image restoration parts are done in a coupled way, allowing the motion segmentation part to positively influence the restoration part and vice-versa. This is the key of our approach that allows to deal simultaneously with the problem of restoration and motion segmentation.

The organization of the article is as follows. In Sect. 2, we make some precise recalls about one of our previous approach for denoising a single image [9, 3, 21] The formalism and the methods introduced will be very useful in the sequel. Sect. 3 is then devoted to the presentation of our new approach to deal with the case of noisy images sequence. We formulate the problem into an optimization problem. The model will be clearly explained and theoretically justified in Sect. 3.3. The precise algorithm will be also given and justified. Experimental results obtained on noisy synthetic and real data will then illustrate the capabilities of this new approach in Section 4. We conclude in Sect. 5 by recalling the specificities of that work and giving the future developments.

2 A Variational Method for Image Restoration

In Sect. 2.1, we recall a classical method in image restoration formulated as a minimization problem [9, 4, 3]. Section 2.2 presents a suitable algorithm called the half quadratic minimization.

2.1 A Classical Approach for Image Restoration

Let $N(x, y)$ be a given noisy image defined for $(x, y) \in \Omega$ which corresponds to the domain of the image. We search for the restored image as the solution of the following minimization problem:

$$\inf_{I} \underbrace{\int_{\Omega} (I - N)^2 d\Omega}_{\text{term 1}} + \alpha^{\text{r}} \underbrace{\int_{\Omega} \phi(|\nabla I|) d\Omega}_{\text{term 2}} \tag{1}$$

where α^r is a constant and ϕ is a function still to be defined. Notice that if $\phi(x) = x^2$, we recognize the *Tikhonov* regularization term. How can we interpret this minimization? In fact, we search for the function I which will be simultaneously close to the initial image N and smooth (since we want the gradient as small as possible). However, this method is well known to smooth the image isotropically without preserving discontinuities in intensity. The reason is that with the quadratic function, gradients are too much penalized. One solution to prevent the destruction of discontinuities but allows for isotropically smoothing uniform areas, is to change the above quadratic term. This point have been widely discussed [31, 32, 4, 3]. We refer to [9] for a review. The key idea is that for low gradients, isotropic smoothing is performed, and for high gradient, smoothing is only applied in the direction of the isophote and not across it. This condition can be mathematically formalized if we look at the Euler-Lagrange Equation (2), associated to energy (1):

$$2(I - N) - \alpha^r div \left(\frac{\phi'(|\nabla I|)}{|\nabla I|} \nabla I \right) = 0 \tag{2}$$

Let us concentrate on the regularization part associated to the **term** 2 of (1). If we note $\eta = \frac{\nabla I}{|\nabla I|}$, and ξ the normal vector to η, we can show that:

$$div \left(\frac{\phi'(|\nabla I|)}{|\nabla I|} \nabla I \right) = \underbrace{\frac{\phi'(|\nabla I|)}{|\nabla I|} I_{\xi\xi}}_{c_\xi} + \underbrace{\phi''(|\nabla I|) I_{\eta\eta}}_{c_\eta} \tag{3}$$

where $I_{\eta\eta}$ (respectively $I_{\xi\xi}$) denotes the second order derivate in the direction η (respectively ξ). If we want a good restoration as described before, we would like to have the following properties:

$$\lim_{|\nabla I| \to 0} c_\eta = \lim_{|\nabla I| \to 0} c_\xi = a_0 > 0 \tag{4}$$

$$\lim_{|\nabla I| \to \infty} c_\eta = 0 \quad and \quad \lim_{|\nabla I| \to \infty} c_\xi = a_\infty > 0 \tag{5}$$

If c_ξ and c_η are defined as in (3), it appears that the two conditions of (5) can never be verified simultaneously. So, we will only impose for high gradients [9, 4, 3]:

$$\lim_{|\nabla I| \to \infty} c_\eta = \lim_{|\nabla I| \to \infty} c_\xi = 0 \quad and \quad \lim_{|\nabla I| \to \infty} \left(\frac{c_\eta}{c_\xi} \right) = 0 \tag{6}$$

Many functions ϕ have been proposed in the literature that comply to the conditions (4) and (6) (see [9]). From now on, ϕ will be a convex function with linear growth at infinity which verify conditions (4) and (6). For instance, a possible choice could be the hypersurface minimal function proposed by Aubert:

$$\phi(x) = \sqrt{1 + x^2} - 1$$

In that case, existence and unicity of problem (1) has recently been shown in the Sobolev space $W^{1,1}(\Omega)$[4] (See also [33]).

2.2 The Half Quadratic Minimization

The key idea is to introduce a new functional which, although defined over an extended domain, has the same minimum in I as (1) and can be manipulated with linear algebraic methods. The method is based on a theorem inspired from *Geman* and *Reynolds* [13]. If a function $\phi(.)$ complies with some hypotheses, it can be written in the form:

$$\phi(x) = \inf_{d}(dx^2 + \psi(d)) \qquad (7)$$

where d will be called the dual variable associated to x, and where $\psi(.)$ is a strictly convex and decreasing function. We can verify that the functions ϕ such that (4) (6) are true permit to write (7). Consequently, the problem (1) is now to find I and its dual variable d_I minimizing the functional $\mathcal{F}(I, d_I)$ defined by:

$$\mathcal{F}(I, d_I) = \int_{\Omega}(I - N)^2 d\Omega + \alpha^r \int_{\Omega} d_I|\nabla I|^2 + \psi(d_I)d\Omega \qquad (8)$$

It is easy to check that for a fixed I, the functional $\mathcal{F}$ is convex in d_I and for a fixed d_I, it is convex in I. These properties are used to perform the algorithm which consists in minimizing alternatively in I and d_I:

$$I^{n+1} = \underset{I}{\mathrm{argmin}} \quad \mathcal{F}(I, d_I^n) \qquad (9)$$

$$d_B^{n+1} = \underset{d_I}{\mathrm{argmin}} \quad \mathcal{F}(I^{n+1}, d_I) \qquad (10)$$

To perform each minimization, we simply solve the Euler-Lagrange equations, which can be written as:

$$I^{n+1} - N - \alpha^r div(d_I^n \nabla I^{n+1}) = 0 \qquad (11)$$

$$d_I^{n+1} = \frac{\phi'(|\nabla I^{n+1}|)}{|\nabla I^{n+1}|} \qquad (12)$$

Notice that (12) gives explicitly d_I^{n+1} while for (11), for a fixed d_I^n, I^{n+1} is the solution of a linear equation. After discretizing in space, we have that $(I_{i,j}^{n+1})_{(i,j)\in\Omega}$ is solution of a linear system which is solved iteratively by the Gauss-Seidel method for example. We refer to [20] for more details about the discretization.

3 The Case of Noisy Images Sequences

Let $N(x, y, t)$ denotes the noisy images sequence for which the background is assumed to be static. A simple moving object detector can be obtained using a thresholding technique over the *inter-frame difference* between a so-called *reference image* and the image being observed. Decisions can be taken independently point by point [10], or over blocks in order to achieve robustness in noise influence [35]. More complex approaches can also be used [26, 1, 15, 22, 5, 16, 17, 14,

11, 24]. However, in our application, we are not just dealing with a motion segmentation problem neither just a restoration problem. In our case, the so-called *reference image* is built at the same time while observing the image sequence. Also, the motion segmentation and the restoration are done in a coupled way, allowing the motion segmentation part to positively influence the restoration part and vice-versa. This is the key of our approach that allows to deal simultaneously with the problem of restoration and motion segmentation.

We first consider that the data is continuous in time. This permit us to present the optimization problem that we want to study (Section 3.1). In Sect. 3.2, we rewrite the problem when the sequence is given only by a finite set of images. This leads to the Problem 2 that will be rigorously justified in Sect. 3.3. The minimization algorithm and its stability are demonstrated in Sect. 3.4.

3.1 An Optimization Problem

Let $N(x, y, t)$ denotes the noisy images sequence for which the background is assumed to be static. Let us describe the unknown functions and what we would like them ideally to be:

(i) $B(x, y)$, the restored background,

(ii) $C(x, y, t)$, the sequence which will indicate the moving regions. Typically, we would like that $C(x, y, t) = 0$ if the pixel (x, y) belongs to a moving object at time t, and 1 otherwise.

Our aim is to find a functional depending on $B(x, y)$ and $C(x, y, t)$ so that the minimizers verify previous statements. We propose to solve the following problem:

Problem 1. Let $N(x, y, t)$ given. We search for $B(x, y)$ and $C(x, y, t)$ as the solution of the following minimization problem:

$$\inf_{B,C} \Big(\underbrace{\int_t \int_\Omega C^2 (B - N)^2 d\Omega dt}_{\text{term 1}} + \alpha_c \underbrace{\int_t \int_\Omega (C - 1)^2 d\Omega dt}_{\text{term 2}}$$
$$+ \underbrace{\alpha_b^r \int_\Omega \phi_1(|\nabla B|) d\Omega + \alpha_c^r \int_t \int_\Omega \phi_2(|\nabla C|) d\Omega dt}_{\text{term 3}} \Big) \tag{13}$$

where ϕ_1 and ϕ_2 are convex functions that comply conditions (4) and (6) , and $\alpha_c, \alpha_b^r, \alpha_c^r$ are positive constants.

Getting the minimum of the functional means that we want each term to be small, having in mind the phenomena of the compensations.

The **term 3** is a regularization term. Notice that the functions ϕ_1, ϕ_2 have been chosen as in Sect. 2 so that discontinuities may be kept.

If we consider the **term 2**, this means that we want the function $C(x, y, t)$ to be close to one. In our interpretation, this means that we give a preference to the background. This is physically correct since the background is visible most of the time. However, if the data $N(x,y,t)$ is too far from the supposed background $B(x,y)$ at time t, then the difference $(B(x,y) - N(x,y,t))^2$ will be high, and to compensate this value, the minimization process will force $C(x,y,t)$ to be zero. Therefore, the function $C(x,y,t)$ can be interpretated as a movement detection function. Moreover, when searching for $B(x,y)$, we will not take into account $N(x,y,t)$ if $C(x,y,t)$ is small (**term 1**). This exactly means that $B(x,y)$ will be the restored image of the static background.

3.2 The Temporal Discretized Problem

In fact, we have only a finite set of images. Consequently, we are going to rewrite the Problem 1, taking into account that a sequence $S(x,y,t)$ is represented during a finite time by T images noted $S_1(x,y), \ldots, S_T(x,y)$. Using these notations for $N(x,y,t)$ and $C(x,y,t)$ permits to rewrite the Problem 1 in the following form:

Problem 2. Let $N_1, \ldots, N_T$ be the noisy sequence. We search for B and $C_1, \ldots, C_T$ as the solution of the following minimization problem:

$$
\inf_{B, C_1, \ldots, C_T} \Big(\underbrace{\sum_{h=1}^{T} \int_{\Omega} C_h^2 (B - N_h)^2 d\Omega}_{\text{term 1}} + \alpha_c \underbrace{\sum_{h=1}^{T} \int_{\Omega} (C_h - 1)^2 d\Omega}_{\text{term 2}}
$$

$$
+ \underbrace{\alpha_b^r \int_{\Omega} \phi_1(|\nabla B|) d\Omega + \alpha_c^r \sum_{h=1}^{T} \int_{\Omega} \phi_2(|\nabla C_h|) d\Omega}_{\text{term 3}} \Big) \tag{14}
$$

This is the problem that we are going to study.

3.3 A Theoretically Justified Method

This section briefly describes the mathematical background of the Problem 2. We will restrict ourself to very general considerations. A complete more theoretical version is now submitted [18]. Notice however that mathematical tools are general and often used in image processing problems.

The proper space to study the Problem 2 is the space of bounded variations, usually noted $BV(\Omega)$[12]. This space can be considered as a natural extension of the classical Sobolev space $W^{1,1}(\Omega) = \{u \in L^1(\Omega) / \nabla u \in L^1(\Omega)\}$. It can be defined by:

$$
BV(\Omega) = \{u \in L^1(\Omega) / Du \in M(\Omega)\}
$$

where Du stands for the distributional derivative of u and $M(\Omega)$ the measure space. It is usually used for proving results in image processing since it permits to have jumps along curves which is not possible for functions in $W^{1,1}(\Omega)$. We have the following proposition :

Proposition 1. *The minimization Problem 2, posed over the space $BV(\Omega)^{T+1}$ admits a solution in that space. Moreover it is enough to consider the functions $(B, C_1, .., C_T)$ such that:*

$$m_B \leq B \leq M_B \tag{15}$$

$$0 \leq C_h \leq 1 \qquad for \ h = 1..T \tag{16}$$

$$where \quad \begin{cases} m_B = \underset{h \in [0..T], (x,y) \in \Omega}{inf} N_h(x,y) \\ M_B = \underset{h \in [0..T], (x,y) \in \Omega}{sup} N_h(x,y) \end{cases}, \tag{17}$$

This remark will be important for the numerical algorithm.

3.4 The Minimization Algorithm

This section is devoted to the numerical study of the Problem 2. If we try to solve directly the Euler-Lagrange equations associated to (14), we will have to cope with non linear equation. To avoid this difficulty, we are going to use the same techniques as developed in the Sect. 2.2. The idea is to introduce dual variables as defined in (7) each time it is necessary. This is the case for the $T + 1$ restoration terms (**term 3**). Consequently, we introduce the $T + 1$ dual variables noted $d_B, d_{C_1}, \ldots, d_{C_T}$ associated respectively to $B, C_1, \ldots, C_T$. Using same arguments as in Sect. 2.2, we will solve, instead of Problem 2, the following problem:

Problem 3. Let $N_1, \ldots, N_T$ the noisy sequence. We search for $B, d_B, C_1, \ldots, C_T$ and $d_{C_1}, \ldots, d_{C_T}$ as the solution of the following minimization problem:

$$
\underset{B, C_1, \ldots, C_T}{inf} \Big(\sum_{h=1}^{T} \int_\Omega \left[C_h^2 (B - N_h)^2 + \alpha_c (C_h - 1)^2 \right] d\Omega
$$

$$
+ \alpha_b^r \int_\Omega \left[d_B |\nabla B|^2 d\Omega + \Psi_1(d_B) \right] d\Omega
$$

$$
+ \alpha_c^r \sum_{h=1}^{T} \int_\Omega \left[d_{C_h} |\nabla C_h|^2 d\Omega + \Psi_2(d_{C_h}) \right] d\Omega \Big) \tag{18}
$$

We will note in the sequel $\mathcal{E}(B, d_B, C_h, d_{C_h})$ the corresponding functional. The main observation is that the functional $\mathcal{E}$ is quadratic with respect to $B, C_1, \ldots, C_T$, and convex with respect to d_B and $(d_{C_h})_{h=1..T}$.

Given the initial conditions $(B^0, d_B^0, C_h^0, d_{C_h}^0)$, we iteratively solve the following system :

$$B^{n+1} = \underset{B}{\operatorname{argmin}} \quad \mathcal{E}(B, d_B^n, C_h^n, d_{C_h}^n) \tag{19}$$

$$d_B^{n+1} = \underset{d_B}{\operatorname{argmin}} \quad \mathcal{E}(B^{n+1}, d_B, C_h^n, d_{C_h}^n) \tag{20}$$

$$C_h^{n+1} = \underset{C_h}{\operatorname{argmin}} \quad \mathcal{E}(B^{n+1}, d_B^{n+1}, C_h, d_{C_h}^n) \tag{21}$$

$$d_{C_h}^{n+1} = \underset{d_{C_h}}{\operatorname{argmin}} \quad \mathcal{E}(B^{n+1}, d_B^{n+1}, C_h^{n+1}, d_{C_h}) \tag{22}$$

Equalities (21)-(22) are written for $h = 1..T$. The way to obtain each variable like described in (19)-(22) consists in solving the associated Euler-Lagrange equations. As we are going to see, the dual variables d_B^{n+1} and $(d_{C_h}^{n+1})_{h=1..T}$ are given explicitly, while B^{n+1} and $(C_h^{n+1})_{h=1..T}$ are solutions of linear systems. This linear systems will be solved by an iterative method like Gauss-Seidel's. Equations are:

$$\sum_{h=1}^{T} C_h^{n\,2}(B^{n+1} - N_h) - \alpha_b^r div(d_B^n \nabla B^{n+1}) = 0 \tag{23}$$

$$d_B^{n+1} = \frac{\phi_1'(|\nabla B^{n+1}|)}{|\nabla B^{n+1}|} \tag{24}$$

$$C_h^{n+1}\left[\alpha_c + (B^{n+1} - N_h)^2\right] - \alpha_c - 2\alpha_c^r div(d_{C_h}^n \nabla C_h^{n+1}) = 0 \tag{25}$$

$$d_{C_h}^{n+1} = \frac{\phi_2'(|\nabla C_h^{n+1}|)}{|\nabla C_h^{n+1}|} \tag{26}$$

We next prove that the algorithm described by (23) to (26) is unconditionally stable.

Proposition 2. *Let Ω^d be the set of pixels (i,j) in Ω and let $\mathcal{G}^d$ be the space of functions $(B, C_1, \ldots, C_T)$ such that, for all pixels $(i,j) \in \Omega^d$ we have:*

$$m_B \leq B \leq M_B \tag{27}$$

$$0 \leq C_h \leq 1 \qquad for\ h = 1..T \tag{28}$$

$$0 < m_c \leq \sum_{h=1}^{T} C_h \leq T \tag{29}$$

$$where \quad \begin{cases} m_B = \inf_{\substack{(x,y) \\ h=1..T}} N_h(x,y) \\ M_B = \sup_{\substack{(x,y) \\ h=1..T}} N_h(x,y) \end{cases}, \quad m_c = \frac{T\alpha_c^r}{\alpha_c + (M_B - m_B)^2 + 4} \tag{30}$$

Then, for a given $(B^n, C_1^n, \ldots, C_T^n)$ in $\mathcal{G}^d$, there exists a unique $(B^{n+1}, C_1^{n+1}, \ldots, C_T^{n+1})$ in $\mathcal{G}^d$ such that (23)-(26) are satisfied.

The proof is based on the application of the fixed point theorem. We refer to [20] for more details. Anyway, let us remark that the boundaries (27) and (28) can be justified if we consider the continuous case (see (17)). As for condition (29), it is also very natural if we admit the interpretations of the variables C_h : if this condition is false, this would mean that the background is never seen at some points which we refuse.

To conclude this section, we will notice that if $\alpha_c^r = 0$, the functions $(C_h^{n+1})_{h=1..T}$ are in fact obtained explicitly by:

$$C_h^{n+1} = \frac{\alpha_c}{\alpha_c + (B^{n+1} - N_h)^2} \tag{31}$$

As we can imagine, this case permits important reduction of the computational cost since T linear systems are replaced by T explicit expressions. We will discuss in Sect. 4 if it is worth regularizing or not the functions C_h.

4 The Numerical Study

This section aims at showing quantitative and qualitative results about this method. Synthetics noisy sequences will be used to estimate rigorously the capabilities of our approach. The purpose of Sect. 4.1 is the quality of the restoration. The Sect. 4.2 is devoted to the movement detection and its sensibility with respect to noise. We will conclude in Sect. 4.3 by real sequences.

4.1 About the Restoration

To estimate the quality of the restoration, we used the noisy synthetic sequence presented in Fig. 1 (a)(b). Figure 1 (c) is a representation of the noisy background without the moving objects. We mentioned the value of the Signal to Noise Ratio (SNR) usually used in image restoration to quantify the results quality. We refer to [21] for more details. We recall that the higher the SNR is, the best the quality is. Usually used to extract the foreground from the background, the median (see Fig. 1 (d)) appears to be inefficient. The average in time of the sequence (see Fig 1 (e)), although it permits a noise reduction, keeps the trace of the moving objects. The Fig. 1 (f) is the result that we obtained.

To conclude that section, let us mention that we also tried the case $\alpha_c^r = 0$, that is to say we did not regularized the functions C_h. The resulting SNR was 14, to be compared with 14.4 ($\alpha_c^r \neq 0$). This leads to the conclusion that regularizing the functions C_h is not very important. However, this point has to be better investigated and more experimental results have to be considered before to conclude.

4.2 The Sensitivity of Object Detection With Respect to Noise

In this section, we aim at showing the robustness of our method with respect to noise. To this end, we choose a synthetic sequence where an object (denoted ⊚) is translating on a uniform black background (See Fig. 2). Both kind of noise have been experimented : Gaussian and uniform. The Gaussian noise is

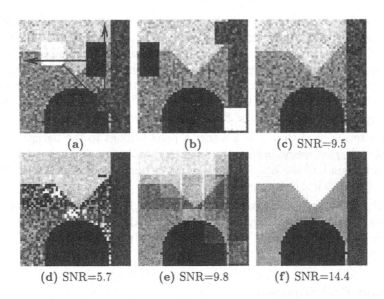

Fig. 1. Results on a synthetic sequence (5 images) **(a)** Description of the sequence (first image) **(b)** Last image of the sequence **(c)** The noisy background without any objects **(d)** Mediane **(e)** Average **(f)** Restored background ($\alpha_c^r \neq 0$)

Fig. 2. The original synthetic sequence used for tests. A white object (noted ⊚) is translating from left to right. 35 images are available.

Gaussian Noise				
σ	SNR(N_h)	$\sigma(B)$	⊚	□
0	0	0	0	0
5	14.7	0.9	0	0
10	9.2	1.8	0	0
15	6.2	3.0	0.1	0
20	4.5	4.5	1.5	0.7
25	3.3	6.3	4.9	3.2
30	2.4	8.4	9.5	7.6

Uniform Noise				
%	SNR(N_h)	$\sigma(B)$	⊚	□
0	0	0	0	0
5	6.8	0.3	2.9	2.2
10	4.3	0.4	5.5	4.5
15	3.3	0.6	8.5	6.7
20	2.3	0.7	11.0	8.6
25	2.0	1.5	14.1	10.8

Table 1. Quantitative measures for tests about robustness to noise (Gaussian and uniform). SNR(N_h)=signal to noise ratio for one image of the data. $\sigma(B)$=root of the variance of the restored background ⊚=percentage of bad detections for the moving object □=percentage of bad detections for the background. See also Fig. 3 for two examples for equivalent noises.

characterized by its variance σ (the average equals to zero), while the uniform noise is defined by a percentage of modified pixels . We recall that a uniform noise of X% means that X% of pixels will be replaced by a value between the minimum and the maximum value of the image with a uniform distribution. Results are reported in Tab. 1 and Fig. 3. Notice that we also wrote the root of the variance of the restored background B which is a good indicator here for estimating the accuracy, since the ideal image is a constant image.

The criterion used to decide whether a pixel belongs to the background or not is : if $C_h(i,j)$>threshold, then the pixel (i,j) of the image number h belongs to the background. Otherwise, its belongs to a moving object. The threshold has been fixed to 0.25 in all experiments.

Finally, notice that same parameters $(\alpha_b^r, \alpha_c, \alpha_c^r)$ have been used for all experiments. Generally speaking, we remarked that the algorithm performs well on a wide variety of sequences with the same set of parameters.

4.3 Some Real Sequences

The first real sequence is presented in Fig. 4 (a). A small noise is introduced by the camera and certainly by the hard weather conditions. Notice the reflections on the ground which is frozen. We show in Fig. 4 (b) the average in time of the sequence. The restored background is shown in Fig. 4 (c). As we can see, it has been very well found and enhanced. Figure 4 (d) is a representation of the function C_h where moving regions have been replaced by the original intensities.

The second sequence is more noisy than the first one. Its description is given in Fig. 5 (a). To evaluate the quality of the restoration, we show a close-up of the same region for one original image (see Fig. 5 (b)), the average in time (see Fig. 5 (c)) and the restored background B (see Fig. 5 (d)). The detection of moving regions is displayed in Fig. 5 (e). Notice that some sparse motion have been detected at the right bottom and to left of the two persons. They correspond to the motion of a bush and the shadow of a tree due to the wind.

5 Conclusion

We have presented in this article an original coupled method for the problem of image sequence restoration and motion segmentation. This original way to restore image sequence has been proved to give very promising result. To complete this work, several ideas are considered : use the motion segmentation part to restore also the moving regions, think about possible extensions for non-static cameras. This is the object of our current work.

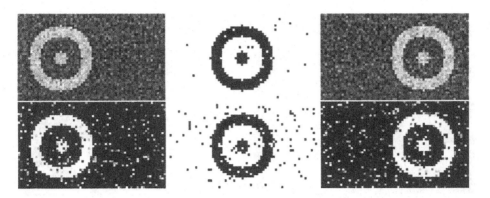

Fig. 3. Results about noise robustness. First row : gaussian noise of variance 20. Second row : uniform noise of percentage 10. Left and Right : images from the sequence. Middle : function C_h.

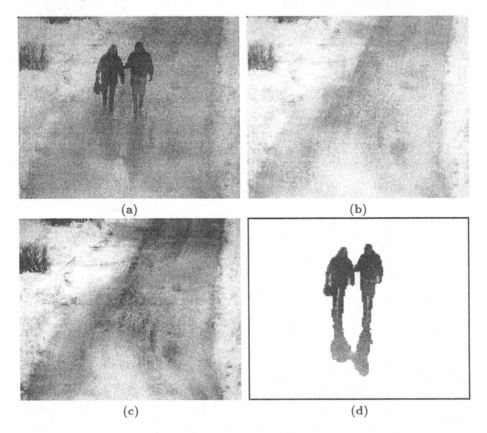

Fig. 4. (a) Description of the sequence (55 images available). Two people are walking from top to bottom (b) The average over the time (c) The restored background B (d) Using function C_h, we replaced moving regions by the data intensity.

560

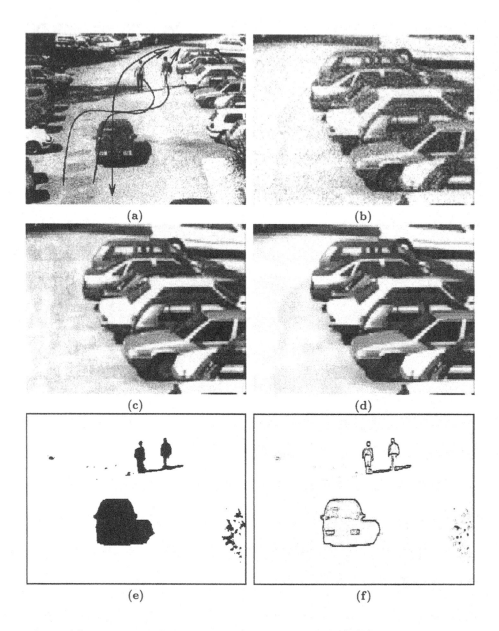

(a)

(b)

(c)

(d)

(e)

(f)

Fig. 5. (a) Description of the sequence (12 images available) (b) Zoom on a upper right part of the original sequence (without objects) (c) Zoom on the mean image (d) Zoom on the restored background B (e) The function C_h thresholded (f) The dual variable d_{c_h}.

References

1. T. Aach and A. Kaup. Bayesian algorithms for adaptive change detection in image sequences using markov random fields. *Signal Processing: Image Communication*, 7:147–160, 1995.
2. L. Alvarez and L. Mazorra. Signal and image restoration using shock filters and anisotropic diffusion. *SIAM Journal of numerical analysis*, 31(2):590–605, Apr. 1994.
3. G. Aubert, M. Barlaud, L. Blanc-Feraud, and P. Charbonnier. Deterministic edge-preserving regularization in computed imaging. *IEEE Trans. Imag. Process.*, 5(12), Feb. 1997.
4. G. Aubert and L. Vese. A variational method in image recovery. *SIAM J. Numer. Anal.*, 34(5):1948–1979, Oct. 1997.
5. J. Boyce. Noise reduction of image sequences using adaptative motion compensated frame averaging. In *IEEE ICASSP*, volume 3, pages 461–464, 1992.
6. J. Brailean and A. Katsaggelos. Simultaneous recursive displacement estimation and restoration of noisy-blurred image sequences. *IEEE Transactions on Image Processing*, 4(9):1236–1251, Sept. 1995.
7. O. Buisson, B. Besserer, S. Boukir, and F. Helt. Deterioration detection for digital film restoration. In *Computer Vision and Pattern Recognition*, pages 78–84, Puerto Rico, June 1997.
8. L. D. Cohen. Auxiliary variables and two-step iterative algorithms in computer vision problems. *ICCV*, 1995.
9. R. Deriche and O. Faugeras. Les EDP en traitement des images et vision par ordinateur. Technical report, INRIA, Nov. 1995. A more complete version of this Research Report has appeared in the French Revue "Traitement du Signal". Volume 13 - No 6 - Special 1996.
10. N. Diehl. Object-oriented motion estimation and segmentation in image sequences. *IEEE Transactions on Image Processing*, 3:1901–1904, Feb. 1990.
11. E. Dubois and S. Sabri. Noise reduction in image sequences using motion-compensated temporal filtering. *IEEE Transactions on Communications*, 32(7):826–831, July 1984.
12. L. C. Evans and R. F. Gariepy. *Measure Theory and Fine Properties of Functions.* CRC, 1992.
13. D. Geman and G. Reynolds. Constrained restoration and the recovery of discontinuities. *IEEE Transactions on Pattern Analysis and Machine Intelligence*, 14(3):367–383, 1993.
14. S. Geman, D. E. McClure, and D. Geman. A nonlinear filter for film restoration and other problems in image processing. *CVGIP : Graphical Models and Image Processing*, 54(4):281–289, July 1992.
15. K. Karmann, A. Brandt, and R. Gerl. Moving object segmentation based on adaptive reference images. *Signal Processing: Theories and Applications*, V:951–954, 1990.
16. A. Kokaram. Reconstruction of severely degraded image sequences. In *International Conference on Image Applications and Processing*, Florence, Italy, 1997.
17. A. C. Kokaram and S. Godsill. A system for reconstruction of missing data in image sequences using sampled 3d ar models and mrf motion priors. In B. Buxton, editor, *Proceedings of the 4th European Conference on Computer Vision*, pages 613–624, Cambridge, UK, Apr. 1996.

562

18. P. Kornprobst, G. Aubert, and R. Deriche. A variational method for image sequences interpretation (submitted). 1997.
19. P. Kornprobst, R. Deriche, and G. Aubert. Image coupling, restoration and enhancement via PDE's. In *International Conference on Image Processing*, volume II of III, pages 458–461, Santa-Barbara,California, Oct. 1997.
20. P. Kornprobst, R. Deriche, and G. Aubert. Image Sequence Restoration : A PDE Based Coupled Method for Image Restoration and Motion Segmentation. Technical Report 3308, INRIA, Nov. 1997.
21. P. Kornprobst, R. Deriche, and G. Aubert. Nonlinear operators in image restoration. In *Proceedings of the International Conference on Computer Vision and Pattern Recognition*, pages 325–331, Puerto-Rico, June 1997. IEEE.
22. S. Liou and R. Jain. Motion detection in spatio-temporal space. *Computer Vision, Graphics and Image Understanding*, (45):227–250, 1989.
23. R. Malladi and J. Sethian. Image processing: Flows under min/max curvature and mean curvature. *Graphical Models and Image Processing*, 58(2):127–141, Mar. 1996.
24. R. Morris. *Image Sequence Restoration using Gibbs Distributions*. PhD thesis, Cambridge University, England, 1995.
25. N. Paragios and R. Deriche. A PDE-based Level Set Approach for Detection and Tracking of Moving Objects. In *Proceedings of the 6th International Conference on Computer Vision*, Bombay,India, Jan. 1998. IEEE Computer Society Press.
26. N. Paragios and G. Tziritas. Detection and localization of moving objects in image sequences. *FORT-Hellas Technical Report, Accepted for publication in Signal Processing: Image Communication*, Oct. 1996.
27. P. Perona and J. Malik. Scale-space and edge detection using anisotropic diffusion. *IEEE Transactions on Pattern Analysis and Machine Intelligence*, 12(7):629–639, July 1990.
28. M. Proesmans, E. Pauwels, and L. V. Gool. *Coupled Geometry-Driven Diffusion Equations for Low-Level Vision*, pages 191–228. Computational imaging and vision. Kluwer Academic Publishers, 1994.
29. L. Rudin and S. Osher. Total variation based image restoration with free local constraints. In *International Conference on Image Processing*, volume I, pages 31–35, Nov. 1994.
30. G. Sapiro, A. Tannenbaum, Y. You, and M. Kaveh. Experiments on geometric image enhancement. In *International Conference on Image Processing*, 1994.
31. C. Schnörr. Unique reconstruction of piecewise-smooth images by minimizing strictly convex nonquadratic functionals. *Journal of Mathematical Imaging and Vision*, 4:189–198, 1994.
32. R. Stevenson, B. Schmitz, and E. Delp. Discontinuity preserving regularization of inverse visual problems. *IEEE Transactions on Systems, Man, and Cybernetics*, 24(3):455–469, Mar. 1994.
33. L. Vese. *Problèmes variationnels et EDP pour l'analyse d'images et l'évolution de courbes*. PhD thesis, Université de Nice Sophia-Antipolis, Nov. 1996.
34. J. Weickert. *Anisotropic Diffusion in Image Processing*. PhD thesis, University of Kaiserslautern, Germany, Laboratory of Technomathematics, Jan. 1996.
35. O. Wenstop. Motion detection from image information. *Proceedings in Scandinavian Conference on Image Analysis*, pages 381–386, 1983.
36. Y. You, M. Kaveh, W. Xu, and A. Tannenbaum. Analysis and Design of Anisotropic Diffusion for Image Processing. In *International Conference on Image Processing*, volume II, pages 497–501, Nov. 1994.

Joint Estimation-Segmentation of Optic Flow

Étienne Mémin[1] and Patrick Pérez[2]

[1] Valoria, Université de Bretagne Sud BP 1104, 56014 Vannes, France and
IRISA 35042 Rennes Cedex; memin@irisa.fr
[2] IRISA/INRIA 35042 Rennes Cedex, France; perez@irisa.fr

Abstract. In this paper we address the intricate issue of jointly recovering the apparent velocity field between two consecutive frames and its underlying partition. We design a global cost functional including robust estimators. These estimators enable to deal with the large deviations occurring in the different energy terms and offer the possibility to introduce a simple coupling between a dense optical flow field and a segmentation. This coupling is also reinforced by a parametric likeness term. The resulting estimation-segmentation model thus involves a tight cooperation between a local estimation process and a global modelization. The minimization of the final cost function is conducted efficiently by a multigrid optimization algorithm.

1 Introduction

Motion estimation and motion-based segmentation are well known to be two tightly interwoven processes in motion analysis. It is obvious that a good estimation of the velocity field (or at least a sensible approximation of it) is required to obtain a good segmentation of the different apparent motions observable in the scene. At the opposite, a good velocity map cannot be obtained without an accurate estimation of the frontiers of the different moving objects. It is therefore natural to consider the resolution of these two motion problems as a whole.

The coupling of motion estimation and segmentation has been considered in various ways the last decade. Two classes of methods may be indeed distinguished. The first class consists in an *unilateral coupling* between some motion cues and a segmentation process. Methods belonging to this class assume that one of the set of variables is known in order to recover the second one. For instance, in [2] the optical flow is first estimated as a dense field and then fixed during all the segmentation process. Segmentation based on the normal flow field relies on the same philosophy [1, 3, 7, 17]. The segmentation problem has been modeled within a number of frameworks: *Markov random field* theory [7, 17], *statistical mixture estimation* framework [3], *minimum description length* paradigm [10] or *region split and merge* methodology [2]. All these methods are based on a regionwise parametric description of the motion cues (i.e., the optical flow field or the normal flow field). More recently, coupled motion-based estimation-segmentation methods have been proposed. They involve a tight coupling between a motion field and a motion-based partition. In that case, the motion field and the associated segmentation map are estimated simultaneously. This is usually done by using a global energy function that ties both entities. In that context, different types of interaction have been proposed. In [18] for instance, the partition frontiers are estimated as a representation of the flow discontinuities. In [6,8], the interaction consists in the cooperation between a dense flow field and a region-wise parametric polynomial flow. The dense optical flow is only encouraged to have some similarity with a piecewise parametric motion field associated to the partition map. In this paper, we present a motion estimation-segmentation method belonging to this latter class. We aim at developping a tight cooperation between a dense optic-flow estimator and a motion based segmentation process.

2 Robust estimation of the optical flow

Many standard optical flow estimators are based on the well known *optical flow constraint* (OFC) equation [13]. This differential equation, issued from a linearization of the brightness constancy assumption, links the spatio-temporal gradients of the luminance to the unknown velocity vector. In order to recover the two components of the velocity vector, a *smoothness* prior on the solution is usually introduced through an additional regularization term [5, 13].

Due to the differential nature of the OFC, this standard modeling does not hold for large displacements. To circumvent the problem, it is usual to consider an incremental estimation of the flow field using a multiresolution setup [5, 11]. This multiresolution framework involving a pyramidal decomposition of the image data is standard and won't be emphasized herein. In the following, we shall assume to be working at a given resolution of this structure. However, one has to keep in mind that the expressions and computations are meant to be reproduced at each resolution level according to a coarse-to-fine strategy. Let us now assume that a rough estimate $w = \{w_s, s \in S\}$ of the unknown velocity field is available (e.g., from an estimation at lower resolution or from a previous estimation), on the rectangular pixel lattice S. Let $f(t) = \{f(s,t), s \in S\}$ be the luminance function at time t. Under the constancy brightness assumption from time t to $t+1$, a small *increment field* $dw \in \Omega \subset (\mathbb{R} \times \mathbb{R})^S$ can be estimated by minimizing the functional $\mathcal{H} \triangleq \mathcal{H}_1 + \alpha\mathcal{H}_2$, with [5]:

$$\mathcal{H}_1(dw) \triangleq \sum_{s \in S} \rho_1[\nabla f(s+w_s, t+1)^T dw_s + f_t(s,t,w_s)], \tag{1}$$

$$\mathcal{H}_2(dw) \triangleq \sum_{<s,r> \in \mathcal{C}} \rho_2\left[\|(w_s + dw_s) - (w_r + dw_r)\|\right], \tag{2}$$

where $\alpha > 0$, $\mathcal{C}$ is the set of neighboring site pairs lying on grid S equipped with some neighborhood system ν, ∇f stands for the spatial gradient of f, $f_t(s,t,w_s) \triangleq f(s + w_s, t + 1) - f(s,t)$ is the displaced frame difference, and functions ρ_1 and ρ_2 are standard *robust M-estimators* (with hyper-parameters σ_1 and σ_2). Functions ρ_1 and ρ_2 penalize both the *deviations* from the data model (i.e., the OFC) and from the first order smoothing prior.

A robust M-estimator ρ is an increasing cost function which compared to quadratic function possesses a saturating property ($\lim_{u \to \infty} \frac{\rho'(u)}{2u} = 0$). It allows to atenuate the influence of large "residual" values [9, 12]. It can be shown that under certain simple conditions (mainly concavity of $\phi(v) \triangleq \rho(\sqrt{v})$), any multi-dimensional minimization problem of the form "find $\arg\min_x \sum_i \rho[g_i(x)]$" can be turned into a dual minimization problem "find $\arg\min_{x,z} \sum_i [\tau z_i g_i(x)^2 + \psi(z_i)]$" involving *auxiliary variables* (or *weights*) z_is continuously lying in $(0, 1]$ and τ is a parameter defined as $\tau \triangleq \lim_{v \to 0+} \phi'(v)$. The function ψ is a decreasing function depending on ρ [9].

The new minimization is then usually led *alternatively* with respect to x and to the z_is. If g_is are affine forms, minimization w.r.t. x is a standard *weighted least squares* problem. In turn x being frozen, the best weights have the following closed form:

$$\hat{z}_i(x) = \frac{\rho'[g_i(x)]}{2\tau g_i(x)} = \frac{1}{\tau}\phi'[g_i(x)^2]. \tag{3}$$

In our case the weights are of two natures: (a) *data outliers weights* (related to the dual formulation of H_1), and (b) *discontinuity weights* (provided by the dual formulation of H_2) lying on the dual edge grid of S. The first set of weights, denoted by $\delta = \{\delta_s, s \in S\}$, allows to attenuate the effect of data for which the OFC is violated. The second one, denoted by $\beta = \{\beta_{sr}, <s, r> \in \mathcal{C}\}$, prevents from over-smoothing in locations exhibiting significant velocity discontinuities. The estimation is now expressed as the global minimization in $(d\boldsymbol{w}, \delta, \beta)$ of $\tilde{\mathcal{H}} \triangleq \tilde{\mathcal{H}}_1 + \alpha\tilde{\mathcal{H}}_2$ where:

$$\tilde{\mathcal{H}}_1(d\boldsymbol{w}, \delta) = \sum_{s \in S} \left[\tau_1 \delta_s \left[\boldsymbol{\nabla} f(s + \boldsymbol{w}_s, t + 1)^T d\boldsymbol{w}_s + f_t(s, t, \boldsymbol{w}_s) \right]^2 + \psi_1(\delta_s) \right], \tag{4}$$

$$\tilde{\mathcal{H}}_2(d\boldsymbol{w}, \beta) = \sum_{<s,r> \in \mathcal{C}} \left[\tau_2 \beta_{sr} \|(\boldsymbol{w}_s + d\boldsymbol{w}_s) - (\boldsymbol{w}_r + d\boldsymbol{w}_r)\|^2 + \psi_2(\beta_{sr}) \right]. \tag{5}$$

More satisfactory robust cost functions being non-convex we end up with a difficult minimization problem to solved. We tackle it using a multigrid strategy that will be briefly described in section 4. Let's first see how this energy function may be coupled with a segmentation device.

3 Motion estimation and segmentation coupling

We now introduce an extension of the model to couple the estimation process with a motion-based partition of the image. Let $\mathcal{P}$ denotes this partition composed of an *unknown* number p of connected regions, $\mathcal{P} = \{\mathcal{R}_1, \ldots, \mathcal{R}_i, \ldots, \mathcal{R}_p\}$. The boundary between regions $\mathcal{R}_i$ and $\mathcal{R}_j$ will be noted $\partial_{i,j}$ and is defined as the set of edge-sites (i.e., lying on the dual edge grid) between $\mathcal{R}_i$ and $\mathcal{R}_j$: $\partial_{i,j} = \{<s, r> \in \mathcal{C} : s \in \mathcal{R}_i, r \in \mathcal{R}_j\}$. The set $\partial\mathcal{P} \triangleq \cup_{i \neq j}\partial_{i,j}$ stands therefore for the frontiers of the partition.

The extension of the energy-based optic flow estimation model is obtained by incorporating two terms to the global energy function $\mathcal{H}$ [1]. The first one, E_{prior}, captures the *a priori* knowledge about the segmentation configuration. The second one, E_{inter}, specifies the mode of interaction between the segmentation and the rest of the estimation model (i.e., velocity field, weights and data).

We have chosen an interaction model which allows an interaction with the velocity field both at the frontiers and inside the regions: the segments will interact with the estimation process through the discontinuity weights, and through a parametric similarity of the motion profile inside each region.

The corresponding cost function component $E_{\text{inter}}(\mathcal{P}, \beta, \mathbf{dw})$ exhibits two terms: The first one is proportional to the sum of β_{sr} mean values over sets $\partial_{i,j}$. It then (a) favors low values (close to zero) of discontinuity weights along the borders and (b) guides the partition boundaries toward the most significant flow discontinuities. The second term enforces a polynomial parametric likeness of the flow field inside each region. The global energy of the extended model is designed as follows:

$$\mathbb{H}(\mathbf{dw}, \mathcal{P}, \delta, \beta) \triangleq \widetilde{\mathcal{H}}(\mathbf{dw}, \delta, \beta) + E_{\text{prior}}(\partial \mathcal{P}) + E_{\text{inter}}(\mathbf{dw}, \mathcal{P}, \beta), \qquad (6)$$

where,

$$E_{\text{inter}}(\mathbf{dw}, \mathcal{P}, \beta) \triangleq \mu_1 \sum_{\partial_{i,j} \in \partial \mathcal{P}} \frac{1}{|\partial_{i,j}|} \sum_{<s,r> \in \partial_{i,j}} \beta_{sr} + \mu_2 \sum_{\mathcal{R}_i \in \mathcal{P}} \sum_{s \in \mathcal{R}_i} \rho_3(\|\mathbf{w}_s + \mathbf{dw}_s - \mathbf{w}_s^{\Theta_i}\|) \qquad (7)$$

with some positive parameters μ_1 and μ_2 and the function ρ_3 being a robust M-estimator with hyper-parameter σ_3. The vector $\mathbf{w}_s^{\Theta_i}$ is the parametric motion model associated to region $\mathcal{R}_i$. In this work, we will consider only the standard six parameter affine model: $\Theta = [a, b, c, d, e, f]^T$ with $\mathbf{w}_s^{\Theta_i} = P_s \Theta_i$, where $P_s \triangleq \begin{pmatrix} 1 & x_s & y_s & 0 & 0 & 0 \\ 0 & 0 & 0 & 1 & x_s & y_s \end{pmatrix}$. This model is usually considered as a good trade-off between model complexity and model efficiency [7]. It has been extensively used in motion analysis. This model conjectures that a given motion region is a projection of a 3D planar patch of surface whose motion is confined to rotations around the optical axis and to translations in its facet plan. According to §2 the interaction term may be rewritten in its dual form as:

$$\widetilde{E}_{\text{inter}}(\mathcal{P}, \beta, \mathbf{dw}, \eta) = \mu_1 \sum_{\partial_{i,j} \in \partial \mathcal{P}} \frac{1}{|\mathcal{C}_{\partial_{i,j}}|} \sum_{<s,r> \in \partial_{i,j}} \beta_{sr} + \mu_2 \sum_{\mathcal{R}_i \in \mathcal{P}} \sum_{s \in \mathcal{R}_i} \tau_3 \eta_s \|\mathbf{w}_s + \mathbf{dw}_s - \mathbf{w}_s^{\Theta_i}\|^2 + \psi_3(\eta_s). \qquad (8)$$

The variables η are auxiliary variables that we will refer to as *parametric likeness weights* throughout the paper. The resulting global energy is $\widetilde{\mathbb{H}}(\mathbf{dw}, \mathcal{P}, \delta, \beta, \eta)$.

---

[1] Even though the superscript remains omitted, we still suppose in the coming developments that some resolution level is concerned.

The segmentation *a priori* term corresponds to a loose geometric constraint in terms of a classical Minimum Description Length (MDL) prior [14].

$$E_{\mathrm{prior}}(\partial \mathcal{P}) \triangleq \lambda |\partial \mathcal{P}| \text{ for some } \lambda > 0. \qquad (9)$$

This energy term favors region with short and smooth border.

The whole energy function has now to be minimized with respect to all the unknowns. A direct minimization of such function is obviously a very intricate problem. As we shall see in the coming section, the optimization may be efficiently conducted through a multigrid minimization strategy.

4 Multigrid optimization

To efficiently cope with the optimization problem w.r.t. $d\boldsymbol{w}$ and $\mathcal{P}$, we design a joint hierarchical "constrained" exploration of the increment configuration space Ω and of the partition configuration space Υ.

The overall optimization is led through a sequence of nested joint configuration subspaces:

$$(\Omega^L \times \Upsilon^L) \subset (\Omega^{L-1} \times \Upsilon^{L-1}) \subset \cdots \subset (\Omega^1 \times \Upsilon^1) \subset (\Omega \times \Upsilon).$$

The subspace Ω^{ℓ} is defined as the set of increment fields $d\boldsymbol{w}$ which are piecewise constant according to a $2^{\ell} \times 2^{\ell}$-block partition of grid S^2. Denote $\mathcal{B}^{\ell} \triangleq \{\mathcal{B}_n^{\ell}, \; n = 1 \ldots N_{\ell}\}$ this partition, the number of blocks being $N_{\ell} = |S|/4^{\ell}$.

Each constrained configuration of Ω^{ℓ} is "equivalent" to a *reduced increment field* $d\boldsymbol{w}^{\ell}$ lying on the grid $S^{\ell} \triangleq \{1, \ldots, N_{\ell}\}$ associated with $\mathcal{B}^{\ell}$. Let Γ^{ℓ} be the set of such reduced configurations and let Φ_1^{ℓ} be the point-to-point mapping from Γ^{ℓ} into Ω^{ℓ}.

In the same way, the partition configuration subspace Υ^{ℓ} is the set of "constrained" partition $\mathcal{P}$ lying on the grid S^{ℓ} (i.e., defined on a $2^{\ell} \times 2^{\ell}$-block partition). Following the same methodology, a point-to-point mapping from a reduced partition configuration space Λ^{ℓ} into Υ^{ℓ} may be easily constructed. Let Φ_2^{ℓ} denote this function.

Constrained optimization in $\Omega^{\ell} \times \Upsilon^{\ell}$ is then equivalent to the minimization of the new energy function:

$$\widetilde{\mathbb{H}}^{\ell}(d\boldsymbol{w}^{\ell}, \mathcal{P}^{\ell}, \delta, \beta, \eta) \triangleq \widetilde{\mathbb{H}}(\Phi_1^{\ell}(d\boldsymbol{w}^{\ell}), \Phi_2^{\ell}(\mathcal{P}^{\ell}), \delta, \beta, \eta) \qquad (10)$$

defined over $\Gamma^{\ell} \times \Lambda^{\ell}$, whereas the auxiliary variables, the data, and the field to be refined remain the same (i.e., defined on the original grid S).

At each resolution, we now have a cascade of optimization problems of reduced complexity:

$$\underset{d\boldsymbol{w}^{\ell}, \mathcal{P}^{\ell}, \delta, \beta, \eta}{\arg \min} \widetilde{\mathbb{H}}^{\ell}(d\boldsymbol{w}^{\ell}, \mathcal{P}^{\ell}, \delta, \beta, \eta), \; \ell = L \ldots 0, \qquad (11)$$

---

[2] Others linear constraints may be also considered [16].

where $dw^\ell \in \Gamma^\ell$ and $\mathcal{P}^\ell \in \Lambda^\ell$ are defined on the reduced grid S^ℓ, and auxiliary variables are attached to S, whatever the grid level.

This cascade of minimization problems is processed in terms of iteratively reweighted least squares within a multigrid coarse-to-fine strategy: the final estimates at level $\ell+1$ have a natural image at level ℓ (through $[\Phi_1^\ell]^{-1} \circ \Phi_1^{\ell+1}$ and $[\Phi_2^\ell]^{-1} \circ \Phi_2^{\ell+1}$), which are used as an initial configuration at level ℓ.

4.1 Multigrid energy derivation

We now go into deeper details about the new multigrid function $\widetilde{\mathbb{H}}^\ell$ which is obviously composed of four terms similar to those of $\widetilde{\mathbb{H}}$: $\widetilde{\mathbb{H}}^\ell = \widetilde{\mathcal{H}}_1^\ell + \alpha\widetilde{\mathcal{H}}_2^\ell + \widetilde{E}_{\text{inter}}^\ell + \widetilde{E}_{\text{prior}}^\ell$.

Data model adequation term: For any $n \in S^\ell$, denote $s_1,\ldots,s_{4^\ell}$ the sites of block $\mathcal{B}_n^\ell$, and define the following blockwise expressions:

$$\delta_n^\ell \triangleq [\delta_{s_1} \cdots \delta_{s_{4^\ell}}]^T, \quad \Psi_1^\ell(\delta_n^\ell) \triangleq \sum_{s\in\mathcal{B}_n^\ell} \psi_1(\delta_s), \quad \Delta_n^\ell \triangleq \text{diag}(\delta_{s_1},\ldots,\delta_{s_{4^\ell}}),$$

$$f_t^\ell(n,w) \triangleq [f_t(s_1,w_{s_1}) \cdots f_t(s_{4^\ell},w_{s_{4^\ell}})]^T, \nabla f^\ell(n,w) \triangleq \left[f_x^\ell(n,w)\ f_y^\ell(n,w)\right]$$

$$f_\bullet^\ell(n,w) \triangleq [f_\bullet(s_1+w_{s_1},t+1) \cdots f_\bullet(s_{4^\ell}+w_{s_{4^\ell}},t+1)]^T, \text{ for } \bullet = x \text{ or } y,$$

Also, we will denote $\langle X|Y\rangle_n \triangleq X^T\Delta_n^\ell Y$ for any two 4^ℓ-row matrices or vectors, and $\|X\|_n^2 \triangleq \langle X|X\rangle_n$ for any 4^ℓ-component column vector. It is then easy to get the following compact expression:

$$\widetilde{\mathcal{H}}_1^\ell(dw^\ell,\delta) = \sum_{n\in S^\ell} \left[\tau_1\|\nabla f^\ell(n,w)dw_n^\ell + f_t^\ell(n,w)\|_n^2 + \Psi_1^\ell(\delta_n^\ell)\right], \quad (12)$$

which is *very similar* to the one of the "parent" energy $\widetilde{\mathcal{H}}_1$ (4). For each block, one gets a blockwise optical flow constraint expression involving aggregated observations.

Smoothing term: Let $\mathcal{C}_n^\ell \triangleq \{<s,r>\in\mathcal{C} : <s,r>\subset\mathcal{B}_n^\ell\}$ be the set of neighboring site pairs included in block $\mathcal{B}_n^\ell$ and $\mathcal{C}_{nm}^\ell \triangleq \{<s,r>\in\mathcal{C} : s\in\mathcal{B}_n^\ell, r\in\mathcal{B}_m^\ell\}$ the set of neighboring site pairs straddling blocks $\mathcal{B}_n^\ell$ and $\mathcal{B}_m^\ell$. These sets $\{\mathcal{C}_n^\ell\}$ and $\{\mathcal{C}_{nm}^\ell\}$ form a partition of $\mathcal{C}$ and reduced grid S^ℓ turns out to be equipped with the *same neighborhood system* as S (i.e., first- or second-order neighborhood system). The corresponding set of neighboring pairs will be denoted by $\mathcal{C}^\ell$. The smoothing term of $\widetilde{\mathcal{H}}^\ell$ is:

$$\widetilde{\mathcal{H}}_2^\ell(dw^\ell,\beta)=\tau_2\left[\sum_{n\in S^\ell}\sum_{<s,r>\in\mathcal{C}_n^\ell}\beta_{sr}\|w_s-w_r\|^2\right.$$

$$\left.+\sum_{<n,m>\in\mathcal{C}^\ell}\sum_{<s,r>\in\mathcal{C}_{nm}^\ell}\beta_{sr}\|(w_s+dw_n^\ell)-(w_r+dw_m^\ell)\|^2\right]+\sum_{<s,r>\in\mathcal{C}}\psi_2(\beta_{sr}) \quad (13)$$

which reduces to:

$$\mathcal{H}_2(\mathbf{0},\beta)+\tau_2\sum_{<n,m>\in\mathcal{C}^\ell}\left[\beta_{nm}^\ell\|\mathbf{dw}_n^\ell-\mathbf{dw}_m^\ell\|^2+2(\mathbf{dw}_n^\ell-\mathbf{dw}_m^\ell)^T\overline{\Delta w}_{nm}^\ell\right],\qquad(14)$$

with $\beta_{nm}^\ell\triangleq\sum_{<s,r>\in\mathcal{C}_{nm}^\ell}\beta_{sr}$ and $\overline{\Delta w}_{nm}^\ell\triangleq\sum_{<s,r>\in\mathcal{C}_{nm}^\ell}\beta_{sr}(\mathbf{w}_s-\mathbf{w}_r)$.

Parametric likeness term: Let us denote $\partial\mathcal{P}^\ell$ the border of partition $\mathcal{P}^\ell$ and let $\partial_{i,j}^\ell\triangleq\Phi_2^\ell(\partial_{i,j})$ be the set of cliques straddling the frontiers resulting from the projection on S of the edge $\partial_{i,j}\subset\partial\mathcal{P}^\ell$ defined on S^ℓ. We have:

$$\widetilde{E}_{\text{inter}}^\ell(\mathbf{dw},\mathcal{P}^\ell,\beta,\eta)=\mu_1\sum_{\partial_{i,j}\in\partial\mathcal{P}^\ell}\frac{1}{|\partial_{i,j}^\ell|}\sum_{<s,r>\in\partial_{i,j}^\ell}\beta_{sr}+$$
$$\mu_2\sum_{\mathcal{R}_i\in\mathcal{P}^\ell}\sum_{n\in\mathcal{R}_i}\sum_{s\in\mathcal{B}_n^\ell}\eta_s\|\mathbf{w}_s+\mathbf{dw}_n^\ell-\mathbf{w}_s^{\Theta_i}\|^2+\psi_3(\eta_s),\qquad(15)$$

which, like previously, reduces to:

$$\widetilde{E}_{\text{inter}}^\ell(\mathbf{0},\mathcal{P}^\ell,\beta,\eta)+\mu_2\sum_{\mathcal{R}_i\in\mathcal{P}^\ell}\sum_{n\in\mathcal{R}_i}\|\mathbf{dw}_n^\ell\|^2 Z_n^\ell+2(\mathbf{dw}_n^\ell)^T\overline{\Delta w}_n^\ell(\Theta_i),\qquad(16)$$

where $Z_n^\ell=\sum_{s\in\mathcal{B}_n^\ell}\eta_s$ and $\overline{\Delta w}_n^\ell(\Theta_i)\triangleq\sum_{s\in\mathcal{B}_n^\ell}\eta_s(\mathbf{w}_s-\mathbf{w}_s^{\Theta_i})$.

Partition a priori term: The corresponding expression of this term is straightforward. It is:

$$E_{\text{prior}}^\ell(\partial\mathcal{P}^\ell)=2^\ell E_{\text{prior}}(\partial\mathcal{P}^\ell)=\lambda 2^\ell|\partial\mathcal{P}^\ell|.\qquad(17)$$

4.2 Energy minimization

In this section we describe how the minimization of the total energy function is led. Due to the nature of the global function, we can devise an iteratively reweighted least squares minimization. The overall optimization process consists in an alternate minimization of the different weights and of the original variables of interest (namely $\mathbf{dw}^\ell$ and $\mathcal{P}^\ell$ and the weights β, δ, and η).

Let us first consider that the partition $\mathcal{P}^\ell$ and the parametric likeness weights are given.

Minimization w.r.t. the motion field and associated weights: We have thus to solve:

$$(\widehat{\mathbf{dw}}^\ell,\hat{\beta},\hat{\delta})=\arg\min\widetilde{\mathcal{H}}_1^\ell+\alpha\widetilde{\mathcal{H}}_2^\ell+\widetilde{E}_{\text{inter}}^\ell.\qquad(18)$$

This optimization is led in terms of iteratively reweighted least squares. The weights and the motion field are successively estimated in a recursive process until convergence. For a given set of weights the incremental field is computed from a weighted least squares estimation. The field being fixed the weights are then directly updated according to (3). To get a deeper insight in the considered minimization let us see exactly what are the updating rules under concern.

Consider that the motion $d\boldsymbol{w}^\ell$ is given. Let $<s, r>$ be a clique in $\mathcal{C}$ and denote by m and n block numbers such that: $s \in \mathcal{B}_n^\ell$ and $r \in \mathcal{B}_n^\ell$. The optimal value of the discontinuity weights β_{sr} is given respectively by:

- if the site pair is inside region $\mathcal{R}_i$ ($<s, r> \subset \mathcal{R}_i$):

$$\hat{\beta}_{sr} = \frac{1}{\tau_2} \phi_2' \left[\|\Delta\boldsymbol{w}_{sr}^\ell\|^2 \right] ; \tag{19}$$

where, $\Delta\boldsymbol{w}_{sr}^\ell \triangleq (\boldsymbol{w}_s + d\boldsymbol{w}_n^\ell) - (\boldsymbol{w}_r + d\boldsymbol{w}_m^\ell)$ as a notational convenience.
- if the site pair straddles the "border" between regions $\mathcal{R}_i$ and $\mathcal{R}_j$ ($<s, r> \in \partial_{i,j}$):

$$\hat{\beta}_{sr} = \frac{1}{\tau_2} \phi_2' \left[\|\Delta\boldsymbol{w}_{sr}^\ell\|^2 + \frac{\mu_1}{\tau_2 |\partial_{i,j}|} \right] . \tag{20}$$

The data weights δ are only involved in $\widetilde{\mathcal{H}}_1$, therefore according to equation (3) and to the definition (1) of $\mathcal{H}_1$, the update rule is:

$$\hat{\delta}_s = \phi_2'[\boldsymbol{\nabla}f(s+\boldsymbol{w}_s, t+1)^T d\boldsymbol{w}_n^\ell + f_t(s, t, \boldsymbol{w}_s)] \tag{21}$$

Considering now that the weights β and δ are frozen, the energy function $\widetilde{\widetilde{\mathbb{H}}}$ is quadratic with respect to $d\boldsymbol{w}^\ell$. Its minimization is equivalent to the resolution of a linear system:

$$\left[\langle \nabla f^\ell(n, \boldsymbol{w})^T | \nabla f^\ell(n, \boldsymbol{w}) \rangle_n + \gamma \mathbb{I}_2 \right] d\boldsymbol{w}_n^\ell + \langle \nabla f^\ell(n, \boldsymbol{w})^T | \boldsymbol{f}_t^\ell(n, \boldsymbol{w}) \rangle_n - \gamma \overline{\boldsymbol{w}}_n^\ell = 0 \tag{22}$$

with

$$\overline{\boldsymbol{w}}_n^\ell \triangleq \frac{\displaystyle\sum_{m \in \nu(n)} \left(\beta_{nm}^\ell d\boldsymbol{w}_m^\ell - \overline{\Delta\boldsymbol{w}}_{nm}^\ell \right) - \frac{\mu_2 \tau_3}{\alpha \tau_1} \overline{\Delta\boldsymbol{w}}_n^\ell(\Theta_i)}{\displaystyle\sum_{m \in \nu(n)} \beta_{nm}^\ell + \frac{\mu_2 \tau_3}{\alpha \tau_1} Z_n^\ell} , \quad \gamma \triangleq \frac{\alpha \tau_2}{\tau_1} \sum_{m \in \nu(n)} \beta_{nm}^\ell + \frac{\mu_2 \tau_3}{\tau_1} Z_n^\ell . \tag{23}$$

The solution of this linear system is searched using *Gauss-Seidel* relaxation method. Until convergence, every site n of the grid S^ℓ is iteratively updated according to:

$$\widehat{d\boldsymbol{w}}_n^\ell = \overline{\boldsymbol{w}}_n^\ell - \frac{\gamma \langle \nabla f^\ell | \nabla f^\ell \overline{\boldsymbol{w}}_n^\ell + \boldsymbol{f}_t^\ell \rangle_n + \det A \, \overline{\boldsymbol{w}}_n^\ell + \mathrm{com}A \langle \nabla f^\ell | \boldsymbol{f}_t^\ell \rangle_n}{\gamma(\gamma + \mathrm{trace}A) + \det A} \tag{24}$$

with

$$A \triangleq \nabla f^{\ell T} \Delta_n^\ell \nabla f^\ell = \begin{bmatrix} \|\boldsymbol{f}_x^\ell\|_n^2 & \langle \boldsymbol{f}_x^\ell | \boldsymbol{f}_y^\ell \rangle_n \\ \langle \boldsymbol{f}_x^\ell | \boldsymbol{f}_y^\ell \rangle_n & \|\boldsymbol{f}_y^\ell\|_n^2 \end{bmatrix},$$

and "det A", "trace A", "com A" stand respectively for the determinant, the trace and the cofactor matrix of A. Note that in the above expressions, $\boldsymbol{f}_x^\ell$, $\boldsymbol{f}_y^\ell$, $\boldsymbol{f}_t^\ell$ vectors, and ∇f^ℓ matrices as well, are displayed without $(n, \boldsymbol{w})$ for the sake of concision.

Minimization w.r.t. the partition and associated weights: Once the incremental motion field $\mathrm{d}\boldsymbol{w}^\ell$ and its associated weights are fixed, one has then to minimize $\widetilde{\mathbb{H}}$ w.r.t. the unknown partition $\mathcal{P}$ and the parametric likeness weights η, respectively. This optimization is conducted in the same alternate minimization spirit.

First the partition being fixed, the parametric weights and the motion parameters (Θ_i) are estimated through an iterated reweighted least squares estimation. For a given region $\mathcal{R}_i \in \mathcal{P}^\ell$, the update of the motion parameter vector is:

$$\widehat{\Theta}_i = \left[\sum_{n \in \mathcal{R}_i} \sum_{s \in \mathcal{B}_n^\ell} \eta_s (P_s^T P_s) \right]^{-1} \sum_{n \in \mathcal{R}_i} \sum_{s \in \mathcal{B}_n^\ell} \eta_s P_s^T (\boldsymbol{w}_s + \mathrm{d}\boldsymbol{w}_n^\ell), \qquad (25)$$

while the parametric likeness updating rule is:

$$\widehat{\eta}_s = \frac{1}{\tau_3} \phi_3'(\|\boldsymbol{w}_s + \mathrm{d}\boldsymbol{w}_n^\ell - \boldsymbol{w}_s^{\Theta_i}\|^2). \qquad (26)$$

Afterwards, the partition $\mathcal{P}^\ell$ has to be estimated. This estimation is done in two distinct steps: a *local deformation step* and a *global deformation step*. The first one consists in moving each point of the border $\partial \mathcal{P}$ within a small neighborhood in order to lower the associated energy terms. The second one consists in considering global transformations of the partition $\mathcal{P}$ such as appearance of new regions or merging of two adjacent regions. Let us carefully describe these two stages.

Local deformations: Iterative local deformations of the regions will be obtained by "moving" border sites of $\mathcal{P}$. This yields a new segmentation $\mathcal{P}'$. Figure 4.2 shows an example of such deformations and settles the notational convention used in the following.

Let us compute the energy difference between two partitions $\mathcal{P}$ and $\mathcal{P}'$. Let us denote $\Delta \partial \mathcal{P}' \triangleq \partial \mathcal{P}' - \partial \mathcal{P}$ the set of boundary pieces of partition $\mathcal{P}'$ that were not included in $\partial \mathcal{P}$ and $\Delta \partial \mathcal{P} \triangleq \partial \mathcal{P} - \partial \mathcal{P}'$ the set of border elements that have disappeared. Furthermore let us introduce the set composed of new portions of region created: $\Delta \mathcal{P}' \triangleq \{\Delta \mathcal{R}_i', \ i = 1 \dots N\}$ (where $\Delta \mathcal{R}_i' = \mathcal{R}_i' - \mathcal{R}_i$) and the dual set of removed region portions $\Delta \mathcal{P} \triangleq \{\Delta \mathcal{R}_i, \ i = 1 \dots N\}$ (where

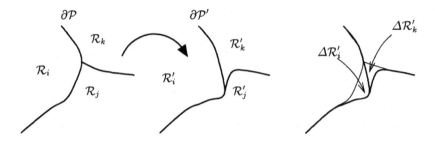

Fig. 1. Example of local deformations of the partition

$\Delta \mathcal{R}_i = \mathcal{R}_i - \mathcal{R}'_i$). Assuming that region-wise motion parameters remain the same (since the deformation is only local) we have:

$$\tilde{\mathbb{H}}^\ell(\mathcal{P}'^\ell) - \tilde{\mathbb{H}}^\ell(\mathcal{P}^\ell) = E_{\text{prior}}(\Delta\partial\mathcal{P}'^\ell) - E_{\text{prior}}(\Delta\partial\mathcal{P}^\ell) + \sum_{\partial_{n,m}\in\Delta\partial\mathcal{P}'^\ell} \frac{\mu_1}{|\partial_{n,m}^\ell|} \sum_{<s,r>\in\partial_{n,m}^\ell} \beta_{sr} - $$

$$\sum_{\partial_{n,m}\in\Delta\partial\mathcal{P}^\ell} \frac{\mu_1}{|\partial_{n,m}^\ell|} \sum_{<s,r>\in\partial_{n,m}^\ell} \beta_{sr} + \sum_{\Delta\mathcal{R}'_i\in\Delta\mathcal{P}'^\ell} \sum_{n\in\Delta\mathcal{R}'_i} \sum_{s\in\mathcal{B}_n^\ell} \rho_3(\|\boldsymbol{w}_s + \mathbf{d}\boldsymbol{w}_n^\ell - \boldsymbol{w}_s^{\Theta_i}\|) - $$

$$\sum_{\Delta\mathcal{R}_j\in\Delta\mathcal{P}^\ell} \sum_{m\in\Delta\mathcal{R}_j} \sum_{s\in\mathcal{B}_m^\ell} \rho_3(\|\boldsymbol{w}_s + \mathbf{d}\boldsymbol{w}_m^\ell - \boldsymbol{w}_s^{\Theta_j}\|). \tag{27}$$

The energy variation corresponding to a local deformation of the partition borders involves only local descriptors and is easily incrementally computed. In practice, a new position is considered for each border element of the current partition $\mathcal{P}^\ell$. If this position corresponds to an energy decrease it is accepted and the partition is updated. In all of our experiences, a border element is allowed to move one site forward or backward in the direction perpendicular to the border. Let us note that these displacements may be quite large (2^ℓ sites) at coarse grid levels. However, we will suppose that our constancy assumption on motion parameters is still valid. This provides large computation time savings since the motion parameters do not have to be re-estimated.

Global deformations: The global deformations concern situations where the topology of the partition map is changed. This includes for example the appearing of new regions or the merging of adjacent regions. Other kinds of global transformations (e.g., rotations, scalings) could be also considered. In this work, only merges and appearance of new regions is considered.

The merging of two adjacent regions consists in removing their common boundary, when this yields a global energy decrease. Let $\mathcal{P}' \triangleq \mathcal{P} - \{\mathcal{R}_i, \mathcal{R}_j\} \cup \{\mathcal{R}_i \cup \mathcal{R}_j\}$ be obtained from $\mathcal{P}$ by the merging of $\mathcal{R}_i$ and $\mathcal{R}_j$. The difference of energy is $\tilde{\mathbb{H}}^\ell(\mathcal{P}) - \tilde{\mathbb{H}}^\ell(\mathcal{P}')$:

$$\sum_{\substack{\mathcal{R}_k \in \\ \mathcal{G}(\mathcal{R}_i) \cap \mathcal{G}(\mathcal{R}_j)}} \left[\left(\frac{\mu_1}{|\partial_{i,k}^\ell \cup \partial_{j,k}^\ell|} - \frac{\mu_1}{|\partial_{i,k}^\ell|} \right) \sum_{<s,r> \in \partial_{i,k}^\ell} \beta_{sr} + \left(\frac{\mu_1}{|\partial_{i,k}^\ell \cup \partial_{j,k}^\ell|} - \frac{\mu_1}{|\partial_{j,k}^\ell|} \right) \sum_{<s,r> \in \partial_{j,k}^\ell} \beta_{sr} \right] +$$

$$\sum_{k \in \{i,j\}} \sum_{n \in \mathcal{R}_k} \sum_{s \in \mathcal{B}_n^\ell} \left[\rho_3(\|w_s + dw_n^\ell - w^{\Theta_{i,j}}\|) - \rho_3(\|w_s + dw_n^\ell - \|w_s^{\Theta_k}\|) \right] - E_{\text{prior}}(\partial_{i,j}),$$

$$(28)$$

where $\mathcal{G}(\mathcal{R}_i)$ denotes the set of adjacent regions of $\mathcal{R}_i$ – with $\mathcal{R}_i \notin \mathcal{G}(\mathcal{R}_i)$. This expression is evaluated for each pair of adjacent regions. The boundary leading to the greatest energy decrease is removed from the partition boundaries set and the corresponding regions are merged. This process is repeated until a complete stability is reached. Let us note that the motion parameter $\Theta_{i,j}$ corresponding to region $\mathcal{R}_i \cup \mathcal{R}_j$ has to be estimated only once (by iterated weighted least squares Equ. (25) and (26)), the first time the merging of the pair is evaluated.

The inclusion of a new region is evaluated according to a Markovian classification of the parametric likeness weights into two classes: $x \in \{0, 1\}$. The first class gathers the *outliers* to the parametric likeness model whereas the second one groups points where the affine model fits well the dense velocity. A standard Markov random field model for supervised image classification is specified through the following energy (formulated here directly in the multigrid formalism):

$$\hat{x}^\ell = \arg\min_{x^\ell} \sum_{n \in S^\ell} \sum_{s \in \mathcal{B}_n^\ell} \frac{1}{2\sigma^2(x^\ell)} \left[m(x^\ell) - \eta_s \right]^2 + 2^{\ell+1}(2^\ell - 1)\lambda \sum_{<n,m> \in \mathcal{C}_{n,m}^\ell} \mathbf{1}(x_n^\ell, x_m^\ell) \quad (29)$$

where $\mathbf{1}(x, y) = 1$ if $x = y$ and $\mathbf{1}(x, y) = 0$ otherwise. The parameters $\sigma(0)$ and $m(0)$ (respectively $\sigma(1)$ and $m(1)$) stand for the standard deviation and the mean of the outlier class (respectively the inlier class). In all the experiences these parameters have been fixed to the same set of values. If a sufficiently large region of outliers is detected by the classification process then it is included as a new region in the partition.

Global deformations obviously involve far more expensive computations than local deformations. Therefore, in practice, they will be only considered at the beginning of each grid level.

A sketchy synopsis of the overall method is presented in Fig. 2 within the multiresolution setup. In this figure, the subscript k represents the resolution level. At the coarser resolution, the flow field is initialized to a null field associated to a partition composed of an unique region (the whole image). At that level, the partition is frozen in order to have a first crude estimate of the optical flow. At finer resolutions, the partition is initialized by a projection of previous segmentation on which global deformation process is run right away.

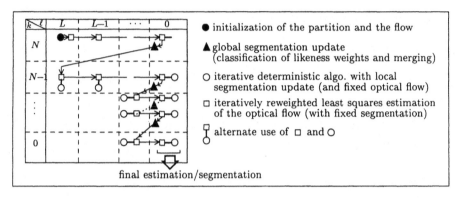

Fig. 2. Schematic synopsis of the complete estimation/segmentation method

5 Experimental results

The experiences have been carried out on synthetic sequence (for which a ground truth on the flow field to recover exists) and two real-world sequences. The first sequence is the well known Yosemite synthetic sequence (Fig. 3). The second test sequence is a Parking lot sequence which involves two cars moving in the foreground while the camera pans the scene. (Fig. 4). The last sequence, named Calendar includes several moving objects (a calendar moving vertically and a toy train pushing a ball) and an horizontal panning of the camera (Fig. 5).

As for the robust estimator, we choose the Leclerc's estimator [14]: $\rho(x) \triangleq 1 - \exp(\frac{x^2}{\sigma^2})$. Let us note that for each sequence, the same set of parameter values have been kept along the multiresolution setup and the multigrid structure. The number of resolution levels was respectively 2 for Calendar and Yosemite and 1 for Parking lot. The number of grid levels were fixed to 6 for Calendar and to 5 for the two others. The other parameters were tuned according to the amplitude of motion present in each sequence.

Flow	$\bar{\mu}$	σ	density
Parametric flow	4.54°	8.37°	100%
Dense flow	4.91°	8.46°	100%
▲ *Estimation/segmentation method* ▲			
Dense flow [15]	5.37°	8.19	100%
▲ *Optic-flow estimation alone* ▲			

Technique	$\bar{\mu}$	σ	density
H. and S. (original)	31.69°	31.18°	100%
H. and S. (modified)	9.78°	16.19°	100%
Uras *et al.*	8.94°	15.61°	100%
Lucas and Kanade	4.28°	11.41°	35.1%
Fleet and Jepson	4.63°	13.42°	34.1%

Table 1. *Comparative results on* Yosemite

Following [4], we provide quantitative comparative results on Yosemite. Angular deviations with respect to the actual flow field have been computed. Tables above list the mean angular error ($\bar{\mu}$) and the associated standard deviation (σ). They gather some of the results presented in [4] and those obtained by the estimation-segmentation method. In the latter case, we report the results for the parametric likeness flow and for the dense flow. Results obtained by the robust multigrid optical flow estimation method [15] without the segmentation coupling are also given.

As may be seen from this table, our method provides almost as good results as those obtained with the best non-dense method. Compared with a single estimation of the optical flow the estimation-segmentation we propose improves the mean of the angular error. Furthermore, through the partition estimation we now have access to a global representation of the scene structure. Indeed, the obtained partition suggests a sensible planar patch representation of the underlying scene (Fig. 3). The parametric likeness field is actually a good approximation

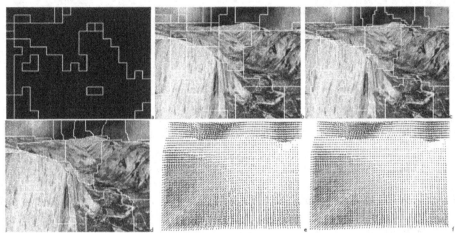

Fig. 3. *Results on* Yosemite (224×288): (a) *partition initialization at the coarsest level* $\ell = 4$, (b, c, d) *final partitions* ($\ell = 4, 2, 0$), (e) *dense optic flow*, (f) *parametric flow.* *(cpu-time~8mn.)*

of the dense estimated flow field. This nice behavior of the method is confirmed by the results obtained on Calendar and Parking lot. For instance, in Calendar some difficult regions (such as the roof of the wagon or the space between the locomotive and the wagon) are fairly well recovered (Fig. 5). These remarks hold also in the Parking lot case where the method retrieves an interesting "structural approximation" of the front car (Fig. 4). We should also outline that the method is not very sensitive to the initialization. More precisely, the method is able to recover meaningful partitions of the flow field from quite "distant" initializations (see for instance Fig. 5 and Fig. 3).

Rough estimates of the computation times (code not hand-optimized) obtained on a Sun Ultra Sparc (200 Mhz) are also given in the captions of figures 3, 4 and 5.

6 Conclusion

In this paper we have presented a method which relies on bilateral coupling between a dense optical flow estimator and a segmentation process. This approach is based on a global energy function where the interaction between the two processes lies both at the borders, through analog line process, and within each region through a parametric modeling of velocities.

The minimization of the global energy function is done using an efficient multigrid approach over both configuration spaces (dense velocity fields and

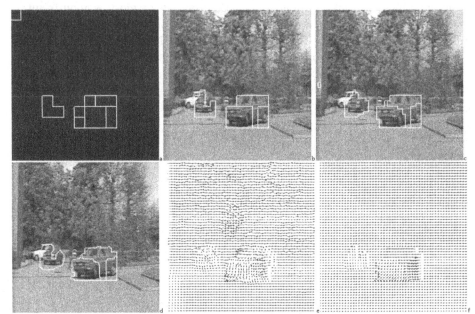

Fig. 4. *Results on* Parking lot (224×224): **(a)** *partition initialization at level* $\ell = 4$, **(b, c, d)** *final partitions* $(\ell = 3, 2, 0)$, **(e)** *dense optic flow*, **(f)** *parametric flow.* (CPU-TIME~*4mn 30s.*)

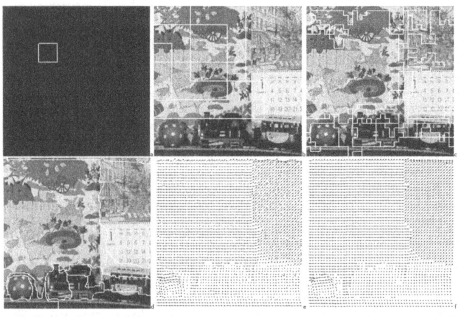

Fig. 5. *Results on* Calendar (256×256): **(a)** *partition initialization at level* $\ell = 4$, **(b,c,d)** *final partitions* $(\ell = 5, 3, 0)$, **(e)** *dense optic flow*, **(f)** *parametric flow.* (CPU-TIME~8mn.)

image partitions). The overall minimization involving only incremental computation is computationally reasonable.

We have experimentally demonstrated that this coupling between a dense optical flow estimator and a segmentation process (i) improves the global quality of the recovered dense flow field and (ii) provides a structural description of the entire motion field, and consequently of the underlying scene.

References

1. E.H. Adelson and J.Y.A. Wang. Representing moving images with layers. *IEEE Trans. Pattern Anal. Machine Intell.*, 5(3):625–638, 1994.
2. G. Adiv. Determining three-dimensional motion and structure from optical flow generated by several moving objects. *IEEE Trans. Pattern Anal. Machine Intell.*, 7:384–401, Jul 1985.
3. S. Ayer and H.S. Sawhney. Layered representation of motion video using robust maximum-likelihood estimation of mixture models and Mdl encoding. In *Proc. Int. Conf. Computer Vision*, pages 777–784, June 1995.
4. J. Barron, D. Fleet, and S. Beauchemin. Performance of optical flow techniques. *Int. J. Computer Vision*, 12(1):43–77, 1994.
5. M. Black and P. Anandan. The robust estimation of multiple motions: Parametric and piecewise-smooth flow fields. *Computer Vision and Image Understanding*, 63(1):75–104, 1996.
6. M. Black and P. Jepson. Estimating optical flow in segmented images using variable-order parametric models with local deformations. *IEEE Trans. Pattern Anal. Machine Intell.*, 18(10):972–986, 1996.
7. P. Bouthemy and E. Francois. Motion segmentation and qualitative dynamic scene analysis from an image sequence. *Int. J. Computer Vision*, 10(2):157–182, 1993.
8. M. M. Chang, A. M. Tekalp, and M. I. Sezan. Simultaneous motion estimation and segmentation. *IEEE Trans. Image Processing*, 6(9):1326–1333, 1997.
9. P. Charbonnier, L. Blanc-Féraud, G. Aubert, and M. Barlaud. Deterministic edge-preserving regularization in computed imaging. *IEEE Trans. Image Processing*, 6(2):298–311, 1997.
10. T. Darrell and A.P. Pentland. Cooperative robust estimation using layers of support. *IEEE Trans. Pattern Anal. Machine Intell.*, 17(5):474–487, 1995.
11. W. Enkelmann. Investigation of multigrid algorithms for the estimation of optical flow fields in image sequences. *Comp. Vision Graph. and Image Proces.*, 43:150–177, 1988.
12. D. Geman and G. Reynolds. Constrained restoration and the recovery of discontinuities. *IEEE Trans. Pattern Anal. Machine Intell.*, 14(3):367–383, 1992.
13. B. Horn and B. Schunck. Determining optical flow. *Artificial Intelligence*, 17:185–203, 1981.
14. Y. Leclerc. Constructing simple stable descriptions for image partitioning. *Int. J. Computer Vision*, 3:73–102, 1989.
15. E. Mémin and P. Pérez. Dense estimation and object-based segmentation of the optical flow with robust techniques. *IEEE Trans. Image Processing*, 5(1), 1998.
16. E. Mémin and P. Pérez. A multigrid approach for hierarchical motion estimation. In *Proc. Int. Conf. Computer Vision*, pages 933–938, 1998.
17. D.W. Murray and H. Buxton. Scene segmentation from visual motion using global optimization. *IEEE Trans. Pattern Anal. Machine Intell.*, 9(2):220–228, Mar 1987.
18. C. Stiller. Object-based estimation of dense motion fields. *IEEE Trans. Image Processing*, 6(2):234–250, 1997.

Recognition
Robotics and Active Vision

Face Recognition Using Active Appearance Models

G.J. Edwards, T.F. Cootes, and C.J. Taylor

Wolfson Image Analysis Unit,
Department of Medical Biophysics,
University of Manchester,
Manchester M13 9PT, U.K.
gje@sv1.smb.man.ac.uk
http://www.wiau.man.ac.uk

Abstract. We present a new framework for interpreting face images and image sequences using an Active Appearance Model (AAM). The AAM contains a statistical, photo-realistic model of the shape and grey-level appearance of faces. This paper demonstrates the use of the AAM's efficient iterative matching scheme for image interpretation. We use the AAM as a basis for face recognition, obtain good results for difficult images. We show how the AAM framework allows identity information to be decoupled from other variation, allowing evidence of identity to be integrated over a sequence. The AAM approach makes optimal use of the evidence from either a single image or image sequence. Since we derive a complete description of a given image our method can be used as the basis for a range of face image interpretation tasks.

1   Introduction

There is currently a great deal of interest in model-based approaches to the interpretation of images [17] [9] [15] [14][8]. The attractions are two-fold: robust interpretation is achieved by constraining solutions to be valid instances of the model example; and the ability to 'explain' an image in terms of a set of model parameters provides a basis for scene interpretation. In order to realise these benefits, the model of object appearance should be as complete as possible - able to synthesise a very close approximation to any image of the target object.

A model-based approach is particularly suited to the task of interpreting faces in images. Faces are highly variable, deformable objects, and manifest very different appearances in images depending on pose, lighting, expression, and the identity of the person. Interpretation of such images requires the ability to understand this variability in order to extract useful information. Currently, the most commonly required information is the identity of the face.

Although model-based methods have proved quite successful, none of the existing methods uses a full, photo-realistic model and attempts to match it directly by minimising the difference between model-synthesised example and the image under interpretation. Although suitable photo-realistic models exist, (e.g. Edwards *et al* [8]), they typically involve a large number of parameters (50-100) in order to deal with the variability due to differences between individuals, and changes in pose, expression, and lighting. Direct optimisation over such a high dimensional space seems daunting.

We show that a direct optimisation approach is feasible and leads to an algorithm which is rapid, accurate, and robust. We do not attempt to solve a general optimisation each time we wish to fit the model to a new image. Instead, we exploit the fact the optimisation problem is similar each time - we can learn these similarities off-line. This allows us to find directions of rapid convergence even though the search space has very high dimensionality. The main features of the approach are described here - full details and experimental validations have been presented elsewhere[4].

We apply this approach to face images and show first that, using the model parameters for classification we can obtain good results for person identification and expression recognition using a very difficult training and test set of still images. We also show how the method can be used in the interpretation of image sequences. The aim is to improve recognition performance by integrating evidence over many frames. Edwards et. al.[7] described how a face appearance model can be partitioned to give sets of parameters that independently vary identity, expression, pose and lighting. We exploit this idea to obtain an estimate of identity which is independent of other sources of variability and can be straightforwardly filtered to produce an optimal estimate of identity. We show that this leads to a stable estimate of ID, even in the presence of considerable noise. We also show how the approach can be used to produce high-resolution visualisation of poor quality sequences.

1.1 Background

Several model-based approaches to the interpretation of face images of have been described. The motivation is to achieve robust performance by using the model to constrain solutions to be valid examples of faces. A model also provides the basis for a broad range of applications by 'explaining' the appearance of a given image in terms of a compact set of model parameters, which may be used to characterise the pose, expression or identity of a face. In order to interpret a new image, an efficient method of finding the best match between image and model is required.

Turk and Pentland [17] use principal component analysis to describe face images in terms of a set of basis functions, or 'eigenfaces'. The eigenface representationis not robust to shape changes, and does not deal well with variability in pose and expression. However, the model can be fit to an image easily using correlation based methods. Ezzat and Poggio [9] synthesise new views of a face from a set of example views. They fit the model to an unseen view by a stochastic optimisation procedure. This is extremely slow, but can be robust because of the quality of the synthesised images. Cootes *et al* [3] describe a 3D model of the grey-level surface, allowing full synthesis of shape and appearance. However, they do not suggest a plausible search algorithm to match the model to a new image. Nastar *at al* [15] describe a related model of the 3D grey-level surface, combining physical and statistical modes of variation. Though they describe a search algorithm, it requires a very good initialisation. Lades *at al* [12] model shape and some grey level information using Gabor jets. However, they do not impose strong shape constraints and cannot easily synthesise a new instance. Cootes *et al* [5] model shape and local grey-level appearance, using Active Shape Models (ASMs) to locate flexible objects in new images. Lanitis *at al* [14] use this approach to interpret face images. Having found the shape using an ASM, the face is warped into a normalised frame, in which a model of the intensities of the shape-free face are used to interpret the image. Edwards *at al* [8] extend this work to produce a combined model of shape and grey-level appearance, but again rely on the ASM to locate faces in new images. Our new approach can be seen as a further extension of this idea, using all the information in the combined appearance model to fit to the image. Covell [6] demonstrates that the parameters of an eigen-feature model can be used to drive shape model points to the correct place. We use a generalisation of this idea. Black and Yacoob [2] use local, hand-crafted models of image flow to track facial features, but do not attempt to model the whole face. Our active appearance model approach is a generalisation of this, in which the image difference patterns corresponding to changes in each model parameter are learnt and used to modify a model estimate.

2 Modelling Face Appearance

In this section we outline how our appearance models of faces were generated. The approach follows that described in Edwards *et al* [8] but includes extra grey-level normalisation steps. Some familiarity with the basic approach is required to understand the new Active Appearance Model algorithm.

The models were generated by combining a model of shape variation with a model of the appearance variations in a shape-normalised frame. We require a training set of labelled images, where landmark points are marked on each example face at key positions to outline the main features.

Given such a set we can generate a statistical model of shape variation (see [5] for details). The labelled points on a single face describe the shape of that face. We align all the sets of points into a common co-ordinate frame and represent each by a vector, $\mathbf{x}$. We then apply a principal component analysis (PCA) to the data. Any example can then be approximated using:

$$\mathbf{x} = \bar{\mathbf{x}} + \mathbf{P}_s \mathbf{b}_s \qquad (1)$$

where $\bar{\mathbf{x}}$ is the mean shape, $\mathbf{P}_s$ is a set of orthogonal *modes of shape variation* and $\mathbf{b}_s$ is a set of shape parameters.

To build a statistical model of the grey-level appearance we warp each example image so that its control points match the mean shape (using a triangulation algorithm). We then sample the grey level information $\mathbf{g}_{im}$ from the *shape-normalised* image over the region covered by the mean shape. To minimise the effect of global lighting variation, we normalise this vector, obtaining $\mathbf{g}$. For details of this method see[4].

By applying PCA to this data we obtain a linear model:

$$\mathbf{g} = \bar{\mathbf{g}} + \mathbf{P}_g \mathbf{b}_g \qquad (2)$$

where $\bar{\mathbf{g}}$ is the mean normalised grey-level vector, $\mathbf{P}_g$ is a set of orthogonal *modes of grey-level variation* and $\mathbf{b}_g$ is a set of grey-level model parameters.

The shape and appearance of any example can thus be summarised by the vectors $\mathbf{b}_s$ and $\mathbf{b}_g$. Since there may be correlations between the shape and grey-level variations, we apply a further PCA to the data as follows. For each example we generate the concatenated vector

Fig. 1. First four modes of appearance variation (+/- 3 sd)

$$b = \begin{pmatrix} W_s b_s \\ b_g \end{pmatrix} = \begin{pmatrix} W_s P_s^T (x - \bar{x}) \\ P_g^T (g - \bar{g}) \end{pmatrix} \tag{3}$$

where W_s is a diagonal matrix of weights for each shape parameter, allowing for the difference in units between the shape and grey models. We apply a PCA on these vectors, giving a further model

$$b = Qc \tag{4}$$

where Q are the eigenvectors of b and c is a vector of *appearance* parameters controlling both the shape and grey-levels of the model. Since the shape and grey-model parameters have zero mean, c does too.

An example image can be synthesised for a given c by generating the shape-free grey-level image from the vector g and warping it using the control points described by x. Full details of the modelling procedure can be found in [4].

We applied the method to build a model of facial appearance. Using a training set of 400 images of faces, each labelled with 122 points around the main features. From this we generated a shape model with 23 parameters, a shape-free grey model with 113 parameters and a combined appearance model which required only 80 parameters required to explain 98% of the observed variation. The model used about 10,000 pixel values to make up the face patch.

Figure 1 shows the effect of varying the first four appearance model parameters.

3 Active Appearance Model Search

Given the photo-realistic face model, we need a method of automatically matching the model to image data. Given a reasonable starting approximation, we require an efficient algorithm for adjusting the model parameters to match the image. In this section we give an overview of such an algorithm. Full technical details are given in [4].

3.1 Overview of AAM Search

Given an image containing a face and the photo-realistic face model, we seek the optimum set of model parameters (and location) that best describes the image data. One metric we can use to describe the match between model and image is simply $\delta\mathbf{I}$, the vector of differences between the grey-level values in the image and a corresponding instance of the model. The quality of the match can be described by $\Delta = |\delta\mathbf{I}|^2$. As a general optimization problem, we would seek to vary the model parameters while minimizing Δ. This represents an enormous task, given that the model space has 80 dimensions. The Active Appearance Model method uses the full vector $\delta\mathbf{I}$ to drive the search, rather than a simple fitness score. We note that each attempt to match the model to a new face image is actually a similar optimisation problem. Solving a general optimization problem from scratch is unnecessary. The AAM attempts to learn something about how to solve this class of problems in advance. By providing a-priori knowledge of how to adjust the model parameters during during image search, an efficient runtime algorithm results. In particular, the AAM uses the spatial pattern in $\delta\mathbf{I}$, to encode information about how the model parameters should be changed in order to achieve a better fit. For example, if the largest differences between a face model and a face image occurred at the sides of the face, that would imply that a parameter that modified the width of the model face should be adjusted.

Cootes *et al.*[4] describe the training algorithm in detail. The method works by learning from an annotated set of training example in which the 'true' model parameters are known. For each example in the training set, a number of known model displacements are applied, and the corresponding difference vector recorded. Once enough training data has been generated, multivariate multiple regression is applied to model the relationship between the model displacement and image difference.

Image search then takes place by placing the model in the image and measuring the difference vector. The learnt regression model is then used to predict a movement of the face model likely to give a better match. The process is iterated to convergence. In our experiments, we implement a multi-resolution version of this algorithm, using lower resolution models in earlier stages of a search to give a wider location range. The model used contained 10,000 pixels at the highest level and 600 pixels at the lowest.

4 Face Recognition using AAM Search

Lanitis et al. [13] describe face recognition using shape and grey-level parameters. In their approach the face is located in an image using Active Shape Model search, and the shape parameters extracted. The face patch is then deformed to the average shape, and the grey-level parameters extracted. The shape and grey-level parameters are used together for classification. As described above, we combine the shape and grey-level parameters and derive Appearance Model parameters, which can be used in a similar classifier, but providing a more compact model than that obtained by considering shape and grey-level separately.

Given a new example of a face, and the extracted model parameters, the aim is to identify the individual in a way which is invariant to confounding factors such as lighting, pose and expression. If there exists a representative training set of face images, it is possible to do this using the Mahalonobis distance measure [11], which enhances the effect of inter-class variation (identity), whilst suppressing the effect of within class variation (pose,lighting,expression). This gives a scaled measure of the distance of an

Fig. 2. Varying the most significant identity parameter(top), and manipulating residual variation without affecting identity(bottom)

example from a particular class. The Mahalanobis distance D_i of the example from class i, is given by

$$D_i = (\mathbf{c} - \bar{\mathbf{c}}_i)\mathbf{C}^{-1}(\mathbf{c} - \bar{\mathbf{c}}_i) \tag{5}$$

where $\mathbf{c}$ is the vector of extracted appearance parameters, $\bar{\mathbf{c}}_i$ is the centroid of the multivariate distribution for class i, and $\mathbf{C}$ is the common within-class covariance matrix for all the training examples. Given sufficient training examples for each individual, the individual within-class covariance matrices $\mathbf{C_i}$ could be used - it is, however, restrictive to assume that such comprehensive training data is available.

4.1   Isolating Sources of Variation

The classifier described earlier assumes that the within-class variation is very similar for each individual, and that the pooled covariance matrix provides a good overall estimate of this variation. Edwards et al. [7] use this assumption to linearly separate the inter-class variability from the intra-class variability using Linear Discriminant Analysis (LDA). The approach seeks to find a linear transformation of the appearance parameters which maximises inter-class variation, based on the pooled within-class and between-class covariance matrices. The identity of a face is given by a vector of *discriminant parameters*, $\mathbf{d}$, which ideally only code information important to identity. The transformation between appearance parameters, $\mathbf{c}$, and discriminant parameters, $\mathbf{d}$ is given by

$$\mathbf{c} = \mathbf{Dd} \tag{6}$$

where $\mathbf{D}$ is a matrix of orthogonal vectors describing the principal types of inter-class variation. Having calculated these inter-class *modes of variation*, Edwards et al. [7] showed that a subspace orthogonal to $\mathbf{D}$ could be constructed which modelled only intra-class variations due to change in pose, expression and lighting.The effect of this decomposition is to create a combined model which is still in the form of Equation 1, but where the parameters, $\mathbf{c}$, are partitioned into those that affect identity and those that describe within-class variation. Figure 2 shows the effect of varying the most significant identity parameter for such a model; also shown is the effect of applying the first mode of the residual (identity-removed) model to an example face. It can be seen that the linear separation is reasonably successful and that the identity remains unchanged.

The 'identity' subspace constructed gives a suitable frame of reference for classifica-

Fig. 3. Original image (right) and best fit (left) given landmark points

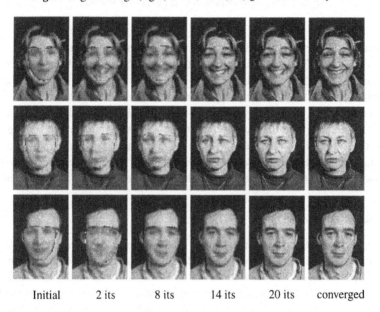

| Initial | 2 its | 8 its | 14 its | 20 its | converged |

Fig. 4. Multi-Resolution search from displaced position

tion. The euclidean distance between images when projected onto this space is a measure of the similarity of ID between the images, since discriminant analysis ensures that the effect of confounding factors such as expression is minimised.

4.2 Search Results

A full analysis of the robustness and accuracy of AAM search is beyond the scope of this paper, but is described elsewhere[4]. In our experiments, we used the face AAM to search for faces in previously unseen images. Figure 3 shows the best fit of the model given the image points marked by hand for three faces. Figure 4 shows frames from a AAM search for each face, each starting with the mean model displaced from the true face centre.

4.3 Recognition Results

The model was used to perform two recognition experiments; recognition of identity, and recognition of expression. In both tests 400 faces were used - 200 for training and

Fig. 5. Typical examples from the experimental set

200 for testing. The set contained images of 20 different individuals captured under a range of conditions. This particular set of faces was chosen for its large range of expression changes as well as limited pose and lighting variation. These factors, the *within class* variability, serve to make the recognition tasks much harder than with controlled expression and pose. Figure 5 shows some typical examples from the set. The active appearance model was used to locate and interpret both the training and test images. In both cases the model was given the initial eye positions, and was then required to fit to the face image using the strategy described in section 3. Thus, for each face, a set of model parameters was extracted, and the results used for classification experiments.

4.4 Recognising Identity

The identity recognition was performed in the identity subspace as described in section 4.1. Each example vector of extracted model parameters was projected onto the ID-subspace. The training set was used to find the centroid, in the ID-subspace for each of the training faces. A test face was then classified according to the nearest centroid of the training set. In order to quantify the performance of the Active Appearance Model for location and interpretation, we compared the results with the best that could be achieved using this classifier with hand annotation. For each example (training and test) the 122 key-landmark points were placed by hand, and the model parameters extracted from the image as described in section 2. Using the above classifier, this method achieved 88% correct recognition. When the active appearance model was applied to the same images, the recognition rate remained at 88%. Although this represents equal performance with hand-annotation, a few of the failures were on different faces from the hand-annotated results. Thus we can conclude that the Active Appearance Model competes with hand annotation; any further improvement in classification rate requires addressing the classifier itself.

4.5 Recognising Expression

In order to test the performance of the Active Appearance Model for expression recognition, we tested the system against 25 human observers. Each observer was shown the set of 400 face images, and asked to classify the expression of each as one of: *happy, sad, afraid, angry, surprised, disgusted, neutral*. We then divided the results into two separate blocks of 200 images each, one used for training the expression classifier, and the other used for testing. Since there was considerable disagreement amongst the human observers as to the correct expression, it was necessary to devise an objective measure of performance for both the humans and the model. A leave-one-out based scheme was devised thus: Taking the 200 test images, each human observer attached a label to each. This label was then compared with the label attached to that image by the 24 *other* observers. One point was scored for every agreement. In principle this could mean a maximum score of 24x200 = 4800 points, however, there were very few cases in which all the human observers agreed, so the actual maximum is much less. In order to give a performance baseline for this data, the score was calculated several times by making random choices alone. The other 200 images were used to train an expression classifier based on the model parameters. This classifier was then tested on the same 200 images as the human observers. The results were as follows:

> Random choices score 660   +/- 150
> Human observer score 2621 +/- 300
> Machine score   1950

Although the machine does not perform as well as any of the human observers, the results encourage further exploration. The AAM search results are extremely accurate, and the ID recognition performance high. This suggests that expression recognition is limited by the simple linear classifier we have used. Further work will address a more sophisticated model of human expression characterisation.

5   Tracking and Identification from Sequences

In many recognition systems, the input data is actually a sequence of images of the same person. In principal, a greater amount of available is information than from a single image, even though any single frame of video may contain much less information than a good quality still image. We seek a principled way of interpreting the extra information available from a sequence. Since faces are deformable objects with highly variable appearance, this is a difficult problem. The task is to combine the image evidence whilst filtering noise, the difficulty is knowing the difference between real temporal changes to the data (eg. the person smiles) and changes simply due to systematic and/or random noise.

The model-based approach offers a potential solution - by projecting the image data into the model frame, we have a means of registering the data from frame to frame. Intuitively, we can imagine different dynamic models for each separate source of variability. In particular, given a sequence of images of the same person we expect the identity to remain constant, whilst lighting, pose and expression vary each with its own dynamics. In fact, most of the variation in the model is due to changes between individuals, variation which does not occur in a sequence. If this variation could be held constant we would expect more robust tracking, since the model would more specifically represent the input data.

Edwards et. al.[7] show that LDA can be used to partition the model into ID and non-ID subspaces as described in section 4.1. This provides the basis for a principled method of integrating evidence of identity over a sequence. If the model parameter for each frame are projected into the identity subspace, the expected variation over the sequence is zero and we can apply an appropriate filter to achieve robust tracking and an optimal estimate of identity over the sequence.

Although useful, the separation between the different types of variation which can be achieved using LDA is not perfect. The method provides a good first-order approximation, but, in reality, the within-class spread takes a different shape for each person. When viewed *for each individual at a time*, there is typically correlation between the identity parameters and the residual parameters, even though for the data *as a whole*, the correlation is minimised.

Ezzat and Poggio [10] describe class-specific normalisation of pose using multiple views of the same person, demonstrating the feasibility of a linear approach. They assume that different views of each individual are available in advance - here, we make no such assumption. We show that the estimation of class-specific variation can be integrated with tracking to make optimal use of both prior and new information in estimating ID and achieving robust tracking.

5.1 Class-Specific Refinement of Recognition from Sequences

In our approach, we reason that the imperfections of LDA when applied to a specific individual can be modelled by observing the behaviour of the model during a sequence. We describe a class-specific linear correction to the result of the global LDA, given a sequence of a face. To illustrate the problem, we consider a simplified synthetic situation in which appearance is described in some 2-dimensional space as shown in figure 6. We imagine a large number of representative training examples for two individuals, person X and person Y projected into this space. The optimum direction of group separation, **d**, and the direction of residual variation **r**, are shown. A perfect discriminant

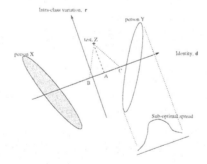

Fig. 6. Limitation of Linear Discriminant Analysis: Best identification possible for single example, Z, is the projection, A. But if Z is an individual who behaves like X or Y, the optimum projections should be C or B respectively.

analysis of identity would allow two faces of different pose, lighting and expression to be normalised to a reference view, and thus the identity compared. It is clear from the diagram that an orthogonal projection onto the identity subspace is not ideal for either person X or person Y. Given a fully representative set of training images for X and Y, we could work out in advance the ideal projection. We do not however, wish (or need) to restrict ourselves to acquiring training data in advance. If we wish to identify an example of person Z, for whom we have only one example image, the best estimate possible is the orthogonal projection, A, since we cannot know from a single example whether Z behaves like X (in which case C would be the correct identity) or like Y (when B would be correct) or indeed, neither. The discriminant analysis produces only a first order approximation to class-specific variation.

In our approach we seek to calculate class-specific corrections from image sequences. The framework used is the Appearance Model, in which faces are represented by a parameter vector c, as in Equation 1.

LDA is applied to obtain a first order global approximation of the linear subspace describing identity, given by an identity vector, d, and the residual linear variation, given by a vector r. A vector of appearance parameters, c can thus be described by

$$c = \bar{c} + Dc + Rr \qquad (7)$$

where D and R are matrices of orthogonal eigenvectors describing identity and residual variation respectively. D and R are orthogonal with respect to each other and the dimensions of d and r sum to the dimension of c. The projection from a vector, b onto d and r is given by

$$d = D^T c \qquad (8)$$

and

$$r = R^T c \qquad (9)$$

Equation 8 gives the orthogonal projection onto the identity subspace, d, the best classification available given a single example. We assume that this projection is not ideal, since it is not class-specific. Given further examples, in particular, from a sequence, we seek to apply a class-specific correction to this projection. It is assumed that the correction of identity required has a linear relationship with the residual parameters, but that this relationship is different for each individual.

Formally, if d_c is the true projection onto the identity subspace, d is the orthogonal projection, r is the projection onto the residual subspace, and $\bar{r}$ is the mean of the residual subspace (average lighting,pose,expression) then,

$$d - d_c = A(r - \bar{r}) \qquad (10)$$

where A is a matrix giving the correction of the identity, given the residual parameters. During a sequence, many examples *of the same face* are seen. We can use these examples to solve Equation 10 in a least-squares sense for the matrix A, by applying linear regression, thus giving the class-specific correction required for the particular individual.

5.2 Tracking Face Sequences

In each frame of an image sequence, an Active Appearance Model can be used to locate the face. The iterative search procedure returns a set of parameters describing the best match found of the model to the data. Baumberg [1] and Rowe et. al. [16] has described a Kalman filter framework used as a optimal recursive estimator of shape from sequences using an Active Shape Model. In order to improve tracking robustness, we propose a similar scheme, but using the full Appearance Model, and based on the decoupling of identity variation from residual variation.

The combined model parameters are projected into the the identity and residual subspaces by Equations 8 and 9. At each frame, t, the identity vector, d_t, and residual vector r_t are recorded. Until enough frames have been recorded to allow linear regression to be applied, the correction matrix, A is set to contain all zeros, so that the corrected estimate of identity, d_c is the same as the orthogonally projected estimate, d. Once regression can be applied, the identity estimate starts to be corrected. Three sets of Kalman filters are used to track the face. Each track 2D-pose, p, ID variation, d_{id}, and non-ID, d_{res}, variation respectively. The 2D-pose and non-ID variation are modelled as random-walk processes, the ID variation is modelled as a random constant, reflecting the expected dynamics of the system. The optimum parameters controlling the operation of Kalman filters can be estimated from the variation seen over the training set. For example, the ID filter is initialised on the mean face, with a estimated uncertainty covering the range of ID seen during training.

6   Tracking Results

In order to test this approach we took a short sequence of an individual reciting the alphabet whilst moving. We then successively degraded the sequence by adding Gaussian noise at 2.5,5,7.5,10,12.5 and 30% average displacement per pixel. Figure 7 shows frames selected from the uncorrupted sequence, together with the result of the Active Appearance Model search overlaid on the image. The subject talks and moves while varying expression. The amount of movement increases towards the end of the sequence.

After 40 frames the adaptive correction and Kalman filtering was switched on. We first show the results for the uncorrupted sequence. Figure 8 shows the value of the raw projection onto the first and second ID parameters. Considerable variation is observed over the sequence. The corrected, and the final, filtered estimates of the ID parameters are shown in figures 9 and 10 respectively. Figures 9 shows that, once the ID correction is switched on (at frame 40), a more stable estimate of ID results. Figure 10 shows that the combination of ID correction and temporal filtering results in an extremely stable estimate of ID. Figure 11 illustrates the stability of the ID estimate with image degradation. The value of the first ID parameter is shown on the y-axis . This is normalised over the total variation in ID-value over the training set. It is seen that the estimate remains reasonably consistent (within +/- 0.03% of the overall variation) at low levels of degradation, becoming unstable at a higher level.

7   Enhanced Visualisation

After tracking many frames of a sequence the estimate of the corrected identity vector stabilises. A corresponding reconstruction of the person can be synthesised. The syn-

Fig. 7. Tracking and identifying a face. Original frames are shown on the top row, reconstruction on the bottom.

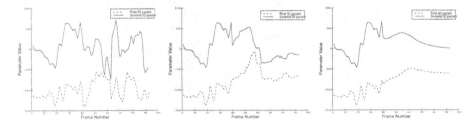

Fig. 8. Raw ID parameters   **Fig. 9.** Corrected ID parameters   **Fig. 10.** Filtered, corrected, ID

thesised image is based on the evidence integrated over the sequence. This provides a means of generating high resolution reconstructions from lower resolution sequences. Figure 12 illustrates an example: The left hand image is a frame from a sequence of 95 images. In the centre image we show an example from the sequence after deliberate Gaussian subsampling to synthesis a low-resolution source image. The reconstruction on the right shows the final estimate of the person based on evidence integrated over the low-resolution sequence.

8   Conclusions

We have described the use of an Active Appearance Model in face recognition. The model uses all the information available from the training data and facilitates the decoupling of model into ID and non-ID parts.

When used for static face identification the AAM proved as reliable as labelling the images by hand. A identification rate of 88% was achieved. When used for expression recognition the systems shows less agreement than human observers but nevertheless encourages further work in this area. A observation of the quality of model fit, and the excellent identity recognition performance suggests that the classifier itself rather than the AAM search limits the expression recognition performance.

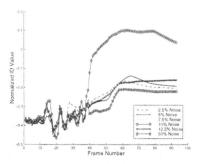

Fig. 11. Tracking Noisy Data. ID estimate remains consistent at increasing noise levels, becoming unstable at 30% noise level.

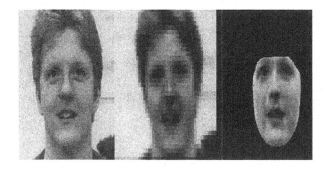

Fig. 12. Synthesising a high-res face from a low-res sequence. Left hand image: an original frame from sequence. Centre image: frame from deliberately blurred sequence. Right hand image: final reconstruction from low-res sequence

We have outlined a technique for improving the stability of face identification and tracking when subject to variation in pose, expression and lighting conditions. The tracking technique makes use of the observed effect of these types of variation in order to provide a better estimate of identity, and thus provides a method of using the extra information available in a sequence to improve classification.

By correctly decoupling the individual sources of variation, it is possible to develop decoupled dynamic models for each. The technique we have described allows the initial approximate decoupling to be updated during a sequence, thus avoiding the need for large numbers of training examples for each individual.

References

1. A. M. Baumberg. *Learning Deformable Models for Tracking Human Motion.* PhD thesis, University of Leeds, 1995.
2. M. J. Black and Y. Yacoob. Recognizing Facial Expressions under Rigid and Non-Rigid Facial Motions. In *International Workshop on Automatic Face and Gesture Recognition 1995*, pages 12–17, Zurich, 1995.

3. T. Cootes and C. Taylor. Modelling object appearance using the grey-level surface. In E. Hancock, editor, 5th *British Machine Vison Conference*, pages 479–488, York, England, September 1994. BMVA Press.

4. T. F. Cootes, G. J. Edwards, and C. J. Taylor. Active appearance models. In *ECCV98 (to appear)*, Freiberg, Germany, 1998.

5. T. F. Cootes, C. J. Taylor, D. H. Cooper, and J. Graham. Active Shape Models - Their Training and Application. *Computer Vision, Graphics and Image Understanding*, 61(1):38–59, 1995.

6. M. Covell. Eigen-points: Control-point Location using Principal Component Analysis. In *International Workshop on Automatic Face and Gesture Recognition 1996*, pages 122–127, Killington, USA, 1996.

7. G. J. Edwards, A. Lanitis, C. J. Taylor, and T. Cootes. Statistical Models of Face Images: Improving Specificity. In *British Machine Vision Conference 1996*, Edinburgh, UK, 1996.

8. G. J. Edwards, C. J. Taylor, and T. Cootes. Learning to Identify and Track Faces in Image Sequences. In *British Machine Vision Conference 1997*, Colchester, UK, 1997.

9. T. Ezzat and T. Poggio. Facial Analysis and Synthesis Using Image-Based Models. In *International Workshop on Automatic Face and Gesture Recognition 1996*, pages 116–121, Killington, Vermont, 1996.

10. T. Ezzat and T. Poggio. Facial Analysis and Synthesis Using Image-Based Models. In *International Workshop on Automatic Face and Gesture Recognition 1996*, pages 116–121, Killington, Vermont, 1996.

11. D. J. Hand. *Discrimination and Classification*. John Wiley and Sons, 1981.

12. M. Lades, J. Vorbruggen, J. Buhmann, J. Lange, C. von der Malsburt, R. Wurtz, and W. Konen. Distortion invariant object recognition in the dynamic link architecture. *IEEE Transactions on Computers*, 42:300–311, 1993.

13. A. Lanitis, C. Taylor, and T. Cootes. A Unified Approach to Coding and Interpreting Face Images. In 5th *International Conference on Computer Vision*, pages 368–373, Cambridge, USA, 1995.

14. A. Lanitis, C. Taylor, and T. Cootes. Automatic Interpretation and Coding of Face Images Using Flexible Models. *IEEE Transactions on Pattern Analysis and Machine Intelligence*, 19(7):743–756, 1997.

15. C. Nastar, B. Moghaddam, and A. Pentland. Generalized Image Matching: Statistical Learning of Physically-Based Deformations. In 4th *European Conference on Computer Vision*, volume 1, pages 589–598, Cambridge, UK, 1996.

16. S. Rowe and A. Blake. Statistical Feature Modelling for Active Contours. In 4th *European Conference on Computer Vision*, volume 2, pages 560–569, Cambridge, UK, 1996.

17. M. Turk and A. Pentland. Eigenfaces for Recognition. *Journal of Cognitive Neuroscience*, 3(1):71–86, 1991.

Face Recognition Using Evolutionary Pursuit

Chengjun Liu and Harry Wechsler

Department of Computer Science, George Mason University,
4400 University Drive, Fairfax, VA 22030-4444, USA
{cliu, wechsler}@cs.gmu.edu

Abstract. This paper describes a novel and adaptive dictionary method for face recognition using genetic algorithms (GAs) in determining the optimal basis for encoding human faces. In analogy to pursuit methods, our novel method is called Evolutionary Pursuit (EP), and it allows for different types of (non-orthogonal) bases. EP processes face images in a lower dimensional whitened PCA subspace. Directed but random rotations of the basis vectors in this subspace are searched by GAs where evolution is driven by a fitness function defined in terms of performance accuracy and class separation (scatter index). Accuracy indicates the extent to which learning has been successful so far, while the scatter index gives an indication of the expected fitness on future trials. As a result, our approach improves the face recognition performance compared to PCA, and shows better generalization abilities than the Fisher Linear Discriminant (FLD) based methods.

1 Introduction

A successful face recognition methodology depends heavily on the particular choice of the features used by the (pattern) classifier [6], [31], [4]. The search for the best feature set corresponds to finding an optimal neural code, biologically characterized as a lattice of receptive fields (RFs) ('kernels') and computationally developed as an optimal basis [26], [2], [30]. Optimization of the visual system then requires searching for such an optimal basis according to the design criteria such as (A) redundancy minimization and decorrelation, (B) minimization of the reconstruction error, (C) maximization of information transmission (infomax) [24], and (D) sparseness of the neural code [26]. Furthermore, to the design criteria listed above one should add as an important functionality the one related to successful pattern classification, referred to by Edelman [13] as neural Darwinism. The rationale behind feature extraction using an optimal basis representation is that most practical methods for both regression and classification use parameterization in the form of a linear combination of basis functions. This leads to a taxonomy based on the type of the basis functions used by a particular method and the corresponding optimization procedure used for parameter estimation. According to this taxonomy, most practical methods use basis function representation — those are called dictionary or kernel methods, where the particular type of chosen basis functions constitutes a kernel. Further distinction is made between non-adaptive methods using fixed (predetermined) basis functions and adaptive dictionary methods where basis functions depend (nonlinearly) on some (tunable) parameters, such that the basis functions themselves (or their parameters) are fit to available data [9].

Representative classes of adaptive dictionary methods include two approaches sharing similar dictionary representations : Projection Pursuit (statistical method) and Multilayer Perceptron (neural network method) [20]. Since most practical methods use nonlinear models, the determination of optimal kernels becomes a nonlinear optimization problem. When the objective function lacks an analytical form suitable for gradient descent or the computation involved is prohibitively expensive one should use (directed) random search techniques for nonlinear optimization and variable selection as those methods characteristic of evolutionary computation and genetic algorithms [17].

Most neural network methods use the same type of basis function, defined as hidden units of a feed forward net and having the same form of activation function (sigmoid or radial basis). In contrast, many statistical adaptive methods do not require the form of all basis functions to be the same. In terms of optimization, statistical methods estimate the basis functions one at a time, hence there is no need for all basis functions to be the same. On the other hand, neural network methods based on gradient descent optimization are more suitable for handling representations with identical basis functions which are updated simultaneously.

Projection Pursuit (PP) regression is an example of an additive model with univariate basis functions [15] [19]. A greedy optimization approach, called back-fitting, is often used to estimate additive approximating functions. The back-fitting algorithm provides a local minimum of the empirical risk encountered during functional approximation by sequentially estimating the individual basis functions of the additive approximating function. Similar to PP in spirit and characteristic of the non-orthogonal and over complete methods is the Matching Pursuit (MP) algorithm [25]. MP decomposes any signal into a linear expansion of waveforms that are selected from a redundant dictionary of functions. These waveforms are chosen in order to best match the signal structure. Using a dictionary of Gabor functions a matching pursuit defines an adaptive time-frequency transform. More recently, Chen and Donoho [7] have described Basis Pursuit as a technique for decomposing a signal into an optimal superposition of dictionary elements using as the optimization criterion the l^1 norm of coefficients.

The search for optimal basis amounts to identifying relevant feature subsets as a result of exploiting non-linear interactions in high dimensional feature spaces. The identification of optimal basis can be approached through the use of Genetic Algorithms (GAs) [17]. GAs work by maintaining a constant-sized population of candidate solutions known as individuals ('chromosomes'). The power of a genetic algorithm lies in its ability to exploit, in a highly efficient manner, information about a large number of individuals. The search underlying GAs is such that breadth and depth — exploration and exploitation — are balanced according to the observed performance of the individuals evolved so far. By allocating more reproductive occurrences to above average individual solutions, the overall effect is to increase the population's average fitness. We advance in this paper an adaptive dictionary method for face recognition using GAs in determining the optimal basis for encoding human faces. In analogy to the pursuit methods referred to earlier our novel method is called Evolutionary Pursuit (EP). The EP method, takes advantage of both statistical and neural methods, and it is described in Sect. 4. EP allows for different types of bases, as some statistical methods do, but it would update the dictionary of choices simultaneously as neural networks do.

As systems that employ several strategies have been shown to offer significant advantages over single-strategy systems, we have developed a hybrid methodology seeking the basis representation for human faces that leads to optimal performance on face recognition tasks. The optimal basis for face recognition is usually defined in terms of 2nd order statistics. PCA related 2nd order methods and their use for face recognition are reviewed in Sect. 2 as they provide the benchmark for comparing our new hybrid and evolutionary methodology for face recognition. Sect. 3 describes the overall strategy for face recognition and the modules involved, while Sect. 4 details the evolutionary pursuit method for deriving the optimal basis and its use for face recognition. Experimental results are given in Sect. 5, while conclusions are presented in Sect. 6.

2 2nd Order Methods and Face Recognition

Principal Component Analysis (PCA), also known as the Karhunen-Loeve expansion, is a classical technique for signal representation [21], [16]. Sirovich and Kirby [32], [22] applied PCA for representing face images. They showed that any particular face can be economically represented along the eigenpictures coordinate space, and that any face can be approximately reconstructed by using just a small collection of eigenpictures and the corresponding projections ('coefficients') along each eigenpicture.

PCA generates a set of orthonormal basis vectors, known as principal components, that maximize the scatter of all projected samples. Let $X = [X_1, X_2, \ldots, X_n]$ be the sample set of the original images. After normalizing the images to unity norm and subtracting the grand mean a new image set $Y = [Y_1, Y_2, \ldots, Y_n]$ is obtained. Each Y_i represents a normalized image with dimensionality N, $Y_i = (y_{i_1}, y_{i_2}, \ldots, y_{i_N})^t$, $(i = 1, 2, \ldots, n)$. The covariance matrix of the normalized image set is defined as

$$\Sigma_Y = \frac{1}{n} \sum_{i=1}^{n} Y_i Y_i^t = \frac{1}{n} Y Y^t \tag{1}$$

and the eigenvector and eigenvalue matrices Φ, Λ are computed as

$$\Sigma_Y \Phi = \Phi \Lambda \tag{2}$$

Note that YY^t is an $N \times N$ matrix while Y^tY is an $n \times n$ matrix. If the sample size n is much smaller than the dimensionality N, then the following method saves some computation [35]

$$(Y^tY)\Psi = \Psi\Lambda_1 \tag{3}$$

$$\Im = Y\Psi \tag{4}$$

where $\Lambda_1 = diag\{\lambda_1, \lambda_2, \ldots, \lambda_n\}$, and $\Im = [\Phi_1, \Phi_2, \ldots, \Phi_n]$. If one assumes that the eigenvalues are sorted in decreasing order, $\lambda_1 \geq \lambda_2 \geq \cdots \geq \lambda_n$, then the first m leading eigenvectors define matrix P

$$P = [\Phi_1, \Phi_2, \ldots, \Phi_m] \tag{5}$$

The new feature set Z with lower dimensionality m $(m \ll N)$ is derived

$$Z = P^tY \tag{6}$$

For pattern recognition, the PCA technique is exploited both directly and indirectly. The direct approaches use the principal components (PCs) as the projection basis, hence preserve the orthogonality of the basis vectors. The indirect methods use PCA primarily as a dimensionality reduction technique for subsequent transformations, and the overall projection basis vectors are usually no longer orthogonal. Unlike signal representation, orthogonality is not a requirement for pattern recognition, and one can expect better performance from non-orthogonal bases over orthogonal ones as they lead to an over complete and robust representational space [12].

Since eigenpictures are fairly good at representing face images, one can also consider using the projections along them as classification features to recognize faces. As a result, Turk and Pentland developed a well known face recognition method, known as eigenfaces, where the eigenfaces correspond to the eigenvectors associated with the dominant eigenvalues of the face covariance matrix. The eigenfaces define a feature space, or "face space", which drastically reduces the dimensionality of the original space, and face detection and identification are carried out in the reduced space [35].

The advantage of direct approaches (PCA only) is their generalization ability [27]. PCA yields projection axes based on the variations from all the training samples, hence these axes are fairly robust for representing both training and testing images (not seen during training). This is the merit of PCA as an optimal technique for signal representation. As a result, the performance during testing will not be very different from that encountered during training. In other words, direct approaches display good generalization ability. The disadvantage of the direct approaches is that they can not distinguish the variations between within and between class scatters, since PCA treats all the training samples equally. As a consequence, by maximizing the scatter measurement, the unwanted within class scatters are also maximized along with the between class scatter maximization. This will lead to poor performance when the within class scatter is big due to lighting, facial expression, pose, and duplicate images.

While PCA is a classical technique for signal representation, Fisher's Linear Discriminant (FLD) is a classical technique for pattern recognition [14], [3]. Several authors have applied this technique for face recognition, gesture recognition, and pattern rejection [8], [11], [1]. Recently Swets and Weng have pointed out that the eigenfaces derived using PCA are only the most expressive features (MEF), which are unrelated to actual face recognition. To derive most discriminating features (MDF), one needs a subsequent FLD projection [33]. Their procedure involves the simultaneous diagonalization of the two within and between class scatter matrices [16]. The MDF space is superior to the MEF space for face recognition only when the training images are representative of the range of face (class) variations; otherwise, the performance difference between the MEF and MDF is not significant. Belhumire, Hespanha, and Kriegman developed a similar approach called fisherfaces by applying first PCA for dimensionality reduction and then FLD for discriminant analysis [3].

The advantage of the indirect methods (combining PCA and FLD) is that they distinguish the different roles of within and between class scatter by applying discriminant analysis, e.g. FLD, and they usually produce non-orthogonal projection axes. But the indirect methods have their disadvantage too, namely poor generalization to new data, because those methods overfit to the training data. As the FLD procedure involves the simultaneous diagonalization of the two within and between class scatter matrices, it is equivalent to two-step operations: first 'whitening' the within class scatter matrix — applying an appropriate transformation that will make the within class scatter matrix equal to unity, and second applying PCA on the new between class scatter matrix [16]. Note that whitening as used here lacks generalization ability when compared to global whitening methods (see Sect. 3.1) which are applied across both within and between scatter matrices defined together as the covariance matrix Σ_Y (see Eq. 1). The purpose of the 'whitening' step here is to normalize the within class scatter to unity, while the second step would then maximize the between class scatter. The robustness of the FLD procedure thus depends on whether or not the within class scatter can capture enough variations for a specific class. When the training samples do not include most of the variations due to lighting, facial expression, pose, and/or duplicate images as those encountered during testing, the 'whitening' step is likely to fit misleading variations, i.e. the normalized within class scatter would best fit the training samples but it would generalize poorly when exposed to new data. As a consequence the performances during testing for such an indirect method will deteriorate. In addition, when the training sample size for each class is small, the within class scatter would usually not capture enough variations. The FLD procedure thus leads to overfitting.

The Evolutionary Pursuit (EP) approach detailed in the following sections would take into consideration of both performance accuracy and generalization capability and evolve balanced results displaying good performance during testing. As a result, EP improves the face recognition performance compared to (direct) PCA (Eigenfaces), and shows better generalization abilities than the FLD based (indirect) methods (MDF/Fisherfaces).

3 Optimal Basis and Face Recognition

Our architecture for face recognition is shown in Fig. 1. The main thrust is to find out an optimal basis along which faces can be projected leading to a compact and efficient face encoding in terms of recognition ability. As discussed in the previous section, PCA first projects the face images into a lower dimensional space. The next step is the whitening transformation and it counteracts the fact that the Mean-Square-Error (MSE) principle underlying PCA preferentially weights low frequencies. Directed but random rotations of the lower dimensional (whitened PCA) space are now driven by evolution and use domain specific knowledge ('fitness'). The fitness behind evolution, the one used to find the optimal basis, considers both recognition rates and the scatter index which are derived using the projections of the face images onto the rotated axes. Evolution is implemented using Evolutionary Pursuit (EP) as a special form of Genetic Algorithms (GAs). Note that the reachable space of EP is increased as a result of using a non-orthonormal (whitening) transformation. One can expect better performance from non-orthogonal bases over orthogonal ones as they lead to an over complete and robust representational space [12]. Note that under the whitening transformation the norms (distances) are not preserved.

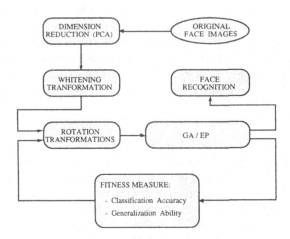

Fig. 1. System Architecture for Face Recognition using Evolutionary Pursuit

3.1 Whitening Transformation

After dimensionality reduction using PCA, the lower dimensional feature set Z (from Eq. 6) is now subjected to the whitening transformation and leads to another feature set V

$$V = \Gamma Z \tag{7}$$

where $\Gamma = diag\{\lambda_1^{-1/2}, \lambda_2^{-1/2}, \ldots, \lambda_m^{-1/2}\}$.

The reason why the whitening procedure can lead to non-orthogonal bases of the overall transformation is as follows. Let Q be a $m \times m$ rotation matrix ($Q^t Q = QQ^t = I$) and apply Q to the feature set V. Combined with Eqs. 6 and 7 one obtains the overall transformation matrix Ξ

$$\Xi = P\Gamma Q \tag{8}$$

Now assume the basis vectors in Ξ are orthogonal (using *proof by contradiction*),

$$\Xi^t \Xi = \Delta \tag{9}$$

where Δ is a diagonal matrix. From Eqs. 8 and 9 it follows that

$$\Gamma^2 = \Delta = cI \tag{10}$$

where c is a constant. Eq. 10 holds only when all the eigenvalues are equal, and when this is not the case the basis vectors in Ξ are not orthogonal. (see Fig. 6).

3.2 Rotation Transformations

The rotation transformations are carried out in the whitened m dimensional space, in which the feature set V lies (see Eq. 7). Let $\Omega = [\varepsilon_1, \varepsilon_2, \ldots, \varepsilon_m]$ be the basis of this space where $\varepsilon_1, \varepsilon_2, \ldots, \varepsilon_m$ are the unit vectors. Our evolutionary pursuit approach would later on search for that (reduced) subset of some basis vectors rotated from $\varepsilon_1, \varepsilon_2, \ldots, \varepsilon_m$ in terms of best discrimination performance. The rotation procedure is carried out by pairwise axes rotation. In particular, let us suppose the basis vectors ε_i and ε_j need to be rotated by α_k, then a new basis $\xi_1, \xi_2, \ldots, \xi_m$ is derived by

$$[\xi_1, \xi_2, \ldots, \xi_m] = [\varepsilon_1, \varepsilon_2, \ldots, \varepsilon_m]Q_k \tag{11}$$

where Q_k is a rotation matrix. There are $M = m(m-1)/2$ rotation angles in total corresponding to the M pairs of basis vectors to be rotated. For the purpose of evolving optimal basis for recognition, it makes no difference if the angles are confined to $(0, \pi/2)$, since the positive directions and the order of axes are not important. The overall rotation matrix Q is defined by

$$Q = Q_1 Q_2 \cdots Q_{m(m-1)/2} \tag{12}$$

3.3 Face Recognition

Let $T = [\Theta_{i_1}, \Theta_{i_2}, \ldots, \Theta_{i_l}]$ be the optimal basis derived by EP (evolutionary pursuit) (see Sect. 4.2). The new feature set U is derived as

$$U = [U_1, U_2, \ldots, U_n] = T^t V \tag{13}$$

where V is the whitened feature set (Eq. 7), and $[U_1, U_2, \ldots, U_n]$ are the feature vectors corresponding to different face images.

Let $U_k^0, (k = 1, 2, \ldots, n)$, be the prototype of class k, the decision rule can be expressed as

$$\|U_i - U_k^0\|_2 = \min_j \|U_i - U_j^0\|_2, \quad U_i \in \omega_k \tag{14}$$

The face image U_i is classified to the class ω_k to which it has the minimum Euclidean distance.

4 Genetic Algorithms (GAs) and Evolutionary Pursuit (EP)

The task for EP is to search through all the rotation axes defined over properly whitened PCA subspaces. Evolution is driven by a fitness function defined in terms of performance accuracy and class separation (scatter index). Accuracy indicates the extent to which learning has been successful so far, while the scatter index gives an indication of the expected fitness on future trials. A large scatter index calls for additional learning so present performance becomes a good indicator on future ('predicted') performance. Predictors on future performance can thus modulate the amount of learning and stop learning, when constant but well behaved performance can be expected from the individual chromosomes. EP defined as above is thus a hybrid between the "filter" and "wrapper" approaches [23] and takes advantage of their comparative merits.

The EP method is implemented using GAs and it has the following advantages. First, directed search in the whitened PCA subspaces which are more reliable than the whitened subspaces of the within class scatter matrix (see MDF for comparison); the reason is that PCA exploits the variations from all the training samples while the within class scatter uses only within class variations. When the sample size of each class is small and the variations are not representative, the whitened subspaces of the within class scatter matrix do not represent the actual unit within class scatter any more. Second, the fitness function consists of two terms: performance accuracy and class separation. These two terms put opposite pressures on the fitness function: the performance accuracy term is similar to the criterion of choosing projection axes with smaller scatter, while the class separation term favors axes with larger scatter. By combining these two terms together (with proper weights), GA can evolve balanced results with good testing performances and generalization abilities.

One should also point out that just using more PCs (principal components) does not necessarily lead to better performance, since some PCs might capture the within class scatter which is unwanted for the purpose of recognition. In our experiments we searched the 20 and 30 dimensional whitened PCA subspaces corresponding to the leading eigenvalues, since it is in those subspaces that most of the variations characteristic of human faces occur.

4.1 Chromosome Representation and Genetic Operators

As is discussed in Sect. 3.2, corresponding to different sets of rotation angles different basis vectors are derived. GAs are used to search among the different rotation transformations and different combinations of basis vectors in order to pick up the best subset of vectors with the most discriminant power. The optimal basis is evolved from a larger vector set $\{\xi_1, \xi_2, \ldots, \xi_m\}$ rotated from a basis $\varepsilon_1, \varepsilon_2, \ldots, \varepsilon_m$ in m dimensional space by a set of rotation angles $\alpha_1, \alpha_2, \ldots, \alpha_{m(m-1)/2}$ with each angle in the range of $(0, \pi/2)$. If the angles are discretized with small enough steps, then we can use GA to search this discretized space. GA requires the solutions to be represented in the form of bit strings or chromosomes. If we use 10 bits (resolution) to represent each angle, then each discretized (angle) interval is less than 0.09 degree, and we need $10*[m(m-1)/2]$ bits to represent all the angles. As we also have m basis vectors (projection axes) to choose from, another m bits should be added to the chromosome to facilitate that choice. Fig. 2 shows the chromosome representation, where $a_i, (i = 1, 2, \ldots, m)$, has the value 0 or 1 and indicates whether the i-th basis vector is chosen or not.

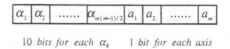

10 *bits for each* α_k 1 *bit for each axis*

Fig. 2. Chromosome Representation of Rotation Angles and Projection Axes

Let N_s be the number of different choices of basis vectors in the search space. The size of genospace, too large to search it exhaustively, is

$$N_s = 2^{5m(m-1)+m} \tag{15}$$

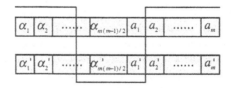

As it searches the genospace, the GA makes its choices via genetic operators as a function of a probability distribution driven by the fitness function. The genetic operators are selection, crossover (or recombination), and mutation [17]. In our experiments, we use (i) proportionate selection: preselection of parents in proportion to their relative fitness; (ii) two points crossover: exchange the sections between the crossover points as shown in Fig. 3; and (iii) fixed probability mutation: each position of a chromosome is given a fixed probability of undergoing mutation (flipping the corresponding bit).

4.2 The Fitness Function

Fitness values guide GA on how to choose offsprings for the next generation from the current parent generation. Let $F \equiv \alpha_1, \alpha_2, \ldots, \alpha_{m(m-1)/2}; a_1, a_2, \ldots, a_m$ represent the parameters to be evolved by GA, then the fitness function $\zeta(F)$ is defined as

$$\zeta(F) = \zeta_a(F) + \lambda \zeta_s(F) \tag{16}$$

where $\zeta_a(F)$ is the performance accuracy term, $\zeta_s(F)$ is the class separation term, and λ is a positive constant. In our experiments, we set $\zeta_a(F)$ to be the number of faces correctly recognized as the top choice after the rotation and selection of a subset of axes, and $\zeta_s(F)$ the scatter measurement among different classes. λ is empirically chosen such that $\zeta_a(F)$ contributes more to the fitness than $\zeta_s(F)$ does. Note that the fitness function defined here has a similar form compared to the cost functional derived from the principle of regularization theory, which is very useful for solving ill-posed problems in computer vision and improving the generalization ability of RBF networks in neural network [34], [29], [18]. Actually, those two terms, $\zeta_a(F)$ and $\zeta_s(F)$, put opposite pressures on the fitness function: the performance accuracy term $\zeta_a(F)$ is similar to the criterion of choosing projection axes with smaller scatter, while the class separation term $\zeta_s(F)$ favors axes with lager scatter. By combining those two terms together (with proper weight λ), GA can evolve balanced results displaying good performance during testing.

Let the rotation angle set be $\alpha_1^{(k)}, \alpha_2^{(k)}, \ldots, \alpha_{m(m-1)/2}^{(k)}$, and the basis vectors after the transformation be $\xi_1^{(k)}, \xi_2^{(k)}, \ldots, \xi_m^{(k)}$ according to Eqs. 11 and 12. If GA chooses l vectors $\eta_1, \eta_2, \ldots, \eta_l$ from $\xi_1^{(k)}, \xi_2^{(k)}, \ldots, \xi_m^{(k)}$, then the new feature set is specified as

$$W = [\eta_1, \eta_2, \ldots, \eta_l]^t V \tag{17}$$

where V is the whitened feature set (see Eq. 7).

Let $\omega_1, \omega_2, \ldots, \omega_L$ and $N_1, N_2, \ldots, N_L$ denote the classes and number of images within each class, respectively. Let $M_1, M_2, \ldots, M_L$ and M_0 be the means of corresponding classes and the grand mean in the new feature space $span[\eta_1, \eta_2, \ldots, \eta_l]$, we then have

$$M_i = \frac{1}{N_i} \sum_{j=1}^{N_i} W_j^{(i)}, \qquad i = 1, 2, \ldots, L \tag{18}$$

where $W_j^{(i)}$, $j = 1, 2, \ldots, N_i$, represent the sample images from class ω_i, and

$$M_0 = \frac{1}{n} \sum_{i=1}^{L} N_i M_i \tag{19}$$

where n is the total number of images for all the classes. Thus, $\zeta_s(F)$ is computed as

$$\zeta_s(F) = \sqrt{\sum_{i=1}^{L} (M_i - M_0)^2} \tag{20}$$

Driven by this fitness function, GA would evolve the optimal solution $F^o \equiv \alpha_1^o, \alpha_2^o, \ldots, \alpha_{m(m-1)/2}^o; a_1^o, a_2^o, \ldots, a_m^o$. Let Q in Eq. 12 represent this particular basis set corresponding to the rotation angles $\alpha_1^o, \alpha_2^o, \ldots, \alpha_{m(m-1)/2}^o$ (remember $\varepsilon_1, \varepsilon_2, \ldots, \varepsilon_m$ are unit vectors), and let the column vectors in Q be $\Theta_1, \Theta_2, \ldots, \Theta_m$

$$Q = [\Theta_1, \Theta_2, \ldots, \Theta_m] \tag{21}$$

Let $\Theta_{i_1}, \Theta_{i_2}, \ldots, \Theta_{i_l}$ be the basis vectors corresponding to $a_1^o, a_2^o, \ldots, a_m^o$, then the optimal basis T can be expressed as

$$T = [\Theta_{i_1}, \Theta_{i_2}, \ldots, \Theta_{i_l}] \tag{22}$$

where $i_j \in \{1, 2, \ldots, m\}$, $i_j \neq i_k$ for $j \neq k$, and $l < m$.

4.3 The Evolutionary Pursuit (EP) Algorithm

The evolutionary pursuit (EP) algorithm works as follows:

1. Compute the eigenvector and eigenvalue matrices of $Y^t Y$ using singular value decomposition (SVD) or Jacobi's method, and derive $\Lambda_1 = diag\{\lambda_1, \lambda_2, \ldots, \lambda_n\}$ and $\Im = [\Phi_1, \Phi_2, \ldots, \Phi_n]$ according to Eqs. 3 and 4. Choose then the first m leading eigenvectors from $\Im$ as basis vectors (Eq. 5) and project the original image set Y onto those vectors to form the feature set Z (Eq. 6) in this reduced PCA subspace.

2. Whiten the feature set Z and derive the new feature set V in the whitened PCA subspace (Eq. 7).

3. Set $[\varepsilon_1, \varepsilon_2, \ldots, \varepsilon_m]$ to be a $m \times m$ unit matrix: $[\varepsilon_1, \varepsilon_2, \ldots, \varepsilon_m] = I_m$.

4. Begin the evolution loop until the stopping criteria (e.g., the maximum number of trials) are reached:

   (a) Sweep the $m(m-1)/2$ pairs of axes according to a fixed order to get the rotation angle set $\alpha_1^{(k)}, \alpha_2^{(k)}, \ldots, \alpha_{m(m-1)/2}^{(k)}$ from the individual chromosome representation (Fig. 2), and rotate the unit basis vectors, $[\varepsilon_1, \varepsilon_2, \ldots, \varepsilon_m]$, in this m dimensional space to derive the new projection axes: $\xi_1^{(k)}, \xi_2^{(k)}, \ldots, \xi_m^{(k)}$ using Eqs. 11 and 12.

   (b) Compute the fitness value (Eq. 16) in the feature space defined by the l projection axes, $\eta_1, \eta_2, \ldots, \eta_l$, chosen from the rotated axes set $\left\{\xi_1^{(k)}, \xi_2^{(k)}, \ldots, \xi_m^{(k)}\right\}$ according to the $a_i's$ from the individual chromosome representation (Fig. 2).

   (c) Find the sets of angles and the subsets of projection axes that maximize the fitness value, and keep these chromosomes as the best solutions so far.

(d) Change the values of rotation angles and the subsets of the projection axes according to GA's genetic operators, and repeat the evolution loop.

5. Carry out recognition using Eqs. 22, 13, and 14, after GA evolves the optimal basis, $\Theta_{i_1}, \Theta_{i_2}, \ldots, \Theta_{i_l}$.

The computational complexity of the algorithm falls mainly into two parts: the PCA computation of step 1 and the evolution loop of step 4. In step 1, the SVD of matrix of size $n \times n$ has the complexity of $O(n^3)$ according to [5], the computation of the eigenvector matrix $\Im$ (Eq. 4) is $O(n^2N)$, and the derivation of the feature set Z (Eq. 6) is $O(mnN)$. In step 4, the rotation transformations of (a) and the fitness value computations of (b) account for most of the computation. In step 4 (a), each rotation transformation changes two column vectors (pairwise axes rotation), and there are $m(m-1)/2$ rotations in total, hence the complexity is $O(m^3)$. In step 4 (b), if we only count the number of multiplications, then Eq. 17 accounts for the major part of the computation with the computational complexity $O(lmn)$. The overall complexity of the evolution procedure also depends on the maximum number of trials.

5 Experimental Results

The experimental data consists of 1107 facial images corresponding to 369 subjects and it comes from the US Army FERET database [28]. 600 out of the 1107 images correspond to 200 subjects with each subject having three images — two of them are the first and the second shot, and the third shot is taken under low illumination (see Fig. 4). For the remaining 169 subjects there are also three images for each subject, but two out of the three images are duplicates taken at a different time (see Fig. 4). Two images of each subject are used for training with the remaining image for testing. The images are cropped to the size of 64 × 96, and the eye coordinates are manually detected.

We implemented the evolutionary pursuit (EP) algorithm with $m = 20$ and $m = 30$, respectively (PCA reduces the dimensionality of the original image space from $N = (64 \times 96)$ to m). The Eigenface and MDF methods were implemented and experimented with as well. Note that once EP found a reduced subset of basis vectors, the same number of projection axes was used by both the eigenface and MDF methods for comparison purposes (see Tables 1, 2 and 3). Table 1 shows comparative training performance, while Tables 2 and 3 give comparative testing performance. In Table 2 and 3, top 1 recognition rate means the accuracy rate for the top response being correct, while top 3 recognition rate represents the accuracy rate for the correct response being included among the first three ranked choices.

When $m = 20$, the evolutionary pursuit approach derived 18 vectors as the optimal basis. Fig. 5 plots the 18 basis vectors, and Fig. 6 shows the non-orthogonality of these vectors. For each row (or column) the unit bar (along the diagonal position) represents the norm of a basis vector, and the other bars represent the dot products of this vector and the other 17 basis vectors. Since the dot products are non-zero, these basis vectors are not orthogonal. When $m = 30$, the EP approach derived 26 vectors as the optimal basis.

Table 1. Comparative **Training Performances** for the Eigenface, MDF, and Evolutionary Pursuit Methods Using **18** and **26** Basis Vectors, respectively

method \features	18	26
Eigenface Method	78.05%	81.30%
MDF Method	100%	100%
Evolutionary Pursuit	83.47%	82.66%

Table 2. Comparative **Testing Performances** for the Eigenface, MDF, and Evolutionary Pursuit Methods when the **20** dimensional whitened PCA subspace is searched by EP ($m = 20$)

method	# features	top 1 recognition rate	top 3 recognition rate
Eigenface Method	18	81.57%	94.58%
MDF Method	18	79.95%	87.80%
Evolutionary Pursuit	18	87.80%	95.93%

Table 3. Comparative **Testing Performances** for the Eigenface, MDF, and Evolutionary Pursuit Methods when the **30** dimensional whitened PCA subspace is searched by EP ($m = 30$)

method	# features	top 1 recognition rate	top 3 recognition rate
Eigenface Method	26	87.26%	95.66%
MDF Method	26	86.45%	93.77%
Evolutionary Pursuit	26	92.14%	97.02%

Table 1 gives the comparative training performances of Eigenface, MDF, and Evolutionary Pursuit methods with 18 and 26 basis vectors, respectively, and one can see that the training performances for MDF method is perfect (100% correct recognition rate). During testing (see Tables 2 and 3) and using 369 test images (not used during training), the performance displayed by the MDF method, however, deteriorates as it lacks a good generalization ability. Both the Eigenface and EP approach display better generalization abilities when compared against MDF. In particular, Table 2 shows that when the 20 dimensional whitened PCA

Fig. 4. Examples of Face Images from FERET Database

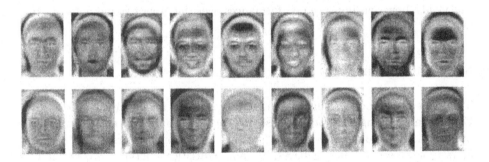

Fig. 5. Optimal Basis (18 Vectors) Derived by the Evolutionary Pursuit (EP) Method

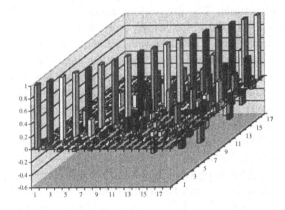

Fig. 6. Non-orthogonality of the Basis Vectors Derived by Evolutionary Pursuit

subspace is searched, the EP approach derives 18 vectors as the optimal basis with top 1 recognition rate 87.80% compared to 81.57% for the Eigenface method and 79.95% for the MDF method. For top 3 recognition rate, the EP approach again comes first and yields 95.93%, compared to 94.58% for Eigenface and 87.80% for MDF method. When the EP approach evolves the optimal basis in the 30 dimensional whitened PCA subspace (see Table 3), it requires only 26 vectors for its optimal basis and achieves 92.14% top 1 recognition rate, compared to 87.26% for Eigenface and 86.45% for the MDF methods. For top 3 recognition rate, the EP approach yields 97.02%, compared to 95.66% for Eigenface and 93.77% for the MDF method.

From Tables 1, 2 and 3 it becomes apparent that MDF does not display good generalization abilities, while PCA and the evolutionary pursuit approach do. The range of training data is quite large as it consists of both original and duplicate images acquired at a later time. As a consequence, during training, MDF performs better than both the Eigenface and evolutionary pursuit (EP) methods because it overfits to a larger extent its classifier to the data. Evolutionary pursuit yields, however, improved performances over the other two methods, during testing.

6 Conclusions

This paper describes an adaptive dictionary method for face recognition using GAs in determining the optimal basis for encoding human faces. In analogy to pursuit methods, our novel method is called Evolutionary Pursuit (EP), and it allows for different types of bases, as some statistical methods do, but it updates the dictionary of choices ('kernels') simultaneously as neural networks do. The main thrust of the EP method is to find out an optimal basis along which faces can be projected leading to a compact and efficient face encoding in terms of recognition ability. EP processes face images in a lower dimensional space defined as PCA projections. The projections are then whitened to counteract the fact that the Mean-Square-Error (MSE) principle underlying PCA preferentially weights low frequencies. The reachable space of EP is increased as a result of using a non-orthonormal (whitening) transformation. One can expect better performance from non-orthogonal bases over orthogonal ones as they lead to an over complete and robust representational space. Directed but random rotations of the lower dimensional (whitened PCA) space are then searched by GAs and use domain specific knowledge ('fitness'). Experimental results show that the EP approach compares favorably against the two methods for face recognition — the Eigenfaces and MDF methods.

The fitness driving evolution considers both recognition rates ('performance accuracy') — empirical risk — and the scatter index — predicted risk — corresponding to the projections of the face images onto the rotated axes. The fitness function is similar to cost functionals implementing regularization methods for ill-posed problems in computer vision. The prediction risk, included as a penalty, is a measure of generalization ability and is driven by the scatter index ('class separation'). The relative contribution of performance accuracy and the scatter index to the fitness function is given through a positive weight parameter λ. The weight parameter indicates the degree of generalization expected from the EP method. In one of the limiting cases, $\lambda \to 0$ implies that only performance accuracy defines fitness and the derived optimal basis will display poor generalization abilities. The other limiting case, $\lambda \to \infty$ implies that now it is the scatter index which fully defines fitness and the derived optimal basis will display poor recognition rates. The weight parameter used for the experimental data presented earlier gives more weight to the empirical risk than to the predicted risk.

As 2nd order statistics provide only partial information on the statistics of both natural images and human faces it becomes necessary to consider higher order statistics as well. Towards that end and in analogy to recent methods such as Independent Component Analysis (ICA) [10] we plan to expand the EP method so it can also consider higher order statistics when deriving the optimal basis — neural code.

Acknowledgments: This work was partially supported by the DoD Counterdrug Technology Development Program, with the U.S. Army Research Laboratory as Technical Agent, under contract DAAL01-97-K-0118.

References

1. S. Baker and S.K. Nayar: Pattern Rejection. Proc. IEEE Conf. Computer Vision and Pattern Recognition (1996) 544–549
2. H.B. Barlow: Unsupervised Learning. Neural Computation 1 (1989) 295–311
3. P.N. Belhumeur, J.P. Hespanha, and D.J. Kriegman: Eigenfaces vs. Fisherfaces: Recognition Using Class Specific Linear Projection. IEEE Trans. Pattern Analysis and Machine Intelligence 19 (1997) 711–720
4. R. Brunelli and T. Poggio: Face Recognition: Features vs. Templates. IEEE Trans. Pattern Analysis and Machine Intelligence 15 (1993) 1042–1053
5. T.F. Chan: An Improved Algorithm for Computing the Singular Value Decomposition. ACM Trans. Math. Software 8 (1982) 72–83
6. R. Chellappa, C.L. Wilson, and S. Sirohey: Human and Machine Recognition of Faces: A Survey. Proc. IEEE 83 (1995) 705–740
7. S. Chen and D. Donoho: Basis Pursuit. Technical Report, Department of Statistics, Stanford University (1996)
8. Y. Cheng, K. Liu, J. Yang, Y. Zhuang, and N. Gu: Human Face Recognition Method Based on the Statistical Model of Small Sample Size. SPIE Proc. Intelligent Robots and Computer Vision X: Algorithms and Technology (1991) 85–95
9. Y. Cherkassky and F. Mulier: Learning from Data : Concepts, Theory and Methods. Wiley (1998) (to appear)
10. P. Comon: Independent Component Analysis — A New Concept?. Signal Processing 36 (1994) 11–20
11. Y. Cui, D. Swets, and J. Weng: Learning-Based Hand Sign Recognition Using SHOSLIF-M. Int'l Conf. on Computer Vision (1995) 45–58
12. J.G. Daugman: An information-theoretic view of analog representation in striate cortex. in Computational Neuroscience, E.L. Schwartz, eds. MIT Press (1990) 403–424

13. G.M. Edelman: Neural Darwinism. Basic Books (1987)
14. R.A. Fisher: The Use of Multiple Measures in Taxonomic Problems. Ann. Eugenics **7** (1936) 179–188
15. J.H. Friedman and W. Stuetzle: Projection Pursuit Regression. J. Amer. Statist. Asso. **76** (1981) 817–823
16. K. Fukunaga: Introduction to Statistical Pattern Recognition, 2nd Edition. Academic Press (1991)
17. D. Goldberg: Genetic Algorithms in Search, Optimization and Machine Learning. Addison-Wesley (1989)
18. S. Haykin: Neural Networks — A Comprehensive Foundation. Macmillan College Publishing Company, Inc. (1994)
19. P.J. Huber: Projection Pursuit. Ann. Stat. **13** (1985) 435–475
20. J. Hwang, S. Lay, M. Maechler, R.D. Martin, and J. Schimert: Regression Modeling in Back-Propagation and Projection Pursuit Learning. IEEE Trans. Neural Networks **5** (1994) 342–353
21. I.T. Jolliffe: Principal Component Analysis. Springer, New York (1986)
22. M. Kirby and L. Sirovich: Application of the Karhunen-Loeve Procedure for the Characterization of Human Faces. IEEE Trans. Pattern Analysis and Machine Intelligence **12** (1990) 103–108
23. R. Kohavi and G. John: Wrappers for Feature Subset selection. Technical Report, Computer Science Department, Stanford University (1995)
24. R. Linsker: Self-organization in a Perceptual Network. Computer **21** (1988) 105–117
25. S.G. Mallat and Z. Zhang: Matching Pursuits With Time-Frequency Dictionaries. IEEE Trans. Signal Processing **41** (1993) 3397–3415
26. B.A. Olshausen and D.J. Field: Emergence of Simple-cell Receptive Field Properties by Learning a Sparse Code for Natural Images. Nature **381** (1996) 607–609
27. P.S. Penev and J.J. Atick: Local Feature Analysis: A general statistical theory for object representation. Network: Computation in Neural Systems **7** (1996) 477–500
28. P.J. Phillips, H. Wechsler, J. Huang, and P. Rauss: The FERET Database and Evaluation Procedure for Face Recognition Algorithms. Image and Vision Computing (1998) (to appear)
29. T. Poggio, V. Torre, and C. Koch: Computational Vision and Regularization Theory. Nature **317** (1985) 314–319
30. D. Ruderman: The statistics of Natural Images. Network : Computation in Neural Systems **5** (1994) 598–605
31. A. Samal and P.A. Iyengar: Automatic Recognition and Analysis of Human Faces and Facial Expression: A Survey. Pattern Recognition **25** (1992) 65–77
32. L. Sirovich and M. Kirby: Low-dimensional Procedure for the Characterization of Human Faces. J. Optical. Soc. Am. A **4** (1987) 519–524
33. D.L. Swets and J. Weng: Using Discriminant Eigenfeatures for Image Retrieval. IEEE Trans. Pattern Analysis and Machine Intelligence **18** (1996) 831–836
34. A.N. Tikhonov and V.Y. Arsenin: Solutions of Ill-posed Problems. W.H. Winston, Washington, DC (1977)
35. M. Turk and A. Pentland: Eigenfaces for Recognition. Journal of Cognitive Neuroscience **3** (1991) 71–86

Recognizing Faces by Weakly Orthogonalizing against Perturbations

Kenji NAGAO and Masaki SOHMA

nagao@mrit.mei.co.jp sohma@mrit.mei.co.jp

Matsushita Research Institute Tokyo, Higashimita, Tama-ku, Kawasaki, 214 JAPAN

Abstract. In this paper, we address the problem of face recognition under drastic changes of the imaging processes through which the facial images are acquired. A new method is proposed. Unlike the conventional algorithms that use only the face features, the present method exploits the statistical information of the variations between the face image sets being compared, in addition to the features of the faces themselves. To incorporate the face and perturbation features for recognition, a technique called *weak orthogonalization* of the two subspaces has been developed that transforms the two overlapped subspaces such that the volume of the intersection of the resulting two subspaces is minimized. Matching is performed in the transformed face space that has thus been weakly orthogonalized against perturbation space. Results using real pictures of the frontal faces from drivers' licenses demonstrate the effectiveness of the new algorithm.

1 Introduction

A considerable amount of literatures have been published in face recognition in recent years. Among those, some of the most successful schemes are based on the Karhunen-Loeve transform (KLT) (or principal component analysis PCA) of the gray level images [5, 6, 7, 3] (see also [2] for frequency domain representation). In this appoach, facial images are compared in a low dimensional subspace [3] called face subspace, included in the whole image vector space, that maximizes the scatters of the projected distribution of faces. This method works very well as long as the imaging conditions for both of the face image sets being compared are similar to each other. However, problems occur when it comes to data sets with large or complicated differences as addressed in the present work (see e.g. figure 1). This is because they do not explicitly take into account how the individual faces change in appearance between the image sets being compared, but such perturbation was handled only implicitly. For example, in the KLT approach, perturbations were excluded by somehow truncating the higher order eigenvectors of the face space in the PCA and matching was performed in the subspaces spanned by the remaining eigenvectors. However, we should note here that perturbations of faces happen independently of the face space configurations, as one would never be able to tell how the imaging conditions, such as lighting directions, and thus the resulting images could change from the canonical appearances. Hence, only using the static face space information is not sufficient for recognizing faces in images with severe deviations. This is also true for other non-subspace approaches such as correlation methods[8]. This is the point that was not considered in previous work and now motivates our research.

Suppose we try to find matches of given faces presented to the camera, let us call this set A, in the registered face images of the database, set B. An example of such pairs of frontal face images is given in figure 1, where the set A is the pictures of the subjects themselves while the set B is obtained through the pictures printed on their plastic drivers' license. Since the imaging processes of both face sets are thus totally different, drastic changes have been introduced between the corresponding face images as shown in the figure. Clearly, such type of face recognition is different from the traditional types that allow only small changes of the appearances. In this paper, we tackle such kind of difficulties of human face recognition, given the pair of frontal facial images with severe variation of the appearances due to the changes of imaging conditions.

To this end, our method exploits perturbation information between image sets explicitly, by introducing *perturbation subspace* and combining it with the face subspace that was used in previous work. A perturbation subspace is a feature space within which any variation between the given pairs of face images is restricted to exist. To incorporate this perturbation subspace with the face space, we develop a technique called *weak orthogonalization* of those two subspaces such that after a weak orthogonalization, the intersection of those two subspaces is minimized, thereby effectively excluding the major components of the perturbations from the face representations. Results on 181 pairs of pictures (362 facial images) of the individuals and their drivers' licenses show the effectiveness of the proposed method for face recogntion under drastic changes of the imaging conditions.

As a related work to our method, recently in [9](see also [1]) a method for face recognition was developed for dealing with image variations due to the changes of lighting, based on Fisher's discriminant analysis. In their work, training images acquired under a variety of lighting conditions were used to construct classes of individual faces, and the optimal projection matrix for classification was computed based on the Fisher ratio criterion.

2   Face and Perturbation Subspaces

The problem can be stated: Given a set of training facial images that are pairs of images of individuals in sets A^l and B^l, identify each face from the test set A^t in the test set B^t, where A^l, A^t and B^l, B^t are resepectively acquired under the same imaging conditions.

We emphasize here again that two kind of differences are included in the face recognition task: one is the difference due to face identity that is described by the face subspace and the other is the change which is brought by different imaging

615

type A   type B

Fig. 1. An example of image pair

The left is the image of the subject himself, type A, while the right image is obtained through a picture printed on his plastic drivers' lisence, type B.

conditions. A perturbation subspace is a feature space for representing the latter change.

As mentioned, the face subspace is designed so that individual faces are discriminated most effectively [5, 6, 7, 3], by taking as its bases the principal components of the face distributions that are the eigenvectors of its covariance matrix: $C_F = \frac{1}{N}\sum_{i=1}^{N}(F_i - M)(F_i - M)^T$. where F_i is the representation of the face labeled i from the sets A^l and/or B^l, M is their mean over i, and N is the number of face images used for the training phase. Similarly, the perturbation subspace is spanned by the principal components obtained as the eigenvectors of the autocorrelation matrix defined below with the large eigenvalues (NOTE: for the sake of simplicity in this paper we may sometimes use the term covariance for the autocorrelation of perturbation ignoring the subtraction operation by its mean in covariance estimation): $C_P = \sum_{i=1}^{N} P_i P_i^T$ where P_i's are sample perturbation vectors that are simply computed by taking the differences of the sets A^l and B^l: $P_i = A_i^l - B_i^l$ where i is a label to individual person, and N is the number of faces used for learning the perturbation space. We assume here that the perturbation of the images happening to individual faces are statistically consistent over the different faces.

Here, now that we use the term subspace for perturbation, the perturbations should be enclosed in a low dimensional space like the face subspace in the high dimensional vector space of the images, which may not be guaranteed in general. However, suppose that for the image sets A and B the respective imaging conditions are somehow fixed, then, as analyzed later in the experiment, the corresponding perturbations constitute a subspace. Thus, such a perturbation subspace might vary depending on the changes of the imaging processes and may have to be computed for every face recognition task.

We also note that since the perturbation defined above is derived simply by the subtraction between face pictures in the set A^l and their corresponding pictures in B^l, if the two face sample spaces of A and B are compatible, from the mathematical definition of a subspace, the resulting perturbation space is simply a subspace of that common face subspace. Thus, at a glance it appears that any feature extracted from the perturbation space is nothing more than an element of that face space, implying that perturbation space may be useless. This is not true, however, because even if the perturbation space is thoroughly contained in the face space, the principal components, i.e., the major axes of those subspaces, might differ from each other. Then, if it is true, we might still have a chance to exclude or suppress the disturbance of perturbations in matching face images. This issue will also be examined empirically later.

3 Weakly Orthogonalizing Face and Perturbation Subspaces

In this section, a method for feature extraction is derived that is suited for recognition, incorporating face and perturbation information introduced so far. Particularly, we focus on the scheme to separate the perturbations from the descriptions of faces.

3.1 Orthogonal Subspace Method Revisited

In 1970's and early 80's, there was once a technical topic called Orthogonal Subspace Methods in statistical pattern classification. This aimed at feature extraction from multiclass patterns suited for classification and recognition. Motivated by the early work of Fukunaga&Koontz[10, 11], they sought ways of transforming patterns to be compared prior to classification such that resulting class subspaces are orthogonal with each other in a mathematical sense [17, 16, 13, 12]. The Fukunaga&Koontz method utilized the mathematical relationship between the two class autocorrelation matrices such that when one whitens the mixture autocorrelation of the two class distributions, one can obtain shared eigen vectors between the resulting two autocorrelations with respective eigenvalues in reversed order.

We reilluminate the orthogonal subspace method based on Fukunaga&Koontz by defining its relaxed concept called *Weakly Orthogonalized* subspaces and by deriving a generalized procedure for performing it.

[Definition: Weakly Orthogonalized Subspaces]
Suppose we are given two distributions $\{X_1\}$ and $\{X_2\}$ with covariance matrices Σ_1 and Σ_2. Let these covariances have SVD's such that $\Sigma_1 = \Phi_1 \Lambda^{(1)} \Phi_1$, $\Sigma_2 = \Phi_2 \Lambda^{(2)} \Phi_2$, where Φ_1, Φ_2 are orthonormal matrices and $\Lambda^{(1)}, \Lambda^{(2)}$ are diagonal matrices such that $\Lambda^{(1)} = diag[\lambda_1^{(1)}, \lambda_2^{(1)}, \lambda_3^{(1)}, \cdots]$, $\Lambda^{(2)} = diag[\lambda_1^{(2)}, \lambda_2^{(2)}, \lambda_3^{(2)}, \cdots]$. Here, if those covariances share the same eigenvectors, i.e., $\Phi_1 = \Phi_2 \equiv \Phi$, and at the same time if the orders of the the the eigenvalues are reversed, i.e., if $\lambda_1^{(1)} \geq \lambda_2^{(1)} \geq \lambda_3^{(1)} \cdots$, then $\lambda_1^{(2)} \leq \lambda_2^{(2)} \leq \lambda_3^{(2)} \cdots$, the we say the two distributions $\{X_1\}$ and $\{X_2\}$ are *weakly orthogonalized*.

As described, this is exactly the state that was performed by Fukunaga&Koontz for two-class classification problem. Although, it has not been used so widely for multiclass classification, when the two classes are associated with the faces and their perturbations, it turns out to be a powerful tool for recognition. Given the second order statistics of face and perturbation, if we have a way to transform these two subspaces into mutually weakly orthogonalized ones, we could effectively reduce the effect of the perturbations contained in the face representations on matching by selecting a subspace that has only small overlaps with the perturbation subspace.

In the following, we show a generalized procedure for such weak orthogonalization by two steps: the first step transforms two covariances into ones sharing eivenvectors (let us call this operation TCSE for short), then the second step reorders the two series of eivenvalues so that their orders are reversed.

3.2 Simultaneous Diagonalization: Yielding Shared Eigenvectors

Suppose we transform two covariances Σ_1, Σ_2 by a non-singular affine transformation L to yield new covariances $L\Sigma_1 L^T, L\Sigma_2 L^T$. It is known that there exists a class of transformations L that can simultaneously diagonalize them. Apparently, the operation of TCSE is almost equivalent to simultaneous diagonalization because: (1) The operation of TCSE is an instance of simultaneous diagonalization. (2)Simultaneous diagonalization includes TCSE in the middle of the procedure, where the resulting diagonal matrix is exactly the eigenvalue matrix resulting from the TCSE operation.

A well known procedure for performing simultaneous diagonalization is the one that makes one of the two matrices, say Σ_1 an identity matrix, and the other, Σ_2, a diagonal matrix $\Lambda^{(2)}$. Specifically,

$$L\Sigma_1 L^T = I \tag{1}$$
$$L\Sigma_2 L^T = \Lambda^{(2)} \tag{2}$$

where matrix L^T is given as the eigenvector matrix of $\Sigma_1^{-1}\Sigma_2$(see e.g.[4]). Apparently, the class of affine transformations that can perform simultaneous diagonalization, and thus TCSE, includes an infinite number of elements. However, the following property regarding the description of this class is noteworthy:

[Proposition]
Suppose a non-singular matrix L simultaneously diagonalizes two covariance matrices Σ_1, Σ_2. Then, any matrix H that can simultaneously diagonalize those two convariances can be written as a product of L and some diagonal matrix D as $H = DL$

(proof of this proposition is found in the appendix). This property implies that the eigenvectors resulting from the TCSE operation are unique with respect to the distribution.

3.3 Diagonal Scaling for Reordering Eigenvalues

When simultaneous diagonalization has been performed on two covariances, we can weakly orthogonalize the two distributions as defined, by further applying a diagonal rescaling matrix to order corresponding eigenvalues in reverse in two covariances. Let affine transformation L diagonalize both Σ_1 and Σ_2:

$$LΣ_1L^T = Λ^{(1)} \tag{3}$$

$$LΣ_2L^T = Λ^{(2)} \tag{4}$$

where $Λ^{(1)}, Λ^{(2)}$ are diagonal matrices such that $Λ_1 = diag[\lambda_1^{(1)}, \lambda_2^{(1)}, \cdots]$, $Λ_2 = diag[\lambda_1^{(2)}, \lambda_2^{(2)}, \cdots]$. Let the rescaling diagonal matrix with positive diagonal components be Υ, premultiplying Υ and postmultiplying $\Upsilon^T (= \Upsilon)$ on both sides of eq's. (3)–(4), we can adjust the amplitude such that:

$$(\Upsilon L)Σ_1(\Upsilon L)^T = \Upsilon Λ^{(1)} \Upsilon^T$$

$$(\Upsilon L)Σ_2(\Upsilon L)^T = \Upsilon Λ^{(2)} \Upsilon^T.$$

To reorder eigenvalues in reverse in the two covariances, we have the following rules to follow:

$$rule1 : \quad \lambda^{(1)'}_i + \lambda^{(2)'}_i = 1 \tag{5}$$

$$rule2 : \quad \lambda^{(1)'^2}_i + \lambda^{(2)'^2}_i = 1 \tag{6}$$

$$rule3 : \quad \lambda^{(1)'^{\frac{1}{2}}}_i + \lambda^{(2)'^{\frac{1}{2}}}_i = 1 \tag{7}$$

$$rule4 : \quad \lambda^{(1)'^n}_i + \lambda^{(2)'^n}_i = 1 \tag{8}$$

$$rule5 : \quad \lambda^{(1)'}_i \cdot \lambda^{(2)'}_i = 1 \tag{9}$$

where primes denote eigenvalues after rescaling, and n in rule4 is an arbitrary real number. Apparently, when the new eigenvalues satisfy any of the above rules, they are ordered in reverse, that is, when $\lambda^{(1)'}_1 \geq \lambda^{(1)'}_2 \geq \cdots$, then $\lambda^{(2)'}_1 \leq \lambda^{(2)'}_2 \leq \cdots$, and, thus, weak orthogonalization has been performed. To carry out the rescaling operation subject to these rules, we just need to apply an appropriate diagonal matrix Υ_i $(i = 1, 2 \cdots)$ as described in the following:

$$\Upsilon_1 = diag[(\lambda_1^{(1)} + \lambda_1^{(2)})^{-\frac{1}{2}}, (\lambda_2^{(1)} + \lambda_2^{(2)})^{-\frac{1}{2}}, \cdots] \tag{10}$$

$$\Upsilon_2 = diag[(\lambda^{(1)^2}_1 + \lambda^{(2)^2}_1)^{-\frac{1}{4}}, (\lambda^{(1)^2}_2 + \lambda^{(2)^2}_2)^{-\frac{1}{4}}, \cdots] \tag{11}$$

$$\Upsilon_3 = diag[(\lambda^{(1)^{\frac{1}{2}}}_1 + \lambda^{(2)^{\frac{1}{2}}}_1)^{-1}, (\lambda^{(1)^{\frac{1}{2}}}_2 + \lambda^{(2)^{\frac{1}{2}}}_2)^{-1}, \cdots] \tag{12}$$

$$\Upsilon_4 = diag[(\lambda^{(1)^n}_1 + \lambda^{(2)^n}_1)^{-\frac{1}{2n}}, (\lambda^{(1)^n}_2 + \lambda^{(2)^n}_2)^{-\frac{1}{2n}}, \cdots] \tag{13}$$

$$\Upsilon_5 = diag[(\lambda_1^{(1)} \lambda_1^{(2)})^{-\frac{1}{2}}, (\lambda_2^{(1)} \lambda_2^{(2)})^{-\frac{1}{2}}, \cdots] \tag{14}$$

Rescaling by rule1 is identical to Fukunaga&Koontz method, that is, to decorrelate the mixture of the face and perturbation distributions. Rule4 is the generalized version of rules 1,2,3, by which the sum of the nth power (n is a real number) of the correponding eigenvalues in both of the covariances are normalized to 1. If one applies the rule5, the transformed covariance matrices are inverses of each other. Thus, by controling the relationship between the corresponding eigenvalues as above, we can order them in reverse between the two covariances and can control the speed of the descent/ascent of the curves of the orderd eigenvalues. Thus, through a simultaneous diagonalization of face and perturbation covariances followed by a diagonal rescaling, we can obtain weakly orthogonalized subspaces, thereby minimizing the size the intersection of the two subspaces.

Summary

A notion called weakly orthogonalized two subspaces has been introduced. This aimed at suppressing the turbulance in recognition due to the perturbations contained in the representation of faces, by reducing the size of the intersection of face and perturbation subspaces. To perform this, a generalized version of Fukunaga&Koontz approach that was for orthogonal subspace method was derived. The generalized procedure consists of a simultaneous diagonalization for obtaining shared eigenvectors and a subsequent diagonal rescaling for ordering the eivenvalues of the face and perturbation covariances in reverse.

4   Recognition Algorithm

Now we can show the core of the algorithm for face recognition that can handle extreme changes of imaging processes, using the technique developed in the previous section. The algorithm is described by two parts: one for training phase for computing the transformation for weak orthogonalization, which is a off-line process, and the other for run time phase of recognition.

Training phase

- step 1-a: Given the face training sets A^l and B^l, estimate covariance C_F of the face distribution using both or either of the two sets.
- step 1-b: Compute the autocorrelation of the perturbations C_P between A^l and B^l as defined in the previous section.
- step 2: Simultaneously diagonalize two matrices C_F, C_P via some appropriate transformation L.
- step 3: Rescale the resulting diagonal elements of both of the transformed covariances using the diagonal transformations Υ described in (10)–(14).
- step 4: Compute the matrix Ψ as a product of Υ and L: $\Psi = \Upsilon L$, which weakly orthogonalizes the face and perturbation subspaces as derived in the previous section.
- step 5 : Transform each of the face vectors in the database B^t using the matrix Ψ and retain the result in the database, where the origin has been set to the mean of all the entry of the database.

Recognition phase

- step 5: Transform the input image of the set A^t by the same transformation Ψ and find the best match in the database.

Step 1-a and 1-b can be performed in parallel. As is true of the case with other subspace based face recognition algorithms, the run time process is computationally very efficient.

5 Experimental Results

In this section, we will present the empirical results of face recognition on two image sets with extreme variation due to the differences of their imaging processes. To examine the effectiveness of the proposed method, the performance has been compared with those of Turk&Pentland's Eigenface approach [5, 7] and another perturbation method based on ML (Maximum Likelihood) estimate (hereafter MLP). As for the density function for the MLP, when we assume that the distribution of the perturbation is normal and is, as described, independent of the face identity, the only parameter we need for describing the common perturbation distribution is the autocorrelation C_P, where the mean is assumed to be zero and the metric for the Gaussian kernel is C_P^{-1}.

5.1 Preliminaries

Three different algorithms were implemented on a Sparc Station SS-UA1. To strictly evaluate the effectiveness of our weak orthogonalization approach against changes of the imaging conditions, variations of the geometrical properties in the images such as the orientation and the size of the faces were normalized prior to the actual training and recognition process. This was done for each image from the sets A and B by first manually specifying the left and right eye centers, and then setting the interocular distance and the direction of eye-to-eye axis, performaing scale and rotation invariance of images. Although the above process includes manual operation, we understand that it can be replaced by an automated process using the techniques for face detection presented in, e.g., [5, 8]. The actual face parts used for the tests were masks for eyes (50x20 pixels), nose(25x25 pixels), and the whole face (45x60 pixels; the area from eyebrows downwards).

5.2 Recognition Experiments

The first experiment tests the recognition performance of Weak Orthogonalization method by a comparison with two other algorithms: Eigenface and MLP, demonstrating the superiority of the proposed method. In the second test of the present method, we check the effect of the selection of the principal components of the transformed face space on recognition performance.

[Test1: comparison with Eigenface and MLP]
Recognition performances of these different algorithms were compared by randomly choosing 80 different pairs of training (A^l, B^l) and test sets (A^t, B^t), where each pair consists of 91 pairs of images from types A and B. The training and test sets had no overlaps. In the following, explanations for using a single pair

of training and test sets are given. Performance evaluations are simply by the results from the iterations on 80 different pairs of the learning and recognition image sets.

Training phase

Training operations were performed for each of the three different algorithms. For the Weak Orthogonalization method: first face covariance C_F was estimated by using the 91 type A images. Similarly, perturbation covariance C_P was estimated, where the differences between types A and B of each face were simply used for perturbation samples. Then, covariances C_F and C_P were simultaneously diagonalized using the affine transformation described in (1)–(2). From these transformed face covariances, 90 principal components were obtained and all of those were used, which means the dimension of the transformed face subspace was 90 (Note that this is exactly the rank of the face sample matrix of which each column face vector has been subtracted by their mean). For the diagonal rescaling, we selected rule 3. As will be described soon, as the number of images used for training was too small, the choice of diagonal rescaling matrix did not make any difference on recognition performance in this experiment. In estimating the covariance of face distribution for Eigenface, the mixture of sets A^l and B^l was used, instead of using C_F computed above. This is because using information from only one type of image set, e.g. set A, is not fair when comparing with weak orthogonalization method that uses information of both types, though original Eigenface used only one of the two comparing sets. For the MLP method, we simply used the same covariance C_P for computing the Mahalanobis distance between the two images as was used for weak orthogonalization method. For both the Eigenface and MLP algorithms, 90 principal components were used. Hence, the dimensions of the extracted feature vectors as well as the used face sample sets, each for computing feature extraction matrix by three different algorithms are the same. For each of the images in the set B^t feature extraction was performed using the three different algorithms and the results were stored in the database.

Recognition phase

Recognition tests were conducted using the remaining 91 pairs of potentially corresponding types A and B (A^t, B^t) images that were not used for the training phase. For each of the images from the set A^t feature extraction was done in the same way as for B^t, and the best match was found using the Euclidean distance between the input (A^t) and database (B^t) facial feature representations that had 90 dimensions.

In figure 2 the correct recognition percentage for the eye part using the three different algorithms are shown, where the horizontal axis simply denotes the different pairs of training and test sets: the top graph shows the results for our weak orthogonalization method, the middle the MLP method, and the bottom the Eigenface method. Here, correct recognition means that the correct pair was found to be the best match. For any of the training and test sets, the weak orthogonalization method performed best. The performance of MLP was always second. Eigenface performed very poorly on this experiment. In table 1,

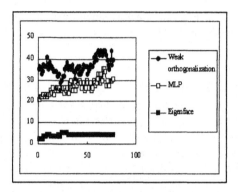

Fig. 2. Comparison with Eigenface and MLP

The correct recognition rates for the eye part are shown, where the horizontal axis denotes simply the different pairs of training and test sets: the top graph is our weak orthogonalization method, the middle the MLP method, and the bottom the Eigenface.

the cumulative percentage of the correct match being ranked within the top 10 ranks for eye images are given. It is seen that the weak orthogonalization method is very stable compared with the other methods.

In table 2, similar results are presented on regions of the nose and the whole face, where the average correct recognition rates are shown, which are also from the 60 different pairs of training and test image sets. From these results, the effectiveness of our weak orthogonalization method is confirmed.

Rank	Weak Orthogonalization	MLP	Eigenface
1	36.3	20.9	2.2
2	49.5	25.3	6.6
3	53.8	31.9	9.9
4	60.4	35.2	11.0
5	61.5	39.6	12.1
6	63.7	42.9	14.3
7	65.9	50.5	18.7
8	68.1	53.8	19.8
9	69.2	57.1	20.9
10	70.3	60.4	24.2

Table 1. Cumulative percentage of correct match within top 10 ranks

The weak orthogonalization method is very stable as compared with the other methods.

[Test2: The effect of the selection of the subspace]

	Weak Orthogonalization	MLP	Eigenface
Eye	36.6	27.0	4.2
Nose	18.6	12.6	3.2
Whole face	41.1	30.9	26.5

Table 2. Correct recognition rates: averages

The average correct recognition rates for nose and whole facial regions as well as eye part are presented, which are also from the 60 different pairs of training and test image sets. On any of the facial regions, weak orthogonalization method performed best.

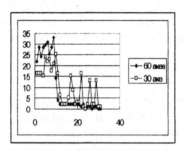

Fig. 3. Effect of the selection of the subspace

The horizontal axis is the order of the componet set (from the lowest to highest) and the vertical axis is the percentage of the correct recognition.

The dependency of the recognition performance of the weak orthogonalization method on the selection of principal components spanning the subspace of the faces was examined using the eye images. Tests were conducted by selecting 60 (and 30) components for spanning the subspace out of the 90 eigenvectors of the face distribution obtained by PCA after the weak orthogonalization operation. The selection was made in consequtive order from the lowest (having largest eigenvalues) 60 components to the highest. Figure 3 shows the results where the horizontal axis is the order of the componet set (from the lowest to the highest) and the vertical axis is the percentage correct recognition. Roughly, we can say that after the 10th order, the performance declined sharply for both of the 60 and 30 axes case. Thus, we tentatively conclude that there is a difference in the recognition power between the principal components after weak orthogonalization, and lowest components appear to have the maximum recognition ability.

[Configurations of weakly orthogonalized face and perturbation subspaces]

In the above tests, for constructing a face subspace that is weakly orthogonalized against perturbation space, we used 91 face image samples and 91 perturbation samples. Since this number was too small as compared with the dimension (1000)

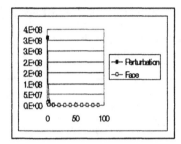

Fig. 4. Eigenvalues assciated with pricipal components

Eigenvalues along the major components of the face (set A^l) and the perturbation subspaces defined as $\{P_i | A_i - B_i\}$ are shown, where the horizontal axis is the order and the vertical axis is the eigenvalues. It can be observed that only a small set of principal components occupy a large part of the variation of the perturbation distribution.

of the eye images, when we performed simultaneous diagonalization, those two subspaces (exactly the spaces for the training sets) were completely orthogonalized in the mathematical sense. This implies that eigenvectors were not shared in practice: for the components of face subspace the eigenvalues for perturbation space were zeros, and vice versa. For this reason, in this paper we could not evaluate the variation of the rescaling methods as it assumes eigenvectors are truly shared.

6 Viability Tests

It may be of readers concern what kind of specific classes of the face recognition problem the present technique may be applied to, as was also addressed in section 2. At present, it is not easy for us to give exact answer to this question. However, we may give indications for this by defining the following two quantitative measures, both of which are computed using the PCA outputs of the training images: K: the degree of concentration of variations of perturbations to lower order components, and V: the degree of overlaps between the face and the perturbation subspaces.

$$K = \frac{1}{N} min[i] \{ \frac{\sum_{j=1}^{i} \sigma_j}{\sum_{j=1}^{N} \sigma_j} > r \} \tag{15}$$

$$V = E\{ log \left[\frac{min\{eval_1^i, eval_2^{f(i)}\} * cosine}{min\{eval_1^i, eval_2^i\}} \right] \} \tag{16}$$

where in the first equation, N is the number of obtained principal components, and $0 < r < 1$, and in the second equation, $eval_1^i$ is the square root of the ith eigenvalue for the first, let say perturbation, subspace, and $eval_2^i$ is the similar eigen property of the second, let say set A, subspace, $f(i)$ is the operation giving the order of component of the second subspace that has the maximum coincidence in direction with the ith component of the first subspace in terms of the consine. The notation $E\{\cdot\}$ denotes the averaging operation over i. Recall that our method assumes that perturbations consistute a subspace which might have some overlaps with face subspace, and also that it is the objective of the method to try to exclude or suppress the disturbance of such perturbations on matching faces. Therefore, we hypothesize that the smaller the values of K and V for the image sets the better our method should perform.

We have made an examination of these measures using the same image sets as those for the face recongition experiments. Figure 4 shows the eigenvalues along the 90 principal components of the eye images (set A) and their perturbation defined as $\{P_i|A_i - B_i\}$. When we set $r = 0.95$, the values of K were 0.23 for the perturbation and 0.22 for the set A. From this, it can be seen that the pertubation distribution can be represented as a small set of major componets, as their associated eigenvalues occupy the most part in the total variance, which allows us to define the perturbation subspace. We have also estimated the degree of overlap between the face and perturbation subspaces using the measure V. This was done for perturbation vs. face set A (P-FA) and perturbation vs. face set B (P-FB), and face set A vs. face set B (FA-FB) was also included for comparison. The results are -1.18 for P-FA, -1.58 for P-FB, and -0.48 for FA-FB. From this, it is observed that the degrees of overlap between perturbation and face subspaces (P-FA, P-FB) are lower than that between the two face subspaces (FA-FB). Thus, both of the measures K and V were low for those given specific image sets A and B used here, which supports the improved recognition performance of the proposed method over the existing techniques as demonstrated in the experiments.

7 Concluding remarks

We have proposed a face recogntion algorithm that can handle extreme changes of appearance due to drastic changes of imaging conditions. In the present method, the statistical information of the perturbation of the face images from the registered corresponding ones are exploited, in addition to the features of the faces themselves that were used in conventional methods. In order to incorporate both of the face and perturbation features for recognition, we developed a technique called weak orthogonalization of the two subspaces that transforms the given two overlapped subspaces such that the volume of the intersection of the resulting two subspaces is minimized. Empirical results using real pictures of the frontal faces from drivers' licenses demonstrated the effectiveness of the new algorithm. The viability of the proposed method for a given specific face recognition task may be evaluated using the measure K: the degree of concentration of the eigenvalues and the measure V: the degree of overlap between the perturbation and face subpaces.

Appendix

Proof of Proposition
Let non-singular matrix A simultaneously diagonalizes two covariances Σ_1, Σ_2:

$$A\Sigma_1 A^T = \Lambda_1 \tag{17}$$

$$A\Sigma_2 A^T = \Lambda_2 \tag{18}$$

Let matrix B be any one that performs similar diagonalization as:

$$B\Sigma_1 B^T = \Omega_1 \tag{19}$$

$$B\Sigma_2 B^T = \Omega_2 \tag{20}$$

Matrix B can be written as a product of A and some matrix C as $B = CA$. Substituting this into (19) and using (17), we have:

$$C\Lambda_1 C^T = \Omega_1 \tag{21}$$

$$C\Lambda_2 C^T = \Omega_2 \tag{22}$$

This can be rewritten as:

$$(C\Lambda_1^{\frac{1}{2}})(C\Lambda_1^{\frac{1}{2}})^T = (\Omega_1^{\frac{1}{2}})(\Omega_1^{\frac{1}{2}})^T \tag{23}$$

$$(C\Lambda_2^{\frac{1}{2}})(C\Lambda_2^{\frac{1}{2}})^T = (\Omega_2^{\frac{1}{2}})(\Omega_1^{\frac{1}{2}})^T \tag{24}$$

From (23), we have $C = \Omega_1^{\frac{1}{2}} U \Lambda_1^{-\frac{1}{2}}$, where U is an orthogonal matrix. Substituting this into (24) and rearranging, we have:

$$U\Lambda_{2/1}U^T = \Omega_{2/1} \tag{25}$$

where $\Lambda_{2/1} = \Lambda_2\Lambda_1^{-1}$ and $\Omega_{2/1} = \Omega_2\Omega_1^{-1}$.
Noting that (25) shows a similarity transformation between $\Lambda_{2/1}$ and $\Omega_{2/1}$ ($U^T = U^{-1}$), we have $\Lambda_{2/1} = \Omega_{2/1}$ and U is an identity matrix. Therefore, we obtain finally $C = \Omega_1^{\frac{1}{2}} \Lambda_1^{-\frac{1}{2}}$, which completes the proof.

References

1. T. Kurita, N. Ohtsu and T. Sato, "A Face Recognition Method Using Higher Order Local Autocorrelation and Multivariate Analysis", In Proc. IEEE ICPR92, pp. 213–216, 1992.
2. S. Akamatsu et. al., "An Accurate and Robust Face Identification Scheme", In Proc. IEEE ICPR92, pp. 217–220, 1992.
3. M. Kirby, L. Sirovich, "Application of the Karhunen-Loeve procedure for the characterization of human faces", *IEEE Trans. Patt. Anal. Machine Intell.*, vol. 12, pp. 103–108, 1990.
4. K. Fukunaga, *Introduction to Statistical Pattern Recognition*, Academic Press 1972.

5. M. Turk, A. Pentland, "Face recognition using eigenfaces", In Proc. IEEE CVPR91, 1991.

6. M. Turk, A. Pentland, "Eigenfaces for recognition", Journal of Cognitive Neuroscience, vol. 3, No. 1, 1991.

7. A. Pentland, B. Moghaddam, T. Starner, "View-based and modular eigenspaces for face recognition", In Proc. IEEE CVPR94, 1994.

8. R. Brunelli, T. Poggio, "Face Recognition: Features versus Template", *IEEE Trans. Patt. Anal. Machine Intell.*, vol. PAMI-8, pp.34–43, 1993.

9. N. Belhumeur, P. Hespanha, J. Kriegman, "Eigenfaces vs. fisherfaces:recognition using class specific linear projection", In Proc. ECCV'96 vol1 pp. 45–58, 1996.

10. K. Fukunaga, W. C. G. Koontz, "Application of the Karhunen-Loeve expansion to feature extraction and ordering", *IEEE Trans. Computers*, Vol. C-19, pp. 311–318, 1970.

11. K. Fukunaga, *Introduction to Statistical Pattern Recognition*, Academic Press 1972.

12. D. H. Foley, J. W. Sammon, "An Optimal Set of Discriminant Vectors", IEEE Trans. Computers, Vol. C-24, NO. 3, pp. 281–289, March 1975.

13. E. Oja, J. Karhunen, "An Analysis of Convergence for a Learning Version of the Subspace Method", J. Math. Anal. Applications 91. pp. 102–111, 1983.

14. E. Oja, *Subspace Methods of Pattern Recognition*, Research Studies Press LTD and John Wiley & Sons Inc., 1983.

15. J. Kittler, "The subspace approach to pattern recognition", in *Progress in cybernetics and systems research*, p. 92, Hamisphere Publ. Co., Washington, 1978.

16. T. Kohonen, P. Lehtio, E. Oja, "Spectral classification of phonemes by learning subspacees", Helsinki University of Technology, Dept. of Technical Physics, Report TKK-F-A348. Also in Proc. IEEE ICASP, pp. 2–4, April 1979.

17. S. Watanabe, N. Pakvasa, "Subspace method of pattern recognition", In Proc. IJCPR pp. 25–32, 1973.

A Probabilistic Approach to Object Recognition Using Local Photometry and Global Geometry

Michael C. Burl[1], Markus Weber[2], and Pietro Perona[2,3]

[1] Jet Propulsion Laboratory
M/S 525-3660, 4800 Oak Grove Drive
Pasadena, CA 91109, U.S.A.
Michael.C.Burl@jpl.nasa.gov
[2] California Institute of Technology
MC 136-93
Pasadena, CA 91125, U.S.A.
{mweber,perona}@vision.caltech.edu
[3] Università di Padova, Italy

Abstract. Many object classes, including human faces, can be modeled as a set of characteristic parts arranged in a variable spatial configuration. We introduce a simplified model of a deformable object class and derive the optimal detector for this model. However, the optimal detector is not realizable except under special circumstances (independent part positions). A cousin of the optimal detector is developed which uses "soft" part detectors with a probabilistic description of the spatial arrangement of the parts. Spatial arrangements are modeled probabilistically using shape statistics to achieve invariance to translation, rotation, and scaling. Improved recognition performance over methods based on "hard" part detectors is demonstrated for the problem of face detection in cluttered scenes.

1 Introduction

Visual recognition of objects (chairs, sneakers, faces, cups, cars) is one of the most challenging problems in computer vision and artificial intelligence. Historically, there has been a progression in recognition research from the particular to the general. Researchers initially worked on the problem of recognizing individual objects; however, during the last five years the emphasis has shifted to recognizing classes of objects which are visually similar.

One line of research has concentrated on exploiting photometric aspects of objects. Matched filtering (template matching) was an initial attempt along these lines. More modern approaches use classification in subspaces of filter responses, where the set of filters is selected based on human receptive fields, principal components analysis [12, 23, 16, 2], linear discriminant analysis, or by training with perceptron-like architectures [22, 20]. These methods allow one to accomodate a broader range of variation in the appearance of the target object than is possible using a simple matched filter.

A second line of research has used geometric constraints between low level object features. Methods such as alignment [11], geometric invariants [15], combinations of views [24, 21], and geometric hashing [26, 19] fit within this category.

Further generalization has been obtained by allowing an object to be represented as a collection of more complex features (or texture patches) connected with a deformable geometrical model. The neocognitron architecture [10] may be seen as an early representative. More recently, Yuille [27] proposed to use deformable templates to be fit to contrast profiles by gradient descent of a suitable energy function. Lades, von der Malsburg and colleagues [13, 25] proposed to use jet-based detectors and deformable meshes for encoding shape. Their work opened a number of interesting questions: (a) how to derive the energy function that encodes shape from a given set of examples, (b) how to initialize automatically the model so that it converges to the desired object despite a cluttered background in the image, and (c) how to handle partial occlusion of the object. Lanitis, Cootes et al. [14, 6, 7] proposed to use principal components analysis (applied to the shape of an object rather than the photometric appearance) to address the first issue. Pope and Lowe [17, 18] used probability theory to model the variation in shape of triples of features. Brunelli and Poggio [1] showed that an ad hoc face detector consisting of individual features linked together with crude geometry constraints outperformed a rigid correlation-based "full-face" detector.

Burl, Leung, and Perona [3, 4] introduced a principled framework for representing object deformations using probabilistic shape models. Local part detectors were used to identify candidate locations for object parts. These candidates were then grouped into object hypotheses and scored based on the spatial arrangement of the parts. This approach was shown to work well for detecting human faces in cluttered backgrounds and with partial occlusion. There is no guarantee, however, that first "hard-detecting" the object parts and then looking for the proper configuration of parts is the best approach. (Under a "hard" detection strategy, if the response of a part detector is above threshold, only the position of the part is recorded; the actual response values are not retained for subsequent processing.)

In this paper, we reconsider from first principles the problem of detecting an object consisting of characteristic parts arranged in a deformable configuration. The key result is that we should employ a "soft-detection" strategy and seek the arrangement of part locations that maximizes the sum of the shape log-likelihood ratio *and* the responses to the part detectors. This criteria, which combines both the local photometry (part match) and the global geometry (shape likelihood) provides a significant improvement over the "hard-detection" strategy used previously.

In Sect. 2 we provide a mathematical model for deformable object classes. The optimal detector for this model is derived from first principles in Sect. 3. We then investigate, in Sect. 4, an approximation to the optimal detector which is invariant to translation, rotation and scaling. In Sect. 5 we present evidence which verifies the practical benefits of our theoretical findings.

2 Deformable Object Classes

We are interested in object classes in which instances from the class can be modeled as a set of characteristic *parts* in a deformable spatial configuration. As an example, consider human faces, which consist of two eyes, a nose, and mouth. These parts appear in an arrangement that depends on an individual's facial geometry, expression, and pose, as well as the viewpoint of the observer.

We do not offer a precise definition of what constitutes an object "part", but we are generally referring to any feature of the object that can be reliably detected and localized using only the local image information. Hence, a part may be defined through a variety of visual cues such as a distinctive photometric pattern, texture, color, motion, or symmetry. Parts may also be defined at multiple scales. A coarse resolution view of the head can be considered a "part" as can a fine resolution view of an eye corner. The parts may be object-specific (eyes, nose, mouth) or generic (blobs, corners, textures).

2.1 Simplified Model

Consider a 2-D object consisting of N photometric parts $P_i(x, y)$, each occuring in the image at a particular spatial location (x_i, y_i). The parts P_i can be thought of as small image patches that are placed down at the appropriate positions. Mathematically, the image T of an object is given by:

$$T(x, y) = \sum_{i=1}^{N} P_i(x - x_i, \, y - y_i) \tag{1}$$

For convenience, we will assume, that the $P_i(x, y)$ are defined for any pair (x, y), but are non-zero only inside a relatively small neighborhood around $(0, 0)$.

Let X be the vector describing the positions of the object parts, i.e.

$$X = \begin{bmatrix} x_1 \ x_2 \ldots x_N \ y_1 \ y_2 \ldots y_N \end{bmatrix}^T \tag{2}$$

An *object class* can now be defined as the set of objects induced by a set of vectors $\{X_k\}$. In particular, we assume that the part positions are distributed according to a joint probability density $p_X(X)$. We will designate the resulting object class as $\mathcal{T}$. To generate an object from this class, we first generate a random vector X according to the density $p_X(X)$. Since this vector determines the part positions, we simply place the corresponding pattern P_i at each of these positions.

Note that no assumption about $p_X(X)$ is made at this time. It should be clear, however, that through $p_X(X)$ we can control properties of the object class, such as the range of meaningful object *shapes*, as well as tolerable ranges of certain transformations, such as rotation, scaling and translation.

3 Derivation of the Optimal Detector

The basic problem can be stated as follows: given an image $\mathcal{I}$ determine whether the image contains an instance from $\mathcal{T}$ (hypothesis ω_1) or whether the image is background-only (hypothesis ω_2). In our previous work we proposed a two-step solution to this problem: (1) apply feature detectors to the image in order to identify candidate locations for each of the object parts and (2) given the candidate locations, find the set of candidates with the most object-like spatial configuration. However, there is nothing to say that first hard-detecting candidate object parts is the right strategy. In the following section, we will directly derive the optimal detector starting from the pixel image $\mathcal{I}$.

3.1 Optimal Detector

The optimal decision statistic is given by the likelihood ratio

$$\Lambda = \frac{p(\mathcal{I}|\omega_1)}{p(\mathcal{I}|\omega_2)} \tag{3}$$

We can rewrite the numerator by conditioning on the spatial positions $\mathbf{X}$ of the object parts. Hence,

$$\Lambda = \frac{\sum_{\mathbf{X}} p(\mathcal{I}|\mathbf{X},\omega_1) \cdot p(\mathbf{X}|\omega_1)}{p(\mathcal{I}|\omega_2)} \tag{4}$$

where the summation goes over all possible configurations of the object parts. Assuming that parts do not overlap, we can divide the image into $N+1$ regions, $\mathcal{I}^0, \mathcal{I}^1, \ldots, \mathcal{I}^N$, where $\mathcal{I}^i$ is an image which is equal to $\mathcal{I}$ in the area occupied by the non-zero portion of part P_i (positioned according to $\mathbf{X}$) and zero otherwise. $\mathcal{I}^0$ denotes the background. Assuming furthermore that the background is independent across regions, we obtain

$$\Lambda = \frac{\sum_{\mathbf{X}} \prod_{i=0}^{N} p(\mathcal{I}^i|\mathbf{X},\omega_1) \cdot p(\mathbf{X}|\omega_1)}{p(\mathcal{I}|\omega_2)} \tag{5}$$

$$= \sum_{\mathbf{X}} \left[\prod_{i=1}^{N} \frac{p(\mathcal{I}^i|\mathbf{X},\omega_1)}{p(\mathcal{I}^i|\omega_2)} \right] \cdot p(\mathbf{X}|\omega_1) \tag{6}$$

$$= \sum_{\mathbf{X}} \left[\prod_{i=1}^{N} \lambda_i(x_i, y_i) \right] \cdot p(\mathbf{X}|\omega_1) \tag{7}$$

Here, the $\lambda_i(x_i, y_i) = \frac{p(\mathcal{I}^i|\mathbf{X},\omega_1)}{p(\mathcal{I}^i|\omega_2)}$ can be interpreted as likelihood ratios expressing the likelihood of part P_i being present in the image at location (x_i, y_i). Note that $\lambda_0(x,y)$ is equal to one, under the hypothesis that the statistics of the background region do not depend on the presence or absence of the object.

We can specialize this derivation by introducing a particular part detection method. For example, assuming that the object is embedded in white Gaussian noise, we can substitute Gaussian class conditional densities and obtain

$$\lambda_i = \frac{\mathcal{N}\left(\mathcal{I}^i;\, \mu_X, \sigma^2 I\right)}{\mathcal{N}\left(\mathcal{I}^i;\, 0, \sigma^2 I\right)} \tag{8}$$

Here, μ_X is the object with parts positioned at X, 0 shall denote a vector of zeros and I is the identity matrix. Expanding the Gaussian densities and combining terms yields:

$$
\begin{aligned}
\lambda_i &= \exp\left(\frac{\mu_X^T \mathcal{I}^i}{\sigma^2} - \frac{\mu_X^T \mu_X}{2\sigma^2}\right) \\
&= \exp\left(-\frac{\mu_X^T \mu_X}{2\sigma^2}\right) \cdot \exp\left(\frac{\mu_X^T \mathcal{I}^i}{\sigma^2}\right) \\
&= c \cdot \exp\left(\frac{\mu_X^T \mathcal{I}^i}{\sigma^2}\right)
\end{aligned} \tag{9}
$$

where σ^2 is the variance of the pixel noise and c depends only on the energy in the object image and is therefore constant independent of X, provided the parts do not overlap. Equation (9) simply restates the well known fact that matched filtering is the optimal part detection strategy under this noise model. Writing A_i for the response image obtained by correlating part i with the image $\mathcal{I}$ and normalizing by σ^2, we finally obtain

$$\Lambda = c \cdot \sum_X \left[\prod_{i=1}^N \exp\left(A_i(x_i, y_i)\right)\right] \cdot p(X) \tag{10}$$

The constant c does not affect the form of the decision rule, so we will omit it from our subsequent equations.

3.2 Independent Part Positions

If the part positions are independent, $p(X)$ can also be expressed as a product

$$p(X) = \prod_{i=1}^N p_i(x_i, y_i) \tag{11}$$

Thus, we have

$$\Lambda = \sum_X \left[\prod_{i=1}^N \lambda_i(x_i, y_i) p_i(x_i, y_i)\right]$$

For the special case of additive white Gaussian noise, we obtain

$$\Lambda = \sum_X \left[\prod_{i=1}^N \exp\left(A_i(x_i, y_i)\right) p_i(x_i, y_i)\right]$$

$$= \sum_{\mathbf{X}} \left[\prod_{i=1}^{N} \exp\left(A_i(x_i, y_i) + \log p_i(x_i, y_i)\right) \right]$$

$$= \prod_{i=1}^{N} \left[\sum_{(x_i, y_i)} \exp\left(A_i(x_i, y_i) + \log p_i(x_i, y_i)\right) \right] \tag{12}$$

Thus, we need to compute the correlation response image (normalized by σ^2) for each object part. To this image, we add the log probability that the part will occur at a given spatial position, take the exponential, and sum over the whole image. This process is repeated for each object part. Finally, the product of scores over all the object parts yields the likelihood ratio.

Note, that the detector is not invariant to translation, rotation, and scaling since the term $p_i(x_i, y_i)$ includes information about the absolute coordinates of the parts.

3.3 Jointly Distributed Part Positions

If the part positions are *not independent*, we must introduce an approximation since summing over all *combinations* of part positions as in (7) is infeasible. The basic idea—similar to a winner-take-all strategy—is to assume that the summation is dominated by one term corresponding to a specific combination $\mathbf{X}_0$ of the part positions. With this assumption, we have

$$\Lambda \approx \Lambda_0 = \prod_{i=1}^{N} \lambda_i(x_i, y_i) \cdot p(\mathbf{X}_0)$$

$$\log \Lambda_0 = \sum_{i=1}^{N} \log \lambda_i(x_i, y_i) + \log p(\mathbf{X}_0) \tag{13}$$

and in the case of additive white Gaussian noise

$$\log \Lambda_0 = \left(\sum_{i=1}^{N} A_i(x_{0i}, y_{0i}) \right) + \log p(\mathbf{X}_0) \tag{14}$$

The strategy now is to find a set of part positions such that the matched filter responses are high and the overall configuration of the parts is consistent with $p(\mathbf{X}|\omega_1)$. Again, the resulting detector is not invariant to translation, rotation, and scaling.

4 TRS-invariant Approximation to the Optimal Detector

The approximate log-likelihood ratio given in (13) can readily be interpreted as a combination of two terms: the first term, $\sum A_i$, measures how well the hypothesized parts in the image match the actual model parts, while the second term, $p(\boldsymbol{X}_0)$, measures how well the hypothesized spatial arrangement matches the ideal model arrangement. The second term, the configuration match, is specified as a probability density over the absolute coordinates of the parts, which in practice is not useful since (a) there is no way to know or estimate this density and (b) this formulation does not provide TRS-invariance.

We can make use of the theory developed in our previous work (see [4] or [5]) to write down a TRS-invariant detector that closely follows the form of (13). In particular, we know how to factor the term $p(\boldsymbol{X}_0)$ into a part that depends purely on shape and a part that depends purely on pose:

$$p_X(\boldsymbol{X}_0) = p_U(\boldsymbol{U}_0(\boldsymbol{X}_0)) \cdot p_\Theta(\boldsymbol{\Theta}_0(\boldsymbol{X}_0)) \tag{15}$$

Here, $\boldsymbol{U}$ denotes the *shape* of the constellation and the vector $\boldsymbol{\Theta}$ captures the pose parameters. Computing $\boldsymbol{U}(\boldsymbol{X})$ corresponds to transforming a constellation $\boldsymbol{X}$ in the image to so-called *shape space* by mapping two part positions (the *base-line pair*) to fixed reference positions. In shape space, the positions of the remaining $N-2$ parts define the shape of the configuration, written as

$$\boldsymbol{U} = \begin{bmatrix} u_3 \, u_4 \ldots u_N \, v_3 \, v_4 \ldots v_N \end{bmatrix}^T \tag{16}$$

If $p_X(\boldsymbol{X})$ is a joint Gaussian density, then the shape density, $p_U(\boldsymbol{U})$, can be computed in closed form as shown by Dryden and Mardia [8]. This established, we can obtain the TRS-invariant detector by dropping the pose information completely and working with shape variables $\boldsymbol{U}_0$, instead of figure space variables $\boldsymbol{X}_0$. The resulting log-likelihood ratio is then

$$\log \Lambda_1 = \sum_{i=1}^{N} A_i(x_{0i}, y_{0i}) + K \cdot \log \frac{p_U(\boldsymbol{U}_0|\omega_1)}{p_U(\boldsymbol{U}_0|\omega_2)} \tag{17}$$

The shape likelihood ratio, rather than just $p_U(\boldsymbol{U}_0)$, is used in place of $p_X(\boldsymbol{X}_0)$ to provide invariance to the choice of baseline features. The likelihood ratio also assigns lower scores to configurations that have higher probabilities of accidental occurrence. The factor of K provides a weighted trade-off between the part match and shape match terms, since the units of measurement for the two terms will no longer agree. (The proper setting for this value can be estimated from training data).

An object hypothesis is now just a set of N coordinates specifying the (hypothesized) spatial positions of the object parts. Any hypothesis can be assigned a score based on (17). It is no longer the case that hypotheses must consist only of points corresponding to the best part matches. The trade-off between having the parts match well and having the shape match well may imply that it is better to accept a slightly worse part match in favor of a better shape match or vice versa.

We do not have a procedure for finding the hypothesis that optimizes $\log \Lambda_1$. One heuristic approach $\mathcal{A}_1$ is to identify candidate part locations at maxima of the part detector responses and combine these into hypotheses using the conditional search procedure described in [4]. However, instead of discarding the response values, these should be summed and combined with the shape likelihood. In this approach, the emphasis is on finding the best part matches and accepting whatever spatial configuration occurs. There is no guarantee that the procedure will maximize $\log \Lambda_1$.

Figure 1 illustrates the gain of approach $\mathcal{A}_1$ over hard detection. The two components of the goodness function (sum of responses and shape log-likelihood) can be seen as dimensions in a two dimensional space. Evaluating the goodness function is equivalent to projecting the data onto a particular direction, which is determined by the trade-off factor K. A technique known as "Fisher's Linear Discriminant" [9] provides us with the direction which maximizes the separability of the two classes. If the sum of the detector responses had no discriminative power, the value of K would tend toward infinity. This would correspond to a horizontal line in the figure. The advantage of soft detection is further illustrated in Fig. 2.

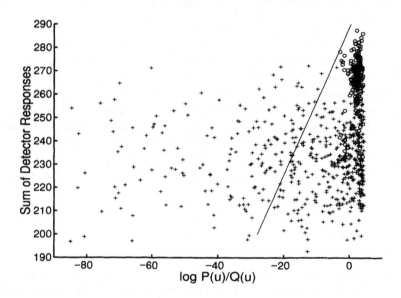

Fig. 1. Illustration of the advantage of *soft* detection. The sum of the detector outputs is plotted against the shape log-likelihood, for a set of face (o) and background (+) samples. Also shown is a line onto which the data should be projected (derived by Fisher's Linear Discriminant method).

A second approach, $\mathcal{A}_2$, is to insist on the best shape match and accept whatever part matches occur. This method is roughly equivalent to using a rigid matched filter for the entire object, but applying it at multiple orientations and scales.

636

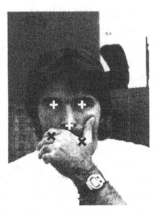

Fig. 2. Two constellations of candidates for part locations are shown. The background constellation (black 'x') yields a greater shape likelihood value than the correct hypothesis (white '+'). However, when the detector response values are taken into consideration, the correct hypothesis will score higher.

Finally, we tested a third approach, $\mathcal{A}_3$, that intuitively seems appealing. Candidate part locations are identified as before in $\mathcal{A}_1$ at local maxima in the part response image. From pairs of candidate parts, the locations of the other parts are estimated to provide an initial hypothesis. (So far, this is equivalent to using a fixed-shape template anchored at the two baseline points). From the initial hypothesis, however, a gradient-style search is employed to find a local maximum of $\log \Lambda_1$. Individual part positions are pulled by two forces. One force tries to maximize the response value while the other force tries to improve the shape of the configuration.

5 Experiments

We conducted a series of experiments aimed at evaluating the improvements over hard detection of object parts, brought about by the different approaches described in the previous section. To test our method, we chose the problem of detecting faces from frontal views. A grayscale image sequence of 400 frames was acquired from a person performing head movements and facial expressions in front of a cluttered background. The images were 320×240 pixels in size, while the face occupied a region of approximately 40 pixels in height. Our face model was comprised of five parts, namely eyes, nose tip and mouth corners.

For the part detectors we applied a correlation based method—similar to a matched filter—acting not on the grayscale image, but on a transformed version of the image that characterizes the dominant local orientation. We found this method, which we previously described in [5], to be more robust against variations in illumination than grayscale correlation. The part detectors were trained

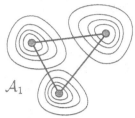 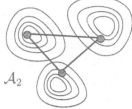 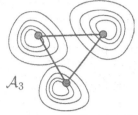

part resp.:	optimal	part resp.:	suboptimal	part resp.: suboptimal
shape:	suboptimal	shape:	optimal	shape: suboptimal
combined:	suboptimal	combined:	suboptimal	combined: optimal

Fig. 3. Pictorial illustration of the three approaches $\mathcal{A}_1$, $\mathcal{A}_2$, and $\mathcal{A}_3$ discussed in the text. For each approach we show a set of three contours which represent the superposition of response functions from three part detectors. With approach $\mathcal{A}_1$ the detector responses are optimal, but the combination of responses and shape is suboptimal. With approach $\mathcal{A}_2$ the shape likelihood is optimal, but the combination is still suboptimal. Only under approach $\mathcal{A}_3$ is the combined likelihood function optimized by seeking a compromise between contributions from the detector responses and shape.

	Best Correct	Best False
Σ Responses	101.1	93.7
Shape Log-LH.	1.457	-0.096
Weighted Total	101.5	93.7

	Best Correct	Best False
Σ Responses	96.4	94.8
Shape Log-LH.	3.460	-3.530
Weighted Total	97.5	93.7

Fig. 4. Examples from the sequence of 400 frames used in the experiments. The highest scoring correct and incorrect constellations are shown for each frame. The tables give the values for shape log-likelihood, sum of detector responses as well as overall goodness function.

on images of a second person. In order to establish ground truth for the part locations, each frame of the sequence was hand-labeled.

Prior to the experiment, shape statistics had been collected from the face of a third person by fitting a joint Gaussian density with full covariance matrix to data extracted from a sequence of 150 images, taken under a semi-controlled pose as discussed in [4].

5.1 Soft Detection vs. Hard Detection

In a first experiment, we found that using the five features described above, recognition on our test sequence under the hard detection paradigm was almost perfect, making it difficult to demonstrate any further improvements. Therefore, in order to render the task more challenging, we based the following experiments on the upper three features (eyes and nose tip) only. In this setting, approach $\mathcal{A}_1$, i.e. combining the part responses with the shape likelihood without any further effort to maximize the overall goodness function (17), yields a significant increase in recognition performance. This result is illustrated in Fig. 5, where ROC (*Receiver Operating Characteristics*) curves are shown for the hard detection method as well as for approach $\mathcal{A}_1$.

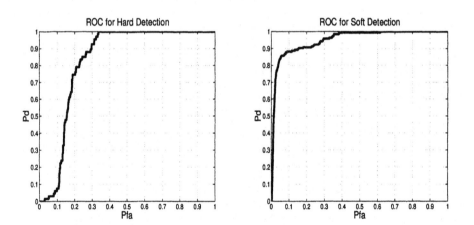

Fig. 5. The two ROC curves show the performance of hard vs. soft detection of features as a trade-off between detection probability, P_d, and probability of false alarm, P_{fa}. The soft detection method $\mathcal{A}_1$ clearly outperforms the hard detection strategy, especially in the low false alarm range.

5.2 Gradient Descent Optimization

Approach $\mathcal{A}_3$ was tested in a second experiment by performing a gradient descent maximization of the goodness criteria with respect to the hypothesized part positions in the image. There are two potential benefits from doing this: improved detection performance and improved localization accuracy of the part positions. A cubic spline interpolation of the detector response images was used in order to provide the minimization algorithm with a continuous and differentiable objective function. Local maxima of the detector response maps were used as initial estimates for the part positions. We found that, on average, optimal part positions were found within a distance of less than one pixel from the initial positions.

Fig. 6 shows the detection performance of the method before and after optimization of (17). There does not seem to be any noticeable improvement over approach $\mathcal{A}_1$. This result is somewhat surprising, but not entirely counterintuitive. This is because by optimizing the goodness criteria, we are improving the score of the constellations from both classes, ω_1 and ω_2. It is not clear that, on average, we are achieving a better separation of the classes in terms of their respective distribution of the goodness criteria. From a different perspective, this is a positive result, because the gradient descent optimization is computationally very expensive, whereas we have already been able to develop a 2 Hz real-time implementation of approach $\mathcal{A}_1$ on a PC with Pentium processor (233 MHz).

Since our part detectors did not exhibit a significant localization error for the test data at hand, we have not been able to determine whether approach $\mathcal{A}_3$ might provide improved localization accuracy.

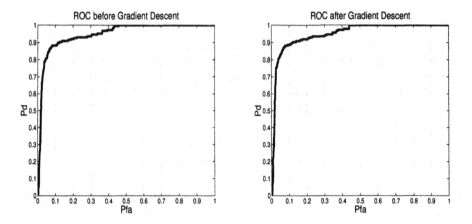

Fig. 6. The ROC performance does not significantly improve after Gradient Descent Optimization of the goodness criteria.

6   Conclusion

We have reconsidered from first principles the problem of detecting deformable object classes of which human faces are a special case. The optimal detector for

640

object class $\mathcal{T}$ was derived for the case of independent part positions. When the part positions are jointly distributed the optimal detector is too complicated to evaluate, but it can be approximated using a winner-take-all simplification. In both cases, the detector is composed of two terms: the first term measures how well the hypothesized parts in the image match the actual model parts, while the second term measures how well the hypothesized spatial arrangement matches the ideal model arrangement.

The configuration match is specified in terms of the absolute positions of the object parts, therefore the optimal detector cannot be used in practice. However, using previous theoretical results, we were able to write an expression that closely follows the form of (13), but only exploits the *shape* of the configuration. The resulting criteria combines the part match with shape match and is invariant to translation, rotation, and scaling.

Although we do not have a procedure for finding the hypothesis that maximizes the overall goodness function, a heuristic approach $\mathcal{A}_1$ worked very well. In this approach, candidate parts are identified and grouped into hypotheses as in the shape-only method, but, in addition, the response values (part matches) are retained and combined with the shape likelihood. A second approach, including a gradient descent optimization of the goodness function with respect to the part position in the image, did not provide significant improvement in recognition performance.

Acknowledgement

The research described in this paper has been carried out in part by the Jet Propulsion Laboratory, California Institute of Technology, under contract with the National Aeronautics and Space Administration. It was funded in part by the NSF Center for Neuromorphic Systems Engineering at Caltech.

References

1. R. Brunelli and T. Poggio. "Face Recognition: Features versus Templates". *IEEE Trans. Pattern Anal. Mach. Intell.*, 15(10):1042–1052, October 1993.
2. M.C. Burl, U.M. Fayyad, P. Perona, P. Smyth, and M.P. Burl. "Automating the hunt for volcanoes on Venus". In *Proc. IEEE Comput. Soc. Conf. Comput. Vision and Pattern Recogn.*, 1994.
3. M.C. Burl, T.K. Leung, and P. Perona. "Face Localization via Shape Statistics". In *Intl. Workshop on Automatic Face and Gesture Recognition*, 1995.
4. M.C. Burl, T.K. Leung, and P. Perona. "Recognition of Planar Object Classes". In *Proc. IEEE Comput. Soc. Conf. Comput. Vision and Pattern Recogn.*, 1996.
5. M.C. Burl, M. Weber, T.K. Leung, and P. Perona. *From Segmentation to Interpretation and Back: Mathematical Methods in Computer Vision*, chapter "Recognition of Visual Object Classes". Springer, in press.
6. T.F. Cootes and C.J. Taylor. "Combining Point Distribution Models with Shape Models Based on Finite Element Analysis". *Image and Vision Computing*, 13(5):403–409, 1995.

7. T.F. Cootes and C.J. Taylor. "Locating Objects of Varying Shape Using Statistical Feature Detectors". In *European Conf. on Computer Vision*, pages 465–474, 1996.
8. I.L. Dryden and K.V. Mardia. "General Shape Distributions in a Plane". *Adv. Appl. Prob.*, 23:259–276, 1991.
9. R.O. Duda and P.E. Hart. *Pattern Classification and Scene Analysis*. John Wiley and Sons, Inc., 1973.
10. K. Fukushima. Neural networks for visual-pattern recognition. *IEICE Trans. Inf. & Syst.*, 74(1):179–190, 1991.
11. D.P. Huttenlocher and S. Ullman. "Object Recognition Using Alignment". In *Proc. 1st Int. Conf. Computer Vision*, pages 102–111, 1987.
12. M. Kirby and L. Sirovich. Applications of the Karhunen-Loeve procedure for the characterization of human faces. *IEEE Trans. Pattern Anal. Mach. Intell.*, 12(1):103–108, Jan 1990.
13. M. Lades, J.C. Vorbruggen, J. Buhmann, J. Lange, C. v.d. Malsburg, R.P. Wurtz, and W. Konen. "Distortion Invariant Object Recognition in the Dynamic Link Architecture". *IEEE Trans. Comput.*, 42(3):300–311, Mar 1993.
14. A. Lanitis, C.J. Taylor, T.F. Cootes, and T. Ahmed. "Automatic Interpretation of Human Faces and Hand Gestures Using Flexible Models". In *International Workshop on Automatic Face- and Gesture-Recognition*, pages 90–103, 1995.
15. J. Mundy and A. Zisserman, editors. *Geometric invariance in computer vision*. MIT Press, Cambridge, Mass., 1992.
16. Hiroshi Murase and Shree Nayar. "Visual Learning and Recognition of 3-D Objects from Appearance". *Int J. of Comp. Vis.*, 14:5–24, 1995.
17. Arthur R. Pope and David G. Lowe. "Modeling Positional Uncertainty in Object Recognition". Technical report, Department of Computer Science, University of British Columbia, 1994. Technical Report # 94-32.
18. Arthur R. Pope and David G. Lowe. "Learning Feature Uncertainty Models for Object Recognition". In *IEEE International Symposium on Computer Vision*, 1995.
19. I. Rigoutsos and R. Hummel. A bayesian approach to model matching with geometric hashing. *Comp. Vis. and Img. Understanding*, 62:11–26, Jul. 1995.
20. H.A. Rowley, S. Baluja, and T. Kanade. Neural network-based face detection. *IEEE Trans. Pattern Anal. Mach. Intell.*, 20(1):23–38, Jan 1998.
21. A. Shashua. "On Geometric and Algebraic Aspects of 3D Affine and Projective Structures from Perspective 2D Views". Technical Report A.I. Memo # 1405, MIT, 1993.
22. K.-K. Sung and T. Poggio. Example-based learning for view-based human face detection. *IEEE Trans. Pattern Anal. Mach. Intell.*, 20(1):39–51, Jan 1998.
23. M. Turk and A. Pentland. "Eigenfaces for Recognition". *J. of Cognitive Neurosci.*, 3(1), 1991.
24. S. Ullman and R. Basri. Recognition by linear combinations of models. *IEEE Trans. Pattern Anal. Mach. Intell.*, 13(10), 1991.
25. L. Wiskott and C. von der Malsburg. "A Neural System for the Recognition of Partially Occluded Objects in Cluttered Scenes". *Int. J. of Pattern Recognition and Artificial Intelligence*, 7(4):935–948, 1993.
26. H.J. Wolfson. "Model-Based Object Recognition by Geometric Hashing". In *Proc. 1st Europ. Conf. Comput. Vision, LNCS-Series Vol. 427, Springer-Verlag*, pages 526–536, 1990.
27. A.L. Yuille. "Deformable Templates for Face Recognition". *J. of Cognitive Neurosci.*, 3(1):59–70, 1991.

Hypothesis Verification
in Model-Based Object Recognition
with a Gaussian Error Model

Frédéric Jurie

LASMEA - CNRS UMR 6602
Université Blaise-Pascal
F-63177 Aubière
France

Abstract. The use of hypothesis verification is recurrent in the model based recognition literature. Small sets of features forming salient groups are paired with model features. Poses can be hypothesised from this small set of feature-to-feature correspondences. The verification of the pose consists in measuring how much model features transformed by the computed pose coincide with image features. When data involved in the initial pairing are noisy the pose is inaccurate and the verification is a difficult problem.

In this paper we propose a robust hypothesis verification algorithm, assuming data error is Gaussian. Previous approaches using gaussian error model start from an initial set of correspondences and try to extend it feature by feature. This solution is not optimal. In this paper, the opposite strategy is adopted. Assuming the right pose belongs to a known volume of the pose space (including the initial pose) we take into account all of the correspondences compatible with this volume and refine iteratively this set of correspondences. This is our main contribution.

We present experimental results obtained with 2D recognition proving that the proposed algorithm is fast and robust.

Keywords : Model-Based Recognition, Pose Verification

1 Introduction

Despite recent advances in computer vision the recognition and localisation of 3D objects from a 2D image of a cluttered scene is still a key problem. The reason for the difficulty to progress mainly lies in the combinatoric aspect of the problem.

This difficulty can be bypassed if the location of the objects in the image is known. In that case, the problem is then to compare efficiently a region of the image to a viewer-centred object database. Recent proposed solutions are, for example, based on principal component analysis [14, 16], modal matching [18] or template matching [4].

But Grimson [9] emphasises that the hard part of the recognition problem is in separating out subsets of correct data from the spurious data that arise from a single object.

Recent researches in this field are focused on the various components of the recognition problem : which features are invariant and discriminant [19], how is it possible to group features into salient parts [13], how to index models [5], how to identify sets of data feature/model feature pairings that are consistent with an object [15] or which similarity measures are relevant [12].

From these researches, we can notice that most of the proposed strategies can be described in terms of prediction - verification schemes. In a pre-processing stage model feature groups having invariant properties are stored in an hash table. Recognition first consists in grouping image features into salient parts. Index keys obtained from these small groups select objects in the model base, producing sets of pairings from indexed models to data features. The transformation aligning a model with the image is usually referred as the pose of the object. Poses obtained by this method are treated as hypotheses realizing a few feature-to-feature correspondences. These hypotheses have to be verified by transforming remaining model features and by trying to match them with image features. Transformations are usually assumed to be affine.

However errors in data generally make the pose incorrect and the verification becomes more difficult (see Fig. 1 for an illustration).

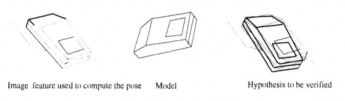

Image feature used to compute the pose   Model   Hypothesis to be verified

Fig. 1. Verification of an inaccurate pose

In that case, as pointed out by [7] the noise in the data will propagate into the pose and will decrease the quality of the correspondences obtained in the verification stage.

This noise effect has been studied assuming bounded error models. Grimson, Huttenlocher and Jacobs [10] provide a precise analysis of affine point matching under uncertainty. They obtain expression for the set of affine-invariant values consistent with a set of four points, where each data point lies in a small disc. Alter and Jacobs [1] model error by assuming that a detected feature point is no more than ϵ pixels from the location of the true point. They propose an expression for the error in the computed image position of a 4th-point (and nth-point)when three matching pairs of image and model points are assumed.

Gandhi and Camps [7] propose an algorithm to select next feature to be matched, after the pose has been computed with a small number of correspondences. Their objective is to find the subset of n model points such that the effect of the data uncertainty in the estimation of the pose is minimised.

Some authors assumed Gaussian error model. Sarachik and Grimson [17] analytically derive the probability of false positive and negative as a function of the number of model features, image features, and occlusions, under the assumption of 2D Gaussian noise.

Beveridge and Riseman [2] present a model based recognition system using 3D pose recovery during matching. Their algorithm is based on a random local search to find the globally optimal correspondence between image and model, with a high probability of success. A current set of correspondences is modified, trying neighbouring sets. The neighbourhood is defined as sets obtained by adding or removing a single pair from the current correspondences set.

In spite of all this research activity, hypothesis verification remains a difficult problem.

2 Overview of the proposed approach

As explained in the introduction, object recognition systems frequently hypothesise model pose from the matching of a small number of model features. A fundamental question is how such hypotheses can be confirmed if poses are inaccurate and if data are cluttered.

The above mentioned approaches generally start from the initial set of correspondences, and try to extend it feature by feature. The pose is refined step by step, guiding for the selection of next features. This solution is not optimal since these algorithms look for only on point at a time. We experimentally observed that in many cases it leads to false solutions, specially if objects are occluded or if data are cluttered.

In this paper, the opposite approach is adopted. Assuming that the right pose belongs to a known volume of the pose space (including the initial pose) we first take into account all of the correspondences compatible with this volume. This set of poses is iteratively reduced, until it can be taken as a single pose. The computed pose (and the related correspondences) is better than when correspondences are added one by one, because influences of each possible correspondences are taken into account together. The transformation aligning models on images is supposed to be affine.

The verification stage have to be as fast as possible, because in case of complex scenes and large number of possible objects, a large number of hypotheses have to be verified. It is expensive to verify each one of these hypotheses. The proposed approach allows hierarchical verification Breuel [3]. : we compute for each possible hypothesis the volume of possible poses, and determine how many correspondences are compatible with this set of poses. This score represent the maximal number of correspondences that a unique pose of the volume may verify. Hypotheses having low score are first discarded. The remaining ones are refined. For purpose of simplicity, we assume that the sub-space is a rectangular volume of the pose space, that we call a "box".

Gaussian error model is used instead of than the usual bounded one (it has been demonstrated [17] that the Gaussian error model has better performances than the bounded error one). Each model feature has its own distribution. By that way the relative stability of features is taken into account for the verification.

As we work with a Gaussian error model, the score of a box doesn't consist in counting the number of correspondences, but relies on the evaluation of the maximal probability of the object to be matched knowing the set of possible poses.

These different steps are summarised as follows :

1. form small groups of features and compute invariant measures.
2. search the knowledge base for compatible objects.
3. for each possible correspondence :
   3.1. use feature pairings to determine the pose P.
   3.2. compute a "box" of the pose space including P that is large enough to compensate for the data errors.
   3.3. compute the probability for each remaining model feature to have a correspondence in the image knowing poses belongs to the "box" of possible transformations, and deduce the maximal probability of the object to be matched.
4. for best hypotheses, refine the box of possible poses so that the match probability is maximal. The size of the box is reduced until it can be considered as a point of the pose space.

This paper only focuses on the verification stage (point 3.3 and 4). In the section 3 we define the Gaussian error model used. Section 4 is devoted to the computation of the probability of feature-to-feature correspondence knowing a pose, and section 5 to the computation of the maximal probability of correspondence knowing possible poses belongs to a box of the pose space. We then study how to combine these individual probabilities to compute the object match probability. Section 7 explained how the the box is refined in order to maximise the object match probability.

3   Gaussian model error

Let f_d denotes a data feature and f_t the transformation of the feature model f by the pose P. Let $\delta = f_d - f_t$.

Data features are assumed to be normally distributed. Let $P(\delta|C)$ the probability of having δ knowing C. C means "f_t and f_d are corresponding features". In a v-dimensional feature space, the v-dimensional normal probability density function with covariance matrix Q is :

$$P(\delta|C) = (2\pi)^{-\frac{v}{2}}|Q|^{-\frac{1}{2}}exp(-\frac{1}{2}(f_t - f_d)^T Q^{-1}(f_t - f_d))$$

If features are image points, the dimensionality is 2 and $f_i = (a_1, a_2)^T$ where (a_1, a_2) is the 2d spatial position of the feature. The dimensionality is 4 for line segments. No assumption is made neither on the dimensionality, neither on the kind of parameters encoding the feature.

For purpose of simplification, in the rest of the paper we do not represent features in their original feature space. We decompose the covariance matrix Q^{-1} as :

$$Q^{-1} = U D^{-1} U^t$$

where U is the orthogonal matrix of eigenvectors of Q and D the diagonal matrix of eigen values. The v eigen values will be denoted $\lambda_1, \cdots, \lambda_v$.

By projecting features in the eigenspace, the normal distribution for the model feature i is much simple :

$$P(\epsilon|C) = (2\pi)^{-\frac{v}{2}} \prod_{j=1}^{j \leq v} \lambda_j^{-\frac{1}{2}} exp(-\frac{1}{2} \sum_{j=1}^{j \leq v} \frac{\epsilon_j^2}{\lambda_j})$$

ϵ denotes the difference $(f_t - f_d)$ projected into the eigenspace ($\epsilon = U\delta$). There is one different covariance matrix per model feature.

4 Probability of a feature-to-feature correspondence knowing the affine transformation P

Denoting $\epsilon = U(f_t - f_d)$ where f_d is the data feature and f_t the transformation in the image reference of the feature f. The probability of having a correspondence between f_t and f_d knowing the pose P is :

$$P(C|P) = P(C|\epsilon) = \frac{P(\epsilon|C)P(C)}{P(\epsilon)} = \alpha exp(-\frac{1}{2} \sum_{j=1}^{j <= v} \frac{\epsilon^2}{\lambda_j})$$

where

$$\alpha = (2\pi)^{-\frac{v}{2}} \prod_{j=1}^{j \leq v} \lambda_j^{-\frac{1}{2}} \frac{P(C)}{P(\epsilon)}$$

$P(\epsilon)$ is modelled during a training stage. This value depends on the kind of feature used. We assumed $P(C) = \frac{N}{NM}$ where N is the number of image features and M the average number of model features.

The pose P is a vector of dimensionality $\mathcal{D}$, where $\mathcal{D}$ denotes the dimensionality of the pose space.

$\epsilon = U(f_t - f_d) = (\epsilon_1, \ldots, \epsilon_v)^T$ is a linear combination of U, f_d and f_t. Then we can write : $\forall j \in [1, \ldots, v] \epsilon_j = N H_j \cdot P$ where vector $N H_j$ is a linear combination of U, f_d and f.

With these notations, we have :

$$P(C|P) = \alpha exp(-\frac{1}{2} \sum_{j=1}^{j <= v} \frac{(N H_j \cdot P)^2}{\lambda_j}) \tag{1}$$

The product $NH_j \cdot P$ can be geometrically interpreted as the distance from transformation P to the hyperplane H_j of the pose space. Hyperplanes H_j are define by their normals NH_j:

$$P \in H_j \text{ if } NH_j \cdot P = 0$$

The probability of the correspondence is then the weighted sum of squared distances from this transformation P to the H_j hyper planes. This geometric property is exploited in the next section.

5 Maximal probability of correspondence, assuming poses belongs a known box of the pose space

The maximal probability of correspondence, knowing that the transformation belongs to to a box (cubic volume) of the pose space, is denoted $P(C|BOX)$

The computation of this probability requires the maximisation of the quadratic function (1), subject to linear inequality constraints (the box of the pose space). This is a problem which can be solved in a finite number of steps with quadratic programming techniques.

One common approach uses the *Lagrange Multipliers* combined with active set methods [6].

But active set methods are highly time consuming. For example, if the transformation is an orthographic scaled projection (weak perspective) the dimension of the pose space is 8, and supposing the size of the active set is 8, a 16x16 linear system is to be solved at each iteration.

Accordingly we propose a more efficient algorithm allowing to compute an approximation of this maximal value.

It consists in the 3 following steps (detailed just after the enumeration) :

1. let V the affine manifold generated by the v hyper-planes H_j given by a pair of matched features (see end of previous section for details). We first compute the position of the pose $P_0 \in V$ such that $\forall P \in V, d(c, P_0) \le d(c, P)$ were c is the centre of the box and $d()$ the Euclidean distance.
2. if P_0 is not in the box then P_{min} is taken as the intersection of the line (c, P_0) with the convex hull of the box $(P_{min} = P_0$ if P_0 is included in the box).
3. if P_{min} is not in the box, its position is iteratively adjusted to minimise the distance $D(P)$ with $D(P) = \sum_{j=1}^{j<=v} \frac{(NH_j \cdot P)^2}{\lambda_j}$

These 3 steps are represented in Fig 2. Let us describe them more precisely.

Determination of P_0 The transformation P_0 defined by : $P_0 \in V$ such that $\forall P \in V, d(c, P_0) \le d(c, P)$ where c is the centre of the box, can be computed by means of a Lagrangian method.

The function to be minimised is (with $P = (P_1, \ldots, p_v)^T$ and $c = (c_1, \ldots, c_v)^T$) :

$$f(P) = \sum_{k=1}^{k \le \mathcal{D}} (p_k - c_k)^2$$

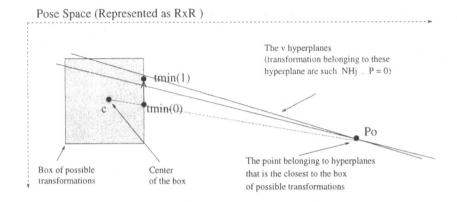

subject to the manifold defined by the four hyper-planes $H^j, j \in [0, \ldots, v]$. Then the minimum is obtained when :

$$\Box\left(f(t) - \sum_{j=1}^{j \le v} \ell^j H^j \times P\right) = 0$$

where ℓ^j are Lagrange Multipliers and $\Box = (\nabla_t, \nabla_\ell)^t$.

Improving P_{min} As shown in Fig. 2, P_{min} is first taken as being the intersection of (c, P_0) and the convex hull of the box. This point is not the minimum of the objective function. That is why we try to improve P_{min}, knowing the minimum belongs to the hull of the box (otherwise P_0 would be in the box). We use the *alternating variable strategy* in which at iteration $k(k \in [1, \ldots, \mathcal{D}])$ the variable p_k is refined in attempt to reduce the objective function. At this iteration other variables are unchanged. The direction where P_{min} should be moved is given by $\frac{\partial f}{\partial p_k}$. In our experiments, $\mathcal{D}$ iterations were enough to ensure an acceptable approximation (never than 1% below the optimal value). We observed that algorithm is more than 100 times faster than the active set method.

Correspondence probability Then the probability of the match is finally :

$$P(C|BOX) = \alpha exp\left(-\frac{1}{2} \sum_{j=1}^{j <= v} \frac{(NH_j \times P_{min})^2}{\lambda_j}\right)$$

Remark : If the dimensionality of the feature space is higher than the dimensionality of the pose space ($v \geq \mathcal{D}$ then P_0 is straightly obtained by a least square technique.

6 From feature correspondences to object correspondences

In this section we study how to derive the full model probability of correspondence from the individual feature probabilities of correspondence.

6.1 Gathering model feature correspondences into the full model match probability $P(M|P)$

We assume that the probability of having a occurrence of the model M in an image subject to a pose P only depends on which model features are matched. If the model size is $\mathcal{M}$ (the number of model features), there are $2^{\mathcal{M}}$ possible configurations denoted γ :

$$P(M|P) = \sum_{\gamma \in \Gamma} P(M|P,\gamma)P(\gamma|P)$$

Configurations can be grouped according to their number of matches. Let $E^k, k \leq \mathcal{M}$ the set of configurations matching k model segments. Then $E^k = \bigcup_{j=1}^{j < C_{\mathcal{M}}^k} \gamma_j^k$, and $\Gamma = \bigcup_{i=1}^{i \leq \mathcal{M}} E^i$, the set of all possible exhaustive and mutually exclusive configurations. Then :

$$P(M|P) = \sum_{\gamma \in \Gamma} P(M|P,\gamma)P(\gamma|P) = \sum_{k=1}^{k \leq \mathcal{M}} \sum_{j=1}^{j \leq C_{\mathcal{M}}^k} P(M|P,\gamma_j^k)P(\gamma_j^k|P)$$

We can simplify this formula, as M and P are conditionally independent given γ :

$$P(M|P) = \sum_{k=1}^{k \leq \mathcal{M}} \sum_{j=1}^{j \leq C_{\mathcal{M}}^k} P(M|\gamma_j^k)P(\gamma_j^k|P)$$

The size of Γ is so large than $P(M|\gamma)$ would be difficult to learn. We simplify this expression considering that the most significant parameter for computing this probability is the number of image features matched.

That is to say :

$$\forall k \in \{1\ldots\mathcal{M}\}, \forall i \in [1\ldots C_{\mathcal{M}}^k] P(M|\gamma_i^k) = P(M| \bigcup_{i=1}^{i \leq C_{\mathcal{M}}^k} \gamma_i^k) = P(M|E^k)$$

The probability $P(M|P)$ can therefore be written :

$$P(M|P) = \sum_{k=1}^{k \leq m} P(M|E^k) \sum_{j=1}^{j \leq C_{\mathcal{M}}^k} P(\gamma_j^k|P) \tag{2}$$

$P(M|E^k)$ is the probability of having model M knowing that k of its features are matched. It has been computed during a learning stage.

The computation of $P(E^k|P) = \sum_{j=1}^{j \leq C_{\mathcal{M}}^k} P(\gamma_j^k|P)$ is more tedious. The event E^k is the union of C_m^k different configurations. $P(\gamma_j^k|P)$ is the probability of that combination, given a set of correspondences. This probability can be written as a function of individual feature correspondences :

$$P(\gamma_j^k|P) = \prod_{i=1}^{i \leq \mathcal{M}} P(m_i \overset{b(i)}{\to})$$

where $b(i)$ is a Boolean variable meaning that the model segment m_i is be (or is not) supposed to be matched in that combination $(m \overset{0}{\to}= m \not\to, m \overset{1}{\to}= m \to)$[1] If we suppose that $m_i \overset{b(i)}{\to}, i \in \{1, \ldots, \mathcal{M}\}$ are independent events, we have $P(\gamma_j^k|P) = \prod_{i=1}^{i \leq \mathcal{M}} P(m_i \overset{b(i)}{\to}|P)$.

In that case $P(E^k|P)$ is a sum of products long to be computed. We propose to use an approximation of that sum, by only taking into account its maximal terms. As each term is a product of positive values, the maximal product is obtained with maximal values. This simplification is very easy to implement : we sort probabilities $P(m_i \overset{b(i)}{\to}|P)$, and affect the k highest probabilities to the k segments that are to be matched in the configuration. Other probabilities are affected to unmatched segments.

If we suppose that I is an index function such that $\forall (k,l) \in \{0, \ldots, \mathcal{M}\}^2$, $P(m_{I(l)} \to |P) > P(m_{I(k)} \to |P) \Rightarrow k < l$
Then

$$P(E^k|P) = P(m_0 \overset{b(0)}{\to}, \ldots, m_i \overset{b(i)}{\to}, \ldots, m_{\mathcal{M}} \overset{b(\mathcal{M})}{\to}|P)$$
$$>= \prod_{j=1}^{j <= i} P(m_{I(j)} \to |P) \prod_{j=i+1}^{j <= \mathcal{M}} (1 - P(m_{I(j)} \not\to |P)) = Papprox(E^k|P)$$

All the experiments presented in that paper have been obtained with the exact values $P(E|P)$ and $Papprox(E|P)$. We always obtain exactly the same results in both case.

6.2 Distinct correspondences

A model segment may be associated with more than one scene segment ; conversely a scene segment may be associated with more than one model segment.

This problem has been treated by several authors like Gavrila and Groen [8] or Huttenlocher and Cass [11] for cases of bounded error models. What is needed is a criterion to select candidate solutions that take into account that one scene segment can correspond to more than one model segment. The solution proposed is based on the maximum number of distinct segment correspondences

---

[1] The fact that a model segment m is matched is denoted $m \to$ (respectively $m \not\to$ if the segment is not matched).

between the model and the scene segment. This involves computing all the possible subsets. It is efficient to determine the number of different scene points and different model points involved in the correspondence and to choose the minimum of them.

Those authors indicate that this criterion give a higher count than when using the maximum number of distinct correspondences criterion, but they explain that this is compensated by the straightforward computation of this criterion.

This criterion cannot be exploited within our framework because what we need is not the number of distinct matches, but the probability that a given model segment is matched.

If we note $P(m \rightarrow |P)$ the probability that the image feature m is matched with a data feature knowing the pose P, and $P(m \rightarrow s|P)$ the probability that "model feature m is matched with image feature s knowing the pose P", then we define :

$$P(m \rightarrow |P) = P(\cup_{j=1}^{j \leq \mathcal{N}} m \rightarrow s_j |P)$$

where $\mathcal{N}$ is the number of image features. This probability is easy to compute if we suppose that individual match events are independent. For example if a model segment can be matched with 2 image segments with the probabilities 0.7 and 0.8, then the probability that this segment is matched is 0.7+0.8-0.7*0.8=.94.

7 Searching the best pose into a box of the pose space

An upper bounds of $P(M|P)$ knowing P belongs to a box of transformations (denoted $P(M|BOX)$) can be obtained by introducing values $P(C|BOX)$ instead of $P(C|P)$ in equation (2). We have $\forall P \in BOX, P(M|P) \leq P(M|BOX)$ because "a best pose" is computed individually for each model feature with no guaranty that these computed pose are equal. (It is possible to find distinct poses in the box aligning each model feature to an image feature, while there is no pose aligning correctly all the model features.)

The value $P(M|BOX)$ is however very informative and permits to make a rough selection between possibles poses, but the "real" best pose is still to be computed. We assume that when the box becomes small it can be treated as a single pose.

To reduce the size of the box around the highest values of $P(M|BOX)$, we use a recursive division of the initial box.

Recursive subdivision consists in recursively splitting the box in two parts, alternating axes. It is illustrated in the Fig. 3

This process can be seen as a tree search. The root node corresponds to the initial box. Leaves are the smallest regions taken into account.

That is why we used a N-search algorithm. N branches are explored at the same time and no backtracking is required. The maximum number of boxes evaluated is below Nh where h denotes the number of levels.

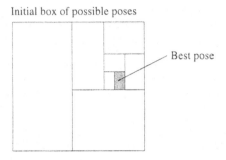

Fig. 3. Recursive division of the initial box (the pose space is represented as R^2)

The probabilistic evaluation of sub-boxes $P(M|BOX)$ guide the search : only the best N sub-boxes are kept in the next level of division. During all our experiments N was set to 5.

8 Computing the initial box

The initial box is supposed to be large enough to compensate for the data errors. If we assume the error model is Gaussian the initial box should have an infinite size.

For practical reasons we adopt a more manageable definition : the size of the initial box is such that there is at least p chance it includes the correct pose. The convex volume of the feature space bounded by $P(C|\epsilon) = p$ leads to a convex volume of the pose space. The initial box is taken as the smallest box including this volume.

In our experiments the box has a constant size, centred on the initial pose.

9 Application to recognition

The pose verification algorithm presented in that paper have been integrated a recognition applications. The 10 small objects shown in the Fig. 4 (stored in a viewer-centred database) have to be recognised in cluttered noisy images.

The 10 objects are modelled by 600 2D views. A view is a collection of line segments. Recognition first consists in indexing the knowledge base with geometric invariants. In our experiments invariants are relative angles in groups of co-terminating line segments. For each image several hundred of hypothesised 2D poses (2D affine transformations) are to be verified. It takes less than 6 seconds even for images having more than 350 line segments (about 55 ms to verify one pose)[2].

Fig. 5 and 6 show typical results. Each experiment is represented by 4 images. The two first represent successively image and line segments. Third one shown

---

[2] times are measured on a HP-700 workstation

Fig. 4. The 10 objects used in our experiments

the best verification obtained. The selected model is aligned on the image by applying the best pose. The last one represents the corresponding initial pose (the pose computed from the initial set of correspondences). One can observe that the verification is performed correctly even if the initial pose is very inaccurate. This explains why the correct object and the correct pose have been chosen from the 600 views.

10 Conclusions

In this paper, we have proposed a robust solution to the pose verification problem, when the pose is inaccurate because obtained from a few feature-to-feature noisy correspondences.

It consists it refining a set of feasible transformations so that the probability of object match knowing the pose is maximal.

The proposed algorithm has been integrated into a recognition application with line segments. However it can be directly used with different features and different recognition strategies.

We experimentally prove that it is fast, robust to data noise and robust to occlusions. The robustness is partly due to the probabilistic framework used to describe data-to-model correspondences. Convergence to the optimal pose would not be possible assuming bounded error model.

But the robustness is mainly due to the strategy used : rather than increasing the initial set of correspondences (as it was done in previous approaches using gaussian error model), we propose to refine the set of the correspondences compatibles with the initial set.

References

1. T.D. Alter and D.W. Jacobs. Error propagation in full 3d from 2d object recognition. In *Proc. IEEE Conference on Computer Vision and Pattern Recognition*, pages 892–898, Seatle, Washington, 1994.

2. J.R. Beveridge and E.M. Riseman. Optimal geometric model matching under full 3d perspective. *Computer Vision and Image Understanding*, 61(3):351–364, 1995.

3. T.M. Breuel. Fast recognition using adaptive subdivisions of transformation space. In *Proc. IEEE Conference on Computer Vision and Pattern Recognition*, pages 445–451, Champain, Illinois, 1992.

4. R. Brunelli and D. Falavigna. Person identification using multiple cues. *IEEE Transactions on Pattern Analysis and Machine Intelligence*, 17(10):955–966, October 1995.

5. A.C. Califano and R. Mohan. Mulidimensional indexing for recognizing visual shapes. *IEEE Transactions on Pattern Analysis and Machine Intelligence*, 16(4):373–392, April 1994.

6. R. Fletcher. *Practical Methods of Optimization*. John Wiley and Sons, New York, wiley-interscience publications edition, 1987.

7. T.L. Gandhi and O.I. Camps. Robust feature selection for object recognition using uncertain 2d image data. In *Proc. IEEE Conference on Computer Vision and Pattern Recognition*, pages 281–287, Seatle, Washington, 1994.

8. D.M. Gavrila and F.C.A. Groen. 3d object recognition from 2d images using geometric hashing. *Pattern Recognition Letters*, 13:263–278, 1992.

9. W.E.L. Grimson. The combinatorics of heuristic search term for object recognition in cluttered environment. *IEEE Transactions on Pattern Analysis and Machine Intelligence*, 13(9):920–935, September 1991.

10. W.E.L Grimson, D.P. Huttenlocher, and D.W. Jacobs. A study of affine matching with bounded sensor error. In *Proc. European Conference on Computer Vision*, pages 291–306, Santa Margherita Ligure, Italy, 1992.

11. D.P. Huttenlocher and T.A. Cass. Measuring the quality of hypotheses in model-based recognition. In *Proc. European Conference on Computer Vision*, pages 773–777, Santa Margherita Ligure, Italy, 1992.

12. D.P Huttenlocher, G.A. Klanderman, and W.J Rucklidge. Comparing images using the hausdorff distance. *IEEE Transactions on Pattern Analysis and Machine Intelligence*, 15(9):850–863, 1993.

13. D.W. Jacobs. Robust and efficient detection of salient convex groups. 18(1):541–548, January 1996.

14. H. Murase and S.K. Nayar. Visual learning and recognition od 3d object from appearance. *International Journal of Computer Vision*, 18(14):5–24, 1995.

15. C.F. Olson. Time and space efficient pose clustering. In *Proc. IEEE Conference on Computer Vision and Pattern Recognition*, pages 251–258, Seatle, Washington, 1994.

16. A.P. Pentland, B. Moghadam, and T. Starner. View-based and modular eigenspaces for face recognition. In *Proc. IEEE Conference on Computer Vision and Pattern Recognition*, pages 84–91, Seatle, Washington, 1994.

17. K.B. Sarachik and W.E.L. Grimson. Gaussian error models for object recognition. In *Proc. IEEE Conference on Computer Vision and Pattern Recognition*, pages 400–406, New-York, 1993.

18. S. Sclaroff and A.P. Pentland. Modal matching for correspondence and recognition. *IEEE Transactions on Pattern Analysis and Machine Intelligence*, 17:545–561, 6 1995.

19. B.M. ter Haar Romeny, L.M.J. Florack, A.H. Salden, and M.A. Viergever. Higher order differential structure of images. *Image and Vision Computing*, 12(6):317–325, 1994.

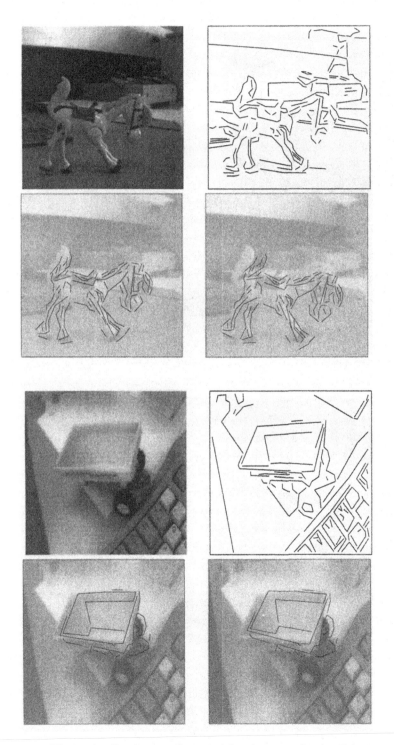

Fig. 5. Application to 2D recognition (see text for details)

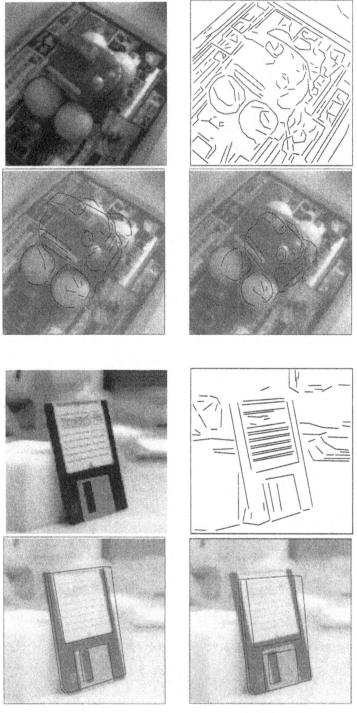

Fig. 6. Application to 2D recognition (see text for details)

Continuous Audio-Visual Speech Recognition

Juergen Luettin[1] and Stéphane Dupont[2,1]

[1] IDIAP — Dalle Molle Institute for Perceptual Artificial Intelligence, Rue du Simplon 4, CH-1920 Martigny, Switzerland, luettin@idiap.ch
[2] Faculté Polytechnique de Mons — TCTS 31, Bld. Dolez, B-7000 Mons, Belgium, dupont@tcts.fpms.ac.be

Abstract. We address the problem of robust lip tracking, visual speech feature extraction, and sensor integration for audio-visual speech recognition applications. An appearance based model of the articulators, which represents linguistically important features, is learned from example images and is used to locate, track, and recover visual speech information. We tackle the problem of joint temporal modelling of the acoustic and visual speech signals by applying Multi-Stream hidden Markov models. This approach allows the use of different temporal topologies and levels of stream integration and hence enables to model temporal dependencies more accurately. The system has been evaluated for a continuously spoken digit recognition task of 37 subjects.

1 Introduction

Human speech perception is inherently a multi-modal process, which involves the analysis of the uttered acoustic signal and which includes higher level knowledge sources such as grammar, semantics, and pragmatics. One information source which is mainly used in the presence of acoustic noise is lipreading or so-called speechreading. It is well known that seeing the talker's face in addition to audition can improve speech intelligibility, particularly in noisy environments.

Automatic speech recognition (ASR) has been an active research area for several decades, but in spite of the enormous efforts, the performance of current ASR systems is far from the performance achieved by humans. Most state-of-the-art ASR systems make use of the acoustic signal only and ignore the visual speech cues. They are therefore susceptible to acoustic noise [15], and essentially all real-world applications are subject to some kind of noise. Much research effort in ASR has therefore been directed towards systems for noisy speech environments and the robustness of speech recognition systems has been identified as one of the biggest challenges in future research [9].

2 Visual Speech Feature Extraction

Facial feature extraction is a difficult problem due to large appearance differences across persons and due to appearance variability during speech production.

Different illumination conditions and different face positions cause further difficulties in image analysis. For a real-world application, whether it is in a car, an office, or a factory, the system has to be able to deal with these kinds of image variability.

The main approaches for extracting visual speech information from image sequences can be grouped into *image based, geometric feature based, visual motion based*, and *model based* approaches. In the *image based* approach [34, 6, 30], the grey-level image containing the mouth is either used directly or after some pre-processing as feature vector. The advantage of this method is that no data is disregarded. The disadvantage is that it is left to the classifier to learn the nontrivial task of finding the generalisation for image variability (translation, scaling, 3D rotation, illumination) and linguistic variability (inter/intra speaker variability). The *visual motion based* approach [25] assumes that visual motion during speech production contains relevant speech information. This information is likely to be robust to different speakers and to different skin reflectance, however, the algorithms usually do not calculate the actual flow field but the visual flow field. A further difficulty consists in the extraction of relevant and robust features from the flow field. The *geometric feature based* approach [27] assumes that certain measures such as the height or width of the mouth opening are important features. Their automatic extraction is however not trivial and most of these systems have used semi-automatic methods or have painted the lips of the talker to facilitate feature extraction. In the *model based* approach a model of the visible speech articulators, usually the lip contours, is built and its configuration is described by a small set of parameters. The advantage is that important features can be represented in a low dimensional space and can often be made invariant to translation, scaling, rotation, and lighting. A disadvantage is that the particular model used may not consider all relevant speech information. Some of the most successful *model based* approaches have been based on colour information [8, 29, 2], although it was found that individual chromaticity models are necessary for each subject if the method is being used for several persons [29]. In comparison, our system [23] is based on grey-level information only. A technique which enables lip tracking from different head poses and the recovery of 3D lip shape from the 2D view has been described in [2].

The system presented here falls into the category of *model based* feature extraction. An important issue is to choose an appropriate description of the visible articulators. We are modelling a physical process, so we could describe this process in terms of physical movements and positions of the articulators that determine the vocal tract. Specifically, for visual analysis, we could attempt to estimate muscle action from the image such as in [25, 13]. However, the musculature of the face is complex, 3D information is not present, muscle motion is not directly observable, and there are at least thirteen groups of muscles involved in the lip movements alone [18]. We have chosen to use an *appearance based model* of the visual articulators [23] based on point distribution models [11].

2.1 Shape Modelling

The lip shape is represented by the coordinates of a point distribution model, outlining the inner and outer lip contour: $\mathbf{x} = (x_0, y_0, x_1, y_1, \ldots, x_{N_s-1}, y_{N_s-1})^T$ where (x_j, y_j) are the coordinates of the jth point. A shape is approximated by a weighted sum of basis shapes which are obtained by a Karhunen-Loéve expansion

$$\mathbf{x} = \bar{\mathbf{x}} + \mathbf{P_s b_s} \tag{1}$$

where $\mathbf{P_s} = (\mathbf{p}_{s1}, \mathbf{p}_{s2}, \ldots, \mathbf{p}_{sT_s})$ is the matrix of the first T_s ($T_s < N_s$) column eigenvectors corresponding to the largest eigenvalues and $\mathbf{b_s} = (b_{s1}, b_{s2}, \ldots, b_{sT_s})$ a vector containing the weights for the eigenvectors.

The approach assumes that the principal modes are linearly independent, although there might be non-linear dependencies present. For objects with non-linear behaviour, linear models reduce the specificity of the model and can generate implausible shapes, which lead to less robust image search. They also require more modes of variation than the true number of degrees of freedom of the object. The specificity of a model can however be improved by a nonlinear process, e.g. by nonlinear PCA.

2.2 Intensity Modelling

Intensity modelling serves two purposes: Firstly, it is used as a mean for a robust image representation to be used for image search in locating and tracking lips; secondly, it provides visual linguistic features for speech recognition. We therefore need to define dominant image features of the lip contours which we try to match with a certain representation of our model, but which also carry important speech information. Our solution to this problem is as follows. One dimensional grey-level profiles $\mathbf{g}_{ij}$ of length N_p are sampled perpendicular to the contour and centred at point j, as described in [10]. The profiles of all model points are concatenated to construct a global profile vector $\mathbf{h}_i = (\mathbf{g}_{i0}, \mathbf{g}_{i1}, \ldots, \mathbf{g}_{iN_s-1})^T$ of dimension $N_i = N_s N_p$. Similar to shape modelling, the model intensity can be approximated by a weighted sum of basis intensities using a K-L expansion

$$\mathbf{h} = \bar{\mathbf{h}} + \mathbf{P}_i \mathbf{b}_i, \tag{2}$$

where $\mathbf{P}_i = (\mathbf{p}_{i1}, \mathbf{p}_{i2}, \ldots, \mathbf{p}_{iT_i})$ is the $N_i \times T_i$ matrix of the first T_i ($T_i < N_i$) column eigenvectors corresponding to the largest eigenvalues and $\mathbf{b}_i$ a vector containing the weights for each eigenvector. This approach is related to the *local grey-level models* described in [22] and to the *eigen-lips* reported in [6].

We define image search as finding the shape of the model which maximises the posterior probability (MAP) of the model given the observed image O_i:

$$\mathbf{b}_s^* = \arg\max_{\mathbf{b}_s} P(\mathbf{b}_s | O_i) = \arg\max_{\mathbf{b}_s} \frac{P(O_i | \mathbf{b}_s) P(\mathbf{b}_s)}{P(O_i)} \tag{3}$$

$P(O_i)$ is independent of $\mathbf{b}_s$ and can therefore be ignored in the calculation of $\mathbf{b}_s^*$. We assume equal prior shape probabilities $P(\mathbf{b}_s)$ within certain limits $\mathbf{b}_{smax}$ (e.g.

$\pm\,3$ *s.d.*) and zero probability otherwise. This reduces the MAP to the likelihood function which is defined as

$$P(O_i|\mathbf{b}_s) = E_i^2 = (\mathbf{h} - \overline{\mathbf{h}})^T(\mathbf{h} - \overline{\mathbf{h}}) - \mathbf{b}_i^T\mathbf{b}_i \tag{4}$$

where $\mathbf{b}_i$ can be obtained using

$$\mathbf{b}_i = \mathbf{P_i}^T(\mathbf{h} - \overline{\mathbf{h}}) \tag{5}$$

and where $\mathbf{h}$ represents the intensity profile of the image corresponding to the model configuration $\mathbf{b}_s$.

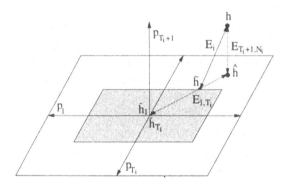

Fig. 1. A simple model for $T_i = 2$ and $N_i = 3$ with mean $\overline{\mathbf{h}} = (\overline{h}_1, \overline{h}_T)^T$ and two eigenvectors $\mathbf{p}_1, \mathbf{p}_{T_i}$. The *best fit* $\hat{\mathbf{h}}$ is the projection of $\mathbf{h}$ onto the surface spanned by $\mathbf{p}_1$ and $\mathbf{p}_{T_i}$ which results in the residual error E_{T_i+1,N_i}. Constraining all parameters b_i to stay within a certain limit $\mathbf{b}_{imax}$ (shaded area) results in the *limited fit* $\tilde{\mathbf{h}}$ and the residual error E_i.

Cootes et al. [10] have used the following measure to estimate how well the model fits the profile:

$$E_c^2 = \sum_{j=1}^{T_i} \frac{b_{ij}^2}{\lambda_j} + \frac{E_i^2}{0.5\lambda_{T_i}} \tag{6}$$

where λ_i is the eigenvalue corresponding to the ith eigenvector with $\lambda_i \leq \lambda_{i+1}$. This measure considers both the distances between the considered modes from the mean $E_{1,T}$ (first term) and the distance not explained by the considered modes $E_{T+1,N}$ (second term). The notation $E_{n,m}$ refers to the residual error for the modes n to m. The relative weighting of both terms assumes that the sum of squares of residuals are Gaussian distributed and have a variance of $0.5\lambda_{T_i}$. It has been shown [26] that the optimal value for $0.5\lambda_{T_i}$ is the arithmetic mean of the eigenvalues $(\lambda_{T_i+1}, \ldots, \lambda_{N_i})$. Since this measure penalises values far from the mean, it is unlikely to be appropriate for the application of lip localisation and tracking, where the intensities vary considerably for different subjects and

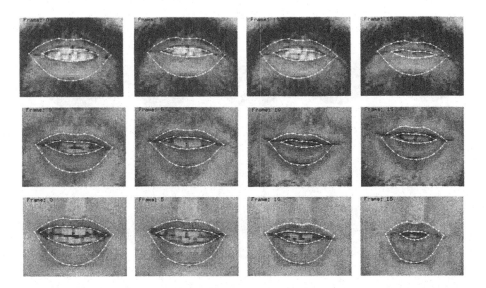

Fig. 2. Examples of lip tracking results. The examples demonstrate the robustness of the algorithm for appearance variability across subjects (e.g. beards) and appearance variability during speech (e.g. visibility of teeth).

mouth opening. In this case it is more desirable to assign equal prior probabilities to instances within a certain limit and to constrain the model parameters to stay within these limits. This strategy was implemented here, by using the sum of residual square errors E_i^2 as distance measure but forcing all intensity modes to stay within certain limits $\mathbf{b}_{imax}$.

Figure 1 illustrates the different error measures for a simple model with two modes of variation. Along the directions $\mathbf{p}_i$ for which $i \leq T_i$, the weights b_i are not considered in the error function E_i, but they are constrained to lie within the limits $\mathbf{b}_{imax}$ (e.g. ± 3 s.d.). For the point $\mathbf{h}$ the *best fit* $\hat{\mathbf{h}}$ is the projection of $\mathbf{h}$ onto the surface spanned by $\mathbf{p}_1$ and $\mathbf{p}_{T_i}$, resulting in the residual error E_{T_i+1,N_i}. The *limited fit* $\tilde{h}$ is obtained by limiting the weight vectors which results in the residual error E_i. Examples of tracking results are shown in Fig. 2.

2.3 Feature Extraction

Psychological studies suggest that the inner and outer lip contour are important visual speech features. The shape parameters $\mathbf{b}_s$ obtained from the tracking results are therefore used as features for the speech recognition system. Translation, rotation and scale parameters are disregarded since they are unlikely to provide speech information. The shape features are invariant to translation, rotation (2D), scale, and illumination.

Lip shape information provides only part of the visual speech information. Other information is contained in the visibility of teeth and tongue, protrusion, and finer details. The intensity parameters $\mathbf{b}_i$ of the lip model are therefore used

"one"

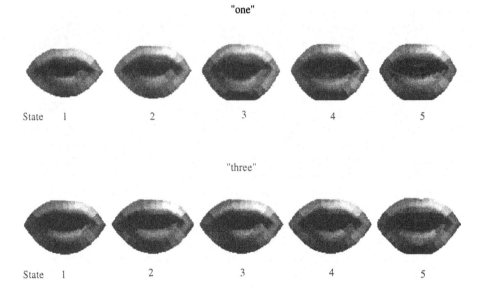

State   1   2   3   4   5

"three"

State   1   2   3   4   5

Fig. 3. Learned sequence of quasi-stationary states for the words "one" and "two" learned by the HMM. The images represent the mean shape and intensities learned from training data of 11 subjects. The images represent the lips, the mouth opening, and the skin region around the lips.

as features to provide information complementary to the shape features. The intensity of a 2D image reflects its actual 3D shape and provides information not covered by the shape model. In general, the intensity image depends on the shape of the object, its reflectance properties, the light source, and the viewing angle. For a Lambertian surface the image radiance or brightness $I_r(x, y)$ at a particular point in the image is proportional to the irradiance or illumination $I_i(x, y)$ at that point. The radiance depends on the irradiance of the illumination source $I_i(x, y)$ and the angle θ between the surface normal and the direction toward the illumination source:

$$I_r(x, y) = \frac{1}{\pi} I_i(x, y) \cos \theta \qquad \text{for } \theta \geq 0. \tag{7}$$

This equation directly relates the 3D shape to intensity and is fundamental to the methods for recovering shape from shading [20]. The recovery of 3D shape from shading is possible under certain constraints, i.e. it is normally assumed that the angle of the illumination source is known and that the surface is smooth. For our application of the face image, the shape from shading problem becomes very difficult. The illumination source is generally not known, the surface is disrupted at the oral opening, the oral opening itself is not smooth, and the reflectance properties of facial parts are not homogeneous and generally not known. Here, the motivation behind the use of intensity information is therefore not to reconstruct the 3D shape but to use it to implicitly represent 3D information and to represent information about the position and configuration of facial parts based on their individual brightness.

Much visual speech information is contained in the dynamics of lip movements rather than the actual shape or intensity. Furthermore, dynamic information is likely to be more robust to linguistic variability, i.e. intensity values of the lips and skin will remain fairly constant during speech, while intensity values of the mouth opening will vary during speech. On the other hand, intensity values of the lips and skin will vary between speakers, but temporal intensity changes might be similar for different speakers and robust to illumination. Similar comparisons can be made with shape parameters. Dynamic parameters of the shape and intensity vectors were therefore used as additional features.

The feature extraction method described here has been compared with several image based approaches (low pass filtering, PCA, optical flow) by Gray et al. [16] and was found to outperform all of these methods. It was also found that the performance of image-based approaches can be considerably improved by the use of the lip tracking results to normalise the images prior to processing.

Figure 3 displays learned hidden Markov models (HMMs) for the words "one" and "two" using extracted visual shape and intensity features from example utterances of 11 subjects. The images represent the mean images synthesised by the shape features and intensity features of HMMs with one Gaussian distribution per state.

3   Audio-Visual Sensor Integration

How humans integrate visual and acoustic information is not well understood. Several models for human integration have been proposed in the literature. They can be divided into early integration (EI) and late integration (LI) models [31]. In the EI model, integration is performed in the feature space to form a composite feature vector of acoustic and visual features. Classification is based on this composite feature vector. The model makes the assumption of conditional dependence between the modes and is therefore more general than the LI model. It can furthermore account for temporal dependencies between the modes, such as the voice-onset-time[1] (VOT) , which are important for the discrimination of certain phonemes. In the LI model, each modality is first pre-classified independently of each other. The final classification is based on the fusion of the outputs of both modalities by estimating their joint occurrence. In comparison with the EI scheme, this method assumes that both data streams are conditionally independent. Furthermore, temporal information between the channels is lost in this approach. AVSR systems based on EI models have for example been described in [6, 32] and systems based on LI models in [27, 30]. Although it is still not well known how humans integrate different modalities, it is generally agreed that integration occurs before speech is categorised phonetically [5, 31]. Furthermore, several studies have shown that consonants which differ by the

---

[1] The time delay between the burst sound and the movement of the vocal folds

VOT such as "bi" and "pi", are distinguished based on the evidence of both modalities [12, 17]. It was concluded that integration, therefore, must take place before phonetic categorisation. In acoustic speech perception, on the other hand, there is much evidence that humans perform partial recognition across different acoustic frequency bands [14, 1] which assumes conditional independence across bands. The auditory system seems to perform partial recognition which is independent across channels, whereas audio-visual perception seems to be based on some kind of early integration, which assumes conditional dependence between both modalities. These two hypotheses are controversial since the audio-visual theory of early integration assumes that no partial categorisation is made prior to the integration of both modalities.

The approach described here follows Fletcher's theory of conditional independence [14, 1], but it also allows the modelling of different levels of synchrony/asynchrony between the streams and can therefore account for speech features like the VOT, which otherwise can only be modelled by an EI integration model. Tomlinson et al. [32] have already addressed the issue of asynchrony between the visual and acoustic streams by the use of HMM decomposition. Under the independence assumption, composite models were defined from independently trained audio and visual models. Although our work is strongly related with [32], it allows to consider different recombination formalisms and enables the decoding of continuous speech. Moreover, the scope of asynchrony between the two streams was here extended from the phone level to the word level.

The bimodal speech signal can be considered as an observation vector consisting of acoustic and visual features. According to Bayesian decision theory, a maximum posterior probability classifier (MAP) can be denoted by

$$\Lambda^* = \arg\max_{\Lambda} P(\Lambda|\mathbf{O}^a, \mathbf{O}^v) = \frac{P(\mathbf{O}^a, \mathbf{O}^v|\Lambda)P(\Lambda)}{P(\mathbf{O}^a, \mathbf{O}^v)} \tag{8}$$

where Λ represents a particular word string, $\mathbf{O}^a$ represents the sequence of acoustic feature vectors $\mathbf{O}^a = \mathbf{o}^a(1), \mathbf{o}^a(2), \ldots, \mathbf{o}^a(T)$ and $\mathbf{O}^v$ the sequence of visual feature vectors $\mathbf{O}^v = \mathbf{o}^v(1), \mathbf{o}^v(2), \ldots, \mathbf{o}^v(T)$. If the two modalities are independent, the likelihood $P(\mathbf{O}^a, \mathbf{O}^v|\Lambda_i)$ becomes

$$P(\mathbf{O}^a, \mathbf{O}^v|\Lambda) = P(\mathbf{O}^a|\Lambda)P(\mathbf{O}^v|\Lambda). \tag{9}$$

Previous AVSR systems based on conditional independence have essentially addressed the problem of isolated word recognition. Most of these contributions were mainly focused on finding an appropriate automatic weighting scheme so as to guarantee good performance in a wide range of acoustic signal-to-noise ratios. Compared to isolated word recognition, the problem of continuous speech recognition is more tricky as we do not want to wait until the end of the spoken utterance before recombining the streams. This introduces a time delay and it also requires to generate N-best hypothesis lists for the two streams. Indeed, one can only recombine the scores from identical hypothesis. As the best hypothesis for the acoustic stream is not necessarily the same as the best hypothesis for the visual stream, techniques such as N-best lists are required. Identical hypothesis must then be matched to recombine the scores from the two streams. An alternative approach would be to generate an N-best list for one of the two streams, to compute the score of these best hypothesis for the other stream, and finally to recombine the scores.

The Multi-Stream approach, proposed in this work, does not require to use such an N-best scheme. As we will show, it is an interesting candidate for multimodal continuous speech recognition as it allows for: (1) synchronous multimodal continuous speech recognition, (2) asynchrony of the visual and acoustic streams with the possibility to define phonological resynchronisation points, (3) specific audio and video word or sub-word HMM topologies.

3.1 Multi-Stream Statistical Model

The Multi-Stream approach [4, 3] used in this work is a principled way for merging different sources of information using cooperative HMMs[2]. If the streams are supposed to be entirely synchronous, they may be accommodated simply. However, it is often the case that the streams are not synchronous, that they do not even have the same frame rate, and it might be necessary to define models that do not have the same topology. The Multi-Stream approach allows to deal with this. In this framework, the input streams are processed independently of each other up to certain anchor points where they have to synchronise and recombine their partial segment-based likelihoods. While the phonological level of recombination has to be defined a priori, the optimal temporal anchor points are obtained automatically during recognition.

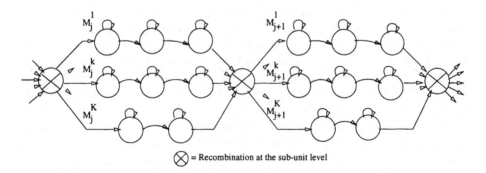

$\bigotimes$ = Recombination at the sub-unit level

Fig. 4. General form of a K-stream model with anchor-points between speech units, forcing synchrony between the streams.

An observation sequence $\mathbf{O}$, representing the utterance to be recognised, is assumed to be composed of K input streams X_k (possibly with different frame rates). A hypothesised model M associated with $\mathbf{O}$ is built by concatenating

---

[2] A different framework for more general networks has also been proposed in [21].

J sub-unit models M_j $(j = 1, \ldots, J)$ associated with the phonological level at which we want to perform the recombination of the input streams (e.g., syllables). To allow the processing of each of the input streams independently of each other up to the pre-defined sub-unit boundaries each sub-unit model M_j is composed of parallel models M_j^k (possibly with different topologies). These models are forced to recombine their respective segmental scores at some temporal anchor points. The resulting model is illustrated in Fig. 4. In this model we note that:

- The parallel HMMs, associated with each of the input streams, do not necessarily have the same topology.
- The recombination state ($\otimes$ in Figure 4) is not a regular HMM state since it will be responsible for recombining probabilities (or likelihoods) accumulated over the same temporal segment for all the streams.

The recombination has to be done for all possible segmentation points. The problem appears to be similar to the continuous speech recognition problem where all of the concurrent word segmentations, as well as all of the phone segmentations, must be hypothesised. However, as recombination concerns sub-unit paths that must begin at the same time, and as the best state path is not the same for all of the sub-stream models, (even if the topologies are the same), it is necessary to keep track of the dynamic programming paths for all of the sub-unit starting points. Hence, an approach such as the asynchronous two-level dynamic programming, or a synchronous formulation of it, is required.

Alternatively, composite models can be used in the same spirit as HMM decomposition [33]. The HMM decomposition algorithm is a time-synchronous Viterbi search which allows the decomposition of a single stream (speech signal) into two independent components (typically speech and noise), each component being modelled by its own set of HMMs. Composite states are defined for each of the combined model states of the different components. This allows to use a classical Viterbi decoding as far as observation probabilities for the combined states can be computed. This idea was exploited in this work to replace the multi-dimensional search (required for decoding using the model in Figure 4) by a one-dimensional search. Composite sub-unit models are built up from corresponding sub-unit models from each stream. This allows to implement independent search within sub-units as well as inter-units synchrony constraints.

As discussed in [3], the training and recognition problems (including automatic segmentation and recombination) can be coined into different statistical formalisms based on likelihoods or posterior probabilities and using linear or nonlinear recombination schemes. During recognition, we will have to find the best sentence model according to (8).

In this work, recombination of the independent likelihoods is done linearly, by multiplying segment likelihoods from the two streams, thus assuming conditional independence of the visual and acoustic streams. This was done according to:

$$P(\mathbf{O}^a, \mathbf{O}^v | \Lambda) = P(\mathbf{O}^a | \Lambda^a)^w P(\mathbf{O}^v | \Lambda^v)^{(1-w)}, \tag{10}$$

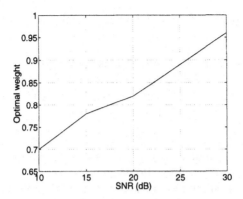

Fig. 5. Mapping between the optimal recombination weight w and the acoustic SNR.

The weighting factor w represents the reliability of the modalities which generally depends on the presence of acoustic or visual noise. Here we estimate the optimal weighting factor on the development set which is subject to the same noise as the test set. Another possibility is to estimate the sound-noise ratio (SNR) from the test data and adjust the weighting factor accordingly. Figure 5 displays the mapping between the SNR and the weighting factor found in our experiments. It can be seen that the optimal weight is related almost linearly to the SNR ratio and can easily be estimated from it.

4 Speech Recognition Experiments

The M2VTS audio-visual database [28] was used for all experiments. This database is publicly available and hence allows the comparison of algorithms by other researchers. It contains 185 recordings of 37 subjects (12 females and 25 males). Each recording contains the acoustic and the video signal of the continuously pronounced French digits from zero to nine. Five recordings have been taken of each speaker, at one week intervals to account for minor face changes like beards. For each person, the shot with the largest imperfection was labelled as shot 5. This shot differs from the others in face variation (head tilted, unshaved beards), voice variation (poor voice SNR) or shot imperfections (poor focus, different zoom factor). Additional imperfections apart from those of shot 5 are due to some people who were smiling while speaking. The video sequences consist of 286*360 pixel colour images with a 25 Hz frame rate and the audio track was recorded at a 48 kHz sampling frequency and 16 bit PCM coding. The database contains a total of over 27,000 colour images which were converted to grey-level images for the experiments reported here.

Although the M2VTS database is one of the largest databases of its type, it is still relatively small compared to reference audio databases used in the field of speech recognition. To increase the significance level of our experiments, we used a jack-knife approach. Five different cuts of the database were used. Each cut consisted of:

- 3 pronunciations from the 37 speakers as training set.
- 1 pronunciation from the 37 speakers as development set. It was used to optimise the weighting coefficients between audio and video streams.
- 1 pronunciation from the 37 speakers as test set.

This procedure allowed to use the whole database as test set (185 utterances) by developing five independent speech recognition systems for each of the compared approaches. These systems could be qualified as multi-speaker (but speaker dependent) continuous digit recognition systems. We note here that the digit sequence to be recognised is always the same (digits from '0' to '9'). This somewhat simplify the task of the speech recognition system which always "see" the pronounced words in the same context.

4.1 Acoustic Speech Recognition

The audio stream was first down sampled to 8 kHz. We used perceptual linear prediction (PLP) parameters [19] computed every 10 ms on 30 ms sample frames. The complete feature vectors consisted of 25 parameters: 12 PLP coefficients, 12 ΔPLP coefficients and the Δenergy.

We used left-right digit HMMs with between 3 and 9 independent states, depending on the digit mean duration. This yielded a total of 52 states. The digit sequences were first segmented into digits using standard Viterbi alignment with a HMM based recogniser trained on the SWISS-FRENCH POLYPHONE database [7] of 5000 speakers. Each M2VTS digit was then linearly segmented according to the number of states of the corresponding HMM model. This segmentation was used to train the HMM states which were represented by a mixture of two multidimensional Gaussian distributions with diagonal covariance matrices, yielding to 5200 parameters.

System training and tests were then performed according to the database partitioning described earlier using the Viterbi algorithm. Results are summarised in Figure 8 for clean speech as well as for speech corrupted by additive white noise with different signal-to-noise ratios. As can be observed, recognition performance is severely affected by additive noise, even at such moderate noise levels.

4.2 Visual Speech Recognition

The most dominant 12 shape features and 12 intensity features, described earlier, were used for the recogniser. These features were complemented by 24 temporal difference parameters (delta parameters). We used the same HMM topologies and the same initial segmentation as for the previously described acoustic-based recognition system. In this case, the HMM-states were represented by a single multidimensional Gaussian distribution with diagonal covariance matrix.

The mean error rate for the five database cuts defined earlier was 44.0%. Since the visual signal only provides partial information, the error rate for the video-based system was considerably lower than for the audio-based system. This is mainly due to the high visual similarity of certain digits like "quatre", "cinq", "six", and "sept", which accounted for about half of the errors. Most of the other errors were deletion errors (i.g. fewer words than the actual number of words were recognised) which are also likely to be due to the high similarity of visually confusable digit models. A more detailed analysis can be found in [24].

4.3 Audio-Visual Speech Recognition

Audio-Visual speech recognition was experimentally investigated and 2 kinds of model topologies were compared. These were based on the HMM word topologies used in the two previous sections. The differences between the models lay in the possible asynchrony of the visual stream with respect to the acoustic stream.

The first model (MODEL 1) did not allow for any asynchrony between the two streams. It corresponds to a Multi-Stream model with recombination at the state level and allows to use fusion criteria that can weight differently the two streams according to their respective reliability.

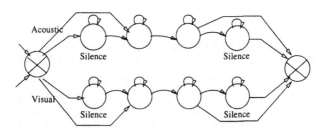

Fig. 6. Multi-Stream model for Audio-Visual speech recognition with optional silence states.

The second model (MODEL 2) was a Multi-Stream model with recombination of the streams at the word level. This model thus allows the dynamic programming paths to be independent from the beginning up to the end of the words. This relaxes the assumption of piecewise stationarity by allowing the stationarity of the two streams to occur on different time regions, while still forcing the modalities to resynchronise at word boundaries. This also accounts for the possible asynchrony of the streams inherent to the production mechanism. Indeed, lip movements and changes in the vocal tract shape are only synchronous up to a certain point.

MODEL 2 also allows the transition from silence to speech and from speech to silence to occur at different time instants for the two streams[3]. Indeed, lip

---
[3] 'Visual silence' could be defined as a portion of the visual signal that doesn't carry any relevant linguistic information.

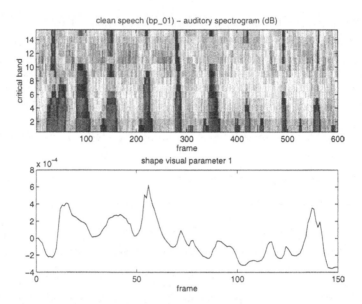

Fig. 7. Acoustic spectrogram (evolution of the critical band energies) and evolution of the first visual shape parameter for a portion ('0' to '8') of an M2VTS utterance.

movement can occur before and after sound production and conversely. Figure 7 shows in parallel a speech spectrogram as well as the evolution of the first visual shape parameter, mainly representing the changes in the position of the lower lip contour [23]. It can clearly be seen that the two signals are partially in synchrony and partially asynchronous. Ideally, we would like to have a model which forces the streams to be synchronous where synchrony occurs and asynchronous where the signals are typically in asynchrony. MODEL 2 is presented in Figure 6.

Table 1. Word error rate of acoustic-, visual- and acoustic-visual-based (MODEL 2) speech recognition systems on clean speech.

System	Video	Audio	Audio-Visual
Error rate	43.9%	3.4%	2.6%

We used the same parameterisation schemes as in the two previous sections. However, as the visual frame rate (25 Hz) is a quarter of the acoustic frame rate, visual vectors were added at the frame level (by copying frames), so that both signals were synchronously available.

Results are summarised in Figure 8 for different levels of noise degradation. In the case of clean speech, using visual information, in addition to the acoustic signal, does not yield significant performance improvements (see Table 1). The

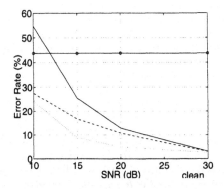

Fig. 8. This graph presents the results obtained after embedded training for the visual models, the acoustic models, and the two audio-visual models. All models were trained on clean speech only. The solid line represents the acoustic system, the dashed line MODEL1 and the dotted line MODEL2. The horizontal line represents the performance of the visual-only system.

confidence level of the hypothesis test was 0.95. In the case of speech corrupted with additive stationary Gaussian white noise, significant performance improvement can be obtained by using the visual stream as an additional information source. The results also clearly show that we can get a significant performance improvement with MODEL2 compared to MODEL1 by allowing the acoustic and visual decoding paths to be asynchronous and by the inclusion of "silence models".

5 Conclusions

We have described an approach based on appearance based models for robust lip tracking and feature extraction. This method allows robust lip tracking in grey-level images for a broad range of subjects and without the need of lipstick or other visual aids. Visual speech information is compactly represented in the form of shape and intensity parameters. Visual speech recognition experiments have demonstrated that this technique leads to robust multi-speaker continuous speech recognition.

We have presented a framework for the fusion of acoustic and visual information for speech recognition based on the Multi-Stream approach. Several significant advances have been achieved by this approach. Firstly, the method enables synchronous audio-visual decoding of continuous speech and we have presented one of the first continuous audio-visual speech recognition experiments. Secondly, it allows for asynchronous modelling of the two streams, which is inherent in the acoustic and visual speech signal and which has been shown to lead to more accurate modelling and to improved performance. Thirdly, the approach allows to design specific audio-visual word or sub-word topologies, including "silence models", which leads to more accurate audio-visual models.

Acknowledgements

We would like to thank Hervé Bourlard for his support and for many useful discussions.

References

1. J. B. Allen. How do humans process and recognize speech? *IEEE Transactions on Speech and Audio Processing*, 2(4):567–577, 1994.
2. S. Basu, N. Oliver, and A. Pentland. 3D Modeling and Tracking of Human Lip Motion. In *IEEE International Conference on Computer Vision*, 1998.
3. H. Bourlard, S. Dupont, and C. Riss. Multi-stream speech recognition. Technical Report IDIAP-RR 96-07, IDIAP, 1996.
4. H. Bourlard, and S. Dupont. Sub-band-based Speech Recognition. In *IEEE Int. Conf. on Acoust., Speech, and Signal Processing*, pages 1251–1254, 1997.
5. L. Braida. Crossmodal integration in the identification of consonants. *Quarterly Journal of Experimental Psychology*, 43A(3):647–677, 1991.
6. C. Bregler and S. M. Omohundro. Nonlinear manifold learning for visual speech recognition. In *IEEE International Conference on Computer Vision*, pages 494–499. IEEE, Piscataway, NJ, USA, 1995.
7. G. Chollet, J. L. Cochard, A. Constantinescu, and P. Langlais. Swiss French Polyphone and Polyvar : Telephone speech databases to study intra and inter speaker variability. Technical report, IDIAP, Martigny, 1995.
8. T. Coianiz, L. Torresani, and B. Capril. 2D deformable models for visual speech analysis. In David G. Stork and Marcus E. Hennecke, editors, *Speechreading by Humans and Machines*, volume 150 of *NATO ASI Series, Series F: Computer and Systems Sciences*, pages 391–398. Springer Verlag, Berlin, 1996.
9. R. Cole, L. Hirschmann, L Atlas, and et al. The challenge of spoken language processing: research directions for the nineties. *IEEE Trans. on Speech and Audio Processing*, 3(1):1–20, 1995.
10. T. F. Cootes, A. Hill, C. J. Taylor, and J. Haslam. Use of active shape models for locating structures in medical images. *Image and Vision Computing*, 12:355–365, Jul-Aug 1994.
11. T. F. Cootes, C. J. Taylor, D. H. Cooper, and J. Graham. Active shape models - their training and application. *Computer Vision and Image Understanding*, 61:38–59, Jan 1995.
12. N. P. Erber and C. L. De Filippo. Voice-mouth synthesis of tactual/visual perception of /pa, ba, ma/. *Journal of the Acoustical Society of America*, 64:1015–1019, 1978.
13. I. A. Essa and A. P. Pentland. Facial expression recognition using a dynamic model and motion energy. In *Proc. 5th Int. Conf. on Computer Vision*, pages 360–367. IEEE Computer Society Press, July 1995.
14. H. Fletcher. *Speech and Hearing in Communication*. Krieger, New York, 1953.
15. Y. Gong. Speech recognition in noisy environments: A survey. *Speech Communication*, 16:261–291, 1995.
16. M. S. Gray, J. R. Movellan, and T. J. Sejnowski. Dynamic features for visual speechreading: A systematic comparison. In M. C. Mozer, M. I. Jordan, and T. Petsche, editors, *Advances in Neural Information Processing Systems*, volume 9. MIT Press, Cambridge, MA, 1997.

17. K. P. Green and J. L. Miller. On the role of visual rate information in phonetic perception. *Perception & Psychophysics*, 38(3):269–276, 1985.
18. W. J. Hardcastle. *Physiology of Speech Production*. Academic Press, New York, NY, 1976.
19. H. Hermansky. Perceptual linear predictive (PLP) analysis of speech. *Journal of the Acoustical Society of America*, 87:1738–1752, 1990.
20. B. K. P. Horn. *Robot Vision*. McGraw-Hill, New York, 1986.
21. M. I. Jordan and Z. Ghahramani and L. K. Saul". Hidden Markov Decision Trees. In M. C. Mozer, M. I. Jordan, and T. Petsche, editors, *Advances in Neural Information Processing Systems*, volume 9. MIT Press, Cambridge, MA, 1997.
22. A. Lanitis, C. J. Taylor, and T. F. Cootes. Automatic interpretation and coding of face images using flexible models. *IEEE Trans. Pattern Analysis and Machine Intelligence*, 19(7):743–756, 1997.
23. J. Luettin and N. A. Thacker. Speechreading using probabilistic models. *Computer Vision and Image Understanding*, 65(2):163–178, February 1997.
24. J. Luettin. *Visual Speech and Speaker Recognition*. PhD thesis, University of Sheffield, 1997.
25. K. Mase and A. Pentland. Automatic lipreading by optical flow analysis. *Systems and Computers in Japan*, 22(6), 1991.
26. B. Moghaddam and A. Pentland. Probabilistic visual learning for object detection. In *IEEE International Conference on Computer Vision*, pages 786–793. IEEE, Piscataway, NJ, USA, 1995.
27. E. D. Petajan. Automatic lipreading to enhance speech recognition. In *Proc. IEEE Conf. on Computer Vision and Pattern Recognition*, pages 40–47, 1985.
28. S. Pigeon and L. Vandendorpe. The M2VTS multimodal face database. In *Proceedings of the First International Conference on Audio- and Video-Based Biometric Person Authentication*, Lecture Notes in Computer Science. Springer Verlag, 1997.
29. M. U. Ramos Sanchez, J. Matas, and J. Kittler. Statistical chromaticity models for lip tracking with B-splines. In *Proceedings of the First International Conference on Audio- and Video-based Biometric Person Authentication*, Lecture Notes in Computer Science, pages 69–76. Springer Verlag, 1997.
30. P. L. Silsbee and A. C. Bovik. Computer lipreading for improved accuracy in automatic speech recognition. *IEEE Transactions on Speech and Audio Processing*, 4(5):337–351, 1996.
31. A. Q. Summerfield. Lipreading and audio-visual speech perception. *Philosophical Transactions of the Royal Society of London, Series B*, 335:71–78, 1992.
32. M. J. Tomlinson, M. J. Russell, and N. M. Brooke. Integrating audio and visual information to provide highly robust speech recognition. In *Proc. IEEE Int. Conf. on Acoust., Speech, and Signal Processing*, volume 2, pages 821–824, 1996.
33. A. Varga and R. Moore. Hidden markov model decomposition of speech and noise. In *Proc. IEEE Int. Conf. on Acoust., Speech, and Signal Processing*, pages 845–848, 1990.
34. B. P. Yuhas, M. H. Goldstein, T. J. Sejnowski, and R. E. Jenkins. Neural network models of sensory integration for improved vowel recognition. *Proc. IEEE*, 78(10):1658–1668, October 1990.

Finding Surface Correspondence for Object Recognition and Registration Using Pairwise Geometric Histograms

A. P. Ashbrook, R. B. Fisher, C. Robertson and N. Werghi

Department of Artificial Intelligence
The University of Edinburgh
5, Forrest Hill, Edinburgh, EH1 2QL
Telephone: +44 131 650 4504
Fax: +44 131 650 6899
anthonya@dai.ed.ac.uk

Abstract. Pairwise geometric histograms have been demonstrated as an effective descriptor of arbitrary 2-dimensional shape which enable robust and efficient object recognition in complex scenes. In this paper we describe how the approach can be extended to allow the representation and classification of arbitrary $2\frac{1}{2}$- and 3-dimensional surface shape. This novel representation can be used in important vision tasks such as the recognition of objects with complex free-form surfaces and the registration of surfaces for building 3-dimensional models from multiple views. We apply this new representation to both of these tasks and present some promising results.

1 Introduction

Finding a correspondence between two or more surfaces is a frequently encountered problem in many computer vision tasks. When surface based descriptions are used for object recognition, the hypothesis that a particular object is in a scene is confirmed by finding a good correspondence between scene and model surfaces [6]. When constructing geometric models of objects by merging multiple range images taken from different viewpoints, the surfaces described by each range image require registration into a common coordinate frame [3, 1]. This can be done by finding the correspondence between portions of the object's surface which is common to two or more views.

In this paper we present a novel representation for arbitrary $2\frac{1}{2}$- and 3-dimensional surface data which enables correspondences to be found reliably and efficiently. The representation is based on pairwise geometric histograms which have previously been demonstrated as a representation for 2-dimensional shape data for object recognition applications [4].

The approach that we are proposing determines whether two surfaces have a correspondence as follows:

1. Each of the surfaces is approximated by a triangular mesh. The details of this approximation and the algorithms we have employed for this are presented in Section 3.1.
2. Each triangular mesh facet is represented by a pairwise geometric histogram which records the relationship between this facet and the surrounding facets within some specified neighbourhood. This representation is discussed in Section 3.2.
3. Correspondences between individual facets are found by matching their respective geometric histograms. These *local* correspondences provide hypotheses for the correspondence between the two surfaces. The metric employed for matching geometric histograms is described in Section 4.
4. The *global* surface correspondence is found by finding consistent local hypotheses using a probabilistic Hough transform. This is discussed in Section 5.

2 Background

A number of approaches to the problem surface registration have been developed from the "iterated closest point" (ICP) algorithm proposed by Besl and McKay [2]. These algorithms have been popular for registering multiple views of an object for model construction and for refining pose in object recognition tasks. The central idea behind this algorithm is that by forming correspondences between points on one surface and their nearest neighbours on another and then minimising the distances between them, the registration of the two surfaces is improved. If this process is iterated the registration of the surfaces often converges. The approach is computationally expensive because of its use of raw surface point data and because of the iterative nature of the algorithm. A more serious problem is that the algorithm is not guaranteed to converge, sometimes getting caught in local minima, and typically requires good initial alignment of the surfaces to get a reasonable solution. One of the advantages of the ICP approach is that, because it uses all of the surface data available, when it does converge the registration can be very accurate. The algorithm is also suitable for arbitrary classes of surface.

Other researchers have used interest points on the surface instead of all of the surface data and formed correspondences by matching geometric descriptors of those points. Thirion [13] proposes the use of extremal points on 3-dimensional surfaces which can be characterised by a number of properties such as their curvature. Interest points with similar properties are treated as potential correspondents and the transformation that aligns the surfaces is determined from triplets of corresponding pairs. Recently, Johnson and Hebert [9] have proposed a novel interest point descriptor which allows point correspondences to be formed between surfaces. In their approach the interest points are defined by the vertices of a polygonal mesh fitted to the surface. At each vertex the geometric relationship with all of the other mesh vertices are recorded in a 2-dimensional *spin-image* which is invariant to rigid transformations of the surface. Interest point correspondences are found by identifying points with similar spin-images.

Local surface features such as edges and surface patches have also been used to determine the correspondence between two surfaces [5]. Initially all features on the first surface are considered as potential correspondents of features of the same class on the second surface. The number of potential correspondences is then quickly reduced using approaches based on geometric constraints such as the interpretation tree. Each pair of matched features provides a constraint on the transformation that aligns the surfaces and these are used to determine the best global alignment. The motivation for using features is to reduce the amount of data to be processed whilst maintaining valuable information needed to perform matching and constrain the alignment transformation. The disadvantage is that a particular choice of features can limit the scope of the algorithm to particular classes of surfaces.

3   A Novel Surface Shape Representation

3.1   Surface Reconstruction and Approximation

Initially a given surface S, acquired using a range sensor, is described by a set of points samples $P = \{p_1, \ldots, p_N\}$. The points may represent a single view of the surface or a number of different views, for example from different viewpoints around an object. The point set is then used to construct a triangular mesh approximation $\hat{S}$ to the original surface, where $\hat{S} = \{t_1, \ldots, t_M\}$ and t_i is a triangular facet of the mesh.

It is important to clarify at this stage that the only requirement of the mesh is that it is a good approximation of the surface shape. No assumptions are made about the actual distribution of facets over the surface as this is unlikely to be repeatable. To minimise the amount of memory and computation needed to solve the correspondence problem, the mesh should also contain the smallest number of facets needed to give a good approximation of the surface.

A number of algorithms have been proposed for reconstructing a triangular faceted mesh from a set of points. In the work presented here an initial, regular mesh was constructed from the sampled point data using a reconstruction algorithm by Hoppe *et al* [8]. The resulting regular mesh was then refined to minimise the number of facets whilst maintaining most of the surface shape using a surface simplification algorithm by Garland and Heckbert [7].

There are a number of advantages in using a triangular mesh to approximate the surface to be represented instead of more complex features such as quadric patches, the most obvious being efficiency. Constructing a mesh is also significantly more straightforward than segmenting a surface into more complex features. A second important issue is scope. Any surface can be approximated by a triangular mesh but selecting a fixed set of features can impose limitations on the types of surfaces that can be described. Another important issue is that of stability. If surface patches are assigned to different classes based on their shape then borderline cases can result in sudden changes in the representation because of slightly different viewing conditions or noise.

The disadvantage of using a triangular mesh is that it requires many facets to describe surfaces with high curvature to a high degree of accuracy. By statistically modelling the shape error introduced by the triangular shape approximation, it is still possible to obtain a good shape representation when only a relatively small number of facets are used.

3.2 Histogram Construction

A pairwise geometric histogram h_i is constructed for each triangular facet t_i in a given mesh which describes its pairwise relationship with each of the other surrounding facets within a predefined distance. This distance controls degree to which the representation is a local description of shape. The histogram is defined such that it encodes the surrounding shape geometry in a manner which is invariant to rigid transformations of the surface data and which is stable in the presence of surface clutter and missing surface data.

Figure 1(a) shows the measurements used to characterise the relationship between facet t_i and one of its neighbouring facets t_j. These measurements are the relative angle, α, between the facet normals and the range of perpendicular distances, d, from the plane in which facet t_i lies to all points on facet t_j. These measurements are accumulated in a 2-dimensional frequency histogram, weighted by the product of the areas of the two facets as shown in Figure 1(b). The weight of the entry is spread along the perpendicular distance axis in proportion to the area of the facet t_j at each distance. To compensate for the difference between the measurements taken from the mesh and the true measurements for the original surface, the entry is blurred into the histogram. For the work presented here a Gaussian blurring function has been used, but we intend to investigate more appropriate error models in the future. Certainly the scale of the blurring function relates to the coarseness of the mesh. The complete pairwise geometric histogram for facet t_i is constructed by accumulating these entries for each of the neighbouring facets.

For clarity, an example of a pairwise geometric histogram is presented in Figure 2(a). This has been constructed for the highlighted facet on the hemispherical mesh presented in Figure 2(b). Note that the representation only depends upon the surface shape and not on the placement of facets over the surface. This independence on the placement of the facets is important because recovering exactly the same mesh for the same surface under different viewing conditions is very unlikely, particularly if there is some surface occlusion.

4 Generating Correspondence Hypotheses

Given two surface meshes, $\hat{S}^A$ and $\hat{S}^B$, the geometric histogram representation allows correspondences between all facets, t_i^A and t_j^B, from each of the meshes to be determined. A match for facet t_i^A is determined by finding the best match between its respective pairwise geometric histogram and all of the histograms

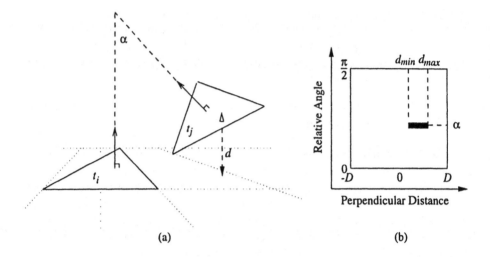

Fig. 1. (a) The geometric measurements used to characterise the relationship between two facets t_i and t_j. (b) The entry made into the pairwise geometric histogram to represent this relationship.

representing the facets in surface $\hat{S}^B$. These *local* correspondences are treated as hypotheses for the correspondence between the two surfaces S^A and S^B.

The similarity, D_{ij}, between two pairwise geometric histograms h_i and h_j is defined using the Bhattacharyya metric. This is given by the expression:

$$D_{ij} = \sum_{\alpha,d} \sqrt{h_i(\alpha,d)}\sqrt{h_j(\alpha,d)} \tag{1}$$

The Bhattacharyya metric is appropriate when the error on the data can be described using a Poisson distribution. This is a reasonable assumption for measured frequency distributions such as a geometric histogram [12]. A derivation of this metric is presented in Appendix A.

5 Hypothesis Verification

Each pair of matched mesh facets provides evidence that the surfaces to which they belong have the same shape, at least locally, and can therefore be registered. The transformation that aligns the paired facets also provides a constraint on the transformation that aligns the complete surfaces. The problem then is to determine whether there is enough evidence to support these hypotheses and, if so, to determine the transformation that aligns the surface data.

We have used an approach taken by other researchers in which N-tuples of matched features, in our case paired mesh facets, are used to estimate the

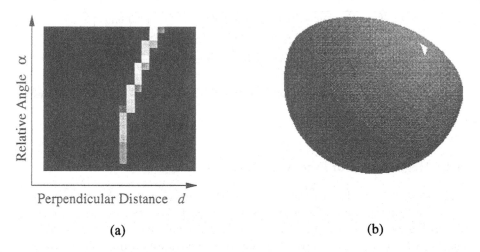

Fig. 2. (a) The geometric histogram that characterises the relationship between highlighted facet and the other facets in the mesh in (b).

alignment transformation. These estimates are then accumulated in a Hough transform resulting in a peak where there is consistency. As an improvement to this scheme we have adopted a probabilistic approach in which the error on the estimated transformation is integrated into the Hough accumulator [11]. This error is determined by statistically modelling the error between the facets and the true surface and propagating this error through the transformation estimator.

Initially 2-tuples of paired facets are used to estimate the rotation component of the alignment transformation and votes are placed in a 3-dimensional Hough transform. The number of 2-tuples can be very large so only a proportion of the largest paired facets are used. If a significant peak is found in this space then 3-tuples of paired facets are used to estimate the translation component of the alignment transformation. Again, only a proportion of the largest facets are used to allow fast operation. If a significant peak is found in the translation space then the hypothesis that the surfaces can be registered is accepted.

6 Experiments

Two applications of the proposed surface representation are presented here. The first application is the registration of two different views of an object with a complex surface. The second application is the identification and localisation of known objects in a scene. All of the data were acquired using a laser stripe range scanner with an accuracy of approximately 0.1mm. The pairwise geometric histogram parameters selected for both of these experiments are presented in Table 1.

680

Quantisation of Relative Angle Axis	20 bins
Quantisation of Perpendicular Distance Axis	20 bins
Maximum Perpendicular Distance	± 100mm
Maximum Relative Angle	$\frac{\pi}{2}$ radians

Table 1. The pairwise geometric histogram parameters used in the experiments presented here.

6.1 Registration of Free-form Surfaces

In this experiment the objective is to find the correspondence between two surfaces constructed from different views of an object. The surface meshes, presented in Figure 3, describe the surface of a farm animal model and consist of 1000 facets each. It should be noted that the model has quite complex, free-form surfaces which are difficult to describe using features such as quadric patches or edges.

Fig. 3. The triangular meshes for two different views of the surface of a farm animal model.

Figure 4(a) presents the two surfaces in their registered positions. Certainly, from a qualitative point of view, the registration seems to have been successful. This is emphasised by the inter-meshing of the two surfaces on the rear leg of the model shown in close-up in Figure 4(b). The fact that this inter-meshing is not visible over all of the surface suggests that there is some registration error, however.

Only the largest 5% of the facets were matched and used to determine the alignment transformation. The entire registration process took approximately 4 minutes 24 seconds on a 200MHz Sun Ultra. A breakdown of these times is presented in Table 2.

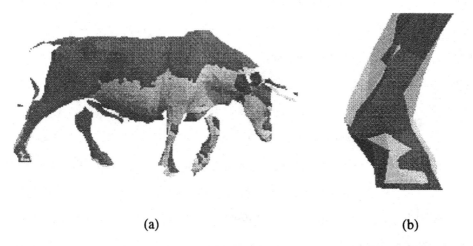

(a)   (b)

Fig. 4. (a) The two meshed surfaces in their registered positions. (b) A close-up of the rear leg of the model. The light and dark shades of grey represent the two different surfaces.

Triangular Mesh Construction	110 seconds
Geometric Histogram Construction	212 seconds
Geometric Histogram Matching	6 seconds
Resolving Hypotheses	126 seconds

Table 2. A breakdown of the time to complete the registration for each of the main algorithm stages.

6.2   Object Recognition and Pose Estimation

The objective of this experiment is to identify known objects in a scene and estimate the pose of those objects. The object models, presented in Figure 5, have been constructed from multiple views to produce a complete 3-dimensional description of all of the surfaces. Each model is represented by 1000 facets.

Figure 6 presents a scene containing two of the known models. The scene has been captured with a single range image and represented by 1000 facets.

The classification of each of the scene facets is presented in Figure 7. In each of the three images the scene facets which best match a facet from the respective model have been drawn. It can be seen that most of the facets have been classified as belonging to the correct models. Most of the incorrectly classified facets lie very close to surface discontinuities where the recovery of the surface normal is very poor. This is largely due to the mesh construction algorithm which has problems preserving discontinuities in the range data. There are also some problems with the classification of the underside of the cylinder model. This is likely to be because this surface is almost parallel to the viewing direction which makes recovery of the surface normal prone to error.

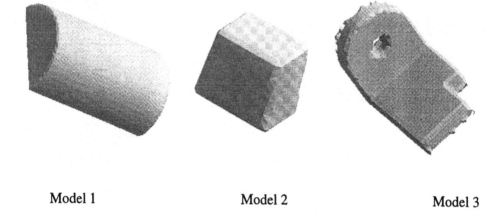

Model 1   Model 2   Model 3

Fig. 5. The three model objects used in the recognition experiment.

Figure 8 presents the results of the recognition of pose estimation process. The original scene data is shown in the darker shade and the recognised models are shown in their estimated positions in the lighter shade. The algorithm has both determined the objects present in the scene and formed a reasonable estimation of their positions.

All of the facets were matched and then the largest 5% from each class were used to determine the model poses. The entire object recognition process took approximately 14 minutes 3 seconds on a 200MHz Sun Ultra. A breakdown of these times is presented in Table 3.

Triangular Mesh Construction	54 seconds
Geometric Histogram Construction	96 seconds
Geometric Histogram Matching	329 seconds
Resolving Hypotheses	364 seconds

Table 3. A breakdown of the time to complete the recognition process for each of the main algorithm stages.

7 Conclusions

The problem of finding a correspondence between two or more surfaces has been investigated by a number of researchers and several solutions have been proposed. The most reliable approaches are based on finding point-feature or

Fig. 6. The scene data used in the recognition experiment.

surface-feature correspondences between the surfaces being registered and using these to estimate the transformation that aligns the complete surfaces.

In this paper we have proposed a novel representation for surface data which enables local surface correspondences to be determined. This representation is invariant to rigid transformations of the surface data and, because of its statistical nature, allows errors in the approximation of the surfaces by triangular meshes to be modelled.

Having established local correspondences we have shown that the transformation that aligns complete surfaces can be determined using a Hough voting scheme. The advantage of using Hough voting is that it is possible to model transformation errors present in the local correspondences by adopting a probabilistic Hough transform.

To demonstrate the effectiveness of the new representation and the algorithm that determines the alignment transformation, we have presented two experiments. In the first experiment two surfaces of a complex curved surfaced object taken from different viewpoints are successfully registered. In the second experiment, known objects are successfully identified and located in a scene.

Acknowledgements

The work presented in this paper was funded by a UK EPSRC grant GR/H86905. The author would also like to thank Dr. Peter Rockett for the derivation of the Bhattacharyya distance presented in Appendix A.

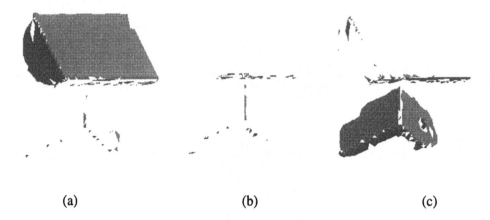

(a)   (b)   (c)

Fig. 7. (a),(b) & (c) present the scene facets which best match facets in Models 1, 2 & 3 respectively.

A   Derivation of the Similarity Metric

In this section the derivation of a statistical metric for comparing binned measurements is presented. Given a random variable X, a statistical measure of the distance D between the endpoints $X = x$ and $X = x + \delta x$ of a short line is obtained by normalising by the standard deviation σ.

$$D = \frac{\delta x}{\sigma} \tag{2}$$

In general then, the statistical distance between any two points $X = s$ and $X = m$ can be determined by the definite integral:

$$D = \int_s^m \frac{dx}{\sigma} \tag{3}$$

For N independent measurements the statistical distance is given by a sum of squared components:

$$D^2 = \sum_i \left(\int_{s_i}^{m_i} \frac{dx_i}{\sigma_i} \right)^2 \tag{4}$$

It is well known that binned data conforms to a Poisson distribution and that the variance of a Poisson variable is equal to its mean. A statistical distance metric for binned data is then obtained by substitution of $\sigma_i = \sqrt{x_i}$.

$$D^2 = \sum_i \left(\int_{s_i}^{m_i} \frac{dx_i}{\sqrt{x_i}} \right)^2 \tag{5}$$

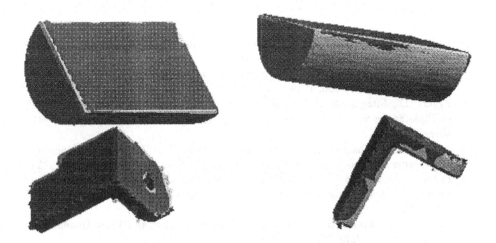

Fig. 8. The identification and localisation of the two objects in the scene. The scene data is presented in the darker shade and the models in the lighter shade. The second image presents the scene from a different view-point.

$$= 4 \sum_i (\sqrt{s_i} - \sqrt{m_i})^2 \tag{6}$$

Removing the constant factor in this expression gives the statistical metric proposed by Matusita [10] which is known as the Matusita distance.

$$D_{matusita} = \sum_i (\sqrt{s_i} - \sqrt{m_i})^2 \tag{7}$$

Expanding this expression gives:

$$D_{matusita} = \sum_i s_i + \sum_i m_i - \sum_i \sqrt{s_i}\sqrt{m_i} \tag{8}$$

If both m and s are normalised, or when using this metric to compare a single *scene* histogram with a set of normalised *model* histograms, this is simply:

$$D_{matusita} = const - \sum_i \sqrt{s_i}\sqrt{m_i} \tag{9}$$

Removing the constant results in the Bhattacharyya distance.

$$D_{bhattacharyya} = \sum_i \sqrt{s_i}\sqrt{m_i} \tag{10}$$

References

1. Bergevin, R., Laurendeau, D. and Poussart, D., "Registering Range Views of Multipart Objects", CVIU, 61(1), pp1-16, 1995.
2. Besl, P. J. and McKay, N. D., "A method for registration of 3-D shapes", IEEE PAMI, 14(2), pp 239-256, 1992.
3. Eggert, D., Fitzgibbon, A. W. and Fisher, R. B., "Simultaneous registration of multiple range views for use in reverse engineering", Proc. ICPR96, pp243-247, Vienna, 1996.
4. Evans, A. C., Thacker, N. A. and Mayhew, J. E. W., "The Use of Geometric Histograms for Model-Based Object Recognition", Proc. BMVC93, pp429, 1993.
5. Faugeras, O. D. and Hebert, M., "A 3-D Recognition and Positioning Algorithm using Geometric Matching between Primitive Surfaces", Proc. 8th IJCAI, pp-996-1002, 1983.
6. Fisher, R. B., "From Surfaces to Objects: Computer Vision and Three Dimensional Scene Analysis", John Wiley & Sons, 1989.
7. Garland, M. and Heckbert, P. S., "Surface Simplification using Quadric Error Metrics", SIGGRAPH97, pp209-216, 1997.
8. Hoppe, H., DeRose, T., Duchamp, T., McDonald, J. and Stuetzle, W., "Surface Reconstruction from Unorganised Points", Computer Graphics, 26(2), pp71-78, 1992.
9. Johnson, A. E. and Hebert, M., "Recognizing Objects by Matching Oriented Points", Proc. CVPR97, pp684-689, 1997.
10. Matusita, K., "Decision Rules Based on Distance for Problems of Fit, Two Samples and Estimation", Ann. Mathematical Statistics, Vol. 26, pp. 631-641, 1955.
11. Stephens, R. S., "A Probabilistic Approach to the Hough Transform", Proc. BMVC90, pp55-59, 1990.
12. Thacker, N. A., Aherne, F. J. and Rockett, P. I., "The Bhattacharyya Metric as an Absolute Similarity Measure for Frequency Coded Data", STIPR97, 1st International Workshop on Statistical Techniques in Pattern Recognition, Prague, Czech Republic, 1997.
13. Thirion, J., "New Feature Points based on Geometric Invariants for 3D Image Registration", IJCV, 18(2), pp121-137, 1996.

Integrating Iconic and Structured Matching

R. B. Fisher and A. MacKirdy

Department of Artificial Intelligence, Edinburgh University
5 Forrest Hill, Edinburgh EH1 2QL, Scotland, UK
rbf@dai.ed.ac.uk
http://www.dai.ed.ac.uk/daidb/staff/Robert_Fisher.html

Abstract. Several investigations [11, 16, 19–21] have recently been undertaken into object recognition based on matching image intensity neighborhoods rather than geometric matching of features extracted from the images. These projects have used small subwindows or complete image regions and matching has been based on the similarity of extracted descriptors to previously stored descriptors. One characteristic common to these approaches is the representation of objects as a whole, rather than as a structured ensemble. This paper describes an extension to these approaches wherein a set of related features recognized at an earlier iteration also contribute to the complete object recognition. The paper describes an iconic, or image-based, matching approach that incorporates an element of geometric matching and shows that use of the subfeatures improves matching efficiency, position accuracy and completeness.

1 Introduction

Symbolic matching algorithms have been popular and well-explored (*e.g.* [9]). They depend for their success on a combinatorial search process to establish feature correspondence and thus have an "all-or-nothing" behavior. To improve reliability and efficiency the use of a subcomponent hierarchy in matching algorithms has also been common in the symbolic domain, for both machine vision (*e.g.* [17, 4, 6, 7]) and biological vision (*e.g.* [13, 3]). In contrast, image template matching has been used in restricted domains for many years (*e.g.* [1], pg 65). The template matching approach has problems with rotation and scale invariance, and has requires much image computation. With the use of the log-polar representation [18, 22], the invariance problems can be overcome and the recent great increase in computational power of standard processors has reduced the computation time. As a consequence of these two factors, several investigations [11, 16, 19–21] have recently been undertaken into object recognition based on matching images (or some non-symbolic representation of them) directly rather than geometric matching of symbolic features extracted from the images.

We have been investigating [10, 11] the capabilities of iconic, or image-based, approaches to object recognition (described in some detail in Section 2) as have other research groups. Rao and Ballard [16] used a number of filters, derivatives of gaussians at several different scales, to build an n-dimensional feature vector. The feature vectors are input into a simple neural network which associates each vector with one of a number of objects. Their system is able to distinguish between a large number of objects under varying pose, by learning a set of poses. However, their system is unable to distinguish between objects with similar global frequency responses and the global filtering approach does not represent the spatial distribution of features necessary for distinguishing subtle appearance differences. Schiele and Crowley [19] have matched 2D histograms of pairs of image properties (mainly gradient-based) and achieved good matching results using a χ^2 metric, but their approach also ignores the global organization of the image features. Seibert and Waxman [20] used an ART network to match feature vectors extracted from log-polar processed images. Their features were interest points extracted from binary images of single isolated objects. 2D image-based recognition was linked into a 3D aspect and multiple competing identity object recognition network. Siebert and Eising [21] used the log-polar architecture with a difference-of gaussians receptive field and their matching scheme used templates applied directly to the log-polar image. An alternative approach [2] uses log-log sampling in the fourier domain but it is not considered here as it confounds the structural information exploited in our approach.

There has been much work on property-based image indexing from databases (*e.g.* [14]) but most of it has not used image geometry other than [8], which uses graph-like models of human and animal limb relationships. Mundy *et al* [15] have compared an iconic and a projective invariant object recognition system on a small database of simple parts and found that the iconic approach had a higher false-positive rate and lower false-negative rates. In part this was due to the iconic system not having a verification stage. The computation rate was also affected as the model base grew. On the other hand, their invariant approach was limited by the ability to model only simple shapes, but did cope better with illumination problems. One of the questions addressed in our research is how the associated model evidence affects the false-positive rate.

Another approach has been to represent families of similar objects by a weighted set of eigenvectors, with the recognition mechanism comparing the projection weights of a sample image to the eigenvectors in a database (*e.g.* [24]). In this case, object geometry is implicit in the representation, so the technique investigated here is inappropriate. Tistarelli [23] investigated the combination of the active space-variant sensor (as used here) with the eigenvector approach, and concluded that the accuracy of recognition can be much improved while simultaneously reducing the database size.

This paper describes an iconic matching approach that incorporates a simplified geometric model and shows that use of the subfeature matching promotes matching efficiency, position accuracy and correctness. More details can be found in [12].

The motivation for this research comes from the intuition that *if* I am looking at a feature and have some moderate evidence that it is a given model (*e.g.* "it might be an eye") *and* I have seen other nearby related features (*e.g.* another eye and a nose in the correct relative orientation and placement) *then* this feature is more likely to be the hypothesized object. The accuracy will increased by the response from the correct orientation and placement of the other features with respect to the current feature. The better the predicted and actual associated labels match, the more accurate the current match is likely to be.

2 Overview of the iconic recognition process

We have used a foveated (R, θ) log-polar coordinate system [22] for retino-centric coordinates, with 20 bands, each containing 48 sectors. The receptive fields (*i.e.* the area of the (i, j) image from which they take input) of each pixel in the (R, θ) representation increase (logarithmically by 1.2) as R grows larger in order to cover the entire foveated area. The receptive fields in the innermost bands take their input from only one or a few pixels, averaging the value. This gives high resolution around the foveation point. Receptive fields in the outermost bands average large numbers of pixels, giving lower resolution. Receptive fields overlap by about 33% to avoid gaps, leading to some blurring. The polar representation is attractive because it maps rotation and scaling into translation, and this feature is used in the matching algorithm described below to deliver scale and rotation invariance.

The main representations are:

1. **The World** - a large static (r, g, b) image (here 512^2) within which the iconic matcher saccades and extracts smaller (here 128^2) foveated views.
2. **The Image Stack** - Foveating the world image maps part of the raw (r, g, b) image to (R, θ) space, to form the first part of the image stack.

   The feature extraction process extracts 42 log-polar images registered with the current foveated image [10]. The images consist of 3 scales (extracted from the $\frac{1}{2}$, 1 and 2 size images) of 14 feature types: the red/green/blue intensity component images, two on- and off-center-surround features, four radial and orthogonal on- and off- bars, four orientations of edges and an unoriented corner measure. Each receptive field in each of the feature planes gives a measure of the strength of the given property at the corresponding spatial image location. The feature images are extracted by applying a small neighborhood operator at each location in the foveated image.
3. **The Model Base** - a set of models that may be matched to the current image stack. The iconic portion of each model has the same format and contents as the image stack. Each feature plane has a weight associated with it, indicating how useful the feature is in identifying this object. The structured portion of each model may have a list of associated models (*e.g.* an eye may link to a likely nearby nose position). This list has of the form { (*model_type, relative_position, relative_orientation, relative_scale, importance_weight*) }. These links can also be used to form an iconic geometric model (described in Section 3). Models are created by a learning process using pictures that are representative of the class. A model is normally registered on a feature that will attract the attention system [11]. Models are learned at three scales (50%, 100% and 200%) because not all features will be visible at all scales.

4. **The Interest Map** - The interest map [11] is an image structure registered with the world. Its contents record a value representing the interestingness of a given point in the scene. Interestingness values increase as center-surround and corner image features are found and as models are identified (as these predict locations of likely associated models). Interestingness values decrease at parts of the image that have been explored. Details of the calculation of the interest map is given in [11].

The scene is explored in a saccade-like process by selecting the current highest interest point as the next location to foveate.

The matching process uses a modified multi-variate cross-correlation function:

$$V_f = f(\sum_{k=1}^{42} \rho_k w_k + w_0) \tag{1}$$

where ρ_k is the single channel match score (using the standard statistical cross-correlation between 2 feature images at each given rotation and scale offset) and w_k are weights which are learned by a perceptron learning algorithm. These weights reflect the relative importance of the feature correlation scores in determining object identity. The bias w_0 reflects the *a priori* probability of data belonging to this class (defaults to 0). $f(x)$ is the sigmoid function $1/(1 + e^{-x})$. The matching process compares the stack of 42 iconic feature images to entries in a model database. In order to achieve rotation and scale invariance, the log-polar images are shifted in a convolution-like process. One shift direction is equivalent to a scale change, the other is equivalent to a rotation (well known properties of the log-polar transform). The shift process, for example, allows alignment of a rotated model with a database entry, thus improving correspondence. To achieve translation invariance, the matcher outer loop has a saccade-like process that shifts foveation to the next highest point in the attention map. As models are created by foveation at high interest points, using these points to direct foveation increases the chances of aligning a model image with the corresponding image in a test scene. Thus, the highest model score (greater than a "recognition threshold") is the recognized model, the current saccade position is the object's position and the rotation and scale at which the best match occurs is the estimated model orientation and size.

While this is an unusual approach to object recognition, its advantages are: the primal-sketch-like features provide an element of illumination invariance, the correlation matching allows a graceful degradation of correspondence and thus an element of generalization and the log-polar representation allows rotation and scale invariance. Its disadvantages include: an unconventional, idiosyncratic and generally unexplored architecture, moderate computation time per foveation position (a second per saccade and model), and somewhat heuristic feature extraction processes.

The architecture does allow exploration of the questions addressed in this paper: **is it possible to integrate geometric models within an iconic** image matching paradigm? If so, does it provide any benefit in terms of speed, spatial accuracy or recognition completeness?

3 Integrating substructures into matching

To extend the architecture summarized in Section 2, five data structures or processes needed to be developed:

1. Structured model representation,
2. Subcomponent evidence recording,
3. Subcomponent evidence location,
4. Extended matching function, and
5. Interest map update.

These points are discussed in the following subsections.

3.1 Structured model representation

The models need to be extended to include other models associated with the current model. The associated models include subcomponents (such as an eye as being a subcomponent of a face) as well as more generally associated objects (such as a keyboard and a monitor).

Each augmented model becomes:

> model type
> 42 feature (R, θ) feature planes
> 42 feature evidence combination weights ω_k plus ω_0
> a set of N associated models:
> $$\mathcal{A} = \{\, a_i \,\} = \{\, (\text{ associated model type}_i,$$
> relative position t_i, relative orientation ψ_i and scale σ_i,
> relative importance γ_i) }

Each related model is normally also a proper full model, containing its own 42 feature planes, as well as its own associated models, which may or may not refer back to the initial model.

3.2 Subcomponent evidence recording

The Stable Feature Frame (SFF) [5] represents the system's visual memory. It is registered on the world rather than the gaze location and incrementally records a stable, non-retinocentric view of the world. It contains defoveated (r, g, b) data obtained during the system's visual exploration, plus a list $\{s_j\} = \{(M_j, t_j, \psi_j, \sigma_j, V_j)\}$ of recognized image structures (i.e. model instances) M_j, their image locations t_j, estimated orientation ψ_j, estimated scale σ_j and matching scores V_j.

3.3 Subcomponent evidence location

When matching at the current foveation position t_f, initially only the 42 feature planes are involved. The matching algorithm computes a feature-based match at t_f with score V_f (using Eqn (1)) and an estimated model scale σ_f and rotation ψ_f. For each associated subcomponent i with relative position t_i, relative orientation ψ_i and relative scale σ_i, one can predict where in the scene the associated models are likely to be found:

$$t_{pi} = t_f + \sigma_f \mathcal{R}(\psi_f) t_i \qquad (2)$$

their expected scale:

$$\sigma_{pi} = \sigma_i \sigma_f$$

and their expected orientation:

$$\psi_{pi} = \psi_f + \psi_i$$

The SFF can then be searched for model instances of the correct type that are within a search window of the predicted position, and that have a scale and orientation that are within a tolerance of the predicted position, scale and orientation.

3.4 Extended match evaluation function

The match evaluation score originally used only the match score V_f provided by correlating the 42 feature planes and combining their match scores (see Eqn (1)). With the associated model matching scores, the overall matching function has been extended to be:

$$\alpha V_f + (1 - \alpha) V_a$$

where V_a is the associated model evidence and $\alpha = 0.7$ (chosen arbitrarily).

The associated model evidence V_a is given by:

$$V_a = \sum_{a_i \in A} \gamma_i \, max_{s_j \in SFF} \{ \, h(pred(a_i), s_j) \, \}$$

where $pred(x)$ is the predicted properties of the observed model, as given by the formulas in Section 3.3, γ_i is the relative importance of each associated model, a_i is an associated model and s_j is a previously found model instance recorded in the stable feature frame (SFF). Thus, the more associated models that are successfully found, the larger is the combined evidence score V_a.

The associated model goodness evaluation $h()$ is given by:

$$h((..., t_{pi}, ...), (..., t_j, ...)) = M_j e^{-\beta d(t_{pi}, t_j)}$$

where M_j is the associated model's match evaluation score, $d()$ is a position dissimilarity metric and β is a scaling factor.

The position dissimilarity function $d()$ is evaluated by:

$$d(t_{pi}, t_j) = \frac{\| t_{pi} - t_j \|}{\| \frac{1}{2}(t_{pi} + t_j) - t_f \|}$$

which has a small value if the distance between the predicted t_{pi} and observed t_i model positions is small relative to the distance of the matched models from the foveation point t_f. This relative distance is important because the accuracy of position location declines as models are located distant from the foveation point (in part due to the averaging effects of the log-polar representation). An orientation and scale dissimilarity metric could also be incorporated into $h()$.

3.5 Interest map update

The original interest map was updated by computing an interest function at each of the 3 scales on the 14 features. Activity from high-interest features was combined with activity from opponent color features and then defoveated into the existing interest map. Details of the interest map calculation are given in [11].

If a model is successfully recognized, this means that there may be other nearby associated models. Section 3.3 discussed how the position of these associated models was predicted and how the previously recognized instances of the models were located. However, not all of the associated models may have been found so far. Therefore, it makes sense to look for these other models in the predicted locations (t_{pi}) that had no successful match. The appropriate mechanism for causing this search is to increase the level of activation in the interest map at the predicted locations. The uncertainty in match position and scale grows as the predicted position becomes more distant from the foveation point. Therefore, the interest map is updated according to this function:

$$Imap(x) + = \alpha e^{-\tau \delta(x)}$$

where x are points near the predicted position t_{pi}, t_f is the foveation point, $\alpha = 250$, $\tau = 100$ and

$$\delta(x) = \frac{\| t_{pi} - x \|^2}{\| t_{pi} - t_f \|^2}$$

The interest map is updated only if no associated model has been previously found at the predicted point t_{pi}. Determining whether a model has been found there uses the mechanism discussed in Section 3.4.

4 Experiments

The claim of the paper is that use of the subcomponent evidence improves the speed, positional accuracy and completeness of recognition. We demonstrate this by running the iconic recognition system with and without the subcomponent evidence process enabled. The recognition system is iconic, so only objects transformed by translation, scaling and rotation about the optical axis are appropriate. The experiments used a set of images containing frontal views of faces as the experimental scenes, with eyes, nose and mouths as the associated models. Faces have standard substructure and face images are commonly obtainable. Note, we are making no claims about this system as a face recognizer, or identifier system.

The model database contained (for these comparison experiments) 4 models: eye, nose, mouth and full face. When the subcomponent mechanism was not used, the interest map was not updated with the predicted associated model positions and the SFF was not searched for associated model matches. All other components of the system were identical including the model base. The time per saccade was virtually identical, with or without the subcomponent process.

All experiments started with a foveation at the center of the image (which was always on the face). The stopping criteria were when either all features were found, or the system had completed 20 saccades.

Table 2 summarizes the measurements taken from the experiments without and with subcomponent evidence, using 7 test images. Table 1 (left) describes the contents of the five feature columns of Table 2, and Table 1 (right) describes the contents of the rightmost summary column of the data tables. Italicized entries in Table 2 denote incorrect recognitions. The feature column boxes record on which saccade the feature was found, how many pixels error there were between the estimated feature position and what we thought was the correct registration point (correct matches only), the match score for the correct recognition and the number of false recognitions of that feature. (As eyes were indistinguishable, false recognitions of eyes are listed only for the left eye.) The rightmost column lists the number of saccades needed until the last feature was found, the total number of correct features found, the average position error in pixels of the correctly found features, and the total number of mismatched features.

The results for image C6 need a special explanation: in this case the initial foveation point was very close to the registration point for the face model, so the face was immediately recognized. This results in a large inhibition region (to prevent re-saccading back to already recognized features) suppressing the recognition of other nearby features. Consequently, it was hard to recognize any other nearby features. This is why the right eye and nose were never found and why it took a long time to saccade to the mouth.

With regard to the three qualities claimed, the evidence shows that:

speed - in all images except C6 (which searched a long time to find the 3rd model at the edge of the inhibition region), the number of saccades to recognize all features was less in the subcomponent evidence case.

position - For the 17 features recognized by both systems, the average subcomponent case position error was smaller (13.5 *versus* 16.7 pixels).

completeness - more features were correctly found (30 *versus* 17 out of 35 possible), and fewer incorrect features were found (12 *versus* 17).

The results on other images (results not shown here) have slight variations, but the same general properties still hold. Thus, we claim that the use of subcomponent evidence increases the speed, positional accuracy and completeness of recognition.

A side effect of the subcomponent evidence mechanism is that recognition scores of the correctly found features are often reduced. This arises because the recognition score now requires associated model evidence in order to obtain top scores. As initial feature recognitions will *not* have many previously found associated features, their recognition scores will be lower. Also, features recognized with inaccurate positions reduce the match scores in proportion to the position error.

Figure 1 shows the saccade path on the FCE5 image (left) without and (right) with subcomponent evidence. The search is clearly much more focussed with subcomponent evidence.

Saccade found	Match score	Max. saccades	Total correct features found
Offset error	False instances	Average offset	Total mismatches

Table 1. Key to the entries in Table 2.

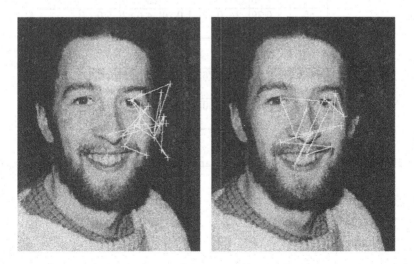

Fig. 1. Saccades on FCE5 without (left) and with (right) use of subcomponent evidence.

a)

Image	left eye	right eye	nose	mouth	face	Summary
c1	4 1.00	1 1.00	5 1.00	3 1.00	7 1.00	7 2
	16 2		1	1	22 0	19 4
c3	1 1.00	7 1.00	8 1.00	4 1.00	3 1.00	8 4
	14 1		12 1	11 0	26 0	15.8 2
c4	10 1.00	2 1.00	1 1.00	8 1.00	12 0.99	12 3
	16 1	19	13 0	1	1	16 3
c5	10 1.00	12 1.00	1 1.00			12 3
	2 1	28	0 0			10 1
c6	5 1.00			2 0.86	1 0.98	5 3
	32 0			34 1	27 0	31 1
fce5	9 1.0	9 1.0	3 1.0		5 0.79	20 1
	1	9	2		2	9 5
bebie1	1 1.00		18 1.00		2 0.94	18 1
	3 0		1		1	3 2

b)

Image	left eye	right eye	nose	mouth	face	Summary
c1	3 0.71	4 0.76	6 0.82	5 0.79	7 0.91	7 5
	9 2	14	9 0	7 0	10 0	7.8 2
c3	1 0.70	2 0.76	3 0.76	4 0.83	5 0.89	5 5
	14 0	14	16 0	12 0	5 0	15.6 0
c4	4 0.71	9 0.81	10 0.82	7 0.77		10 4
	19 0	25	20 1	23 0		17.2 1
c5	3 0.79	2 0.72	1 0.70	4 0.82	5 0.74	5 5
	7 1	17	7 0	5 0	9 0	9 1
c6	2 0.83			18 0.80	1 0.68	18 3
	25 0			9 3	27 0	20.3 3
fce5	13 0.83	12 0.76	14 0.81	11 0.75	15 0.92	15 5
	4 2	5	4 2	6	2	4 4
bebie1	1 0.70	6 0.80		5 0.75	9 0.86	9 4
	3 1	10		22 0	8 0	8.6 1

Table 2. Results of testing (a) *without* and (b) *with* full subcomponent evidence.

Fig. 2. Test images for reported experiment (c1, c3, c4, c5, c6, fce5, bebie1)

5 Discussion

The claim made earlier in the paper is that the use of the simplified geometrical model and the associated subcomponent recognition processes improves the recognition process in several ways:

- **recognition speed** - in most cases, the number of saccades needed to recognize the features in the scene was reduced.
- **position accuracy** - the average error in the estimated position of the feature was reduced.
- **recognition correctness** - more features were correctly found and fewer incorrect features were found.

The experimental evidence supports this claim.

Sometimes, when a model has been incorrectly recognized (*e.g.* recognizing a squint eye with the mouth model), then prediction can lead the process to search several non-feature positions before returning to true feature positions. Adding a cumulative evidence process to the attention mechanism could help reduce the effect of this.

At the moment, the models do not distinguish between left and right eyes. This reduces matching accuracy but means that a single recognized eye will predict two possible positions for the second eye and the recognition will also expect to find evidence from 2 positions. The multiple prediction is reasonable, but the model representation that we use should be extended to allow mutually exclusive alternatives.

References

1. DH Ballard and CM Brown. Computer Vision, Prentice-Hall, New Jersey, 1982.
2. J Ben-Arie and Z Wang. Pictorial recognition using affine-invariant spectral signatures. Proc. Int Conf on Comp. Vis. and Pat. Rec., pp 35–39, San Jose, Puerto Rico, 1997.
3. I Biederman. Recognition-by-components: A theory of human image understanding. Psychological Review. vol 4, pp 115-147, 1987.
4. RA Brooks. Symbolic reasoning among 3D models and 2-D images. Artificial Intelligence Journal, vol 17, pp 285–348, 1981.
5. JA Feldman. Four frames suffice: a provisional model of vision and space. Behavioral Brain Sciences Vol 8, pp 265-313, 1985.
6. RB Fisher. From Surfaces to Objects: Computer Vision and Three Dimensional Scene Analysis. John Wiley, UK, 1989.

7. RB Fisher. Hierarchical Matching Beats The Non-Wildcard and Interpretation Tree Model Matching Algorithms. Proc. 1993 British Machine Vision Association Conf., pp 589-598, Surrey, 1993.
8. D. A. Forsyth and M. M. Fleck. Identifying nude pictures. In IEEE Workshop on the Applic. of Comp. Vis. pp 103-108, 1996.
9. W. E. L. Grimson. Object Recognition By Computer: The Role of Geometric Constraints. MIT Press, 1990.
10. TD Grove. Attention directed iconic object matching. M.Sc. dissertation, Dept. of Artificial Intelligence, University of Edinburgh, 1995.
11. TD Grove, RB Fisher. Attention in Iconic Object Matching. Proc. British Machine Vision Conference BMVC96, Edinburgh, pp 293-302, September 1996.
12. A MacKirdy. Full Subcomponent Evidence and Further Parallelism in an Iconic Object Recognition System. BSc Honours Dissertation, Dept. of Artificial Intelligence, Univ. of Edinburgh, 1997.
13. D Marr. Vision. W.H. Freeman and Company, 1980.
14. K Messer, J Kittler, M Kraaijveld. Selecting features for neural networks to aid an iconic search through an image database. Proc. IEE 6th Int. Conf. on Image Proc and Its Applic, pp 428-432, 1997.
15. J Mundy, A Liu, N Pillow, A Zisserman, S Abdallah, S Utcke, S Nayar and C Rothwell. An experimental comparison of appearance and geometric model based recognition. in Proc. Int Workshop on Object Representations in Comp. Vis, 1996. In assoc. with ECCV 1996.
16. RPN Rao and DH Ballard. Object indexing using an iconic sparse distributed memory. Technical Report TR 559, Computer Science Dept., U. Rochester, 1995.
17. LG Roberts. Machine Perception of Three-Dimensional Solids, in Tippett, J. T. (ed.), Optical and Electro-Optical Information Processing, MIT Press, Ch. 9, Cambridge, Massachusetts, pp 159-197, 1965.
18. G Sandini and M Tistarelli. Vision and Space-Variant Sensing. In (ed. H. Wechsler), Neural Networks for Perception, Vol 1: Human and Machine Perception, Academic Press, Ch II.9, pp 398-425, 1992.
19. B Schiele and JL Crowley. Object Recognition Using Multidimensional Receptive Field Histograms. Proc. 1996 Eur. Conf. on Comp. Vision, Vol 2, pp 610-619, 1996.
20. M Seibert and AM Waxman. Learning and Recognizing 3D Objects from Multiple Views in a Neural System. in (ed. H. Wechsler), Neural Networks for Perception, Vol 1: Human and Machine Perception, Academic Press, Ch II.12, pp 426-444, 1992.
21. JP Siebert and I Eising. Scale-space recognition based on the retino-cortical transform. Proc. IEE Conf on Image Processing and its Applications, Edinburgh, 1995.
22. J van der Spiegel, G Kreider, C Claeys, I Debusschere, G Sandini, P Dario, F Fantini, P Belluti, and G Soncini. A foveated retina-like sensor using CCD technology. In C. Mead and M. Ismail, editors, Analog VLSI Implementation of Neural Systems, Ch 8, pp 189-212. Kluwer Academic Publishers, Boston, 1989.
23. M Tistarelli. Active/Space-Variant Object Recognition. Image and Vision Computing, Vol. 13, No 3, pp 215-226, 1995.
24. MA Turk and AP Pentland. Eigenfaces for Recognition. J. Cognitive Neuroscience, vol 3 no 1, pp 71-86, 1991.

Combining Multiple Views and Temporal Associations for 3-D Object Recognition

Amin Massad, Bärbel Mertsching, and Steffen Schmalz

University of Hamburg, Dep. of Computer Science, AG IMA
Vogt-Kölln-Str. 30, D-22527 Hamburg, Germany
mertsching@informatik.uni-hamburg.de

Abstract. This article describes an architecture for the recognition of three-dimensional objects on the basis of viewer centred representations and temporal associations. Considering evidence from psychophysics, neurophysiology, as well as computer science we have decided to use a viewer centred approach for the representation of three-dimensional objects. Even though this concept quite naturally suggests utilizing the temporal order of the views for learning and recognition, this aspect is often neglected. Therefore we will pay special attention to the evaluation of the temporal information and embed it into the conceptual framework of biological findings and computational advantages. The proposed recognition system consists of four stages and includes different kinds of artificial neural networks: Preprocessing is done by a Gabor-based wavelet transform. A Dynamic Link Matching algorithm, extended by several modifications, forms the second stage. It implements recognition and learning of the view classes. The temporal order of the views is recorded by a STORE network which transforms the output for a presented sequence of views into an item-and-order coding. A subsequent Gaussian-ARTMAP architecture is used for the classification of the sequences and for their mapping onto object classes by means of supervised learning. The results achieved with this system show its capability to autonomously learn and to recognize considerably similar objects. Furthermore the given examples illustrate the benefits for object recognition stemming from the utilization of the temporal context. Ambiguous views become manageable and a higher degree of robustness against misclassifications can be accomplished.

1 Introduction

The utilization of image processing seems promising for the development of machines capable of circumspect, flexible, or even autonomous interactions with their environment. As scenes are usually composed of objects, artificial image understanding needs the implementation of a functioning object recognition system. The latter is the main topic of the presented work which aims at the recognition of real three-dimensional objects. Special attention is given to the evaluation of the temporal dimension for the representation as well as for the recognition. Hereby, ambiguous views become manageable and a higher degree of robustness can be achieved for the recognition process.

Recent studies in psychophysics and neurophysiology stress the advantages and plausibility of viewer centred representations in contrast to object centred models. These biological findings together with computational aspects give reason for the usage of a view-based representation scheme as presented here.

Another important concern is the realization of a system equipped with learning abilities to ensure adaptability to newly perceived views of known objects and to allow the addition of previously unknown objects. With respect to the desired properties of the solution, we focus on a universality regarding the kind of objects, features, and restrictions.

Facing the complexity of the subject we only can propose one possible way based on a sufficient number of arguments. Accordingly, the selection, interpretation, evaluation, and connection of various approaches are regarded as main components of this study.

2 Representing 3-D Objects

2.1 Viewer Centred vs. Object Centred Representations

The implementation of an object recognition necessarily requires the definition of a representation scheme for the objects, which does not only determine the type of storage but even the manner of the recognition process. Special attention shall be paid to the representation schemes because of considerable contradictions between the concepts of object centred and viewer centred descriptions. Object centred models store a single representation for each object (e. g. Marr and Nishihara 1978; Biederman 1985; Thompson and Mundy 1987; Lowe 1986). Accordingly, such a representation has to be three-dimensional and often resembles models used in computer graphics, esp. CAD. In contrast, viewer centred models contain collections of representations for the different perspectives under which the object appears to a (virtual) viewer. Thus a self-contained description of an object is embodied in the combination of its views, which can be three-dimensional as well as two-dimensional. Concerning invariance it has been argued for the usage of object centred models. Likewise the anticipation of a combinatorial explosion, caused by the multitude of imaginable views, lead to the rejection of viewer centred representations. Object centred models have the one purpose in common: the description of objects by high level features which provide stability over all perspectives. These features, however, involve a high degree of complexity and computational efforts. As a matter of fact, a great number of representation schemes is merely designed for theoretical treatments without being implemented, not even for testing purposes.

Recent studies in computer science as well as in psychology and neurophysiology support the notion of viewer centred models by not only refuting the fear of a combinatorial explosion but even stating several advantages over object centred representations. Therefore a short review of the relevant work will be given together with the corresponding implications.

Ullman and Basri (1991) propose a viewer centred model based on two-dimensional views: It is not restricted to rigid transformations, does not involve the explicit reconstruction and representation of the three-dimensional structure for storing the objects. Another noteworthy aspect is the proof that under certain assumptions all the views of a three-dimensional object, which may arise by affine transformations, can be derived from the linear combination of a few 2D views. On the other hand this method presupposes the visibility of all object points from every perspective. Even though these assumptions must be regarded as hardly realizable for real scenes or automated model acquisition, the scheme gives impressive hints of the potential information content of two-dimensional views.

An early implementation of a view based recognition system by means of an artificial neural network is presented by Poggio and Edelman (1990). They postulate that for every object an appropriate function can be found which is capable of transforming all possible views into a single standard view. The approximations of these functions are expected to be evolved by *RBF* networks (*Radial Basis Functions*) after separately training them on different views of their corresponding object. Recognition involves the application of the transformation functions to the input view and the comparison of the resulting outputs with the stored standard views. Because of the necessity of a constant number of feature points together with an exact correspondence relation between image and model, the previously mentioned drawbacks also hold for this approach.

In contrast, the *CLF* network (*Conjunctions of Localized Features*) suggested by Edelman and Weinshall (1991) does not need the computation of an explicit correspondence but uses topological feature maps. While CLF networks have the capability to simulate error rates and recognition measures found in psychological tests, they seem to be inadequate for general image processing purposes because of their generalization method, which is mainly based on gaussian blurring of the stored model representations. Therefore, preliminary experiments with real images instead of artificially designed objects showed the tendency towards improper matches with models containing a higher number of feature points. This systematic fault is caused by single feature points in the input image overlapping with several widened model points simultaneously and can only be circumvented by a constant number of feature points over all views and all objects as it was the case in the study of Edelman and Weinshall.

More realistic input images are processed by the *VIEWNET* architecture (*View Information Encoded with NETworks*) described by Grossberg and Bradski (1995). The view based model includes a biologically motivated preprocessing chain to convert the input images into a representation invariant under illumination changes, translation, plane rotation, and scaling. The classification of the resulting patterns is done by a Fuzzy-ARTMAP network (cf. Carpenter et al. 1992), an artificial neural network stemming from the adaptive resonance theory (ART). While this study hints at the advantages resulting from the consideration of view sequences instead of single images, it still neglects the order in which the views appear.

Such an evaluation of the serial information can be found in Seibert and Waxman (1992). Their system is able to create transition matrices from view sequences and thus offers a method for the automated construction of aspect graphs as defined by Koenderink and van Doorn (1979). However, the edges of an aspect graph indicate the transition between merely two views. The assembly of longer sequences requires the implicit assumption of transitivity along edges. Although the connections are augmented by the relative frequency of the according transition, detailed information about longer sequences is not provided because of the missing serial relations.

Viewer centred representations not only give rise to these successful technical implementations but even have a close relationship to biological findings. Yet, the existence of so-called *canonical* and *accidental views* has diverging interpretations. Supporters of object centred representations might argue that accidental

models. These biological findings together with computational aspects give reason for the usage of a view-based representation scheme as presented here.

Another important concern is the realization of a system equipped with learning abilities to ensure adaptability to newly perceived views of known objects and to allow the addition of previously unknown objects. With respect to the desired properties of the solution, we focus on a universality regarding the kind of objects, features, and restrictions.

Facing the complexity of the subject we only can propose one possible way based on a sufficient number of arguments. Accordingly, the selection, interpretation, evaluation, and connection of various approaches are regarded as main components of this study.

2 Representing 3-D Objects

2.1 Viewer Centred vs. Object Centred Representations

The implementation of an object recognition necessarily requires the definition of a representation scheme for the objects, which does not only determine the type of storage but even the manner of the recognition process. Special attention shall be paid to the representation schemes because of considerable contradictions between the concepts of object centred and viewer centred descriptions. Object centred models store a single representation for each object (e. g. Marr and Nishihara 1978; Biederman 1985; Thompson and Mundy 1987; Lowe 1986). Accordingly, such a representation has to be three-dimensional and often resembles models used in computer graphics, esp. CAD. In contrast, viewer centred models contain collections of representations for the different perspectives under which the object appears to a (virtual) viewer. Thus a self-contained description of an object is embodied in the combination of its views, which can be three-dimensional as well as two-dimensional. Concerning invariance it has been argued for the usage of object centred models. Likewise the anticipation of a combinatorial explosion, caused by the multitude of imaginable views, lead to the rejection of viewer centred representations. Object centred models have the one purpose in common: the description of objects by high level features which provide stability over all perspectives. These features, however, involve a high degree of complexity and computational efforts. As a matter of fact, a great number of representation schemes is merely designed for theoretical treatments without being implemented, not even for testing purposes.

Recent studies in computer science as well as in psychology and neurophysiology support the notion of viewer centred models by not only refuting the fear of a combinatorial explosion but even stating several advantages over object centred representations. Therefore a short review of the relevant work will be given together with the corresponding implications.

Ullman and Basri (1991) propose a viewer centred model based on two-dimensional views: It is not restricted to rigid transformations, does not involve the explicit reconstruction and representation of the three-dimensional structure for storing the objects. Another noteworthy aspect is the proof that under certain assumptions all the views of a three-dimensional object, which may arise by affine transformations, can be derived from the linear combination of a few 2D views. On the other hand this method presupposes the visibility of all object points from every perspective. Even though these assumptions must be regarded as

interventions. Given the example of a car, a rotation about the horizontal axis (fortunately) occurs less often than a turning about its vertical axis and may therefore be regarded as an exception.

There are several neurophysical and psychological experiments hinting at the utilization of temporal associations in biology. Miyashita (1988) reports the training of macaque monkeys with a set of 97 randomly generated fractal images. Conducting *delayed matching to sample (DMS)* tasks the animals had to decide whether two consecutively presented patterns were the same or not. Training was performed over quite a long period of time by presenting a circular repetition of the images and thus maintaining the order of the training set. Subsequent single cell recordings in the inferotemporal cortex exhibited neurons with effective stimuli formed by clusters of consecutive patterns of the training set. Accordingly these randomly generated patterns established associations not for their geometric similarity but for their temporal connections. This conclusion is affirmed by further experiments of Sakai and Miyashita (1991) who managed to create associations between any pairs of shapes on the basis of a consecutive presentation.

Psychophysical evidence for the existence of temporal associations can be found in Wallis (in press). His study makes use of training sequences which are artificially created by the combination of consecutive faces belonging to different persons. Assuming the development of temporal associations, one would suppose interconnections between the views of a sequence possibly leading to the fusion of a single virtual face. In fact, recognition errors showed more often a confusion between faces belonging to a common artificial sequence than between faces of different sequences. In other words the subjects formed associations between views because of their coincident appearance and not because of their similarity.

Summarizing the findings about temporal associations, Stryker (1991) deduces a powerful scheme which seems to supersede the need for mechanisms of geometric transformations or hierarchical connections of so-called trigger features. As previously mentioned for viewer centred representations, he considers temporal associations to be a trade-off between memory and computation providing a means for the brain to accomplish perceptual constancy.

3 Recognizing 3-D Objects from View Sequences

3.1 Overview of the Recognition System

The design of our object recognition system is based on the combination of viewer centred representations and temporal associations. According to the notion of viewer centred representations discussed in Sect. 2.1, it is possible to store three-dimensional objects as collections of two-dimensional views and to achieve an invariant object recognition by the connection of several variant view classes with broadly tuned outputs. Hence the need arises for mechanisms capable of generalizing across a range of vantage points, which is a task suggesting the use of artificial neural networks. However, objects do not come into sight as single views, instead they are naturally embedded into a temporal context. The stated advantages of a hypothesized continuity for a view based recognition propose the utilization of temporal information by the integration of view sequences into the representation scheme. Therefore the model will be augmented by mechanisms with the capacity to record the temporal order of successive views and to divide these sequences into classes. Thus object classes can be built upon collections of sequence classes. By defining a single view to be a special case of a (very short) sequence, one can drop the additional shortcut connections between views and object classes as depicted in Fig. 2.

Obviously the use of long sequences yields a high number of possible sequence classes. In anticipation of an objection to a combinatorial explosion, it is important to notice that in practice only a very limited subset of the theoretically possible sequences will appear. Constraints originate from natural laws or conditions: gravity, for example, affects the viewer as well as the objects and considerably restricts the motions under which objects can be perceived; living beings show characteristic movements determinded by morphology or learnt behaviour. Matsakis et al. (1990) report investigations of cosmonauts of the space station MIR obtaining improved capabilities in mental rotation experiments under weightlessness. They presume the improvements to be effected by learning and to be partly caused by physiological processes in conjunction with the lost sense of gravity which make it easier to mentally relate the positions of object and viewer. Evidence for the relevancy of certain kinds of movements can be found in Perrett et al. (1990) where neurophysiological experiments exhibited cells of the macaque temporal cortex selectively reacting on complex movements or actions. Furthermore the number of cells coding compatible movements (e. g. the left profile of a person walking to left) was noticeably higher than the number of cells representing unusual movements (e. g. the left profile of a person moving to the right, i. e. walking backwards). Similarly Sumi (1984) reports higher recognition rates for normally presented biological motion stimuli than for inverted sequences.

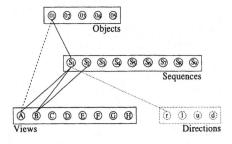

Fig. 2: Relations between the elements of the representation scheme, which comprises classes of views, sequences and objects. The system can be extended by direction classes indicating whether a rotation is right-, left-, up-, or downwards.

Moreover, the number of sequence classes can be reduced by the inclusion of mechanisms for invariance against modifications of the temporal patterns. The proposed system does explicitly not aim at storing all possible view sequences into the object model, instead it is designed to employ its learning capabilities in order to extract characteristics of the objects from the presented training sequences, to weigh them, and to use them for future recognition tasks.

Although spatial information is not necessarily required for the object recognition intended here, it should be included later to complete the concept of the object model: We suggest to seek the useful spatial information of an object in the relationship of its views. For this the sequence classes could be augmented by a small number of detectors indicating some basic directions of rotation about the main axes. Assuming mutually exclusive direction classes, such a modelling will be in agreement with the results of mental rotation experiments (cf. Metzler and Shepard 1974) in which the subjects have more difficulties in the simultaneous rotation of three-dimensional objects about more than one axis than in rotations about a single main axis.

Based on the proposed representation scheme the structure of the recognition system is implemented as depicted in Fig. 3. The process starts with the extraction of local features resulting from a Gaborjet transform applied to the input images. The inclusion of a visual attention algorithm to select a subset of these features for further processing would be beyond the scope of this article and is therefore preliminarily integrated as relatively simple method for the selection of a window around the interesting object within the input scene.

Usually the following steps employ a kind of coordinate transform and the computation of global features in order to yield an invariant representation as the foundation of a subsequent view classification. In Sect. 3.3 we will discuss why such a technique has serious drawbacks. Therefore we have chosen another approach which combines several of the processing steps and profits from the consideration of the topological information coded in feature maps. This so-called *Dynamic Link Matching (DLM)* has its origin in von der Malsburg (1981), however several extensions had to be applied to this basic concept before it could be used in the given context for the foundation of view classes.

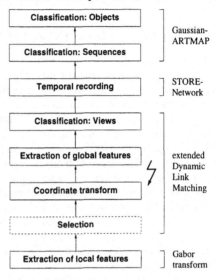

Fig. 3: Simplified block diagram of the recognition system depicting the relations of the processing steps to the implemented algorithms.

The temporal recording of the view classes is done by a STORE network according to Bradski et al. (1992) which transforms the patterns into an *item-and-order coding* as described in Sect. 3.4. A Gaussian-ARTMAP architecture, which was introduced by Williamson (1996), divides the outputs from the STORE network into sequence classes and maps them onto object classes by means of a supervised training method. Section 3.5 deals with the details of this stage.

3.2   Feature Extraction: Gaborjet Transform

In principle, the generality of the DLM algorithm allows to use every kind of input that is organized in feature maps. Even though DLM is designed to tolerate variations of the feature positions, it is necessary to find features which are stable under a large range of varying conditions and on the other hand not too widespread in order to reduce the number of initial ambiguities. Würtz (1994) suggests the usage of a Gabor-wavelet transform because Gabor filters are well known to have computational advantages and to give a theoretical account for findings about biological visual systems. Accordingly, preprocessing is implemented as the convolution of the input images with a number of n_{dir} different oriented kernels on n_{lev} resolution levels defined as

$$(\mathcal{F}\psi_{\boldsymbol{k}})(\boldsymbol{\omega}) = \exp\left(-\frac{\sigma^2\,(\boldsymbol{\omega} - \boldsymbol{k})^2}{2k^2}\right) - \exp\left(-\frac{\sigma^2\,(\boldsymbol{\omega}^2 + \boldsymbol{k}^2)}{2k^2}\right) \text{ with } \boldsymbol{k} = \begin{pmatrix} k_{lev}\cos\phi_{dir} \\ k_{lev}\sin\phi_{dir} \end{pmatrix}$$

where $k_{lev} = n_{lev}/\sqrt{2}^{lev}$, $\phi_{dir} = \pi \cdot dir/n_{dir}$, and $\mathcal{F}$ denotes the Fourier transform. The resulting amplitudes of the filter outputs form a feature vector f, called Gaborjet, of the dimension $n_{dir} \cdot n_{lev} = 12 \cdot 2$. An additional subsampling yields patterns of the size 64×64 pixels from the input images of 256×256 pixels.

3.3 Classifying Views: Extended Dynamic Link Matching

It is common practice to transform the input patterns into a special representation invariant against certain kinds of mathematically defined operations (e. g. the magnitudes of the Fourier transform or a centred log-polar transform) or to predetermine a transforming function (e. g. an affine transform) and compute its parameters for the mapping of the current input image onto the stored patterns. However, the success and the applicability of these approaches are limited because an appropriate formal description for real scenes is still to be found. Serious problems arise for example from noise, occlusions, distortions, non-rigid objects, changes of illumination or background. In its most general formulation matching consists in mapping local features of the input pattern onto corresponding features of a trained pattern and thus yielding a global transformation between both patterns. In this process ambiguities of local features have to be solved by the consideration of neighbouring features. Therefore, special attention is paid to the information contained by the topological structure of the patterns.

Konen et al. (1994) present a neural formulation of such a match process, called *Dynamic Link Matching*, which uses topography as a guideline on the assumption that a transformation needed to map a local feature of the stored pattern onto its counterpart in the input pattern is very likely to be applicable to match the neighbours onto their counterparts. The system consists of two layers, the image layer X representing the current input pattern and the model layer Y storing the pattern against which the input is to be matched. The neurons of each layer are labeled by local features. Both layers are connected by interlayer links J_{ba} carrying information about the correspondence between each cell b of layer Y and each cell a of layer X. These connections, called *dynamic links*, model a kind of working memory with rapid weight changes and can be understood as a measure for the probability that a cell a is the correct correspondence for b. Additionally, the wiring contains static intralayer weights in both layers which couple each cell with its local neighbours by excitatory connections and with more distant cells by inhibitory connections. The process for self-organization of the dynamic links has two formulations, a description of the neural activity by dynamic equations and a simplified algorithm based on the blob equilibrium solution, which proves the emergence of a connected active region in each layer. Our discussion will be focussed on this *Fast DLM (FDLM)* algorithm outlined in Fig. 4.

This basic DLM concept was usually applied to sets of quite dissimilar objects whereas our application has additionally to cope with similar views depicting the same objects under different perspectives. By separately applying the DLM to every model, we frequently obtained high correspondences between a given input image and several models. Neither the correlation value of the blob regions

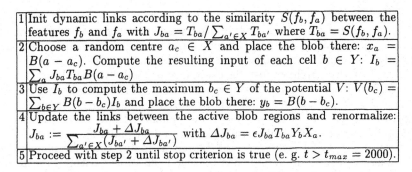

1	Init dynamic links according to the similarity $S(f_b, f_a)$ between the features f_b and f_a with $J_{ba} = T_{ba}/\sum_{a' \in X} T_{ba'}$ where $T_{ba} = S(f_b, f_a)$.
2	Choose a random centre $a_c \in X$ and place the blob there: $x_a = B(a - a_c)$. Compute the resulting input of each cell $b \in Y$: $I_b = \sum_a J_{ba} T_{ba} B(a - a_c)$
3	Use I_b to compute the maximum $b_c \in Y$ of the potential V: $V(b_c) = \sum_{b \in Y} B(b - b_c) I_b$ and place the blob there: $y_b = B(b - b_c)$.
4	Update the links between the active blob regions and renormalize: $J_{ba} := \dfrac{J_{ba} + \Delta J_{ba}}{\sum_{a' \in X}(J_{ba'} + \Delta J_{ba'})}$ with $\Delta J_{ba} = \epsilon J_{ba} T_{ba} Y_b X_a$.
5	Proceed with step 2 until stop criterion is true (e. g. $t > t_{max} = 2000$).

Fig. 4: Fast Dynamic Link Matching according to Konen et al. (1994). The blob solution B can be of arbitrary and simple shape, e. g. a rectangular window function.

nor the structure of the dynamic links allowed the definition of a measure to discern between them. Therefore, the algorithm has to be modified to competitively match all stored models against the current input. In contrast to Wiskott and von der Malsburg (1996) we will maintain the principle of the FDLM algorithm. The scheme of Fig. 4 is extended to consider m layers Y_m simultaneously, where m denotes the number of stored models. Step 3 now has to compute the maximum of V over all models m. Only the layer $Y_{m'}$ containing the region of highest activation will form a blob and update its weights to the current blob in X (step 4).

The modification makes it possible to define a useful recognition measure $r^m(t)$ for a model m and an iteration step t by

$$r^m(t_0) = 1 \qquad \dot{r}^m(t) = \lambda_r r^m \left(F^m - \max_{m'} \left(r^{m'} F^{m'} \right) \right)$$

where F^m denotes the „fitness" of the layer m, computed as total activity of all its cells, and λ_r is a time constant. The right equation expresses a competition between the model with the highest fitness and all the weaker models, which will be further suppressed by the last term becoming negative. During the recognition process the recognition value of the best fitting model approaches one while the remaining values decrease to zero. A speed up of recognition is achieved by ignoring models which have dropped under a threshold $r^m(t) < \theta_r$. Additionally, we demand a certain significance of the maximum found in step 3 before admitting the weight updates of step 4, i. e. there has to be a sufficient distance to the second best value $V(b_c')$. A precondition defined as $V(b_c)/V(b_c') \geq k$ (e. g. $k = 1.1$) intensifies the competition and ensures that connections are only made between characteristic regions and not between areas belonging to several models (e. g. some background pixels which are inaccurately included in the models).

A full connectivity between the model layers Y^m and the input layer X yields large matrices $J_{b^m a}$ for the links and $T_{b^m a}$ for the similarity values. To save memory and to reduce computation Wiskott and von der Malsburg (1996) propose to restrict the receptive field of each cell b to patches of the size $w_{patch} \cdot h_{patch}$, which are evenly distributed over the image layer. In addition to the primarily intended increase of performance, this restriction has great advantages for the arrangement of the generated correspondences: The feature extraction can roughly be interpreted as a kind of edge detector, therefore the DLM process sometimes finds implicit symmetries (e. g. by matching opponent parts of a lengthy edge and thus creating a intersection of the links) which are then gradually extended over the complete image. The local bounding of the weights prevents such effects by initially excluding connections between too distant features.

The size of the patches must be chosen very carefully: On the one hand performance depends on small sizes, on the other hand the patches have to be large enough to allow displacements of the stored model in larger input scenes. For that reason the size of the patches is individually computed for each model according to its size (note: smaller models need larger patches).

Generally the model layers Y^m will be much smaller than the image layer X, for example when the system has to search an object within a scene. In this case the results of the DLM can be further enhanced by the introduction of an attention window which limits the positions of blobs in layer X to the region of a presumed object. After a predefined number of iterations (e. g. $t_w = 800$) we set the region of interest by considering the model m' with the highest recognition value and computing the centre $(\bar{a}_x, \bar{a}_y)$ of the window on the basis of its link matrix $J_{b^{m'}a}$ as $\bar{a}_{x/y} = \sum'_{b^m} \sum_{a_{x/y}} a_{x/y} \cdot J_{b^{m'}a_{x/y}}$, height and width of the window are deduced from the standard deviations $(2\sigma_{a_x}, 2\sigma_{a_y})$.

The extended DLM algorithm described above forms the first stage of the matching process. For a given input image it returns the best fitting model from the set of known views. In a second stage we have to test whether the selected model is sufficiently similar to the input. If this is true we will update the model else we will create a new model to hold the current view. The definition of an appropriate similarity measure is facilitated by the DLM algorithm and can be derived from the smoothness of the correspondence grids as depicted in Fig. 5. We have implemented two different distortion measures yielding comparable results, one based on the normalized standard deviation of the node distances and another indicating the perpendicularity of the grid by summing up the deviations of the angles from 90 degrees.

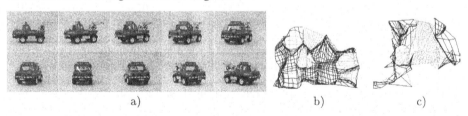

a)   b)   c)

Fig. 5: Two different kinds of correspondence grids as exhibited while training of view sequences. Each node corresponds to a cell of the model layer Y, edges connect neighbouring neurons. The positions of the nodes indicate the best corresponding location within the image layer X. This correspondence is based on the correlation values C_{ba} between a model neuron b and an image neuron a. In order to reduce small irregularities an additional smoothing has been applied to the grid. Nodes b with no sufficiently correlated cell within X are positioned by interpolation with their matching neighbours and connected by light-grey edges. **a)** Example of a view sequence taken from object 1. **b)** Regular correspondence grid stemming from the match of view 4 onto the previously learnt model view 2. **c)** Irregular grid originating from the match of view 9 onto view 2 for the lack of a more similar candidate within the model database.

If the second stage requires the update of an existing model an adaptation of this model to the current input will be performed by placing the feature vector located at (b_x, b_y) to $(b_x, b_y)' := (b_x, b_y) + \lambda[(c_x, c_y) - (b_x, b_y)]$ where λ denotes the learn rate and (c_x, c_y) is the position of the cell b within the correspondence grid.

3.4 Recording View Sequences: Sustained Temporal Order Network

We have chosen to represent the temporal order of the view sequences by a *STORE* (Sustained Temporal Order REcurrent) model according to Bradski et al. (1992). The network is capable of encoding the invariant temporal order of sequential events (e. g. regardless of their durations and interstimulus intervals). Basically it transforms the input sequences into an item-and-order coding which encodes the events that have occurred and the temporal order in which they have occurred. This coding ensures that the presentation of new events will not invalidate the previously learnt patterns. We are especially interested in the possibility to use a network of the ART architecture for the following classification because this design facilitates fast learning and provides a solution for the stability-plasticity-dilemma of artificial neural networks. Both aspects can be regarded as advantages over other kinds of temporal representations realized by time shifter networks or the frequently applied JORDAN and ELMAN nets.

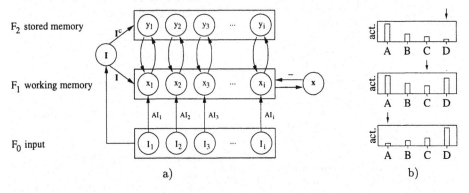

a)   b)

Fig. 6: a) STORE architecture according to Bradski et al. (1992). The bold-faced letters denote the sums $\mathbf{I} = \sum_k I_k$, $\mathbf{I}^c = 1 - \mathbf{I}$, and $\mathbf{x} = \sum_k x_k$; A is an arbitrary factor controlling the shape of the generated gradient. **b)** Representing temporal information by means of an *item-and-order coding*. Top: *Primacy* gradient for small A. Middle: *Bowing* gradient for $0 < A < 1$. Bottom: *Recency* gradient for $A \geq 1$ of the sequence $A \to B \to C \to D$. The arrow indicates the position at which the bowing starts.

Figure 6a shows the structure of a STORE network. The layer F_1 implements a short term memory (STM) which represents the temporal order of the input sequence by its activities x_i and is regarded as the output of the STORE architecture. The negative feedback of the total layer activity $\mathbf{x}$ ensures a partial normalization in order to model psychological findings of a limited STM capacity. The second layer F_2 consists of neurons which track the activities of the F_1-cells and function as a kind of memory. Changes in both layers occur mutually exclusive in dependence of the gain control $\mathbf{I}$ which indicates whether an input is present or not. The factor A applied to the inputs controls the shape of STM gradients as depicted in Fig. 6b. The following stage of our system will receive recency gradients as inputs by setting $A = 1.1$.

3.5 Classifying Sequences and Objects: Gaussian ARTMAP

A Gaussian ARTMAP network as introduced by Williamson (1996) is used for incremental learning of the sequences and their mapping onto object classes. This architecture implements a combination of a Gaussian classifier and an ART neural network which remedies known deficiencies of other ARTMAP architectures, especially Fuzzy ARTMAP (Sarle 1995). It is more resistant to noise, prevents the proliferation of the generated classes, achieves independence of the order in which the patterns are trained, and pays attention to the statistical distribution of the patterns stored within the classes.

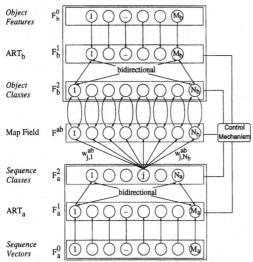

Gaussian ARTMAP (Fig. 7) is based on the concept of the Gaussian ART architecture, which defines its classes by Gaussian distributions. Such a class j is represented by trainable M-dimensional vectors storing the mean μ_j and standard deviation σ_j together with a scalar n_j counting the number of coded samples. The ART choice function and the match function are computed by means of the a priori probabilities and their normalization to unit height, respectively.

The map field is trained to map a class J of F_a^2 onto its predicted class K in F_b^2, a function which is generally a many-to-one assignment. If a class J is chosen during training that maps onto an incorrect prediction $K' \neq K$ a mechanism called match tracking will be invoked. As a consequence

Fig. 7: Gaussian ARTMAP architecture consisting of two Gaussian ART nets and a map field. ARTₐ receives at F_a^0 the STORE patterns as input and divides them into classes represented by the cells of F_a^2. Similarly ARTᵦ yields object classes at F_b^2 from object features.

of match tracking, the class J will be reset in order to let ARTₐ bring up another class which obtains a correct mapping or is an untrained class that will be recruited for the storage of the current input pattern.

4 Results and Discussion

4.1 Demonstration of the Learn- and Recognition-Process

In the first example we illustrate the learn-process. Learning of the first object has already been mentioned by Fig. 5; therefore we present the sequence of Fig. 9a now. The system is supposed to perform a gradual update of the set of model views by means of the extended DLM algorithm. To make the interpretation of the view classes easier, the combination of more than one input image into a view class is prevented by demanding very low distortion measures.

Figure 8a shows the results. The greyed entries mark the stored view which is returned by the extended DLM algorithm as the view best matching the

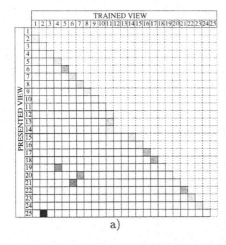

class	views	class	views	class	views
1	1	7	9, 10	13	18
2	2, 3	8	11, 12	14	19, 20
3	4, 5	9	13, 14	15	21
4	6	10	15	16	22, 23
5	7	11	16	17	24, 25
6	8	12	17		

a)   b)

Fig. 8: a) Distortion measures of the first stage matches occurring during the successive learning of object 2. **b)** Assignments of views to classes resulting from the learn-process.

Fig. 9: Objects used for training. Each object was presented as a sequence of 25 views which shows a complete rotation of the object about the vertical axis. Object 1 is depicted in Fig. 5a. **a)** Object 2. **b)** Object 3.

current input (first matching stage). The grey level corresponds to the distortion measure assigned to the grid of this match. Dotted fields in the upper right part denote views which have not been included into the set of model views yet. As expected most matches lie on the main diagonal of the table and indicate highest similarity with the directly preceding view which has just been stored into the model database.

The mean of the distortion measures on the diagonal is 0.98, whereas especially aberrant matches show higher values. If one sets the admissible distortion to a value less than the mean, the system will be allowed to combine similar views into a common view class as shown by Fig. 8b. It is noteworthy that slightly changed distortion mea-

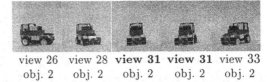

view 26	view 28	**view 31**	**view 31**	view 33
obj. 2	obj. 2	obj. 2	obj. 2	obj. 2

Fig. 10: Example of the classification of a view sequence belonging to object 2. The resulting view classes and their assignment to objects are shown below.

sures can result from the adaptation of the stored views to one another dependent on the chosen learn rate.

The following example will demonstrate the processes of learning and recognition for three similar objects. Note that the resemblance between the objects intentionally sets the system a difficult task. Therefore, we have to expect that some misclassifications will occur on the view level. They elucidate why it is necessary to consider sequences instead of single views.

The system was trained for the objects depicted in Fig. 5a and Fig. 9. Learning created a total of 55 view classes for the storage of 75 training views. The classes are almost evenly spread over the three objects (17, 18, 20 classes respectively). The presentation of the test sequence illustrated in Fig. 10 demonstrates the advantages of the temporal context. Despite of an ambiguous view (view 31) appearing twice in the sequence, the knowledge about the preceding views still allows a reliable recognition of the object.

Fig. 11: Example of the classification of view sequence belonging to object 3. **a)** Presented test sequence of object 3. **b)** Representatives of the view classes matching each view of a). The second and the fourth view have been erroneously mapped onto similar views of other objects. The third image yields a wrong view class of the corresponding object. **c)** Classification output, which is stable despite of the misclassified views.

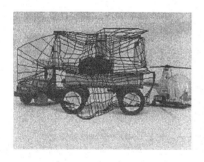

Fig. 12: Example for the recognition of object 3 within a cluttered scene. The correspondence grid is overlayed over the scene.

In addition to the manageability of uncertain views, an object recognition based on sequences facilitates an improved tolerance against misclassifications of single views: Figure 11 shows a test sequence of object 3 together with the views matching each input image. Although two of five views (2nd and 4th view) are mapped onto an incorrect object, the outputs resulting from the sequence classification yield the actual object class over all inputs.

A test with cluttered scenes is depicted in Fig. 12. After approx. 2000 iteration steps the correspondence grid is unfolded and positioned over the known object. Some distortions can be noted. However, they are restricted to the boundary nodes and still allow to localize the object within the scene. The effects of occlusion can be handled similarily. Further investigations of these aspects are currently in progress.

4.2 Comparison with Related Work

We have presented an image processing system for the recognition of three-dimensional objects which is based on the approach of viewer centred representations and on the utilization of temporal associations between the views.

To our knowledge the outlined architecture is unique with respect to the combination of its modules while particular elements were adapted from different known approaches. However, most implementations of viewer centred representations include a direct mapping of view classes onto objects and neglect the temporal order of the image sequences. As an example of such a system we have already mentioned the VIEWNET architecture of Grossberg and Bradski (1995). Figure 13 depicts the trained weights of some view classes generated by the Fuzzy-ARTMAP classifier of the VIEWNET system.

Due to an insufficient position invariance, training creates many similar classes (e. g. class 1, 2, 4, 7, and 9) and causes a proliferation of the number of classes. Moreover, the usage of the Fuzzy-AND operation produces serious „deletion effects": The rotation of an object shows several similar images in succession matching the same class. This class is then trained to store the intersection of the subsequent views. Hence, the rotation of the plane yields classes which represent a virtual

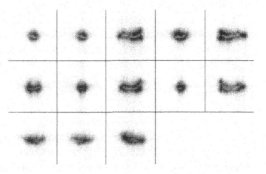

Fig. 13: View classes created by a VIEWNET architecture. The system has been trained for the views of an airplane as depicted in Fig. 1.

image formed by the central region of the object. However, the implied instability of the view classes will obviously impede a reliable definition of sequence classes.

The Dynamic Link Matching developed by von der Malsburg et al. deals with the achievement of position invariance and robustness against distortion but requires that all model views are of the same size and manually aligned (e. g. the application to face recognition needed the eyes in all the stored faces to be placed at corresponding positions). Furthermore, recent publications focus on the computationally more expensive formulation of the DLM in terms of dynamical equations whereas our system still relies on the faster FDLM algorithm. Above all, the DLM architectures contain no mechanism for an automated learning of the models. The only report of an automatic model acquisition is given by von der Malsburg and Reiser (1995) where the attempt is made to map all the views of an object onto a single model view. However, the applicability of this approach seems questionable and is not in agreement with the concept of viewer centred representations proposed here.

With respect to the classification of sequences a comparable system can be found in Bradski and Grossberg (1993), which is based on a Fuzzy-ART network. This implementation has the same drawback of a deletion effect analogous with the one explained in the context of view classes: If a sequence misses out a view even once, this view will be deleted from the stored sequence class and will never be added to this class again.

Darrell and Pentland (1993) present a system for the processing of view sequences. The employed image processing algorithms, however, are quite simple. Moreover, training and recognition require an alignment, called dynamic time warping, of the current input sequence and all the known sequences.

4.3 Further Development

We are planning to increase the performance of the system with respect to speed as well as concerning its recognition capabilities. Another important aspect is the development of a benchmark test which provides an appropriate image database for a quantitative comparison of efficiency and accuracy. Currently none of the mentioned references offers such a set of input patterns applicable for testing our recognition system. The test sets either do not contain sequences or images without interior structure of the objects.

The results, presented here, indicate that some misclassifications originate from the subsampling rates. As the usage of an increased resolution comes along with considerably longer response times, certain mechanisms for a speed-up must be implemented. The replacement of the fixed stop criterion of the DLM by a measure which dynamically ends the recognition process seems promising. Furthermore, the use of additional features is possible without changing the architecture and should be investigated in the future. Another extension will be the embedding of the recognition system into an active stereo vision environment. Extracting information about motion and depth will enable the segmentation of the scene into regions of interest and thus speed up the recognition process. Moreover, by tracking the objects the system will be allowed to observe moving objects on its own instead of being dependent on artificially created training sequences.

References

Biederman, I. (1985): Human image understanding: Recent research and a theory. *Comput. Vision Graphics Image Processing* 32: 29–73.

Bradski, G.; Carpenter, G. and Grossberg, S. (1992): Working memory networks for learning temporal order with application to three-dimensional visual object recognition. *Neural Comput.* 4: 270–286.

Bradski, G. and Grossberg, S. (1993): Fast learning VIEWNET architectures for recognizing 3-D objects from multiple 2-D views. Technical Report CAS/CNS-TR-93-053, Boston Univ., Boston, MA.

Carpenter, G.; Grossberg, S.; Markuzon, N.; Reynolds, J. and Rosen, D. (1992): Fuzzy ARTMAP: A neural network architecture for incremental supervised learning of analog multidimensional maps. *IEEE Trans. Neural Networks* 3(5): 698–713.

Darrell, T. and Pentland, A. (1993): Recognition of space-time gestures using a distributed representation. In R. Mammone (ed.), *Artificial neural networks for speech and vision*. London: Chapman & Hall, pp. 502–519.

Edelman, S. and Weinshall, D. (1991): A self-organizing multiple-view representation of 3D objects. *Biol. Cybern.* 64: 209–219.

Grossberg, S. and Bradski, G. (1995): VIEWNET architectures for invariant 3-D object recognition from multiple views. In B. Bouchon-meunier; R. Yager and L. Zadeh (eds.), *Fuzzy logic and soft computing*. Singapore: World Scientific Publishing.

Koenderink, J. and van Doorn, A. (1979): The internal representation of solid shape with respect to vision. *Biol. Cybern.* 32: 211–216.

Konen, W.; Maurer, T. and von der Malsburg, C. (1994): A fast link matching algorithm for invariant pattern recognition. *Neural Networks* 7: 1019–1030.

Lowe, D. G. (1986): *Perceptual organization and visual recognition*. Boston: Kluwer.

Marr, D. and Nishihara, H. K. (1978): Representation and recognition of the spatial organization of three-dimensional shapes. *Proc. R. Soc. Lond.* 200: 269–294.

Matsakis, Y.; Berthoz, A.; Lipschits, M. and Gurfinkel, V. (1990): Mental rotation of three-dimensional shapes in microgravity. In *Proc. Fourth European Symposium on Life Sciences in Space*. ESA, pp. 625–629.

Metzler, J. and Shepard, R. (1974): Transformational studies of the internal representaion of three-dimensional objects. In R. Solso (ed.), *Theories in cognitive psychology: The Loyola Symposium*. Erlbaum.

Miyashita, Y. (1988): Neuronal correlate of visual associative long-term memory in the primate temporal cortex. *Nature* 335: 817–820.

Perrett, D.; Harries, M.; Benson, P.; Chitty, A. and Mistlin, A. (1990): Retrieval of structure from rigid and biological motion: An analysis of the visual responses of neurones in the Macaque temporal cortex. In A. Blake and T. Troscianko (eds.), *AI and the Eye*, chap. 8. Wiley & Sons, pp. 181–200.

Perrett, D.; Oram, M.; Harries, M.; Bevan, R.; Hietanen, J.; Benson, P. and Thomas, S. (1991): Viewer-centred and object-centred coding of heads in the macaque tempral cortex. *Experimental Brain Research* 86: 159–173.

Poggio, T. and Edelman, S. (1990): A network that learns to recognize three-dimensional objects. *Nature* 343: 263–266.

Sakai, K. and Miyashita, Y. (1991): Neural organization for the long-term memory of paired associates. *Nature* 354: 152–155.

Sarle, W. (1995): Why statisticians should not FART. ftp://ftp.sas.com/pub/ neural/fart.doc.

Seibert, M. and Waxman, A. (1992): Adaptive 3-D object recognition from multiple views. *IEEE Trans. Pattern Anal. and Machine Intel.* 14(2): 107–124.

Stryker, M. P. (1991): Temporal associations. *Nature* 354: 108–109.

Sumi, S. (1984): Upside-down presentation of the Johansson moving light-spot pattern. *Perception* 13: 283–286.

Tanaka, K. (1996): Inferotemporal cortex and object vision. *Annu. Rev. Neurosci.* 19: 109–139.

Thompson, D. W. and Mundy, J. L. (1987): Three dimensional model matching from an unconstrained viewpoint. In *Proc. IEEE Int. Conf. Robotics and Automation*. Raleigh, NC: IEEE, pp. 208–220.

Ullman, S. and Basri, R. (1991): Recognition by linear combinations of models. *IEEE Trans. Pattern Anal. and Machine Intel.* 13(10): 992–1006.

von der Malsburg, C. (1981): The correlation theory of brain function. Internal report, Max-Planck-Institut für Biophysikalische Chemie, Göttingen.

von der Malsburg, C. and Reiser, K. (1995): Pose invariant object recognition in a neural system. In *Proc. Int. Conf. on Artificial Neural Networks ICANN*. pp. 127–132.

Wallis, G. (in press): Temporal order in human object recognition learning. *To appear in Journal of Biological Systems* .

Williamson, J. (1996): Gaussian ARTMAP: A neural network for fast incremental learning of noisy multidimensional maps. *Neural Networks* 9(5): 881–897.

Wiskott, L. and von der Malsburg, C. (1996): Face recognition by Dynamic Link Matching. Internal Report IR-INI 96-05, Inst. f. Neuroinformatik, Ruhr-Univ. Bochum.

Würtz, R. (1994): *Multilayer dynamic link networks for establishing image point correspondences and visual object recognition*. Ph.D. thesis, Ruhr-Univ. Bochum.

Model-Based Recognition of 3D Objects from One View

Isaac Weiss* and Manjit Ray

Center for Automation Research, University of Maryland,
College Park, MD 20742-3275, USA
weiss@cfar.umd.edu

Abstract. In this work we treat major problems of object recognition which have previously received little attention. Among them are the loss of depth information in the projection from 3D to 2D, and the complexity of finding feature correspondences in general cases. This treatment enables us to recognize objects in difficult real-world situations.

It is well known that there are no geometric invariants of a projection from 3D to 2D. However, given some modeling assumptions about the 3D object, such invariants can be found. The modeling assumptions can be either a particular model or a generic assumption about a class of models. Here we deal with both situations. We find invariant connections between a 2D image and a 3D model under general projective projection. We give a geometric interpretation of the method as an invariant model in 3D invariant space, illuminated by invariant light rays, converging to an invariant camera center in the same space. We demonstrate the method on real images.

This work differs from related work in the following ways: 1) Most work in invariants has concentrated on transformations of the same dimensionality, mainly 2D to 2D projections. We deal here with the problem of projecting a 3D object onto a 2D image, which is of greater relevance to object recognition. 2) Much of the previous work is done on multiple images, such as the work on camera calibration. This usually requires knowledge of the correspondence between images. We concentrate on single images, but we also apply our method to finding correspondences in multiple images without prior knowledge or expensive search.

Keywords: object recognition, model based vision, invariants

1 Introduction

Almost all the work on invariants so far has been concerned with transformations between spaces of equal dimensionality, e.g. [31,32,19]. In the single-view case, invariants were found for the projection of a planar shape onto the image,

---
* The author is grateful for the support of the Air Force Office of Scientific Research under grant F49620-92-J-0332, the Defense Advanced Research Projects Agency (DARPA Order No. E655) and Air Force Wright Laboratory under Grant F49620-96-1-0355, and the Office of Naval Research under Grant N00014-95-1-0521.

although the planar shape was embedded in 3D. For real 3D objects, most of the work has involved multiple views with known correspondence, which amounts to a 3D to 3D projection. Yet, humans have little problem recognizing a 3D object from a single 2D image.

This recognition ability cannot be based on pure geometry, since it has been shown (e.g. [6]) that there are no geometric invariants of a projection from 3D to 2D. Thus, when we only have 2D geometric information, we need to use some modeling assumptions to recover the 3D shape.

There are several possibilities for a modelling assumption. The simplest one is having a library of specific 3D models. In theory there could be many models that project into the same image, so an object cannot be identified uniquely. In practice, however, in most cases there is only one or very few models in the database that would project to the same image, so it is possible to recognize them.

Another possibility is to have more generic assumptions, rather than specific models. One such assumption can be that the visible object is symmetric in 3D. More general assuptions for curved objects were studied in [36]. In this paper we deal mainly with the two assumptions mentioned above, namely specific models and symmetry. To a lesser extent we use other assumptions, such as that a vanishing point in a 2D image indicates parallel lines in 3D.

The outline of our recognition method is as follows. We define a 3D invariant space, namely a space with three invariant coordinates I_1, I_2, I_3. Given a 3D model, we can extract a set of such invariant triplets from it, so it can be represented as a set of points in the invariant space. Given an image of the model, the depth information is lost so the invariant point cannot be recovered. However, we show that we can draw a set of "invariant light rays" in 3D, each ray passing through a 3D invariant model point (Fig. 1). When enough rays intersect the model points in 3D, we can safely assume that the model is indeed the one visible in the image. We do not need to search for correspondences. We can also see that the rays converge at a point in the invariant space that represents the location of the camera center with respect to the model. Thus it is easy to find the pose of the model. Given this, we can project the original (non-invariant) model onto the image. That makes it possible to perform a more exact match between the model projection and the given image of the object.

In summary, the invariant modeling assumption and the object descriptors make it possible to perform recognition regardless of viewpoint and with no need for a search for correspondence.

The use of modeling for shape recovery from single images is of course not new. However, most of the earlier work was not concerned with viewpoint invariance. Some recent research does use invariance in modeling. However, most of it uses very specific modeling assumptions that cannot be applied to general shapes. A major example is the assumption that the objects are composed of "general cylinders" [4,37] of various forms. The invariance and generality of this assumption are limited. A subset of this is the assumption that the object is a surface of revolution [38]. Another assumption is that various corners visible in the image are right-angled in 3D [11]. Yet another approach is to assume that it is sufficient to characterize an object by special local properties such as tangencies and inflection points [30]. Of course this ignores the information available between the inflection points.

The above examples represent only a small part of the quite active research on invariants. However, unlike our interest here, most of the recent activity is concerned not with single images but with multiple images. These methods can recover the 3D geometry without modeling. However, they require knowledge of the correspondence between features in the different images. Correspondence is a difficult and generally unsolved problem, leading to a high-dimensional search space. Among such methods are those using the trilinear tensor [22,2,18]. They require finding a substantial number of corresponding points and lines in at least three images. This can be accomplished only for very small disparities. Much of the multiple image work is intended for camera calibration, e.g [9,17,29], rather than object recognition. Techniques for multiple images have been applied to a single image, when "repetitive" or symmetric structures can be found in it [8,38,23]. These parts can be viewed as separate images, but the correspondence between their features still needs to be found. We can deal with both symmetric and non-symmetric objects in a single image, without correspondence.

Work that directly connects 2D and 3D quantitative invariants was done in [12] and [26]. That work comsidered affine point-sets only, while here we derive the projective case as well. They did not use modeling assumptions, and therefore a 3D shape could not be recognized uniquely.

There is also considerable research on curves. Differential projective geometry was used for plane curves in e.g. [33,19,34,5,20,28]. More specialized approaches, including the use of pairs of co-planar conics, can be found in [25,27,3,21,16,13]. More general 3D curves were studied in [36].

2 Point Set Invariants

2.1 General Dependencies among Invariants

Here we describe our method of connecting 3D and 2D invariants by applying it to point sets. We rederive all the results in [26] in a much simpler way, using elementary algebra rather than algebraic geometry. We then add the new projective case.

We denote 3D world coordinates by $\mathbf{X}$, and 2D image coordinates by $\mathbf{x}$. We have five points $\mathbf{X}_i$, $i = 1, \ldots, 5$ in 3D space, of which at least the first four are not coplanar. They are projected into $\mathbf{x}_i$ in the image. The correspondence is assumed to be known for now. In a 3D projective or affine space, five points cannot be linearly independent. We can express the fifth point as a linear combination of the first four:

$$\mathbf{X}_5 = a\mathbf{X}_1 + b\mathbf{X}_2 + c\mathbf{X}_3 + d\mathbf{X}_4 \tag{1}$$

In the projective case the coefficients a, b, c, d are not uniquely determined because the point coordinates can be multiplied by an arbitrary factor. In the affine case, the coefficients are constrained by the requirement that the fourth homogeneous coordinate is always 1, again leaving only three independent coefficients. Because the projection from 3D to 2D is linear (in homogeneous coordinates), the same dependence holds in 2D:

$$\mathbf{x}_5 = a\mathbf{x}_1 + b\mathbf{x}_2 + c\mathbf{x}_3 + d\mathbf{x}_4$$

Since determinants are relative invariants of a projective or affine transformation, we look at the determinants formed by these points in both 3D and 2D. Any four of the five points in 3D, expressed in four homogeneous coordinates, can form a determinant M_i. We can give the determinant the same index as the fifth point that was left out. For example,

$$M_1 = |\mathbf{X}_2, \mathbf{X}_3, \mathbf{X}_4, \mathbf{X}_5|$$

Similarly, in the 2D projection, any three of the five points can form a determinant m_{ij}, with indices equal to those of the points that were left out, e.g.

$$m_{12} = |\mathbf{x}_3, \mathbf{x}_4, \mathbf{x}_5|$$

Since the points are not independent, neither are the determinants. Substituting the linear dependence (1) in M_1 above we obtain

$$M_1 = a|\mathbf{X}_2, \mathbf{X}_3, \mathbf{X}_4, \mathbf{X}_1| + b|\mathbf{X}_2, \mathbf{X}_3, \mathbf{X}_4, \mathbf{X}_2| + c|\mathbf{X}_2, \mathbf{X}_3, \mathbf{X}_4, \mathbf{X}_3| + d|\mathbf{X}_2, \mathbf{X}_3, \mathbf{X}_4, \mathbf{X}_4|$$

As is well known, a determinant with two equal columns vanishes. Also, when columns are interchanged in a determinant, the sign of the determinant is reversed. Therefore we obtain

$$M_1 = a|\mathbf{X}_2, \mathbf{X}_3, \mathbf{X}_4, \mathbf{X}_1| = -a|\mathbf{X}_1, \mathbf{X}_2, \mathbf{X}_3, \mathbf{X}_4| = -aM_5$$

Similarly for the other determinants, with a simplified notation:

$$M_2 = |1,3,4,5| = b|1,3,4,2| = b|1,2,3,4| = bM_5$$
$$M_3 = |1,2,4,5| = c|1,2,4,3| = -c|1,2,3,4| = -cM_5$$
$$M_4 = |1,2,3,5| = d|1,2,3,4| = dM_5$$

The coefficients a, b, c, d can now be expressed as invariants, using the above relations:

$$a = -\frac{M_1}{M_5}, \qquad b = \frac{M_2}{M_5}, \qquad c = -\frac{M_3}{M_5}, \qquad d = \frac{M_4}{M_5} \qquad (2)$$

This is the standard solution for a, b, c, d as unknowns in eq. (1).

Similar relations hold in the 2D projection:

$$m_{12} = |3,4,5| = a|3,4,1| + b|3,4,2| = a|1,3,4| + b|2,3,4| = am_{25} + bm_{15} \quad (3)$$

$$m_{13} = |2,4,5| = a|2,4,1| + c|2,4,3| = am_{35} - cm_{15} \quad (4)$$

$$m_{14} = |2,3,5| = a|2,3,1| + d|2,3,4| = am_{45} + dm_{15} \quad (5)$$

Other relations are linearly dependent on these.

2.2 Relation between 3D and 2D Invariants — Affine Case

In the affine case the coefficients a, b, c, d are absolute invariants. Therefore we can substitute the a, b, c, d found in 3D, eq. (2), directly into the 2D equations above. We obtain three relations between the 3D and the 2D invariants:

$$M_5 m_{12} + M_1 m_{25} - M_2 m_{15} = 0 \qquad (6)$$
$$M_5 m_{13} + M_1 m_{35} - M_3 m_{15} = 0 \qquad (7)$$
$$M_5 m_{14} + M_1 m_{45} - M_4 m_{15} = 0 \qquad (8)$$

These relations are obviously invariant to any affine transformation in both 3D and 2D. A 3D transformation will merely multiply all the M_i by the same constant factor, which drops out of the equations. A 2D affine transformation multiplies all the m_{ij} by the same constant factor, which again drops out. However, in the projective case each point can be independently multiplied by an arbitrary factor λ_i, which does not in general drop out. Thus the above relation is affine but not projective invariant.

The above relations become linearly dependent so that only two of them are meaningful. To see this, we first note a relationship between the M_i which exists only in the affine case. We can write a determinant involving all five points as

$$\begin{vmatrix} x_1 & x_2 & x_3 & x_4 & x_5 \\ y_1 & y_2 & y_3 & y_4 & y_5 \\ z_1 & z_2 & z_3 & z_4 & z_5 \\ 1 & 1 & 1 & 1 & 1 \\ 1 & 1 & 1 & 1 & 1 \end{vmatrix} = 0$$

The M_i are minors of this determinant so we can write the above equation as

$$M_1 - M_2 + M_3 - M_4 + M_5 = 0 \qquad (9)$$

This is equivalent to writing $a + b + c + d = 1$ in eq. (1), which ensures that the last coordinate equals 1.

Similar relations can be derived in 2D. We have

$$\begin{vmatrix} x_2 & x_3 & x_4 & x_5 \\ y_2 & y_3 & y_4 & y_5 \\ 1 & 1 & 1 & 1 \\ 1 & 1 & 1 & 1 \end{vmatrix} = 0$$

leading to the relation

$$m_{12} - m_{13} + m_{14} - m_{15} = 0$$

Similarly, from the determinant involving points 1,2,3,4 we obtain the relation

$$m_{15} - m_{25} + m_{35} - m_{45} = 0$$

We now look at the following linear combination of the invariant relations, eqs. (6),(7),(8):

$$(6)-(7)+(8) = M_5(m_{12}-m_{13}+m_{14})+M_1(m_{25}-m_{35}+m_{45})+(-M_2+M_3-M_4)m_{15} = 0$$

Using the two relations above between the m_{ij} we obtain

$$m_{15}(M_1 - M_2 + M_3 - M_4 + M_5) = 0$$

which is an identity, due the the relation between the M_i above. Thus, only two invariant relations, say (6),(7), are independent.

Similar results for this particular case can be obtained using Grassmannians, Schubert cycles and wedge-products [26]. These methods are hard to extend much beyond this point.

2.3 Relations between 3D and 2D Absolute Affine Invariants

It is easy now to derive the relation between the 3D and 2D absolute invariants. We define the 3D absolute invariants

$$I_1 = \frac{M_1}{M_5}, \quad I_2 = \frac{M_2}{M_5}, \quad I_3 = \frac{M_3}{M_5}$$

and the 2D absolute invariants

$$i_{12} = \frac{m_{12}}{m_{15}}, \quad i_{13} = \frac{m_{13}}{m_{15}}, \quad i_{25} = \frac{m_{25}}{m_{15}}, \quad i_{35} = \frac{m_{35}}{m_{15}}$$

and obtain the following theorem:

Theorem 1. *Given five points $\mathbf{X}_i$ in 3D, at least four of which are non-coplanar, the relation between their 3D and 2D absolute affine invariants is given by*

$$i_{12} + I_1 i_{25} - I_2 = 0 \tag{10}$$

$$i_{13} + I_1 i_{35} - I_3 = 0 \tag{11}$$

Proof: Divide eqs. (6),(7) by M_5 and m_{15} (assuming these do not vanish).

Given the 2D projection of a five-point set, we have thus obtained two equations for the three unknown 3D invariants I_1, I_2, I_3. Since all three invariants are needed to recover the five points in 3D (up to an affine transformation), we can recover the 3D quintuple only up to one free parameter.

A geometric interpretation and applications are described in the next section.

2.4 Points and Directions

Rather than dealing with a point, we can deal with a *direction*, namely a unit vector in 3D pointing in a certain direction. This can represent a direction of a major axis of the model or a direction of the camera axis.

A direction is equivalent to a point on the infinite plane and can be written as $(x, y, z, 0)$, i.e. with a vanishing fourth coordinate. It will remain at infinity under affine transformation. Thus, the derivation leading to eqs. (6),(7),(8) remains valid. However, eq. (9) needs to be modified. For a direction $\mathbf{X}_4$ we can write the determinant

$$\begin{vmatrix} x_1 & x_2 & x_3 & x_4 & x_5 \\ y_1 & y_2 & y_3 & y_4 & y_5 \\ z_1 & z_2 & z_3 & z_4 & z_5 \\ 1 & 1 & 1 & 0 & 1 \\ 1 & 1 & 1 & 0 & 1 \end{vmatrix} = 0$$

in which M_i are the minors and we immediately obtain

$$M_1 - M_2 + M_3 + M_5 = 0$$

The constraints on m_{ij} also change, but it is easy to show that we again obtain a linear dependency among eqs. (6),(7),(8). Thus, Theorem 1 is still valid. A direction vector can be multiplied by an arbitrary constant, but $\mathbf{X}_4, \mathbf{x}_4$ are common to all terms in the equations and thus their factors drop out.

2.5   The Projective Case

Our method is easily extended to the projective case, yielding new simple results such as Theorem 2 below. This case is more difficult because in "real" (Cartesian) coordinates the projective transformation is non-linear, causing other approaches [1,15] to be quite cumbersome.

We start with the 3D quantities. To obtain invariants we need at least six points, having three projective invariants. We now have two linear dependencies rather than one:

$$\lambda_5 \mathbf{X}_5 = a\lambda_1 \mathbf{X}_1 + b\lambda_2 \mathbf{X}_2 + c\lambda_3 \mathbf{X}_3 + d\lambda_4 \mathbf{X}_4$$

$$\lambda_6 \mathbf{X}_6 = a'\lambda_1 \mathbf{X}_1 + b'\lambda_2 \mathbf{X}_2 + c'\lambda_3 \mathbf{X}_3 + d'\lambda_4 \mathbf{X}_4$$

with λ_i being arbitrary scalar factors. We now have two sets of four equations with four unknowns each. The two sets of unknowns are $a\lambda_1/\lambda_5, \cdots, d\lambda_4/\lambda_5$ and $a'\lambda_1/\lambda_6, \cdots, d'\lambda_4/\lambda_6$. The solutions are similar to eqs. (2):

$$a\frac{\lambda_1}{\lambda_5} = -\frac{M_1}{M_5}, \qquad b\frac{\lambda_2}{\lambda_5} = \frac{M_2}{M_5}, \qquad c\frac{\lambda_3}{\lambda_5} = -\frac{M_3}{M_5}, \qquad d\frac{\lambda_4}{\lambda_5} = \frac{M_4}{M_5} \qquad (12)$$

$$a'\frac{\lambda_1}{\lambda_6} = -\frac{M_1'}{M_5}, \qquad b'\frac{\lambda_2}{\lambda_6} = \frac{M_2'}{M_5}, \qquad c'\frac{\lambda_3}{\lambda_6} = -\frac{M_3'}{M_5}, \qquad d'\frac{\lambda_4}{\lambda_6} = \frac{M_4'}{M_5} \qquad (13)$$

with M_i' denoting determinants in which $\mathbf{X}_5$ is replaced by $\mathbf{X}_6$. Unlike the affine case, these solutions are not invariant. However, we can find cross ratios of them which are absolute projective invariants, i.e. cross ratios that eliminate all the λ_i:

$$I_1 = \frac{ab'}{a'b} = \frac{M_1 M_2'}{M_1' M_2}, \quad I_2 = \frac{ac'}{a'c} = \frac{M_1 M_3'}{M_1' M_3}, \quad I_3 = \frac{ad'}{a'd} = \frac{M_1 M_4'}{M_1' M_4} \qquad (14)$$

We turn now to the 2D quantities. Our unknown quantities can be written in terms of 2D relative invariants, similarly to eqs. (3),(4),(5), with the first unknown being a free parameter μ:

$$a\frac{\lambda_1}{\lambda_5} = \mu$$

$$b\frac{\lambda_2}{\lambda_5} = \frac{1}{m_{15}}(m_{12} - \mu m_{25})$$

$$c\frac{\lambda_3}{\lambda_5} = \frac{-1}{m_{15}}(m_{13} - \mu m_{35})$$

$$d\frac{\lambda_4}{\lambda_5} = \frac{1}{m_{15}}(m_{14} - \mu m_{45})$$

Similar equations hold for a', b', c', d', with μ', m'_{ij}, λ_6 replacing μ, m_{ij}, λ_5.

We can now eliminate the λ_i on the left hand sides above using the same cross ratios as in the 3D case, eq. (14). We obtain

$$I_1 = \frac{ab'}{a'b} = \frac{\mu(m'_{12} - \mu'm_{25})}{\mu'(m_{12} - \mu m_{25})}$$

$$I_2 = \frac{ac'}{a'c} = \frac{\mu(m'_{13} - \mu'm_{35})}{\mu'(m_{13} - \mu m_{35})}$$

$$I_3 = \frac{ad'}{a'd} = \frac{\mu(m'_{14} - \mu'm_{45})}{\mu'(m_{14} - \mu m_{45})}$$

This is a simple quadric surface in invariant space, parametrized by μ, μ':

$$\mu m'_{12} - I_1\mu'm_{12} + \mu\mu'(I_1 - 1)m_{25} = 0$$
$$\mu m'_{13} - I_2\mu'm_{13} + \mu\mu'(I_2 - 1)m_{35} = 0$$
$$\mu m'_{14} - I_3\mu'm_{14} + \mu\mu'(I_3 - 1)m_{45} = 0$$

It is easy to eliminate the terms proportional to μ, μ'. The remaining (last above) equation is devided by $\mu\mu'm_{12}m'_{13}m'_{14}m_{25}$. Defining now the 2D projective invariant cross ratios

$$i_1 = \frac{m'_{12}m_{14}}{m_{12}m'_{14}} \qquad i_2 = \frac{m'_{12}m_{35}}{m'_{13}m_{25}} \qquad i_3 = \frac{m'_{12}m_{13}}{m_{12}m'_{13}} \qquad i_4 = \frac{m'_{12}m_{45}}{m'_{14}m_{25}}$$

we finally obtain:

Theorem 2. *The 3D absolute projective invariants of six generic points in 3D are given in terms of 2D invariants as*

$$I_3(I_2-1)i_1i_2 - I_3(I_1-1)i_1 - I_1(I_2-1)i_2 = I_2(I_3-1)i_3i_4 - I_2(I_1-1)i_3 - I_1(I_3-1)i_4$$
$$(15)$$

3 Applications

We will apply the above results to recognize 3D objects invariantly. For this purpose, we build a 3D invariant space in which recognition will take place. Each 3D 5-tuple is represented as a point in this space, with invariant coordinates I_1, I_2, I_3 (Fig 1). A 3D model is represented by a set of points in this space. (There is also some way of identifying these points as part of the same model.) The problem now is how to match the image to the model. We will distinguish several applications. They will be described using the affine approximation, but we will show later that the projective case needs only a small modification, requiring only 5-tuples.

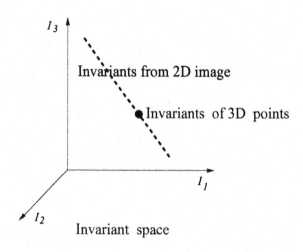

Fig. 1. Invariant space

1) **Single image.** Since the depth information is lost in this case, we cannot recognize an object without having a model. The simplest model can consist of five points in space, giving rise to three invariants I_1, I_2, I_3. These can be represented as a point in the 3D invariant space. (Of course a realistic model will consist of many such points). To recognize the model in the image, we extract 5-tuples of features from the image and calculate their 2D invariants $i_{\alpha\beta}$. Using Theorem 1 (or 2), we have two equations relating the three 3D invariants I_1, I_2, I_3. Geometrically, we obtain a space line in our 3D invariant space. If a 5-tuple in the 2D image is a projection of some 5-tuple in 3D, then the line obtained from this 2D 5-tuple will pass through the point in invariant space representing the 3D 5-tuple (Fig. 1). That is, we have found the correspondence between the 2D and 3D 5-tuples. A different view of the 5-tuple will give rise to a different line in 3D, but still passing through the same point. To recognize objects we thus look for instances in which lines obtained from the image pass through points representing models in the invariant 3D space.

2) **Multiple images.** Although we concentrate on single views, multiple view applications are also valuable. For instance it helps in the symmetry case (described next) which can be regarded as multiple views. Here we do not need a model to recover the depth information, only for the identification. We use our method to find correspondences between the images. We first extract a 5-tuple of features from one of the images and transform it into a line in the 3D invariant space.

Next, we look at a different image, in which objects are seen from a different viewpoint. Again we draw a line in the same 3D space of invariants as before. If this line meets the first line in 3D then the two 5-tuples have the same 3D invariants I_i. These are the coordinates of the intersection point. This means that the two 5-tuples are affine equivalent. (We later generalize to the projective case). This in turn indicates that we may have two different views of the same 5-tuple. Again, we have found a correspondence between 5-tuples, this time between two views.

With n 5-tuples, the total number of lines in the invariant space is $O(n)$. We can find line intersections in a way similar to that used in Hough space, namely divide the space into bins and see if a certain bin has more than one line going through it. We do not need to check all bins; we only need to go along the known lines. A hierarchical scale space approach can be used to make the process more efficient. This brings our total complexity closer to $O(n)$ rather than $O(n^2)$ as in previous methods.

Based on the above discussion, our recognition algorithm involves the following steps:

i) Feature extraction. Find candidate 5-tuples that are potentially affine (or projective) equivalent. Various clues can be used to prune unpromising sets, e.g. non-matching links that are visible between the points, or parallelism.

ii) Invariant description. For each 5-tuple that remains from (1), calculate the two equations for the three 3D invariants, namely plot a line in a 3D invariant space. Find all lines that meet in 3D. Each intersection represents the 3D affine invariants of two affine equivalent 5-tuples. An object will be represented by several such intersection points.

iii) Recognition. We now have invariant 3D point sets representing various visible objects. Similarly, the models in the database can be represented by point sets in the same invariant 3D space. We can use several 5-tuples in each model, obtaining several points representing the model in the invariant space. Identification is now straightforward. If an object's point set falls on a model's point set in the invariant space, than the object is identified with the model. No search is needed for the right model, because the invariant point sets of the models can be indexed according to their coordinates. No search is needed for the viewpoint or pose either because of the invariance. As many points as practical need to be used to increase reliability.

iv) Verification. This step is independent of the invariants method. It overcomes any errors that we may have in calculating the determinants I_i. Using the 2D coordinates of the images, and the correspondence found in (ii), we calculate the 3D coordinates of the features. Now we can find the 3D transformation (pose) that produces the best fit between the 3D object and the model identified in (iii), using least squares fitting. The identification is rejected if the fitting error is too big. We may try to fit several models to each object to find the best fit.

3) **Single image, symmetric models.** The problem encountered earlier in the single-image case was the unknown parameter along the space line, resulting from the missing depth information. Instead of using a model as was done in case (1), we can use a modeling *assumption*. One modeling assumption that we use is symmetry. Most man-made objects are symmetric, e.g. vehicles, tanks, airplanes and buildings. Symmetry is also found in human and animal bodies. The symmetry is observed explicitly only in a frontal view. In any other view the symmetry is observed as a skew-symmetry. Many researchers have used skew-symmetry for recognition, but with serious limitations. They usually assume that the skew-symmetry itself is known, i.e. we know which feature in one half of the object corresponds to which feature in the symmetric half. In other words, they assume that the correspondence problem has already been solved. Here we make no such assumption but detect the skew-symmetric objects in an image.

The two halves of a skew-symmetric object are affine equivalent. Therefore we can apply the algorithm described above which was designed to find affine equivalent 5-tuples. Having found matching 5-tuples, we have to verify that they are halves of the same object. The lines connecting corresponding points in a symmetric object are parallel in 3D, therefore they will be parallel in an affine projection, and this is easy to check.

The verification step (iv) is easier because of the symmetry assumption. The skew-symmetric object that we have found can be rectified, using an affine transformation, to obtain a standard view in which the object is (non-skew) symmetric. It can then be matched directly with a database of symmetric models.

4 Implementation Issues

Experiments performed so far with the method seem very encouraging. We have used only a small number of models, but the robustness to errors seems quite good, so that we can safely add more models.

During the implementation, a number of problems had to be overcome. We briefly summarize some of them here, along with their solutions.

1) Low level image processing. It is not the goal of this research to develop new methods of feature extraction. Rather, we use the model-based approach to overcome the problems inherent in feature detection. Nevertheless, the inadequacies of feature detection are so great that we must do some preprocessing before using our method. The positions of feature points are very inaccurate, so we have concentrated on finding lines and their intersections rather than points. However, we usually have far too many lines, most of which are irrelevant to the object (Fig. 2).

Solution: We keep only those lines that lie along *principal directions*. Most man-made objects such as vehicles and buildings have a small number of directions, e.g. major axes, to which most prominent lines are parallel. These are relatively easy to find. Fig. 3 (left) shows the lines left after the above pruning.

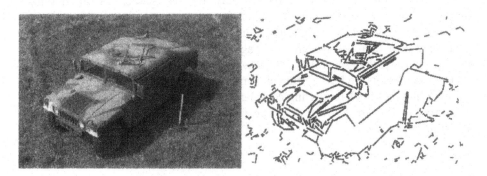

Fig. 2. Image and detected lines

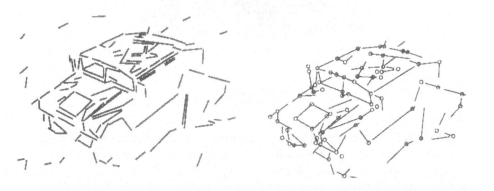

Fig. 3. Lines along principal directions (left), corner features (right).

2) Large numbers of 5-tuples. With the number of features in the hundreds, the number of all possible quintuples is on the order of 100^5, which is quite prohibitive.

Solution: We use only *connected* quintuples, i.e. 5-tuples whose member points are connected to each other by visible lines. Four points may be connected to form a (3D) corner, with one central point connected to three others, and the connections lying along principal directions. The fifth point can be any point connected to these four. Thus the number of possible quintuples (and invariants) is reduced to on the order of 10^3. Fig. 3 (right) shows the resulting corners.

3) Perspectivity. The affine (orthographic) approximation that we initially assumed was found to be inadequate in many cases. We had to use the full perspective treatment. However, this normally requires 7-point sets rather than the 5-point sets we have been using, which increases complexity significantly.

Solution: We use *vanishing points,* namely the points at which the lines along a principal direction intersect in the image. This is based on a (quite common) assumption that when several lines intersect in an image, they probably intersect in 3D as well. Thus we have obtained some known correspondences between 2D and 3D points without increasing complexity. The invariant calculation is quite insensitive to the exact location of the vanishing points. Fig. 4 illustrates the vanishing point method.

Fig. 4. Vanishing points

4) Finding intersections. Finding the point–line intersections in the 3D invariant space needs to be done efficiently, with low complexity. Given a line, we want to search for intersecting points only in the neighborhood of this line. For this purpose we can borrow methods from GIS (Geographic Information Systems). These types of problems have been solved there in the 2D case using quadtrees. We can extend these methods to 3D using octrees.

5   Experimental Results

5.1   Single Views

We show here results obtained from two different images of a HMMWV vehicle.

The first step is building a 3D model in the invariant space described earlier. We start from a "real" 3D model of a vehicle (downloaded from the Internet;

Fig. 5), and choose a "base" of four corner points on it. These can be assigned the coordinates of a standard affine coordinate base, namely

$$\mathbf{X}_1 = (1,0,0,1), \ \mathbf{X}_2 = (0,1,0,1), \ \mathbf{X}_3 = (0,0,1,1), \ \mathbf{X}_4 = (0,0,0,1)$$

The original model can be transformed by a unique affine transformation so that the four base points will take on the above values. This has no effect on our treatment since it is invariant. Doing that, any fifth point of the model is transformed to a point with some coordinates $\mathbf{X} = (X, Y, Z, 1)$.

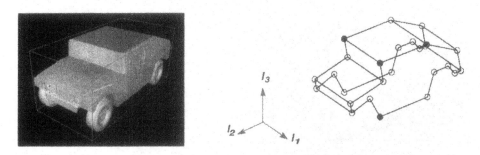

Fig. 5. Original and invariant models

It is easy to see that these new coordinates are in fact invariants. One way is to explicitly calculate the invariants as given earlier, to obtain

$$I_1 = X, \quad I_2 = Y, \quad I_3 = Z$$

Another way is to note that such a base is a standard, or canonical base that can always be obtained from any given affine transformed version of the model. That makes it an invariant base and any quantity expressed with respect to it is thus invariant.

The model we thus obtain in invariant space is shown in Fig 5 (right).

Next, given one view of the vehicle, we calculate the lines in 3D invariant space according to Theorem 2. The results for each view are shown in Fig 6.

An intersection of a line with a point in 3D means that a correspondence has been found between the 5-point set in the image, which gave rise to the line, and a 5-point set in the 3D model that gave rise to the point. In theory, we need only 6–7 feature correspondences. This is enough to calculate the pose (or camera coordinates). We can then project the model on the image and do a more detailed match. However, more intersections give higher reliability.

Reliability: We have obtained rather good results for the intersections (Fig. 6). Out of 13 lines that were supposed to intersect, 10 intersected within the error circles marked in the figure, two missed and one was a "coincidental" intersection. We have introduced an artificial error of 10% in the positions of the feature points, and have still obtained an acceptable number of 7–8 intersections.

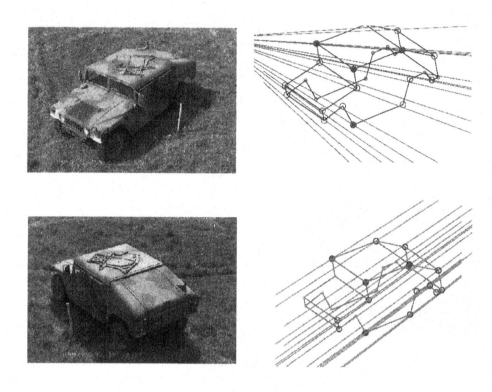

Fig. 6. Intersections in invariant space between image lines and model points, for each view.

The lines converge to a point representing the position of the camera center in invariant space, making it easy to calculate the pose. Thus the lines are in fact a representation of the light rays in invariant space.

5.2 Two Views

We have applied the method described above to find a correspondence between two views, without a model. Applications include: (1) "stereo" with widely differing images, such as the two views above; (ii) 3D model construction from 2D images.

The correspondences are found by drawing the lines in 3D invariant space generated by each image, and then finding the intersections between the space lines. A line intersection indicates that there is a correspondence between the appropriate 5-point sets from the two images. The intersection point is also a point of the unknown invariant 3D model.

6 Summary

We summarize our object recognition method as follows.
- Build a model in invariant 3D space.
- From 5-tuples in the image, draw lines in 3D space.
- Find intersections of the above lines with model points, tentatively identifying one or a few models.
- Find the pose and project the tentative model(s) on the image.
- Perform final matching and identification between the projected model(s) and the image.

References

1. E. Barrett. Personal communication.
2. P. Beardsley, P. Torr, and A. Zisserman. 3D Model Aquisition from Extended Image Sequences. *Proc. European Conf. on Computer Vision*, 683–695, 1996.
3. J. Ben-Arie, Z. Wang, and R. Rao. Iconic Recognition with Affine-Invariant Spectral Signatures. *Proc. ICPR A*, 672–676, 1996.
4. T.O. Binford and T.S. Levitt. Model-Based Recognition of Objects in Complex Scenes. *Proc. DARPA Image Understanding Workshop*, 89–100, 1996.
5. A. Bruckstein, E. Rivlin, and I. Weiss. Scale Space Invariants for Recognition. *Machine Vision and Applications*, **15**:335–344, 1997.
6. J.B. Burns, R. Weiss, and E.M. Riseman. View Variation of Point Set and Line Segment Features. *Proc. DARPA Image Understanding Workshop*, 650–659, 1990.
7. S. Carlsson. Relative Positioning from Model Indexing, *Image Vision Comut.*, **12**:179–186, 1994.
8. R.W. Curwen and J.L. Mundy. Grouping Planar Projective Symmetries. *Proc. DARPA Image Understanding Workshop*, 595–605, 1997.
9. R. Deriche, Z. Zhang, Q.T. Luong, and O.D. Faugeras. Robust Recovery of the Epipolar Geometry for an Uncalibrated Stereo Rig. *Proc. European Conf. on Computer Vision*, A567–576, 1994.
10. H. Guggenheimer. *Differential Geometry*. Dover, New York, 1963.
11. J.P. Hopcroft, D.P. Huttenlocher, and P.C. Wayner. Affine Invariants for Model-Based Recognition. In *Geometric Invariance in Machine Vision*, eds. J.L. Mundy and A. Zisserman, MIT Press, Cambridge, MA, 1992.
12. D. Jacobs. Space Efficient 3D Model Indexing. *Proc. IEEE Conf. on Computer Vision and Pattern Recognition*, 439–444, 1992.
13. D. Jacobs and R. Basri. 3-D to 2-D Recognition with Regions. *Proc. IEEE Conf. on Computer Vision and Pattern Recognition*, 547–553, 1997.
14. D. Keren, R. Rivlin, I. Shimshoni, and I. Weiss. Recognizing 3D Objects using Tactile Sensing and Curve Invariants. University of Maryland Technical Report CS-TR-3812, 1997.
15. S.J. Maybank. Relation between 3D Invariants and 2D Invariants. *Image Vision Comut.*, **16**:13–20, 1998.
16. P. Meer and I. Weiss. Point/Line Correspondence under Projective Transformations. *Proc. ICPR A*, 399-402, 1992.

732

17. R. Mohr, L. Quan, and F. Veillon. Relative 3D Reconstruction using Multiple Uncalibrated Images. *Intl. J. Robotics Research*, **14**:619–632, 1995.

18. S. Peleg, A. Shashua, D. Weinshall, M. Werman, and M. Irani. Multi-Sensor Representation of Extended Scenes using Multi-View Geometry. *Proc. DARPA Image Understanding Workshop*, 79–83, 1997.

19. E. Rivlin and I. Weiss. Local Invariants for Recognition. *IEEE Transactions on Pattern Analysis and Machine Intelligence*, **16**:226–238, 1995.

20. E. Rivlin and I. Weiss. Recognizing Objects Using Deformation Invariants. *Computer Vision and Image Understanding*, **65**:95–108, 1997.

21. C.A. Rothwell. *Object Recognition through Invariant Indexing*. Oxford University Press, Oxford, 1995.

22. A. Shashua and N. Navab. Relative Affine Structure: Canonical Model for 3D from 2D Geometry and Applications. *IEEE Transactions on Pattern Analysis and Machine Intelligence*, **18**:873–883, 1996.

23. J. Sato and R. Cipolla. Affine Integral Invariants for Extracting Symmetry Axes. *Image and Vision Computing*, **15**:627–635, 1997.

24. G. Sparr. Projective Invariants for Affine Shapes of Point Configurations. *Proc. 1st Workshop on Invariance*, 151–170, 1991.

25. C.E. Springer. *Geometry and Analysis of Projective Spaces*. Freeman, San Francisco, 1994.

26. P.F. Stiller, C.A. Asmuth, and C.S. Wan. Invariant Indexing and Single View Recognition. *Proc. DARPA Image Understanding Workshop*, 1423–1428, 1994.

27. B. Strumpel. *Algorithms in Invariant Theory*. Springer Verlag, New York, 1993.

28. L. Van Gool, T. Moons, E. Pauwels, and A. Oosterlinck. Vision and Lie's Approach to Invariance. *Image and Vision Computing*, **13**:259–277, 1995.

29. T. Vieville, O. Faugeras, and Q.T. Luong. Motion of Points and Lines in the Uncalibrated Case. *Intl. J. Computer Vision*, **17**:7–41, 1996.

30. B. Vijayakumar, D.J. Kriegman, and J. Ponce. Structure and Motion of Curved 3D Objects from Monocular Silhouettes. *Proc. IEEE Conf. on Computer Vision and Pattern Recognition*, 327–334, 1996.

31. I. Weiss. Geometric Invariants of Shapes. *Proc. DARPA Image Understanding Workshop*, 1125–1134, 1988.

32. I. Weiss. Noise Resistant Invariants of Curves. *IEEE Transactions on Pattern Analysis and Machine Intelligence*, **15**:943–948, 1993.

33. I. Weiss. Geometric Invariants and Object Recognition. *Intl. J. Computer Vision*, **10**:207–231, 1993.

34. I. Weiss. Local Projective and Affine Invariants. *Annals of Mathematics and Artificial Intelligence*, **13**:203-225, 1995.

35. I. Weiss. 3D Curve Reconstruction from Uncalibrated Cameras. University of Maryland CS-TR-3605. Also in *Proc. ICPR A*, 323–327, 1996.

36. I. Weiss. Model-based Recognition of 3D Curves from One View. *Journal of Mathematical Imaging and Vision*, in press, 1997.

37. M. Zerroug and R. Nevatia. Using Invariance and Quasi-invariance for the Segmentation and Recovery of Curved Objects. *In Lecture Notes in Computer Science 825*, Springer-Verlag, Berlin, 1994.

38. A. Zisserman, D.A. Forsyth, J.L. Mundy, C.A. Rothwell, J. Liu, and N. Pillow. 3D Object Recognition using Invariance. *Artificial Intelligence* **78**:239–288, 1995.

A Two-Stage Probabilistic Approach
for Object Recognition

Stan Z. Li[1] and Joachim Hornegger[2]

[1] Nanyang Technological University
School of EEE, Nanyang Avenue, Singapore 639798
szli@szli.eee.ntu.ac.sg
http://markov.eee.ntu.ac.sg:8000/~szli/
[2] Stanford University, Robotics Laboratory
Gates Building 134, Stanford, CA 94305-9010, USA
jh@Robotics.Stanford.EDU

Abstract. Assume that some objects are present in an image but can be seen only partially and are overlapping each other. To recognize the objects, we have to firstly separate the objects from one another, and then match them against the modeled objects using partial observation. This paper presents a probabilistic approach for solving this problem. Firstly, the task is formulated as a two-stage optimal estimation process. The first stage, *matching*, separates different objects and finds feature correspondences between the scene and each potential model object. The second stage, *recognition*, resolves inconsistencies among the results of matching to different objects and identifies object categories. Both the matching and recognition are formulated in terms of the maximum *a posteriori* (MAP) principle. Secondly, contextual constraints, which play an important role in solving the problem, are incorporated in the probabilistic formulation. Specifically, between-object constraints are encoded in the prior distribution modeled as a Markov random field, and within-object constraints are encoded in the likelihood distribution modeled as a Gaussian. They are combined into the posterior distribution which defines the MAP solution. Experimental results are presented for matching and recognizing jigsaw objects under partial occlusion, rotation, translation and scaling.

1 Introduction

Model-based *object recognition* is a high level vision task which identifies the category of each object in the scene with reference to the model objects. There are two broad types of approaches: templet-based and feature-based. In the templet-based approach, an object is represented by a templet which may be in the form of its bitmap or the entire outline; the observation is matched to the templet based on some distance measure. This approach has been used in numerous applications such as character recognition and face recognition in which objects are well observed in the image.

Currently, the templet-based approach does not seem to offer a proper solution to the partial matching problem. A basic assumption in the templet-based approach is that the object can be observed entirely. The assumption is invalidated when objects are only partially observable due to mutual occlusions. The templet-based approach is not inherently ready to handle this situation: While it allows local deformations, it is unable to perform with missing parts. This is because of its lack of the ability to represent an object by local features.

The feature-based approach is complementary to the templet-based approach in this regard. Here, an object model is represented by local object features, such as points, line segments or regions, subject to various constraints [3, 8, 6, 17]. *Object Matching* is performed to establish correspondences between local features in the scene (image) and those in each model object. Because it is based on the local features of an object rather than the global information of it, it is more appropriate to handle the partialness and ovelappingness, and hence provides an alternative for object recognition. This paper is aimed to investigate a formal mathematical framework for object recognition using partial observation.

From a pattern recognition viewpoint, an object is considered as a pattern of mutually or contextually constrained features. The use of contextual constraints is essential in the interpretation of visual patterns. An feature itself makes little sense when considered independently of the rest. It should be interpreted in relation to other image features in the spatial and visual context. At a higher level, a scene is interpreted based on various contextual constraints between features.

An interesting situation is when a scene contains many, possibly mutually occluded, objects, which is the case dealt with in this paper. In this situation, both the following two sources of contextual constraints are required to resolve ambiguities in the model-based matching and recognition, in our opinion: *between-object constraints* (BOCs) and *within-object constraints* (WOCs). The particular structure of an object itself is described by the WOCs of the object. Such constraints are used to identify an instance of that object in the scene. The BOCs, which describe constraints on features belonging to different objects, are used to differentiate different objects in the scene. In a sense, within-object constraints are used for evaluating similarities whereas between-object constraints are for evaluating dissimilarities. An interpretation is achieved based on the two types of constraints.

In matching and recognition, as in other image analysis tasks, exact and perfect solutions hardly exist due to various uncertainties such as occlusion and unknown transformations from model objects to the scene. Therefore, we usually look for some solution which optimally satisfies the considered constraints. A paradigm is prediction-verification [1]. It is able to solve the matching problem efficiently. In terms of statistics, we may define the optimal solution to be the most probable one. The maximum *a posteriori* (MAP) principle is a statistical criteria used in many applications and in fact has been the most popular choice in statistical image analysis.

Markov random field (MRF) theory provides a convenient and consistent way for modeling image features under contextual constraints [4, 14, 12], also for object recognition [15, 5, 12, 9]. MRFs and MAP together give rise to the MAP-

MRF framework. This framework, advocated by Geman and Geman (1984) and others, enables us to develop algorithms for a variety of vision problems systematically using rational principles rather than relying on *ad hoc* heuristics.

Scene-model matching is generally performed by considering one model object at a time, and when there are multiple model objects, multiple matching results are generated. Because the matching to each model is done independently of the other models, inconsistencies can exist among the results of matching to the different objects, and must be resolved to obtain consistent and unambiguous solutions. Our formulation of a two-stage estimation offers a solution in terms of the MAP principle.

In this paper, we develop a statistically optimal formulation for object matching and recognition of a scene containing multiple overlapping objects. Matching and recognition are posed as labeling problems and are performed in two consecutive stages, each solving an MAP-MRF estimation problem. The first stage matches the features extracted from the scene against those of each model object by maximizing the posterior distribution of the labeling. This finds feature correspondences between the scene to the model objects, and separates overlapping objects from one other. It produces multiple MAP matching results, each for one model object. Inconsistencies in these results are resolved by the second estimation stage, MAP recognition. In this latter stage, the MAP matching results produced by the previous stage are examined as a whole, inconsistencies among them are resolved, and all the objects are identified unambiguously finally.

The contextual constraints are imposed in probability terms. The BOCs are encoded in the prior distribution modeled as a Markov random field (MRF). This differentiates between different objects and between an object and the background. In a way, this is similar to the line-process model [7] for differentiating edge and non-edge elements. The WOCs are encoded in the likelihood distribution modeled as a Gaussian. It compares the similarity between a model object and its corresponding part in the scene. The BOCs and the WOCs are combined into the posterior distribution. An optimal solution, either for matching or for recognition is defined as the most probable configuration in the MAP sense.

The rest of the paper is organized as follows: In Section 2, the optimal solutions for matching and recognition are formulated, which illustrates how to use probabilistic tools to incorporate various contextual constraints and how to resolve ambiguities arising from matching to individual model objects. Experiments are presented in Section 3 for matching and recognition of a scene containing multiple free-form jigsaw objects under rotations, translations, scale changes and occlusions.

2 Two Stage MAP-MRF Estimation

Object matching and recognition, like many other image analysis problems, can be posed as labeling problems. Let $\mathcal{S} = \{1, \ldots, m\}$ be a set of m sites corresponding to the features in the scene, and $\mathcal{L} = \{1, \ldots, M\}$ be a set of M labels corresponding to the features in a model object. What types of features to use to represent an object is a problem not addressed in this paper. We assume some features have been chosen which present invariance in some feature properties and relations. An example of representation is given in the experiments section for curved objects like jigsaw, which can be referred to now by the unfamiliar reader.

In addition to the M labels in $\mathcal{L}$, we introduce a virtual label, called the NULL and numbered 0. It represents everything not in the above label set $\mathcal{L}$, including features due to un-modeled objects as well as noise. By this, the label set is augmented into $\mathcal{L}^+ = \{0, 1, \dots, M\}$. Labeling is to assign a label from $\mathcal{L}^+$ to each site in S. Without confusion, we still use the notation $\mathcal{L}$ to denote the augmented label set unless there is a necessity to differentiate. A labeling configuration, denoted by $f = \{f_1, \dots, f_m\}$, a mapping from the set of sites to the set of labels, i.e. $f : S \to \mathcal{L}$, in which $f_i \in \mathcal{L}$ is the object feature matched to the image feature i. When there are more than one object, a label represents not only an object feature but also the object category.

Given the observed data d, we define the optimal labeling f^* to be the one which maximizes the posterior. The posterior is a Gibbs distribution $P(F = f \mid d) \propto \mathrm{e}^{-E(f)}$ with the posterior energy

$$E(f) \triangleq U(f \mid d) = U(f) + U(d \mid f) \tag{1}$$

The energy is a sum of the prior energy $U(f)$ (the energy in the prior distribution) and the likelihood energy $U(d \mid f)$ (the energy in the distribution of d). Hence, the MAP solution is equivalently found by minimizing the posterior energy $f^* = \arg\min_{f \in \mathbb{F}} E(f)$. An MAP estimation is performed in each of the two stages.

2.1 Stage 1: MAP Matching

This stage performs MAP matching to each model object by minimizing the energy $E(f)$ of a posterior distribution in which the prior is modeled by Markov random fields (MRFs) and the likelihood by Gaussian.

The prior is modeled as an MRF which is a Gibbs distribution $P(f) = Z^{-1} \times \mathrm{e}^{-U(f)}$ where Z is the normalizing constant. The energy $U(f)$ is of the form $U(f) = \sum_{c \in \mathcal{C}} V_c(f)$ where $\mathcal{C}$ is the set of "cliques" for a neighborhood system $\mathcal{N}$ and $V_c(f)$ are the clique potential functions. In object matching, one may restrict the scope of interaction by defining the neighborhood set of i as the set of the other features which are within a distance r from feature i, $\mathcal{N}_i = \{i' \in S \mid [\mathrm{dist}(\mathrm{feature}_{i'}, \mathrm{feature}_i)]^2 \le r,\ i' \ne i\}$. The function "dist" is a suitably defined function for the distance between features. For point features, it can be chosen as the Euclidean distance between two points. It is tricky as how to define a distance between non-point features; e.g. for straight lines, a simple definition would be the distance between the midpoints of two straight lines. The distance threshold r may be chosen reasonably to be the maximum diameter of the model object currently under consideration.

The prior energy $U(f)$ is of the form $U(f) = \sum_{c \in \mathcal{C}} V_c(f)$ where $\mathcal{C}$ is the set of "cliques" and $V_c(f)$ are the clique potential functions. In essence, a Gibbs distribution is featured by two things: it belongs to the exponential family and its energy is defined on clique potentials. When cliques containing up to two sites are considered, the energy has the following form

$$U(f) = \sum_{\{i\} \in \mathcal{C}_1} V_1(f_i) + \sum_{\{i,i'\} \in \mathcal{C}_2} V_2(f_i, f_{i'}) = \sum_{i \in \mathcal{S}} V_1(f_i) + \sum_{i \in \mathcal{S}} \sum_{i' \in \mathcal{N}_i} V_2(f_i, f_{i'}) \quad (2)$$

where $\mathcal{C}_1 = \{\{i\} \mid i \in \mathcal{S}\}$ and $\mathcal{C}_2 = \{\{i,i'\} \mid i' \in \mathcal{N}_i, i \in \mathcal{S}\}$ are the sets of single- and pair-site cliques, respectively, and V_1 and V_2 are single- and pair-site potential functions. In defining $\mathcal{C}_2$, we assume that $\{a, b\}$ is an ordered set and so $\{i, i'\} \neq \{i', i\}$. The clique potentials are defined as

$$V_1(f_i) = \begin{cases} 0 & \text{if } f_i \neq 0 \\ v_{10} & \text{if } f_i = 0 \end{cases}, \quad V_2(f_i, f_{i'}) = \begin{cases} 0 & \text{if } f_i \neq 0 \text{ and } f_{i'} \neq 0 \\ v_{20} & \text{if } f_i = 0 \text{ or } f_{i'} = 0 \end{cases} \quad (3)$$

where $v_{10} > 0$ and $v_{20} > 0$ are penalty constants for NULL labels.

The pair-site clique potentials $V_2(f_i, f_{i'})$ encode between-object constraints by treating the two situations differently: (i) when both features are due to the considered object ($f_i \neq 0$ and $f_{i'} \neq 0$), and (ii) when one of the features is due to the background or another object ($f_i = 0$ or $f_{i'} = 0$). This differentiates between the considered model object and another object, and between the considered model object and the background. A dissimilarity between the classes of the two features is thus evaluated. The potentials associate label pairs belonging to the considered object (more closely related) with a lower cost, and associates label pairs belonging to different objects (less closely related) with a higher cost. Therefore, the use of the properties of the pairwise interactions plays a crucial role in separating overlapping objects.

The likelihood distribution $p(d \mid f)$ describes the statistical properties of model features seen in the scene and is therefore conditioned on pure non-NULL matches $f_i \neq 0$. It depends on how the visible features are observed, and this in turn depends on the underlying transformations and noise, which is regardless of the neighborhood system $\mathcal{N}$. Denote D_1 for unary properties and D_2 for binary relations between the features of a model object. Assume (i) that the truth $D = \{D_1, D_2\}$ of the model features and the data d are composed of types of features which are invariant under the considered class of transformations (their selections are application-specific); (ii) that they are related via the observation models $d_1(i) = D_1(f_i) + e_1(i)$ and $d_2(i, i') = D_2(f_i, f_{i'}) + e_2(i, i')$ where e is additive independent zero mean Gaussian noise.[1] Then the likelihood function is a Gibbs distribution with the energy

$$U(d \mid f) = \sum_{i \in \mathcal{S}, f_i \neq 0} V_1(d_1(i) \mid f_i) + \sum_{i \in \mathcal{S}, f_i \neq 0} \sum_{i' \in \mathcal{S} \setminus i, f_{i'} \neq 0} V_2(d_2(i, i') \mid f_i, f_{i'}) \quad (4)$$

---

[1] The assumptions of the independent Gaussian noise may not be accurate but offers an approximation when an accurate observation model is not available.

where $\mathcal{S}_{\setminus i} \triangleq \mathcal{S} - \{i\}$, and the summations are restricted to the non-NULL matches $f_i \neq 0$ and $f_{i'} \neq 0$. The likelihood potentials are

$$V_1(d_1(i) \mid f_i) = \sum_{k=1}^{K_1} [d_1^{(k)}(i) - D_1^{(k)}(f_i)]^2 / \{2[\sigma_1^{(k)}]^2\} \qquad (5)$$

and

$$V_2(d_2(i,i') \mid f_i, f_{i'}) = \sum_{k=1}^{K_2} [d_2^{(k)}(i,i') - D_2^{(k)}(f_i, f_{i'})]^2 / \{2[\sigma_2^{(k)}]^2\} \qquad (6)$$

where the vectors $D_1(f_i)$ and $D_2(f_i, f_{i'})$ are the "conditional mean" (conditioned on f) for the random vectors $d_1(i)$ and $d_2(i,i')$, respectively; K_1 and K_2 are the numbers unary properties and binary relations; $[\sigma_n^{(k)}]^2$ ($k = 1, \ldots, K_n$ and $n = 1, 2$) are the variances of the corresponding noise components.

The likelihood potentials are defined for image features belonging only to the model object under consideration ($f_i \neq 0$ and $f_{i'} \neq 0$). Therefore they encode the within-object constraints. They are used to evaluate the similarity between the model object and its corresponding part in the scene.

The constraints on both the labeling *a priori* and the observed data are incorporated into the posterior distribution with the posterior energy

$$\begin{aligned} U(f \mid d) = &\sum_{i \in \mathcal{S}} V_1(f_i) + \sum_{i \in \mathcal{S}} \sum_{i' \in \mathcal{N}_i} V_2(f_i, f_{i'}) + \\ &\sum_{i \in \mathcal{S}: f_i \neq 0} V_1(d_1(i) \mid f_i) + \\ &\sum_{i \in \mathcal{S}: f_i \neq 0} \sum_{i' \in \mathcal{S}_{\setminus i}: f_{i'} \neq 0} V_2(d_2(i,i') \mid f_i, f_{i'}) \end{aligned} \qquad (7)$$

Hence, the between-object constraints and the within-object constraints are combined into the posterior energy. The MAP matching is the configuration which minimizes $U(f \mid d)$.

One model object is considered at a time. Minimizing $U(f \mid d)$ for a model object results in a mapping from $\mathcal{S}$ to $\mathcal{L}^+$ for that object. The result tells us two things: (i) (separation) image features belonging (the "in-subset") and not belonging to the considered object, and (ii) (matching) correspondences between the features in the "in-subset" and the features of the model object.

The parameters MRF v_{10} and v_{20} and the likelihood parameter $\sigma^{(k)}$ have to be determined in order to completely define the MAP solution. This is done by using a supervised learning algorithm [12].

The present model can be compared to the coupled MRF model of [7] in that there are two coupled MRFs, one for line processes (edges) and one for intensities; and a line process variable can be on or off depending on the difference between the two neighboring intensities. The concept of "line process" in the present model is the relational bond between features in the scene. When $f_i \neq 0$ and $f_{i'} \neq 0$, i and i' are relationally constrained to each other; otherwise when $f_i = 0$ or $f_{i'} = 0$, the relational bond between i and i' is broken. The differences are: the present model makes use of relational measurements of any orders because contextual constraints play a stronger role in high level problems, whereas the model in [7] uses only unary observation. Moreover, in the present model, the

$i =$	1	2	3	4	5	6	7	8	9	10	11	12
$f^{(1)}$	0	0	0	0	0	0	0	0	0	0	0	0
$f^{(2)}$	0	0	0	0	0	0	0	$10^{(2)}$	$9^{(2)}$	$7^{(2)}$	0	0
$f^{(3)}$	0	0	0	0	0	0	0	0	0	$3^{(3)}$	$4^{(3)}$	0
$f^{(4)}$	0	0	0	$5^{(4)}$	$4^{(4)}$	$3^{(4)}$	$2^{(4)}$	$1^{(4)}$	0	0	0	0
$f^{(5)}$	0	0	0	0	0	0	0	$7^{(5)}$	$6^{(5)}$	$5^{(5)}$	$4^{(5)}$	$3^{(5)}$
$f^{(all)}$	0	0	0	$5^{(4)}$	$4^{(4)}$	$3^{(4)}$	$2^{(4)}$	$7^{(5)}$	$6^{(5)}$	$5^{(5)}$	$4^{(5)}$	$3^{(5)}$

Table 1. Matching and recognition of an image containing $m = 12$ features to $L = 5$ objects.

neighborhood system is non-homogeneous and anisotropic, as opposed to the image case in which pixels are equi-spaced.

The MAP matching of the scene is performed to each potential object one by one. In this case, the complexity of the search is linear in the number of models. Some fast screening heuristics may be imposed to quickly rule out unlikely models, but this is discussed in this paper. We concentrate on the MAP formalism.

2.2 Stage 2: MAP Recognition

After matching to each potential object one by one, we obtain a number of MAP solutions. However, inconsistencies may exist among them: Assuming that there are L potential model objects, we have L MAP solutions, $f^{(1)}, \ldots, f^{(L)}$ where $f^{(\alpha)} = \{f_1^{(\alpha)}, \ldots, f_m^{(\alpha)}\}$ is the MAP labeling f^* for matching the scene to model object $\alpha \in \{1, \ldots, L\}$ obtained in stage 1, and $f_i^{(\alpha)}$ denotes feature number $I = f_i$ of object α. Since each $f^{(\alpha)}$ is the optimal labeling of the scene in terms only of model object α but not of the other objects, inconsistencies may exist among the L results in the sense below.

A feature $i \in S$ in the scene may have been matched to more than one model feature in different objects; that is, there may exist more than one $\alpha \in \{1, \ldots, L\}$ for which $f_i^{(\alpha)} \neq 0$. Table 1 illustrates an example of results for matching an image with $m = 12$ features to $L = 5$ model objects, where $f^{(\alpha)}$ ($\alpha = 1, \ldots, 5$) are the MAP solutions for matching to the five objects. For example, image feature $i = 8$ has been matched to $10^{(2)}$ (feature No. 10 of object 2), $1^{(4)}$ and $7^{(5)}$. However, any feature in the scene should be matched to at most one non-NULL model feature; that is, for a specific i, there should be that either $f_i^{(\alpha)} = 0$ for all α or $f_i^{(\alpha)} \neq 0$ for just one α value. When this is not the case, the inconsistencies should be resolved in order to unambiguously identify the object category to which each image feature uniquely belongs. A possible consistent final result is given as $f^{(all)}$ in the table.

The recognition stage is to make the matching results consistent and to identify the categories of objects in the scene. Again, this stage is also formulated as an MAP estimation. Denote object α as $\mathcal{O}^{(\alpha)}$. The posterior derived previously for matching to $\mathcal{O}^{(\alpha)}$ can be explicitly expressed as $P(f \mid d, \mathcal{O}^{(\alpha)})$. Denoting the posterior probability for matching to all the L objects as $P(f \mid d, \mathcal{O}^{(all)})$ where $\mathcal{O}^{(all)}$ is short for $\mathcal{O}^{(1)}, \cdots, \mathcal{O}^{(L)}$, the MAP recognition is then defined as $f^* = \arg\max_{f \in \mathbb{F}^{(all)}} P(f \mid d, \mathcal{O}^{(all)})$. The configuration space $\mathbb{F}^{(all)}$ consists of $(1 + \sum_{\alpha=1}^{L} M^{(\alpha)})^m$ elements, where $M^{(\alpha)}$ is the number of labels in model α, when all the labels in all the models are admissible.

The posterior, $P(f \mid d, \mathcal{O}^{(all)}) \propto P(f \mid \mathcal{O}^{(all)})p(d \mid f, \mathcal{O}^{(all)})$, is a Gibbs distribution because of the Markov property of the labels. Similar to that in the matching stage, the prior energy is

$$U(f \mid \mathcal{O}^{(all)}) = \sum_{i \in S} V_1(f_i \mid \mathcal{O}^{(all)}) + \sum_{i \in S} \sum_{i' \in \mathcal{N}_i} V_2(f_i, f_{i'} \mid \mathcal{O}^{(all)}) \tag{8}$$

and the likelihood energy is

$$U(d \mid f, \mathcal{O}^{(all)}) = \sum_{i \in S, f_i \neq 0} V_1(d_1(i) \mid f_i, \mathcal{O}^{(all)}) +$$
$$\sum_{i \in S, f_i \neq 0} \sum_{i' \in S_{\backslash i}, f_{i'} \neq 0} V_2(d_2(i, i') \mid f_i, f_{i'}, \mathcal{O}^{(all)}) \tag{9}$$

The single-site potential are defined as $V_1(f_i^{(\alpha)} \mid \mathcal{O}^{(all)}) = V_1(f_i^{(\alpha)} \mid \mathcal{O}^{(\alpha)})$ which is the same as that in (3) for matching to a single model object α. The pair-site potential are defined as

$$V_2(f_i^{(\alpha)}, f_{i'}^{(\alpha')} \mid \mathcal{O}^{(all)}) = \begin{cases} V_2(f_i^{(\alpha)}, f_{i'}^{(\alpha')} \mid \mathcal{O}^{(\alpha)}, \mathcal{O}^{(\alpha')}) & \text{if } \alpha = \alpha' \\ v_{20} & \text{otherwise} \end{cases} \tag{10}$$

where $V_2(f_i^{(\alpha)}, f_{i'}^{(\alpha')} \mid \mathcal{O}^{(\alpha)}, \mathcal{O}^{(\alpha')}) = V_2(f_i, f_{i'})$ is the same as that in (3). The above definitions are a straightforward extension of (3): In (3), features due to other objects (as opposed to the one currently under consideration) are all labeled as NULL ; (10) simply takes this principle into consideration for recognizing multiple objects. Using (3), we obtain

$$V_2(f_i^{(\alpha)}, f_{i'}^{(\alpha')} \mid \mathcal{O}^{(all)}) = \begin{cases} 0 & \text{if } (\alpha = \alpha') \text{ and } (f_i^{(\alpha)} \neq 0) \text{ and } (f_{i'}^{(\alpha')} \neq 0) \\ v_{20} & \text{otherwise} \end{cases}$$
$$\tag{11}$$

The single-site likelihood potentials are $V_1(d_1(i) \mid f_i^{(\alpha)}, \mathcal{O}^{(all)}) = V_1(d_1(i) \mid f_i^{(\alpha)}, \mathcal{O}^{(\alpha)})$ which is the same as (5). The pair-site likelihood potentials are

$$V_2(d_2(i, i') \mid f_i^{(\alpha)}, f_{i'}^{(\alpha')}, \mathcal{O}^{(all)}) = \begin{cases} V_2(d_2(i, i') \mid f_i^{(\alpha)}, f_{i'}^{(\alpha')}, \mathcal{O}^{(\alpha)}, \mathcal{O}^{(\alpha')}) \\ \qquad\qquad\qquad\qquad\qquad\qquad \text{if } \alpha = \alpha' \\ 0 \qquad\qquad\qquad\qquad\qquad\qquad \text{otherwise} \end{cases}$$
$$\tag{12}$$

where $V_2(d_2(i, i') \mid f_i^{(\alpha)}, f_{i'}^{(\alpha')}, \mathcal{O}^{(\alpha)}, \mathcal{O}^{(\alpha')}) = V_2(d_2(i, i') \mid f_i, f_{i'})$ is the same as (6). The posterior energy is obtained as $U(f \mid d, \mathcal{O}^{(all)}) = U(f \mid \mathcal{O}^{(all)}) + U(d \mid f, \mathcal{O}^{(all)})$.

When L MAP matching solutions are available, the configuration space $\mathbb{F}^{(all)}$ can be reduced to a great extent. Let $\mathcal{S}' \subset \mathcal{S}$ be the set of sites which were previously matched to more than one non-NULL label, $\mathcal{S}' = \{i \in \mathcal{S} \mid f_i^{(\alpha)} \neq 0$ for more than one different $\alpha\}$. For the case of Table 1, $\mathcal{S}' = \{8, 9, 10, 11\}$. Only those labels in $i \in \mathcal{S}'$ are subject to changes in the recognition stage. Therefore, the configuration space can be reduced to $\mathbb{F}^{(all)} = \mathcal{L}_1^{(all)} \times \mathcal{L}_2^{(all)} \times \cdots \times \mathcal{L}_m^{(all)}$ where $\mathcal{L}_i^{(all)}$ is constructed in the following way:

- For $i \in \mathcal{S}'$, $\mathcal{L}_i^{(all)}$ consists of all the non-NULL labels previously assigned to i, $\{f_i^{(\alpha)^*} \neq 0 \mid \alpha = 1, \ldots, L\}$, plus the NULL label; e.g. $\mathcal{L}_8^{(all)} = \{0, 10^{(2)}, 1^{(4)}, 7^{(5)}\}$ for Table 1.
- For $i \notin \mathcal{S}'$, $\mathcal{L}_i^{(all)}$ consists of the non-NULL label if there is a non-NULL label, or $\mathcal{L}_i^{(all)} = \{0\}$ otherwise; e.g. $\mathcal{L}_6^{(all)} = \{3^{(4)}\}$, and $\mathcal{L}_3^{(all)} = \{0\}$.

Each involved object α contributes one or zero label to $\mathcal{L}_i^{(all)}$, as opposed to $M^{(\alpha)}$ labels before the reduction, and therefore the size of $\mathcal{L}_i^{(all)}$ is at most $L + 1$ as opposed to $1 + \sum_{\alpha=1}^{L} M^{(\alpha)}$ before. The size of $\mathcal{L}_i^{(all)}$ is one for $i \notin \mathcal{S}'$. Therefore, the MAP recognition is thus reduced to the following: (i) It is performed over the reduced configuration space $\mathbb{F}_{\mathcal{S}'}^{(all)} = \prod_{i \in \mathcal{S}'} \mathcal{L}_i^{(all)}$; (ii) it is to maximize the *conditional* posterior $f_{\mathcal{S}'}^* = \arg\max_{f_{\mathcal{S}'} \in \mathbb{F}_{\mathcal{S}'}^{(all)}} P(f_{\mathcal{S}'} \mid d, f_{\mathcal{S}-\mathcal{S}'}, \mathcal{O}^{(all)})$ where $f_{\mathcal{S}'} = \{f_i \mid i \in \mathcal{S}'\}$ is the set of labels to be updated, and $f_{\mathcal{S}-\mathcal{S}'} = \{f_i \mid i \in \mathcal{S} - \mathcal{S}'\}$ is the set of labels which are fixed during the maximization. It is equivalently to minimize the conditional posterior energy $U(f_{\mathcal{S}'} \mid d, f_{\mathcal{S}-\mathcal{S}'}, \mathcal{O}^{(all)})$.

After the reduction, only one or just a small number of labels remain admissible for each site and the search space becomes very small. For example, for the case of Table 1, the reduced label sets of size larger than one are $\mathcal{L}_8^{(all)} = \{0, 10^{(2)}, 1^{(4)}, 7^{(5)}\}$, $\mathcal{L}_9^{(all)} = \{0, 9^{(2)}, 6^{(5)}\}$, $\mathcal{L}_{10}^{(all)} = \{0, 7^{(2)}, 3^{(3)}, 5^{(5)}\}$, $\mathcal{L}_9^{(all)} = \{0, 4^{(3)}, 4^{(5)}\}$, and the sizes of $\mathcal{L}_i^{(all)}$ are one for $i \notin \mathcal{S}'$; the previous size of $\sum_{\alpha=1}^{5}(M^{(\alpha)} + 1)^{12}$ configurations (say, $M^{(\alpha)} = 10$) is then reduced to $4 \times 3 \times 4 \times 3 = 144$, so small that an exhaustive search may be plausible.

2.3 Minimization Methods

The optimization in MAP matching and recognition is combinatorial. While an optimum is sought in a global sense, many optimization algorithms are based on local information. Many algorithms are available for this [12]. The ICM algorithm [2] iteratively maximizes local conditional distributions in a way as a "greedy method". Global optimizers such as simulated annealing (SA) [11, 7] also iterate based on local energy changes. Relaxation labeling algorithms [10, 16] provide yet another choice. It is desirable to find globally good solution with an MAP estimation. Denote object α as $\mathcal{O}^{(\alpha)}$. The posterior derived previously for matching to $\mathcal{O}^{(\alpha)}$ can be explicitly expressed as $P(f \mid d, \mathcal{O}^{(\alpha)})$. Denoting the posterior probability for matching to all the L objects as $P(f \mid d, \mathcal{O}^{(all)})$ where $\mathcal{O}^{(all)}$ is short for $\mathcal{O}^{(1)}, \cdots, \mathcal{O}^{(L)}$, the MAP recognition is then defined as $f^* = \arg\max_{f \in \mathbb{F}^{(all)}} P(f \mid d, \mathcal{O}^{(all)})$. The configuration space $\mathbb{F}^{(all)}$ consists of $(1 + \sum_{\alpha=1}^{L} M^{(\alpha)})^m$ elements, where $M^{(\alpha)}$ is the number of labels in model α, when all the labels in all the models are admissible.

The posterior, $P(f \mid d, \mathcal{O}^{(all)}) \propto P(f \mid \mathcal{O}^{(all)}) p(d \mid f, \mathcal{O}^{(all)})$, is a Gibbs distribution because of the Markov property of the labels. Similar to that in the matching stage, the prior energy is

$$U(f \mid \mathcal{O}^{(all)}) = \sum_{i \in S} V_1(f_i \mid \mathcal{O}^{(all)}) + \sum_{i \in S} \sum_{i' \in \mathcal{N}_i} V_2(f_i, f_{i'} \mid \mathcal{O}^{(all)}) \qquad (8)$$

and the likelihood energy is

$$U(d \mid f, \mathcal{O}^{(all)}) = \sum_{i \in S, f_i \neq 0} V_1(d_1(i) \mid f_i, \mathcal{O}^{(all)}) +$$
$$\sum_{i \in S, f_i \neq 0} \sum_{i' \in S \setminus i, f_{i'} \neq 0} V_2(d_2(i, i') \mid f_i, f_{i'}, \mathcal{O}^{(all)}) \qquad (9)$$

The single-site potential are defined as $V_1(f_i^{(\alpha)} \mid \mathcal{O}^{(all)}) = V_1(f_i^{(\alpha)} \mid \mathcal{O}^{(\alpha)})$ which is the same as that in (3) for matching to a single model object α. The pair-site potential are defined as

$$V_2(f_i^{(\alpha)}, f_{i'}^{(\alpha')} \mid \mathcal{O}^{(all)}) = \begin{cases} V_2(f_i^{(\alpha)}, f_{i'}^{(\alpha')} \mid \mathcal{O}^{(\alpha)}, \mathcal{O}^{(\alpha')}) & \text{if } \alpha = \alpha' \\ v_{20} & \text{otherwise} \end{cases} . \qquad (10)$$

where $V_2(f_i^{(\alpha)}, f_{i'}^{(\alpha')} \mid \mathcal{O}^{(\alpha)}, \mathcal{O}^{(\alpha')}) = V_2(f_i, f_{i'})$ is the same as that in (3). The above definitions are a straightforward extension of (3): In (3), features due to other objects (as opposed to the one currently under consideration) are all labeled as NULL ; (10) simply takes this principle into consideration for recognizing multiple objects. Using (3), we obtain

$$V_2(f_i^{(\alpha)}, f_{i'}^{(\alpha')} \mid \mathcal{O}^{(all)}) = \begin{cases} 0 & \text{if } (\alpha = \alpha') \text{ and } (f_i^{(\alpha)} \neq 0) \text{ and } (f_{i'}^{(\alpha')} \neq 0) \\ v_{20} & \text{otherwise} \end{cases}$$
$$(11)$$

The single-site likelihood potentials are $V_1(d_1(i) \mid f_i^{(\alpha)}, \mathcal{O}^{(all)}) = V_1(d_1(i) \mid f_i^{(\alpha)}, \mathcal{O}^{(\alpha)})$ which is the same as (5). The pair-site likelihood potentials are

$$V_2(d_2(i, i') \mid f_i^{(\alpha)}, f_{i'}^{(\alpha')}, \mathcal{O}^{(all)}) = \begin{cases} V_2(d_2(i, i') \mid f_i^{(\alpha)}, f_{i'}^{(\alpha')}, \mathcal{O}^{(\alpha)}, \mathcal{O}^{(\alpha')}) & \\ & \text{if } \alpha = \alpha' \\ 0 & \\ & \text{otherwise} \end{cases}$$
$$(12)$$

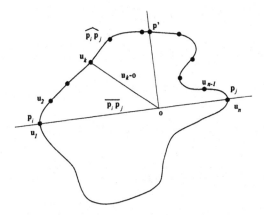

Fig. 2. Deriving similarity invariants for each curve segment bounded by two feature points p_i and p_j.

3.1 Invariant Features

A similarity invariant representation is used to encode constraints on the feature points $(d_1(i))$ and on the curve segments between the feature points $(d_2(i,j))$. The invariant unary property $d_1(i)$ is chosen to be the sign of the curvature $\kappa(p_i)$ for corner i. Similarity invariant relations $d_2(i,j)$ are derived to describe the curve segment between the pair of corner i and j, as follows: Consider the curve segment $\widehat{p_i p_j}$ between p_i and p_j and the straight line $\overline{p_i p_j}$ that passes through the points, as illustrated in Fig.2. The ratio of the arc-length $\widehat{p_i p_j}$ and the chord-length $\overline{p_i p_j}$: $d_2^{(1)}(i,j) = \frac{\text{arclength}(\widehat{p_i p_j})}{\text{chordlength}(\overline{p_i p_j})}$ is an invariant scalar. The ratio of curvature at p_i and p_j: $d_2^{(2)}(i,j) = \frac{\kappa(p_i)}{\kappa(p_j)}$ is also an invariant scalar. Two n-position-vectors of invariants are derived to utilize the constraints on the curve segment: First, find the mid-point, denoted by p', of $\widehat{p_i p_j}$ such that curve segments $\widehat{p_i p'}$ and $\widehat{p' p_j}$ have the equal arc-length. Next, find the point, denoted by o, on $\overline{p_i p_j}$ such that line $\overline{op'}$ is perpendicular to $\overline{op_j}$. Both p' and o are unique for $\widehat{p_i p_j}$. Then sample the curve segment at the n equally spaced (in arc-length) points $u_1, \ldots, u_n$. This is equivalent to inserting $n-2$ points between p_i and p_j. The vector of normalized radii is defined as $d_2^{(3)}(i,j) = [r_k]_{k=1}^n$ where $r_k = \frac{\|u_k - o\|}{\|op'\|}$ is similarity invariant. The vector of angles is defined as $d_2^{(4)}(i,j) = [\theta_k]_{k=1}^n$ where $\theta_k = \angle u_k o p_i$ is also similarity invariant. Now, $d_2(i,j)$ consists of four types ($K_2 = 4$) of $2n + 2$ similarity invariant scalars.

3.2 Matching and Recognition

In the matching stage, an image curve is matched against each of the eight model jigsaws. Fig.3 shows the solutions of matching one of the image boundary curves (in solid) to each of the eight model jigsaws, *i.e.* the MAP estimates

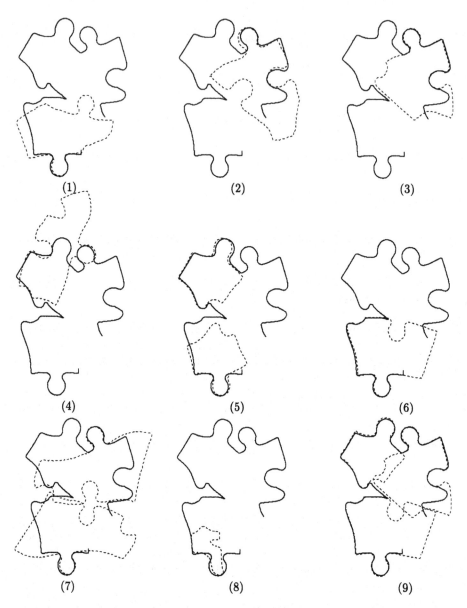

Fig. 3. Results from matching and recognition stages. (1) MAP solution $f^{(1)*}$ for matching the boundary curve (in solid) to model jigsaw No.1 (in dashed). The overlay of the model jigsaw on the input boundary curve indicates the correspondence. (2)–(8) MAP solutions for matching the boundary curve to models Nos.2–8. (9) The final MAP recognition result where the three recognized model jigsaws are overlayed on the input boundary curve.

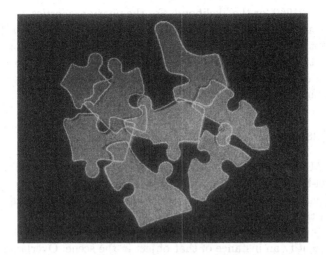

Fig. 4. The overall matching and recognition result.

$f^{(\alpha)^*} = \max_f P(f \mid d, \mathcal{O}^{(\alpha)})$ for $\alpha = 1, \ldots, 8$, where each model jigsaw (in dashed) is aligned to the curve. The overlapping portion indicates the correspondences whereas the image corners in the non-overlapping portion of the scene are assigned the NULL label.

The matching stage does two things: (i) It classifies the corners in the scene into two groups, non-NULL and NULL , or in other words, those belonging to the considered object and those not. (ii) For the non-NULL group, it gives the corresponding model corners. Therefore, the matching stage not only finds the feature correspondences between the scene and the considered model, but also does the separation of feature belonging to the considered object from those not.

Despite the ambiguities caused by the common structure of round extrusions and intrusions, the MAP matching has successfully distinguished the right model using information about the other part of the model. Also, it allows multiple instances of any model object, as in $f^{(5)^*}$ and $f^{(7)^*}$ of Fig.3 where each contains two instances of a model.

Although each MAP matching result is reasonable by itself, it may be inconsistent with others. For example, $f^{(2)^*}$, $f^{(3)^*}$ and $f^{(7)^*}$ in Fig.3 compete for a common part. This is mostly due to the common structures mentioned above. The inconsistencies have to be resolved. The MAP recognition stage identifies the best model class for each corner in the scene. The final recognition result is shown in the lower-right corner of Fig.3. Fig.4 shows the overall result for matching and recognizing the three boundary curves in the scene to all the models.

There are a number of parameters involved in the definition of the MAP solutions. Parameters $v_{20} = 0.7$ is fixed for all the experiments. Parameters $[\sigma_2^{(k)}]^2$ in the likelihood are estimated by using a supervised learning procedure [12]. The estimated values are $1/\sigma_2^{(1)} = 0.00025$, $1/\sigma_2^{(2)} = 0$, $1/\sigma_2^{(3)} = 0.02240$

and $1/\sigma_2^{(4)} = 0.21060$ for the likelihood. For the unary properties, we set $v_{10} = 0$ for the prior and $V_1(d_1(i) \mid f_i) = 0$ for the likelihood. The reason for setting $v_{10} = 0$ is that the influence of the single-site prior on the result is insignificant as compared to the pair-site one. The reason for $V_1(d_1(i) \mid f_i) = 0$ (in other words, we set $\sigma_1^k = \infty$) is because we are unable to compute unary constraints which are both invariant and reliable.

4 Conclusions

A two stage MAP estimation approach has been presented for solving the problems of model-based object separation, feature correspondence and object recognition using partial and overlapping observation. Contextual constraints are considered important for solving the problem. The particular structure of an object itself is described by the within-object constraints of the object. Such constraints are used to identify an instance of that object in the scene. Overlapping objects are separated by using the between-object constraints which differentiate between features belonging to an object and those not belonging to. The MAP estimate problem is formulated by taking both types of contextual constraints into consideration. Currently, the within-object constraints are mainly imposed by the likelihood, *i.e.* the distribution of properties and relations conditioned on non-NULL labels. How to use MRFs to encode within-model constraints into the prior distribution in a more efficient way is a topic in future research.

References

1. N. Ayache and O. D. Faugeras. "HYPER: A new approach for the representation and positioning of two-dimensional objects". *IEEE Transactions on Pattern Analysis and Machine Intelligence*, 8(1):44–54, January 1986.
2. J. Besag. "On the statistical analysis of dirty pictures" (with discussions). *Journal of the Royal Statistical Society, Series B*, 48:259–302, 1986.
3. P. J. Besl and R. C. Jain. "Three-Dimensional object recognition". *Computing Surveys*, 17(1):75–145, March 1985.
4. R. Chellappa and A. Jain, editors. *Markov Random Fields: Theory and Applications*. Academic Press, 1993.
5. P. R. Cooper. "Parallel structure recognition with uncertainty: Coupled segmentation and matching". In *Proceedings of IEEE International Conference on Computer Vision*, pages 287–290, 1990.
6. O. Faugeras. *Three-Dimensional Computer Vision – A Geometric Viewpoint*. MIT Press, Cambridge, MA, 1993.
7. S. Geman and D. Geman. "Stochastic relaxation, Gibbs distribution and the Bayesian restoration of images". *IEEE Transactions on Pattern Analysis and Machine Intelligence*, 6(6):721–741, November 1984.
8. W. E. L. Grimson. *Object Recognition by Computer – The Role of Geometric Constraints*. MIT Press, Cambridge, MA, 1990.
9. J. Hornegger and H. Niemann. "Statistical learning, localization and identification of objects". In *Proceedings of IEEE International Conference on Computer Vision*, pages 914–919, MIT, MA, 1995.

10. R. A. Hummel and S. W. Zucker. "On the foundations of relaxation labeling process". *IEEE Transactions on Pattern Analysis and Machine Intelligence*, 5(3):267–286, May 1983.

11. S. Kirkpatrick, C. D. Gellatt, and M. P. Vecchi. "Optimization by simulated annealing". *Science*, 220:671–680, 1983.

12. S. Z. Li. *Markov Random Field Modeling in Computer Vision*. Springer-Verlag, New York, 1995.

13. S. Z. Li, H. Wang, K. L. Chan, and M. Petrou. "Minimization of MRF energy with relaxation labeling". *Journal of Mathematical Imaging and Vision*, 7:149–161, 1997.

14. K. V. Mardia and G. K. Kanji, editors. *Statistics and Images: 1*. Advances in Applied Statistics. Carfax, 1993.

15. J. W. Modestino and J. Zhang. "A Markov random field model-based approach to image interpretation". *IEEE Transactions on Pattern Analysis and Machine Intelligence*, 14(6):606–615, 1992.

16. C. Peterson and B. Soderberg. "A new method for mapping optimization problems onto neural networks". *International Journal of Neural Systems*, 1(1):3–22, 1989.

17. Ullman. *High-Level Vision: Object Recognition and Visual Cognition*. MIT Press, 1996.

Combining Geometric and Probabilistic Structure for Active Recognition of 3D Objects

Stéphane HERBIN

Ecole Normale Supérieure de Cachan
Centre de Mathématiques et de Leurs Applications
CNRS, URA 1611
61, Av. du Président Wilson
94235 Cachan Cedex, France
Stephane.Herbin@cmla.ens-cachan.fr

Abstract. Direct perception is incomplete: objects may show ambiguous appearances, and sensors have a limited sensitivity. Consequently, the recognition of complex 3D objects necessitates an exploratory phase to be able to deal with complex scenes or objects.

The variation of object appearance when the viewpoint is modified or when the sensor parameters are changed is an idiosyncratic feature which can be organized in the form of an *aspect graph*.

Standard geometric aspect graphs are difficult to build. This article presents a generalized probabilistic version of this concept. When fitted with a Markov chain dependance, the aspect graph acquires a quantitative predictive power. Tri-dimensional object recognition becomes translated into a problem of Markov chain discrimination. The asymptotic theory of hypothesis testing, in its relation to the theory of large deviations, gives then a global evaluation of the statistical complexity of the recognition problem.

Keywords: 3D object recognition, active vision, aspect graphs, Markov chains, statistical hypothesis testing.

Introduction

Aspect graphs have been extensively studied in a theoretical way. Their practical use, however, has not been clearly demonstrated. Furthermore, their original dynamic nature has not been used directly, except in a few projects.

This article aims at showing that the dynamic nature of aspect transitions can be genuinely exploited for the recognition of 3D objects when fitted with a probabilistic model.

The general organization of the paper will be the following. In a first section, the possible application of aspect graphs as a modelling tool for object recognition will be described. Their limitations will lead us to define in a second section a probabilistic extension of the aspect graph by embedding it in a Markov chain representation. A third section will present the mathematical results stemming from the theory of large deviations in its application to hypothesis testing. In a fourth section, the mathematical features will be computed and tested on a few examples. A small review of related work is presented in the fifth section.

1 Classical aspect graphs

One of the main difficulties of vision, and presumably its foremost idiosyncratic feature, is the dimensional discrepancy between the sensors — usually 2D retinas — and the observed world of 3D objects. This characteristic generates two kinds of problems: 1) the objects are only accessible as appearences which may be *ambiguous*; 2) since objects cannot be apprehended as a whole, visual systems have to deal with a *multiplicity* of appearences related to a same object.

The final objective of visual systems description, and especially those dedicated to recognition, is to find practical or theoretical means of dealing with the appearences of objects. Many approaches have been studied in the literature: among them, the theory of *aspect graphs* has proposed an original way of reducing the multiplicity of appearances down to a global combinatorial structure. This section presents the conceptual fundation of this approach, its possible application to object recognition and its limitations.

1.1 Transitions between stable views

The multiplicity of appearences can be indexed by a state in a finite-dimension control space. The collection of a tri-dimensional object geometric appearences, for instance, may be referenced by a position in a two-dimensional manifold — the view sphere — when the viewing model is an othographic projection.

In general, the mapping between the control space and the set of appearences is locally continuous, except for some very specific areas which segment the control space in connected regions, usually called view cells. In each view cell the object appearences are considered similar or equivalent. The similarity class of appearences is called an *aspect*.

The set of aspects can be organized as a *graph* structure which represents the dissimilarity relations between view cells. The standard aspect graph example is provided by the occluding contour variation of a piece-wise smooth object. The apparent contour, which is the set of points on the object surface that have a high order contact with the viewing direction or belong to an edge, projects onto the retina as a differentiable curve except on a finite number of points. The occluding contour varies abruptly, "catastrophically", for some view directions, revealing a discontinuity in the set of appearences [19, 18]. These catastrophic transitions are called visual events.

Two contours are declared similar or of same qualitative type if they can be transformed one into another by a one to one differentiable mapping. This similarity relation defines equivalence classes of *structurally stable* views, corresponding to the segmentation of the view sphere by the catastrophe loci. Rigorous theoretic description of the aspect graphs for piece-wise smooth objects have been given [26], and some algorithms for their construction in the case of objects described as polyhedron, solids of revolution, parametric and algebraic surfaces.

The significance of the geometric approach to aspect graphs is essentially theoretic. It provides a mathematical justification of view categorization through the detection of differentiable mapping singularities. It gives a description of the aspect structure as a graph of connected view cells. It unifies the multiplicity of appearences into a global object. These three properties indicate the possibility of considering a formal description of vision both viewer-centered — since aspect graphs refer to the distribution of appearences — and object centered — since it organizes globally the appearences in a single formal object.

Conceptually, therefore, aspect graphs are appealing mathematical objects. Besides the complexity of their construction, an important question remains to state how useful they can be in practice. This paper will concentrate thereafter on the problem of visual object recognition and show that some extensions of the standard aspect graph concept are necessary in order to make it tractable.

1.2 Aspect graphs for object recognition

The long term objective of the work presented in this paper is to describe the characteristics of a *genuinely visual* model of object recognition. Since, as it has been briefly mentioned, aspect graphs conciliate in a way the traditionnally antagonistic viewer and object centered approaches, it could be a good idea to see how they could be used to recognize objects.

The origin of aspect graphs lies in the dynamic nature of vision: the variations of aspects can only revealed by moving or modifying something in an observer visual system. An aspect graph, therefore, should not be considered as an object model since it does not consist in an objective substitute. It reveals as much of the object as of the way it is perceived, and points out the intrinsic incompleteness of vision.

A classical or geometric aspect graph is specific of an object both by the nature of its aspects and by the structure of its variations. Therefore, aspect graphs should be exploited *dynamically* in order to use fully all the information it contains, especially the structural repartition of view cells. The natural way of using classical aspect graphs for object recognition would be to move in the control space, *i.e.* change continuously the viewpoint, and detect the aspect transitions that could be considered characteristic of the object observed.

An aspect, in the classical geometric framework, is defined as the maximal set of structurally stable curves, *i.e.* the class of occluding contours that can be transformed by a diffeomorphism. The key feature of an aspect, therefore, is the distribution of singular points along the occluding contour. Transitions between aspect are detected as birth or death of singularities of the object outline.

The aspect transitions are organized in a graph structure where each node refers to an aspect. In order to recognize an object, it is enough to detect empirically what is the graph related to the object observed by collecting a sequence of aspects until a recognition decision can be made. It is assumed in this scheme that a given object can be fully characterized by the graph structure of its aspects.

We can now state what could be the most important elements of a recognition system based on aspect graph discrimination. It shoud be characterized by:

- Visual features: occluding contour singularities.
- Data structure: distribution of singular points.
- Control parameters: view point direction.
- Recognition principle: graph structure discrimination.

1.3 Difficulties

The elementary recognition scheme described above, although conceptually appealing, has to face many difficulties. There are mainly two series of obstacles to its practical use: aspect graphs are too complex to build *and* to use, and in many cases, the concept itself of aspect graph do not bring enough reliable discriminating information for recognition.

The complexity of aspect graphs The construction of aspect graphs, although theoretically solved for many classes of objects, is computationnaly expensive. Most of the thorough studies have concentrated on a single object [24, 35], revealing the difficulties of designing an automatic procedure.

An evaluation of the intrinsic complexity of aspect graphs has been performed by S. Petitjean [23] for piecewise-smooth algebraic surfaces. For an object made of n quadrics, for instance, the number of aspects exact upper bound is a polynome of degree n^{12} when an orthographic projection is used. This huge bound may explain why aspect graphs are difficult to build in the case of complex objects, and intractable in practice.

Besides this intrinsic complexity, one may suspect that the direct use of the graph structure is also a difficult problem. The question of deciding whether two graphs are isomorphic has never been proved to be NP-complete, but no algorithm in polynomial time has ever been found either [12, 17]. In the othographic case, however, the aspect graph is planar, which implies that a faster algorithm can be used. In the general case, and since the number of aspects is huge, even for a simple object, the recognition principle cannot lie only in a graph structure discrimination.

The limitations of classical aspect graphs The "classical" concept of aspect graph itself may not be adequate for object recognition because of three reasons.

Firstly, the notion of singular point on the contour comes from a continuous, and even differentiable, approach of vision processes. In practice, most of the available signals are in the form of pixel arrays, where the notion of singular point is ill defined. If aspects can be built from a theoretical object model, it seems difficult to detect them empirically on images obtained from a digital camera retina, for instance.

Secondly, the control space contains a unique parameter, although in general multi-dimensional: the viewpoint direction and position. Classical aspect graphs are based essentially on geometric features of the objects. Information such as color, texture or photometry, are not used and may have in some occasions a greater discriminating power.

Thirdly, the graph structure may not hold enough discriminating information. **Fig.** 1 illustrates this problem.

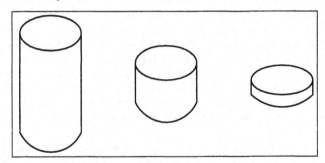

Fig. 1. Three different objects from the same viewpoint having the same geometric aspect graph.

The three objects have the same simple aspect graph but are clearly distinguishable since, for instance, they would not be naturally grasped in the same manner. This fact implies that something more must be added to the classical geometric approach to aspect graphs to efficiently and reliably use them for recognition purposes.

2   Probabilistic aspect graphs

The first section has proposed a way of using aspect graphs for object recognition based on its original dynamic nature, and pointed out several limitations of the approach.

This section intends to show that some of the previously exposed difficulties can be removed if a probabilistic model is fitted to the graph structure in the form of a Markov dependence.

2.1 Probable aspects

Research in computer vision have been mostly interested until now in a geometric or topological description of phenomena: this step was necessary in order to make the intuitions more formal and rigorous, and allowed the practical use of rather abstract mathematical fields. The recent development of geometric invariants is one of the most prominent examples.

Geometric theories are essentially qualitative: they do not get along very well with metric measurements. Recently, however, several studies dealing with quantitative concepts have been conducted. They concern the definition of geometric robustness and utility. thanks to a concept of canonical or generic object view.

A canonical view can be characterized according to two dimensions: stability and likelihood. The definition of a view likelihood relies on a very simple and rather intuitive phenomenon: the probability distribution of an angle defined by two intersecting lines has a maximum when the viewing direction is perpendicular to the plane defined by the the two lines, if the view sphere is uniformly sampled [2, 5]. This "peaking effect" defines therefore a most probable view and has been exploited in [31] to recognize very simple polyhedrons. Another definition of generic view based on a notion of bayesian stability was proposed in [10].

The two concepts of likelihood and stability of views have been generalized in [37] and used in [13] to determine the canonical views of some simple smooth objects from their occluding contour. It was shown it these papers using some formal definitions that stable views are the most likely observed ones. More generally, canonical viewpoints are orthogonal to the first two 3D object inertia axes.

The practical use of these notions of stability and likelihood is difficult: the complexity of analytical results increases drastically with the complexity of the objects. Furthermore, and more fundamentally, the definition of a canonical view using a stability criterion is contradictory with the definition of an aspect as a set of views referenced by a region in the control space delimited by a set of catastrophic hypersurfaces. One can represent an aspect by the most stable view as a prototype, but the stability criterion does not say anything about the overall aspect organization and on their potentially predictive capacity.

The general framework studied in this paper is to allow the system to generate dynamically new object appearances by modifying its viewpoint or other control parameters. The key feature is the structure of the appearance variation. Therefore, what should be embedded in a probabilistic environment is the collection of aspects themselves, and not the set of views or appearances. The origin of an aspect is, of course, of geometric nature, but the only accessible reality is an already categorized view, in other words, the aspect itself.

The reduction of the object geometry to a probability distribution on categorized visual data allows one to integrate roughly some uncertainty on the appearence variations. It also gives a quantification of the utility of views. Some aspects will be more often observed than others depending on the object geometry; the conditional probability of aspect occurence can be converted into a likelihood. The next section will explain in more details how the aspect probability structure can be analyzed statistically.

2.2 Markov representation of aspect graphs

Visual aspects are categories of object appearances. The graph structure that comes with them, deduced from the visual events organizing their variations, can be considered as a primitive predictive tool. The graph connectivity foretells what are the expected visual events, and thus what are the possible observable aspects.

The probabilistic description of aspects gives a quantitative measure of their empirical utility. In the same way, it is possible to embed the graph structure into a probabilistic environment in order to provide some utility measure of the visual events themselves. Some events will happen more likely than others, will be more stable, will give a better and more robust characterization of the object observed.

The true origin of visual events is vision dynamics. Aspect change can only be detected if something has been actively modified, if the viewpoint has been forced to move. Said informally, it is necessary to act if you want that something happens.

It is possible to be more formal, however. If s_t represents an observed aspect at a given discrete time t, and if an action a_t from a control space is produced, the probability that an event of the form $s_t \rightarrow s_{t+1}$ for an object o_k can be described as a probability transition: $\Pr[s_{t+1} \mid s_t, a_t, o_k]$.

This last expression simply means that the probability of observing a given visual event depends on the type of object observed, on the type of viewing parameter modification, and on the current aspect observed. This probabilistic interpretation of a visual event leads to a modelling of an aspect graph as a controlled Markov chain, specific to a given object.

This probabilistic aspect graph can be simplified by assuming that the the actions are drawn from a stationnary probability distribution $\mu(a)$. A homogeneous Markov chain can then be derived from this law as:

$$\mathbf{P}_k[s_{t+1} \mid s_t] = \int_a \Pr[s_{t+1} \mid s_t, a, o_k] \, d\mu(a)$$

An object can now be modelled as a Markov chain describing the probabilistic evolution of its aspects.

At this point, it should be necessary to be a bit more precise about what I would call a *model* of an object. The probabilistic formulation of an aspect graph, as I have mentioned it above, cannot be considered as an approximate substitute of some reality. It characterizes only the *a priori* structural relations of appearences when some viewing parameters are modified according to a stationnary stochastic action law, and when the views are categorized by a fixed process. An object model must be understood as a prediction or anticipation of a sensory actuality when an observer interacts with it.

The Markovian dependence is able to take into account two different series of features: empirical measures of event utility, leading to the definition of a likelihood, and definition of visual events. The transitions with probability equal to zero and those with positive probability do not have the same interpretation. Indeed, the first ones reveal the structural organization of events, whereas the second ones measure their relative frequencies, *i.e.* their informative capacity. This double nature of the probability transitions will be used more precisely in a next section for the actual recognition of objects and the measure of recognition problem complexity.

2.3 Construction as estimation

If a Markov representation of aspect graph is used, a natural method for the determination of the model is an empirical estimation. The exact aspect graph construction translates into a problem of statistical learning. The complexity to deal with is of another kind: problem of dimension, learning time, approximation and generalization errors. This new type of complexity is usually more manageable and quantizable.

The dynamic nature of aspect graphs is captured by the notion of stochastic process. The construction of a probabilistic aspect graph will simply consist in sampling the Markov chain by generating a random sequence of actions drawn from the stationnary control law $\mu(a)$. For each object o_k all there is to do is to detect the aspect transitions $s' \to s$ and collect the frequencies $n_k(s, s')$. The corresponding probability transition will be obtained by using the standard maximum likelihood estimator [3]. From a computing point of view, an estimated aspect graphs will therefore consist in a array of integers, with many coefficients equal to zero.

There are two types of questions related to the estimation of Markov representation of aspect graphs: 1) when the learning time is unbounded, when can it be decided to stop the estimation in order to achieve a given level of confidence; 2) when the learnig time is limited, what to do with the available samples. These two questions have been studied in [15] and will be presented in a forthcoming paper. The rest of the paper is devoted to a mathematical analysis and characterization of a 3D object recognition based on Markov representations of aspect graphs.

2.4   Generalized aspects

So far, the only type of action that has been explicitly mentioned was a modification of the viewpoint, according to the classical geometric approach. It has also been pointed ou that the concept of singular point was ill defined in the context of pixel-based sensory data. Another notion of singular point, however, can be defined by introducing a *scale* of analysis.

The definition of a generalized singular point on a contour, controlled by a scale of analysis, has been proposed in a previous paper [14], following classical work on edge detection. It was emphasized that no optimal intrinsic analysis scale can be found in order to characterize a given digital curve. A shape should be analyzed at all scales. The philosophy of *scale space theory* [9, 20, 21, 11] claims precisely that the global spectrum of local extrema obtained by spatial filtering at all scales brings useful information. This means that — if we relate it to our problem of *active* recognition — scale should be considered as a control parameter, and should be actively modified.

The concept of scale of analysis, which was introduced rather naturally in order to give a a definition of a singular point on a digital contour, is in fact the prototype of a new kind of appearance variety. In other words, the variations of object appearance when the viewpoint is modified and when the scale of analysis is changed are not different in essence. The scale can be added to the control space as another dimension. From the observer, moving the viewpoint or changing the scale of analysis produces aspect transitions which are undistinguishable.

Some notion of scale in relation to aspect graphs has been proposed in [8]. The scale was not used however as a free control feature but as a parameter able to deal with some kind of "geometric noise".

3   Active recognition as a statistical inference

Markov chain representations of aspect graphs are generated by sampling a stationnary action law in a given control space. This control space may not contain only specifications of the viewpoint, but also parameters characterizing the description of appearences such as scales of pattern analysis.

Tri-dimensional object recognition translates now into a problem of Markov chain discrimination. A classical approach to this problem is to generate an empirical trajectory of a given observed chain and produce a statistical inference from the sequence of collected states — in our case a sequence of aspects.

The observation of certain aspect transitions will be rare or even impossible for some objects: they will be *selective*. When the visual features and the categorized appearances are well adapted to a given recognition problem, several aspects will be able to reshape the set of hypothetical objects by rejecting those that could not be associated with some observed aspects or transitions. In the extreme case, some observed aspect transitions will be able to index directly a given object by rejecting all the others.

The general recognition principle will be the following: the system samples the Markov chain corresponding to a given object by generating new random actions. When a selective transition is observed, a set of rejecting decision can be made in order to restrict the set of hypotheses. If it is required to take a decision based on the available data, a test is performed according to a likelihood ratio.

In this recognition scheme, two different statistical regimes compete. The first one is a function of a set of likelihood values which is modified by interacting with the environment, the second uses *a priori* discriminating data to select dynamically the set of potentially observable objects. This section is intended to formalize this scheme and to give several mathematical tools to analyze it.

3.1 Hypothesis testing of positive Markov chains

The decision principle for the recognition scheme that will be presented in this paper consists in testing whether a given object is more likely to be observed than any other. The decision will be based on the computation of all the likelihood ratios for all couples of objects once the sequence of aspects has been collected. We restrict the study in this subsection to the case of Markov representation of aspect graphs described by positive stochastic matrices.

A hypothesis test $D_T^{\Phi}(k, k')$ for a couple of objects o_k and $o_{k'}$ is a random variable taking values in $\{0, 1\}$. It takes the value 1 if it is estimated that the object o_k is more likely to be observed than object $o_{k'}$ according to the sequence of aspects $\Phi_T = (S_0, S_1, ..., S_T)$, and 0 otherwise.

Globally, it will be decided that the observed object is o_{k^*} if:

$$\forall k \neq k^*, \quad D_T^{\Phi}(k^*, k) = 1.$$

If not, no decision will be taken (the hypotheses are rejected). This decision scheme implies that the important features to study are the comparisons of two objects.

As it is customary, we define the errors of first and second kind $\alpha_T(k, k')$ et $\beta_T(k, k')$ as:

$$\alpha_T(k, k') = \mathbf{P}_k \left[D_T^{\Phi}(k, k') = 0 \right] \text{ and } \beta_T(k, k') = \mathbf{P}_{k'} \left[D_T^{\Phi}(k, k') = 1 \right]$$

which measure the mean error of rejecting the true hypothesis, and the mean error of accepting the wrong one.

The Markov representation of an aspect graph will be written as a stochastic matrix $p_k(i, j)$ if it is related to the object o_k. The columns of the matrix will be considered as the conditional probabilities: $p_k(i, j) = \mathbf{P}_k[S_t = i \,|\, S_{t-1} = j]$ if S_t is the random variable describing the observed aspect at time t. We define now the random variables $Y_t(k, k')$ as:

$$Y_t(k, k') = r_{kk'}(S_t, S_{t-1}) = \log \left[\frac{p_{k'}(S_t, S_{t-1})}{p_k(S_t, S_{t-1})} \right]$$

They can be considered as the individual contribution of each new generated action to the log-likelihood ratio between the objects o_k and $o_{k'}$. These contributions are then summed and normalized in:

$$L_T(k, k') = \frac{1}{T} \sum_{t=1}^{T} Y_t(k, k') \tag{1}$$

If a fixed threshold λ is given, the likelihood ratio test consists in deciding that the object o_k is more likely observed than $o_{k'}$ if

$$L_T(k, k') < \lambda$$

The first and second kind errors are then defined as $\alpha_T(k, k') = \mathbf{P}_k [L_T(k, k') \in [\lambda, +\infty[]$ and $\beta_T(k, k') = \mathbf{P}_{k'} [L_T(k, k') \in] - \infty, \lambda[]$.

The law of large numbers applied to Markov chains allows one to state, if the object o_k is observed, that:

$$L_T(k, k') \xrightarrow[T \to \infty]{} \sum_{j=1}^{|S|} \mu_k(j) \sum_{i=1}^{|S|} p_k(i, j) \log \left(\frac{p_{k'}(i, j)}{p_k(i, j)} \right) = -K(\mathbf{P}_k \,|\, \mathbf{P}_{k'}) < 0 \tag{2}$$

where $\mu_k(j)$ is the invariant measure of the Markov chain $p_k(i, j)$. The coefficient $K(\mathbf{P}_k \,|\, \mathbf{P}_{k'})$ plays the role of an entropy between the two chains and gives an idea of what should be the useful interval for the threshold λ used to compare the normalized log-likelihood ratio.

A better characterization of the likelihood ratio test will use asymptotic results from the theory of large deviations. Indeed, in a recognition problem, what we are really interested in is the errors behavior. One can prove [22, 16, 6]:

> **Theorem 1** *The likelihood ratio test for the positive Markov chains $\mathbf{P}_k$ and $\mathbf{P}_{k'}$ and a fixed threshold $\lambda \in] - K(\mathbf{P}_k \,|\, \mathbf{P}_{k'}), K(\mathbf{P}_{k'} \,|\, \mathbf{P}_k)[$ has first and second kind errors $\alpha_T(k, k')$ and $\beta_T(k, k')$ verifying:*
>
> $$\lim_{T \to \infty} \frac{1}{T} \log \alpha_T(k, k') = -\Lambda_{kk'}(\lambda) < 0$$
>
> $$\lim_{T \to \infty} \frac{1}{T} \log \beta_T(k, k') = \lambda - \Lambda_{kk'}(\lambda) < 0$$
>
> *where the rate function $\Lambda_{kk'}(\lambda)$ is defined as*
>
> $$\Lambda_{kk'}(\lambda) = \sup_{x \in [0,1]} (x\lambda - \chi_{kk'}(x)) \tag{3}$$
>
> *The function $\chi_{kk'}$ is given by $\chi_{kk'}(x) = \log \rho(\Pi_k(r_{kk'}, x))$ where $\rho(.)$ is the Perron-Frobenius eigen value of the matrix $\Pi_k(r_{kk'}, x) = \{p_k(i, j).\exp[x.r_{kk'}(i, j)]\}_{i,j \in S}$ and $r_{kk'}(i, j) = \log[p_{k'}(i, j)/p_k(i, j)]$.*

This theorem states that the likelihood ratio test generates errors going to zero exponentially fast. The logarithmic speed of convergence is characterized by the rate function $\Lambda_{kk'}(\lambda)$ which can be computed when the stochastic matrices are known.

When the decision threshold λ is zero, the speed of convergence of the two errors are equal. One can show easily that, in this case, the Bayes risk is optimal regarding its converging rate. The rate function corresponding to a zero threshold $\Lambda_{kk'}(0)$ is often called also Chernoff information or bound.

3.2 General case: Non negative stochastic matrices

The asymptotic results presented above require strictly positive stochastic matrices. In practice, the generic structure of aspect graphs has many impossible transitions. The corresponding incidence matrices contain therefore many null coefficients. The stochastic matrices will be in general sparse, although irreducible since all aspects communicate. Likelihood ratios will be defined only for the set of common positive probability transitions.

We define now the set of positive probability transitions for a given object o_k as:

$$\mathcal{T}_k = \{(i,j) \in \mathcal{S}^2 \,/\, p_k(i,j) > 0\}.$$

where $\mathcal{S}$ is the set of observable aspects. The transitions in this set will be called *admissible* for the object o_k. Using a conditionning by the set of admissible transitions for two objects, the decision can be divided into two terms:

$$D_T^\Phi(k,k') = \begin{cases} C_T^\Phi(k,k') & \text{if} \quad \Phi_T \in \mathcal{T}_{kk'}^T \\ S_T^\Phi(k,k') & \text{if} \quad \Phi_T \notin \mathcal{T}_{kk'}^T \end{cases}$$

where $\mathcal{T}_{kk'} = \mathcal{T}_k \cap \mathcal{T}_{k'}$.

The first term, the *comparative* part, is defined for the admissible transitions of two objects ($\Phi_T \in \mathcal{T}_{kk'}^T$). The second term, *selective*, takes a decision as soon as a selective transition has been observed. The errors can be written as:

$$\alpha_T(k,k') = \alpha_T^C(k,k')\mathbf{P}_k[\Phi_T \in \mathcal{T}_{kk'}^T] + \alpha_T^S(k,k')\mathbf{P}_k[\Phi_T \notin \mathcal{T}_{kk'}^T]$$

$$\beta_T(k,k') = \beta_T^C(k,k')\mathbf{P}_{k'}[\Phi_T \in \mathcal{T}_{kk'}^T] + \beta_T^S(k,k')\mathbf{P}_{k'}[\Phi_T \notin \mathcal{T}_{kk'}^T]$$

The selective part of the decision, $S_T^\Phi(k,k')$, do not produce any error: when a selective transition has been observed, a secure rejection decision can be taken if the set of admissible transitions has been perfectly identified. The errors, thus, come from the comparative term of the decision.

The global evaluation of the errors behavior necessitates another mathematical result. It is possible to compute the exit logarithmic speed of a Markov chain from a set of transitions [29]:

> **Theorem 2** *Let $\mathcal{T} \subset \mathcal{S}^2$ be a transition subset of a given Markov chain $\mathbf{P}_k$ having states in $\mathcal{S}$, and Φ_T a trajectory of length $T+1$. There exists a number $\rho_k(\mathcal{T}) < 1$ such that:*
>
> $$\lim_{T \to \infty} \frac{1}{T} \log \mathbf{P}_k[\Phi_T \in \mathcal{T}^T] = \log \rho_k(\mathcal{T}) < 0$$
>
> *This number is the Perron-Frobenius eigenvalue of the matrix $p_k(i,j)$ where the coefficients belonging to $\mathcal{S}^2 \setminus \mathcal{T}$ have been set to zero.*

With this result, it is easy to evaluate the global asymptotic behavior of the errors when the trajectory length goes to infinity:

$$\alpha_T(k,k') = \alpha_T^C(k,k')\mathbf{P}_k[\Phi_T \in \mathcal{T}_{kk'}^T] = A_T.e^{-v_\alpha T} \tag{4}$$

$$\beta_T(k,k') = \beta_T^C(k,k')\mathbf{P}_{k'}[\Phi_T \in \mathcal{T}_{kk'}^T] = B_T.e^{-v_\beta T} \tag{5}$$

Fig. 2. Example of four 3D objects. The two objects on the left are militar planes, the two on the right are civil planes.

where $\lim_{T\to\infty} \frac{1}{T}\log A_T = \lim_{T\to\infty} \frac{1}{T}\log B_T = 0$. The global logarithmic speeds of convergence can be computed as the sum of two terms:

$$v_\alpha = \Lambda'_{kk'}(\lambda) - \log \rho_k(\mathcal{T}_{kk'}) > 0$$
$$v_\beta = \Lambda'_{kk'}(\lambda) - \lambda - \log \rho_{k'}(\mathcal{T}_{kk'}) > 0$$

where the rate function $\Lambda'_{kk'}(\lambda)$ will be computed using the formula (3) on the Markov chains conditionned by the set of admissible transitions $\mathcal{T}_{kk'}$.

These asymptotic results give a global characterization of a 3D object recognition problem. The complexity of the problem can be measured by a single number: the error logarithmic speed of convergence to zero. This number is the sum of two terms.

The first one, $\Lambda'_{kk'}(\lambda)$, is a quantitative measure of the occurence of aspects. Thanks to this number we are able to quantify the difference between two objects having the same geometric aspect graph, but with different view frequencies. The simple recognition problem presented in the first section in **Fig. 1** can now be solved and quantified.

The second term, $-\log \rho_k(\mathcal{T}_{kk'})$, characterizes the differences between two sets of visual events. The bigger this term, the more likely recognition will be produced by structural comparisons as the classical aspect graph approach to object recognition would have produced.

4 Experiments

The theoretical elements presented above will be applied to a simulated problem of 3D object recognition. The objects tested are rather complex polyhedric representations of planes (**Fig. 2**). Three different couples will be tested: two militar planes, the civil planes and a couple formed by a militar and a civil planes. Note that the civil planes differ mainly on the relative sizes of their components.

The method used to define an object aspect requires the choice of a total number of aspects. [14, 15] present in more details the algorithms used. This paper concentrates on the conceptual foundation of an active recognition based on sampling randomly an action or control space, and on its the mathematical analysis.

The problem of recognizing 3D objects has been translated into that of discriminating Markov representations of probabilistic aspect graphs. The complexity of the problem has been characterized globally by its asymptotic behavior, which can be quantized by a logarithmic speed of convergence of the error to zero.

The computation of the recognition complexity measure depends only on the stochastic matrices and on their structure. The simulations have tested essentially the values of this measure when the number of aspects for a given problem varies. Several empirical measures of the actual recognition errors have been performed to evaluate the confidence that can be expected from the asymptotic results.

4.1 Aspect graph structure

The stochastic matrices representing the probabilistic interpretation of aspect graphs will be generally rather sparse. They have a dominant diagonal ($\forall i \neq j, p_k(i,i) \gg p_k(i,j)$) and contain a great ratio of probability transition with a zero value, *i.e.* selective transitions. The distribution of probability transitions can be divided into two modes: one of them concerns the diagonal elements of the matrices and are all above 0.2. This means that the Markov chain will stay in the same state during a rather long time and then move to another state. This should not be surprising since aspects have been defined as structurally stable classes of appearances.

In the theoretical presentation above, the key role of selective transitions has been emphasized since they have an infinite rejecting capacity. It can be observed that, when the number of aspects increases, the number of admissible transitions increases only linearly or sub-linearly: matrices tend to get sparser and their structure becomes more specific to the object they refer to.

Graph connectivity of admissible and selective transitions have interesting features: they exhibit a phenomenon of saturation (**Fig.** 3). When the number of aspects increases, the average graph degree, *i.e.* the average number of connections per node, increases also but with a sub-linear regime, indicating a decreasing connectivity. The average degree of the comparative transition graph, *i.e.* transitions which are common to two objects, reaches a maximum whereas the average degree of the selective transition graph increases more regularly.

The connectivity variation of the stochastic matrices when the number of aspects increases shows that the graph of transitions become more and more structurally discriminating. The comparative transitions increase their number until reaching a limit value after which they get distributed among the newly created aspects without generating new efficient selective transitions.

Several differences are noticeable between the three couples of objects tested. Although they exhibit the same global behavior, their quantitative characteristics show that the number of selective transitions is significantly smaller for the civil planes. This result is not really surprising since, "visually", they appear rather similar. The civil planes are less selectively distinguishable than the two other couples. This result should be confirmed by computing the recognition complexity measures provided by the large deviation theory.

4.2 Active recognition complexity

During the recognition phase, two statistical regimes compete: the first one waits until a selective transition is observed, the second one modifies incrementally the log-likelihood and takes a decision based on its final value.

The recognition complexity depends on the type of object observed, on the number of aspects, on the decision threshold and on the strategy of action sampling $\mu(a)$. In the simulations presented here the action law is a uniform random sampling corresponding to a brownian motion on the view sphere, and the decision threshold is fixed to 0.

Two numbers characterize the recognition complexity: the logarithmic speed of exiting the set of comparative transitions $-\log \rho_k(\mathcal{T}_{k'})$ and the Chernoff bound $\Lambda'_{kk'}(0)$. The sum of these two terms gives the global logarithmic speed of convergence of both the first and second kind errors $v_\alpha(k,k')$.

The graphics of **Fig.** 4 confirm the expected complexity difference between the problem of discriminating the civil planes and the two other couples of objects. Both the logarithmic exit speed and the Chernoff bound have smaller values. The global logarithmic speed of convergence increases almost linearly with the number of aspects.

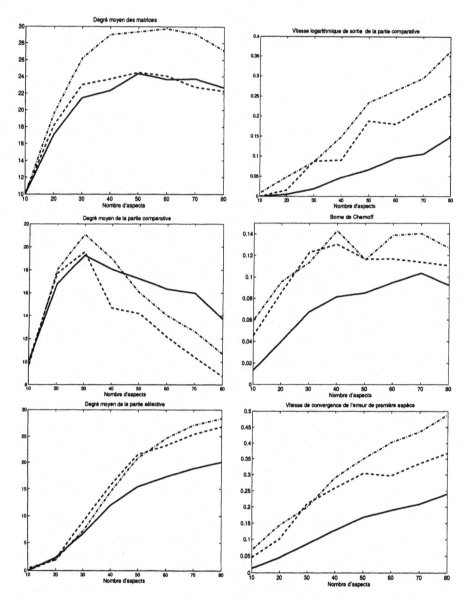

Fig. 3. Average degree of the global (top), comparative (middle) and selective (bottom) transition graphs for the couples of civil (solid line), militar (dashed line) and mixed (dotted line) planes.

Fig. 4. Logaruthmic speed of exiting from the set of comparative transitions $-\log \rho_k(k')$ (top), Chernoff bound (middle) and logarithmic speed of convergence of the error (bottom) for the couples of civil (solid line), militar (dashed line) and mixed (dotted line) planes.

The relative difference between the civil and the militar is about 40% when 50 aspects are used.

The variation of the two terms forming the global logarithmic convergence speed of the errors are not identical. When the number of aspects reaches about 40, the increase is due mainly to the logarithmic speed of exiting the comparative transitions. The Chernoff bound saturates at a value corresponding approximately to the transition graph average degree saturation of **Fig.** 3: the statistical selective regime becomes the prominent one.

4.3 Recognition performances

The theoretical results presented above gave an asymptotic characterization of the error behavior. In practice, the asymptotic regime, which corresponds to a stationnary one with Markov chains, is seldom reached since the trajectories generated will generally be short.

Fig. 5 shows the error behavior for the different couples of objects tested and for various trajectory lengths. In a logarithmic scale, the errors decrease approximately lineraly towards zero. The expected quantitaive difference between the civil plane problem and the other two is clearly noticeable.

The asymptotic results, however, must be used with care, especially if one wants to employ numerical values. **Fig.** 6 shows the error behavior for the civil plane problem and compares it with its rate function value. On this graphic, the empirical measures show worse performances than would have been expected if the chain had reached its stationnary regime. This difference can be explained by the fact that the rate function only qualifies the logarithmic speed of convergence: the functions A_T and B_T of (4) and (5) are unknown and may be influencial for short recognition trajectories.

Another critical parameter when studying Markov chains are their second largest eigenvalue which characterize the speed of convergence towards the stationnary regime. In the examples presented in this paper, the action law produced trajectories similar to brownian motions, generating Markov chains with a second largest eigenvalue around 0.95, which is a rather large value since the speed of convergence will be proportional to 0.95^T.

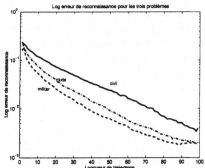

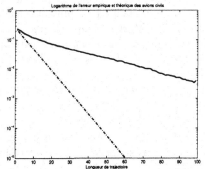

Fig. 5. Logarithmic error for the couples of civil (solid line), militar (dashed line) and mixed (semi-dashed line) planes and 50 aspects.

Fig. 6. Comparison between the theoretical (dashed line) and empirical (solid line) error behavior for the couple of civil planes and 50 aspects.

5 Related work

A few studies have been interested in designing recognition systems dealing with an active paradigm. Most of them describe exploratory strategies able to discover the most discriminating point of view or set of features, and *then* perform recognition. This question can be related to the general problem of sensor planning [32]. Recognition applications have been described in [34, 38, 36, 7, 33].

Recognition based on the active accumulation of pieces of evidence, although it has a long history in the case of 2D patterns, has been less extensively studied in computer vision. [27] describe a system able to solve simple taks by seeking actively and optimally information in a scene. They use a Bayes net to control the way the evidences are handled to perform the task. The actual use of their method for 3D vision is not clear. [25] describes a strategy using two cooperative processes — locating and identifying — to detect the presence of objects in a scene. [30] proposes a general formalism for the specific selection of useful features, and a dynamic procedure to combine them. When a hypothesis is rejected, the system changes its viewpoint or extracts another set of features. The accumulation of pieces of evidence is obtained by restricted the set of potentially observable objects. [1] proposes an evaluation of the information contained in a view by computing a likelihood conditionned to a parametric object model. The likelihood is incrementally updated using a combination of probabilities.

The series of studies most related to the work presented here is [28] and more recently [4]. They describe a system able to learn aspects and to use incrementally a sequence of aspects in a recognition phase. The system is decribed using very complex coupled differential equations with many critical parameters which role seem difficult to analyze precisely. They do not provide either a clear evaluation of recognition performances.

6 Conclusion and future work

This article has shown how active vision can be used for object recognition, and has pointed out that recognition is inherently active.

A general approach combining both "objective" and "subjective" features has been proposed. It is based on the detection of visual events when an agent interacts with the environment and on their statistical purposive accumulation. A set of mathematical tools has been provided in order to analyze and quantify the behavior and the performances of the recognition procedure.

The general stochastic representation of an aspect graph probabilistic interpretation is a *controlled* Markov chain. The recognition procedure presented in this paper used a stationnary action law: one possible extension of the model is to develop more intelligent strategies in order to seek more directly, for instance, the most discriminating aspect transitions. Object recognition becomes translated into a problem of controlled Markov process discrimination, where the action law is purposively controlled by the system.

Acknowledgements

The content of this paper described part of Ph.D work directed by Robert Azencott. The author was supported by a studentship from the CNRS.

References

1. T. Arbel and F.P. Ferrie. Informative views and sequential recognition. In *Proc. Fourth European Conference on Computer Vision, Cambridge, England, April 14-18*, pages I:469–481. 1996.
2. J. Ben-Arie. The probabilistic peaking effect of viewed angles and distances with applications to 3-D object recognition. *IEEE Transactions on Pattern Analysis and Machine Intelligence*, 12(8):760–774, 1990.

3. P. Billingsley. *Statistical Inference for Markov Processes*. The University of Chicago Press, Chicago, London, 1961.
4. G. Bradski and S. Grossberg. Fast learning VIEWNET architectures for recognizing three-dimensional objects from multiple two-dimensional views. *Neural Networks*, 8(7/8):1053–1080, 1995.
5. J.B. Burns, R.S. Weiss, and E.M. Riseman. View variation of point-set and line-segment features. *IEEE Transactions on Pattern Analysis and Machine Intelligence*, 15(1):51–68, 1993.
6. A. Dembo and O. Zeitouni. *Large Deviations Techniques and Applications*. Jones and Bartlett Publishers, Boston, 1993.
7. S.J. Dickinson, H.I. Christensen, J. Tsotsos, and G. Olofsson. Active object recognition integrating attention and viewpoint control. In J-O. Eklundh, editor, *Proc. Third European Conference on Computer Vision, Stockholm, Sweden, May 2-6*, number 801 in Lecture Notes in Computer Science, pages 3–14. Springer Verlag, Berlin, 1994.
8. David W. Eggert, Kevin W. Bowyer, Charles R. Dyer, Henrik I. Christensen, and Dmitry B. Goldgof. The scale space aspect graph. *IEEE Transactions on Pattern Analysis and Machine Intelligence*, 15(11):1114–1130, November 1993.
9. L.M.J. Florack, B.M. ter Haar Romeny, J.J. Koenderink, and M.A. Viergever. Scale and the differential structure of images. *Image and Vision Computing*, 10:376–388, 1992.
10. W.T. Freeman. Exploiting the generic viewpoint assumption. *International Journal of Computer Vision*, 20(3):243, 1996.
11. J. Gårding and T. Lindeberg. Direct computation of shape cues using scale-adapted spatial derivative operators. *International Journal of Computer Vision*, 17(2):163–191, February 1996.
12. M.R. Garey and D.S. Johnson. *Computers and Intractability — A guide to the theory of NP-completeness*. W.H. Freeman, San Francisco, 1979.
13. Y. Gdalyahu and D. Weinshall. Measures for silhouettes resemblance and representative silhouettes of curved objects. In B.F. Buxton and R. Cipolla, editors, *Proc. Fourth European Conference on Computer Vision, Cambridge, England, April 14-18*, volume 1065 of *Lecture Notes in Computer Science*, pages 363–375. Springer Verlag, Berlin, Heidelberg, New York, 1996.
14. S. Herbin. Recognizing 3D objects by generating random actions. In *Proc. IEEE Computer Society Conference on Computer Vision and Pattern Recognition, San Francisco, CA, June 18-20*, pages 35–40, 1996.
15. S. Herbin. *Eléments pour la formalisation d'une reconnaissance active — application à la vision tri-dimensionnelle*. Thèse de mathématiques appliquées, Ecole Normale Supérieure de Cachan, Juillet 1997. In french.
16. D. Kazakos. Asymptotic error probability expressions for multihypothesis testing using multisensor data. *IEEE Transactions on Systems, Man, and Cybernetics*, 21(5):1101–1114, 1991.
17. J. Köbler, U. Schöning, and J. Torn. *The Graph Isomorphism Problem: Its Structural Complexity*. Birkhauser, Cambridge, MA, 1993.
18. J. Koenderink. *Solid Shape*. MIT Press, Cambridge Ma, 1990.
19. J.J. Koenderink and A.J. van Doorn. The singularities of the visual mapping. *Biological Cybernetics*, 24:51–59, 1976.
20. T. Lindeberg. Scale-space theory: A basic tool for analysing structures at different scales. *Journal of Applied Statistics*, 21(2):224–270, 1994.
21. T. Lindeberg. *Scale-Space Theory in Computer Vision*. 1994.

22. S. Natarajan. Large deviations, hypotheses testing, and source coding for finite markov chains. *IEEE Transactions on Information Theory*, 31(3):360–365, 1985.

23. S. Petitjean. The enumerative geometry of projective algebraic surfaces and the complexity of aspect graphs. *International Journal of Computer Vision*, 19(3):261–287, 1996.

24. S. Petitjean, J. Ponce, and D. Kriegman. Computing exact aspect graphs of curved objects: algebraic surfaces. *International Journal of Computer Vision*, 9(3):231–255, 1992.

25. R.P.N. Rao and D.H. Ballard. An active vision architecture based on iconic representations. *Artificial Intelligence*, 78(1-2):461–505, October 1995.

26. J.H. Rieger. On the complexity and computation of view graphs of piecewise-smooth algebraic surfaces. Technical Report FBI_HH_M_228/93, Hamburg Univerität, 1993.

27. R.D. Rimey and C.M. Brown. Control of selective perception using bayes nets and decision-theory. *International Journal of Computer Vision*, 12(2-3):173–207, April 1994.

28. M. Seibert and A.M. Waxman. Adapative 3D-object recognition from multiple views. *IEEE Transactions on Pattern Analysis and Machine Intelligence*, 11:107–124, 1992.

29. E Seneta. *Non-negative matrices and Markov chains*. Springer Verlag, New York, second edition, 1981.

30. L.G. Shapiro and M.S. Costa. Appearance-based 3D object recognition. In M. Hebert, J. Ponce, T.E. Boult, A. Gross, and D. Forsyth, editors, *Proc. International Workshop on 3-D Object Representation in Computer Vision, New York City, NY, USA, 5-7 Dec 1994*, volume 994 of *Lecture Notes in Computer Science*, pages 51–64. Springer Verlag, Berlin, 1995.

31. I. Shimshoni and J. Ponce. Probabilistic 3D object recognition. In *Proc. Fifth International Conference on Computer Vision, Cambridge, MA, USA, June 20-22*, pages 488–493, 1995.

32. K.A. Tarabanis, P.K. Allen, and R.Y. Tsai. A survey of sensor planning in computer vision. *IEEE Transactions in Robotics and Automation*, 11(1):86–104, February 1995.

33. M. Tistarelli. Active space-variant object recognition. *Image and Vision Computing*, 13(3):215–226, April 1995.

34. J.K. Tsotsos. On the relative complexity of active vs. passive visual search. *International Journal of Computer Vision*, 7(2):127–141, January 1992.

35. T. van Effelterre. *Calcul exact du graphe d'aspect de solides de révolution*. Thèse de doctorat, Université de Rennes I, 1995.

36. S. Vinther and R. Cipolla. Active 3D object recognition using 3D affine invariants. In J-O. Eklundh, editor, *Proc. Third European Conference on Computer Vision, Stockholm, Sweden, May 2-6*, number 801 in Lecture Notes in Computer Science, pages 15–24. Springer Verlag, Berlin, 1994.

37. D. Weinshall, M. Werman, and N. Tishby. Stability and likelihood of views of three dimensional objects. In J-O. Eklundh, editor, *Proc. Third European Conference on Computer Vision, Stockholm, Sweden, May 2-6*, number 800 in Lecture Notes in Computer Science, pages 24–35. Springer Verlag, Berlin, 1994.

38. D. Wilkes and J.K. Tsotsos. Active object recognition. In *Proc. IEEE Computer Society Conference on Computer Vision and Pattern Recognition, Champaign, IL, June 15-18*, pages 136–141, 1992.

Spatial Dependence in the Observation of Visual Contours

John MacCormick and Andrew Blake

Department of Engineering Science, University of Oxford,
Parks Road, Oxford OX1 3PJ, UK
{jmac,ab}@robots.ox.ac.uk,
http://www.robots.ox.ac.uk/~ab/

Abstract. Two challenging problems in object recognition are: to output structures that can be interpreted statistically; and to degrade gracefully under occlusion. This paper proposes a new method for addressing both problems simultaneously. Specifically, a likelihood ratio termed the Markov discriminant is used to make statistical inferences about partially occluded objects. The Markov discriminant is based on a probabilistic model of occlusion which introduces spatial dependence between observations on the object boundary. This model is a Markov random field, which acts as the prior for Bayesian estimation of the posterior using Markov chain Monte Carlo (MCMC) simulation. The method takes as its starting point a "contour discriminant" designed to differentiate between a target and random background clutter.

1 Introduction: detecting occluded objects

In some object recognition applications, it is sufficient for the output to consist of a single hypothesis. In other cases, however, the output must be statistically meaningful. Ideally the output should be a list of potential target configurations with their relative probabilities, or perhaps some other representation of the posterior distribution of target configurations. This permits data fusion with the outputs of other sensors, complex hypothesis tests, and the formulation of optimal strategies for performing high-level tasks. As a simple example, consider the task of spraying weeds while avoiding genuine plants. Given a cost function that specifies the penalties incurred by spraying a plant or missing a weed, it is easy to calculate the best strategy provided that the recognition system outputs probabilistic information. The initialisation of tracking systems is another example where statistical output could be used, since the resources of the tracking system can be distributed over the probable targets in a way that maximises some performance criteria.

This paper suggests a way of achieving statistically meaningful output for a certain subset of object recognition problems. It is assumed there is only one class of target objects to be localised (this can be thought of as recognition with a database of just one object). However, there may be more than one such target in the scene to be analysed, and some of the targets may be partially occluded.

A typical example is shown in figure 1, where the problem is to localise the coffee mugs in the two images. Our objective in this paper is to design a system which reports the presence of the unoccluded mugs, and in addition detects the occluded mug *with an appropriate degree of confidence.* Note that a heuristically-based recognition system (relying, for example, on the number of a certain type of feature matches) might have difficulty even with the left-hand image since the two targets might have very different scores. This problem is amplified in the right-hand image, where one mug is partially occluded: the heuristic scores of the two targets are very unlikely to reflect the actual relative probabilities that targets are present in those two configurations.

(a) cups with no occlusion   (b) one cup partially occluded

Fig. 1. *Can a localisation system produce meaningful results from scenes like these? A heuristically-based system may or may not be able to detect both mugs in both images after appropriate tuning. However, the real challenge is to report a realistic probability that the partially occluded mug in (b) is indeed a target. Heuristic scoring functions are of little use in answering this challenge.*

An essential component of systems which can output relative probabilities is a stochastic model of how the measured image features are generated. Several authors have suggested such models though most require a certain degree of heuristic input. Examples include [5, 7, 8, 13], but none of these address the specific problem of interest in this paper, which is to obtain realistic inferences despite occlusion. Amir and Lindenbaum [1] proposed a powerful method for assessing partially occluded targets, which used graph partitioning and "grouping cues" to draw inferences on whether missing edge information is due to occlusion. Although their model was designed entirely in terms of elementary probabilities, the output was chiefly useful for identifying a single best hypothesis. Indeed, the likelihoods for plausible configurations tended to differ by many orders of magnitude, possibly due to the assumption of independence between grouping cue measures.[1] Another effective approach was suggested by Rothwell [12]. This

---

[1] If this is indeed the reason for this effect, then it makes an interesting comparison with the contour discriminants discussed in this paper, since the Markov discrimi-

used image topology, and T-junctions in particular, to assess whether missing boundaries were genuine occlusions. It is not clear to what extent the "verification scores" of [12] can be used for statistical inferences, but in any case, the methodology presented here uses measurements based on a different set of image features. Hence the outputs of each system could in principle be fused to achieve even better performance.

The solution proposed here uses an approach involving a likelihood ratio termed a *contour discriminant*[9] to produce realistic probabilistic outputs. The next section reviews contour discriminants and explains why independence assumptions render the method inadequate for assessing partially occluded targets. Subsequent sections introduce the *Markov discriminant*, and describe experiments which demonstrate it has the desired properties.

2 Contour discriminants

In [9] a new method of localising objects was introduced. It used a likelihood ratio termed a *contour discriminant* to assess whether hypothesised configurations of the target were likely to have been caused by the target itself or by random background clutter. Good results were achieved in experiments, in that the configuration with the highest discriminant was almost always a genuine target. In scenes containing more than one target, strong peaks in the contour discriminant were observed at every target, and in fact conditions were stated under which the values of the contour discriminant could be used to infer the posterior distribution for the presence of targets in the scene. Figure 2 explains how each hypothesised configuration is measured before its discriminant is calculated.

To understand the motivation behind the contour discriminant, suppose we are given a scene to analyse and are asked to consider two well-separated[2] configurations w_1 and w_2; each configuration is measured by the method of figure 2, obtaining z_1 and z_2 respectively. The objective is to infer from the measurements, and any prior knowledge, the probability that w_i is $\overline{w}$, the configuration of the true target. (For notational simplicity this section is phrased in terms of a two-hypothesis test, but everything generalises straightforwardly to the multi-hypothesis case.) It was shown in [9] that one way to approach this problem is to define a *contour discriminant* $D(w)$ by[3]

$$D(w) = \frac{F(\mathbf{z} \mid w = \overline{w})}{F(\mathbf{z} \mid w \neq \overline{w})}, \tag{1}$$

where F is the pdf of a probabilistic process producing the measurements $\mathbf{z}$ at configuration w. It then turns out that the probabilities for each w_i being

---

nant is designed to eliminate a certain independence assumption from the contour discriminant framework.

[2] A technical assumption which means the contours do not overlap significantly.

[3] If a prior on the configurations w is available, we can incorporate it by simply multiplying the discriminant by the value of the prior. The technical details of doing this were discussed in [9], but throughout this paper we assume for simplicity that the prior on configurations is uniform.

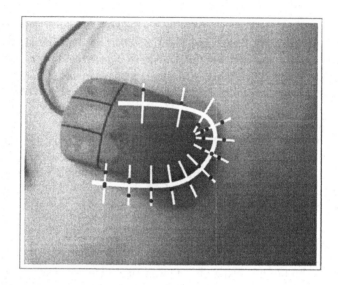

Fig. 2. *Measurement methodology and independence assumption. The thick white line is a mouse-shaped contour in some hypothesised configuration. The thin lines are measurement lines, along which a one-dimensional feature detector is applied. Black dots show the output of the feature detector; it is these outputs which are modelled probabilistically by the method of [9]. The independence discriminant assumes outputs on different lines are independent, whereas the Markov discriminant introduced in this paper uses a more sophisticated approach.*

the true configuration of the target are in the ratio $D(w_1) : D(w_2)$. Note that here $\mathbf{z}$ is a vector whose number of elements is not known in advance, listing all measurements on all N measurement lines at the configuration w. The list of measurements on the nth line is denoted z_n, and because the contour discriminant assumes the outputs of different lines are independent, the discriminant can be written

$$D(w) = \prod_{n=1}^{N} d(z_n), \qquad (2)$$

where $d(z_n)$ is a likelihood ratio analogous to (1) but for an individual measurement line. That is,

$$d(z_n) = f(z_n | w = \overline{w}) / f(z_n | w \neq \overline{w}),$$

where f is the pdf of the probabilistic process generating features on a *single* measurement line. Note that this implies $F(\mathbf{z}) = \prod_{n=1}^{N} f(z_n)$. The precise model giving rise to f is not relevant to this paper, and is described in [9]. Only one detail about f is important for this discussion: given that $w = \overline{w}$, it is assumed that there is a fixed probability q that each measurement line is occluded, and it is further assumed that these occlusion events occur *independently on each measurement line*. The importance of this fact is that it is a weakness of the contour discriminant, and this paper suggests a way to remove that weakness. To emphasise this, we will refer to the discriminant defined by (2) as the *independence discriminant*. A new expression which does not rely on the independence assumption will be introduced later and called the *Markov discriminant*.

To understand why this assumption can lead to unrealistic results, suppose a small but significant portion of the target outline is occluded — up to seven or eight measurement lines, for instance. Then the discriminant D is reduced dramatically, since according to our model of the feature formation process, seven or eight unlikely events have occurred independently. An example is shown in figure 3. In fact, only one unlikely event has occurred — a single interval of contour was occluded — but the values of the independence discriminant do not reflect this.

(a) output using independence discriminant on unoccluded mugs

(b) output using independence discriminant with one mug partially occluded

Fig. 3. *Relative values of the independence discriminant are not realistic for partial occlusions. The independence discriminant performs adequately in (a), producing peaks in the posterior with similar magnitudes at each target. However the results in (b), in which one target is partially occluded, are not at all realistic. The displayed intensity of each contour in these figures is proportional to the log of its discriminant. The right-hand peak in (b) is actually 10^{-8} times weaker than the left-hand peak and would be invisible on a linear scale. Note carefully the sense in which the contour discriminant has failed. Both mugs are successfully detected, as there are strong peaks in the discriminant at each target. However, the magnitudes of these peaks are not realistic when interpreted as relative probabilities.*

3 The Markov discriminant

To solve the problem seen in figure 3, we need a model reflecting the fact that occlusion events on nearby measurement lines are not independent. More specifically, the incorporation of such a model in a Bayesian framework will require a prior expressing the type and amount of occlusion expected. The approach taken here is to express the prior as a Markov random field (MRF), regarding the measurement lines round the contour as the sites of the MRF. The possible states of each site are "visible" and "occluded". Formally, suppose there are N measurement lines and denote the state of site n by s_n. We adopt the convention that $s_n = 1$ if site n is occluded, and $s_n = 0$ if site n is visible. An entire state vector $(s_1, \ldots s_N)$ will normally be denoted just by $\mathbf{s}$, and the set of all possible $\mathbf{s}$'s is written S — note that S has 2^N elements, and that typically N is between 10 and 100. The prior on S is denoted Θ, and the next section describes how the values of $\Theta(\mathbf{s})$ were determined in our examples.

Meanwhile, we continue the derivation of a new discriminant. The model for the formation of edge features on measurement lines is as follows:

1. A (generally small, possibly empty) subset of the measurement lines is selected as the occluded measurement lines, according to the prior Θ described in the next section. In other words, we draw a value of the occlusion state vector $\mathbf{s}$ from the prior $\Theta(\mathbf{s})$.
2. On each unoccluded measurement line, the feature generation process proceeds independently with the pdf $f(\cdot | w = \overline{w})$ described in the previous section, except that now the occlusion probability q is set to zero.
3. On each occluded measurement line, the feature generation process proceeds independently with the pdf $f(\cdot | w \neq \overline{w})$ described in the previous section.

Let $\tilde{F}$ be the new observation density arising from the model just described. For a given value of $\mathbf{s}$, we have

$$\tilde{F}(\mathbf{z} \,|\, w = \overline{w}, \mathbf{s}) = \left(\prod_{n \,|\, s_n = 0} f(z_n \,|\, w = \overline{w}) \right) \left(\prod_{n \,|\, s_n = 1} f(z_n \,|\, w \neq \overline{w}) \right).$$

Of course, to obtain an expression which can be used in calculating a new discriminant, we must sum over all values of $\mathbf{s}$, weighting by the prior probabilities $\Theta(\mathbf{s})$. This gives

$$\tilde{F}(\mathbf{z} \,|\, w = \overline{w}) = \sum_{\mathbf{s} \in S} \left(\prod_{n \,|\, s_n = 0} f(z_n \,|\, w = \overline{w}) \right) \left(\prod_{n \,|\, s_n = 1} f(z_n \,|\, w \neq \overline{w}) \right) \Theta(\mathbf{s}).$$

The denominator of the new discriminant is the same as the old one (1), so the second factor here cancels out and we get the following expression for the new discriminant:

$$\tilde{D}(w) = \sum_{\mathbf{s} \in S} \left(\prod_{n \,|\, s_n = 0} \frac{f(z_n \,|\, w = \overline{w})}{f(z_n \,|\, w \neq \overline{w})} \right) \Theta(\mathbf{s}) = \sum_{\mathbf{s} \in S} \left(\prod_{n \,|\, s_n = 0} d(z_n) \right) \Theta(\mathbf{s}).$$

To distinguish $\tilde{D}$ from the old (independence) discriminant D, we call $\tilde{D}$ the *Markov discriminant*. Although $\tilde{D}$ is a likelihood ratio and not a probability density, it will simplify our discussions to abuse notation slightly and write

$$\tilde{D}(w|\mathbf{s}) = \prod_{n \,|\, s_n=0} d(z_n), \tag{3}$$

so that the expression for the Markov discriminant is just

$$\tilde{D}(w) = \sum_{\mathbf{s} \in \mathcal{S}} \tilde{D}(w|\mathbf{s})\Theta(\mathbf{s}). \tag{4}$$

There is a crucial difficulty in calculating the Markov discriminant: the sum in (4) contains 2^N elements (recall N is the number of measurement lines) — far too many to be enumerated explicitly for typical values of N which are 10–100. Hence we must resort to a simulation technique, or equivalently, a Monte Carlo integration. The standard factored sampling method [4] would be to draw samples $\mathbf{s}^{(1)}, \ldots \mathbf{s}^{(K)}$ from Θ, and estimate (4) as

$$\frac{1}{K} \sum_{k=1}^{K} \tilde{D}(w|\mathbf{s}^{(k)}). \tag{5}$$

In fact, the convergence of this method is generally not rapid enough for practical estimation of the Markov discriminant. The results in this paper were instead calculated using an importance sampling technique described in section 7.

4 Prior for occlusions

As explained in the last section, the prior that models the types of occlusion expected will be expressed as a Markov random field whose sites are the measurement lines and whose state at each site is either "visible" or "occluded". Recall the notation for this: $\mathbf{s} = (s_1, \ldots s_N)$ is a state vector of the MRF, with $s_n = 1$ if the nth measurement line is occluded and 0 otherwise. The set of all possible $\mathbf{s}$'s is $\mathcal{S}$.

Our objective in this section is to define a prior Θ on $\mathcal{S}$. As explained in texts on Markov random fields (see [14], for example), there is a one-to-one correspondence between priors Θ and energy functions H. This correspondence is given by

$$\Theta(\mathbf{s}) = Z^{-1} \exp(-H(\mathbf{s})), \quad Z = \sum_{\mathbf{s}' \in \mathcal{S}} \exp(-H(\mathbf{s}')). \tag{6}$$

Configurations with higher energy have lower prior probability, as in thermodynamics. The method for designing such a prior has two steps. First, fix the functional form of a suitable energy function by incorporating intuitive notions of its desirable properties, and second, select or learn any parameters to achieve good behaviour for a given target object. The intuitive ideas to be incorporated by the first step are:

(a) Extensive occlusion is relatively unlikely.

(b) The occlusion is more likely to occur in a small number of contiguous intervals than in many separated intervals.

These are expressed by an energy function H of the form

$$H = \alpha \sum_{n=1}^{N} s_n - \beta \sum_{n=1}^{N} s_n s_{n+1}, \tag{7}$$

where α and β are positive real parameters to be determined later.[4] The first term in this expression penalises every occluded site, thus incorporating the intuitive idea (a) above. The second term encourages occlusion at adjacent sites, incorporating intuitive idea (b). It can be made even more explicit that idea (b) really has been captured here. Let $O = \sum s_i$ be the number of occluded sites and let I be the number of contiguous occluded intervals. Then penalising each of these quantities in the energy function would suggest adopting $H = \alpha' O + \beta' I$, for some α', β'. But observe that $I = O - P$, where $P = \sum s_i s_{i+1}$ is the number of adjacent pairs of occluded sites. Hence $H = (\alpha' + \beta')O - \beta' P$, exactly as in (7) if we take $\alpha = \alpha' + \beta'$ and $\beta = \beta'$.

The choice of precisely how to incorporate the two intuitive ideas is of course rather arbitrary. The above choice was guided by the desirability of simplicity. Note that the first term of (7) is the sum of single-site potentials, and the second term is the sum of pair potentials. This can be immediately recognised as the energy for an Ising model, and the graph of its neighbourhood system is a "necklace" — this is sometimes called a cyclic Markov random field [6]. Quantities of interest can now be calculated easily. For example, it turns out the probability of occlusion given that the two neighbours of a site are visible is given by

$$\text{Prob}(s_n = 1 \mid s_{n-1} = s_{n+1} = 0) = (1 + \exp(\alpha))^{-1},$$

and the probability of an occluded site between two other occluded sites is

$$\text{Prob}(s_n = 1 \mid s_{n-1} = s_{n+1} = 1) = (1 + \exp(\alpha - 2\beta))^{-1}.$$

In the examples shown here, the parameters were chosen so that the expected number of occluded sites is 5% of the total number of sites, and the expected number of contiguous intervals of occluded sites is 0.7; this corresponds to $\alpha = 5.33$ and $\beta = 5.0$. Alternatively, the values of α, β could, in principle, be learned from training data.

It is worth addressing one further question here: is it possible to specify α and β as a function of N, the total number of sites, in such a way that some desirable statistical properties are constant? If so, then this more general approach would be preferable to finding suitable α, β numerically for each new class of target. Unfortunately, this turns out to be a rather difficult problem. Statistical physicists are interested in the same question, and attempts to answer it have

---

[4] To avoid messy notation, we have adopted the convention $s_{N+1} = s_1$.

led to the deep and beautiful theory of renormalisation group transformations [2]. Vision researchers have also used renormalisation theory, though in a completely different context to this paper [3,10]. Some unpublished work by Nicholls suggests that numerical schemes for altering the parameters α, β may be of some use, but this is unnecessary for the limited range of examples addressed here.[5]

5 Realistic assessment of multiple targets

The first subsection below gives a broad outline and explanation of the result shown in figure 4. The second subsection gives precise details of how the experiment was carried out.

5.1 Explanation of results

Recall our objective in introducing the Markov discriminant: to obtain roughly equal peaks in the discriminant when evaluated at true target configurations, regardless of whether a small portion of the outline is occluded.

To test this we applied the method to two nearly identical scenes, figures 1(a) and (b). The first scene shows two coffee mugs with their handles visible; the second shows the same scene but this time the handle of the right-hand mug is occluded by a hand which is about to pick up the mug. Figures 3(a) and (b) show the posterior distribution as calculated by the independence discriminant. (The next subsection describes in detail exactly what these figures represent and how they were created.) When neither mug is occluded, the two peaks in the distribution differ by a factor of about 22 — not a particularly realistic result but at least the peaks have similar orders of magnitude. However, when the right-hand mug has its handle occluded (figure 3d), the independence discriminant evaluates the corresponding peak in the posterior as being approximately 10^{-8} times smaller in magnitude than the peak for the left-hand mug! This is essentially because 8 measurement lines were occluded, and since the non-detection probability q was set to 0.1, the independence discriminant considers that 8 independent events of probability 0.1 have occurred.

Next the Markov discriminant was applied to the same two scenes (figure 4). As before, when neither mug is occluded the two peaks in the posterior are of similar magnitude. However, figure 4(b) shows that the two peaks still have a similar magnitude even when the handle of the right-hand mug is occluded. This is because, according to the Markov random field prior we used on the occlusion status vectors of the measurement lines, the event that 8 consecutive measurement lines are occluded is not considered particularly unlikely.

More precise details of the relative values of the peaks in the posterior distributions are given in figure 5. Note that these numbers can actually be used for the type of statistical inferences we speculated about in the introduction. For

---

[5] We are indebted to Geoff Nicholls who pointed out the connection to renormalisation group theory and suggested relevant literature.

(a) output using Markov discriminant   (b) output using Markov discriminant
with on unoccluded mugs   with one mug partially occluded

Fig. 4. *The Markov discriminant produces more realistic posterior probabilities. When both mugs are unoccluded (a), the peak posterior probability at the left-hand mug is about 3 times that at the right-hand mug. When the right-hand mug is occluded (b), the peaks differ by a factor of about 4. Both these results are more realistic than those calculated by the independence discriminant (figure 3), but the improvement is particularly marked in the case of partial occlusion.*

	ratio of independence discr	ratio of Markov discr
both mugs visible	22	0.31
one mug partially occluded	5.8×10^{-8}	0.24

Fig. 5. *Relative heights of peaks in posterior distributions shown in figures 3 and 4. The figures shown are the peak value of the discriminant at the right-hand mug divided by the peak value at the left-hand mug. The ratios of peak values for the Markov discriminant are much more realistic than those given by the independence discriminant.*

example, suppose for simplicity we have prior knowledge that precisely one mug is present in the scene. Let w_1 be the configuration at the left-hand peak in the posterior and w_2 the configuration at the right-hand peak. Then

$$\text{Prob}(w_1 = \overline{w}) = \frac{\tilde{D}(w_1)}{\tilde{D}(w_1) + \tilde{D}(w_2)} = 0.81.$$

Similar calculations can be made with more realistic priors on the number of mugs present in the scene.

5.2 Experimental details

The coffee mug template was taken from the scene in figure 6(a); note that this is a different mug and background to those used for the experiment. The prior used for mug configurations had the following properties: uniform distribution over the two Euclidean translation parameters; rotation in the plane by an angle whose mean is zero and standard deviation 3°; scaling in the x-direction by a normally distributed factor whose mean is 1 and standard deviation 0.1; scaling in the y-direction by a normally distributed factor whose mean is 1 and standard deviation 0.05. For each scene, the same 10000 samples were drawn from this prior, and the independence contour discriminant evaluated for each one. The 100 configurations with the highest independence discriminants were recorded for further investigation, and the remainder discarded. This approach was taken mainly for a practical reason: it takes several seconds to estimate the Markov discriminant, whereas the independence discriminant has a closed-form formula which can be calculated in milliseconds.

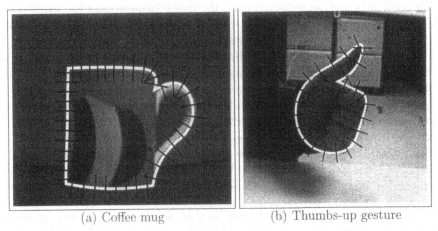

(a) Coffee mug   (b) Thumbs-up gesture

Fig. 6. *Templates for experiments. (a) There are 44 measurement lines, which means 44 sites in the cyclic MRF used to specify the prior on which parts of the contour will be occluded. (b) Note that the signaller is wearing long-sleeved clothing so there are detectable edges on the wrist area.*

The Markov discriminants of the selected 100 configurations were then estimated by the importance sampling method described in section 7. In the plots of the posterior distributions shown in figures 1, 3, and 4, the total mass of each contour (intensity × width) is proportional to the log of the contour discriminant.

6   Improved discrimination with a single target

The main motivation for introducing the Markov discriminant was to obtain more realistic relative values in the peaks of the posterior distribution when two or more targets are present. However experiments showed that in some cases the performance of the method was significantly improved even when only a single target was present.

Figure 7 shows an example of this behaviour, where the discriminant approach is being used to search for a "thumbs-up" signal in a static grey-scale image. The template thumb-signal is shown in figure 6(b); note that there is good contrast on the wrist because the signaller is wearing long-sleeved clothing. The experiment involved searching for a thumb-signal when the signaller might be wearing short sleeves, in which case no edges would be detected on the wrist. This absence of edge features is actually a generalised form of occlusion.

On around 90% of images tested, both the independence discriminant and the Markov discriminant correctly identified the single target as the strongest peak in the posterior. However, occasionally some background clutter is scored higher than the true configuration by the independence discriminant, as in figure 7(a). Of course, the reason the independence discriminant fails is that it finds no edges on the wrist area and consequently gives the true configuration a low likelihood. By evaluating the contours using the Markov discriminant instead, this situation can be rectified: in figure 7(b), for example, the peak at the correct configuration is 5 times stronger than the one at the spurious hypothesis.

The reason for the improved discrimination is as follows. Recall that the independence discriminant is calculated by multiplying together the likelihood ratios $d(z_n)$ of the measurements on each individual measurement line. Therefore, the positioning of "unlikely" measurement lines (i.e. those which do not resemble the target) is irrelevant. For instance, a configuration with three very unlikely measurement lines will score the same regardless of whether these three lines are adjacent or separated from each other by intervening sites. The Markov discriminant, on the other hand, takes precisely this type of positioning into account: consecutive (or even nearby) unlikely measurement lines do not incur as great a penalty as separated ones. Consider figures 7 as an example: the two competing configurations have a similar number of poorly-scoring measurement lines, but on the true configuration these are all on the wrist, on consecutive lines. The Markov discriminant takes this into account and gives this configuration a higher likelihood.

7 Faster convergence using importance sampling

Because it is a product of up to N individual ratios, the likelihood ratio $\tilde{D}(w|\mathbf{s})$ defined by (3) is very sharply peaked when regarded as a function of $\mathbf{s}$. Hence the factored sampling estimate (5) is dominated by the few samples near a strong peak in $\tilde{D}(w|\mathbf{s})$, and the majority of samples contribute virtually nothing to the estimate. A standard method to reduce the variance of factored sampling estimates is called *importance sampling*[6] [11]. The basic idea is to spend more time sampling near the peaks of $\tilde{D}(w|\mathbf{s})$, and compensate for this by weighting the calculation appropriately. More specifically, suppose the samples $\mathbf{s}^{(1)}, \ldots \mathbf{s}^{(K)}$

---

[6] In the specific case of statistical mechanical Gibbs samplers, importance sampling is sometimes called non-Boltzmann sampling. An accessible survey of the techniques involved is given in [2].

 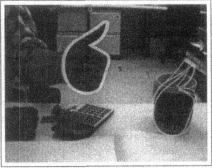

(a) independence discriminant   (b) Markov discriminant

Fig. 7. *Improved discrimination with a single target.* *Note the reason for the in-dependence discriminant's failure here: the thumbs-up template had strong edges on the wrist, which are not present in this scene. However, the Markov discriminant recognises that this generalised "occlusion" of three consecutive measurement lines on the wrist is not particularly unlikely, and therefore does not penalise the true configuration unduly.*

are drawn from an importance distribution $\Theta'(\mathbf{s})$ on $\mathcal{S}$. Then as $K \to \infty$ the quantity (4) can be estimated by

$$\frac{1}{K} \sum_{k=1}^{K} \left(\tilde{D}(w|\mathbf{s}^{(k)}) \times \frac{\Theta(\mathbf{s}^{(k)})}{\Theta'(\mathbf{s}^{(k)})} \right). \tag{8}$$

This is true for essentially any choice of $\Theta'(\mathbf{s})$, but of course the idea is to obtain faster convergence and to this end Θ' should be chosen so that a higher proportion of the samples contribute significantly to the estimate.

In the particular case of this paper, our choice of Θ' is guided by the following observation: the likelihood ratios $d(z_n)$ of the individual measurement lines give very useful guidance on likely sites of occlusion. Consider a site i for which the value of $d(z_i)$ happens to be very low. Then it is very plausible that the target boundary was occluded at this site. Hence the importance function Θ' should be biased towards the possibility that site i is occluded. We will say in this case that site i is "encouraged" to be occluded. Of course this choice can be justified by a purely numerical argument. According to (3), the contributions $\tilde{D}(w|\mathbf{s})$ to the Markov discriminant are proportional to the product of the $d(z_n)$ over *only those lines which were not occluded*. Thus if it happens that for some i the value of $d(z_i)$ is negligible, contributions to the discriminant will be non-negligible only for values of $\mathbf{s}$ that specify the ith site is occluded. Hence we are led to the following conclusion: if, for a fixed configuration w, there is a site i for which $d(z_i)$ is small, then the importance distribution $\Theta'(\mathbf{s})$ should strongly favour values of $\mathbf{s}$ with $s_i = 1$ (i.e. site i is occluded).

First we discuss the situation when only one site is "encouraged" in this way — the importance sampling method can easily be extended to encourage multiple sites but the notation becomes more complicated. Note that a different encouraged site i is selected for each configuration w. In our implementation this was done by selecting the central site of the longest contiguous low-scoring interval of contour. A measurement line was labelled as low-scoring if the likelihood ratio $d(z_n)$ was less than a parameter λ. In the rare event that no measurement line was low-scoring according to this definition, we selected the one with the lowest value of $d(z_n)$. For the examples shown here we took $\lambda = 0.2$, which corresponds to an occlusion probability of $5/6$.

The importance function for one encouraged site will be denoted Θ' and is a distribution of the Gibbs form (6) with energy denoted by H'. To define H', we must fix in advance a parameter $\gamma > 0$, which determines to what extent occlusion will be favoured at an encouraged site — this choice is discussed briefly below. Then, for a given configuration w, we select by the heuristic above a site i whose occlusion will be encouraged and define the energy of the importance function by

$$H'(\mathbf{s}) = H(\mathbf{s}) - \gamma s_i,$$

where $H(\mathbf{s})$ is the energy of the occlusion prior $\Theta(\mathbf{s})$ defined earlier. Observe that this choice does indeed "encourage" occlusion at the site i: when $s_i = 1$, the value of H' is reduced by γ, resulting in a more probable configuration.

Note that in order to perform importance sampling using (8), we must have an expression for $\Theta(\mathbf{s})/\Theta'(\mathbf{s})$. In this case, if we let Z' be the partition function — as defined by (6) — of the Gibbs distribution with energy H', we have

$$\frac{\Theta(\mathbf{s})}{\Theta'(\mathbf{s})} = \frac{\exp(-H)}{Z} \Big/ \frac{\exp(-H')}{Z'}$$

$$= \frac{Z'}{Z} \exp(-\gamma s_i). \tag{9}$$

It remains to explain how to calculate Z'/Z. It turns out that for the simple 1-dimensional, 2-state MRFs used in this paper, all the partition functions can be calculated exactly from a recursive formula, but the ratio Z'/Z can also be estimated for much more general MRFs by a Monte Carlo integration. We omit the details, but some related techniques are described in [2]. Note that although we preselected a specific site i at which occlusion would be encouraged, the value of Z' does not depend on i. This is because there is an obvious isomorphism between the MRF at which site i is encouraged and the MRF at which site j is encouraged — just rotate the "necklace" by $i - j$ sites.

Now suppose we wished to improve this importance sampling approach by using an importance function which encouraged occlusion at two different sites i and j. The argument works as before: the importance function Θ'' is of Gibbs form with energy $H'' = H + \gamma(s_i + s_j)$, and a formula analogous to (9) holds:

$$\frac{\Theta(\mathbf{s})}{\Theta''(\mathbf{s})} = \frac{Z''}{Z} \exp(-\gamma(s_i + s_j)).$$

There is no longer an isomorphism between different choices of (i, j) — in fact the partition function of the importance distribution depends on $|i - j|$. However, for a given value of $|i - j|$, the ratio Z''/Z can be calculated by either of the techniques mentioned above, so the method still works provided the $\lceil N/2 \rceil$ values needed are pre-computed. (Recall that N is the number of sites in the MRF, which is the number of measurement lines on the contour.) This approach can be extended to arbitrary numbers of "encouraged" sites, but the amount of pre-calculation necessary increases as $\binom{N}{E}$ where E is the number of encouraged sites.

The method is valid with any fixed value of γ, but once again the idea is to choose a value which causes (8) to converge quickly. If Monte Carlo integration is being used to estimate the partition function ratios, then an additional requirement is that these should also converge at an acceptable rate. We have not investigated the issue of how to choose an optimal γ, but empirical tests showed that $\gamma \approx \beta$ worked well. All results presented here took $\gamma = 4.5$. Similar comments apply to the parameter λ: the method is valid for any value, and empirical tests showed that $\lambda = 0.2$ is effective in speeding convergence.

The effectiveness of importance sampling with Θ' and Θ'' is shown in figure 8. Standard factored sampling and the importance sampling method were applied to the best 50 configurations of the unoccluded mug experiment. Each point on the graph is the standard error of 20 estimates of the Markov discriminant, and each of these 20 estimates was calculated from equation (8) with $K = 20000$. On average, the standard error of the importance sampling estimate is reduced by 60% if one site at a time is encouraged, and by 85% if pairs of sites are encouraged.

8 Conclusion

Occlusion is a perennial problem for anyone working in object localisation. This paper introduced a new way of obtaining realistic inferences about partially occluded targets. Specifically, it addressed the problem of how to adjust the contour discriminant of [9] so that the posterior probabilities of occluded targets are not over-penalised. This was done by removing the assumption that occlusion events on different measurement lines are independent: instead, the measurement lines are treated as sites in a Markov random field whose behaviour is chosen to represent the types of occlusion expected in practice. Using this MRF as the prior for a Bayesian approach, a new discriminant termed the Markov discriminant was derived.

The paper demonstrated two situations where the Markov discriminant produces far more realistic output than the previously introduced independence discriminant. Firstly, it was shown that if the Markov discriminant is used to analyse a scene with one unoccluded target and one partially occluded target, the two peaks in the posterior distribution of target configurations have similar magnitudes (see table 5). This is in marked contrast to an identical analysis using the independence discriminant, where the posterior peaks differ by several orders of magnitude. Secondly, it was shown the Markov discriminant can significantly

780

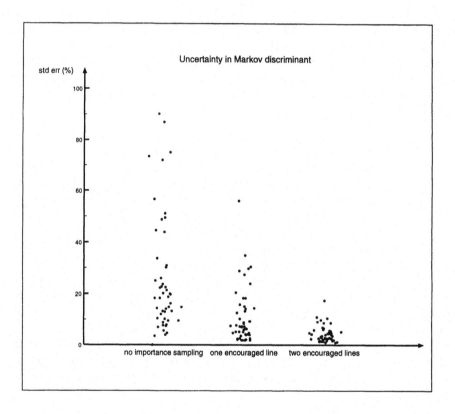

Fig. 8. *Importance sampling improves convergence of the MCMC estimates.*
*The Markov discriminant of the best 50 configurations from the unoccluded coffee mug
experiment were estimated in three different ways: (1) standard factored sampling (i.e.
no importance sampling) (2) importance sampling with one "encouraged" measurement
line selected for each configuration as described in the text (3) importance sampling with
two encouraged measurement lines. The uncertainty was found empirically by estimating the discriminant value 20 times for each configuration. On the y-axis is shown the
standard error of the 20 estimates, expressed as a percentage of their mean.*

improve differentiation between partially occluded targets and background clutter (figure 7). This is because the Markov discriminant takes account of which
types of occlusion have good support from the prior.

There is an important open problem associated with the method, related
to the accuracy and speed of the estimates of the Markov discriminant. The
improved performance was gained at the expense of introducing Monte Carlo
simulation which takes seconds rather than milliseconds, and therefore precludes
the use of the Markov discriminant in real time situations. The details given in
section 7 show how importance sampling can be used to speed convergence, but
even with these improvements it can take over 5 seconds on a desk-top workstation to obtain an estimate with relative error less than 10%. Uncertainties of this
magnitude are acceptable for the outputs described here, but better accuracy

might be required for more precise statistical inferences. A related problem is therefore the choice of which configurations to analyse with the Markov discriminant, since it is essential that all significant peaks in the posterior are evaluated. Hence one avenue of future work on this topic will be to investigate ways of judiciously choosing when to use MCMC, and for how long.

The success of the Markov discriminant shows it is possible to apply rigorous probabilistic modelling and Bayesian methods to the classic problem of occlusion. Moreover it represents a significant advance in the potential of recognition systems to provide meaningful statistical information to higher-level systems. It remains to be seen, however, whether any of the current recognition paradigms can realise this potential.

References

1. A. Amir and M. Lindenbaum. Grouping based non-additive verification. Technical Report 9518, Center for Intelligent Systems, Technion, 1996.
2. D. Chandler. *Introduction to Statistical Mechanics*. Oxford University Press, 1987.
3. B. Gidas. A renormalisation group approach to image processing problems. *IEEE Trans. Pattern Analysis and Machine Intelligence*, 11(2):164–180, 1989.
4. U. Grenander. *Lectures in Pattern Theory I, II and III*. Springer, 1976–1981.
5. W.E.L. Grimson, D.P. Huttenlocher, and D.W. Jacobs. A study of affine matching with bounded sensor error. In *Proc. 2nd European Conf. Computer Vision*, pages 291–306, 1992.
6. J.T. Kent, K.V. Mardia, and A.N. Walder. Conditional cyclic Markov random fields. *Adv. Appl. Prob.*, 28:1–12, 1996.
7. T.K. Leung, M.C. Burl, and P. Perona. Finding faces in cluttered scenes using random graph matching. In *Proc. IEEE PAMI Conf.*, pages 637–644, Cambridge, June 1995.
8. D.G. Lowe. Robust model-based motion tracking through the integration of search and estimation. *Int. J. Computer Vision*, 8(2):113–122, 1992.
9. J.P. MacCormick and A. Blake. A probabilistic contour discriminant for object localisation. In *Proc. 8th Int. Conf. Computer Vision*, Jan 1998.
10. P. Perez and F Heitz. Restriction of a Markov random field on a graph and multiresolution statistical image modelling. *IEEE Trans. Information Theory*, 42(1):180–190, 1996.
11. B.D. Ripley. *Stochastic simulation*. New York: Wiley, 1987.
12. C. Rothwell. Reasoning about occlusions during hypothesis verification. In *Proc. 4th European Conf. Computer Vision*, pages 599–609, April 1996.
13. I. Shimshoni and J. Ponce. Probabilistic 3D object recognition. In *Proc. 5th Int. Conf. Computer Vision*, pages 488–493, 1995.
14. G. Winkler. *Image analysis, random fields and dynamic Monte Carlo methods*. Springer, 1995.

Handling Uncertainty in 3D Object Recognition Using Bayesian Networks

B. Krebs, M. Burkhardt and B. Korn
email:{B.Krebs, M.Burkhardt, B.Korn}@tu-bs.de

Institute for Robotics and Computer Control, Technical University Braunschweig,
Hamburger Str. 267, D-38114 Braunschweig, F.R.G.

Abstract. In this paper we show how the uncertainty within a 3d recognition process can be modeled using Bayesian nets. Reliable object features in terms of object rims are introduced to allow a robust recognition of industrial free-form objects. Dependencies between observed features and the objects are modeled within the Bayesian net. An algorithm to build the Bayesian net from a set of CAD models is introduced. In the recognition, entering evidence into the Bayesian net reduces the set of possible object hypotheses. Furthermore, the expected change of the joint probability distribution allows an integration of decision reasoning in the Bayesian propagation. The selection of the optimal, next action is incorporated into the Bayesian nets to reduce the uncertainty.

1 Introduction

The task to perform recognition for a 3d scene is a highly complex process which involves various types of sensor processing and interpretation algorithms. A human observer identifies the objects by the knowledge of what he expects to see. If an unknown object occurs the observer may try to find a clue by looking from different directions or may try to detect specific features to solve the ambiguity. Thus, the cognitive process of recognition should be described rather as a task-triangle than a simple bottom-up or top-down process (Figure 1). Based on the

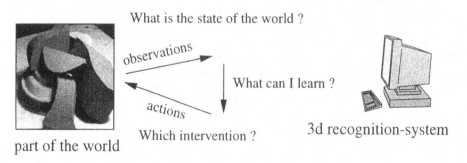

Fig. 1. The task-triangle which has to be modeled in a recognition system.

observations of the world (from sensor data) an interpretation of the scene is established. Since the sensor information may be incomplete or misleading this interpretation has to be considered as uncertain. The observer decides on an action to obtain a better interpretation of the scene. As a result of the observer's intervention the knowledge of the state of the world increases.

All available a priori knowledge has to be integrated to make 3d recognition system reliable. Not only reliable object features (what I expect to see) but also the dependencies between the observations of the object feature (what are the expected relations of the observations) have to be specified. Hence, the domain of observations with their uncertainties has to be modeled and classical probability calculus and decision theory has to be used to guarantee a consistent representation. Now, the recognition task becomes a task to minimize the uncertainty in the scene interpretation.

In section 2 we define reliable free-form object features. This features are treated as elemental observations which are modeled with their dependencies to the objects in a Bayesian net (section 3). Since information from a single view may be insufficient to get reliable results an *active recognition system* has to implement the task-triangle in Figure 1. Dependent on the current evidence appropriate actions have to be executed to acquire more information about the scene. Rimey and Brown showed that evidence values from Bayesian nets can also be used for selecting next actions [19]. However, the decision reasoning is still done with explicit *goodness functions*. We show that the whole decision process can be encoded in a Bayesian net incorporating cost-benefit analysis to select the optimal action of a set of admissible actions.

Early approaches to integrate e.g. viewpoint selection into Bayesian nets don't use the general approach for decision reasoning proposed in this paper which allows a more flexible and more powerful design of various decision schemes [5, 6]. Thus, Bayesian nets and decision theoretic techniques provide a sound formal basis for representation and control in a selective perception system.

2   Rim Curves for Object Identification

The definition of reliable features for free-form objects is a major research field in CAD based vision (CBV). Features based on differential properties are very vulnerable with respect to noise. Some authors proposed to model small, local surface portions, e.g. in terms of "splashes" [21]. Other approaches represented surfaces with a tessellated graph (e.g. [7, 10]) or with point samples (e.g. [2, 4]). Nevertheless, all these algorithm involve complex computations because surface identification is a two dimensional search problem (3 DOF).

Nevertheless, usual industrial objects do not consist of an overall smooth surface but contain rims, edges, and holes. Using these *object rims* the matching problem is reduced to a one dimensional search (1 DOF). A rim is defined as a 3d space curve separating two adjacent surfaces at a discontinuity. The object rims are represented by 3d B-spline curves. A 3d curve can be identified by curvature

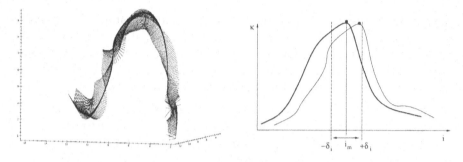

Fig. 2. Matching of subcurves around a curvature extremum.

and torsion values which are invariant with respect to 3d transformations. Rim curves describing surface discontinuities can be efficiently computed from CAD data ([8]) and range images as well ([14]) allowing an robust CAD based vision system. For a 3d space curve at each curve point p_i a Frenet-Frame F_i is defined by

$$F_i = \left[t_i = \frac{\dot{p}_i}{\|\dot{p}_i\|} \ , \ b_i = \frac{\dot{p}_i \times \ddot{p}_i}{\|\dot{p}_i \times \ddot{p}_i\|} \ , \ m_i = t_i \times b_i \right] \tag{1}$$

which allows the computation of the curvature $\kappa = \frac{d\alpha}{ds}$ and torsion $\tau = \frac{d\beta}{ds}$:

$$d\alpha_i = arccos \left(\frac{< t_i, t_{i+1} >}{|t_i| |t_{i+1}|} \right) \quad , \quad d\beta_i = arccos \left(\frac{< b_i, b_{i+1} >}{|b_i| |b_{i+1}|} \right) . \tag{2}$$

Thus, an equidistanly sampled 3d B-spline is uniquely represented by two feature sequence:

$$f_{s_\kappa} = [d\alpha_0, \ldots, d\alpha_{n_s}] \quad , \quad f_{s_\tau} = [d\beta_0, \ldots, d\beta_{n_s}]. \tag{3}$$

The *similarity* between two feature sequences f_s and f_c is defined by

$$s(i,j) = \begin{cases} 1 & (f_s[i] - f_c[i+j])^2 \le \varepsilon_{max} \\ 0 & else \end{cases} \tag{4}$$

$$s_f(i) = \sum_j s(i,j). \tag{5}$$

Since curvature and torsion are significant for a 3d curve an extracted curve can be identified by the *combined similarity*:

$$s(i) = \frac{\gamma_1 s^\kappa(i) + \gamma_2 s^\tau(i)}{\gamma_1 + \gamma_2} \quad \gamma_1, \gamma_2 \in [0,1] \tag{6}$$

whereas γ_1, γ_2 determine whether curvature or torsion is more discriminant. In our case curvature is more important because the rim curve lay within the object surfaces, i.e. $\gamma_1 = 0.8, \gamma_2 = 0.2$. The best match is described by the *maximum of similarity*

$$i_{max} = \max_{i \in [0, n_c - n_s]} s(i) \tag{7}$$

with the *matching evidence*

$$e_m = \frac{s(i_{max})}{n_c} \in [0,1] \tag{8}$$

the rim curves are divided into *subcurves* to guarantee locality (*Local Feature Focus*) and to handle different curve length. Subcurves are selected around a curvature extremum. This allows a simple matching by only computing the similarity around the maxima at the index i_m (Figure 2), i.e. the index j for computing the subcurve's similarity is only taken from the interval $j \in [i_m - \delta_i, i_m + \delta_i]$ within the subcurve in equation (4) and (5).

Subcurves have to be distinct to allow a reliable subcurve identification. Therefore, in an off-line preprocessing the set of all subcurves $\acute{S}$ is computed from a given set of CAD objects ([8]). All subcurves which are similar, i.e. $e_m > \varepsilon_1$, are represented by the subcurve with the highest maximum to form the set of *significant subcurves* $S = \{S_0, \ldots, S_n\}$. If an extracted subcurve S_c is identified by the matching with $e_c = \max_{S_i \in S} e(S_c, S_i) \geq \varepsilon_m$ then the transformation T_f to map the model subcurve S_i onto the extracted subcurve S_c is computed by a least square minimization [11].

3 Bayesian Nets for 3d Recognition

The uncertainty in the recognition process has two major sources. On the one hand erroneous sensor data leads to an erroneous feature extraction or to noisy feature values. Reasoning with Bayes rules for low level feature computation

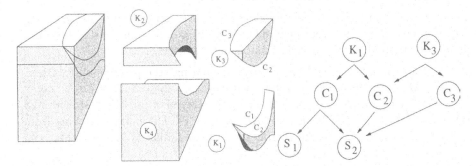

Fig. 3. Dependencies between subcurves, curves and objects define a Bayesian net.

from sensor data has been successfully applied (e.g. [1,9]).

On the other hand uncertainty may result from a misclassification between an object and extracted features or from an inseparability between objects which have similar features. To cope with these problems the statistical behavior of the features has to be modeled within the recognition process. Using *Bayesian nets* not only the statistical behavior of the feature values but also the dependencies between features and objects can be used.

A Bayesian net is a acyclic directed graph (DAG) where the nodes represent a random variable with a fixed set of states and the directed links represent the dependencies between the nodes. For the 3d object recognition example each node represents a hidden cause or an observed feature with the states present (=y) or not present(=n).

In most object recognition systems using Bayesian nets the nodes represent subparts of an object [3, 16, 19]. However, observable features need not to coincide with object subparts, i.e. features from the same subpart are not statistical independent as it is assumed by constructing objects from subparts. Furthermore, general free-form objects can not be constructed from a simple set of primitives.

Thus, constructing a Bayesian net the dependencies between observations and not between geometrical primitives have to be modeled. Furthermore, the leaf nodes in a Bayesian net have to be independent. The first step is to define reliable object features which can easily be extracted from sensor data and CAD data. In the previous section subcurves of object rims are defined to provide simple and robust features to identify industrial free-form objects. The match of a subcurve with the matching evidence e_m (8) represents an observation and the evidence is entered into the corresponding leaf node of the Bayesian net.

Nevertheless, a major problem using Bayesian nets for recognition is the encoding of the object's locations. Sakar and Boyer proposed the Perceptual Inference Network (PIN) which is a special Bayesian net propagating not only belief values but also position information [20]. But their methods involve highly complex propagation algorithms. Hence, the PIN is reduced to a tree-like structure and is used for reasoning in 2d gray level images only.

We propose to model only relational properties of objects and features in a Bayesian net. The nodes represent subsets of object's hypotheses and the links point from more discriminative to more general subsets.

The Bayesian net can be constructed by "simulating" the possible observations in the CAD data. In a first step for each object in the database a root node, a node with no parents, is introduced in the Bayesian net. In a second step rim curves are extracted from the CAD models [8]. The curve matching from the previous section allows the computation of the similarity between these rim curves. A high matching evidence

$$e_m > \varepsilon_e \qquad (9)$$

indicates a dependency between the two curves. The threshold ε_e indicates the ability to separate different types of curves depending on the uncertainty of the sensor data. The value is determined by experiments with real data and in our case is set to $\varepsilon_e = 0.90$. All similar curves are mapped onto a single node. Links between the root nodes and the curve nodes are established if a high matching evidence is found by equation (9).

Subsequently, the curves are divided into subcurves to allow object identification even if only a part of a curve is visible. Only *significant subcurves* are mapped onto leaf nodes in the Bayesian net to guarantee the independence of the leaf nodes. Similar subcurves given by equation (9) are represented only by a single subcurve, i.e. are represented by the subcurve with the highest curvature maximum.

If a significant subcurve is similar to a curve by equation (9), i.e. if the significant subcurve $S_i \in C_n$ is similar to the subcurve $S_j \in C_m$, then there is a link between (S_i, C_n) and (S_i, C_m). The nodes representing subcurves are the expected observations. All the other nodes represent the hidden causes containing a set of likely object hypotheses. Therefore, the proposed Bayesian net contains three node layers describing subcurves, curves and objects (Figure 3). The propagation of detected features can be performed without considering the positions of the subcurves.

To complete the network specification we have to specify the prior and the conditional probabilities at the nodes. If prior knowledge of the probabilities of occurrence for the objects in the scenes is available then the priors must represent the expected probability of occurrence. In the absence of any prior knowledge we assume equal prior probabilities:

$$P(O_i = n) = P(O_i = y) = \frac{1}{2} \tag{10}$$

The conditional probability at a node represents the conditional belief that a child node is caused by the parent node, i.e. a set of hypotheses sharing a curve causes the observation of a specific subcurve. The matching evidence (8) determines the *likelihood*

$$L(C|S) := e_m \tag{11}$$

that the observation of a specific subcurve S was caused by a curve C and the likelihood $L(O|C)$ of the curve C to have been caused by the object O.

The conditional probability table at each node with parents describes the strength of the links to the parents. If evidence is entered into a node N the evidence must be distributed to the parents $pa(N) = P = \{N_0, \ldots, N_l\}$. Hence, the correct conditional probabilities $P(N|P^*)$ for all states in a node N dependent on all combinations of the states in the parent nodes have to be specified. A likelihood value represents only the strength to a single parent. The whole conditional probability table is computed by the "*noisy or*" operation [12, 18].

Each event $C_i = present = y$ causes $S = present = y$ unless an inhibitor prevents it, and the probability for that is

$$q_i = 1 - L(C_i|S). \tag{12}$$

That is, $P(S = n|C_i = y) = q_i$ assuming all inhibitors to be independent. The conditional probabilities are defined by:

$$P(S = n|C_0, \ldots, C_n) = \prod_{j \in Y} q_j \tag{13}$$

where Y is the set of indices for variables in the state *present* $= y$ [12]. The conditional probabilities $P(C|O^*)$ are computed likewise.

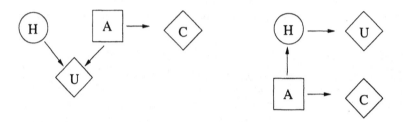

Fig. 4. There are two different types of actions: an action with has no impact on the probability distribution (left) and an action changing the probability of H (right).

4 Decision Reasoning in Uncertainty

To take decisions under uncertainty the global goal is to reduce the uncertainty within the recognition process. The recognition has to decide in a quest for more information which action to take. Let the knowledge be represented in one variable called a hypothesis H with a probability distribution $P(H)$, i.e. given a hypothesis with n_h exclusive states with a probability value each. The driving force for the evaluation of the information value is the variable H, i.e. the decision process is called *hypotheses driven* [12].

Given a set of admissible actions $A = \{a_0, \ldots, a_n\}$ and a *utility table* $U(a, h)$ which describes the utility of each action to reduce the uncertainty if the state $h \in H$ is true. The *value of information* $V(a)$ for each action is the expected

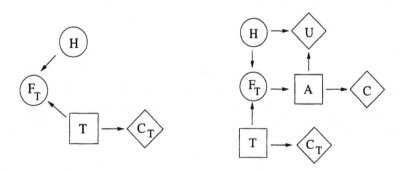

Fig. 5. A test action is an intervening action connected to a node which carries the test outcome as states (left Figure). A test can be easily combined with any arbitrary action (right Figure).

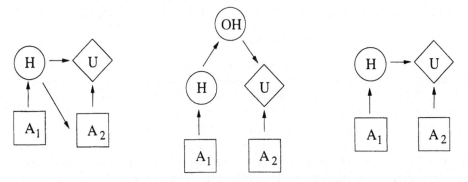

Fig. 6. Decision reasoning with known results (left), uncertain results (middle) and unknown results (right) from action $a_1 \in A_1$.

utility $EU(a)$ of the action:

$$V(a) = EU(a) = \sum_{h \in H} U(a,h)P(h). \qquad (14)$$

The *value of information* V for the whole decision process is a function of the distribution of H defined by the *expected utility* EU of performing the *optimal action* $opt(A) \in A$:

$$V(P(H)) = EU(P(H)) = \max_{a \in A} \sum_{h \in H} U(a,h)P(h). \qquad (15)$$

The optimal action $opt(A)$ is the argument which maximizes the value of information V:

$$opt(A) = \arg\max V(a). \qquad (16)$$

Introducing costs for each action the *expected gain* $g(a)$ of an action is defined by

$$g(a) = \max(V(a) - c(a), 0) \in [0,1] \qquad (17)$$

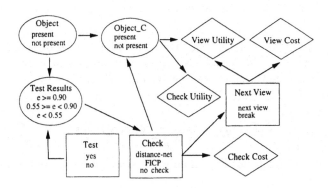

Fig. 7. An example task net to select the optimal action for 3d object recognition.

and the optimal action $opt_g(A)$ maximizes now the expected gain with

$$opt_g(A) = \arg \max g(a). \tag{18}$$

This decision problem can be mapped conveniently on a Bayesian net with a *influence graph* [12]: A two state utility node U is connected with the hypothesis. The decision table is mapped on the conditional probability table of U. The action's costs are mapped likewise onto a utility node C. The set of actions is mapped on a n state decision node A and the cost node C is connected to it. Now, we have only to distinguish between *intervening* and *non-intervening* actions (Figure 4). The execution of a non-intervening action doesn't change the probability distribution in the hypothesis H whereas the execution of a intervening action does, i.e. the decision node A is connected to the utility node U or the hypotheses node H is connected to the decision node A. The *expected utility* of a non-intervening actions is

$$EU(a|e) = \sum_{h \in H} U(a,h)P(h|e). \tag{19}$$

The optimal action for a non-intervening actions can be computed by an Bayesian net (see left Figure 4) with:

$$opt(A) = \arg \max(P(U = y|a,e) + C(a)). \tag{20}$$

Several sets of non-intervening actions can be computed independently and the optimal action is the Cartesian product of the separated optimal actions [12].

The *expected utility* of a intervening actions is

$$EU(a|e) = \sum_{h \in H} U(h)P(h|a,e). \tag{21}$$

The optimal action for an intervening actions can be computed by an Bayesian net (see right Figure 4) with:

$$opt(A) = \arg \max \left[\frac{P(a|U = y, e)}{P(a|e)} + C(a) \right]. \tag{22}$$

Several sets of intervening actions must be solved by simulating each action [12].

Now we have to consider a sequence of actions, e.g. taking a test before executing an action. The outcome of the test has a direct influence of the merit of an action. Furthermore, a test action is an intervening action and may influence the probability of the hypothesis H, i.e. the evidence whether an object is "present" or not. If a test T with cost $c(T)$ yields the outcome t then the value of the new information is

$$V(P(H|t)) = \max_{a \in A} \sum_{h \in H} U(a,h)P(h|t). \tag{23}$$

Since the outcome of T is not known only the *expected information value* $EV(T)$ can be considered:

$$EV(T) = \sum_{t \in T} V(P(H|t))P(t). \tag{24}$$

The expected gain $g(T) \in [0, 1]$ performing the test T is

$$g(T) = \max(EV(T) - V(P(H)) - c(T), 0). \tag{25}$$

A test is easily incorporated into a Bayesian net (see left Figure 5). A chance node F_T with a state for each test result is connected to a decision node T containing the test actions. After performing the test evidence for the outcome t is entered into the net. Deciding which action to execute by first taking a test can be easily combined in one Bayesian net and no further computation is necessary (see right Figure 5). Taking a test is only profitable if the decision to select an action is changed through the outcome of the test. Hence, not only the impact of taking test T onto the selection of an action from A but also the decision whether to take the test can be computed by equation (22).

The procedure to select an action after taking a test uses a single look-ahead and is called the *myopic* approach (e.g. [12, 19]). Nevertheless, the results from an action my either be uncertain or unknown. Therefore, the look-ahead has to be performed over a sequence of actions to allow non-myopic action selection; e.g. the utility of two subsequent actions may be greater than the utility of each single action. Deciding on a sequence of actions $(a_1 \in A_1, a_2 \in A_2)$ three different cases can be distinguished: the results from action a_1 are known, myopic strategy (Figure 6 left), the results are known but are uncertain (Figure 6 middle) or are unknown, non-myopic strategy (Figure 6 right). This can be implemented in a Bayesian net as well by changing the order of the summation/maximization. The utility for the myopic case $MEU_1(A_2|a_1)$, the uncertain case $MEU_2(A_2|a_1)$ and the non-myopic case $MEU_3(A_2|a_1)$ computes to:

$$MEU_1(A_2|a_1) = \sum_h \max_{a_2} \ U(a_2, h)P(h|a_1) \tag{26}$$

$$MEU_2(A_2|a_1) = \sum_o \max_{a_2} \ (\sum_h U(a_2, h)P(o, h|a_1)) \tag{27}$$

$$MEU_3(A_2|a_1) = \max_{a_2} \sum_h U(h, a_1)P(h|a_1) \tag{28}$$

whereby the summation performs a marginalization over all unknows. Since a non-myopic decision reasoning is more uncertain the following equation holds:

$$MEU_3 \leq MEU_2 \leq MEU_1 \tag{29}$$

This theoretical background allows to build highly complex decision schemes. Furthermore, the selection and execution of actions can be easily incorporated within the evidence propagation scheme allowing an interaction of scene interpretation and e.g. sensor actions in the recognition.

5 Recognition Results

The range images are acquired with a sensor based on the coded light approach (CLA) which is a well-known active triangulation method. The Bayesian net was

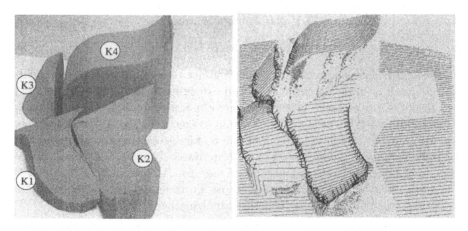

Fig. 8. An example view of a scene with four objects (left) and the extracted 3d spline curves in the corresponding range image (right).

implemented using the HUGIN software system [17]. The proposed algorithms are implemented on a SUN Sparc V. The modelbase of significant subcurves is either extracted from CAD models or learned in a previous range data extraction for each single object.

The decision reasoning is done with a task net depicted in Figure 7. The task net has a sequence of three different action types. First a test is performed which checks whether any reliable evidence for each interpretation (object node in the Bayesian net) has arrived. The thresholds are taken from the matching evidence threshold ε_e in equation (9). If the evidence is greater than ε_e the object is identified and *single object hypotheses* are created which carry a position information. Each single hypothesis is validated by a Fuzzy ICP algorithm [15]. If the evidence lies between 0.55 and ε_e a different Bayesian net encoding distance information is used [13]. After performing the validation actions the system checks whether new information by new range images is necessary.

An recognition example for CAD models is depicted in Figure 8. The propaga-

Table 1. Results for single and final match of CAD models

object	single e_m	#S_i	matched
$P(K1{=}y)$	0.7634	16	5
$P(K2{=}y)$	0.8673	24	6
$P(K3{=}y)$	0.6735	17	4
$P(K4{=}y)$	0.4534	8	1

object	final e_m	#S_i	views
K1	0.76	5 of 16	1
K2	0.86	6 of 24	1
K3	0.88	4 of 17	2
K4	0.76	2 of 8	3

tion results of a single view and after a view sequence are listed in table 1. The propagation results after a single view yield that the objects "K2", "K1" and "K3" have a high evidences because many subcurves are correctly matched. The

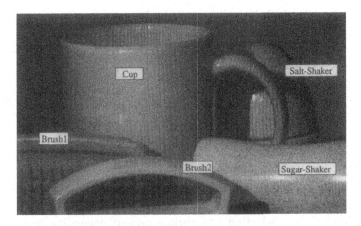

Fig. 9. An example view of every day objects.

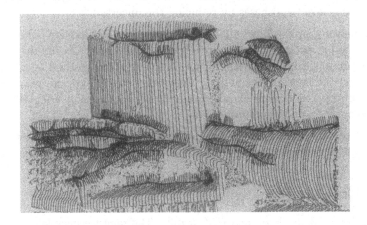

Fig. 10. The extracted 3d spline curves in the corresponding range image.

evidence for object "K4" allows no statement about the finding of the object in the scene because a evidence value about 0.5 is not significant. The sensor data is highly corrupted, thus no correct subcurves are found. After evaluating more views the object "K4" is correctly identified by using the task net from Figure 7 as shown in the table 1.

In Figure 9 a sample of every-day objects is analyzed. The model curves are learned in a previous off-line step for each object. The achieved matching evidence is shown in table 2. Since the edges of the objects for the learned example ar not as crisp as in the CAD example matching evidence is lower. Furthermore, the reflections on the surface disturb the curve extraction. Thus, more views are necessary to identify the objects.

The results show that common objects can be recognized with a database either

Table 2. Matching results for learned subcurves

object	single e_m	#S_i	matched
P(Cup=y)	0.7834	5	2
P(Brush1=y)	0.8073	8	3
P(Brush2=y)	0.54	4	1
P(Sugar-Shaker=y)	0.6	6	1
P(Salt-Shaker=y)	0.57	3	1

object	final e_m	#S_i	views
Cup	0.78	2 of 5	1
Brush1	0.80	6 of 8	1
Brush2	0.88	4 of 4	2
Sugar-Shaker	0.77	2 of 6	5
Salt-Shaker	0.76	2 of 3	7

from CAD descriptions or learned from previous views.

We showed that the separation of position independent from position dependent know-ledge solves a major problem introducing Bayesian nets in recognition systems. Furthermore, selecting appropriate actions depending on the already acquired evidence can be incorporated in the Bayesian nets. The recognition process adapts to the actual information via a task net which minimizes the set of mutual exclusive hypotheses by reducing the uncertainty.

Using influence graphs allows to build highly complex decision schemes even with non-myopic action selection providing a much more flexible decision reasoning within a vision system than any other proposed method (e.g.[5, 6, 19]). Furthermore, the concept of handling uncertainty with Bayesian networks and selecting appropriate actions is quite general and can be easily adapted to other field of recognition and computer vision.

Using features from 3d rim curves provide sufficient information to allow a robust and efficient identification and pose estimation of industrial free-form objects.

References

1. K. L. Boyer, M. j. Mirza, and G. Ganguly. The robust sequential estimator: A general approach and its application to surface organisation in range data. *IEEE Transactions on Pattern Analysis and Machine Intelligence*, 16(10):987–1001, 1994.
2. K. Brunnstroem and A. J. Stoddart. Genetic algorithms for free-form surface matching. In *Proc. International Conference on Pattern Recognition, Vienna, Austria*, 1996.
3. D. M. Chelberg. Uncertainty in interpretation of range imagery. In *Proc. International Conference on Computer Vison, Osaka, Japan*, pages 634–657, 1990.
4. C. S. Chua and R. Jarvis. 3d free-form surface registration and object recognition. *Int. J. of Computer Vision*, 17:77–99, 1996.
5. D. Dijan, P. Probet, and P. Rives. Active sensing using bayes nets. In *Proc.International Conference on Advanced Robotics*, pages 895–902, 1995.
6. D. Dijan, P. Rives, and P. Probet. Training bayes nets for model-based recognition. In *Proc.International Conference on Control, Automation, Robotics and Computer Vision, Singapore*, pages 375–379, 1996.
7. C. Dorai and A. K. Jain. Recognition of 3-d free-form objects. In *Proc. International Conference on Pattern Recognition, Vienna, Austria*, 1996.
8. G. E. Farin. *Curves and Surfaces for Computer Aided Geometric Design, a Practical Guide 3rd. ed.* Academic Press, New York, 1993.

9. K. Goldberg and M. Mason. Bayesian grasping. In *Proc. IEEE International Conference on Robotics and Automation, Cincinnati, Ohio*, pages 1264–1269, 1990.
10. K. Higuchi, M. Hebert, and K. Ikeuchi. Bulding 3-d models from unregisterd range images. In *Proc. IEEE International Conference on Robotics and Automation, San Diego, California*, pages 2248–2253, 1994.
11. B. K. P. Horn. Closed-form solution of absolute orientation using unit quaternions. *J. Opt. Soc. of America*, 4(4):629–642, 1987.
12. F. V. Jensen. *An Introduction to Bayesian Networks*. UCL Press, 1996.
13. B. Krebs, B. Korn, and M. Burkhardt. A task driven 3d object recognition system using bayesian networks. In *Proc. International Conference on Computer Vison, Bombay, India*, pages 527–532, 1998.
14. B. Krebs, B. Korn, and F.M. Wahl. 3d b-spline curve matching for model based object recognition. In *Proc. International Conference on Image Processing, Santa Barbara, USA*, pages 716–719, 1997.
15. B. Krebs, P. Sieverding, and B. Korn. A fuzzy icp algorithm for 3d free form object recognition. In *Proc. International Conference on Pattern Recognition, Vienna, Austria*, pages 539–543, 1996.
16. W. B. Mann and T. O. Binford. An example of 3d interpretation of images using bayesian networks. In *DARPA Image Understanding Workshop*, pages 793–801, 1992.
17. K. G. Olesen, S. L. Lauritzen, and F. V. Jensen. Hugin: A system creating adaptive causual probabilistic networks. In *Proc. International Conference on Uncertainty in Artificial Intelligence*, pages 223–229, 1992.
18. J. Pearl. *Probababilistic Reasoning in Intelligent Systems*. Morgan Kaufmann, 1998.
19. R. D. Rimey and C. M. Brown. Control of selective perception using bayes nets and decision theory. *Int. J. of Computer Vision*, 12(2/3):173–208, 1994.
20. S. Sakar and K. L. Boyer. *Computing Perceptual Organization in Computer Vision*. World Scientific, 1994.
21. F. Stein and G.Medioni. Structural indexing: Efficient 3-d object recognition. *IEEE Transactions on Pattern Analysis and Machine Intelligence*, 14(2):125–145, 1992.

Optimal Robot Self-Localization
and Reliability Evaluation*

Kenichi Kanatani and Naoya Ohta

Department of Computer Science, Gunma University
Kiryu, Gunma 376-8515 Japan
{kanatani|ohta}@cs.gunma-u.ac.jp

Abstract. We discuss optimal estimation of the current location of a robot by matching an image of the scene taken by the robot with the model of the environment. We first present a theoretical accuracy bound and then give a method that attains that bound, which can be viewed as describing the probability distribution of the current location. Using real images, we demonstrate that our method is superior to the naive least-squares method. We also confirm the theoretical predictions of our theory by applying the bootstrap procedure.

1   Introduction

For a robot to navigate autonomously, it must have a geometric model of the environment; it may be given as data or constructed by the robot itself from vision and sensor data. Here, we consider the case in which a robot already has a three-dimensional map of the environment and study the problem of identifying its current location in the world model. In theory, the current location can be computed by tracing the history of motion from a known initial position, e.g., integrating the rotation of the wheels or incrementally correcting the position by estimating robot motion from images [8]. However, the accuracy of the computed location quickly deteriorates as errors (due to slippage of the wheels, vibration of the camera, etc.) are accumulated in the course of integration. At some point, therefore, we need to estimate the current location by some direct means.

A typical method for self-localization is computing the current position of the camera by matching feature points detected in the images with their corresponding positions in the world model. A direct method is stereo vision, by which the 3-D locations of the feature points can be computed relative to the cameras [1]. This fails, however, if the feature points are located very far away as compared with the baseline of the stereo system. In an outdoor environment, feature points easily discernible from a wide range of positions are usually those located very far away (e.g., towers and mountain tops). Hence, we need a method for computing the current position by matching a single image with the world model.

---

* This work was in part supported by the Ministry of Education, Science, Sports and Culture, Japan under a Grant in Aid for Scientific Research C(2) (No. 09680352).

The problem of matching image and model features is inseparable from the problem of computing the 3-D position; we first hypothesize a matching based on known clues (e.g., brightness, color, shape, etc.) and then validate the resulting 3-D position (e.g., by comparing it with that obtained by integrating the history of motion, examining the image if features that should be observed from that position actually exist, etc.) [10, 11]. Hence, computing the 3-D position for given matching between image and model features is crucial whether the matching is correct or not.

Computing the 3-D relationship between image and model features has been studied by many researchers in the past in the form known as "PnP", in which the goal is to compute the 3-D positions of the feature points relative to the camera, given a 3-D configuration of the feature points relative to each other. Here, we are interested in computing the absolute position of the camera, given absolute 3-D positions of feature points.

If the robot motion is constrained to be on a horizontal surface (e.g., the ground or a floor), a simple method based on elementary geometry of circles is well known for this purpose [7]. It can also be applied to three-dimensional motion by replacing circles by spheres [9]. But this technique uses only pairwise relative orientations of the lines of sight defined by the feature points; their absolute positions in the image are not used. Using minimal information has the advantage that it can be adapted to mismatch removal: we pick out multiple minimal sets of data and choose the solution supported by majority voting [4]. For assumed matching, however, it is obviously better to fuse all available information in an optimal manner. Such a method also exists [2], but so far the main concern has been *methods* for estimation; little attention has been given on *theoretical optimality* and *reliability of the solution*.

The aim of this paper is *not* to propose yet another new solution technique. Rather, we focus on *statistical* aspects. We first introduce a model of noise and view the problem as statistical estimation. Then, we present a *theoretical accuracy bound* that can be evaluated independently of particular solution techniques involved. Next, we give a computational scheme that attains that bound; such a method alone can be called "optimal".

Since the solution attains the accuracy bound, we can view it as quantitatively describing the "probability distribution" of the current location of the robot. We show that we can compute this distribution without any knowledge about the magnitude of image noise. This computation helps validate the hypothesized matching: if the evaluated distribution spreads out widely, the hypothesis is very questionable. We confirm the theoretical predictions of our theory by using real images and applying the bootstrap procedure [3].

2 Statistical Self-Localization

We regard the camera imaging geometry as perspective projection and define an XYZ camera coordinate system in such a way that its origin is at the center of projection and its optical axis is along the Z-axis (Fig. 1(a)). Letting f be the

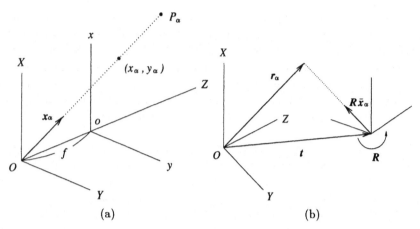

Fig. 1. (a) Camera imaging geometry. (b) The camera coordinate system and the world coordinate system.

focal length, we identify the plane $Z = f$ with the image plane, on which we define an xy image coordinate system in such a way that the origin is on the optical axis and the x- and y-axes are parallel to the X- and Y-axes, respectively.

We regard observed image coordinates (x_α, y_α) (in pixels) as perturbed from their true values $(\bar{x}_\alpha, \bar{y}_\alpha)$ by noise and write

$$x_\alpha = \bar{x}_\alpha + \Delta x_\alpha, \qquad y_\alpha = \bar{y}_\alpha + \Delta y_\alpha. \tag{1}$$

We regard Δx_α and Δy_α as (generally correlated) Gaussian random variables of mean 0, independent for each α.

Suppose the camera coordinate system is in a position defined by translating the world coordinate system by t and rotating it by R with respect to the world coordinate system (Fig. 1(b)). We call $\{t, R\}$ the *motion parameters*. Our goal is formally stated as follows:

Problem 1. Given image coordinates (x_α, y_α), $\alpha = 1, ..., N$, of feature points whose *3-D* positions r_α, $\alpha = 1, ..., N$, with respect to the world coordinate system are known, optimally compute the motion parameters $\{t, R\}$ and their probability distribution.

We represent a point with image coordinates (x, y) by the following three-dimensional vector:

$$x = \begin{pmatrix} x/f \\ y/f \\ 1 \end{pmatrix}. \tag{2}$$

This vector indicates the line of sight starting from the camera coordinate origin and passing through the corresponding point in the scene (Fig. 1(a)). Let x_α and $\bar{x}_\alpha$ be the αth observed point and its true position, respectively. The error

$\Delta x_\alpha = x_\alpha - \bar{x}_\alpha$ is a three-dimensional vector. We define its covariance matrix by

$$V[x_\alpha] = E[\Delta x_\alpha \Delta x_\alpha^\top], \tag{3}$$

where $E[\cdot]$ denotes expectation and the superscript $\top$ denotes transpose. Since the Z component of Δx_α is identically 0, the covariance matrix $V[x_\alpha]$ is singular; its third row and third column consist of 0s.

The covariance matrix $V[x_\alpha]$ measures the uncertainty of detecting the feature point x_α, but in practice it is usually very difficult to predict it precisely. However, it is often possible to predict the relative likelihood of noise. Here, we assume that the covariance matrix is known only *up to scale* and write

$$V[x_\alpha] = \epsilon^2 V_0[x_\alpha]. \tag{4}$$

We assume that $V_0[x_\alpha]$ is known but the constant ϵ is unknown; we call ϵ the *noise level*, and $V_0[x_\alpha]$ (generally different from point to point) the *normalized covariance matrix* [6].

For example, if Δx_α and Δy_α are subject to an isotropic and identical Gaussian distribution of mean 0 and variance σ^2, we have

$$\epsilon = \frac{\sigma}{f}, \qquad V_0[x_\alpha] = \mathrm{diag}(1, 1, 0), \tag{5}$$

where $\mathrm{diag}(\lambda_1, \lambda_2, \lambda_3)$ denotes the diagonal matrix with diagonal elements λ_1, λ_2, and λ_3 in that order.

The vector $\bar{x}_\alpha$ is defined with respect to the camera coordinate system. If it is described with respect to the world coordinate system, it becomes $R\bar{x}_\alpha$ (Fig. 1(b)). Hence, letting Z_α be the depth of the αth feature point in the scene from the camera coordinate origin, we obtain the following relationship:

$$r_\alpha = t + Z_\alpha R\bar{x}_\alpha. \tag{6}$$

Such a depth Z_α exists if and only if vector $r_\alpha - t$ is parallel to vector $R\bar{x}_\alpha$. Hence, Problem 1 reduces to the following statistical estimation:

Problem 2. Given $\{r_\alpha\}$, estimate the motion parameters $\{t, R\}$ that satisfy

$$(t - r_\alpha) \times R\bar{x}_\alpha = 0, \qquad \alpha = 1, ..., N, \tag{7}$$

from the noisy data $\{x_\alpha\}$. At the same time, compute the probability distribution of the estimated motion parameters $\{t, R\}$.

3 Theoretical Accuracy Bound

Let $\{\hat{t}, \hat{R}\}$ be an estimator of the true motion parameters $\{\bar{t}, \bar{R}\}$. The deviation of translation can be measured by the "difference"

$$\Delta t = \hat{t} - \bar{t} \tag{8}$$

of the estimator $\hat{t}$ from its true value $\bar{t}$. The deviation of rotation can be measured by the "quotient" $\hat{R}\bar{R}^{\top}$, i.e., the rotation of $\hat{R}$ relative to $\bar{R}$. Let l (unit vector) and $\Delta\Omega$ be, respectively, the axis and angle of the relative rotation $\hat{R}\bar{R}^{\top}$, and define

$$\Delta\Omega = \Delta\Omega l. \tag{9}$$

We define the covariance matrices of the estimator $\{\hat{t}, \hat{R}\}$ as follows:

$$V[\hat{t}] = E[\Delta t \Delta t^{\top}], \qquad V[\hat{t}, \hat{R}] = E[\Delta t \Delta\Omega^{\top}],$$

$$V[\hat{R}, \hat{t}] = E[\Delta\Omega \Delta t^{\top}], \qquad V[\hat{R}] = E[\Delta\Omega \Delta\Omega^{\top}]. \tag{10}$$

Applying the theory of Kanatani [6], we can obtain the following lower bound, which Kanatani called the *Cramer-Rao lower bound* in analogy with the corresponding bound in traditional statistical estimation:

$$\begin{pmatrix} V[\hat{t}] & V[\hat{t}, \hat{R}] \\ V[\hat{R}, \hat{t}] & V[\hat{R}] \end{pmatrix} \succ \epsilon^2 \begin{pmatrix} \sum_{\alpha=1}^{N} \bar{A}_\alpha^{\top} \bar{W}_\alpha \bar{A}_\alpha & \sum_{\alpha=1}^{N} \bar{A}_\alpha^{\top} \bar{W}_\alpha \bar{B}_\alpha \\ \sum_{\alpha=1}^{N} \bar{B}_\alpha^{\top} \bar{W}_\alpha \bar{A}_\alpha & \sum_{\alpha=1}^{N} \bar{B}_\alpha^{\top} \bar{W}_\alpha \bar{B}_\alpha \end{pmatrix}^{-1}. \tag{11}$$

Here, $U \succ V$ means that $U - V$ is a positive semi-definite symmetric matrix. The matrices $\bar{A}_\alpha$, $\bar{B}_\alpha$, and $\bar{W}_\alpha$ are defined as follows (I is the unit matrix):

$$\bar{A}_\alpha = -(\bar{R}\bar{x}_\alpha) \times I, \qquad \bar{B}_\alpha = (\bar{t}_\alpha - r_\alpha, \bar{R}_\alpha\bar{x}_\alpha)I - \bar{R}\bar{x}_\alpha(\bar{t} - r_\alpha)^{\top}, \tag{12}$$

$$\bar{W}_\alpha = \left((\bar{t} - r_\alpha) \times \bar{R}V_0[x_\alpha]\bar{R}^{\top} \times (\bar{t} - r_\alpha)\right)^{-}. \tag{13}$$

Throughout this paper, the inner product of vectors u and v is denoted by (u, v). The product $v \times U$ of a vector v and a matrix U is the matrix whose columns are the vector products of v and the columns of U. The product $U \times v$ of a matrix U and a vector v is the matrix whose rows are the vector products of the rows of U and vector v. The operation $(\cdot)^{-}$ designates the (Moore-Penrose) generalized inverse.

4 Optimal Estimation

Applying the general theory of Kanatani [6], we can obtain a computational scheme for solving Problem 2 in such a way that the resulting solution attains the accuracy bound (11) in the first order (i.e., ignoring terms of $O(\epsilon^4)$): we minimize the sum of squared *Mahalanobis distances*

$$J = \sum_{\alpha=1}^{N} (\bar{x}_\alpha - x_\alpha, V_0[x_\alpha]^{-}(\bar{x}_\alpha - x_\alpha)) \tag{14}$$

with respect to $\{\bar{x}_\alpha\}$ subject to the constraint (7). The solution is given by

$$\bar{x}_\alpha = x_\alpha - V_0[x_\alpha]R^{\top}\left((t - r_\alpha) \times W_\alpha \times (t - r_\alpha)\right)Rx_\alpha, \tag{15}$$

$$W_\alpha = \left((t - r_\alpha) \times R V_0[x_\alpha] R^\top \times (t - r_\alpha) \right)_2^-, \qquad (16)$$

where the operation $(\cdot)_r^-$ designates the *rank-constrained* (Moore-Penrose) generalized inverse computed by transforming it into the canonical form, replacing its eigenvalues except the r largest ones by 0, and computing the (Moore-Penrose) generalized inverse (this operation is necessary for preventing numerical instability [6]).

Substituting eq. (15) into eq. (14), we obtain the following expression to be minimized with respect to the motion parameters $\{t, R\}$ alone:

$$J = \sum_{\alpha=1}^{N} ((t - r_\alpha) \times Rx_\alpha, W_\alpha \left((t - r_\alpha) \times Rx_\alpha \right)). \qquad (17)$$

The unknown noise level ϵ can be estimated *a posteriori*. Let $\hat{J}$ be the *residual*, i.e., the minimum of J. Since $\hat{J}/\epsilon^2$ is subject to a χ^2 distribution with $2N - 6$ degrees of freedom in the first order [6], we obtain an unbiased estimator of the squared noise level ϵ^2 in the following form:

$$\hat{\epsilon}^2 = \frac{\hat{J}}{2N - 6}. \qquad (18)$$

Because the solution $\{\hat{t}, \hat{R}\}$ of the minimization (17) attains the accuracy bound (11) in the first order, we can evaluate their covariance matrices by optimally estimating the true positions $\{\bar{x}_\alpha\}$ (we discuss this in the next section) and substituting the solution $\{\hat{t}, \hat{R}\}$ and the estimator (18) for their true values $\{\bar{t}, \bar{R}\}$ and ϵ^2 in eqs. (11). Using the covariance matrix $V[\hat{t}]$ in eqs. (11), we can estimate the probability distribution of the current location in the following form:

$$p(r) = \frac{1}{(2\pi |V[\hat{t}]|)^{3/2}} e^{-(r - \hat{t}, V[\hat{t}]^{-1}(r - \hat{t}))/2}. \qquad (19)$$

We conduct the minimization (17) by modified Newton iterations. If rotation R is perturbed by a small rotation represented by the vector $\Delta\Omega$ defined by eq. (9), the perturbed rotation has the expression

$$R + \Delta\Omega \times R + \frac{1}{2}\Delta\Omega\Delta\Omega^\top R - \frac{1}{2}\|\Delta\Omega\|^2 R + O(\Delta\Omega)^3, \qquad (20)$$

where $\|u\|$ denotes the norm of a vector u and $O(u, v, ...)^k$ designates terms of order k or higher in the elements of vectors u, v, ... Substituting eq. (20) and $t + \Delta t$ for R and t, respectively, in eq. (17) and expanding it with respect to Δt and Ω, we obtain the following expression:

$$J + (\nabla_t J, \Delta t) + (\nabla_R J, \Delta\Omega) + \frac{1}{2}(\Delta t, \nabla_{tt}^2 J, \Delta t)$$

$$+ (\Delta t, \nabla_{tR}^2 J, \Delta\Omega) + \frac{1}{2}(\Delta\Omega, \nabla_{RR}^2 J, \Delta\Omega) + O(\Delta t, \Delta\Omega)^3. \qquad (21)$$

Differentiating this with respect to Δt and $\Delta\Omega$, letting the resulting expressions equal zero, and ignoring terms of $O(\Delta t, \Delta\Omega)^3$, we obtain the following simultaneous linear equations:

$$\begin{pmatrix} \nabla^2_{tt}J & \nabla^2_{tR}J \\ (\nabla^2_{tR}J)^\top & \nabla^2_{RR}J \end{pmatrix} \begin{pmatrix} \Delta t \\ \Delta\Omega \end{pmatrix} = -\begin{pmatrix} \nabla_t J \\ \nabla_R J \end{pmatrix}. \tag{22}$$

Starting from an initial guess $\{t, R\}$, we solve eq. (22) for the increments $\{\Delta t, \Delta\Omega\}$ and update the solution in the form $t \leftarrow t + \Delta t$ and $R \leftarrow \mathcal{R}(\Delta\Omega)R$, where $\mathcal{R}(\Delta\Omega)$ designates the rotation matrix by angle $\|\Delta\Omega\|$ around axis $\Delta\Omega$:

$$\mathcal{R}(\Delta\Omega) = \cos\Delta\Omega I + (1 - \cos\Delta\Omega)ll^\top + \sin\Delta\Omega l \times I. \tag{23}$$

We iterate this until $\|\Delta t\| < \epsilon_t$ and $\|\Delta\Omega\| < \epsilon_R$ for specified thresholds ϵ_t and ϵ_R.

We compute the initial guess $\{t, R\}$ by a structure-from-motion algorithm. First, we hypothetically place a reference camera coordinate system in a known position in the world model and compute the image coordinates of the feature points viewed from that position (we need not actually generate a graphics image). From the correspondences of image coordinates between this reference image and the actually observed image, we can reconstruct the 3-D motion of the camera and the 3-D positions of the feature points up to scale; since we know the absolute positions of the feature points, we can easily adjust the scale a posteriori. Here, we adopt the statistically optimal algorithm of Kanatani [5] using a technique called *renormalization*.

5 Example 1

Fig. 2(a) is a real image of a toy house. We manually input the feature points marked by white dots and used the noise model of eqs. (5). The computation converged after five iterations for thresholds $\epsilon_t = 0.01$cm (the height of the house is 8cm) and $\epsilon_R = 0.01°$. Fig. 2(b) displays the house and the estimated camera coordinate axes viewed from an angle.

We evaluated the reliability of the computed solution $\{\hat{t}, \hat{R}\}$ in the following two ways:

- Theoretical analysis.
- Random noise simulation.

The former is straightforward: since our method attains the accuracy bound (11) in the first order, we can evaluate the reliability of the solution by approximating the true values by their estimates in eq. (11).

A well known method for the latter is *bootstrap* [3], which can be applied to any solution method. Here, we adopt the following procedure. We first optimally correct the observed positions $\{x_\alpha\}$ into $\{\hat{x}_\alpha\}$ so that constraint (7) exactly holds. From eq. (15), this optimal correction is done as follows:

$$\hat{x}_\alpha = x_\alpha - V_0[x_\alpha]\hat{R}^\top \left((\hat{t} - r_\alpha) \times \hat{W}_\alpha \times (\hat{t} - r_\alpha)\right) \hat{R}x_\alpha, \tag{24}$$

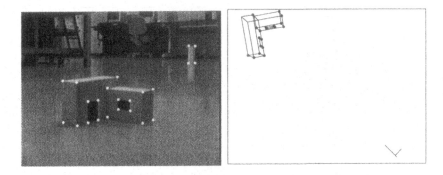

Fig. 2. (a) A real image of a toy house. (b) Estimated current location.

$$\hat{W}_\alpha = \left((\hat{t} - r_\alpha) \times \hat{R} V_0[x_\alpha] \hat{R}^\top \times (\hat{t} - r_\alpha) \right)_2^-. \tag{25}$$

Estimating the noise variance by eq. (18), we generate random Gaussian noise that has the estimated variance and add it to the corrected positions independently. Then, we compute the motion parameters $\{t^*, R^*\}$ and the angle $\Delta\Omega^*$ and axis l^* of the relative rotation $\hat{R}^* \hat{R}^\top$.

Fig. 3 shows three-dimensional plots of the error vectors $\Delta t^* = t^* - \hat{t}$ and $\Delta\Omega^* = \Delta\Omega^* l^*$ for 100 trials. The ellipsoids in the figures are respectively defined by

$$(\Delta t^*, V[\hat{t}]^{-1} \Delta t^*) = 1, \qquad (\Delta\Omega^*, V[\hat{R}]^{-1} \Delta\Omega^*) = 1, \tag{26}$$

where $V[\hat{t}]$ and $V[\hat{R}]$ are computed by approximating $\bar{R}$, $\{\bar{x}_\alpha\}$, and ϵ^2 by $\hat{R}$, $\{\hat{x}_\alpha\}$, and $\hat{\epsilon}^2$ on the right-hand side of eq. (11). These ellipsoids indicate the standard deviation of the errors in each orientation [6]. The cubes in the figures are displayed as a reference.

We compared our method with the naive least-squares method; we simply replaced the matrix W_α by the unit matrix I. Fig. 4 shows the result that corresponds to Fig. 3 (the ellipsoids and the cubes are the same as in Fig. 3).

Comparing Figs. 3 and 4, we can confirm that our method improves the accuracy of the solution as compared with the least-squares method. We can also see that errors for our method distribute around the ellipsoids, indicating that our method already attains the theoretical accuracy bound; no further improvement is possible.

The above visual observation can be given quantitative measures. We define the *bootstrap standard deviations* by

$$S_t^* = \sqrt{\frac{1}{B} \sum_{b=1}^B \|\Delta t_b^*\|^2}, \qquad S_R^* = \sqrt{\frac{1}{B} \sum_{b=1}^B (\Delta\Omega_b^*)^2}, \tag{27}$$

where B is the number of bootstrap samples and the subscript b labels each sample. The corresponding standard deviations for the (estimated) theoretical

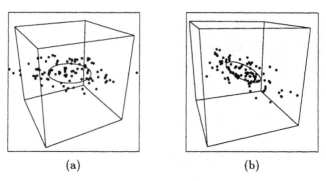

Fig. 3. Bootstrap errors (our method): (a) translation; (b) rotation.

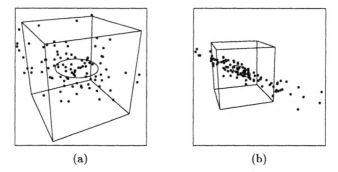

Fig. 4. Bootstrap errors (least squares): (a) translation; (b) rotation.

lower bound are

$$S_t = \sqrt{\mathrm{tr}V[\hat{t}]}, \qquad S_R = \sqrt{\mathrm{tr}V[\hat{R}]}, \tag{28}$$

respectively. Table 1 lists the values of S_t^* and S_R^* for our method and the least-squares method ($B = 1000$) together with their theoretical lower bounds S_t and S_R. We can see from this that our method is indeed superior to the least-squares method and that the accuracy of our solution is very close to the theoretical lower bound.

This observation confirms that we can evaluate the probability distribution of the estimated location by (approximately) evaluating the theoretical accuracy bound given by eq. (11).

6   Example 2

Fig. 5(a) is a real image of a real building for which a design plan is available. We manually input the feature points marked by white dots and used the noise model of eq. (5). The computation converged after four iterations for thresholds $\epsilon_t = 0.1$cm and $\epsilon_R = 0.01°$.

Table 1. Bootstrap standard deviations and the theoretical lower bounds.

	Translation	Rotation
Our method	0.16cm	0.16°
Least squares	0.25cm	0.45°
Lower bounds	0.16cm	0.15°

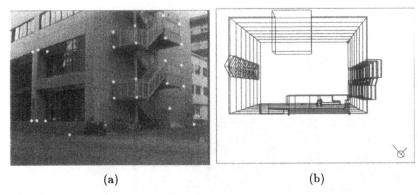

(a)   (b)

Fig. 5. (a) A real image of a real building. (b) Estimated current location and its reliability.

Fig. 5(b) displays the building and the estimated camera coordinate axes viewed from above; the ellipse in the figure indicates the ellipsoid corresponding to those in Figs. 3(a) and 4(a) enlarged by three times. We also evaluated the reliability of the solution by both theoretical analysis and bootstrap. Table 2 is the result corresponding to Table 1. We can again confirm that our method is superior to the least-squares method and that our method almost attains the theoretical bound, which can be viewed as describing the probability distribution of the estimated location.

7 Example 3

If the robot is constrained to be on a horizontal plane, the computation is considerably simplified. Fig. 6(a) is a real image of a city scene. We manually spotted nine features at the bottoms of the white vertical bars in the figure and computed the viewer location by matching the positions of the bars to their corresponding locations in the city map. The initial guess was computed by the method of circle geometry [7, 9]; the computation converged after five iterations for thresholds ϵ_t = 0.01m and ϵ_R = 0.01°.

Fig. 6(b) shows the estimated current location superimposed on the city map. The ellipse in the figure is the two-dimensional version of the ellipsoids in Figs. 3(a) and 4(a). The white dot indicates the place where we actually took

Table 2. Bootstrap standard deviations and the theoretical lower bounds.

	Translation	Rotation
Our method	44.1cm	1.31°
Least squares	47.3cm	1.39°
Lower bounds	43.7cm	1.29°

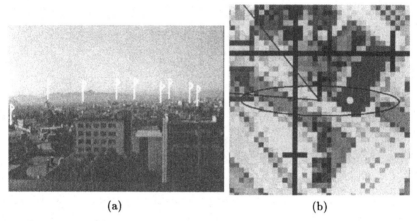

(a)   (b)

Fig. 6. (a) A real image of a city scene. (b) Estimated current location.

the picture of Fig. 6(a), and it is within the ellipse. Fig. 7 shows the angle of view from the estimated location superimposed on the city map; the locations of the feature points are marked by white dots.

Figs. 8(a) and (b) show 100 bootstrap errors in the estimated location plotted in the same way as Figs. 3(a) and 4(b) (we omit errors in rotation; they are very small). Table 3 corresponds to Tables 1 and 2 (this time $B = 10000$); our method is still superior to the least-squares method, although the difference is not so marked as in the three-dimensional case. At any rate, our method almost attains the theoretical bound, which can be viewed as describing the probability distribution of the estimated location.

8   Concluding Remarks

We have discussed optimal estimation of the current location of a robot by matching an image of the scene taken by the robot with the model of the environment. We have first presented a theoretical accuracy bound defined independently of solution techniques and then given a method that attains it; our method is truly "optimal" in that sense. Since the solution attains the accuracy bound, we can view it as describing the probability distribution of the estimated location; the computation does not require any knowledge about the noise magnitude. Using real images, we have demonstrated that our method is superior to

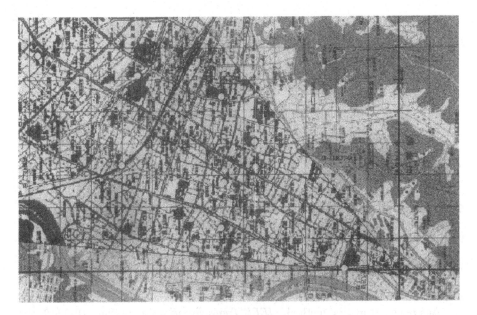

Fig. 7. Estimated angle of view.

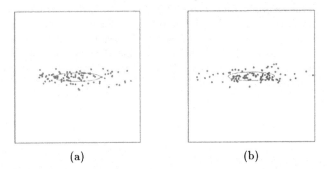

(a)   (b)

Fig. 8. Bootstrap errors in the estimated location: (a) our method; (b) least squares.

the naive least-squares method. We have also confirmed the theoretical predictions of our theory by applying the bootstrap procedure.

References

1. N. Ayache and O. D. Faugeras, "Building, registrating, and fusing noisy visual maps," *Int. J. Robotics Research*, **7**-6 (1988), 45–65.
2. M. Betke and L. Gurvits, "Mobile robot localization using landmarks," *IEEE Trans. Robotics Automation*, **13**-2 (1997), 251–263.
3. B. Efron and R. J. Tibshirani, *An Introduction to Bootstrap*, Chapman-Hall, New York, 1993.

Table 3. Bootstrap standard deviations and the theoretical lower bounds.

	Translation	Rotation
Our method	37.1m	0.78°
Least squares	37.9m	0.79°
Lower bounds	37.3m	0.78°

4. M. A. Fischler and R. C. Bolles, "Random sample consensus: A paradigm for model fitting with applications to image analysis and automated cartography," *Comm. ACM*, **24**-6 (1981), 381–395.

5. K. Kanatani, "Renormalization for motion analysis: Statistically optimal algorithm," *IEICE Trans. Inf. & Syst.*, **E77-D**-11 (1994), 1233–1239.

6. K. Kanatani, *Statistical Optimization for Geometric Computation: Theory and Practice*, Elsevier, Amsterdam 1996.

7. K. Sugihara, "Some location problems for robot navigation using a single camera," *Comput. Vis. Gr. Image Process.*, **42** (1988), 112–129.

8. R. E. Suorsa and B. Sridhar, "A parallel implementation of a multisensor feature-based range-estimation method," *IEEE Trans. Robotics Automation*, **10**-6 (1994), 755–768.

9. K. T. Sutherland and W. B. Thompson, "Localizing in unconstrained environment: Dealing with the errors," *IEEE Trans. Robotics Automation*, **10**-6 (1994), 740–754.

10. R. Talluri and J. K. Aggarwal, "Mobile robot self-location using model-image feature correspondence," *IEEE Trans. Robotics Automation*, **12**-1 (1996), 63–77.

11. Y. Yagi, Y. Nishimitsu and M. Yachida, "Map-based navigation for a mobile robot with ominidirectional image sensor COPIS," *IEEE Trans. Robotics Automation*, **11**-5 (1995), 634–648.

Mobile Robot Localisation Using Active Vision

Andrew J Davison and David W Murray

Department of Engineering Science, University of Oxford,
Parks Road, Oxford OX1 3PJ, UK
[ajd|dwm]@robots.ox.ac.uk

Abstract. Active cameras provide a mobile robot with the capability to fixate and track features over a wide field of view. However, their use emphasises serial attention focussing on a succession of scene features, raising the question of how this should be best achieved to provide localisation information. This paper describes a fully automatic system, able to detect, store and track suitable landmark features during goal-directed navigation. The robot chooses which of the available set of landmarks to track at a certain time to best improve its position knowledge, and decides when it is time to search for new features. Localisation performance improves on that achieved using odometry alone and shows significant advantages over passive structure-from-motion techniques. Rigorous consideration is given to the propagation of uncertainty in the estimation of the positions of the robot and scene features as the robot moves, fixates and shifts fixation. The paper shows how the estimates of these quantities are inherently coupled in any map-building system, and how features can reliably be re-found after periods of neglect, mitigating the "motion drift" problem often encountered in structure-from-motion algorithms.

1 Introduction

Active cameras potentially provide a navigating vehicle with the ability to fixate and track features over extended periods of time, and wide fields of view. While it is relatively straightforward to apply fixating vision to tactical, short-term navigation tasks such as servoing around obstacles where the fixation point does not change [6], the problem of using serial fixation on a succession of features to provide global localisation information for strategic navigation is more involved.

In this paper, we demonstrate a system which is able to detect, store and track suitable landmark features during goal-directed navigation. The features used are arbitrary points of high contrast which are abundant in any typical environment. The robot chooses which of the available set of landmarks to track at a certain time to best improve its position knowledge, and decides when to change fixation point and when to search for new features with the aim of maintaining a useful 3D map. When suitable landmarks have been detected, the robot is able to refer to them at any time to calculate its position, or to track one of them during a movement to provide continuous information. The method has significant advantages over the passive structure-from-motion techniques used in a number of navigation systems [1–4]. Parts of our approach could be considered as an transfer to the visual domain of methodology used in directable sonar work [5].

Navigating in unknown surroundings inherently couples the processes of building a map of the area and calculating the robot's location relative to that map. With this in mind, a single filter is used to maintain estimates of all the quantities of interest and the covariances between them. This approach differs from many previous approaches to robot navigation and structure-from-motion (e.g. [3, 4]) where separate filters are used for the robot position and that of each of the features. In the work in this paper, the goal is to provide the robot with a sparse map of features which can be used for localisation over extended periods during which the same areas may be traversed many times and the same features will be observed. Only full uncertainty propagation will lead to the localisation performance we should expect in these circumstances, as will be shown in the experiments described later. Our approach allows features to be re-found and re-registered reliably after periods of neglect. This alleviates the problem of "motion drift" often encountered in structure-from-motion, where, for instance, the start and end points of a closed path are not recognised as such [3].

When deciding upon the exact form of the filter, the issue of coordinate frames and their significance was considered in detail. Consider navigation around a restricted area such as a room: certainly there is no need to know about position or orientation relative the world as a whole, but just about the relative location of certain features of the room (walls, doors, etc.). This initially suggested a completely robot-centred approach to navigation, attractive as is minimises the problem of representation. However, such an approach cannot explicitly answer questions such as "how far has the robot moved between points A and B on its trajectory?", important in goal-directed performance. Our approach explicitly estimates the vehicle and feature positions relative to a world frame while maintaining covariances between all the estimates. This provides a way to answer these questions while retaining all the functionality of the robot-centred method, since it is possible at any stage to re-zero the coordinate frame to the robot, as we will show in Section 3.6. The extra information held in the explicit robot state and its covariances with the feature estimates codes the registration information between an arbitrary world coordinate frame or map and the structure of the feature map the robot has built itself.

2 Vehicle and Head Geometry

2.1 Vehicle Geometry and Kinematics

The robot used in this work (Figure 1) has three wheels: two run freely on a fixed transverse axis at the front, while the third, located centrally at the rear, is both steerable and driven. A high performance four-axis active stereo head [7] is mounted with its vertical pan axis directly above the point halfway between the front wheels. The fiduciary "head centre" is defined to lie where the pan axis intersects the horizontal plane containing the elevation axis. This point, fixed relative to the vehicle regardless of head movements, is used to define the vehicle's location relative to a world coordinate frame. The robot vehicle is assumed to

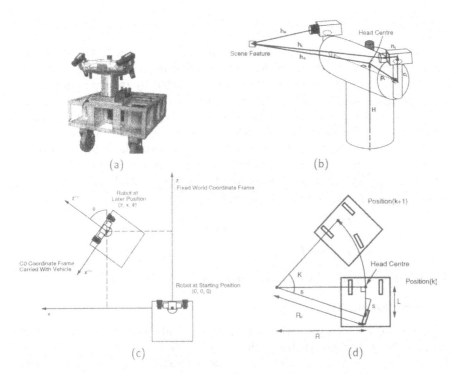

Fig. 1. Head and vehicle geometry. In (c) the vehicle's location in the world coordinate frame is specified with the coordinates (z, x, ϕ). The $C0$ coordinate frame is carried with the vehicle.

move at all times on the horizontal xz ground-plane. Its position and orientation are specified by the coordinates (z, x, ϕ). ϕ is the robot's orientation relative to the world z-axis. The robot-centred frame $C0$ is defined to have its origin on the ground plane directly under the head centre, with its z-axis pointing to the front of the robot, x-axis to the left, and y-axis upwards. In normal operation, at the start of its motion the vehicle's location in the world frame is defined as $z = 0$, $x = 0$, $\phi = 0$, and the world and vehicle frames coincide.

The control inputs determining the vehicle motion are the steering angle s and velocity v of the rear driving wheel. With no slippage, setting a steering angle of s at the rear wheel means that points on the vehicle will travel in circular paths centred on the centre of rotation at the intersection of the wheel axes, as shown in Figure 1(d). In particular, the head centre and rear driving wheel move in paths of radius $R = L/\tan(s)$ and $R_d = L/\sin(s)$ respectively. During a period Δt in which both v and s are held constant, the angle in radians through which the vehicle moves along its circular trajectory is $K = v\Delta t/R_d$, after which the new location of the head centre becomes

$$z(t + \Delta t) = z(t) + R(t)\,(\cos\phi(t)\sin K + \sin\phi(t)(\cos K - 1))$$
$$x(t + \Delta t) = x(t) + R(t)\,(\sin\phi(t)\sin K - \cos\phi(t)(\cos K - 1))$$

$$\phi(t + \Delta t) = \phi(t) + K .$$

These are exact expressions and do not require Δt to be small. (Note that for straight line motion ($s = 0$, R and R_d infinite) a limiting form is used.) The robot will of course not move precisely in the way predicted by the equations due to factors including slipping of the wheels and the non-zero time taken to respond to commands. This uncertainty is modelled as a Gaussian variation in v and s from the demanded values. The steering angle s, was given a constant standard deviation σ_s of around $4°$, and the velocity input v a standard deviation which was proportional to the velocity demand itself: $\sigma_v = \sigma_f v$, with $\sigma_f \approx 0.10$.

Naming the estimated position vector $\mathbf{f}_v$ and the control vector $\mathbf{u}$, the covariance matrix Q of $\mathbf{f}_v$ can be calculated as

$$\mathbf{f}_v = \begin{pmatrix} z(t + \Delta t) \\ x(t + \Delta t) \\ \phi(t + \Delta t) \end{pmatrix} \quad , \quad \mathbf{u} = \begin{pmatrix} v \\ s \end{pmatrix} \quad , \quad \mathsf{Q} = \frac{\partial \mathbf{f}_v}{\partial \mathbf{u}} \mathsf{U} \frac{\partial \mathbf{f}_v}{\partial \mathbf{u}}^\mathsf{T} , \quad (1)$$

where U is the diagonal covariance matrix of $\mathbf{u}$.

2.2 Head Geometry

Fixating a feature with the active head provides a 3D measurement of its location from stereo and knowledge of the head odometry (Figure 1(b)). Locating a feature at position u_L, v_L in the left camera's image and u_R, v_R in the right one, its 3D position $\mathbf{h}_G$ relative the the head centre can be calculated in the $C0$ vehicle-centred frame. Using knowledge of the head's joint angles, the vectors $\mathbf{p}_L, \mathbf{c}_L, \mathbf{n}_L$ and $\mathbf{p}_R, \mathbf{c}_R, \mathbf{n}_R$ are formed and summed to obtain the vector locations of the two optic centres with respect to the head centre. $\mathbf{h}_G$ can then be expressed as either:

$$\mathbf{h}_G = \mathbf{p}_L + \mathbf{c}_L + \mathbf{n}_L + \mathbf{h}_L \quad \text{or} \quad \mathbf{h}_G = \mathbf{p}_R + \mathbf{c}_R + \mathbf{n}_R + \mathbf{h}_R .$$

Vectors $\mathbf{h}_L$ and $\mathbf{h}_R$ can be found up to scale in the vehicle-centred coordinate frame:

$$\mathbf{h}_L{}^{C0} \propto \mathsf{M}^{\mathrm{COL}} \mathsf{C}_L^{-1} (u_L, v_L, 1)^\mathsf{T} \quad \text{and} \quad \mathbf{h}_R{}^{C0} \propto \mathsf{M}^{\mathrm{COR}} \mathsf{C}_R^{-1} (u_R, v_R, 1)^\mathsf{T} ,$$

where $\mathsf{M}^{\mathrm{COL}}$ and $\mathsf{M}^{\mathrm{COR}}$ are the (known) rotation matrices transforming from the left and right camera-centred coordinate systems into the vehicle coordinate system, and $\mathsf{C}_{L,R}$ are the (known) camera calibration matrices.

The feature position relative to the head centre, $\mathbf{h}_G$, is found by back-projecting the two rays defined by $\mathbf{h}_L$ and $\mathbf{h}_R$ and finding their intersection in 3D space — in the presence of noise, the midpoint of their mutually perpendicular bisector is used.

3 The Map-Building and Localisation Algorithm

3.1 The State Vector and its Covariance

Current estimates of the locations of the vehicle and the scene features which are known about are stored in the system state vector $\hat{\mathbf{x}}$, and the uncertainty of the estimates in the covariance matrix P. These are partitioned as follows:

$$\hat{\mathbf{x}} = \begin{pmatrix} \hat{\mathbf{x}}_v \\ \hat{\mathbf{y}}_1 \\ \hat{\mathbf{y}}_2 \\ \vdots \end{pmatrix} \quad , \quad \mathbf{P} = \begin{bmatrix} P_{xx} & P_{xy_1} & P_{xy_2} & \cdots \\ P_{y_1x} & P_{y_1y_1} & P_{y_1y_2} & \cdots \\ P_{y_2x} & P_{y_2y_1} & P_{y_2y_2} & \cdots \\ \vdots & \vdots & \vdots \end{bmatrix} . \tag{2}$$

$\hat{\mathbf{x}}$ has $3(n+1)$ elements, where n is the number of known features. P is symmetric, with size $3(n+1) \times 3(n+1)$. $\hat{\mathbf{x}}_v$ is the vehicle position estimate, and $\hat{\mathbf{y}}_i$ the estimated 3D location of the ith feature:

$$\hat{\mathbf{x}}_v = (\hat{z}, \ \hat{x}, \ \hat{\phi})^{\mathsf{T}} \quad , \quad \hat{\mathbf{y}}_i = (\hat{X}_i, \ \hat{Y}_i, \ \hat{Z}_i)^{\mathsf{T}} .$$

3.2 Moving and Making Predictions

The robot's motion is discretised into steps of time interval Δt, with an incrementing label k affixed to each. Δt is set to be the smallest interval at which changes are made to the vehicle control inputs v and s, allowing the motion model of Section 2.1 to be used. After a step of movement, a new state estimate and covariance are produced:

$$\hat{\mathbf{x}}(k+1|k) = \begin{pmatrix} \mathbf{f}_v(\mathbf{x}_v(k|k), \mathbf{u}(k)) \\ \hat{\mathbf{y}}_1(k|k) \\ \hat{\mathbf{y}}_2(k|k) \\ \vdots \end{pmatrix} \tag{3}$$

$$\mathbf{P}(k+1|k) = \begin{bmatrix} \frac{\partial \mathbf{f}_v}{\partial \mathbf{x}_v}P_{xx}(k|k)\frac{\partial \mathbf{f}_v}{\partial \mathbf{x}_v}^{\mathsf{T}} + Q(k) & \frac{\partial \mathbf{f}_v}{\partial \mathbf{x}_v}P_{xy_1}(k|k) & \frac{\partial \mathbf{f}_v}{\partial \mathbf{x}_v}P_{xy_2}(k|k) & \cdots \\ P_{y_1x}(k|k)\frac{\partial \mathbf{f}_v}{\partial \mathbf{x}_v}^{\mathsf{T}} & P_{y_1y_1}(k|k) & P_{y_1y_2}(k|k) & \cdots \\ P_{y_2x}(k|k)\frac{\partial \mathbf{f}_v}{\partial \mathbf{x}_v}^{\mathsf{T}} & P_{y_2y_1}(k|k) & P_{y_2y_2}(k|k) & \cdots \\ \vdots & \vdots & \vdots \end{bmatrix}, \tag{4}$$

where $\mathbf{f}_v$ and $Q(k)$ are as defined in Equation 1. This new covariance matrix is formulated from the usual EKF prediction rule $P(k+1|k) = \frac{\partial \mathbf{f}}{\partial \mathbf{x}}P(k|k)\frac{\partial \mathbf{f}}{\partial \mathbf{x}}^{\mathsf{T}} + Q(k)$, where $\frac{\partial \mathbf{f}}{\partial \mathbf{x}}$ is the full state transition Jacobian:

$$\frac{\partial \mathbf{f}}{\partial \mathbf{x}} = \begin{bmatrix} \frac{\partial \mathbf{f}_v}{\partial \mathbf{x}_v} & 0 & 0 & \cdots \\ 0 & I & 0 & \cdots \\ 0 & 0 & I & \cdots \\ \vdots & \vdots & \vdots \end{bmatrix} .$$

3.3 Updating the State Vector After a Measurement

When the location of a feature is measured, as described in Section 2.2 we obtain a measurement in the vehicle frame $C0$ of the vector $\mathbf{h}_G$ from the head centre to the feature. The function giving the predicted cartesian components of this measurement is:

$$\mathbf{h}_{Gi} = \begin{pmatrix} h_{Gix} \\ h_{Giy} \\ h_{Giz} \end{pmatrix} = \begin{pmatrix} \cos\phi(X_i - x) - \sin\phi(Z_i - z) \\ Y_i - H \\ \sin\phi(X_i - x) + \cos\phi(Z_i - z) \end{pmatrix}. \tag{5}$$

Before processing measurements, however, they are transformed into an angular form:

$$\mathbf{h}_i = (\alpha_i \ , \ e_i \ , \ \gamma_i)^\mathsf{T} = (\tan^{-1}\frac{h_{Gix}}{h_{Giz}} \ , \ \tan^{-1}\frac{h_{Giy}}{h_{Gi\rho}} \ , \ \tan^{-1}\frac{I}{2h_{Gi}})^\mathsf{T}, \tag{6}$$

where h_{Gi} is the length of vector $\mathbf{h}_{Gi}$ and $h_{Gi\rho} = \sqrt{h_{Gix}^2 + h_{Giz}^2}$ is its projection onto the xz plane. I is the inter-ocular separation of the active head. These angles represent the pan, elevation and vergence angles respectively of an ideal active head positioned at the head centre and fixating the feature, "ideal" here meaning a head that does not have the offsets that the real head has (in terms of Figure 1(b) this would mean that vectors $\mathbf{n}$ and $\mathbf{c}$ would be zero, with $\mathbf{p}$ purely along the elevation axis). Now α_i, e_i and γ_i will be very close to the actual pan, elevation and vergence angles of the real active head at fixation, but accuracy is gained by taking account of all the head offsets in this way.

The reason for using an angular measurement representation at all is that it allows measurement noise to be represented as a constant, diagonal matrix. The largest error in measurements is in the accuracy with which features can be located in the image centre — the rule used is that a successful fixation lock-on has been achived when the feature is located within a radius of two pixels from the principal point in both images. This represents an angular uncertainty of around 0.3°, and Gaussian errors of this standard deviation are assigned to α_i, e_i and γ_i. The angular errors in measurements from the head axis encoders are much smaller than this and can be neglected. The measurement noise covariance matrix is therefore:

$$R = \begin{bmatrix} \Delta\alpha^2 & 0 & 0 \\ 0 & \Delta e^2 & 0 \\ 0 & 0 & \Delta\gamma^2 \end{bmatrix}. \tag{7}$$

With a diagonal R, measurements α_i, e_i and γ_i are independent. This has two advantages: first, potential problems with bias are removed from the filter update by representing measurements in a form where the noise can closely be modelled as Gaussian. Second, the measurement vector $\mathbf{h}_i$ can be decoupled, and scalar measurement values used to update the filter in sequence. This is computationally beneficial since it is now not necessary to invert any matrices in the update calculation. For each scalar part of the measurement h_i (where h_i is one of α_i, e_i, γ_i for the current feature of interest), the Jacobian

$$\frac{\partial h_i}{\partial \mathbf{x}} = \left(\frac{\partial h_i}{\partial \mathbf{x}_v} \ 0 \dots 0 \ \frac{\partial h_i}{\partial \mathbf{y}_i} \ 0 \dots \right).$$

is formed. This row matrix has non-zero elements only at locations corresponding to the state of the vehicle and the feature in question, since $h_i = h_i(\mathbf{x}_v, \mathbf{y}_i)$. The scalar innovation variance S is calculated as:

$$S = \frac{\partial h_i}{\partial \mathbf{x}} \mathrm{P} \frac{\partial h_i}{\partial \mathbf{x}}^\top + R = \frac{\partial h_i}{\partial \mathbf{x}_v} \mathrm{P}_{xx} \frac{\partial h_i}{\partial \mathbf{x}_v}^\top + 2\frac{\partial h_i}{\partial \mathbf{x}_v} \mathrm{P}_{xy_i} \frac{\partial h_i}{\partial \mathbf{y}_i}^\top + \frac{\partial h_i}{\partial \mathbf{y}_i} \mathrm{P}_{y_i y_i} \frac{\partial h_i}{\partial \mathbf{y}_i}^\top + R,$$
(8)

where P_{xx}, P_{xy_i} and $\mathrm{P}_{y_i y_i}$ are 3×3 blocks of the current state covariance matrix P, and R is the scalar measurement noise variance ($\Delta\alpha^2$, Δe^2 or $\Delta\gamma^2$) of the measurement. The Kalman gain W can then be calculated and the filter update performed in the usual way:

$$W = \mathrm{P}\frac{\partial h_i}{\partial \mathbf{x}} S^{-1} = S^{-1} \begin{pmatrix} \mathrm{P}_{xx} \\ \mathrm{P}_{y_1 x} \\ \mathrm{P}_{y_2 x} \\ \vdots \end{pmatrix} \frac{\partial h_i}{\partial \mathbf{x}_v} + S^{-1} \begin{pmatrix} \mathrm{P}_{xy_i} \\ \mathrm{P}_{y_1 y_i} \\ \mathrm{P}_{y_2 y_i} \\ \vdots \end{pmatrix} \frac{\partial h_i}{\partial \mathbf{y}_i}$$
(9)

$$\hat{\mathbf{x}}_{new} = \hat{\mathbf{x}}_{old} + W(z_i - h_i)$$
(10)

$$\mathrm{P}_{new} = \mathrm{P}_{old} - WSW^\top .$$
(11)

z_i is the actual measurement of the quantity obtained from the head, and h_i is the prediction. This update is carried out sequentially for each scalar element of the measurement.

3.4 Initialising a New Feature

When an unknown feature is observed for the first time, a vector measurement $\mathbf{h}_G$ is obtained of its position relative to the head centre, and its state is initialised to

$$\mathbf{y}_i = \begin{pmatrix} x + h_{Gix} \cos\phi + h_{Giz} \sin\phi \\ H + h_{Giy} \\ z - h_{Gix} \sin\phi + h_{Giz} \cos\phi \end{pmatrix} .$$
(12)

Jacobians $\frac{\partial \mathbf{y}_i}{\partial \mathbf{x}_v}$ and $\frac{\partial \mathbf{y}_i}{\partial \mathbf{h}_G}$ are calculated and used to update the total state vector and covariance (assuming for example's sake that two features are known and the new one becomes the third):

$$\mathbf{x}_{new} = \begin{pmatrix} \mathbf{x}_v \\ \mathbf{y}_1 \\ \mathbf{y}_2 \\ \mathbf{y}_i \end{pmatrix}$$
(13)

$$\mathrm{P}_{new} = \begin{bmatrix} \mathrm{P}_{xx} & \mathrm{P}_{xy_1} & \mathrm{P}_{xy_2} & \mathrm{P}_{xx}\frac{\partial \mathbf{y}_i}{\partial \mathbf{x}_v}^\top \\ \mathrm{P}_{y_1 x} & \mathrm{P}_{y_1 y_1} & \mathrm{P}_{y_1 y_2} & \mathrm{P}_{y_1 x}\frac{\partial \mathbf{y}_i}{\partial \mathbf{x}_v}^\top \\ \mathrm{P}_{y_2 x} & \mathrm{P}_{y_2 y_1} & \mathrm{P}_{y_2 y_2} & \mathrm{P}_{y_2 x}\frac{\partial \mathbf{y}_i}{\partial \mathbf{x}_v}^\top \\ \frac{\partial \mathbf{y}_i}{\partial \mathbf{x}_v}\mathrm{P}_{xx} & \frac{\partial \mathbf{y}_i}{\partial \mathbf{x}_v}\mathrm{P}_{xy_1} & \frac{\partial \mathbf{y}_i}{\partial \mathbf{x}_v}\mathrm{P}_{xy_2} & \frac{\partial \mathbf{y}_i}{\partial \mathbf{x}_v}\mathrm{P}_{xx}\frac{\partial \mathbf{y}_i}{\partial \mathbf{x}_v}^\top + \frac{\partial \mathbf{y}_i}{\partial \mathbf{h}_G}R_L\frac{\partial \mathbf{y}_i}{\partial \mathbf{h}_G}^\top \end{bmatrix}$$
(14)

where R_L is the measurement noise R transformed into cartesian measurement space.

3.5 Deleting a Feature

A similar Jacobian calculation shows that that deleting a feature from the state vector and covariance matrix is a simple case of removing the rows and columns which contain it. An example in a system where the second of three known features is deleted:

$$
\begin{pmatrix} \mathbf{x}_v \\ \mathbf{y}_1 \\ \mathbf{y}_2 \\ \mathbf{y}_3 \end{pmatrix} \rightarrow \begin{pmatrix} \mathbf{x}_v \\ \mathbf{y}_1 \\ \mathbf{y}_3 \end{pmatrix} \quad , \quad \begin{bmatrix} P_{xx} & P_{xy_1} & P_{xy_2} & P_{xy_3} \\ P_{y_1x} & P_{y_1y_1} & P_{y_1y_2} & P_{y_1y_3} \\ P_{y_2x} & P_{y_2y_1} & P_{y_2y_2} & P_{y_2y_3} \\ P_{y_3x} & P_{y_3y_1} & P_{y_3y_2} & P_{y_3y_3} \end{bmatrix} \rightarrow \begin{bmatrix} P_{xx} & P_{xy_1} & P_{xy_3} \\ P_{y_1x} & P_{y_1y_1} & P_{y_1y_3} \\ P_{y_3x} & P_{y_3y_1} & P_{y_3y_3} \end{bmatrix} . \quad (15)
$$

3.6 Zeroing the Coordinate Frame

As mentioned in the introduction, it is possible to re-zero the world coordinate frame at the current vehicle position. The new state becomes:

$$
\mathbf{x}_{new} = \begin{pmatrix} \mathbf{x}_{vnew} \\ \mathbf{y}_{1new} \\ \mathbf{y}_{2new} \\ \vdots \end{pmatrix} = \begin{pmatrix} \mathbf{0} \\ \mathbf{h}_{G1} + \mathbf{H} \\ \mathbf{h}_{G2} + \mathbf{H} \\ \vdots \end{pmatrix} , \quad (16)
$$

where $\mathbf{h}_{Gi}$ is the current vector from the head centre to feature i as given in Equation 5, and $\mathbf{H}$ is the constant vector describing the vertical offset from the ground plane to the head centre. To calculate the new state covariance we form the sparse Jacobian matrix:

$$
\frac{\partial \mathbf{x}_{new}}{\partial \mathbf{x}_{old}} = \begin{bmatrix} 0 & 0 & 0 & \dots \\ \frac{\partial \mathbf{h}_{G1}}{\partial \mathbf{x}_v} & \frac{\partial \mathbf{h}_{G1}}{\partial \mathbf{y}_1} & 0 & \dots \\ \frac{\partial \mathbf{h}_{G2}}{\partial \mathbf{x}_v} & 0 & \frac{\partial \mathbf{h}_{G2}}{\partial \mathbf{y}_2} & \dots \\ \vdots & \vdots & \vdots & \end{bmatrix} , \quad (17)
$$

and calculate $P_{new} = \frac{\partial \mathbf{x}_{new}}{\partial \mathbf{x}_{old}} P_{old} \frac{\partial \mathbf{x}_{new}}{\partial \mathbf{x}_{old}}^{\mathsf{T}}$.

4 Implementation

All visual processing and the localisation filter are implemented in C++ on a 100 MHz Pentium PC operating under Linux. The PC hosts a Matrox Meteor for stereo image capture, a Delta-Tau PMAC controller to direct the head, and a proprietary Transputer controller to drive the vehicle.

As the robot drives at speeds of up to 20cms^{-1}, a feature may be tracked at fixation at a frequency of 5Hz: the system predicts, moves the active head to fixation, obtains a measurement and incorporates it into the filter in a time less than 0.2s. Alternatively, the robot may stop and make sequential measurements of several features. The main factor limiting speed of operation is the time required to carry out expensive correlation searches (see Section 5.2) on this general purpose hardware. If the robot's position is very uncertain (possibly after failed measurements), search regions become large, search times long, and the robot velocity and the frequency of measurements are automatically reduced accordingly.

Maintaining the large state vector and covariance becomes comparably computationally costly only with a large number (≈ 25) of features. We have developed a method (not described here) whereby execution speed is not compromised by this, even with very large numbers of features, by postponing the full, but exact, update of the whole state until the robot has stopped moving and has some unutilised processing time.

5 Features

5.1 Detecting and Initialising Features

Visual landmarks should be stationary, point features which are easily distinguishable from their surroundings. In this work we use the operator of Shi and Tomasi [8] to selects regions of high interest, and represent the features as 15×15 pixel patches. Typical features found in this way are shown in Figures 2(a) and Figure 5.

To initialise a new feature, the patch operator is applied in the left camera image. For the best patch found, an epipolar line is generated in the right image (using knowledge of the head geometry), and the nearby region searched. If a good stereo match is found, the two pairs of image coordinates (u_L, v_L) and (u_R, v_R) allow the feature's 3D location in the vehicle-centred coordinate frame to be calculated. The head is driven to fixate the feature, (with symmetric left and right head vergence angles enforced to remove redundancy), and re-measured, being easily found now near the centre of the images. Making all measurements at fixation reduces the need for accurate knowledge of the camera focal lengths. The feature is then initialised in the map as detailed in Section 3.4.

Typical indoor environments provide many features which are suitable for tracking, as well as some which, because of partial occlusion or reflection, are not. While no attempt is made to discern these bad features at the initialisation stage, they can be rejected later because they will not be tracked under the constraints of the filter (see Section 5.3).

5.2 Measuring and Tracking Features

The Kalman Filter approach means that a prediction is available of any measurement to be made, and a prediction covariance. When measuring a known feature with the active head, use of the prediction is essential to drive the cameras to the expected fixation angles to make the feature visible. The prediction covariance is then used to produce search areas in the two images within which the feature must lie with a high probability.

Having calculated $\mathbf{h}_{Gi}$, the predicted vector from the head centre to the feature, as in Equation 5, along with its covariance, the system drives the head to fixation and calculates in camera centred coordinates the vectors $\mathbf{h}_L$ and $\mathbf{h}_R$ from the camera optic centres to the feature and their covariances P_{h_L} and P_{h_R}. Both of these vectors will have zero x and y components since at fixation the z-axis-defining optic axes pass through the feature. Considering the left camera, image projection is defined by the the usual equations:

$$u_L = -fk_u(h_{Lx}/h_{Lz}) + u_0 \quad \text{and} \quad v_L = -fk_v(h_{Ly}/h_{Lz}) + v_0 . \quad (18)$$

The covariance matrix of the image vector $\mathbf{u}_L = (u_L \ v_L)^\mathsf{T}$ is given by $\mathsf{U}_L = \frac{\partial \mathbf{u}_L}{\partial \mathbf{h}_L} P_{h_L} \frac{\partial \mathbf{u}_L}{\partial \mathbf{h}_L}^\mathsf{T}$. The value of the Jacobian at $h_{Lx} = h_{Ly} = 0$ is

$$\frac{\partial \mathbf{u}_L}{\partial \mathbf{h}_L} = \begin{bmatrix} \frac{-fk_u}{h_{Lz}} & 0 & 0 \\ 0 & \frac{-fk_v}{h_{Lz}} & 0 \end{bmatrix} .$$

Specifying a number of standard deviations (typically 3), U_L defines an ellipse in the left image which is searched for the feature patch using normalized cross-correlation The same procedure is followed in the right image. Limiting our search for feature patches to these areas not only maximises computational efficiency but also minimises the chance of obtaining mismatches. Figure 2(b,c) shows examples of the elliptical search regions, and (d-g) shows a feature tracked by the head over a large robot motion.

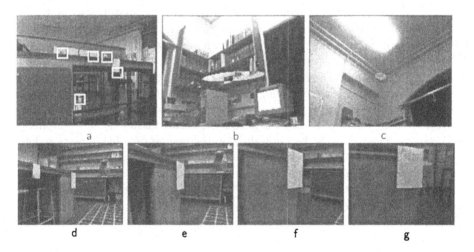

Fig. 2. (a) Typical features detected using Shi and Tomasi. (b,c) Examples of image search ellipses with large and small uncertainty. (d-g) Continuous fixation of a feature by the head.

5.3 Selecting Between Features and Maintaining the Map

As discussed in the introduction, when moving through an unfamiliar world the visual system needs to perform the joint roles of building a useful map and telling

the robot where it is on that map. A strategy is needed to direct attention to where it is most needed, since during its motion the robot is able to track just one feature at a time. Three issues need to be considered, viz:
1. Which of the current set of known features should be tracked?
2. Is it time to label any features as not useful and abandon them?
3. Is it time to look for new features?

Since the features are simple image patches, they are not expected to be recognisable from all viewpoints. The expected visibility of a feature is defined based on the difference in angle and distance between the robot's current estimated viewpoint and the viewpoint from which it first identified the feature (angle differences of up to 45° and distance ratios of up to 1.4 being tolerated). Using different types of feature, different visibility criteria would be appropriate (we are currently investigating using 3D planar patches as features).

In answer to Question 3 then, the robot uses the heuristic that new features should be found if less than two are currently visible. The system attempts to initialise three widely-spaced new features by examining regions to the left, right and straight ahead. More purposive approaches to finding new features in optimal positions have been considered, but in most environments the critical factor is finding reliable features at all. There may not be anything to see in an "optimal" position. Once features have been found, an intelligent choice can be made about which is best to observe from an information point-of-view. To answer Question 2, a feature is abandoned if, after at least 10 attempted measurements from viewpoints from which it should be visible, more than half have failed. Features not corresponding to true point features, having very low viewpoint-invariance, or which are frequently occluded, are quickly rejected and deleted from the map.

To tackle Question 1, the principle of making a measurement where the ability to predict is least, as discussed in recent work by Whaite and Ferrie [9], is used. Given a choice of measurements in a system where the uncertainty in estimates of the parameters of interest is known, it makes sense to make the one where we are least certain of the result, since this will in a sense "squash" the total uncertainty, viewed as a multi-dimensional ellipsoid, along the longest axis available.

Whenever the robot is to make a measurement of a feature, a predicted measurement $\mathbf{h}$ is formed and the innovation covariance matrix S is calculated. This matrix describes how much the actual measurement is expected to vary from the prediction. To produce scalar numbers to use as the basis for decisions about which feature to observe, the volume V_S in (α, e, γ) space of the ellipsoid represented by S at the 3σ level can be calculated for each visible feature. That having the highest V_S is chosen for tracking. The highest possible integrity in the whole map / robot estimation is retained in this way.

The most striking result of this criterion seen in experiments is that it demands frequent changes of tracked feature. Once one or two measurements have been made of a feature, the criterion tells us that there is not much more information to be gleaned from it at the current time, and it is best to switch

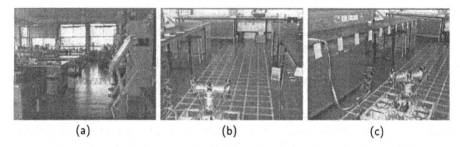

Fig. 3. (a) The laboratory used in experiments. (b) The corridor-like bay where ground-truth measurements could be referenced to a 20cm grid (not used by the vision system). (c) The set of regularly-spaced reference features used in the ground-truth experiment.

attention to another. This is a result of the way that tracking one point feature, even with perfect measurements, does not fully constrain the robot's motion — uncertainty is always growing in some direction.

6 Experiments

6.1 Comparison with Ground Truth

To evaluate the localisation and map-building accuracy of the system, a corridor-like area of a large laboratory was laid with a grid and a set of features in known positions was set up in a regularly-spaced line (see Figure 3). Starting from the grid origin, the robot was driven forward in a nominally straight line. Every second feature in the line was initialised and tracked for a short while on this outward journey, the robot stopping at frequent intervals so that ground-truth measurements could be made of its position relative to the grid, and orientation using an on-board laser pointer. The robot then reversed back down the corridor, tracking the features it had *not* previously seen. Once it had returned to near its starting position, it drove forward again, now attempting to re-measure features found early on, thus completing the loop on the motion and establishing that a reliable map had been formed. It will be shown how much better the single filter approach performs than the multiple-filters methods seen in the literature.

Results directly generated by the full system are shown in Figure 4 superimposed on the measured ground truth. The robot's position was tracked well by the filter as it moved forward and back, but it can be seen that drift started to occur; in particular by the 4th picture, when the robot was close again to its starting position, the filter estimated the robot's position as $z = -0.11$m, $x = 0.26$m, $\phi = -0.08$rad when the true position was $z = 0.01$m, $x = 0.02$m, $\phi = 0.02$rad. This discrepancy is to be expected, since the robot had continually been tracking new features without referring to previously known ones (motion drift). However, the filter had correctly montitored this uncertainty: in the next step (5th picture), measurements had been made of feature 0. This, the very first feature measured, had a position which was very well known in the world coordinate frame since the robot's position had been very certain at this time. Making these measurements therefore locked down the vehicle uncertainty and a

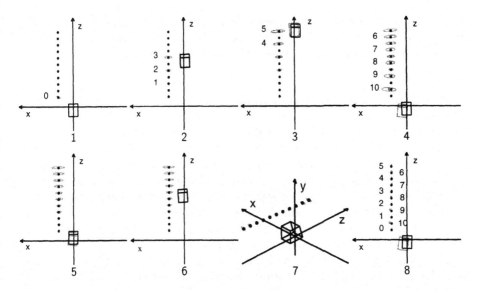

Fig. 4. Experiment with regularly-spaced landmarks: estimated positions of the robot ($\hat{x}_v$) and features ($\hat{y}_i$) in grey, along with 3σ ellipses for the point covariances $P_{y_i y_i}$, are shown superimposed on the true positions (from manual measurement) in black as the robot moved forward and back. The feature spacing was 40cm, and the robot moved about 5m from its origin. Feature labels show the order they were tracked in.

much better estimate was produced: estimated position $z = 0.31$m, $x = 0.04$m, $\phi = -0.08$rad, true position $z = 0.39$m, $x = 0.02$m, $\phi = 0.00$rad. The covariance matrices of the robot state before and after the measurements were:

$$P_{xx}(4) = \begin{bmatrix} 0.0039 & -0.0095 & 0.0036 \\ -0.0095 & 0.0461 & -0.0134 \\ 0.0036 & -0.0134 & 0.0051 \end{bmatrix}, \quad P_{xx}(5) = \begin{bmatrix} 0.0016 & -0.0004 & 0.0016 \\ -0.0004 & 0.0002 & -0.0004 \\ 0.0016 & -0.0004 & 0.0018 \end{bmatrix}$$

The estimates of the locations of all the other features were also immediately improved. The remaining discrepancy in the z and ϕ estimates reflects the fact that measuring one feature does not fully constrain the robot location: it can be seen that these estimates improved when the robot had re-measured more features by the 6th picture. The 7th picture shows the state from the 6th picture zeroed with respect to the robot as in Section 3.6 and displayed at an angle to show the three-dimensionality of the map generated.

In the 8th picture, results are shown from a repeat of the experiment demonstrating the failure of methods using separate filters for the robot and feature states to achieve re-registration with original features. With our implementation, these methods are simulated by simply zeroing all off-diagonal blocks of the total covariance matrix P after each prediction and update (this can be shown to be equivalent to the most sensible approach using multiple filters). The picture shows the state once the robot had returned to near its starting position, and it can be seen that while similar drift was observed in the robot and feature estimates as above, correct account was not taken of this and the covariances were underestimated (the feature uncertainty ellipses being too small to see). An attempt to re-measure feature 0 from this position failed because it did not lie within the image search ellipse generated. The method has no ability to recover from this situation.

6.2 A Fully Automatic Experiment

We present results from a fully automatic run where the robot drove up and down the corridor-like bay with no initial knowledge of the world. The instructions given to the robot were to head in sequence from its starting point at $(z, x) = (0, 0)$ to the waypoints $(6, 0.4)$, $(6, 0)$, and finally $(0, 0)$ again (in metre units). When heading for a particular waypoint, the robot continuously controls its steering angle s according to a simple law described in [6]. A particular waypoint is said to have been reached when the robot's estimated position is within 30cm of it, and the robot starts to steer for the next one.

The robot's progress is shown in frames cut from a video in Figure 5, along with saved views of the first 16 features detected and initialised into the map as in Section 5.3. The output of the filter appears in Figure 6, where those features are annotated. Some of these features did not survive very long before being abandoned as not useful (numbers 4 and 5 in particular not surviving past very early measurement attempts and not being displayed in Figure 6). Others, such as 0, 12 and 14 proved to be very durable, being easy to see and match from all positions from which they are expected to be visible. It can be seen that many of the best features found lie near the ends of the corridor, particularly the large number found near the cluttered back wall (11–15, etc.). The active approach really comes into its own during sharp turns such as that being carried out in the 5th picture, where features such as these could be tracked continuously, using the full range of movement of the neck axis, while the robot made a turn of 180°. The angle of turn can be estimated accurately at a time when odometry data is unreliable.

Outward Journey: the sequence of features selected to be tracked in the early stages of the run (up to the 3rd picture in Figure 6)) was 0, 2, 1, 0, 2, 1, 3, 5, 4, 7, 6, 8, 3, 6, 8, 7, 3, 7, 8, 3, 9 — we see frequent switching between a certain set of features until some go out of visibility and it is necessary to find new ones.

Return to Origin: in the 6th picture of Figure 6, the robot had reached its goal, the final waypoint being a return to its starting point. The robot had successfully refound original features on its return journey, in particular feature 0 whose position was very well known. The choice of feature criterion described in Section 5.3 had demanded re-measurement of these features as soon as they became visible again, reflecting the drift occurring between the robot position estimate and the world coordinate frame. The robot's true position relative to the grid was measured here, being $z = 0.06$m, $x = -0.12$m, $\phi = 3.05$rad, compared to the estimated position $z = 0.15$m, $x = -0.03$m, $\phi = 2.99$rad.

Repeat Journey: the experiment was continued by commanding the robot back out to $(z, x) = (6, 0)$, then home again to $(0, 0)$. In these further runs, the

Fig. 5. The robot navigating autonomously up and down the corridor. The lower four images are example fixated views of four of the features initialised as landmarks. Their numbering corresponds with that used in Figure 6.

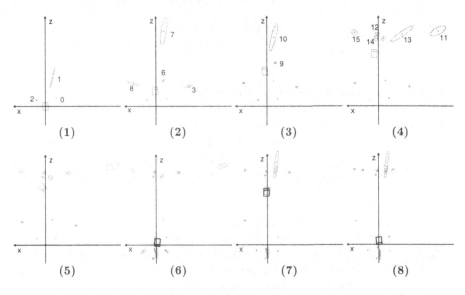

Fig. 6. The map built in autonomous navigation up and down a corridor. Grey shows the estimated locations of the vehicle and features, and black (where measured) the true vehicle position. The furthest features lie at $z \approx 8$m.

system needed to do far less map-building since a large number of features was already known about along the trajectory. At (6, 0), shown in the 7th picture, the robot's true position was $z = 5.68$m, $x = 0.12$m, $\phi = 0.02$rad, and estimated state was $z = 5.83$m, $x = 0.00$m, $\phi = -0.02$rad. At (0, 0) again, shown in the 8th picture, the true position of $z = 0.17$m, $x = -0.07$m, $\phi = -3.03$rad compared with the estimate $z = 0.18$m, $x = 0.00$m, $\phi = -3.06$rad. This is very impressive localisation performance considering that the robot had travelled a total distance of some 24m by this stage.

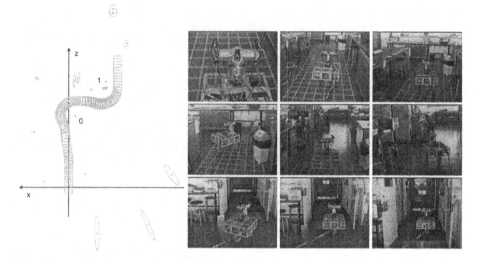

Fig. 7. The estimated trajectory and frames cut from a video as the robot navigated autonomously around two known landmarks and out of the laboratory door.

6.3 Incorporating Prior Map Knowledge

In a real application of an autonomous robot, it is likely that some prior knowledge about the world will be provided, or indeed that this will be necessary to the robot's ability to perform a useful task. In particular, our system as described does not give the robot the capability to detect obstacles along a requested route. It is not intended that the map of features used as landmarks be dense enough to use as a basis for obstacle avoidance.

Prior knowledge of a feature can be incorporated into the map by initialising its location into the state vector at the start of motion, and providing the system with the feature description (i.e. an image patch). If the feature location is precisely known, this is correctly managed by the filter by simply setting all covariance elements relating to that feature to zero — otherwise, some non-zero measurement uncertainty could be initialised. No special treatment needs to be accorded to the feature after this. Having perfect features in the scene means that the robot is able to remain true to the world coordinate frame over a wider area than otherwise.

In addition, extra labels can be attached to features initialised in this way to aid navigation, as we demonstrate in experiment here. The locations of two features lying on the corners of a zig-zag path were given to the robot as prior knowledge, along with instructions to steer to the left of the first and to the right of the second on its way to a final location at $(z, x) = (9, -3.5)$. This is information that could be assigned to automatically detected features by additional visual modules such as a free-space detector.

Figure 7 shows the locations of the known features 0 and 1, the map of other features which was formed, and the estimated robot trajectory as it negotiated the corners to pass out of the laboratory door. Steering around the known features was accomplished with a similar steering law to that used to steer to a waypoint, but with the aim of avoidance by a safe radius of 1m [6]. It can be seen that features detected in the vicinity of the known ones (especially 1) are also well known. Small "kinks" in the trajectory are noticeable where the robot first made successful measurements of the known features and made relatively large re-registration adjustments to its position estimates.

7   Conclusions

This paper has shown how a robot can use active vision to provide continuous and accurate global localisation information by serially fixating its cameras on arbitrary features in the scene. A map of landmarks is automatically built and maintained, and extended periods of navigation are permitted by the robot's ability to identify the same features again and again, mitigating the problem of motion drift.

The system provides a framework into which goal-directed visual capabilities can be inserted, as demonstrated in experiments. In future work, it is planned to add modules which enable a wide variety of purposive manoeuvres, such as automatic free-space detection to permit obstacle avoidance, or target recognition to provide goals automatically.

Potential improvements to the localisation system itself are chiefly concerned with allowing different sorts of scene feature to be used as landmarks: the additional use of line segments or planar patch features would extend robustness by making reliable landmarks easy to find and track in any environment.

References

1. N. Ayache. *Artificial Vision for Mobile Robots: Stereo Vision and Multisensory Perception*. MIT Press, Cambridge MA, 1991.
2. P. A. Beardsley, I. D. Reid, A. Zisserman, and D. W. Murray. Active visual navigation using non-metric structure. In *Proc 5th Int Conf on Computer Vision, Boston MA*, pages 58–65. IEEE Computer Society Press, 1995.
3. J.-Y. Bouget and P. Perona. Visual navigation using a single camera. In *Proc 5th Int Conf on Computer Vision, Boston MA*, pages 645–652. IEEE Computer Society Press.
4. C. G. Harris and J. M. Pike. 3D positional integration from image sequences. In *Proc 3rd Alvey Vision Conf, Cambridge UK*, pages 233–236, 1987.
5. J. J. Leonard and H. F. Durrant-Whyte. *Directed Sonar Navigation*. Kluwer Academic Press, 1992.
6. D. W. Murray, I. D. Reid, and A. J. Davison. Steering and navigation behaviours using fixation. In *Proc 7th British Machine Vision Conf, Edinburgh*, pages 635–644, 1996.
7. P. M. Sharkey, D. W. Murray, S. Vandevelde, I. D. Reid, and P. F. McLauchlan. A modular head/eye platform for real-time reactive vision. *Mechatronics*, 3(4):517–535, 1993.
8. Jianbo Shi and Carlo Tomasi. Good features to track. In *Proc of the IEEE Conf. on Computer Vision and Pattern Recognition*, pages 593–600, 1994.
9. P. Whaite and F. P. Ferrie. Autonomous exploration: Driven by uncertainty. *IEEE Transactions on Pattern Analysis and Machine Intelligence*, 19(3):193–205, 1997.

Structure from Motion

From Reference Frames to Reference Planes: Multi-view Parallax Geometry and Applications⋆

M. Irani[1], P. Anandan[2], and D. Weinshall[3]

[1] Dept. of Applied Math and CS, The Weizmann Inst. of Science, Rehovot, Israel,
irani@wisdom.weizmann.ac.il
[2] Microsoft Research, One Microsoft Way, Redmond, WA 98052, USA,
anandan@microsoft.com,
[3] Institute of Computer Science Hebrew University 91904 Jerusalem, Israel
daphna@cs.huji.ac.il

Abstract. This paper presents a new framework for analyzing the geometry of multiple 3D scene points from *multiple* uncalibrated images, based on decomposing the projection of these points on the images into two stages: (i) the projection of the scene points onto a (real or virtual) physical reference planar surface in the scene; this creates a virtual "image" on the reference plane, and (ii) the re-projection of the virtual image onto the actual image plane of the camera. The positions of the virtual image points are directly related to the 3D locations of the scene points and the camera centers relative to the reference plane alone. All dependency on the internal camera calibration parameters and the orientation of the camera are folded into homographies relating each image plane to the reference plane.

Bi-linear and tri-linear constraints involving multiple points and views are given a concrete physical interpretation in terms of geometric relations on the physical reference plane. In particular, the possible dualities in the relations between scene points and camera centers are shown to have simple and symmetric mathematical forms. In contrast to the *plane+parallax* (p+p) representation, which also uses a reference plane, the approach described here removes the dependency on a reference image plane and extends the analysis to multiple views. This leads to simpler geometric relations and complete symmetry in multi-point multi-view duality.

The simple and intuitive expressions derived in the reference-plane based formulation lead to useful applications in 3D scene analysis. In particular, simpler tri-focal constraints are derived that lead to simple methods for New View Synthesis. Moreover, the separation and compact packing of the *unknown* camera calibration and orientation into the 2D projection transformation (a homography) allows also partial reconstruction using partial calibration information.

Keywords: Multi-point multi-view geometry, uncalibrated images, new view synthesis, duality of cameras and scene points, plane+parallax, trilinearity.

⋆ M. Irani is supported in part by DARPA through ARL Contract DAAL01-97-K-0101

1 Introduction

The analysis of 3D scenes from multiple *perspective* images has been a topic of considerable interest in the vision literature. Given two calibrated cameras, their relative orientations can be determined by applying the epipolar constraint to the observed image points, and the 3D structure of the scene can be recovered relative to the coordinate frame of a reference camera (referred to here as the *reference frame*–e.g., see [13, 6]). This is done by using the *epipolar constraint* and recovering the "Essential Matrix" E which depends on the rotation R and translation T between the two cameras. Constraints directly involving the image positions of a point in three calibrated views of a point have also been derived [19].

If the calibration of the cameras is unavailable, then it is known that reconstruction is still possible from two views, but only up to a 3D projective transformation [4]. In this case the *epipolar constraint* still holds, but the Essential Matrix is replaced by the "Fundamental Matrix", which also incorporates the unknown camera calibration information. The 3D scene points, the camera centers and their image positions are represented in 3D and 2D projective spaces (using homogeneous projective coordinates). In this case, the **reference frame** reconstruction may either be a reference camera coordinate frame [8], or as defined by a set of 5 basis points in the 3D world [14]. A complete set of constraints relating the image positions of multiple points in multiple views have been derived [5, 15]. Alternatively, given a projective coordinate system specified by 5 basis points, the set of constraints directly relating the projective coordinates of the camera centers to the image measurements (in 2D projective coordinates) and their dual constraints relating to the projective coordinates of the 3D scene points have also been derived [2, 20].

Alternatively, multiple uncalibrated images can be handled using the "plane + parallax" (P+P) approach, which analyzes the parallax displacements of a point between two views relative to a (real or virtual) physical planar surface Π in the scene [16, 12, 11]. The magnitude of the parallax displacement is called the "*relative-affine structure*" in [16]. [12] shows that this quantity depends both on the "Height" H of P from Π and its depth Z relative to the reference camera. Since the *relative-affine-structure* measure is relative to both the *reference frame* (through Z) and the reference plane (through H), we refer to the P+P framework also as the **reference-frame + reference-plane** formulation. The P+P has the practical advantage that it avoids the inherent ambiguities associated with estimating the relative orientation (rotation + translation) between the cameras; this is because it requires only estimating the homography induced by the reference plane between the two views, which folds together the rotation and translation. Also, when the scene is "flat", the F matrix estimation is unstable, whereas the planar homography can be reliably recovered [18].

In this paper, we remove the dependency on the *reference frame* of the analysis of multi-point multi-view geometry. We break down the projection from 3D to 2D into 2 operations: the projection of the 3D world onto the 2D reference plane Π, followed by a 2D projective transformation (homography) which maps the reference plane to the image plane. Given the "virtual images" formed by the projection onto the reference plane, we derive algebraic and geometric relations involving the image locations of multiple points in multiple views in these virtual images. The positions of virtual image points are directly related to the 3D locations of the scene points and the camera centers relative to the reference plane alone. All dependency on the internal camera calibration parameters and the orientation of the camera are folded into homographies relating each image plane to the reference plane. We obtain a structure measure that depends *only* on the heights of the scene points relative to the reference plane

In this paper, we derive a complete set dual relationships involving 2 and 3 points in 2 and 3 views. On the reference plane the multi-point multi-view geometry is simple and intuitive. These relations are directly related to physical points on the reference plane such as the *epipole* and the *dual-epipole*[9]. We identify these points, and also two new entities called the *tri-focal line* and the *dual trifocal-line* which are analogous to the epipole and the dual-epipole when considering three-view and three-point geometries on the reference plane. Structures such as the fundamental matrix and the trilinear tensor have a rather simple form and depend only on the epipoles, and nothing else. The symmetry between points and cameras is complete, and they can be simply switched around to get from the epipolar geometry to the dual-epipolar geometry.

The simple and intuitive expressions derived in the reference-plane based formulation in this paper lead to useful applications in 3D scene analysis. In particular, simpler tri-focal constraints are derived, and these lead to simple methods for New View Synthesis. Also, the separation and compact packing of the *unknown* camera calibration and orientation into the 2D projection transformation (a homography) that relates the image plane to the reference plane, leads to potentially powerful reconstruction and calibration algorithms. For instance, based on minimal partial domain information, partial calibration and partial reconstruction can be achieved. This is also briefly discussed in this paper.

The remainder of this paper is organized as follows: Section 2 introduces our notations, and describes the two-view geometric and algebraic constraints (bilinearity and parallax) in the reference plane representation. Section 3 describes duality (between scene points and camera centers) on the reference plane. Section 4 examines the relations involving 3 views and the corresponding dual relations. Section 5 discusses applications of this representation and shows initial results for one particular application, namely new-view synthesis.

2 Two View Geometry on the Reference Plane

Figure 1 illustrates the two stage decomposition of the image formation process. Figure 1a shows the projection of one scene point from two camera centers onto the reference plane Π. Figure 1b shows the re-projection from the plane to one of the camera image planes (the "reference frame"). In this and in all subsequent figures in this paper, we adopt the following notations: P denotes scene points in 3D, C denotes camera centers; i, j, k are indices used for scene points (e.g.,

832

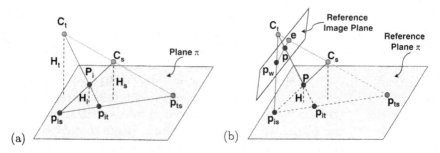

(a) (b)

Fig. 1. The reference plane representation: (a) the projection of the
points onto the reference plane itself, removing the dependency on the reference image plane. p_{ts} is the epipole, and the red line is the epipolar line. (b)
the re-projection of the reference plane image onto a reference image frame
(camera "t").

P_i) and r, s, t are indices used for camera centers (e.g., C_r). Also, p_{it} denotes the
projection of the scene point P_i through camera center C_t. It is the intersection
of the ray $P_i C_t$ with the reference plane Π. Similarly p_{is} is the intersection of
$P_i C_s$ with the reference plane. We define p_{it} and p_{is} as the "virtual-images" of
P_i on the reference plane from cameras C_t and C_s respectively. We define the
intersection of $C_t C_s$ with Π as the **epipole** on Π. We use p_{ts} to denote the
epipole. Note that the location of the epipole p_{ts} on the reference plane Π is is
independent of the orientations and the internal calibration parameters of the
cameras s and t.

To derive the algebraic constraints involving multiple points in multiple
views, we define a coordinate system (x, y, Z) relative to the reference plane
Π, where (x, y) are parallel to Π and Z is perpendicular to it. For points on
the reference plane, we define $Z = 1$, for other points we define $Z = H + 1$,
where H denotes the height (i.e., the perpendicular distance) of the point from
the plane Π. Thus, $P_i = (x_i, y_i, Z_i)$, where $Z_i = H_i + 1$, denotes the 3D coordinates of the scene point P_i. Similarly $C_t = (x_t, y_t, Z_t)^T$, where $Z_t = H_t + 1$, and
and $C_s = (x_s, y_s, Z_s)^T$, where $Z_s = H_s + 1$. The points p_{it}, p_{is} and p_{ts} on the
reference plane are the intersections of the lines $C_t P_i$, $C_s P_i$, and $C_t C_s$ with the
reference plane Π:

$$p_{it} = \begin{pmatrix} x_{it} \\ y_{it} \\ 1 \end{pmatrix} = \begin{pmatrix} \frac{H_i x_t - H_t x_i}{H_i - H_t} \\ \frac{H_i y_t - H_t y_i}{H_i - H_t} \\ 1 \end{pmatrix} \qquad p_{is} = \begin{pmatrix} x_{it} \\ y_{it} \\ 1 \end{pmatrix} = \begin{pmatrix} \frac{H_i x_s - H_s x_i}{H_i - H_s} \\ \frac{H_i y_s - H_s y_i}{H_i - H_s} \\ 1 \end{pmatrix} \quad (1)$$

$$p_{ts} = \begin{pmatrix} x_{ts} \\ y_{ts} \\ 1 \end{pmatrix} = \begin{pmatrix} \frac{H_s x_t - H_t x_s}{H_s - H_t} \\ \frac{H_s y_t - H_t y_s}{H_s - H_t} \\ 1 \end{pmatrix} \quad (2)$$

Note that the expressions given above do not involve any of the camera internal
calibration parameters or the orientations of the image planes. Also note that

there is only a single epipole, which is unlike the case of the reference-frame based formulation, which involves two epipoles, one on each image frame.

The points p_{it}, p_{is} and p_{ts} on the reference plane are related to their corresponding points on an image plane (e.g., a reference image) via a single 2D projective transformation, which is the homography between that image plane and the plane Π. Figure 1b shows the re-projection onto the reference image t — the points p, p_w, and e are the projections of the image points p_{it}, p_{is}, and the epipole p_{ts} respectively.

There are two basic results concerning two views of a point as observed on the reference plane Π. The first is the expression for the "parallax" on the reference plane, and the second is the bilinear constraint involving the two image locations of the scene point and the epipole. These are described below.

Parallax on the Reference Plane: Given the expressions in Equations 1 and 2 , it can be easily verified that

$$p_{is} - p_{it} = \gamma(p_{is} - p_{ts}), \tag{3}$$

where $\gamma = \frac{H_i(H_t - H_s)}{(H_t - H_i)H_s}$

Note that this expression for parallax (Equation 3) involves only the heights of the scene point and of the camera centers relative to the reference plane Π. It *does not* include any quantities relative to any of the camera coordinate systems (e.g., the *reference frame*) such as Z or T_Z as before. Also, the parallax magnitude γ does not depend on the x, y locations of either the camera centers or the scene point[1].

The Bilinear Constraint: Equation 3 implies that p_{it}, p_{is}, *and* p_{ts} *are collinear.* Similar to the definition of the epipolar line on the image plane, the line containing these three points on Π is the intersection of the epipolar plane containing P_i, C_t, and C_s with Π. Thus, this is the *epipolar* line as observed on the reference-plane. The collinearity of these three points can be expressed as $p_{it}^T F p_{is} = 0$ where $F = \begin{bmatrix} 0 & 1 & -y_{ts} \\ -1 & 0 & x_{ts} \\ y_{ts} & -x_{ts} & 0 \end{bmatrix}$ is the "Fundamental Matrix". As opposed to the reference frame based formulation, where the fundamental matrix depends on the camera rotations and the internal calibration parameters of the camera, here it depends only on the epipole. Moreover, the epipole is *explicit* in the F matrix here, whereas, it is *implicit* in the standard formulation.

---

[1] The expression for $\gamma = \frac{HT_Z}{Zd_\pi}$ in the P+P case can be related to the current expression as follows: Consider a *virtual* camera centered at C_t, whose image plane is the plane Π, and its optical axis coincides with the H direction. Then $H = H_i$, $Z = H_t - H_i$, $T_Z = H_t - H_s$ and $d_\pi = H_s$.

What happens when the epipole goes to ∞? In Equation 2, it can be seen that when $H_s = H_t$, the epipole p_{ts} goes to ∞. In this case,

$$p_{ts} = \begin{pmatrix} x_{ts} \\ y_{ts} \\ 0 \end{pmatrix} = \begin{pmatrix} x_t - x_s \\ y_t - y_s \\ 0 \end{pmatrix},$$

and the expression for parallax can be rewritten as: $(p_{is} - p_{it}) = \frac{H_i}{(H_t - H_i)} p_{ts}$. In other words, all the parallax vectors are parallel to each other (i.e., meet at ∞). The Fundamental Matrix $F = \begin{bmatrix} 0 & 0 & -y_{ts} \\ 0 & 0 & x_{ts} \\ y_{ts} & -x_{ts} & 0 \end{bmatrix}$. We can, of course, unify the finite and the infinite case by using 2D projective notations. However, in this paper we choose to use 2D Euclidean coordinate representations, in order to emphasize the *physical meaning* of the various observed and derived quantities. Moreover, the parallax expression in Equation 3, which involves metric relations is meaningless in a projective coordinate representation.

Also, when $H_t = H_i$ or $H_s = H_i$, then p_{it} or p_{is} go to ∞ respectively. This occurs when, fortuitously, the plane Π is chosen to be parallel to the optic ray from the scene point to one of the cameras. In this case, the corresponding image point cannot be observed on the reference plane, and our analysis does not apply.

3 Duality on the Reference Plane

In this section, we derive a set of dual relations on the reference-plane by switching the roles of camera centers and scene points as was previously done in [2, 20].

Consider two points P_i and P_j and one camera center C_t. Consider the intersection of the rays $P_i P_j$, $P_i C_t$ and $P_j C_t$ with the reference plane Π (see Figure 2a). These occur respectively at p_{ij}, p_{it} and p_{jt}. In a manner analogous to the "epipolar plane" (defined by 2 camera centers and a scene point), we define the plane containing P_i, P_j and C_t (2 scene points and a camera center) as the "*dual* epipolar plane". By the same analogy, we define its intersection with Π (i.e., the line connecting p_{it}, p_{jt} and p_{ij}) as the "*dual* epipolar line", and p_{ij} as the "*dual* epipole". Note that the dual-epipole, the dual-epipolar lines, and the dual-epipolar planes relate to a pair of scene points over multiple views, in the same way the epipole, the epipolar lines, and the epipolar planes relate to multiple scene points over a pair of views.

By applying the duality of scene points and camera centers, we can derive the dual of the bilinear constraint and the parallax expressions in algebraic form. They are:

Dual Parallax: $\qquad\qquad p_{it} - p_{jt} = \gamma_d(p_{it} - p_{ij})$, where $\gamma_d = \frac{H_t(H_j - H_i)}{(H_j - H_t)H_i}$,

and

Dual Bilinearity Constraint: $\qquad\qquad p_{it}{}^T F_d p_{jt} = 0,$

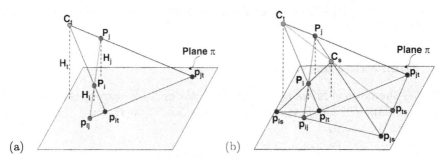

Fig. 2. Duality on the reference plane: (a) the dual-epipolar geometry associated with two points in one view. p_{ij} is the *dual*-epipole, and the blue line going through p_{ij} is the *dual*-epipolar line. (b) both sets of epipolar lines (shown in red) and dual-epipolar lines (shown in blue) that arise when considering two points in two views.

where $F_d = \begin{bmatrix} 0 & 1 & -y_{ij} \\ -1 & 0 & x_{ij} \\ y_{ij} & -x_{ij} & 0 \end{bmatrix}$ is (defined as) the "*Dual* Fundamental Matrix".

The duality of the bilinear constraint has been previously explored - e.g., Carlsson[2] and Weinshall, *et al.*[20] derive dual bilinear and trilinear relations in terms of the projective coordinate representations of the scene points, camera centers, and image points. Here, however, we derive these relations in the context of the reference plane images, and provide physical meaning to the dual relations. Also, Irani and Anandan [9] pointed out the dual epipole in the context of the plane+parallax representation. In that case, since the projection on a camera image plane ("reference frame") is included in the formulation, there exists an asymmetry in the various constraints and their dual constraints. Here, *complete* symmetry is achieved by projecting all the observed quantities onto the reference plane itself.

Figure 2b completes the picture by considering two points (P_i, P_j) in two views (C_t, C_s). This configuration gives rise to one set of epipolar lines (corresponding to each scene point) going through the epipole p_{ts}, and one set of *dual*-epipolar lines (corresponding to each camera) going through the *dual*-epipole p_{ij}.

4   Three View Geometry on the Reference Plane

In this section we extend our treatment to three views. [5] shows that there are no additional *independent* constraints that can be derived in more than three views. In this section we present a geometric interpretation of the three-view constraints in terms of physical quantities on the reference plane Π. We derive the algebraic three-view constraints and show that they have a very simple mathematical form. We will also show that the tensor-representation of these constraints in the reference-plane has a very simple mathematical form when compared to the tensors in the standard formulations[15, 7, 5].

4.1 Geometric Observations

Figure 3 shows three views p_{is}, p_{it}, and p_{ir} of a point P_i as projected onto the reference plane Π. The new camera center is labeled as C_r, and the two new epipoles as p_{rt} and p_{sr}[2].

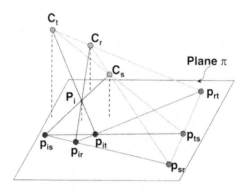

Fig. 3. Geometry of three views on the reference plane – a 3D view. The 3 red lines are the epipolar lines of pairs of views, and the turquoise line the <u>trifocal-line</u>. The 6 points on Π lie on 4 lines forming a "complete quadrilateral".

Taken pairwise at a time, the three views give rise to three epipolar constraints:

$$\underline{p_{it}, p_{is}, p_{ts} \text{ are collinear.}} \qquad \underline{p_{is}, p_{ir}, p_{sr} \text{ are collinear.}}$$
$$\underline{p_{ir}, p_{it}, p_{rt} \text{ are collinear.}}$$

There is, however, a fourth collinearity constraint, namely:

$$\text{The epipoles } \underline{p_{ts}, p_{sr}, p_{rt} \text{ are collinear.}}$$

This line is simply the intersection of the plane containing the three camera centers C_t, C_s and C_r with Π (see Figure 3). This plane is referred to as the *tri-focal plane*. Based on this definition we define the line connecting the three epipoles as the "tri-focal line".

The fact that the six points lie on four lines is fundamental to the projection of three views of a point onto a reference plane Π. Note that this figure on the

---

[2] Note that geometrically this figure is identical to Figure 2b, but the labeling of the point is different. The scene point P_j in Figure 2b has been replaced by a camera center C_r. In fact, this is because of the complete symmetry between scene points and camera centers in our representation.

plane (Figure 4a) is known as the "complete quadrilateral" and plays a central role in plane projective geometry [3].

Given the three cameras, every point in the scene forms a triangle (e.g., with vertices p_{it}, p_{is} and p_{ir}. Different points (e.g., indexed i, j, etc.) will form different triangles, all of which share the same tri-focal line (see Figure 4b). In other words, all these triangles are perspective from the tri-focal line[3].

4.2 The Trifocal Ratio

Each pair of views from the three views provides an expression for parallax similar to Equation 3. For example, consider:

$$p_{is} - p_{it} = \frac{H_i(H_t - H_s)}{(H_t - H_i)H_s}(p_{is} - p_{ts})$$
$$p_{ir} - p_{it} = \frac{H_i(H_t - H_r)}{(H_t - H_i)H_r}(p_{ir} - p_{rt})$$

$$(4)$$

From these equations we can eliminate $H_i/(H_t - H_i)$ to obtain:

$$\frac{||p_{is} - p_{it}||}{||p_{is} - p_{ts}||} = \lambda_{rst}\frac{||p_{ir} - p_{it}||}{||p_{ir} - p_{rt}||}$$

$$(5)$$

where $\lambda_{rst} = \frac{(H_t - H_s)}{H_s}\frac{H_r}{(H_t - H_r)}$. The above equation is true upto a sign change. Note that λ_{rst} does not depend on the point i. In other words, for every scene point, the locations of its image from the three views on the reference plane is related by the same Equation 5.

This constraint is further explored in Section 4.3.

Given two "images" of the point P_i on Π, e.g., p_{is} and p_{ir}, and the corresponding epipoles, p_{rt} and p_{ts}, we can determine the location of the third "image" p_{it} by intersecting the two epipolar lines $p_{is}p_{ts}$ and $p_{ir}p_{rt}$ (see Figure 4a).

There are, however, two cases in which the three epipolar lines collapse into a single line (and hence, their intersection is not unique). These are the same situations noted in [5, 15], but here we examine it in the context of the reference-plane images. The first is the case when the three camera centers are collinear (see Figure 5) - in this case the three epipoles collapse into a single point (denoted as e in Figure 5). The three epipolar lines also collapse into a single line, and therefore p_{it} cannot be determined by the intersection of the epipolar lines. However, given the common epipole e and λ_{rst}, p_{it} can be recovered from p_{is} and p_{ir} using Equation 5. In fact, in this case, λ_{rst} is the *cross ratio* of these four points (the three image points and the epipole).

---

[3] It is known in plane-projective geometry that if two triangles are perspective from a line they are also perspective from a point [3] – this is the converse of the Desargues' Theorem. Given the two triangles corresponding to i and j as in Figure 4b, then the point of perspectivity is in fact the *dual-epipole* p_{ij}.

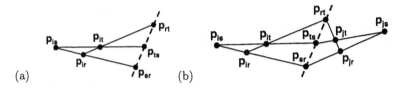

Fig. 4. Three view geometry on the reference plane: (a) the complete quadrilateral formed by the image of a single point in three views and the trifocal-line (shown as a dashed line) containing the three epipoles. (b) different triangles due to different scene points share the same trifocal-line.

Another interesting case is when the scene point P_i lies on the "tri-focal plane" of the three cameras. In this case the three image points p_{it}, p_{is} and p_{ir} all lie on the tri-focal line itself, i.e., once again the three epipolar lines collapse onto the tri-focal line. Hence we cannot use the intersection of epipolar lines to determine p_{it}. In this case too, p_{it} can be determined by Equation 5, using λ_{rst}.

The ratio λ_{rst} has a special significance. If we consider the tri-focal line, we can show (by replacing P_i with C_r in Equation 3)that:

$$p_{sr} - p_{rt} = \lambda_{rst}(p_{sr} - p_{ts}) \tag{6}$$

(Hence, the name *"trifocal-ratio"*.) In other words, in the general case:

$$\begin{aligned} \lambda_{rst} &= \frac{||p_{sr} - p_{rt}||}{||p_{sr} - p_{ts}||} \\ &= \frac{||p_{is} - p_{it}||}{||p_{is} - p_{ts}||} \frac{||p_{ir} - p_{rt}||}{||p_{ir} - p_{it}||} \end{aligned} \tag{7}$$

Note that in the singular case, when the epipoles collapse, the ratio of the distances between the epipoles (the top equation) is undefined, but the bottom equation is still valid and can be used.

4.3 The Trifocal Tensor

Returning to Equation 5, we can write down component equalities as follows:

$$\frac{x_{is} - x_{it}}{x_{is} - x_{ts}} = \frac{y_{is} - y_{it}}{y_{is} - y_{ts}} = \lambda_{rst}\frac{x_{ir} - x_{it}}{x_{ir} - x_{rt}} = \lambda_{rst}\frac{y_{ir} - y_{it}}{y_{ir} - y_{rt}} \tag{8}$$

By taking two of these equalities at a time and cross-multiplying by the denominators we can get six linear constraints. Of these two are the same as the bilinear (epipolar) constraints involving only two views at a time. The other four, which involve all three views are:

$$\begin{aligned} (x_{is} - x_{it})(x_{ir} - x_{rt}) &= \lambda_{rst}(x_{ir} - x_{it})(x_{is} - x_{ts}) \\ (x_{is} - x_{it})(y_{ir} - y_{rt}) &= \lambda_{rst}(y_{ir} - y_{it})(x_{is} - x_{ts}) \\ (y_{is} - y_{it})(x_{ir} - x_{rt}) &= \lambda_{rst}(x_{ir} - x_{it})(y_{is} - y_{ts}) \\ (y_{is} - y_{it})(y_{ir} - y_{rt}) &= \lambda_{rst}(y_{ir} - y_{it})(y_{is} - y_{ts}) \end{aligned} \tag{9}$$

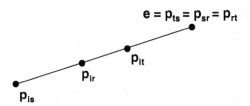

Fig. 5. The Epipolar Lines Collapse

Note that these three view constraints are actually only *bilinear* in the image locations of the scene point (as opposed to the trilinear constraints in [15])). This is because by considering the projection of the points on the reference plane itself, we eliminate the homographies induced between the views (which appear in [16]).

The trilinear forms given in Equation 9 can be unified into a single tensor equation in a manner analogous to [17]:

$$(s^\alpha p_{it})(r^\beta p_{rt}) - \lambda_{rst}(r^\beta p_{it})(s^\alpha p_{ts}) = 0 \qquad (10)$$

where

$$s = \begin{bmatrix} -1 & 0 & x_{is} \\ 0 & -1 & y_{is} \end{bmatrix}, \quad r = \begin{bmatrix} -1 & 0 & x_{ir} \\ 0 & -1 & y_{ir} \end{bmatrix}$$

and $\alpha, \beta = 1, 2$ indicate the row indices of s and r (e.g., $s^1 = [-1 \ \ 0 \ \ x_{is}])^4$.

Based on further algebraic manipulation, Equation 10 can be rewritten as:

$$\forall \alpha, \beta = 1, 2 \quad 0 = \sum_{a=1}^{3} \sum_{b=1}^{3} \sum_{c=1}^{3} (p_{it})_a (r^\beta)_b (s^\alpha)_c \left((p_{rt})_b \delta_{ac} - \lambda_{rst}(p_{ts})_c \delta_{ab} \right)$$

$$= \sum_{a=1}^{3} \sum_{b=1}^{3} \sum_{c=1}^{3} (p_{it})_a (r^\beta)_b (s^\alpha)_c (T^{rst})_{abc} \qquad (11)$$

where δ follows the standard definition: $\delta_{pq} = 1$ if $p = q$ and 0 otherwise. T^{rst} is $3 \times 3 \times 3$ tensor

$$(T^{rst})_{abc} = ((p_{rt})_b \delta_{ac} - \lambda_{rst}(p_{ts})_c \delta_{ab})$$

In the above equations, $(p_{it})_1, (p_{it})_2, (p_{it})_3$, etc. denote the first (i.e., x), the second (i.e., y), and the third (i.e, 1) components of p_{it}, etc. Similarly $(T^{rst})_{abc}$ denotes the entry indexed by a, b, c in the Tensor.

---

[4] Note that as in [17], s^1 is the vertical line on Π passing through p_{is} and s^2 is the horizontal line on Π passing through p_{is}. Similarly r^1 and r^2 are the vertical and horizontal lines on Π passing through p_{ir}. Also, as in [17] the relationships in Equation 10 are valid for any line passing through p_{is} and any other line passing through p_{ir}. In other words, Equation 10 captures the same point-line-line relationship described in [17] and [5].

Note that the elements of T^{rst} depend on the two epipoles p_{rt} and p_{ts} and λ_{rst}. This is in contrast to the general form of the trifocal tensor – for example, the trilinear tensor in [15] also depends on the homographies due to the plane Π between the different cameras and the tensor described in [5] which depends on the camera projection matrices. As in the case of the Fundamental Matrix F in our formulation, the epipoles are explicit within the Tensor T, whereas in the general formulation, the tensor is implicitly related to the epipole. Given the Tensor T^{rst} we can recover the two epipoles p_{rt} and p_{ts} and the trifocal-ration λ_{rst}; using Equation 6 we can recover the third epipole p_{sr}.

4.4 Duals of the Three View Constraints

3 Scene Points + 1 Camera: As in the case of two-view analysis, the duality between scene points and camera centers also applies to three-view analysis. By switching the roles of scene points and camera centers in Figure 3 (i.e., $P_i \rightarrow C_t, C_t \rightarrow P_i, C_s \rightarrow P_j, C_r \rightarrow P_k$) we can derive new constraints involving one camera center and three points. The resulting geometric configuration is also a *complete quadrilateral*, but with a different labeling of the points. Figure 6a indicates the labeling corresponding to *one view of three points*. In this case the *dual*-trifocal-line contains the *dual-epipoles* p_{ij}, p_{jk}, and p_{ki}. The three-view constraint given in Equation 5 is replaced by

$$\frac{\|p_{jt} - p_{it}\|}{\|p_{jt} - p_{ij}\|} = \lambda_{ijk} \frac{\|p_{kt} - p_{it}\|}{\|p_{kt} - p_{ki}\|} \tag{12}$$

where $\lambda_{ijk} = \frac{(H_j - H_i)}{H_j} \frac{H_k}{(H_k - H_i)}$, is the *dual* to the *trifocal-ratio* λ_{rst}. Dual to the other forms of the three-view constraints, (e.g., Equation 9) can also be obtained by the same substitution of indices (i.e. $i \rightarrow t, t \rightarrow i, s \rightarrow j, r \rightarrow k$), leading to the *dual*-tensor form:

$$(T^{ijk})_{abc} = ((p_{ki})_b \delta_{ac} - \lambda_{ijk}(p_{ij})_c \delta_{ab}))$$

and the corresponding constraint set:

$$\forall \alpha, \beta = 1, 2 \quad 0 = \sum_{a=1}^{3} \sum_{b=1}^{3} \sum_{c=1}^{3} (p_{it})_a (k^\beta)_b (j^\alpha)_c (T^{ijk})_{abc} \tag{13}$$

where the definitions of the 2×3 matrices k and s are analogous to the definitions of r and s given earlier. Note that the the three-view constraints and their dual, the three-point constraints are completely symmetric. The dual-tensor depends on the *dual-epipoles* and the *dual* to the *trifocal-ratio*,

Other Combinations of 3+1 Points: The complete symmetry between scene points and camera centers implies that we can arbitrarily choose the label (either as a scene point or as a camera center) for each of the four 3D points in Figure 3. So far, we have considered two choices: <u>3 camera center + 1 scene point</u>,

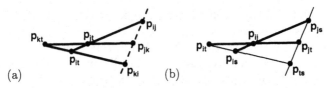

Fig. 6. Duals to the Three View Geometry: (a) the complete quadrilateral formed by 3 points + 1 camera center. (b) the quadrilateral formed by 2 points + 2 cameras. Note that the epipolar-lines (thin lines) intersect at an *epipole*, the dual-epipolar lines (thick lines) intersect at a *dual-epipole*, and an epipolar line intersects a dual-epipolar line at an *image-point*.

and 3 scene points + 1 camera center. The basic structure is that four points are divided into a group of 3 and a single point. We can obtain other duals by choosing the four points to consist of 2 camera centers + 2 scene points and grouping them as 2 camera centers and a scene point + 1 scene point or as 2 scene points and a camera center + 1 camera center.

In Figure 6b we show the resulting quadrilateral corresponding to the first of these groupings. Since the configuration shown in this figure is based on 2 camera centers and 2 scene points, the six points on the quadrilateral consist of four image points, one epipole, and one dual-epipole. Note that the two epipolar lines intersect at an *epipole*, the two dual-epipolar lines intersect at a *dual-epipole*, and each epipolar line intersects each dual-epipolar line at an image point.

Unlike the 3D world, where there are two types of points, camera centers and scene points, on the reference-plane, there are three-types of points – epipoles, dual-epipoles, and image points. Each of these form the center of a radial field of lines that go through that point, all three have completely dual-roles on Π.

5 Applications

The simple and intuitive expressions derived in the reference-plane based formulation in this paper lead to useful applications in 3D scene analysis. In particular, the simpler (bilinear) tri-focal constraints with the identified tri-focal ratio lead to a simple method for New View Synthesis. Initial experimental results are shown in this section. Moreover, the separation and compact packing of the *unknown* camera calibration and orientation into the 2D projection transformation (a homography) that relates the image plane to the reference plane, leads to potentially powerful reconstruction and calibration algorithms. These are briefly discussed in this section.

5.1 New View Generation Using the Three-View Constraints

In this section we show that the reference-plane based formulation provides a simple and intuitive way to generate new views from a given set of views.

We first show some results, followed by an explanation how they were obtained.

Figure 7a and 7b display two images taken by a hand-held camera. The scene contained toys which were placed on a rug on the floor. The camera translated and rotated between the two views. The 3D parallax effects due to the camera translation are apparent in the change of the 2D distance (on the image) between the clown's hat and the upper-right corner of the rug.

Figure 7c is a new *synthesized* view of the scene, as if obtained from a *virtual* camera positioned farther to the left of the scene relative to the two original views (and rotated, to compensate for the translation). Note the smaller distance between the clown's hat and the corner of the rug. For comparison and verification, Figure 7d shows an *actual* view obtained from the same viewing direction and orientation. Also, note the differences between the actual and synthesized view. There are image distortions where the flow was inaccurate (at depth discontinuities, e.g., on the rug around the clowns head, and near the ears of the smaller doll). Also, the synthesized view is missing the left part of the rug, as this portion of the rug was not viewed in any of the 2 input images.

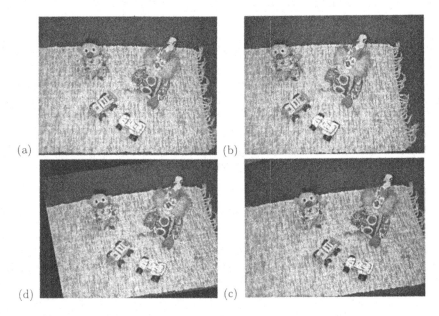

(a) (b) (d) (c)

Fig. 7. *New View Synthesis.*
(a) and (b) show two images taken by a hand-held camera. The camera translated and rotated between the two views. The 3D parallax effects due to the camera translation are apparent by the change in the 2D distance (on the image) between the clown's hat and the upper-right corner of the rug. (c) A new synthesized view of the scene, Note the smaller distance between the clown's hat and the corner of the rug. (d) an actual view obtained from the same viewing direction and orientation. Note the differences between the actual and synthesized view: There are image distortions where the flow was inaccurate (e.g., on the rug around the clowns head, and near the ears of the smaller doll). Also, the synthesized view is missing the left part of the rug, as this portion of the rug was not viewed in any of the 2 input images, (a and b).

Below is a brief description of how the synthesized view was generated. To work directly with quantities on the reference plane Π would require partial calibration information about the input views. But as explained below, new view synthesis is possible even without such information.

Step I: One of the two input images (camera "s") is first *warped* towards the other input image (camera "t"; the *reference image*) via a 2D projective transformation to align the *images* of the plane Π in the two input image s and t. (Π is the plane of the rug, in our case). The corresponding 2D projective transformation is computed *automatically*, without any prior or additional information, using a 2D registration technique described in [10]. This method locks onto a *dominant* 2D parametric transformation between a pair of images, even in the presence of moving objects or other outliers (such as the toys, in our case). For more details see [10].

Note that after such 2D warping, the two plane-stabilized images are in full alignment in all image regions which correspond to the rug, and are misaligned in all other (i.e., out-of-plane) image points (i.e., the toys). The farther a scene point is from the planar surface (rug), the larger its residual misalignment. We refer to these as planar-parallax displacements (see [11, 12, 9]).

Note that the plane-stabilized sequence is in fact a 2D re-projection of the corresponding "virtual images" on the reference plane Π onto the reference image plane, t (See Figure 1.b). Therefore, a "quadrilateral" on Π will project to a "quadrilateral" on the image plane; different triangles on Π corresponding to different scene points and sharing a common tri-focal line will preserve this relation on the reference image plane t. It can be shown that for any quadrilateral, there exists some λ'_{rst} such that Equation (7) holds. In fact, it can be shown that

$$\lambda'_{rst} = \frac{T_Z{}^{ts}}{H_s} \frac{H_r}{T_Z{}^{tr}}, \tag{14}$$

where $T_Z{}^{ts}$ is the component of the translation between cameras t and s along the optical (Z) axis of the reference camera t. Similarly $T_Z{}^{tr}$ for the third camera r. H_s and H_r are as before (i.e., heights relative to Π).

Step II: Dense flow is estimated between the two plane-stabilized images (using the method described in [12]). Note that after plane stabilization, the flow field between the two images reduces to a *radial epipolar field* centered at the epipole (see Equation (3); see also [11, 12, 9]). The cancellation of the plane homography removes all effects of camera rotation and changes in calibration. This allows to compute the flow field between a plane-stabilized image pair more reliably than general flow, as it is constrained to satisfy a global epipolar constraint.

Step III: We estimate the epipole (p_{ts}) from the radial flow field between the two input plane-stabilized images.

We then specify: (i) the *virtual* epipole (e.g., p_{rt}) between the reference image and the *virtual* "plane-stabilized" image, (ii) a *virtual* tri-focal ratio λ'_{rst} in the reference frame. Given the virtual tri-focal ratio λ'_{rst}, the virtual epipole p_{rt}, the actual epipole p_{ts}, and the dense flow field between the two plane-stabilized images (between p_{it}'s and corresponding p_{is}'s), we can estimate all image points in the virtual (plane-stabilized) image (namely, all p_{ir}'s) using Equation 8.

The virtual tri-focal ratio λ'_{rst} and the virtual epipole p_{rt} can either be specified directly (e.g., via Equation (14)), or else by specifying the location of two or more image points in the virtual (plane-stabilized) view, and estimate them accordingly.

Step IV: Note that the synthesized *plane-stabilized* image is the same for *any* camera centered at C_r. In other words, it is independent of the internal parameters and the orientation of that camera. By specifying a homography that relates the image plane of the virtual camera to the stabilized image from the reference view, we have the complete flexibility to generate an image obtained by *any* camera situated at C_r. This is done by *unwarping* the synthesized plane-stabilized image via the corresponding 2D projective transformation.

5.2 3D Reconstruction and Camera Calibration

Given uncalibrated images, any approach for obtaining Euclidean (or Affine) reconstruction requires some type of calibration. One of the benefits of our approach is that this process is factored into two separate stages, each of which has a simple and intuitive solution. First, given the input images, the "virtual-images" on Π must be determined. This can be done by taking advantage of the P+P method[12]–(i) determine the planar homography for Π *between* an arbitrarily chosen reference image and each other image, and (ii) determine the homography between the reference image and Π. Note that the parallax Equation 3 is valid even if the image locations on Π are known only upto a 2D *affine* transformation. This means that just by indicating two sets of parallel lines (that are in different orientations) Π, the 3D Heights relative to the reference plane can be recovered. From this information, the parallax magnitude γ (in Equation 3) can be determined. (Note that by specifying the 2D coordinates of four points on the reference plane, the homography can fully determined, leading to Euclidean reconstruction.)

Given γ and the height of one 3D scene point relative to Π the Heights of all other points can be determined upto a global scale factor. Both these calibration steps are simple and intuitive and require minimal specification of information. The resulting reconstruction is with respect to the reference plane Π and does not involve the camera reference frames.

The foregoing outline for a reconstruction method assumes that the correspondences of each point across the multiple-views can be estimated. This involves computing the parallax flow-field(s), and the epipole(s)– these can be done in the same manner as described in [11, 12]. It is worth noting, however, the removal of the planar homography allows the parallax computation to be more robust and accurate [11, 12].

References

1. S. Avidan and A. Shashua. Novel view synthesis in tensor space. In *IEEE Conference on Computer Vision and Pattern Recognition*, pages 1034–1040, San-Juan, June 1997.
2. S. Carlsson. Duality of reconstruction and positioning from projective views. In *Workshop on Representations of Visual Scenes*, 1995.
3. H.S.M Coxeter, editor. *Projective Geometry*. Springer Verlag, 1987.
4. O.D. Faugeras. What can be seen in three dimensions with an uncalibrated stereo rig? In *European Conference on Computer Vision*, pages 563–578, Santa Margarita Ligure, May 1992.
5. O.D. Faugeras and B. Mourrain. On the geometry and algebra of the point and line correspondences between n images. In *International Conference on Computer Vision*, pages 951–956, Cambridge, MA, June 1995.
6. Olivier Faugeras. *Three-Dimensional Computer Vision – A Geometric Viewpoint*. MIT Press, Cambridge, MA, 1996.
7. Richard Hartley. Lines and poins in three views – a unified approach. In *DARPA Image Understanding Workshop Proceedings*, 1994.
8. Richard Hartley. Euclidean Reconstruction from Uncalibrated Views. In *Applications of Invariance in Computer Vision*, J.L. Mundy, D. Forsyth, and A. Zisserman (Eds.), Springer-Verlag, 1993.
9. M. Irani and P. Anandan. Parallax geometry of pairs of points for 3d scene analysis. In *European Conference on Computer Vision*, Cambridge, UK, April 1996.
10. M. Irani, B. Rousso, and S. Peleg. Computing occluding and transparent motions. *International Journal of Computer Vision*, 12(1):5–16, January 1994.
11. M. Irani, B. Rousso, and P. peleg. Recovery of ego-motion using region alignment. *IEEE Trans. on Pattern Analysis and Machine Intelligence*, 19(3):268–272, March 1997.
12. R. Kumar, P. Anandan, and K. Hanna. Direct recovery of shape from multiple views: a parallax based approach. In *Proc 12th ICPR*, 1994.
13. H.C. Longuet-Higgins. A computer algorithm for reconstructing a scene from two projections. *Nature*, 293:133–135, 1981.
14. R. Mohr. Accurate Projective Reconstruction In *Applications of Invariance in Computer Vision*, J.L. Mundy, D. Forsyth, and A. Zisserman, (Eds.), Springer-Verlag, 1993.
15. A. Shashua. Algebraic functions for recognition. *IEEE Transactions on Pattern Analysis and Machine Intelligence*, 17:779–789, 1995.
16. A. Shashua and N. Navab. Relative affine structure: Theory and application to 3d reconstruction from perspective views. In *IEEE Conference on Computer Vision and Pattern Recognition*, pages 483–489, Seattle, Wa., June 1994.
17. A. Shashua and P. Ananadan Trilinear Constraints revisited: generalized trilinear constraints and the tensor brightness constraint. IUW, Feb. 1996.
18. P.H.S. Torr. Motion Segmentation and Outlier Detection. *PhD Thesis: Report No. OUEL 1987/93*, Univ. of Oxford, UK, 1993.
19. M. Spetsakis and J. Aloimonos. A unified theory of structure from motion. *DARPA Image Understanding Workshop*, pp.271-283, Pittsburgh, PA, 1990 .
20. D. Weinshall, M.Werman, and A. Shashua. Shape descriptors: Bilinear, trilinear and quadlinear relations for multi-point geometry, and linear projective reconstruction algorithms. In *Workshop on Representations of Visual Scenes*, 1995.

Duality, Rigidity and Planar Parallax

A. Criminisi, I. Reid and A. Zisserman

Department of Engineering Science, Oxford University
Parks Road, Oxford, OX1 3PJ, UK
tel: +1865 273148
fax: +1865 273908
e-mail: [criminis,ian,az]@robots.ox.ac.uk

Abstract. We investigate the geometry of two views of seven points, four of which are coplanar, and the geometry of three views of six points, four of which are coplanar. We prove that the two are dual, and that the fundamental geometric constraints in each case are encapsulated by a planar homology. The work unifies a number of previously diverse results related to planar parallax, duality and planar homologies.

In addition, we make a number of practical contributions, including formulae for computing the distance of the cameras from a distinguished world plane and formulae for structure computations. We show that the trifocal tensor is obtained uniquely from three views of six points, four of which are coplanar, and give a simple interpretation of the trifocal geometry.

We give examples of these computations on real images.

1 Introduction

In recent work Carlsson and Weinshall *et al.* [2, 3, 18, 19] have demonstrated the fundamental duality of the 3D reconstruction problem. They show that for points and camera in *general position*, the problem of computing camera positions from n points in m views is mathematically equivalent to the problem of reconstructing $m + 4$ points in $n - 4$ views.

In this paper we investigate the case where the points are not in general position, but where four of the space points are coplanar (which we refer to as the plane + points configuration). We show that in this case there exists an additional dual relationship which is described by a *planar homology* [13, 17], which encapsulates the fundamental geometric constraints which can be obtained. A summary of the duality results contrasted with the general position cases is shown in table 1.

The plane + points configuration has received significant attention in the past, not least because it arises frequently in everyday scenes. A useful and popular approach to the problem decomposes the image motion into a planar homographic transfer plus a residual image parallax vector [7, 8, 12]. This decomposition has the advantage that it partially factors out dependence on the camera relative rotation and internal parameters. Furthermore it can be shown

m views	n pts	general position	coplanar
2	7	$3n + 7 = 28$ d.o.f. $2mn = 28$ constraints F determined up to a 3-fold ambiguity no further constraints	$3n - 1 + 7 = 27$ d.o.f. $2mn = 28$ constraints F determined uniquely motion constraint (one) in addition $\exists$ *homology*: maps between views, *vertex* is epipole, i.e. intersection of plane and camera baseline, *axis* is intersection of plane with plane containing remaining three points.
3	6	$3n + 18 = 36$ d.o.f. $2mn = 36$ constraints T determined up to a 3-fold ambiguity no further constraints	$3n - 1 + 18 = 35$ d.o.f. $2mn = 36$ constraints T determined uniquely structure constraint (one) in addition $\exists$ *homology*: maps between points, *vertex* is intersection of plane and line joining the remaining two points, *axis* is intersection of plane and plane containing the camera centres.

Table 1. Camera/point duality results for (i) points in general position and (ii) four points lying on a distinguished plane. The fundamental matrix F has 7 degrees of freedom (d.o.f.) and the trifocal tensor T has 18 d.o.f.

[7] that the relative structure of points, and the rigidity of a scene, can be determined directly from the image measurements – i.e. the parallax vectors – without needing to compute the epipolar geometry. We show that these constraints, and other equivalent and dual ones, are consequences of the planar homology.

In fact, the work here unifies a number of previously diverse results related to planar parallax [7, 8, 12], duality [2, 3, 18, 19] and planar homologies [17]. In addition to this theoretical contribution, we make a number of practical contributions, including formulae for computing the distance of the cameras from a distinguished world plane, formulae for structure computations, and we derive the trifocal tensor [6, 15, 16] in the plane + points case, showing that it is obtained uniquely.

The remainder of the paper is organised as follows. We begin with a discussion of background material – notation, parallax geometry and, planar homologies.

We then turn to the geometry of two views, seven points, four of which are coplanar. We show that there exists a homology on the plane relating the two views and derive necessary conditions for the homology directly in terms of the parallax measurements. In section 4 we show the duality of the geometry of three views, six points (four coplanar) to the two view, seven point case, and hence obtain analogous necessary conditions. We also derive the trifocal tensor and show that it is over-constrained. In section 5 we derive expressions for the height of the cameras from the distinguished plane and the structure of points in terms of affine invariants, and give examples of various applications. We conclude with a discussion and directions for future study in section 6.

2 Background

2.1 Notation

We denote 3D points in general position by upper case bold symbols (e.g. $\mathbf{P}$) and image positions and vectors by lower case bold symbols (e.g. $\mathbf{p}$, $\boldsymbol{\mu}_p$) and scalars by lower case normal symbols (e.g. d, h_p). Matrices are denoted by typewriter style capitals (e.g. A, B).

The area of a triangle on a plane with vertices $\mathbf{p}$, $\mathbf{q}$, and $\mathbf{r}$ is denoted $A_{\mathbf{pqr}}$, and can be determined via the formula $A_{\mathbf{pqr}} = \frac{1}{2}|\mathbf{pqr}|$ where the points $\mathbf{p}$, $\mathbf{q}$, and $\mathbf{r}$ are represented as homogeneous 3-vectors with last component equal to one.

Numbered subscripts are used to distinguish different views, with the first camera centre given by $\mathbf{O}_1$, the second by $\mathbf{O}_2$ and the third by $\mathbf{O}_3$. The projection of an image point onto the distinguished world plane from the ith view is denoted $\mathbf{p}_i$.

2.2 Planar parallax

The underlying parallax geometry is shown in figure 1. The distinguished world plane induces a homography between the views meaning that the images of points on the plane can be transferred via the homography between views 1 and 2. The homography can be determined from a minimum of four correspondences in the two views of points (or lines) on the distinguished plane [11].

The parallax vector in the first view is the vector joining the image of a world point $\mathbf{P}$ with the transferred location of $\mathbf{P}$'s image in the other view (i.e. the image of $\mathbf{p}_2$). Furthermore, since the three planes (distinguished world plane and two image planes) are equivalent up to a plane projectivity, we can also measure parallax in the second view, or – if we know the image to world plane homographies – on the distinguished world plane. In fact it is particularly elegant to work with the world plane. In this case all dependence on the rotational and internal parameters of the cameras is removed (aggregated into the image plane to world plane homographies) leaving only a dependence on the camera centres.

Since the clarity of the underlying geometry is greatly increased, we depict all relevant points and vectors on the world plane in all of our figures. However the computations in general do *not* require the image to world homographies to be known.

The parallax vector is directed towards (or away from) the epipole, so two such vectors are sufficient to compute its position, and the full epipolar geometry follows [1, 9, 10]. The magnitude of the parallax vector is related to the distance of the world point and cameras from the world plane. Although others have described this function in detail [7, 8, 12], we re-derive the relationship in section 5.

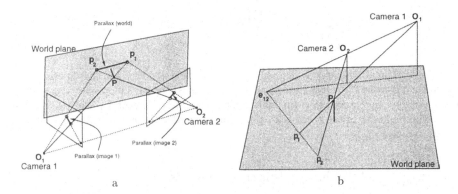

Fig. 1. Parallax geometry: (a) general configuration; (b) viewed on the distinguished plane. The parallax vector $< \mathbf{p}_1, \mathbf{p}_2 >$ passes through the epipole $\mathbf{e}_{12}$.

2.3 Planar homologies

A *planar homology* is a plane projective transformation with five degrees of freedom, having a line of fixed points, called the *axis* and a distinct fixed point not on the axis known as the *vertex* (figure 2). Algebraically, such a transformation has one distinct eigenvalue, with corresponding eigenvector being the vertex, and two repeated eigenvalues, whose corresponding eigenvectors span the axis. Planar homologies arise naturally in an image when two planes related by a perspectivity in 3-space are imaged [17].

If two triangles on a plane are related such that the lines joining their corresponding vertices are concurrent, then they are said to be in a *Desargues configuration*, and Desargues' Theorem states that the intersections of their corresponding sides are collinear [13] (figures 4, 6). Such triangles are related by a planar homology, with the common point of intersection being the vertex of the transformation, and the axis being the line containing the intersections of corresponding sides. Conversely, any triple of points in correspondence under a homology must be in a Desargues configuration.

The projective transformation representing the homology can be parametrized directly in terms of the 3-vector representing the axis $\mathbf{a}$, the 3-vector representing

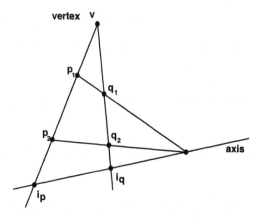

Fig. 2. A planar homology is defined by a vertex and an axis. Its characteristic invariant is given by the cross-ratio $< \mathbf{v}, \mathbf{p_1}, \mathbf{p_2}, \mathbf{i}_p >$ where $\mathbf{p_1}$ and $\mathbf{p_2}$ are *any* pair of corresponding points and $\mathbf{i}_p$ is the intersection of the line through $\mathbf{p_1}$ and $\mathbf{p_2}$ and the axis. The point $\mathbf{p_1}$ is projected onto the point $\mathbf{p_2}$ under the homology, and similarly for $\mathbf{q_1}$ and $\mathbf{q_2}$.

the vertex $\mathbf{v}$, and the characteristic cross-ratio μ as:

$$H = I + (\mu - 1)\frac{\mathbf{v}\mathbf{a}^{\top}}{\mathbf{v}.\mathbf{a}}$$

Having five degrees of freedom (the scales of $\mathbf{v}$ and $\mathbf{a}$ have no effect), a homology can be determined by 2.5 point correspondences. Three point correspondences therefore, provide an additional constraint. In the next section we derive the link between homologies and the structure and motion.

3 Geometry of two views

We consider the case of imaging seven points, four of which are coplanar from two distinct viewpoints. Each of the three points $\mathbf{P}, \mathbf{Q}$ and $\mathbf{R}$ not on the plane gives rise to a parallax vector, which is depicted on the world plane in figure 3.

The plane $\mathbf{PQR}$ intersects the world plane in a line, and the camera baseline intersects the world plane in a point. It can be seen by inspection of figures 3 and 4 that the geometry under consideration (seven points, two views) leads directly to a Desargues configuration in which the epipole is the vertex of the homology and the intersection of plane $\mathbf{PQR}$ with the world plane is the axis of the homology. The two triangles in the Desargues configuration are the two images of the space triangle $\mathbf{PQR}$. This key observation underpins the results which follow.

As stated in the previous section, a homology has five degrees of freedom, and therefore three point correspondences over-determine the homology. The extra constraint available can be used as a test for the rigidity of the scene and is equivalent to the epipolar constraint.

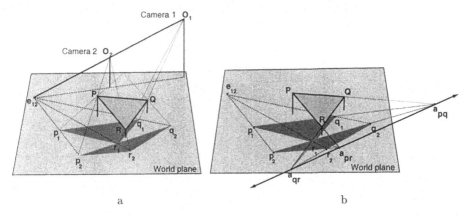

Fig. 3. (a) The geometry of three points in two views. The triangle $\mathbf{p}_i\mathbf{q}_i\mathbf{r}_i$ is the "shadow" of $\mathbf{PQR}$ under the camera $\mathbf{O}_i$; (b) The axis of the homology is given by the intersection of the plane $\mathbf{PQR}$ with the world plane, and the vertex (epipole e_{12}) by the intersection of the baseline with the world plane.

Clearly the constraint can be tested geometrically by using point correspondences either to construct the intersections of corresponding sides and testing their collinearity, or testing the concurrence of the parallax vectors. Alternatively an algebraic test could, for example, compute the epipole using two point correspondences, use the epipole plus the three point correspondences to solve for a general homography, then test the homography to determine if it is a homology.

The former has the disadvantage of requiring the construction of features which may be far removed from the measured image features themselves, while the latter gives little insight into the underlying geometry.

Below we derive novel bilinear and trilinear constraints which are necessary conditions on the homology. We refer to these as *motion constraints* and they are equivalent to the epipolar constraint, but have the advantage that the computations involve only those features which can be measured directly, namely the parallax vectors.

3.1 Motion constraints

Here we give necessary conditions for the homology (which are therefore necessary for scene rigidity in two views) in the form of an identity involving only areas computable from the parallax vectors. Two such conditions and their symmetric forms can be determined. The first is derived from the collinearity of the points $\mathbf{a}_{qr}$, $\mathbf{a}_{pr}$ and $\mathbf{a}_{pq}$ and leads to a constraint which is trilinear in the areas. The second is derived from the collinearity of the epipole $\mathbf{e}_{12}$ and corresponding points and is bilinear in the areas. The results are summarised in table 2.

The areas $A_{\mathbf{pqr}}$ can be computed either in the image or on the distinguished plane. The latter requires knowledge of the world to image homography, the former only the homography between images.

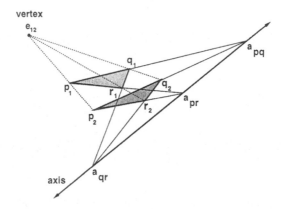

Fig. 4. Three points in two views relative to a known plane leads directly to a Desargues configuration on the plane.

Violation of any of (1) – (5) is a clear indication that there has been non-rigid motion between the views. However if any (or all) of the points $\mathbf{P}, \mathbf{Q}, \mathbf{R}$ moves in its own epipolar planes then the equations are still satisfied and non-rigidity is not detected.

	MOTION CONSTRAINTS	
T_1	$A_{p_1p_2r_1}A_{q_1q_2p_1}A_{q_1r_1r_2} = A_{p_1p_2q_1}A_{q_1q_2r_1}A_{p_1r_1r_2}$	(1)
T_2	$A_{p_2p_1r_2}A_{q_2q_1p_2}A_{q_2r_2r_1} = A_{p_2p_1q_2}A_{q_2q_1r_2}A_{p_2r_2r_1}$	(2)
B_1	$A_{r_2p_1p_2}A_{r_1q_1q_2} = A_{r_1p_1p_2}A_{r_2q_1q_2}$	(3)
B_2	$A_{p_2r_1r_2}A_{p_1q_1q_2} = A_{p_1r_1r_2}A_{p_2q_1q_2}$	(4)
B_3	$A_{q_2p_1p_2}A_{q_1r_1r_2} = A_{q_1p_1p_2}A_{q_2r_1r_2}$	(5)

Table 2. Two view bilinear (B_i) and trilinear (T_i) motion constraints equivalent to the epipolar constraint.

4 Geometry of three views

We now consider the geometry of six points, four of which are coplanar, in three views. This is the situation addressed by Irani and Anandan [7]. The geometry is shown in figure 5.

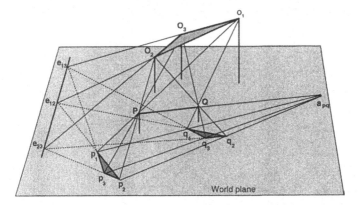

Fig. 5. The geometry of three views with two points off the plane. The three epipoles are collinear, lying on the line which is the intersection of the plane $O_1O_2O_3$ with the world plane. The point a_{pq} is the intersection of the line $\mathbf{PQ}$ with the world plane.

We begin by demonstrating the duality of this case to the two view case in section 3, and obtain a *structural constraint* directly from the measured image features. We then derive the trifocal tensor for the three view, six point (four coplanar) case. Since the trifocal tensor is over-constrained by six points, four of which are coplanar, we also obtain another form of the structure constraint.

4.1 Duality

It is clear by inspection of figure 5 that the three view geometry is dual to that of figure 3 in which we have directly exchanged points off the plane for camera positions. The vertex of the homology is given by the intersection of the line $\mathbf{PQ}$ with the world plane, and the axis by the intersection of the trifocal plane containing the three camera centres O_1, O_2, O_3 with the world plane (figure 6).

Having established the duality of the two situations, we are now in a position to invoke duality in order to prove further results. We make the substitutions:

2 views	e_{12}	p_1	p_2	r_1	r_2	q_1	q_2	a_{pr}	a_{pq}	a_{qr}
3 views	a_{pq}	p_1	q_1	p_2	q_2	p_3	q_3	e_{12}	e_{13}	e_{23}

and the dual trilinear and bilinear constraints given in table 3 follow. Note that the bilinear constraints (8) – (10) are exactly the constraints given by Irani and Anandan [7]. The trilinear constraints are new.

4.2 The trifocal tensor

In this section it is shown that the trifocal tensor is uniquely determined from three views of six points, four of which are coplanar. We begin with a familiar

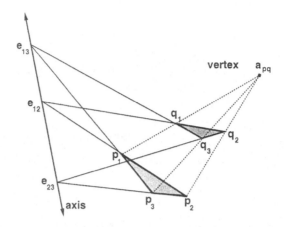

Fig. 6. The planar geometry in the three view two point case is also clearly a Desargues configuration and point correspondences $p_1 \to q_1$, $p_2 \to q_2$ and $p_3 \to q_3$ are related by a homology. This situation is clearly dual to that in figure 4.

	STRUCTURAL CONSTRAINTS	
T_1	$A_{p_1q_1p_2}A_{p_3q_3p_1}A_{p_3p_2q_2} = A_{p_1q_1p_3}A_{p_3q_3p_2}A_{p_1p_2q_2}$	(6)
T_2	$A_{q_1p_1q_2}A_{q_3p_3q_1}A_{q_3q_2p_2} = A_{q_1p_1q_3}A_{q_3p_3q_2}A_{q_1q_2p_2}$	(7)
B_1	$A_{q_2p_1q_1}A_{p_2p_3q_3} = A_{p_2p_1q_1}A_{q_2p_3q_3}$	(8)
B_2	$A_{q_1p_2q_2}A_{p_1p_3q_3} = A_{p_1p_2q_2}A_{q_1p_3q_3}$	(9)
B_3	$A_{q_3p_1q_1}A_{p_3p_2q_2} = A_{p_3p_1q_1}A_{q_3p_2q_2}$	(10)

Table 3. Three view bilinear (B_i) and trilinear (T_i) structure constraints.

form of the trifocal tensor (after [5]) in which we consider the image projection matrices and image point locations. We then show how the form of the tensor is simplified when we consider all geometric objects (lines, points, etc) projected onto the distinguished plane.

Image form: In order to discriminate between points (and epipoles) in images, as opposed to their projections onto the distinguished plane, we use primes to indicate the image in which the points appear; i.e. the images of **P** in views 1, 2 and 3 are, respectively, **p**, **p**′ and **p**″. Suppose the homographies induced by the plane of the points are A and B, so that **p**′ = A**p** and **p**″ = B**p** for images of points on the plane. These homographies are computed from the images of the four coplanar points.

The images of the first camera centre in the second and third images, denoted $\mathbf{e}'$ and $\mathbf{e}''$ respectively, are the epipoles. They are determined using parallax vectors, as described in section 3, so that $F_{12} = [\mathbf{e}']_\times A$, and $F_{13} = [\mathbf{e}'']_\times B$. It can be shown that the three camera projection matrices can be chosen as

$$P = [I \mid 0], \quad P' = [A \mid \mathbf{e}'], \quad P'' = [B \mid \lambda \mathbf{e}''] \tag{11}$$

up to a homography of 3-space, where λ is an unknown scalar. This unknown scalar is determined by line transfer.

The line through the (non-coplanar) points $\mathbf{P}$, $\mathbf{Q}$, is imaged as $\mathbf{l} = \mathbf{p} \times \mathbf{q}$, $\mathbf{l}' = \mathbf{p}' \times \mathbf{q}'$, $\mathbf{l}'' = \mathbf{p}'' \times \mathbf{q}''$ in the first, second and third views respectively. It is then straightforward to show that lines transfer as follows (we could alternatively consider point transfer):

$$\mathbf{l} = \lambda(\mathbf{e}''.\mathbf{l}'')A^\top \mathbf{l}' - (\mathbf{e}'.\mathbf{l}')B^\top \mathbf{l}'' \tag{12}$$

The scalar λ is the only unknown in this equation. It is determined by taking the vector product with $\mathbf{l}$.

$$\lambda(\mathbf{e}''.\mathbf{l}'')\mathbf{l} \times (A^\top \mathbf{l}') = (\mathbf{e}'.\mathbf{l}')\mathbf{l} \times (B^\top \mathbf{l}'') \tag{13}$$

This provides two equations in the one unknown λ and so we can solve uniquely for the trifocal tensor and obtain one further constraint, namely the rigidity condition that the imaged intersection of the line through $\mathbf{P}, \mathbf{Q}$ is the same when computed from views one and two ($\mathbf{l} \times (A^\top \mathbf{l}')$) as from views one and three ($\mathbf{l} \times (B^\top \mathbf{l}'')$). This is yet another form of the constraints (6) – (10). The scale factor lambda is obtained by normalising both sides of (13):

$$\lambda = \frac{\|(\mathbf{e}'.\mathbf{l}')\mathbf{l} \times (B^\top \mathbf{l}'')\|}{\|(\mathbf{e}''.\mathbf{l}'')\mathbf{l} \times (A^\top \mathbf{l}')\|} \tag{14}$$

Distinguished plane form: On the distinguished plane $A = B = I$, so the equivalent of (12) for point transfer is

$$\mathbf{r}_3 = \lambda \mathbf{e}_{13}(\mathbf{l}_2.\mathbf{r}_1) - (\mathbf{e}_{12}.\mathbf{l}_2)\mathbf{r}_1 \tag{15}$$

where $\mathbf{r}_1$, $\mathbf{r}_2$, $\mathbf{r}_3$ are the distinguished plane images of a general 3D point $\mathbf{R}$, and $\mathbf{l}_2$ is any line through $\mathbf{r}_2$. This equation depends only on the positions of the epipoles on the distinguished plane, with all dependence on camera internals and relative rotations having been factored out into the image to plane homographies.

Additionally the projection matrices have the very simple form

$$P_1 = [I \mid 0], \quad P_2 = [I \mid \mathbf{e}_{12}], \quad P_3 = [I \mid \lambda \mathbf{e}_{13}] \tag{16}$$

Hence, representing a general 3D point as $\mathbf{R} = \begin{bmatrix} \mathbf{r}_1 \\ \rho \end{bmatrix}$, we determine the distingished plane images to be:

$$\mathbf{r}_1 = P_1\mathbf{R}, \quad , \mathbf{r}_2 = P_2\mathbf{R} = \mathbf{r}_1 + \rho \mathbf{e}_{12}, \quad \mathbf{r}_3 = P_3\mathbf{R} = \mathbf{r}_1 + \rho\lambda \mathbf{e}_{13} \tag{17}$$

We now give an interpretation of ρ and λ on the distinguished plane (see figure 7).

The ratio λ depends only on the camera centres, not on the points, and can be determined as $\lambda = d(\mathbf{e}_{12}, \mathbf{e}_{23})/d(\mathbf{e}_{13}, \mathbf{e}_{23})$ where $d()$ is the distance between the points on the distinguished plane. The parameter ρ is the relative affine invariant of Shashua [14], and is related to the point depth. On the distinguished plane it is obtained as $\rho = d(\mathbf{r}_2, \mathbf{r}_1)/d(\mathbf{r}_2, \mathbf{e}_{12})$.

So point transfer using the trifocal tensor simply involves computing the ratio ρ from $\mathbf{r}_1$, $\mathbf{r}_2$ and $\mathbf{e}_{12}$ and employing λ to define the transferred point $\mathbf{r}_3$ on the line between $\mathbf{e}_{13}$ and $\mathbf{r}_1$ as $\mathbf{r}_3 = \mathbf{r}_1 + \rho\lambda\mathbf{e}_{13}$ in (17). This is identical to the point transfer of (15), as can be seen by considering similar triangles in figure 7. In the case that the three camera centres are collinear there is no degeneracy in point/line transfer. The ratio λ is still defined and can be obtained using the distinguished plane equivalent of (14).

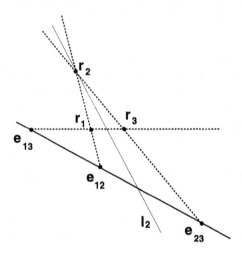

Fig. 7. Point transfer: the ratios of the distances between $\mathbf{r}_1$, $\mathbf{r}_2$ and $\mathbf{e}_{12}$ and the three epipoles define the transfer of the point $\mathbf{r}_1$ to $\mathbf{r}_3$.

5 Structural computations and applications

In this section we discuss a number of useful structural computations which can be achieved using ratios of areas. We require *affine* measurements on the world plane, which can be obtained either from four world plane points known up to an affinity (and hence the image to world plane homographies), or from the inter-image homography and vanishing line of the world plane in each image. In either case we obtain results for the scene structure without resorting first to computing the epipolar geometry. A significant novel aspect of the formulae given in sections 5.1 and 5.2 is that the vanishing point for the direction of measurement need not be known.

The results are derived for the two view, seven point case. However because of the fundamental duality proved in section 4.1, they are equally valid (with appropriate symbol substitutions) in the three view, six point case. For example (22) can be used to compute the height of a third point given two other known heights in the two view, seven point case; dually, in the three view, six point case, it can be used to obtain the height of a third camera given the other two camera heights.

We begin by re-deriving the basic parallax relationship for the case where the parallax is measured on the distinguished world plane (18).

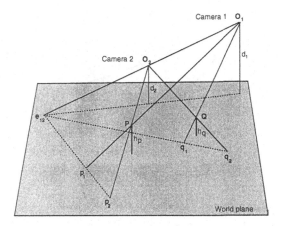

Fig. 8. Parallax geometry of two points.

Considering figure 8 and writing $\mathbf{p}_1 = \mathbf{O}_1 + \frac{d_1}{d_1 - h}(\mathbf{P} - \mathbf{O}_1)$, $\mathbf{p}_2 = \mathbf{O}_2 + \frac{d_2}{d_2 - h}(\mathbf{P} - \mathbf{O}_2)$ and $\mathbf{e}_{12} = \mathbf{O}_2 + \frac{d_2}{d_2 - h}(\mathbf{O}_1 - \mathbf{O}_2)$. Then eliminating $\mathbf{O}_1$ and $\mathbf{O}_2$ yields

$$\mu_p = \frac{h_p}{d_2 - h_p} \frac{\Delta_d}{d_1}(\mathbf{p}_1 - \mathbf{e}_{12}) \qquad (18)$$

where $\mu_p = \mathbf{p}_2 - \mathbf{p}_1$ is the planar parallax vector and $\Delta_d = d_1 - d_2$ is the component of camera translation towards the plane.

Let γ be the ratio of the distance of a point to the plane and the point to the first camera (measured in the same direction), i.e $\gamma_p = \frac{h_p}{d_1 - h_p}$ and $\gamma_q = \frac{h_q}{d_1 - h_q}$ then combining the basic parallax equation (18) for two points $\mathbf{P}$ and $\mathbf{Q}$ gives

$$\gamma_q \mu_p - \gamma_p \mu_q = \gamma_p \gamma_q \frac{\Delta_d}{d_2}(\mathbf{p}_2 - \mathbf{q}_2) \qquad (19)$$

Finally, taking the cross product of both sides of the equation with $\mathbf{p}_2 - \mathbf{q}_2$ and taking magnitudes yields an expression for $\frac{\gamma_q}{\gamma_p}$ as a ratio of areas (see figure 9) of the form

$$\frac{\gamma_q}{\gamma_p} = \frac{|\mu_q \times (\mathbf{p_2} - \mathbf{q_2})|}{|\mu_p \times (\mathbf{p_2} - \mathbf{q_2})|} = \frac{A_{\mathbf{q_1 q_2 p_2}}}{A_{\mathbf{p_1 p_2 q_2}}} \tag{20}$$

This ratio is computable solely from the parallax measurements, and is clearly affine invariant, being a ratio of areas. Our derivation is equivalent to Irani and Anandan's construction [7], but note that in our formulation we have used only affine constructs (no perpendicularity has been assumed and the formulae are homogeneous).

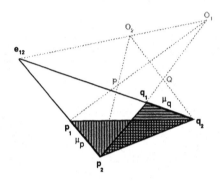

Fig. 9. The relative structure $\frac{\gamma_q}{\gamma_p}$ can be expressed as a ratio of areas.

5.1 Camera distance to world plane

Here we show that: given the parallax vectors of two world points $\mathbf{P}$ and $\mathbf{Q}$, the Euclidean distances of these points from the world plane (measured in the same but arbitrary direction), h_p and h_q, and affine measurements on the world plane, then we can determine the Euclidean distance of either camera to the world plane (measured in the same direction as h_p and h_q).

We can rearrange (20) to give an expression for the distance of the first camera from the plane (a similar formula can be derived for the second camera):

$$d_1 = \frac{h_p h_q (A_{\mathbf{p_1 p_2 q_2}} - A_{\mathbf{q_1 q_2 p_2}})}{h_q A_{\mathbf{p_1 p_2 q_2}} - h_p A_{\mathbf{q_1 q_2 p_2}}} \tag{21}$$

In figure 11 we have used the formulae to compute the heights of the camera above the floor as 566cm and 586cm (left and right views respectively).

5.2 Measuring the structure of other points

Here we show that: given the parallax vectors of three world points $\mathbf{P}$, $\mathbf{Q}$ and $\mathbf{R}$, the Euclidean distances of two of these points from the world plane (measured in the same but arbitrary direction), h_p and h_q ($h_p \neq h_q$), and affine measurements on the world plane, then we can determine the Euclidean distance of the third point from the plane (measured in the same direction as h_p and h_q).

From (20) we have that $\gamma_r = \gamma_p \frac{A_{r_1 r_2 p_1}}{A_{p_1 p_2 r_1}}$ and $\gamma_r = \gamma_q \frac{A_{r_1 r_2 q_1}}{A_{q_1 q_2 r_1}}$. After eliminating the camera distance d between these equations we obtain an expression for h_r:

$$
h_r = \frac{|M_1|}{|M_2|}, \quad M_1 = h_p h_q \begin{bmatrix} A_{r_1 r_2 q_1} & A_{q_1 q_2 r_1} \\ A_{r_1 r_2 p_1} & A_{p_1 p_2 r_1} \end{bmatrix}, \quad M_2 = \begin{bmatrix} A_{r_1 r_2 q_1} & A_{q_1 q_2 r_1} & A_{q_1 q_2 r_1} \\ h_p & 0 & -h_q \\ A_{p_1 p_2 r_1} & A_{p_1 p_2 r_1} & A_{r_1 r_2 p_1} \end{bmatrix}
$$
$$(22)$$

Note that if h_p and h_q are equal then the formulae above degenerate, however this situation can be avoided in practice. The degeneracy is understood in terms of the geometry as follows: in general we obtain projective structure (since F is determined uniquely). If in addition $h_p \neq h_q$, the line **PQ** intersects π_∞ in a point which can be identified in both images (details omitted). This point and the vanishing line of the world plane, $\mathbf{l}_\infty$, determine π_∞, hence we can obtain affine structure. When $h_p = h_q$ then the line **PQ** intersects π_∞ on $\mathbf{l}_\infty$ and so no additional information about π_∞ is obtained; it is determined only up to a one parameter family (the pencil of planes with $\mathbf{l}_\infty$ as its axis).

Figure 10 shows an example in which point heights have been estimated. The floor tiling and the perpendicular heights of two other points were measured by hand with a tape measure. A second example is shown in Figure 11. As before, we have used the patterned floor tiling to compute the image to world plane homography, and measured the heights of two points with a tape measure as reference heights.

6 Discussion

We have considered the geometry of two views of seven points, four of which are coplanar, and the geometry of three views of six points, four of which are coplanar. These configurations were shown to be dual to one another and that the fundamental geometric constraints are captured by a planar homology relating the images of points across views. Consequently a number of previously diverse results related to planar parallax, duality and planar homologies have been unified.

The constraints derived from the homology are easily computed from directly measured image features, and have been tested on real imagery. Formulae for determining the height of the cameras from the world plane, and the heights of points from the plane have been developed and tested on real imagery. We are currently evaluating the accuracy of the method. In particular we are investigating how uncertainty and errors in image measurements propagate to 3D measurements [4]. A subject of further investigation will be the sensitivity of the structure and motion constraints.

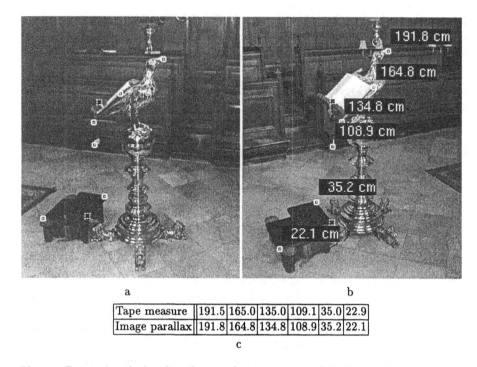

Tape measure	191.5	165.0	135.0	109.1	35.0	22.9
Image parallax	191.8	164.8	134.8	108.9	35.2	22.1

c

Fig. 10. Estimating the heights of points from two views of the lecturn in The Queen's College chapel. The heights of the reference points, shown black on white, were measured by hand ($\pm 0.5cm$) to be 150cm (top edge of lecturn), and 35cm (height of foot stool). In (c), all heights are given in centimetres. The error between the computed and measured heights is always less than one centimetre.

Fig. 11. Estimating the heights of points from two views of The Queen's College dining hall. The heights of the reference points, shown black on white, were measured by hand ($\pm 0.5cm$) to be 76cm (table top), and 230cm (fireplace). The step was computed to be 11.4cm high and measured by hand as 11.0cm.

Acknowledgements The work has been supported by Technology Foresight Grant AMVIR, Esprit Project IMPROOFS and by an EPSRC Advanced Reareach Fellowship. We are grateful to A. Fitzgibbon and F. Schaffalitzky for assistance and discussions.

References

1. P. A. Beardsley, D. Sinclair, and A. Zisserman. Ego-motion from six points. Insight meeting, Catholic University Leuven, Feb 1992.
2. Carlsson S. Duality of reconstruction and positioning from projective views. In *ICCV Workshop on Representation of Visual Scenes, Boston*, 1995.
3. Carlsson S. and Weinshall D. Dual computation of projective shape and camera positions from multiple images. *Int'l J. of Computer Vision*, 1998. in Press.
4. A. Criminisi, I. Reid, and A. Zisserman. A plane measuring device. In *Proc. BMVC*, UK, September 1997.
5. R. I. Hartley. Lines and points in three views – a unified approach. In *ARPA Image Understanding Workshop, Monterrey*, 1994.
6. R. I. Hartley. A linear method for reconstruction from lines and points. In *Proc. ICCV*, pages 882–887, 1995.
7. M. Irani and P. Anandan. Parallax geometry of pairs of points for 3d scene analysis. In B. Buxton and R. Cipolla, editors, *Proc. ECCV*, pages 17–30. Springer, 1996.
8. R. Kumar, P. Anandan, M. Irani, J. Bergen, and K. Hanna. Representation of scenes from collections of images. In *ICCV Workshop on the Representation of Visual Scenes*, 1995.
9. Q.-T. Luong and T. Viéville. Canonic representations for the geometries of multiple projective views. In *Proc. ECCV*, pages 589–599, May 1994.
10. R. Mohr. Projective geometry and computer vision. In Chen, Pau, and Wang, editors, *Handbook of Pattern Recognition and Computer Vision*. 1992.
11. J. Mundy and A. Zisserman. *Geometric Invariance in Computer Vision*. MIT Press, 1992.
12. H. S. Sawhney. Simplifying motion and structure analysis using planar parallax and image warping. In *Proc. CVPR*, 1994.
13. J. Semple and G. Kneebone. *Algebraic Projective Geometry*. Oxford University Press, 1979.
14. A. Shashua. On geometric and algebraic aspects of 3d affine and projective structures from perspective 2d views. In J. Mundy, A. Zisserman, and D. Forsyth, editors, *Applications of Invariance in Computer Vision LNCS 825*, pages 127–143. Springer-Verlag, 1994.
15. A. Shashua. Trilinearity in visual recognition by alignment. In *Proc. ECCV*, volume 1, pages 479–484, May 1994.
16. M. E. Spetsakis and J. Aloimonos. Structure from motion using line correspondences. *Intl. J. of Computer Vision*, 4(3):171–183, 1990.
17. Van Gool L., Proesmans M., and Zisserman A. Grouping and invariants using planar homologies. In Mohr, R. and Chengke, W., editors, *Europe-China workshop on Geometrical Modelling and Invariants for Computer Vision*, pages 182–189. Xidan University Press, Xi'an, China, 1995.
18. D. Weinshall, M. Werman, and A. Shashua. Duality of multi-point and multi-frame geometry: Fundamental shape matrices and tensors. In B. Buxton and R. Cipolla, editors, *Proc. ECCV*, pages 217–227. Springer-Verlag, 1996.
19. Werman M., Weinshall D., and Shashua A. Shape tensors for efficient and learnable indexing. In *ICCV Workshop on Representation of Visual Scenes, Boston*, 1995.

On Degeneracy of Linear Reconstruction from Three Views: Linear Line Complex and Applications

Gideon P. Stein[1] and Amnon Shashua[2]

[1] Artificial Intelligence Laboratory, MIT
Cambridge, MA 02139, USA
gideon@ai.mit.edu
http://www.ai.mit.edu/people/gideon/gideon.html
[2] Institute of Computer Science, Hebrew University of Jerusalem
Jerusalem 91904, Israel
shashua@cs.huji.ac.il
http://www.cs.huji.ac.il/~shashua/

Abstract. This paper investigates the linear degeneracies of projective structure estimation from line features across three views. We show that the rank of the linear system of equations for recovering the trilinear tensor of three views reduces to 23 (instead of 26) when the scene is a Linear Line Complex (set of lines in space intersecting at a common line). The LLC situation is only linearly degenerate, and one can obtain a unique solution when the admissibility constraints of the tensor are accounted for.

The line configuration described by an LLC, rather than being some obscure case, is in fact quite typical. It includes, as a particular example, the case of a camera moving down a hallway in an office environment or down an urban street. Furthermore, an LLC situation may occur as an artifact such as in direct estimation from spatio-temporal derivatives of image brightness. Therefore, an investigation into degeneracies and their remedy is important also in practice.

1 Introduction

It is known that point and line image features across three perspective views can generally give rise to a linear system of equations for a unique solution for 3D structure and camera motion. The structure and motion parameters are represented by a $3 \times 3 \times 3$ tensor. The image measurements of matching points and lines provide constraints, trilinear in image coordinates, that as a whole make a linear system of equations for the (unknown) coefficients of the tensor. Finally, the tensor has only 18 degrees of freedom, i.e., the 27 coefficients are subject to non-linear admissibility constraints. In the presence of errors in image measurements, one often starts with the linear solution and improves it further by employing a numerical Gauss-Newton style iterative procedure until a solution that satisfies the admissibility constraints is obtained. (See Appendix for more details).

In this paper we investigate the cases in which the linear solution is degenerate. As it happens, the degeneracy occurs in typical real situations. We show that when the sample of features is taken from a configuration of lines that have a common intersection, known as a Linear Line Complex (LLC), then the rank of the linear system reduces from 26 (in the general case) to 23 — yet, there exists a *unique* solution for the tensor when the non-linear admissibility constraints are accounted for[1]. An LLC includes in particular the case of lines on parallel planes whose degeneracy was observed in [21].

To appreciate the practical importance of investigating LLC configurations, consider a few typical outdoor and indoor scene examples depicted in Fig.1. In Fig.1a the common intersecting line is the edge of the building. All horizontal lines on the two faces of the building meet the edge in the image plane, and the vertical lines meet the edge at infinity. Note also that the vertical line representing the lamp-post also meets the edge of the building (at infinity) thereby included in the LLC configuration. This leaves very few lines (the sidewalk and the oblique line of the lamp-post) not part of the LLC. Imagine a robot moving down the hallway in Fig.1b. The lines are either in the direction of motion or lie on a set of planes that are perpendicular to the direction of motion. The lines on the parallel planes all intersect a common line on the plane at infinity. As we will see the lines in the direction of motion are also degenerate.

Finally, an LLC situation occurs also as an artifact in direct estimation of the Tensor from spatio-temporal derivatives of image brightness [18]. The spatio-temporal derivatives provide an axis of certainty (a one-dimensional uncertainty) for the location of the matching points in views 1,2 relative to points in the reference view 0. The uncertainty axes in views 1,2 are parallel which means that the information gathered from a *general* scene by means of first-order spatio-temporal derivatives is at most comparable to the information gathered from an LLC configuration of discrete matching lines.

Given our main result, an attempt to reconstruct structure and motion from the image line information of the scenes in Fig. 1 using conventional approaches would be at best unstable. The linear system of equations is singular or near singular, and would most likely not serve as a reasonable starting solution for the subsequent Gauss-Newton iterations. Therefore an investigation into degeneracies caused by an LLC and their remedy is important also in practice.

The remainder of the paper is organized as follows. Section 2 contains the main results which include the statement of degeneracy of the linear system forming a null space of dimension 4, and the statement of uniqueness by incorporating the admissibility constraints with a simple constructive algorithm for obtaining a unique solution from an LLC configuration. In Section 3 we verify the theory and the algorithm with experiments with real images. We use a schematized version of the real scene shown in Fig. 1a because it allows for a wider

---

[1] This in contrast to *critical line configurations* from which a unique solution is not possible, see [9, 3, 10]

set of experiments. One can accurately find both line and point correspondences and can therefore perform the motion estimation using line correspondences and then verify the results against motion estimates obtained using points.

Notations in general, and tensorial notations in particular, theory and background of the Trilinear Tensor with its contraction and slicing properties and admissibility constraints, are discussed in the Appendix.

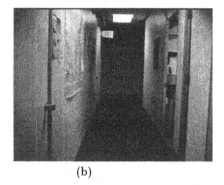

(a)   (b)

Fig. 1. *Typical urban indoor and outdoor scenes. The lines in the images form a Linear Line Complex. See text for more details.*

2   Linear Line Complex Scene Structure

Consider the tensor T_i^{jk} applied to the point-line-line configuration:

$$s_j' s_k''(p^i T_i^{jk}) = 0,$$

where p is a point in image 1 and s', s'' are lines coincident with the matching point p', p'' in image 2 and 3, respectively. Note that $p^i T_i^{jk}$ is a 3×3 matrix determined by p, which we will denote by B_p, i.e., in matrix notation $s''^\top B_p s' = 0$ for all pairs of lines coincident with p', p''. Assume that there exists a matrix B, independent of p, such that $s''^\top B s' = 0$, then clearly the tensor T_i^{jk} is not unique: slice the tensor into three matrices $(T_1^{jk}, T_2^{jk}, T_3^{jk})$, then the tensors $(B, 0, 0), (0, B, 0)$ and $(0, 0, B)$ (and their linear combinations) all satisfy the constraint $s_j' s_k'' p^i T_i^{jk} = 0$. Hence, such a matrix B does not exist in general. We may, nevertheless, ask *whether there exists a special configuration of points and lines in space for which such a matrix B is valid?* Such a configuration is a Linear Line Complex (LLC):

Theorem 1. *Let S be a set of lines in 3D which have a common intersecting line L (i.e., $S \wedge L = 0$ for all $S \in \mathcal{S}$). Let Q be a set of lines in 3D that intersect the line joining the two camera centers. Then, there exists a unique matrix B*

865

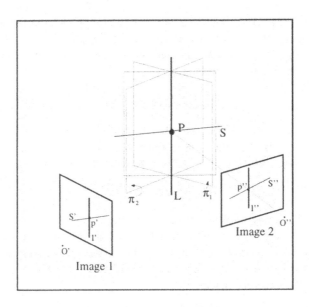

Fig. 2. *Figure to accompany theorem 1.*

satisfying $s''^{\mathsf{T}} B s' = 0$ *for all pairs of projections* s', s'' *of lines* $S \in \mathcal{S}$ *onto two distinct views. The matrix* B *also satisfies* $q''^{\mathsf{T}} B q' = 0$ *for all pairs of projections* q', q'' *of lines* $Q \in \mathcal{Q}$.

Proof: Let P be the intersection of a line $S \in \mathcal{S}$ with L and denote its projections by p', p'' onto views 1,2 respectively (see Fig. 2). Choose any plane π from the pencil of planes meeting at the line L, and let H_{π} be the corresponding 2D projective mapping (homography matrix) of points in view 1 to points in view 2 via (projections of) the plane π. Since π contains the line L, then

$$H_{\pi} p' \cong p''.$$

Let l', l'' be the projections of L, then p' is the intersection of s' and l', thus,

$$H_{\pi}[l']_x s' \cong p'',$$

where $[l']_x$ denotes the skew-symmetric matrix of cross products, i.e., $l' \times s' = [l']_x s'$. Likewise, s'' is coincident with p'', then

$$s''^{\mathsf{T}} H_{\pi}[l']_x s' = 0.$$

Denote $B_\pi = H_\pi[l']_x$. We show next that B_π is unique, i.e., independent of the choice of π. Let π_1, π_2 be two distinct planes of the pencil and let H_{π_1}, H_{π_2} be their corresponding homography matrices. It is known that any two homography matrices between two fixed views satisfy,

$$H_{\pi_2} \cong \lambda H_{\pi_1} + e''n^\mathsf{T}$$

where e'' is the projection of the optical center of camera 1 onto the image plane of camera 2 (the epipole), and n is a free vector. Because π_1, π_2 intersect at L, then, $H_{\pi_1}u \cong H_{\pi_2}u$ for all $u^\mathsf{T}l' = 0$, thus $n \cong l'$ and we have:

$$H_{\pi_2} \cong \lambda H_{\pi_1} + e''l'^\mathsf{T},$$

and from which it clearly follows that $B_{\pi_1} = B_{\pi_2}$.

Let D be the intersection of a line $Q \in \mathcal{Q}$ with the plane π and denote its projections by d', d'' onto views 1 and 2. The image line q' passes through the point d' and through the epipole e' and therefore: $q' \cong e' \times d'$. and similarly $q'' \cong e'' \times d''$. We can then write:

$$
\begin{aligned}
q''^\mathsf{T} B q' &= (e'' \times d'')^\mathsf{T} H[l']_x (e' \times d') \\
&= (e'' \times d'')^\mathsf{T} H(d' \cdot l')e' - (e'' \times d'')^\mathsf{T} H(l' \cdot e')d' \\
&= (d' \cdot l')(e'' \times d'')^\mathsf{T} e'' - (l' \cdot e')(e'' \times d'')^\mathsf{T} d'' \\
&= 0
\end{aligned}
\tag{1}
$$

where we used the identity:

$$a \times (b \times c) = (c \cdot a)b - (a \cdot b)c \tag{2}$$

and the fact that the homography H maps d' to d'' and e' to e''. $\square$

Corollary 1. *The rank of the estimation matrix of the tensor from image measurements of lines across three views of a Linear Line Complex structure is at most 23.*

Proof: Let the tensor T_i^{jk} be sliced into three matrices $(T_1^{jk}, T_2^{jk}, T_3^{jk})$, then the tensors $(B, 0, 0), (0, B, 0)$ and $(0, 0, B)$ (and their linear combinations) span the tensors of the form:

$$T_i^{jk} = \delta_i b^{jk}$$

where δ is a free vector of the family. Then,

$$s_j' s_k'' p^i T_i^{jk} = (p^i \delta_i)(s_j' s_k'' b^{jk}) = 0.$$

Since $\delta_i b^{jk}$ does not include the general form of trilinear tensors (eqn. 4), the null space of the estimation matrix includes at least four distinct vectors: the true tensor describing the relative location of the three cameras, and the three 'ghost' tensors $(B, 0, 0), (0, B, 0)$ and $(0, 0, B)$. Thus, the rank is at most $27 - 4 = 23$. $\square$

The ambiguity can be further reduced by incorporating the tensor admissibility constraints (see Appendix) as detailed below.

Theorem 2. *The ambiguity of Tensor estimation from measurements coming from an LLC structure is* **at most** *an 8-fold ambiguity.*

Proof: We assume the correlation matrix slicing of the tensor into the three standard correlation matrices $(T_1^{jk}, T_2^{jk}, T_3^{jk})$ (see Appendix). Let W be the $N \times 27$, $N \geq 27$, estimation matrix for linear estimation of the tensor, i.e., $Wv = 0$ where v is the tensor whose elements are spread as a 27 element vector, and v is spanned by the four-dimensional null space of $W^T W$. Let v_1, v_2, v_3 be the three 'ghost' tensors corresponding to $(B, 0, 0), (0, B, 0)$ and $(0, 0, B)$, respectively. Let v_0 be the (one dimensional) null space of

$$W^T W - v_1 v_1^T - v_2 v_2^T - v_3 v_3^T .$$

Since the null space span the admissible tensors, the three standard correlation matrices (T_1, T_2, T_3) of the admissible tensors are spanned by the tensors $v_0, ..., v_3$, i.e.,

$$T_1 = \hat{T}_1 + \alpha_1 B$$
$$T_2 = \hat{T}_2 + \alpha_2 B$$
$$T_3 = \hat{T}_3 + \alpha_3 B$$

where $\hat{T}_i$, $i = 1, 2, 3$, are the standard correlation matrices of the tensor v_0, and α_i are scalars. As part of the admissibility constraints (see Appendix), the standard correlation matrices T_i must be of rank 2, thus α_i are generalized eigenvalues of $\hat{T}_i$ and B, and since B is of rank 2, the characteristic equation for each α_i is of second order. Thus, we have at most 8 distinct solutions for T_i. $\Box$

Empirical Observation 1 *Only one of the 8 solutions satisfies all the admissibility constraints.*

Explanation: the rank-2 constraint of the standard correlation matrices is closed under linear superposition (see Appendix). Numerical experiments show that only one out of the 8 possible solutions for the generalized eigenvalues α_1, α_2 and α_3 produces standard correlation matrices T_1, T_2, T_3 whose linear superpositions produce rank-2 matrices. $\Box$

2.1 Algorithm for recovering structure and motion in the LLC case

1. Using robust estimation techniques determine the line correspondences which belong to the LLC and compute the matrix B (see theorem 1). Here one might use a robust version of the 8 point algorithm [7].
2. From the matrix B create the 3 'ghost' tensors: $v_1 = (B, 0, 0), v_2 = (0, B, 0)$ and $v_3 = (0, 0, B)$.
3. Using the point-line-line correspondences from the 3 views compute W, the $N \times 27$, $N \geq 27$ estimation matrix for the linear estimation of the tensor.
4. Find v_0, the 4th vector spanning the (row) null space of W orthogonal to v_1, v_2 and v_3 by finding the null space of:

$$W^T W - v_1 v_1^T - v_2 v_2^T - v_3 v_3^T .$$

In practice take the eigenvector corresponding to the smallest eigenvalue.

5. Find scalars α_i such that the vector:

$$v = v_0 + \sum_{i=1}^{3} \alpha_i v_i$$

is an admissible tensor (see theorem 2). This is done in two stages:

(a) Let $\hat{T}_i$, T_i , $i = 1, 2, 3$, be the standard correlation matrices of the tensors v_0 and v respectively. Then:

$$T_I = \hat{T}_i + \alpha_i B$$

Enforce the constraint that T_i is of rank-2 to find α_i. Since the matrix B is of rank-2 this is quadratic constraint resulting in up to 2 solutions for each α_i for a total of $2^3 = 8$ solutions.

(b) Prune the number of solutions down to one by enforcing the stronger admissibility constraint that any linear superposition of matrices T_i must be of rank-2. This is done by generating K random sets of linear coefficients δ_i such that $\sum \delta_i^2 = 1$ and computing the determinant of the linear superposition: $\sum \delta_i T_i$ for each of the 8 possible solutions. The solution that consistently gives $\det(\delta_i T_i) \simeq 0$ is the correct solution.

3 Experiments

3.1 The experimental procedure

Fig.3a,3b, and 3c show the three input images used for the experiments. The scene is composed of two faces of a cube and another plane on the left which is parallel to the vertical edge of the cube. This is a schematic model of a typical urban scene with an edge of a building such as in Fig 1a.

Corresponding point features were manually extracted. The feature points were saddle points formed by the corners of two black squares which can be found with subpixel accuracy. The point features were grouped into four groups: Points from the left and right faces of the cube form one group each. Points on the planar surface were grouped into two vertical sets of features.

Line features were created by taking pairs of points. If no pair of points has members from more than one group (for example Fig. 3) then we limit ourselves to a Linear Line Complex since all the 3D lines in the scene intersect the edge of the cube. By adding pairs that span two groups we can add lines that do not belong to the LLC. By judiciously choosing pairs we can add lines that are close or far from being part of the LLC (see Fig. 3d). We can also choose pairs of points that define lines passing through the epipoles. This flexibility allows us to verify all the claims in theorem 1.

Hardware notes The images were captured using a Pulnix TM9701 progressive scan camera with a $2/3_{inch}$ CCD and an 8.5_{mm} lens. The image resolution was $640 \times 480_{pixels}$.

To achieve the results presented here we had to take into account radial lens distortion. Only the first term of radial distortion was used. The radial distortion parameter, $K_1 = 6e - 7$ was found using the method described in [19]. We note that that parameter value also minimized the error terms in equation 3.

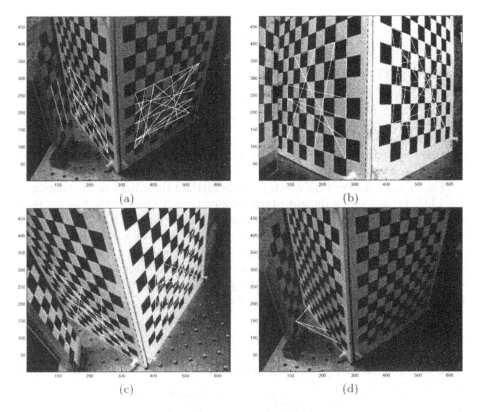

(a)

(b)

(c)

(d)

Fig. 3. *The three input images used. All the lines marked are part of a linear line complex. They all intersect the line defined by the edge of the cube. Vertical lines intersect the edge at the point at infinity. The LLC was computed using images (b) and (c). The dashed lines in (b) and (c) are the projection of the common intersection line into the images. The results show it aligns very well with the edge of the true cube. (d) Three line which are not part of the LLC that are used in the experiments.*

3.2 Determining the LLC

The three input images (Figures 3a,3b, and 3c) will be denoted image 1, 2 and 3 respectively. We chose $N = 28$ pairs of points which defined lines all belonging to the LLC. These are overlaid as white lines in the figures. For each image pair (1,2), (2,3) and (1,3) we used the 8 point algorithm [7] applied to the line correspondences to compute the matrices B_{12}, B_{23} and B_{13} that minimize:

$$E_{12} = \frac{1}{N} \sum_{i=1}^{N} (s_i B_{12} s_i')^2 \qquad (3)$$

$$E_{23} = \frac{1}{N} \sum_{i=1}^{N} (s_i B_{23} s_i'')^2$$

$$E_{13} = \frac{1}{N} \sum_{i=1}^{N} (s_i B_{13} s_i'')^2$$

respectively. The coordinates of the lines s, s', s'' have been scaled as described in [7]. From theorem 1, the left and right null spaces of B_{23} (for example) are the projections of the line L in images 2 and 3. The dashed black line in figures (3b), and (3c) show the lines corresponding to the null spaces overlaid on the input images. They align well with the edge of the cube verifying the theory and showing that the matrix B can be recovered accurately. Similar results were found using the other image pairs.

Fig.3d shows image 1 on which we have overlaid three lines not belonging to the LLC. Table 1 shows the error terms of equations 3 when all the line are from the LLC and when we add one of the lines shown in figure 3d. When the extra line is far away from the common line of intersection the error is large. Even when the line nearly intersects the edge of the cube the error is still significant. Therefore if most of the line come from an LLC robust methods can be used to detect outliers. Other experiments, not reported here, use lines that pass through the epipole to verify the second half of theorem 1.

Table 1. *Values of the error cost function for estimating the LLC when all the lines belong to the LLC (none) and when we add a line which passes close to or far from the common line of intersection (the edge of the cube).*

Extra Line	E_{23}	E_{12}	E_{13}
None	0.000055	0.00064	0.000079
Close	0.0019	0.0016	0.00054
Middle	0.0065	0.0038	0.0017
Far	0.0119	0.0919	0.0062

3.3 Recovering motion and structure

We computed the motion tensor from the three views using four methods. First we used the linear method for a set of 131 point correspondences. Then we used the linear method for a set of 34 non degenerate line correspondences. Next we applied the linear method in a naive way to the set-of 28 line correspondences from an LLC. In other words we ignored the fact that the lines come from an LLC. Finally we estimated the tensor from the 28 degenerate lines using the algorithm described in section 2.1.

Condition of the estimation matrix Figure 4a (top) shows the four smallest singular values of the estimation matrix W used to compute the tensor from 34 non-degenerate lines. The smallest eigenvalue is considerably smaller than the others indicating that the null space of the matrix is of $rank = 1$ and the problem is well conditioned. Figure 4a (middle) shows the 5 smallest singular values for the estimation matrix computed from 28 lines belonging to an LLC. The 4 smallest singular values are about equal and are considerably smaller than the next smallest. This indicates that the null space of W is of $rank = 4$ as expected from theorem 1. Simply taking the eigenvector corresponding to the smallest eigenvalue would be a mistake.

Figure 4b shows the projection of the vectors v_1, v_2 and v_3 on the eigenvectors of the estimation matrix $W^T W$. The projections onto the eigenvectors corresponding to the first 23 eigenvalues are close to zero verifying that the vectors v_1, v_2 and v_3 are orthogonal to the first 23 eigenvectors. This verifies part of theorem 2 which states that the vectors v_1, v_2 and v_3 are in the null space of $W^T W$ (the remaining four eigenvectors).

Following the algorithm described in section 2.1 we compute the eigenvalues and eigenvectors of the matrix

$$W^T W - v_1 v_1^T - v_2 v_2^T - v_3 v_3^T .$$

Figure 4a (bottom) shows the three smallest eigenvalues. The smallest eigenvalues is significantly smaller than the next smallest value indicating that the null space is now of $rank = 1$.

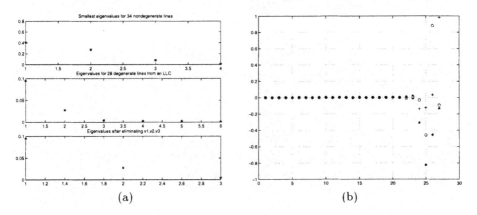

(a)   (b)

Fig. 4. *(a) The smallest singular values of the estimation matrix W for a degenerate and non degenerate set of lines. (b) With a degenerate set of lines, the vectors v_1, v_2 and v_3 were projected onto the 27 eigenvectors of $W^T W$. The values for the first 23 eigenvectors are close to zero verifying that the vectors v_1, v_2 and v_3 are orthogonal to the first 23 eigenvectors and are therefore in the null space of $W^T W$. (See theorem 2.)*

Reprojection of lines using the tensor After recovering the tensor one can use the tensor to reproject a line given in two images into the third image. In order to test the tensor estimates we used ten additional lines shown in figure

5. Three of the lines lie in the LLC on the left face of the cube. The other 7 do not lie on the LLC.

Figures 5b,c,d show the reprojection results (dashed lines) together with the original lines (solid lines) overlaid on image 1. One can see that if the set of lines used to estimate the tensor all belong to an LLC then other lines in the LLC reproject more or less correctly but the reprojection of lines not in the LLC is incorrect (Fig. 5c). On the other hand, reprojection using the tensor computed by taking into account the degeneracy (Fig. 5d) gives results as good as if we had a non-degenerate set of lines to estimate the tensor (Fig. 5b).

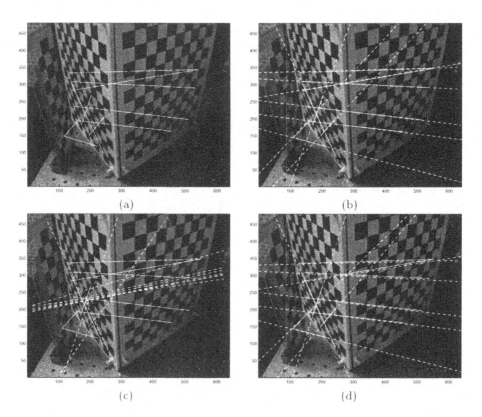

(a) (b)

(c) (d)

Fig. 5. *(a) Ten additional lines are used to test the recovered tensors. Three of the lines lie on the left face of the cube and are therefore the part of the LLC. The other 7 are not. The test lines from images (2) and (3) are reprojected back into image (1) using the recovered tensors. Solid lines are the true locations. Dashed lines are the reprojected lines. (b) The tensor was computed using a set of 34 non degenerate lines. (c) The tensor was computed using a degenerate set of 28 lines using the standard method. Since it does not take into account the degeneracy the tensor fails to correctly reproject the lines. The only lines in (c) that reproject correctly are those that belong to the LLC. (d) Using the new algorithm for the degenerate case the computed tensor correctly reprojects all the lines.*

4 Summary

We have shown that linear methods for estimating motion and 3D structure from lines lead to a degenerate set of equations in the case of a Linear Line Complex. The LLC, a configuration of lines that all intersect a common line in $\mathcal{P}^3$, is in fact a common configuration of lines occuring frequently in man-made environments. This degeneracy is due to a bilinear constraint on lines in two views where the constraint equation has a form similar to the epipolar constraint but where lines replace points and the epipoles are replaced by the image of the common line of intersection in the two views. This constraint can be used to determine whether a set of lines belongs to an LLC and enables us to reject a outliers using *least median of squares* or other robust estimation methods.

An LLC is not degenerate for non-linear methods in general. The theoretical analysis leads to a modification of the linear methods that can recover the structure and motion in the LLC case. We have proven that the motion can be recovered up to 8 discrete solutions. Empirical evidence shows that the number of solutions can be reduced further to a single solution one.

We have implemented the algorithm, and experiments with real images verify the theoretical analysis. Although the results using the modified linear algorithm compare favorably with the results obtained using a non-degenerate set of lines, the system at this point is not robust. For example, it requires that lens distortion be taken into account. Further engineering would be involved in making a practical system.

Acknowledgments

A.S. wishes to thank Steve Maybank, Shai Avidan and Nassir Navab for helpful comments and acknowledge the financial support from US-IS Binational Science Foundation 94-00120/2, the European ACTS project AC074 "Vanguard", and from DARPA through ARL Contract DAAL01-97-0101. G.S. would like acknowledge the financial support from ONR contracts N00014-94-1-0128 and DARPA contracts N00014-94-01-0994, N00014-97-0363.

References

1. S. Avidan and A. Shashua. Tensorial transfer: On the representation of $n > 3$ views of a 3D scene. In *Proceedings of the ARPA Image Understanding Workshop*, Palm Springs, CA, February 1996.
2. S. Avidan and A. Shashua. View synthesis in tensor space. In *Proceedings of the IEEE Conference on Computer Vision and Pattern Recognition*, Puerto Rico, June 1997.
3. T. Buchanan. On the critical set for photogrammetric reconstruction using line tokens in p3(c). *Geometriae Dedicata*, 44:223–232, 1992.
4. O.D. Faugeras and B. Mourrain. On the geometry and algebra of the point and line correspondences between N images. In *Proceedings of the International Conference on Computer Vision*, Cambridge, MA, June 1995.

5. O.D. Faugeras and T. Papadopoulo. A nonlinear method for estimating the projective geometry of three views. To be published ICCV 98, January 1998.
6. R. Hartley. Lines and points in three views — a unified approach. In *Proceedings of the ARPA Image Understanding Workshop*, Monterey, CA, November 1994.
7. R. Hartley. A linear method for reconstruction from lines and points. In *Proceedings of the International Conference on Computer Vision*, pages 882–887, Cambridge, MA, June 1995.
8. A. Heyden. Reconstruction from image sequences by means of relative depths. In *Proceedings of the International Conference on Computer Vision*, pages 1058–1063, Cambridge, MA, June 1995.
9. S.J. Maybank. The critical line concruence for reconstruction from three images. *Applicable Algebra in Engineering Communication and Computing (AAECC)*, 6:89–113, 1995.
10. N. Navab, O.D. Faugeras, and T. Vieville. The critical sets of lines for camera displacement estimation: A mixed Euclidean-projective and constructive approach. In *Proceedings of the International Conference on Computer Vision*, Berlin, Germany, May 1993.
11. A. Shashua. Algebraic functions for recognition. *IEEE Transactions on Pattern Analysis and Machine Intelligence*, 17(8):779–789, 1995.
12. A. Shashua. Trilinear tensor: The fundamental construct of multiple-view geometry and its applications. Submitted for journal publication, 1997.
13. A. Shashua and P. Anandan. The generalized trilinear constraints and the uncertainty tensor. In *Proceedings of the ARPA Image Understanding Workshop*, Palm Springs, CA, February 1996.
14. A. Shashua and S. Avidan. The rank4 constraint in multiple view geometry. In *Proceedings of the European Conference on Computer Vision*, Cambridge, UK, April 1996.
15. A. Shashua and M. Werman. Trilinearity of three perspective views and its associated tensor. In *Proceedings of the International Conference on Computer Vision*, June 1995.
16. M.E. Spetsakis and J. Aloimonos. Structure from motion using line correspondences. *International Journal of Computer Vision*, 4(3):171–183, 1990.
17. M.E. Spetsakis and J. Aloimonos. A unified theory of structure from motion. In *Proceedings of the ARPA Image Understanding Workshop*, 1990.
18. G. Stein and A. Shashua. Model based brightness constraints: On direct estimation of structure and motion. In *Proceedings of the IEEE Conference on Computer Vision and Pattern Recognition*, Puerto Rico, June 1997.
19. G. Stein. Lens distortion calibration using point correspondences. In *Proceedings of the IEEE Conference on Computer Vision and Pattern Recognition*, Puerto Rico, June 1997.
20. B. Triggs. Matching constraints and the joint image. In *Proceedings of the International Conference on Computer Vision*, pages 338–343, Cambridge, MA, June 1995.
21. J. Weng, T.S. Huang, and N. Ahuja. Motion and structure from line correspondences: Closed form solution, uniqueness and optimization. *IEEE Transactions on Pattern Analysis and Machine Intelligence*, 14(3), 1992.

A   Mathematical Background and the Trilinear Tensor

Let x be a point in 3D space and its projection in a pair of images be p and p'. Then $p = [I; 0]x$ and $p' \cong Ax$, where $\cong$ denotes equality up to scale. The left

3×3 minor of A stands for a 2D projective transformation of the chosen plane at infinity and the fourth column of A stands for the epipole (the projection of the center of camera 0 on the image plane of camera 1). In particular, in a calibrated setting the 2D projective transformation is the rotational component of camera motion and the epipole is the translational component of camera motion.

We will occasionally use tensorial notations as described next. We use the covariant-contravariant summation convention: a point is an object whose co-ordinates are specified with superscripts, i.e., $p^i = (p^1, p^2, ...)$. These are called contravariant vectors. An element in the dual space (representing hyperplanes — lines in $\mathcal{P}^2$), is called a covariant vector and is represented by subscripts, i.e., $s_j = (s_1, s_2, ...)$. Indices repeated in covariant and contravariant forms are summed over, i.e., $p^i s_i = p^1 s_1 + p^2 s_2 + ... + p^n s_n$. This is known as a contraction. An outer-product of two 1-valence tensors (vectors), $a_i b^j$, is a 2-valence tensor (matrix) c_i^j whose i, j entries are $a_i b^j$ — note that in matrix form $C = b a^{\mathsf{T}}$.

Matching image points across three views will be denoted by p, p', p''; the homogeneous coordinates will be referred to as p^i, p'^j, p''^k, or alternatively as non-homogeneous image coordinates $(x, y), (x', y'), (x'', y'')$ — hence, $p^i = (x, y, 1)$, etc.

Three views, $p = [I; 0]\boldsymbol{x}, p' \cong A\boldsymbol{x}$ and $p'' \cong B\boldsymbol{x}$, are known to produce four trilinear forms whose coefficients are arranged in a tensor representing a bilinear function of the camera matrices A, B:

$$T_i^{jk} = v'^j b_i^k - v''^k a_i^j \tag{4}$$

where $A = [a_i^j, v'^j]$ (a_i^j is the 3×3 left minor and v' is the fourth column of A) and $B = [b_i^k, v''^k]$. The tensor acts on a triplet of matching points in the following way:

$$p^i s_j^\mu r_k^\rho T_i^{jk} = 0 \tag{5}$$

where s_j^μ are any two lines (s_j^1 and s_j^2) intersecting at p', and r_k^ρ are any two lines intersecting p''. Since the free indices are μ, ρ each in the range 1,2, we have 4 trilinear equations (unique up to linear combinations). If we choose the *standard* form where s^μ (and r^ρ) represent vertical and horizontal scan lines, i.e.,

$$s_j^\mu = \begin{bmatrix} -1 & 0 & x' \\ 0 & -1 & y' \end{bmatrix}$$

then the four trilinear forms, referred to as *trilinearities* [11], have the following explicit form:

$$x'' T_i^{13} p^i - x'' x' T_i^{33} p^i + x' T_i^{31} p^i - T_i^{11} p^i = 0,$$
$$y'' T_i^{13} p^i - y'' x' T_i^{33} p^i + x' T_i^{32} p^i - T_i^{12} p^i = 0,$$
$$x'' T_i^{23} p^i - x'' y' T_i^{33} p^i + y' T_i^{31} p^i - T_i^{21} p^i = 0,$$
$$y'' T_i^{23} p^i - y'' y' T_i^{33} p^i + y' T_i^{32} p^i - T_i^{22} p^i = 0.$$

These constraints were first derived in [11]; the tensorial derivation leading to eqns. 4 and 5 was first derived in [13]. The trilinear tensor has been well known in disguise in the context of Euclidean line correspondences and was not identified at the time as a tensor but as a collection of three matrices (a particular contraction of the tensor, correlation contractions, as explained next) [16, 17, 21]. The link between the two and the generalization to projective space was identified later by Hartley [6, 7]. Additional work in this area can be found in [15, 4, 20, 8, 14, 1], and applications in [2, 18].

The tensor has certain contraction properties and can be sliced in three principled ways into matrices with distinct geometric properties. These properties is what makes the tensor distinct from simply being a collection of three matrices and will be briefly discussed next — further details can be found in [12].

A.1 Contraction Properties and Tensor Slices

Consider the matrix arising from the contraction,

$$\delta_k T_i^{jk} \tag{6}$$

which is a 3×3 matrix, we denote by E, obtained by the linear combination $E = \delta_1 T_i^{j1} + \delta_2 T_i^{j2} + \delta_3 T_i^{j3}$ (which is what is meant by a contraction), and δ_k is an *arbitrary* covariant vector. The matrix E has a general meaning introduced in [15]:

Proposition 1 (Homography Contractions). *The contraction $\delta_k T_i^{jk}$ for some arbitrary δ_k is a homography matrix from image one onto image two determined by the plane containing the third camera center C'' and the line δ_k in the third image plane. Generally, the rank of E is 3. Likewise, the contraction $\delta_j T_i^{jk}$ is a homography matrix from image one onto image three.*

For proof see [15]. Clearly, since δ is spanned by three vectors, we can generate up to at most three distinct homography matrices by contractions of the tensor. We define the *Standard Homography Slicing* as the homography contractions associated by selecting δ be $(1, 0, 0)$ or $(0, 1, 0)$ or $(0, 0, 1)$, thus the three standard homography slices between image one and two are T_i^{j1}, T_i^{j2} and T_i^{j3}, and we denote them by E_1, E_2, E_3 respectively, and likewise the three standard homography slices between image one and three are T_i^{1k}, T_i^{2k} and T_i^{3k}, and we denote them by W_1, W_2, W_3 respectively.

Similarly, consider the contraction

$$\delta^i T_i^{jk} \tag{7}$$

which is a 3×3 matrix, we denote by T, and where δ^i is an *arbitrary* contravariant vector. The matrix T has a general meaning is well, as detailed below [12]:

Proposition 2. *The contraction $\delta^i T_i^{jk}$ for some arbitrary δ^i is a rank 2 correlation matrix from image two onto image three, that maps the dual image plane (the space of lines in image two) onto a set of collinear points in image three that form the epipolar line corresponding to the point δ^i in image one. The null space of the correlation matrix is the epipolar line of δ^i in image two. Similarly,* *the transpose of T is a correlation from image three onto image two with the null space being the epipolar line in image three corresponding to the point δ^i in image one.*

For proof see [12]. We define the *Standard Correlation Slicing* as the correlation contractions associated with selecting δ be $(1,0,0)$ or $(0,1,0)$ or $(0,0,1)$, thus the three standard correlation slices are T_1^{jk}, T_2^{jk} and T_3^{jk}, and we denote them by T_1, T_2, T_3, respectively. The three standard correlations date back to the work on structure from motion of lines across three views [16, 21] where these matrices were first introduced.

A.2 Tensor Admissibility Constraints

The 27 coefficients T_i^{jk} are not independent. One can easily show that the tensor is determined by only 18 parameters; and from the contraction properties discussed above that the constraints among the 27 coefficients, referred to as *admissibility constraints*, are grouped into three classes. Both will be discussed briefly below (further details in [12]).

18 Parameters The tensor

$$T_i^{jk} = v'^j b_i^k - v''^k a_i^j$$

is determined by 24 parameters given by the two camera matrices, each has 12 parameters. Two additional parameters drop out because we can scale v' and accordingly b_i^k without changing the tensor, and likewise scale v'' and accordingly a_i^j. An additional parameter drops out because of the global scale factor (tensor is determined up to overall scale). Thus, we readily see there can be at most 21 parameters defining the tensor. We can drop out three more parameters by noticing that the matrices a_i^j and b_i^k belong to a family of homography matrices that leaves the tensor unchanged (uniqueness proof in [11]), as detailed below:

$$
\begin{aligned}
T_i^{jk} &= v'^j b_i^k - v''^k a_i^j \\
&= v'^j (b_i^k + \alpha_i v''^k) - v''^k (a_i^j + \alpha_i v'^j) \\
&= T_i^{jk} + \alpha_i v'^j v''^k - \alpha_i v'^j v''^k \\
&= T_i^{jk}
\end{aligned}
$$

hence, we have three free parameters α_i (in geometric terms there is a free choice of reference plane in space). We can select α_i such that the matrix b_i^k will have a vanishing column (this corresponds to selecting a reference plane coplanar with the center of projection of the third view). Therefore, the new matrices a_i^j and b_i^k have only 15 non-vanishing entries, and we have reduced the number of parameters from 21 to 18.

Admissibility Constraints We may deduce from the Correlation Contractions discussed above the following three groups of constraints that the 27 coefficients must satisfy:

1. Rank$(\delta^i T_i^{jk})=2$ for all choices of δ. The three standard correlation slices T_1, T_2, T_3 are of rank 2 each and this property is *closed* under all linear combinations.
2. Rank(null(T_1),null(T_2),null$(T_3))=2$. This follows from the fact the the null space of $\delta^i T_i^{jk}$ is the epipolar line in the second image corresponding to the point δ in the first image — since all epipolar lines are concurrent, their rank is 2.
3. Rank(null(T_1^{T}),null(T_2^{T}),null$(T_3^{\mathsf{T}}))=2$. These are epipolar lines in third image, thus their rank is 2 as well.

One can easily show that no subset of these constraints is sufficient to describe an admissible tensor of the form of eqn. 4. In practice, in the presence of errors in image measurements one often starts with the Linear solution (that might not satisfy the admissibility constraints) and improves it further by employing a numerical Gauss-Newton style iterative procedure until a solution that satisfies the admissibility constraints is obtained (for example, [5]).

Author Index

Lecture Notes in Computer Science

For information about Vols. 1–1340

please contact your bookseller or Springer-Verlag

Vol. 1377: H.-J. Schek, F. Saltor, I. Ramos, G. Alonso (Eds.), Advances in Database Technology – EDBT'98. Proceedings, 1998. XII, 515 pages. 1998.

Vol. 1378: M. Nivat (Ed.), Foundations of Software Science and Computation Structures. Proceedings, 1998. X, 289 pages. 1998.

Vol. 1379: T. Nipkow (Ed.), Rewriting Techniques and Applications. Proceedings, 1998. X, 343 pages. 1998.

Vol. 1380: C.L. Lucchesi, A.V. Moura (Eds.), LATIN'98: Theoretical Informatics. Proceedings, 1998. XI, 391 pages. 1998.

Vol. 1381: C. Hankin (Ed.), Programming Languages and Systems. Proceedings, 1998. X, 283 pages. 1998.

Vol. 1382: E. Astesiano (Ed.), Fundamental Approaches to Software Engineering. Proceedings, 1998. XII, 331 pages. 1998.

Vol. 1383: K. Koskimies (Ed.), Compiler Construction. Proceedings, 1998. X, 309 pages. 1998.

Vol. 1384: B. Steffen (Ed.), Tools and Algorithms for the Construction and Analysis of Systems. Proceedings, 1998. XIII, 457 pages. 1998.

Vol. 1385: T. Margaria, B. Steffen, R. Rückert, J. Posegga (Eds.), Services and Visualization. Proceedings, 1997/1998. XII, 323 pages. 1998.

Vol. 1386: T.A. Henzinger, S. Sastry (Eds.), Hybrid Systems: Computation and Control. Proceedings, 1998. VIII, 417 pages. 1998.

Vol. 1387: C. Lee Giles, M. Gori (Eds.), Adaptive Processing of Sequences and Data Structures. Proceedings, 1997. XII, 434 pages. 1998. (Subseries LNAI).

Vol. 1388: J. Rolim (Ed.), Parallel and Distributed Processing. Proceedings, 1998. XVII, 1168 pages. 1998.

Vol. 1389: K. Tombre, A.K. Chhabra (Eds.), Graphics Recognition. Proceedings, 1997. XII, 421 pages. 1998.

Vol. 1390: C. Scheideler, Universal Routing Strategies for Interconnection Networks. XVII, 234 pages. 1998.

Vol. 1391: W. Banzhaf, R. Poli, M. Schoenauer, T.C. Fogarty (Eds.), Genetic Programming. Proceedings, 1998. X, 232 pages. 1998.

Vol. 1392: A. Barth, M. Breu, A. Endres, A. de Kemp (Eds.), Digital Libraries in Computer Science: The MeDoc Approach. VIII, 239 pages. 1998.

Vol. 1393: D. Bert (Ed.), B'98: Recent Advances in the Development and Use of the B Method. Proceedings, 1998. VIII, 313 pages. 1998.

Vol. 1394: X. Wu. R. Kotagiri, K.B. Korb (Eds.), Research and Development in Knowledge Discovery and Data Mining. Proceedings, 1998. XVI, 424 pages. 1998. (Subseries LNAI).

Vol. 1395: H. Kitano (Ed.), RoboCup-97: Robot Soccer World Cup I. XIV, 520 pages. 1998. (Subseries LNAI).

Vol. 1396: E. Okamoto, G. Davida, M. Mambo (Eds.), Information Security. Proceedings, 1997. XII, 357 pages. 1998.

Vol. 1397: H. de Swart (Ed.), Automated Reasoning with Analytic Tableaux and Related Methods. Proceedings, 1998. X, 325 pages. 1998. (Subseries LNAI).

Vol. 1398: C. Nédellec, C. Rouveirol (Eds.), Machine Learning: ECML-98. Proceedings, 1998. XII, 420 pages. 1998. (Subseries LNAI).

Vol. 1399: O. Etzion, S. Jajodia, S. Sripada (Eds.), Temporal Databases: Research and Practice. X, 429 pages. 1998.

Vol. 1400: M. Lenz, B. Bartsch-Spörl, H.-D. Burkhard, S. Wess (Eds.), Case-Based Reasoning Technology. XVIII, 405 pages. 1998. (Subseries LNAI).

Vol. 1401: P. Sloot, M. Bubak, B. Hertzberger (Eds.), High-Performance Computing and Networking. Proceedings, 1998. XX, 1309 pages. 1998.

Vol. 1402: W. Lamersdorf, M. Merz (Eds.), Trends in Distributed Systems for Electronic Commerce. Proceedings, 1998. XII, 255 pages. 1998.

Vol. 1403: K. Nyberg (Ed.), Advances in Cryptology – EUROCRYPT '98. Proceedings, 1998. X, 607 pages. 1998.

Vol. 1404: C. Freksa, C. Habel. K.F. Wender (Eds.), Spatial Cognition. VIII, 491 pages. 1998. (Subseries LNAI).

Vol. 1406: H. Burkhardt, B. Neumann (Eds.), Computer Vision – ECCV'98. Vol. I. Proceedings, 1998. XVI, 927 pages. 1998.

Vol. 1407: H. Burkhardt, B. Neumann (Eds.), Computer Vision – ECCV'98. Vol. II. Proceedings, 1998. XVI, 881 pages. 1998.

Vol. 1409: T. Schaub, The Automation of Reasoning with Incomplete Information. XI, 159 pages. 1998. (Subseries LNAI).

Vol. 1411: L. Asplund (Ed.), Reliable Software Technologies – Ada-Europe. Proceedings, 1998. XI, 297 pages. 1998.

Vol. 1413: B. Pernici, C. Thanos (Eds.), Advanced Information Systems Engineering. Proceedings, 1998. X, 423 pages. 1998.

Vol. 1414: M. Nielsen, W. Thomas (Eds.), Computer Science Logic. Selected Papers, 1997. VIII, 511 pages. 1998.

Vol. 1415: J. Mira, A.P. del Pobil, M.Ali (Eds.), Methodology and Tools in Knowledge-Based Systems. Vol. I. Proceedings, 1998. XXIV, 887 pages. 1998. (Subseries LNAI).

Vol. 1416: A.P. del Pobil, J. Mira, M.Ali (Eds.), Tasks and Methods in Applied Artificial Intelligence. Vol.II. Proceedings, 1998. XXIII, 943 pages. 1998. (Subseries LNAI).

Vol. 1417: S. Yalamanchili, J. Duato (Eds.), Parallel Computer Routing and Communication. Proceedings, 1997. XII, 309 pages. 1998.

Vol. 1418: R. Mercer, E. Neufeld (Eds.), Advances in Artificial Intelligence. Proceedings, 1998. XII, 467 pages. 1998. (Subseries LNAI).

Vol. 1422: J. Jeuring (Ed.), Mathematics of Program Construction. Proceedings, 1998. X, 383 pages. 1998.

Vol. 1425: D. Hutchison, R. Schäfer (Eds.), Multimedia Applications, Services and Techniques – ECMAST'98. Proceedings, 1998. XVI, 531 pages. 1998.

Vol. 1427: A.J. Hu, M.Y. Vardi (Eds.), Computer Aided Verification. Proceedings, 1998. IX, 552 pages. 1998.

Vol. 1430: S. Trigila, A. Mullery, M. Campolargo, H. Vanderstraeten, M. Mampaey (Eds.), Intelligence in Services and Networks: Technology for Ubiquitous Telecom Services. Proceedings, 1998. XII, 550 pages. 1998.